EXPLORING
WINE

EXPLORING
WINE

COMPLETELY REVISED THIRD EDITION

STEVEN KOLPAN   BRIAN H. SMITH   MICHAEL A. WEISS

THE CULINARY INSTITUTE OF AMERICA

WILEY

JOHN WILEY AND SONS, INC.

The Culinary Institute of America
President: Dr. Tim Ryan '77
Vice-President, Dean of Culinary Education: Mark Erickson '77
Senior Director, Educational Enterprises: Susan Cussen
Director of Publishing: Nathalie Fischer

Published by John Wiley & Sons, Inc., Hoboken, New Jersey

Published simultaneously in Canada

For general information on our other products and services or for technical support, please contact our Customer Care Department within the United States at (800) 762-2974, outside the United States at (317) 572-3993 or fax (317) 572-4002.

Wiley also publishes its books in a variety of electronic formats. Some content that appears in print may not be available in electronic books. For more information about Wiley products, visit our web site at www.wiley.com.

Design by Memo Productions, NY

Library of Congress Cataloging-in-Publication Data:
Kolpan, Steven.
Exploring wine : completely revised third edition
Steven Kolpan, Brian H. Smith, Michael A. Weiss. — 3rd ed.

     p. cm.

  Includes bibliographical references and index.

  ISBN 978-0-471-77063-3 (cloth)

  1. Wine and Wine Making. I. Kolpan, Steven. II. Smith, Brian H. III. Weiss, Michael A.
  IV. Culinary Institute of America. V. Title.

  TP548.K578 2010
  641.2'2—dc22   2009014016

Printed in China

10 9 8 7 6 5 4 3 2 1

To the memory of Brian Smith. Brian loved wine.
Brian loved life.

To my friends and loved ones, a toast to
life and love, and to the wisdom and pleasures
we find in a glass of wine.

— Steven Kolpan

To the many varied members of the extended wine
family I have grown to know over the years.
I offer my deepest gratitude for all you have done
to help me understand and enjoy wine. I could
not have done it without your support and friendship.

To my children, Lauren and Drew.
Grab life, live fully, and be happy.

— Brian Smith

To my teacher Thinley Norbu Rinpoche, my sangha,
my wife Jenny, mother Sabina, father Csoki (Jack),
brother Richard, and friends.

I thank the compassionate people in the
wine world and beyond who have nurtured me.

— Michael Weiss

ETTENTAL

Jer...
20...

Laurent-P

CHAMPAG

CONTENTS

MONT

2006

Fortune see...
they came fo...
founded in...
begin produ...
our golden...

DRY RED WINE
NAOUSSA
APPELLATION OF ORIGIN NAOUSSA OF HIGH QUALITY
2006
VINTAGE

ELLBOUN

PETITE SIRAH
CALIFORNIA

Aigle les l...
APPELLATION D'...

EXPLORING
WINE

FOREWORD

I SPEND MUCH OF MY TIME presenting my family's wines to chefs and sommeliers all across the country, and I am always struck by how many wine buyers today were students of professors Steven Kolpan, Brian Smith, and Michael Weiss at The Culinary Institute of America. These three men are major influences on the new generation of tastemakers. I am honored to write a foreword to the third edition of their book *Exploring Wine*.

This is a great book. The writing is lively. The content is rich. It is a textbook, a reference book, a wine lover's guidebook, a wine professional's manual. It is highly opinionated, which makes it particularly entertaining. It contains many insights into wine lists, explains how wines are priced, and suggests alternatives to Chardonnay and Cabernet, which makes it extremely helpful for wine professionals and consumers alike.

I have both the first and second editions on my bookshelf at home and am excited to add this third edition to my personal library. Wine is a living, breathing, evolving pleasure and so too must wine books change and evolve. This edition expands on new and exciting wine-producing areas, appellations that did not exist when the first edition

came out, advances in viticulture and winemaking techniques, innovative food and wine pairings, and the changing nature of wine lists.

It is completely up-to-date in terms of wine consumption, wine attitudes, and the development of a genuine American wine culture thanks to the establishment of vineyards and wineries in all fifty states, such that we are well on the road to becoming the largest wine-consuming nation on earth.

Exploring Wine is a grand tour. I was particularly fascinated by the section on Spain. I am embarrassed to admit that I know very little about Spanish wines, and I drank in the overview with the enthusiasm of a novice. The new edition covers many more wine regions than the previous books. It also goes into further depth on the wine regions, grape types, suggested wines, and wine and food pairings.

I was most impressed with the chapter on America. Even as someone thoroughly entrenched in California wine, I found it relevant and provocative. Perhaps most important, I can vouch for the veracity of the book as it drills down, kind of like the images on Google Earth, from North America, to California, Sonoma County, Russian River, and then to our winery's specific growing area, Green Valley, right down to the specifics of the soil type.

Kolpan, Smith, and Weiss teach twelve hundred students a year, who then fan out across the country (and around the world; there are more international students at The Culinary Institute of America than ever), bringing with them the wealth of knowledge contained in this book. Here is their curriculum. Drink it in.

Joy Sterling
CEO, Iron Horse Vineyards
Sebastopol, California

BONARDA

QU

OSS(

CO

TA REGAL

Vina Robl

2001

SYRAH

ESTATE BOTTLED

Cambria®

2005

SYRAH

BenMa

ROSSO

ONTALC

NE DI ORIGINE C

CIACCI

Cuvée

BELLAVI

Franciacort

PART 1
FUNDAMENTALS: GROWING GRAPES, MAKING WINE, AND TASTING WINE

WINE IS ANCIENT, and yet the beverage we enjoy today is thoroughly modern. It has been enjoyed for eight thousand years, through the great civilizations of Mesopotamia, Greece, and Egypt, to the Roman Empire, and on into medieval Europe and the boundless opportunities of the New World. Today, the student of **WINE** is likely to see more developments in **VITICULTURE** and **VINIFICATION** than at any other time in wine's existence. Technology has allowed grape growers and **WINEMAKERS** to control the formerly uncontrollable and to improve even the greatest of all wines.

The first part of this book is dedicated to exploring what wine is and how **GRAPES** become wine, starting with the simplest definitions. The notion that wine comes from grapes is at once exact and misleading; there are thousands of different grape varieties with countless variations in flavor and chemical composition. Chapters 1 and 2 discuss the major grape varieties and the basics of winemaking. Chapter 3 explores what it means to taste wine and lays the foundations for developing your own method of tasting wines.

The modern, technological era of wine is very recent, no more than a blip in the life pulse of wine's history. For thousands of years, farmers and merchants relied on the favor and the mercy of the gods to bless them with a pleasing wine. Sometimes they got what they prayed for, without ever knowing why. In other years they were not quite so blessed.

Wine can and does make itself. Placed in its simplest context, wine is nothing more than alcoholic grape juice. For thousands of years, it was undoubtedly used only in that context. As evidence of a bountiful harvest and as a magical liquid that had gone through a mysterious transformation, it was used in dedications to deities of all kinds in all religions. It remains a symbol in the principal celebrations of Christianity and Judaism. It has been given to the sick and ailing and still finds a place in some hospital diets. Most important, once it was known that a beverage containing **ALCOHOL** is less likely to cause disease, wine became the daily beverage of all classes of people in countries where it could be made, in preference to the local water source.

But if modern wine drinkers had access to even the best of these ancient wines, we would most likely be unimpressed by their **STYLE** and character, for wine has changed dramatically. In some parts of the world, even as recently as the middle of the twentieth century, the notion of what constituted good wine was very different from today's standards.

What has not changed is the romance associated with wine. A fine bottle of wine makes a grand meal even grander, and many a simple picnic has become an unforgettable meal in the company of even the simplest wine. Good wine magnifies the pleasure we find in good food and good company.

trellis

PINOT NOIR

SAUVIGNON BLANC

VINIFERA

CLIMATE

CANOPY

acidity

ripeness

RIESLING

ZINFANDEL

PINOT GRIS

GRENACHE

VIOGNIER

shiraz

THE RIGHT STUFF: GRAPE GROWING AND GRAPE TYPES

How do we know when a wine is good? Such a question may appear daunting, but at some point any student of wine confronts this issue. Certainly the people who make the wines that we enjoy grapple with the question on an ongoing basis. While this is not the only answer, the grape variety, where those grapes come from, and the grape grower's and winemaker's commitment to quality make a difference to what we experience in the mouth.

Questions about quality are certainly relevant. In the past twenty to thirty years or so, the dominant trend has been toward decreased production of JUG WINES, or poor-quality table wines, and an increased emphasis on high-quality wines. In the Old World winemaking countries (especially France, Italy, Spain, Portugal, and Germany), this means that more wines are being produced within strict government regulatory systems, often referred to as appellation (or naming) systems. At the same time, some Old World grape growers and wine producers are working together to produce nontraditional wines made from "international" varietals to serve the world wine market—Cabernet Sauvignon in Italy, Chardonnay in Spain, Syrah in Greece.

In the New World countries, where appellation systems are not so meticulously detailed, the move to higher-quality wines means a greater concentration on wines made from single grape varieties or from blends of certain varieties known to complement each other. In all cases, higher quality means that more wines are produced for

retail in BOTTLE and MAGNUM (two-bottle) sizes with a CORK, screwcap, or synthetic-material closure, with decreased marketing of gallon jugs or five-LITER boxes of "GENERIC" or "semi-generic" wines (such as "Crackling Chablis" or "Hearty Burgundy," both made from high-yielding VINEYARDS of mostly cheaper-by-the-ton grape types in California's Central Valley).

Here are some of the ways in which we might objectively establish consideration of a wine's quality:

· The wine should offer VARIETAL CHARACTER: distinct TASTE and flavor characteristics that are typical of the grape variety or varieties used to make the wine.
· The wine's style, taste, and flavors should reflect the place of origin of the grapes. A Merlot wine produced from the vineyards of Napa Valley, California, *should* taste different from a Merlot wine produced from the vineyards of the Pomerol district of Bordeaux, France.
· There should be no unpleasant or OFF aromas or flavors.

To begin understanding grape flavors and regional influences, in this chapter we will survey the general environmental issues to be considered before planting a vineyard. We will then go on to describe the overall life of a vineyard and its annual cycle, with particular emphasis on vineyard management. Lastly, we will profile some of the major grape varieties and the characteristics of the wines made from each, and offer short descriptions of several "minor" grapes.

CLIMATE

THE STANDARD USED to determine the suitability of any area for wine grapes is a minimum annual average temperature of 50°F/10°C. Below that figure, summers are probably too cool to sufficiently ripen the grapes, or winters may be so severe that the VINES would suffer serious damage from the cold.

To grow grapes that will make good wine, a moderate, temperate climate is best, and the areas around the globe that are most suitable are usually found between the 30th and 50th parallels north and south of the equator. Within these broad bands, there are both MARITIME CLIMATES, such as Oregon in the United States or Médoc in Bordeaux, and CONTINENTAL CLIMATES, such as the Columbia Valley of Washington State or the northern Rhône Valley in France. Maritime climates exhibit a narrow range of mean temperatures, while Continental climates experience greater extremes from summer to winter, and even from day to night.

Within that broad climatic picture, there are many dif-

Steeply inclined vineyard slopes in the cool growing region of the Saar Valley in Germany

ferent influences, such as exposure to the sun, airflow, and temperature swings, resulting in some areas that are considered cool and other areas considered hot. Generally speaking, the climate of an overall region might be defined as the macroclimate, while the mesoclimate would represent the climatic influence over a whole vineyard, and the MICROCLIMATE would be specific to a small plot of that vineyard. Using this general model, we can find cool microclimates in an otherwise warm macroclimate. Cool climates make distinctly different wines than do warmer climates, since the grapes retain higher levels of acidity during the growing season in a cool climate. That ACIDITY becomes part of the wine, resulting in a profile that is often described as clean, crisp, and PALATE-cleansing. Like any high-acid beverage, acidic wines make the mouth salivate and leave it feeling refreshed. The lower acid profile of warm-climate wines results in bigger, mouth-filling flavors and SOFTER textures that seem to coat the palate and can feel somehow RICHER and more satisfying. This is not to suggest that one style is better than the other; they are simply different.

Regional climates and latitude also influence the length of the growing season: Higher latitudes enjoy longer daylight hours into the fall months, providing a long, gradual, cooler maturation period for the grapes and longer "hang time" on the vine; in the warmer lower latitudes, where the days vary less in length, there is usually quicker ripening.

Because of these climatic effects, most grape growers consider certain grape types to be more suitable to local conditions. The more delicate characteristics found in the white grape Riesling or the red grape PINOT Noir make them more suited to cooler climates, while the more forceful character of the white grape Viognier or the red grape Syrah make them more at home in warmer areas.

SOIL

WHILE IT IS NOT TRUE that vines need poor soil to produce good grapes, many recognized wine areas around the world attribute at least part of their success to low-fertility soils that seem to produce more interesting wines. For some reason, rocky soils with high mineral content, which would have difficulty producing most other crops, deliver wines that show complexity of AROMAS and layers of flavors, with a firm but appealing TEXTURE and a length of flavor that is deeply satisfying. Some of the important considerations in assessing the effect of soil on a wine are fertility, minerality, drainage, and heat retention.

The major soil types for growing wine grapes include:

ALLUVIAL A combination of **CLAY**, silt, sand, and gravel. The soil is formed over long periods of time—sometimes many thousands of years—from successive layers of mineral deposits left by bodies of water, including rivers and oceans.

CALCAREOUS Composed of calcium carbonate and significant levels of limestone and seashell fossils.

CHALK Soft types of porous limestone composed mostly of seashell fossils.

CLAY A mineral-rich soil of small particles that retains water.

GRANITE A hard, granular rock rich in crystal content, especially quartz.

GRAVEL Composed of separate pebbles or rocks.

JORY Volcanic soil composed primarily of basalt, a gray-black, fine-grained volcanic rock. The soil is relatively solid and dense.

LOAM Composed of sand, silt, and clay. The soil is crumbly and has better drainage than clay.

MARL Composed of clay, calcium carbonate, magnesium carbonate, and seashell fossils. The soil is crumbly.

SANDSTONE Sedimentary rock composed of sand, principally quartz. The rock is bound together with minerals, feldspar, mica, and stone fragments by time and pressure.

SCHIST Metamorphic, rocky soil derived from clay and mud, first forming shale and slate, but over time becoming mineral-rich soil that can easily break and shatter.

SHALE The most common sedimentary rock, shale is formed from clay and mud and can break easily, forming sharp chips of rock. Shale exposed to heat and pressure over time becomes slate.

SLATE A rocky soil that retains moisture and heat.

VOLCANIC Rock produced over time from pressurized, hardened volcanic ash.

FERTILITY

LIKE MOST CROPS, grapes will grow very well in fertile soil—sometimes too well, resulting in large quantities of grapes and leaves. While this appears desirable, the opposite is often true, based on the premise of lower **YIELDS**: Fewer grapes on the vine mean higher-quality grapes

overall, because the finite amount of resources available to the vine will be distributed among fewer grapes. It is also possible that the vine will put so much energy into producing leaves that less energy goes to the grapes, or the grapes are shielded from sunlight by too many leaves and do not ripen fully. If the vineyard has fertile soil, such as nutrient-rich clay, marl, or loam, the grape grower can use specific vineyard management techniques that will help reduce the vigor of the vine or dissipate the energy of the plant so that grape quality remains high. For example, the specific **ROOTSTOCK** (see page 10) used to plant the vine can reduce vigor in the plant; pulling off excess leaves during the growing season can concentrate the vine's energy on grapes; and a trellis system that divides the vine's upper portion into two sections will make the plant use its excess energy to produce up to twice as many grapes, but in a controlled situation. (See the section on vineyard management, "Viticulture," on page 13.)

MINERALITY

EXPERIENCE SUGGESTS that soils with high mineral content produce grapes and wines with more **COMPLEX** aromas and flavors. This appears to be due in part to an inverse relationship: High-**PH** soils (above 6.0) result in low-pH wines (under 3.5 for white wines and under 4.0 for reds), enhancing the primary fruit aromas and flavors of the grape with a **STRUCTURE** of acidity that somehow "frames" the wine. A wine with a pH of 3.0 is actually *ten times* more acidic than a wine with a pH of 4.0. This makes

The slate soils of the Juffer Sonnenuhr vineyard in the Mosel region of Germany give a distinctly mineral edge to the wines.

the wine leaner and less obvious, more subtle. In addition, tasting after tasting demonstrates that soils with high levels of rock such as slate, shale, and gravel seem to infuse the wines with an aroma and taste of wet rocks, similar to the smell of gravel after a rainstorm or the aroma of small pebbles in a shallow stream. Again, this provides an extra dimension of aroma and flavor that is reflected in the glass. We will make specific references to soil composition and its effect on wines in the chapters on various regions.

If the soil contains metallic compounds, such as iron, the general pattern is that red grapes are better suited to such soils, and the wines that are produced from iron-rich soils show a greater density of fruit and a firmer structure of acidity and **TANNINS**. (For more information on acidity and tannins, see pages 19 and 65.)

DRAINAGE

THE RATE of water runoff and water absorption by the soil structure can be a crucial factor in the health of the vine and the quality of the grapes. Soils that are compacted and do not allow for drainage to lower levels can easily leave the vine starved of water, which in the short term might give emphasis to fruit character in the grape but in the long term will lead to weakened stems and possible loss of grapes. Soil structures that are loose on the surface but compacted at a short depth below the surface will cause a vine to spread its roots laterally rather than vertically, which may be a problem in cooler climates, where a severe frost could easily penetrate the soil and kill the root system.

Again, experience suggests that the more desirable soil structure is of a friable (crumbly) nature, which allows water to seep far into the soil and encourages the roots to grow down to where they can find sufficient water. A vine that has deep roots is generally healthy and unlikely to suffer in extremes of dry or cold weather. While **IRRIGATION** systems have helped alleviate concerns about water supply for vines in many areas, considerations of soil structure are still relevant, especially in warmer regions where water shortages have been or may become an important factor.

HEAT RETENTION

ONE FURTHER ADVANTAGE of soils with high rock content is that they reflect heat back to the vine. They also absorb heat from the sun during the day; that stored heat can then be used by the plant at night to continue to ripen the grapes or to keep the root system warmer even though the air temperature may drop. In contrast, richer clay and loamy soils can remain cool and moist, even in warm weather, and this seems to retard the maturation of the fruit.

HISTORY

GRAPE GROWERS TODAY are faced with a dizzying array of grape varieties, from the ubiquitous Chardonnay to the obscure Madeleine Angevine. In general, there are two distinct groups of grapes for winemaking: the **VITIS VINIFERA** species, which originally developed in Asia and Europe, and the very large group of native North American species.

LEFT: *Deep limestone soils provide good drainage and mineral content for these vines.* RIGHT: *Heat-retentive rocky soil in a vineyard in Chinchón, near Madrid, Spain*

EASTERN ORIGINS

ALTHOUGH THERE IS archeological evidence of grapes and vine leaves from before the Ice Age, most historians of wine agree that the modern grape used for wine production probably evolved as the species *Vitis vinifera* in what is now Iran around 2000 B.C. *Vitis* is the genus for many vine plants; **VINIFERA** comes from two Latin words meaning "to bear or carry wine." Recognized as a plant that could be easily transplanted and as an economically stable crop, grapevines were often introduced by successive waves of invading tribes into newly dominated territory. In this way, the vine made its way out of the Middle East into the eastern Mediterranean. Starting around 500 B.C., the Greeks introduced grapevines into North Africa and southern Italy, and the Romans took the vines along in their occupation of the western part of Europe as early as the first century B.C.

As the vine was transplanted into different climates, different varieties developed through mutations and deliberate crossbreeding. Subsequently, growers began to categorize the varieties and even cloned new varieties by vegetative propagation, using cuttings or **BUDS** taken from a mother vine. Over time, some ancient varieties have been lost, and new varieties have emerged.

The spread of the vinifera grape varieties continued with the European colonization of other continents, and today hundreds of different varieties of vinifera grapes are grown throughout the world. The major wine grape varieties, grown around the world and widely recognized by wine consumers and professionals, are shown in the table on major wine grapes above.

THE WESTERN PARALLEL

THROUGHOUT ALL THIS PERIOD of time, vines were probably also growing on the North American continent. Certainly in the twelfth century, the Norwegian explorer Leif Eriksson saw enough evidence of vines on the coastal stretches of North America to name the region Vinland. But these vines were, and remain, a completely different family from the vinifera species, with very different characteristics of aroma, flavor, and balance of fruit to acid. In fact, the North American continent is home to several different

MAJOR WINE GRAPE VARIETIES	
WHITE	**RED**
Chardonnay	Cabernet Franc
Chenin Blanc	Cabernet Sauvignon
Gewürztraminer	Gamay
Muscat	Grenache
Müller-Thurgau	Merlot
Pinot Blanc	Nebbiolo
Pinot Gris/Pinot Grigio	Pinot Noir
Riesling	Sangiovese
Sauvignon Blanc	Syrah
Sémillon	Tempranillo
Viognier	Zinfandel

nonvinifera species, with many varieties within each species. The principal species in North America are **VITIS LABRUSCA**, **VITIS RIPARIA**, Vitis aestivalis, and **VITIS ROTUNDIFOLIA**. All these native American species grow wild east of the Rocky Mountains, but there were no vinifera vines growing in North America until they were imported from Europe.

It is reasonable to assume that Native Americans used these native grapes as food and perhaps even made a beverage from them. There is certainly ample evidence to suggest that early European settlers made wines from these grapes, though they quickly realized how different they tasted when compared to the wines made from the grape varieties they had known in Europe. Early attempts by European settlers to grow vinifera vines in the eastern United States were thwarted by cold temperatures and diseases that killed the relatively delicate vines.

It was not until the mid-nineteenth century that the two distinct groupings of European vinifera grapes and North American grapes came together as the solution to the pest **PHYLLOXERA**, which had decimated most of France's vineyards starting in the 1860s and destroyed most of the world's vineyards by just after the turn of the century.

PHYLLOXERA

THE MID-NINETEENTH CENTURY was an age of tremendous discovery, including the realization that science could be put to the service of humans. In the rush to learn and explore, American vines were shipped to Europe as part of a general program of plant material exchange. It was not realized at the time that various plant diseases and insects could be shipped along with the plant material.

Thus, when the American vines were shipped to Europe, either an adult live form or the larval form of some insects went along with the vine, and among those insects was phylloxera, a plant louse then unknown in Europe. Having evolved with the diseases and insects, the American vines had developed immunity to them, but when these vines were planted in French soil, phylloxera rapidly multiplied and spread into existing European vinifera vineyards.

The phylloxera bug has a very complex life cycle and in the different stages of its life, attacks different parts of the vine. In its earlier, aphid stage of development, phylloxera lives on the root system of the vine, sustaining itself by sucking sap from the roots. The bug copes with its waste by injecting it back into the vine's roots. The phylloxera's waste is poisonous to the vinifera family, and any vinifera vine infected by phylloxera will die within a couple of years.

GRAFTING

ALTHOUGH AMERICAN VINES are immune to the effects of phylloxera, European grape growers and winemakers did not want to plant American vines in their vineyards, because they could not accept the very different flavor profile of wine made from American vines. The solution was to GRAFT the desirable fruit character of vinifera onto the root system of sturdy, phylloxera-resistant American species. This is done by cutting a healthy fruit cane from the desired vinifera variety so it will fit into an accommodating notch cut into the selected American rootstock.

Just as grape varieties differ in flavor, vine rootstocks also exhibit different characteristics, and the prospective grape grower must select the correct root type for a particular grape variety and for the soil type and climate. There are hundreds of rootstocks available today for grape growers to choose from, each one developed by crossbreeding or genetic splicing to create a rootstock with a specific set of characteristics. Some rootstocks push the vine plant to be more vigorous, while others promote slower development of the plant. Certain rootstocks are bred to be resistant to extremes of cold or to various viruses or diseases. There are even rootstocks that are not totally resistant to phylloxera, for those areas where growers feel that the louse is not a significant threat.

The development and perfection of grafting techniques took several years, by which time the phylloxera bug had spread throughout the vineyards of France and into Germany and Italy. With grafting, French grape growers could begin to reestablish their vineyards, but that was not the end of phylloxera, which went on to conquer almost every vineyard area in the world.

There are areas that have remained phylloxera-free, either because the soil composition does not allow phylloxera to thrive (for example, the sandy soils of Chile) or because of strict laws governing the movement of machinery, people, and certified-disease-free cuttings (such as in South Australia). There are also regions of relatively new plantings, such as Oregon and Washington State, where growers decided to risk growing vinifera vines on their own root systems. While this may have simplified planting procedures and possibly reduced planting costs, the threat of phylloxera still remains. Beginning in August of 1990, growers in the Willamette Valley in Oregon had to face the reality that phylloxera had begun to appear in their vineyards and had to replant vines using phylloxera-resistant American rootstocks.

Wherever anybody wants to grow vinifera grapes, the only practical solution to phylloxera is to graft the vinifera grape varieties onto American rootstock. Even then, the grape grower may not be safe, as many California grape growers discovered in the late 1980s. Though they had followed recommendations from the University of California, Davis to use a rootstock called AxR1, many vineyards in Napa Valley became infected with phylloxera and vines began to die. It seems that phylloxera has mu-

This newly grafted vine, produced at Lorane Grapevines, King Estate Winery, in Eugene, Oregon, clearly shows the join of the small piece of lighter-colored fruitwood and the darker-colored rootstock.

tated into what is referred to as biotype B, to which AxR1 rootstocks are not resistant. The only solution was to replant the vineyards using more-resistant rootstocks and to hope that the phylloxera bug will not mutate in any significant way for many human generations.

With the AxR1 rootstock discredited, growers and winemakers began to research several other rootstocks and focused even more on selecting specific rootstocks for particular climatic and soil conditions. Among the hundreds of available, the current favorites include 3309, because of its moderate vigor and its ability to do well in cooler climates and thrive in deep but less fertile soils, and 110, with higher vigor and the ability to develop a deep root system in rocky soils. Two old standbys in California are 5C, which does well in deep, loamy clay soils (though there are fears that it too may be susceptible to phylloxera), and St. George, known for its high vigor and ability to do well in dry soils. As with all other vineyard issues, the key to rootstock selection is suitability to the vineyard site.

A NEW FAMILY GROUPING

THE PHYSICAL COMBINATION of an American rootstock grafted to vinifera budding stock was only the beginning. Even in the late 1800s, scientists, particularly in France, had begun experimenting with the cross-pollination of different vine varieties and families. Botanists theorized, quite rightly, that it should be possible to create a phylloxera-resistant vine by CROSSING a vinifera plant with a North American plant. (See the section "Hybrid Grapes," on page 12.)

From these crossings emerged a third group of grape vines called *direct producers*, or French-American HYBRIDS. At one time hybrid vines accounted for several million acres of vineyards in various parts of France. Today that acreage is drastically reduced, though there are still pockets of hybrid vineyards to be found. These vines have, to varying degrees of success, combined the winter-hardiness and phylloxera resistance of American vines with the fruit and flavor characteristics of the vinifera family. New hybrid grape varieties are still being developed in North America, most notably at the Cornell Viticultural Research Station in Geneva, New York.

In North America, hybrid varieties are found mostly in cool growing regions of the United States and in eastern Canada. A few areas in South America, particularly Brazil, also grow hybrid varieties. With one exception, hybrid grapes are not used to produce any *vins de qualité* in France, the exception being the white grape Baco 22A, which is widely used in the production of the base wine that is subsequently distilled into Armagnac BRANDY.

The science of cross-pollinating to create new grape varieties is not restricted to the creation of hybrids by crossbreeding between two vine species. The practice has been very successfully applied *within* the vinifera species to create new vinifera varieties. This is especially true of the work done at Geisenheim in Germany, where new grape varieties are being developed to better cope with the cool climate and growing season of some of Germany's vineyard areas. (See the section on grape types on page 491 in Chapter 11.)

VARIETIES AND CLONES

LONG BEFORE HUMANS started using science to develop new crossings and new varieties, nature had already been hard at work, with new grape types resulting from natural selection, mutation, and cross-pollination. From the work done by Carole Meredith, Ph.D., at the University of California, Davis (Dr. Meredith is now retired), we know that some of today's most famous grapes have somewhat obscure and surprising origins. The Chardonnay grape is a result of a natural cross between the noble and highly respected Pinot Noir (a red grape) and the all but unknown Gouais Blanc (a white grape). We also know that the Cabernet Sauvignon boasts its parentage as Cabernet Franc (red) and Sauvignon Blanc (white), and that Pinot Gris (white) is a mutation of Pinot Noir (red).

Not only is it clear that natural developments led to the emergence of new varieties, but we also find that there are often slight variations *within* a variety, since vines often adapt to new surroundings and climates, taking on slightly different characteristics from the parent plant. The differences are visible on the vine in terms of leaf formation or bud position, and occasionally minor variations in the finished wine become apparent. These slight variations have resulted in what grape growers refer to as different CLONES of the same grape variety. To take a classic example: Chardonnay is the grape used to make white wines in the region of Burgundy in France, but not exactly the same type of Chardonnay is being grown throughout Burgundy. Though all the various

HYBRID GRAPES

Hybrid grape types were first developed in the late 1800s, when scientists realized that they could select specific varieties within different vine species and crossbreed them so that the positive qualities of the selected parent grape types would be emphasized in the new offspring.

The impetus for this hybridization was to create a new family of vines that would be resistant to the phylloxera bug but produce grapes and wines of cleaner, purer fruit character than the native North American varieties. Thus the starting point was to breed vinifera varieties with native North American varieties. From there, it soon became apparent that the resulting hybrid vines could be crossbred with each other to produce new vine types that were resistant to other diseases and problems such as mold and **MILDEW**, or were more winter-hardy and able to withstand extremely cold temperatures.

Crossbreeding of grape types continues today, both between North American and vinifera species, creating hybrids, and within the vinifera species, creating new vinifera varieties. Two of the primary research centers in the world for grape development are the research center at Geisenheim, in the Rheingau region of Germany, and Cornell University's Agricutural Experiment Station at Geneva, in the Finger Lakes region of New York.

In terms of worldwide use, hybrid plantings are relatively small, with almost all commercial vineyards using them located in cooler growing regions, especially in the eastern United States and eastern Canada. In these cool climate regions, the hybrid vines are appreciated for their resistance to harsh winters. Among the hybrid varieties, white grapes are generally far more visible than reds,

especially if the wine is to be marketed as a single-variety wine, though there is still a large market for blended hybrid reds.

Some of the more favored hybrid grapes grown for wine production are:

WHITE	RED
Seyval	De Chaunac
Vidal	Baco Noir
Vignoles	Maréchal Foch
Traminette	Noiret
Chardonel	Frontenac

Of the whites, the Seyval (also known as Seyval Blanc) is appreciated for its ability to produce **LIGHT**, clean, fruity wine when **COLD-FERMENTED** in stainless steel, or a heavier, richer wine that is more intense and more complex when given oak-barrel treatment. The Vidal and Vignoles are also capable of making simple, refreshing, fruity wines, but the grapes really shine when they are left on the vine to be affected by **BOTRYTIS** or allowed to freeze for making Icewine. The varieties then create rich, **SWEET**, **LUSCIOUS** wines with a honeyed aroma and **RIPE** flavors of peaches, **APRICOTS**, and citrus fruits.

Recently, wines made from red hybrids have improved, especially wines made from De Chaunac, Baco Noir, Maréchal Foch, and Frontenac. These wines are mostly vinified as **DRY** wines with moderate levels of alcohol, acidity, tannin, and **BODY**. They rarely achieve the complexity of vinifera-based red wines and are generally not meant for long **AGING**.

---

clones taste of Chardonnay, there are differences in the way the vines grow, and there may be slightly different emphases in the flavor profile of each one. The same pattern is repeated with Pinot Noir within Burgundy or indeed with any grape variety wherever it is grown.

Knowledge of **CLONAL VARIATION** is essential to successful grape growing and winemaking. In the United States, the original plantings of Chardonnay in Oregon were the same clone as grown in California. The California clone prefers a warm climate and short growing season so it turned out to be unsuited to Oregon's cooler and lon-

ger growing season. Not until Oregon growers switched to Burgundian clones did Oregon winemakers begin to produce Chardonnays that matched the region's potential. (For further discussion of Oregon Chardonnay, see page 195.) The same problem occurred in New York's Finger Lakes region, where a clone known locally as the Champagne clone of Pinot Noir was widely planted and produced lightly **FRUITY** but unstructured wines. Only after growers planted Burgundy clones of Pinot Noir have winemakers been able to produce fuller and denser wines, with riper fruit and **DEPTH** of flavor.

Grape growers and winemakers have now embraced the general practice of planting several clones of the same variety, providing the winemaker with several different lots of wine. The winemaker can then use the different nuances of expression of each lot of wine to create a blend that is far more complex but eventually creates a more balanced wine, rather than having an excess of one characteristic over all the others. The overriding consideration, however, would always be whether the clone is suited to the climatic and soil conditions of the vineyard.

VITICULTURE

LIFE OF A VINEYARD

THE RAW MATERIAL that is put in the ground to start a new vineyard most often comes from a nursery that provides certified virus-free and disease-free plants up to one

New plantings in nursery boxes

year old. Even then there is a choice of buying **BENCH-GRAFTED** vines, which have already been grafted at the nursery and then grown for at least a season to produce a root system, or buying American rootstock vines to be planted in the vineyard for one season and then field-grafting vinifera cuttings onto the rooted American vines. Field grafting is a dying art and a skill that few people possess these days, so most commercial vineyards opt for bench-grafted vines.

At this point, a crucial decision has to be made about how wide apart the vines should be spaced. In the past, the question of vine density was influenced by the practical consideration of how much room was needed for maneuvering machinery in the vineyard. In older vineyards, areas that used to be tilled by horse and plow have much narrower spacing than more recently planted vineyards, which may be planted to accommodate motorized tractors. Vine density will determine how many plants there are per acre, influencing the quantity of grapes that each vine will produce.

In deep, fertile soils, wider vine spacing is usually used so that each individual vine can use its natural vigor to produce a greater number of high-quality grapes. In poorer soils, where fertility is lower and each vine will produce fewer grapes, vines are usually spaced closer together. In addition, the spacing will help determine the kind of trellis system that will be used to support the vines, which in turn has a major impact on the cost of the posts and wires that need to be installed to set up the trellis.

With all the replanting because of phylloxera problems, grape growers have used the opportunity to increase the density of plantings, sometimes increasing the number of vines per acre twofold or even threefold. Proponents of close spacing argue that by making vines compete for nutrients, they produce fewer bunches, but the grapes are of higher quality in terms of fruit flavor and balance of components overall. Closer vine density has become a given in many of the best vineyards throughout the world, as the enhanced quality of the fruit (and the finished wine) is palpable.

The grape grower will use the first two or three years after planting to develop the young vine's root system and to train the trunk up toward the trellising system. Fruit that can be harvested for wine will not be available until the vine is three or four years old, and the vine will go on producing usable fruit for as long as it is maintained in a healthy condition, sometimes as long as a hundred years or more. As a vine grows older, the quantity of fruit that it can be relied on to produce will decrease, though the quality will remain very high.

Most commercial vineyards, even at the highest quality level, pursue a replanting program, attempting to have the majority of their vines within an age range of fifteen to forty years old, with some older vines scheduled for replacement by younger vines that are coming into their prime. There are many wine producers throughout the world who specialize in making wines from "old vines." Although there is no universally accepted definition for "old vines," there are several producers (some California Zinfandel winemakers, for example) that pride themselves on making wines from vines that are between sixty and a hundred years old.

If a vine is left untrained, it will grow in an abundant but very random manner. The practice of TRAINING the vines on a trellis provides a support for the weight of the leaves and fruit and makes it easier for the vines to be tended throughout the year. It also allows the grape grower to control the quantity of leaves and grapes that the vine produces, and to place the leaves and grape bunches in specific locations to gain optimal sun exposure or shade. Most of the trellis systems used are variations on three main types: the vertical trellis system, the Geneva double curtain system, and the lyre system.

Different trellising systems are favored in different regions, since soil and climate help determine what kind of trellis to use. The gradient of the slope and the soil's water retention are important considerations, as is the number of daylight hours, since light is vital to the plant's natural chlorophyll to start the process by which the vine converts carbon dioxide and water into sugar and oxygen, with the sugar being stored in the grapes. The natural vigor of the grape type and rootstock and the soil's fertility help determine what kind of trellis system is most desirable.

Whether the grapes are harvested by hand or by machine is another determining factor.

The grape grower also needs to consider exposure to or shading from the sun, air circulation, and optimal growth of foliage. The science and practice of trellising, which includes this element of canopy management, is now so far advanced that for any given grape type, growers know how many leaves are needed for each bunch of grapes to be provided with the right amount of carbohydrates through photosynthesis. In all of the trellising systems, the vines are trained to grow onto a network of wires that are supported by posts along the vine rows. Very often, the wires are movable so that they can be raised as the vine's SHOOTS get longer.

Vertical Trellis System

The vertical trellis system is common in many winemaking countries around the world. Stationary wires near the top of the vine trunk act as the support to train permanent cordons or annual canes horizontally away from the trunk, and movable wires are strung in pairs along the vine rows at different heights. The new shoots are trained upward within the wires, creating a hedgelike effect.

Geneva Double Curtain System

The Geneva double curtain system is typified by a horizontal set of wires on which the pruned canes are trained. A secondary wire is located above this, and when the shoots reach this higher wire, they can be turned outward and downward, forcing the foliage to cascade down from the top wire of the trellis in a curtain effect on both sides.

TOP: *The upright positioning of the new shoots is clearly visible on this vertical trellis.* BOTTOM: *This variation on the lyre trellis system creates a divided canopy with two vertical planes of shoots and leaves.*

This has the effect of opening up the canopy and allowing more sunlight into the center of the vine row, discouraging mold. The downward slope of the vine's shoots also seems to inhibit any new shoot growth, putting more of the vine's energy into fruit development. This trellis system was developed at Cornell University's Agricultural Experiment Station in Geneva, New York, and it is particularly useful for vines planted on fertile soils in cooler climates.

Lyre System

The lyre system is really a double vertical trellis. The vine is trained from the trunk onto two separate, small trellis systems with the new shoots growing upward. The movement of air through the foliage helps reduce moisture buildup among the leaves and grape bunches, reducing the chances of various molds developing on the grapes.

There are many patented variations on these three basic systems. No single trellising system is right for any one place or any one grape type, and grape growers must experiment with many different systems before they find the best combination for any particular site.

AGRICULTURAL PRACTICES: ORGANIC VITICULTURE AND BIODYNAMICS

ALONG WITH SELECTING a trellising system that will work for their site, many grape growers enthusiastically practice and promote various farming practices that they believe are beneficial to the overall health of the planet. Increasingly, grape growers are embracing sustainable and organic agriculture, biodynamics, and **INTEGRATED PEST MANAGEMENT** to grow grapes, and some winemakers are producing totally **ORGANIC WINE**.

While organic viticulture has long been practiced without fanfare in many vineyards in France, in the past twenty years it seems to have taken hold in much of the western United States as well, where it is part of a nationwide movement toward **SUSTAINABLE AGRICULTURE** and healthier food and wine choices. Organic growers do not rely on inorganic **PESTICIDES** and **FUNGICIDES** but use traditional, tried-and-true agricultural techniques that produce fine grapes without polluting the water and land.

As of 2008, about 9,000 acres/3,642 **HECTARES** of California's vineyards have been certified as organic by California Certified Organic Farmers (CCOF) or other certifying agencies. In addition, about ninety growers of nearly 4,000 acres/1,619 hectares of vineyard in Oregon are part of a program called Low Input Viticulture and Enology (LIVE) that promotes a "whole vineyard" philosophy, discourages chemical use in the vineyard, and encourages biodiversity. Such groups abound throughout the United States and the rest of the wine world. This is in addition to a large group of growers and **WINERIES** that employ organic and sustainable practices but have either chosen not to become certified or are in a transitional phase that will result in organic certification.

The major goals of organic growers are:

· To create a sustainable system that addresses the health of the environment, social responsibility, and economic viability.

· To produce grapes and finished wines that express not only varietal character but the unique characteristics of vineyard sites—that is what the French call **TERROIR**.

· To protect the soil for generations to come, as well as the water supply used in the vineyards, both in the soil and on its surface, by severely restricting toxic chemical use, increasing organic matter to improve soils, nourishing the soil with natural material that thrives in the soil (e.g., earthworms), protecting the soil from erosion, and eliminating any imbalance in the soil that might inhibit strong root growth and the absorption of nutrients.

· To enhance energy efficiency in the vineyard by using **COVER CROPS** and compost, and in the wineries by increasing use of energy-efficient mechanisms (several wineries in California, for example, run on solar power).

· To protect and enhance the health of vineyard and winery workers and those communities surrounding vineyards and wineries.

· To recognize and embrace practices that will encourage biodiversity and conservation.

· To serve the growing public demand for wines made from **ORGANICALLY GROWN** or sustainably grown grapes.

Since wine grapes do not have to have the same pristine appearance as table grapes, **SPRAYING** has always been moderate in the vineyards. Now many producers recognize that spraying with synthetic chemicals may not be needed at all, although many of those who have to contend with high-moisture climates feel that spraying against mold and mildew is and will always be necessary.

Major producers who have embraced organic viticulture now use cover crops (such as alfalfa and clover) to diminish weeds in the vineyard, increase soil nutrients, and provide a home for beneficial insects, such as ladybugs, that thrive on unwelcome pests. Integrated pest management also includes the introduction or reintroduction of natural predators such as owls and falcons to control rodent populations that can damage vine trunks and roots. Cover crops can have an effect on water use, too, either competing with the vines for excess water or acting as a mulch to retain more water in the soil. To control fungi and plant diseases, some growers are using elemental sulfur (which is allowed in organic vineyards) instead of spraying dangerous chemicals that, in some cases, can cause cancer among grape pickers and have resulted in birth defects in their children.

Some producers not only grow organic grapes but also make certified organic wine. Unlike the fairly easy transition to organics in the vineyard, organic winemaking is tough going. Wine producers have historically used small to moderate amounts of chemical **STABILIZERS**, and making wines without them can be difficult. It is particularly difficult to make organic white wines, as white grapes do not contain the natural **ANTIOXIDANTS**, such as resveratrol and quercetin, found in red wine grapes, so organic white wines can be prone to **OXIDATION**.

Biodynamics views farms or vineyards as self-sustaining organisms that thrive within the larger surrounding ecosystem. Moving the concept of organics to the next level, biodynamics demands the best holistic farming practices, but coupled with a strong focus on the vibrant seasonal rhythms of the earth and cosmos. All synthetic fertilizers, pesticides, and **HERBICIDES** are prohibited and replaced with homeopathic concoctions that feature cow and horse manure, hay and vegetable compost, and seasonally specific mixtures of medicinal herbs, roots, and tree bark. The idea is that such an approach to agriculture will result in healthy plants and animals while enhancing soil fertility.

While most practitioners of biodynamics are found in Europe, Australia, and New Zealand, there is growing interest in this approach in the United States. Biodynamic farms and vineyard sites are certified by the Demeter Association, founded in Europe in 1928, whose domestic outpost is in Oregon's Willamette Valley. Biodynamic certification standards are stricter than organic certification, especially when it comes to soil additives and treatments. Unique aspects of Demeter certification include:

· Maintenance of a healthy, diverse ecosystem on the farm or vineyard site.
· Use of biodynamic preparations to build soil health.
· Integration of livestock into the farming system, with a requirement that at least 80 percent of livestock feed be produced from farm soils.
· Prohibition of genetically engineered plant materials and organisms.

The "father" of biodynamics in viticulture is Nicolas Joly, who grows grapes and produces wines in the Loire Valley of France (see page 265). Joly and his family own Coulée de Serrant, in the village of Savennières, planted exclusively to Chenin Blanc grapes. First planted by Cistercian monks in 1130, their ancient monastery still stands on the grounds of the estate.

In the mid-1970s, French agricultural agents told Joly (now in his seventies) that his family's approach to viticulture was archaic and that they should adopt the use of chemical fertilizers and insecticides. Joly, a former banker who felt that his family must join the modern age, embraced this high-tech approach to growing grapes, a decision that he soon regretted.

Joly noticed that the color of the soils changed and that the birds, animals, and beneficial insects abandoned Coulée de Serrant. The vineyard had lost its life, and Nicolas Joly began his search for alternatives to compacting the soil with chemicals. In 1984, after much research

Grasses and wildflowers act as nutrient-rich and moisture-holding cover crops between the rows of vines.

and vineyard trials, he found what he was looking for in biodynamics, a holistic approach to sustainable agriculture developed by Austrian philosopher Rudolf Steiner in the 1920s. After just five years of growing vines on his 30-acre estate using a biodynamic regimen, Joly says he "began to see nature reborn." The practices included crop rotation, **PRUNING**, composting, and preparing site- and season-specific soil and photosynthesis-enriching herbal infusions. In 1999, Nicolas Joly published *Wine from Sky to Earth: Growing and Appreciating Biodynamic Wine*, and in 2008 he published *Biodynamic Wine, Demystified*. Both books describe his personal journey with biodynamic viticulture in an inspiring and honest way.

In the United States, the most visible biodynamics activist is Mike Benziger of the Demeter-certified Benziger Family Winery in Sonoma County, California. Other California certified-biodynamic wine producers include Frey Vineyards, McNab Ranch, and Ceago Vineyards. In Oregon, Cooper Mountain Vineyards was the first producer in the Pacific Northwest to be certified as biodynamic. Throughout the world, there are now many vineyards and wineries—certified and uncertified—that have adopted biodynamic practices.

THE VINE CYCLE

THE FOLLOWING DESCRIPTION is necessarily general, and the months mentioned apply only to vineyards in the Northern Hemisphere. Add six months for the Southern Hemisphere; for example, March becomes September. Since grape growing is a never-ending cycle, it is difficult to choose a starting point. This description begins at the point immediately after harvest, as the plant goes into dormancy, and then follows the vine's developments through the subsequent year's harvest.

In many of the classic grape-growing regions of Europe, such as Bordeaux, France, or Piedmont, Italy, the harvest is completed by the end of September or the beginning of October, and once the fruit has been picked, the plant goes into a dormant stage as the leaves turn color and drop. At the same time, the sap falls back toward the trunk and the root system, where it will be protected from cold temperatures, and the canes (branches) that bore fruit during the summer become more brittle.

There are two major tasks to be accomplished in the vineyard during the winter months: to protect the vine from severe cold and to prune it in preparation for fruit production the following spring and summer. If cold weather is a significant factor, some vineyard managers mound earth around the base of each vine to provide an extra layer of insulation for the trunk and root system. In even colder climates, grape growers have been known to untie the vines from the wire support system, lay them on the ground, and cover the entire plant with earth.

Pruning

In most grape-growing areas, pruning is done during the two to three months following harvest. In climates where cold weather sets in very quickly, pruning is delayed until late winter or early spring. This helps delay the bursting of the buds in spring so that they will not be affected by frost. It is the buds at the end of the fruiting cane that break open first, so if the canes are left unpruned in cold climates, the buds at the very tip of the previous year's long canes will develop first and be hit by any damaging frost, while the buds left after pruning will remain undamaged.

Pruning is really a controlling process, since it dictates how many buds will open the next spring, and therefore how many flowers and grapes will develop. Left to its own devices, a vine will produce an abundance of foliage and fruit, but

After harvest and leaf drop, the vines still have all of the cane wood from the previous growing season.

the grape grower tends to follow the old axiom that lower quantity brings higher quality. So pruning is a balancing act between producing a small number of high-quality bunches and producing enough grapes to be profitable.

As the vine is pruned, the vine canes are trained to grow in a certain manner. The three main types of pruning are head-spur pruning, CANE PRUNING, and CORDON-SPUR PRUNING.

HEAD-SPUR PRUNING

This system, which leaves the vine in a small bush shape, is particularly favored by grape growers who want to keep the grape bunches close to the ground, where they can benefit from heat reflected from the soil during the day and from radiated heat given off by the earth in the evening as the air temperature cools. It has traditionally been used in places such as Beaujolais and the Rhône Valley in France. The disadvantage of such a system is that grapes developing close to the ground can be more easily hit by late spring frosts, so it is generally not used in cool climates.

CANE PRUNING

There are many variations on this system, but essentially one, two, or four fruiting canes will be left after pruning. Each cane will have a predetermined number of buds left on it, as decided by the grape grower; each bud will produce new shoots. Throughout the world, the most common type of pruning has been the two-cane system.

CORDON-SPUR PRUNING

This is a combination of the other two methods, with established canes extended along the support system. The vine is then pruned to short spurs, usually having two buds each, along the cordon. The cordon-spur system is particularly suited to mechanical pruning and harvesting and so it is becoming increasingly popular.

Spring Growth and Flowering

After pruning, a vineyard looks its tidiest, with the neatly trimmed vines standing in an orderly array against the stark winter earth. With the warm temperatures of spring, the sap rises, and the buds left by the pruners break open

to produce leaves and new cane growth. This generally happens in April or May, depending on the climate, and by the beginning of June the vine's flowers are visible.

The months of March, April, and May can be hazardous for grape growers anywhere, as the vines are often subjected to sudden late frosts, battering winds, or even hailstorms. Assuming that the vine escapes these hazards and produces flowers, tradition holds that the fruit will be harvested one hundred days after flowering.

Fruit Development

After the flower petals drop, the grape berries are visible, though at this stage the grapes look like tiny green ball bearings. Regardless of whether the vine is a red or white grape type, the grapes stay green until they have reached full size, around the middle of August. At this point the grapes go through VERAISON, or color change, so that the grower begins to see the more familiar yellow-green of white grapes or the deep purple of red grapes.

From June to August, the vineyard manager will continue to monitor the new cane growth, adjusting the trellis wires to support the shoots and removing excess leaves if necessary, either to limit the energy spent on leaf development or to expose the fruit to more sun. At *veraison* many grape growers will also make qualitative decisions about the upcoming harvest and drop the smaller and less developed bunches of grapes onto the ground. This quality-driven practice is known as a "green harvest," and it allows the vine to put its resources into fewer grapes to produce more concentrated flavors.

Though the actual harvest is not far off at this stage, the grapes still taste very sour, since they contain high levels of TARTARIC and MALIC ACIDS and a small amount of CITRIC ACID, as well as energy in the form of sugar. As the sugar continues to reach higher levels in the grapes, the berries take on more and more sweetness and develop their own VARIETAL flavor characteristics.

Harvest

To predict a harvest date, the grape grower begins taking readings of sugar levels and acidity levels (see page 6). It is important to monitor these levels regularly, as they change rapidly depending on the weather. In good years, the weather will stay warm into September, allowing the sugar to build and acidity level to drop. Any rain at this point may be drawn up from the soil by the vine and distributed to the grapes, resulting in a diluted sugar level. Cold temperatures close to harvest will keep the acidity level high and the sugar level low. However, high temperatures at this time can be just as damaging, resulting in either a low acid level in the grapes (which translate into a flat, DULL character in the wine) or an elevated sugar level (which will give the wine too much alcohol or too much sweetness). Prolonged hot temperatures also tend to "bake out" or weaken some of the flavor components, leaving less complex flavor and aroma.

Although the levels of sugar and acidity are important, they are not the most significant factor. What is much more important is that the grapes reach a point of ripeness where they show true varietal characteristics, so that Merlot grapes taste like Merlot fruit and Riesling grapes taste like Riesling. This can be a harrowing time. While it is easy to grow any fruit in a warmer climate, growing wine grapes in a warm climate can often result in elevated sugar

TOP LEFT: *In hot, dry areas such as southern France, vines are typically head-pruned to grow as bushes low to the ground.* TOP MIDDLE: *The buds on this shoot have opened to produce new leaves.* TOP RIGHT: *This vine has been cane-pruned to leave only two canes from the previous season; each cane will be tied to the bottom horizontal wire, and each of the buds left on the cane will produce new shoots next growing season.* BOTTOM LEFT: *Newly set grapes after flowering* BOTTOM MIDDLE: *Pinot Noir grapes at* veraison, *when they change color from green to purple* BOTTOM RIGHT: *The vine flowers at the beginning of June in the Northern Hemisphere.*

levels without full varietal character. If the grape grower waits for complete varietal typicity, the alcohol developed during **FERMENTATION** can sometimes be so high that it masks the true flavor of the wine.

For red grapes, there is also the issue of tannin development and tannin ripeness. Picking red grapes by sugar levels alone will often result in a wine that is plagued by severe **ASTRINGENCY**, or a drying sensation in the mouth, caused by unresolved tannins that were still green and unripe when the grapes were picked. It is this balancing act that is at the very heart of the need to match the vineyard site to the appropriate grape type, so that full ripeness can be achieved during the growing season that nature controls. For this reason, Riesling, a variety that needs a long, cool season with gradual ripening to reach its best expression, is well suited to sites in Germany's northern vineyards, while the faster-ripening Grenache is very much at home in France's warm southern Rhône Valley.

Assuming that the gods smile on the farmers, the harvest of any agricultural product is a joyous time for all involved, as another season's work comes to a close and the fruits of everyone's labor can be seen, touched, and tasted. In the case of wine, as the grape harvest moves into the winery to be transformed into juice and then wine, work in the vineyard continues as the vines move into the dormancy stage, ready for pruning again.

MAJOR WHITE GRAPE VARIETIES

CHARDONNAY

CHARDONNAY BECAME the darling of the worldwide wine industry in the late 1980s, when consumers began to feel comfortable requesting wines by specific grape type. Chardonnay caught on in a big way, and more and more grape growers planted it so that more and more winemakers could produce it. Chardonnay grows just about everywhere in the modern wine world. Unless forbidden by law to appear in the vineyards of a particular wine region of the Old World (such as in Bordeaux, France), Chardonnay vines show up in both cool and warm climates and in both the Northern and Southern hemispheres.

Many people believe that Chardonnay is "the grape that tastes like **OAK**," and that's understandable, because more often than not, Chardonnay is fermented or aged in oak **BARRELS**, or in countries where it is legal, exposed to **OAK CHIPS** or oak essences. Unfortunately, some of the wines made from Chardonnay, including some expensive ones, are over-oaked, which throws off the **BALANCE** of flavors in the wine. Thankfully, these days we taste far fewer wines that taste like lumber and more that taste like fruit.

A well-made Chardonnay should contain flavors of **APPLES** and citrus. Its profile can be anywhere from light, crisp, and **GREEN** or underripe when the grapes are grown in a cool climate, to rich in tropical fruit notes, like pineapple and mango, when the grapes are grown in warmer growing regions. When oak is added to the equation, the wine takes on both sweet **VANILLA** and buttered **TOAST** flavors. Note that not all Chardonnay-based wines are oak-aged or oak-fermented, especially those from cooler climates, and some of these wines, produced in stainless steel and featuring refreshing acidity, are gaining in popularity.

Grape growers and winemakers like to work with Chardonnay for several reasons. First, the vine grows in varied climates and soils, and even though classic Chardonnay-based wines are made from cool-climate grapes, like those that grow in Burgundy, France, or the Russian River Valley of California, acceptable wine is produced from grapes that grow in warm wine regions, such

Chardonnay grapes

as Australia's Hunter Valley. Chardonnay grapes grow best in stony soil that is rich in calcium, but will produce marketable fruit in far more fertile soils.

Second, Chardonnay's yield in the vineyard is pretty flexible. As usual, the best wines begin with low-yielding vines, but quite drinkable Chardonnay can be produced from ripe grapes grown in relative abundance.

Third, Chardonnay grapes produce a base wine that is fairly neutral and needs the signature of the winemaker to create a style for the finished wine. Unlike other fine wines that are highly regarded for their raw materials (grapes) and "noninterventionist" winemaking techniques, successful Chardonnay needs the hand of the winemaker to define its style.

There are artisan Chardonnay winemakers whose signature is unique and whose wines can be quite rare and expensive. More often, however, Chardonnay is the cash cow for a wine producer, and in order to meet consumer expectation, the signature of that producer becomes more of a rubber stamp than an autograph. While the best Chardonnay producers achieve balance and quality in their wines through a delicate touch and restraint, far too many Chardonnay producers pull out all the technical stops and end up with a wine geared to please the palates of a mass audience.

Nevertheless, Chardonnay does deserve its prominent place in the wine world because, at its best, it is responsible for some of the best dry white wines made in both the Old World and the New World; it is also an important component in fine sparkling wines. When grown in a cool climate, Chardonnay will retain enough acidity to keep the wine tasting **FRESH** and to balance the ripe apple flavors that are the benchmark of this grape. The very best examples of cool-climate Chardonnay wines can develop a depth and length of flavor that will make for truly memorable experiences.

Where Chardonnay Grows

FRANCE

Burgundy (see page 311) is considered the ancestral home of fine Old World Chardonnay. The finest white wines of Burgundy are 100 percent Chardonnay, and some of them—even the most affordable ones—can be delicious, even memorable. The three most important major subregions within Burgundy for fine Chardonnay are Chablis

(see page 316), for crisp, green fruit, high-acid, mineral-laden, often unoaked Chardonnay grown in a very cool climate and chalk and limestone soils; Côte de Beaune (see page 322), for rich, complex, balanced, oaked (but restrained) Chardonnay; and Mâconnais (see page 327), which can produce warmer-climate, medium-bodied Chardonnay, some of them simple, several of them with pleasing mineral flavors and complexity.

Chardonnay is one of only three legal grapes in the Champagne region (see page 277)—and the only white grape allowed in this famous sparkling wine. The only other grapes allowed in Champagne are Pinot Noir and Pinot Meunier, both red varieties. What Chardonnay does for Champagne is provide lightness and delicacy, as well as bracing acidity, especially because Champagne is the coldest grape-growing region in all of France.

Although Burgundy and Champagne account for at least 60 percent of the Chardonnay plantings in France, Chardonnay grows in many other wine regions of France, particularly in southern France, where high yields in the vineyards most often result in drinkable, affordable wines.

NORTH AMERICA: THE UNITED STATES AND CANADA

With about 100,000 acres/40,000 hectares planted, more than any other variety in California, Chardonnay grows throughout the vineyards of the state, from the coolest sites to the warmest. There is more Chardonnay planted in the state of California than in any *country* outside the United States. California has adopted the rich, **OAKY**, vanilla style of Chardonnay as its signature, though there are some "leaner" exceptions that strive to bring out the grape's varietal character and the sense of place expressed by the vineyard site.

Wines whose labels read simply "California" Chardonnay can be produced from grapes grown anywhere in the state, and most often the source of the fruit in these wines is the warm Central Valley or, increasingly, the somewhat cooler areas of Monterey County. These wines tend to be full-blown, rich, oaky, with **MATURE**, ripe fruits in the background. If the grapes are sourced in warm climates, these wines can lack the refreshing acidity that cool weather brings. You can easily buy a wine labeled "California" Chardonnay for under $15 in a local wine shop or supermarket.

If you are looking for Chardonnay from California of higher quality (at a higher price), wines produced from grapes grown in the cooler growing regions of California can be good to exquisite. Very fine Chardonnay is produced in places like Napa Valley, Carneros, Sonoma Coast, Russian River Valley, Edna Valley, Santa Maria Valley, and Santa Ynez Valley.

New York State (see page 185) produces fine Chardonnay in both the Finger Lakes and Long Island, which are cooler climates than the vast majority of California's cooler growing regions. Chardonnay from the Finger Lakes does not rely on oak to define its style, as the ripe grapes maintain their refreshing fruit acids, and the finished wines can display a lovely balance of flavors. Chardonnay from cool-climate Long Island can also be impressive, the style a bit oakier than the Finger Lakes, but with balance and zesty fruit. A small amount of very good, high-acid, cool-climate Chardonnay is also produced in New York State's Hudson River Region vineyards and wineries.

In the Pacific Northwest, Washington State (see page 190) produces a wide variety of Chardonnay styles, but Washington concentrates on its red wines as flagships for the state. In Oregon (see page 194), some very good cool-weather Chardonnay is grown and produced, but Chardonnay takes a back seat to Oregon's premier red varietal, Pinot Noir, and its premier white, Pinot Gris. Idaho makes some fine Chardonnay in small amounts.

Chardonnay, from drinkable to extraordinarily good, is made in many other states, from Texas to Rhode Island, from Virginia to Michigan. In addition, Canada (see page 202) produces some fine Chardonnay wines, some of them from single vineyards. Canada's primary Chardonnay region is the Niagara Peninsula in Ontario and secondarily, the Okanagan Valley in British Columbia.

THE SOUTHERN HEMISPHERE: CHILE, ARGENTINA, AUSTRALIA, NEW ZEALAND, SOUTH AFRICA
....
In South America, Chile (see page 208) shows some promise in producing high-quality Chardonnay, especially from grapes grown in the cool-climate Casablanca region. These wines are inexpensive to moderately expensive and deliver delicious, ripe, balanced flavors, without a preponderance of oak.

Argentina (see page 219) makes a small amount of fine Chardonnay, but the majority of the wines that have reached the United States have so far been driven by the market and price points. Still, each year the small selection of fine wines has expanded and improved.

Australia (see page 224) produces rivers of Chardonnay, where the variety is second only to the red grape Shiraz in acres planted. Much of Australia's Chardonnay is produced from grapes grown in the gigantic Southeastern Australia megaregion, which takes up more than 95 percent of the vineyards in the entire country. These wines are relatively inexpensive and easily drinkable, featuring lots of tropical fruit flavors, the vanilla and caramel flavors of oak, high alcohol, and maybe a touch of RESIDUAL SUGAR. These mostly warm-climate wines have more or less defined an "international style" of Chardonnay and are successful in the marketplace.

In addition to mass-produced Chardonnay, Australia also produces some very ELEGANT Chardonnay wines from smaller wine districts, such as the Limestone Coast, Orange, Clare Valley, and the Adelaide Hills.

Australia produces quite a few Chardonnay wines in the unoaked style. These wines are beginning to garner both popular and critical attention, and several wines are FLINTY and mineral-rich, with refreshing green apple acidity.

New Zealand (see page 241) has made its reputation in the export market for its popular Sauvignon Blanc, but actually grows almost as much Chardonnay. Chardonnay from the wine regions of Gisborne and Hawkes Bay, both located on the North Island of the country, can be excellent. Gisborne Chardonnay features flavors akin to peaches and melon while Hawkes Bay Chardonnay displays more citrus flavors—grapefruit and lime. Chardonnay produced from South Island fruit often comes from the Marlborough wine region, which produces juicy, tropical-fruit-driven wines, with fresh, crisp flavors.

As with so many of the wines of South Africa (see page 245), Chardonnay, depending on the producer, can be pleasantly drinkable or deep and complex. The best growers and winemakers in South Africa are making fine wines at fairly affordable prices.

THE REST OF THE WORLD
....
Chardonnay grows in just about any country that makes wine on a commercial basis. Italy has grown Chardonnay successfully for several decades, especially in its northeastern provinces of Veneto, Friuli–Venezia Giulia, and Trentino–Alto Adige. Tuscany and Piedmont also grow and produce Chardonnay. Spain, Portugal, Germany, Austria (where it is called Morillon), Switzerland, Greece, and England each grow a bit of Chardonnay in selected

regions, as do cooler-climate regions of Israel and Lebanon. Eastern Europe grows quite a bit of Chardonnay, and the new wine regions of China and India do, too. Chardonnay seems to be everywhere.

SAUVIGNON BLANC

LIKE THE REST of the white varieties in the wine universe, Sauvignon Blanc lives in the shadow of Chardonnay. But Sauvignon Blanc seems poised, if not to dethrone Chardonnay, at least to lay claim to the respect it deserves as a strong supporting player on the world wine stage.

Think "green." Sauvignon Blanc at its best exhibits high acidity, with flavors and aromas of green apples, green grapes, green herbs, and perhaps just a bit of green **BELL PEPPER**. Sauvignon Blanc is the principal grape of many of the great white wines of Bordeaux and the only grape in some of the Loire Valley's fine white wines. In the coolness of the Loire Valley in France, wines made from Sauvignon

Sauvignon Blanc grapes

Blanc show the character of only-just-ripe green fruit, such as gooseberry or green plums, with very high, piercing acidity. In the warmer areas of Bordeaux (or California), the fruit may be closer to apricots.

Lime, kiwi, green honeydew melon, and tropical fruits such as guava, papaya, and passion fruit make some Sauvignon Blanc wines, especially those from New Zealand and South Africa, smell and taste like a fruit salad in a glass that's been poured over calcium-rich stones. The flavors of Sauvignon Blanc can shift in both subtle and dramatic ways, depending on where the grapes are grown.

In the past, some wines made from Sauvignon Blanc have been criticized for having too much of a grassy, hay-like character. At its worst, Sauvignon Blanc does seem to develop an aroma of cat urine. However, the days of such wines seem to be in the past. Winemakers all over the world are now sensitive to the demands of Sauvignon Blanc and realize that it needs careful nurturing as a grape and as a wine.

In the Loire Valley, local grape growers generally refer to Sauvignon Blanc as "Blanc Fumé," while growers in California, Australia, New Zealand, South Africa, and several other countries refer to wines made from the grape as Sauvignon Blanc or "Fumé Blanc." Either name may appear on the label.

Where Sauvignon Blanc Grows

FRANCE

Classic Old World Sauvignon Blanc, from the Loire Valley, is chiefly represented by the wines Sancerre and Pouilly-Fumé (see page 272). These wines exhibit a high degree of minerality—chalk, limestone, and the brininess of the sea and seashells. The flavors and aromas of citrus fruits, especially lemon and grapefruit, are prominent in Loire Valley Sauvignon Blanc.

In Bordeaux, Sauvignon Blanc is often blended with another grape, Sémillon (see page 290), to produce a distinctive style of white wine (see page 296). These wines tend to be medium- to **FULL-BODIED** and more restrained in their acidity and fruit flavors, as Sémillon is nuttier and more honeyed than the greener-quality Sauvignon Blanc. The classic versions of these Bordeaux blends come from the districts of Pessac-Léognan and Graves (see pages 296 and 297). White wines from Bordeaux labeled as Entre-Deux-Mers (see page 297) or simply Bordeaux tend to be more about the straightforward, crisp flavors of Sauvignon Blanc and are meant for early drinking.

In the Bordeaux district of Sauternes, Sauvignon Blanc is often blended with Sémillon to make one of the most famous sweet wines in the world. Sauternes is based on a heavy percentage (most often 75 percent to 95 percent) of botrytis-affected Sémillon, with just a bit of Sauvignon Blanc added for its refreshing acidity (see page 297).

THE UNITED STATES: CALIFORNIA

In California, Sauvignon Blanc is an important white variety that is sometimes labeled as "Fumé Blanc." In the late 1960s, Robert Mondavi coined this name for a style of Sauvignon Blanc that is fermented and aged in oak barrels. The resulting wine is far richer—and far less "green"—than classic Sauvignon Blanc produced in stainless steel. Today, Fumé Blanc need not be oaked, but the name often connotes wine that is richer and fuller than a wine labeled as Sauvignon Blanc. Some people prefer the more "sophisticated" Fumé Blanc style, while others much prefer the "wild" style of Sauvignon Blanc, and some wine drinkers enjoy both styles, depending on the food they are pairing with the wine.

Sauvignon Blanc from the North Coast of California—especially Napa, Sonoma, and Mendocino counties—is the antithesis of the Chardonnay produced in the same region. Rather than the rich, oaky, vanilla flavors of Chardonnay that can overwhelm simpler foods, the refreshing, straightforward, fruity flavors of Sauvignon Blanc are just the thing for lighter, simpler, spicier foods. California Sauvignon Blanc has emerged as a food-friendly wine, gaining more space on restaurant wine lists and more adherents among American consumers.

Sauvignon Blanc can also make a sweet wine when produced from **LATE-HARVEST** grapes. Late Harvest Sauvignon Blanc is a fairly rare wine, but several California winemakers produce this style.

THE SOUTHERN HEMISPERE: NEW ZEALAND, AUSTRALIA, SOUTH AFRICA, AND CHILE

For years, and until quite recently, classic Sauvignon Blanc was defined by the wines from the villages of the eastern Loire Valley of France, such as Sancerre. Today, things have changed. New Zealand Sauvignon Blanc has become, especially for many younger wine drinkers, the classic expression of this variety. Full of tart lime and tropical aromas and flavors, with grace notes of minerals, grass, and herbs, the best examples of New Zealand Sauvignon Blanc, especially those sourced from the Marlborough region on the northern tip of New Zealand's South Island, are wines to enjoy with a myriad of tasty dishes. A great accompaniment to spicy foods, especially Asian and Latin American flavors, this wine is like a squeeze of fresh lime juice, awakening and brightening flavors throughout the meal.

Australia produces a wide range of Sauvignon Blanc wines, from simple summer sippers to more complex wines, with rich, jammy fruit balanced by a vein of mouthwatering acidity. Australian wine producers, unlike their neighbors in New Zealand, do not generally specialize in Sauvignon Blanc.

One of South Africa's best white wines is its Sauvignon Blanc. When sourced from low-yielding vineyards in the cooler regions, particularly the Stellenbosch area, the wines can be incomparable. Though wines from South Africa can be uneven in quality—the reputation of the producer is paramount in choosing the wines—Sauvignon Blanc seems to be among the most successful varietals exported to foreign markets. With thirst-quenching acidity, a healthy dose of minerality, and green, tropical fruits in the mix, the wines are more fruit-driven than the wines of the Loire Valley, but a bit more restrained in their exuberance and slightly fuller-bodied than the wines of New Zealand.

Chile produces some delightful Sauvignon Blanc, very much in the California style, but with a bit more forward fruit on the palate, especially from grapes grown in the cool Casablanca and Leyda regions.

THE REST OF THE WORLD

Sauvignon Blanc grows all over the world, but without much of the attention that Chardonnay receives. One country that produces fine Sauvignon Blanc is Italy, particularly in the Friuli–Venezia Giulia region. Although perhaps a bit hard to find, Sauvignon Blanc from Friuli is worth the search. Often just labeled as "Sauvignon," these wines are some of the most elegant examples of Sauvignon Blanc produced anywhere in the world, with a grassy background and subtle fruit acids that refresh the palate. Tuscany also produces some well-made Sauvignon Blanc wines.

RIESLING

RIESLING, WHICH IS ENJOYING a renewed popularity in wine markets around the world, is an often-misunderstood variety, because so many people believe that Riesling wines must be sweet. The truth is that Riesling can produce extraordinary wines in every style, from bone-dry to incredibly sweet.

Riesling can be difficult to grow, as it really needs a long, cool growing season to come to perfect ripeness. Riesling ripens late in the growing season, leaving it at the mercy of both spring and fall frosts. Riesling is also extremely sensitive to the soil types of vineyard sites; slate-based soils are best for this variety. When the climate and soil are in harmony, Riesling is perhaps the most *terroir*-expressive of all white varieties.

Depending on where Riesling is grown, the flavor profile of the grape can be as varied as its many vineyard sites. High acid is a hallmark of Riesling, along with citrus—lemon, lime, grapefruit—and peach and pear flavors. On the nose and on the palate, Riesling is rich with minerals—from slate to quartz—and even the smell (though certainly not the flavor) of gasoline or diesel fuel. To make a general statement about Riesling's flavor profile is difficult, as there are so many styles of Riesling in the bottle, and those "same" styles change from vineyard to vineyard, region to region, country to country.

Dramatically high acidity is the benchmark of fine Riesling. The vein of acidity that runs through fine Riesling wines will emphasize the green fruit flavors in the drier styles and cut the **UNCTUOUS**, syrupy qualities of the sweeter wines. In all styles, fine Riesling is mouthwatering and refreshing because of the acidity that defines the variety.

While most Riesling wines, especially drier versions, are drunk relatively young to celebrate their fresh, green flavors, the high level of acidity that refreshes these young wines also helps preserve the wine; it is not uncommon to drink Rieslings that are more than ten years old. Sweeter versions, in which the residual sugar in the wine conspires with the acidity to preserve the wine even longer, can deliver pleasure twenty or thirty years past the original **VINTAGE**.

Where Riesling Grows

GERMANY

In Germany (see page 487), Riesling is the most important variety, the grape by which overall German wine quality is judged. German Riesling, taking advantage of a cool-to-cold climate, ripens slowly and is able to develop complex flavors that are partially based on minerals in the soil.

One of the classic growing regions for Riesling in Germany is the Mosel region (formerly Mosel-Saar-Ruwer, named for the Mosel River and its two tributaries). Mosel features dramatically steep vineyards on south-facing slopes covered in slate stones, within a cold climate moderated by the mirror-effect of the sun's rays on the rivers. Mosel Rieslings are very high in acid, with citrus or green fruit flavors, and tend to be light- to medium-bodied.

The other classic Riesling regions in Germany are located near or within the confines of the Rhine River and are represented by the Rheingau, Rheinhessen, and Pfalz zones. Of the three regions, the Rheingau is best known for the quality of its Riesling wines, with Pfalz Riesling a close second. The three Rhine regions are considerably warmer than the Mosel and so produce wines that are richer, riper, fuller-bodied, and somewhat lower in acidity.

Riesling grapes

FRANCE

Alsace (see page 274), which borders Germany, is home to a particularly French style of Riesling—full-bodied, dry, and higher in alcohol than most German Rieslings. Alsace Riesling enjoys weather cool enough to ramp up acidity in the grapes, but also many days of sunshine along the eastern side of the Vosges Mountains so that the grapes ripen fully. Alsace Riesling at its best can age well for years in the bottle, while the simpler wines are enjoyable in their youth—within two to five years of vintage.

There are sweet versions of Riesling produced in Alsace. Look for the label terms VENDANGE TARDIVE (late harvest, which can be anywhere from semisweet to quite sweet) or SÉLECTION DE GRAINS NOBLES (botrytis-affected, which produces lusciously sweet wines). As with the best Rieslings of Germany, Alsace wines, even when produced in a sweet style, feature a serious vein of acidity that refreshes the palate.

AUSTRIA

Close by the riverbanks of the Danube, Austria grows Riesling grapes that translate into some very elegant wines. One of the best wine regions in Austria for Riesling is Wachau, west of Vienna, which owes its cooling breezes to the Danube River, and where the vineyards are planted on steep slopes.

Austria produces Riesling in as many styles and quality levels as Germany. The best Austrian Rieslings, especially those labeled *Smaragd*—the highest-quality wines from the Wachau region—are fruit- and mineral-driven wines that, like the best wines of Germany and Alsace, can pair with hearty, rich foods and are certainly ageworthy.

NORTH AMERICA: THE UNITED STATES AND CANADA

With the exception of high-quality Riesling made by a literal handful of artisan winemakers in cooler pockets of the state, California is not known for quality Riesling. Overall, the state is just too warm to produce fine Riesling wines, especially when the coolest regions are wed to the far more profitable Chardonnay.

Washington State (see page 190) produces more Riesling than any state in the United States, but many of the vines are planted in areas that are relatively warm. The wines are mostly semidry to semisweet and can sometimes lack both the acidity and minerality of classic Riesling. The wines are fine as picnic wines with simple foods and are usually priced as easy-to-sip bargains. Some Washington producers see Riesling as an achievable challenge and are working hard to produce better wines.

The Finger Lakes region of New York State (see page 187) produces a small amount of fine Riesling wines, made from grapes grown on the stony banks of the Cayuga, Keuka, and Seneca lakes. The weather is cold and snowy, with just enough sunshine and reflected warmth from the lakes to produce high-acid wines that are similar to the style of Germany's Mosel.

A minuscule amount of fresh, crisp, fruit-driven Riesling is produced in the state of Idaho from vineyards planted along the Snake River, and it is very good.

Canada, with its cold climate, produces some fine Riesling wines in several styles, from bone-dry to sweet to its specialty, Icewine, especially from Riesling grapes grown on the Niagara Peninsula of Ontario and in the Okanagan Valley of British Columbia. Canada is the largest producer of Icewine in the world.

AUSTRALIA

Australia is interpreting Riesling for the New World audience: acid- and fruit-driven dry to semidry food-friendly wines with crisp, refreshing flavors at inexpensive to moderate prices. Many of the wines are bottled with easy-to-use screwcaps. Most Australian Riesling is produced for early consumption and immediate enjoyment, with a select few able to improve over time in the bottle.

Riesling from Australia tends to be lighter on the palate, with lime, ripe peaches, and tropical fruits in the background. Many of the wines have a bit of spice—nutmeg and ginger—that balances the luscious fruit flavors.

GEWÜRZTRAMINER

GEWÜRZTRAMINER PRODUCES very attractive wines, offering everything that Riesling does, but with more emphatic fruit character and an unmistakable touch of cinnamon spice, scents of honeysuckle and rose petal, and the distinctive aroma of lychee fruit. Gewürztraminer is traditionally linked to the vineyards of Alsace, France, where, along with Riesling, Gewürztraminer is one of the jewels in the crown of Alsace wines.

The best Gewürztraminer vineyard sites are located in cool-weather regions and rely on low yields in those vineyards to amplify the natural, appealing gifts that nature has bestowed upon the Gewürztraminer grape. If grape yields in the vineyard are too high, the finished wine will lack the **PERFUME** and power that define the best wines. If the soils—limestone and chalk are the preferred soil types—are not mineral-rich, then the wine will lack the all-important **SPICY** aromas and flavors; *gewürz* means both "spicy" and "perfumed" in German. If the weather is too warm, the grapes will lack acidity, so the wine will taste flat, flabby, and **UNBALANCED**. However, if the growing region is not sunny, then ripening of the grape will suffer. A cool and sunny climate does not guarantee success, however, as this finicky grape is renowned as a variety that ripens unevenly, even in the best conditions. That makes picking the grapes at the right time—not too early or too late—difficult.

Classic Old World Gewürztraminer is a dry wine, with forward flavors of heady fruit and spice, intermingled and in balance. Alsace is considered the definitive growing region for this style of Gewürztraminer. Other styles seen less frequently include Late Harvest Gewürztraminer, which is produced from extremely ripe grapes, and the extremely rare and lusciously sweet botrytis-affected Gewürztraminer.

New World Gewürztraminer is made in several different styles. It is a hard-to-find wine when made as dry as the Gewürztraminer produced in Alsace, though a grow-

Gewürztraminer grapes

ing number of producers make a classic style. Much of the Gewürztraminer produced in the New World lacks the depth of mineral and spice of the Alsace style, but these fruitier versions can be quite attractive.

Where Gewürztraminer Grows

FRANCE

Alsace is home to the classic Gewürztraminer and has the ideal growing conditions for the Gewürztraminer grape: cool weather and lots of sunshine (see page 274). The wine is full-bodied, intensely **AROMATIC**, and most often dry. The Alsace style tends to be full-blown and full-bodied, with very ripe fruit character and a richly textured fullness in the mouth, but with a tendency toward a slight bitterness at the back of the palate.

Fine Alsace Gewürztraminer can age well for years. The simpler wines can be enjoyed in their youth, about three to five years after the vintage date. There are also sweet versions of Gewürztraminer produced in Alsace. As with Rieslings from Alsace, look for the label terms *Vendange Tardive* or *Sélection de Grains Nobles*.

GERMANY

Gewürztraminer grows mostly in the **ANBAUGEBIETE** (wine regions) of Pfalz (see page 504) and Baden (see page 507). Pfalz Gewürztraminer is rarely as dramatic a wine as its Alsatian counterpart; it is fruitier but less spicy. Baden, which is separated from Alsace by the Rhine River, produces some very elegant, full-bodied Gewürztraminer wines.

AUSTRIA

Here the grape is more likely to be called Traminer, and the wines tend to be less *gewürz* (spicy), except perhaps in the wine region of Steiermark, where the wines are both floral and full of spice. Other wine regions produce mostly sweet versions.

ITALY

The Alto Adige region is a bilingual area—Italian and German, as it was formerly part of Austria (see page 411). Alto Adige (Südtirol in German) is the birthplace of this grape. Here it is called either Traminer Aromatico (Italian) or Gewürztraminer (German). Most of it grows around the town of Tramin, and the wines tend to be medium-bodied, floral, but not very spicy in the nose and on the palate. We rarely see Gewürztraminer from Italy in the U.S. market.

THE UNITED STATES AND CANADA

In 1986, there were about 4,000 acres/1,600 hectares of Gewürztraminer in the United States, but today there are less than 2,000 acres/800 hectares cultivated. The reason? Gewürztraminer, which needs a cool climate, is expensive and labor-intensive to grow and will not bring nearly as much money per ton as cool-climate Chardonnay or Sauvignon Blanc. In California, Gewürztraminer is planted in the cooler parts of Mendocino, the Russian River, and Monterey County. The wines are mostly off-dry, with a few truly dry wines, especially from the Anderson Valley in Mendocino County. The Finger Lakes region of New York State produces a small amount of Gewürztraminer, as do Washington State and Oregon.

Canada does not specialize in Gewürztraminer, but there are several good examples produced in the Okanagan Valley of British Columbia, including a small selection of some fine Icewines, for which grapes are picked in late December or early January.

PINOT GRIS/PINOT GRIGIO

PINOT GRIGIO IS NOT really an Italian grape. The grape is Pinot Gris (the "Gray" Pinot), found most prominently in Alsace, France. In the vineyard, it is hard to tell if the grape is Pinot Gris or Pinot Noir until after color-changing *veraison*, as the leaves and grape shapes are identical. Pinot Gris is a variant of the Pinot Noir grape (as is Pinot Blanc). Although Alsatians think of it as a white grape, most Italians think of Pinot Gris as red, but in the end this may be a difference without a distinction, as the grape is treated as a white grape in the winemaking process. With just a little bit of SKIN CONTACT during fermentation, Pinot Gris can show a bit of pleasantly bronze to almost-pink COLOR in the wine.

Depending on their origins, wines made from Pinot Gris can be light- to medium-bodied and refreshing, as in Italy, or medium- to full-bodied with more emphatic flavor, as in Alsace. The fuller-bodied versions also exhibit a telltale richness of texture that is almost agreeably oily on the palate. At its best, Pinot Gris should exhibit spice, honey, honeysuckle, and nuttiness on the nose and tropical flavors on the palate, with just a touch of mineral. To achieve such concentration of flavor, fine Pinot Gris relies on low yields in the vineyard. If conditions are right at the end of the growing season, Pinot Gris grapes can be left on the vine to develop botrytis mold for the production of sweet wines.

TOP: *Pinot Gris (Pinot Grigio) grapes* BOTTOM: *Pinot Gris grapes with botrytis mold*

While Pinot Gris will always have its small number of admirers, it was not until the introduction of wines labeled "Pinot Grigio" that this grape found its place in the sun and on so many dining tables around the world, especially in the United States.

Where Pinot Gris/ Pinot Grigio Grows

FRANCE

Pinot Gris from Alsace defines the wine made from this variety, a full-bodied, assertive white wine that exhibits the classic aromatics and flavor profile of the grape, without a lot of oak overtones but with a medium-to-full body.

GERMANY

In the southern region of Baden, the wine is produced in a style similar to that of neighboring Alsace. The wine is most often labeled as Grauburgunder for dry wines, or Ruländer for sweet versions.

ITALY

There are several quality-driven producers in northeastern Italy, particularly in the province of Alto Adige, which borders Austria, that make clean, Alpine-crisp wines. In the Friuli–Venezia Giulia province of Italy, which borders Slovenia, Pinot Grigio tends to be richer and fuller-bodied. Tuscany produces Pinot Grigio in a fruit-driven, fairly simple style.

THE UNITED STATES: OREGON AND CALIFORNIA

Oregon, where the wine is most often labeled as "Pinot Gris," sets the benchmark for this varietal in the New World. At their best, the wines are complex, luscious, and full-bodied, with mineral- and fruit-driven flavors, without the intrusion of oak, that create a great marriage with a wide range of foods.

The most important Cal-Italian white grape in the Golden State, California produces quite a bit of Pinot Grigio (and a bit of "Pinot Gris"). Quality ranges from drinkable to excellent.

AUSTRALIA AND NEW ZEALAND

Artisan wine producers in both Australia and New Zealand are focusing on Pinot Grigio as a quality varietal, and the wines are beginning to appear in the American market. At the same time, there are many producers of market-driven Pinot Grigio in both countries.

VIOGNIER

The number of acres planted to this grape around the world has risen dramatically as a result of increased interest in Rhône grape varieties in general, and it is no surprise that Viognier wines have become so popular, since they positively explode with ripe, exotic fruit and floral aromas and flavors such as peach, mango, and papaya. The grape's natural acidity levels are rather low, a factor that simply means that the wines are best enjoyed fairly soon after bottling.

To thrive, the Viognier grape needs a warm climate. Yields in the vineyard should be low, otherwise the complex flavors of the wine will turn simple. The best Viognier wines are not oak-and-alcohol bombs but subtle wines with several layers of aroma and flavor.

Where Viognier Grows

FRANCE

The northern Rhône Valley produces Viognier wines of wondrous depth and structure, particularly Condrieu and

Viognier grapes

Château Grillet (see page 334). With an almost lanolin-like oiliness that coats the palate, it is not all that unusual to age these whites for four to seven years, but they are especially good to drink when young and fresh. In the southern Rhône Valley, Viognier is used mostly in blended wines.

Wine producers in southern France are making lots of varietal-labeled Viognier. These are good entry-level Viognier wines and are relatively inexpensive.

THE NEW WORLD

New World Viognier is characterized by luscious fruit and an appealing, rich viscosity and a silky texture.

Some of the best American Viogniers have a perfumed apricot and peach **NOSE** and a background of tropical fruit flavors. Good Viognier wines are produced from grapes grown in Washington, Texas, and Virginia, as well as California, where vineyards devoted to Viognier now exceed 1,500 acres/600 hectares.

Australia, New Zealand, and South Africa all produce varietal-labeled Viognier, but these are rarities in the export market. Consumers are more likely to find a blended white wine, usually comprised of Viognier, Marsanne, and Rousanne. A small amount of single-varietal Viognier is produced in Chile.

OTHER IMPORTANT WHITE GRAPE VARIETIES

CHENIN BLANC

CHENIN BLANC SEEMS to find its best expression in the Loire Valley of France, where the cool climate seems to provide perfect growing conditions. Wines made from Chenin Blanc are usually light in body, with **DELICATE** flavors and just a hint of implicit sweetness; they may exhibit aromas of melons or honey with a **NUTTY** overtone, and some smell a bit like beeswax. The tendency of the grape to maintain high acid levels keeps the wines fresh

and clean, especially when made semisweet to sweet, as they sometimes are in the Loire Valley.

In the United States, there are a handful of Chenin Blanc producers, but the grape has been largely relegated to a **BLENDING** role, mostly in inexpensive wines. Chenin Blanc is grown and produced widely in South Africa, where, particularly in its drier versions, it is often known as "Steen."

PINOT BLANC/ PINOT BIANCO

WINES MADE FROM PINOT BLANC often come across as light- to medium-bodied, with characteristics similar to those of Chardonnay, but they are simpler wines, much less obvious in flavor and elegance. The classic growing area for Pinot Blanc is Alsace, France. Good Pinot Blanc wines are produced in the Trentino–Alto Adige region of Italy (where it is called Pinot Bianco), as well as in Baden and Württemberg in Germany (where it is called Weissburgunder). A bit of Pinot Blanc, some of it quite good, is produced in California.

TOP: *Chenin Blanc grapes* BOTTOM: *Pinot Blanc grapes*

MUSCAT/MOSCATO

THERE ARE MANY CLONES of the Muscat grape, and most of them are associated with sweet wines. While Muscat is made as a fine sweet wine in places around the Mediterranean basin and California, dry versions of Muscat can be found in Alsace and Portugal. The grape is called Moscato in Italy and is used to make Asti (formerly Asti Spumante), a very fruity, light, sparkling wine in northern Italy. Sweet Greek wines made from Muscat, especially Muscat of Samos, are enjoyed internationally.

In all cases, the fruity character of the Muscat grape shines through, grapey and delicate in the lighter versions of northern Italy and California, full and luscious in the bigger, dry versions from Alsace. The sweeter wines usually display a greater richness in the glass and on the palate.

SÉMILLON

SÉMILLON IS a much-overlooked grape that produces some truly outstanding wines. As a dry wine, it has medium to full body and flavor intensity, with aromas of lanolin and peaches or ripe apricots. The sweet versions are more VISCOUS and more concentrated in their fruit character.

Sémillon is grown throughout the Graves region in Bordeaux, France, where it is blended with Sauvignon Blanc to make dry white wines. In Sauternes and Barsac, it is often affected by botrytis and is a major component in the sweet white wines of those areas. Depending on the vintage, it is sometimes the only grape used to make the glorious sweet Sauternes wine Château d'Yquem. It has been produced for decades as a dry wine in Australia, particularly in the Hunter Valley, often resulting in a wine of great depth and exceptional aging ability. Sweet wines are also produced in Australia, and the Australians popularized the dry "SemChard," a blend with Chardonnay.

Sémillon is also produced in California and Washington State as a single-varietal wine, as part of a blend with Sauvignon Blanc, or in a "SemChard" blend.

MÜLLER-THURGAU

DEVELOPED BY Professor Hermann Müller at the Geisenheim research station in Germany from a cross between Riesling and Chasselas, the Müller-Thurgau grape provides growers with an early-ripening, very fruity

LEFT: *Sémillon grapes* RIGHT: *Sémillon grapes with botrytis*

variety. It is a grape variety that offers many of the attractive, delicate aromas and flavors of the Riesling variety but with a shorter growing season, making it a more dependable ripener in cooler climates. It produces wines with attractive fruitiness and a hint of sweetness, but without the depth and breeding of the Riesling grape.

Until the early to mid-1990s, Müller-Thurgau was the most planted grape in Germany, but it has since been eclipsed by Riesling. Likewise, it was the most planted grape in New Zealand, until it was overtaken by Chardonnay and Sauvignon Blanc. Müller-Thurgau is still an important grape in these countries, as well as in the Trentino–Alto Adige region of Italy and in England.

ALBARIÑO/ALVARINHO

THIS GRAPE is known as Albariño in the Galicia region of northwestern Spain and as Alvarinho in the Vinho Verde appellation in Minho, a region of northern Portugal. In both countries, this cool-climate grape thrives, producing fresh, fruity wines with very high acidity. In Galicia in particular, where Albariño is often produced as a single-varietal wine with a varietal label, this grape has brought recognition to Spain as a producer of fine white wines, since the best versions offer vibrant fruit character of apricot and peach with attractive orange blossom aromas.

GRÜNER VELTLINER

ALONGSIDE RIESLING, this grape has brought fully deserved recognition to Austria as a producer of elegant and well-structured white wines. Grüner Veltliner is grown principally in the Kamptal, Kremstal, and Wachau regions and occupies a far greater percentage of all vine plantings in Austria than does Riesling, so we will continue to see many more of these wines in the future. Grüner Veltliner wines have a smooth texture and medium weight, a ripe stone fruit character, and an oddly attractive white pepper and cooked lentil aroma.

MARSANNE AND ROUSSANNE

MARSANNE IS MOSTLY associated with warmer climates, in which it can produce fruity, medium-bodied wines, but generally with lower acidity, a hint of an **EARTHY**, nutty, or truffle aroma, and a distinct note of orange peel or even marmalade when aged. It has most often been supported by the Roussanne grape in blends but is increasingly proving that it can make fine wines as a varietal on its own.

Roussanne can produce fine wines, typified by moderate to high acidity and an aromatic stone fruit character, but because of its low yields, it has too often been relegated to the role of adding fresh, clean fruit qualities to the great red wines of the Rhône Valley. When it is used as the primary grape for a white wine, most Roussanne wines achieve balance when blended with a bit of Marsanne.

The classic growing region for Marsanne and Roussanne is France's Rhône Valley, but the grapes also grow in other wine regions of southern France, Switzerland, Australia (particularly in Victoria), and in California.

MELON DE BOURGOGNE

BETTER KNOWN by its nickname, Muscadet, this grape has long been the mainstay of the vineyards in northwest France, especially the western end of the Loire Valley, where the grape's nickname has become the name of the region's most famous wine. Muscadet is usually a simple, straightforward, high-acid wine with green fruit characteristics, an excellent accompaniment to the wide array of simply prepared seafood of the region. It also responds well to prolonged contact with the **LEES** (**YEAST** sediment) after fermentation, which gives the wine a little more weight and smoothness. These wines are called Muscadet **SUR LIE**.

In addition to plantings in northwest France, some Melon is planted in California (where it was misidentified as Pinot Blanc for quite some time).

SECONDARY WHITE GRAPE VARIETIES

ALIGOTÉ Used in Burgundy in France for lesser-quality wines.

ANSONICA Also known as Inzolia, an important white grape in Sicily's white wines, as well as a component of the fortified wine Marsala.

ARINTO Also known as Pedernã, a high-acid grape from Portugal; often the anchor in blended white wines from warm climates.

ARNEIS An important grape, brought back from near extinction in Piedmont, Italy, where it makes a delicious medium-bodied wine. Also planted in California and the Pacific Northwest.

ASSYRTIKO The most important grape on the island of Santorini, Greece, producing acidic fruit-driven wines with good minerality.

BOAL One of the grapes used to make sweet Madeira wines (also spelled "Bual").

CHASSELAS In Switzerland, the short growing season of this grape makes it attractive to many grape growers, though the wines produced from it are generally simple, light wines, bordering on neutral.

COLOMBARD Fairly neutral in flavor, but a high-acid grape, grown in Western France mostly for brandy production. Very large acreage in California for bulk wine production and for inexpensive sparkling wines.

CORTESE Grown in northern Italy to make light, refreshing wines, especially Gavi in Piedmont.

FALANGHINA From Campania, Italy, it produces fruit-driven, light- to medium-bodied wines that are increasingly appreciated in export markets.

FIANO Mostly found in Campania; best known for producing the full-bodied, floral, almost spicy wine Fiano di Avellino.

FOLLE BLANCHE In the western Loire Valley of France, where it is known as Gros Plant, this grape makes fresh, **TART**, simple wines. It is also a staple in making the base wines for distillation into brandies such as Cognac and Armagnac.

FURMINT Used in the Tokaji region of Hungary to produce dry as well as sweet, botrytis-affected wines.

GARGANEGA The major grape in Soave from northern Italy.

GARNACHA BLANCA/GRENACHE BLANC Used for wines produced in Catalonia, Spain, and the southern Rhône Valley in France.

GODELLO The most important grape in the Valdeorras region of Spain. Known as Gouveio in Portugal. It produces aromatic, medium-bodied, fruit-driven wines.

GRECO BIANCO Grown in southern Italy, transplanted from Greece more than 2,500 years ago. It is best known for Greco di Tufo from Campania.

HONDARRIBI ZURI Used for the light, refreshing Spanish Basque wine Chacolí (Txacoli in the Basque language, Euskara), from Guetaria or Vizcaya.

MACABEO One of the grapes used in most blends to make Spanish sparkling wines (Cava), and part of the blend for some Roussillon whites in southern France, where it is called Maccabéo. It is the same grape as Viura, used in the production of white wines of Rioja in northern Spain.

MALVASIA Used to make the sweet versions of Madeira, and also planted widely in Italy to make fragrant dry and sweet wines. Widely planted in California to add fruitiness to jug wines.

MUSCADELLE Planted in the Entre-Deux-Mers and Graves regions of Bordeaux to add grapey fruitiness to the dry and sweet wines produced there. Also used to make sweet fortified wines in Victoria, Australia.

PALOMINO FINO The most widely used grape in the production of **SHERRY** in southern Spain.

PARELLADA Used in Catalonia, Spain, as a blending grape for sparkling Cava, but also on its own or in a blend as a fresh, delicate white.

PETITE ARVINE Grown in the Valais region of Switzerland and Valle d'Aosta, Italy, producing both fine dry and sweet wines.

PROSECCO Grown primarily in the Veneto region of Italy, the grape gives its name to the refreshing, dry to off-dry, mostly sparkling wine.

RKATSITELI Planted widely in Russia to produce fragrant, light wines with a hint of sweetness. Small amount of acreage in the Finger Lakes of New York State.

SCHEUREBE One of the most successful vinifera crossings from Germany, producing soft, fruit-forward, usually simple wines.

SERCIAL Most famous for the driest, lightest versions of Madeira, a Portuguese fortified wine, which, at its best, can age for many years.

THOMPSON SEEDLESS Widely planted in California and Australia for producing neutral base wines for blending in jug-wine production. Also used for table grapes and raisin production.

TORRONTÉS Produces Argentina's intensely aromatic, floral, spicy, medium-bodied dry wines.

TREBBIANO This is Italy's most widely planted white grape, though its wines are generally fairly neutral. It is the same grape known as Ugni Blanc in France, where it is primarily used to make the base wines for distillation into brandies such as Cognac and Armagnac.

VERDEJO The most important grape in the Rueda region of Spain, where it produces fragrant, fruity, very pleasant wines.

VERDELHO Used to make the off-dry version of Madeira.

Also grown in Australia, where it produces a fresh and fruity but simple dry or off-dry wine.

VERDICCHIO A grape of central Italy's Marche region that, handled well, can produce fresh, exciting, and fruity wines, as well as wines of some substance with a little wood treatment or yeast contact.

VERMENTINO A grape found throughout Italy. The best wines made from Vermentino are usually produced in Sardinia and Tuscany.

VERNACCIA There are actually several Italian grapes called by this name, but best known is the Vernaccia of Tuscany, used in Vernaccia di San Gimignano, a medium-bodied, fruity white with good acidity.

XAREL-LO One of the grapes used for blending to make most Spanish sparkling Cava and fine still wines.

MAJOR RED GRAPE VARIETIES

CABERNET SAUVIGNON

IT SEEMS THAT Cabernet Sauvignon grows everywhere, and that perception is not far from wrong. Almost any recognized wine region that is moderately warm to hot grows Cabernet Sauvignon, and red wine drinkers can't seem to get enough of this varietal. Why is it that Cabernet Sauvignon has captured the hearts, minds, and palates of millions of wine consumers and taken over hundreds of thousands of vineyard acres?

For one thing, wherever you grow it, Cabernet Sauvignon makes a wine that is recognizable, true to its varietal character. With vibrant aromas of black cherries, black currants, black plums, black olives, and **EUCALYPTUS** in a young wine, and hints of cedar and cigar box **BOUQUET** as it ages, Cabernet Sauvignon produces reliable, even predictable, full-bodied wine, with high degrees of both tannins and acidity.

The popularity of Cabernet Sauvignon is both its strength and its weakness. Without the commanding presence of this varietal, there simply would not be a successful wine industry and wine culture in Bordeaux, France, or the Napa Valley of California, or the Maipo Valley of Chile. Cabernet Sauvignon has put these regions on the world's wine map, but it has also diminished the impor-

tant traditional varietals of countries such as Italy and Spain, among others. Why is Cabernet Sauvignon so successful in the vineyards and wineries of so many of the world's wine regions and so popular with wine consumers, from the neophyte to the auction-conscious collector?

For grape growers, Cabernet Sauvignon is a smart choice; it grows in almost every wine-producing country of the world and adapts well to a wide variety of climates and soils. As a grape, Cabernet Sauvignon is very small, with one of the highest ratios of **SKIN** to juice, medium to high acidity, and intense black currant aromas and flavors that can be masked by high levels of tannin. The grape has a thick skin and is resistant to many of the plant viruses and diseases that plague less hardy varieties. For winemakers, the variety is also pliable. Depending on the desired style of the finished wine, Cabernet Sauvignon does well with either short or long maceration—exposure of the juice to

Cabernet Sauvignon grapes

the tannin-laden skins—anywhere from three days to longer than three weeks. The longer the maceration, the more tannins are evident in the young wine, which adds to the structure and potential longevity of the wine; a short maceration most often produces soft, easy-to-drink wines.

And Cabernet Sauvignon seems to have an affinity for oak, especially the assertive spicy vanilla flavors of new oak barrels. The **BARRIQUES** used to age Cabernet Sauvignon are most often 60 gallons/225 liters, and if all of the barrels are new, the result can be a dramatic, over-the-top, overtly alcoholic but smooth, sweet black cherry–like wine. Some of the best Cabernet Sauvignon wines are made using a regimen of new and used barrels to tone down the oak flavors in the finished wine, but the producers of these wines often do so at their own peril. Why? Because many of the most influential wine writers and critics who assign numerical scores (like 92 out of a possible 100 points, or heaven forbid, 82 out of 100) seem to favor wines that feature the overwhelming flavors of new oak. These writers and critics are powerful, not only because their opinions are published in the wine press, but also because their scores and their direct quotes about a wine often accompany a "neck hanger"—an in-store mini-ad that promotes the wine in a retail environment and influences the wine consumer.

Yet another reason for Cabernet Sauvignon's worldwide success is its ability to blend with other grapes that usually make softer, more approachable wines, diminishing Cabernet Sauvignon's aggressive qualities, its hard edges. With Cabernet Sauvignon as its anchor, a wine blended with, for example, 15 to 25 percent Merlot, Cabernet Franc, or both (and maybe an even smaller percentage of wines made from Malbec and Petit Verdot grapes) is a classic mix that started in Bordeaux and found its way around the world. Many esteemed Napa Valley Cabernet Sauvignons contain between 5 percent and 25 percent Merlot or Cabernet Franc (for a varietal name to grace a label in the United States, the wine in the bottle must be made from at least 75 percent of that named varietal; see page 116).

Cabernet Sauvignon's ability to blend with other wines takes the creative handcuffs off the winemaker, who can create his or her own style of Cabernet Sauvignon partially based on the chosen blend. And winemakers are not limited to the classic Bordeaux blending model. Just some examples: In Tuscany, Italy, literally hundreds of Super Tuscan wines (see page 390) are based on blends of Cabernet Sauvignon and Sangiovese, the most important traditional grape of the region. In several wine regions of Spain (see page 415), blends of Cabernet Sauvignon and Tempranillo are increasingly common. Australia (see page 224) is well-known for making a wide range of blended wines from Cabernet Sauvignon and Shiraz.

When produced as a single-variety red wine, Cabernet Sauvignon can be everything that white wine drinkers hate about red wine. At its worst, it may appear to be harsh and astringent (from the tannins), sour (from the acidity), very dry and drying on the palate, and too strongly flavored (if you can get beyond the tannins to taste anything). However, for those who enjoy red wines, it is important to note that there are also some fine examples of 100 percent Cabernet Sauvignon wines, some offering distinctive cassis fruit character with a background of **MINT** or eucalyptus and notes of cedar and thyme.

Because Cabernet Sauvignon is so flexible, there are almost as many styles of wine as there are winemakers. However, even though the wines vary stylistically, Cabernet Sauvignon is still one of the easiest wines to identify, as it exhibits its varietal character, whether it is a $10 Cabernet Sauvignon or a $200 Cabernet Sauvignon. Then what makes that $200 wine so special? The reason is that the best wines made primarily from the Cabernet Sauvignon grape display a sense of place, not just varietal character. What you are paying for is the "address" of the wine—its *terroir*—not only the grape that appears on the label.

In Bordeaux, you can pay a lot for the character of the soil and the heralded history of the estate (the "château") on which the grape is grown. In the New World, a "California Cabernet Sauvignon" should taste decidedly different from a "Napa Valley Cabernet Sauvignon," which should taste different from a "Rutherford Cabernet Sauvignon" (Rutherford is a town within the Napa Valley), and a single-vineyard "Rutherford Cabernet Sauvignon" should taste even more special than a wine made from grapes grown on more than one Rutherford vineyard or vineyard block. At each heightened level of perceived quality, the price goes up, and the difference between the California Cabernet Sauvignon and the single-vineyard Rutherford Cabernet Sauvignon can easily be more than $100.

Cabernet Sauvignon is bold and brawny and powerful, and its dark, brooding color and complex nature make a statement that may appeal to those looking for a definition of what a "**BIG** red wine" should be. While other red wines may have their adherents and boosters, the preeminent position of Cabernet Sauvignon remains unchallenged, at least for the immediate future.

Where Cabernet Sauvignon Grows

FRANCE

The Left Bank of Bordeaux is the quintessential classic region for both Cabernet Sauvignon vineyards and some world-famous Cabernet Sauvignon–based wines (see page 292). Specifically, most well-known are the subregions (and some of the most famous Cabernet Sauvignon–based wines) Haut-Médoc (Château Latour, Château Lafite-Rothschild, Château Mouton Rothschild, Château Margaux) and Graves/Pessac-Léognan (Château Haut-Brion).

Wines made from the vineyards in these Bordeaux subregions are most often judicious blends of Cabernet Sauvignon, Merlot, and Cabernet Franc, with grace notes sometimes provided by Malbec and Petit Verdot.

Outside Bordeaux, Southwest France grows a lot of Cabernet Sauvignon grapes and produces quite a bit of pretty good wine dominated by the variety. The Mediterranean provinces of Languedoc-Roussillon (see page 343) in south central France are awash in high-yielding Cabernet Sauvignon vineyards, where a huge volume of drinkable, mostly varietal-labeled Cabernet Sauvignon is produced.

ITALY

Cabernet Sauvignon has been planted sporadically in the vineyards of Italy for hundreds of years, but today the variety is purposefully planted in the majority of Italy's twenty provinces. In the cooler regions of the northeast—Veneto, Friuli–Venezia Giulia and Trentino–Alto Adige—there is a lot of wine produced. In Italy's other wine regions, Cabernet Sauvignon is sometimes produced as a single-varietal wine or as a Cabernet Sauvignon–Merlot blend. Often it is blended with wines made from indigenous varietals.

The most heralded blend is Cabernet Sauvignon and Sangiovese, made famous by the much sought-after and often expensive Super Tuscans. Sangiovese is the backbone of virtually all the traditional wines of Tuscany—most famously Chianti and Brunello di Montalcino—and Cabernet Sauvignon turns out to be a successful partner in many of the region's nontraditional blended wines. Some of the best-known examples in which Cabernet Sauvignon dominates the blend include Solaia, Sassicaia, Ornellaia, Excelsus, and Tinscvil.

In Lombardy and Emilia-Romagna, it is easy to find Cabernet Sauvignon–based wines, often blended with Merlot and Cabernet Franc. Some interesting, often delicious, wines are now being produced in southern Italy, where Cabernet Sauvignon may be blended with indigenous varietals, such as Aglianico, Nero d'Avola, and Gaglioppo. On the island of Sardinia, successful blends of Cabernet Sauvignon and Cannonau (the local name for the Grenache grape) are produced.

SPAIN

Cabernet Sauvignon is making its presence known in Spain, often blended with Tempranillo, in the wine regions Ribera del Duero and Rioja, among others. In the Penedès region of Catalonia, anchored by Barcelona, the historic and cultural influence of France is expressed in the choice of grapes to make wine, and Cabernet Sauvignon is one of the most important red grapes of the region. It is not uncommon to find varietal Cabernet Sauvignon or a Cabernet Sauvignon–Merlot blend produced in Penedès or neighboring wine regions, but it is just as common to find a Tempranillo–Cabernet Sauvignon blend. Also in Catalonia, the small but prestigious region of Priorato produces Cabernet Sauvignon–based wines as either single-varietal wines or blended with the indigenous varietals Cariñena (Carignan) or Garnacha (Grenache).

THE REST OF THE OLD WORLD

Cabernet Sauvignon grows in just about every wine-producing nation of the Old World, including Portugal, Greece, Bulgaria, Hungary, Romania, and even the warmer parts of Switzerland, Austria, and Germany. Cabernet Sauvignon is the most important red variety in the wines of Israel and high-quality wines from Lebanon, especially the esteemed Château Musar. Cabernet Sauvignon also grows in both India and China.

THE UNITED STATES: CALIFORNIA

Cabernet Sauvignon is the most widely planted red wine grape in the vineyards of California (see page 111). Due to a near-perfect match of climate and variety, Cabernet Sauvignon has become the signature grape for both the best "artisan" single-vineyard wines of the Napa Valley and the "industrial" vineyards of the Central Valley, as well as every peak and valley in between these extremes. Whichever Cabernet Sauvignon you choose, and at whatever price point, it still captures "sunshine in a bottle" and shows off its varietal character, a jammy, sweet attack of voluptuous black fruit, with a dry FINISH.

As in Bordeaux, varietal-labeled Cabernet Sauvignon from California will often contain a healthy dose of Merlot or Cabernet Franc or both in the finished blend, allowing the individual wine producer to tweak the wine to meet his or her own standards of balance and quality. Or just as often, the winemaker can anticipate taste preferences of the American wine consumer with such tweaks.

Cabernet Sauvignon has defined California's red wine industry, just as Chardonnay has defined it for white wine. The public has embraced California's Cabernet Sauvignon wines, whether from the shelves of supermarkets or the wine lists of the world's most expensive restaurants.

OTHER STATES AND THE REST OF NORTH AMERICA

Cabernet Sauvignon maintains a serious presence in the warmer parts of Washington State's Columbia Valley, such as the Red Mountain and Yakima Valley regions. Although the Merlot grape is the most planted red varietal in this moderately cool–climate state, Cabernet Sauvignon's ability to tough it out in cool weather allows producers to make some attractive wines.

In Oregon, there are about 600 acres/240 hectares of Cabernet Sauvignon planted mostly in the Rogue Valley and Umpqua Valley, but Oregon Cabernet Sauvignon lives in the shadow thrown by the state's premier red varietal, Pinot Noir.

New York State's Long Island wine regions grow and produce some very fine Cabernet Sauvignon, but in such small amounts that they rarely leave the New York metro area. Colorado, Idaho, New Mexico, Texas, and Virginia are among the many other Cabernet Sauvignon–producing states.

Canada, because of its cold temperatures, produces a lot more Cabernet Franc than Cabernet Sauvignon, but Mexico can produce some drinkable-to-very-good Cabernet Sauvignon, especially in the Baja Peninsula.

SOUTH AMERICA: CHILE AND ARGENTINA

Without Cabernet Sauvignon, there probably would be no Chilean wine industry. Chile produces a lot of Cabernet Sauvignon for the export market, and in the 1990s developed a reputation for true-to-varietal-type wines at bargain prices. You can still buy inexpensive Chilean Cabernet Sauvignon produced from mostly high-yielding vineyards, but you can also find *terroir*-driven, single-vineyard wines from the Maipo, Colchagua, Aconcagua, and Curicó wine regions, with high prices to match their pedigree.

In the Mendoza region of Argentina, there is some varietal Cabernet Sauvignon produced, but Cabernet Sauvignon is most often reserved for blending with the nation's premier red wine, Malbec. At their best, Argentine Cabernet Sauvignon and blends can exhibit assertive aromatics and complex flavors that make for some age-worthy wines.

AUSTRALIA, NEW ZEALAND, AND SOUTH AFRICA

Although Shiraz (Syrah) is the most important grape in the vineyards of Australia, the nation's wine regions produce a lot of full-bodied, jammy Cabernet Sauvignon too, and just like Shiraz, do so at every conceivable price. Cabernet Sauvignon–Shiraz blends are also quite popular and can be delicious.

Some of the best Australian Cabernet Sauvignon originates in the vineyards of South Australia, Victoria, and Western Australia.

New Zealand produces some fine Cabernet Sauvignon as well as Cabernet Sauvignon–Merlot blends, mostly from vineyards in the Hawkes Bay region, located on the southern tip of the nation's North Island.

Several wine producers in the Stellenbosch region of South Africa make some very fine Cabernet Sauvignon, sometimes blended with Merlot.

MERLOT

MANY WINE CONSUMERS have turned to Merlot as their preferred single-variety red wine (although they also seem to fall in and out of love with the grape on a regular basis). The Merlot grape is bigger than the Cabernet Sauvignon grape and has a lot more juice in proportion to its skin surface area. It is a thinner-skinned grape, with lower tannin levels and lower acid levels. Measure for measure,

Merlot almost always produces a softer, smoother, fruitier, more accessible wine than Cabernet Sauvignon.

Until the 1980s, Merlot, especially in the New World, was viewed primarily as a blender, most often used to soften the tannins and acidity of Cabernet Sauvignon. Today, although Merlot is still a fine blending wine for Cabernet Sauvignon, Merlot, as its own varietal, is successful around the world, pleasing wine consumers in the Old World, but especially in the New World, and specifically in the United States.

These days, Merlot wines feature aromas and flavors of ripe, sweet chocolate-covered black cherries tinged with oaky vanilla overtones, complete with a silky, voluptuous texture. Most wines made from Merlot are predictable fun and don't require a lot of thought and analysis to enjoy. The exceptions are some of the best wines produced in the classic Merlot grape–growing region Pomerol, on the cooler Right Bank of Bordeaux (the famous Château Pétrus is often 95 percent Merlot). There are a select group of Merlot producers in California and Washington State that also produce some memorable, even powerful, wines.

Aside from the small amount of exceptional Merlot wines that can age gracefully for years, most Merlot is best consumed within a few years of its vintage date. Unless it is a great wine from a great estate, it is not only unnecessary to age Merlot, in most cases it's a bad idea. Merlot usually lacks the tannins, acids, and overall structure that allow a wine to seriously improve with time.

Because Merlot is so popular, and because it ripens in cooler climates more readily than Cabernet Sauvignon, it is planted in almost all of the wine regions of the world, except in the absolute coldest places. Merlot grows in vineyards from Switzerland to Slovenia, from New Zealand to New York, from Austria to Australia, from Croatia to China, from South America to South Africa.

Where Merlot Grows

FRANCE

Merlot is the most planted grape in the Bordeaux region of France, and as the world clamors for soft, easy-to-drink reds, its varietal star is ascending here. While it plays a supporting role in the wines from the Left Bank of Bordeaux (including the Haut-Médoc and Graves regions), it is the star varietal on the Right Bank (including Pomerol and St-Émilion) and in the satellite appellations that produce accessible, less-expensive Bordeaux wines.

Merlot is the third-most-planted red grape in all of France, and its popularity is growing every year. It is grown throughout Provence and the southwest, and in the southern province of Languedoc, among many others. It may be used as the main grape or as a blender in these regions. There are many relatively inexpensive French wines made from 100 percent Merlot.

ITALY

Merlot is an important grape in Italy, with plantings growing exponentially over the last decade or so. The northeastern regions of Veneto and Trentino–Alto Adige mostly produce wines from vineyards with high yields, but they are easy to drink and affordable. In the same area, Friuli produces its share of workhorse wine but also some elegant examples of Merlot.

In the vineyards of Tuscany, Merlot has become an important grape for producing dozens of Super Tuscans, both varietal-labeled wines and blends, usually with the

Merlot grapes

Sangiovese grape as either the anchor or the seasoning for the finished wine. Sometimes Cabernet Sauvignon is blended with Merlot or with Merlot and Sangiovese to create these very popular—and often very expensive—Super Tuscans.

THE REST OF EUROPE

Merlot is planted in the warmer vineyard sites of Austria, Hungary, Romania, Bulgaria, and Moldova. In these countries the wines produced from the Merlot grape or from Merlot–Cabernet Sauvignon blends are drinkable and affordable. But it is in Switzerland's Italian-speaking Ticino region where Merlot positively dominates, producing some predictable quaffs and a few glorious wines.

THE UNITED STATES: CALIFORNIA AND WASHINGTON STATE

California produces wines that are fruit-forward with sweet blackberry flavors, and most often low in acids and tannins. Styles range from light and fruity to massive and complex, but almost always silky, satiny, and smooth on the palate.

A lot of Merlot is planted in the warm Central Valley, known these days for producing near-unlimited amounts of "fighting varietals"—relatively inexpensive California wines that "fight" for shelf space in supermarkets and high-volume wine retailers. These are simple, easy-to-drink, affordable wines that work well with a burger, a sandwich, or a slice of pizza; they are not meant to impress connoisseurs.

Merlot with more character is derived from the vineyards of California's cooler North Coast wine district, especially Napa, Sonoma, and Mendocino counties. These wines are darker in color, more concentrated in flavor, and feature ripe-to-overripe fruit flavors in an often full-bodied to massive high-alcohol wine. Some of these wines, especially those from Oakville, Rutherford, Stags Leap District, and Howell Mountain, all within the Napa Valley appellation, can be very expensive and hard to find. In Sonoma County, the vineyards and wineries of Sonoma Valley, Alexander Valley, Bennett Valley, and Knights Valley also produce some fine Merlot wines.

Washington State has developed quite a reputation for the quality of its Merlot wines, both on the small-producer "boutique" level and the grand scale. Growers in the Columbia Valley and Walla Walla Valley have to work hard to make sure all is right in the vineyard and have to hope

for winters that are not too frigid. In Washington, Merlot is second only to Chardonnay in total acres planted, and it is the most important red grape in the entire Pacific Northwest wine industry.

AUSTRALIA AND NEW ZEALAND

Although plantings of Merlot are increasing every year in Australia, it is a grape that has yet to really catch on as the basis for varietal-labeled wines (only 4 to 5 percent of its vineyards are planted with Merlot). Add to this the tradition of blending Shiraz—not Merlot—with Cabernet Sauvignon, and Australia has a bit of a learning curve to get over when it comes to producing Merlot on a large scale.

Most of Australia is quite warm, ideal for Cabernet Sauvignon but not cool enough for Merlot, so SITE SELECTION will become a very important issue if this variety is to have a happy future.

New Zealand is cooler than Australia, and the southern tip of the North Island may be an ideal climate to grow Merlot. Indeed, Merlot is New Zealand's third most planted grape (Sauvignon Blanc and Chardonnay are first and second, respectively, making Merlot the most-planted red grape in the nation). About half of the Merlot plantings are in Hawkes Bay, with about 30 percent in the Auckland wine district. On the northern tip of the South Island, Merlot appears to have a serious future in the warmer spots in the Marlborough wine region, currently known only for its white wines, particularly Sauvignon Blanc.

PINOT NOIR

PINOT NOIR IS a difficult grape to grow successfully. It is a thin-skinned grape that traditionally needs a long, cool growing season. Cool weather allows Pinot Noir to develop attractively high levels of acidity, although it can make ideal ripening difficult. Because the grape is light-colored and thin-skinned, tannins are usually soft and subtle. When all of the elements of nature collide successfully, Pinot Noir vineyards can provide the raw material for glorious medium-bodied wines. But these elements strike a delicate balance that, when things go wrong in the vineyard, can just as easily create wines that are unpleasant, sometimes with green, unripe flavors, sometimes with flavors of cooked and stewed fruits, overripe and foul.

There is no real consensus about what kind of soil is best

for growing Pinot Noir, but most growers point to soils rich in either limestone or clay. The soils of Champagne are rich in chalk, but in most growing years the grapes ripen just enough for use in sparkling wine and would be considered "green," or underripe, for still wines. What almost all growers do agree on is that the soil must be well drained and not overly fertile, to keep yields low.

Growing Pinot Noir is not for everybody. Indeed, people who happily grow Chardonnay, Cabernet Sauvignon, and other less-tricky varietals are often intimidated by the idea of growing Pinot Noir. It isn't so much that these growers are incapable of doing a good job in the vineyards and in the winery, it's that everybody has their own opinions on what "a good job" is when it comes to judging wines made from this grape.

Pinot Noir is a very finicky grape that defies definition when it comes to style and expectation in the finished wine. Pinot Noir celebrates both its sense of place and the human touch; depending on where it is grown and who is growing it, this varietal may produce a wine very unlike its nearest neighbor or the most distant vineyards. Pinot

Pinot Noir grapes

Noir is probably the most *terroir*-driven of all red wines (it's Riesling for whites).

Fine Pinot Noir is a wine of medium-intense fruitiness, just enough tannin to give it structure, high acidity for delicacy and freshness, a floral and herbal aroma, red berry or CHERRY flavors, and a silky texture that is truly beguiling. At its worst, the floral aroma will decay into the euphemistically named barnyard aroma (an unattractive feral animal smell), the wine's delicacy becomes lightness, the fruitiness just is not there, and the acidity only provides a sour taste.

With Pinot Noir you usually get what you pay for—an axiom that is perhaps truer for this varietal than for any other. Bargain-priced Pinot Noir made for early drinking can be charming in its simplicity, tasting of strawberries and, to a lesser extent, cranberries and red raspberries. Moving up the quality ladder, the wines take on more complexity, with a mix of spiced strawberries and black cherries, and noticeably higher acidity on the palate. The most complex examples of fine Pinot Noir will demonstrate aromas and tastes of both red and black fruits, with earthbound aromas of mushroom, LEATHER, CHARRED wood, SMOKE, and moist soil. These wines can age from five to ten years and even longer, and are usually rare and expensive.

More a cliché than a statement of certifiable fact is that the best wines made from Pinot Noir should mimic wines from Burgundy, France, where the grape has been cultivated for at least six hundred years and possibly more than sixteen hundred. Pinot Noir is celebrated in Burgundy and is by law the only red grape allowed to be grown on its best vineyard sites. It may be a good idea that good Pinot Noir should taste like fine Burgundy, but it is also an idea that is nearly impossible to put into practice because the beauty of great red Burgundy is that each one tastes different. So, to define good Pinot Noir based on "the Burgundy model" is an almost meaningless generalization. When it comes to Pinot Noir, one size does not fit all.

Where Pinot Noir Grows

FRANCE: BURGUNDY AND CHAMPAGNE

In Burgundy, the only red grape planted in the northern subregions of Côte de Nuits and Côte de Beaune (collectively known as "Côte d'Or"; see page 318) is Pinot Noir. The Côte d'Or, especially the Côte de Nuits, is home to some of the most famous and sought-after Pinot Noir vineyards in the world. Here, *terroir* carries the day, as wines produced from a small vineyard, or a small part of a larger vineyard, will taste noticeably different—not necessarily better or worse, but different—from a vineyard site less than a thousand feet down the road or up a hill.

There is also a lot of good Pinot Noir from Burgundy at more affordable prices than the most-prized reds from the Côte d'Or, produced a bit farther south in the Côte Chalonnaise subregion (see page 326).

In the Champagne region (see page 277), Pinot Noir is one of only three grapes; the other two are the red Pinot Meunier and the white Chardonnay. These are the only legal grapes in Champagne, and most Champagnes are made from a blend of wines made from varying percentages of these grapes. Champagne is the coldest wine region in all of France, and Pinot Noir usually ripens just enough to produce a wine that is high in acidity that meshes beautifully with bubbles to refresh the palate. Since most Champagne is a white sparkling wine, there is very little skin contact—the skin is where all the color is—when Pinot Noir grapes are fermented. Some fine ROSÉ Champagnes rely on skin contact with Pinot Noir or Pinot Meunier to produce a pink sparkling wine.

THE REST OF EUROPE

Pinot Noir also grows in Germany (see page 487), where it is known as Spätburgunder, and in Austria (see page 508), where the grape is often called Blauburgunder. In Italy (see page 351), where it is most often called Pinot Nero, the variety is grown in Lombardy as an essential constituent of the excellent sparkler, Franciacorta. Pinot Noir is also widely planted in the Alto Adige region, where it produces fine still wine, and there is some good Pinot Noir produced in Tuscany. Switzerland (see page 512) grows the grape and makes some light versions of the wine, but mostly Pinot Noir is blended with Gamay to make the country's most famous red, Dôle.

THE UNITED STATES: CALIFORNIA, OREGON, AND NEW YORK STATE

California (see page 111) had to navigate a massive learning curve to succeed with Pinot Noir, and even today, great California Pinot Noir is a rarity, but a sublime one. The coolest regions are some of the premier growing regions for Pinot Noir: Carneros, which is a shared appellation between Napa and Sonoma counties, the Russian River Valley (and especially its subregion, Green Valley) in Sonoma County, the Anderson Valley in Mendocino, the Santa Maria Valley in Santa Barbara, Santa Ynez Valley in San Luis Obispo, and Mount Harlan in San Benito.

The complaint against California's Pinot Noir has been that the wines lack balance, are too jammy, too alcoholic, too "big," too Cabernet-like. California winemakers still produce some of these wines, but more and more Pinot Noir is being made with a gentle touch, made with restraint. The future of high-quality, carefully selected California Pinot Noir seems assured. Over the medium-to-long term, the prospect of climate change and global warming in California may have a negative impact on growing high-quality Pinot Noir grapes.

Oregon (see page 194) is on the same latitude as Burgundy, and although the entire state produces a bit more than 1 percent of the nation's wine, it has developed a well-earned reputation for its Pinot Noir. In particular, the Willamette Valley is considered one of the best places in the New World for growing this grape. The finest of these wines are delicate but substantive, and beautifully balanced. The overwhelming majority of Oregon Pinot Noir winemakers are artisans, producing small amounts of very fine wines. As in California, prices run the gamut from bargains to very expensive, and quality runs from good basic varietal character to very special and rare, true to vineyard *terroir* and vintage conditions.

New York State grows a small amount of Pinot Noir, most of it in the cool Finger Lakes and Hudson River regions. In the Finger Lakes, the grape is an important component in sparkling wines, and little by little good varietal Pinot Noir is being produced on a small scale. In the Hudson River Region, a tiny amount of high quality Pinot Noir is produced.

THE SOUTHERN HEMISPHERE: CHILE, NEW ZEALAND, AUSTRALIA

Pinot Noir seems to have a bright future in the Southern Hemisphere. Chile's coastal Casablanca Valley (see page 216), which is best-known for nurturing Chardonnay and Sauvignon Blanc, also provides a good home for Pinot Noir, producing wines that strike a balance between delicacy and juicy ripeness and are very appealing.

Pinot Noir looks promising in New Zealand (see page 241). In the Martinborough region, on the southern tip of its North Island, and in Central Otago, on the southern tip of its South Island, cool-climate New Zealand is growing and producing some very exciting and delicious Pinot Noir. Central Otago is actually the coldest place in the Southern Hemisphere to grow this varietal, and the results are highly encouraging.

Australia (see page 224) produces a handful of good Pinot Noir wines, with the Yarra Valley, located on the outskirts of Melbourne in the state of Victoria, showing real promise. Only about 2 percent of vineyard plantings in Australia are Pinot Noir, and much of the fruit is utilized quite successfully as part of the blend for **MÉTHODE CHAMPENOISE** sparkling wines.

SYRAH/SHIRAZ

SYRAH AND SHIRAZ are actually the same grape, but with different names. "Syrah" is the Old World name for the grape, while "Shiraz" is definitely a New World name, closely identified with, but not limited to, Australia. Grape growers, winemakers, and wine consumers have embraced this varietal with enthusiasm.

There is more Syrah planted in France than anywhere on earth (about 100,000 acres/40,000 hectares), and Australia plants at least 70,000 acres/28,000 hectares of Shiraz, securing second place. The United States and

Syrah (Shiraz) grapes

Argentina—both use "Syrah" or "Shiraz" on their wine labels—are in a virtual tie for third place with about 12,000 acres/4,800 hectares planted in each country. The popularity of Syrah or Shiraz is growing, however it's labeled, and plantings are increasing dramatically worldwide.

In Europe, the classic growing region for Syrah is the northern Rhône Valley of France. The Rhône Valley is the coolest place in the world for growing Syrah, but its heat-retaining slopes composed of granite soils help make ripening of the grape possible.

In the New World, Shiraz and Australia have become nearly synonymous. Original vine cuttings for Shiraz were brought from the Rhône Valley to Australia in the nineteenth century, and vineyards are located in various parts of the states of South Australia and New South Wales, with fewer plantings in the cooler states of Victoria and Western Australia. Overall, Australia's vineyards are the warmest sites in the world for growing Shiraz.

There are many different styles of Syrah/Shiraz wines in the marketplace. The wine can be fashioned as a light- to medium-bodied easy sipper or as a massive red wine. In between these two extremes, a full gamut of Syrah/Shiraz styles, from sunny simplicity to extraordinarily earthy elegance, abound. As a bonus, add to these multiple personalities of Syrah/Shiraz the fact that it is an excellent blending grape with numerous other varietals, especially Grenache, Mourvèdre, and Cabernet Sauvignon.

Where Syrah/Shiraz Grows

FRANCE: THE RHÔNE VALLEY AND LANGUEDOC-ROUSSILLON

As we mentioned earlier, the northern Rhône Valley defines classic Old World Syrah. The steep slopes, rich in granite soil, provide just enough sunshine and warmth for full ripening, but not too much. So, at their best, the Rhône wines made from Syrah are redolent of black fruits, complex earthy aromas, a lovely tannin-acid balance, and a kick of black pepper in the nose and on the palate. Depending on what district the grapes are grown in, the wines can be lighter or darker in color, medium or full in body, with flavors that span from jammy to roasted fruits.

Wines from the Hermitage and Côte-Rôtie districts are perhaps the most famous Syrah wines in the world, producing strong, sturdy wines of deep purple color, capable of aging for many years. Syrah thrives here, providing a lot of tannins but retaining enough acidity to keep the wines tasting fresh. The best examples offer dark plum aromas and flavors, a **PEPPERY** spiciness on the palate, and a hint of the aroma and flavor of smoked or cured meats.

The Languedoc-Roussillon area (see page 343), the "Midi" of the south of France, actually has twice as many Syrah vines planted as the Rhône Valley. Here an endless stream of drinkable and affordable varietal-labeled Syrah and Syrah blends are produced from very warm vineyard sites.

THE REST OF EUROPE

Syrah is planted in the Valais region of Switzerland; Swiss Syrah can be very tasty, but is virtually invisible in the U.S. market. We do find small patches of Syrah planted all over Italy, where there are some producers making 100 percent Syrah wines, but most blend with Italian varietals, especially Sangiovese in Tuscany and Nero d'Avola in Sicily. Several of these Italian wines are sold in the United States.

There is quite a bit of Syrah planted in the Catalonia region of Spain, as well as significant plantings in Greece.

THE UNITED STATES: CALIFORNIA AND WASHINGTON STATE

In the United States, the grape is grown and the wine is made under either name, Syrah or Shiraz. California has been planting Syrah in earnest since the 1970s. California Syrah is now much sought-after by wine consumers, and some of them enjoy Syrah as an alternative to the more predictable Merlot and Cabernet Sauvignon.

Today, Syrah is being planted in California's best wine-growing regions; the challenge is to find vineyard sites that are not too warm so that the finished wine is not a high-alcohol, full-bodied heady fruit bomb. The best California Syrah wines, made from vineyards located in cooler coastal regions, can be excellent and tend to follow the Rhône model of Syrah. Wines of restrained earthy power, they are great with hearty foods.

Washington State has enthusiastically embraced Syrah. Here, Syrah thrives in the cooler climes of the Columbia Valley, Walla Walla Valley, and especially the Yakima Valley. The best wines are deceptively soft and **SUPPLE**, with ripe, even sweet fruit flavors, but with balanced tannins and acidity—wines that are enjoyable now or ten years from now.

AUSTRALIA

Australia has been growing Shiraz since the early 1800s, and for most of that time it was considered to be a reliable but undistinguished varietal; the future was all about Cabernet Sauvignon and Chardonnay. Starting in about 1990, Shiraz came out of its shell, and successfully. With an international marketing push and with some very good wines that fit in perfectly with the New World wine drinker's shift from delicate wines to big, brawny reds, people began to enjoy drinking Shiraz. Shiraz also fits the new, less-formal bistro-style dining that is permeating New World cultures. Australian wine producers even produce sparkling Shiraz, some of it very good.

Australian Shiraz continues its success in the international market and has spurred interest in the Shiraz category in general. A possible problem on the horizon for Australia and its premier grape is the issue of climate change and global warming. At the time of this writing, much of Australia's vineyards were suffering the effects of five consecutive years of drought and a serious problem with obtaining enough water for irrigation.

ZINFANDEL

ZINFANDEL IS OFTEN thought of as *the* California grape. While Zinfandel grapes grow in several American states, and Italy, Australia, Chile, Mexico, and South Africa also produce small amounts of Zinfandel, it is California that defines Zinfandel for wine drinkers.

Zinfandel is an adaptable grape for winemakers. Decades ago, Zinfandel was a mainstay of many inexpensive blended jug wines produced in California, since it was recognized as providing huge amounts of ripe **BERRY** flavors and lots of sugar for sweetness and alcohol. Later, Zinfandel became famous in the production of the light **BLUSH** or pink wines called White Zinfandel, which are fruity, simple, but honest wines.

Bob Trinchero of Sutter Home Winery introduced White Zinfandel in 1972, and much of the American wine-drinking public, including many new wine consumers, responded en masse to the concept and the flavor of the wine. From 1975 to 1994, off-dry to semisweet White Zinfandel was the most popular varietal-labeled wine in the world. White Zinfandel is no longer quite so popular, having been eclipsed by Chardonnay and other varietals, but Sutter Home still sells more White Zinfandel than any other California winery.

Today, Zinfandel grapes are respected for their ability to produce classic, full-bodied red wines with a woodsy, wild-berry character and a distinctive spicy quality, particularly from the Sierra Foothills and North Coast areas of California. The best examples of Zinfandel—deep, dark, rich, earthy red wine—begin in warmer vineyard sites. Zinfandel thrives on heat, and this is one of the few varieties that can actually benefit from a bit of over-ripening. The best climate combination for Zinfandel is a summer filled with really hot days (from 90°F/32°C and up) and pretty cool nights (a drop to as low as 40°F/4°C), enabling the grower to preserve both high degrees of ripeness and sufficient acidity in the grapes. California has at least 50,000 acres/20,000 hectares of Zinfandel vines planted, and the best vineyards fit this ideal climate profile.

In California, there are quite a few acres of "old vines." Old-vine Zinfandel, made from grapevines planted in poorer soil, sometimes dry-farmed (no **DRIP IRRIGATION**), often organically grown, and with naturally lower yields, produce wines of compelling complexity and depth. Sometimes the term "Old Vines" (or "Old Vine") will appear on a label; there is no legal meaning for the term.

Depending on the style of the finished wine, Zinfandel

Zinfandel grapes

can exhibit a wide variety of aromas: red fruits in a lighter wine, dried black fruits in a full-bodied version; a hint of black pepper in a young Zinfandel, with dark chocolate in a mature, Port-style Zinfandel. Basically, what you want to look for in any good glass of Zinfandel is the assertive aromas of fruits—red raspberries, cranberries, strawberries in the lightest versions; black cherries, black plums, even raisins and black figs in the brooding, big Zinfandels. A pleasant smattering of herbs provides some grace notes, as do oak-barrel inspired spice and vanilla.

Internationally, Italy is by far the most important producer of Zinfandel, but under its Italian name, Primitivo. Researchers using DNA analysis have identified Zinfandel as being the same as the Primitivo grape of southern Italy. No matter its patrimony, it is California that has focused on Zinfandel and has placed Zinfandel on the world's current wine map.

Where Zinfandel Grows

THE UNITED STATES: CALIFORNIA

Zinfandel is the second-most-planted red grape in California (Cabernet Sauvignon is first), and depending on where and when it was planted, results in the grapes and finished wines can be dramatically different.

Sonoma County grows a lot of Zinfandel and producers here make some excellent wines, especially in the Dry Creek Valley wine district. Warm days and cool nights give Dry Creek Zinfandel a perfect platform to excel. The slightly warmer Alexander Valley is also a fine place to grow the grape. Sonoma is home to several single-vineyard Zinfandel wines, which display their sense of place with delicious dignity.

The Napa Valley can produce some extraordinary Zinfandel, but here Zinfandel lives in the shadow of Cabernet Sauvignon. Old-vine Zinfandel from the vineyards of the Redwood Valley of Mendocino County make some of the state's best wines. Paso Robles has some old vines, too, and has made quite a reputation for itself with artisan Zinfandel from the boulder-strewn Paso Robles soils. In Santa Cruz, Paul Draper of Ridge Vineyards makes what many consider to be the finest Zinfandel wines produced in California, and these wines really are singular and remarkable.

The Sierra Foothills wine region is synonymous with Zinfandel; more than 80 percent of the vineyards are dedicated to the grape. There is quite a bit of old-vine Zinfandel here, and the wines from both the small and larger producers can be earthy, complex, and memorable.

In the very warm Central Valley, quite a bit of Zinfandel is grown, and some of it ends up in White Zinfandel or in bargain-brand Zinfandels; some is used for blending into other varietal-labeled wines. But the Lodi district in this area, where the breezes from the delta cool things off, produces some very fine Zinfandel, some of it from old vines.

ITALY

In Italy, the grape is called Primitivo, and the wine world never took notice of it until 1994, when researchers at the University of California, Davis proved that Primitivo and Zinfandel have the same DNA. Prior to this, Primitivo, grown in southern Italy, was used by the Italian wine industry to "bulk up" inferior wines produced in northern Italy. Since the DNA discovery, the southern province of Puglia has begun to specialize in Primitivo, and most of these wines are quite satisfying.

GRENACHE

GRENACHE (called Garnacha in Spain) is one of the most widely planted red varieties in the world, with most of those grapes growing in Spain (at least 225,000 acres/90,000 hectares) and France (about 125,000 acres/50,000 hectares). There is quite a bit planted in Italy (where it is sometimes known as Cannonau), and substantial amounts are found in Australia and California.

A grape that thrives in warmer climates, Grenache produces soft, smooth, round wines with mouthfuls of ripe, sweet, red plum flavors. Like Syrah, with which it is often blended in the Rhône Valley of France, it can attain high sugar levels when ripe, providing the wines with alcohol levels in the 13, 14, even 15 percent range. A major disadvantage is that some clones are prone to oxidation as a grape, as juice, and as wine, which often means that the wines turn out with a distinct orange-brown note in the color. The advantage of wines that oxidize quickly is that they are usually softer and more accessible when young.

In order for Grenache to achieve greatness, it must be treated well in the vineyard. Low yields are key, and avoiding over-ripeness and too-high sugar levels is very important if the grapes are to make a fine wine. When best

practices are followed in the vineyard and in the winery, Grenache, either on its own or in a blend, can create a fine, fruit-forward wine with a unique, earthy elegance.

Where Grenache Grows

Until fairly recently, the only place that Grenache has received anything close to a full measure of respect is in the southern Rhône Valley of France, where it is the dominant grape and the anchor of the famous blended wine Châteauneuf-du-Pape (see page 340), among many others. But lately, things have been looking up for Grenache.

Some very good varietal-label Grenache and blends are being produced from grapes grown in Australia and in California. The New World has copied the Old World, blending Grenache with Syrah and another important red grape of the Rhône Valley, Mourvèdre. It is not uncommon to see New World wines, especially from Australia, labeled as "GSM," a blend of Grenache, Syrah, and Mourvèdre.

In Spain, where it has always been taken for granted as a workhorse, old-vine Garnacha grapes are producing magnificent wines in the Priorato region (see page 434), even as it continues to be an important constituent in the red wines of Rioja (see page 431), but subservient to the more esteemed Tempranillo grape. In the Navarra region (see page 430), Garnacha makes some of the loveliest dry rosé wines in the world, just as Grenache does in the Tavel

Grenache grapes

region (see page 342) of the southern Rhône valley. On the Italian island of Sardinia (see page 375), Cannonau can produce some delicious, earthy red wines.

OTHER IMPORTANT RED GRAPE VARIETIES

CABERNET FRANC

RELATED TO CABERNET SAUVIGNON, Cabernet Franc is also a small grape with high acidity, but it has a less intense flavor profile and a distinctive mineral, ashlike aroma. With the exception of the Loire Valley in France, where for decades it has been the dominant grape in the red wines Chinon, Bourgueil, and Saumur-Champigny, Cabernet Franc is more often used to blend with Cabernet Sauvignon and Merlot, as in Bordeaux. Quite a few producers in California, the Pacific Northwest, and the eastern United States have had good success making varietal wines from Cabernet Franc.

As a blending grape, Cabernet Franc is prized for its acidity, distinctive aroma, and strawberry-like fruit qualities. As a single-variety wine, it is usually medium-bodied, with fresh acidity and moderate-to-high intensity of flavor, balanced tannins, and bright red berry characteristics with a mineral, gravelly streak.

GAMAY

IN THE WINE LEXICON, the Gamay grape and wine from the Beaujolais region of France are almost synonymous. Once vilified by Philip the Bold as "that filthy grape" and banished by him from the northern stretches of Burgundy forever, Gamay now thrives in the Beaujolais region. The wines made from Gamay vary in intensity, but most of them are low in tannin, light, fresh, and fruity, with a sort of fruit-punch flavor. Were it not for the fresh, **BRIGHT** ruby color, they would be more in the style of many white wines than red, making them the perfect red wine for outdoor barbecues, picnics, and summertime drinking.

Gamay is the only red grape planted in the Beaujolais region of France. There is quite a bit of Gamay planted in Switzerland, and a small amount of acreage is dedicated to Gamay in California, New York State, and Canada.

MOURVÈDRE

THIS DARK PURPLE GRAPE thrives in warmer climates as in Spain, southern France, California, and Australia, and it is used in all those regions to add rich, plummy fruit character, color, and extra tannin structure to blended red wines. In Spain, where it is an important grape in the wine regions of Catalonia and and the Jumilla *denominación* in southern Spain, it is usually called Monastrell (Mourvèdre used to be referred to as Mataro in Australia). With the strong revival of interest in Mediterranean grape types, many Australian

TOP: *Gamay grapes* BOTTOM: *Pinot Meunier grapes*

and Californian wine producers are marketing single-variety wines, or offering blends of Mourvèdre along with its usual partners, Syrah and Grenache.

PINOT MEUNIER

THIS GRAPE IS often thought of as the other red grape permitted in the blend to make Champagne in France, although it is the most widely planted of all the Champagne varieties. It is very useful in providing the softer red berry fruit aromas and flavors that round out the whole blend. As sparkling wine production has increased in parts of the New World, more and more growers have planted Pinot Meunier as a complement to their Pinot Noir and Chardonnay to emulate the classic true Champagne blend. A handful of sparkling wine producers in California and Australia also produce Pinot Meunier as a red varietal wine.

BARBERA

THE MOST-PLANTED GRAPE in Piedmont, Italy, and the second-most-planted red grape in that nation, Barbera produces medium- to full-bodied wines with a dark ruby color, vibrant red and dark berry characteristics, and very, very pleasing acidity. A few producers have also produced much more substantial wines from specific vineyard plots and by using oak aging. Barbera also once occupied significant acreage in California for jug wine production but is now enjoying a bit of a new lease on life as a single-variety wine. It is also found in Argentina.

NEBBIOLO

THE GRAPE RESPONSIBLE for producing the "king and queen" of Italian wines, Barolo and Barbaresco, the most esteemed red wines from the Piedmont region of Italy (see page 363), Nebbiolo is truly a noble grape. It is capable, in good vintages, of producing big, full-bodied wines that, when young, have high tannin levels but are likely to evolve into elegant, velvety-smooth wines with flavors of ripe and dried fruit, overtones of tea, and a distinct aroma of tar and leather. Some Nebbiolo wines have a more noticeable **WOOD** and vanilla character if they are aged in small oak barrels as opposed to the more traditional large oak casks.

Aside from the Piedmont, where it also provides the base for Ghemme, Gattinara, and Roero wines, Nebbiolo is widely planted in the Valtellina region of Lombardy, Italy, where it is known as Chiavennesca. There is also a bit of Nebbiolo planted in California.

SANGIOVESE

FOR MANY YEARS, this grape remained relatively obscure, since its reputation was mainly based on its role as the majority grape in the blend used to make Chianti. Both within Italy and elsewhere, it is now recognized as capable of producing very fine wines that are prized for their distinctive floral and herbal aromas and sour cherry flavors.

Sangiovese, although the most-planted red grape in all of Italy, defines the classic red wines of Tuscany, Italy; the most famous example is Brunello di Montalcino, which must be 100 percent Sangiovese. Other famous Sangiovese-based Tuscan reds include Chianti and Chianti Classico, Vino Nobile di Montepulciano, Carmignano, and Morellino di Scansano. Many of the modern, nontraditional wines of Tuscany—the Super Tuscans—feature Sangiovese on its own or in a blend with international varietals. As with all grape varieties, there are numerous clones of Sangiovese, including Sangioveto, Brunello, Prugnolo, and Morellino.

In the 1980s and 1990s, a fair amount of Sangiovese was planted in California, but although the wines produced from those grapes were pleasant, they lacked traditional Sangiovese character. Based on the California experience, it appears that Sangiovese is at home in Italy but does not travel well.

TEMPRANILLO

OVER THE PAST several years, Tempranillo has received the recognition it has long deserved as the key to some of the finest wines produced in northern Spain, where it produces wines with sturdiness, a **BACKBONE** of acidity and tannin, and a depth of dark fruit flavors, such as plum and blackberry.

The most important growing areas for Tempranillo in Spain are Rioja, Ribera del Duero, and Catalonia. In Portugal, where it is known as Tinto Roriz, the grape is an important constituent in both dry red wines and the famous fortified wine Porto. There is a small amount of acreage dedicated to Tempranillo in California and in Australia.

TOURIGA NACIONAL

This is the most prized and highly respected of all the grapes used in the production of Porto wines from the hot, baked Douro region of Portugal. Touriga Nacional is particularly admired for the dense, ripe, dark fruit qualities, high sugar content, and ripe tannin structure that ensure long, slow development in the bottle over ten years at least, if not twenty, thirty, or more. It is also used on a regular basis in the production of dry red wines from Douro and from the Dão region, also in Portugal.

MALBEC

In the right (that is, fairly warm) climate, this grape has long been prized for its ability to produce wines with a rich, ripe plum character, solid structure, and overtones of dried leaves and potpourri. The most-prized versions continue to come from Cahors in France and especially from the Mendoza region of Argentina, where it has become that nation's most important varietal. There is more Malbec planted in Argentina than in any other country.

In cooler climates, Malbec is appreciated for its ability to add color, dense fruit, and acidity to the basic Bordeaux-style blend of Cabernet Sauvignon and Merlot. As such, it has been increasingly adopted for blending by Cabernet Sauvignon winemakers in California and Australia.

Some French regions use the names Cot, Pressac, or Auxerrois for this grape.

PINOTAGE

This grape type was developed in South Africa as a vinifera cross between the hot-climate Cinsaut and the cooler-climate Pinot Noir in the hope of creating a more elegant and acidic grape still capable of offering plenty of ripe fruit as a wine. Overall the cross has been successful, but it produces good wine only when harvested at low yields and handling with extreme care in the winery. The best Pinotage wines show deep purple color, ripe dark berry fruit, and high, cleansing acidity.

SECONDARY RED GRAPE VARIETIES

AGIORGITIKO An important grape of Greece, grown chiefly on the peninsula of Peloponnese, producing the fine red wine Nemea.

AGLIANICO Native to Greece, this grape is planted throughout southern Italy, where it produces full-bodied wines; its best regions are Basilicata and Campania. There are some plantings in California.

ALICANTE BOUSCHET Widely grown in Spain for lesser-quality wine production. Once widely grown in California for the same purpose, but has decreased in acreage. Some renewed interest in California for producing Rhône-style wines.

BAGA Important in Portugal as a single-variety wine from Bairrada, or in a blend from the Beiras or Dão regions. High in tannins and acidity.

BLAUFRÄNKISCH Austria's leading quality red variety, it produces varietal wines and blends with good structure, forward fruit, and medium body. Known as Lemberger in Germany and Washington State.

BONARDA A very popular grape in Argentina, produced as a varietal wine and in blends. Needs a warm climate and ripens late in the season.

BRACHETTO This Italian grape produces pale red wines, usually sweet, sparkling or semi-sparkling style. The best come from the Acqui district of Piedmont.

CARIGNAN A grape that thrives in warmer climates such as California or southern France, where it is mostly used in blended wines. Known as Cariñena or Mazuelo in Spain.

CARMENÈRE A popular red grape of Chile, both on its own and in blended wines, providing color and soft, ripe berry fruit. Originally a blending grape of Bordeaux, where today very little Carmenère remains.

CINSAUT One of the grapes used in blends in the southern Rhône Valley of France. Some acreage in California. Widely planted in South Africa. (Sometimes spelled "Cinsault.")

CORVINA The most aromatic and acidic grape in the blend (with Rondinella or Molinara) to make Valpolicella and Bardolino in Veneto, Italy. When dried, the grape is the most important component in Amarone.

DOLCETTO Produces a delightful medium-bodied wine with black cherry and red fruit flavors in the Piedmont region of Italy. Also grown in California, where it was, and sometimes still is, labeled as Charbono.

GROLLEAU Grown mostly in the Loire Valley for rosé wines or sparkling wines.

LAGREIN Grown in Trentino-Alto Adige, Italy, Lagrein produces a medium-bodied, fruit-driven wine that is enjoyably drinkable in its youth.

LAMBRUSCO Grown in the Emilia-Romagna region of Italy for the production of gently sparkling red wines, dry or sweet. Widely exported.

MENCIA A grape attracting notice primarily for the fresh, black fruit-driven wines produced in Spain's Bierzo region. Known as Jaen in Portugal.

NEGROAMARO An important grape for the wines of both Puglia and Sardinia, Italy. The wine is dark in color, tannic, and usually full-bodied.

NERO D'AVOLA From Sicily, producing medium- to full-bodied red wines of deep color and flavors of black fruits. Some plantings in Australia.

PETITE SIRAH Found mostly in California, this grape was often confused with Syrah, but it is a distinct variety in its own right: Durif, a natural cross of Syrah with Peloursin. Petite Sirah wines are quite full-bodied.

PETIT VERDOT One of the grapes authorized for use in the blends of red Bordeaux wines. Also being planted in California and Australia for blending.

PRIMITIVO Widely grown in southern Italy, and acknowledged to have the same genetic makeup as Zinfandel.

SAGRANTINO From Umbria, Italy, Sagrantino produces powerful wines with assertive fruit and tannins. The best examples come from the commune Montefalco.

TANNAT In the Basque region of France, Tannat is the dominant grape in the wine Madiran. A high-tannin grape, it is the single most important variety in Uruguay, where it has attracted international attention.

XINOMAVRO From Greece, meaning "acidic and black." Wines made from Xinomavro include the full-bodied Naoussa from Greek Macedonia.

ZWEIGELT Austria's most-planted grape, it produces moderately complex, fruit-driven wines that are gaining in international popularity.

SUMMARY

GRAPES COME IN MANY different varieties, far too numerous to list in this book. The grape varieties listed and described here are many of those that have received the most attention from grape growers, winemakers, and wine consumers around the world. Grape varieties are chosen by growers for their suitability to local growing conditions, for the flavors they offer, and for the marketability of the wines they produce. As with most plants, grapevines need to be tended, and growers will select the most appropriate pruning method and trellising system to obtain optimal flavor and yield.

RÉMUAGE

PRESSING

DOSAGE

OAK

HARVEST

botrytis

vinification

YEAST

TANNIN

VAT

malolactic

FERMENTATION

barrel

VINTAGE

AGING

FINING

HOW WINE IS MADE

ONE OF THE MOST FASCINATING THINGS about wine, for both the novice and the experienced wine consumer, is the broad array of wine styles available around the world and even within any single geographic area. Wines come in numerous colors and shades, generally categorized within the broad ranges of white, blush (rosé), and red. Wines can be sparkling or still. Some wines are intended for aging, while others are much more enjoyable within months of being bottled. Many wines are light and delicate on the palate, while others are fuller and richer, with more complex flavors. There are sweet wines and wines that are not sweet, high-alcohol wines and low-alcohol wines. There are even wines that have had alcohol added to them (**FORTIFIED**) and some that have had flavorings added (**AROMATIZED**).

This chapter will introduce the reader to the many choices faced by winemakers in producing the style of wine they believe will please the consumer. Having learned the basics of winemaking, or *vinification*, you will then be ready to study the basics of wine tasting and to apply your newly developed skills to understand the different wine styles of the major wine-producing countries.

Reduced to the simplest terms, there are four major influences on the final characteristics of a wine. These are:
- The grape variety used to make the wine
- The climate in the vineyard, including weather conditions during the growing season
- The soil in the vineyard
- The winemaker and vineyard manager, who make decisions all through the grape-growing and winemaking process

Chapter 1 looked at different grape varieties and discussed the general effects of climate and soil. More specific and localized influences of soil and climate will be discussed at greater length in the chapters about different regions. This chapter will concentrate on the fourth influence—the activity of the winemaker.

Wine and winemaking are both exceptionally simple and excruciatingly complex. At its most basic, wine is nothing more than the fermented juice of a fruit, usually grapes. Grape juice becomes wine when its sugar content is converted into alcohol by the action of yeast.

The vast majority of wine in the world is produced from grapes, though other fruits can also be used. Grapes have the optimal proportion of sugar to water and, more than any other fruit, develop a whitish, powdery coating on the skin at harvest time. This coating, called **BLOOM**, is largely composed of millions of microorganisms, many of which are "wild" or "natural" yeast cells. The yeast on a grape skin includes a high proportion of **SACCHAROMYCES CEREVISIAE**, which, in its various forms, is considered the best yeast strain for converting grape sugars to alcohol.

Modern winemaking is a complex process that is controlled by detailed knowledge of organic chemistry and

microbiology, as well as by the winemaker's skill, artistry, and judgment. But wine can also be viewed as a natural substance that people have been making since ancient times. All that ancient peoples needed to do was to put grapes into a large container and lightly crush the fruit, in order to break the skin of the grapes. This allowed the sugar and liquid inside to come into contact with the yeast cells on the skin of the grapes, which in turn would convert the sugar to alcohol. Carbon dioxide would be released into the atmosphere in the process.

WINE IS ALCOHOLIC GRAPE JUICE

SUGAR + YEAST = ALCOHOL + CARBON DIOXIDE
- Sugars are provided by the ripe grapes.
- Yeasts are either from the naturally occurring covering of microflora on the skin of grapes or are added to the grape juice by the winemaker.
- The alcohol stays in the wine.
- Carbon dioxide gas escapes into the atmosphere.

THE COLOR OF WINE

ONE OF THE PRIMARY CONSIDERATIONS of wine consumers and of winemakers is the color of a wine. The ancients discovered that grapes, left to their own devices, produce an alcoholic liquid. They also found that though the juice of red grapes is the same color as the juice of white grapes, if the grape skins were left as part of the winemaking process, red- or black-skinned grapes would produce a dark red wine, while white or yellow grapes would produce a yellow-green or straw-colored wine. Historically, this is where winemaking begins to show some complexity, and it is important for today's consumer and wine lover to comprehend that the color of the grape variety sometimes plays an important role in determining the style of a wine, especially if the grape skins are allowed any contact with the grape juice during the winemaking process.

Once ancient winemakers identified the connection between grape-skin color and wine color, it was easy for them to control the exact color of the wine. If the grape skins are left in contact with the grape juice for any length of time, pigments from the skin dissolve into the juice, with the alcohol produced during fermentation acting as a solvent. Early winemakers learned that by using a press to squeeze the juice from white grapes, they could produce a very light-colored white wine. Perhaps more significant was the fact that the same result could be achieved by gently pressing red grapes and extracting only the clear juice to make a white wine with some of the fruit-flavor characteristics of red wine. (During pressing of any grape, the juice absorbs yeast cells from the grape skins, so fermentation can proceed as usual, regardless of whether the grape skins continue to remain part of the process.) To make a red wine, the grape skins—which can span the color spectrum from the lightest ruby to the deepest purple-black—are left in contact with the grape juice during fermentation.

THE MODERN APPROACH

MODERN WINEMAKING all around the world is based on two things: the very simple principle of yeast converting sugar to alcohol, and the recognition that different grape varieties contribute various characteristics, including

Pinot Gris grapes, with their typically slightly red skins. The color of the juice is clear.

FAMOUS WHITE WINES MADE FROM RED GRAPES

True French Champagne is produced using one white grape variety (Chardonnay) and two red grape varieties (Pinot Noir and Pinot Meunier). Without the inclusion of the clear juice from the two red grape varieties, the wine would be a less complex, lighter style of wine.

BLANC DE NOIRS sparkling wines from California and other areas in the United States are produced from red grapes, often Pinot Noir and Pinot Meunier. Some Blanc de Noirs sparkling wines are slightly pink or salmon-colored; others are much closer to a white-wine color. Again, sparkling wines made using only white grapes are generally lighter and more delicate in style.

White Zinfandel from California is made from the red Zinfandel grape. Some White Zinfandel wines are slightly pink in color; others are white. The same applies to wines labeled White Merlot, Cabernet Blanc, or Blanc de Pinot Noir. Some may indeed be white, but they are all made from red grapes, giving them a noticeable red-fruit flavor characteristic.

TOP: *True French Champagne is typically made from a blend of one white and two red grape types.* BOTTOM: *White Zinfandel is the most widely marketed of pink wines made from red grapes.*

color, to wine. A wine's character is strongly influenced by the choice of grape variety and the vineyard site, as we have already discussed in the previous chapter. But once the grapes are harvested, modern winemakers employ several different processes to achieve distinct styles of wine. The most important of these are:

· Pressing or crushing the grapes (almost all wines)
· Controlled fermentation (almost all wines)
· **MALOLACTIC FERMENTATION** (some wines)
· Aging (some wines)
· **CLARIFICATION** (almost all wines)

These processes will be described as they apply to the production of white, red, and rosé wines. We will then look at the special considerations given to the production of sweet wines, fortified wines, aromatized wines, and sparkling wines. Before that, however, we need to make note of how grapes are harvested, how winemakers assess the ripeness of grapes in the vineyard, and why and how winemakers estimate the level of sugar and acid in the grapes before harvest.

HARVESTING

THE VINTAGE

IN ENGLISH-SPEAKING COUNTRIES around the world, the harvesting of grapes is called the "vintage," from the French word **VENDANGE**, meaning "wine harvest." When people refer to wine as being from the 2010 vintage, they are indicating that the grapes used to make the wine were harvested in the year 2010. If the phrase "a good vintage" is used to describe a wine, the observer is simply indicating that the climatic conditions that prevailed that year were such that the grapes were harvested in excellent condition and the resulting wine should be very good. If a wine is produced from grapes of a single year's harvest, the vintage date usually appears somewhere on the label.

Not all wines are made from a single vintage. Those wines that do not have a vintage date on the label are called **NONVINTAGE** or multivintage wines and are usually blends of several wines from different vintages. The intent behind a nonvintage wine is to provide the consumer with a product that will taste the same every time. The philoso-

phy behind a vintage-dated wine is to take the grapes from one single harvest and to make the best wine possible given the growing conditions in that vineyard that year. In other words, a vintage-dated wine is the winemaker's bottled expression of the combination of climate, soil, and grape variety from a single year.

DECIDING WHEN TO HARVEST

THE WINEMAKER AND GRAPE GROWER decide the optimal time to harvest the grapes based on an assessment of the grapes' varietal flavors and a chemical analysis of the sugar and acid levels of the grapes. By sampling grapes from many different areas of the vineyard, it is possible to get an accurate picture of the ripeness of the grapes in the entire vineyard. However, picking simply "by the numbers" can have disastrous results, since it is easily possible for grapes in a hot climate to reach high sugar levels before true varietal character has been achieved. If grapes are not fully ripe, they still contain "green" flavors and a **BITTER** taste, and they tend to have a hard edge to them. Tasting an unripe grape would be similar to eating an unripe plum or a green banana. The fully ripe stage of a grape occurs only when the grape has developed the complete set of volatile organic compounds that provide that particular variety with its signature aromas and flavors. For example, Riesling would not be Riesling without its full array of monoterpene compounds, which include linalool (providing a floral, perfumed aroma), citronellol (lending a lemon-lime aroma), and terpineol (adding a petroleum aroma). Experienced grape growers and winemakers know to wait patiently for the telltale aromas and flavors to become apparent.

The chemical analysis reveals the sugar and acidity levels in the grapes, as well as the pH. For the winemaker these are important readings, as the sugar level will dictate the alcohol content and the sweetness of the finished wine, and the acidity is an important component for balance in the final flavor profile of the wine. The pH is an indicator of the concentration of the hydrogen ions in a solution; solutions with a greater concentration of hydrogen ions are more strongly acidic. Measurements of pH are expressed on a scale of 0 to 14, with a number lower than 7 indicating acidity (the lower the number, the more acid the solution) and a number higher than 7 indicating alkalinity (with 14 representing the greatest level of alkalinity). A lower pH also indicates that the grape juice and the resulting wine will resist **BACTERIAL SPOILAGE** better, as most microbes generally grow less well in acidic environments.

As the vine is exposed to sunlight over the growing season, photosynthesis gradually produces a greater concentration of sugar in the grapes. At the same time, heat and humidity affect the fruit's acid content. In general, hot, dry conditions drive the acid levels down. The cooler the climate, the higher the acidity; the warmer the climate, the higher the sugar content.

The decision of when to harvest is not simply a matter of selecting a date; it also means deciding whether to pick during the day or at night. Cooler nighttime temperatures will drive the acid up, and in some regions the extra acidity achieved by this strategy will make the difference between a balanced wine and an unbalanced one. Cooler temperatures during picking also slow down the rate of oxidation and decrease the rate at which color will leach from the skins into the juice. Many winemakers go to great lengths to be sure that the grapes are as cold as possible, using nighttime harvesting and refrigerated containers to get the grapes from the vineyard to the winery where they will immediately be placed in cold storage or be pressed so that the juice can be stored in a refrigerated tank.

The relationship between sugar and acidity in the grapes at harvest will be reflected in the resulting taste components in the wine. Most important, the sugar content of the grapes at harvest will determine the maximum level of alcohol that can be produced during fermentation.

MEASURING SUGAR LEVELS

ALL WINEMAKERS ARE INTERESTED in the sugar content of the grapes or grape juice. The sugar content of grape juice is measured with a hydrometer, a calibrated instrument that is dropped into the grape juice: The higher the hydrometer floats, the greater the juice's **SPECIFIC GRAVITY**, and hence, the greater the concentration of sugar in the juice. The scale used to calibrate the hydrometer varies from country to country. Since wine labels sometimes refer to sugar levels, it will be useful here to review the different scales used to measure sugar content.

In North America, the **BRIX** scale (also called the Balling scale) expresses the sugar content of the grape juice as a percentage of the liquid's total weight. When winemakers know the Brix measurement of the grape juice, they can estimate the total amount of alcohol that the sugar in the juice will produce and make a decision as to how much sugar could be left unfermented in the wine to provide sweetness.

In France, the **BAUMÉ** scale has been and still is used as the measurement of sugar in the juice. Here the hydrometer is calibrated to indicate the amount of alcohol that the sugar content of the juice could produce if all of the sugar were fermented to alcohol.

In Germany, the **OECHSLE** scale, measured in degrees, represents the number of grams by which the weight of one liter of grape juice exceeds the weight of one liter of water, again giving an indication of how much alcohol could be produced from the sugar content or how much of the sugar could be left in the wine to give it a sweet taste.

PICKING

WHEN THE GRAPES are ready to be harvested, they may be picked by hand or harvested by **MECHANICAL HARVESTER**. Both methods have their advocates. Those who prefer handpicking claim that the grapes are more carefully handled, because good pickers select only the fully ripe bunches as they progress through the vineyard. Certainly for those grape growers with vineyards on steep hillsides, handpicking is almost mandatory, since machines cannot work the steep slopes.

Handpicking supporters also point to the fact that pickers can be instructed to use small plastic bins to collect the grapes, limiting the weight of grapes in each bin and minimizing the likelihood that some grapes will be crushed under the weight of others. The individual bins are then transported to the winery for processing.

However, the size of a vineyard will be a limiting, and perhaps deciding, factor. In New World areas that have been newly planted, many vineyards are extremely large, and their sheer size makes handpicking less viable.

Those who use mechanical harvesters suggest that their grapes exhibit more uniform quality characteristics, since they have been harvested rapidly and within a short time period. It is also possible to harvest at night using a mechanical harvester. This can be an advantage in a hot growing area, where cooler grape temperatures at night mean less extraction of bitter components, such as tannin, from the skins. Cooler grapes also mean a reduced likelihood of spontaneous, uncontrolled fermentation. Critics of mechanical harvesters that beat the vines with rods or use a vacuum machine to remove the grapes claim that this can cause the skin of the grapes to break open, resulting in bruised fruit, unclean flavors, and oxidized juice.

Once harvested, the grapes proceed to the pressing or crushing stage, depending on whether they are being made into white or red wine.

In many parts of the winemaking world, cool weather patterns in some years result in sugar levels that are lower than desired or needed. If the winemaker wants the wine to reach a certain alcohol level, it is permissible in some of these regions to add regular beet or cane sugar to the juice before or during fermentation. In other words, the practice of adding sugar, referred to as **CHAPTALIZATION**, is intended to produce a higher level of alcohol in the wine. It is not intended as a method for producing sweet wines.

Chaptalization originated in France and is named after Jean-Antoine Chaptal, a scientist and minister of the interior under Napoléon I. Chaptal encouraged winemakers to use the scientific principle that the alcoholic strength of wine could be increased by adding sugar to the fermenting juice. French winemakers continue to rely on this method today, though the practice is forbidden by national, state, or local law in Italy, Spain, Australia, and California. In cooler climates such as New York or Oregon, chaptaliza-

tion may be desirable in order to give the wine sufficient body and structure to carry the flavors of the wine. In general, a wine that is low in alcohol does not present all of its flavors to full advantage.

Note that some of the areas that forbid chaptalization have warm or even hot growing conditions anyway. Also, these areas have several other legal methods to ensure that there is enough alcohol in the final product. For example, the **GOVERNO** process, used in some parts of Italy, allows winemakers to add a small percentage of dried grapes to an already fermented wine. The introduction of the concentrated sugar in the dried grapes causes the wine to referment, increasing the alcohol content and, coincidentally, providing a higher level of glycerol in the wine, which creates a richer, smoother texture and fuller body.

YEAST SELECTION

THERE HAS BEEN MUCH DEBATE among winemakers in recent years about the use of natural yeasts, those occurring naturally on the grape skin at harvest time, as opposed to specifically selected pure yeast strains, which are purchased and added to the grapes or grape juice to begin fermentation. There are proponents of both, and while this debate is too complex to detail here, the issue highlights the fact that fermenting with different strains of yeast will result in different characteristics in the finished wine.

The principal function of yeast is to convert the sugar molecules into alcohol and **CARBON DIOXIDE**, and naturally occurring species and selected strains are equally capable of doing this. However, most natural yeast strains are relatively intolerant of higher alcohol levels and are usually sluggish at high sugar concentrations. Even with selected yeast strains there are variations in how they behave, with some allowing for higher levels of alcohol to be produced, while using others might result in lower levels of

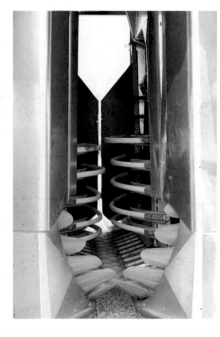

LEFT: *A standard mechanical harvester rides over the vine row, and the harvested grapes are blown out through the chute at top left.*
RIGHT: *Inside view shows the bent fiberglass rods that shake the branches to release the grapes, and the belt below that captures them.*

glycerol, which would create the impression of lighter body in the wine and possibly a perception of greater acidity.

If there is a problem with using natural yeasts, it is that the bloom on the grape skins contains many other microorganisms in addition to *Saccharomyces cerevisiae*, or wine yeast. Several kinds of undesirable bacteria or yeast strains may be present on grape skins, and in large enough quantities that they can spoil the fermentation process from the beginning, leaving the winemaker with something closer to **VINEGAR** than wine.

However, some of the world's most respected and highly prized wines continue to be made using natural yeasts without any problems. There is also a trend toward winemakers developing their own yeast strains, broadly based on the **WILD YEASTS.** These proprietary yeasts combine the best of both worlds: a yeast strain close to its natural state that can be controlled by the winemaker. Other winemakers prefer to inoculate their grapes or juice with a pure, certified, bacteria-free yeast strain whose characteristics and influence on the final wine are known ahead of time.

If a winemaker chooses to use a pure, selected strain of yeast, any natural yeasts that are present can be rendered inactive by the judicious addition of **SULFUR DIOXIDE** to the grapes or juice. The selected yeast strains are more tolerant of higher levels of sulfur and can perform their function of fermentation while the naturally present yeasts remain inactive.

WHITE WINE PRODUCTION

PRESSING

WHITE WINES CAN BE MADE from white or red grapes, as the color of the juice in red and white grapes is the same: light yellow. In either case, the general process requires rapid processing of the grapes to extract the juice as quickly as possible and place the juice (sometimes referred to as "**MUST**") in a closed container. Throughout the whole winemaking process (see the chart on page 58), the winemaker needs to carefully control the amount of oxygen that is allowed to come into contact with the juice or wine. Although small amounts of oxygen might be desirable to stimulate yeast activity or to develop flavors

ADDING SULFUR DIOXIDE TO INHIBIT BACTERIAL GROWTH

Almost every bottle of wine sold in the United States carries the statement "contains sulfites" on the label. This does not mean that winemakers add chemicals to wine with no concern for the customer or the environment.

Sulfur is a basic element, and in its dioxide form is an excellent antioxidant used in the processing of many natural foods such as dried fruit, packed seafood, and bottled fruit juice. Sulfur dioxide also blocks the metabolic processes of many bacteria, thus preventing their development and spread. In addition, in wine production, sulfur dioxide renders inactive the naturally occurring yeasts and other microorganisms that collect on the skin of the grape before harvest, making it possible to use one pure selected strain of yeast that is added to the juice to start fermentation. By using added yeast strains rather than relying on the naturally present yeasts, winemakers have more control over the fermentation, thereby reducing the likelihood that something will go wrong with the process. Most winemakers would point out that sulfur dioxide is a naturally occurring by-product of the fermentation process, which means that all wines contain some level of sulfur whether the winemaker adds it or not.

Addition of sulfites is closely monitored by ever more conscientious wine producers, and wine chemists are constantly searching for ways to avoid using any chemicals. It is better understood now, for example, that grapes with high acidity provide a natural barrier to bacterial growth, thereby reducing the need for sulfites to be added to the juice or wine. There is also more use of natural, inert gases such as nitrogen, used as a "blanket" to keep air out of the wine, and there is more understanding of the antibacterial role of the carbon dioxide created during fermentation. All of this has meant a gradual decrease in the overall use of sulfur dioxide.

during fermentation and aging, it is generally considered that air is the enemy of wine, and contact between the two needs to be carefully regulated. Just as rusting is an oxidation process—oxygen in the air attacks metal—oxygen can attack wine during fermentation, prematurely aging it and changing its character.

At the winery building, the grapes are most often channeled mechanically through a destemming machine, which separates the grapes from the stems. This machine may also crush the grapes, though the term *crush* may be too harsh. What the machine really does is break the skin of the grapes, making juice extraction quicker and easier.

The romantic notion of vineyard workers stripping off their shoes, rolling up their trouser legs, and jumping into a large wooden tank filled with grapes in order to tread them is no longer common these days (see photo on page 77). Even the use of wooden-slatted presses similar to cider presses has decreased dramatically, giving way to horizontal pneumatic presses that can apply very gentle pressure to the grapes. Inside the horizontal steel drum is a rubber membrane that can be inflated to gently press the grapes against the inside surface of the closed cylinder. In addition, the steel drum is rotated on its horizontal axis, which provides more even pressure.

The efficiency of this type of pneumatic press is based on a very simple principle: The more gently the grapes are pressed, the better the quality of the juice. This is because the best juice, with the purest varietal flavors and the best ratio of sugar to acidity, comes from the band of pulp between the grape SEEDS and the skin. The harder the grapes are pressed, the more likely it is that unwanted harsh and bitter flavors will be extracted from pulp in areas nearest the seeds and close to the skin.

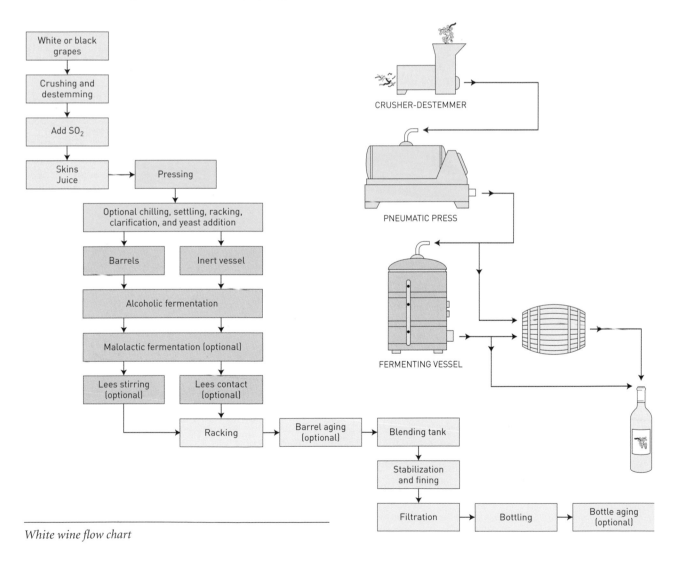

White wine flow chart

TOP LEFT: *Grape bunches being loaded into the destemmer* TOP RIGHT: *Removed stems will most likely be returned to the vineyard as compost.* BOTTOM LEFT: *The modern* **BASKET PRESS** *employs pneumatic principles from the commonly used horizontal press.* CENTER RIGHT: *The old-fashioned basket press is still used by some winemakers.* BOTTOM RIGHT: *Clear juice drips into the collection pan from a horizontal pneumatic press.*

However, this principle has a necessary corollary: The more gently the grapes are pressed, the lower the quantity of juice extracted. This inverse relationship of quality to quantity runs all the way through the grape-growing and winemaking process. A winemaker who wants to produce the best wine possible will not be able to make it in huge quantities. This obviously means that availability of certain wines is limited, and this relative rarity allows some winemakers to charge more for their wine. That is why some wines, such as Château Pétrus, Henschke's Hill of Grace, and Dom Pérignon, are so expensive. Alternatively, if a winemaker wants to increase production without growing or buying more grapes, quality will suffer.

After pressing for white wine production, most winemakers allow the must to sit overnight, sometimes in a refrigerated tank, to encourage any particles of pulp or skin to settle out. It is also possible to **CENTRIFUGE** the must to render it absolutely clear of solid matter.

CONTROLLED FERMENTATION FOR WHITE WINE PRODUCTION

SOME WINEMAKERS who want a fuller-bodied and more strongly flavored white wine allow the juice of white grapes to sit in contact with the skins for a short period of time. This skin-contact time extracts more of the flavor components and more yellow pigments from the skins.

Containers

When the winemaker is ready to let fermentation begin, the juice is pumped into the container of choice, which may be any of the following:

- An open-top cement tank
- A closed, glass-lined cement tank
- A large, refrigerated stainless steel tank
- A cured fiberglass tank
- A large, upright wooden vat
- A large wooden barrel
- A small wooden barrel

The choice of container is often driven by economics. Maybe one winemaker can afford the latest stainless steel tank that holds thousands of gallons of juice and comes with all the latest gadgets, such as temperature control, while her colleague has inherited from her father and grandfather large wooden barrels that hold 132 or 264 gallons/500 or 1,000 liters. Or it may be that the winemaker simply does not have enough juice to fill a large tank, and small 60-gallon/225-liter barrels might be more desirable, though they may be just as expensive. However, even if money is no object, the choice of container depends largely on the style of wine that the winemaker wants to produce. Modern commercial winemakers most frequently choose stainless steel vats for fermentation, though certain regions around the world still favor the use of wooden barrels.

While there are exceptions to the following generalizations, the table below highlights the differences between a wine fermented in stainless steel and the same wine fermented in a small wooden barrel. Although slightly different techniques are used to make wine in stainless steel as opposed to wooden barrels, it would be true that, even if every step of the process were exactly the same, the wine from the two containers would be noticeably different. Principally this is true because wood does not provide a neutral container: A wooden barrel imparts some of its characteristics to the wine. Most obviously, the wine is infused with the aroma and taste of wood; also, the wine may extract varying levels of tannins and vanillin from the wood, especially if it is an oak barrel, and both of these substances will affect the taste and flavor of the final wine. The tannins from wood, along with any tannins from the grape skins, may initially taste bitter and harsh, but they provide some structure to the wine (i.e., they give a sense of firmness and even a feeling of height on the palate) and are usually balanced by softer elements in the wine. Vanillin may be one of those elements, smelling and tasting soft and sweet, like vanilla essence. (For more information on tannins and taste, see "Tannins," on page 65. For more information on the effects of wood, see the section "Aging," starting on page 69.)

STAINLESS STEEL VERSUS WOOD

STAINLESS STEEL	SMALL WOODEN BARREL
Light- to medium-body wine	Usually fuller, richer style
Crisp, clean style	More rounded, softer
Simple, aromatic fruit flavors	More complex, multidimensional

Because a small wooden barrel allows for a greater surface area of contact in relation to the volume of wine, a smaller barrel imparts more wood character to a wine than a larger barrel. Similarly, new wooden barrels provide much more wood character, and barrels that have been used for four to five years or longer are essentially neutral containers.

Requirements of Fermentation

Once the juice is in the container, fermentation begins, either with natural yeasts or with the selected yeasts added to the juice. For the yeasts to be active, the temperature of the fermenting juice needs to be controlled carefully. If the temperature rises above 90°F/32°C or falls below 38°F/3°C, fermentation is likely to stop, as the yeasts cannot function

at these extremely high or low temperatures. The temperature during fermentation will also have an effect on the eventual style and flavor of the wine. Generally, cool fermentations proceed at a very slow, gentle pace, producing wines with noticeably clean, crisp, aromatic characteristics, such as Riesling from the Mosel Valley in Germany. Hotter fermentations are much quicker and more vigorous, producing fuller-flavored and more complex, heavier wines, such as the red Châteauneuf-du-Pape of the Rhône Valley in France. The increasing use of stainless steel tanks makes it easier to maintain cool, even temperatures, most often by pumping a coolant through a **JACKET** on the outside of the tank. Obviously, it is much less practical to try to cool a wooden barrel.

The fermentation of any wine proceeds until one of three things happens:

LEFT: *Stainless steel tanks provide a cool and clean, sanitary environment for fermentation.* TOP RIGHT: *Old, large wooden casks may have no wood characteristics to impart to the wine, but they make seasoned, reliable fermentation vessels.* BOTTOM RIGHT: *Small wooden barrels like these hold about 60 gallons and are used to enhance the wine with nuances of smokiness, spice, wood, and a touch of sweetness.*

ALCOHOL LEVELS IN WINE

Across the entire range of wines, alcohol levels vary dramatically, from less than 7 percent alcohol by volume in some whites to as much as 16 percent in some reds, 15 percent in a sweet white Sauternes from Bordeaux, and 21 percent in some Sherries and Ports that have been fortified by the addition of brandy.

Over the past decade, the average alcohol content of wine has increased dramatically from around 12 percent to perhaps 13.5 percent. This is probably a result of climate change on a broad scale. Some consumers appear to accept the higher alcohol levels, while others find that the alcohol is overpowering and the wine is unbalanced.

In reaction to higher alcohol levels, one famous retailer in Sacramento, California, Corti Brothers, announced that they would no longer stock any nonfortified wine that was higher than 14.5 percent.

TOP: *With so much sugar in the grapes, this Sauternes has reached a standard level of 13.5 percent alcohol but still has enough residual sugar to be a sweet dessert wine.* BOTTOM: *This Zinfandel has been fermented completely dry, with all of the sugars converted to a very high 16.1 percent alcohol by volume.*

- All of the sugar is converted to alcohol, resulting in what is called a dry wine, meaning a wine that is not perceptibly sweet because it has little or no grape sugar left in it.
- The alcohol level gets so high that the yeast cells can no longer function; this usually occurs at around 15 percent alcohol by volume, though some yeast strains have been developed to withstand higher and higher levels of alcohol. When the yeasts fail in the presence of high alcohol, all the natural sugar from the grapes may have been converted to alcohol, creating a dry, high-alcohol wine, or some sugar may remain unconverted, resulting in a sweet, high-alcohol wine.
- The winemaker intervenes and stops the fermentation before all of the sugar has been converted to alcohol, either by adding a high-alcohol spirit such as brandy (fortification) or by rapidly chilling the fermenting wine and then removing the yeast cells from the wine using a centrifuge or a sterile filtration system. Fortification is most often used to stop fermentation in order to leave a high level of residual sugar in the wine, creating a high-alcohol, very sweet wine. Chilling the wine and removing the yeast cells is more likely to be used to produce a wine of moderate alcohol content (11 to 11.5 percent alcohol by volume) that has a small amount of residual sugar to leave a slightly sweet taste in the final wine.

When the fermentation has stopped, grape juice has become wine. Left in the tank or barrel, the yeasts and other solid matter will sink to the bottom of the container, forming the lees. Some wines are left in contact with the lees to pick up yeast aroma and flavor. Also, as the yeast cells begin to break down, extra amino acids and proteins are released into the wine, giving it a smoother, richer texture. If left undisturbed, the SEDIMENT remains in a reductive (i.e., nonoxidative) state, protected from bacterial spoilage by the lingering presence of carbon dioxide from the fermentation. If bottled directly from the lees, as is done with Muscadet from the Loire Valley in France, the wine can have a slightly SPRITZY, or PÉTILLANT, quality. However, some producers take a different route with the lees, deliberately establishing a more oxidative environment with the practice of BÂTONNAGE, or stirring the lees back into the wine to extract even more yeast aroma and flavor.

For some white wines, there will be the additional process of aging the wine (see the section "Aging," on page 69).

The final steps are to ensure that the wine is bright, clean, and clear (see the section "Clarification," on page 72).

RED WINE PRODUCTION

CRUSHING OR PRESSING?

THE MOST OBVIOUS DIFFERENCE between white and red wine production is that to make red wine, the grapes have to be red and the skins have to be part of the process (see the chart on page 64), since the skins provide the pigments that make the wine appear red. The pigments can be extracted just before fermentation, using a hot or cold maceration technique to dissolve them, along with flavors and tannins, from the skins. If this is the route taken, the grapes can be pressed at this stage, essentially leaving the winemaker with red juice for fermentation. Alternatively, and more traditionally, the red grapes are destemmed and crushed (the skins are broken), but they are *not* pressed, and the mixture of juice, fruit pulp, skins, and seeds is pumped into vats for fermentation. In this scenario, the red grape solids will be pressed later in the process, usu-

ally after the fermentation has been completed, or after the winemaker is satisfied that the skins have provided enough color to the wine.

For the winemaker who wants to produce a red wine with a more intense hue, an option is to keep the grapes cold and to press them slightly, and then to draw off a small portion of the clear juice, leaving a smaller quantity of juice in proportion to the quantity of skins.

Many winemakers have expcrimented with variations on all of these themes, including the choices of whether to destem the grapes and whether to crush the fruit or leave it whole. Some who make red wine feel that they can produce a more substantial wine by putting whole bunches, including stems, into the fermentation vat, or by using whole grapes (destemmed but not crushed) in the fermentation.

The danger with whole-bunch fermentation is that the stems may contain harsh, bitter PHENOLIC compounds, especially tannins, which will have a negative impact on the taste and flavor profile of the wine. However, if the grapes have been left on the vine long enough to achieve full varietal ripeness, the tannins in the stems may have become soft and ripe enough to become a positive contribution to the wine's overall structure and longevity.

Like whole-bunch fermentation, whole-berry fermentation is also considered to provide a fuller structure and more complex flavors, while crushed grapes with no stems are more likely to result in a less complex wine.

Many wineries practice some form of hand sorting before destemming or crushing, to be sure that only the best bunches of grapes are being used.

CONTROLLED FERMENTATION FOR RED WINE PRODUCTION

AGAIN, THE WINEMAKER may choose to use natural yeasts or to introduce a specific strain of pure yeast to start the fermentation. Many of the same considerations of which container to use for fermentation apply as much to red wine as to white wine, but there is the further consideration of how to maximize color and flavor extraction. Although cement tanks may seem archaic, some winemakers favor them because of the easy access they provide, allowing for extra manipulation of the grape skins during red wine fermentation to extract more color and flavor. This concept of working the grape solids has also been automated, and there is now widespread use of

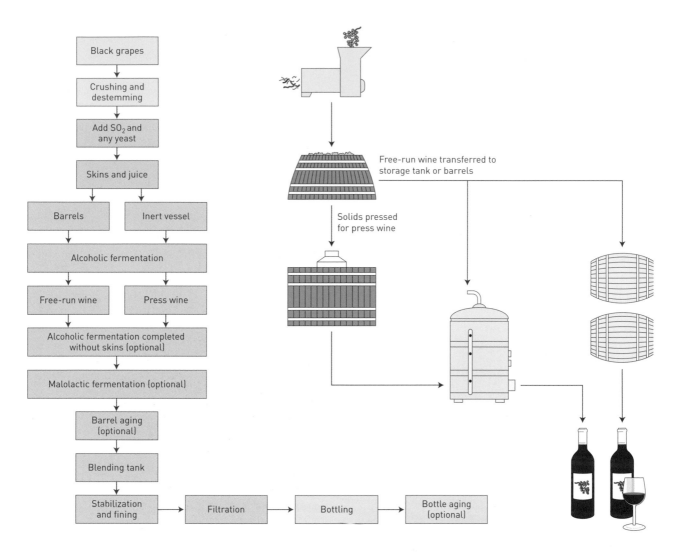

the rotofermenter, essentially a rotating horizontal stainless steel tank with a screw through the center that can be activated from time to time to move the solids around.

Assuming that the fermenting red wine includes grape skins and fruit solids in a vertical tank, those solids are forced upward in the container by the escaping carbon dioxide. If the mass of grape solids is left to sit on the surface of the wine, it will dry out, and there will be much less extraction of color and flavor. To ensure full extraction, wine producers have to make certain that the CAP of grape solids and skins is broken up and resubmerged into the wine. This can be achieved in different ways, but the choice of container and the grape variety being fermented will be factors in how the cap is managed.

One of the simplest methods is to draw wine off from

TOP: *Red wine flow chart* BOTTOM: *A bank of rotofermenters with a horizontal press in the foreground, which can be positioned under any of the fermenters to press the red grape skins at any time during or after fermentation*

the bottom of a large tank and then pump it into the top of the same tank. This action breaks up the cap and pushes it back down into the wine so that the heat and alcohol in the fermenting wine will continue to leach color and flavor from the solids. This method is particularly suited to thick-skinned varieties, such as Cabernet Sauvignon, fermented in upright stainless steel tanks.

For a thin-skinned variety, it is generally preferable to have the fermenting juice in an open-top container so that a plunger can be used to repeatedly push the cap back down into the wine, almost like churning butter. This is a preferred method for a variety such as Pinot Noir, since the skins of this grape contain fewer pigments and flavoring compounds, so they have to be worked more to get a desirable level of color, tannins, and flavor. Whichever method is used, **PUMPING OVER** or pushing down, the procedure often will be done three times a day during the fermentation process.

As with white wine production, modern technology allows winemakers to monitor the fermentation closely, even giving them the option of removing the red grape skins as soon as they feel that enough pigments, tannins, and flavor components have been extracted from the skins. This may occur before the fermentation ends.

It is important to note that color is not the only thing that is extracted from red grape skins. They also contain naturally occurring tannins (the amount depends on the specific grape variety), and winemakers work hard to ensure that their red wines contain a level of tannin that is in balance with the other components in the wine.

TANNINS

Tannins are present in grape skins as well as in tea leaves and coffee beans. Different grape varieties contain different concentrations of tannins in the skin, and red grape varieties contain more tannins than white varieties. Tannins are also found in the seeds and stems of grapes, as well as in wooden barrels used for fermentation or aging of wines.

Tannins have a noticeably bitter taste and a **ROUGH**, astringent feel, causing the mouth to dry out. It's a bit like chewing an aspirin. Why would winemakers want to have tannins in the wine if they taste so awful?

Tannins are useful to the winemaker for two main reasons:

1   They are a natural preservative. If a winemaker has made a wine that is supposed to develop and improve with age (often a red), the presence of tannins in the wine increases the likelihood that the wine will remain sound through the aging process.

2   Tannins have a natural affinity for protein. They act as a catalyst with any protein-containing fining agent added to the wine—the tannin molecules are attracted to the fining agent, causing a mass of colloidal matter to collect and sink down through the wine, pulling other particles with it as it sinks. (For more information on fining agents and colloids, see the section "Clarification," on page 72.)

From the taster's point of view, this affinity with protein can also be used to advantage. If a red wine is high in tannins, pairing that wine with a red meat cooked rare will mean that the protein in the meat helps attenuate the tannins in the wine, thereby allowing the fruit flavors of the wine to be more noticeable.

White wines aged in wood can have noticeable levels of tannins as well, although the perception is different: Wood tannins create a rougher effect toward the back of the mouth, whereas grape tannins are usually more noticeable between the top gum and upper lip.

Management of tannins in the vineyard and in the winery is now much better understood, and makers of high-quality wine work hard to ensure that tannin-rich grapes are fully ripe, since ripe tannins taste much less harsh than green tannins. In the winery, tannins can be softened by heating the must in contact with the red grape skins and solids. The effect of the heat on the tannin molecules is that they polymerize, creating longer chains of molecules, which are perceived as having a softer texture in the mouth. Since color is also extracted during hot maceration, it is possible to get enough color into the juice so that fermentation can take place without the skins, allowing the winemaker to concentrate on the soft, fruit qualities of the wine without worrying about extracting more tannins during fermentation.

The fermentation will proceed until one of the conditions mentioned in the section on white wine production occurs—conversion of all sugars to alcohol, achievement of a sufficiently high alcohol level, or intervention by the winemaker. Most red wines are fermented to complete dryness, with little or no residual sugar remaining.

Whether the red grape skins are removed during fermentation or left in until fermentation is complete, the skins are usually retrieved at some point in order to press them. What is extracted is called **PRESS WINE**; this is more concentrated in flavors, tannins, pigments, and body, and is lower in acidity. The press wine is reserved and later may be blended back into the rest of the wine to achieve the desired style and flavor. The remaining skins can be used as fertilizer in the vineyard.

Carbonic Maceration

For centuries, the wine producers of Beaujolais (see page 328) have employed an alternative method of red wine fermentation called **CARBONIC MACERATION**. Because this method results in a lighter, easy-drinking style of wine, it has recently been adopted by many winemakers in other parts of the world. It is also possible to ferment a portion of any wine using carbonic maceration to create a lighter style that can then be blended with the other portion that has been fermented by the more traditional method.

Carbonic maceration occurs when whole, unbroken red grapes are placed in a closed container that is then saturated with carbon dioxide. Generally, the weight of the grapes in the container causes the bottom 10 to 15 percent of the grapes to be crushed. The sugar in those grapes is transformed by the natural yeasts on the grape skins into alcohol and carbon dioxide.

Each individual uncrushed grape in the upper part of the closed container undergoes its own mini-fermentation *inside* the grape. The grape absorbs the carbon dioxide, and enzymes inside the grape convert the stored sugar to alcohol and more carbon dioxide. The creation of the extra carbon dioxide would ordinarily allow the grape to continue this process for some time. However, at around 2 to 3 percent alcohol, the cell structure of the grape begins to break down, and the fermenting juice is released into the tank to continue fermentation with the rest of the wine.

Carbonic maceration does not involve any physical movement of the grape solids during fermentation to extract extra color or tannins from the skins. The result is a

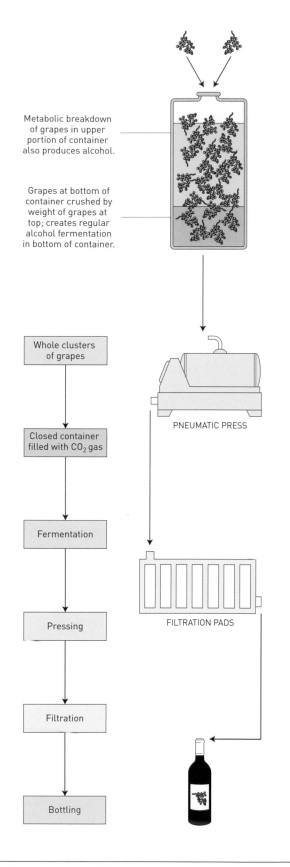

Metabolic breakdown of grapes in upper portion of container also produces alcohol.

Grapes at bottom of container crushed by weight of grapes at top; creates regular alcohol fermentation in bottom of container.

PNEUMATIC PRESS

Whole clusters of grapes

Closed container filled with CO_2 gas

Fermentation

Pressing

Filtration

Bottling

FILTRATION PADS

Carbonic maceration flow chart

light-colored red wine that is low in tannins. Wines produced this way, such as Beaujolais from France and Gamay from North America, are enjoyed particularly for their fresh fruit flavors.

ROSÉ WINE PRODUCTION

GOOD-QUALITY ROSÉ WINES are produced by allowing red grape skins to remain in limited contact with the grape juice before fermentation starts, thereby creating a pink-tinted juice. The skins are then removed from the process, and the pink juice is treated in the same manner as white juice.

It is legal in some countries to produce a pink wine by blending a small amount of red wine with a large amount of white wine.

For all intents and purposes, the terms *pink, rosé,* and *blush* mean the same thing. All refer to pink-tinted wines.

SCIENCE AND TECHNOLOGY

THOUGH TRULY GREAT WINE is made in the vineyard, not everybody can have the best vineyard location, or sometimes other factors such as climate do not cooperate in producing the best that the site has to offer. For many people who are new to grape growing, it may take years to realize that the plot of land that looked good on paper simply does not provide great-quality grapes. What, then, do you do when nature is not providing the raw material to make the kind of wine you want?

That is the nub of a major problem. There are many grape growers and winemakers who have entered the wine business with an idea of the kind of wine they want to make and then try to make a plot of land fit their dream. On a visit to a new vineyard planting in the Monterey area of California, the tour guide pointed to an expanse of new plantings and proclaimed, "This will be our *grand cru* vineyard!" The problem is clear.

There are steps that can be taken in the vineyard to improve the situation, such as different trellising, different rootstocks, different density of plantings, etc. But many winemakers resort to science and technology in the winery. That is not to condemn the use of science and technology in general. The advent of temperature-controlled stainless steel fermentation is a very welcome advancement. The main concern is when science and technology are invoked to correct a problem that would not have occurred if the grapes were not grown in the "wrong" location in the first place.

However, winemakers face challenging times. Climate change has already made grape growers and winemakers consider changing location. But when that is not possible, perhaps the only resort is to work in the winery to correct problems. The most common problems encountered are high or low levels of acidity or alcohol, and **VOLATILE ACIDITY**. In addition, there are ways to adjust color in wines, and even ways to remove aromas and flavors, such as smoke taint from proximity to a forest fire.

ACIDITY ADJUSTMENT

HIGHER LEVELS OF ACIDITY are easily achieved by adding an acid, usually tartaric or citric acid, to the wine, though it is generally agreed that the earlier the addition is made, the more likely it is that the added acidity will be better integrated into the wine. Last-minute additions of acid are usually detectable on the palate, with the extra acidity seemingly disjointed from the rest of the wine.

Decreasing the acidity level can be achieved by physical or chemical means. One option is to induce the wine's natural tartaric acid to precipitate out of the wine. Chilling the wine encourages the formation of **TARTRATE** crystals, which can then be removed. Alternatively, potassium carbonate or **CALCIUM CARBONATE** can be added to the wine; this renders the tartrates insoluble, so that they drop out of the wine.

One major method used to reduce acidity is the process known as malolactic fermentation. This process can take place simultaneously with the basic alcohol fermentation, or it may follow the alcohol fermentation. It can occur naturally, without any intervention from the winemaker, or it can be induced intentionally.

The agents that cause malolactic fermentation are bacteria, usually of the genus *Leuconostoc,* part of the family of lactobacilli familiar to people who enjoy yogurt. If a winemaker wants to create a malolactic fermentation, the bacteria can be purchased and added to the wine. Once introduced into the winery environment, these bacteria may survive and continue to be present in and around the winery, in which case malolactic fermentation can occur in subsequent years without any action from the winemaker.

After the bacteria are introduced to the wine, they act upon the malic acid in the wine, converting it to lactic acid. The overall effects are to convert the sharp, harsh malic acid to softer, smoother LACTIC ACID (the acid in milk products), changing the taste and flavor profile of the wine. The total measurable acidity of the wine is also reduced.

Most red wines and some white wines (particularly Chardonnay wines from cooler climates) go through malolactic fermentation, making them generally smoother and softer on the palate.

In the area of reducing acidity levels, a more recent application of physics is the use of electrodialysis, by which an electric current is passed through the wine, affecting the electric charge of the mineral ions in the wine. As the wine reaches an ion selective membrane, ions of the offending acid are removed from the wine. This has been especially helpful in correcting levels of volatile acidity in wines, and removing unwanted ALDEHYDES and ESTERS.

GRAPE ACIDS

Three major acids are found in grapes, though the actual content of each acid varies from variety to variety and from climate to climate. The three acids are:
- Tartaric acid, found primarily in grapes
- Malic acid, as in green apples (such as Granny Smith)
- Citric acid, as in lemons and grapefruit

These three acids all have a sharp, piercing taste, and all cause the mouth to salivate. Malic acid does taste like Granny Smith apples and even has some of the slight drying effect at the front of the mouth. Citric acid has the same effect as biting into a lemon. Tartaric acid is slightly less sharp and has a more noticeable drying effect throughout the mouth. (For more information on the effect of acids on taste, see above.)

ALCOHOL ADJUSTMENT

WE KNOW THAT ALCOHOL LEVELS can be increased by the addition of sugar before or during fermentation, or by the addition of alcoholic grape spirit (brandy) to produce a fortified wine. All other additions of alcohol to increase alcohol levels are at least frowned upon, if not illegal. But the usual problem with alcohol levels today is that they are too high, a factor of poor site selection to begin with, or a consequence of climate change.

The simplest adjustment for alcohol reduction is to add water. However, the water will also dilute every other aspect of the wine, which would be undesirable. The most commonly used technology is reverse osmosis, which also depends on the use of a semipermeable membrane selected to hold back a specific part of a liquid as the liquid is passed through it. In this case, wine passes through the membrane, and alcohol is held back.

COLOR ADJUSTMENT

SOME WINEMAKERS BELIEVE that consumers are influenced in their choice of wine by the actual hue of the wine in the glass, and the general preferences seem to be for white wines to appear paler and red wines to be darker. Science and technology can be used to achieve whatever shade of color is desired.

In making white wines paler, any number of chemical additions will reduce the intensity of color, but these chemical methods have other negative side effects. For example, higher doses of sulfur dioxide will reduce color intensity in wines but can also give the wine an undesired sulfur aroma and taste. The most neutral method is charcoal filtration, which is used throughout the entire beverage industry.

For color intensification in red wines, normal winemaking practices include the variety of ways used to keep the skins in contact with the juice during fermentation (see pages 63–65). But more extreme measures include bleeding some of the clear juice from the red grapes before fermentation has begun to reduce the amount of liquid in proportion to the quantity of grape skins. Color intensification is also a side effect of cryoextraction (see page 76).

REMOVING UNWANTED AROMAS AND FLAVORS

THE PHYSICAL PROCESSES of electrodialysis and reverse osmosis described above can also be used to remove unwanted aromas and flavors that occur in the wine through no fault of the grape grower or winemaker. The most important application here has been to remove smoke taint caused by forest fires near vineyards, especially in California and Australia in recent years. The work of companies like Enologix, Vinovation, and Winesecrets has been invaluable in this regard. However, such companies have also been criticized for promoting the attitude among winemakers that a wine can be made to be whatever is desired.

While the correction of accidental faults is admirable, some critics question the desirability and validity of the substantiated claim that wine-technology companies, working with grape growers and winemakers throughout the season and post-season, can create a 95-point wine. It seems that such wines are chemistry-lab creations, not the wondrous product of man and nature collaborating to let the wine make itself.

BLENDING

THERE ARE MANY REGIONS in the world where blending is an integral part of the winemaking process, allowing a winemaker to marry the individual characteristics of separately made wines in order to create something that is much more than the sum of its parts. The blending components used in this process can be extremely varied, derived from different grape types, different clones, different soils, different climates, or different years. It is important to note that blending usually takes place after each individual wine component has been made as a separate wine. In other words, blending is not achieved by putting different grapes into the same fermentation process.

The best examples of this approach would be any of the Bordeaux grape variety blends produced anywhere in the world. When a château in Bordeaux or Francis Ford Coppola's Rubicon Estate in Napa or the Rustenberg Estate in South Africa sets about making a wine from the three grape varieties of Cabernet Sauvignon, Merlot, and Cabernet Franc, they do not harvest all three varieties together and throw everything into one big pot to ferment.

Since each of those three varieties ripens differently, they are harvested separately and made into wine separately. Several barrels of each different variety are made separately and given a few months aging, and only then is each barrel tasted and decisions made as to what percentage of each type to blend together for finishing and bottling.

Blending is therefore a way of adjusting what nature and man have produced. Some years the Merlot will turn out better than the other wines, so the winemaker uses more of it in the blend. The same is true of Champagne and other sparkling wines around the world that use more than one grape variety. Each variety is made separately and then blended to the desired flavor profile before being bottled for the second fermentation (see page 78).

AGING

ONCE THE WINE IS MADE, it is either prepared for bottling or stored at the winery and allowed to age, or mature. The decision of whether to age a wine at the winery

Wooden barrels are preferred for aging certain types of wine. The barrels alone in this aging warehouse would cost over $1 million.

depends mainly on the style of the wine, although winemakers sometimes bottle wines before they are ready, either because there is a high demand for the product or because the company needs to generate sales.

Ideally, of course, the decision to age is driven purely by the style considerations of the wine. It is a common belief that all wines improve with age. This is not true. Only a small percentage of the world's wines derive any benefit from aging, and even then, aging a wine is very much a gamble.

The vast majority of all wines produced are made in a style that renders them most enjoyable when young. In fact, better than 90 percent of the world's wine is consumed within two years of its vintage date. They are liked for their attractive, fresh, clean fruit flavors and aromas, which will only diminish as time goes on. Winemakers all around the world produce huge quantities of this type of wine, and most consumers buy it and enjoy it. Only a very small percentage of wine consumers have the money, the facility, and the time to buy wine with the intention of aging it.

Most wines, then, do not go through any aging process. When a winery decides to age a wine before releasing it to the public, it is because the winemaker feels that the wine will somehow improve by being held back and kept in a suitable container. A red wine aged at the winery will lose some of its harsh, youthful abrasiveness (often derived from the combination of tannins and intense, just-ripe fruit flavors) and develop a softer, more harmonious profile that is much more appealing to the consumer. A very small percentage of white wines are aged to develop more complexity and a smoother texture.

If a wine is to be aged, the winemaker must first decide what kind of container to store it in. Should the wine be left in the container in which it was fermented, possibly in contact with the yeast sediment from the fermentation process? Or should the wine be moved into a clean container, and if so, what kind? The container options for storing wine during aging are basically the same as the options for fermenting the wine. However, it may also be desirable to age the wine in bottles at the winery, or a combination of containers may be used, simultaneously or successively.

If the principal objective is to soften the texture of a white wine, this can be achieved by leaving the wine in contact with its yeast cells in the original container, occasionally stirring the yeast sediment back into the wine. This is easier in a small container, such as a wooden barrel, but it can also be done in a stainless steel tank. The presence of nutrients in the yeast sediment is also a source of

WHAT KIND OF BARREL?

When deciding on the type of container in which to age or ferment wine, the first consideration is: What kind of material? For many winemakers, the natural choice, especially for aging complex wines, is wood. Then a series of considerations come into play. What kind of wood? Traditional wisdom says that oak is the best wood to use, though winemakers around the globe have used and continue to use chestnut or (in California) redwood.

Where, then, to get the oak? Again, traditional wisdom suggests that French is best, but some winemakers prefer American, Italian, or Slavonian oak. If from France, where exactly in France? Five main forests in France supply most of the oak for wine containers: Nevers, Limousin, Vosges, Tronçais, and Allier. As to which is better, every winemaker and French barrel maker will give a different opinion.

After deciding to go with a particular French forest, what size container? The size that is becoming increasingly popular around the world is the barrique, which is approximately 60 gallons/225 liters. There are many other sizes and shapes available. The main consideration is: How much surface-area contact should the wine have with the wood? Since the smaller barrels contain a smaller quantity of wine, the overall effect of the oak on the wine is greater.

There are also many coopers, or barrel makers, each with their own special trade secrets, who claim to make

barrels better than anyone else's. Among the various considerations are how the wood is split or sawed; how the wood is dried; how long the wood is seasoned; how thick the staves are; how the staves are bent; and so forth.

Once a cooper is selected, the winemaker needs to specify how the barrels should be toasted (fired) on the inside. The options are light, medium, and dark toast. If the barrel is dark-toasted, the influence of the oak will not be so harsh, but the wine will pick up toasty aromas and flavors.

The barrels are delivered. Does the wine just go straight into them? The winemaker still has to decide whether all of the wine should have oak treatment, or just half of the wine, or maybe a third or less—and whether the wine goes into all new barrels or only some into new barrels (if so, how much?) and some into used barrels (and should the used barrels be one, two, or three years old, or a combination of one, two, and three?).

Obviously, the oak influence is very strong in a brand-new barrel and decreases with every year the barrel is used. Some winemakers have gotten some oak influence out of seven-year-old barrels, but very, very little. After that, the barrel will still be usable as a storage container, as long as it is kept in good condition.

Once the winemaker has all the oak influence desired from the barrel, is it just thrown away? It could be, but it could also be sold to another winemaker who wants less oak influence, or it could get sent to a cooper to shave one-quarter to one-eighth of an inch from the inside of the barrel, revealing virgin wood on the inside and effectively creating a brand-new barrel, which, of course, may be retoasted.

How much will this fancy French barrel cost? In 2010, a single good, new French-oak *barrique* cost around $1,500. **AMERICAN OAK** barrels cost about half that.

FROM LEFT TO RIGHT: *Making a wooden barrel, placing the rings at one end first. Fitting rings to the opposite end of the barrel. Firing or toasting the inside of the barrel. The head, ready for placement on the barrel. Using a machine to shave the inside of a used barrel to expose raw wood*

energy for the bacteria that drive malolactic fermentation, so leaving the wine in contact with the yeast sediment is a way of encouraging this additional fermentation, which contributes greater softness to the wine.

If the objective is to give a white wine more complexity, this is more often achieved in small wooden barrels. The barrel will impart wood aromas and flavors, and possibly a darker yellow color, to the wine; the wine will extract vanillin from oak barrels (if that is what is being used); and it is commonly assumed that the small barrel will allow some exchange of oxygen into and out of the barrel (though this notion has been contested), causing a limited degree of oxidation and development of the wine's aromas and flavors. Wines left in contact with yeast sediment will also take on yeast aromas and flavors.

Aging of red wines is almost always done in small oak barrels to allow some oxidation, to extract vanillin from the oak, to develop oak aromas and flavors, and to give the original grape variety's flavors and aromas time to develop and emerge. After aging in the barrel, the wine may be aged in the bottle before release, both to enhance the wine's character and to minimize what is called BOTTLE SHOCK—the transfer of the wine from barrels to the bottle seems to "numb" the wine, temporarily masking its positive characteristics.

BARREL ALTERNATIVES

SCIENCE AND TECHNOLOGY have recently offered potential solutions to a serious economic problem for winemakers—the cost of new oak barrels. If the cost of barrels is prohibitive, there are two major ways to try to achieve barrel characteristics with lower costs. Oak staves can be lowered into a stainless steel tank of wine, thereby providing an oak "lining" intended to approximate the effect of an oak barrel. Given the size of the vat, the overall effect will never be the same because the volume of wine in direct contact with oak in the tank is proportionately much smaller than it is in a small oak barrel. However, since the winemaker has a choice of using just one stave or as many as can fit in the tank, this provides the option of creating a small amount of oak influence at relatively low cost.

An alternative to the alternative is to throw quantities of oak chips into the wine in the stainless steel vat. Given the varieties of oak that exist and the varying degrees of toasted qualities that the chips can be subjected to, it is possible to make endless variations of "brew mixtures" of oak chips, just like the endless varieties of teas or coffees that exist in bags or pods these days.

Again, the main criticism is that the effect will never be the same using oak chips compared with using a real barrel. In particular, critics suggest that elements such as sweetness and smokiness will become more volatile through the chipping process and will therefore be far more noticeable in the wine. There will be a relatively low presence of structural tannins to give the wine height and substance. However, for many styles of wine on the modern market, oak chips may be a very satisfactory way of achieving wood character at low cost.

CLARIFICATION

CONSUMERS AROUND THE WORLD expect wine to be clear and free of any particles or haze, so most commercially produced wines go through some kind of clarification process. Some clarification methods are thought to leave the wine with more of its character intact than other methods: Such techniques are usually slow and labor-intensive. As such, they are more suitable for smaller quantities of wine. Other methods allow large quantities of wine to be processed in a short period of time, though it is often suggested that these methods strip the wine of some of its character.

The principal clarification methods used today are (from slowest to quickest):

- Time and gravity, or RACKING (moving from one container to another)
- FINING (adding a catalytic agent to precipitate solids), followed by racking
- Refrigeration or COLD STABILIZATION, followed by racking
- Filtration, using various types of pads
- Centrifuge (a machine that spins solids out of the wine)

RACKING

WINEMAKERS WHO ARE NOT RUSHED (by their sales department or by bank loan officers) may simply leave the wine to sit so that gravity will slowly pull any solid matter to the bottom of the container. The wine can then be gently racked, or siphoned, separating it from the sediment, which collects on the bottom of the container. However, there are some dangers in this method: Leaving the wine to sit increases the risk of contact with air; the wine may begin to lose its fresh flavor; the sediment may begin to decompose and spoil the wine. It is also possible that some solid matter will remain in a hazy suspension in the wine and will never drop out.

FINING

THE RACKING PROCESS can be accelerated by adding a fining agent to the wine that will cause any solid particles to clump together and fall to the bottom of the container. This happens for a variety of reasons. Some fining agents used are high in protein, and the solids in wine, particularly any tannins, have a natural affinity for proteins. Alternatively, the fining agent may have the opposite electrical charge from that of the suspended solids and, since opposites attract, the solids are attracted to the fining agent. Lastly, some fining agents neutralize the tiny electrical charges that keep certain particles apart. Many natural fining agents are still used, such as egg whites (ALBUMEN), gelatin, ISINGLASS (a gelatinous, gluey substance obtained from fish bladders), and BENTONITE (a colloidal clay mined in many parts of the world, including Wyoming). Bentonite works particularly well, since it attracts any protein in the wine, and the protein in turn attracts any tannins in the wine. Egg whites have particular limitations and are more suited for use in small containers of wine, such as *barriques*. After fining, the wine is racked off the sediment before decomposition occurs.

REFRIGERATION

WITH THE CORRECT EQUIPMENT, winemakers can refrigerate large quantities of wine, which encourages much of the solid material to precipitate to the bottom of the container. Again, following precipitation of all solids, the wine is racked off the sediment.

FILTRATION

A MORE RAPID and more certain method of clearing the wine of all foreign matter is to pump it through a series of pads. The more traditional (and cheaper) pad is made of cellulose and is capable of holding back a large amount of undesirable solids. Increasingly, winemakers are turning to micropore filters as a more reliable system. Since even a single microscopic organism can spoil an entire batch of wine, many winemakers appreciate the reassurance afforded by using at least one filtration process on their wine. Critics of filtration charge that it can rob the wine of some of its color and flavor components. Those who believe this sometimes label their wines as "unfiltered."

CENTRIFUGE

A CENTRIFUGE PROVIDES a rapid and surefire way of clearing the wine of all solid particles, as it spins the wine at high speed and any solids are literally flung out of the wine. This method is very efficient at clarifying large quantities of wine but, like filtration, it has been criticized for removing color and flavor components.

SWEET WINES

A SWEET WINE IS ONE that contains residual (i.e., unfermented) sugar. Most of the famous sweet wines of the world are white, and the greatest, such as the Sauternes wines from the Bordeaux region of France or the BEERENAUSLESE wines of Germany, all derive their sweetness from sugar that was present in the grape at harvest. While this is true in any sweet wine made to high standards anywhere in the world, there are many bulk, inexpensive

The cellulose pads in this filtration system show the solids and color pigments left on the pads after filtering red wine.

sweet wines whose sugar content has been increased by adding a sweetening agent after fermentation.

The discussion here concerns those sweet wines whose sugar content is from natural grape sugars. Some of these wines are only slightly sweet, while others are very rich, luscious, and extremely sweet. The principal strategies for sweet wine production are controlled fermentation, the addition of reserved juice, and the use of late-harvest grapes, raisins, botrytis-affected grapes, or frozen grapes.

CONTROLLED FERMENTATION

THE MOST COMMON WAY for slightly sweet wines to achieve their sweetness is for the winemaker to halt the fermentation before all of the naturally present grape sugars have been converted to alcohol. Good examples of such wines are many of the Riesling, Gewürztraminer, or Chenin Blanc wines from various parts of the United States or Australia. The residual sugar in most of these wines is around 1.5 to 2 grams per liter, giving a light but noticeable impression of sweetness on the palate.

RESERVED JUICE

AN INTERESTING ALTERNATIVE is the use of what German winemakers call *Süssreserve* (literally "sweet reserve," or sweet grape juice that has not fermented). After the grapes have been pressed, but before fermentation, some winemakers put aside a portion of the juice and sterilize it or centrifuge it so that it will not ferment. The rest of the juice is allowed to ferment possibly to complete dryness, and then the *Süssreserve* is added to the wine to enhance its sweetness and fruitiness. In this instance, the *Süssreserve* is considered to be a natural source of grape sugars and not an added sweetening agent. Any use of *Süssreserve* would not be mentioned on the label, and it is generally avoided by the more scrupulous, quality-minded producers.

LATE HARVEST

BY LEAVING GRAPES ON THE VINE for an extended period of time, into October or even November in the Northern Hemisphere, the sugar will become more con-

centrated, and the grapes will develop richer, riper flavors. In many instances, some of the grapes will begin to shrivel on the vine, concentrating the sugar even more and allowing for the development of higher levels of glycerol. As a result, wines made from late-harvest grapes are often more viscous and intensely sweet, with very high levels of residual sugar and aromas of raisins or other dried fruits.

RAISINS

IN MANY DIFFERENT PARTS of the world, grapes are picked and then allowed to shrivel by placing them on drying mats or racks before fermentation. This has been practiced in Greece and Cyprus for centuries, as well as in the Jura region of France, where the wines are called *vins de paille* (the French word *paille* means "straw"; the grapes are left out to dry on straw mats). In the Veneto region of Italy, this practice is still used for the production of *recioto* and Amarone wines. Again, the resulting wines are usually noticeably more viscous and concentrated in flavor, with aromas of raisins and dried fruits, and at least a hint of residual sugar.

BOTRYTIS

ONE OF THE MORE UNUSUAL, intriguing, risky, and complex methods of producing a sweet wine relies on a naturally occurring mold, *Botrytis cinerea*. Botrytis is one of a family of molds that commonly attack the grapes in a vineyard. All of these molds are simply looking for somewhere to live and something to eat, and a ripening or ripe bunch of grapes is an ideal location. Of all the molds in this family, botrytis is the only one that is considered

The term Trockenbeerenauslese *on a bottle of German wine indicates the grapes were all botrytis-affected, making a luscious, sweet wine.*

beneficial: All of the other molds have to be prevented or removed, as they will completely ruin the affected grapes.

If a winemaker wants botrytis to affect the grapes, there are certain climatic conditions that favor its development: cool, moist, even misty mornings, followed by warm, dry afternoons. These conditions should be prevalent over a period of days or weeks if the majority of a vineyard is to be affected.

There are certain grape-growing areas where such conditions can almost be relied on to occur every growing season. Such areas usually include a fairly large body of water and some steeply sloping land. As the night air cools and rolls down the slope to the water, mist forms and enshrouds any nearby vineyards, keeping the grapes cool and damp and allowing the botrytis mold to grow and spread from grape to grape, from bunch to bunch, and from vine to vine. As the air warms up, the mist will be burned off by the sun, and the vineyards will have a chance to dry out. The most famous areas that enjoy these conditions include:

- Sauternes, Barsac, and adjacent areas in Bordeaux
- Tokaj in Hungary
- Napa Valley, pulling fog from San Francisco and San Pablo bays
- Mosel and Rhine vineyards in Germany
- Finger Lakes district in New York

Once the botrytis mold has settled on a bunch of grapes, it needs nutrients to prosper, and it finds most of these in the form of sugars inside the grapes. To reach the sugars, the mold pierces the skin of the grape with its tiny filaments and draws out minute quantities of sugar solution, in turn secreting glycerol that provides a luxurious texture to the wine. During the warmer, drier periods, the water content of the grape evaporates through the microscopic holes made in the grape skin, and the grape dehydrates on the vine. The net result is a very messy-looking, rust-colored grape, but one that contains an extremely high concentration of sugars, acids, and flavors in a much-reduced quantity of liquid.

The wine made from these grapes is extremely rich, viscous, and sweet. It is also, for obvious reasons, produced in very limited quantities. Château d'Yquem, the most famous estate in Sauternes, produces approximately one bottle of wine from eight vines, as opposed to the standard yield for a regular dry wine of three to four bottles of wine per vine. Such figures make for very high prices. For example, a bottle of Château d'Yquem from the 1988, 1989, or 1990 vintage is valued at around $4,100.

It is important to note that if the climatic conditions are right for botrytis, the mold is completely indiscriminate in terms of which grapes it attacks. It can be present on grapes at any stage of maturation, but for the mold to

The vineyards of Château d'Yquem are ideally situated to benefit from the onset of botrytis mold.

be beneficial to the winemaker, it must grow on only fully ripe grapes with fully developed flavor characteristics. In addition, the mold will attack any grape variety, red or white. With very few exceptions, fine botrytis wines are made only from white grapes, but even within the white grape types, certain varieties are considered to be much more suitable for producing botrytis-affected wines.

The best white grapes for making botrytis-affected wines are:

- Riesling, especially in Germany, Australia, and the United States
- Sémillon, especially in Sauternes and Australia
- Sauvignon Blanc, especially in Sauternes, Australia, and the United States
- Chenin Blanc, especially in the Loire Valley
- Vidal and Vignoles (hybrid varieties), especially in the eastern United States and Canada

As in all other areas of winemaking, science and technology have become a fact of life in Sauternes and Barsac. Troubled by the problem of the valuable botrytis degenerating into simple and worthless black **ROT** through the presence of too much water, steps were taken in the 1980s to quickly reduce the water content and save the precious botrytis through cryoextraction. Basically this means applying the natural methodology of Icewine production to already-harvested grapes in the winery. In other words, pick the botrytis-affected grapes and put them in the freezer. This allows you to freeze out excess water content and to press pure botrytis-affected juice.

ICEWINE

NOT TOO LONG AGO, the only Icewine in the world came from Germany and Austria, where it is called Eiswein, but today many more people are interested in making this unusual and highly demanding wine. The major prerequisite for Icewine is that the grapes have to be fully ripe but clean, with no mold or breakage in the skin. The objective is to allow the grapes to be frozen on the vine. This usually occurs around the second or third week of December in the Northern Hemisphere, and most often at around 3 A.M., at which time pickers are asked to carefully cut the whole bunches from the vine, place them in insulated cartons, and transport them as quickly as possible to the winery. The whole bunches are pressed, and because the majority of the water in the grape remains frozen, only a small quantity of highly concentrated sugar solution is pressed out. The ice stays in the press, while the sugar solution is placed in the fermentation vessel.

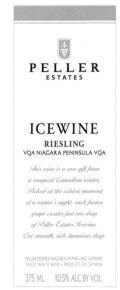

For many people, Icewine represents one of the purest expressions of concentrated grape flavor. It certainly is very sweet, though not necessarily as viscous as a botrytis-affected wine, and not necessarily high in alcohol. Today, many New World areas, especially the eastern United States and Canada, produce Icewine. It is possible to make Icewine by harvesting the grapes and then freezing them (cryoextraction), though regulations forbid this in Germany, Austria, and Canada. In Germany, laws governing *Eiswein* grape harvests stipulate that the temperature must remain at 17.5°F/−8°C for a minimum of six hours before the grapes can be picked.

Icewine from the Niagara Peninsula of Ontario is a highly acclaimed style of sweet wine.

BOTRYTIS

The mold responsible for some of the best sweet wines in the world goes by different names in different countries. Its botanical name is *Botrytis cinerea*, which means "gray mold."

COUNTRY	MOLD NAME
Most English-speaking countries	Botrytis, noble rot
France	Pourriture noble
Germany	Edelfäule
Italy	Muffa nobile

The gray mold is related to many other grape molds that, unlike botrytis, have no beneficial effect at all on the grapes or the wine.

FAMOUS FORTIFIED WINES

WINE LABEL	REGION, COUNTRY
Sherry (Jerez, Xeres)	Jerez, Spain
Porto (Port)	Upper Douro, Portugal
Madeira	Madeira, Portugal
Marsala	Sicily, Italy

A variation on the theme of fortified wines is what the French call a *vin* **DOUX** *naturel*. In this instance, the high-alcohol spirit is added to grape juice before fermentation starts, or very soon after it starts. In other words, the spirit is added directly to grape juice or very-low-alcohol wine, producing a very grapey, sweet, high-alcohol wine. Good examples would be Ratafia from the Champagne region of France, or Pineau des Charentes from the French region that produces Cognac brandy.

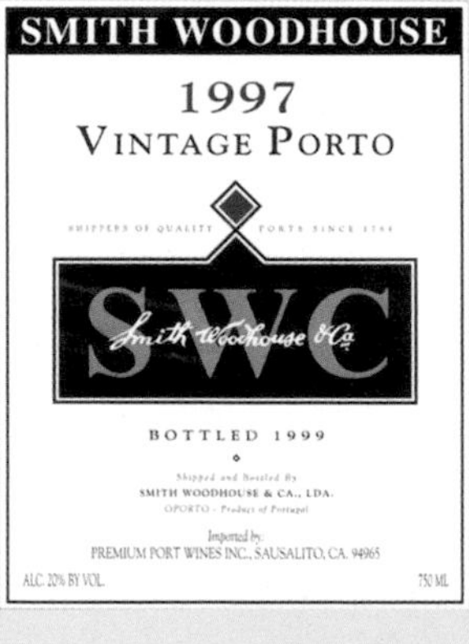

TOP: *La Gitana Manzanilla Sherry is a dry fortified wine from southern Spain.* BOTTOM: **VINTAGE PORTO** *is one of the most famous sweet fortified wines in the world.*

FORTIFIED WINES

SOME FAMOUS WINES ARE CLASSIFIED as fortified wines because their alcohol content has been strengthened, or fortified, by adding a high-alcohol spirit to the wine. The most illustrious examples of such wines are Porto, or Port, from Portugal, and Sherry, also known as Jerez or Xeres, from southern Spain.

It has often been claimed that the original reason for fortifying wines was to stabilize and preserve them, since alcohol does both. There is some truth in this claim, evidenced by the fact that both Porto and Sherry were largely developed by British merchants who shipped the wine fairly long distances as they built the British wine trade. It is also true that in Andalusia, where Sherry is produced, the local inhabitants and winery workers drink a lower-alcohol version of Sherry than that which is exported.

Whatever the reason, fortifying wine means simply that a high-alcohol spirit, usually a locally made brandy or eau-de-vie, is added to the wine during or after fermentation. The difference between adding the spirit during and adding it after fermentation is the difference between a sweet fortified wine and a dry one.

If the spirit is added during fermentation, as is the case in Porto, the addition of the spirit will raise the alcohol content of the fermenting wine to a level at which fermentation will stop—beyond 15 percent alcohol. However, not all of

Traditional foot-treading of grapes for Porto.

the original grape sugars will have been converted to alcohol, leaving residual sugar in the now-sweet fortified wine.

If the spirit is added after fermentation, as is the case in Sherry production, the original grape sugars in the grape juice are all converted to alcohol, producing a dry wine. When the spirit is added to this wine, it becomes a dry fortified wine. In the case of Sherry, producers have the option of sweetening the Sherry at a later stage. (See the section on Sherry on page 442.)

AROMATIZED WINES

PERHAPS LENDING CREDENCE to the notion that, at least historically, fortified wines come from areas where the regular wines are of poor quality, some producers of fortified wines choose to add flavorings to their product. The flavorings usually come in the form of herbs and spices but also may include barks, roots, and flowers. Many of these wines fit into the group known as vermouths, with most of the base wines coming from southern France or southern Italy, both areas known for large production of mediocre bulk wines. Red and white aromatized wines come in both sweet and dry versions.

SPARKLING WINES

WHEN GRAPE JUICE ferments to become wine, carbon dioxide is formed as a by-product and released into the atmosphere. The end result is a still, or nonsparkling, wine. If the winemaker, at some stage of the process, prevents the gas from escaping, the end result is a sparkling wine.

The most famous sparkling wine in the world is Champagne. For most wine-consuming countries, the use of the name Champagne indicates a sparkling wine made from legally specified grape varieties grown on a particular soil structure in specific mesoclimates in the namesake region of northern France. Some other countries, the United States in particular, still use the generic term *champagne* to indicate any wine with bubbles in it.

Ironically, there is much evidence to suggest that sparkling wine was not invented in the Champagne region of France, even though a very famous resident of

Champagne, Dom Pérignon, is often credited with developing the Champagne method. Dom Pérignon (1638–1715) started as a novice at an abbey in Hautvillers in 1668 and eventually became **CELLAR MASTER** there. His name is frequently associated with many innovations connected with sparkling wine production. However, there is no reference to sparkling wine in any of his notes or those of his successors. If he did make sparkling wine, it was probably the misunderstood result of a second fermentation from previously unfermented residual sugar that was present in whatever containers were used to store the wine. He may have made sparkling wine, but it was almost certainly an accident, and it may even have been considered an error.

By the end of the seventeenth century, it is believed, some people living in the Champagne region, possibly including Dom Pérignon, were making sparkling wine by means of the naturally occurring second fermentation after the wine had been bottled, but the second fermentation was not being induced by the addition of extra sugar. It was not until the mid-nineteenth century that it was learned that a second fermentation could be induced by the addition of sugar to the wine, after the work of Jean-Antoine Chaptal, in 1801, and that of Professor André François, who in 1836 invented the **GLUCO-OENOMÈTRE** to provide an easy calculation of how much sugar was needed to create extra alcohol. Even then, it was not until Pasteur's groundbreaking work in 1857 that the relationship between sugar and yeast was fully understood.

Dom Pérignon is believed to have made many refinements to the winemaking process in Champagne, though he did not invent sparkling wine.

Although Dom Pérignon's role may have been embellished, he remains an important figure in many ways. He is believed to have contributed greatly to the knowledge of how to get white wine from red grapes. He is also thought to have contributed to the understanding of the benefits to be derived from blending wines from different grape types and from different vineyards in order to create a more complex, more interesting final product. He probably was instrumental in adopting the use of strong English glass to bottle the wine before the second fermentation—an important step, since many of the weaker bottles that had been used were likely to explode under the pressure created by trapping the carbon dioxide in the bottle. Having found a strong enough bottle, he is also credited with re-introducing the use of cork as a secure closure for the bottles, as opposed to the hemp-and-oil stoppers widely used at the time.

Just as important, he was known to use a rudimentary form of disgorging, or **DÉGORGEMENT** (see page 84), though his technique was probably practiced by most of his contemporaries as a convenient way of at least partially removing the collected yeast sediment immediately prior to consumption. At the beginning of the nineteenth century, another famous Champagne character developed a significant step that provided a way of completely eliminating all of the yeast sediment that was left after the second fermentation. Even though at that time the method of producing Champagne did not include the intentional addition of sugar and yeast to create the second fermentation, an indomitable and famous widow named Veuve Clicquot (the name Veuve Clicquot means "the widow Clicquot") found that she could obtain a perfectly clear bottle of wine by using a process called **RIDDLING** or **RÉMUAGE** (see page 83) prior to *dégorgement*.

Veuve Clicquot is credited with developing the system of rémuage *to make it easier to remove the yeast sediment from bottles of sparkling wine after the second fermentation in the bottle.*

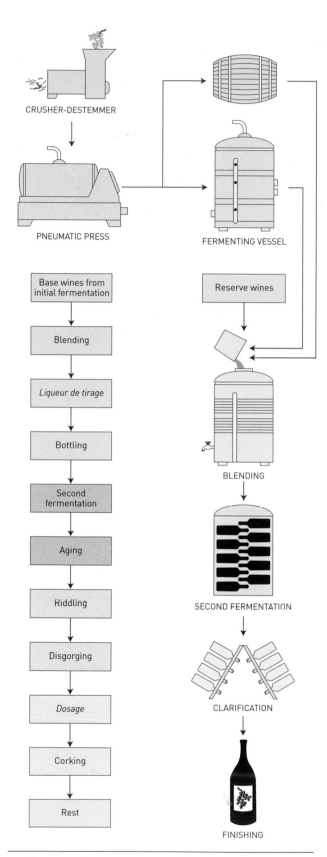

CRUSHER-DESTEMMER

PNEUMATIC PRESS

FERMENTING VESSEL

Base wines from initial fermentation

Blending

Liqueur de tirage

Bottling

Second fermentation

Aging

Riddling

Disgorging

Dosage

Corking

Rest

Reserve wines

BLENDING

SECOND FERMENTATION

CLARIFICATION

FINISHING

Sparkling wine flow chart

With the assistance of her *chef de cave*, Antoine Müller, Veuve Clicquot perfected the methods of working the sediment to the mouth of the bottle and then removing it without any appreciable loss in gas pressure (which would rid the wine of its precious bubbles).

The fame and respect earned by the sparkling wine producers of the Champagne region in France are reflected in the fact that many producers of sparkling wine around the world have adopted the methods of production developed over centuries. Three major methods are employed in making sparkling wine today:

- *Méthode champenoise* (the traditional method of second fermentation in the bottle)
- **TRANSFER METHOD** (a modified version of the *méthode champenoise*)
- **CHARMAT** (or tank) method (carbon dioxide is trapped in the tank)

MÉTHODE CHAMPENOISE

THE WORD CHAMPENOISE refers to something or somebody coming from or belonging to the region of Champagne. True French Champagne producers are very protective of their heritage and of the terms and words that they believe are uniquely theirs. They have gone to great lengths in recent years to prevent non-Champagne producers from using the words *Champagne* or *méthode champenoise* in the labeling or marketing of any non-Champagne product. The fervor with which today's French Champagne producers apply their protective efforts derives from a singular history that has inarguably provided immeasurable pleasure to millions of people.

It is important to understand that from the second fermentation through the aging, release for sale, and service of the wine, true *méthode champenoise* sparkling wines stay in the same bottle. This entire process can last anywhere from eighteen to forty months, with some exceptional wines spending even longer in the aging stage. (See the section on late-disgorged Champagne in Chapter 7, on page 285.) The pillars of the Champagne method are time and quality. It is a protracted, labor-intensive technique and is usually reserved for higher-quality grape varieties.

Initial Fermentation

Since almost all sparkling wine is white, the following commentary is restricted to the production of white sparkling wines. Sparkling wine starts its life in the same way as any other wine: White or red grapes are pressed, rapidly and gently, to provide a clear grape juice, which is then put through the fermentation process, creating a dry white wine of 10.5 to 11 percent alcohol by volume. As with still wines, the choice of container for the initial fermentation process will have an effect on the eventual flavor characteristics of the sparkling wine. Most base wines that later become sparkling wines are fermented in stainless steel.

Blending

The majority of all Champagnes and other sparkling wines are nonvintage wines, blends of wines from several years' harvests. After a new batch of wine has been made from the most recent harvest, it is used as the primary base wine to which several other wines from previous years will be added to create a standard blend that will eventually become the sparkling wine. The resulting wine offers the same characteristics and flavors as previous nonvintage bottlings from that producer. The intention is to offer a consistent product from bottling to bottling. The task of blending is enormously complex and challenging, requiring exceptional skill to marry together numerous wines into a final base wine whose character will change as it becomes sparkling wine, but will continue to reflect the style of the individual producer.

While some rosé sparkling wines are made by skin contact with red grapes, most are produced by adding still red wine to the base wine prior to the second fermentation.

A small percentage of sparkling wines are vintage-dated wines, produced from grapes harvested in a single year. For these wines, the focus is not on year-to-year consistency, but on the unique qualities expressed by the vintage.

Bottling

The next stage in the *méthode champenoise* is to add a mixture of sugar and yeast, called the LIQUEUR DE TIRAGE, to the blended wine while it is still in the tank, and then to bottle the wine. Each bottle of wine is usually capped with a crown cap, very much like a beer-bottle cap, though a few sparkling wine producers continue to use a cork secured with an *agrafe* (metal clasp) to close the bottle at this stage.

The bottles are then stored on their sides, preferably in a cool, constant-temperature environment, such as an

Rows of sparkling wine bottles in A-frame racks (pupitres) *ready for hand-riddling*

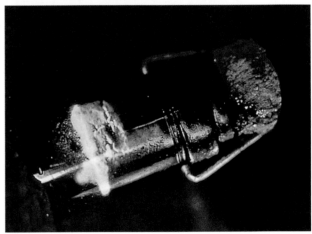

underground *cave*, or **CELLAR**. During this time, the *liqueur de tirage* will work to cause a second fermentation in the bottle. The carbon dioxide created by the second fermentation remains trapped in the bottle. This second fermentation will take only one to two weeks to complete, depending on temperature. All of the additional sugar will be converted to alcohol, resulting in a completely dry wine with an additional 1 to 2 percent alcohol by volume, bringing the total alcohol by volume to approximately 12 to 12.5 percent.

The bottles remain in storage, on their side, for many more months. Producers of high-quality sparkling wines try to leave the bottles untouched for at least twelve months. In the case of high-quality Champagnes (from France), this period may be as long as three years, or even six years for the very finest. During this time, the spent yeast cells from the second fermentation will lie as sediment along the lower side of the bottle, in contact with the wine in the bottle. The yeast cells are slowly destroyed

CLOCKWISE FROM TOP: *Freezing the yeast sediment in inverted bottles of sparkling wine. The yeast sediment in the neck of the bottle. Adding the final* dosage *after disgorging or* dégorgement.

by their own enzymes, a process referred to as **AUTOLYSIS**. The slow breakdown of the yeast cells creates extra amino acids and proteins that provide a richer, smoother texture to the wine. The extended contact with the yeast also provides new opportunities for flavor development in the wine. This yeast contact time is of major importance in determining the style and character of the final sparkling wine. With a longer contact time, the wine develops more yeast characteristics, which will be noticeable in the aroma and flavor of the wine when it is opened. The most common descriptions of a wine with long yeast contact are that the wine has a "toasty," "biscuity," or "mealy" (as in freshly milled grains) aroma and flavor.

There is another important aspect to the length of time that the bottle remains in storage at this stage, following the second fermentation. A by-product of the second fermentation is carbon dioxide, which is trapped in the bottle. There appears to be a correlation between the length of time in storage after the second fermentation and the size, consistency, and persistence of the bubbles that form when the bottle is opened. The process of autolysis also releases fatty acids that increase the surface tension of each tiny bubble, making it harder to break that surface. In a sparkling wine that is left only a short time on its lees, not enough fatty acids are released and the bubbles remain weak on the surface. When the bottle is opened, smaller, weak bubbles combine into larger bubbles, creating a less impressive, less sparkling effect.

The longer the wine remains undisturbed, the more thoroughly the carbon dioxide becomes incorporated into the wine, and the more slowly it will be released from the wine as bubbles of gas in the glass—assuming that the bottle has been opened and the wine poured in the appropriate manner. (See the section on Champagne service on page 663.)

This stage of sparkling wine production underscores an extremely important point with respect to production of all wines, not only sparkling ones. There are some steps in wine production that most winemakers would agree are preferable because they result in a better wine. Some of these steps, such as storage, take time—lots of time. And time, as the saying goes, is money. It requires a huge outlay on the part of any producer to, for example, harvest grapes in September, make the wine, bottle it in January of the following year, and then leave the wine untouched until January or February of the next year—and even then the wine is not ready for distribution or sale.

During all this time the wine has not earned one penny, but production costs continue to mount.

The Champagne method ends with two final steps: *rémuage* (or riddling), working the yeast sediment into the neck of the bottle, and *dégorgement* (disgorging), removing the sediment from the bottle.

Rémuage (Riddling)

After the second fermentation in the bottle, and after the aging period on the yeast sediment in the bottle, the bottles are taken from their resting place and inserted into large A-frame wooden racks, called *pupitres* (see photo on page 81), with the necks of the bottles pointing slightly downward. At this stage many of the yeast cells have become stuck to the side of the bottle, so the objective is for the *remueur*, or riddler, to maneuver the sediment into one manageable lump inside the bottle, and then to work the sediment down the inside, into the bottle neck and onto the stopper in the mouth of the bottle.

In order to do this, the following series of steps are performed repeatedly on each bottle over time:
· Manually grasp the bottom of each bottle.
· Shake the bottle slightly to dislodge any stuck yeast cells.
· Turn the bottle approximately one-eighth of a turn.
· Raise the bottom of the bottle slightly.
· Drop the bottle back into the hole in the rack.

Gradually this handling of the bottle coerces all of the sediment into the neck of the bottle, at which point the bottle is almost completely inverted in the rack.

When Veuve Clicquot first developed the riddling system, every step was done by hand, meaning that the complete process would take anywhere from six to eight weeks for a batch of about five thousand bottles. Some producers still use this hands-on method, but today, most large producers of *méthode champenoise* sparkling wine use modern, automated methods to riddle the wine. In these systems, the bottles are placed upside down in large metal crates, called *gyropalettes*, which are mounted on two large mechanical arms. In seven to ten days, through a series of rocking motions, these machines can riddle as many bottles as would take the *remueur* six to eight weeks to complete. There are also semiautomatic devices called *girasols*, in which a hexagonal metal basket with a base shaped like

SWEETNESS STYLES
FOR SPARKLING WINES

CATEGORY	SWEETNESS LEVEL
Extra-brut	Bone dry; no *dosage*, or minimal *dosage* added
Brut	Dry; small amount of *dosage* added
Extra-dry	Medium dry; noticeable sweetness
Sec	Medium sweet
Demi-sec	Sweet
Doux	Very sweet

an upside-down cone is filled with inverted bottles and occasionally rotated back and forth.

The most recent refinement to the riddling process is the use of yeast beads, called *billes*, added as the yeast component of the *liqueur de tirage* to induce the second fermentation. The yeast works from inside an alginate bead to convert the sugar to alcohol and carbon dioxide, and even allows for interaction of the wine with the yeast during aging. However, when it comes to removing the used yeast, the beads simply roll into the neck when the bottle is inverted, with no riddling needed.

Corks for sparkling wines are perfectly cylindrical before being inserted into the bottles, after which they take on their familiar mushroom shape.

Dégorgement (Disgorging)

Again, when Veuve Clicquot first developed her methods, all disgorging was done by hand, bottle by bottle. The bottles were taken from their inverted position on the riddling rack and, using a pair of pliers, the stopper was removed from each bottle, allowing just a very small amount of wine to escape. When done properly, all of the sediment was carried away as well. Obviously, this method was haphazard at best. A major refinement came when Veuve Clicquot realized that the whole bottle of wine should be as cold as possible, thereby reducing the carbon dioxide pressure in the bottle, and also reducing the tendency of the gas to escape when opening the bottle. (This is a very useful point to remember when opening any bottle of sparkling wine—always make sure it is well chilled.)

A modern refinement of this method is to freeze a small amount of wine in the inverted neck of each bottle. When the stopper is removed, the gas pressure in the bottle is enough to propel the ice pellet (and all of the yeast sediment, which is trapped in the pellet) from the bottle. In modern facilities, each of these steps is now automated with large machines, which perform all of these functions in a very short amount of time. (See photos on page 82.)

Final Dosage, or
Liqueur d'Expédition

While the stopper is off the bottle, most producers of sparkling wine add a small amount of wine and liquid sugar—the final **DOSAGE**—to the bottle before inserting the cork.

The amount of sugar added determines the style of the sparkling wine. The terms listed in the table above are the official sweetness designations for Champagne from France. Many of these terms, especially **BRUT**, have been adopted by other regions that produce sparkling wine, with approximately the same meaning. After the final *dosage,* the bottles of wine are allowed to rest for three to six months before being released for sale.

TRANSFER METHOD

ANOTHER METHOD OF MAKING sparkling wine, the transfer method, is similar to the *méthode champenoise,* up to and including the second fermentation in the bottle. However, the transfer process differs radically from the *méthode champenoise* after the fermentation in the bottle is complete. In an effort to save time, money, and labor, the sparkling wine is transferred, under pressure, from the bottle to a tank where it is filtered in order to get rid of the sediment. Then the *dosage* is added and the wine is re-bottled. This process does away with both *rémuage* and *dégorgement* and produces a less expensive, and some would say lower-quality, sparkling wine. However, there is no evidence to prove that transfer method wines are inherently inferior. If care is taken with every step of the process and the wine is aged long enough, a transfer method wine could be every bit as good as a *méthode champenoise* wine.

CHARMAT (TANK) METHOD

A FAR CRY FROM EITHER the *méthode champenoise* or the less-expensive transfer process, the *charmat* method is simple, direct, and inexpensive. Still wine is placed in a closed, pressurized tank, and sugar and yeast are added to it to create a sparkling wine. The wine is filtered and clarified in bulk, and then bottled. Many critics claim that the *charmat,* or tank, method is inherently inferior to *méthode champenoise* and will never produce a high-quality wine. Theoretically, if wine was left in contact with the lees in the tank for long enough after the second fermentation, the tank method could produce many of the same characteristics as *méthode champenoise*. However, this has never been tested because of the impracticality of keeping wine in a production tank for such a long time.

Many sparklers are produced all around the world using the *charmat* method, including the world-famous Asti and Prosecco wines, with fresh and floral aromas and delicate, fruity flavors. Indeed, the bulk method, with its emphasis on cool fermentation in stainless steel tanks, is ideally suited to producing fresh, fruity wines that emphasize grape character.

SUMMARY

WINEMAKING IS BOTH AN ART and a science. Pure scientific knowledge is applied in different humanistic, artistic ways to the same basic raw materials to achieve a broad and fascinating array of wine styles. The true art of the winemaker lies in the intuitive knowledge of what to do in different circumstances to achieve the desired result. At harvest time each year, the winemaker is presented with a completely different set of circumstances for each grape type, given that the growing conditions in any two years will probably never be identical. For every vintage, winemakers set out to make the best wine they can from the raw materials that come from the vineyards, and to do this they make a series of choices that determine how the wine will be made. They make judgments about pressing, about skin contact time, and about acidity and sugar levels. They decide whether a wine should age, how long it should age, and what kinds of containers should be used.

Chapter 3 will delve into the different goals and techniques of tasting. The subsequent, regionally themed chapters will bring together knowledge of grape varieties and winemaking practices to develop a greater understanding of the prominent styles of wine from the major wine-producing areas in the Old World and the New World.

acidic

SWEET HOT AROMA

BOUQUET

BUTTERY BODY

CRISP appearance

BITTER

color CLARITY MINERAL

VEGETAL

BALANCE FRUITY

CHAPTER 3

TASTING WINE

A TRUE AESTHETIC EXPERIENCE lies *within* a bottle of wine. No matter how appealing the bottle and label, it's what's inside the bottle that counts. To some neophyte wine drinkers, tasting may seem complicated and intimidating, but *tasting* is just a catchall phrase that means capturing, evaluating, and hopefully enjoying the characteristics of a specific wine.

The basic purpose of wine tasting is, of course, to determine whether or not the taster takes pleasure in a particular wine. We respond to the wine ORGANOLEPTICALLY by using all of our major senses—sight, smell, touch, taste, and even sound—to experience and evaluate the wine. Tasting is *aural,* starting with the popping of the cork and the splashing of wine in the glass. Tasting is *visual,* as the color hints at the depth, power, or style of the wine, and the *perlage*—the steady stream of tiny bubbles—indicates quality in a fine sparkling wine. Tasting is *olfactory,* as the associative memory attaches significance or emotions to the smells that go beyond simple grapes. Tasting is *tactile,* as the mouth reacts to the interplay of temperature, tannins, acids, sugar, alcohol, and bubbles. Depending on the surroundings, the company, the mindset and emotions of the taster, and, of course, the quality of the wine, tasting may even be an inspirational experience.

Tasting wine is, at best, an inexact science, since it is based largely on personal preference. With some experience, however, any wine taster's responses can be quantified and shared. A beginning wine taster should not be intimidated by the vast range of descriptive terms available (some of them helpful, some of them examples of useless "wine-speak"), but should taste at a level that provides personal comfort. For an individual's first few wine tastings, "light red" or "dark red" may suffice for describing the color, and if no smells are immediately identifiable, the taster has no reason to worry. He or she can still articulate the main flavors, sweetness level, and intensity of the wine, and answer this fundamental question: "Is the wine enjoyable?"

While vacationing in a wine region, we may venture into a tasting room, have a quick taste, decide "this stuff is okay," and buy a couple of bottles as a souvenir of the experience. This is the least formal kind of tasting and perhaps the most pleasurable. It is a judgment based on individual preference, and the taster never thinks of it as a formal tasting.

In a formal professional tasting, on the other hand, where the purpose is to market wines to restaurants and wine merchants, a wine importer or SOMMELIER may be risking a large amount of money on decisions made in a few minutes.

Naturally, there are many other circumstances between these two extremes, but it is clear that we taste wine in different ways on different occasions, and for different reasons.

WHEN TO TASTE WINE

SEVERAL STUDIES HAVE SHOWN that the tasting is most likely to achieve the best results earlier in the day, around 9 A.M. or 10 A.M., when the eyes, nose, tongue, and brain are at their most alert, and tasters are most likely to make an accurate, reliable, and consistent assessment. As the day wears on and taste detectors and aroma receptors are bombarded by a sensual assault, and as the brain suffers from at least some fatigue, the ability to remain sharp and decisive in identifying aromas, tastes, and flavors diminishes.

Tasting early in the day is recommended, but that doesn't mean we cannot taste later. By practical necessity, wine events are frequently held in the afternoon or evening, and we still can respond well to the challenges of tasting. The ability to overcome the natural fatigue of the day indicates that it is possible to train "the muscles" used in tasting—the olfactory bulb, the tongue, and, most important, the brain. We can become *better* tasters if we apply ourselves. That means that we keep ourselves alert to opportunities to *sense everything*. When it rains, smell the earth; when you peel an eggplant, smell the skin, then taste it; when you go to a café or bakery for your morning coffee and perhaps a pastry, stand in different places and breathe and smell; chew a tea leaf. Breathe in everything, and remember it.

A FORMAL WINE TASTING: SETTING AND PROCEDURE

THE FOLLOWING ARE the ideal conditions for a formal tasting. Obviously it may be impossible to meet all these criteria on all occasions.

· The tasting room should be a comfortable temperature, well ventilated, and free of any distracting smells.
· It is best to judge the true color of the wine by natural daylight in a room with several good-sized windows. If

I have found that most people, I would say a good 75 percent of people, are good tasters, if they are interested and put their mind to it. They also have to have a good memory. Taste depends on being interested in what you taste, trying to define in words what you taste, and having a memory to recall similar taste experiences. It also helps if you get guidance initially on how to taste. Sight, smell, and taste are all closely interconnected, but a taster must be guided initially to bring to tasting the discipline without which it is easy to overlook details essential to bring the maximum of one's faculties to the task. It is also essential to make notes, even if those notes are not kept. As with all other sensory experiences, verbalizing your experiences helps you define them. The environment is also important. There should not be any odd smells. A calm environment, well lighted and not too hot or too cold, without any smells, is essential. The time of day is also important. Professional tasters try to taste only in the morning, when they are rested, after a small breakfast, preferably no later than ten o'clock. An experienced guide is desirable, because certain off tastes have some definite origin that an experienced taster can identify and anchor in your mind for future reference. I have found, by and large, that women are often more perceptive than men. I have also noticed that personal preferences intrude on tasters' abilities. Thus, tasters who do not like sweet wines will not be good at critically tasting them. Another phenomenon is age. As people get older they seem to prefer softer and sweeter tastes, just as they did when young. Though one cannot generalize on this subject, there is no doubt that you must be in good physical health to taste well. Here, as in everything else, experience makes the master.

Peter M. F. Sichel,
Fourth Generation Wine Merchant, Grower, and Exporter; President, Franz W. Sichel Foundation

The single most important ability to develop when embarking on this adventure of wine tasting is to teach yourself how to recognize quality. When I was a young sommelier, I had no mentor, no professional direction other than my own common sense. I was thirsty for the counsel of anyone with some depth of experience in wine. While working in a formal dining room, I had the privilege one evening of serving André Gagey, the director of the esteemed Burgundy house Louis Jadot. With enthusiasm and innocence I asked him. "Mr. Gagey, could you please tell me how you taste wine?" To my eternal gratitude he gave the question some thought and then answered, "When I first approach a wine, I always ask myself, Is this a good wine?" I will always remember his kindness in giving me the best advice I've ever received on how to taste wine. "Is this a good wine?" is, on the surface, a simple question. But it presupposes that you have garnered experience in judging balance and typicity, can assess a wine in its unyielding youth, and most important, can make a quality call independent of any critical press. No wine critic is going to be standing behind your shoulder when you recommend wine to a guest in your dining room—you must make the opinion on your own. Also, to all the enthusiastic blind tasters out there, the ability to deduce what a wine is is impressive but utterly unrelated to assessing quality, in my humble opinion.

Here is an easy checklist of questions to ask yourself as you taste to purchase, whether for yourself or for a hotel/restaurant property: Is this wine a good example of type, or is it a new example of type? Can I sell this to my guests? Is there a market for this wine, or can I create one? Is it delicious—will it deliver pleasure at the table? Is there a good price/value relationship, and what will I have to sell it for? And finally, once again, is this a good wine? This simple methodology practiced faithfully will become second nature and will keep your palate honest.

Madeline Triffon,
Master Sommelier; Wine Director for the Matt Prentice Restaurant Group, Detroit, Michigan

artificial light is used, incandescent is preferable to fluorescent. A white tablecloth, place mat, or tasting sheet provides a neutral background. This is important in judging the color of the wine and the attendant properties. (See the section on color on page 52.)

· Glassware should be clear, unadorned, and free of any soapy residue. It should be polished with a lint-free cloth, hand-rinsed, or run through an extra rinse cycle without detergent. The best glasses to use to "nose" a wine tend to have a wide bowl and a tapered top; standard "tasters" are just fine for most tastings. It can be instructive (and fun) to taste wines in glasses made especially for a particular style of wine, grape type, or region. This is not just a party trick. The concentration of aromatics and flavors, and our ability to perceive them really do differ in different glasses.

· Spittoons should be provided; they can be simple large paper cups or larger buckets. The palate tires over time, and if much wine is consumed during a formal tasting, the taster cannot stay sharp and the senses are numbed. Spitting takes a bit of practice and some getting used to, but it does not interfere with the appreciation of the nose and flavor elements of the wine. Spitting is a necessary part of formal wine tasting and only enhances our ability to appreciate the wines.

· A pitcher of water and a water glass should also be provided for clearing the palate between wines. Local tap water or a still mineral water may be used as long as neither has a strong chlorine or mineral flavor.

· Service staff should be briefed about each of the wines to be poured, and they should be equipped with CORK-SCREWS and white cloth napkins. The person in charge of service should keep a running inventory of the number of bottles of each wine poured. It is best to have one person coordinate the issuing of the wines so that servers do not confuse types.

· Decanted wines (see page 659) should be organized with a bottle of the wine in front of the decanter, so that the label is prominent (unless this is a BLIND TASTING). A small sticker with the wine's number or name could also be affixed to each decanter to avoid the possibility of pouring the wrong wine.

· A paper mat with numbered circles indicating the position of each glass should be provided.

· Tasting sheets should be provided for recording the identities and descriptions of the numbered glasses and the wines.

- Promotional or informational materials for the wines may be placed at the table, along with a pencil and perhaps a notepad for preliminary notes. Such materials usually address the most frequently asked questions about the wines being tasted. Historical, geographic, and technical data on the vineyard and winemaking process help the taster understand the conditions that created each of the wines in the tasting.
- If bread or crackers are provided for the purpose of neutralizing the palate, they should have as little flavor as possible. In particular, salty or sweet bread or crackers should be avoided.
- A reception desk is used as a central point to collect invitations or business cards, check identification to ensure that participants are of legal drinking age, and assign seat or table numbers at very large tastings.

TASTING PROCEDURE

THE POURING OF WINES at a formal tasting is coordinated by one person or team, whose concerns are the order in which the wines are served, when to open them, at what temperature they are served, and the amount poured.

The usual procedure is to serve the less powerful dry whites and sparkling wines before the more tannic reds. Rosés may be served in between whites and reds, with sweet and fortified wines served at the end of the sequence of wines to be tasted. This is done so that the taster's palate is not overwhelmed by the initial wines and may still appreciate those at the end of the tasting.

Sparkling wines should be opened as close to the time of the actual tasting as possible in order to preserve the lively action of the bubbles. Still wines may be opened a half hour in advance so that any change in nose and taste is minimized. Realistically, there is no one formula to determine how long in advance a given wine should be opened before service. Some wines are best uncorked hours before service, while others would be less interesting with that much aeration. An ideal situation would be to contact the producer or the winery and ask advice or to consult someone familiar with the wine. Wines poured for a large group may also be "nosed" or tasted beforehand to make sure there are no unpleasant odors and that the wine is in sound condition.

Sparkling, white, rosé, and some light-bodied red wines are usually chilled; they should not be poured too far in advance so that they do not get too warm. Full-bodied red wines are served at room temperature and may be poured in advance. (For the correct SERVING TEMPERATURES for wines, see the sections on pages 649–651.) If a speaker is conducting a tasting, she or he may request that no wines be poured in advance. The speaker may instruct the staff to coordinate the serving of wines to specified times in the seminar or may just give the word when a wine is to be poured.

A tasting portion (a "pour") is generally about 1–1.25 ounces/3–5 centiliters, so a bottle should easily provide sixteen to twenty-five tasting portions. If a small number of wines are to be tasted with food, tasting portions may be larger.

The servers should pour the wines at the location where the tasters are seated; they should not bring glasses already filled. The person in charge should give a demonstration of how the bottles are to be held, the amount of the pour, and how to use a napkin to wipe the lip of the bottle so that no wine splashes onto the tasting mat.

> Though we spend our lives tasting and smelling things, most people approach wine tasting as though other new and mysterious principles need to be applied. Instead, imagine that your job is to identify as many of the flavors in a given wine as you can. Then try to decide which flavors are the predominant ones. And most important, do not be in a hurry. Let the good wines hang out, in your mouth and in your mind, until you understand everything in the wine that you can. Or better yet, just enjoy it.
>
> Though blind tasting seems mysterious to most people, it is simply based upon a few principles and a strong dollop of experience. Determine the fruit flavors of a wine and think of cold-climate fruits (such as apples and pears) coming from cool areas and richer, riper fruits (such as pineapples and plums) coming from warmer climates. Learn how to tell the herbal, coconut-like flavors of American oak from the complex spices of French oak barrels. Most important, decide which varietal taste you like, memorize it, and compare it to every wine you taste.
>
> Doug Frost,
> *Master Sommelier, Master of Wine,*
> *Author, Journalist, Consultant, Educator*

THE THREE BASIC STEPS TO TASTING WINE

APPEARANCE

A WINE'S APPEARANCE is the first clue to its taste. The hue should be inviting and true to the wine's varietal, geographic, or stylistic type. Descriptions of color may be as general as "red" or "white" or as specific as "pale garnet with pinkish-blue highlights" or "pale yellow with a green tinge and watery RIM." In any case, color is the first indicator we evaluate when we taste wine. Even before smelling and actually tasting the wine, we can learn much about the wine's character from its color. As an example, intensity of color is often an indication of a wine's power. Very often, opaque, dark red wines are heavier on the palate than translucent, lighter reds; paler white wines are usually from cooler growing areas or vintages beset by wet and cool conditions close to harvest.

To determine a wine's true color, hold the tasting glass by its stem against a white background and tilt the glass to about a 45-degree angle. On first glance, notice the general color category of the wine. Is it a white, rosé, or red wine? Within these three broad categories a second glance will help define the hue and shading of the wine's color.

A good rule of thumb is that most of the paler white wines, such as a fresh Muscadet from the Loire Valley of France, are among the lightest in flavor intensity. In a mediocre wine, however, a pale, watery color might also be the result of a too-high yield of grapes in the vineyard, which reduces not only the color but the flavor as well. A pale color with green highlights usually indicates a wine from a cooler growing area, often promising a good vein of acidity in its flavor. Younger white wines tend to be paler, as the wines gain color with age; for example, a rich golden color is much appreciated in complex, oak-aged Chardonnay-based wines. Straw yellow is a common in-between color, usually indicating a wine of moderate flavor intensity and appropriate age. Wines with a "buttercup yellow" shade will show more powerful flavors or aged characteristics, or the wine may be sweet. White wines that have a deep yellow hue may come from warmer climes, be oak-aged, or come from a grape variety that exhibits more color, such as Gewürztraminer.

Red wines get their color from contact with the grape skins; the darker the skins and the longer the contact with the grape must (juice and skins), the deeper the color. Moderate to warmer climates tend to produce darker-hued red wines. Red wines may range from purple, garnet, black cherry, or ruby in young wines to mahogany, orange-red, and brownish colors in older wine. Young red wines usually show a medium ruby color at the heart of the wine and paler orange hues toward the outer edge. As red wines age, suspended pigments and tannins fall out and create sediment in the wine. Because of this process, and because of the BROWNING caused by slow oxidation, red wines lose their vibrant red and purple hues as they become older. Each varietal has the potential to pass through a spectrum of different shades of red from youth to maturity.

Rosé or "blush" wines may range from salmon to light pink to pale red. Their depth of color depends mostly on the grape types used and the length of skin contact during the winemaking process.

As they age, whites, rosés, and reds all start to brown; this browning will first be visible at the edge of the meniscus (around the rim of the surface) of the wine. When the browning becomes apparent nearer the center part of the bowl, the wine is usually past its prime and may be referred to as "oxidized." Oxidized wines have a nutty smell and taste, akin to that of Sherry. Some wine lovers enjoy *slightly* oxidized wines, but in general too much oxidation interferes with the true smell and taste characteristics of the wine. (Of course, fortified wines, as well as very old sweet wines, may exhibit a tawny shade of brown, but this hue is appropriate to those wines. Fortified wines, such as Sherry and Madeira, are purposely oxidized during the winemaking process.)

Beaujolais will demonstrate a light purple hue with pinkish-purplish highlights and translucence in its youth. It is not meant to be drunk more than a few years beyond its vintage, and any significant sign of browning in the wine is a sign of trouble. On the other hand, in its youth a Cabernet Sauvignon from Napa Valley will have a deep black cherry color and will be totally opaque; it will be harsh and tannic at this stage. As it ages, losing tannins and throwing sediment, a lighter color and a decidedly brown rim will be noticeable. An experienced taster can sometimes pinpoint the age of a wine by the graduations of color in the glass.

When describing a wine's color, the challenge is to use terms that are easy to understand. The University of

Chardonnay from Chassagne-Montrachet, Burgundy, five years old and twenty-five years old. White wines gain color with age.

Sauvignon Blanc from California, three years old, nine years old, fourteen years old, and botrytis-affected (half bottle). Notice how the older white and botrytis-affected wines are deeper in color.

Riesling from the Mosel and Rhine regions of Germany. The younger Mosel wine is lighter in color, with a green tinge. The bottles reflect the style difference, with Mosel wines traditionally in green bottles and the Rhine wines in brown bottles.

The color of rosé wines will vary by length of time of skin contact. From left to right, an American White Zinfandel, a Portuguese example (Baga) from Bairrada, and a Bandol wine from Provence, France.

American reds. From left to right, a Pinot Noir, a Syrah, and a Gamay Beaujolais. The color difference is due to the variety, with the Syrah, which is the most tannic, having the darkest and most opaque hue.

A Sangiovese-based Tuscan red from Italy and a Tempranillo-based Ribera del Duero from Spain.

Fortified wines, Sherry styles. From left to right, fino, amontillado, and oloroso.

Fortified wines, Porto and Madeira styles. From left to right, ruby, tawny, and vintage Portos, and a 5 Year Old Malmsey from Madeira.

Sparkling wines. From left to right, Blanc de Blancs, Blanc de Noirs, and Rosé.

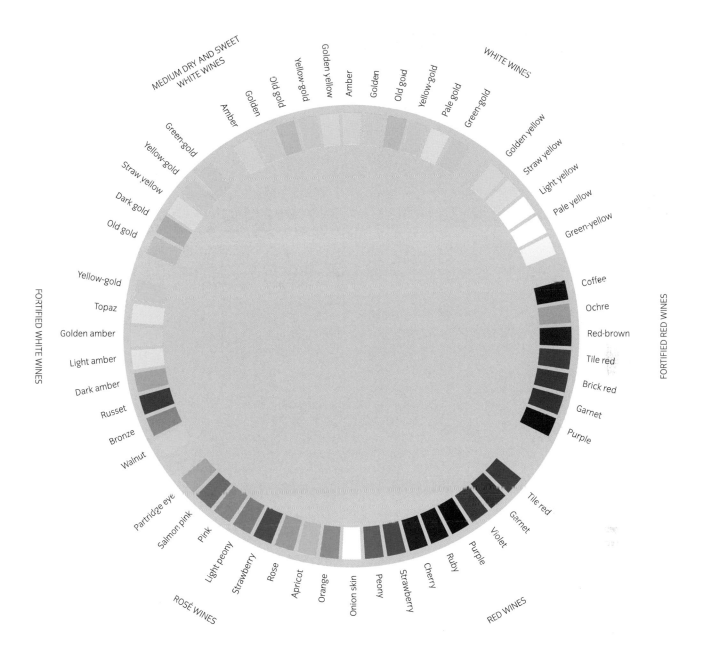

MEDIUM DRY AND SWEET WHITE WINES

Amber
Golden
Old gold
Yellow-gold
Golden yellow
Amber
Golden
Old gold
Yellow-gold
Pale gold
Green-gold

WHITE WINES

Golden yellow
Straw yellow
Light yellow
Pale yellow
Green-yellow

Green-gold
Yellow-gold
Straw yellow
Dark gold
Old gold

FORTIFIED WHITE WINES

Yellow-gold
Topaz
Golden amber
Light amber
Dark amber
Russet
Bronze
Walnut

Coffee
Ochre
Red-brown
Tile red
Brick red
Garnet
Purple

FORTIFIED RED WINES

Partridge eye
Salmon pink
Pink
Light peony
Strawberry
Rose
Apricot
Orange
Onion skin
Peony
Strawberry
Cherry
Ruby
Purple
Violet
Garnet
Tile red

ROSÉ WINES

RED WINES

California, Davis Color Wheel (see above), for example, uses terms such as "garnet," "tile red," **BRICK** red," "purple," "coffee," "cherry," and "strawberry" to describe red wine. Each term allows the taster to visualize the color of the wine described. You may choose to use terms that are easily recognized by the audience. For instance, the terms "cranberry juice," "sun-dried tomato," or "ancho chile" may be more familiar than references to gemstones, flowers, or tiles. Describing colors in wines is subjective, and the Davis Color Wheel is just another helpful tool used in wine communication.

The taster should also make note of the wine's clarity. The expectation of most tasters is that the wine should be bright and clean; radiant or star-bright clarity is preferred to lackluster cloudiness. Most wine is filtered to achieve clarity and stability. (For a discussion of filtration, see page 73.) Some winemakers, however, believe that this process strips the wine of its character. As a point of pride, many of

University of California, Davis Color Wheel

these producers print the word *unfiltered* on the bottle label. Unfiltered wines sometimes meet with customer resistance, since consumers want their wines to be bright and clear. While unfiltered wines are gaining in popularity (especially among influential wine writers and critics), proponents of filtering believe that the process has no adverse effects.

Also, in white or red wines small, tasteless crystalline deposits called tartrates sometimes accumulate on the cork. These deposits are sometimes in the bottle of wine as well, and by pouring slowly the server may avoid stirring them up so that no crystals interfere with a wine's appearance and lessen its attractiveness. (Some producers, especially in Germany, refer to these as "wine diamonds.") The taster should also determine whether the wine contains suspended particles or sediment. A hazy color, from suspended particles, is the first warning sign that the wine may have been stored improperly or has been aged too long. However, it is important to remember that older red wines may have quite a bit of sediment and may need decanting to bring out their true clarity.

LEGS, sometimes called "tears," may be seen running down the side of the glass after the glass is swirled. These rivulets result from higher levels of alcohol in the wine and hint at the degree of the wine's power.

When the wine is poured, or after swirling, some still wines will reveal small bubbles that are usually the result of leftover carbon dioxide from the fermentation process. These faintly spritzy wines—such as many Vinho Verde wines from Portugal—are often intentionally produced this way to provide a pleasant, cleansing effect on the palate. When judging the **APPEARANCE** of true sparkling wines, it is the smaller bubbles and their persistence and multiple streams (the *perlage*) and the foam or head (the *mousse*) at the top of the glass that are the first signs of quality.

SMELL

OUR SENSE OF SMELL enables us to identify hundreds of substances. Smelling the wine is a skill that requires practice and a familiarity with the kinds of scents that frequently are evident in wine. For example, Sauvignon Blanc frequently smells of green plums and gooseberries, and Chardonnay of apples, so a serious wine student should smell and taste those foods before and during a training session with those wines.

To enhance sensitivity to smells, go to the spice rack and sniff the cinnamon, clove, and mint separately. Take a walk in the woods and compare the scents of dead brown leaves and live green leaves. Go to a florist and try to distinguish the unique smells of roses, violets, and magnolias. Pick up a pebble from a stream or lake and put it right under a nostril so that the mineral or wet rock smell will be

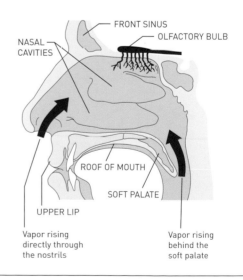

We can smell aromas through the nostrils and in a retronasal manner as vapors rise through the back of the palate.

easier to recognize in a wine. These methods may help you become more proficient at identifying different smells.

How to Smell

Aroma messages are received both through the nostrils and retronasally, through the back of the throat. These smell and taste centers—the tongue, nose, and retronasal passage—form the palate.

You should smell a wine before and after swirling in the glass, because swirling aerates the wine, bringing out its volatile elements or "nose." To swirl a wine properly, hold the stem of the wineglass between thumb and forefinger and move the glass gently in a small circle. Generally speaking, you should not aerate sparkling wines, as swirling breaks the bubbles in the wine.

A popular method of smelling a wine is first to give it a gentle sniff, then inhale more deeply, and finally inhale so heartily that you are virtually attempting to "taste" the wine with your nose. Others reverse this sniffing strategy, inhaling deeply first.

Whatever strategy for smelling wine you prefer, the important thing is to try to recognize and record first impressions, since nasal fatigue, a decreased sensitivity to smell, is bound to occur over time. Just as people who wear perfume cannot really smell the perfume on their bodies after a while, over time our noses habituate themselves to the smells emanating from the wineglass.

Note the intensity of the wine's nose. Is it shy or powerful? Weak or intoxicating? CLOSED and DUMB are two terms

Culinary Institute of America students smell fruits, flowers, vegetables, herbs, spices, and other elements to recognize aromas and bouquets of wine.

used when tasters are stymied by a lack of smells. The nose of a wine may be shy at first and then, as it is exposed to air, open up, releasing more of the volatile elements in the wine. After it is poured, a simple jug wine will not really change much at all, no matter how much time passes, but a fine wine will go through waves of change in the nature and intensity of its smells; this contributes to identifying it as "complex." The attraction and pleasure of just smelling such a wine is why some disciplined tasters prolong this stage and do not put the wine to their lips until many minutes pass.

What Smells Indicate

How can wine, made only from grapes, smell like banana, rose, or bitter almond? The volatile substances that are the roots of these analogous smells result from aldehydes, esters, terpenes, alcohols, and other chemicals. For example, piperonal smells of peach; a banana or pear smell indicates the presence of isoamyl acetate; a tea rose smell is from phenylethyl acetate; phenylpropionic aldehyde gives the scent of lilac; and acetoin smells of almonds. Recognizing and naming the properties of these chemicals is not as much fun as just trying to recognize the different smells. With experience, an aware taster will find that these associative smells are indicators of certain grape types, wine regions, winemaking techniques, and other important factors.

Everyone has a different "taste memory," so for some wine tasters recognition of certain smells is easier than for others. Every person has a different threshold at which he or she can distinguish a particular smell. Companies market smell kits that can be used to sensitize tasters to certain smells and to check the hunches of the taster's nose ("Was that really black currant I smelled?"). Also, dried spices or flowers can be put in a solution, or fruit jams can be used, to help train the nose to develop a memory bank of smells (see photo at left). Note that a cold will block the olfactory cleft and make both smelling and tasting difficult.

Aroma versus Bouquet

The smell of a young wine is called its AROMA. The *primary smell* is that of the grape type; experienced wine tasters can smell lychee nuts in a glass and know the wine is probably a Gewürztraminer and definitely not a Muscadet. The *secondary smell* is that of the wine after the fermentation process; an example of a secondary smell is the lactic

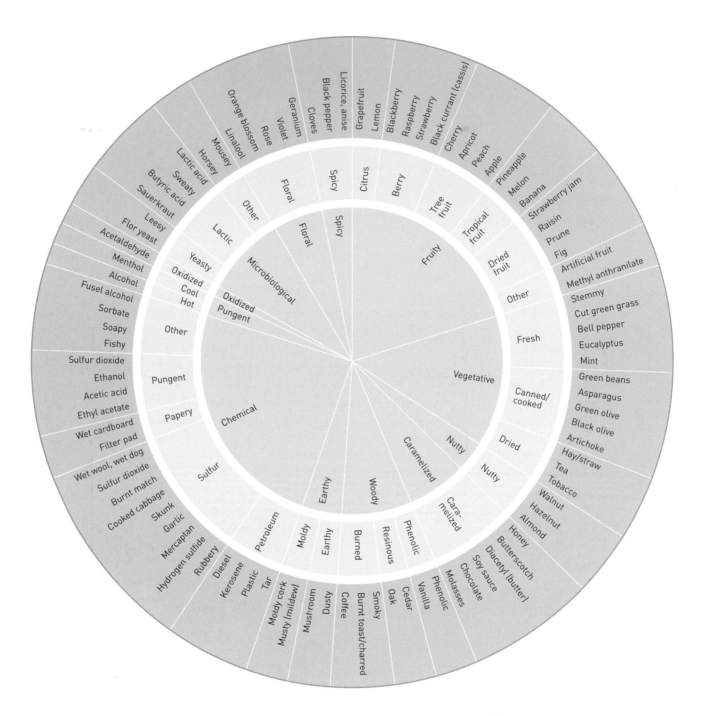

or creamy smell that is characteristic of a wine that has undergone malolactic fermentation. Aroma should not be confused with bouquet, the *tertiary smell* of a wine, which develops with age. Bouquet is the product of the aging process of the alcohols, acids, esters, enzymes, and other chemical compounds in the wine, both in the cask and in the bottle. Nutty smells are always present in the bouquet of wines that are oxidized, such as Vin Santo of Italy, Madeira from Portugal, or Sherry from Spain. The most ardent tasters can fill an entire page writing about the complexities of an aged wine's bouquet.

Unfortunately, there is no surefire way to predict exactly what the bouquet of an aged wine will be like based on the aroma of the young wine. Pronounced primary grape

University of California, Davis Aroma Wheel, developed by Ann Noble

smells and other smells, such as oak or alcohol, only suggest what the wine may achieve when time integrates those distinct parts into a more harmonious bouquet.

The UC Davis Aroma Wheel (see facing page) gives some of the terms used for smelling wines and their sources, but these are not the only terms that can be used to describe the smell of wine. Just about any mental association made from smelling wine is proper and correct. Indeed, there can be real delight in the phenomenon of a smell evoking a memory.

Smells That Indicate a Bad Wine

A hydrogen sulfide smell is similar to the odor of rotten eggs and is created as yeast cells decompose and interact with any excess sulfur dioxide in the wine.

Mercaptans, formed by a breakdown of sulfur, impart the smell of garlic, onion, or rubber to a wine, irritating the nose of the taster.

The chemical smell of iodine or a MUSTY quality are attributed to the use of rotten grapes. However, a very slight iodine smell may be the result of a wine's being made near the sea or the use of grapes affected by botrytis and is not a fault.

The smell of a so-called CORKED wine is strong and reminiscent of musty, wet cardboard or a MOLDY newspaper, and is most often due to the presence of the chemical 2, 4, 6 trichloranisole (TCA) in the wine. TCA, a product of the

An indoor tasting at Iron Horse Ranch and Winery

marriage of airborne fungi and chlorphenol compounds, or the result of bleaching corks with a chlorine-based solvent to sterilize them, has led to a worldwide problem with cork taint, from the least expensive to the most expensive wines in the world. The amount of TCA that can ruin a wine is infinitesimal—the equivalent of about a teaspoonful poured into the entire Pacific Ocean.

Small amounts of ACETIC ACID or ethyl acetate occur naturally in wine, but bacteria can ruin a wine by increasing the amount of those substances. Any more than 0.0005 fluid ounces per quart/150 milligrams per liter of ethyl acetate and 0.002 fluid ounces per quart/700 milligrams per liter of acetic acid will produce a wine that has an unpleasantly high level of volatile acidity. If acetic acid is present, the wine will smell vinegary and have a harsh, sour taste. If ethyl acetate is the problem, the wine will smell of nail polish remover.

If there are unpleasant odors, a small taste of wine should be sampled. It is much easier to deal with a problem wine before all the tasters are seated than to have to remove glasses and replace wine in the middle of a tasting or seminar.

TASTE

Tasting the Wine

Salty, sour, sweet, and bitter are the four main tastes the tongue can experience. (*Umami*, a fifth taste, refers to the taste of foods high in glutamic acid, such as shiitake mushrooms, parmesan cheese, anchovies, or soy sauce. *Umami* means "savory" in Japanese.) Taste messages are sent to the brain from the papillae, or taste buds, on the surface of the tongue. The taste buds most sensitive to bitterness are concentrated at the back of the tongue, with those most sensitive to sweetness concentrated at the tip, those sensitive to acidity found in greatest number on the sides of the tongue, and those most receptive to salt dispersed along the sides and front. In addition, there are areas of the tongue that are relatively sensitive to all five tastes, and areas that are almost totally insensitive to taste.

The flow of saliva in the mouth is affected when tasting wine. Wines high in acid always increase saliva flow, while very astringent or tannic wines leave the mouth feeling dried out.

One tastes a wine by moving it around the whole mouth. In this way, the wine is warmed and hits more

The sense of smell, the sense of taste...what joys they can be! Why not expand them? Just as the senses of sight and hearing can vary from person to person, so can the senses of smell and taste.

We can readily test our eyesight and hearing. We can usually correct weakness with glasses or hearing aids. But what about the senses of smell and taste? Notice they are two different senses, yet they work together. Yet these too vary with each person. Do you wonder where your palate would rank on a sensory scale? First of all, test yourself a bit. Go through your spice rack and, without looking at the labels, smell each spice and herb. Write down your responses. Don't worry if you get some wrong; practice, and soon you will learn to identify them by their fragrance alone. Just as we learn any new language, learning food descriptors is simply flavor and aroma recognition and retention. Once you feel solid with the spice rack, move on to smelling and tasting fresh herbs in order to identify and remember these. Then go on to fruit, vegetables, and so on, until your vocabulary and recall are quite good.

I use these techniques to help with wine tasting. I have found this method helps in describing a wine beyond fruity or dry or round. Coffee beans, beeswax, and so many other aromas will broaden your skills and expand your flavor and aroma recognition. You can include outdoor aromas as well, such as dried leaves, peat moss, hay, green grass, oak, eucalyptus, and so on.

If you could describe a person as being of medium height with brown hair, you have a vague picture that could describe millions of people. Yet to say a well-groomed, bearded man of thirty-five, tanned, stout, just under six feet tall, with intense blue eyes, a prominent nose, and waxy reddish-brown hair describes the same person in a more recognizable, perhaps memorable way. The same is true with wine. By using flavor terms, you can remember the specific traits of any wine. The more specific the wine description, the easier it will be to remember.

When people tell me with a big smile of a great wine they had the previous night but say they cannot remember the name of it, I think, What a shame the memory is gone forever! Why not keep a tiny notebook to jot down a name, a varietal, a vintage, and a descriptor or two, and if you like it or not? Why not expand your library of knowledge and retention at the same time? This way, that lovely experience, those glorious flavors, could be found and enjoyed again. It is also a great way to learn more about your palate, your likes, your dislikes, and your personal journey with this delicious food of the soul we call wine.

Holly Peterson-Mondavi,
Chef and Educator, Napa Valley, California

taste buds, and the aroma molecules enter the retronasal passage, making flavors more evident. Ten to thirty seconds is a normal amount of time to swirl about an ounce of wine in the mouth before spitting. (It is always best to leave some of the wine in the tasting glass, in case you are instructed to taste, or want to taste, a particular wine again.) Quickly swallowing some wine may provide refreshment and pleasure, but to truly taste a wine takes a conscious effort. With practice, the process of wine tasting becomes second nature.

The first taste of the wine is the "attack," followed by the "middle palate" and then the "finish." The attack refers to how powerful the wine is and what sensations are felt during the first five seconds after the wine enters the mouth. The middle palate is the evolution of those sensations as well as the development of new ones over the next ten seconds. The finish is the **AFTERTASTE** of flavors and the length of time those flavors can be sensed on the palate.

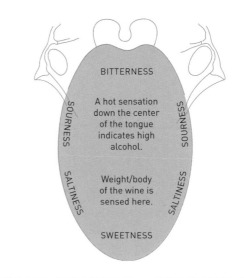

BITTERNESS

SOURNESS SOURNESS

A hot sensation down the center of the tongue indicates high alcohol.

Weight/body of the wine is sensed here.

SALTINESS SALTINESS

SWEETNESS

Tongue sensitivity

A wine that feels "hot" on the taster's tongue has a high level of alcohol that may be out of balance with the rest of the wine. A wine that lacks sufficient acidity to balance the other elements, such as fruitiness, sweetness, oak, and alcohol, is said to be "flat" or "flabby." Imbalanced wines are inconsistent with the ideal of a fine wine, which is harmony of taste and nose. In the finest wines, the sum of the flavor elements is greater than their parts.

How much perceived fruitiness, acidity, alcohol, or oak should there be? A wine should strike a balance of flavor components but be true to the grape type and the growing region it represents. A serious wine taster will become acquainted with the traditional tastes of the major grapes and wine regions of the world. This is a task that may take a lifetime, but the pursuit of knowledge and the attendant tastings can provide great pleasure. A wine-tasting novice may not enjoy the green, high-acid flavors of Sancerre, a Sauvignon Blanc–based wine from the Loire Valley of France, and may dislike the mineral nose even more. A taster familiar with the wine, however, will expect the mineral nose and the green-fruit acidity on the palate, and will be disappointed if they are not present in the glass.

Finish

Jean Anthelme Brillat-Savarin (1755–1826, the author of *The Physiology of Taste*, published in France in 1825, and translated into English by M. F. K. Fisher in 1949) said of tasting, "While the wine is in one's mouth, one receives a pleasing but imperfect impression; it is only when one has finished swallowing that one can really appreciate the taste and discern the bouquet particular to each type of wine; and then a few more moments are required before the gourmet can say that's good, passable, or bad."

The finish or aftertaste of a wine is judged based on how long the flavors persist on the palate after spitting or swallowing, and whether the lingering flavors are pleasant or not. White wines should have a finish underscored by acidity; otherwise they are described as flabby. Reds can be expected to have higher tannin levels. Since harmony is the goal, are the acidity, sweetness, alcohol, or tannins so excessive that they dominate the finish? Any flavors or aromas that can be detected in the aftertaste should be noted. Depending on the wine, a finish of less than ten seconds is considered short, but may still be pleasant. A finish of ten to about thirty seconds is considered medium, and more

The first thing I tell students in my wine-tasting classes is that I can't teach them how to taste. Tasting is a skill that you acquire, like any other skill, through practice. The only other way to learn is to do it. I impart techniques that I've found useful, but whether anyone actually learns how to taste is up to them. For me, the key to developing tasting accuracy and a deeper enjoyment of wine involves two separate acts. First, we follow a systematic pattern of looking, smelling, assessing the wine on the palate, and writing notes. This requires concentration, focus, and an ability to suspend judgment. We train our eyes, nose, and mouth to simply record the information that the wine transmits: colors, aromas, flavors, and tactile impressions. I spend a lot of time asking the students to concentrate on the aromatic impression the wine makes, because I've found this to be the most difficult and also the most essential aspect of the tasting process. The second step involves analysis. Interpreting the information requires an understanding of grape varieties, the effects of climate and weather, and techniques of fermentation and maturation, as well as age and quality assessments. For most people, of course, the furthest they would like to go is to know with greater certainty why some wines appeal to them more than others and how they can improve their chances of finding these wines. Even here we concentrate a good bit on breaking each wine down into its component parts and analyzing what the sensory characteristics represent, because increased enjoyment does seem to flow from greater understanding.

Sandy Block,
Master of Wine, Educator;
Vice President of Beverage Operations,
Legal Sea Foods, Boston, Massachusetts

than thirty seconds is considered long. Length of finish is the final measure of a great wine. Whether it is a short, refreshing, tart finish in a young white (Canadian Pinot Gris, for example) or a long, complex finish in an aged red (Syrah-rich Hermitage from the Rhône Valley of France), the finish is a taster's final impression and prompts reflection on the overall quality of a wine.

THE COMPONENTS OF WINE

FINDING PLEASURE in wine depends on the wine's many components being in balance, but the notion of "balance" can vary according to an individual's preferences. Using a couple of simple experiments, a taster may roughly define his or her preferences and practice identifying components. Start with a small glass of water and add a couple of tablespoons of lemon juice. Then start adding sugar a little at a time, tasting after each addition to determine when the mixture tastes good. The amount of sugar added is a personal preference. The same process could be reversed, starting with sugar and water, then adding the citrus. To sample tannins, try black tea steeped for a long time and served at room temperature. One glass could be mixed with lemon juice and varying amounts of sugar. Next, try the black tea with milk or cream and sugar, and notice how the impression of tannin is less powerful on the palate.

Another factor to consider is how the components of a given wine are likely to mesh in the future. A young wine may be very aggressive in tannins, oak, and alcohol. However, if there is enough richness of fruit and acidity, an experienced taster will realize that in the future, the power of the tannins and alcohol will diminish, hopefully to bring the wine into balance. The taster may appreciate the wine based not only on its present appeal but also on its potential *future* taste or its development.

When tasting wine, a taster can attempt to isolate the following major components:

ALCOHOL The alcohol in the wine should be in balance with the other components, because too much makes the wine taste hot. The perception of heat in a young wine may diminish with age as other flavors evolve. Wines higher in alcohol may have a perceived hint of sweetness from the GLYCERIN they contain.

RESIDUAL SUGAR How much residual sugar is there? Many people confuse a wine that is fruity, one that has just a bit of residual sugar, with a wine that is sweet. The more residual sugar, the sweeter the wine.

OAK Not all wines are fermented or aged in a barrel. If oak is in the taste, how prominent is its flavor? Does it mask the fruit or perhaps a defect in the wine? Toasted scents are apparent in all types of oak, with American oak contributing an impression of spice and coconut while French and Eastern European varieties display more of a vanilla flavor.

TANNINS Wood tannins are sensed more toward the back and roof of the mouth, while grape-skin tannins are sensed more at the front of the mouth, on the gums, and on the inside of the cheeks. Tannins taste bitter and can make the mouth pucker and dry the palate. "Astringency" is the term used to describe this drying effect.

ACIDITY The main acid in wine is tartaric acid (grapes are higher in tartaric acid than other fruits). The hard taste of tartaric acid is accompanied by the green apple taste of malic acid and the citrus taste of citric acid. Gluconic acid occurs mostly when rotten or oxidized grapes are included in a wine. While all of these acids occur naturally in the grape, there are three other acids that occur because of bacteria or fermentation. Lactic acid has a sour cream taste, while succinic acid has a tart, fruity taste, and acetic acid is vinegary. Acidity keeps a wine fresh as it ages and provides balance to the fruit and alcohol components.

I am often asked, "What is your favorite wine?" I'm usually reluctant to answer that question because I am more interested in seeing people develop their own palate. It's like painting. I might prefer Monet; you might like Jackson Pollack. It could be argued they are both great, but they are certainly worlds apart from each other.

So, taste lots of wines and keep track of what you like. Soon you will probably see a pattern in discovering what your favorites are.

Boots Brounstein,
Proprietor, Diamond Creek Vineyards,
Napa Valley, California

CARBON DIOXIDE When judging bubbles, look for size (tiny is better) and the number of *cordons* or streams (more is better). The bubbles will also form a mousse or foam on the surface of the wine, which may be described as "fine" or "thick." The feel of bubbles foaming is pleasant at cool temperatures but may be unpleasant when the wine is warmer. Some still wines may contain a slight amount of fizz that is created during fermentation and retained as flavor and texture elements in the wine. This slight effervescence may be found in some Vinho Verde wines of Portugal and some northern Italian wines, such as Gavi.

VARIETAL CHARACTER Are any specific tastes of a grape type apparent?

OFF FLAVORS Are there any unpleasant flavors, such as rancidity, rotten eggs, or mold?

AROMAS How powerful are the wine's aromas, both nasal and retronasal? Are there floral or fruit indicators, such as violets or raspberries? Or perhaps **VEGETAL** or spicy aromas, such as bell pepper, black olive, or cinnamon? Are there any other indicators? The taster should focus on the flavors and aromas that are there, not those that are *supposed* to be there. For example, if a taster who thinks a wine could be based on Cabernet Sauvignon perceives the classic bell pepper aroma and tannin effect on the palate, he or she may easily imagine the black currant flavors that should be there, even if they are not.

BODY Body is the perceived weight of the wine in the mouth. It can be described as "watery," "very light," "light," "medium," "full," or "very full," or a combination of these terms, such as "medium/full." As the weight of the wine progresses from light to full, the idea of the coating of the palate comes into play. A very light wine may actually cleanse and enliven the palate, while a full-bodied oak-aged wine may come close to deadening the palate.

TEXTURE The impressions of a wine's texture on the palate may be expressed as "velvet" or "satin" for wines with a smooth or rich mouthfeel, but without harsh alcohol or tannic sensations. "Loose-knit" might refer to a wine whose taste components are not individually well-defined and do not combine to make a balanced wine.

The tasting process and terms associated with it are tools that help us define our preferences and share them. When wine and food are combined at a meal, the atmosphere and company in which the wine is drunk can also elevate or negate the enjoyment, but when tasting wine as a serious or professional activity, we should do our best to ignore the outside world and focus on the world in the glass. Become one with the wine.

TYPES OF TASTINGS

GENERAL TASTING

IN A GENERAL TASTING, wines of different styles are tasted. A good starting point is to taste a light-bodied dry white and then a fuller-bodied white wine. Or try a bone-dry white, then a semidry wine, and finally a sweet wine. Light purple, translucent reds could be compared with darker red wines and with an older wine displaying shades of reddish brown.

As an example of a general white wine tasting, a dry, light-bodied Muscadet from the Loire Valley of France might be followed by a dry, medium-bodied Albariño from Galicia, Spain; next could be a dry, full-bodied barrel-fermented Chardonnay from California, then a semidry Riesling from New York or Washington State, ending with a sweet Recioto di Soave white from Veneto, Italy. Gaining experience in general tastings is a good way to develop confidence about perceiving the weight or body of a wine and the difference between dry, semidry, and sweet.

VERTICAL TASTING

IN A VERTICAL TASTING, the same wine or similar wines are tasted through a series of vintages. The general rule in a vertical tasting is to start with the youngest, most powerful wines and proceed chronologically to the older vintages. These tastings allow participants to focus on the distinct style of the producer or wine region. When the soil types and grape varieties are constant, the dynamics of the growing conditions of the vintage and the aging process can be isolated.

An example of a vertical tasting would be a series of vintage Portos from 2004, 2001, 1994, 1991, 1990, 1985, 1977, 1970, 1963, and 1955. A further control could be to taste wines from just one producer to avoid stylistic differences between firms. Porto is known to age well, but there are many other ageworthy wines that could be tasted, such as those made from the Cabernet Sauvignon grape. In a vertical tasting of red wines, tasters will observe that the wines become less harsh and their flavors more integrated and harmonious over time. Such a tasting will also show that experts are making educated guesses when they try to project how much longer an old wine will remain enjoyable before its demise.

HORIZONTAL TASTING

IN A HORIZONTAL TASTING, the quality of a specific vintage is assessed by concentrating on one region or grape type and focusing on the styles produced.

As an example, try California Cabernet Sauvignons of the 2007 vintage from the Stags Leap District, Rutherford, Howell Mountain, and Mount Veeder viticultural areas of Napa Valley, along with examples from the Alexander Valley in Sonoma County, from Monterey County, and from the Paso Robles district in San Luis Obispo County.

BLIND TASTING

IN A BLIND TASTING, the taster attempts to discern what the wine is by using information and experience obtained from years of studying the major grape types and regions of the world and how they interact. A knowledge of producers and vintages is also required for this difficult task. The advantage of tasting blind is that it is good training for the palate and mind, and the taster cannot presuppose the nature or quality of a wine. It forces the taster to rely on his or her senses and any lessons learned from previous tastings.

SEMIBLIND TASTING

A SEMIBLIND TASTING is when tasters have a limited amount of information, such as the country or grape type, and taste wines without knowing such vital information as vintage, producer, or product. The advantage of this kind of tasting is that judgments are not prejudiced, and the most appealing wines will show well.

COMPARATIVE TASTING

IN A COMPARATIVE TASTING, similar styles of wine are tasted together and compared with each other.

An example of this type of tasting would be a group of powerful reds, which might include a Barolo from Italy, a Châteauneuf-du-Pape from France, a Ribera del Duero from Spain, a Bairrada from Portugal, a Shiraz from Australia, and a Malbec from Argentina.

TASTING CIRCLES

RESTAURANTS AND HOTELS often form tasting circles that meet regularly, sometimes tasting in silence so as to avoid unduly affecting one another's opinions. Participants then declare their top choices in each flight, or set of wines that will be tasted together, such as California Chardonnays between $10 and $20, or those over $20. It is strongly recommended that some kitchen staff be included in the tasting circle team, for the dialogue between the kitchen and dining room staff on wine acquisitions and food pairing will be appreciated by the customers, who will experience a harmony of wine and food rather than competition or discord.

WALK-AROUND TASTINGS

ANOTHER TYPE OF TASTING often found at wine festivals or organized especially for the trade is the walk-around tasting, usually held in a large room where participants go to different tables or booths, sampling a wine or two from each location. At such tastings, each taster is provided with one glass as she or he enters. Each table is equipped with water pitchers for rinsing glasses and cleansing the palate, as well as a spit bucket. Tasters may have a hundred or more wines available to sample, so spitting is essential.

Having a tasting strategy can be useful at large walk-around tastings. Try tasting the lighter and drier wines before those that are heavy or sweet, so that the palate is not overwhelmed in the early stages of the tasting. For example, tasting a sweet wine just before a dry or semidry wine would strongly affect how those wines are perceived; in particular, the hint of sweetness in a semidry wine would not be easily detected after tasting one that is much sweeter. A two-and-a-half-hour tasting might be broken down into three segments, with the first hour devoted to white wines and dry sparkling wines, the next hour to dry reds, and the remaining time to sweet and fortified wines.

TASTING SHEETS

UNLESS THE TASTING is blind, in which case the names of the wines are never revealed in advance, tasting sheets with the name of the product, producer, area, and vintage should be provided. Each wine should be numbered on the sheet, with the corresponding number on the decanter or bottle of wine, so that the sequence of tasting is clear. The sheet may be informal, with some room to make general comments, or it may be quite specific, with labeled categories such as "color," "nose," "taste," "body," and "finish" and boxes for personal comments and a numerical rating. Other tasting sheets may list descriptors of nose and taste, with a box to check off each relevant descriptor. This latter method serves as a guide for the tasters, giving them choices instead of asking for evaluations and relative numerical ratings.

SUMMARY

THE REASONS FOR TASTING WINE vary, but it is an acquired skill that in the begining requires discipline but will in time become a practice that leads to relaxation and pleasure. The tasting terms mentioned and illustrated in this chapter provide a framework that helps define individual preferences and creates a common language to share perceptions about wine; as such, wine terms should be used only as a tool for communication, never for intimidation. Don't get hooked on wine-speak, but instead develop your own vocabulary for communicating your interest and passion for wine.

Because of the strong connection between the senses and our personal memory or feelings, opening our senses to a glass of wine may allow us to remember something long forgotten or inspire a vision of the future. The practical side of tasting wine is a necessary skill for anybody in the wine business, but we should never forget the artists, playwrights, and poets who have exhorted us over the centuries to enjoy all its pleasures.

The Culinary Institute of America

Wine Tasting Sheet

Topic: _____ Date: _____

Wine	Color Depth Hue Clarity	Nose Aroma Bouquet	Body In Glass In Mouth Sugar/Alcohol	Taste Components	Finish Duration New Flavors	Restaurant and/or Food
1.						
2.						
3.						
4.						
5.						
6.						
7.						
8.						

A basic tasting sheet with a reference for possible food pairings or restaurant

SUGGESTED TASTING SHEET FOR SPARKLING WINES

Modeled after the work of Georges Hardy, Station Enotechnique de Champagne, Epernay

Vintage: _____ Producer: _____

Appellation: _____ Style: _____

VISUAL EVALUATION	
Foam	
Bubbles	
Color	
EVALUATION BY NOSE	
Aromas	
Overall quality	
EVALUATION BY PALATE	
Sugar/acid balance	
Body	
Development of flavors	
Overall quality	
GENERAL CONCLUSIONS	

SUMMARY
Give a mark between 1 and 20 for each category

Visual	Olfactory	Taste	Quality of Vinification	Overall Appeal	TOTAL

Wine Type (White/Rosé/Red)			Appellation:
			Type:

Laboratory Observations and Conclusion — Date of Analysis

Specific Gravity	Total Acidity
Alcohol	Fixed Acidity
Residual Sugar	Volatile Acidity
Potential Alcohol	(corrected for sulfuric acid)
Total SO_2	
Free SO_2	
pH	
color index P/x	
Index of permangranate	

Method of Vinification

Visual Examination	Surface of the Liquid		Brilliant—dull Clean—iridescent—oily
	Color	White Wine	Pale with green or yellow tints—pale yellow—straw yellow—canary yellow—gold—amber
		Rosé Wine	Pale with violet or rose tints—gray—light rose—deep rose—partridge eye—onion skin
		Red Wine	Red with crimson or violet tints—cherry red—ruby—garnet red—red brown—tile red—mahogany—tawny
		Color Hue	Frank—oxidized—cloudy
	Aspect		Crystalline—brilliant—limpid—hazy—cloudy—turgid—lead—gray/white—opaque, with or without deposit
	Legs/Tears		Quick or slow to form—nonexistent—slight—heavy

Temperature of the Wine			Any Factor Hindering the Tasting
Olfactory Examination	First Impression		Pleasant—ordinary—unpleasant
	Aroma	Intensity	Powerful—adequate—feeble—nonexistent
		Quality	Very fine—racy—distinguished—fine—ordinary—common—not very pleasant—unpleasant
		Character	Primary—secondary—tertiary—floral—fruity—vegetal—spicy—animal—oxidized
		Length	Long—average—short
	Abnormal odors		CO_2—SO_2—H_2S—mercaptan—strongly oxidized—woody—lactic acid—acescence—phenolic—corky Flaw { temporary—permanent / slight—serious
	Details		
Any Factor Hindering or Stopping the Continuation of the Tasting			

Gustatory Examination	First Impression			
	Flavors and Sensations	**Sweetness**	Sugar	Heavy—very sweet—sweet—dry—brut
			Glycerine and alcohol	Soft—unctuous—velvety—smooth—rough—dried out
		Acidity	Excessive	Acid—green—tart—nervy—acidulous
			Balanced	Fresh—lively—supple—smooth
			Insufficient	Flat—flabby
		Body	Alcoholic strength	Light—sufficient—generous—heady—hot
			Flesh	Fat—round—full—thin—meager
			Tannin	Rich—balanced—insufficient—astringent—bitter
		Aromas in the mouth	Intensity	Powerful—average—weak—long—short
			Quality	Very fine—elegant—pleasant—common—faded
			Nature	Floral—fruity—vegetable—spicy—wood—chemical—animal—other—young—developed—complex
	Inherent or Abnormal Flavors	*Terroir*		Marked—noticeable—faint—nonexistent
		Sickness		Grease—turned—aldehydes—sweet—sour—rancid—acetic acid—lactic acid
		Accident		Stagnant—mold—lees—woody—cork—metallic—H_2S—herbaceous—acrid
	Final Impression	**Balance**		Harmonious—bold—correct—unbalanced—Xs acid, Xs sugar, Xs tannin, Xs alcohol
		Aftertaste		Straightforward—unpleasant
		Resistance of taste and aroma		> 8 sec 5–7 sec 4–5 sec < 3 sec
				very long long medium short
Conclusions	**Conformity to Appellation or Type**			
	Score out of 20			
	Summary of Tasting (character of wine—future, readiness for drinking)			

A detailed tasting sheet by A. Castell for the Institut National des Appellations d'Origine (INAO) provides descriptive choices for the taster.

TERR
d'O

Magnificá

Sam
Don
August & Sylvia
Mary Ann

Hanze
SONOMA VALL

SINCE
1791
Nederbu
PINOTAGE

CARDINAL
ZIN

ONTEVINA
WINERY
Established: 1970

PART 2
WINES OF THE NEW WORLD

IN THE SPACE of less than four decades, the North American continent has emerged from relative obscurity as a wine producer to a position of prominence as a major producer of quality wines. Also, the United States has become a country with a true wine culture, as wine is now produced in all fifty states, and the nation's wine drinkers have made the United States a major consumer of wine from all over the world.

While it may not possess the *terroir* of Burgundy, the romance of Tuscany, or the rustic spirit of Rioja, California is still one of the most exciting and vital wine-producing regions in the world. In a country where **PROHIBITION** virtually wiped out the possibility of an American fine wine industry, and where the public's taste in the immediate post-Prohibition years was largely limited to inexpensive jug wines, what has happened in California's vineyards and wineries in the past forty years is nothing short of revolutionary.

The recent history of wine in California is a compelling story, a complex and rapidly unfolding narrative, but California's meteoric rise in the wine world has not occurred without its share of fits, starts, and serious threats to its continued well-being. On balance, however, the story of wine, *especially of fine wine*, in post-Prohibition California is one of a miraculous rise to prominence.

California, a behemoth in the North American wine industry, has set the pace for producing wines at every conceivable quality and price level, and we will discuss California in Chapter 4. It is not only California, however, that produces great wine in the United States. Washington State, Oregon, New York State, and Virginia, among several other states, have garnered national and international attention for the consistent quality of the wines produced in their vineyards and wineries.

Chapter 5 is dedicated to the wines of other U.S. states, and to the wines of the other two nations that complete North America: Canada and Mexico. Mexico is not a major player on the international wine scene, but their wines deserve attention. Canada has become an important producer of wine, especially much sought-after wines made from cool-climate vineyards.

SONOMA

russian river valley

paso robles

MENDOCINO

RUTHERFORD

PACIFIC OCEAN

SAN LUIS OBISPO

meritage

SANTA MARIA VALLEY

CARNEROS

MOUNTAINS

VALLEYS

OAKVILLE

NAPA

UNITED STATES: CALIFORNIA

CHAPTER

4

THE UNITED STATES HAS EMERGED from relative obscurity as a wine-producing country only forty years ago to a prominent position today as a major producer of quality wines. Of all the fifty states, California is the single largest producer of wine, accounting for at least 90 percent of the nation's wine production.

In this chapter, we will discuss the United States, its current wine culture and wine laws, and then focus on California. Admittedly, there is a tendency, even within the United States, to think only of California as producing good wine, but increasingly the international press focuses deserved attention on other areas of the United States as well as on Canada and Mexico. So we will discuss California, the largest producer in North America, in this chapter, and then focus on the rest of North America in the next chapter.

UNITED STATES

As A WINE-PRODUCING and wine-consuming nation, the United States is a collection of contradictions and inconsistencies. Although estimates for 2008 show the nation was the fourth-largest producer of wine in the world (see Table on page 112), the same year it ranked only thirtieth in annual per capita consumption. On the other hand, the total amount of wine consumed in the United States, as of 2007, places the nation third in total consumption (see Table on page 112). And if current trends continue, by the time you read this, it is quite possible that the United States will be the number one wine consumer, or very close to number one in the world, by dollars spent on wine. The United States is the sixth-largest wine-exporting nation, claiming about 6 percent of the world wine market.

While many U.S. wineries are proud to advertise the fact that their wines have been served at White House dinners, the controls imposed by the government on labeling and merchandising wines have been widely ridiculed. The United States was the first nation in the world to require health warning labels on every bottle of wine sold, while American wines exported to many other nations *are not permitted* to carry the warning label by the importing nations' laws. The federal regulatory agency for wine is the **ALCOHOL AND TOBACCO TAX AND TRADE BUREAU** of the Treasury, or TTB.

Many Americans see the consumption of wine as one aspect of living well, yet there is also a strong sentiment throughout the nation that drinking is wrong. Many physicians recommend a glass of wine or two per day for their patients' overall health, but there are many people who regard someone who drinks one or two glasses of wine *every day* as an alcoholic. And for all of the United States' consumerism, an attitude that encourages anybody to

TOP TEN WINE-PRODUCING NATIONS, 2008 (ESTIMATED)

RANK	COUNTRY	GALLONS	HECTOLITERS
1	France	1,277,760,000	48,400,000
2	Italy	1,266,698,000	47,981,000
3	Spain	916,080,000	34,700,000
4	United States	528,897,000	20,034,000
5	Argentina	397,214,000	15,046,000
6	China	316,800,000	12,000,000
7	Germany	270,890,000	10,261,000
8	South Africa	259,776,000	9,840,000
9	Australia	253,968,000	9,620,000
10	Chile	217,193,000	8,227,000

Source: Office International de la Vigne et du Vin

buy and use the newest, most complicated, and technologically advanced machinery without knowing anything about how it works, there persists a bizarre notion in the country that in order to buy and enjoy wine, you have to know quite a lot about it.

WINE IN THE UNITED STATES TODAY

OF THE TOTAL U.S. POPULATION, approximately one-third does not drink alcohol at all. Of the remaining two-thirds, a little more than half are defined as regular wine drinkers, with the definition of *regular* being one glass of wine *per week*. Yet the dedicated wine drinker in the United States drinks one glass of wine, sometimes two or three, *per day*. Taking the entire population, including minors, as a base, per capita annual consumption of wine in the United States has increased modestly from about 2.1 gallons/7.95 liters in 1986 to about 2.31 gallons/8.75 liters in 2006, to an estimated 2.96 gallons/11.2 liters in 2008.

This last figure equates to the consumption of about one bottle of wine per month per capita. By some estimates, however, as much as 90 percent of all the wine consumed in the United States is consumed by less than 15 percent of the wine-drinking population, which means that a small core of wine drinkers are consuming not one bottle per month, but a bottle of wine per week, if not more.

The profile of the American wine drinker is far different from the profile of the average European wine consumer. The 2006 per capita annual wine consumption figures for France and Italy (see the table on facing page) were 16 gallons/60.13 liters and 12.71 gallons/48.16 liters, respectively, but even Italy's figures were eclipsed by tiny Luxembourg's 14.75 gallons/55.85 liters.

In Europe, however, despite its much higher per capita wine consumption than the United States, wine consumption is dramatically down. In 1990, the French consumed 19.27 gallons/72.94 liters of wine per person and Italians consumed 16.37 gallons/61.97 liters per person. Worldwide, consumption has dropped to below one gallon/3.5 liters per person, the lowest level recorded since 1975, when statisticians began to collect such data.

So the United States is bucking the international trend toward lower wine consumption. Although U.S. per capita consumption has not risen dramatically, it has continued to rise. The truly dramatic difference is in the overall wine consumption by volume; the idea that the United States is poised to become the number one wine consumer in the world would have been unthinkable even ten years ago.

In addition to all of the news about wine consumption in the United States, we cannot ignore another interesting, and formerly unthinkable, fact about drinking in the nation. Wine is now the number one choice in alcoholic beverages for Americans, eclipsing both beer and spirits.

TOP TEN WINE-CONSUMING INDUSTRIAL NATIONS BY TOTAL VOLUME CONSUMED, 2007 (ESTIMATED)

RANK	COUNTRY	GALLONS	HECTOLITERS
1	France	849,261,600	32,169,000
2	Italy	710,160,000	26,900,000
3	United States	699,600,000	26,500,000
4	Germany	532,012,800	20,152,000
5	China	359,040,000	13,600,000
6	Spain	350,354,400	13,270,000
7	United Kingdom	319,440,000	12,100,000
8	Argentina	294,782,400	11,166,000
9	Russia	277,200,000	10,500,000
10	Romania	145,965,600	5,529,000

Source: The Wine Institute, based on data provided by the Office International de la Vigne et du Vin

TOP WINE-CONSUMING INDUSTRIAL NATIONS PER CAPITA, 2006

RANK	COUNTRY	GALLONS	LITERS
1	France	16	60.13
2	Luxembourg	14.75	55.85
3	Italy	12.71	48.16
4	Portugal	12.32	46.67
5	Slovenia	11.44	43.37
6	Croatia	11.16	42.27
7	Switzerland	10.52	39.87
8	Spain	9.15	34.66
9	Hungary	8.73	33.06
31	United States	2.31	8.75

Source: The Wine Institute, based on data provided by the Office International de la Vigne et du Vin

THE EVOLUTION OF THE AMERICAN WINE DRINKER

TODAY, WINE DRINKERS in America consume just about equal amounts of white and red wine. This situation is very different from the consumption patterns of forty or fifty years ago, when more Americans drank heavy red wines, especially sweet wines in a Porto or Sherry style. But as our tastes in food have moved to lighter fare, so our preferences for wine have changed. Today, white wines, especially Chardonnay, but also Sauvignon Blanc and Riesling, are major players, but there have been dramatic increases in red wine consumption, too. This trend followed the widespread distribution of reports in the early 1990s that moderate consumption of wine, especially red wine, might play a role in keeping cholesterol levels low and in inhibiting the development of certain forms of cancer. As a result, Cabernet Sauvignon and Merlot have become major varietals for all wine-producing nations, and planting of Pinot Noir, Zinfandel, and red Rhône varieties such as Syrah have also increased in response to greater demand, especially in the United States.

This is true at all age levels for legal drinkers, and the largest growth in wine consumption appears to be among the segment of the public identified by marketers as the "millenials," the generation of people brought up in the 1980s. This demographic seems to enjoy wine, and wine with food, and have been tracked as being quite adventurous in their wine choices, enthusiastically trying wines from different regions of the world.

Although the United States has truly developed an appreciation for wine and and has created a wine culture, a cultural difference with Europe remains. Although wine consumption is falling in Europe, it is still true that people at all socioeconomic levels drink wine—and not just one glass of wine per week, but a glass or two of wine at dinner just about every day. In other words, virtually everybody drinks wine in the Old World wine-producing countries. In America, the higher a person's level of education and income, or the higher he or she aspires, the more likely he or she is to drink wine.

The American wine industry gears almost all of its marketing strategies to attracting the upscale consumer, and in particular, the upscale *male* consumer. This makes little sense, because women make more than 60 percent of the wine purchases in the United States. Likewise, if the American wine industry wants to continue to increase the sale and consumption of wine, it should try to broaden the base of wine consumers by appealing to a wider swath of American society, including women, minorities, and Americans with strong ethnic identities, and not just try to sell more wine to existing wine drinkers.

THE EVOLUTION OF THE AMERICAN WINE PRODUCER

JUST AS AMERICAN WINE CONSUMERS have changed over time, so the American wine producer has learned, adapted, and improved to the point where several states are now major producers of high-quality wines. Part of the American psyche and character is an unswerving need to learn and understand, to experiment and improve, and this is as true for wine as it is for aeronautics or computer software. American winemakers and researchers have made some major contributions to the world of wine knowledge. To understand these contributions, we first need to look at how the industry evolved.

For all of the early attempts at grape growing and winemaking on the East and West coasts of the United States, and notwithstanding the awards and gold medals from World's Fairs from the late 1800s through the early 1900s, serious world-class winemaking on anything approaching

POPULAR WINES THROUGH THE YEARS

1960s Cold Duck sparkling red, Porto-style fortified wines, Gallo Hearty Burgundy

1970s Ackermann's Sparkling Rosé and Rosé d'Anjou, Mateus, Lancers, Sichel Blue Nun, Gallo Chablis

1980s Riunite, Bartles & Jaymes wine coolers, Sutter Home White Zinfandel, Kendall-Jackson Chardonnay

1990s Chardonnays, Merlots, Cabernet Sauvignons, sparkling white wines, Rhône varietals, flavored wines

THE PRESENT Chardonnay and Cabernet Sauvignon are the most popular varietals. Merlot is still strong; Zinfandel is very popular; Sauvignon Blanc and Riesling are gaining more recognition; and there is an increasing interest in Pinot Noir as well as red and white Rhône varietals. Good-quality box wines and wine bottles with screw caps have emerged, as have California Cult Cabernets and wines from Italy, Australia, Chile, Argentina, New Zealand, and South Africa. At least 70 percent of wine consumed by Americans is produced in the United States; all fifty states produce wines, many of high quality.

---

a large scale did not emerge in the United States until the 1950s and 1960s. Prohibition lasted from 1920 to 1933. Even after its repeal and the formation three years later of the Wine Institute, an organization created "to educate the American public about wine," many states, counties, towns, and villages retained some form of prohibition or restrictive licensing, and a similar situation existed in Canada. The beginning of the Great Depression was not the best time to borrow money to start up new wineries. In the early 1940s, American industry concentrated on helping win a war, and it was not until the 1950s that the social and economic climate became ripe for any real development in wine production in the United States.

The first new winery to open in Napa Valley following Prohibition was Joe Heitz's in 1962, twenty-nine years after its repeal. Soon after, Heitz was followed by the late Robert Mondavi, who split from his family-run Charles Krug Winery business to open his own winery in 1966. At that time, two European immigrants, Charles Fournier from France and Dr. Konstantin Frank from Ukraine, were pioneering the use of vinifera grape varieties in New York

State. Since that time, research and development have proceeded at a steady pace. Much of that development can be seen through the evolution of the standard label on bottles of North American wine.

NAMING THE WINE

THERE ARE THREE MAIN TYPES of names used on North American wine labels: generic, proprietary, and varietal (see descriptions below). This is in distinct contrast to the age-old practice in European wine countries, where many of the wines are named for the place where the grapes grow. There are also various descriptive terms used on North American labels. Some of these terms are defined in law, some are not.

Generic Labels

Generic labels (actually categorized as *semi-generic* by the TTB) have been in use for many years in North America. The word *generic* refers to the fact that the name used reflects a type of wine. All of the generic names used on American wine labels are European place names, borrowed by American winemakers, presumably in the belief or hope that their wine is of the same type as the wines from that place. In practice, however, wines carrying these names bear little or no resemblance to the wines from the original place in Europe. The wines are drinkable and affordable, and these days are as likely to be packaged in a five-liter box as in the traditional glass jug.

The following are the most common examples of generic names used in America.

A generic (legally known as semi-generic) wine label

BURGUNDY Used in North America to name any usually soft red wine.

CHABLIS Used in North America to name any usually medium-dry white wine.

CHAMPAGNE Used in North America to name any white wine with bubbles in it.

RHINE Used in North America to name any medium-sweet white wine.

SAUTERNE Used in North America to name any sweet white wine. (Notice that in crossing the Atlantic, the name "Sauternes," a place in Bordeaux, France, lost the final *s*.)

Other generic names include Chianti, Claret, Haut Sauterne, Hock, Madeira, Malaga, Marsala, Moselle, Port, Sherry, and Tokay.

Until the early 1990s, generic-label wines were the most popular category of wine in the United States, ceding that place to varietal labels in 1994. Understandably, generic labels were a point of contention between American winemakers and European winemakers, whose wines actually were produced from grapes grown in the often-famous places whose names were appropriated for mass-produced, inferior wines. Under the terms of an agreement between the United States and the European Union, reached in March 2006, American producers of generic-label wines may continue to produce them, but no new generic labels will be approved by the TTB.

Proprietary Labels

Throughout the twentieth century and still today, wine producers in North America have used proprietary names to label their wines. A proprietary name is one that is often trademarked or copyrighted, and is reserved for the sole use of one company. Early examples were as curious as the current crop of proprietary names, ranging from prototypes such as Thunderbird and Night Train to the more recent Opus One, Rubicon, and Sutter Home's Fré label for its nonalcoholic wines. The essential purpose of the proprietary label is to provide brand recognition and encourage customer loyalty.

Producers of high-quality wines in the United States today are dealing with a small but highly educated group of consumers who are likely to know what they are buying when they purchase Opus One or Rubicon. These buyers will probably know what grape varieties were used, where they were grown, and who made the wine.

There has been an interesting development in proprietary wine labels with the introduction in 1998 of the **MERITAGE** category (rhymes with *heritage*), which designates a red or white wine made in the style of red and white wines of Bordeaux, using the grapes traditionally used by Bordeaux winemakers. These grapes are mostly various combinations of Cabernet Sauvignon, Merlot, and Cabernet Franc for the red wines, and Sauvignon Blanc and Sémillon for the whites. Wines that fit this category are sometimes labeled as Meritage (if the winery belongs to the Meritage Alliance, formerly the Meritage Association) and sometimes labeled with proprietary names. Sometimes both the proprietary name (for example, Magnificat) and the word *Meritage* appear on the label. The category has proved quite successful for red wines, but not so successful for whites.

Varietal Labels

Presumably in an attempt to bring more integrity and authenticity to wine names (as well as to gain name differentiation), some U.S. producers, led by the Wente family in California in 1936, took the unprecedented step of giving their wines varietal names. This means that the wine is named for the grape variety used to make the wine.

 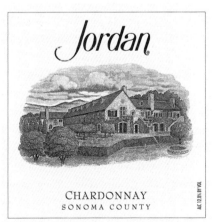

LEFT: *A proprietary label, "The Mariner," a mostly–Cabernet Sauvignon blend with Merlot. Note that it is a Meritage wine, based on the blending model of Bordeaux, France.* RIGHT: *A varietal label, in this case, for Chardonnay*

Interestingly, the introduction of varietal labels has created the need and a demand for a large body of legislation to control when and how certain terms can be used on the label. (See the following section on label laws.) The most commonly used varietal names in North America are:

WHITES

CHARDONNAY It is considered *the* white wine, seemingly made everywhere. It is the most important white grape in Burgundy, France.

RIESLING The white grape most closely identified with Germany and the Alsace region in France.

SAUVIGNON BLANC A white variety made famous in Bordeaux and the Loire Valley of France.

REDS

CABERNET SAUVIGNON The red variety was popularized by Bordeaux wine producers and is perhaps the most widely known in the world.

MERLOT Favored by some producers and consumers for its character, which is softer and fruitier than Cabernet.

PINOT NOIR The red grape nearly synonymous with the Burgundy region of France, popularized in 2004 by the film *Sideways*.

SYRAH This is an increasingly popular red variety, prominent in the Rhône Valley of France.

ZINFANDEL Named simply Zinfandel if the wine is red but called White Zinfandel if the wine is blush or white in color.

Other Label Terms

ESTATE-BOTTLED This term indicates that the activities of growing the grapes, making the wine, and bottling the finished product were essentially or substantially under the control of the same person or company. It is therefore assumed to ensure authenticity. The vineyards and winery must be located within any appellation on the label (for example, Napa Valley).

RESERVE Beware! This term is widely used to suggest wine blended from special vineyards, or wine aged longer than usual. In fact, according to federal regulations, this term may be used by any vintage-dated, varietal-labeled wine. Ironically, the word **RESERVE** often appears on labels of a producer's least expensive, least special wines. Reputable producers use the term to indicate a specially aged or selected wine.

LATE HARVEST This indicates that grapes were left on the vine to ripen for a longer time than usual to develop higher sugar content. The resulting wine, almost always a white, will be very sweet.

BOTRYTIS When this term appears on the label, it indicates that the grapes have been affected by the fungus of the same name. (See the section on botrytis in Chapter 2, "How Wine Is Made," on page 74.) The resulting concentration of sugar in the grapes will make for an intensely sweet wine.

THE LAWS BEHIND THE LABELS

Varietal Names

As soon as winemakers started using varietal grape names to label a wine, the U.S. government stepped in, demanding to know exactly how much of the grape named on the label was in the wine. (By contrast, it is patently absurd that the U.S. government waited until 2006, and only under pressure from the European Union, to rule on the use or misuse of terms such as *Chablis* or *Burgundy* by U.S. winemakers when the wines are obviously not from those places.) The immediate solution adopted by the federal bureaucracy was to demand that at least 51 percent of the wine in a bottle labeled as Chardonnay be made from Chardonnay grapes. In other words, up to 49 percent of the wine could be made from any other grape variety, thereby dramatically reducing, even nullifying, the Chardonnay character of the wine.

An example of an estate-bottled wine label

Quality-minded U.S. winemakers have always used 100 percent Chardonnay grapes in that wine, since the addition of even 3 or 5 percent of another grape variety noticeably alters the flavor of the wine. Those wine producers successfully lobbied for legislation to increase the minimum percentage of the named grape, and since 1993, legislation in the United States has required that *a minimum of 75 percent of the named grape variety* be used in the production of a wine with a varietal label.

The 25 percent leeway allows producers to blend in a second, third, or fourth grape when the winemaker considers that the wine will be improved by those additions. A good example is Cabernet Sauvignon. A wine made from 100 percent Cabernet Sauvignon is often too tannic and too intense for many consumers. A standard way of making the wine more appealing is to blend in wine from grape varieties that are known to have softer, less-aggressive characteristics. In the case of Cabernet Sauvignon, Merlot is often used as a blending grape, and so is Cabernet Franc. The winemaker is not required to state on the label the exact percentage of any of the grapes used in a blend, but is not prohibited from doing so.

Any state is free to amend the federal legislation to require that a higher percentage of the named varietal be used, as in Oregon, where at least 90 percent of the grapes must be of the named varietal (except in the case of Cabernet Sauvignon, where 75 percent remains the minimum).

Place Names

It is obvious that the makers of any product have competitors, and one way to gain an edge on the competition is to create some kind of differentiation and highlight it on the label. In the case of wine, one of the notable differences is the location of the vineyard, reflecting the belief that grapes grown in one location have characteristics different from those grown in another. These differences are the accumulated effect of exposure to the sun, amount of rainfall, length of daylight exposure, average temperatures, soil types, and so forth. (For more information on this, see the section "Heat Summation," on page 180.)

When some California winemakers wanted to suggest to the consumer that the use of grapes from Napa Valley made their wine somehow better than wine made from grapes grown elsewhere in California, the words "Napa Valley" began to appear on wine labels. The wine thus became not just Chardonnay, but Napa Valley Chardonnay.

The same kind of place-name differentiation is applied to Cheddar-type cheese made in the United States, where New York State, Vermont, and Wisconsin all vie for recognition as premium producers of Cheddar (even though Cheddar is the name of a place in England where that type of cheese was originally produced).

As soon as producers started using Napa Valley as a label term, regulators stepped in to control the meaning of such terms. Currently, the law states that if a place name is used on a label, that place name must be a state name, a county name, or an appellation or AVA (**AMERICAN VITICULTURAL AREA**) approved by the TTB (or prior to 2002, approved by the Bureau of Alcohol, Tobacco, and Firearms [**BATF**]). If the name used on the label is a state or county, the law requires that *at least 75 percent of the grapes must come from that place.* In California, Oregon, and Washington State, if the state name appears on the label, the wine must be made from grapes grown only in that state. If an appellation name—an AVA—appears on a label (Napa Valley, Finger Lakes, and Atlas Peak are just three examples of the more than two hundred approved AVAs), *at least 85 percent of the grapes used to produce the wine must have been grown and harvested in the named AVA.* Both Oregon and Washington State have gone beyond that requirement, to demand that 100 percent of any wine bearing a place name come from that place, be it state, county, town, or AVA. (For more on how the appellation system works in the United States, see the section "Appellation System,"

A Syrah produced by Saintsbury from grapes grown in the Sonoma Valley AVA. By law, at least 75 percent of these grapes must be Syrah, and at least 85 percent must be grown and harvested in the Sonoma Valley AVA. Note that the AVA refers to where the grapes are grown, not necessarily where the winery is located.

AMERICAN CONTRIBUTIONS

THIS SECTION WILL LOOK AT SOME of the contributions made by Americans to the greater understanding of wine and how it is made. In particular, we will look at the concepts of **HEAT SUMMATION**, wood aging, vine spacing, and the appellation system in the New World. This is not to suggest that only Americans have made advances in these areas, but they have certainly made significant contributions.

Heat Summation

We have already suggested that world-class winemaking in America did not become a realizable dream until the 1950s. At that time, American winemakers were smart enough to recognize that the Old World countries had already had almost two thousand years of practice making wine and already had the right grapes growing in the right places. That was achieved more through trial and error than any other method. If a particular grape variety was not successful in one region, it was torn out and replaced with another. As a result, Cabernet Sauvignon and Merlot grow in Bordeaux, France; Nebbiolo grows in Piedmont, Italy; Riesling grows in Mosel, Germany; and so forth. (See the relevant sections in Part 3.)

American winemakers knew they could not wait two thousand years to come up with the right answers. They wanted results, and wanted them far more quickly. Maynard Amerine had already done research in the 1930s in the graduate program at the University of California, Davis that associated specific grape varieties with certain climatic conditions, specifically with the amount of heat exposure for the grapes, since there appears to be a direct relationship between the amount of heat exposure and the degree of ripeness of the grape at harvest.

Starting with the assumption that the minimum average annual temperature required to ripen a grape through the growing season is 50°F/10°C, the UC Davis team began measuring daily temperatures between April 1 and October 31 in numerous locations throughout the California grape-growing regions. Over several years of data collection, they established a formula to determine the average amount of heat accumulation in any one area over and above the minimum required average temperature. That formula (for the Fahrenheit scale) is:

on page 120.) It is important to note that the AVA refers to where the grapes are grown, not necessarily where the winery is located.

If a single vineyard or ranch is named in addition to an appellation, the vineyard *must lie completely within* the named appellation, and 95 percent of any named variety must come from that vineyard. (For more complete information on the federal regulations regarding minimum percentages, see Appendix B, beginning on page 733.)

Vintage Date

The other major legally defined term on U.S. wine labels is the vintage date. If a label on the bottle states a year, *at least 95 percent* of the wine must have been produced from grapes harvested in the stated year.

LEFT: *A single-vineyard label. At least 95 percent of the grapes must have been harvested from the Chicken Ranch Vineyard, which must be wholly situated within the Rutherford AVA, a sub-AVA of the Napa Valley AVA.* RIGHT: *By law, at least 95 percent of the grapes used to produce this wine were harvested in 2002. At least 75 percent were Merlot, and at least 85 percent were grown and harvested in the Oakville AVA, a sub-AVA of the larger Napa Valley AVA.*

Daily average temperature − 50 = number of **DEGREE DAYS**.

Example: On June 2, the high temperature in that region for the day is 88°F. The low temperature is 60°F. The average temperature is 74°F. So: 74 − 50 = 24 degree days.

When that calculation is made every day from April 1 to October 31, and the number of degree days taken each day are added together, the result is a total number of degree days for that region. Regions throughout California were then classified according to the range of degree days measured, with Region 1 being the coolest and Region 5 the hottest.

Over the same period of time, UC Davis had conducted extensive research into the growing patterns of different vine varieties grown in different climates. They were then able to match specific grape variety recommendations to each climatic region. The principal recommendations are:

REGION 1 Chardonnay, Pinot Noir, Riesling, Gewürztraminer, Pinot Gris/Pinot Grigio

REGION 2 Cabernet Sauvignon, Sauvignon Blanc, Merlot, Cabernet Franc

REGION 3 Zinfandel, Barbera, Syrah, Gamay, Petite Sirah, Sangiovese, Viognier

REGION 4 Thompson Seedless, Malvasia

REGION 5 Thompson Seedless, dessert table grapes

The only role of UC Davis in creating this list is to provide recommendations. Grape growers remain free to plant any grape variety on any piece of land they choose.

The collective data from all of this research show that the cooler regions (regions 1 and 2) are all located near the coast. Those cool regions are exactly the ones most people associate with high-quality wines from California, including Napa, Sonoma, Carneros, Anderson Valley in Mendocino, Paso Robles in San Luis Obispo, and Santa Maria Valley in Santa Barbara.

The table at the left gives a comparison of degree days for some of the notable locations in North America, the Southern Hemisphere, and Europe. It is well recognized that the degree-day system is not perfect and that many other factors are involved in choosing which grape variety to plant. For example, the system measures only heat summation over a period of time, but it does not provide information on how much heat is accumulated at what point in the season. It takes no account of rainfall, in terms of either quantity or timing. There is no reference to latitude, the length of the growing season, or the number of daylight hours. It certainly avoids the question of soil, which Europeans have long regarded as a major factor in wine quality. Despite these shortcomings, the heat summation system brought grape growing and winemaking in California to a state of maturity much sooner than would have been the case without such a system.

In an era of global climate change, we can expect to see both subtle and not-so-subtle temperature shifts from

HEAT UNITS IN GROWING SEASON

	IN DEGREE DAYS (CELSIUS) 10°C BASE	IN DEGREE DAYS (FAHRENHEIT) 50°F BASE
FRANCE		
Chablis	950	1,710
Loire	950–1,100	1,710–1,980
Champagne	1,050	1,890
Beaujolais	1,150	2,070
Côte d'Or	1,180	2,150
Alsace	1,230	2,230
Médoc	1,350–1,400	2,430–2,520
Hermitage	1,450	2,610
GERMANY		
Mosel–Saar–Ruwer	950–1,150	1,710–2,070
Baden	1,050	1,890
Rheinhessen	1,050–1,100	1,890–1,980
Rheingau	1,050–1,200	1,890–2,160
Pfalz	1,200–1,250	2,160–2,250
CALIFORNIA		
Monterey	1,200–1,300	2,160–2,340
Santa Clara	1,250–1,300	2,250–2,340
Livermore Valley	1,250–1,400	2,250–2,520
Napa	1,300–2,000	2,340–3,600
Sonoma	1,200–1,725	2,160–3,100
CHILE		
Maipo Valley	1,350–1,400	2,430–2,520
SOUTH AFRICA		
Stellenbosch	1,300–1,400	2,340–2,520
Paarl	1,400–1,450	2,520–2,610
NEW ZEALAND		
Canterbury	900–1,100	1,620–1,980
Auckland	1,300–1,350	2,340–2,430
AUSTRALIA		
Coonawarra	1,150–1,250	2,070–2,250
McLaren Vale	1,300–1,400	2,340–2,520

Source: D. Jackson and D. Schuster, Grape Growing and Wine Making. Orinda, CA: Altarinda Books, 1981.

region to region. We would also expect that recommendations for grape growing based on heat summation will follow those shifts, especially as wine-growing regions become warmer.

Wood Aging

Chapter 2 gave some examples of how the choice of a wooden barrel for making or aging wine might affect the final outcome. Much of the experimentation associated with wood aging was begun in the United States by winemakers such as Robert Mondavi, who were not satisfied with blanket statements from Old World winemakers to the effect that one wood was better than another, but with no explanation. In fact, it quickly became clear to many Americans that most Bordeaux winemakers were not aware that a different type of barrel was used in Burgundy, nor did they care.

Several wineries in the United States conduct aging experiments that attempt to demonstrate the effects of different types of wood on wine and of different lengths of time aging in wood. Such experimentation is now common to many large wineries in California, and yet we cannot help but be struck by the enormous investment of money and time these experiments demand. Thousands of gallons of wine are involved for long periods of time, and some of that wine may never be sold. Thousands of barrels from various forests and cooperages, and barrels of various ages, will be used, all as part of the effort to understand more about wood aging so that American winemakers can produce better wine.

Vine Spacing

The experimentation noted in connection with wood continues in other areas, notably in vineyard management. Larger wineries with vast vineyard holdings are most heavily involved in experiments to ascertain the optimal spacing for vines, but small- to moderate-size growers and producers also participate. This may seem simplistic on the surface, but there are endless variations involved in such experiments, all of them taking up land whose real-estate value may be extremely high. A winery may experiment with Merlot vines by spacing the vines two feet apart and five feet between the rows, then three feet between the vines and six feet between the rows, and so forth. Then, of course, they might have the same spac-

ing variations for Cabernet Sauvignon and for ten other grape varieties. With these experiments, wineries hope to establish guidelines for vine spacing that will eventually result in improved yields and improved grape and wine quality in the future.

With the replanting that has taken place since the disastrous effects of phylloxera in Napa and Sonoma (see page 150), many grape growers have undertaken vine-spacing experiments, resulting in very different-looking vineyards. Many vineyards are now much more densely planted than before, with some having increased the number of vines per acre by as much as 100 percent. This does not necessarily mean more tons of grapes per acre; rather, by asking each vine to produce less, the quality of the grapes will improve and the resulting wine will be better.

Appellation System: American Viticultural Areas (AVAs)

The appellation system is not, of course, an American invention, although among New World countries, the United States has led the way in defining what appellations are. As the name implies, appellations in the United States are based in concept on the **APPELLATION D'ORIGINE CONTRÔLÉE SYSTEM** that governs French grape growing and winemaking (see page 262). The U.S. system is not as extensive as the French system, however. In France, the appellation system controls not only the delineation of any named area, but also factors such as which grape varieties may be grown there, how many tons of grapes per acre may be harvested, minimum aging requirements, and minimum alcohol levels. In the United States, the appellation system is restricted to a geographic definition of the named area.

To gain AVA status in the United States, the grape growers or winemakers of any region are required to petition the TTB. The petition must explain why and how the region is identifiable as a separate grape-growing area and how it is distinct from any surrounding land. Usually, the petition will cite such factors as history, climate, soil, elevation, water table, and so forth.

Of all the AVAs that have been approved in the United States, the most famous is undoubtedly Napa Valley in California. Ironically, Napa Valley was not the first AVA in the United States (that honor went to Augusta, Missouri, in 1980, with Napa Valley being the second shortly thereafter), nor is it the best-defined. As appellations go, Napa Valley is a relatively large area, encompassing many different climate regions, a varied topography, and numerous soil types.

In the past twenty years, the number of AVAs has grown dramatically, to the point where, as of 2010, there were more than 200 distinct and defined grape-growing areas, 115 of them in California. By the time you read this sentence, there are bound to be more. The system now involves the recognition of large umbrella appellations as well as various levels of subappellations. For example, the North Coast AVA groups together the counties of Napa, Sonoma, Lake, Mendocino, Solano, and Marin. Similarly, the North Coast appellation falls within the appellation of California, and California is surrounded by the mega-appellation of America. In addition to the large appellation of North Coast, there are also the large appellations of Central Coast and San Francisco Bay Area, which are further split into counties and then into specific appellations. A simple but effective model to understand the appellation system is to use concentric circles to represent small subappellations inside larger appellations inside state appellations.

The development of subappellations in both Sonoma County and Napa County, along with several other counties in California, underscores an important tenet of the appellation system. Smaller appellations are drafted and adopted to make more specific delineations. The smaller the appellation, the more likely it is that all of the grapes from that appellation will have similar characteristics. Thus it is true to say that smaller appellations usually produce more specific wines, and some people would suggest that greater specificity leads to better quality.

At least thirty-five states now boast fully defined and registered AVAs, although only California's system (and increasingly, Oregon's) has the degree of complexity described above.

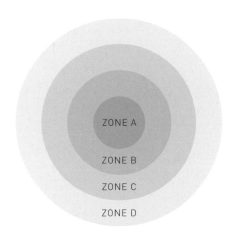

A concentric-circle model shows how smaller appellations fit within larger ones. For example, Zone D might be California, Zone C could be North Coast, Zone B could be Napa Valley, and Zone A might be Stags Leap District. An alternative application of the model would make Zone D North Coast, Zone C Sonoma County, Zone B Russian River Valley, and Zone A Chalk Hill.

CALIFORNIA

CALIFORNIA IS ONE of the most exciting and vital wine-producing regions in the world. In a country where Prohibition (1920–1933) almost wiped out the possibility of an American fine wine industry, and where the public's taste in the post-Prohibition years was for a long time limited to inexpensive, generic jug wines, in the past thirty to forty years, California's vineyards and wineries have witnessed a revolution in fine wine.

The relatively recent history of California wine is a compelling story, a complex and rapidly unfolding narrative, but California's meteoric rise in the wine world has not occurred without its share of fits, starts, dramatic shifts in winery and vineyard ownership, and serious threats to its continued well-being. On balance, however, the story of California wine after Prohibition is one of a miraculous rise.

HISTORY

FRANCISCAN MONKS BEGAN the settlement of Alta California in Mexico by establishing a mission at San Diego in 1769. The friars established coastal and valley missions throughout California over the next fifty to sixty years. The purpose of these Franciscan missions was to convert the native Indians of the coastal valleys to Christianity, and the monks were largely successful in spreading the Word of Christ. Indians and padres alike raised cattle, sheep, grains, and vegetables and planted orchards.

In 1779, what was perhaps California's first vineyard was planted at Mission San Juan Capistrano under the auspices of Father Junipero Serra, the architect of the mission system in California; its first wine, made from the Criolla grape, was produced in 1782. Father Serra made sure that almost all of the missions had their own vineyards, with the largest vineyard and basic winemaking facilities at Mission San Gabriel, due east of Los Angeles.

Even as the missions were being built by Spain and the Catholic Church, California was attracting European immigrants from France, Germany, Italy, and Hungary, many of whom were accustomed to wine as a daily beverage with their meals. Small home vineyards were planted and thrived, especially in the immigrant neighborhoods of the Los Angeles area.

In 1823, Father José Altimira established the Sonoma Mission. Here, the Franciscans produced four types of wine, all made from the "Mission" (Criolla) grape: a sweet red, which nobody seemed to favor; an undistinguished dry red; a dry white made only from the free-run juice of the black grape; and a sweet white, made by the addition of grape spirit to unfermented grape must and aged for several years in huge barrels. This fortified wine is Angelica, which at its best resembles a sweet Madeira, the famous fortified wine of Portugal. Angelica, originally named for the city of Los Angeles, still has some enthusiastic adherents in California, where it continues to be made in small quantities.

In 1833, pressured by the rise of the Mexican independence movement, which was led by Antonio de Santa Anna and was radically anti-ecclesiastic, the mission system of California was dismantled. General Mariano Guadalupe Vallejo, on orders from the governor of California, José Figueroa, secularized the Sonoma Mission, soon to become the Sonoma Pueblo. Vallejo was supposed to oversee the transfer of the land to the Indians but instead granted land to his family members, military cronies, and friends. The Santa Anna government, itself mired in corruption, did nothing to stop Vallejo. The Sonoma Pueblo comprised more than 700 square miles/1,813 square kilometers of land, including the entire Napa Valley.

As the missions were dismantled, the first fine wine grapes were planted in California. Jean-Louis Vignes brought some Cabernet Sauvignon cuttings from his native Bordeaux and planted them in Los Angeles, producing wine from them circa 1837. Further north, in the Santa Clara Valley, Charles LeFranc planted Cabernet Sauvignon, Merlot, and other French varietals in 1853, endeavoring to make a blended Bordeaux-style wine.

LeFranc referenced Bordeaux's famous Château Margaux as the benchmark for his wine.

In the mid-1820s, George Calvert Yount, a North Carolina native, arrived in California. Yount was a frontier explorer who trapped and hunted for food and trade throughout the West. He passed through the Napa Valley in 1831, finally settling in the Sonoma Pueblo in 1834. Yount made a point of getting to know General Vallejo, who by now controlled virtually all the lands and commerce of the pueblo.

Yount made himself useful to Vallejo in several ways. He taught the Indians to build their own homes, but more important to Vallejo, Yount could be counted on to assist in Vallejo's sometimes brutal control of the pueblo natives.

Yount wanted a land grant from Vallejo, but he was not a baptized Catholic, which was essential to hold land in the Sonoma Pueblo. In 1835, Yount traveled to San Rafael, where he was baptized Jorge Concepción. On March 23, 1836, Vallejo granted Yount the Caymus Rancho: 12,000 acres/5,000 hectares of undeveloped land in the Napa Valley. The southern border of the ranch began just below what is now Yountville and extended to just about a mile below St. Helena. Yount built himself a log cabin, planted vegetables, acquired cattle, and hunted the grizzly bears that roamed the valley, sometimes killing eight bears in a day. Yount befriended the local Napa Indians (the Wappo), who became his workforce. In exchange, Yount helped defend their tiny *rancherías* from marauders.

In 1839, George Yount transplanted cuttings and vines from General Vallejo's vineyards to his Caymus Rancho. In doing so, he planted the first grapes in the Napa Valley.

Good Times

Gold was discovered at Sutter's Mill in 1848, and California became a material Garden of Eden. In 1857, a Hungarian nobleman, Count Agoston Haraszthy, who imported vine cuttings, founded Sonoma's Buena Vista Winery. Haraszthy preached to all who would listen his vision of the California wine industry. First, growers needed to plant better grapes. Second, newly minted *vignerons* must learn how the greatest wines of Europe were made. Third, California's wine producers had to create a sophisticated system for selling their wines in the United States and abroad. Haraszthy, sometimes called the father of the modern California wine industry, is just as often called less charitable names (he lost a lot of money in the wine business, much of it said not to be his own), but his was a voice that heralded the future, and he is remembered for understanding the potential for fine wine production on a large scale in California. In 2007, Buena Vista Winery celebrated its 150th anniversary.

The years between 1860 and 1900 were heady times for the California wine industry, especially in the Napa Valley. In 1861, Charles Krug established his winery in Napa Valley's St. Helena (the winery is now owned by the Peter Mondavi family); in 1862, not far from Krug, Jacob Schram established his winery, now famous as Schramsberg, the prominent Napa sparkling wine producer (presently owned by the Davies family); in 1876, Beringer Vineyards was founded in St. Helena by the Beringer brothers (Beringer is now owned by the Australian beverage conglomerate Foster's); in 1879, Finnish sea captain and fur trader Gustave Niebaum founded Inglenook in the Napa Valley town of Rutherford (the vineyards and winery, today known as Rubicon Estate, are now owned by film director Francis Ford Coppola and his family); in 1882, the Christian Brothers founded their famous winery (the historic Christian Brothers Greystone winery is home to the Napa Valley campus of The Culinary Institute of America); in 1882, Alfred Tubbs established Chateau Montelena, just north of Calistoga in Napa (now owned by the Barrett family); in 1885, Rossini of Howell Mountain was

TOP ROW, FROM LEFT: *A view of Greystone from the Charles Krug vineyards, which were established in 1861. Greystone, now home to the Napa Valley campus of The Culinary Institute of America, was the winery of the Christian Brothers beginning in 1882. The Charles Krug winery, established in 1861, was purchased by Cesare Mondavi and his sons, Peter and Robert, in 1943. Robert Mondavi left to start his own winery in 1966. Today, Krug is solely owned by the Peter Mondavi family. Robert Mondavi died in 2008.* BOTTOM ROW, CLOCKWISE FROM LEFT: *Jacob Schram's historic home, built in 1862, is now part of the estate of the sparkling-wine producer Schramsberg, founded by Jamie Davies and Jack Davies in 1966. Jack Davies died in 1998 and Jamie Davies died in 2008. The home built by the Beringer brothers, both German immigrants, in 1876 is now a visitors center at the Beringer winery. BV (Beaulieu Vineyard), located in the Napa Valley town of Rutherford, made its early reputation on the high quality of its Georges de Latour Private Reserve Cabernet Sauvignon. Morning fog rolling in from San Pablo Bay to Napa Valley's Mayacamas Mountains*

founded (and is now home to Burgess Cellars, owned by Tom Burgess); and in 1889, the Mayacamas winery was built around its vineyards on Mount Veeder (owned by Robert and Elinor Travers).

In Sonoma County, the Simi family began making wine in Healdsburg in 1881 (Simi Winery is now owned by Constellation, the largest wine and beverage conglomerate in the world). In 1882, the extraordinary 400-acre/160-hectare Italian Swiss Colony was established at the far northern reaches of Sonoma County, in Asti, with the ability to produce more than a half million gallons of wine annually (the Italian Swiss Colony brand is also owned by Constellation, but not the original vineyards).

At the same time that Napa and Sonoma were booming, Leland Stanford, who made millions of dollars in the railroad business, established the Stanford winery in 1871 in Alameda County, and later the 3,500-acre/1,400-hectare Vina Ranch. At his death, Stanford's winery had a capacity of 2 million gallons/80,000 hectoliters. Stanford University sits on a former vineyard in Palo Alto.

In 1900, Georges de Latour, freshly arrived from France, established Beaulieu Vineyard (BV) in Rutherford (now owned by mutinational wine and spirits giant Diageo); its nearest neighbor was Inglenook (the brand, but not the vineyards or winery, is owned by The Wine Group). It was BV that put Napa Valley Cabernet Sauvignon on the map, as de Latour recognized that he could capitalize on the reputation of Bordeaux and the appropriate growing conditions for Cabernet at BV. Inglenook followed the lead of BV, as did most of the finest pre-Prohibition wineries of the central Napa Valley.

Bad Times

Just before 1890, the phylloxera epidemic that had begun in France arrived in California. (For further details, see the sections on pages 9–10.) The phylloxera louse, an aphid that attacked the roots of ungrafted vinifera vines or rootstock, destroyed more than 10,000 acres/4,000 hectares of vines in the Napa Valley from 1890 to 1892, leaving barely 2,000 acres/800 hectares of vineyard untouched. By 1915, phylloxera had destroyed about 250,000 acres/100,000 hectares of vineyards in the state of California.

In 1919, Congress passed the Eighteenth Amendment to the Constitution: Prohibition. While it was still legal to consume alcoholic beverages, the production, sale, and possession of these beverages was illegal. Many vineyards,

still reeling from phylloxera, were allowed to go to seed, and other cash crops, such as prune plums, were planted where grapevines once stood.

In a nod to its Italian-American constituency, Congress allowed "male heads of household" to make 50 gallons/190 liters of "fermented grape juice" annually for personal and family consumption. In addition to companies such as BV getting lucrative and exclusive contracts to produce sacramental wines for the Catholic Church, some wineries survived and even thrived during Prohibition by shipping grapes east in refrigerated railroad cars.

Good Times Begin Again

By 1933, when Prohibition was repealed (by passage of the Nineteenth Amendment, which ended the federal prohibition but still allowed states, counties, or municipalities to remain "dry"), the California fine wine industry was largely decimated, but American wine drinkers had developed a taste for good homemade wine at a decent price, whether they made the wine themselves or bought it. After Prohibition, it became clear that the immediate future of the California wine industry lay in sterile, filtered, processed wines that were well made and drinkable. The goal was to achieve consistency, not greatness. The Gallo brothers, Ernest (1909–2007) and Julio (1910–1993), seizing on a brilliantly perceived vision of opportunity, began their then-modest winery in a Modesto warehouse in 1933.

Gallo wines and their imitators were the perfect beverages to get the California wine industry back on its feet. Post-Prohibition vineyards and wineries were in a state of chaos. Most wineries wcre unsanitary, filled with mold and bacteria, and the wines reflected these problems. With the help of the University of California, Davis, the industry began to make "jug" wines: affordable, drinkable, safe, reliable, technically sound, predictable, nonvintage wines made from unspecified varieties and carrying generic labels (Chablis, Burgundy, etc.).

At the same time the Gallo brothers were prospering and jug wine was booming, the fine wine industry was taking baby steps back to health. BV brought in André Tchelistcheff (1901–1994), a Russian-born enologist who not only knew how to make fine wine but also understood the chemistry of mold and microorganisms and how they negatively affect wines. He shared his knowledge with his employers at BV, and as a consultant with other serious fine wine producers in the Napa Valley and beyond.

Following Tchelistcheff's lead, John Daniel Jr. revived the original Inglenook of Napa Valley in 1938, Jack and Mary Taylor did the same for Mayacamas in 1941, and the eclectic Martin Ray started his own winery in the Santa Cruz Mountains in 1942 (Martin Ray is now a brand whose winery and vineyards are located in the Russian River Valley of Sonoma County). Frank Bartholomew rescued Buena Vista in 1943, and Lee Stewart founded Souverain in that same year (the Souverain property—but not the brand name—was acquired by Francis Ford Coppola in late 2005). San Francisco industrialist and former ambassador to Italy James Zellerbach dreamed of Burgundy and planted Chardonnay and Pinot Noir at his Hanzell property in 1952. Hanzell introduced several

TOP: *A ninety-year-old dry-farmed organic head-pruned vine is still commercially productive on the low-yield vineyards of the historic Inglenook estate, now Rubicon Estate, owned by film director Francis Ford Coppola and located in the town of Rutherford in the Napa Valley.* BOTTOM: *Before there was Opus One, there was Insignia. With its first vintage in 1974, the Joseph Phelps winery created the first Napa Valley proprietary blend in the Bordeaux style.*

innovations to the California wine industry: temperature-controlled stainless steel fermentation tanks, the use of French oak for aging wine, and scientifically controlled malolactic fermentation (Hanzell has been privately owned by the de Brye family since 1965). Also in that year, Fred and Eleanor McCrea produced their first Stony Hill wines (Stony Hill is still owned by the McCrea family). In 1959, three Stanford engineers started up the abandoned Ridge Vineyards (Akahiko Otsuka of Japan purchased Ridge in 1986).

Beginning in the 1960s, with the California wine boom still fifteen years away, a couple of benchmarks were achieved. In 1961, Joe and Alice Heitz started Heitz Wine Cellars outside St. Helena; in 1966, they made the first vintage of a now-famous wine from a single vineyard in Oakville, Martha's Vineyard Cabernet Sauvignon, and people began to line up outside their little building on Highway 29. Heitz Wine Cellars is still owned by the Heitz family; David Heitz is the winemaker.

Robert Mondavi, perhaps the most important person in the history of the modern California fine wine industry, persuaded his family to buy the Charles Krug Winery in 1943. Because of serious disagreements within the Mondavi family about their wine business, Robert later decided that he wanted to have his own Napa Valley winery. In 1966, after a fractious lawsuit for his share of Krug, he built the first new post-Prohibition winery in the Napa Valley, the Robert Mondavi Winery, located on Highway 29 in the town of Oakville. The name Robert Mondavi became synonymous with the California wine revolution and its headquarters in the Napa Valley. In 2004, in a move that stunned the California wine industry, the Robert Mondavi Winery and its affiliated companies, including half-ownership of Opus One (the other half being owned by Château Mouton Rothschild of Bordeaux, France), were purchased by Constellation for $1.3 billion.

Also in 1966, the late Richard Graff produced the first Chalone wine, a Pinot Noir, while Charles Carpy and friends opened Freemark Abbey just outside of St. Helena, and Jack and Jamie Davies began to make fine sparkling wine at Schramsberg. During the late 1960s, Diamond Creek, Fetzer, Chappellet, Davis Bynum, and Cuvaison also were founded. As the country entered the 1970s, Americans were beginning to become curious about wine—but they were far more interested in white wine than red wine, and most fine restaurants still featured and promoted French wines on their wine lists.

Starting in the 1970s, many of the wineries we are now familiar with burst upon the California wine scene: Kenwood, Stag's Leap Wine Cellars, Clos Du Val, Far Niente, Burgess, Shafer, Acacia, La Crema, Kistler, Caymus, Cakebread, Joseph Phelps, Duckhorn, Ravenswood, Clos du Bois, Jekel, Grgich Hills, Firestone, Dehlinger, DeLoach, Conn Creek, Chateau St. Jean, Carneros Creek, Gallo-Sonoma (now Gallo Family Vineyards), Domaine Chandon, Jordan, Franciscan, Fisher, and Zaca Mesa, among many others. Quite a few of them were started by men and women successful in other businesses, some of them very wealthy. In 1976, a tasting in Paris of "California versus France," with all-French judges, was held, and California won both the red and white tastings in the "Judgment of Paris." (See the section on this tasting on page 136.) There was no turning back; California wines were hot.

The decade culminated in 1979, when Robert Mondavi and Baron Philippe de Rothschild of Bordeaux's esteemed Château Mouton Rothschild announced a partnership to make a Napa Valley Cabernet Sauvignon–based blended wine, using American vineyards and French winemaking skills and techniques. That wine is Opus One, and the creation of this wine opened the floodgates of the Napa Valley to serious foreign and American investment in vineyards and wineries throughout California.

Since the 1980s, the California wine industry has been riding a roller coaster of phenomenal successes: White Zinfandel (created by Bob Trinchero of Sutter Home Winery), the vogue of red wine for health, a very prosperous economy in the mid- to late 1990s and into the cusp of the current millennium come to mind. More recently, there has been tremendous consumer interest in Pinot Noir from California (credit the 2004 film *Sideways* for this, at least in part), and a desire to taste the expensive Cult Cabernets of the Napa Valley. California Zinfandel, this time in its original red color, is enjoying an ongoing love affair with consumers, and at all price points too. There have been some failures as well, such as the planting of thousands of doomed acres of Cabernet Sauvignon and Merlot in Monterey, the wine cooler fad, the promoting of Sangiovese and several other grapes as "the next big thing" in California varietals. Still, the successes of the modern California wine industry far outweigh the failures.

The industry has done a good job of promoting California wines on the national and international level, increasing exports of wine dramatically (now far more than $1 billion per year). In 2008, 20 percent of California wine was exported, a total of 43.5 million CASES of wine, the equivalent of more than half a billion bottles. Especially as the value of the dollar has often shrunk against the value of the euro and the British pound, the price of California wines has become more attractive to the European export market, which accounts for more than half of total exports. There has been a significant jump in California wine exports to Canada (up 11 percent in 2008) and to countries in Asia, especially Hong Kong (export volume up 244 percent in 2008) and the sleeping giant of the international wine industry, China (sales increased to $22 million in 2008, a jump of 34 percent).

In the United States, nine out of every ten bottles of wine produced is made in California, and Americans continue to show a true patriotic spirit when it comes to California wines: More than 70 percent of all wines sold in the United States are from California.

The California wine industry has endured many internal battles, especially as regards the perceived price-to-quality relationship of its wines and the impact of that perception on consumers. Branding has become increasingly important in the wine industry, and California is no exception. With an ever-increasing number of drinkable varietal-labeled California wines sold at bargain-basement prices, there is downward pressure on the prices of almost all California's popular brands. Perhaps the best example is "Two Buck Chuck," the Charles Shaw brand of wines produced by Bronco Wine Company, which sells for between $2 and $3 exclusively at Trader Joe's stores across the United States. In blind tastings at several wine competititons, "Chuck" has beaten wines selling for more than $50.

A compelling issue in the California wine industry is ownership of several *marquee* wine brands by large corporations, some of them U.S.–based conglomerates, some of them multinational and under foreign ownership. In some cases, a large corporation will own several wineries and have one chief winemaker in charge of the diverse brands. This situation, which includes shifting grapes from company-owned vineyards and juice to company-owned wineries, tends to create a certain sameness in the taste characteristics of the multiple brands. The wines are often "engineered" to satisfy current consumer preference, and essential differences in style become largely a matter of price. Wines in the *fighting varietal* segment of the market—the wines you are likely to find on the shelves of supermarkets and large retailers—achieve certain well-researched flavor profiles to please the consumer. More expensive wines sometimes, but certainly not always, show a bit more individuality.

Lately, it seems that large wine brands are being acquired by even larger companies, and then those companies are acquired by the some of the largest wine companies in the world. Brands are bought and sold among these companies, and in the process, some famous wine brands are eliminated or relegated to obscurity while others are pumped up and highlighted. Below is a partial list of the major players in California multiwinery ownership, along with some of their better-known brands. Many of these companies also own wineries and well-known wine brands all over the world, and their California brands represent only a small portion of their corporate portfolios. There are, however, companies that have built their wine empires from scratch over generations, such as Gallo, Bronco, Trinchero, Jackson Family, and Don Sebastiani and Sons.

We can practically guarantee that by the time you read this, some of the brands listed below will have been resold to other large companies, either to privately held or public corporations. The major players and their best-known premier California wine brands include:

E. & J. GALLO WINERY (privately held, based in California; estimated annual sales in the United States: 80 million cases): Gallo Family Vineyards, Louis M. Martini, William Hill, Mirassou, Rancho Zabaco, Anapamu, Barefoot Cellars, Bridlewood, Frei Brothers, Indigo Hills, MacMurray Ranch, Marcelina, Redwood Creek, Turning Leaf, Carlo Rossi, Livingston Cellars, Peter Vella

CONSTELLATION WINES (publicly traded, based in Canandaigua, New York; estimated annual sales in the United States: 70 million cases): Robert Mondavi, Franciscan Oakville Estates, Mount Veeder, Simi, Estancia, Ravenswood, Woodbridge by Robert Mondavi, Toasted Head, Talus, Vendange, Rex Goliath, Turner Road, Papio, Trove, Black Box, Blackstone, Dunnewood, Clos du Bois, Haywood, Wild Horse, partner with Mouton Rothschild in Opus One

THE WINE GROUP (privately held, based in California; estimated annual sales in the United States: 60 million cases): Concannon, Glen Ellen, Corbett Canyon, MJ Vallejo, Franzia, Paul Masson, Almadén, Inglenook

BRONCO WINE COMPANY (privately held, based in California; estimated annual sales in the United States: 36 million cases): Charles Shaw, ForestVille, Estrella, Montpelier, Grand Cru, Silver Ridge, Fox Hollow, Hacienda, Black Mountain, Crane Lake, Napa Ridge, Napa Creek, Salmon Creek

FOSTER'S WINE ESTATES (publicly traded, based in Australia; estimated annual sales in the United States: 20 million cases): Beringer, Chateau Souverain, Chateau St. Jean, Stags' Leap Winery, Etude, Meridian, St. Clement, Carmenet, Cellar No. 8, Talomas, Taz, Bohemian, White Lie

TRINCHERO FAMILY ESTATES (privately held, based in California; estimated annual sales in the United States: 12 million cases): Sutter Home, Montevina, Trinchero, Trinity Oaks, Folie à Deux, Three Thieves, Ménage à Trois, Jargon, Bandit, Fre

BROWN-FORMAN (publicly traded, based in Kentucky; estimated annual sales in the United States: 7 million cases): Fetzer, Sonoma-Cutrer, Bonterra, Jekel, Korbel, Bel Arbor, Five Rivers, Mariah, Sanctuary, Little Black Dress, Virgin Vines Wines

JACKSON FAMILY FARMS (privately held, based in California; estimated annual sales in the United States: 6 million cases): Kendall-Jackson, Cambria, Matanzas Creek, La Crema, Cardinale, Atalon, Acadia, Lokoya, Arrowood, Edmeades, La Jota, Jackson Ridge, Carmel Road, Stonestreet, Archipel, Verité, Pelton House, Hartford Family, Freemark Abbey, Murphy-Goode, Anakota, Robert Pepi, Byron, Camelot

DIAGEO CHATEAU & ESTATE WINES (publicly traded, based in Great Britain; estimated annual sales in the United States: 5 million cases): Beaulieu Vineyard (BV), Sterling, Chalone, Edna Valley, Acacia, Jade Mountain, Provenance, Echelon, Dynamite, Blossom Hill, Monterey Vineyard, Rosenblum Cellars

Kendall-Jackson is the flagship brand for a large company owned by the Jackson family. Among its fifty-plus wine brands are such famous labels as Byron, Cambria, Edmeades, Freemark Abbey, La Crema, Matanzas Creek, and Murphy-Goode.

DON SEBASTIANI & SONS (privately held, based in California; estimated annual sales in the United States: 2 million cases): Smoking Loon, Pepperwood Grove, Aquinas, Mia's Playground, Screw Kappa Napa, Kono Baru, Plungerhead, Hey Mambo, The White Knight, Used Automobile Parts

TERLATO WINE GROUP (privately held, based in Illinois; estimated annual sales in the United States: not available): Sanford, Chimney Rock, Cuvaison, Markham, Rutherford Hills, Alderbrook, Hanna, Rochioli, Glass Mountain

OTHER MAJOR PLAYERS Ste. Michelle Wine Estates, Heck Estates, Pacific Wine Partners, Remy Cointreau USA, Delicato Vineyards, Vincor USA, C. Mondavi & Sons, Ironstone Winery, J. Lohr Winery, Francis Ford Coppola Presents, Bogle Vineyards, Ascentia Wine Estates (Buena Vista Carneros, Gary Farrell, Geyser Peak, Atlas Peak, and XYZin wineries, all formerly owned by Constellation)

Also, American wine consumers are having a love affair with varietal-labeled "box wines" from California. These wines provide more than decent quality at a highly affordable price. Add to that the ease of the box—no corkscrew needed and the wine remains fresh in the fridge or on the kitchen shelf for at least a couple of weeks—and it appears that box wines are here to stay. This is good news for large-scale wine producers, especially in years when there is a glut of grapes or juice in the commodity spot market, but it creates real challenges for small artisanal producers who can't compete based on price and must rely on a small percentage of consumers who perceive their boutique wines to be worth the money.

The good news for California's smaller wineries is the relatively new market in direct shipping and Internet sales. It was not long ago that wines could not be shipped out of state, and Internet sales were largely illegal. Today, the possibility of combined sales based on direct shipments and online commerce has created a lucrative new market for California wineries, both big and small. The advantage for the small wine producer who may not have national distribution kicks in when someone—say, from Vermont or from Texas—visits the winery, tastes the wine, loves it, and places an order on the spot. The wine is shipped home to that visitor, who soon shares his or her new wine discovery with friends, and they go online to purchase the wine. Many California wineries, as well as wineries from many other wine-producing states, now maintain sophisticated websites and make it relatively easy for consumers to purchase wine online.

Especially at the retail level and particularly in supermarkets and big-box stores that sell California wine (Costco, a huge network of membership warehouse stores, is the nation's leading wine retailer), cutthroat pricing has become the norm for many wines. In the short term, this is good news for the wine consumer, but is it sustainable? Only time will tell, but as California producers compete among themselves and fend off competition from foreign wine nations, particularly Australia, Chile, and Argentina, something may have to give in the price-to-quality relationship. And that something just might be dictated by the weather.

The California wine industry is beginning to see the impact of global climate change in its vineyards and in its finished wines. Alcohol levels—based on sugar levels in the grapes, which are in turn based on the amount of heat in the growing region—have gone through the roof, and several producers are now utilizing technologies that either add water to their wine to dilute alcohol or diminish alcohol without the addition of water. Fine wines traditionally have not been—at least overtly—technologically manipulated. These wines are not generally made in oppressively hot climates; the best wines are produced in regions that are quite cool to moderately warm. In California, this has usually meant coastal growing areas that benefit from the cooling influence of the Pacific Ocean.

LEFT: *Cuvaison is part of the Terlato Wine Group, which owns at least ten prestigious California wineries and imports many other fine wines.* **RIGHT:** *"Box wines" of good quality have become quite popular in the United States and abroad. Black Box is owned by Constellation, the world's largest wine producer.*

The impact that climate change and global warming may have on the California wine industry cannot be emphasized enough. Wine grapes are among the most temperature-sensitive crops grown in the world. Climate models for California are alarming. The scientific community in general, and in particular climatologists, agree that as early as the year 2030, cool coastal areas will become substantially warmer, and northern California will suffer from increased rain and the mountains from decreased snow. The higher temperatures and the decrease in the snowpack will put tremendous pressure on California's water storage systems. This is a major problem in vineyards that rely on drip irrigation, as most California vineyards do. Barring genetic manipulation of grapes (of course, that research is already going on), much of California may become a fine wine wasteland, producing just-drinkable wines dressed up with fancy labels.

Even with all of the current and future challenges facing the California wine industry—both economic and environmental—one thing is true: Today, wines from California's more than 2,700 wineries, especially the overwhelming majority of wines produced from grapes grown in the coastal regions of the state, are as good as or better than they have ever been, and the best producers in California are absolutely dedicated to making the finest wines they can.

OVERVIEW OF CALIFORNIA WINE REGIONS

CALIFORNIA IS MADE UP of many wine regions, large and small, and a current overview of the most important appellations in California allows us to explore the total picture that is California wine. Where appropriate, the discussion includes the multicounty and single-county appellations as well as the larger AVAs and smaller AVAs in the important California wine regions.

The first appellation to explore, North Coast, is a perfect example of the vitality and quality of the modern California wine industry.

North Coast

The North Coast includes the following constituent appellations and AVA's: Napa, Sonoma, Mendocino, Lake, Marin, and Solano counties.

NAPA COUNTY

The blanket AVA in the county is Napa Valley. All of the following AVAs are, legally, sub-AVAs of the Napa Valley AVA. This means that producers from these smaller AVAs are allowed to use either the name of that AVA (e.g., Rutherford) or the always commercially viable Napa Valley AVA on their wine labels.

The names of the sixteen AVAs located within the larger Napa Valley AVA are:

Atlas Peak, Calistoga, Carneros or Los Carneros (AVA shared with Sonoma County), Chiles Valley, Diamond Mountain District, Howell Mountain, Mount Veeder, North Coast (Napa is a constituent county of this multi-county AVA), Oak Knoll District of Napa Valley, Oakville, Rutherford, Spring Mountain District, St. Helena, Stags Leap District, Wild Horse Valley (shared with Solano County), and Yountville.

NAPA VALLEY

When we think of California wine, what's the first place that comes to mind? Inevitably, it's the Napa Valley, which became an AVA in 1983. As Bordeaux is to France and

An example of a North Coast AVA wine label

California

Major AVAs

North Coast AVAs
- Anderson Valley
- Redwood Valley
- Potter Valley
- Mendocino
- Mendocino Ridge
- Sonoma Coast
- Clear Lake
- Guenoc Valley
- Dry Creek Valley
- Alexander Valley
- Knights Valley
- Russian River Valley
- Sonoma Valley
- Napa Valley
- Los Carneros

Interior/ Central Valley AVAs
- Solano County Green Valley
- Suisun Valley
- Clarksburg
- Lodi
- El Dorado
- Shenandoah Valley
- Fiddletown

Central Coast AVAs
- Livermore Valley
- Santa Cruz Mountains
- Monterey
- Santa Clara Valley
- Mount Harlan
- Chalone
- Santa Lucia Highlands
- Carmel Valley
- Arroyo Seco
- San Lucas
- York Mountain
- Paso Robles
- Edna Valley
- Arroyo Grande Valley
- Santa Maria Valley
- Santa Ynez Valley
- Temecula Valley
- San Pasqual Valley

OREGON

CASCADE RANGE

COAST RANGES

Crescent City

Clear Lake Res.

Goose Lake

Weed

Alturas

Klamath

Pit

Eureka

Weaverville

Shasta Lake

Eagle Lake

Honey Lake

Redding

Lake Almanor

Garberville

Red Bluff

Quincy

Redwood Valley · Potter Valley

Fort Bragg

Willows

Downieville

Lake Oroville

Mendocino

Anderson Valley

Clear Lake

Knights Valley

Nevada City

Lake Tahoe

Mendocino Ridge

Yuba City

Sonoma Coast

Guenoc Valley

Napa Valley

El Dorado

Alexander Valley

Clarksburg

Sacramento

Dry Creek Valley

Lodi

Fiddletown

Russian River Valley

Shenandoah Valley

Sonoma Valley

Suisun Valley

Bridgeport

Los Carneros

Solano County Green Valley

Stockton

San Francisco

Oakland

Tuolumne

Mono Lake

San Mateo

Livermore Valley

Modesto

NEVADA

Redwood City

Freemont

Palo Alto

San Jose

Merced

Santa Clara Valley

Madera

Independence

Santa Cruz Mountains

Hollister

CALIFORNIA

Santa Cruz

Mount Harlan

Fresno

Death Valley Junction

Salinas

Visalia

Monterey

Chalone

Kings

DEATH VALLEY

Carmel Valley

Hanford

Santa Lucia Highlands

Big Sur

Tulare

Arroyo Seco

Coalinga

San Lucas

San Miguel

Delano

Baker

Paso Robles

York Mountain

San Luis Obispo

Bakersfield

Edna Valley

MOJAVE

Arroyo Grande Valley

Mojave

Needles

Santa Maria

DESERT

Barstow

PACIFIC OCEAN

Santa Maria Valley

Lompoc

Santa Ynez Valley

Santa Barbara

Ventura

Santa Clara

COAST RANGES

Glendale

Pasadena

San Miguel

Santa Monica

Los Angeles

Santa Rosa

Santa Cruz

Palm Springs

Anaheim

Long Beach

Santa Ana

Blythe

CHANNEL ISLANDS

Salton Sea

San Nicolas

Santa Catalina

Temecula Valley

Gulf of Santa Catalina

Brawley

El Centro

San Pasqual Valley

El Cajon

San Clemente

San Diego

National City

ARIZONA

MEXICO

Los Angeles Aqueduct

Kern

California Aqueduct

SAN JOAQUIN VALLEY

SIERRA NEVADA

Colorado River Aqueduct

San Luis Rey

N

0   25   50   75   100 Miles

0   25 50 75   100 Kilometers

Tuscany is to Italy, so the Napa Valley is to California. Unlike Bordeaux and Tuscany, however, which respectively produce an appreciable percentage of France's and Italy's premium wines, the Napa Valley, with 44,000 acres/18,000 hectares planted, produces only about 4 to 5 percent of California's wines. As a matter of fact, the entire North Coast AVA, which includes the superstar California appellations of Napa, Sonoma, and Mendocino counties, produces about 15 percent of California's total wine output. An equally important fact is that on an annual basis wines produced in the Napa Valley account for at least 20 percent of the total value of all of California's wines.

There are more than 450 wineries in the Napa Valley, most of them producing fine wines on a small-to-medium scale. There are also more than 700 farmers, some of whom also make wines but most grow grapes to sell to Napa's wineries. Despite, or perhaps because of, the limited amount of wine produced, there is no denying that the American and foreign wine-loving public identifies Napa Valley as the seat of quality in California. While it is true that not every varietal wine produced in the Napa Valley is world-class, there is no doubt that if the gods of the vintage cooperate, a wine labeled as Napa Valley Cabernet Sauvignon is going to be a fine wine.

Among all the best-known American Viticultural Areas in California, the Napa Valley is the most geographically inclusive, which can, in the long run, potentially damage the integrity and value of the AVA. In their rush to get federal approval for Napa Valley as an AVA (see map on page 132) back in the early 1980s, Napa-area growers and producers may have compromised too much, too soon. The original proposal was to restrict the Napa Valley AVA to the Napa River watershed, but this was challenged by grape growers as far north and east as Pope Valley on both historical and commercial grounds. The result is that the approved Napa Valley appellation covers the whole of Napa County except for Lake Berryessa and Napa's northeastern corner. Napa Valley as an appellation has less meaning than some purists might like. Approvals and pending approvals of numerous subappellations are an imperfect attempt to rectify the situation.

Napa Valley is justifiably famous for its wines and wine culture, and it attracts millions of visitors each year to celebrate the vine. The Napa Valley and its sixteen subappellations make up an extraordinarily diverse wine region. Soils, drainage, climates, elevations, age of vines, and viticultural and vinicultural practices vary widely across the region.

The valley floor runs approximately 30 miles/48 kilometers, from the city of Napa in the south to Calistoga in the north. It is bounded on the west side by the Mayacamas Mountains (which separate Napa from Sonoma) and on the east side by the smaller ridge of the Vaca Hills, which rise above the Silverado Trail.

Soils on the floor of the Napa Valley are deep, fertile, and dominated by clay but also contain alluvial deposits of sand, silt, minerals, and gravel. These are some of the youngest soils in the Napa Valley. Older volcanic soils, formed by the eruptions of the Mayacamas and Vaca ranges, are found in the mountain and hillside vineyards that surround the valley. These soils are thinner, less fertile, and

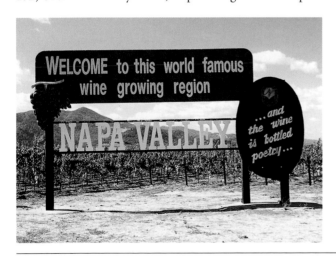

LEFT: *Napa Valley welcome sign, located off Highway 29, with a quote attributed to author Robert Louis Stevenson, from his travel memoir* Silverado Squatters, *published in 1883* RIGHT: *A twenty-foot-high bronze and wood sculpture created by artist Gino Miles welcomes visitors to the entrance of California's Napa Valley.*

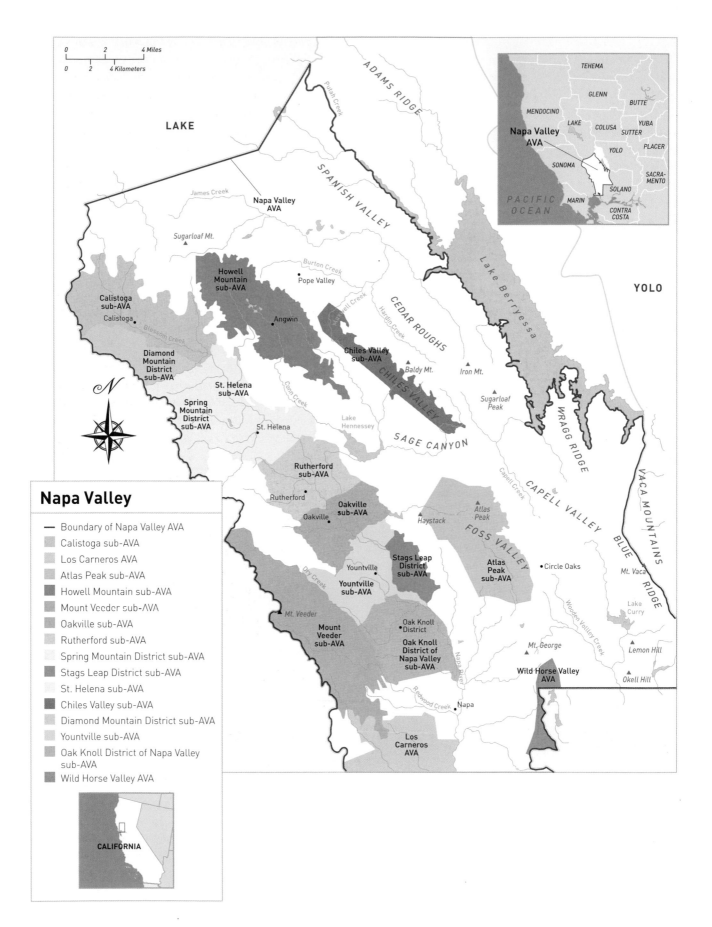

Napa Valley

- — Boundary of Napa Valley AVA
- Calistoga sub-AVA
- Los Carneros AVA
- Atlas Peak sub-AVA
- Howell Mountain sub-AVA
- Mount Veeder sub-AVA
- Oakville sub-AVA
- Rutherford sub-AVA
- Spring Mountain District sub-AVA
- Stags Leap District sub-AVA
- St. Helena sub-AVA
- Chiles Valley sub-AVA
- Diamond Mountain District sub-AVA
- Yountville sub-AVA
- Oak Knoll District of Napa Valley sub-AVA
- Wild Horse Valley AVA

CALIFORNIA

generally better-drained than the soils of the valley floor. In the far north, Calistoga, with its famous hot springs and mud baths, provides ample proof that volcanic action is not dormant in Napa Valley.

Given its size, it is not surprising that several different climatic zones exist within the valley. A general overview suggests that cool ocean air and fog are pulled from the Golden Gate Bridge into the San Pablo Bay and then north up the Napa Valley floor. The result is that the fog-sheltered vineyards of southern Napa usually remain cooler than those in the north.

Because of the valley's bowl-like shape, fog from both the San Pablo Bay and San Francisco Bay rolls into the Napa Valley early in the morning hours to enshroud the Carneros district and northern Napa. Because of its proximity to the bays, Carneros is cooler and the fog burns off slowly, sticking around until close to 1 P.M. In the warmer central Napa Valley and warmest northern valley, the fog burns off far more quickly and is usually gone before 11 A.M.

Southern Napa Valley is far cooler than northern Napa Valley: Carneros is at least 10°F/6°C cooler than Calistoga during the summer months, and each represents the extremes of climate for growing grapes for fine wines. You do not want Carneros any cooler nor Calistoga any warmer. The valley floor absorbs much summer heat but also attracts the breezes of the Pacific Ocean, creating a cooling fog during early to mid-morning. Sunshine benefits the grapes in Napa's western vineyards during the morning, while having the most impact in eastern vineyards during the afternoon. Napa's mountainside vineyards located both east and west, and above the fog line, enjoy cool breezes during the late afternoon and evening, countering the release of heat from the valley floor.

Red wines—mostly Cabernet Sauvignon—produced from the fertile floor of the Napa Valley are generally richer and riper, with higher alcohol levels, than the wines produced from less-fertile hillside and mountainside vineyards. The latter tend to display higher acidity, with just-ripe tannins, somewhat lower alcohol levels, and a higher degree of overall complexity and structure.

Undoubtedly, Napa includes the most famous names—past and present—connected with California wine: Robert Mondavi, Charles Krug, the former Inglenook (now Rubicon Estate), Beaulieu Vineyard (BV), Louis M. Martini, Beringer, Mayacamas, Sterling Vineyards, Christian Brothers, Joseph Phelps, Diamond Creek, Heitz Cellars, Chateau Montelena, Clos Du Val, Cakebread, and Stag's Leap Wine Cellars. The Napa Valley and some of its subappellations—Rutherford, Oakville, St. Helena, Yountville—have become well-known in the wine lexicon. Even Napa's roads, such as the Silverado Trail and the appropriately named Zinfandel Lane, are known far beyond Napa's borders.

LEFT: *The Louis M. Martini Winery in St. Helena has been in business since 1922. It moved to the Napa Valley in 1934, immediately following the repeal of Prohibition. To date, its only winemakers have been Louis M. Martini; his son, Louis P. Martini; and the current winemaker, grandson Michael Martini. Martini's Monte Rosso Vineyard in the Mayacamas Mountains of the Sonoma Valley AVA is legendary for Cabernet Sauvignon and "Gnarly Vines" Zinfandel.* RIGHT: *The Clos Pegase winery in Calistoga, commissioned by owner Jan Shrem and designed by postmodern architect Michael Graves, is in Shrem's words "a temple to wine and art." Some of Shrem's extensive art collection is housed there. The winery is best known for its "Hommage" Cabernet Sauvignon blend.*

Although fine examples of Merlot, Zinfandel, Cabernet Franc, Syrah, Chardonnay, Sauvignon Blanc, and Viognier are produced in the Napa Valley AVA, there is one grape that rules (at least outside of the Carneros district) and has made its reputation: Cabernet Sauvignon. In its best vintages, Napa "Cab" must be included among the world's great red wines. Luscious but not fat or flabby, fruit-driven but complex, accessible but ageworthy, sunny but not simple, full-bodied with delicate nuances, and with a remarkable balance of alcohol to fruit and tannin to acidity, Napa Cab can be an extraordinary wine.

Napa is also home to some world-famous Cabernet blends, sometimes known as "Meritage" (rhymes with "heritage") or Meritage-style wines (see "What Is a Meritage Wine?" on facing page). Following the lead of the famous châteaux of the Cabernet-rich Haut-Médoc and Graves districts of Bordeaux (see pages 301 and 304), several Napa wine producers are making expensive Cabernet-based blended wines, the components and percentages of which vary from vintage to vintage. The usual blending grapes are Merlot and Cabernet Franc. These wines, some of which sell at retail for far more than $100 per bottle, have received high levels of critical acclaim; most of them are sold only to the best restaurants and shops, and only in small quantities. Some of the best-known Meritage-style wines produced in the Napa Valley include:

- Anthology: Conn Creek
- Argos: Dutch Henry
- Cain Five, Cain Concept, Cain Cuvée: Cain
- Cardinale: Kendall-Jackson
- Claret: Atlas Peak Vineyards
- Claret, Diamond Mountain District Red: Ramey
- Dominus, Napanook: Dominus Estate
- Double T Red: Trefethen
- Eloge: Anderson's Conn Valley Vineyards
- Élu: St. Supéry
- Generations: Charles Krug
- Hommage: Clos Pegase
- Howell Mountain Red: Duckhorn (more Merlot than Cabernet)
- Insignia: Joseph Phelps
- J. Daniel Cuvée: Lail Vineyards
- King of the Gypsies: Behrens & Hitchcock
- Magnificat: Franciscan Oakville Estate
- Opus One: Robert Mondavi Winery and Baron Philippe de Rothschild partnership
- The Oracle: Miner Family Vineyards

- Orropas: St. Clement
- Persistence: Reynolds Family Winery
- The Poet, M. Coz, CE2V: Cosentino
- Quintessa: Agustin Huneeus
- Rubicon: Rubicon Estate
- Tapestry Reserve: BV (Beaulieu Vineyard)
- Terzetto: Volker Eisele Family Estate
- Trifecta: Beaucanon Estate
- Trilogy: Flora Springs

The following wineries, arranged alphabetically, are some of the producers of wines made from grapes grown in the Napa Valley AVA (mostly, but not exclusively, Cabernet Sauvignon, Merlot, Cabernet Franc, Zinfandel, Chardonnay, and Sauvignon Blanc). Most, but not all, maintain wineries in the Napa Valley; some own wineries elsewhere but produce wine from Napa Valley fruit.

Abreu, Acacia, Adler Fels, Adobe Road, Aetna Springs, Altamura, American Roots, Amizetta, Amusant, Anderson's Conn Valley, Andretti, Angelo, Aquinas, Araujo, Artesa, Atalon, Atlas Peak, August Briggs, Azalea Springs, Baldacci, Ballentine, Barlow, Bayview, Beaucannon, Beaulieu Vineyard (BV), Behrens & Hitchcock, Bell, Benessere, Bennett Family, Beringer, Bighorn, Black Coyote, Blockheadia, Bouchaine, Bourassa, Bridgeway, Bryant Family, Buehler, B Wise, Cafaro, Cain, Cakebread, Calistoga Cellars, Cardinale, Cartlidge & Browne, Casa Nuestra, Cavus, Caymus, C. Beck, Ceja, Chanticleer, Chappellet, Charles Creek, Charles Krug, Chateau Montelena, Chateau Potelle, Chimney Rock, Cliff Lede, Clos Du Val, Clos Pegase, Colgin, Conn Creek, Corison, Cosentino, Coup de Foudre, Crichton Hall, Cuvaison, Dalla Valle, Dancing Horse, David Arthur, Davis Family, Del Bondio, Delectus, Diamond Creek, Dickerson, Dolce, Domaine Carneros, Domaine Chandon, Dominus, Downing Family, Duckhorn, Dunn, Dutch Henry, Dyer, Edgewood, Ehlers, Elkhorn Peak, Elodian, El Molino, Elyse, Enkidu, Etude, Farella-Park, Far Niente, Fife, Flora Springs, Folie à Deux, Forman, Four Bears, Franciscan, Frank Family, Franus, Frazier, Freemark Abbey, Frog's Leap, Gain Bay, Ghost Pines, Girard, Grace Family, Green and Red, Grgich Hills, Groth, Gustavo Thrace, Hagafen, Hall, Harlan Estate, Harrison, Hartwell, Havens, Hawkstone, Hayman & Hill, Heitz, Hendry, Hess Collection, Honig, Irony, J. Davies, Jade Mountain, Jana, Jarvis, Joel Gott, Joseph Phelps, Judd's Hill, Karl Lawrence, Kendall-Jackson, Kent Rasmussen, Kitchak, Kongsgaard, Kuleto Estate, La Jota, Lail, Laird Family, Lamborn,

WHAT IS A MERITAGE WINE?

If a winemaker wants to produce a red wine that emulates a Bordeaux blend—say 50 percent Cabernet Sauvignon, 45 percent Merlot, and 5 percent Cabernet Franc—what is he or she going to call it? Since it's not 75 percent of any particular grape variety, the wine can't be called by the name of a grape, and in fact U.S. wine laws dictate that it be called simply "Red Wine" or "Red Table Wine." Not too sexy.

In 1988, some frustrated Napa Valley winemakers who wanted to produce Bordeaux-style blended wines got together to address this issue. Agustin Huneeus of Franciscan Winery, Mitch Cosentino of Cosentino Winery, and Julie Garvey of Flora Springs Winery knew that they couldn't call the wines "Bordeaux Blend," as the French would go crazy and the U.S. government agency

that approves labels (at the time, the Bureau of Alcohol, Tobacco, and Firearms) wouldn't go for it. Besides, these winemakers and others that they attracted wanted to create a uniquely American name for their Old World–New World winemaking concept. They formed a loosely-knit association of about twenty members and announced a contest to give their "concept" wines a legal, proprietary brand name. The group received more than six thousand entries, and chose one submitted by a young Californian, Neil Edgar, who came up with the name "Meritage" (rhymes with "heritage"). Neil's prize would be two bottles of the first ten vintages of each Meritage Association member's wine.

The first Meritage wine was produced by Mitch Cosentino: the 1986 vintage of The Poet. Today, there are two hundred Meritage members, most of them in California, but with member wineries in twenty states, including New York State, New

Jersey, Arizona, Colorado, Michigan, New Mexico, and Virginia, and even members from Argentina, Australia, Canada, Mexico, and Israel. (For a full list of wine producers, go to www.mertiagealliance.org.) In 2008, the Meritage Association celebrated its twentieth anniversary. In May 2009 the group was renamed the Meritage Alliance.

What, then, constitutes a Meritage wine? First of all, the wine must be made from a blend of at least two traditional Bordeaux grapes—Cabernet Sauvignon, Merlot, Cabernet Franc, Malbec, and Petit Verdot for reds, Sauvignon Blanc and Sémillon for whites (more than 80 percent of Meritage wines are red). Second, no varietal can exceed 90 percent of the blend. This is probably why some of the most famous "Bordeaux blend" wines—Opus One, Rubicon, Insignia, and others—are not official members of the Meritage Alliance, as these wines often exceed 90 percent Cabernet Sauvignon.

NAPA MEETS (AND BEATS) FRANCE: THE 1976 PARIS TASTING

The bicentennial year for the United States, 1976, was a watershed for the international reputation of California wines, especially the wines from the Napa Valley and one Stags Leap District wine in particular. In 1976, Steven Spurrier—a well-known British wine writer and educator, wine bar owner, and wine merchant with a home base in Paris—proposed a blind tasting of five California Cabernets and five Chardonnays, pitting them against five red Bordeaux (all from the Médoc and Graves districts) and five white Burgundies (all from the Côte de Beaune district).

The tasting was held at the Inter-Continental Hotel in Paris. As a condition of France's participation, all of the judges were French, and the panel included well-regarded journalists, academicians, merchants, government officials, restaurateurs, and wine producers.

The results of the Paris tasting were like a sound bite heard around the world. Incredibly, the French judges picked a Napa Valley Cabernet Sauvignon (Warren Winiarski's 1973 Stag's Leap Wine Cellars) as the best red of the tasting and a Napa Valley/Alexander Valley Chardonnay as the best white of the tasting (Chateau Montelena 1973 Chardonnay, made by Miljenko "Mike" Grgich). The judges, who consistently mistook French wines for California wines during the tasting—and vice versa—were quite upset by this turn of events, but there was no going back: California's best had beaten France's best. All of the winning wines from California were made mostly from Napa Valley grapes, except for one; those grapes were grown on an old single vineyard in the Santa Cruz Mountains, Monte Bello.

The official results of the 1976 Paris tasting (note that the tasting was held before the introduction of the AVA system to California):

WHITE WINE

1. Chateau Montelena Chardonnay, California, 1973
2. Domaine Roulot Meursault-Charmes Premier Cru, Burgundy, France, 1973
3. Chalone Vineyard Chardonnay, California, 1974
4. Spring Mountain Vineyards Chardonnay, California, 1973
5. Joseph Drouhin Beaune Clos des Mouches Premier Cru, Burgundy, France, 1973
6. Freemark Abbey Chardonnay, California, 1972
7. Ramonet-Prudhon Bâtard-Montrachet Grand Cru, Burgundy, France, 1973
8. Domaine Leflaive Puligny-Montrachet Les Pucelles Premier Cru, Burgundy, France, 1973
9. Veedercrest Vineyards Chardonnay, California, 1972
10. David Bruce Chardonnay, California, 1973

RED WINE

1. Stag's Leap Wine Cellars Cabernet Sauvignon, California, 1973
2. Château Mouton Rothschild, Pauillac, Bordeaux, France, 1970
3. Château Haut-Brion, Graves, Bordeaux, France, 1970
4. Château Montrose, St-Estèphe, Bordeaux, France, 1970
5. Ridge Vineyards Monte Bello Cabernet Sauvignon, California, 1971
6. Château Léoville-Las-Cases, St-Julien, Bordeaux, France, 1971
7. Mayacamas Vineyards Cabernet Sauvignon, California, 1971
8. Clos Du Val Cabernet Sauvignon, California, 1972
9. Heitz Cellars Martha's Vineyard Cabernet Sauvignon, California, 1970
10. Freemark Abbey Cabernet Sauvignon, California, 1969

On May 24, 2006, to celebrate the thirtieth anniversary of the Paris tasting, Steven Spurrier organized simultaneous tastings in London and in the Napa Valley. This time, the judges were not all French, but a mix of American, British, and French (including Christian Vanneque, who was a judge in the 1976 tasting). All of the California producers were happy to submit their wines for the 2006 tasting. None of the Bordeaux producers extended the same courtesy; Spurrier either had to purchase the wines or accept donations from collectors.

This time around, the judges were told which red wines were from California and which were from Bordeaux. Each wine was awarded a total amount of points based on the total scores of all of the judges. The results of the 2006 red wine tasting were astonishing: Not one Bordeaux wine made the Top Five. The results of the tasting also confirmed that California's best Cabernet Sauvignons are ageworthy wines. But another fact, a bit more subtle than the blockbuster headlines, emerged, too. Note that the number one wine was not a Napa Valley Cabernet Sauvignon, but the 1971 Ridge Monte Bello Cabernet Sauvignon, made by Paul Draper in California's Santa Cruz Mountains.

2006 TASTING RESULTS: RED WINES

1   Ridge Vineyards Monte Bello Cabernet Sauvignon, California, 1971 (137 points)
2   Stag's Leap Wine Cellars Cabernet Sauvignon, California, 1973 (119 points)
3·4 A tie between Mayacamas Vineyards Cabernet Sauvignon, California, 1971, and Heitz Cellars Martha's Vineyard Cabernet Sauvignon, California, 1970 (112 points)
5   Clos Du Val Cabernet Sauvignon, California, 1972 (106 points)
6   Château Mouton Rothschild, Pauillac, Bordeaux, France, 1970 (105 points)
7   Château Montrose, St. Estèphe, Bordeaux, France, 1970 (92 points)
8   Château Haut-Brion, Graves, Bordeaux, France, 1970 (82 points)
9   Château Léoville-Las-Cases, St-Julien, Bordeaux, France, 1971 (66 points)
10 Freemark Abbey Cabernet Sauvignon, California, 1969 (59 points)
Total points: California: 639; France: 345

White wines were tasted in their then-current vintages, and again were separated by provenance: The judges knew they were tasting either California Chardonnay or French white Burgundy. In the 2006 tasting, white wines were not officially ranked against each other, as some of the wines tasted in 1976 were not represented in the 2006 tasting. (If the wines had been ranked, the winner would have been Domaine Leflaive Puligny-Montrachet Les Pucelles, Burgundy, France, 2002.) Overall, the whites ran a statistical dead heat.

Total points: California: 378; France: 378

In 2008, a feature film based on the 1976 Paris tasting, *Bottle Shock*, was released, to mostly tepid critical reviews.

LEFT: *The 1973 vintage of Stag's Leap Wine Cellars Cabernet Sauvignon won first place among the red wines in the Paris tasting, defeating some fine red Bordeaux wines.* RIGHT: *The thirtieth anniversary of the Paris tasting was celebrated with a reenactment of the 1976 tasting. This time, the winner among the reds was the 1971 Ridge Vineyards Monte Bello Cabernet Sauvignon.*

Lang & Reed, Larkmead, Leaping Lizard, Ledgewood Creek, Lewis, Liparita, Livingston-Moffett, Lokoya, Long, Louis M. Martini, Luna, Mad Hatter, Mahoney, Markham, Martin Ray, Mayacamas, Mayo, McKenzie-Mueller, Merryvalc, Michael Pozzan, Miner Family, Monticello, Mount Veeder, Mumm Napa, Napa Cellars, Napa Creek, Napa Family, Napa Ridge, Newton, Neyers, Nichelini, Nicholis, Nickel & Nickel, Oakford, Oakville Ranch, Opus One, Pahlmeyer, Palmeri, Paradigm, Parcel 41, Patz & Hall, P. B. Hein, PEJU Province, Perfecta, Philip Togni, Pine Ridge, Plumpjack, Prager, Pride, Provenance, Q Napa, Quail Ridge, Quintessa, Ravenswood, Raymond, Regusci, Reynolds Family, Richard Partridge, Rios, Robert Biale, Robert Craig, Robert Foley, Robert Keenan, Robert Mondavi, Robert Pecota, Robert Sinskey, Rombauer, Round Hill, Rubicon Estate, Rudd, Rutherford Vintners, Saddleback, Saintsbury, Schramsberg, Screaming Eagle, Selene, Sequoia Grove, Serdonis, Shafer, Shoofly, Shypoke, Signorello, Silverado, Silver Oak, Sky, Smith-Madrone, SoloRosa, Spelletich, Spottswoode, Staglin, St. Clement, Stelzner, Sterling, Stonegate, Stonehedge, Stony Hill, Storybook Mountain, St. Supéry, Stag's Leap Wine Cellars, Stags' Leap Winery, Stratford, Sullivan, Sumners, Sutter Home, Swanson, Terremoto, Textbook, Toad Hall, Tom Eddy, Tor, Trefethen, Tria, Trinchero, Truchard, Tudal, Tuocay, Turley, Turnbull, T-Vine, Twenty Bench, Two Hands, Van Asperen, Viader, Villa Mt. Eden, Vine Cliff, Vineyard 7 & 8, Volker Eisele, Von Strasser, Voss, V. Sattui, Whitehall, William Hill, York Creek, X, and ZD.

CARNEROS

Carneros, the first subappellation of the Napa Valley, was approved in 1983, right after the original, cumbersome Napa Valley AVA was granted. The area straddles boundaries between Napa County and Sonoma County. With its 7,000 acres/3,000 hectares planted in a much cooler climate

The dramatic sweep of Carneros vineyards

than in most of the rest of the Napa Valley, Carneros was the first growing region granted AVA status based on climate. Grape growers in the Carneros district and the wineries that purchased the grapes moved swiftly to establish their own identity, and with great success. The players were so confident that they could go it alone without any reference to Napa that they had no qualms about proposed Carneros AVA boundaries crossing into Sonoma County (at that time Sonoma was virtually unknown compared to Napa).

Pioneering work in Chardonnay and Pinot Noir plantings was done in Carneros by Louis M. Martini and his son, Louis P. Martini, at their legendary La Loma Vineyard as early as 1942. Still, Carneros was something of a protected secret until the 1980s, when it was "discovered." The characteristic independence of Carneros wine growers and their refusal to participate in commercial and political rivalries with each other—insisting that Carneros become part of neither Napa nor Sonoma—ensured the integrity of Carneros as an AVA (see maps on pages 130 and 132). As if to amplify the spirit of working together in Carneros, wineries and growers formed the Carneros Wine Alliance (formerly called the Carneros Quality Alliance), dedicated to "telling the story" of Carneros and its wines and to advocate for financial, social, and environmental stability in the AVA. About thirty-five wineries and forty growers are members of the Carneros Wine Alliance.

Carneros (officially named Los Carneros but rarely referred to by this name) is a very cool district and since the 1980s has become increasingly identified with outstanding Pinot Noir and Chardonnay wines. Now, in the early part of the twenty-first century, other areas, such as the Russian River Valley and the southern Central Coast, are heralded as equally good, or even better, districts for growing these two grapes. Carneros, however, continues to hold its own, as amply demonstrated by the long-term loyalty of its grape growers and wine producers.

Carneros is more about its vineyards than any particular wineries located in the AVA, and it is the quality of its vineyards that has made its reputation. High-quality wine producers line up to purchase grapes from such well-known Carneros properties as Hyde, Hudson, Sangiacomo, Truchard, and Winery Lake and are willing to pay a premium to feature the name of the vineyard on their wine label.

In the 1980s, the burgeoning premium sparkling wine industry, whose workhorse grapes are Pinot Noir and Chardonnay, quickly recognized the potential of the Carneros district, and many producers purchased

vineyard land there or developed long-term contracts with established growers. Those who established wineries for sparkling wine production in Carneros include Domaine Carneros (the parent company is Taittinger, of Champagne, France) and Gloria Ferrer (the parent company is Freixenet, of Spain). Cordoníu Napa, now renamed Artesa (parent company Cordoníu, of Spain) made an extraordinary postmodern architectural statement with its underground winery in Carneros but has since all but given up the sparkling wine business in California, and it has retrofitted its Carneros winery to produce red and white **TABLE WINES**. This is the case, to a lesser or greater extent, with almost all of the sparkling wine producers focused on Carneros. Domaine Carneros, Gloria Ferrer, Artesa, and Domaine Chandon, whose winery is in the Yountville AVA of Napa, are following market trends toward high-quality Chardonnay and Pinot Noir table wines—produced from Carneros fruit.

In the mid-1990s, several producers, led by Robert Sinskey, Michael Havens, Sterling Vineyards, Truchard, Cuvaison, Ravenswood, and Clos Pegase, among others, planted Merlot in the clay-rich, Merlot-friendly soils of Carneros. Many people thought that what happened to Cabernet Sauvignon plantings in Carneros—unripe green fruit, herbal flavors due to cold weather—would happen to Merlot as well. It appears they were wrong. In the warmer parts of the Napa Valley, Merlot ripens more rapidly than Cabernet Sauvignon, producing grapes that have more than adequate sugars but not much acidity. In cool-climate Carneros, the extra "hang time" on the vine seems to have agreed with Merlot, often producing grapes with a greater depth of flavor and more complexity.

Currently, several producers are growing Syrah in the northernmost part of Carneros and are getting some stunning results. Syrah is native to the Rhône Valley (see page

332), and the finest Syrah wines are produced from grapes grown in the coolest districts of the northern Rhône. Early results indicate that Syrah can flourish in the cool Carneros vineyards. Still, Chardonnay and Pinot Noir are the viticultural backbone of Carneros.

The following wineries are some of the best-known producers of wines produced from grapes (mostly, but not exclusively, Pinot Noir and Chardonnay) grown in the Carneros AVA:

Acacia, Ardiri, Artesa, B. R. Cohn, BV, Benessere, Benziger Family, Beringer, Blue, Bouchaine, Buena Vista, Cakebread, Carneros, Carneros Creek, Castle, Ceja, Charles Krug, Cline, Clos Du Val, Clos Pegase, Connor/Brennan, Cuvaison, Diamond Oaks, Domaine Carneros, Domaine Chandon, Dutch Henry, Etude, Fleur de California, Frank Family, Franus, Frog's Leap, Gloria Ferrer, Hartford, Havens, Jacuzzi, Joseph Phelps, Kent Rasmussen, Kistler, La Crema, Laird Family, Landmark, Laurier, Livingston-Moffett, MacRostie, Mahoney, Merryvale, Neyers, Nickel & Nickel, Patz & Hall, Paul Hobbs, Pine Ridge, Provenance, Ramey, Robert Mondavi, Robert Sinskey, Robert Stemmler, Robledo, Roche, Rombauer, Saintsbury, Salexis, Schug, Selene, Sequoia Grove, Shafer, St. Clement, St. Francis, Steele, Sterling, Tantalus, Toad Hall, Truchard, Tulocay, V. Sattui, Valley of the Moon, Viansa, Voss, Whitehall Lane, and ZD.

HOWELL MOUNTAIN

In 1984, Howell Mountain, whose only town, Angwin, was founded by prohibitionist Seventh-Day Adventists in 1909, was awarded AVA status. Although vineyards had been sited on Howell Mountain since the late nineteenth century—in fact, beginning in 1880, the legendary Charles Krug was one of the first producers to seriously explore the vineyard potential of this district, situated in the extreme northeast of Napa County—it was not until Randy Dunn, former winemaker for Caymus winery, produced opulent Cabernet Sauvignon on his mountainside vineyard and Paul Draper, winemaker for Ridge Vineyards, made extraordinary Zinfandel from the Park-Muscadine vineyard that Howell Mountain garnered attention for its *terroir*-driven wines.

The 600 acres/240 hectares are planted in Howell Mountain at elevations that rise to just under 2,200 feet/725 meters, which ensures a good balance of acidity in the grapes with southern and western exposures for afternoon and late afternoon sun to warm the vineyards. (In order to qualify for AVA status, vineyards must be located at least 1,400 feet/420 meters above sea level.)

Randy Dunn, swearing by extended maceration and swearing at the overuse of new oak, makes two of the earliest and most long-lived Cabernet Sauvignon wines in the Napa Valley: one with a Howell Mountain appellation, one with a Napa Valley appellation. Both Dunn Vineyard wines are 100 percent Cabernet Sauvignon. Dunn's wines are sold mostly by subscription—there is a long waiting list for any wine produced by Dunn—and to a few select restaurant accounts. He now owns the Park-Muscadine vineyard and sells those Zinfandel grapes to other well-respected producers, such as Storybook Mountain. Zinfandel is the grape with the most history on Howell Mountain, and Howell Mountain Zin can be glorious in its tarry earthiness.

One of the finest Merlot wines in all of California was made by Beringer's now-retired winemaker, Ed Sbragia, from grapes grown on the soils of Howell Mountain's Bancroft Ranch. In 1994, Sbragia produced 200 cases of

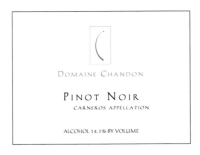

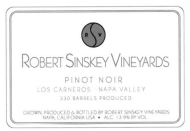

TOP: *Domaine Chandon, owned by the world's largest Champagne producer, Moët et Chandon, has extensive vineyard holdings in Carneros. Note that this is a still wine made from Pinot Noir, the premier red grape of Carneros.* BOTTOM: *This label indicates that the grapes were grown only on the Napa side of Carneros (Carneros is a shared appellation of Napa and Sonoma counties). Robert Sinskey also expresses his production in the number of barrels made; 330 barrels translates to about 7,500 cases of wine, about 90,000 bottles.*

ATALON

Keyes Vineyard

ALC. 14.4% BY VOL.

MERLOT
NAPA VALLEY
HOWELL MOUNTAIN

ABOVE LEFT: *Randy Dunn makes artisanal* terroir-*driven Cabernet Sauvignon from his Howell Mountain vineyards at the small winery adjoining his mountain home.* ABOVE RIGHT: *Atalon produces fine Howell Mountain Merlot.* BELOW: *The vineyards of the Stags Leap District lie at the base of mammoth rock outcroppings. Stags Leap is a bit cooler and at higher elevations than the two other well-known Cabernet Sauvignon districts in the Napa Valley, Rutherford and Oakville. The differences in climate and elevation make for Cabernet Sauvignon wines with a unique signature.*

Cabernet Sauvignon from the same vineyard site; it sold out immediately at $100 per bottle, and prices have escalated since. Sbragia's successors at Beringer continue to produce the wine.

Just shy of the legal altitude minimum of the Howell Mountain AVA, Viader produces its famous Cabernet Sauvignon, considered one of the Napa Valley's "Cult Cabernets," at 1,200 to 1,300 feet/367 to 398 meters above the valley floor. Viader also produces a Syrah, and V, a Petit Verdot–Cabernet blend.

The following wineries are some of the best-known producers of wines produced from grapes (mostly, but not exclusively, Zinfandel, Cabernet Sauvignon, and Merlot) grown in the Howell Mountain AVA: Atalon, Atlas Peak, Beringer, Black Sears, Cakebread, Cliff Lede, D. R. Stephens, Duckhorn, Dunn, Elyse, Forman, Howell Mountain Vineyards, Ladera, Lail, La Jota, Lamborn, Liparita, Lokoya, Nickel & Nickel, Robert Craig, Robert Foley, Roberts & Rogers, Rocking Horse, St. Clement, Stephen & Walker Trust, Storybook, Summit Lake, Turley, and V. Sattui.

STAGS LEAP DISTRICT

Napa Valley's Stags Leap District, most of which lies just east of the Silverado Trail, received AVA status in 1989 and is known as one of the best spots in California for Cabernet Sauvignon. The earliest planting of Cabernet Sauvignon, the Fay Vineyard, which remains a benchmark today, was planted here as late as the 1960s, with the overwhelming majority of Cabernet plantings happening in the 1970s. Today, there are a total of 1,350 acres/540 hectares planted.

Following the lead of Norman Fay, who decided to plant the grapes on soils that had supported hay and promiscuous plantings of prune plums, vegetables, and grapevines, came other Stags Leap Cab pioneers: Richard Stelzner, who began as a grape grower and then formed Stelzner Vineyards; Warren Winiarski of Stag's Leap Wine Cellars; Carl Doumani of Stags' Leap Winery; and Bernard Portet of Clos Du Val, all in 1972. They were followed in 1978 by John Shafer, of Shafer Vineyards, and Gary Andrus, who founded Pine Ridge Winery.

Stanley Anderson of S. Anderson Vineyards (1979) expanded the district; S. Anderson is the northernmost vineyard in the Stags Leap District, lying just north of the Yountville crossroad. In 1980, Sheldon Wilson bought the Chimney Rock golf course, brought in bulldozers to reduce the course to nine holes, and planted 75 acres of vines, mostly Cabernet Sauvignon. In 2000, under the direction of the current owner, international wine-industry legend Anthony Terlato, the rest of the golf course was bulldozed and planted to fifty more acres of Cabernet Sauvignon grapes. Silverado Vineyards (founded in 1981 by the daughter of Walt Disney) and Robert Mondavi Winery expanded the district yet again when they planted Sauvignon Blanc vines to the west of Silverado Trail, making the Napa River the western boundary of the district.

Even with the expansion of the Stags Leap District, the entire AVA is only a mile wide and three miles long. "SLD," as it is often called, is home to about twenty wineries and a dozen growers.

Merlot is planted on weightier, denser clay soils, but Cabernet Sauvignon is the signature grape of the Stags Leap District. The grape typically grows best in lighter, well-drained soils that envelop the dramatically beautiful hills, formed from volcanic outcroppings. Stags Leap District Cab is distinctive: aromas of violets and black cherries, a sensual, almost satiny texture with ripe tannins and a complex if surprisingly delicate finish on the palate.

Both older and more recent vintages of classic Cabernet Sauvignon wines from the Stags Leap District are some of the best-known connoisseur's wines—dubbed "cult wines"—from California. They include Baldacci Family, Chimney Rock Reserve, Cliff Lede, Clos Du Val SLD, Hartwell Vineyards, Ilsley Estate, Pine Ridge, Regusci, Robert Sinskey RSV, Shafer Vineyards Hillside Select,

Shafer Hillside Select Cabernet Sauvignon, made from grapes grown on Shafer's Stags Leap District property, has now reached the status of a "cult" wine: critically acclaimed, expensive, hard to find, and in great demand by connoisseurs and restaurateurs.

MOUNT VEEDER WINE HISTORY: THE CHRISTIAN BROTHERS

••••••••••••••••••••••••

During most of the nineteenth century, Mount Veeder was known as the Napa Redwoods, a resort community. In 1903, German-born Theodore Gier, a highly successful wine producer in Livermore and wine merchant in Oakland, purchased hundreds of acres of land for vineyards and built the first winery on Mount Veeder. Gier was a controversial man whose sympathies for his homeland during and after World War I got him into trouble; at one time, all of his holdings were seized by the U. S. government.

In 1928, Gier was able to sell his Mount Veeder winery and vineyards to the Christian Brothers, a religious order formed to provide free secular and religious education to the children of poor families. They established the Mont La Salle Vineyards and winery (named for their founder, Jean-Baptiste de la Salle) as a means to support their charitable work.

By 1937, the Christian Brothers were producing 200,000 gallons of wine. When they introduced a fine Christian Brothers brandy in 1940, the order became a powerhouse in the California wine industry. By the 1980s, the Christian Brothers, under the guidance of their cellar master, Brother Timothy, owned 2,100 acres/840 hectares of vineyard, half of it in the Napa Valley. In addition to the Mont La Salle winery, the order purchased Greystone in St. Helena, mostly for brandy production, and also owned aging cellars in Fresno. Total production capacity at this time was 40 million gallons.

By the late 1980s, the Christian Brothers wine empire had almost completely unraveled, because of intense competition and because the quality of their brandy was eclipsed. The order sold its wine and brandy production facilities, at a time when it was producing more than a million cases of brandy per year. By 1994, there were no Christian Brothers production facilities in the Napa Valley, and the name Christian Brothers was used for mostly inexpensive fortified wines and brandies that are still produced in the Central Valley.

The Christian Brothers also signed a fifty-year lease for the old Gier-built winery with their Swiss neighbor, Donald Hess, owner of the Hess Collection. The Hess Collection owns thousands of acres of vineyards on Mount Veeder and beyond. The facility houses the refurbished Gier winery, as well as an extraordinary collection of modern and postmodern artworks owned by Donald Hess.

The historic Greystone winery is now owned by The Culinary Institute of America, serving as the Institute's West Coast campus. Brother Timothy, at one time the most famous winemaker in California due to his inclusion in Christian Brothers advertisements, who was a wellspring of Napa Valley wine history, lived at the La Salle Institute on Mount Veeder until his death at 94 years old, in 2004.

Brother Timothy (1910–2004) was the winemaker for Christian Brothers, the religious order to which he dedicated his life. He became one of the most famous, most respected, and legendary winemakers in the Napa Valley.

Silverado Vineyards Solo, Stags' Leap Winery Estate Grown, Stelzner Reserve Barrel Select, and three wines from Stag's Leap Wine Cellars: Fay Vineyard, Cask 23, and SLV.

Other wineries located in the Stags Leap District or producing wine from Stags Leap District fruit include Cavus, J. R. Wagner Family, Malk Family, Martin Ray, Pillar Rock, Quixote, Reynolds Family, Taylor Family, Traverso, and White Rock.

In 2007, Warren Winiarski, then 79 years old, stunned the Napa Valley wine industry when he sold his heralded Stag's Leap Wine Cellars to a partnership of Ste. Michelle Estates (based in Washington State) and Piero Antinori (Tuscany, Italy) for $185 million. In acquiring the iconic vineyards and winery, the new partnership promises to carry on Winiarski's commitment to quality.

MOUNT VEEDER

At 2,700 feet/823 meters, Mount Veeder is the highest peak in the Mayacamas Mountains, which rise west of the town of Yountville in southwestern Napa. The region received AVA status in 1990 and has 1,000 acres/400 hectares planted. The Mayacamas Mountains separate Napa

County from Sonoma County. In 1968, Bob and Elinor Travers bought the historic Mayacamas Vineyards, located 2,000 feet/660 meters up Mount Veeder, including the original stone winery, which was built in 1889. As of 2008, Bob Travers is still the winemaker at Mayacamas. He established the reputation of the winery with the rustic but long-lived estate Cabernet Sauvignon wines he produced starting in the 1970s. In the mid-1980s, Travers turned his attention to estate Chardonnay, and as he did with Cab, Travers makes a unique mountain-grown wine. The Chardonnay employs no malolactic fermentation, only minimal oak treatment, and improves in the bottle with at least four or five years of age.

HESS
COLLECTION

MOUNT VEEDER ~ NAPA VALLEY
CABERNET SAUVIGNON

ESTATE GROWN

RED WINE

On Mount Veeder we find The Hess Collection, which is not only an estate winery but a museum-quality modern art gallery of works curated by Donald Hess. The Hess Collection's Mount Veeder wines—Cabernet Sauvignon, The Lion, Chardonnay, and 19 Block Cuvée, a blend of Cabernet Sauvignon, Malbec, Syrah, and Merlot—speak to the unique spice and wild berry qualities imparted by the mountainside vineyards in this AVA.

Over the years, the outstanding wines of Mayacamas and The Hess Collection have slowly been joined by a handful of neighbors, such as Sky Vineyards (great Zinfandel with labels to match) and Chateau Potelle (Zinfandel). Napa winemakers also look to Mount Veeder as a source of grapes for some very special wines. Patz & Hall makes a very fine Mount Veeder Chardonnay from the Carr Vineyard, Robert Craig makes a very good Cab from purchased grapes, and both Peter Franus and George Hendry make rustic Zinfandel from the Brandlin Ranch vineyard, owned by Hendry. Lokoya, owned by Kendall-Jackson principal Jess Jackson, specializes in estate Cabernet Sauvignon wines from mountain vineyards; Lokoya's Mount Veeder Cabernet Sauvignon sells at retail for more than $100.

Atlas Peak's mountainside vineyards

The following wineries are some of the best-known producers of wines produced from grapes (mostly, but not exclusively, Cabernet Sauvignon and Chardonnay) grown in the Mount Veeder AVA:

Calafia, Chateau Potelle, Domaine Chandon, Franus, The Hess Collection, Jade Mountain, Kendall-Jackson, Lagier-Meredith, Lokoya, Mayacamas, Mount Veeder Winery, Robert Craig, Sky, and V. Sattui.

ATLAS PEAK

The Atlas Peak AVA is located mostly in Napa's Foss Valley, sited high above the stone foothills of Stags Leap and across the valley floor from Mount Veeder. Standing on Atlas Peak on a reasonably clear day, you can easily see downtown San Francisco, which is about 70 miles/112 kilometers away. The high-altitude vineyards here, high enough to escape the late morning and afternoon fog so prevalent on the valley floor, receive instead sunlight throughout the afternoon, followed by a precipitous drop in temperature during the evening hours. The climate helps provide excellent ripeness and acidity in the grapes. The star of the AVA is Cabernet Sauvignon, but very good Zinfandel, Syrah, and Chardonnay are produced from grapes grown on Atlas Peak. AVA status was granted in 1992, and the region has 1,500 acres/600 hectares planted.

Atlas Peak Vineyards, after a decade-long commitment to Sangiovese-based wines by owner Piero Antinori, the famous producer of wines from Tuscany, now produces Cabernet Sauvignon and Chardonnay here, under the Antica label. Other wineries located in the Atlas Peak AVA include: Ardente, Astrale e Terra, Bialla, Cobblestone, Dominari, Elan, Hill Family, Jocelyn Lonen, Krupp Brothers, Pahlmeyer, Rivera, Veraison, and William Hill.

SPRING MOUNTAIN DISTRICT

The Spring Mountain District AVA, with 1,000 acres/400 hectares planted, lies above and to the west of the city of St. Helena, starting at Sulphur Canyon at 400 feet/123 me-

ters and rising to Ritchie Creek at 2,500 feet/825 meters, bordering Sonoma County. In 1943, Fred and Eleanor McCrea pioneered post-Prohibition Spring Mountain wines with the creation of the famous Stony Hill Vineyard, whose Chardonnay was so extraordinary and available in such small quantities that it was sold by subscription. Today, Stony Hill is still a classic producer of fine wines. In 1993, Spring Mountain District was granted AVA status.

The slopes of Spring Mountain are home to many small vineyards focused largely on Cabernet Sauvignon. Smith-Madrone Winery continues to produce one of the finest estate-bottled Riesling wines in California.

At the apex of Spring Mountain are some of the finest vineyards in the entire viticultural area, owned by Pride Mountain, whose former winemaker and vineyard manager, Bob Foley, is a master of Merlot as well as Cabernet

TOP: *Pride Mountain, a high-elevation vineyard sited primarily in the Spring Mountain District AVA, produces one of the finest Merlot wines in the Napa Valley.* BOTTOM: *A sex pheromone trap at Pride Mountain that attracts and snares the bees that thrive in the vineyards. The traps are highly effective.*

Sauvignon and Chardonnay. Cain Cellars was the first California estate winery to blend all five Bordeaux varietals (Cabernet Sauvignon, Merlot, Cabernet Franc, Petit Verdot, and Malbec), producing the idiosyncratic Cain Five, starting in 1985.

The following wineries are some of the best-known producers of wines produced from grapes grown in the Spring Mountain District AVA:

Atchley, Barnett, Behrens & Hitchcock, Beringer, Cain, Fife, Lynch, Marston, Newton, Paloma, Peacock, Philip Togni, Pride Mountain, Ridge, Robert Keenan, School House, Smith-Madrone, St. Clement, Stony Hill, Vineyard 7 & 8, and York Creek.

RUTHERFORD AND OAKVILLE

Why do we group these two AVAs together? The answer is one grape in two words: Cabernet Sauvignon. Oakville and Rutherford are contiguous viticultural areas; Oakville is Rutherford's southeastern border, Rutherford

is Oakville's northwestern border. Both are situated in the central Napa Valley, and both were granted AVA status in 1994. Oakville, truly on the valley floor, is a little cooler than Rutherford; Rutherford has a bit more elevation than Oakville and a bit more heat. Cabernet ripens beautifully in the vineyards of both AVAs, but a bit quicker in Rutherford. Both Oakville and Rutherford produce full-bodied, rich, complex wines that will age gracefully, with Rutherford getting the edge for long aging due to a bit more tannin development.

Oakville Cab at its best is redolent of fresh herbs, with a strong hint of mint and sage. Some of the wines are produced from grapes planted closer to the Napa River. These grapes are harvested later, and the wines show off elements of coffee and tobacco, balanced by black currants and sweet cherries, with moderately assertive tannins. Rutherford Cabernet Sauvignon is more plum and cherry flavors with a background of the herb and mint that defines Oakville. Tannins are quite dramatic in Rutherford Cab, with a bitter chocolate bite followed by opulent fruit.

Oakville has a broader stretch along the floor of the Napa Valley and a more varied soil structure than Rutherford, which relies on fairly rich and loamy soils. Because of this stretch, Oakville also has a number of different mesoclimates and microclimates. Although Cabernet is king in Oakville, excellent soil and climate pockets for Sauvignon Blanc, Merlot, Zinfandel, and even Chardonnay abound here. The Oakville AVA contains about forty resident wineries that work the 5,000 acres/2,000 hectares of vineyards.

Starting in 1880, Rutherford has been historically defined by the Cabernets of the original Inglenook (now Rubicon Estate) and Beaulieu (BV). Cabernet continues to rule Rutherford today on most of its 4,000 acres/1,600 hectares of vineyards. There are excellent exceptions to this rule: Tiny amounts of Merlot and Zinfandel are grown on Rutherford soils.

About 3,000 acres/1,200 hectares in Rutherford are planted with Cabernet Sauvignon (the grapes are worth about $36 million on an annual basis), with 550 acres/220 hectares of Merlot and about 120 acres/48 hectares of Cabernet Franc. Less than 300 acres/120 hectares are planted with Chardonnay. Of the 137 property owners in Rutherford, 111 have vineyards; 53 of those vineyards are less than 25 acres/10 hectares, and only 8 are more than 100 acres/40 hectares. There are nearly sixty wineries in Rutherford, and almost all of these wineries produce Cabernet Sauvignon wines.

There is general agreement that the west side of the Oakville and Rutherford AVAs contains the "Rutherford Bench." Two elevated alluvial fans—known as "benchlands"—created over centuries by the Napa River, create deep, loamy, well-drained soils. Starting just north of Yountville and extending six miles north to just south of St. Helena, the Rutherford Bench is home to some of the most famous Cabernet Sauvignon vineyard sites in California: Bella Oaks, Martha's Vineyard, Bosché, BV, Rubicon Estate, Grgich Hills, Opus One, Cakebread, Far Niente, and Livingston-Moffett, among others. The benchlands are what defines "Rutherford Dust," the mint/eucalyptus, mineral-driven taste of the Cabernet Sauvignon wines produced from the benchland vineyards.

Longtime wine producers, residents, and amateur geologists argue for the existence of geological benches—natural terraces—in both Oakville and Rutherford, and claim that the different soil structures that make up these gently sloping benches influence drainage and land use. Others deny the existence of any such benches, or perhaps vehemently defend the idea of a Rutherford Bench while vehemently denying the idea of an Oakville Bench. These debates will continue, but nothing will change the fact that vineyards in both Rutherford and Oakville produce some of the finest wines in all of Napa and indeed all of California. If there are any quality distinctions to be made between the two districts, they are mostly those stylistic choices imposed by the grape growers and the winemakers.

The following wineries are some of the best-known producers of wines (mostly, but not exclusively, Cabernet Sauvignon) grown in the Oakville AVA:

Cardinale, Cosentino, Dalla Valle, Downing Family, Emilio's Terrace, Far Niente, Girard, Groth, Harlan Estate, Maybach, Michael Pozzan, Miner Family, Nickel & Nickel, Oakford, Oakville Ranch, Opus One, Pahlmeyer, Plumpjack, Robert Mondavi, Rudd, Saddleback, Screaming Eagle, Silver Oak, Swanson, Tor, Turnbull, Vine Cliff, and Voss.

The following wineries are some of the best-known producers of wines (mostly, but not exclusively, Cabernet Sauvignon) grown in the Rutherford AVA:

Beaucanon, Beaulieu Vineyard (BV), Bell, Cakebread, Caymus, Conn Creek, David Arthur, Del Bondio, Frog's Leap, Grace Family, Grgich Hills, Hall, Harrison, Heitz, Honig, Livingston-Moffett, Mumm Cuvée Napa, Peju Province, Quail Ridge, Quintessa, Raymond, Rocking Horse, Round Pond, Rubicon Estate, Rutherford Grove, Rutherford Hill, Scarecrow, Sequoia Grove, St. Supéry,

Staglin Family, Sullivan, Trinchero, Villa Mt. Eden, Voss, Whitehall Lane, and ZD Wines.

WILD HORSE VALLEY

Wild Horse Valley, situated in the extreme southeastern corner of Napa County, is shared as an AVA with Solano County, which was, after much argument, included in the formation of the multicounty North Coast AVA in 1983. Most of Wild Horse Valley lies in Solano, and it would appear that this still-developing AVA was granted status in 1996 as part of the Napa Valley for commercial reasons. Wild Horse Valley is even cooler than Carneros, and is considered an ideal location for Pinot Noir and Chardonnay. David Mahaffey's Heron Lake Winery, currently the only winery in this AVA, produces about 600 cases of much sought-after Pinot Noir and Chardonnay each year from 125 acres/50 hectares.

CHILES VALLEY

The power of petition and the gumption of two small estate wine producers, Jay Heminway and Volker Eisele, resulted in Chiles Valley receiving AVA status in 1999. Although part of the larger Napa Valley AVA, Chiles Valley is actually a separate valley that lies east of Rutherford at a somewhat higher elevation. Chiles Valley, with 1,000 acres/400 hectares of grapes, is cooler than most other Napa Valley AVAs. Coincidentally, 10 miles/16 kilometers to the northwest of Chiles Valley, Pope Valley is also geographically separate from Napa Valley but somehow has been included in the general blanket Napa Valley AVA.

Volker Eisele, well known in the Napa Valley for leading the controversial but successful fight to create a valley-wide agricultural preserve, makes wonderfully rustic, artisanal Cabernet Sauvignon. Chiles Valley is also home to top Zinfandel producer Green & Red, owned by Jay Heminway. His Chiles Canyon Vineyards Zin is consistently one of California's best. Nichelini, founded in the Chiles Valley in 1890, is second only to Wente (founded in Livermore in 1887) as the oldest continuously operating family-owned winery in California. One of the most favored vineyard sites in Chiles Valley is the Martini Ghost Pines Ranch, now owned by Gallo.

Other notable wineries located in the Chiles Valley AVA include Brown Estate, Catacula Lake, Eagle & Rose, Jessup, RustRidge, and Stonegate.

YOUNTVILLE

Yountville, recognized as an AVA in 1999, is bordered by Oakville to the north, Stags Leap District to the east, the foothills of Mount Veeder to the west, and Oak Knoll District of Napa Valley AVA to the south.

Yountville has 4,000 acres/1,600 hectares planted, and Cabernet Sauvignon is the star, with Chardonnay in a strong supporting role. Yountville Cabernet is personified by the former Napanook vineyard (the source of much classic Inglenook Cask Cabernet Sauvignon). Napanook is now home to Dominus Estate and its postmodern winery, both owned by Christian Moueix of the world-renowned Château Pétrus in the Pomerol district of Bordeaux, France (see page 307). Moueix originally entered into partnership with the daughters of John Daniel Jr., who owned all of Inglenook until 1964 and willed the 122-acre/49-hect-

are Napanook to his adult children, Robin Lail and Marcia Smith. The partnership with Moueix began only three years after Robert Mondavi and Baron Philip de Rothschild formed Opus One. In 1994, Moueix purchased the Daniel daughters' interest in Dominus.

The most famous winery in Yountville is Domaine Chandon, owned by Champagne house Moët & Chandon. Chandon produces about 500,000 cases of *méthode champenoise* sparkling wine and varietal Pinot Noir and Chardonnay from their 1,110 acres/444 hectares in Napa and Sonoma, and from purchased grapes.

The tiny town of Yountville is also a very special place to eat. We would be remiss if we did not mention the pleasurable breakfasts at Gordon's, where homemade muffins, scones, and omelets head the bill. Dining in Yountville is every bit as special, if not more so. Domaine Chandon maintains a fine classical French restaurant. The former chef at Chandon, Philippe Jeanty, owns Bistro Jeanty, where the menu is truly authentic French bistro. Finally, chef Thomas Keller's world-famous, once-in-a-lifetime dining experience, The French Laundry, is located in Yountville. It is an amazing restaurant, and Keller may just be the most innovative chef in the United States. Make reservations literally months in advance. If you can't snag a reservation, try Keller's bistro, Bouchon, or the excellent—and very busy—Mustards Grill.

The following are some of the best-known wineries and vineyards in the Yountville AVA:

TOP LEFT: *Volker Eisele makes about 1,500 cases of artisanal, age-worthy Cabernet Sauvignon from his certified organic 60-acre vineyard in Chiles Valley. Eisele was a leader in declaring and maintaining the Napa Valley as a conservation district, limiting sprawl and nonfarming commercial exploitation of the valley.* TOP RIGHT: *Freshly picked Pinot Noir grapes from Carneros arriving in Yountville at the Domaine Chandon crusher*

Bell, Buccella, Chanticleer, Domaine Chandon, Dominus Estate, Gemstone, Goosecross, Hopper Creek, Kapscándy Family, Keever, Laird Family, L'Angevin, Paradigm, Rocca Family, Taylor Family, and Thomas Michael.

ST. HELENA AND CALISTOGA

St. Helena is home to some of Napa's most heralded wineries and vineyards. AVA recognition came in 1999. Bordered on the north by the Calistoga AVA and on the south by Rutherford's Zinfandel Lane, St. Helena encompasses the historic Beringer, Charles Krug, Louis M. Martini, and Sutter Home wineries, as well as Markham, Merryvale, Spottswoode, and Grace Family. Cabernet Sauvignon and Zinfandel ripen beautifully in this viticultural area, as does Sauvignon Blanc. Total area under vine is 1,400 acres/560 hectares.

St. Helena is also home to Greystone, originally a Christian Brothers winery and now the Napa Valley outpost of The Culinary Institute of America. In addition to its educational programs, Greystone features its popular and critically acclaimed Wine Spectator Restaurant and vegetable and flower gardens.

The following are some of the best-known wineries and vineyards in the St. Helena and Calistoga AVA:

Abreu, Anderson's Conn Valley, Andrew Geoffrey, Andrew Lane, August Briggs, Ballentine, Benessere, Blockheadia, Buehler, Calafia, Charles Krug, Chateau Montelena, Chiarello Family, Clos Pegase, Corison, Duckhorn, Ehlers, Flora Springs, Folie à Deux, Freemark Abbey, Grace Family, Hall, Heitz, Joseph Phelps, Kent Rasmussen, Lang & Reed, Merryvale, One, Spottswoode,

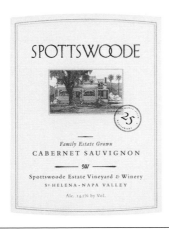

The certified organic 40-acre Spottswoode Estate in St. Helena is owned by Mary Novak and her daughters. Spottswoode is best known for its Cabernet Sauvignon and Sauvignon Blanc wines.

Titus, V. Sattui, Van Asperen, Venge, Vineyard 29, and Wolf Family.

DIAMOND MOUNTAIN DISTRICT

Although the Diamond Mountain District, located in the Mayacamas Mountain range in northwestern Napa Valley, covers more than 5,000 acres/2,000 hectares, only 10 percent of the rocky soil in this high altitude AVA is planted to vineyards. Because of that altitude, Diamond Mountain is not impacted by the fog that is so important for the vineyards on the floor of the Napa Valley.

Diamond Mountain soils are volcanic and well-drained, and because of its high elevation, vineyards here benefit from extended sun exposure. The signature grape of the Diamond Mountain District is Cabernet Sauvignon, which produces full-bodied, powerful, complex wines with hard tannins; these are wines meant for aging. In addition to Cabernet Sauvignon, Zinfandel and Cabernet Franc do quite well in Diamond Mountain soils, and AVA recognition came in 2001.

Diamond Mountain was first put on the quality-wine map by Al Brounstein and his wife, Boots, who founded Diamond Creek Vineyards. In 1967, the Brounsteins purchased 70 acres/28 hectares of land on Diamond Mountain and planted Cabernet Sauvignon vineyards with vine cuttings from Bordeaux that Brounstein smuggled into California. Al Brounstein identified three distinct vineyard blocks on his property: Red Rock Terrace (seven acres that face north, composed of loamy soils), Gravelly Meadow (five acres of flat lands with gravel and sand soils), and Volcanic Hill (eight acres facing south, composed of volcanic ash). In the best vintages, Brounstein would also bottle wine made from his Lake Vineyard (about 1 acre/0.4 hectares). Beginning in 1972, Brounstein produced wines from the different vineyard blocks, and each wine expresses the *terroir* of its site. Diamond Creek is a Cabernet Sauvignon–only winery, and the wines, produced on a minuscule scale, command very high prices. Al Brounstein, much respected as a wine producer and philanthropist, died in 2007 at the age of 86.

The following are some of the best-known wineries and vineyards in the Diamond Mountain District AVA:

PHYLLOXERA: FROM DISASTER TO OPPORTUNITY

• •

As early as 1985, many producers knew that the seeds of disaster were taking root around Napa and Sonoma. Vines were sick and dying, and the culprit was phylloxera.

Grudgingly, growers accepted that the AxR1 rootstock, so highly recommended by the University of California, Davis as resistant to phylloxera, was not, in fact, immune. Scientists identified a new strain of phylloxera, biotype B, which AxR1 cannot withstand. It is also likely that the vinifera branch of the AxR1 parentage has proven to be a weak link, contributing to AxR1's susceptibility to biotype B phylloxera. The only solution: replant entire vineyards on different rootstocks.

At least twelve counties in California showed signs of infestation by phylloxera by the 1990s. The hardest-hit counties were Napa and Sonoma, and Monterey showed increased symptoms. Both Sonoma and Monterey saw an even more rapid spread of phylloxera following the heavy rains of early 1995, since the floodwaters carried phylloxera from infested vineyards to previously unaffected sites. Phylloxera had been already so well established in Napa County that the floodwaters there had minimal effect on its spread. The replanting that started in 1987 in Napa and Sonoma was complete by 2004–2005. Replanting costs ran to millions of dollars.

According to the Napa County Cooperative Extension of the University of California, the monitoring agency for post-phylloxera replanting, in the 1990s about 65 percent of phylloxera-infected vines in Napa and Sonoma were planted on the AxR1 rootstock. That amounted to about 22,000 acres/8,800 hectares in each county, at a replanting cost of around $30,000 per acre/$75,000 per hectare. More than 15,000 acres/6,000 hectares were replanted in Napa County specifically because of the biotype B phylloxera, and almost 7,000 acres/2,800 hectares in Sonoma County.

Since the only practical remedy was to replant, many growers took the opportunity to reassess which variety to grow, what rootstock to plant on, and what spacing and trellising to use. What appeared at first to be a major blow to the industry turned into an opportunity to further improve the quality of California wines by adopting more appropriate grape varieties and matching varieties and even clones to optimal sites, soils, and microclimates. Replanted vineyards are also using higher-density planting patterns. Higher-density plantings have resulted in fewer but higher-quality grapes on each vine and an overall increase in yield per acre. As a preventive measure, vineyards have been replanted using a wide array of rootstocks, rather than relying so heavily on one type. Thus, if one rootstock develops any vulnerability to phylloxera, the problem will not be so widespread or so dramatic.

Replanting of red varieties in Napa and Sonoma counties concentrated on Merlot and Cabernet Sauvignon. Other red varieties showing an increase of acreage were Pinot Noir, especially in Napa, and Zinfandel and Cabernet Franc in both counties. For white varieties, the overwhelming preference was for Chardonnay, while Sauvignon Blanc maintained a reasonable rate of replanting.

Many producers decided to take a completely different route, planting grapes most closely identified with the Rhône Valley. Even prior to the spread of phylloxera, the Rhone Rangers had great success making wine from the grapes native to the Rhône Valley in southern France, a distinctly warm region whose grapes may well be better suited to some of California's climates than Chardonnay ever was.

Rhône grapes used in California for red wine production include Syrah, Petite Sirah, Mourvèdre, Grenache, and Carignan. White varietals include Viognier, Roussanne, and Marsanne.

A phylloxera-devastated vineyard in Napa Valley's Oakville district, which has since been replanted. Note the healthy vineyards in the distance.

ESTATE GROWN NAPA VALLEY
CABERNET SAUVIGNON
OAK KNOLL DISTRICT OF NAPA VALLEY

Andrew Geoffrey, Azalea Springs, Constant, Diamond Creek, Diamond Terrace, Dyer, Graeser, GTS, J. Davies/ Schramsberg, Lokoya, Reverie on Diamond Mountain, Stonegate, Teachworth, Terisa, and Von Strasser.

OAK KNOLL DISTRICT OF NAPA VALLEY

This AVA is located in southern Napa Valley, just north of Carneros, with 3,500 acres/1,400 hectares of vines. Like Carneros, the Oak Knoll District benefits from the cooling fog and ocean breezes provided by the San Pablo Bay.

Not quite as cool as Carneros, but cooler than the rest of Napa Valley, Oak Knoll's vineyards are home to several varieties—chief among them Merlot, but also Chardonnay. Janet Trefethen, who led the petition drive for AVA status for the Oak Knoll District (granted in 2004), is perhaps best known for her Trefethen Riesling, a grape that really needs a cool climate.

The Oak Knoll District is home to about twenty wineries and about thirty vineyards. Many Napa Valley wine producers line up to buy fruit from Oak Knoll growers, especially when it comes to Chardonnay and Merlot grapes.

In addition to Trefethen, other wineries that make their home in the Oak Knoll District of Napa Valley include:

Andretti, Blackbird, Boyd Family, Etude, Frisinger, Kate's Vineyard, Laird Family, Luna, Modus Operandi, Monticello/ Corley Family, O'Brien, Silverado Hill, Smith Wooton, Steltzner, StoneFly, Strata, Terremota, and Van Der Heyden.

SONOMA COUNTY

The fourteen AVAs of Sonoma County are Alexander Valley, Bennett Valley (a sub-AVA of the Sonoma Valley AVA), Carneros (AVA shared with Napa County; a sub-AVA of Sonoma Valley; see page 138), Chalk Hill (a sub-AVA of the Russian River Valley AVA), Dry Creek Valley, Green Valley of Russian River Valley (a sub-AVA of the Russian River Valley AVA), Knights Valley, North Coast (Sonoma is a constituent county of this multicounty AVA), Northern Sonoma (a blanket AVA that covers most of Sonoma County's AVAs, except for the Sonoma Valley AVA and its sub-AVAs), Rockpile (a sub-AVA of Dry Creek Valley), Russian River Valley, Sonoma Coast, Sonoma Mountain (a sub-AVA of the Sonoma Valley AVA), and Sonoma Valley.

Sonoma County is roughly twice as large as Napa County and has more acres of vinifera grapes under vine than any other single coastal county in California, about 55,000 acres/22,000 hectares. Sonoma is a bit less showy than Napa, with fewer millionaire industrialists turned wine producers and many more multigenerational farms and farmers. Sonoma wine producers know they have extraordinary vineyard sites, and the best of them make wines with great depth, elegance, and heart.

Sonoma's growers and producers are justifiably proud of their wines, and the truth is that although Sonoma wines are far less hyped in the wine industry and wine media, it would be absurd to rank Napa first and Sonoma second in terms of quality. On balance, Sonoma produces far better Chardonnay, Sauvignon Blanc, Pinot Noir, Zinfandel, and Syrah than the Napa Valley, yielding first place only to Napa Valley Cabernet Sauvignon and perhaps Merlot.

LEFT: *The Sebastiani winery was founded in 1904 by Samuele Sebastiani. Note the family tree on this label. In Sonoma County, the Sebastiani family name is at least as famous as Mondavi is in Napa. In late 2008, Sebastiani was sold to the Foley Wine Group.* RIGHT: *Chateau St. Jean includes all five of the traditional Bordeaux varietals in its Cinq Cépages. Produced since 1990, it has become one of the most sought-after wines from Sonoma County.*

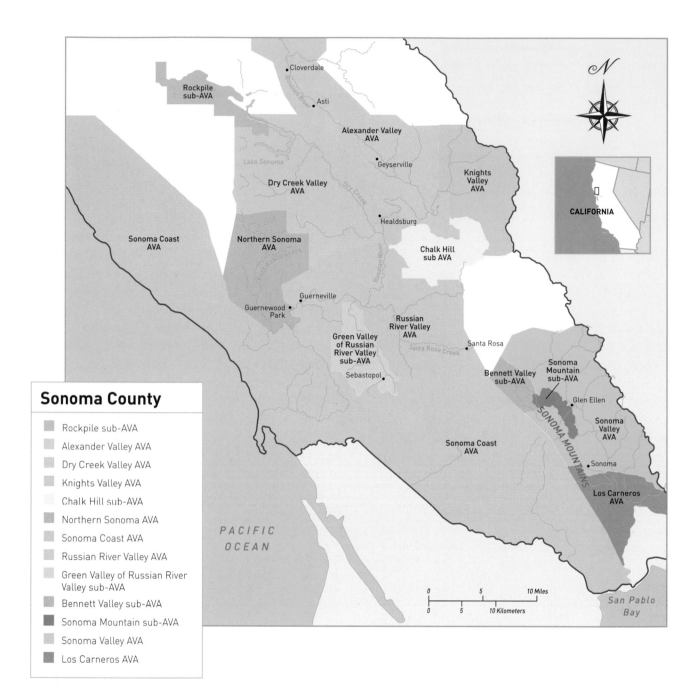

Sonoma County

- Rockpile sub-AVA
- Alexander Valley AVA
- Dry Creek Valley AVA
- Knights Valley AVA
- Chalk Hill sub-AVA
- Northern Sonoma AVA
- Sonoma Coast AVA
- Russian River Valley AVA
- Green Valley of Russian River Valley sub-AVA
- Bennett Valley sub-AVA
- Sonoma Mountain sub-AVA
- Sonoma Valley AVA
- Los Carneros AVA

What is increasingly clear about the best wines made from Sonoma fruit is that the AVA system works better in Sonoma County than in Napa County. The reason is that Sonoma's best-known viticultural areas, such as Russian River Valley, Alexander Valley, Dry Creek Valley, and of course that part of Carneros that is within Sonoma Valley, are increasingly identified with certain grapes, and there is a true attempt to make wines from those signature grapes with a sense of area identity. Russian River Chardonnay and Pinot Noir, Alexander Valley Cabernet Sauvignon

and single-vineyard Chardonnay, and Dry Creek Valley Zinfandel are perfect examples of what makes Sonoma's best wines so exciting and so *terroir*-driven. It really comes as no surprise that while the Alcohol and Tobacco Tax and Trade Bureau (TTB) has been petitioned on numerous occasions to expand the boundaries of certain commercially successful AVAs, the only AVA that has ever petitioned the TTB to reduce its size, in the name of quality and the spirit of *terroir*, is Sonoma's Russian River Valley. The exceptions to this varietal-specific tradition are the two mega-AVAs—Northern Sonoma and Sonoma Coast, which were approved for largely commercial reasons and are largely meaningless.

Because Sonoma County's vineyards are mostly planted in valleys with a much shallower north-to-south slope than Napa's, there are more-dramatic shifts in weather patterns from AVA to AVA. The extreme southwest of Sonoma County, bordered by the Pacific Ocean, though part of the Sonoma Coast AVA is traditionally considered too cold to ripen grapes for wine production. Those vineyards planted within a few miles of the Pacific coast must be planted on south-facing hillsides in order to be protected from the ocean's winds. These sites and the vineyards planted along the Russian River are very cool. As vineyards move inland, a dramatic climatic shift occurs and viticultural districts become quite hot; very little of Sonoma is moderately warm. Soils range from volcanic deposits full of large heat-reflecting rocks to the sandy loams found along the banks of the Russian River.

SONOMA VALLEY

Sonoma Valley, along with the Santa Clara Valley, is where the northern California wine industry originated (see "History," on page 121), and fittingly, it was one of the earliest to gain AVA status, in 1982. Unlike the Napa Valley AVA, which encompasses almost all of Napa County, the Sonoma Valley AVA, although quite large at 161 square miles/258 square kilometers, runs only from the San Pablo Bay in the south to the Santa Rosa city limits in the north, and from the Sonoma Mountains in the west to the Napa County line/Mayacamas Mountains in the east. About half of Sonoma County's 28,000 acres/11,200 hectares of vineyard are actually planted in the Sonoma Valley AVA (16,000 acres/6,000 hectares).

In contrast to the situation in Sonoma County's smaller viticultural areas, such as Alexander Valley and the Russian River Valley, there is no one varietal that dominates in Sonoma Valley. However, there are stellar examples of wines made from the major varietals throughout the "Valley of the Moon," produced with as many topographical and climatic exceptions as there are rules. In very general terms, Chardonnay and Pinot Noir seem to do best at the extreme south end of the valley, where it encompasses Carneros. Cabernet Sauvignon prospers in the eastern hills closest to Napa, and Zinfandel grows beautifully in the western hills. Everywhere, exceptions abound, such as Kistler's extraordinary Chardonnay grown in the eastern hills. The Rhinefarm Vineyard, owned by Gundlach-Bundschu and harvested every year without exception since 1858, is located at the extreme southeast of Sonoma Valley and grows just about every varietal that makes premium wine in California.

LEFT: *Located in the Sonoma Valley AVA, Monte Rosso, with its copper-red volcanic soils, is one of the most beautiful mountain vineyard sites in the world. Purchased by the Louis M. Martini Winery in 1936, Monte Rosso produces extraordinary Cabernet Sauvignon and Zinfandel from its old, "gnarly" vines.* MIDDLE: *Winemaker Michael Martini measuring sugar levels in the Cabernet Sauvignon grape must at Monte Rosso. Michael is a third-generation Martini family winemaker, succeeding his father and grandfather.* RIGHT: *In 1952, James Zellerbach planted Chardonnay and Pinot Noir in his Hanzell vineyards. Hanzell introduced several innovations to the California wine industry: temperature-controlled stainless steel fermentation tanks, the use of French oak for aging wine, and scientifically controlled malolactic fermentation. The wines can be superb.*

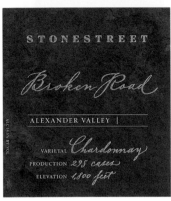

The two star grapes that define the fine wines produced in the Alexander Valley are Cabernet Sauvignon and Chardonnay, with increasingly significant pockets of high-quality Merlot, Zinfandel, and Sauvignon Blanc playing supporting roles. Total vineyard land is 15,000 acres/6,000 hectares. Alexander Valley Cabernet Sauvignon features aromas of herbs and bell peppers, revealing the cool nights and mornings in the valley. These "green" characteristics are most often balanced by grace notes of cherry, plum, and black currant. Normally less tannic and a bit less structured than Cab from the Napa Valley, the Alexander Valley wines are supple, with true depth and concentration of fruit, which is what most lovers of California Cabernet Sauvignon seek. Its AVA status was granted in 1984.

Chardonnay from Alexander Valley is typically very ripe and juicy, with tropical fruit and pear flavors, but some winemakers opt for a leaner, more classic style of Chardonnay. Alexander Valley Chardonnay ripens easily because of the relatively warm climate and nutrient-dense soils. Chardonnay vines here are vigorous, but in a way that yields a lot more high-quality fruit than energy-sapping vegetation. That is why some of the most esteemed single vineyards, such as the Robert Young and Belle Terre estates (both of which find their way into separate bottlings of vineyard-designated Chateau St. Jean Chardonnay), can yield between 5 and 6 tons per acre/11,500 and 12,750 kilograms per hectare without diminishing quality.

The Merlot grape produces a fine varietal wine at Alexander Valley Vineyards and the former Chateau Souverain (the estate—but not the brand name) is now owned by Francis Ford Coppola and is utilized well in Clos du Bois Marlstone, a Bordeaux blend. The best-known Zinfandel estate in Alexander Valley is Ridge Geyserville.

For three generations, the Wetzel family has produced excellent estate-bottled wines from their Alexander Valley Vineyards property in Healdsburg. The property was purchased in 1963 and the winery began in 1975. Now producing 100,000 cases of wine annually, the Wetzels are best known for their Cabernet Sauvignon, Merlot, Chardonnay, Syrah, and Zinfandel (especially their Sin Zin). Most of the Wetzel's wines retail for about $20 to $25; they are undoubtedly among the best bargains in the Alexander Valley AVA. The quality of the wine is superb.

In 2007, Jess Jackson, owner of the ubiquitous Kendall-Jackson brand of wines, as well as Vérité and Stonestreet wineries in the Alexander Valley, petitioned for a separate Alexander Mountain AVA. Jackson owns 900 acres of high-elevation vineyards on Alexander Mountain, and the wineries are situated at the base of the mountain.

The following are some of the best-known wineries, vineyards, and producers in the Alexander Valley AVA:

Alexander Valley Vineyards, Angeline, Archipel, Atelier, Bandiera, Bella, Canyon Road, Chameleon, Chauffe-Eau, Clos du Bois, deLorimier, Diamond Oaks, Dutcher Crossing, Elaine Maria, Eric Guerra, Field, Field Stone, Francis Ford Coppola Presents Rosso & Bianco, Frei Brothers, Geyser Peak, Icaria, Jordan, Kendall-Jackson, Laurier, Ledson, Legacy, Marietta, Murphy-Goode, Pedroncelli, Pellegrini, Rodney Strong, Rusina, Sausal, Silver Oak, Simi, Sommer, Souverain, Stonestreet, Stryker, Stuhlmuller, Terisa, Trentadue, Vérité, and Windsor.

RUSSIAN RIVER VALLEY

The Russian River Valley is quite large—just about 150 square miles/240 square kilometers—and includes two notable sub-AVAs, Green Valley (official AVA name: Green Valley of Russian River Valley) and Chalk Hill. Set in central Sonoma County, all three AVAs—Russian River Valley and its two sub-AVAs—were recognized the same year, in 1983. The Russian River Valley AVA, with 10,000 acres/4,000 hectares planted, starts at Sebastopol in the southwest and extends to Healdsburg at the extreme northeast. The southern sections of the AVA, especially those close to the banks of the Russian River, which runs through the center of the viticultural district, and the Pacific Ocean, which lies to the west, maintain a cool and damp climate, extending a beneficial cooling fog to the vineyards north and east. Prior to the late 1970s and early 1980s, before the premium varietal market began to have a huge influence on the vineyards of California in general and Sonoma County in particular, the cooler areas of the district were considered too cool to grow most of the varieties used in popularly priced blended jug wines.

When Chardonnay took hold of the northern California white wine industry, clearly the cool, damp climate of the southwestern Russian River Valley was one of the places to grow the varietal. As it became clear that there was going to be a market for the most finicky red varietal, Pinot Noir, again the Russian River Valley seemed to be the ideal place to plant vines. Today, many wine professionals and connoisseurs believe that this viticultural area produces the finest and most *terroir*-driven Pinot Noir wines in all of California, and perhaps the entire country. Carneros and Anderson Valley are its only intrastate competitors for such accolades, and Oregon's Willamette Valley is its only American competitor outside of California.

Wines made from Russian River Pinot Noir are truly distinctive. Nowhere else in California does Pinot Noir achieve such depth of concentration, intensity, and richness while maintaining a certain delicacy and brightness that does not fatigue the palate. Chardonnay from this AVA is reliably good to excellent, but in the glass it does not differ much from the best wines of Sonoma Valley or Alexander Valley.

Some of the most renowned producers of Chardonnay and Pinot Noir are situated in the Russian River Valley, and several of them are multigeneration family grape growers, such as Rochioli, Martini & Prati, and Martinelli, who produce their own wines, mostly with superior results. An almost well-kept secret is the great Zinfandel, Gewürztraminer, and Sauvignon Blanc being made in the warmer areas of this AVA. Foppiano and Hop Kiln, among other producers, produce exciting Petite Sirah here from a varietal that has rarely been given the respect it deserves when made in this restrained style.

The following are some of the best-known wineries, vineyards, and producers in the Russian River Valley AVA:

Acorn, Albini Family, Amicitia, Angeline, Arista, Arrowood, Balletto, Bannister, Bearboat, Benovia, Bogle, Branham, Brogan, Carol Shelton, Castalia, Castle, Chasseur, Christie Estate, Christopher Creek, Clos du Bois, Crane Canyon, Crinella, D'Argenzio, Davis Bynum, Davis Family, De Loach, DeBurca, Dehlinger, DeNatale, Derbes, Destino, Domaine St. George, DuMOL, DuNah, Dutch Bill Creek, Elaine Maria, Emeritus, Eric Guerra, Fanucchi, Foppiano, Freeman, Frei Brothers, Gamba, Gary Farrell, George, Geyser Peak, Goldschmidt, Hanna, Hartman

Lane, Harvest Moon, Hayman & Hill, Holdredge, Hook & Ladder, Hop Kiln, Inman Family, Inspiration, Iridesse, J, J. Keverson, J Lynne, John Tyler/Bacigalupi, Joseph Swan, Keegan, Kistler, Kitchak, Korbel, Kosta Browne, La Crema, Lauterbach, Limerick Lane, Littorai, Longboard, Lynmar, Macrae Family, Magito, Malm, Mantra, Mark West, Martin Ray, Martinelli, McIlroy, Merriam, Merry Edwards, Mietz, Moshin, Mossback, Mueller, Old World, Oriel, Ottimino, Papapietro Perry, Paradise Ridge, Paul Hobbs, Pax, Pedroncelli, Pellegrini, Philip Staley, Portalupi, Porter Creek, Porter-Bass, Rabbit Ridge, Radio-Coteau, River Ridge, Robert Rue, Rochioli, Rodney Strong, Roshambo, Russian Hill, Russian River Vineyards, Rutz, Sapphire Hill, Sauvignon Republic, Selby, Sellards, Sheldon, Shibumi Knoll, Siduri, Sonoma-Cutrer, Stephen & Walker Trust, St. Rose, Suncé, Taft Street, Tara Bella, Teira, Three Alarm, Thumbprint, Toad Hollow, Trecini, TR Elliott, Valdez, Villa Pompei, Vision, Walker Station, Walter Hansel, WesMar, Westover, Williams Selyem, Willowbrook, Windsor, Woodenhead, and ZMOR.

GREEN VALLEY OF RUSSIAN RIVER VALLEY

Originally named Sonoma County Green Valley, this is one of two subappellations of the Russian River Valley AVA. This very cool and very foggy AVA located in the western part of the Russian River Valley is best known for excellent Chardonnay and Pinot Noir vineyard sites, due in part to its soil, "Goldridge," which drains well and is mineral rich. Green Valley is located only thirteen miles from the Pacific Ocean, and that accounts for the climate and fog that nurtures the 3,750 acres/1,500 hectares of vines.

In 1976, Barry Sterling, who worked in international corporate law in San Francisco, and his wife, Audrey, bought Iron Horse Ranch and Vineyards. The estate, house, and vineyards were in desperate need of renovation, and the Sterlings eagerly took on the project, working with founding winemaker Forrest Tancer. Today, the Sterlings' daughter, Joy, and Joy's brother, Laurence, are in charge of the winery. Dave Munksgard is the winemaker. Iron Horse Vineyards produces elegant estate-bottled wines from their Green Valley vineyards: Chardonnay—including an "unoaked" version—Pinot Noir, and Pinot Noir Rosé. Iron Horse is best known for its line of seven different estate-bottled vintage-dated sparkling wines and custom cuvées produced by the *méthode champenoise*.

The Sterling family petitioned for the Green Valley AVA even before the Russian River Valley AVA was granted. Not long after the establishment of Iron Horse, Marimar Torres, of the famous Spanish wine family (see page 433), planted vineyards and built a winery in Green Valley, Marimar Estate, which produces Pinot Noir and Chardonnay. Dutton Ranch, the source of several fine Chardonnay and Pinot Noir wines, including the famous and expensive wines produced by Steve Kistler, is located here.

The following are some of the best-known wineries, vineyards, and producers in the Green Valley of Russian River Valley AVA, best known for, but not limited to, Chardonnay and Pinot Noir:

Atascadero Creek, August West, Battaglini Estate, Dutton Estate and Sebastopol Vineyards, Dutton-Goldfield, Eric Ross, Graton Ridge, Hartford Family, Iron Horse, Landmark, Marimar Estate, Occidental Road, Orogeny, Peters Family, Salinia, Scherrer, Taft Street, Tandem, and Topolos.

CHALK HILL

Chalk Hill is the other subappellation of the Russian River Valley, located in the eastern quadrant of the parent AVA. It has 1,000 acres/400 hectares planted. Home to Chalk Hill Estate Winery and its 300-acre/120-hectare estate, this district is known for fine Chardonnay, although we have tasted increasingly fine Sauvignon Blanc, Cabernet Sauvignon, and Merlot from Chalk Hill. Rodney Strong's Chalk Hill Chardonnay is a fine example of how the chalk soil of this district can be expressed in a fine wine.

The following are some of the best-known wineries, vineyards, and producers in the Chalk Hill AVA:

Albini Family, Balverne, Chalk Hill Estate, Chateau Felice, Diamond Oaks, Guerrero Fernandez, J Vineyards, Mossback, Rodney Strong, and Terremoto.

DRY CREEK VALLEY

With the exception of Gallo's huge Frei Ranch, Dry Creek Valley is dominated by dozens of small producers and grape growers. Adjacent to the town of Healdsburg, Dry Creek Valley is Zinfandel country and has been since Italian immigrants who settled this narrow valley began to grow Zinfandel in 1870. The climate in Dry Creek Valley seems ideally suited to this varietal, which needs cool mornings and intensely warm afternoons to develop the desired raspberry, black cherry, and spicy flavor profile in the best Zin. Zinfandel is as important a signature grape in the Dry Creek Valley as Cabernet Sauvignon is in the Napa Valley. Its AVA status was secured in 1983 and total vineyard acreage is 10,000 acres/4,000 hectares.

Sauvignon Blanc also does well here, especially on the irrigated valley floor; the wines are clean, crisp, and typically herbal and grassy, a style that many identify as classic. Producers have also had generally good luck with Cabernet Sauvignon, Syrah, Sangiovese, Petite Sirah, and other warm-weather red varietals. Here and there, some fine Chardonnay emerges from cooler vineyard parcels, too.

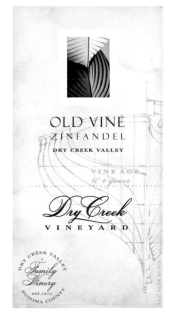

ROCKPILE

Rockpile is a high-elevation AVA (and a sub-AVA of Dry Creek Valley that gained its separate recognition in 2002). The entire growing region is at least 800 feet/244 meters above sea level, and climbs as high as 1,900 feet/581 meters. With over 15,000 acres in the AVA, only about 10 percent (160 acres/60 hectares) are planted with vineyards mostly focused on Zinfandel, as well as Cabernet Sauvignon, Syrah, and Petite Sirah. The terrain of Rockpile, as its AVA name indicates, is rocky and rugged, and there are no resident wineries here. This has not stopped wine producers from securing grapes from Rockpile and making terrific wines, such as Rosenblum Rockpile Road Vineyard Zinfandel and Martin Family Rockpile Cabernet Sauvignon.

The following are some of the best-known wineries, vineyards, and producers in the Dry Creek Valley AVA and its sub-AVA, Rockpile, best known for, but not limited to, Zinfandel and Sauvignon Blanc:

Alderbrook, Amphora, A. Rafanelli Armida, Banyan, Bella, Brogan, C 5, Carol Shelton, Collier Falls, David Coffaro, Deux Amis, Dogwood, Dry Creek Vineyard, Dutcher Crossing, Duxoup, Everett Ridge, Ferrari-Carano, Forchini, Forth, Frei Brothers, Frick, Fritz, Gallo, Handley, Lake Sonoma, Lambert Ridge, MacPhail Family, Manzanita Creek, Martin Family, Mazzocco, McCray Ridge, Michel Schlumberger, Mill Creek, Muscardini, Mutt Lynch, Nalle, Optima, Owl Ridge, Pedroncelli, Peterson, Pezzi-King, Preston, Puccioni, Quivira, Rancho Zabaco, Raymond Burr, Ridge Lytton Springs, Rosenblum, Rusina, Seghesio, Stephen & Walker Trust, Teldeschi, Travieso, William Wheeler, and Windsor.

KNIGHTS VALLEY

Knights Valley is the warmest AVA in Sonoma County, teetering on a perch that separates Sonoma County from Napa Valley. The hills of Knights Valley lie beyond the cooling, foggy influence of the Pacific Ocean. This AVA's volcanic soils coupled

with its warm weather make an ideal home for Cabernet Sauvignon. About 2,000 acres/800 hectares are under vine, and its status was granted in 1983.

The most famous winery in Knights Valley is owned by Peter Michael, who makes the wonderfully rich Cabernet

---

LEFT: *Frick Winery in Dry Creek Valley was founded in 1976 with the proceeds from the sale of Bill Frick and Judith Gannon's 1957 Chevrolet. Here is the two-acre Owl Hill Vineyard, from which Bill Frick produces Syrah.* MIDDLE: *Dry Creek Vineyard produces several different Zinfandel wines, including single-vineyard bottlings. One of their best wines is their Old Vine Zinfandel. Note that the vines are at least eighty years old.* RIGHT: *Rosenblum produces several vineyard-designated Zinfandels, including the Rockpile Road Vineyard bottling.*

SONOMA COAST

Much like the Northern Sonoma AVA, which was approved to accommodate Gallo's vineyard holdings, the excessively large Sonoma Coast AVA—750 square miles/1,200 square kilometers—was originally created in 1987 to encompass the three "estate" properties of Sonoma-Cutrer: the Les Pierres, Russian River Ranches, and Cutrer vineyards.

The Sonoma Coast AVA, the county's largest viticultural area with 7,000 acres/2,800 hectares of vines, which begins just north of the Sonoma County Green Valley AVA and extends south to the Carneros border, is focused on cool-climate vineyards. It really is an outrageous interpretation of what an appellation should be. Perhaps the definition of "estate-bottled" needs to be changed, so that any properties owned by the producer can be included as part of the "estate." This seems a better alternative than creating appellations out of whole cloth to meet the marketing needs of powerful producers.

Of course, within such a large growing area, there are bound to be quality producers, and some of California's finest Chardonnay and Pinot Noir is produced within the confines of Sonoma Coast. Alesia, Aston, Belle Glos, Clos du Bois, David Bruce, De Loach, Failla, Flowers, Francis Coppola, Freestone, Gazzi, Hartford Family, Joseph Phelps,

Sauvignon–based Meritage-style wine Les Pavots. Knights Valley is known best, however, for three wines produced by Beringer Vineyards. The wines, all exceptional, are Cabernet Sauvignon Knights Valley, Alluvium (a red Meritage), and Alluvium Blanc (a white Meritage). Beringer owns about 540 acres/220 hectares in Knights Valley, the source for all three wines. Other wineries and producers in the AVA include Adobe Road, Anakota, Ehret Family, Hans Fahden, Pelton House, Pride Mountain, and Zacherle.

Anakota's Helena Montana vineyard in the Knights Valley AVA

THE RHONE RANGERS

••

Randall Grahm of Bonny Doon Vineyard was the first "Rhone Ranger," producing single-varietal and blended wines from grapes native to the Rhône Valley, starting in the mid-1980s. Since that time, more than 250 California wine producers have tried their hand at making Rhône-style varietals, some with great success. There is no doubt that since the early 1990s Rhône-style wines have become an increasingly important part of California's wine industry.

In the mid-1990s, the Rhone Rangers incorporated as a nonprofit educational organization to spread the word about American-grown Rhône varietals and the wines that are produced from those grapes. For a winery to be a member of the Rhone Rangers, its Rhône-style wine must be made from at least 75 percent traditional Rhône grapes. The Rhone Rangers now have about two hundred California winemakers as members.

The Rhone Rangers recognize twenty-two varieties as being true to their heritage. The red grapes are Carignan, Cinsaut, Counoise, Grenache, Mourvèdre, Muscardin, Petite Sirah (known as Durif in the Rhône Valley), Picpoul Noir, Syrah, Terret Noir, and Vaccarèse. Of these, the most important in California is Syrah (about 19,000 acres/7,600 hectares planted), followed by Grenache (about 7,600 acres/3,040 hectares planted), and Petite Sirah (about 6,000 acres/2,400 hectares planted).

The white grapes are Bourbolenc, Clairette Blanc, Grenache Blanc, Marsanne, Muscat Blanc à Petits Grains, Picardin, Picpoul, Roussanne, Ugni Blanc, and Viognier. Of these, the most important in California is Viognier (about 2,300 acres/920 hectares planted), followed by Roussanne (about 200 acres/80 hectares planted).

California's Rhône-style wines are produced as both single-varietal wines and as blends. Syrah is the current star as a red varietal wine, but there are quite a few Syrah-Grenache-Mourvèdre blends produced too. Petite Sirah is its own varietal, but just as often, it finds its way into blends with both Rhône varietals and non-Rhône varietals, especially Zinfandel. For whites, Viognier has long been the star, mostly as a single varietal.

For more information on the Rhone Rangers of California, go to www.rhonerangers.org.

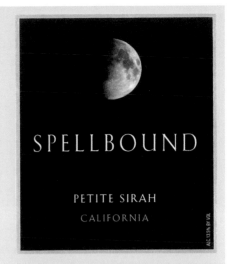

Bonny Doon's Le Cigare Volant is a full-bodied blend of red Rhone Ranger grapes: Grenache, Syrah, and Mourvèdre. Syrah is the most popular of all of the single-varietal Rhone Ranger wines. Winemakers in the Paso Robles AVA in San Luis Obispo County, such as Vina Robles, produce very fine Syrah wines. Viognier is the premier white varietal among the Rhone Ranger grapes. Toasted Head Viognier, sourced in the Dunnigan Hills AVA in California's Yolo County, is a good value.

THE CAL-ITALIANS: SO FAR, A MIXED BAG

Sangiovese was one of the vines brought to California by Agoston Haraszthy in 1862, and it became the base for the jug wines of the Italian Swiss Colony, especially its Tipo Chianti. Starting after Prohibition, Italian Swiss Colony, wanting to take advantage of higher-yielding varietals such as Zinfandel and Carignan, destroyed or grafted its Sangiovese vines to these more popular grape types. By 1980 there was literally no Sangiovese planted in California, and prior to 1989, when growers on the North Coast of California started to pay attention to phylloxera and vineyards began to be replanted, there was a total of 59 acres/30 hectares. By the year 2000, there were 2,500 acres/1,000 hectares of Sangiovese vines, with about half of those planted in Napa, Sonoma, and Mendocino counties.

Today, there are dozens of California producers making wines with Sangiovese. The early proponents were Seghesio, making Chianti Station red from vines planted in 1910 at Italian Swiss Colony in Geyserville; Robert Pepi, who made Colline di Sassi; and Ferrari-Carano, making a Sangiovese-Cabernet-Merlot blend, Siena, which is in very high demand. Until 2002, Shafer produced an outstanding Sangiovese-based wine, Firebreak.

Many producers believed that Sangiovese and other Italian varietals would form the basis for a high level of consumer interest in "Cal-Italian" wines. That has not happened, and several producers, including Shafer and Atlas Peak, owned by Tuscan wine legend Piero Antinori, have abandoned their Sangiovese projects, replanting the vines to more popular or soil-and-climate-appropriate varietals, especially Cabernet Sauvignon.

BARBERA
Amador County

Barbera, native to Italy's Piedmont region, is a Cal-Italian grape that makes a light-to medium-bodied wine in California and is extremely food-friendly and budget-friendly. The most commercially promising white grape is Pinot Grigio, native to Italy's northeast regions, which makes light to medium-bodied, refreshing, dry wines in California. Moscato (also Piemontese) is usually made in a low-alcohol, sweet version.

Montevina in Amador County, owned by the Trinchero family, is a leading producer of Cal-Italian varietal wines.

Keller Estate, Kistler, MacRostie, Marcassin, Marimar, Oriel, Patz & Hall, Peters Family, Radio-Coteau, Ramey, Schug, Williams-Selyem and several other producers make very fine vineyard-designated wines bearing the Sonoma Coast AVA.

MENDOCINO COUNTY

The thirteen AVAs of Mendocino County (including two pending approval) are Anderson Valley, Cole Ranch, Covelo, Dos Rios, McDowell Valley, Mendocino (a blanket AVA that covers almost all of Mendocino County's vineyards), Mendocino Ridge, North Coast (Mendocino is a constituent county of this multicounty AVA), Potter Valley, Redwood Valley, Sanel Valley (AVA status pending), Ukiah Valley (AVA status pending), and Yorkville Highlands.

Some of California's best table wines and sparkling wines are made in Mendocino County, but many of these are still well-kept secrets. Aside from one very well-known and very large producer, Fetzer (with more than 3.5 million cases of wine produced every year), many wine-savvy folks are still completely inexperienced in the pleasures of Mendocino wines. The great majority of Mendocino's wine producers are proud local farmers who go to great lengths to display the name Mendocino County or the name of one of Mendocino's AVAs prominently on their labels—just what one would expect from a unique area that, after the Civil War, developed its own language, Boontling, named after Mendocino's commercial center, Boonville. Boontling is studied by scholars to this day.

Most of Mendocino County's major vineyards are sited along the Russian River, with the exception of most Anderson Valley vineyards, planted on shallow terraces, or benches, created by the Navarro River. The northern half of Mendocino is not considered to be very good

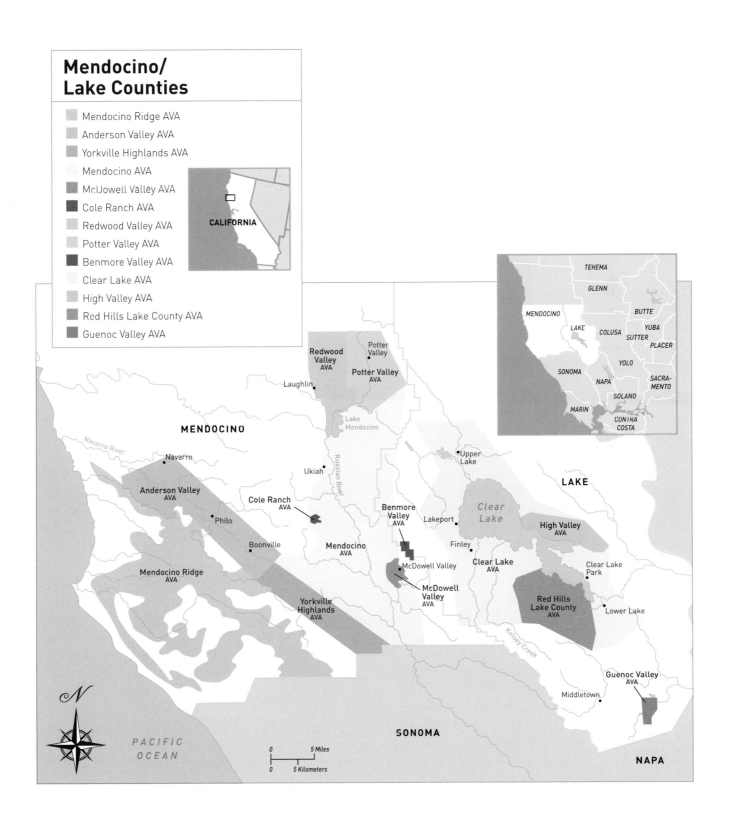

Mendocino/ Lake Counties

- Mendocino Ridge AVA
- Anderson Valley AVA
- Yorkville Highlands AVA
- Mendocino AVA
- McDowell Valley AVA
- Cole Ranch AVA
- Redwood Valley AVA
- Potter Valley AVA
- Benmore Valley AVA
- Clear Lake AVA
- High Valley AVA
- Red Hills Lake County AVA
- Guenoc Valley AVA

CALIFORNIA

TEHEMA

GLENN

MENDOCINO

BUTTE

LAKE

COLUSA

SUTTER

YUBA

PLACER

YOLO

SONOMA

NAPA

SACRA-MENTO

SOLANO

MARIN

CONTRA COSTA

MENDOCINO

Navarro River

Navarro

Anderson Valley AVA

Philo

Boonville

Mendocino Ridge AVA

Yorkville Highlands AVA

PACIFIC OCEAN

Redwood Valley AVA

Potter Valley

Potter Valley AVA

Laughlin

Lake Mendocino

Ukiah

Cole Ranch AVA

Russian River

Mendocino AVA

Benmore Valley AVA

Lakeport

McDowell Valley

McDowell Valley AVA

Upper Lake

Clear Lake

Finley

Clear Lake AVA

LAKE

High Valley AVA

Clear Lake Park

Red Hills Lake County AVA

Lower Lake

Kelsey Creek

Guenoc Valley AVA

Middletown

SONOMA

NAPA

N

0   5 Miles

0   5 Kilometers

vineyard land, and is already planted with the county's official number one cash crop: marijuana (wine grapes are Mendocino's number two cash crop). However, the two newest (and tiniest) AVAs in Mendocino County are located in northern Mendocino—Dos Rios (AVA approved in 2005) and Covelo (2006). Dos Rios has one winery,

Vin de Tevis, with six acres of vineyards. Covelo has no winery and a total of two acres under vine. Both AVAs were granted because of their unique, cool-breeze-in-the-hot-sun microclimates. Time will tell if these AVAs have much impact.

Starting in 2001, some of Mendocino County's forward-looking and well-known producers came together to make a "signature" wine, "Coro Mendocino." The idea of the program is that any winery in Mendocino County can make Coro but must first adhere to the rules. Coro Mendocino must be made exclusively from Mendocino fruit and must contain at least 40 percent Zinfandel; no other grape may dominate the blend. Other approved Mendocino "heritage" grapes, such as Syrah, Petite Sirah, Sangiovese, Charbono, Grenache, and Carignan must be included. Each winemaker is given 10 percent of the blend to play with, and may include any other grapes he or she chooses. All Coro Mendocino wines have the same label, the only difference being the name of the producer and a signed statement about the wine

from the winemaker. All Coro Mendocino wines sell for $35.

Coro Mendocino is the only regional-identity wine program of its kind in the United States, and mirrors the approach of many famous European appellations. Producers of Coro Mendocino include Brutocao, Dunnewood, Eaglepoint Ranch, Fetzer, Golden, Graziano, McDowell

---

TOP: *Coro Mendocino is the only regional-identity wine program in the United States. Coro is made by several different Mendocino producers, including Parducci, but all the wines have the same Coro label, and all must include Mendocino "heritage" grapes. Coro means "chorus" in both Italian and Spanish.*

Valley Vineyards, McFadden, McNab Ridge, Pacific Star, and Parducci.

Mendocino is an official AVA and is currently the single-county appellation of choice for many of the wines produced from the 15,500 acres/6,200 hectares of vineyards and more than seventy wineries situated in the southern half of the county. The vineyards and wineries of Mendocino make a satellite pattern around the town of Hopland to the south and Redwood Valley to the north, with most of the vineyards planted to the east and west of the borders, and only a few north of Redwood Valley and even fewer south of Hopland. Lake County lies to the east of Ukiah.

The Mendocino AVA encompasses several smaller AVAs of Mendocino County: Anderson Valley, Cole Ranch, Dos Rios, McDowell Valley, Potter Valley, Redwood Valley, and Yorkville Highlands. Applications for the Sanel Valley AVA and Ukiah Valley AVA are pending, and these two new AVAs would be found within the much larger blanket Mendocino AVA.

ANDERSON VALLEY

The Anderson Valley AVA begins west of Ukiah and stretches for about 30 miles/48 kilometers to the Pacific Ocean. The area closest to the sea (about 10 miles/16 kilometers away) forms the coolest part of Mendocino, a quintessential Region 1 (see "Heat Summation," on page 118). As the valley moves inland, it creates a cool Region 2 vine-growing environment. Because of the climate in the Anderson Valley AVA—the temperature can vary as much as 50°F/10°C in one day—the coastal sites are perfect for growing high-acid Chardonnay and Pinot Noir for sparkling wines, and the inland sites commend themselves to the same grapes, but for table wines. In addition, Gewürztraminer and Riesling wines from Anderson Valley are quite tasty, with unique *terroir*-driven character. Zinfandel does extremely well here when grown on highly specific sites facing away from strong wind currents. The Anderson Valley has 1,400 acres/560 hectares planted, and its AVA status was granted in 1983.

Roederer Estate is a prestigious sparkling-wine producer in Mendocino's Anderson Valley. The winery and its vineyards are wholly owned by the French holding company of Champagne Louis Roederer. Roederer Estate produces more than 70,000 cases of estate-bottled *méthode champenoise* wine. All the grapes are sourced from Roederer's 324 acres/130 hectares of Anderson Valley Chardonnay and Pinot Noir, and the wine is produced at Roederer's state-of-the-art winery. The quality of Roederer Estate Brut, Rosé, and vintage-dated L'Ermitage is extraordinary.

Scharffenberger, also owned by Champagne Louis Roederer, makes fine sparklers from its 100 acres/40 hectares of Anderson Valley Pinot Noir and Chardonnay vineyards and other sources.

At Navarro Vineyards, the Bennett-Cahn family has been making wines in the Anderson Valley since 1974. Known for the quality of their dry Gewürztraminer—one of the best produced in California—Navarro also produces very good Riesling, Chardonnay, and Pinot Noir.

Milla Handley is one of California's best unhyped winemakers. She produces very fine Anderson Valley Brut and Rosé sparkling wines, Both sparklers are vintage-dated, complex, delicious, and refreshing. She also makes Chardonnay, Gewürztraminer, Riesling, Sauvignon Blanc, Pinot Gris, Pinot Blanc, Pinot Noir, Syrah, Viognier, and Zinfandel. Most of the wines are produced from her own certified organic vineyards in Mendocino and in Dry Creek Valley (Sonoma); Handley's total production is about 15,000 cases.

The following are some of the best-known wineries, vineyards, and producers in the Anderson Valley AVA:

Baxter, Black Kite, Breggo, Brutocao, Cakebread, Christine Woods, Claudia Springs, Demuth, Drew, Edmeades, Elke, Esterlina, Goldeneye, Greenwood Ridge, Handley, Harmonique, Jim Ball, La Crema, Lazy Creek, Londer, Maple Creek, Mariah, Mark Moretti, Navarro, Oak Arbor, Philo Ridge, Roederer Estate, Sayler-Tait, Scharffenberger, Standish, and Toulouse.

MCDOWELL VALLEY

This is a single-winery AVA, which was granted in 1983. In 1979, the Keehn family, Mendocino grape farmers, decided to make wine from the 370 acres/148 hectares of vineyard they had owned since 1970. The Keehn ranch was located just due east of Hopland, and the owners built their McDowell Valley winery to make wine from the seventeen different varietals planted on their estate. McDowell became known for its Rhône-style wines made

from old vines, Les Vieux Cépages. The current plantings have grown to 700 acres/280 hectares. By 1993, production had reached 50,000 cases at McDowell, but the winemaking was problematic; too many varieties, too many wines. Some of the wines were quite good, others not very good at all. In 1993, the Keehns sold their winery to a family member who had worked in the vineyards since he was twelve years old—William Crawford. Today, Crawford and McDowell Valley Vineyards continue to focus on the Rhône Valley as a model for McDowell Valley.

COLE RANCH

Cole Ranch is a tiny single-vineyard AVA of 62 acres/25 hectares. There is no winery in the AVA, though the region has been recognized since 1983. In 1973, the Cole family planted their vineyards, situated at the base of the Anderson Valley, just east of Boonville and south of Ukiah. Cole Ranch, now owned by Esterlina Winery in nearby Anderson Valley, plants Cabernet Sauvignon, Merlot, and Riesling at about 1,500 feet/457 meters.

POTTER VALLEY

The Potter Valley AVA is located in the northeastern sector of Mendocino, bordering Lake County, making it and the Redwood Valley AVA, its western neighbor, the most northerly major AVAs within the broader North Coast viticultural area. Because of the relatively cool climate, Merlot and Sauvignon Blanc do well in Potter Valley's 1,000 acres/400 hectares of vineyards, and so do Chardonnay and Riesling. Some sparkling winemakers utilize Potter Valley Chardonnay and Pinot Noir because of the high acid levels the grapes can reach and retain here, when the overnight temperatures drop dramatically. Potter Valley vines grow on the valley floor, protected by the hills that encompass the area. It has been recognized as an AVA since 1983.

The esteemed Napa Valley producer Chateau Montelena produces a Potter Valley Riesling (available only in their tasting room). There are two wineries here—McFadden and Naughty Boy—but custom-crush wineries are easily found in the adjoining Redwood Valley AVA.

REDWOOD VALLEY

Home to the original 250 acres of Fetzer Vineyards, which began in 1968, the Redwood Valley AVA features quality-driven vineyards and wineries, including Lolonis, Fife, and Frey. Since Redwood Valley, which became an AVA in 1996, is cooler than Ukiah to its south, its grapes mature somewhat later and achieve an excellent balance of color, tannin, and acid. Fetzer, Lolonis, and Frey pride themselves on organic practices in the vineyards, and total plantings in the AVA cover 2,500 acres/1,000 hectares. Lolonis was the first certified organic vineyard in California.

The Lolonis family began growing grapes in 1920 in Redwood Valley. Today, they have about 400 certified organic acres under vine and produce 35,000 cases of wine, including Zinfandel, Fumé Blanc, Chardonnay, Cabernet Sauvignon, and Orpheus, a deep, dark, rich Petite Sirah. Special bottlings are named for Lolonis family members: Petros (Merlot), Tryfon (Zinfandel), and two late-harvest whites, Eugenia (Sauvignon Blanc) and Antigone (Chardonnay). Lolonis also produces the very popular, very affordable, and very drinkable Ladybug Red and Ladybug White wines. The ladybug is the Lolonis symbol, as they use ladybugs to diminish the population of unwanted pests in their Redwood Valley vineyards, not chemicals. Lolonis continues to sell fruit to the best producers in Mendocino, including Fetzer, Parducci, and Jed Steele.

The following are some of the best-known wineries and producers in the Redwood Valley AVA:

Anderson/Molloy, Barra, Claudia Springs, Cole Bailey, Domaine Saint Gregory, Elizabeth, Fife, Frey, Gabrielli, Girasole, Giuseppe, Graziano, Handley, Lolonis/Ladybug, Mid Mountain, and Silversmith.

MENDOCINO RIDGE

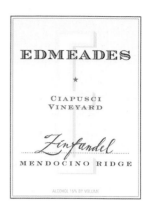

This is the quintessential Mendocino AVA, perfectly reflecting the spirit of many of the county's growers and producers. Unique among AVAs, the Mendocino Ridge AVA (granted in 1998) is based not on a contiguous growing district, soil type, fog pattern, microclimate, or history, but strictly on elevation. Thus, inclusion in this AVA has but one criterion: vineyards must be planted at least 1,200 feet/365 meters above sea level, or as the locals call them, "Islands in the Sky." As drawn, the AVA is huge, about 400 square miles/640 square kilometers and at least 250,000 acres/100,000 hectares. Currently, however, only seven outstanding but noncontiguous vineyards making up a total of about 75 acres/30 hectares pass the test for inclusion in Mendocino Ridge: the Greenwood Ridge estate, which is best known for mountain-grown Cabernet Sauvignon, and the DuPratt, Zeni, Ciapusci, Perli, Alden, and Mariah vineyards, all of which are famous for Zinfandel. Edmeades, the elite Zinfandel-only shop of Kendall-Jackson, sources much of its fruit from these estates, and its winery is located here, along with Drew, Greenwood Ridge, and Mariah wineries.

YORKVILLE HIGHLANDS

In 1995 a petition was submitted to establish the Yorkville Highlands AVA, and it was granted five years later, in 2000. This is a large AVA but only has 400 acres/160 hectares planted. The delimited area begins at Cloverdale, on the Sonoma/Mendocino border, and extends northwest

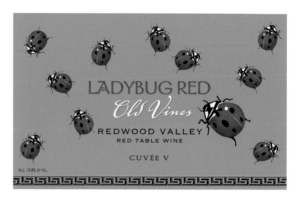

The ladybug is the symbol of the family-owned Lolonis winery in Redwood Valley. Lolonis farms about four hundred certified organic vineyards, and tens of thousands of ladybugs are introduced to the vineyards each year to diminish the presence of unwanted pests.

along Highway 128 to Boonville, stopping just south of Anderson Valley. Basically, this is an extension of Sonoma County's Alexander Valley into Mendocino County but the soils are different: loam and clay soils on the Sonoma side, gravelly soil on the Mendocino side. This wine-growing region shows promise with Pinot Noir because of cool nights, but also Sauvignon Blanc, Cabernet Sauvignon, and Merlot due to warm days.

The best-known wineries in the Yorkville Highlands AVA include Bink, Le Vin, Lone Oak, Maple Creek, Marietta, Meyer Family, Route 128, Wattle Creek, and Yorkville.

LAKE COUNTY

The six AVAs of Lake County are:

Benmore Valley, Clear Lake, Guenoc Valley, High Valley, North Coast (Lake County is a constituent county of this multicounty AVA), and Red Hills Lake County.

Until Prohibition became the law of the land in 1920, Lake County was a promising red- wine–producing district and contained seventy-five wineries, making it one of the most important wine regions in California. By the time Prohibition was repealed, pears and walnuts were the crop of choice in Lake County. However, in the last ten years or so, Lake County has become the fastest growing part of the North Coast AVA. Today, there are at least twenty-eight wineries currently in operation, and 8,800 acres/3,520 hectares of vineyard, planted with Sauvignon Blanc, Zinfandel, Cabernet Sauvignon, Chardonnay, and Merlot. Since 1998, there has been a tripling of grape acreage in Lake County and a quadrupling of wineries. Growers in Lake County are likely to sell their crops to producers who will make varietal wines with the sometimes more profitable and better-recognized multicounty North Coast AVA on the label.

CLEAR LAKE AND RED HILLS LAKE COUNTY

Clear Lake is named for California's largest freshwater lake and is by far the largest AVA in Lake County, encompassing more than half of the county's vineyard acreage. The Clear Lake AVA was granted in 1984. With a total of about 8,000 planted acres/3,200 planted hectares in the AVA, the biggest player here is Kendall-Jackson.

Red Hills is a sub-AVA (granted 2004) of the Clear Lake AVA and is located at the base of an ancient, dormant volcano, Mount Konocti. Its deep-red volcanic soils and relatively warm climate nourish about 3,000 acres/1,200

hectares of vines, mostly Zinfandel, Syrah, Cabernet Franc, Merlot, and Petite Sirah.

Clear Lake and Red Hills area wineries include Barclay & Browning, Brassfield Estate, Gregory Graham, High Valley, Kendall-Jackson, Monte Lago, Ployez, Shannon Ridge, Steele, and Wildhurst.

GUENOC VALLEY

The AVA (granted in 1981) is controlled by a single winery, the Langtry Estate/Guenoc Winery, originally owned by the Magoon family, which is the first winery whose name became not only a brand but an AVA. In 1963, brothers Orville and Eaton Magoon swapped 23 acres/9 hectares of oceanfront property in Hawaii for 23,000 acres/9,200 hectares of land in Lake County, including the home and vineyard lands owned by the legendary British actress Lillie Langtry, who produced good wines from her vineyards until 1906. The Magoon brothers and their mother, Genevieve, decided to revive some 350 acres/140 hectares of the vineyards, and they started to produce wine in 1976. In 1981, the Magoons built a winery, and today Guenoc, which has gone through several ownership and management changes, produces about 150,000 cases of wine. The winery is best known for its Langtry Estate wines (Guenoc Valley AVA and Lake County appellation) and its Guenoc wines (Lake County and California appellations).

BENMORE VALLEY

This is is another single-owner AVA, in this case Sonoma Valley winery Geyser Peak, which has planted Chardonnay and Syrah on the border of the Russian River drainage basin and the Clear Lake basin in southwest Lake County. Benmore Valley received its AVA status in 1991. The AVA contains no wineries.

HIGH VALLEY

This AVA certainly lives up to its name, as the valley begins at 1,600 feet/490 meters and goes as high as 3,000 feet/910 meters. Here, the valley floor is cooler than

previously discussed Monterey AVA, these appellations are:

ARROYO SECO Granted AVA status in 1983, its 9,000 acres/3,600 hectares of vines are suited mostly to Chardonnay, Riesling, Gewürztraminer, and Pinot Noir. Chardonnay and Riesling in particular show off lush, tropical fruit and bracing acidity. Wineries located in the Arroyo Seco AVA include Carmel Road, Cobblestone, Hangtime, J. Lohr, Jekel, McIntyre, Meador, and Ventana.

CHALONE Granted AVA status in 1982, its 300 acres/120 hectares of vines were developed solely by the Chalone Vineyard winery, much respected for *terroir*-driven Chardonnay, Pinot Noir, and a very fine Pinot Blanc. The high-altitude AVA is sited on the Gavilan Mountains and stretches across Monterey and San Benito counties. Two other wineries have joined Chalone: Brosseau and Michaud.

SANTA LUCIA HIGHLANDS Granted AVA status in 1987, its 2,300 acres/920 hectares of vines show much success with Chardonnay and, increasingly, Pinot Noir. Cabernet Sauvignon and Merlot do well at higher elevations, because of more intense and sustained sunlight and less fog. Quality-conscious wineries in the Santa Lucia Highlands AVA include Hahn, La Rochelle, Lucia, Manzoni, Mer Soleil, Morgan, Paraiso, Pisoni, ROAR, Smith & Hook, Tondre, and Tudor.

MOUNT HARLAN Granted AVA status in 1990, with 74 acres/30 hectares of vines, this small appellation in San Benito County was developed solely by the Calera winery to define the four Pinot Noir vineyards for which it is justly famous: Jensen, Mills, Reed, and Selleck. Josh Jensen, founder and owner of Calera, went looking for Burgundy in California and found it in the limestone soils and isolated terrain of San Benito County's

Gavilan Mountains. The Calera winery also makes fine Chardonnay and Viognier, both from small Mount Harlan vineyards. Josh Jensen certainly deserves all of the accolades his wines have received; they are stellar in quality and singular in character.

SAN LUCAS Granted AVA status in 1987, its 5,000 acres/2,000 hectares of vines planted in the warm-weather vineyards of the southern Salinas Valley are dedicated mostly to Cabernet Sauvignon, Merlot, Chardonnay, and Sauvignon Blanc. Created by Almadén, which had planted 1,300 acres/520 hectares here, San Lucas is the source of reliable fruit for several inexpensive "fighting varietals," all of which carry the California appellation. Lockwood and Shale Ridge are the two resident wineries in the AVA.

In 2004, a sub-AVA, San Bernabe, at the northern end of the San Lucas AVA, was established to accommodate the Delicato family's 5,000-acre/2,000-hectare vineyard, the largest contiguous vineyard site in California.

SANTA CRUZ MOUNTAINS

Within the other counties of the "North Central Coast," the AVA that draws the most attention is one shared by San Mateo, Santa Clara, and Santa Cruz counties. The appellation is Santa Cruz Mountains, granted AVA status in 1982. This very large appellation (110,000 acres/44,000 hectares) has a very small number of plantings, only about 1,500 acres/600 hectares, starting at 800 feet/250 meters above sea level, and topping out at 2,000 feet/625 meters. Growers must compete with the suburban sprawl of San Francisco, extremely expensive prices for land that is isolated in rugged mountains, and even earthquakes. To complete the picture, several vineyards in the AVA have

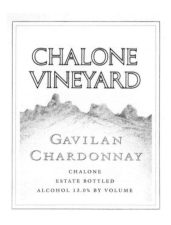

TOP: *Josh Jensen's single-vineyard Pinot Noir wines are stellar examples of the* terroir *expressed by the rugged terrain of the vineyards in the Mount Harlan AVA.*

fallen victim to PIERCE'S DISEASE (see page 178). Yet, grape growers and wine producers with both sheer will and talent have made the Santa Cruz Mountains AVA one of the most important regions of California for artisanal wines of great character.

Generally cool, the Santa Cruz Mountains AVA has wide-ranging microclimates, with the coolest weather provided by the Pacific Ocean and at lower altitudes. Overall, the Santa Cruz Mountains AVA is generally hospitable to Chardonnay, Cabernet Sauvignon, Pinot Noir, and Zinfandel. Quality is largely vintage-dependent because of the unpredictable weather. Probably the most highly regarded wines from this AVA are Cabernet Sauvignon from the esteemed Ridge Monte Bello vineyards, as well as David Bruce Pinot Noir and Chardonnay.

Randall Grahm is owner and winemaker of Bonny Doon Vineyard, located in the Santa Cruz Mountains AVA, and California's original Rhone Ranger (see page 161). In 1986, Grahm released the first vintage of Le Cigare Volant (which refers to the flying saucer many locals claimed to have seen in the southern Rhône Valley), his New World homage to the famous Châteauneuf-du-Pape, which is a blend of southern Rhône varietals. Grahm became famous for his idiosyncratic Rhône-style wines, and was first called the "Rhone Ranger" (named after the famous masked cowboy hero, the Lone Ranger, popular on radio, television, and comic books in the 1950s) in 1988. It was Randall Grahm who began the Rhône revolution in California.

The Ben Lomond Mountain AVA (granted 1987), located solely in Santa Cruz County, is located within the far western reaches of the Santa Cruz Mountains AVA. A historically important California wine region, with vineyards first planted circa 1860, Ben Lomond Mountain has more recently had more than its share of setbacks, due largely to widespread Pierce's Disease (see page 178) in its vineyards, forcing some vineyard owners to move to more hospitable ground. Beauregard Vineyards has so far weathered the storm and continues to plant about 60 acres. Beauregard is the only winery that consistently displays the Ben Lomond Mountain AVA on its label.

Bargetto, Beauregard, Bonny Doon, Cinnabar, David Bruce, Fernwood, Gatos Locos, Kathryn Kennedy, Martin Ranch, McHenry, Mount Eden, Organic Wine Works, Pelican Ranch, Rhys, Ridge, Roudon-Smith, Soquel, Storrs, and Thomas Fogarty are some of the better-known, quality-driven producers who make wine in the Santa Cruz Mountains and Ben Lomond Mountain AVAs.

LIVERMORE VALLEY AND THE SAN FRANCISCO BAY

As the city of San Francisco has grown, many bedroom communities have sprung up around it, some of them a considerable distance from the city itself. A number of these San Francisco suburbs, such as the cities of Livermore and Pleasanton in Alameda County, located about thirty miles east of San Francisco, were created from former agricultural lands. The fast-paced development of these communities has threatened the existence of the 3,000 acres/1,200 hectares of vineyards in the historic Livermore Valley appellation, which was one of the first wine regions to receive AVA status, in 1982, based largely on afternoon ocean winds and fog, as well as its gravelly soil.

Livermore Valley is largely defined by two historic family-owned wineries, both started in the 1880s and still active today: Wente and Concannon. Wente produces about 300,000 cases of wine, much of it for export (Wente was the first California producer to sell wine in China), and Concannon (now owned by Wente) produces about 30,000 cases, mostly for domestic consumption. The Wentes were among the first commercial producers of Chardonnay in California in the early 1960s, and the Wente clone of Chardonnay is the most planted in the state. Little by little, Wente and Concannon were joined by several other small family-owned wineries in Livermore Valley. There are now about forty wineries in the AVA.

Livermore Valley is widely known for the quality of its Sauvignon Blanc and Petite Sirah wines, but also makes

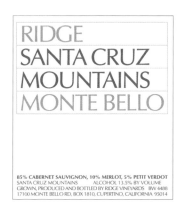

Ridge Monte Bello Cabernet Sauvignon has been considered one of the truly great California wines for almost forty years. Paul Draper is the winemaker. The Monte Bello vineyard is sited in the Santa Cruz Mountains AVA.

some very fine Sauvignon Blanc/Sémillon blends, as well as Cabernet Sauvignon and Cabernet-based blends, Syrah, Zinfandel, and the current regional specialty, Merlot.

In addition to Wente and Concannon, some of the better-known wineries and producers in the Livermore Valley AVA include Bent Creek, Big White House, Bodegas Aguirre, Chouinard, Darcie Kent, Eagle Ridge, Fenestra, John Christopher, Murietta's Well (Wente's Meritage label), Retzlaff, Rios-Lovell, Rosenblum, Steven Kent, Tamas, Thomas Coyne, White Crane, and Wood Family.

San Francisco Bay, included in the official Central Coast AVA, was granted its own AVA status in 1999 at the urging of the Wente family, as a kind of quality center of the "North Central Coast." It is a huge area of 2,450 square miles/3,920 square kilometers with about 120 wineries contained within it, but very few of the wines feature this AVA name on the label. The appellation, distinguished by the cooling impact of the Bay on the vineyards (although no shoreline is included in the AVA), appears to have more commercial than viticultural purpose. It allows the producers and growers to separate themselves from the Central Coast or California appellations most often found on bottles produced from this region's fruit. Perhaps the thinking is that if we

read Central Coast on a label, we think Monterey, and if we read California on a label, we think inexpensive, but when we read San Francisco Bay on a label, we think of the beautiful city. The appellation name is sure to help Wente and other producers who have their eyes set on the international market.

Wineries that feature the San Francisco Bay AVA on their labels include Chouinard, Clos de la Tech, Little Valley, Page Mill, Poetic Cellars, Rosenblum, Rhys, Thomas Coyne, and Westover.

CENTRAL COAST: THE SOUTH

SAN LUIS OBISPO AND SANTA BARBARA COUNTIES

Despite their southerly location, the coastal areas of San Luis Obispo County and Santa Barbara County have cool coastal stretches, and some of the Pacific Ocean fog is drawn inland through the valley openings so that special microclimates exist in certain spots in the valleys. Ironically, given that vines and wine were introduced to this part of California by Spanish missionaries long before Napa ever thought of growing vines, modern, post-Prohibition winemaking is a very recent activity here.

San Luis Obispo, the more northerly county, is home to five appellations: Central Coast (the "blanket" AVA); Edna Valley, the oldest (AVA approved in 1982); Paso Robles, the largest (AVA approved in 1983); York Mountain, the smallest (AVA approved in 1983); and Arroyo Grande Valley, the newest (AVA approved in 1990).

Of the four San Luis Obispo viticultural areas, the York Mountain AVA is probably the easiest to define, not only because of its small size (30 acres/12 hectares planted), but also because of a single unifying feature—York Mountain is extremely cool. The AVA is located in the Templeton Gap, at a high elevation east of the Santa Lucia Mountains and west of Paso Robles. Templeton Gap acts as a funnel to draw cold air in from the ocean throughout the growing season. Not surprisingly, Chardonnay is well represented here, as is Pinot Noir and Syrah. Originally, this was a single-winery AVA; the owner of York Creek Vineyards is now Martin & Weinrich, only the third owner of the winery, which was founded in 1882. The two other wineries are Shadow Canyon and Stephen's Cellar, named for Stephen Goldman, one of the original petitioners for the York Mountain AVA.

Wineries that often source their grapes in the York Mountain AVA include Calcareous, David Bruce, Silver Mountain, Shadow Canyon, Stephen's Cellar, and York Creek Vineyards.

Situated to the south of York Mountain and closer to the coastline, the Edna Valley AVA's 2,300 acres/920 hectares of vineyard and Arroyo Grande Valley AVA's 420 acres/168 hectares enjoy a more maritime climate. Chardonnay dominates in both appellations, particularly the full-bodied rich wines from the Edna Valley. Pinot Noir and Rhône varietals show promise in the Edna Valley. Arroyo Grande Valley, a bit further to the south, has shown promise with Pinot Noir and Zinfandel as well

as very good Chardonnay (the Edna valley is often too cool for full ripening).

Well-known wineries and producers in the Edna Valley AVA and the Arroyo Grande Valley AVA include:

Alban, Au Bon Climat, Baileyana, Bianchi, Bozzano, Carpe Diem, Claiborne and Churchill, Domaine Alfred, Edna Valley Vineyard, Hangtime, Kynsi, Laetitia, Martin & Weyrich, Saucelito, Stephen Ross, Talley, Wolff, and York Mountain Winery.

The Paso Robles AVA (granted in 1983) has become a major producer of quality wines in California. Located in San Luis Obispo County, north of Santa Barbara and south of Monterey, Paso Robles is a coastal AVA with a wide variety of soil types and microclimates. Zinfandel has taken a strong stand here, as have red Rhône varietals (especially Syrah), but Cabernet Sauvignon and Merlot are still the most planted varieties in Paso Robles, accounting for more than 60 percent of the nearly 18,500 acres/7,400 hectares of vines.

What makes this wine region shine are the artisan-produced and *terroir*-driven wines that define a rustic elegance, an earthy sophistication, a complex grace. The flavors of the best Paso Robles wines are singular and even unfamiliar; these are not cookie-cutter wines.

Paso Robles is identified as a single AVA, but along the Salinas River there is an east-west divide that breaks Paso Robles into at least two very different viticultural designations. On the east side, the fertile soils are composed of layers of stratified layers of clay, gravel, and sand, derived from alluvial sediments. With easy access to rivers and creeks, these soils are efficiently irrigated, and the vines do not have to struggle to sink their roots deep to drink.

The soils on the west side of the river (locally known as Westside) are significantly different from the east side. Chalk soils (rare in California, but essential to the character of the wines of Champagne and Chablis in France, and Jerez in Spain) define the west. Westside soils have less access to water, and the vines are stressed, with roots burrowing through rock. There are many historic head-pruned and dry-farmed Westside vineyards, including Rancho San Ignacio, established by concert pianist and president of Poland Ignace Paderewski in the early 1920s, which he planted with Petite Sirah and Zinfandel. In 2009, a petition for a proposed Paso Robles Westside AVA was not granted by the TTB.

Just as important as the soils in Paso Robles is the climate. It is not unusual to encounter a 40°F/4.4°C difference during the course of a day: warm, clear, cloudless days, followed by a cooling marine layer after sunset. In the winter, cooler areas can dip down to well below freezing, and just about all of the vineyards are completely dormant by December. One of the coolest areas is known as the Templeton Gap, centered around the town of Templeton, which gets some wicked winds to cool the area dramatically. The Templeton Gap traverses both east and west vineyards, and due to the winds can create wines of bracing acidity and structure.

In 1990, there were about 20 wineries in the Paso Robles AVA; today there are more than 170, making a wide variety of wines. The largest producer in this AVA is J. Lohr (with

LEFT TO RIGHT: *Pharaoh Moans produces only 300 cases of this fine, artisanal Syrah, produced from the chalk soils of Paso Robles vineyards. Zinfandel is the special focus of Peachy Canyon Winery, which produces eight different Zinfandels, including several single-vineyard bottlings. Au Bon Climat produces an excellent Chardonnay from Arroyo Grande Valley vineyards. Gary Eberle is known as "the grandfather of Paso Robles" because of his early and sustained commitment to the Paso Robles wine region.*

a focus on Cabernet Sauvignon, Syrah, and Zinfandel; J. Lohr also owns vineyards in Arroyo Seco and Monterey). The best-known wineries in the Paso Robles AVA include the following:

- Adelaida is known for its Syrah and Zinfandel.
- Eberle produces estate-bottled artisan wines. Gary Eberle is known as "the Grandfather of Paso Robles" because of his vision and commitment to this wine region. Eberle Cabernet Sauvignon, Syrah, Zinfandel, and Côtes-du-Rôbles are terrifc.
- EOS produces estate-bottled wines, with excellent Zinfandel and Petite Sirah.
- Justin Vineyards focuses on Syrah, Cabernet Sauvignon, and its justifiably famous Cabernet blend, Isosceles.
- Peachy Canyon is known for its estate-bottled, single-vineyard Zinfandels.
- Tablas Creek is a joint venture between wine importer/exporter Robert Haas and the Perrin family of Château de Beaucastel in the Rhône Valley of France. The vines are planted with cuttings from Beaucastel and the focus is strongly on Rhône varietals and blends.
- Turley Wine Cellars; Larry Turley is known for producing great Zinfandel from some of California's oldest vines, and his single-vineyard Pesenti Zin from eighty-five year-old vines is a great example.

Other wineries making fine wines in the Paso Robles AVA or from fruit grown in the AVA include Alban, Andrew Murray, Anglim, Baretto, Bianchi, Byington, Calcareous, Carmody McKnight, Castoro, Cerro Caliente, Cinquain, Clautiere, Clayhouse, Daniel Gehrs, Dark Star, Dunning, Eagle Castle, Edmunds St. John, Edward Sellers, Estancia, Garretson, Graveyard, Gugliemo, Halter Ranch, Hearthstone, Hunt, Jeff Runquist, Joseph Filippi, Kenneth Volk, Kiamie, L'Aventure Bella Luna, Linne Calodo, Maddalena, Maloy O'Neill, Martin & Weyrich, Meridian, Midlife Crisis, Midnight, Niner, Norman, Orchid Hill, Oso Libre, Page Springs, Pomar Junction, Rabbit Ridge, Red Soles, Rhombus, RiverStar, Robert Hall, Rosenblum, Rotta, San Antonio, Saxum, Sextant, Silver Horse, Solaire by Robert Mondavi, Still Waters, Sylvester, Talley, Thunderbolt Junction, Toad Hollow, Tobin James, Victor Hugo, Villa Creek, Vina Robles, WCP, Wild Horse, and York Mountain.

Santa Barbara County, to the south of San Luis Obispo, has three AVAs: Santa Maria Valley (AVA status granted 1981), Santa Ynez Valley (1983), and Santa Rita Hills (2001; a sub-AVA of Santa Ynez Valley, which now appears as "Sta. Rita Hills" on labels, due to a legal tussle with the large Chilean wine producer, Santa Rita, settled in 2006). Chardonnay and Pinot Noir dominate in Santa Barbara County, with excellent plantings of Rhone Ranger grapes, especially Syrah, and some smaller plantings of Cabernet Sauvignon and Merlot further inland. There are now more than sixty wineries in the county and over 21,000 acres of vineyard.

This is *Sideways* wine country, as the 2004 movie that did so much for California Pinot Noir (and so little for Merlot) was filmed at the wineries and in the vineyards of Santa Barbara County, especially the Santa Rita Hills AVA.

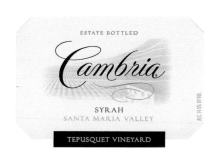

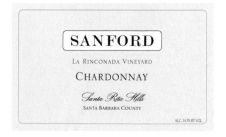

In the narrow, long Santa Ynez Valley AVA, Pinot Noir and Chardonnay rule in the cooler western end, while Sauvignon Blanc, Cabernet Sauvignon, and Merlot are found more in the eastern end. At higher elevations in the east, plantings of Syrah make excellent wines. Santa Ynez Valley is a perfect example of how the Pacific Ocean influences the coastal vineyards of California. The part of Santa Ynez that is less than 10 miles/16 kilometers from the ocean is too cool for grapes to ripen; at about 15 miles/24 kilometers, the conditions are perfect for Chardonnay and Pinot Noir. By the time you are 20 miles/32 kilometers from the coast, Santa Ynez becomes Cabernet Sauvignon and Merlot country. As elevation rises to about 800 feet, daily temperature fluctuates dramatically, with lots of warm sunshine, but also windy days and cool nights, perfect for Santa Ynez Valley Syrah. About 10,000 acres/4,000 hectares of vineyards are planted in this AVA.

The Santa Rita Hills AVA is almost wholly contained within the Santa Ynez Valley AVA. With the Santa Rosa Hills bordering the AVA in the south and the Purisma Hills in the north, the Santa Rita Hills enjoy the cool breezes of the Pacific and rocky soil, both fine conditions for growing Pinot Noir and Chardonnay. Syrah does quite well here, too. A fairly small AVA, Santa Rita Hills has about 1,700 acres/680 hectares of vineyards.

The 135-acre/54-hectare Sanford & Benedict vineyard in the Santa Rita Hills AVA has been a premium source of Pinot Noir and Chardonnay for Sanford, Au Bon Climat, Bonnacorsi, Cold Heaven, Di Bruno, Foxen, Hitching Post, Kynis, Longoria, and Whitcraft wineries, among others. Sanford & Benedict, the first estate vineyard in the AVA, and the Sanford winery were purchased by the Terlato Wine Group in 2007.

Other wineries growing grapes or producing wines in the Santa Rita Hills AVA include Ampelos, Coup de Foudre, Drew Family, Foley, Sea Smoke, and Summerland.

The Santa Maria Valley AVA has more than thirty wineries in residence and about 7,500 acres/3,000 hectares of vineyards. The growing season is long here, due to the powerful sun tempered by scant rainfall, lots of fog, and strong Pacific winds. Most vineyards are planted on slopes that begin at about 200 feet/62 meters above sea level and top out at about 800 feet/248 meters, helping drain the soils. Grapes from this AVA are some of the most expensive in California, especially those that are grown in Santa Maria Valley's most famous vineyards: Bien Nacido, Sierra Madre, and Tepusquet.

Bien Nacido Vineyards, owned by the Miller family, is about 2,000 acres and is the source for some of the best wines—Chardonnay, Pinot Noir, Syrah, Pinot Blanc, and Merlot—made by several wineries, including bottlings by Alta Maria, Au Bon Climat, Bernardus, Byron, Fess Parker, Foxen, Gary Farrell, Hitching Post, Jaffurs, Landmark, Longoria, Ojai, Qupé, Steele, Stephen Ross, Testarossa, Villa Mt. Eden, and Whitcraft. The influence of the Miller family on the Santa Maria Valley as a superior quality wine region cannot be overestimated.

The historic 1,400-acre/560-hectare Tepusquet Vineyard is owned by Cambria (Kendall-Jackson); the winery produces vineyard-designated Syrah and Viognier. Sierra Madre Vineyard is owned by the Circle family, and its 175 acres/70 hectares is mostly planted to Chardonnay and Pinot Noir. Producers sourcing fruit here include many of those who buy fruit from Bien Nacido Vineyards plus David Bruce, Edna Valley, Gainey, Kenneth Volk, Lane Tanner, LaZarre, Paul Lato, Row Eleven, Rusack, and Wild Horse.

The dedicated farmers and producers of Santa Barbara County set a high benchmark for California wines made from Pinot Noir, Chardonnay, and increasingly, Syrah.

South Coast

The mega-appellation for the southern region of California is the South Coast AVA (granted 1985), which includes all of Orange County as well as western parts of Riverside, San Bernardino, and San Diego counties. With 3,000 acres/1,200 hectares of vineyards and more than eighty wineries, this region produces some of California's more idiosyncratic wines. Due to a very warm climate, somewhat lessened by ocean breezes, and a difficult bout of Pierce's Disease, the Chardonnay grapes that previously defined the South Coast have mostly been replaced with Cabernet Sauvignon and Rhone Ranger varietals, as well as the even more exotic Sangiovese, Trebbiano, and Tempranillo.

San Bernardino is physically the largest county in the United States, more than 20,000 square miles/32,000 square kilometers of mostly desert lands and temperatures that can exceed 100°F/38°C. In 1954, there were 25,000 acres/10,000 hectares of wine grapes in the county; today there are about 1,000 acres/400 hectares, most of them planted to red grapes such as Grenache, Mourvèdre, Zinfandel, Carignane, and Alicante Bouschet. There is one AVA in San Bernardino County, Cucamonga Valley

In addition to Zinfandel, Cabernet Sauvignon, and Merlot, red Italian varietals—Cal-Italians—are being planted here with good results, especially Barbera and Sangiovese. Syrah, Grenache, Viognier, Marsanne, Roussanne, and other Rhone Ranger varietals appear to have a future in this region as well. Producers here seem to dance to the beat of a different drum. Frog's Tooth Vineyard, for example, produces a great red Tempranillo. Stevenot makes a crisp, refreshing dry white Verdelho.

There are about two hundred wineries in this vast region (2.5 million acres/1 million hectares). Some are tiny, most are small, a few are big, and just about all of them are worth seeking out in shops and restaurants, in person or online. Well-known producers in Amador County and/or the Sierra Foothills AVA include:

Amador Foothill, Black Sheep, Boeger, Chathom, Clos du Lac/Greenstone, Deaver, Drytown, Easton, Frog's Tooth, Grey Fox, Ironstone, Iverson, Jeff Rinquist, Jewel, Karly, Lang, Lava Cap, Lucas, Montevina, Mount Aukum, Paradise Ridge, Perry Creek, Renaissance, Sierra Vista, Silver Fox, Sobon, Stevenot, Stonehouse, Story, Talus, and Van Ruiten, among many other artisanal wineries.

YOLO COUNTY AND SACRAMENTO COUNTY

The three official AVAs centered around California's delta region of the Central Valley are Clarksburg, its sub-AVA Merritt Island, and the Dunnigan Hills AVA. These districts receive soft breezes off San Francisco Bay and so enjoy more moderate climatic conditions than most of the rest of the Central Valley.

CLARKSBURG

This AVA, with 9,000 acres/3,600 hectares planted, is not far from the city of Sacramento and is best known for growing good, dependable Chenin Blanc and Petite Sirah for a variety of producers, some of whom choose Clarksburg as their appellation of choice but most of whom use California as the appellation on the label. The climate here is warm, but cool Pacific breezes make their way into the Sacramento Delta by late afternoon. Soils are generally poorly drained and clay-based. These fertile soils allow for the growing of nearly thirty different grape varieties, but growing conditions seem to favor Chenin Blanc and Petite Sirah above all others. AVA status was granted in 1984.

Bogle, the first winery established in the Clarksburg AVA, produces well in excess of 100,000 cases of well-made, value-driven wines annually. The Bogle family farms more than 1,200 acres of vineyard in the Clarksburg AVA, but they also source grapes from other regions, including Lodi and Amador County. Bogle Petite Sirah and Old Vines Zinfandel are particularly good. Most Bogle wines use the California appellation on their labels.

Other wineries and producers in the Clarksburg AVA include Carvalho, Dancing Coyote, Dry Creek, Ehrhardt, Frasinetti, Heringer, River Grove, Saddleback, Scribner Bend, Six Hands, Todd Taylor, and Wilson.

MERRITT ISLAND

Located in Yolo County, Merritt Island received its own AVA in 1983, because even though it is contained within the Clarksburg AVA, its sandy loam soils and cooler island climate are different from the soils in the rest of Clarksburg. The Bogle family's winery is actually located on Merritt Island.

DUNNIGAN HILLS

The R. H. Phillips winery owned most of the acreage (of the total 1,500 acres/600 hectares planted) in this north-

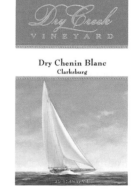

west Yolo County AVA. The R. H. Phillips brand (now owned by wine giant Constellation) is well-known for innovative packaging and bottle design, as well as good varietal character in its wines, night harvesting of its grapes (to maintain acidity), and very fair prices. R. H. Phillips' other brands include the EXP and Toasted Head lines of wines. Constellation closed the R. H. Phillips winery in 2008, shifting production to its Woodbridge, California, winery. Constellation still farms the 1,700 acres of vineyards in Dunnigan Hills. Currently, the only winery in the AVA is Crew Wine Company, whose Matchbook Tempranillo is an intriguing wine, made from the most important red grape of Spain, but grown in the Dunnigan Hills. Its AVA status was approved in 1993.

CENTRAL VALLEY

The Central Valley is about 450 miles long, running south from Sacramento to Bakersfield. It is an amazingly beautiful agricultural area, inhabited by American agribusiness, as well as family farms and vineyards. Although nearly 70 percent of California's wine is produced from Central Valley grapes (Gallo is located in Modesto; Gallo *is* Modesto), the valley is so vast, fertile, and productive that wine grapes account for a small fraction of total cropland. In a region that produces 25 percent of America's rice and virtually all of the nation's raisins, olives, almonds, canning tomatoes, garlic, walnuts, plums, prunes, nectarines, and lemons, wine grapes might go unnoticed if the California wine industry were not a $90+ billion business.

The two major valleys that form the larger Central Valley are the Sacramento River Valley and the San Joaquin River Valley. The Sacramento River Valley, because it receives its rain much earlier in the growing season, is famous for producing rice. Since the San Joaquin Valley stays drier longer, it is able to grow raisins, table grapes, and wine grapes, especially Thompson Seedless, used for raisins and budget wines. Because it is so hot in the Central Valley, and because state-subsidized reservoirs and federally subsidized canals provide water to farms, the tradition of grape growing has been to plant any grapes anywhere in the valley's fertile soils. Barring some unforeseen disaster, there will always be a bumper crop of whatever grapes the farmer plants, although the grapes may maintain only a faint echo of their true varietal essence. For generic jug or box wines this is not a problem, and so the interior lands of the San Joaquin Valley are known for growing high-yielding grape varieties, such as Chenin Blanc, Colombard, Carignan, and of course, Thompson Seedless. The vines, looking more like trees, can be huge, and yields easily can run 10–15 tons per acre/11,000–17,000 kilograms per hectare.

So how is it that the Central Valley is now home to a wide variety of premium wine grapes, with even some fine single-vineyard Zinfandel wines coming out of this area? The answer is the Lodi AVA (approved 1986, 90,000 acres/36,000 hectares planted), situated close to where the Sacramento River has cut a swath through the coastal ranges, creating an opportunity for cooler ocean air to reach the delta, which is a large part of the 500-square-mile/800-square-kilometer Lodi appellation. The AVA runs south from Sacramento, stopping just before Stockton. Most of Lodi is located in San Joaquin County and the rest of it in Sacramento County.

Lodi, once home to grower-owned **COOPERATIVES**, is now home to some very large winery operations, including the seminal Woodbridge by Robert Mondavi winery, making millions of cases of good, basic, varietal wines at affordable prices. Following the lead of Robert Mondavi, who was born in Lodi, large wineries and vineyards have been established by other major players in the California premium wine industry, including Delicato, Sutter Home, and Turner Road (owned by wine behemoth Constellation). As for the source of grapes demanded by these huge wineries, there are more than eight hundred grape growers toiling in Lodi vineyards.

While the majority of the "big-brand" wines produced from Lodi fruit are labeled with the California appellation, there is a trend among producers both large and small to highlight the Lodi AVA on the label. In fact, more than a hundred wine labels now feature Lodi as the appellation of choice. At least partial credit for this

Delicato, a large third-generation family-owned winery, sources its grapes throughout the Central Valley, with a focus on the Lodi AVA. The wines are of good quality and are good values.

WILLAMETTE

OKANAGAN

ICEWINE

FINGER LAKES

WALLA WALLA

OLD MISSION

ROGUE VALLEY

BAJA CALIFORNIA

SUPER TEXAN

RIESLING

SENECA

PINOT

YAKIMA

NIAGARA PENINSULA

BEYOND CALIFORNIA: WINES OF NORTH AMERICA

UNITED STATES

THERE IS NO DOUBT that California leads the way as the state producing the most wine in the United States. But every state now has some kind of wine industry, and at least thirty-five states can boast at least one AVA. Eleven states merit some mention here.

NORTHEASTERN UNITED STATES

New York State

CLIMATE AND GRAPES

In a general sense, the climate of New York State's grape-growing areas can be classified as Region 1 and 2 in the UC Davis heat summation system. This immediately identifies New York as a cool-climate grape-growing area, with the possibility of some warmer microclimates for specific vineyard sites. The conventional wisdom about New York is that it is very well suited to white grapes, especially Chardonnay and Riesling in the vinifera family, and Seyval Blanc, Vidal, and Vignoles in the hybrid family. However, things have changed, and New York's premier

areas, the Finger Lakes and Long Island, have recently produced some stunning red wines, particularly from Pinot Noir, Cabernet Franc, and Cabernet Sauvignon.

This success does not come easily. Such wines are often the result of relatively low yields of 2.5–3.5 tons per acre/30–45 hectoliters per hectare, which is considerably less than in some western states. Low yields and the tender loving care that the vines demand throughout the growing season require an inordinate amount of hard work. The lingering threat of winter cold in some years still makes many New York State grape growers hesitant to work with vinifera grape varieties, which are generally not hardy enough to withstand such temperatures without a lot of labor-intensive care. Many growers prefer to work with hybrid varieties, which are more winter-hardy and disease-resistant. Some growers and producers continue to work with the extremely hardy native varieties, such as Concord, Catawba, and Niagara.

WINE STYLES

The days when New York State produced mostly sweet red wines, such as the kosher brands Manischewitz and Royal Kedem and the nonkosher brands Richard's Wild Irish Rose (from Canandaigua Wines) and Lake Niagara (from Widmer), are long gone. The range of wines currently produced in New York State is now much broader,

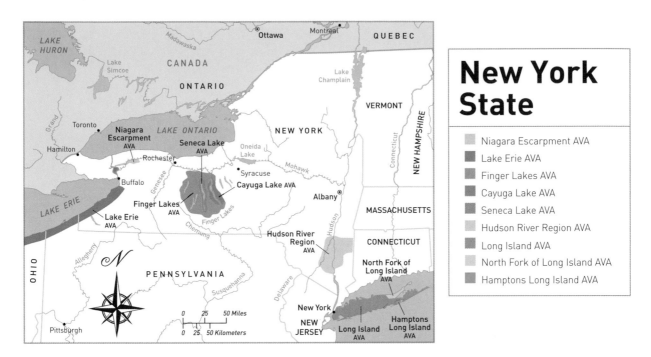

including light, fresh Rieslings and Seyval Blancs, fuller Chardonnays, crisp sparkling wines, and full, dry Cabernet Francs and Cabernet Sauvignons.

It comes as a surprise to most people to learn that New York State is the third-largest wine-producing state in the nation, behind California and Washington, with more than 230 wineries. More important, the quality of New York State wines is high enough to compete at a national and international level. Again, it is important to judge this region's wines not in direct comparison with wines from elsewhere, but simply as wine. Using that as the sole criterion, New York State has nothing to be ashamed of and much of which it can be proud. As in any developing wine region, it takes time for the vines to age and for winemakers to find the best sites and to identify the best clones of varieties that will make the best wine possible. New York now seems to have found its course and is well on its way to a more solidly defined future of quality vinifera production of both whites and reds.

REGIONS

There are nine appellations (AVAs) in New York State. As with many of the recognized regions in Europe, what makes grape growing possible in an otherwise marginal climate is the existence of large bodies of water. In each case, the appellation relies on lakes, rivers, or the ocean to moderate the air temperature and make it possible for the early, tender buds and shoots to survive and for the grapes to reach full ripeness with optimal flavor development.

NIAGARA ESCARPMENT

Recognizing the long-standing influence that the entire Niagara region has exerted on climates, soils, and agriculture, New York State recently recognized this thin ribbon of vineyard land stretching east and west around the city of Lockport. Using the beneficial influences of the lakes and the protective slope of the land, orchards have long been a feature of this area, so it is no surprise that it would be recognized as its own AVA for wine production. Native grape varieties and hybrids outnumber vinifera varieties, but a few brave souls, such as the proprietors of Arrowhead Spring Vineyards and Warm Lake Estate, are making a name for their vinifera wines.

LAKE ERIE

Located in the western corner of the state, this is the largest of New York State's AVAs in terms of vineyard acreage, though it produces relatively little wine, since most of the grapes are old native North American varieties that are used in juice and jelly production. The appellation continues southwest along the shore of Lake Erie, through Pennsylvania, and into Ohio. The climate is strongly influenced by Lake Erie in a number of ways. By the time cold air has traversed the lake, the air has become much warmer, and it then hovers between the lake and the Allegheny

Plateau, which rises to the south of the lake, keeping warm air in the vineyard area. Heavy snows, referred to as "lake-effect snow," are beneficial to the vines during the winter, since the snow acts as a layer of insulation against very low temperatures.

In the spring, the lake stays cold longer than the ground does, keeping the air temperature lower than it otherwise might be. This retards the development of the buds, which helps reduce the possibility of damage by a sudden late cold spell or frost. In the fall, the lake stays warmer than the surrounding ground, keeping the air temperature higher and allowing the grapes to continue to ripen in the warmer air.

Of the vinifera producers, Woodbury is the most prominent, winning numerous awards for its Chardonnay.

FINGER LAKES

Though smaller in land area than the Lake Erie AVA, the Finger Lakes region produces far more wine than any other appellation in New York, containing as it does about half of all the state's wineries. Finger Lakes has a larger percentage of its vineyards planted with hybrid and vinifera grapes for wine production than Lake Erie, which has most of its vineyards planted with native varieties for juice and jelly production. Most of the wineries in Finger Lakes are clustered around Keuka Lake, Seneca Lake, and Cayuga Lake to take full advantage of the temperature moderation these lakes provide and the rolling hillsides, which help angle the vineyards into the sun and allow the coldest air to sink down the slope below the vineyards, minimizing the risk of frost damage. The lakes, formed by glacial action during the ice age, are extremely deep in parts (up to 200 feet/60 meters), increasing their temperature-moderating ability. The Finger Lakes AVA also includes two sub-appellations, Cayuga Lake and Seneca Lake.

The area owes much of its fame to some prominent names in the wine business of the northeastern United States. For many years, the area's wine production was dominated by the giant Taylor Wine Company in Hammondsport, at the southern end of Keuka Lake. The influence of Taylor is now much less, but during its heyday, Taylor's Gold Seal label gained a reputation as one of New York State's finest sparkling wines. Today, the Taylor Wine Company and several other prominent and well-established New York wine brands, such as Great Western, Gold Seal, and Widmer, are owned by the multinational wine company, Constellation, and they are still recognized for their contributions to the evolution of the modern New York wine industry. For example, Charles Fournier, an immigrant from the Champagne region of France who worked for Great Western, and Dr. Konstantin Frank, a Russian immigrant, pioneered the planting of vinifera grape varieties in the region and recognized the potential of the land surrounding the lakes.

Today, the Frank name is carried on by Dr. Frank's grandson, Fred Frank, and the sparkling wine tradition is continuing with fine products from such companies as Chateau Frank and Hermann Wiemer. The Konstantin Frank Winery produces a unique and flavorful dry white made from the Rkatsiteli grape.

Not surprisingly, Chardonnay and Riesling are the most successful white vinifera varieties, and Vignoles and Seyval Blanc are prominent as white hybrid varieties. The production of red wine used to be smaller but has grown rapidly with the recognition that in carefully chosen sites, cool-climate reds such as Pinot Noir and Cabernet Franc can ripen well enough in the Finger Lakes climate to win some major national and international awards.

CAYUGA LAKE

The growers and producers of Cayuga Lake feel that the slate and shale deposits underlying this area make their growing conditions distinct enough to be singled out as a separate AVA. Because of the higher mineral content of the soil, the wines tend to have a noticeably higher level of crispness, while the lake's lower altitude and slightly warmer temperatures produce ripe fruit with excellent structure. A prominent producer is Knapp Vineyards, now owned by Glenora.

SENECA LAKE

One of the major driving forces here is Cabernet Franc. The grape has not been widely recognized as a single-variety wine in New World nations, but there have always been well-made Cabernet Franc wines produced in the cool climate of the Loire Valley in France. Perhaps it was only a matter of time before it was recognized as a variety with a personality that can be fully expressed in other cool climates outside of France.

There is also a lot of excitement surrounding other red wines from Seneca, such as Pinot Noir, always a temperamental grape, as well as Cabernet Sauvignon and Merlot. There has even been talk of Syrah and Sangiovese! As expected, Chardonnay and Riesling continue to excel.

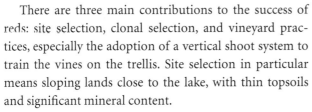

There are three main contributions to the success of reds: site selection, clonal selection, and vineyard practices, especially the adoption of a vertical shoot system to train the vines on the trellis. Site selection in particular means sloping lands close to the lake, with thin topsoils and significant mineral content.

Recognized producers include a clutch of relative newcomers such as Standing Stone, Lamoureaux Landing, Anthony Road, Fox Run, Shalestone, Red Newt, and Lakewood Vineyards.

HUDSON RIVER REGION

The Hudson River area boasts some of the oldest vineyards and wineries in America. There is evidence that Huguenot settlers planted grapes and made wine near New Paltz during the sixteenth century, and the Brotherhood winery has now incorporated the phrase "America's Oldest Winery" into its official name. There are older wineries in America,

but they closed during Prohibition, whereas Brotherhood has been in continuous operation since it opened, producing **SACRAMENTAL WINES** through the Prohibition era.

The history of grape growing and winemaking in this area is closely linked to the Concord grape and to other native varieties that have long been used to make juices, jellies, and Manischewitz and Royal Kedem wines. The picture is very different now, with many acres planted with hybrid varieties, particularly at Benmarl, Cascade Mountain, and Clinton Vineyards. In the late 1970s, Clinton Vineyards planted some Chardonnay but has since abandoned the variety. In the 1980s and 1990s, West Park Wine Cellars, Millbrook Vineyards, and Whitecliff Vineyard also planted Chardonnay, with greater success.

The climate is heavily influenced by the broad expanse of the Hudson River, which provides a moderating influence by pulling Atlantic water and air up into the valley during the summer months. This confluence of summer

---

TOP LEFT: *These Seneca Lake vineyards were planted in 1972 by vinifera pioneer Charles Fournier. They are now owned by Tom and Marti Macinski of Standing Stone Vineyards.* **TOP RIGHT**: *Tocai Friulano grapes nearing ripeness at Millbrook Vineyards.* **BOTTOM LEFT**: *The three-million-year-old rock reflects the minerality in the Shalestone vineyard.* **BOTTOM RIGHT**: *Pinot Noir grapes at Millbrook Vineyards*

heat and cooling influence is conducive to good ripening conditions for vinifera and hybrid varieties. The most notable progress in vinifera production has been at Millbrook Vineyards, which successfully produces wines from Tocai Friulano, Chardonnay, Pinot Noir, and Cabernet Franc grown on the property. A relatively new venture, Whitecliff Vineyards has also shown some promise, particularly with its Gamay, Cabernet Franc, Chardonnay, and a pleasant Pinot Grigio.

LONG ISLAND

The entire island was designated as an AVA in 2001, long after the smaller AVAs at the eastern end of the island came into existence. The appellation allows a few wineries outside of North Fork and the Hamptons to use the Long Island name.

NORTH FORK OF LONG ISLAND

Out on the eastern end of Long Island, as potato farms disappeared in the 1970s, a few visionary people such as Alex and Louisa Hargrave began buying the old farmland to  plant grapes. The Hargraves were followed by many others who shared their dream of growing vinifera grapes in New York. The prevailing belief at the time was that the climate in the rest of the state gave white vinifera varieties the best chance of success, whereas the slightly more moderate climate of Long Island suggested that red vinifera could finally be planted in greater quantities and brought to full ripeness.

Certainly in good summers, the Long Island vineyards fit comfortably into a Region 2 climate zone, and when the climate cooperates by providing enough warm weather in September and October to ripen the grapes to their fullest, grape growers have had enough success with Cabernet Sauvignon and Merlot to claim to be North America's equivalent of Bordeaux. While that claim may be an exaggeration, there are enough similarities that Bordeaux winemakers have shown an interest in consulting with some of the wineries on Long Island. As the vines have aged, there has been a steady increase in the depth of fruit and the quality of the red wines, especially when the vineyards are able to bask in the comfort of an Indian summer. Within the North Fork of Long Island AVA, the more prominent wineries are Castello di Borghese (formerly Hargrave), Palmer, Pindar, Schneider, Bedell, Pellegrini, Lenz, and Gristina.

HAMPTONS LONG ISLAND

This smaller AVA in the southern part of the island has had a more checkered career, with financial woes closing some of the early starters. There are currently three major wineries, Duck Walk, Channing Daughters, and Wölffer Estate, all producing a wide range of vinifera wines.

MIDWEST

Michigan

With over forty wineries and four AVAs, Michigan is fast becoming an important wine state. There are around 14,000 acres/5,500 hectares of grapes planted, but only about 1,500 acres/600 hectares are used for wine production, with the rest going to juice. The impressive thing is that almost all of the wine-production vineyards are planted with cool-climate vinifera varieties, with only a small percentage of hybrids like Vidal and Chambourcin. With its distinctly cool climate, the wines are typically clean and fresh, but the protective warmth provided by Lake Michigan results in attractively ripe flavors.

Riesling, Pinot Gris, and Chardonnay are particularly favored. Inevitably, Pinot Noir has been tried but it tends

TOP: *Whitecliff Vineyards uses netting to keep hungry birds away. The namesake white cliffs of the Shawangunk Mountains are in the background.* BOTTOM: *Bedell Cellars produces good Merlot on the North Fork of Long Island.*

to lack structure and flavor. However, sparkling-wine producers like Larry Mawby have used Pinot Noir to great effect in their sparklers.

The state's AVAs are split evenly between the southwestern corner and the northwestern part of the state. In the southeast are the Lake Michigan Shore AVA, south of the city of Saint Joseph, and Fennville AVA, around the town of Fennville. The northwestern AVAs demonstrate just how important lake-derived warmth can be at northern latitudes, as both Leelanau Peninsula AVA and Old Mission AVA stretch northward into the surrounding waters of Lake Michigan above Traverse City. Riesling from these two areas is particularly impressive, and Cabernet Franc shows great promise.

NORTHWESTERN UNITED STATES

Washington State

Of the northwestern states, Washington is the only one that can boast any substantial wine production before the 1970s. As early as the 1930s and 1940s, Washington State was producing large quantities of wine from native American grapes and other fruits, especially for the production of sweet, fortified wines of the Sherry and Porto type. In a sense, it is appropriate that Washington's very first vinifera vines were planted in the 1850s by French settlers in the

CLOCKWISE FROM TOP LEFT: *The serene setting for Riesling vineyards on Northern Michigan's Old Mission Peninsula. Like their wines, Willow Vineyards' sign is understated. Larry Mawby's whimsical names for his sparkling wines, such as "Sex" and "Wet," are reflected in the winery sign at the front gate.*

Walla Walla Valley. Although that area saw little vineyard development for more than a hundred years, it is now the site of a lot of expansion and experimentation. Today, any remaining acres of native grapes are used for juice or jelly production, while 31,000 acres/12,545 hectares of vinifera grapes produce in excess of 20 million gallons/758,000 hectoliters of wine. This represents a dramatic increase in acreage and production from a decade ago, though it still pales in comparison to California's almost 600 million gallons/22.7 million hectoliters. Today, the industry continues to grow, and Washington State is now home to over 540 wineries, compared with 163 in 2000.

Working with the Washington Wine Commission, the industry has taken important steps to demonstrate its commitment to quality. Starting with the 2000 vintage, the Washington Wine Quality Alliance was created to allow member wineries to use a specially created alliance logo on their bottles and in their advertising in return for following three very simple but very important guidelines. First, if any AVA name, any county name, or the state name is used on the label, 100 percent of the grapes must come from that named place. Second, all wines carrying a Washington place name must be made from 100 percent vinifera grapes and contain no **ADDITIVES** to flavor the wine or change the color or aroma. Third, the term "reserve" may be used only for wines that are made from 100 percent Washington grapes, and can be applied to a maximum of 10 percent of the winery's total production of any variety or 3,000 cases of that variety, whichever is the greater amount.

In effect, these laudable guidelines eliminate the use of generic labels bearing foreign place names such as Chablis and Burgundy, reinforce the principles that wine is a natural product and that the place of origin of the grapes matters, and give meaning and validity to the use of the term "reserve," whereas before there were no guidelines and wineries were free to call their entire production "reserve."

CLIMATE

Washington State contains two distinct climatic regions for grape growing, separated by the Cascade Mountains. On the western side of these mountains, toward the coast, a maritime climate experiences substantially more rainfall, and there are smaller swings between high and low temperatures. On the eastern side of the mountains, the continental climate approximates semidesert conditions, with much less rainfall, warmer days, and cooler nights. The lower rainfall means that vineyards must be irrigated, but it also means that there is less chance that rain at harvest time will increase the water content and lower the sugar content of the grapes, which would result in a thinner wine. The warm days make for good sugar and flavor development, while the cool nights help keep acid levels high, maintaining clean, crisp, but ripe flavors in the wines. Overall, the climate is cooler than in California, but the summer daylight hours are longer (an average of 17.5 hours), and the growing season is also longer, allowing all grape types to mature slowly and to reach full ripeness in most years. It is in the eastern part of the state that most of the grapes are grown and where most appellations have been approved.

WINE STYLES

Since Washington State concentrates almost entirely on vinifera grape growing, the wines are usually labeled by varietal names that are easily recognizable by American wine consumers. The naturally crisp, fruity style favored by the climate is enhanced by cool fermentation in stainless steel tanks for many of the white wines, especially Riesling, Sémillon, and Sauvignon Blanc. Occasionally, wood fermentation and wood aging is practiced on the latter two, and Chardonnay may be wood fermented and wood aged.

In red wines, Cabernet Sauvignon and Merlot can develop full, ripe fruit flavors in the vineyard, backed up by a substantial backbone of acid and tannin levels, which winemakers successfully balance with oak flavors from aging. So far, the reds have shown attractive, vibrant flavors when young, and a potential to develop, sometimes over two

Even as the days get cooler at the end of the growing season, grapes enjoy extended daylight hours in Washington State's Columbia Valley.

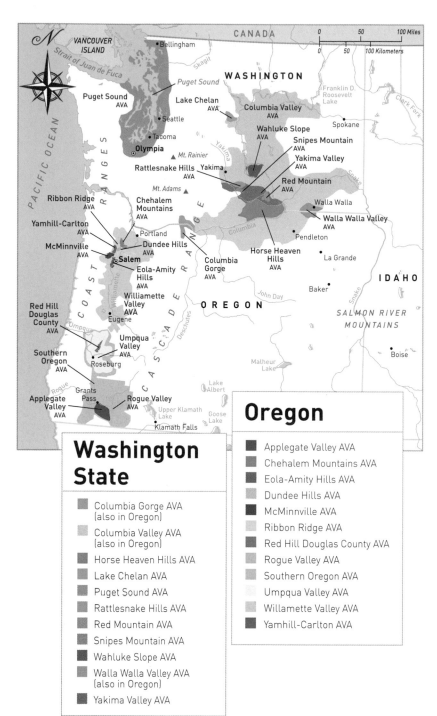

Washington State

- ■ Columbia Gorge AVA (also in Oregon)
- ■ Columbia Valley AVA (also in Oregon)
- ■ Horse Heaven Hills AVA
- ■ Lake Chelan AVA
- ■ Puget Sound AVA
- ■ Rattlesnake Hills AVA
- ■ Red Mountain AVA
- ■ Snipes Mountain AVA
- ■ Wahluke Slope AVA
- ■ Walla Walla Valley AVA (also in Oregon)
- ■ Yakima Valley AVA

Oregon

- ■ Applegate Valley AVA
- ■ Chehalem Mountains AVA
- ■ Eola-Amity Hills AVA
- ■ Dundee Hills AVA
- ■ McMinnville AVA
- ■ Ribbon Ridge AVA
- ■ Red Hill Douglas County AVA
- ■ Rogue Valley AVA
- ■ Southern Oregon AVA
- ■ Umpqua Valley AVA
- ■ Willamette Valley AVA
- ■ Yamhill-Carlton AVA

decades. In addition to the expected concentration on red Bordeaux grape types, there has been significant interest in the last five years in red Rhône varieties, especially Syrah, and in some Italian grape types.

REGIONS

There are eleven AVAs in Washington State, ranging from Region 1 through Region 3 in the UC Davis heat summation system. The largest appellation is Columbia Valley, and most of the state's other appellations fall within Columbia Valley. The major exception is Puget Sound on the western side of the Cascade Mountains around the cities of Seattle, Tacoma, and Olympia. The state's grape growers and winemakers continue to be involved in discussions to develop subappellations, an understandable evolution in an area that is growing so rapidly and learning more and more about the potential of specific sites for certain grape types. Growers and producers concentrate on Riesling, Sauvignon Blanc, Sémillon, Chenin Blanc, Cabernet Sauvignon, Merlot, Syrah, and Chardonnay.

COLUMBIA VALLEY

This is a huge AVA, covering 10.5 million acres/4.2 million hectares with only 7,000 acres/2,755 hectares currently planted with vineyards. The region encompasses six smaller subappellations and also extends southward into the state of Oregon. By any measure, Columbia Valley is an oddity as an appellation. First, it covers many acres of land that are not and may never be vineyards, but the appellation was originally drawn to include some outlying vineyard areas. The land in between simply got included. Second, its size is somewhat at odds with the whole concept of appellations, which attempts in most places to identify small tracts of land that produce grapes and wines of definable regional character. To suggest that a wine is "typically Columbia Valley–style" would not convey much meaning. Third, some would argue that grapes should not be grown at all in the semi-arid, almost desert conditions of this region. It is only the technology of modern irrigation systems that allows the grapes to grow at all.

Nevertheless, with irrigation, long growing seasons, and careful trellis selection, Columbia Valley vineyards are capable of producing consistently high yields of high-quality fruit, resulting in wines that are much admired around the world.

YAKIMA VALLEY

Within the larger Columbia Valley, the Yakima Valley appellation runs east to west from Yakima to Kennewick and covers the valley floor of the Yakima River and the surrounding foothills of the Toppenish Ridge and the Ahtanum Ridge. Temperatures here are generally cooler than in the Columbia Valley, though there are a couple of hot spots at the eastern and western extremes, both of them appropriately including the word *red* in their name. Red Willow Vineyard at the western end of the valley has emerged as an important site for growing several varieties, particularly Syrah, which has given Columbia Winery more than a decade of success. At the eastern end of the valley is Red Mountain, which recently earned its own appellation. Also within the Yakima Valley appellation are the Rattlesnake Hills AVA and the Snipes Mountain AVA.

RED MOUNTAIN

The broad slopes here, to the north of the Yakima River just around Richland, offer excellent southern exposure. Friable, mineral soils that encourage deep penetration of the root system and good airflow have given excellent results with Cabernet Sauvignon for several years, providing wines with dense, ripe fruit flavors and a lean, firm structure with enough acidity to keep the flavors fresh and firm, but without harsh tannins, allowing better development and aging of the wines.

RATTLESNAKE HILLS

Concentrating on the red varieties of Cabernet Sauvignon, Cabernet Franc, Syrah, and Merlot, this area has been a reliable source for many wineries, providing them with grapes of full varietal character. The south-facing slopes and higher elevation, up to 3,000 feet/914 meters, combine to give full ripeness with balanced acidity.

SNIPES MOUNTAIN

Distinguished by large, ancient river rock pebbles in the soil, this newly designated south-facing area promises to deliver more stellar wines from its plantings of mostly Cabernet Sauvignon and Syrah.

HORSE HEAVEN HILLS

Again, south-facing slopes and good elevation, up to 1,800 feet/549 meters, mediate against damage from frost, allowing for some intense varietal character to be achieved in red and white varieties, from Riesling to Cabernet Sauvignon. Like Rattlesnake Hills, grapes from these vineyards are highly prized by the region's winemakers.

WAHLUKE SLOPE

A particularly hot and dry area where irrigation is essential, the Wahluke Slope produces fruit of exceptional ripeness with full intensity of flavor. Not surprisingly, the usual red varieties dominate, but there is some Sauvignon Blanc and Chardonnay.

LAKE CHELAN

The newest of Washington State's appellations is also the most northerly, sitting at the eastern end of Lake Chelan where it meets the Columbia River. Developed originally as a vacation area and favorite second-home location, the newly approved appellation has shown great promise for cooler-climate white grape varieties such as Riesling and Chardonnay.

WALLA WALLA VALLEY

The Walla Walla River forms the basis for this appellation in the southeast corner of the state, with part of its acreage extending south into Oregon and its eastern edge rising rapidly into the Blue Mountains. In 2000, the appellation boundary was extended to include all of the area that has

The Wahluke Slope provides a warm microclimate on a broad, gentle, south-facing slope.

deposits of the same glacial silt loam that distinguishes this valley, and the new appellation now includes some of the older and historically important vineyard properties that inexplicably had been left out of the original appellation. The warmer valley floor has proven very successful for Cabernet Sauvignon and Merlot, while the cooler hillsides show promise for Riesling and Gewürztraminer. Among the best producers are the highly noted Leonetti Cellar, Woodward Canyon (with thirty years of success with Cabernet Sauvignon under its belt), L'Ecole No. 41, Glen Fiona (concentrating on Rhône styles), Cayuse Cellars, and Walla Walla Vintners.

COLUMBIA GORGE

This new AVA is adjacent to the southeastern end of the Columbia Valley appellation in a transition zone from dry-and-warm to moist-and-cool. The cooler maritime influences in the Gorge make the area more suitable to white varieties such as Chardonnay, Pinot Gris, Riesling, and Gewürztraminer.

PUGET SOUND

This appellation covers a large area from Mount Baker and the San Juan Islands north of Seattle to as far south as Olympia at the base of Puget Sound, which separates the Olympic Peninsula from the mainland. There are twenty-five wineries in this appellation, though most of them are very small. They include several wineries started by hob-

Cobblestone vineyards of Cayuse Cellars in Walla Walla

byists, often using other fruits as well as grapes, and they range from those who use their own fruit to those who truck in grapes from the interior appellations. The area includes three outstanding wineries: Andrew Will, Quilceda Creek, and McCrea Cellars.

Oregon

There are currently over three hundred wineries in Oregon, with around 44,000 acres/18,000 hectares of vinifera grape types. The wine industry received a major boost in the 1960s with the immigration of California winemakers looking for the challenge of cooler, marginal climates associated with specific grape types. As such, there has always been somewhat of an air of rebellion and individuality surrounding Oregon wine, though this has certainly not hampered the drive to produce wines of very high caliber; in fact, that attitude has probably helped push Oregon wines solidly into the realm of excellence.

The preoccupation with specific grape types in certain locations has helped build Oregon's reputation as a producer of occasionally fine Pinot Noir. But the concentration of the international press on Pinot Noir is a disservice to the other grapes that can do very well here, such as Pinot Gris, Riesling, Chardonnay, and Gewürztraminer.

Perhaps as part of their individualistic attitude, many of the pioneer growers planted their new vineyards on their own roots, rather than grafting the vinifera vines onto American rootstock. This proved to be an unwise decision: Phylloxera was first identified in vineyards in northern Oregon in 1990; by 1995, thirteen vineyards were positively identified as infected, and by 1999, the number had risen to forty-five. Replanting of infected vineyards on resistant rootstock has followed, and using resistant rootstock in new vineyards has become the norm. On a more positive note, several Oregon vineyards have become active leaders in sustainable agriculture by participating in a number of different programs. From the 2008 vintage onward, the Oregon Wine Board launched the Oregon Certified Sustainable (OCS) logo to be used on labels by wineries that participate in any of the national and international sustainable-agriculture programs such as LIVE (Low Input Viticulture and Enology), Demeter Certified Biodynamic, Oregon Tilth, and Vinea: The Winegrowers' Sustainable Trust, all of which promote biodiversity and a broad concern for the environment in all stages of grape growing and winemaking.

CLIMATE

While Washington State has its semiarid conditions in the Columbia Valley, the climate in Oregon's major grape-growing regions is much more maritime, producing more marginal conditions for successful grape growing. The main grape-growing regions in Oregon are situated on the western side of the Cascade Mountains in river valleys that run mostly north-south, only about 60 miles/100 kilometers from the Pacific Ocean, with cooler temperatures and more rainfall than other West Coast grape-growing regions. The soaring Cascade Mountains cause the moisture-laden air to leave most of the precipitation on their western side, where all but a few of the vineyards are located, and the most heavily planted areas experience around 40 inches/100 centimeters of rain per year, most of it falling in the autumn and winter months.

Moving southward from Portland, through Eugene and Grant's Pass to the California border, the rainfall tapers off until it averages only 20 inches/50 centimeters per year in central and southern Oregon. This means that winemakers in the northern areas have more to contend with in terms of molds associated with moist air, and they have to carefully weigh the risks and benefits of leaving grapes out in the vineyards in the fall months, when the risk of serious rain becomes greater. Those who are willing to take that risk are sometimes repaid with an Indian summer that helps bring the grapes to full varietal character.

On the western side of the vineyards, there is a small coastal range of mountains that keeps the worst of the Pacific storms away and helps trap warm summer air in the vineyards. Temperatures vary in the same way that the rainfall does, with cooler temperatures in the northern growing regions that favor Pinot Noir, Riesling, Pinot Gris, and Chardonnay, and warmer temperatures further south near Grant's Pass, where growers have had good success with Syrah, Cabernet Sauvignon, and Merlot.

WINE STYLES

As in Washington State, a small amount of wine is produced using fruit other than grapes. Otherwise, wine production is all from vinifera varieties. Oregon does not allow generic labeling of wine, and wines labeled as varietal must be made from at least 90 percent of the named variety (except Cabernet Sauvignon, for which the minimum is 75 percent). Because their region is cool, Oregon

growers and producers have concentrated on grape varieties recommended for Region 1 and have had great success with Pinot Noir. In years with enough sun and warmth, Oregon's Pinot Noirs develop vibrant purple hues and attractive cherry fruit aromas and flavors, with a good structural backbone of tannin and acidity, typical of well-made cool-climate Pinot Noir wines. In recent years, the style of the Pinot Noirs has become more defined, offering more suppleness and smooth texture, as some of the developmental winemaking problems have been ironed out.

Chardonnay was slow to receive the same kind of acclaim, probably because most growers started with the same clone of Chardonnay that had been widely used in California's warmer climate, which meant that the grapes never really developed the varietal character typical of a cool climate. New plantings of Burgundian cool-climate clones have had much more success, with leaner structure, crisper acidity, and a greater depth and complexity of apple, citrus, pear, and melon flavors. The negative reaction to Oregon's original versions of unripe Chardonnay has

---

TOP: *Freshly harvested Pinot Noir grapes* BOTTOM: *Pinot Gris has captured the attention of Oregon's producers and consumers everywhere.*

had a lingering effect, though. Growers are still hesitant to plant it, with the result that Chardonnay still occupies less than 1,000 acres/405 hectares in Oregon, compared with Pinot Noir's almost 8,000 acres/3,237 hectares.

In the absence of commendable Chardonnay, Pinot Gris became the white wine darling of the northern Oregon industry, offering ripe, slightly tropical fruit flavors, in a dry style, with a richness of texture close to some Alsace Pinot Gris wines but without the excessive exotic fruit character that typifies those wines. Some growers and producers have also received acclaim for Riesling, Chenin Blanc, Müller-Thurgau, Pinot Gris, and Gewürztraminer.

Further south, the warmer climate offers the opportunity to grow a broader variety of grapes, especially Cabernet Sauvignon and Merlot, and some growers have even experimented with plantings of Tempranillo and Syrah.

REGIONS

There are sixteen AVAs either entirely or partially within Oregon. Almost all of them are named after river valleys or hills, demonstrating the importance of climate and soil conditions provided by those valleys, with deeper and more complex soil profiles on the valley slopes and hills, along with better sun exposure and frost and wind protection. Twelve of the appellations lie completely within Orgeon, while small portions of the Columbia Valley, Columbia Gorge, and Walla Walla Valley appellations extend from Washington State into Oregon, and part of the Snake River Valley extends from Idaho into eastern Oregon.

WILLAMETTE VALLEY
Centered on the Willamette River and stretching south from the Columbia River at Portland to Cottage Grove,

just south of Eugene, this is the largest and best-known of Oregon's AVAs. It is home to most of the state's wineries, including many of its finest, such as Ponzi, Serene, Sokol-Blosser, Adelsheim, and Eyrie. Both Robert Drouhin of Burgundy and Brian Croser of Australia's Petaluma winery have purchased property here to plant vineyards and establish wineries. All of these names represent an impressive mix of some of the early pioneers and the newcomers. What is particularly impressive is that foreigners, well schooled for centuries in the fine art of growing and making Pinot Noir, have seen fit to invest heavily in this area, a tribute to the pioneers who first recognized it as an area with potential. Many parts of the appellation show a distinct red tinge to the soil, a result of iron deposits that are considered to be an important element in the development of structure and body in Pinot Noir wines.

In general, the valley can be described as a series of hills and smaller valleys, providing some excellent south- and east-facing slopes and a good mix of clay and loam soils, as well as excellent airflow and water drainage. The mix of soils and microclimates in those smaller valleys has inevitably led to the establishment of six subappellations within the larger Willamette Valley AVA. Throughout the Willamette Valley, Pinot Noir and Pinot Gris have established a reputation as a monarchical pair that deserves the loving loyalty of growers, winemakers, and consumers. The six subappellations that have emerged from within the Willamette Valley are Chehalem Mountains, Dundee Hills, Eola-Amity Hills, McMinnville, Ribbon Ridge, and Yamhill-Carlton District.

CHEHALEM MOUNTAINS
A complex mix of deep volcanic soils with iron content, sandstone spotted with quartz, and fine-grained loess provides a patchwork of soils within this subappellation, allowing for a variety of grape types that can be grown successfully. Pinot Noir and Pinot Gris still dominate. Most of the vineyards are in the southwest corner of this sprawling subappellation, with some of the highest elevations in Oregon, from 200 to 1,600 feet/60 to 488 meters.

DUNDEE HILLS
The Dundee Hills, around the town of Dundee, are home to land that is particularly favorable for Pinot Noir, with

Some of Domaine Drouhin's vines catching the last rays of the sun in the Willamette Valley.

a rich, loamy-clay soil formed from volcanic basalt. The result is wines of deep complexity and elegance, with a distinct mineral character.

EOLA-AMITY HILLS

The Eola-Amity Hills, around McCoy, are also considered a fine site for Pinot Noir and Pinot Gris. Relatively shallow volcanic and sedimentary soils provide some complexity of mineral character, while cool nighttime temperatures keep the fruit characteristics fresh and lively.

MCMINNVILLE

This area has become somewhat of a mecca for Pinot Noir lovers, with the always sold-out annual Pinot Noir festival attracting many to McMinnville every year, where the pains and pleasures of making this wine are ardently discussed. The wines from here always show clean, red berry fruit character with good acidity and tannin levels.

RIBBON RIDGE

An extension of the Chehalem Mountain subappellation, this area rejoices in a warm, temperate climate that more often results in a fuller, richer style than Chehalem, which emphasizes ripe fruit.

YAMHILL-CARLTON DISTRICT

The Yamhill Foothills to the north are based mostly on sandstone soils, creating wines with good berry fruit notes and lower acidity for wines of immediate appeal.

SOUTHERN OREGON

This relatively new appellation, recognized in 2004, is intended as an umbrella appellation for all the appellations south of the Willamette Valley. Its range of varied soils and climate reinforce the notion that it is intended primarily as a catchall appellation to allow blending of wines from grapes grown in two or three of its constituent subappellations.

UMPQUA VALLEY

This appellation lies immediately to the south of the Willamette Valley and is separated from it by the Calapooya Divide, which reaches a height of more than 3,000 feet/925 meters. Like the Willamette Valley, the Umpqua Valley AVA is centered on its namesake river and covers a landscape of small valleys and hillsides. The Umpqua appellation is very much a transition zone, especially in terms of climate, with cooler, wetter conditions in the northern sector where the favorite grapes tend to be Pinot Noir, Pinot Gris, Riesling, Chardonnay, and Gewürztraminer. Warmer, drier conditions in the south mean that growers are more likely to experiment with Cabernet Sauvignon, Merlot, Syrah, and Tempranillo.

Umpqua has a slightly longer history of grape growing and was the site of Oregon's first modern-era winery (Hillcrest Vineyards, founded in 1962), but subsequent growth was slow. Of the early pioneers, Hillcrest is still in operation and produces some of the state's best Pinot Noir and Chardonnay, as well as some very fine Riesling and one of Oregon's rare Zinfandels. The Henry Estate winery, another pioneer from 1978, continues to produce stylish Gewürztraminer and Pinot Gris. Within the last decade, there has been substantial growth, with new plantings and new wineries coming on the scene. Much of this is a reaction to expensive land in Willamette, but it also reflects a desire to take advantage of the unique microclimates that Umpqua offers.

RED HILL DOUGLAS COUNTY

A distinct enclave within the Umpqua Valley, this subappellation is blessed with high elevations, from 800 to 1,200 feet/244 to 366 meters, and a cool climate, with maritime influence. Its cool climate and volcanic red soils, similar to the Dundee Hills, make it highly suited to Pinot Noir, Pinot Gris, and Chardonnay.

LEFT: *Steeply planted sections of the Dundee Hills* RIGHT: *Bethel Heights vineyards in the Eola-Amity Hills*

ROGUE VALLEY

Established in 1992, eight years after the Willamette and Umpqua Valley appellations, this appellation still seems to drift, albeit enthusiastically, in different directions as it discovers its many possibilities. It may be that it is too diverse for its own good, and insiders are already talking about the need for more subappellations based on the three river systems (Rogue, Illinois, and Applegate) that flow through the area. Located in the southern part of Oregon, close to California, the climate of the overall appellation is generally warmer, since it has not only the Cascade Mountains to the east and the Coastal Range to the west, but also the Siskiyou Mountains to the south, thereby creating a heat trap that allows high-elevation vineyards to produce some promising Cabernet Sauvignon and Merlot wines. However, there are warmer areas and cooler ones, and the soils vary from granite to sand and silt.

Within the Rogue Valley appellation, the Rogue River valley runs generally to the northwest and is the warmest zone, favoring the planting of Cabernet and Merlot, and even promises good results with Rhône or Italian varieties. The Illinois River valley offers a different climate, its proximity to the ocean providing cooler sites for Pinot Noir, Pinot Gris, and Chardonnay.

APPLEGATE VALLEY

Essentially a subappellation of the Rogue Valley AVA, the Applegate Valley AVA stretches north from the California border for about fifty miles. Recognized for its warmer climate, growers concentrate on Cabernet, Merlot, and Syrah. Cool nights help maintain high acidity in the wines.

COLUMBIA VALLEY

Situated east of the Cascade Mountains, the Oregon vineyards in the southernmost portion of the Columbia Valley have to contend with the dry, semidesert conditions that most Washington State vineyards deal with. There are now fifty wineries in the Oregon portion. Some vineyards enjoy cooler conditions similar to parts of the Columbia Gorge and concentrate on Chardonnay, Riesling, and Gewürztraminer. In the warmer, drier areas, Cabernet Sauvignon, Merlot, and Syrah are the more likely choices.

WALLA WALLA VALLEY

The Oregon portion of this appellation has seen considerable growth in the number of vineyards planted, with the number now at thirty-one. Of those, the Seven Hills Vineyard continues its excellent reputation for Bordeaux and Rhône grape varieties that are eagerly sought by both Oregon and Washington wineries.

COLUMBIA GORGE

Many wine and grape people have been attracted to this diverse area, as evidenced by the thirteen wineries and twenty-six vineyards that dot the Oregon side of the appellation. Cooler maritime influences in the west favor the typical cool-climate varieties, while the warmer, drier eastern section is planted with Bordeaux and Rhône varieties.

SNAKE RIVER VALLEY

Located in the extreme eastern portion of Oregon, this appellation spreads into southwestern Idaho where most of the acreage is located. As in the Idaho portion, cool-climate varieties are favored in the Oregon section because of the short growing season, high elevations (2,000 to 3,000 feet/610 to 914 meters), and the extreme variations between daytime and nighttime temperatures.

Idaho

CLIMATE

The main grape-growing area in Idaho is just across the border from Oregon in the Snake River Valley in the southwestern corner of the state. This area offers the most moderate climate, with the rest of the state generally being typically continental, with very cold, sometimes harsh winters and hot, dry summers. There is little rainfall in the Snake River area, and irrigation is necessary. However, the biggest challenge is the abrupt arrival of cold fall weather, which cuts short the growing season and makes it difficult to achieve full ripeness and flavor development.

WINE STYLES

Region 1 grapes are the most suitable, but even Chardonnay can have difficulty developing full varietal character. Riesling, Gewürztraminer, and Chenin Blanc have performed better, showing crisp, clean flavors and tart acidity.

Grape growing and winemaking take place mostly in the western end of the Snake River Valley (AVA approved in 2007). Ste. Chapelle is the largest producer, and Hells Canyon is a leading boutique.

SOUTHWESTERN UNITED STATES

COVERING A BROAD RANGE of climates and microclimates, the whole southwestern corner of the United States has witnessed a revitalization of its wine industry, based mostly on careful selection of vinifera grape types according to climate and soil suitability. Many people believe that this area of the United States is too hot and dry for successful grape growing. That sentiment is perhaps reinforced by recent weather patterns, with some areas in the southwest experiencing extended periods over 90°F and, in some cases, several consecutive days over 100°F. The danger for grape growers is not just the shortage of water that usually accompanies such weather patterns, but the likelihood that the vine will simply shut down in extreme temperatures. The result is that out of extremely hot seasons come wines that, ironically, are not overripe but show signs of underdevelopment. There are increasing challenges to finding ways to counteract these extremes of climate. The usual solution is higher elevations to avoid vine shutdown and to ensure cooler temperatures and thus obtain suitable acidity levels in the grapes and the wines. Water shortages are a persistent problem, with increased competition between agricultural needs and residential demands.

Texas

With slow but gradual growth, Texas now has approximately 4,000 acres/1,600 hectares of vineyards planted, with vinifera varieties in the majority. The state also has eight AVAs. In general, the Texas wine industry is dominated by a few very large wineries, such as Ste. Genevieve, Llano Estacado, and Fall Creek, backed up by a number of much smaller enterprises. The climatic extremes of Texas present some serious challenges to grape growing, with the range of weather hazards including hail, spring and fall frosts, and high humidity, which promotes molds and mildew in the grape bunches. A general criticism would be that yields remain high, sometimes over 8 tons per acre/100 hectoliters per hectare, a factor that will almost always result in good, marketable wine, but not great wines that reflect the individuality of any specific grape type from a particular place.

In the western part of the state, there are a number of wineries in the cool Texas High Plains AVA, around the town of Lubbock, at elevations that average 3,500 feet/1,075 meters. The most prominent wineries in the High Plains AVA are Llano Estacado and Pheasant Ridge, both producing some fine examples of crisp, fruity vinifera whites such as Riesling and Chardonnay, and lean but stylish Cabernet Sauvignon. In addition, well-established vineyards such as Newsom Vineyards produce grapes that winemakers across the state are willing to pay high prices for.

LEFT: *Evening at Flat Creek Vineyards in the Texas Hill Country* RIGHT: *An older vine at the well-established Bell Mountain Vineyards*

HAWKES BAY

WAIRARAPA

COONAWARRA

STELLENBOSCH

casablanca

ACONCAGUA

CARMENÈRE

HUNTER VALLEY

McLAREN VALE

MARLBOROUGH

TORRONTÉS

MALBEC

MAIPO

BAROSSA

mendoza

pinotage

THE SOUTHERN HEMISPHERE

CHAPTER

6

THE MOST IMPORTANT winemaking countries of the Southern Hemisphere are Chile and Argentina in South America, Australia and New Zealand in Oceania, and South Africa. The global wine industry has embraced the wines of the Southern Hemisphere, as it contains some of the most dynamic wine regions in the world. These regions have far exceeded any reasonably optimistic production and export goals for quality wines.

At the same time that Brazil's wine industry seems to be finding its way in fits and starts, Uruguay has found a signature grape—the red Tannat—that is attracting attention in the export market. World-weary wine watchers have reason to celebrate the fact that both Argentina and South Africa, after a dormant period—for lack of an organized export program in Argentina and diminishing quality in South Africa—are now again producing fine wines for export.

The white and sparkling wines of all the Southern Hemisphere countries have a distinct advantage over those of the Northern Hemisphere: They can appear in the marketplace about six months earlier. The Southern Hemisphere harvest is in the warm months of February and March, instead of September and October. In other words, the first vintage 2011 wines reach Northern Hemisphere stores in fall 2011, instead of spring 2012. Reds also appear earlier, but only light reds or *nouveau*-style wines would show up in the export market during the harvest year.

Another advantage is that Southern Hemisphere producers use varietal labels, and the average consumer looking for good value in wine is more comfortable buying a wine labeled Chardonnay than a wine labeled with an unknown, often unpronounceable place name. Consumer-friendly labeling helps sell the wines of the Southern Hemisphere.

Not so long ago, Southern Hemisphere wines were thought of as abundant in quantity but poor in quality. However, in the late 1970s and early 1980s, many winemakers began to move away from fortified and jug wines toward premium table wines made from popular varieties. As the quality-to-price ratio improved, many Southern Hemisphere wines gained both visibility and market acceptance. The potential for further growth, in both acreage and quality, is confirmed by the very large amount of capital investment by European and American wine companies pouring into Chile, Argentina, Australia, New Zealand, and South Africa.

A disadvantage for grape growers and wine producers in the Southern Hemisphere is a tendency toward irregular and unreliable weather patterns, making harvest predictions difficult. The countries of the Southern Hemisphere, with far less landmass than those of the Northern Hemisphere, are all affected by the westerlies, winds that blow across the surrounding oceans. Precipitation often occurs offshore, before it can reach the vineyards, so many areas must be irrigated. Most Southern Hemisphere vineyard areas were established by the sea, where European

this has been a problem in Chile, as quality was sacrificed for quantity. The modern Chilean wine industry, however, with its emphasis on exports, has been radically redefined by a new attitude that stresses balanced yields in the vineyards and better quality in the wines.

History

Vinifera vines were introduced to Chile by the Spanish explorer Cortés, circa 1523. Some commercial vineyards were planted as early as 1554, and there has been continuous wine production in the area surrounding Chile's capital, Santiago, for at least four centuries. Even though Spain, in a vain attempt to protect its export market, tried to ban new vineyards in Chile during the late seventeenth century, by the early eighteenth century Chile developed a reputation for producing large quantities of inexpensive but drinkable wines.

In the 1830s, the Chilean government established the Quinta Normal, an experimental nursery for a wide range of plants, including vinifera cuttings. The development of this agricultural station was a turning point in the Chilean wine industry, because it allowed Chile to isolate cuttings of vinifera vines just at the time when phylloxera was ravaging Europe.

During the nineteenth century, the gentry of Chile established vinifera vineyards, more often than not employing expatriate French winemakers who had been either financially wiped out or terrified by the phylloxera epidemic in their native country. The Chilean wine industry was quite

LEFT: *An old vine, between eighty and a hundred years old, untouched by phylloxera and still bearing fruit, at the Torres vineyard in Chile's Curicó Valley* TOP RIGHT: *The Torres Manso de Velasco old vines vineyard* BOTTOM RIGHT: *Mugron, the bending of the vine to plant a new vine, without the use of nursery rootstock. When the vine takes root, it is cut from the parent. This type of planting can be done in both Chile and South Australia because they have never experienced an outbreak of phylloxera, so vines can be planted on their own roots.*

healthy, especially in light of phylloxera in Europe, and began to be taxed heavily as the twentieth century arrived.

Because of the burden of taxation and political instability, by 1980 almost half of Chile's vines had been pulled out of the ground. By 1985, bulk wine brought the equivalent of 5 cents per liter, and by 1990, two-thirds of the nation's vineyards had been replanted with stone fruits. Political instability, especially Chile's bloody transition from the socialism of the late Salvador Allende to the military dictatorship of the late General Pinochet in the late twentieth century, was detrimental not only to basic human rights, but also to the country's vineyards. The return of the vineyards from collective to private ownership (beginning in 1982, when the vineyards were all but worthless, largely due to abandonment because of high taxes) has not been without some major problems. However, since 1987, when the government lifted price controls and decreased draconian taxes, more than 70,000 acres/28,000 hectares of new vineyards have been planted with premium vinifera grapes, with an eye to an ever-expanding export market, especially the United States. Currently, Chile has vineyard plantings of about 292,500 acres/117,000 hectares.

While French varieties are planted for the international market, the local, everyday wine consumed by Chileans is Viño Pippero, made mostly from Pais grapes. In a concerted effort to curb alcoholism, the government limits local consumption to a generous 10 gallons/40 liters per capita yearly, even though actual per capita consumption is about 4.25 gallons/16 liters, which ranks about twenty-eighth in the world. Liberal production and grape-yield quotas are enforced, and excess production is distilled into industrial alcohol.

Red Wines

Chile is primarily red wine country, perhaps due to the nation's Spanish cultural roots. The wines can be charming, with forward fruit and aromas and flavors of red currants, strawberries, blackberries, and red plums. Chile's Cabernet Sauvignon and Merlot wines are extremely popular in the North American export market. Until recently, the wines were seen as one-dimensional bargains, delivering varietal character at an affordable price but most often lacking the complexity of the finer wines of Bordeaux and California's North Coast. These wines are food-friendly and approachable at an early age, with limited cellaring potential.

Although Chile entered the export market by successfully providing drinkable red wines at highly affordable prices, Chile has not confined itself to bargain wines. While it is still easy to find dozens of inexpensive red wines from Chile, there are now some compelling wines with international reputations being produced, often, but not always, in partnership with internationally recognized American or European wine producers. When these wines, which start at retail prices of about $25 and top out at close to $100, were first introduced to the international retail wine market, the reaction was something akin to sticker shock, but when the wines were tasted seriously, it was hard to argue with their pricing.

For Chile to establish itself in the luxury tier of export wines, ironically it has to overcome its reputation as a supplier of bargain brands to responsive consumers looking for value. Just because someone enjoys an inexpensive Chilean Cabernet Sauvignon at home, it does not mean that she or he will be willing to spend more than $100 for a fine

LEFT: *The most important grape in Chile is Cabernet Sauvignon. Chile's reputation rests on good, affordable varietal wines, such as this Cassilero del Diablo by Concha y Toro.* **MIDDLE:** *In Chile, Merlot is both a varietal-labeled wine and also blended with Cabernet Sauvignon.* **RIGHT:** *Carmenère is an important varietal in Chile, producing single-varietal wines and blends with Cabernet and Merlot.*

THE NEW CHILE: WORLD-CLASS WINES AT WORLD-CLASS PRICES

Chile made its reputation in the export market for value-driven red wines, mostly Cabernet Sauvignon and Merlot. Starting in the late 1990s, a new class of red wines began to appear: beautifully made and expensive wines from prized vineyard sites, with prices to match. The response of the North American consumer has so far been decidedly mixed, and some of the wines have had to lower their initial high prices to gain a foothold in the United States retail and restaurant wine market. Currently, when a restaurant customer is willing to spend more than $100 for a bottle of wine, the first country of origin the customer thinks of is usually not Chile. The following are some of the ultra-premium Chilean reds:

- **Alpha M**, made by the well-respected Chilean vintner Aurelio Mantes from Cabernet Sauvignon with a bit of Merlot and Cabernet Franc sourced from the La Finca de Apalta estate in the Aconcagua Valley. Introduced in 1996 at a retail price of about $60, Montes made about 800 cases; only 150 reached the U.S. market, where it sold out quickly. This ageworthy wine now sells for about $80, and Montes produces about 9,000 cases.

- **Seña** was a partnership between the Robert Mondavi Winery and the Chadwick family of Viña Errazuriz. Seña is now wholly owned by Eduardo Chadwick. Seña retails for about $75 and is a blend of Colchagua Valley Cabernet Sauvignon, Merlot, and Carmenère. Only 2,000 cases of the inaugural 1995 vintage were produced, almost all for the U.S. market.

- **Veramonte** is owned by wine giant Constellation and is run by its founder and former owner, Agustin Huneeus, owner of Napa Valley's Quintessa and the former chairman of California's Franciscan Estates (see page 135), and his son, also named Agustin. Huneeus is Chilean by birth and has a long history in the Chilean premium wine industry. Veramonte focuses on Casablanca as the best region to produce wines from Cabernet Sauvignon, Chardonnay, and Merlot, and constructed a state-of-the-art winery there, complete with Casablanca's first hospitality and wine education center. Veramonte's varietal wines sell for less than $15 in the United States and have received both critical and popular attention. Veramonte's Primus, a blend of Merlot, Cabernet Sauvignon, and Carmenère, is an excellent wine that sells at an affordable price, usually less than $20 per bottle.

- **Almaviva** is a blend of Cabernet Sauvignon, Carmenère, and sometimes Cabernet Franc, produced by Concha y Toro in partnership with the esteemed Château Mouton Rothschild of Bordeaux. A new $5 million winery was built in the Maipo Valley to produce Almaviva, and the grapes were sourced from Concha y Toro's finest vineyard in Puente Alto, the source for its famous and much-heralded **Don Melchor** Cabernet Sauvignon. The retail price of Almaviva and Don Melchor: each about $75. Concha y Toro also produces a fantastic "Marques de Casa Concha" Cabernet Sauvignon, made from grapes grown in their Puente Alto vineyards, which retails for less than $20.

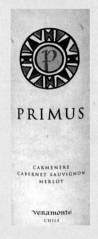

- **Le Dix de Los Vascos** is 100 percent Cabernet Sauvignon; the inaugural 1996 and 1997 vintages were released in 1999. Los Vascos, whose vineyards are sited in the Colchagua Valley, has been wholly owned by Baron Eric de Rothschild of Château Lafite Rothschild since 1988. Le Dix de Los Vascos is only released in superior vintage years, and no more than 3,000 cases are produced in each vintage. Retail price: $45. Also produced: a fine Los Vascos Grande Reserve (100 percent Cabernet Sauvignon) that sells for less than $20.
- **Casa Lapostolle** is owned by Alexandra Marnier-Lapostolle, scion of the family that created Grand Marnier liqueur. The strategy is to produce accessible wine in the $10 to $20 range from large vineyard holdings in the Colchagua Valley, but also more expensive wines from the tiny dry-farmed, old vine Apalta vineyards in the valley. Lapostolle's ultra-premium red wine, Clos Apalta, is a blend of Carmenère, Merlot, and Cabernet Sauvignon that sells for about $70. The winery is a $12 million state-of-the-art facility; the consulting winemaker is Bordeaux enologist Michel Rolland.
- **Cordillera**, a Chilean Rhone Ranger, has been made since 1988 from a small, low-yielding hillside planting of Carinena (Carignane), blended with a bit of Syrah. The grapes are grown on an estate in the Linares district of the Curicó Valley owned by Miguel Torres of the famous Spanish wine family. The price is about $80, but the wine is difficult to find in the United States. Another single-vineyard wine produced by Torres, also in the Curicó Valley, is **Manso de Velasco**, which is 100 percent Cabernet Sauvignon, easier to find, and sells for about $40. Torres also produces a single-vineyard Chardonnay here, as well as a sparkling wine.

Chilean Cabernet Sauvignon in a restaurant. Chile must find its rightful place on the luxury products radar screen for its fine wines to succeed with a sizeable audience.

The single most important varietal in Chile is Cabernet Sauvignon; it is the grape that defines the Chilean wine industry. In 2008, plantings of Cabernet Sauvignon accounted for about 102,500 acres/41,000 hectares, or about 35 percent of total wine grapes planted in Chile. Merlot, which is produced as its own varietal wine and is often blended with Cabernet Sauvignon, accounts for about 12 percent of plantings.

Carmenère is an important red grape in Chile, although its origins are in the vineyards of Bordeaux, where it once was used as a blending grape. There is practically no Carmenère left in Bordeaux, but it does account for about 7 percent of plantings in Chile, where it is produced as a varietal wine but is also favored as a blender with Cabernet Sauvignon. At one time, Carmenère was mistakenly identified as Merlot in Chile's vineyards (some say it was on purpose, as Merlot is a more marketable varietal name in export markets), but that confusion appears to have largely resolved itself.

Other important red wine grapes in Chile are Syrah, Pinot Noir, and Cabernet Franc. There are about 2,500 acres/1,000 hectares of Malbec planted, but that grape is far more important in Argentina (see page 219).

White Wines

Chile's white wines span the spectrum of styles, from oxidized wines heavy with the flavors of the local *rauli* casks (made from beech) and little acidity and fruit to delicate, fresh, high-tech white wines made by cool fermentation. Modern winemakers now rarely use *rauli* casks, and then only for storage. They are far more likely to use the smaller **ALLIER** and **TRONÇAIS** French oak *barriques* or American oak barrels for aging. Many of Chile's white wines don't use oak at all, however, especially its Sauvignon Blanc, opting for the fresh aromas and flavors provided by cool fermentations in stainless steel.

Even more critical than winemaking technology to the success of Chilean white wines is the proper siting of white wine vineyards. Until the late 1990s these vineyards were sited alongside successful Cabernet Sauvignon vineyards, and little attention was paid to the flabbiness of the white wines coming from such warm environs. During the last twenty years, however, there has been a growing recognition that Chile can in fact make fine white wines, but the vineyards for these wines must be located closer to the Pacific Coast. The Casablanca Valley is now the premier region for Chilean whites, especially Sauvignon Blanc. The Leyda region, located within the larger San Antonio Valley, with its first vineyards planted in 1998 and less than 3 miles/4.5 kilometers from the Pacific Ocean, is even cooler than Casablanca and produces sometimes stunning Sauvignon Blanc and Chardonnay from its low-yielding, granite-based soils.

There is actually a little bit more Sauvignon Blanc (including some Sauvignonasse in the census, we would imagine) than Chardonnay planted in Chile, but not by much. Each variety accounts for about 21,500 acres/8,600 hectares, or about 7 percent each of total plantings. There is also quite a bit of Muscat planted in Chile (for sweet and fortified wines) and very small amounts of Riesling, Viognier, and Gewürztraminer.

Just as Carmenère used to be identified as Merlot, Sauvignon Blanc in Chile suffered its own identity crisis. For quite a while, up to the beginning of the twenty-first century, true Sauvignon Blanc was virtually nonexistent in Chile. What was labeled as Sauvignon Blanc was actually Sauvignonasse (the name means "Sauvignon-like"), a variety biologically related to Italy's Friulano (see page 409) and not at all related to Sauvignon Blanc. There is still a healthy amount of Sauvignonasse planted in Chile, and most of that wine sells for less than $10, so if you like it, drink it, and don't worry about it.

In the production of both red and white wines, Chile has had and continues to have three problems, two of which are not difficult to surmount: permitting too-high yields in the vineyards and harvesting grapes from vines that are too young. There is much evidence that as the country's modern wine industry matures, Chilean growers and producers are grappling with these problems, and improvements can be seen everywhere. The third difficulty, lack of diversity in vineyard sites, is a long-term problem that began when wealthy Chileans, many of them copper and coal barons, established their vineyards close to the capital city of Santiago. Just as producers of white wines need to look to Chile's southern Pacific coastline, so do growers of red grapes and producers of red wines. In the past ten years, several growers and producers have confronted this challenge. Not content to ride the Cabernet-and-Merlot wave that its traditional vineyard sites and winemaking technology provide, winemakers have been siting their vines much more carefully and are beginning to produce fine examples of Syrah and Pinot Noir, as well as Sauvignon Blanc and Chardonnay.

Chilean producers have also been focusing on single-vineyard sites and separate vineyard blocks to produce wines with unique characteristics and reds for long aging. Chile has long been accused of creating cookie-cutter wines to satisfy a thirsty, thrifty public, and those wines continue to serve an important purpose—providing drinkable, affordable wine on a mass scale. However, in the long run, what people who care about fine wine are willing to pay for is site and vintage character; varietal character is a given. Chile must diversify its vineyard sites if it is to maintain its well-earned position as a New World wine leader. Chile has proven and continues to prove that it can produce singular wines from the best growing sites, thus ensuring the future of its wine industry in an increasingly competitive, quality-driven world wine market.

Wine Laws and Traditions

Traditionally, the best wines of Chile have been varietal-proprietary wines. Following the name of the variety on the label, the producer is free to use a different name and criterion for each high-end product. For example, Santa Rita uses Medalla Real, while Concha y Toro (Chile's largest winery, which exports 90 percent of their estate wines) uses both Marques de Casa Concha and Don Melchor as quality designations for two of their best varietal wines (e.g., Don Melchor Cabernet Sauvignon).

Wines labeled as varietal must be made from at least 75 percent of that variety. If the name of a particular wine region appears on a label, at least 75 percent of the grapes must have been grown in that region. For vintage-dated wines, at least 75 percent of the grapes must have been harvested during that vintage year. The term *reserva especial* seems to have no meaning. Estate bottling is osten-

SINGLE VINEYARD
DON MAXIMIANO ESTATE

Varietal: *Sauvignon Blanc*
Comments: *From a single vineyard site, a wine that is a true expression of its unique location.* Vintage:

ERRAZURIZ

Sauvignon Blanc, especially from Chile's Casablanca Valley and the Leyda region, can be superb.

sibly controlled, and the wine must be grown, produced, and bottled by the "estate," or named producer.

Chilean wine laws stipulate that export white wines must attain a minimum alcohol level of 12 percent and reds 11.5 percent. While *reserva especial* is strictly a marketing term, there are aging requirements for wines labeled with similar terms: for *especial*, it is two years; for *reserva*, it is four years; and for *gran vino*, it is six years minimum. *Finas* are varietal-labeled wines made from government-recognized grape types, mostly vinifera, such as Cabernet Sauvignon or Sauvignon Blanc.

Wine Regions

THE CENTRAL VALLEY AND RAPEL VALLEY VITICULTURAL REGIONS

The majority of Chile's premium wines are made from grapes grown between 32 degrees and 38 degrees south latitude, placing the vineyards in the south-central part of the country where the towering Andes having tremendous influence on growing conditions (see map on page 209).

The city of Santiago is at the northern end of the fertile basin between the Andes and the high plateaus of the coastal Cordillera mountain range. This basin comprises the Central Valley (Valle Central) and its subregion, the Rapel Valley, which, along with their hillsides, provide most of the grapes for Chile's fine wines. Here, temperatures can reach 90°F/32°C during the day, with lots of uninterrupted sunshine; temperatures can plummet at night. The Andes Mountains provide favorable air currents, good drainage, and sources of water, including the Aconcagua and Maule Rivers. However, most of the commercial vineyards in these regions are irrigated. Valle Central is Chile's oldest wine region and its most traditional.

Valle Central and the Rapel Valley include the appellations (from north to south) of Aconcagua Valley, Casablanca Valley, San Antonio Valley, Maipo Valley, Cachapoal Valley, Colchagua Valley, Curicó Valley, and Maule Valley.

CENTRAL VALLEY APPELLATIONS

The Aconcagua Valley is towered over by Mt. Aconcagua, the highest mountain in the Americas. The mountain peak

The Max 1 Estate in Chile's Aconcagua Valley, owned by the Errazuriz winery

snow, which melts in warm weather, is an important source of water for vineyards, although drip irrigation is becoming common here. There are less than 2,500 acres/1,000 hectares of vineyard in the Aconcagua Valley, and about half of it is Cabernet Sauvignon. Increasingly, when Aconcagua Valley appears on a wine label, it is an outward sign of quality, especially for Cabernet Sauvignon, Merlot, and Syrah.

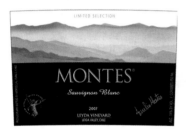

The Casablanca Valley is best-known for producing high quality Sauvignon Blanc, Chardonnay, and increasingly, Pinot Noir. It is close by the Pacific and about 90 miles/144 kilometers from Santiago. At lower elevations it is so cold that windmills are used to keep the early-morning air warm enough to prevent frost damage to the fruit. About twenty years ago, when the Chilean wine industry was focused on warm-weather red grapes, the Casablanca Valley was barren of vineyards. Today, thanks to the pioneering efforts of wine producer Pablo Morandé and others, there are 10,000 acres/4,000 hectares of vines planted in the Casablanca Valley, with Chardonnay and Sauvignon Blanc accounting for more than 70 percent of plantings.

The San Antonio Valley, which includes the very cool–climate Leyda Valley appellation, is beginning to develop a reputation for artisanal Chardonnay, Sauvignon Blanc, and Pinot Noir. Leyda Valley Sauvignon Blanc is a true and rare gem. Drip irrigation is a common practice here, but water supply can be a problem. Some producers have had to build their own dams and aqueducts to ensure a reliable water source for the vineyards. So far, there are about 3,000 acres/1,200 hectares of working vineyard in the entire San Antonio Valley, but Chilean wineries are purchasing land for vineyards at a rapid pace, as the world takes notice of the quality of the wines produced here.

The Maipo Valley, in the shadow of Santiago, a city of about 6 million people, is Chile's most famous wine region, and it is here that Cabernet Sauvignon rules, with about 65 percent of total plantings. Maipo is considered a desirable growing area, because its mild winter and spring seasons mean that frost is not a problem. Its dry summer and autumn seasons reduce the risk of mildew in the vineyards. There are many large and established wineries here, as well as new, small boutique growers and wineries, focused on organic or biodynamic viticulture.

Producers informally divide the Maipo Valley into three subregions. Alto Maipo, at about 2,130 feet/650 meters above sea level, is closest to the Andes Mountains, while Central Maipo lies at the valley floor, at 1,800–2,400 feet/550–650 meters above sea level, and Pacific Maipo is closest to the ocean, situated below 1,800 feet/550 meters above sea level. It is not unusual for producers to blend

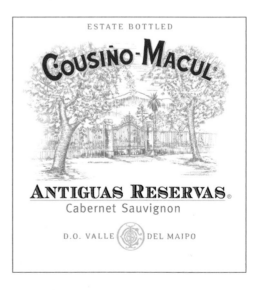

TOP: *A single-vineyard, single-block Casablanca Valley Sauvignon Blanc. An arrow on the label points to Block 28 of El Triángulo vineyard.* **MIDDLE**: *Aurelio Montes, dean of Chilean winemakers, produces a relatively small amount of Sauvignon Blanc from a low-yielding vineyard in the Leyda Valley.* **BOTTOM**: *Amaral, owned by MontGras winery, produces unoaked Chardonnay and Sauvignon Blanc from their 1,500-acre/600-hectare estate in Chile's San Antonio Valley.* **RIGHT**: *Cousiño-Macul is one of the oldest and finest wineries in Chile's Maipo Valley. In 1860, Luis Cousiño brought vine cuttings from Bordeaux to his estate in Chile. Cousiño-Macul is owned by the sixth generation of the Cousiño family.*

wines made from grapes in the Alto, Central, and Pacific Maipo subregions to achieve the best results in their finished wines.

RAPEL VALLEY APPELLATIONS

Rapel Valley, about 60 miles/100 kilometers south of Santiago, is a desirable region for the production of red wines, and until fairly recently its fate seemed to be sealed as a reliable source of Cabernet and Merlot grapes for Maipo Valley wineries. But in the mid-1990s, Rapel, and especially its Colchagua Valley subregion, became the darling of boutique wineries, large producers, and high-quality international wine partnerships, such as Casa Lapostolle, Los Vascos, Montes, MontGras, Louis Felipe Edwards, Seña, Viu Manent, and Viña Morande. Foreign investment is increasing at an astonishing clip throughout the Rapel Valley, indicating that both production and export numbers will be increasing in this area.

The Cachapoal Valley, a subappellation of the Rapel Valley, is an arid area, completely reliant on drip irrigation to nurture its 17,500 acres/7,000 hectares of vineyards, about 60 percent planted to Cabernet Sauvignon. The warm climate produces seriously ripe grapes and full-bodied, fruit-forward red wines. On the cooler hillsides of the valley, a small amount of Chardonnay and Sauvignon Blanc is planted, mostly for blending into white wines produced from grapes grown in cooler climates.

The Colchagua Valley, the other subappellation of Rapel Valley, is quickly becoming the Napa Valley of Chile (in the viticultural sense, not the tourist sense). The region lies closer to the Pacific Coast than to the Andes and benefits from the cool fog and even cooler ocean breezes that roll into the vineyards. Larger than its northern appellation partner, Cachapoal Valley, Colchagua, with more than 50,000 acres/20,000 hectares planted, focuses on Cabernet Sauvignon (60 percent of plantings), Merlot (20 percent), and Carmenère (15 percent). Some of the nation's best producers own wineries and vineyards here, mostly in the southeastern section of the valley.

Curicó Valley is one of Chile's largest wine districts, and vinifera grapes were first planted here in the mid-nineteenth century. Many Chilean wine producers own vineyards here, and some maintain wineries in Curicó. In the 1970s, Miguel Torres of Spain planted his flag in Curicó, attracted by its Mediterranean climate, which provided a long, dry growing season but with sufficient rainfall, and the well-drained soils. Many wine producers followed the lead of Torres, so much so that wine production is now Curicó's primary industry. Vineyards tend to be large here, and thirty-two different varieties are planted in those vineyards, with Cabernet Sauvignon, Sauvignon Blanc, Merlot, and Chardonnay accounting for about 80 percent of plantings.

Maule is the largest vineyard area in Chile, growing close to 45 percent of total plantings. There is more Cabernet Sauvignon planted here than any other variety, with about 23,375 acres/9,350 hectares, but more than 20,000 acres/8,000 hectares of the Pais grape still remains in Maule vineyards. Pais is the grape of Chile's *corriente* wines, inexpensive and indifferent red wines meant for domestic consumption and not exported. Merlot, Carmenère, and Sauvignon Blanc account for a total of about 18,750 acres/7,500 hectares of plantings. Maule is a region that produces grapes that mostly feed wines produced with more prestigious appellation names, such as the Maipo Valley. Maule soils contain more clay and less sand than the Maipo region, and the climate is Mediterranean and humid. Maule's cooler microclimates lie at the foot of the Andes mountain range, and it is here that white grapes are planted.

Some of the many quality producers of Chile include:
ANTIYAL AND KUYEN The wines under these two labels are the products of, respectively, biodynamic and organic vineyards. Both wines are made by Alvaro Espinoza, a true artisan who has long been dedicated to fine wines

LEFT: *Santa Rita is a large wine producer. Its 120 line of wines is inexpensive. The 120 Merlot is sourced in the Rapel Valley.*
RIGHT: *MontGras, owned by brothers Hernán and Eduardo Gras, produces excellent wines in Chile's Colchagua Valley. Quatro is a blend of four grapes: Cabernet Sauvignon, Malbec, Merlot, and Carmenère.*

grown in the most sustainable manner. Espinoza was one of the first Chilean winemakers to produce a varietal Carmenère.

CARMEN Chile's oldest existing winery, established in 1850, produces a fine line of varietal "Reserve" wines, as well as the well-regarded Gold Reserve Cabernet Sauvignon.

CONCHA Y TORO Now the biggest and one of the best, featuring vineyards from every viticultural region, this producer makes great Cabernet Sauvignon, especially the Almaviva, Don Melchor, and Marques de Casa Concha bottlings; Carmín de Peumo Carmenère; Amelia Chardonnay; Terrunyo Chardonnay and Syrah; the wide range of affordable Casillero del Diablo varietals, but especially the Riserva Privada Cabernet-Syrah blend; very reasonably priced Trio blends, Frontera, and Xplorador wines.

CONO SUR Owned by Concha y Toro, with a large presence in the European export market, this producer makes a very fine Pinot Noir, called Ocio, from vineyards in the Casablanca Valley, as well as its 20 Barrels line, and wines produced from varieties that are unusual for Chile, such as Viognier, Riesling, and Gewürztraminer.

COUSIÑO-MACUL One of Chile's finest wineries, it produces wines only from its own estate vineyards, and

the Finis Terrae blend of Cabernet Sauvignon and Merlot is terrific, as is the Cabernet Sauvignon Antigua Reserva. The Lota Cabernet Sauvignon–Merlot blend is outstanding.

ERRAZURIZ The winery is owned by Eduardo Chadwick and his family, who also own the popularly priced Caliterra brand. Errazuriz is best known for its wines sourced from their estates in the Aconcagua Valley: Don Maximiano Founder's Reserve, a Cabernet Sauvignon blend; the Specialties, single-vineyard and wild yeast–fermented varietals; and the Max Riserva line of varietal wines.

MONTES Aurelio Montes made the reputation of the Curicó and Aconcagua regions, first with his varietal Malbec, then his La Finca Cabernet Sauvignon, and then, with the consultation of British "flying winemaker" Hugh Ryman, the very expensive Alpha M. The Montes Folly is one of the best Syrah wines produced in Chile, and his Cherub rosé of Syrah is fun to drink. Montes also produces more affordable wines in his Alpha, Limited Selection, and Classic series.

SANTA RITA This was one of the initial producers to make a splash in the American export market (Undurraga was first), with its 120 line of inexpensive varietals (named for the 120 men of Bernardo O'Higgins, who hid in the Santa Rita cellars while liberating Chile). Santa Rita now owns the historic Carmen winery and vineyards, and was an early partner with Château Lafite Rothschild in Los Vascos. Santa Rita produces some excellent wines in their Casa Real, Medella Real, Reserva, and single-vineyard bottlings.

VALDIVIESO This is Chile's largest producer of sparkling wine, but more recently attention has been focused on still wines, especially the multivintage, variously blended, numbered batches of Caballo Loco, and Éclat, a blend of Carignan and Syrah. Single-vineyard wines can be impressive, too.

WILLIAM FÈVRE CHILE This is owned by a well-known producer of fine Chablis in Burgundy, France. Fèvre has a state-of-the-art winery and wants to make world-class Chardonnay and Pinot Noir from fruit grown in the mountains of the Maipo Valley region.

Other good to excellent Chilean wine producers with representation in the American market include:

Agricola La Viña, Alamaeda, Alfasi, Amaral, Anakena, Antu, Arboleda, Aresti, Botalcura, Calina, Caliterra,

Canepa, Casa Amada, Casa Blanca, Casa Silva, Chateau La Joya, Chocolan, Chono, De Martino, Echeverria, Emiliana, Erasmo, Guelbenzu, Henriquez Hermanos, Intrigo, Kingston Family, La Fortuna, La Palma, La Playa, Las Casas del Toqui, Leyda, Los Maquis, Luis Felipe Edwards, Lurton, Matetic, Miguel Torres, MontGras, Morandé, Odfjell, Porta, Portal del Alto, Requingua, San Pedro, Santa Alicia, Santa Amelia, Santa Carolina, Santa Ema, Santa Marvista, Segu Olie, Sergio Traverso, Stony Hollow, Tabali, Tarapaca, Terra Andina, TerraMater, Terranoble, Two Brothers, Undurraga, Valle Andino, Villarica, Viña Altair, Viña Cachagua, Viña Garcés Silva, Viu Manent, and Walnut Crest.

ARGENTINA

ARGENTINA (see map on page 209), a country of about 41 million people, with 550,000 acres/222,000 hectares under vine, ranks fifth in the world in wine production. Argentina's thirsty domestic market consumes about 80 percent of its total production, with a per capita consumption of about 11 gallons/29 liters per year, which ranks tenth in the world. The homegrown industry is very successful on its own turf. Argentina is the ninth largest wine exporter in the world, with about a 2 percent share of the world wine market,

On the international stage, quality is the paramount issue in Argentina. Not so long ago, Argentina was best known for bulk exports of grape must and concentrate, produced from high-yielding vineyards in warmer areas. This practice continues, but not on the scale of previous years. The musts and concentrates are exported for blending, and the finished wines are often labeled as products of the importing country. The United Kingdom, Japan, and Venezuela have been major customers for this bulk material. At the same time, Argentina's finer wines, its *vinos finos,* are quickly gaining respect and market share in North America and Western Europe because of their high quality and affordability. Cooler fermentation and the export market's demands are inducing a less oaky, less alcoholic, fresher range of wines.

Perhaps the single greatest problem Argentina has had in raising the quality standards of its wine industry is one that has plagued it for some time: The yields in Argentina's vineyards have been just too high. Taking a page from the book of its neighbor Chile, which is largely focused on reduced yields and quality-wine production for the export market, Argentina has refocused its efforts on producing fine wine to serve both a demanding domestic market and a burgeoning export market.

The road to quality has been a bumpy one for the Argentine wine industry. Starting about twenty-five years ago, Argentina began a program of pulling out vineyards that either were poorly sited for the varieties being grown or were growing grapes that ended up making wine of very low quality. This move to improve quality had the full backing of the Argentine government and wine industry. By the year 2000, more than one-third of Argentina's vines had been ripped out of the ground, but wine production fell by only 10 percent. A quick check of the math shows that in this period of "improvement," yields actually increased from the equivalent of 135 cases of wine per acre/300 cases per hectare to 160 cases per acre/400 cases per hectare.

However, after the folly of the vine-pulling scheme, the best wine producers in Argentina got increasingly serious about enhancing the image of their nation's wine industry, and they appear to have succeeded, as each year brings better news about the quality of Argentine wines. Especially in the export market, where Argentina had been particularly weak, annual figures of export volume and the value of fine wines have been skyrocketing.

Argentina's wine industry now has the collective consciousness needed to compete in a quality-driven export market, and it has all the raw materials necessary to do a good job. For example, while Argentina's climate is dry, irrigation is a cinch compared with Chile because of the melting snow pack of the Andes Mountains.

LEFT: *Bodega y Cavas de Weinert is a premier producer in Argentina.* RIGHT: *"Crios" means "offspring," and the three hands represent winemaker Susana Balbo and her two children, as well as the care given to Balbo's younger wines. Torrontés is an important white varietal in Argentina, and the high-elevation Cafayate district of the Salta region is the best place to grow it.*

In the past, this advantage had been turned into a negative, because irrigation can mean the proliferation of more grapes and diluted, characterless wine. Today, the leaders of Argentina's quality wine industry are demonstrating that they know how to control water use to grow a balanced crop of quality grapes and to produce better wines.

And Argentine winemakers, such as the pioneering Nicolas Catena (owner of Catena, Bodegas Esmeralda, and Alamos) and Bernardo Weinert, (owner of the classic quality-driven winery Weinert), have taken their place on the world stage. Catena makes superb wines that have caught the attention of the export market and the wine press, and he is totally focused on quality at all price levels, from value-driven, mass-market budget varietals to his most personal project, Catena Alta, whose production is minuscule; the wines sell for about $50 per bottle. Weinert is revered for the quality of its wines and the family's commitment to making the best wines possible.

Another extraordinary winemaker and spokeswoman for quality in the Argentine wine industry is Susana Balbo of Dominio del Plata winery. Her Crios, Susana Balbo, BenMarco, and Nosotros labels express her passion and superior winemaking skills. Her partner and husband, Pedro Marchevsky, is the viticulturist in charge of the vineyards, where grapes are grown in the most sustainable ways possible. Balbo commands worldwide attention for her dedication to quality winemaking.

Grape Types in Argentina: Malbec and Torrontés

While Argentina grows a wide range of international varieties, it is not Cabernet Sauvignon or Chardonnay that have emerged as Argentina's signature grapes. Rather, Argentina has focused—and very successfully—on the Malbec grape, a red variety known mostly (if at all) as the primary grape of the southern French wine Cahors. Malbec was planted in Argentina for the first time in the mid-nineteenth century, and was planted throughout the country, at first producing high-alcohol reds, fortified wines, and brandies. As the Argentine wine industry matured and began to look for a signature grape, Malbec was their choice, and it was a good one.

Malbec is produced in many styles, from simple, light- to medium-bodied reds, to complex wines capable of long aging—from inexpensive, drinkable stuff to very expensive wines that appear on the best wine lists. Malbec is also made as a dry rosé, and there is even a bit of sparkling Malbec. Sometimes Cabernet Sauvignon and Malbec are blended together. In the export market, Malbec has taken off primarily as a full-bodied wine to accompany hearty dishes. Malbec can be quite a bargain, but even at higher prices it almost always delivers good value for money. Argentines, proud of another one of their leading agricultural products, have been known to say, "We don't have a cuisine; we have beef." And that amusing maxim works just fine for the hearty Malbec, as it is the perfect accompaniment to beef, stews, game, and mature cheeses.

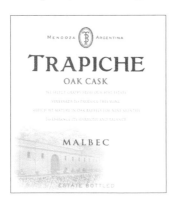

LEFT: *Trapiche exports more wine around the world than any other Argentine producer.* **MIDDLE:** *Kaiken Malbec is produced by Aurelio Montes, arguably the most famous winemaker in Chile, who, like the wild goose (kaiken), crosses the Andes to make this wine in Argentina.* **RIGHT:** *La Posta produces a fine Bonarda, a grape with Italian roots. Bonarda from Argentina is still an undiscovered gem.*

Reflecting its Spanish and Italian heritage, Argentina also produces wines from the Tempranillo grape, the most important red grape of Spain, as well as Bonarda and Sangiovese, both of which have Italian roots. Bonarda has yet to make a splash in the U. S. market, but Bonarda from Argentina, especially old-vine Bonarda, can be a lovely medium- to full-bodied, fruit-forward red wine with balanced tannins. Sangiovese is consumed mostly in the domestic market.

When it comes to white grapes, although Argentina produces some very good Chardonnay, Sauvignon Blanc, Viognier, and even some Riesling and Gewürztraminer, its most interesting grape is Torrontés. This variety has been shown to be a different grape than the Torrontés grape planted in Spain, and Argentine Torrontés is a unique, perfumed, exotic wine featuring aromas of roses and jasmine. For Torrontés to succeed as a varietal wine, it needs low yields in the vineyards and protection from excessive heat, as acids in the grape are only moderate. When the forces of nature and the care of humans conspire to make a fine Torrontés, it is a perfect accompaniment to empanadas, but also to Indian curries and Chinese, Vietnamese, and Thai food.

Wine Regions

The majority, 80 percent, of all Argentine wines are produced in the gigantic Mendoza region, which in terms of sheer size—60,000 square miles/96,000 square kilometers—is the largest wine region in the entire Southern Hemisphere, and perhaps the world. More than 30,000 grape growers are at work here, tending about 365,000 acres/146,000 hectares of vineyards. Malbec, Argentina's premier red grape, is the most important grape for quality wines, followed closely by Cabernet Sauvignon; both can be made as truly elegant wines in Argentina. Other red grapes include Merlot, the esteemed Spanish variety Tempranillo, and the Italian varieties Bonarda and Sangiovese. White varieties include Chardonnay, Chenin Blanc, Sauvignon Blanc, and the star of Argentina's white wines, Torrontés. Mendoza is warmer than Chile's Central Valley, but with low humidity and plenty of sunshine. There is very little rainfall, but the Andes Mountains act almost as an irrigation spigot.

Being so large, Mendoza is informally divided into five subregions based on climate, altitude, and soil composition. Each subregion is referred to as an "oasis" in Argentina.

The five areas are Northern Mendoza, Eastern Mendoza, Mendoza River Area, Uco Valley, and Southern Mendoza.

Northern Mendoza, the smallest of the five subregions, relies on the Mendoza River as a water source for the vineyards. Altitude ranges from about 2,000 to 2,300 feet/600 to 700 meters above sea level. Northern Mendoza focuses on white grapes, especially Chardonnay, Sauvignon Blanc, and Torrontés. Red grapes include Syrah, Cabernet Sauvignon, Bonarda, and Malbec.

Eastern Mendoza is a major vineyard and winery oasis. Altitude ranges from about 2,000 to 2,500 feet/600 to 750 meters above sea level, and there are several different types of soil, from clay to desert sands. Sandy soils, which drain water efficiently, are the most prized for vineyard sites in Eastern Mendoza. Diurnal climate patterns, with hot weather during the day and very cool temperatures at night, make this area attractive for large-scale grape growing. White grapes planted in Eastern Mendoza include Chardonnay, Sauvignon Blanc, Chenin Blanc, Torrontés, and Viognier; reds include Sangiovese, Syrah, Bonarda, and Tempranillo.

TOP: *Salentein is a quality-driven producer. This Pinot Noir is produced from high-altitude vineyards, at 4,265 feet/1,300 meters above sea level, on Salentein's La Pampa estate in the Uco Valley of Mendoza.* **BOTTOM:** *Huarpe is one of the finest producers in Argentina. Guayquil is a red blend of Malbec, Cabernet Sauvignon, Petit Verdot, Bonarda, and Tannat. The wine is unfiltered and only 600 cases are produced.*

The Mendoza River Area, which begins just to the south of the city of Mendoza, features some smaller, old-vine vineyards planted at altitudes beginning at about 2,150 feet/650 meters and soaring to 3,500 feet/1,060 meters. Soils are well-drained in this area, and the premier grape is Malbec. One of Argentina's first commercial wine regions, the Mendoza River Area has attracted quite a bit of foreign investment in vineyards and wineries, beginning in 1990 and growing ever since.

The Uco Valley, also one of Argentina's earliest commercial wine regions, is best known for Malbec, Pinot Noir, Sauvignon Blanc, and Sémillon plantings, and features high altitude vineyards, some as high as 4,600 feet/1,400 meters. Producers consider Uco Valley as a good source of grapes for some of Argentina's most ageworthy red wines.

Southern Mendoza, located between latitudes 34.5 degrees and 35 degrees south, is known as the primary grower of Chenin Blanc grapes, with a smattering of other varieties planted.

OTHER WINE REGIONS

San Juan, with about 92,500 acres/37,000 hectares of vineyards, is, after Mendoza, Argentina's second-most-prolific wine-producing region. The oasis is composed of five valleys: Tulum, Ullum-Zonda, Calingasta, Iglesia, and Fertil. Tulum, close by the San Juan River, is the most important for wine production. At 2,080 feet/630 meters above sea level, rainfall in Tulum is limited. The average annual temperature is about 63°F/17°C. Malbec, Cabernet Sauvignon, Merlot, and Bonarda are the most-planted varieties, but San Juan is also gaining international recognition for the high quality of its Syrah.

La Rioja is a very warm region where the grapes must be protected, via a dense leaf pergola, from the power of the sun. Torrontés is the primary grape here, and it, like many other grapes grown in La Rioja, finds its way into fortified wines and brandies.

Salta, with less than 5,000 acres/2,000 hectares under vine, produces a small percentage of the nation's wines, but the quality is generally good. With vineyards planted at high altitudes—as high as 7,900 feet/2,400 meters in its Colomé Valley—Salta has become a reliable source of Torrontés grapes, especially from the Cafayate district, as well as some Cabernet Sauvignon and Malbec.

Catamarca is very warm, and its valleys rise to about 5,600 feet/1,700 meters above sea level. Soils are sandy and stone-laden, and 5,750 acres/2,300 hectares of vineyards are largely dedicated to Torrontés, with some red varieties grown as well. Catamarca grapes often end up in Argentine brandies.

Neuquén, with about 2,500 acres/1,000 hectares of vineyards, several new state-of-the-art wineries, and a healthy Patagonian wine-and-food tourism industry, seems to be a model for the future of Argentine wine. Conditions in the vineyards—adequate rainfall, an average temperature of 68°F/20°C, plenty of sunshine and mild breezes—allow the grapes to ripen slowly. Malbec is the most important variety grown here, followed by Merlot, Cabernet Sauvignon, Pinot Noir, and Syrah.

Rio Negro, also in Patagonia, focuses on grapes grown in its High Valley (latitude 40 degrees south and 1,220 feet/370 meters above sea level), which features a continental climate. Winter is cold while summer is warm and dry, but with fairly low humidity and constant mountain breezes. Best known for Sémillon and Sauvignon Blanc, red wines produced from Rio Negro High Valley vineyards, particularly Malbec and Merlot, can also be quite good.

Wine Laws

Argentina's Instituto Nacional de Viniviticultura (INV), the federal regulatory body, controls pruning methods, harvesting schedules, transport of grapes, release dates of finished wines, minimum and maximum alcohol percentages, and the planting of new vines. The INV also sets domestic prices, which passively discourages fine wine production for the domestic market but could encourage the export market. Neither appellation nor varietal labeling is regulated, but *vinos finos,* Argentina's best wines, which account for about 20 percent of total production, are under strict government and industry controls. As in so many other countries where the climate is warm, chaptalization is forbidden in Argentina.

In addition to the fine wines made by Nicolas Catena, Bernardo Weinert, and Susana Balbo (see page 220), Argentina's quality wineries include:

Accordeón, Achàval Ferrer, Alamos, Alma Negra, AltaVista, Altos de Medrano, Altos Las Hormigas, Amancaya, Andeluna, Antigal, Balbi, Bodega de Desierto, Bodega Noemia de Patagonia, Borbore, Budini, Caro, Chacra, Chandon, Cheval des Andes, Cobos, Colomé, Doña Paula, Dös Lomos, Durigutti, El Origen, El Portillo, Enrique Foster, Escorihuela, Esmeralda, Fabre Montmayou,

Familia Rutini, Familia Zuccardi, Felix Lavaque, Finca Flichman, Gascón, Gusto, High Altitude, Huarpe, Kaiken, La Boca, La Linda, La Posta del Viñatero, Lo Tengo, Luca, Luigi Bosca, Lurton, Mapema, Mariposa, Masi Tupungato, Maza Tonconogy, Medrano, Melipal, Mendel, Monteflores, Morichetti, Ñandú, Nativo Cocodrilo, Navarrita, Navarro Correas, Nieto Cadus, Noemia de Patagonia, Norton, NQN, O. Fournier, Pannotia, Pascual Toso, Poesia, Pulenta, Punto Final, Reginato, Ruca Malen, Sagta, Salentein, Santa Cecilia, Santa Julia, Septima, Sur de Los Andes, Tahuan, Tapiz, Terra Rosa/Laurel Glen, Terrazas de Los Andes, Tierra Brisa, Tikal, Tilia, Tomero, Trapiche, Trivento, Trumpeter, Uxmal, Vale La Pena, and Valentín Bianchi.

BRAZIL AND URUGUAY

Brazil

In 1500, Pedro Àlvares Cabral of Portugal explored Brazil, and vines have been planted here since 1532. It was not until the 1970s, however, that high-quality wines began to be produced in Brazil. The warm, humid climate made growing vinifera, such as the Criolla, difficult, so native American grapes and hybrids have been planted since the mid-1800s. Isabella, sometimes called Albany Surprise, is an important hybrid grown in Brazil. In fact, hybrids account for more than a third of of all vine plantings in the 225,000 acres/90,000 hectares of vineyards in Brazil.

Thirty years ago, Brazil was the third- or fourth-largest wine producer in the world, making undistinguished

plonk for blending into even-less-distinguished international plonk. Its slip to the fifteenth-largest producer in 2007 speaks volumes about how the wine world has changed and how Brazil has not kept up with those changes. The international market is no longer interested in bulk wines made from hybrid grapes, and Brazil's domestic market is weak. Per capita consumption in this country of about 190 million people is less than 0.5 gallon/1.75 liters, about fiftieth in the world.

As the twenty-first century takes shape, Brazil's wine industry is trying hard to make up for lost time. Prior to the present day, Brazil's last great moment in the international wine trade was the nineteenth century, when Italian immigrants brought Italian varietals and a thirst for wine to Brazil. But today, things are slowly changing for the better in Brazil.

In 1998, the Brazilian Wine Institute (Ibravin) was established to put Brazilian wines on the world map, to encourage domestic consumption, and to share technological and commercial advances throughout the wine industry. With an infusion of interest and funds from both domestic and foreign sources, Brazil has begun to employ modern practices in its vineyards, wineries, and marketing efforts. By 2007, the hard work of Ibravin had begun to pay off, as domestic wine consumption of Brazilian wines has grown little by little—but perhaps more important, the wines of Brazil are now exported to at least twenty foreign countries (compared with only two export markets in 1998).

The major grape-growing and winemaking region of Brazil is the Rio Grande do Sul in the far southeast of the country. The formal wine regions of this area are Serra

LEFT: *The Panceri winery in Brazil. Panceri produces wines from international varieties in the Santa Catarina Mountains.*
RIGHT: *A Brazilian Merlot from the Campanha subregion of the Rio Grande do Sul.*

Gaúcha, Serra do Sudueste, Campanha, and São Joaquim. There is plenty of rainfall here, and drip irrigation is unnecessary. Of these, the Serra Gaúcha region, with its 200,000 acres/80,000 hectares of vineyards, is the most important, as it accounts for almost 90 percent of Brazil's wine production.

Red vinifera varieties planted in southern Brazil include Cabernet Sauvignon, Merlot, Cabernet Franc, Pinot Noir, Tannat, and Ancelotta (normally found in Central Italy). White varieties include Riesling Itálico, Chardonnay, Prosecco, Muscat, and Malvasia.

In the São Francisco Valley in northeast Brazil, a basic tenet of traditional wine orthodoxy—that good wine can be produced only at latitudes between 30 degrees and 50 degrees—has been turned on its head. This region is located at latitude 9 degrees south, making it part of the tropics. The expectation is that anything resembling quality wine could not be produced from vineyards planted here, but due to advances in technology in vineyard management—including a total reliance on drip irrigation—and improved refrigeration during the winemaking process, the São Francisco Valley now boasts the largest tropical vineyard (5,000 acres/2,000 hectares) in the world. The wine world is watching, because due to a year-round growing season with average temperature fluctuation only between 68°F/20°C and 88°F/31°C, harvesting is basically continuous, with two harvests per year the norm. Other major "new latitudes" wine regions include India (see page 550).

The modern wine industry in Brazil has received the most attention for its sparkling wines, but more white, rosé, and red wines are appearing in export markets, thanks in part to a solid proliferation of *churrascarias* (Brazilian barbecue restaurants) in foreign countries. These restaurants want to serve Brazilian wines with their dishes, and the public response has been positive. We can expect to see a wider variety of Brazilian wines in the North American wine market in the near future.

Brazilian wine producers with an export program include Ariano, Bouza, Casa Valduga, Dal Pizzol, Irmãos Molon, Panceri, Perini, Pizzato, and Salton.

Uruguay

Uruguay, located south of Brazil and northeast of Buenos Aires, Argentina, is a nation of about 3.8 million people, with an annual per capita wine consumption of about 7 gallons/27 liters. Uruguay is the thirtieth-largest wine-producing nation in the world (fourth-largest in South America). Uruguay has close to three hundred wineries, most of them small and family owned, and total vineyard plantings are less than 30,000 acres/12,000 hectares.

Vineyards in Uruguay are planted mostly on flat lands, and the soils are a mixture of clay and loam. Although the country has sixteen officially designated wine regions, better than 90 percent of Uruguay's wine originates in the vineyards surrounding its capital city, Montevideo.

Although Uruguay produces wines from well-known international varieties, one grape in particular seems to thrive in Uruguay: Tannat. Best known as the grape of Madiran from southwest France, Tannat wines from Uruguay are beginning to generate a buzz in international markets. True to its name, Tannat usually produces a dark wine that is quite tannic in its youth and needs time to settle down. In Uruguay, Tannat is often blended with Merlot and often goes through carbonic maceration in the winery (see page 66) to soften the aggressive tannins. Young Tannat wines from Uruguay tend to be softer and more fruit-forward than their Old World counterparts, but still they are formidable, full-bodied wines.

As of 2008, only about twenty wineries in Uruguay were involved in the export trade, and about half of those serve the North American market, so Uruguayan wines may be hard to find, but they are worth seeking out, especially Tannat. Producers with a presence in the North American market include Carrau, Casa Magrez, Castel Pujol, Catamayor, Don Prospero, H. Stagnari, Monte de Luz, Pisano, Quara, and Viñedo de los Ventos.

OCEANIA

AUSTRALIA

BY 2006 AUSTRALIA was well on its way to achieving its goals of becoming one of the world's largest producers and exporters of wine, ranking as the world's sixth-largest wine producer, with a total production of around 375 million gallons/14.2 million hectoliters from a total of about 210,000 acres/166,000 hectares of vines. It seemed at the time that Australian wine producers could do no wrong. But then came a couple of reality checks. The fact that wine is a natural agricultural product was emphasized by

ongoing drought conditions in some wine areas through the first decade of the twenty-first century, causing shutdown in the vines, and reduced crops. In addition, wine exports took a dive as too much bulk wine and low-end wine began to hit the market, and consumers pulled back from their favorite Australian brands. So there has been a natural correction in the market, and a realization on the part of some of the larger Australian wine corporations that growth cannot go on forever, particularly in a world where there is a global glut of wine at all quality levels. The combined effect of natural and market corrections was that in 2008 Australia's production was down to 330 million gallons/12.5 million hectoliters, and the final figures for 2009 are expected to show a further fall to 264 million gallons/10 million hectoliters.

Disastrously low harvest levels in Hunter Valley in 2008 and bushfires that destroyed vineyards and wineries in Victoria in 2009 have only added to the gloomy picture, prompting calls for government assistance from the industry in general. Not seen since the 1970s, Australia could now be looking at a government-funded program to uproot excess acres of vineyards, especially in the area where the states of New South Wales, South Australia, and Victoria meet.

Still, the glory years allowed Australia's wineries to expand and invest in modern high-tech equipment, producing wines with clean flavors and easily identifiable varietal character. Indeed, Australia's commitment to technological innovation has been well established for several decades, leading the way with rotofermenters and screwcap closures. Penfolds, one of the nation's most reputable

TOP: *The Yarra Valley, with the Great Dividing Range in the background* **BOTTOM:** *The scale of Australian wine production is evident from these 1-million-liter/264,000-gallon fermentation tanks. The Yellow Tail winemaking facility has one hundred of these tanks.*

producers of fine, ageworthy red wines, is now experimenting with specially developed glass stoppers for its red wine program. And Australia is no stranger to the multinational megacorporations, which own several wineries, providing much-needed capital for vital equipment such

THE TASTING CELLAR

as temperature-controlled fermentation vats and drip irrigation systems. Such equipment is mandatory to produce the kind of fresh varietal flavors that Australia is famous for and to combat the ongoing problems of drought and climate change.

There are about nineteen million people in Australia, and wine consumption is reasonably high, about 7.4 gallons/28 liters per capita annually. Although domestic consumption has slipped a little in recent years, consumers in Australia have shown the same trend as in other countries, toward higher-quality products. Like other wine-producing nations in the Southern Hemisphere, such as New Zealand and Chile, Australia can send its vintage wines to markets in the Northern Hemisphere six months before its northern competitors, because harvest takes place in the first four months of the year.

Contemporary Australia

It is not always appreciated that the nation of Australia is approximately the same size as the United States of America, providing a huge diversity of soils and climates and the opportunity to grow almost all of the major varietals. Australia's major disadvantage is that more than half the country is desert, and many other areas have low rainfall and hot weather. So although high sugar levels in the grapes are almost never a problem, low acid levels can be a problem. Chaptalization is illegal in Australia, but acidification, usually with tartaric acid, is common. Mechanical picking at night and keeping the unfermented must cool also help maintain acidity and freshness in the wines. The cooler areas, which are all in the southern portion of the continent

and close to the coasts, provide the best climates for viticulture, benefiting from the effects of the Antarctic Ocean. The state of South Australia produces almost half of Australia's wines, and the other southeastern states New South Wales and Victoria produce almost all of the rest. Western Australia accounts for only 5 percent of all wines produced, and Tasmania's contribution is less than 1 percent.

The Murray River and its tributary the Murrumbidgee provide much-needed irrigation for many of the drier areas in southeastern Australia, as the average rainfall is less than 30 inches/75 centimeters.

The Great Dividing Range, about 7,300 feet/2,400 meters at its highest point, and other hills and mountains help provide a cooler climate for growing wine grapes, particularly in New South Wales and southern Victoria. The melting snows provide irrigation, and cloud cover can reduce the scorching of the grapes in some areas. Beneficial, cool maritime breezes in some of the newer and cooler growing areas have allowed for the production of balanced and crisp dry wines.

The emergence of corporate control in the Australian wine industry has led to an interesting situation regarding the origin of grapes for wine production. The larger wine

LEFT: *Throughout Australia, wineries maintain public tasting and sales rooms.* RIGHT: *Kangaroos may look cute to some, but most grape growers view them as a nuisance since they love ripe grapes.*

companies think nothing of trucking grapes or juice hundreds of miles from the harvest area to a large winemaking facility somewhere else, often in another state. It is also common for a large company's Chardonnay or any other varietal wine to be a blend of grapes from two or three different regions.

The Australian "varietal-first" approach to winemaking is defensible. The objective of such an approach is to produce well-made, affordable, and enjoyable wine that is liked and consumed by a broad cross section of the wine-consuming public in many different nations around the world. Nobody can deny that Australia has been successful in achieving that objective. Despite the recent downturn in production and exports, the world's consumers are all now very familiar with the bold, assertive fruit-forward nature of most Australian wines.

For those who are still intrigued by small-site individuality, Australia offers that as well, both from the large corporate-owned wineries and from smaller boutique operations. The joy of corporate success is that it provides the revenue that allows the winemaker to have the luxury of producing a specialty wine from a small, distinctive vineyard in a prime growing area where the yield may be only 1–2 tons per acre/14–28 hectoliters per hectare. As the entire Australian wine industry continues to grow, there will be an increased emphasis by some winemakers on good site selection and growing methods to produce not only the best fruit but also the most intriguing wine that is reflective of the grape variety and the site where those grapes were grown.

Phylloxera remains a minor problem in the vineyards of Australia, although it takes a gigantic effort on the part of the agricultural authorities to maintain that situation.

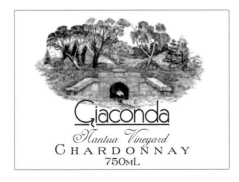

Giaconda Winery's Chardonnay from the Nantua Vineyard in Beechworth, Victoria, is an example of small-site individuality.

Some of Victoria's vineyards are grafted because of the presence of phylloxera, but the surrounding areas practice very strict quarantine methods to prevent the spread of the pest. Visitors to some Victoria vineyards are required to wear footwear protection, and all machinery and boots must be sprayed on leaving the area. On the state line between Victoria and South Australia there are checkpoints where all cars must stop to be inspected for the possible transfer of agricultural pests.

Wine Laws

The Australian Wine and Brandy Corporation operates the Universal Recording System, an auditing system that is used to track the harvesting and movement of grapes made into wine, a necessary component when grapes and juice may be trucked thousands of miles. The corporation also enforces Australia's Label Integrity Programme (LIP), which guarantees the following:

- A minimum of 85 percent of the grape variety stated on the label must be used.
- If two different types of grapes are used in a blended wine and neither grape represents 85 percent of the blend, both grapes must be mentioned on the label in order of descending proportion (e.g., a wine labeled Cabernet/Shiraz has more Cabernet than Shiraz).
- Generic labels (e.g., Chablis) are not permitted.
- If the name of a growing area, state, region, or sub-region is placed on the label, a minimum of 85 percent of the grapes must come from that place (e.g., Southeastern Australia or Barossa Valley).
- If a vintage is stated on the label, a minimum of 95 percent of the grapes must have been harvested during that vintage.
- If the term "show reserve" is used on the label, the wine must have won a medal at a tasting competition (most Australian winemakers take competitions very seriously).
- If the term "reserve bin" or "bin [number]" appears on the label, it usually distinguishes a premium or higher-quality wine. For example, some producers make several Shiraz-based wines but with several different bin numbers at different prices, indicating that a particular bin is of higher quality than another.
- If the term "wood-matured" appears on the label, it indicates that the wine spent time in new or relatively young casks and thus has an oaky taste.

Australia has developed a system of wine laws that define geographic areas, similar to the American Viticultural Area (AVA) system in the United States. Like that system, the Australian Geographic Indication system has been fraught with controversy in its initial stages and is still evolving. The biggest arguments have been centered on the geographic boundaries and what constitutes the defining features of any delineated area. Although Coonawarra is one of the oldest and most recognized areas for grape growing in Australia, every proposed geographic boundary was met with challenges from growers who were left outside of the proposed boundary but claimed a long-standing right to use of the name. Eventually such arguments were worked out, and Coonawarra is now officially defined.

The framework for the Geographic Indication system is as follows:

- One "super-area" named Southeastern Australia covers all of Tasmania, Victoria, New South Wales, the southern portion of South Australia, and the southern portion of Queensland. In other words, Southeastern Australia is a catchall category, ideal for those occasions when the larger corporations truck grapes from several sources to be blended into a midrange, mid-priced wine. The geographic indication Southeastern Australia is seen frequently on labels in wine markets all around the world.

- The six states and two territories of Australia constitute the next level of labeling. The Northern Territory has no grape-growing and winemaking ventures to speak of, and Queensland's winemaking activities are limited to serving the domestic market. The Australian Capital Territory is included in the southern New South Wales zone (see page 231).

- For Geographic Indication (appellation) purposes, the states of New South Wales, Victoria, Western Australia, and South Australia are divided into zones, which are then subdivided into regions and subregions, although the region and subregion names are more likely to show up on a label than zone names. (For the most important region and subregion names, see the maps on pages 232 and 240 to the relevant sections below on each state.)

Grape Types

By the end of the 1990s Australia had completed its switch from producing mostly sweet fortified wines and brandies to making dry white and red still wines and dry sparkling wines. Part of the transition had included a large number of generically labeled wines that were often based on the same grapes as had been used for the fortified wines and brandies. Because of this, the varietal landscape in Australia used to include various Muscats and large plantings of Trebbiano, Palomino, Doradillo, Colombard, Crouchen, and Chenin Blanc. Today the picture is dramatically different, with the usual heroes dominating and reduced quantities of the old varieties.

What has also changed is the carefree approach to naming grapes. For example, the name Riesling was once freely borrowed to describe many different varieties. Fortunately, those days are gone, and Australian wine producers are now generally using the same varietal terms as everyone else to label their wines. The major exception is Syrah, which the Australians refer to as Shiraz.

Throughout the first decade of the twenty-first century, Australia has consistently produced more red wine than white, with that trend fueled by major growth in the export of Shiraz wines, and a worldwide preference for red wines in general. The unusual circumstances of the 2007 harvest, with reduced crops, especially for Shiraz, resulted in a larger percentage of white wine being produced.

LEFT: *According to the Australian wine laws, at least 85 percent of the grapes for this wine must be Cabernet Sauvignon, and at least 85 percent of those grapes must come from Margaret River.* RIGHT: *The label for this wine shows that the origin of the grapes is the state of Victoria.*

WHITE VARIETIES

As usual, Chardonnay is the dominant white variety, with 18.5 percent of total acreage. Its adaptability to different climates and soils and its responsiveness to different wine-making practices will ensure its continued presence on the Australian scene. Australian Chardonnay is still prized

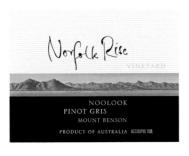

for its open, ripe fruitiness and bold style, with a generous, even lavish pineapple quality and soft, American oak notes. However, the newer vineyard areas offer leaner styles from cooler climates, such as Padthaway and Piccadilly Valley in South Australia and Margaret River in Western Australia. Part of the interest in Chardonnay is due to increased use as a component in blended *méthode champenoise* sparkling wines.

More than any other country, Australia has a history of producing Sémillon as a single-variety wine, and acreage continues to increase, even though the variety's share of total acreage has fallen to 3.5 percent. It is particularly prevalent in the Hunter Valley of New South Wales, where it makes superb, ageworthy wines. It is also important as a blending partner with Sauvignon Blanc in Western Australia's Margaret River region.

Riesling has great potential in certain parts of Australia where cool climates and long growing seasons prevail, and Australia has produced some truly great Rieslings with fine citrus qualities and the occasional hint of mineral complexity. Despite the difficulty of marketing Riesling, acreage of the variety continues to increase. Styles range from dry, lean grapefruity versions to bright, opulent lime to concentrated, luscious botrytis-affected wines. Most of Australia's Riesling is planted in South Australia, particularly in the Barossa, Clare, and Eden Valleys.

At 2.6 percent of all plantings, Sauvignon Blanc continues to increase in acreage as greater knowledge is gained about suitable sites with mineral-rich soils and cold climates. Margaret River in Western Australia continues to show promise, as does the Yarra Valley in Victoria.

Offering fresh fruit and crisp acidity from cool climates, Verdelho continues to carve out a niche for itself, and Pinot Gris has increased significantly in acreage, perhaps as a response to the worldwide fascination with this grape variety.

RED VARIETIES

Shiraz (the true Syrah from the Rhône Valley of France) remains the stereotypical Australian red grape type—bold, in-your-face, ripe, generous fruit—and has maintained its position as the most widely planted red grape, occupying a quarter of all Australia's vineyards—a remarkable achievment. Despite its ubiquitous nature, there are considerable stylistic differences to be found between the Shiraz wines from Hunter Valley and those from the Barossa Valley, McLaren Vale, or Victoria, but what usually defines Australian Shiraz is a smooth texture with ripe, dark fruit character, a mouth-filling opulence, and a touch of peppery spiciness, born of barrel fermentation.

In the late 1980s and early 1990s, Shiraz was challenged by Cabernet Sauvignon. It is still the second-most-planted red grape, at 16 percent of plantings, and despite a decrease in acreage. What makes Australian Cabernet Sauvignon particularly attractive is the ability to achieve

TOP: *Vasse Felix produces a Sémillon–Sauvignon Blanc blend from the Margaret River region.* BOTTOM: *From the Mount Benson region in South Australia, Pipers Brook winery produces this "Norfolk Rise" Pinot Gris.* RIGHT: *This seventy-year-old Shiraz vine in the Barossa Valley is evidence of Australia's long-term commitment to this grape.*

SHIRAZ: AUSTRALIA'S WORLD-CLASS WINE

If there is one varietal that defines the highest qualities of the modern Australian wine industry, it is Shiraz. At its best, Shiraz is a stellar red wine, able to age at least as long and well as many of the world's finest Bordeaux and Napa Valley Cabernet Sauvignon wines—and without losing its fruit flavors and satiny texture, much like great Burgundy. Even Australia's budget Shiraz wines impart lush, smooth, easy-drinking enjoyment when paired with a wide variety of foods.

By now, wine connoisseurs, collectors, and wine auction houses are familiar with the classic Penfolds Grange and the two Henschke Shiraz bottlings, Hill of Grace and Mount Edelstone. But how many know about Bailey's 1920s Old Block, Eldenton, Pike's, Rockford Basket Press, Peter Lehmann Stonewell, Tyrell's Vat 9, Hardy's Eileen Hardy, Mitchelton Reserve, Bannockburn, and Jasper Hill Emily's Paddock? All of these wines are 100 percent Shiraz, and all, in their best vintages, are cellar-keeping classics.

Although Australian Shiraz (the exotic nomenclature is from the original Persian name for the grape) is the same Syrah clone planted in the Hermitage and Côte-Rôtie districts of the northern Rhône Valley in France, as late as the 1980s Australian growers and producers were being urged to replant even old-vine Shiraz plots over to Cabernet Sauvignon. Some did, but quite a few did not heed this wrong-headed advice. During this not-so-long-ago era, the Cabernet/Shiraz (more Cab than Shiraz) and Shiraz/Cabernet (more Shiraz than Cab) blends were born, and with mostly great results. Because the blend worked so well, and because young-vine, relatively high-yield Shiraz makes such an approachable, fruit-driven wine, it has taken quite a while for Merlot to catch on in Australia, either as a separate varietal or for blending with Cabernet Sauvignon.

You can buy good Shiraz and Shiraz blends for about $15 to $20. The wine will be a great choice for dinner and will age nicely for two to five years. If you want to buy a wine to lay down in your cellar, you may have to pay well in excess of $45 for those that are readily available in the marketplace, and *really* serious dollars for wines made in limited quantities and shipped on allocation. The only place you should expect to see classic vintages of Grange, Hill of Grace, and other stunners is on the auction block.

Whether you buy Shiraz as an easy-to-find, great-tasting value-driven wine or as a wine to present to your newborn baby on her graduation from college twenty-one years hence, one fact is clear: Shiraz from Australia has by leaps and bounds become a recognized and renowned wine that can take its place on the world stage as an equal to the finest wines produced in the Old World or the New World.

ripe berry and currant characteristics in the wine without so much of the rough, harsh tannins that make the wines unpleasant in their youth. South Australia has done particularly well with the variety, with Coonawarra standing out as the region that produces ripe, complex, and age-worthy Cabernets. Western Australia's Mount Barker has also defined its own leaner style.

It comes as a bit of a surprise to many people to find that Grenache has been grown for a long time in Australia; it used to be a component in the production of sweet red Porto-style wines. Since the dramatic decline of that side of the industry, Grenache has found a place next to Shiraz as a ripe, jammy style of wine. Many of the plantings that remain are forty years old (and older), providing rich, concentrated flavors, particularly in the Barossa Valley

and McLaren Vale in South Australia. On a similar note, Mourvèdre (sometimes referred to in Australia as Mataro) has followed a similar course as Grenache. It can be found as a single-variety wine but is more likely to be used as a blending agent with Shiraz or Grenache, much as it is used in France's southern Rhône Valley and in California.

Some fine Grenache wines are produced in Barossa.

Like most wine-producing nations, Australia has its fair share of winemakers who have been smitten by Pinot Noir, and, as elsewhere, only a few have succeeded at making wines that draw attention. It is the cooler areas that show the most promise for still red wines bottled as Pinot Noir, and for sparkling base wines. Those areas are concentrated in the southern part of Victoria and in Tasmania.

For anybody who watched the evolution of the world wine market in the 1990s, it seemed inevitable that Merlot would draw attention to itself in Australia. That was borne out by the variety's increase in acreage through the next ten years, so that by 2007 Merlot was the third-most-planted red grape in Australia, and the fourth-most-planted grape overall. It has proven itself as a single-variety wine and as a useful component in blends with Cabernet Sauvignon.

Wine Regions

NEW SOUTH WALES

Although some areas of New South Wales (see map on page 232) are very hot, cloud cover helps moderate heat in the vineyards, which are planted on the volcanic soils of the Great Dividing Range, which runs in a north-north-east to south-southwest direction, separating the coastal stretch from the inland area. Newly expanded vineyard regions from Tumbarumba in the south to Mudgee in the north along the western side of the range take advantage of higher elevation on the hillside slopes to moderate the temperatures and to provide airflow, producing a number of crisp, even elegant wines. In addition to this exciting development, the state is home to the massive Riverina and Murray Darling regions, both of which depend on irrigation to supply huge quantities of average wine for the wine-in-a-box market and supermarket brands. New South Wales is second only to South Australia in acreage under vine and total wine production, producing about 30 percent of all Australia's wines. The currently approved zones, regions, and subregions in New South Wales are listed in the table at right (also see map on page 232).

HUNTER VALLEY

The Hunter Valley is the best-known wine region in New South Wales and one of Australia's oldest winemaking names. The Brokenback Range provides a cooling influence, along with afternoon clouds to help moderate the heat. But the area is beset with challenges. Lack of easy

access to water for irrigation in the southern Lower Hunter Valley and an ongoing drought situation continue to make grape growing there difficult, and yet, ironically, air humidity is so high that the Lower Hunter Valley has one of the most frequent fungicide spraying regimes. The volcanic soil is rich in parts, sometimes too rich for grapevines, which tend to prefer more mineral soil structures. But the soil types vary dramatically within the Hunter Valley, so that the occasional pocket of granite, volcanic clay, or alluvial sand will produce grapes of outstanding quality.

"Hunter honey" is the compliment paid to the excellent Sémillon produced: It is clean and crisp when young, with bright melon, grapefruit, and orange character; as it ages, it shows the complexity of lanolin and marmalade, but retains a citrus-like freshness. Notwithstanding the enormous success that producers such as Tyrell's, Rothbury Estate, and Rosemount have had with Chardonnay from this region, the Hunter Valley is a curious site in which to grow Chardonnay, and yet there is lots of it. Its acceptance is based either on cooler vineyard sites at higher elevations in the Brokenback Range or on masterful winemaking, the

NEW SOUTH WALES: CURRENTLY APPROVED ZONES, REGIONS, AND SUBREGIONS

ZONES	REGIONS	SUBREGIONS
Big Rivers	Murray Darling (also stretches across into Victoria)	
	Swan Hill	
	Riverina	
	Perricoota	
Central Ranges	Cowra	
	Orange	
	Mudgee	
Hunter Valley	Hunter	Broke Fordwich
Northern Rivers	Hastings River	
Northern Slopes	New England	
South Coast	Shoalhaven Coast	
	Sydney	
	Southern Highlands	
Southern New South Wales	Canberra District (mostly the Australian Capital Territory)	
	Hilltops	
	Tumbarumba	
	Gundagai	
Western Plains		

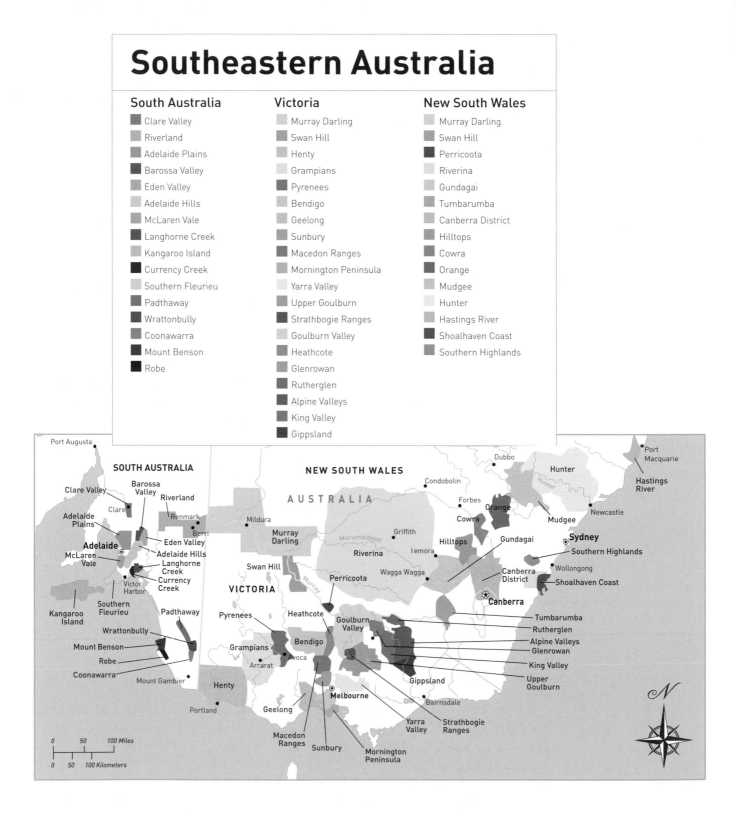

Southeastern Australia

South Australia

- Clare Valley
- Riverland
- Adelaide Plains
- Barossa Valley
- Eden Valley
- Adelaide Hills
- McLaren Vale
- Langhorne Creek
- Kangaroo Island
- Currency Creek
- Southern Fleurieu
- Padthaway
- Wrattonbully
- Coonawarra
- Mount Benson
- Robe

Victoria

- Murray Darling
- Swan Hill
- Henty
- Grampians
- Pyrenees
- Bendigo
- Geelong
- Sunbury
- Macedon Ranges
- Mornington Peninsula
- Yarra Valley
- Upper Goulburn
- Strathbogie Ranges
- Goulburn Valley
- Heathcote
- Glenrowan
- Rutherglen
- Alpine Valleys
- King Valley
- Gippsland

New South Wales

- Murray Darling
- Swan Hill
- Perricoota
- Riverina
- Gundagai
- Tumbarumba
- Canberra District
- Hilltops
- Cowra
- Orange
- Mudgee
- Hunter
- Hastings River
- Shoalhaven Coast
- Southern Highlands

Chardonnay grape being a particularly accommodating variety. Generally, Hunter Valley Chardonnay is broader in profile than most other versions, with big, ripe flavors and lower acidity, unless it is helped along by a judicious addition of Sémillon to spike up the acidity.

More understandable is the long-standing tradition of Shiraz and its recent venture into Verdelho as a single-variety wine. Hunter Valley Shiraz generally displays ripe red berry flavors, concentrated in the best years and made more complex by rich chocolate aromas. Their firm tannins allow them to age and develop a typical leathery, tobacco character. The Verdelho wines are excitingly fresh and aromatic, best within the first year after bottling, and it is notable that more acreage has been planted to meet growing demand for this fresh, vibrant wine.

REGIONS TO WATCH

In the Central Ranges zone to the southwest of Hunter Valley, the cooling influence of the Great Dividing Range presents a different picture, depending on elevation and latitude. Full, bold, structured reds, especially Shiraz and Cabernet Sauvignon, have brought fame to Mudgee, while the lower elevations around Cowra result in softer, milder versions of the same varieties. Chardonnay from Cowra also exhibits the same properties. However, a portion of the harvest is still used as a crutch to boost some of the lighter Hunter Valley wines. Between Mudgee and Cowra lies the Orange region whose elevation is significantly higher than Cowra. Along with the southerly regions of Hilltops and Canberra District, the concentration here

The Brokenback Mountain Range in Hunter Valley

is on bright fruit, lively acidity, with balanced structure, which gives hope to the prophets of Riesling and Pinot Noir, in addition to the mainstay varieties.

VICTORIA

Swiss immigrants pioneered winemaking in Victoria, which was Australia's premier wine region before the phylloxera epidemic in 1875 and today is Australia's third-largest producer with about 15 percent of total production. The range of wine styles is exceptionally broad for a relatively small state. Very warm temperatures in summer and fall have traditionally suited the production of sweet fortified wines in the historic region of Rutherglen on the northern border with New South Wales. Conversely, annual average rainfall of about 22 inches/55 centime-

VICTORIA: CURRENTLY APPROVED ZONES, REGIONS, AND SUBREGIONS

ZONES	REGIONS	SUBREGIONS
Central Victoria	Bendigo	
	Goulburn Valley	
	Heathcote	
	Strathbogie Ranges	
	Upper Goulburn	
	Gippsland	
North East Victoria	Rutherglen	
	Alpine Valleys	
	Beechworth	
	Glenrowan	
	King Valley	
North West Victoria	Murray Darling (also stretches across into NSW)	
	Swan Hill (also stretches across into NSW)	
Port Phillip	Geelong	
	Mornington Peninsula	
	Sunbury	
	Yarra Valley	
	Macedon Ranges	
Western Victoria	Grampians	Great Western
	Henty	
	Pyrenees	

ters and cooler temperatures in the southern coastal stretches encourage premium wine production, while the warmer northern region of Murray Darling (straddling the border with New South Wales) relies on irrigation from the river, and the large yields of grapes from there are more often used for cask or bulk wines. The distinguishing factor here is once again the Great Dividing Range as it rounds out in the final curve of the comma in a southwesterly and westward direction from New South Wales. The Murray River rises in northeastern Victoria and then forms the boundary between New South Wales and Victoria as it flows northwest and then turns southwest through South Australia to empty into the ocean south of Adelaide (see map on page 232). The approved zones, regions, and subregions of Victoria are listed in the table on page 233. A discussion of some of Victoria's more important regions follows.

GLENROWAN

This area is known for dessert wines and for muscular, sturdy Shiraz and Cabernet with opulent fruit character. Arid conditions help shrivel the grapes while still on the vine to produce unique versions of concentrated late-harvest Muscat and Muscadelle, as well as fortified wines.

RUTHERGLEN

Similar to Glenrowan, Rutherglen enjoys a reputation for its fortified Liqueur Muscat, which may be barrel aged for up to fifty years. A new emphasis on lighter-style white table wines from this region is a reaction to current fashion, but consumer response has not been favorable. The Cabernet Sauvignon and Shiraz remain impressive, with depth and fleshy, sumptuous fruit, perhaps lacking in finesse but undoubtedly packing a punch.

BENDIGO

Cabernet and Shiraz produced from certain vineyards here show great depth and class, with deep purple hues, smooth texture on the palate, and eucalyptus notes on the nose.

GOULBURN VALLEY

Australia's historic Chateau Tahbilk was first produced here in 1860. Tahbilk continues to make wine as it always has, in the most traditional way. Its no-compromise wines need plenty of bottle age, and the original winery is one of the treasures of the Australian National Trust. Today, better than half of the world's Marsanne grapes, native to the Rhône Valley of France, are planted here. Michelton is a popular Marsanne producer of the region.

GRAMPIANS

This region used to be dominated by the production of Seppelt's Great Western *méthode champenoise* sparkling wine. However, concentration today is on varietal table wines of finesse and elegance, from Cabernet Sauvignon and Shiraz to Riesling and Chardonnay. This is possible because of the distinctly cooler climates, as compared with Bendigo and Goulburn Valley.

YARRA VALLEY

One of Australia's most promising wine regions, Yarra Valley is one of the cooler vineyard areas on the mainland. Located east of Melbourne, Yarra features both adequate rainfall and mineral-rich soils, good for the production of high-quality Riesling, Chardonnay, Shiraz, Cabernet, and arguably Australia's best Pinot Noir. Domaine Chandon of California produces very fine sparkling wine here, exported under the Greenpoint label, and Coldstream Hills produces elegant Pinot Noir and Chardonnay. Yarra Ridge Winery produces a full range of wines, of which the Pinot Noir, Cabernet Sauvignon, and Shiraz stand out, especially in the reserve versions.

MORNINGTON PENINSULA

With a climate similar to Yarra Valley, a number of wineries in the Mornington Peninsula do an excellent job with Chardonnay, Pinot Noir, Riesling, and Pinot Gris, emphasizing freshness and length of clean flavors. Depending on the warmth and length of the growing season, there are also some excellent examples of Bordeaux blends.

Vine clippings in the Yarra Valley

TASMANIA

One of the world's coolest viticultural areas, at latitudes 41 degrees to 43 degrees south, most of this island's vineyards are isolated and small compared with those of the rest of Australia. At one time, the French Champagne house Louis Roederer had joined forces with a local producer, Heemskerk, to produce sparkling wines under the Jansz label. Those wines garnered much praise for their style, elegance, and depth, their toasty aromas and flavors over crisp fruit character. Roederer has since pulled out of that project, and the Jansz label has been sold to Yalumba, though they continue to source grapes from the same Tasmanian vineyards.

What brought Roederer to Tasmania was the prospect of using the cool climate to grow the triumvirate of grapes that Champagne uses to produce exceptional sparkling wine. They were right, and many others such as Clover Hill and Pipers Brook followed. The sparkling-wine movement led others to assume, rightly so, that areas on the island must be suitable for still wine production from Chardonnay and Pinot Noir, as well as other grape types such as Riesling, Gewürztraminer, and Pinot Gris.

To date, there are no approved zones, regions, or subregions in Tasmania, but when there eventually are, they will probably recognize the importance of a region in the south around the city of Hobart that has a distinctly cool climate and concentrates on growing the usual cool-climate varieties. In contrast, in the northern region around Launceston where the climate is more complex, Cabernet Sauvignon can ripen sufficiently well to produce deeply colored and well-extracted wines, as proven by Pipers Brook.

Pipers Brook Ninth Island wines from Tasmania have received high praise.

SOUTH AUSTRALIA

This region, which currently produces around 45 percent of Australia's wine, includes areas that have never been attacked by phylloxera, and it is not uncommon to find fine wines from Riesling and Shiraz vines that are more than a hundred years old. With the first vines planted around South Australia's major city of Adelaide in 1837, the region produces what is arguably Australia's finest wine. In the 1950s, Max Schubert, then winemaker for Penfolds, produced the Shiraz-based Grange (originally named Grange Hermitage), which continues to rank as one of the world's best red wines. Grange can age for thirty to forty years, depending on the vintage, and is one of the best expressions of the full-bodied and fruit-rich Shiraz grape.

From the warmer areas north of Adelaide to the southernmost region of Mount Gambier, South Australia offers a myriad of climates and soils to support a broad range

SOUTH AUSTRALIA: CURRENTLY APPROVED ZONES, REGIONS, AND SUBREGIONS

ZONES	REGIONS	SUBREGIONS
Adelaide Superzone includes Barossa, Fleurieu, and Mount Lofty ranges		
Barossa	Barossa Valley	
	Eden Valley	High Eden
Far North	Southern Flinders Ranges	
Fleurieu	Langhorne Creek	
	McLaren Vale	
	Currency Creek	
	Kangaroo Island	
	Southern Fleurieu	
Limestone Coast	Mount Benson	
	Coonawarra	
	Padthaway	
	Wrattonbully	
	Robe	
Lower Murray	Riverland	
Mount Lofty Ranges	Adelaide Hills	Piccadilly Valley
		Lenswood
	Clare Valley	
	Adelaide Plains	
The Peninsulas		

of grape types and wine styles. South Australia's most important wine-producing regions include Adelaide Hills, Barossa Valley, Eden Valley, McLaren Vale, Langhorne Creek, Coonawarra, Clare Valley, and Padthaway. (The complete list of approved zones, regions, and subregions of South Australia is shown in the table on page 235.)

ADELAIDE HILLS

With elevations from 1,250 to 2,380 feet/420 to 775 meters, this region receives an average of 30 inches/75 centimeters of rain per year, but precipitation can be highly variable from vintage to vintage. Like many regions around the world, the Adelaide Hills underscore the unreliability of generalizations. It is always tempting to assume that, in the Southern Hemisphere, the northern areas are warmer and therefore are suited to producing full-bodied red wines like Cabernet Sauvignon and Shiraz, while the southern areas lend themselves to crisper Chardonnays or even Rieslings. But within the Adelaide Hills, the central part includes the subregion Piccadilly Valley, which produces some of South Australia's very best and most elegant Chardonnay, while both the northern and south-

ern parts of the Adelaide Hills are known for bold, assertive reds. Piccadilly Valley's reputation for fine wines also extends to Pinot Noir and Sauvignon Blanc. Some of the Pinot Noir and Chardonnay are used for sparkling-wine production.

CLARE VALLEY

The name Clare Valley has been synonymous with Riesling, producing a very fine, slightly austere style that warms with age, becoming softer and richer, but still with crisp, finishing acidity. In warmer microclimates, Shiraz and Cabernet Sauvignon seem to reverse that profile, being robust, fruity, and concentrated when young and developing a graceful, silky elegance as they age. The Mitchell winery and Annie's Lane are especially impressive.

BAROSSA VALLEY

Along with the Hunter Valley in New South Wales, South Australia's Barossa Valley is one of Australia's most famous wine regions. Settled by German immigrants, the Barossa Valley once boasted many acres of older Riesling vines that produced fine, full-flavored wines with abundant tropical, passion-fruit flavors. But the realities of climate have trumped cultural allegiance, and the modern industry shows a preference for Shiraz as its focus. This is not surprising, since Shiraz has been a mainstay of the Barossa landscape since the mid-1800s, and the region

TOP LEFT: *The famous Lenswood vineyards in the Adelaide Hills region of South Australia* **TOP RIGHT:** *Clare Valley vineyards* **BOTTOM:** *Henschke produces a fine Chardonnay from the Lenswood Vineyard in the Adelaide Hills.*

retains some plots of very old vines that produce wines of extraordinary structure, depth, and ripeness: The best of them is still Penfolds Grange. However, Barossa is not standing still. There has been plenty of interest in other red Rhône grape varieties, especially Grenache, and Riesling is finding favor again in the cooler subregion of High Eden.

A very welcome innovation has been regional acceptance of the Barossa Old Vine Charter, which specifies a minimum age for vines if producers want to include certain descriptive phrases on the label. For the term Barossa Old Vines, the vines must be at least 35 years of age, Survivor Vines at least 70 years old, Centurion Vines at least 100 years, and Ancestor Vines at least 125 years old. Most interestingly, other regions have expressed a desire to adopt the charter for their own use, possibly paving the way to a national standard.

EDEN VALLEY

The Barossa Valley region extends only up to the 1,312-foot/400-meter mark in elevation on the eastern side; beyond that, the Eden Valley takes over, offering cooler climates at higher elevations. Accordingly, Eden Valley Riesling is leaner and finer, with higher acid content and more citrus character. A wide variety of soils, microclimates, and exposures means that Cabernet Sauvignon shows its riper fruit character in some vineyard sites, while other plots emphasize the menthol side of Cabernet. In general, the sites chosen for Shiraz promote a full, fruity ripeness, but some special plots offer a more complete picture. A dedication to careful site selection has resulted in the finest Shiraz made in the Eden Valley—Henschke's Hill of Grace, which many connoisseurs consider to be Grange's equal. Henschke's Mount Edelstone Shiraz, also from Eden Valley, also stands very high in the classic Shiraz rankings.

MCLAREN VALE

Within the Fleurieu zone, McLaren Vale has earned a special reputation for amply ripe but finely structured and concentrated Shiraz and Cabernet Sauvignon. But a reluctance to gamble on a relatively unknown place name and the Australian industry's obsessive preoccupation with blending means that some of McLaren Vale's best ends up in broader regional blends. As more of the region's smaller wineries find access to the export market, expect that picture to change.

LANGHORNE CREEK

As an inland cousin to McLaren Vale, Langhorne Creek

TOP: *Barossa Valley vineyards greet the morning sun.* BOTTOM RIGHT: *Yalumba sources grapes from the Menzies vineyard for Coonawarra Cabernet Sauvignon.*

Cabernet—dense black currant fruit with hints of eucalyptus and cigar box aromas and an ability to develop complexity and nuances over several years of aging.

The famous terra rossa soils have been both a blessing and a bane for the Coonawarra region. They consist of rich organic matter in loamy soils over a bed of deep limestone laid down as the ocean receded more than a half million years ago. They provide an excellent base for grapes such as Cabernet Sauvignon that mature over a long period of time. However, they were also at the heart of the controversy over what actually constitutes Coonawarra as an official geographic indication. Now that the controversy has been settled, the vineyard managers and winemakers can concentrate on demonstrating the full potential of the Coonawarra region.

That potential goes beyond Cabernet Sauvignon and includes possibly promising futures for other grapes such as Chardonnay and Shiraz. The juxtaposition of Shiraz and Cabernet is not surprising, but the success of some growers with Chardonnay and even Riesling underscores the innate suitability of Coonawarra to fine wine production.

finds itself in a similar situation, producing excellent Cabernet and Shiraz, but little of it is bottled specifying the place name.

PADTHAWAY

Like a troublesome teenager, Padthaway has been difficult to understand. Initially pioneered as a red wine region, based on its perceived similarity to Coonawarra, it is Chardonnay that has become the varietal champion, exhibiting the ripe stone fruit character of a warm but not hot region, and enough citrus character and acidity to retain finesse and length on the palate. The suitability of the region for Chardonnay has recently been reinforced by a small number of very elegant Pinot Noirs being produced. Hopefully, the number of those will increase too.

COONAWARRA

Lying within the large Limestone Coast zone, Coonawarra, the "Bordeaux of Australia," is a flat strip of land 1-by-8 miles/1.6-by-13 kilometers in size, with terra rossa soil—a calcareous-limestone porous base covered with red topsoil. Most growers and winemakers agree that these particular soil conditions seem exceptionally well suited to producing some of Australia's finest Cabernet Sauvignon grapes, along with other red Bordeaux varieties (Cabernet Franc, Merlot, Malbec) for blending. With the almost Continental but cool climate of the region, there is magic in Coonawarra

WRATTONBULLY

While the controversy about Coonawarra's boundaries raged, vineyard development continued around its proposed borders, notably in the Wrattonbully region immediately to the north, where similar soil conditions can be found. While Coonawarra may have history and fame on its side, Wrattonbully has a similarly conducive climate, the same limestone soil base, and the future to demonstrate its ability to produce world-class wines. We can fully expect to see some fine Bordeaux blends from this relatively new region.

WRATTONBULLY

Smith & Hooper

———————

CABERNET SAUVIGNON
MERLOT

———————

FINE WINE OF AUSTRALIA
750ML

TOP: *The famous limestone subsoil and terra rossa topsoil of Coonawarra* **BOTTOM:** *Smith & Hooper have faith in the Wrattonbully region as a source of fine Cabernet Sauvignon and Merlot.*

WESTERN AUSTRALIA

Perth is the capital of this state, whose eastern half is desert. Western Australia has produced some impressive wines, stressing low yields in the best vineyard sites. Production levels are still low compared with the other states and territories, with only 8 percent of the national total coming from Western Australia. (The approved zones, regions, and subregions are listed in the following table.)

WESTERN AUSTRALIA: CURRENTLY APPROVED ZONES, REGIONS, AND SUBREGIONS

ZONES	REGIONS	SUBREGIONS
Eastern Plains, Inland and North of Western Australia		
West Australian South East		
Coastal South West Australia	Blackwood Valley	
	Geographe	
	Great Southern	Albany
		Denmark
		Frankland River
		Mount Barker
		Porongurup
	Margaret River	
	Manjimup	
	Pemberton	
Central Western Australia		
Greater Perth	Peel	
	Perth Hills	
	Swan District	Swan Valley

North of the city of Perth, the Swan District, at the base of the Darling Ranges, was historically important for jug and fortified wines, because of its warm climate. Investment by large corporations has resulted in some sizeable fermentation plants using temperature-controlled fermentation tanks, but world-class wine will never be produced here.

Vineyard development through the 1990s was in the more southerly, cooler areas south of Perth, in the southwest corner of the nation, and this is where the more important regions are located.

MARGARET RIVER

The Margaret River is sandwiched between Cape Leeuwin and Cape Naturaliste on the Indian Ocean, part of a strip of gravel soils on sandy loam and granite. The coastal location in and around a river system, coupled with its gravelly mineral soils and overall temperate maritime climate, immediately invites comparison with Bordeaux, France. Not surprisingly, Cabernet Sauvignon as a single varietal or blended with Cabernet Franc or Merlot has established a track record in the Margaret River region. Sémillon and Sauvignon Blanc, separately or together, are similarly impressive, with the typically herbaceous characteristics to be expected in a maritime climate. In some of the cooler districts, Chardonnay also does very well. Leeuwin Estate and Cape Mentelle are the best-known producers in the Margaret River region.

GREAT SOUTHERN

This region lies at the southernmost tip of the state, and is heavily influenced by its coastal location. This is one of the coolest regions in Western Australia, where loam soils and long ripening conditions allow for the making of quality Rieslings that age well. Chardonnay is also suited to the cooler regions. Within the Great Southern region, the Mount Barker subregion averages about 30 inches/75 centimeters of rain and boasts elevations of 1,000 feet/330

Vineyards in the Margaret River region of Western Australia

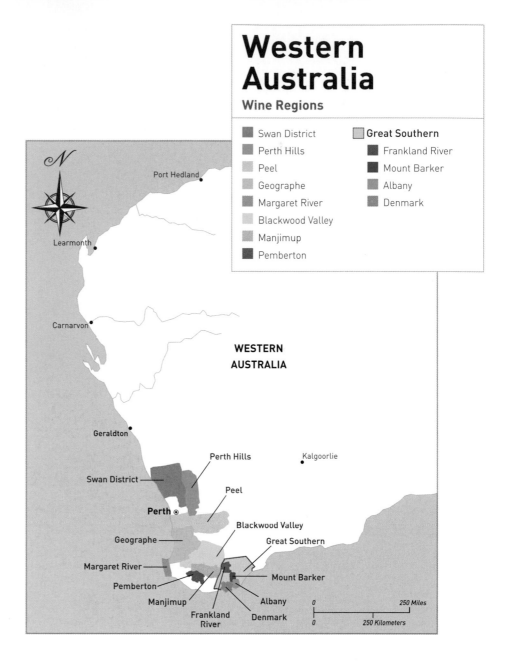

Western Australia
Wine Regions

- Swan District
- Perth Hills
- Peel
- Geographe
- Margaret River
- Blackwood Valley
- Manjimup
- Pemberton
- Great Southern
- Frankland River
- Mount Barker
- Albany
- Denmark

Port Hedland

Learmonth

Carnarvon

WESTERN
AUSTRALIA

Geraldton

Kalgoorlie

Perth Hills

Swan District

Perth

Peel

Blackwood Valley

Geographe

Great Southern

Margaret River

Mount Barker

Pemberton

Manjimup

Albany

Frankland
River

Denmark

0   250 Miles

0   250 Kilometers

meters. Here, Cabernet Sauvignon and Shiraz produce some impressive wines from warmer vineyards. Mount Barker's neighbors Porongurup and Frankland River also show promise for these grape types.

GEOGRAPHE

With the Indian Ocean as its influence and a variety of soils from the coast to the inland areas, Geographe is home to a mix of grape types, and the region perhaps is still looking for its identity and focus. Nevertheless, Sauvignon Blanc, Chardonnay, and Verdelho can all be pleasant and even exciting, while the usual reds (Cabernet Sauvignon, Shiraz, and Merlot) produce bold, satisfying wines.

When buying Australian wines, good value is just about guaranteed. The wines, like almost all of the wines of the New World, feature varietal labels, and the wines are true to the taste characteristics of each varietal. At the same time, Australia is developing its own style with certain grape types and varietal blends. Like Chile, the other export leader in the Southern Hemisphere, Australia is beginning to export a small amount of select wines from single vineyards with distinguished pedigrees, and these wines are expensive. Still, if we define value as high quality at a reasonable price, these boutique Australian wines qualify as good values.

Australia's export market is dominated by Great Britain,

NEW ZEALAND

Contemporary New Zealand

New Zealand has modern winemaking equipment and technology, good soils, and cool climate, so it can compete on the basis of quality with the finest traditional wine regions of the world. On that basis, New Zealand rose to rank twenty-third in worldwide wine production, having experienced significant increases in acreage and production since 2000, while leading European nations have seen their total production decrease.

Consisting of the North and South Islands, New Zealand stretches 932 miles/1,553 kilometers, from 34 degrees to 47 degrees south latitude. Vineyard lands on the North and South Islands total approximately 64,000 acres/26,000 hectares, an increase of almost 150 percent since 2000. Climatically, the northern section of the North Island experiences the warmest temperatures, while the southern part of the South Island is recognized as the southernmost grape-growing area in the world and sees distinctly cool, even cold temperatures. In the warmer north, grape harvest usually begins in February, but in the cooler south, the grapes may have to wait until late April to be ripe enough for harvesting.

The islands are small enough that all areas are affected by the maritime climate, creating generally hospitable weather patterns for viticulture. The most prized growing areas in New Zealand are those with relatively less rain, less-fertile soils, good drainage, long and cool growing seasons, and plenty of sunshine. These ideal conditions provide grapes with good levels of acidity and adequate sugar levels. New Zealand is best known for wonderfully unique styles of Sauvignon Blanc and other cool-climate wines like Riesling and Pinot Noir. In the cooler parts, these grapes fare well because of long hours of daylight, even into the fall months, and significant temperature variation from day to night, with warm daytime temperatures for grape ripening and much cooler temperatures at night for acid retention.

History

Historically, New Zealand has not been a wine-conscious nation. Until about forty years ago, restaurants could not legally sell wine with food, and no alcohol could be consumed after 6:30 P.M.; even today, New Zealand still maintains dry

but the United States and Canada are becoming increasingly important clients. On the back of extraordinary growth during the 1990s, Australian exports to the world increased by 60 percent between 2000 and 2007, and the value of its exports doubled in the same time period. Australia continues to offer the full range of wine styles, something for everybody's palate and everybody's wallet. American wine consumers can easily find Chardonnay, Sauvignon Blanc, Riesling, Sémillon, Sémillon/Chardonnay blends, and Marsanne; on the red side, Cabernet Sauvignon, Shiraz, Cabernet Sauvignon/Shiraz blends, Shiraz/Cabernet blends, Grenache, Pinot Noir, and Merlot are quite available. Australia also exports some fine sparkling wines, made by the *méthode champenoise*, and some interesting, well-made Porto-style fortified wines.

Australia's best export wines include those made by Bridgewater Mill, Brown Bros., Cape Mentelle, Charles Melton, Château Reynella, Château Tahbilk, Coldstream Hills, Croser, D'Arenberg, Hardys, Henschke, Jacob's Creek, Leasingham, Leeuwin Estate, Lindemans, Mildara, Mitchell, Mitchelton, Mountadam, Orlando, Padthaway Estate, Penfolds, Petaluma, Peter Lehmann, Piper's Brook, Rosemount, Rothbury Estate, Saltram, Seaview, Seppelt, Shaw and Smith, Stonehaven, Taltarni, Tyrrell's, Wolf Blass, Wyndham, Wynns, and Yalumba.

The vineyards of Goundrey Wines, one of the pioneers of the Mount Barker subregion within Great Southern

parishes. Just before the turn of the century, New Zealand's first commercial wines were made with the American hybrid Isabella, which was also known locally as Albany Surprise. Other hybrids, such as Baco Noir and Seibel, were a major part of the young industry. These grapes were mostly used to make low-quality fortified wines.

In the early 1900s, farmers from Germany brought cuttings of Müller-Thurgau grapevines to New Zealand, as climatic conditions promised success with this variety. New Zealand imposed prohibition from the early to mid-1900s; shortly after this decree, an outbreak of phylloxera wiped out most of the vines. By 1923, only 180 acres/72 hectares of vines remained. After prohibition ended, Yugoslav immigrants from Dalmatia started replanting and new wineries were built, but local taste was geared toward fortified and sweet wines.

By 1960, there were only 1,000 acres/400 hectares of vines in all of New Zealand, but a new appreciation for table wines began to emerge. Between the years 1970 and 1983, national consumption figures shifted, from 70 percent dessert wines to 70 percent table wines. Although a good deal of wine made in the 1970s was of the Liebfraumilch style, straightforward and fruity, and made from blends of Müller-Thurgau, plantings of Sauvignon Blanc also began in the early 1970s.

In the 1980s, the New Zealand government paid farmers the equivalent of about U.S.$800 per acre/U.S.$2,000 per hectare to uproot unpopular grape varieties. Many farmers used the money to upgrade their vineyards with French varieties that have export potential. Today, 90 percent of New Zealand's vineyards are planted with vinifera vines.

Grape Types

As of 2007, with 41 percent of all plantings, Sauvignon Blanc has eclipsed Chardonnay as the most planted vinifera grape in New Zealand, covering 26,000 acres/10,491 hectares. Sauvignon Blanc's rise to preeminence has been nothing short of startling, with a 322 percent increase in acreage between 2000 and 2007. Just as notable has been the increased acreage for Pinot Noir, increasing 294 percent between 2000 and 2007, to a total of 10,970 acres/4,441 hectares. In comparison, Chardonnay's growth in acreage for the same period is a paltry 37 percent.

Along with the obvious leaders, other varieties like Pinot Gris, Riesling, Merlot, and even Syrah have seen major growth spurts in terms of new vineyard plantings.

Only Cabernet Sauvignon and Sémillon have decreased in acreage, recognizing the lack of suitable climates for Cabernet Sauvignon as a single-varietal wine (reinforced by Merlot's increased acreage) and the lack of market success for Sémillon.

Like other Southern Hemisphere growing areas, New Zealand has a natural advantage in the world market, especially the white wine market, since its grape harvest is in the first half of the year, and their new-vintage wines appear on the shelves six months before those of their Northern Hemisphere counterparts.

Wine Laws

Currently, wine producers of New Zealand are able to operate with a minimum of governmental regulation. Wine quality is guaranteed by intense competition, especially in the export market. A free-trade agreement with Australia promises increased investment and a larger market for New Zealand wines. What regulations there are seem to be in line with those of other wine-producing nations. Official boundaries and rules for districts and regions are still being formalized, but other specific laws with regard to labeling are worth noting, such as:

- If a place is named on the label, at least 75 percent of the grapes must come from that place. By this measure, generic label terms, such as Burgundy or Chablis, cannot be used for New Zealand wines.
- If a grape is named on the label, at least 75 percent of the grapes must be the named variety. However, if the wine is to be sold in any member nation of the European Union, the wine must be made from at least 85 percent of the named variety.
- If more than one grape variety is named on a label, the grapes must be listed in order of percentage used, from highest to lowest.

Wine Regions

NORTH ISLAND

The North Island is the more populated of the two islands, with about 70 percent of New Zealand's population of 4.2 million.

AUCKLAND

The Auckland wine region, which is mostly west and north

of the major city of Auckland, used to have three-fourths of the nation's vines. Because of rising land costs and urbanization, as well as a shift away from Auckland's poorly drained, heavy clay soils, only 2 percent of the country's vines are now planted there.

Still, some of New Zealand's largest producers, such as Montana, Babich, and Villa Maria, all have offices and production facilities in the Auckland region. Grape-crushing and winemaking facilities for other large producers, such as Fenton Estate, Coopers Creek, and Kumeu River, are also located in this appellation.

Subregions of Auckland continue to develop, especially the Kumeu region and the fashionably hip Waiheke Island. However, within the total national production, their output is minimal.

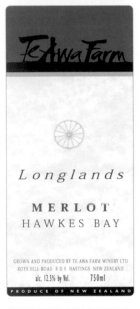

WAIKATO AND BAY OF PLENTY

Located just south of Auckland, these regions produce a small amount of wine, but most of the grapes are sourced from Gisborne, Hawkes Bay, and Marlborough. The best-known producers are Morton Estate and de Redcliffe Estates.

HAWKES BAY

Southeast of Auckland, this region grew almost 20 percent from 2000 to 2007, with about 11,500 acres/4,600 hectares under vine. It is an important region for the production of Merlot-Cabernet blends, Cabernet Sauvignon, and some Shiraz and other Rhône

TOP: *Bordeaux blends like this one have brought fame to the Waiheke Island subappellation.* MIDDLE: *Merlot has produced some fine wines in Hawkes Bay.* BOTTOM: *Hawkes Bay produces a fuller style of Chardonnay.*

varities. Compared with many other New Zealand wine regions, Hawkes Bay has less rain, more sun, and lighter soils with good drainage. One of the most promising viticultural regions, it was the work of one man that put Hawkes Bay on the world wine map: John Buck of Te Mata Estate. Te Mata is known for its exquisite Cabernet Sauvignon from the Awatea vineyard and especially its Coleraine, a classic Bordeaux blend of Cabernet Sauvignon, Merlot, and Cabernet Franc, very much in the style of the best Meritage wines from California.

GISBORNE

Sheltered by mountains to the west, this region enjoys low rainfall and plenty of sunshine. In fact, it is the first wine region in the world to see the new sun every day, since it is located on the easternmost tip of the North Island. Gisborne is now New Zealand's third largest wine region, with a total of just over 5,000 acres/2,000 hectares, and has achieved renown for its Chardonnay, as well as some interesting versions of Riesling, Chenin Blanc, and Gewürztraminer.

WAIRARAPA

Formerly Wellington or Martinborough, Wairarapa has good drainage, sunshine, and low rainfall in autumn. The Pinot Noir and Chardonnay wines from the stone-drained gravelly silt soil of Wairarapa vineyards have received substantial praise, reflected in the 150 percent increase in vineyard acreage between 2000 and 2007, with much of that increase dedicated to those two varieties. Martinborough Vineyards, Ata Rangi, Dry River, Palliser Estates, and Te Kairanga produce some fine wines.

SOUTH ISLAND

As late as 1989, the South Island had only 26 percent of total vine plantings; today one of its regions alone has more than half of all New Zealand's vineyard acreage. That region is Marlborough, and the frenzy of South Island growth can be attributed largely to one grape that when planted on these stony soils makes a truly unique style of wine: Marlborough Sauvignon Blanc. These wines have drawn worldwide acclaim, because of their clean gooseberry, grassy, tropical-fruit nose; their ripe fruitiness; and their lively citrus attack on the palate.

Kaitaia
Whangarei
NORTH ISLAND
Northland
Auckland
Auckland ✪
Thames
Bay of Plenty
Bay of Plenty
Hamilton
Waikato
Rotorua
New Plymouth
Gisborne
Gisborne
Napier
Hastings
Hawke Bay
Hawkes Bay
Wanganui
Palmerston North
Wairarapa
Nelson
Nelson
Wellington
Westport
Blenheim
PACIFIC OCEAN
Greymouth
SOUTH ISLAND
Marlborough
TASMAN SEA
Pegasus Bay
Lake Wakatipu
Canterbury
Christchurch
Lake Te Anau
Canterbury Bight
Queenstown
Central Otago
Dunedin
Invercargil
STEWART ISLAND

0   250   500 Miles
0   250   500 Kilometers

MARLBOROUGH

Montana Winery began to plant Sauvignon Blanc in Marlborough in 1976. Although there was some evidence that Marlborough would provide a good home for Sauvignon Blanc and Chardonnay grapes, Montana's reason for planting in Marlborough was far more practical: Hawkes Bay had become too expensive to undertake a large-scale land purchase and vineyard development. Montana released its first Sauvignon Blanc wines in 1980, to enthusiastic reviews and excellent consumer response. From 10,000 acres/4,000 hectares in 2000, Marlborough now has more than 32,000 acres/13,000 hectares under vine, mostly on stony and gravelly soils. In addition to Sauvignon Blanc, Marlborough also is home to Chardonnay, Pinot Noir, and Riesling.

If it was Montana that put Marlborough Sauvignon Blanc on the world wine map, it was Cloudy Bay Sauvignon Blanc that defined the category, winning rave reviews for its early vintages that offered the seemingly impossible combination of ripe fruit balanced by searing acidity.

Cloudy Bay (now a subsidiary of Clicquot, Inc., the corporate parent of Veuve Clicquot Champagne), along with Montana, Selaks, Corbans, and other Marlborough producers, is able to make wines that are balanced between green, crisp flavors and ripe, soft flavors, with a touch of gooseberry and even passion fruit on the palate and subtle but unmistakable citrus, melon, and lime zest complexity.

Marlborough, centered around the city of Blenheim, has long, sunny summers and moderate rainfall, 30 inches/75 centimeters per year. The slow ripening period in Marlborough and its Wairau Valley and Awatere Valley subregions is a result of lots of sunshine without scorching heat throughout spring, summer, and fall. Chardonnay is made in a lighter style here than in Hawkes Bay, and Riesling is made in both fruity and crisp styles as well as in late-harvest and botrytis-affected styles.

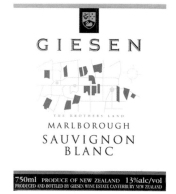

There is also an active *méthode champenoise* sparkling-wine industry in Marlborough, with foreign investment provided by Champagne houses such as Deutz, in a joint venture with Montana, which also has its own highly successful Lindauer sparkling wine. Cloudy Bay's Pelorus sparkler is also well regarded.

NELSON

Located about 45 miles/75 kilometers east of Marlborough, Nelson's rain shadow and cool climate are best suited to the usual cool-climate varieties such as Sauvignon Blanc, Riesling, Pinot Noir, and Chardonnay. An impressive increase of 285 percent in vineyard acreage between 2000 and 2007 brought the total number of acres to 1,930/780 hectares, though still only 3 percent of the national total.

CANTERBURY

With its subregions of Waipara, Burnham, and Banks Peninsula, the Canterbury region extends along the east coast of the South Island, sheltered by mountains to the

Sauvignon Blanc put Marlborough on the wine map.

west. Bright summer sun and a long, cool growing season favor Chardonnay and Pinot Noir, along with Riesling and Sauvignon Blanc. Even though Canterbury lost its position of fourth-largest producing region to Central Otago, it has still seen substantial growth, based on the promise of its cool growing season to deliver clean, fresh, ripe flavors along with delicacy and finesse.

CENTRAL OTAGO

This region enjoys a far more Continental climate than the other wine regions of New Zealand, with drier summers and cold winters. Careful vineyard siting is the key in Otago, and those who venture here are blessed with higher levels of mineral content in the soils than anywhere else in New Zealand. Not surprisingly perhaps, Pinot Noir has become the darling of the region, and the wines from here have received considerable acclaim from many quarters for their vivacious qualities of ripe cherry and berry fruit, fresh acidity, and a lingering mineral streak.

Based on fascination with Pinot Noir, Central Otago has seen a huge 400 percent increase in vineyard land over the past six years, and is now New Zealand's fourth-largest region, with 3,500 acres/1,400 hectares. Those growers who have not followed the Pinot Noir dream concentrate on Chardonnay, Riesling, and Pinot Gris.

TOP: *Canterbury's cool climate is very well suited to Riesling.*
BOTTOM: *Central Otago has become another mecca for Pinot Noir enthusiasts.*

SOUTH AFRICA

SITTING BY THE WATER'S EDGE of downtown Cape Town, you cannot help but be moved by the tranquil setting—sailboats bobbing on small whitecaps, a gentle sun glinting off blue ocean and white city buildings. And yet, minutes away is the other downtown—a thriving, bustling, cosmopolitan city that rivals any in the world for amenities and attractions. Later that same evening, high on the hills of Durbanville, you can look down on the city of Cape Town, nestled like a jewel in the safety of its magnificent natural harbor. And even when the dulcet amber glow of sunset is threatened by the gathering gloom of towering thunderclouds laden with moisture from ocean winds, there is still a vibrant natural beauty in the juxtaposition of brooding darkness and the last vestiges of dusk. Just a few miles farther inland lie majestic mountains like Simonsberg and Middelberg, soaring sentinels over the foothills and valleys that dot the landscape.

South Africa is a land of contrasts, especially within the hundred miles from the east, south, and west coastlines that define this wine land. It is situated at a crossroads of climatic and cultural influences that have helped define South African history and its wines. Climatically, both the Atlantic and Indian Oceans impact the region, bringing dry or moist, hot or cold air, depending on the season and the prevailing winds.

HISTORY

MODERN SOUTH AFRICAN HISTORY has centered on its ugly period of apartheid and racial hegemony, but all that changed with the political and social changes brought about by the heroic actions of Nelson Mandela and members of the African National Congress. However, despite governmental and social programs to bring diversity to the grape-growing and winemaking industries, there is still much work to do in South Africa if all its citizens are to share in the gifts of a hard-fought democracy.

In previous centuries, the area was developed by Dutch traders, who needed a rest stop on their journey to the east. Subsequently, the British wrested control of the Cape away from the Dutch, and British traders established colonies to provision the endless stream of ships. Even the French in-

fluence was felt when the religiously persecuted Huguenots who had fled to the Netherlands from France were again displaced by the Dutch and offered land grants and safe passage to South Africa. The Dutch and English influences are still very evident in the languages and customs of the land, while the French Protestant influence is very strong in places like the cultural enclave of Franschhoek.

With respect to wine, the French influence is seen in many of the vine types imported to South Africa over the centuries and in the stylistic imprint of many of its wines. The English and Dutch influence is more evident in the establishment of a centuries-old wine industry that was originally designed to feed the growing demand of the fortified wine trade and served the Sherry and Porto imitators in those nations and in their colonies around the world. Today that organization and infrastructure are being used to position modern South African wines in the world market.

For many consumers, South Africa appears to be a newcomer to the wine world, but the history of South African wine spans three centuries. And, just as the origi-

nal settlers had to deal with the double duty of providing for the international traders and providing for themselves, the South African wine industry now finds itself stuck between catering to the world wine market with the usual international wine types like Chardonnay and Cabernet Sauvignon and maintaining its own unique vine varieties and wine styles.

South Africa's modern history left its wine industry with a serious problem that has only recently been overcome. The social and political practices of apartheid had resulted in sanctions on and resistance to almost all the products of the country, including wine. By virtue of its failed apartheid policy, South Africa was isolated from the international community of nations, and its wine industry was kept out of touch with state-of-the-art production methods and contemporary trends in viticulture. By 2010 that picture had thankfully changed, with South African grape growers and winemakers receiving lots of advice from friends around the world and able to acquire the very best technology and equipment in the fields and in the wineries.

TOP LEFT: *Only the sign in English betrays the fact this is Franschhoek, not Paris.* BOTTOM LEFT: *A vineyard in the Stellenbosch wine region* RIGHT: *Signs of Dutch presence are seen in the early house architecture of South Africa.*

CONTEMPORARY SOUTH AFRICA

SOUTH AFRICA, a country of about 50 million people, produces about 3 percent of the world's wines and is the world's ninth-largest wine producer. With about 250,000 acres/100,000 hectares under vine, South Africa produces about 193 million gallons/7.3 million hectoliters of wine per year. These statistics border on the extraordinary when we realize that all of South Africa's vineyards and wineries are concentrated within 100 miles/166 kilometers of Cape Town, the major port city at the extreme southern tip of the nation. The nation's export strategy has been to move out of the market for bulk and fortified wines and brandy and into that of high-quality vinifera wines. The strategy is a sound one, but it has been, and continues to be, a bumpy ride.

The South African wine industry is still battling problems. Having played catch-up to the rest of the world post-apartheid, South Africa seems too often to be caught in the swing of wine fashions, constantly trying to keep up with having the "right" ratio of white to red grape types and the "right" varieties planted to cater to whatever the worldwide consumer is drinking at any point in time. Still, some long-term trends suggest that the South African wine industry is getting more in step with consumer preferences. In 2000, South Africa's total vineyard acreage was split 64 percent white to 36 percent red; by 2007 that had changed to 56 percent white and 44 percent red.

Grape Types

Reluctantly perhaps, South Africa has had to come to terms with its two grape demons—Chenin Blanc and Pinotage. Even with decreased acreage, now down to 19 percent, Chenin Blanc is still the most widely planted grape in the nation, occupying more land here than in any other nation. That odd statistic is a legacy of South Africa's previous status as a supplier of fortified wines to the British, and Chenin Blanc was an easy grape to grow on the warm plains of the colony.

The only other grape to show decreased acreage is South Africa's very own Pinotage, a cross between the warm-climate Cinsaut and the cool-climate Pinot Noir. Like that odd combination of parents, Pinotage seems incapable of figuring out what it wants to be as a wine,

sometimes being made in a simple, light, fruity style, and other times showing full extract of flavors enhanced by new wood. However, neither personality has captured the world's attention.

In all other regards, South Africa currently concentrates on the standard international roster of grape types, with Cabernet Sauvignon (19 percent) and Shiraz (10 percent) being the second- and third-most-planted grape types, followed by Chardonnay (9 percent), Sauvignon Blanc (8 percent), and Merlot (7 percent). Of those, the most interesting developments have followed New Zealand's success with Sauvignon Blanc and Australia's success with Shiraz. South Africa has successfully shown that with careful vineyard site selection they can find cool climates to show off the zingy side of Sauvignon Blanc and the full, fruity aspect of Shiraz.

Wine Laws

In 1973, the South Africa Wines of Origin (WO) system was adopted. Like other appellation systems, the regulations set minimum standards for the use of grape variety names, vintage dates, and place names on labels, as follows:

- A vintage date on the label means that at least 85 percent of all the grapes must have been harvested in the stated year.
- A grape variety name on the label means that at least 85 percent of all the grapes used to make the wine must be the stated variety.
- A place name on the label means that 100 percent of the grapes must have been grown in that place.

Cabernet Sauvignon is typical of the international grape varieties grown in South Africa.

Of the 193 million gallons/7.3 million hectoliters of wine currently produced in South Africa, only half of that volume qualifies as Wine of Origin from one of the following defined categories, in decreasing order of size: Geographical Unit, Region, District, Ward, Wine Estate.

The geographical units, or GUs, are the equivalent of mega-appellations, while the districts and wards are sub-appellations of the regions. The two major GUs defined to date are Western Cape and Northern Cape, each of which includes a number of regions or districts. A third GU, KwaZulu-Natal, is located on the east coast of the nation, south of Mozambique, but it has no regions or districts within it. To date, the wines from the Northern Cape and from KwaZulu-Natal have not reached the international market, so our comments will be restricted to the more important wine areas of the Western Cape.

The defining criteria for regions are fairly broad, consisting mostly of a broad geographic or historic name, while a district is a more distinct entity. To qualify as a ward, the requirements are far stricter, requiring, for example, a single unifying soil structure. Wine estates can be made up of several vineyards, but they must all be connected and be farmed as one unit.

Not all districts are contained within regions. If a wine comes from a region, district, or ward, the place of origin will be on the label, usually with the phrase "Wine of Origin" or the abbreviation "WO." In addition, if the wine comes from a single wine estate, it will be identified as "Estate Wine," and the label will list the WO.

Wine Regions

WESTERN CAPE GUs

This area, centered on Cape Town, contains all of South Africa's historically important wine names that still have relevance in the modern wine world, as well as the emerging wine names that have won international attention. The five regions in this area are Boberg, Breede River Valley, Coastal Region, Klein Karoo, and Olifantsrivier (see map opposite). Boberg is a unique appellation applied to the fortified wines produced around the towns of Paarl and Tulbagh. Of the remaining four, Breede River Valley and the Coastal Region contain all of the significant regions, districts, or wards, and we will concentrate our attention there.

BREEDE RIVER VALLEY

Within this region, the districts of Breedekloof and Worcester constitute an amazing 20 percent of the entire nation's vineyards, producing a whopping 30 percent of all South African wines. However, very little if any ever makes onto a store shelf outside of South Africa. This is because most of the vineyards in the two districts are dedicated to growing grapes for brandy production or for lower-end wines.

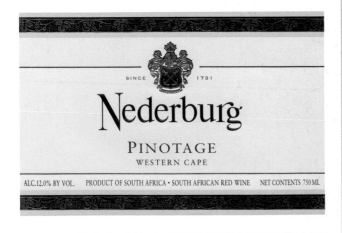

This Pinotage label indicates that the grapes came from several locations within the Western Cape.

BREEDE RIVER VALLEY

REGION	DISTRICT	WARD
Breede River Valley	Robertson	Agterkliphoogte
		Boesmansrivier
		Bonnievale
		Eilandia
		Hoopsrivier
		Klaasvoogds
		Le Chasseur
		McGregor
		Vinkrivier
	Worcester	Aan-de-Doorns
		Hex River Valley
		Nuy
		Scherpenheuvel
	Breedekloof	Goudini
		Slanghoek
	Swellendam	Buffeljags
		Stormsvlei

South Africa
Main Wine of Origin Regions, Districts, and Wards

Western Cape

Coastal Region
- Swartland
- Tulbagh
- Paarl
- Stellenbosch
- Constantia (ward)
- Darling
- Durbanville (ward)
- Tygerberg
- Cape Point

Breede River Valley Region
- Worcester
- Robertson
- Swellendam
- Breedekloof

Klein Karoo Region

Olifantsrivier Region

Other Districts
- Overberg
- Walker Bay
- Cape Agulhas

ROBERTSON

Cool winds from the southeast and a calcareous soil base have combined to make Robertson a unique pocket of grape growing in an otherwise hot, fertile riverbed. The wine pioneers who adventured here have been proven right as seen in their lively, fruity Sauvignon Blancs and Chardonnays, as well as complex and structured Cabernet Sauvignon single-varietal wines and blends. All of this is achieved by careful site selection and vineyard management to produce grapes with ripe flavors balanced by clean acidity.

COASTAL REGION

The Coastal Region fans out northward and eastward from Cape Town to include the inland towns of Paarl, Stellenbosch, and Tulbagh. The region also extends a little southward to include the famous Constantia ward and the Cape Point district. The odd fortified wine region of

Boberg (Paarl plus Tulbagh) is included within the Coastal Region (see map on page 249).

Among the districts and wards of the Coastal Region, Paarl, Stellenbosch, and Constantia have traditionally captured all of the attention. However, we have included commentary on a number of other districts and wards that merit consideration as worthy producers of quality wines.

STELLENBOSCH

Stellenbosch is a well-known district with the greatest number of famous-name wine estates: Allesverloren, Alto, Bonfoi, La Bonheur, Jacobsdal, Kanonkop, La Motte, L'Ormarins, Meerendal, Meerlust, Middelvlei, Mulderbosch, Overgaauw, Rietvallei, Rustenberg, Rust-en-Vrede, Simonsig, Theuniskraal, and Uitkyk.

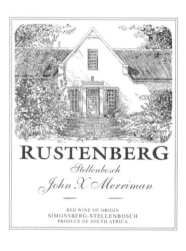

Stellenbosch has about fifty different soil types and so many climatic variations that it is hard to generalize about its pan-Mediterranean weather patterns. However, cool ocean air from the south makes its way through the imposing mountain ranges like the Simonsberg mountain and the Drakenstein hills, both of which create significant differences in climate and soil conditions. Two of Stellenbosch's best wards are located in the vicinity of these hills, namely Simonsberg-Stellenbosch and the Jonkershoek Valley. The Stellenbosch region and its wards have won high acclaim for fruity but lean cool-climate wines like Sauvignon Blanc, Chenin Blanc, and Chardonnay, while complex and sinewy Cabernet Sauvignons can be very impressive.

CONSTANTIA

The Constantia ward had been virtually ignored until the wine boom of the early 1990s, which is ironic, considering that Constantia is home to the oldest Cape vineyard region. It is also the home of the first and most famous vineyard lands in South Africa, Groot Constantia, which is still

LEFT: *Rustenberg is one of several wine estates in the Stellenbosch district. The John X Merriman wine is a Bordeaux blend.* **RIGHT, TOP:** *Aubrey Bruwer of the Life From Stone Vineyard likes to get close to the source of his wines' character.* **RIGHT, BOTTOM:** *The Simonsberg Mountain is a major factor in the different microclimates found in the Simonsberg-Stellenbosch Ward.*

COASTAL REGION

REGION	DISTRICT	WARD
Coastal Region	Cape Point	—
	—	Constantia
	Darling	Groenekloof
	Paarl	Franschhoek Valley
		Simonsberg-Paarl
		Voor Paardeberg
		Wellington
	Tygerberg	Durbanville
		Philadelphia
	Stellenbosch	Banghoek
		Bottelary
		Devon Valley
		Jonkershoek Valley
		Papegaaiberg
		Polkadraai Hills
		Simonsberg-Stellenbosch
	Swartland	Malmesbury
		Riebeekberg
	Tulbagh	

a working vineyard and winery, now owned and operated by the government. It is also a major tourist attraction.

Constantia's vineyards are sited on the granite slopes of Constantia Mountain, bordered by the ocean on two sides, and the climate is mid-Mediterranean, but with a lot of rainfall, up to 47 inches/120 centimeters per year. Now part of Cape Town's southwestern suburbs, Constantia is a promising area for Cabernet Sauvignon from Groot Constantia; Sauvignon Blanc, Cabernet Sauvignon, Riesling, and dessert Muscat wines from neighboring, privately owned Klein Constantia vineyards; and mouth-filling Sauvignon

Blanc and Chardonnay from Buitenverwachting (which means "beyond expectation" in Afrikaans).

PAARL

With a history and heritage of producing fortified wines (the fortified-wine Region of Boberg includes Paarl), the Paarl region has had a difficult time injecting itself into the modern wine consciousness. However, perseverance and careful site selection have produced impressive results, especially with regard to fuller-style Bordeaux varietals and Rhône-style wines.

The French influence has been particularly strong in the Franschhoek ward, where a more nuanced style of wine is produced by such French-sounding producers as Dieu Donné and La Motte. That said, the Boekenhoutskloof winery also produces an impressive array of wines from this ward. There are a few cooler sites provided by the influence of the Simonsberg mountain in the Simonsberg-Paarl ward, allowing for some cooler climate profiles in the Chardonnays produced there. And the Wellington ward holds its own with some medal-winning Bordeaux- and Rhône-style wines.

LEFT: *Buitenverwachting (Beyond Expectation) is one of the famed estates of the Constantia ward.* **RIGHT**: *The Nederberg Estate is famous in the Paarl district.*

DARLING

Blessed with a maritime climate derived from its location just north of Cape Town near the Atlantic Ocean, the Darling district has impressed many with its cool-climate wines, especially from the Groenekloof ward. Sauvignon Blanc and Chardonnay display excellent profiles of ripe fruit and clean, bracing acidity.

TYGERBERG

A little further south from Darling is the Tygerberg district, struggling to survive the onslaught of suburban sprawl from Cape Town, but so far winning the fight. The cool ocean influence and even cooler overnight temperatures have resulted in very stylish Sauvignon Blanc wines, as well as elegant red Bordeaux styles from Cabernet Sauvignon and Merlot blends. The wards of Durbanville and Philadelphia have been especially successful.

OTHER PROMISING AREAS

Given the historical tendency for the grape-growing and winemaking business of South Africa to be located near Cape Town, in relatively comfortable climates concentrating on fortified wine styles, it is no surprise that the quest for fine wine sites has pushed some tenacious pioneers into more remote, cooler regions. That has been especially evident in the relentless push southward, but there also a few surprises that bear the right kind of vinous fruit for success. Listed below are a few of South Africa's unpolished gems.

CAPE AGULHAS DISTRICT   As the southernmost point in the nation, it is no surprise that a few wine pioneers have paved the way here with the standard cool-climate varieties and have already won praise for their wines, especially from the Elim Ward.

TOP: *The DeGrendel winery has done well with its Tygerberg/ Tijgerberg Sauvignon Blanc.* **BOTTOM:** *The Klein Constantia Estate uses the Marlbrook label for its Bordeaux blend.*

WALKER BAY DISTRICT   Located near the town of Hermanus on the south coast, the Walker Bay District, with its wards of Hemel-en-Aarde Valley and Upper Hemel-en-Aarde Valley, has impressed many with the depth of clean flavors in cool-climate varieties such as Sauvignon Blanc, Riesling, and Pinot Noir, something that very few other wine areas have been able to achieve.

OVERBERG DISTRICT   Some unique outcroppings of sandstone and a long, cool growing season have attracted many grape growers to this area, especially to the Elgin Ward, where they have produced some outstanding Sauvignon Blancs, Rieslings, and Pinot Noirs.

TULBAGH DISTRICT   Given its history as a center of fortified wines, it is difficult to believe that this area might make sparkling wine to compete on the world market, but a few brave souls have placed great faith in an odd climate-inversion phenomenon that creates pockets of cool air suitable for fine sparkling-wine production. Leading the way with the highly successful Krone Borealis sparkler has been Krone Vineyards, in association with Mumm Champagne.

SUMMARY

WINES PRODUCED in the Southern Hemisphere have become an increasingly important part of the international wine scene. In the United States, wine imports from Chile, Argentina, New Zealand, and Australia have increased significantly from 2000 to 2010. There's no mystery as to why these wines enjoy such popularity in the contemporary marketplace: They provide good value and increasingly provide excellent quality. In addition, as with most wines of the New World, relatively easy-to-understand varietal labels help consumers buy the wine with ease.

Shiraz from Australia, Sauvignon Blanc from New Zealand, and Malbec from Argentina are unique and important wines in the international market and a refreshing break from the standard New World Chardonnay and Cabernet Sauvignon wines that have become commonplace. Argentina has all the natural resources to make great wines, and when we taste a fine Argentine red, we can only hope that there will be a lot more where that one came from; we think there will be. However, Australia in particular has been hit with a reality check, and that reality is that there is too much lower- to middle-quality wine in the world. Having fallen into the high-volume, low-end wine game, Australia has seen its exports cut dramatically. On the other hand, New Zealand geared its wine strategy to high-end sales, and their exporting status has not been so negatively affected.

Chilean wine producers, whose Cabernet Sauvignon and Cabernet blends continue to be popular, are beginning to explore not only varietal character, but also the largely unknown *terroir* of Chile. By producing wines of extremely high quality from unique vineyard sites, often with the assistance of foreign capital and expertise, Chile has taken a worldly giant step.

South Africa—which, after all, is in many ways a young country with a young wine industry—has begun to live up to its marvelous potential, offering the world its own versions of the international varieties, along with a couple of specialty items. There is every reason to think that South Africa will continue to hold its place as an important international producer of premium wines. The good plant material is still in the ground, and the human energy is still in the wineries.

The vineyards of the Durbanville ward in South Africa

BARCA VELHA 1983

RUBESCO

PRODOTTO

IN ITALIA

GATTINARA

·EST·
1822

FON
PO
BIN

VinSanto

Φ

PARÉS
BALTÀ

AN FEIXE
BLANC SELECCIÓ

PART 3
WINES OF THE
OLD WORLD

FOR MANY WINE LOVERS, both novices and the more experienced, Old World wine conjures up myriad romantic images. All of the images would be "old" in some way: old bottles, old winemakers, old vines, old cellars. But such images themselves are not only old, they are tarnished and inexact. In the past fifty years, Old World wine-producing countries have seen more change than during the previous eight millennia. The changes have been rapid and have brought previously insular communities roaring headlong into the global twenty-first century.

With the undeniable presence of aggressive winemakers in the New World and an ever-more-educated consumer, Old World winemakers have been faced with the challenge of change or perish. Not everybody has risen to the task.

The new millennium dawned with the bright light and promise of a golden age for European wines. In the twenty-seven nations that now make up the European Union, total vineyard area in 2000 was at a record 10 million acres/4 million hectares. Positive steps had been taken to eliminate corruption, prosecute illegal activities, reduce production, and improve quality. Never before had there been such a varied availability of high-quality wines at competitive prices. But the light has faded, the bubble has burst, and some European wines are suffering. Vineyard acreage has decreased to 9.5 million acres/3.85 million hectares. While Spanish, Portuguese, and Greek wines have found favor in new markets around the world, other European nations have experienced severe cutbacks in their sales abroad. Germany and Austria have shown some positive movement, but that was not too difficult since their sales records were not spectacular. It is the old guard nations of Italy and, especially, France that have suffered the most.

France has lost significant market share to New World producers that offer consumers the easy appeal of clean fruit and straightforward flavors. They may not be wines of place, but they please the consumer.

The conclusion by the European Union is that Europe is producing too much, so they have drawn up plans to pull vines and to remove subsidies that prop up inefficient production. The predictable results have been strikes and protests, some of which have been violent. It is easy to agree with the EU proposals if one believes in quality, but it is also hard not to sympathize with the plight of the small wine producer who has been producing wines the same way for centuries. Specific issues of legislation and related problems will be addressed in the chapters on each nation.

Despite this gloomy scenario, there have been dramatic improvements. Many of the vines are new, the winemakers are certainly new, the machinery and equipment are new, and some would even say that the wine made there is somehow new. Part 3 will look at the major wine-producing countries of the European continent and the Mediterranean basin, the countries and civilizations that distributed the vine over thousands of years and nurtured and perpetuated the age-old mysteries of winemaking. The discussion will concentrate on the current state of grape growing and winemaking in those countries, most of which have undergone dramatic changes in recent years.

Where old laws have been relaxed or repealed, Old World grape growers and winemakers are more open to developing their own innovations as well as importing ideas from outside. Various areas have experimented with heating and cooling the must or grape juice before fermentation starts to extract more color or to bond the tannin molecules into longer molecular chains, resulting in a softer overall texture on the palate. In the vineyard, obsolete vine varieties have been replaced, and vineyard areas have been expanded. In some areas, vine spacing, the trellising system, or the pruning system have been changed, and all of this in countries where the vine had been grown in the same manner for thousands of years.

France, Italy, Germany, Spain, Portugal, Austria, and Greece all have appellation laws that are similar in structure and intent. In a general sense, the philosophy and policy of the European Union legislators has been to create two broad categories of wine: ordinary wine and quality wine. However, the clamor to revitalize the image and sales figures of European wines led to a debate about the real and intended functions of any wine legislation and whether or not such legislation is too limiting. That debate resulted in the introduction in August 2009 of European Union reforms to labeling laws and wine categorization. As vague as some of the language and details seem to be, there is a significant shift away from intimations of quality toward place name protection. Most significantly, the new legislation allows for EU wines at any level to be labeled with a grape variety name, if the producer so chooses, and a vintage date, if applicable. This is a radical departure from the old philosophy of "primacy of place" that had dominated European wine-label terminology for so long and comes as a welcome attempt to allow European wines to compete directly with New World wines, whose labels promote grape variety above all else.

The new reforms provide subsidies to encourage the elimination of sub-par vineyard areas and eliminate subsidies that encouraged some producers to make low-quality wines, knowing that they would be paid when the wine was sent for "crisis distillation" into industrial alcohol.

Lastly, the reforms eliminate the old category of "Table Wine," replacing it with the even simpler designation "Wine." Even wines at this most basic level will be allowed to carry a grape variety name and vintage date, as well as an indication such as "Product of Greece." Further, the old "Quality Wine" categories have been replaced with two new groupings that emphasize protection of place name while still permitting the use of a grape variety on the label. The English-language versions of the two new categories are "Protected Designation of Origin," and "Protected Geographic Indication," with the basic difference being that the former requires that 100 percent of the grapes used to make wine come from the named place, while only 85 percent of the grapes must be from the named place for the second category.

Until 2011, the European Union legislation allows current terms to remain in use, or in conjunction with the new terms. The table opposite shows variations in language that will be used and how the old categories relate to the new.

These EU labeling regulations will continue to be supplemented by national laws, so that the INSTITUT NATIONAL DES APPELLATIONS D'ORIGINE (INAO) of France, for example, can continue to insist that its AOP wines must also comply with regulations regarding specific grape types to be used, yields per hectare, or grape-growing and winemaking methodologies. This new era that promises to make European wines more competitive presents an excellent opportunity for all European nations to reassess the philosophy and direction of their national appellation laws and to draft guidelines that allow for innovation while maintaining tradition and prestige. In each of the chapters on European nations that follow, we will make reference to both the old and new language.

When studying the appellation laws of the various countries, it is helpful to remember that the categories in each country fit the above framework, which is based on the French system. At the same time, however, it must be pointed out that the objective of the appellation system of any country is to ensure authenticity by legislating that certain grapes are grown in a certain place to produce a wine. An appellation system cannot guarantee quality, since quality is a perception of the consumer. However, the very existence of an appellation system encourages the production of quality wines.

Legislated appellation systems pose age-old questions. Should tradition and custom be respected by insisting on old ways and methods enshrined in law? Or should legislation be flexible enough to allow the introduction of new

COMPARISON OF PLACE NAME PROTECTION SYSTEMS IN EUROPEAN WINEMAKING COUNTRIES

England	France	Italy	Spain	Portugal	Germany
Protected Designation of Origin (PDO)	Appellation d'Origine Protégée (AOP)	Denominazione di Origine Protetta (DOP)	Denominación de Origen Protegida (DOP)	Denominação de Origem Protegida (DOP)	Geschützte Ursprung-bezeichnung (gU)
Formerly known as — *these terms can still be used on labels until 2011*					
	APPELLATION D'ORIGINE CONTRÔLÉE (AOC)	Denominazione di Origine Controllata (DOC)	Denominación de Origen (DO)	Denominação de Origem Controlada (DOC)	Pradikatswein and Qualitätswein
Protected Geographic Indication (PGI)	Indication Géographique Protégée (IGP)	Indicazione Geografica Protetta (IGP)	Indicación Geográfica Protegida (IGP)	Indicação Geográfica Protegida (IGP)	Geschützte geographische Angabe (ggA)
Formerly known as — *these terms can still be used on labels until 2011*					
	Vin de Pays	Indicazione Geografica Tipica (IGT)	Viño de la Tierra	Vinho de Mesa Regional	Landwein
Wine	Vin	Vino	Viño	Vinho	Wein
Formerly known as					
	Vin de Table	Vino da Tavola	Viño de Mesa	Vinho de Mesa	Tafelwein

grape types, new trellissing systems, or new winemaking techniques into a region whose lifeblood has been wine for hundreds of years?

Both Spain and Portugal have taken advantage of grants and tax incentives from the European Union to modernize their vineyards and their wineries. At the same time, their governments have shown remarkable cooperation, working with regional authorities to modernize wine laws. The results have been astonishing, but there are still questions. In particular, the Spanish authorities might be criticized for acting too quickly, creating numerous appellation equivalents in areas where a lesser designation might have sufficed.

German legislators have been confronted with nothing short of a revolution from some producers who want to revert to a concept that recognizes a single site as the basis for quality, not sugar levels at harvest. Accordingly, new label language has been proposed to identify recognized vineyard plots as consistently producing wines of superior quality. But label language continues to be a problem with German wines, since different terms will be used depending on whether the wine is dry or sweet.

In Italy, the government never seems to be able to react fast enough to accommodate all of the changes that maverick winemakers want to introduce, yet nobody could deny that some of the world's finest wines have come from those renegade winemakers. However, the rush to nominate more and more wines at the highest level is disturbing because there seems to be no consistent set of criteria used to anoint the latest darling of the Italian scene.

Lastly, the old French **APPELLATION CONTRÔLÉE** system is still under relentless pressure to modernize or suffer the consequences of steadily decreasing sales. So the questions remain. What grape types should be grown where, should specific grape types be mandated in any region, and what level of regulation is needed to maintain quality and authenticity?

Wine consumption in Old World wine-producing countries has always been substantially higher than in the United States. However, per capita consumption in many Old World countries is declining at the same time as production of higher-quality wines in those same countries is increasing. This only adds to the complex problems that have resulted in overproduction at all quality levels. Those problems may become even more acute as Eastern European countries see their economies flourish because of their membership in the European Union. There are exciting possibilities ahead for all Old World wine countries, and a potential for increased pleasures for wine lovers all over the world. However, those possibilities will have to occur within the overall context of maintaining style and quality alongside acceptable levels of production.

LANGUEDOC

BRUT

CHENIN BLANC

TERROIR

SANCERRE

SAUMUR

SAUTERNES

MUSCADET

MONTRACHET

blanc de blancs

CÔTE-RÔTIE

petit verdot

GRAND CRU

GAMAY

premier cru

CHABLIS

FRANCE

THE PRESUMED SUPREMACY of French wines is under attack. Admittedly, those with enough money continue to buy the recognized jewels in the French crown, such as Château Margaux from Bordeaux, Romanée-Conti for a fine red Burgundy, and its white counterpart Le Montrachet. But for the average consumer all around the world, that crown has lost its luster. This is not solely due to international politics in the twenty-first century. It has more to do with the fact that French wines do not have the same appeal as wines of New World nations. Just as people have expanded their culinary repertoire to admire cuisines from around the globe, so have they moved beyond seeing France as a role model for wine and food. Even so, the wines of Champagne, Bordeaux, Burgundy, and the Rhône continue to be held in high regard. The rest of France still has lots to offer the average modern wine consumer, but French winemakers will have to work harder in the future to attract and retain customer loyalty.

But what is it about France that had given its wines such cachet, apparently more so than the wines of other European nations? It is not a question of time. Within and outside Europe, other nations and civilizations have been producing wine for far longer than France has. It seems unlikely that it could be something as simple as climate or even as complex as soil. There are other locations that can boast just as much of a unique character in terms of sunlight, rainfall, temperature swings, drainage, soil porosity, or soil mineral content, as witnessed by the production of great wines in places such as Montalcino in Italy, Ribera del Duero in Spain, or Barossa Valley in Australia.

However, there is one aspect of French wine production that remains far more entrenched and accepted than in other nations, and that is the long-standing presence of classification systems that rank a region's vineyards into a hierarchy of good, excellent, and the greatest. These classification systems even label the vineyards with titles such as **GRAND CRU**, or **PREMIER GRAND CRU**. They imply supremacy and superlative character, and they make the finest French wines easy to categorize and easy to admire.

But wines such as these make up only a small percentage of France's total production. To fully understand French wine, we need to look at the overall pattern of wines produced in France and the national wine laws. From there, we can break up France into its regions and discuss the wines produced there and any specific classifications of vineyards. Mastery of French wines does take time, but it is not difficult. Just follow a simple recipe for success: Identify which grape types are grown in what location (sometimes as specific as a village name) and what kind of wine they make.

Though France is not the oldest wine-producing country, the French have had centuries of trial-and-error experience in matching suitable grape types with the best locations, whereas many of the new regions of the world are just beginning to understand what to plant and where. For this reason, soil types and exposures will be discussed in more detail in this chapter than elsewhere. The *terroir* of a vineyard refers to its soil, exposure to the sun, its drainage of air and water, and its shelter from such elements as wind and rain. It is the understanding of each *terroir* that has allowed French winemakers to produce many of the finest expressions of a grape variety in the world or to blend different grape types from different vineyard sites to make up for what one area and grape type cannot accomplish alone.

OVERALL PATTERN OF FRENCH WINE PRODUCTION

ALMOST EVERY REGION of France grows grapes and makes wine. The major exception is the band of land that stretches from just north of Nantes along the Atlantic coast to the border with Belgium. In this section, Brittany and Normandy produce wonderful sparkling cider, and the region next to Belgium produces great beer. But just about everywhere else in France, the alcoholic beverage of choice is wine.

Within that broad landscape, it is possible to visualize three main sections of wine production, largely differentiated by climate.

In an arc across the north of France, the concentration is on white wine production, as dictated by the cooler climate. White grapes can ripen adequately, but it is not sufficiently

An old basket press provides memories of the old ways.

warm to allow most red grapes full flavor development. In this arc, the three most important areas of wine production are the Loire Valley, Champagne, and Alsace. They all concentrate on producing a high percentage of white and sparkling wine, with small quantities of rosé and red wine.

The middle section, a band from Bordeaux on the west coast to the border with Switzerland in the east, is blessed with climate pockets that allow varieties of red and white grapes to grow well, so that the regions of Bordeaux and Burgundy in particular are known as producers of fine red and white wines.

Lastly, the arc that follows the Mediterranean coast from the Spanish border to the Italian border is hot enough to bring red grapes to full ripeness, whereas most white grapes would suffer in the heat of those regions. As a result, the south of France, including the Rhône Valley, Languedoc, Roussillon, and Provence, can be thought of as red wine country, with only a small production of white wines.

GENERAL PRODUCTION AND CONSUMPTION PATTERNS

ALL FRENCH WINE falls into either of the two broad categories provided for by European Union regulations: Wine and Protected Name Wine. Over the last two decades there has been a dramatic increase in the quantity of French wine in the second category. This was in response to a specific strategy defined by the EU to concentrate on lower production overall and to concentrate on quality rather than quantity. This strategy at the production level reflects a similar phenomenon at the consumption level: French people are consuming less wine every year, and they are consuming better wine every year. However, many critics have charged that just because the label identifies the wine as coming from a protected place name does not mean the consumer will get a quality wine.

We might applaud the French wine industry for uprooting thousands of acres of high-yielding vines like Ugni Blanc and Carignan, which are used to support low-quality wine production, but many of the touted improvements may have simply resulted in the planting of thousands of acres of noble varieties like Cabernet Sauvignon and Chardonnay that would only be used to make mediocre wine but dressed up to look special.

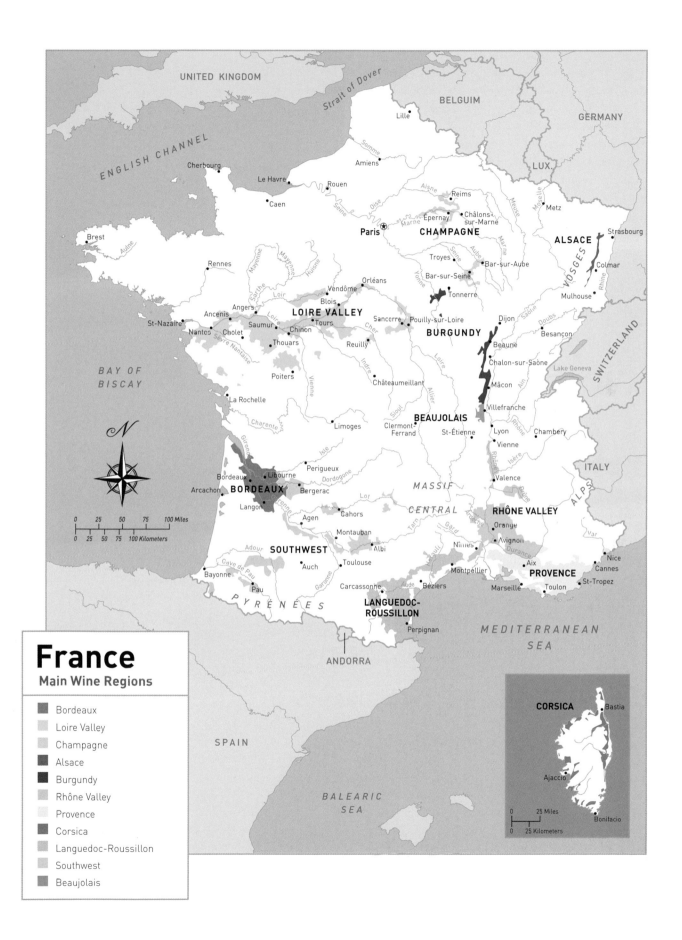

France
Main Wine Regions

- Bordeaux
- Loire Valley
- Champagne
- Alsace
- Burgundy
- Rhône Valley
- Provence
- Corsica
- Languedoc-Roussillon
- Southwest
- Beaujolais

CORSICA

There are similar concerns voiced about the status of France's appellations. The past decades have seen some appellations' boundaries extended to take in areas that were previously excluded on the grounds that they could not produce wines as representative of the appellation because of less-suitable soil types or exposures. Similarly, permitted yields have been increased for many areas and a PLC (*plafond limité de classement*) allows producers to ask permission to produce up to 20 percent over the legally established yields. The additional 20 percent has become a regular practice in most regions. As noted elsewhere, producers with integrity are not seduced by these temptations to make more wine of a lesser quality. They continue to harvest low yields from the best locations and vines, in a manner that would make their ancestors proud.

FRENCH WINE LAWS

SINCE THE NEW MILLENNIUM, France's challenge has been to revamp and revitalize its wine laws to ensure continued authenticity but improved quality, while allowing producers some latitude for innovation and creativity. In other words, how do you hold onto the past and embrace the future at the same time? There are different areas of concern, such as whether to allow the grape variety to be printed on the label, whether new grape varieties should be permitted in historically designated areas, whether restrictions on irrigation should be lifted, and so on. There have been steps forward, with varietal labeling allowed under the new EU laws, and previously banned grapes planted on an experimental basis in Bordeaux. But there remain major questions about how a wine achieves the vaunted status of *appellation protégée*. Theoretically, every wine labeled *appellation protégée* has been produced according to a strict set of rules, and has been tasted by an impartial panel to ensure that the wine reflects the quality and style of the appellation. Many critics have charged that this inexact tasting system allows many poor-quality wines to slip though the cracks to achieve *appellation protégée* status. While producers may be happy that their wines are on the shelves with an *appellation protégée* label, they have slowly come to realize that many of their wines are staying on the shelves because the quality and style do not match what the modern consumer wants.

Concerns about the ease with which French wines achieve appellation status will not be eased simply by the introduction of the new terms *indication géographique protégée* to take in the old VINS DE PAYS group, and *appellation d'origine protégée* to replace the old *appellation d'origine contrôlée*. As good as they may sound, the great fear is that these new label categories will simply replace what is already there, and things will continue exactly as they have been. It would be great to have faith in the ability of any government to achieve what amounts to a re-ranking of *appellation protégée* wines, but recent arguments about classifications in France do not inspire confidence. Admittedly, a major impediment to broad-sweeping changes is the existence of many different interested parties and the ease with which they can convey their position in the modern information age. This has been especially apparent in the ongoing arguments over the classification of châteaux in the St-Émilion district of Bordeaux.

Previously held up as a model of continuous improvement, promoting and demoting châteaux based on past and present performance, the 2006 reclassification of St-Émilion châteaux hit a roadblock when demoted and passed-over producers filed a lawsuit against the proposed amendments. After several legal battles, the entire reclassification was deemed invalid in 2008, with the result that all label references to the classification had to be removed. Further legal arguments were presented until finally the French government intervened in 2009 and declared that the old 1996 classification would stand alongside the proposed promotions of 2006 until a completely new reclassification can be organized.

At the same time as the world watched the legal problems of St-Émilion unravel, the world also witnessed what some have called the duplicity of the major Champagne producers, who, against all previous practices, boldly extended the appellation boundaries to include forty villages that were previously outside of the appellation. Having spent decades and millions of dollars rigorously defending Champagne as a term to be used only for wines produced from specific grapes grown in a very specific area with a unique *terroir*, it turns out that the *terroir* was not so unique after all, and there are other areas that qualify to use the term Champagne. While everyone benefits from the continued supply of Champagne to the world market, it raises questions about the authenticity of the claim that the appellation is indeed unique.

Thus, the previously simmering problems of French wine categorization have come to a boil, but nobody seems to be tending the pot. The old systems remain in

place, limping along, with no clear solution on the horizon. For now, we can offer an overview of the current picture of French wine production and the present state of the *appellation protégée* laws.

As of 2010, French wine production has fallen from approximately 1.4 billion gallons/55 million hectoliters to 1.186 billion gallons/45 million hectoliters of wine. French wine laws, supervised by the Ministry of Agriculture, provide for three categories of wine. In ascending order of quality they are:

- *Vin*
- *Indication géographique protégée* (IGP)
- *Appellation d'origine protégée* (AOP)

The first level is deemed to be fairly ordinary wine, while the second two levels are presumed to be wines of quality. As the new EU laws currently stand, producers of IGP and AOP wines can opt to continue to use the old language or to include the new terminology. For the rest of this chapter, we will adopt the new phrases and initials.

One of the many beautiful châteaux that dot the French wine landscape

Vin

The majority of French *vin* is red and produced in the southern Mediterranean regions of France. There are standard health requirements that apply to the production of any food, but there are no limits set on the total yield of grapes per area of land or volume of juice per quantity of grapes. French *vin* currently constitutes approximately 10 percent of total annual wine production.

Indication Géographique Protégée (IGP)

This category of French wine has continued to innovate in terms of regional designations totaling 152 different regions and zones of production. Total volume has rounded out at about 15 million hectoliters (395 million gallons), concentrating on grape varieties that have international name recognition such as Chardonnay, Cabernet Sauvignon, Merlot, Viognier, and Syrah. In total, these wines make up about 35 percent of total French production. The wines from these relatively new vineyards have

flooded the markets all around the world with competitively priced, varietally labeled wines. Every IGP wine produced must be approved by a regional tasting panel before it can be bottled and marketed. IGP wines must conform to regulations about the defined geographic area of production and be made from any of the recommended (not necessarily required by law) grape varieties for that area. On the label, the phrase *indication géographique protégée* will be followed by a geographic name to indicate where the wine came from. At least 85 percent of the grapes used to make the wine must come from the named region.

There are three levels of geographic area for IGP wines: large regions, departments, and smaller zones. In the large region category, there are six designations:

- Val de Loire, covering the whole of the Loire Valley and beyond
- Comté Tolosan, from Bordeaux to the Pyrenees and east, almost to the Mediterranean
- Pays d'Oc, from Perpignan near Spain to Avignon in the southern Rhône Valley

Vineyards around the village of St-Émilion

- Comtés Rhodaniens, from Mâcon to Avignon and east to the Swiss and Italian borders
- Atlantique, around Bordeaux
- Méditerranée, from the Alpine border with Switzerland to the south coast and Corsica

In addition, there are fifty-two departments (*un département* in France is a geopolitical entity, similar to a province or state) names that can be used to identify IGP wines, plus almost one hundred small zone names. In effect, this hierarchical system mirrors a similar structure that exists for *appellation protégée* wines, where smaller subappellations are contained within larger appellations that together make up a whole region.

Appellation d'Origine Protégée (AOP)

Representing around 55 percent of all French wines, this category and the laws that govern its production are supervised by the Institut National des Appellations d'Origine des Vins et Eaux-de-Vie (INAO). To understand the full philosophy of the French AOP system, it helps to provide a simple translation of the phrase. It literally means "protected naming of origin." In other words, the AOP system is all about where the grapes are grown, reflecting a French preoccupation with the importance of location in general and *terroir* in particular. As a result of this preoccupation, most French AOP wines carry a place name on the label. The place name could be:

- a large region (e.g., Bordeaux or Bourgogne)
- a district (e.g., Médoc or Côte de Beaune)
- a village (e.g., Pauillac or Chassagne-Montrachet)
- a single vineyard site (e.g., Château Latour or Le Montrachet)

To qualify for the use of a specific place name, AOP wines must comply with the following regulations:

- The wine must be made from grapes all grown within the specified location.
- The wine must be made from grape types approved for that location. In some cases, the number of permitted grape types is one; in other cases there is a list of grape types from which producers may choose the ones they want to use.
- The wine must reach a minimum alcohol level. The specific minimum level varies from appellation to appellation.
- There is a maximum yield (quantity of wine produced) specified for each appellation. Generally the smaller and more revered sites have smaller permitted yields, thereby assuring that the higher-quality wines will be made from grapes with more concentrated flavors. The lowest yield in the nation is for the appellation Quarts de Chaume in the Loire Valley, with a maximum yield of 22 hectoliters per hectare (approximately 1.5 tons per acre). Quarts de Chaume falls within the larger appellation of Coteaux du Layon and wines labeled as Coteaux du Layon have a maximum permitted yield of 30 hectoliters per hectare (approximately 2 tons per acre), while the even larger appellation Anjou that contains them both has a maximum permitted yield of 50 hectoliters per hectare, or approximately 3.5 tons per acre.
- Certain viticultural practices are regulated, such as pruning methods or training systems, and vinification techniques are sometimes specified, such as *méthode champenoise* for Champagne and some other French sparkling wines.

- The wine must be tested by taste (to ensure typicality for that appellation) and by a chemical analysis before being bottled and marketed.

Within the category of *appellation protégée*, there is provision in some regions for specific vineyards to be designated as *grand cru* or PREMIER CRU or some equivalent phrase. These highly prized vineyards earn their designation after a prolonged period (sometimes centuries) of demonstrating that they can, on a regular basis, produce better grapes that will create wine of inimitable character. Among the major *appellation protégée* regions of France, the Loire, Champagne, Alsace, Burgundy, Bordeaux, and Beaujolais have some kind of official CRU or *grand cru* system. Only the Rhône Valley does not have any officially recognized *cru* system.

WINE REGIONS OF FRANCE

The Loire Valley

The wines of the Loire Valley hold a fascinating charm—they are a bright, spring day in a bottle! With the overall cool climate of northwestern France, dark grapes have had trouble reaching full ripeness, so most of the wines from the Loire Valley are white. Nevertheless, climate change has had an impact here as everywhere else, and the region offers a broad array of styles, utilizing different grape types according to their suitability to the different soil structures and climates that can be found throughout the vineyards that line the river Loire and its tributaries.

From the fresh, dry, lean whites of the Atlantic region to the botrytis-affected *moëlleux* and *sélection de grains nobles* (both sweet) wines of Anjou to the berry-bright reds of Touraine, there is something for almost everybody here. The hallmark of all the wines is a high, sometimes searing acidity, though it never comes across as simply sour. It is a refreshing, palate-cleansing acidity that is both thirst-quenching and an excellent accompaniment to the rich panoply of seafood, poultry, and fresh vegetables that have made this region the "garden of France."

The valley's central region seems the most natural home in the world for the Chenin Blanc grape. Indeed, nowhere else in the world does this often-ignored grape type reach

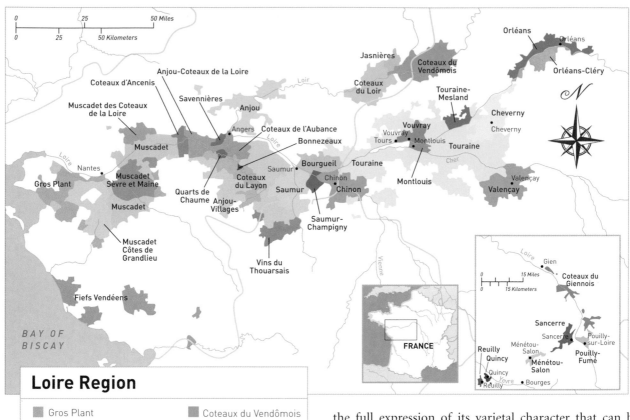

Loire Region

■ Gros Plant	■ Coteaux du Vendômois
■ Muscadet	■ Touraine
■ Muscadet Côtes de Grandlieu	■ Bourgueil
■ Muscadet Sèvre et Maine	■ Saumur-Champigny
■ Muscadet des Coteaux de la Loire	■ Chinon
■ Coteaux d'Ancenis	■ Saumur
■ Anjou-Coteaux de la Loire	■ Montlouis
■ Savennières	■ Vouvray
■ Quarts de Chaume	■ Touraine-Mesland
■ Bonnezeaux	■ Cheverny
■ Coteaux du Layon	■ Valençay
■ Anjou-Villages	■ Orléans
■ Fiefs Vendéens	■ Orléans-Cléry
■ Vins du Thouarsais	■ Coteaux du Giennois
■ Anjou	■ Sancerre
■ Coteaux de l'Aubance	■ Pouilly-Fumé
■ Coteaux du Loir	■ Ménétou-Salon
■ Jasnières	■ Quincy
	■ Reuilly

the full expression of its varietal character that can be found here. Arguably, the Chenin Blanc originated here, mutating from other indigenous varieties. If so, it is one of the strongest arguments ever in favor of regional typicality. And yet, at least two grape variety outcasts from other regions are now firmly established in the Loire Valley: The Melon de Bourgogne and the Gamay both produced less impressive wines in the Burgundy region and were subsequently adopted by Loire growers.

The full roster of grape types grown is extensive, including everything from Chardonnay (of course!) to the rare white Romorantin, and from Cabernet Sauvignon to the mostly unknown red Grolleau. The broad range of grape types is matched by the production in the different Loire districts of almost every wine type—light- to medium-bodied dry whites, sweet whites, dry rosés, semisweet rosés, sparkling whites and rosés, and light- and medium-bodied reds.

WINE REGIONS OF THE WESTERN LOIRE
NANTES

The Nantes, or Atlantic region, in the westernmost part of the Loire, is cool and ideally suited to the Melon de Bourgogne grape, known locally as the Muscadet, which grows well in the mild summers and ripens around mid-

September before the cold, early fall weather sets in. There are three distinct appellations in this region:

- Muscadet, offering the lightest and simplest style of wine
- Muscadet des Coteaux de la Loire, providing wines of a little more fullness, but still very tart and lacking a little in full fruit ripeness
- Muscadet Côtes de Grandlieu, making wines of noticeable weight and structure
- Muscadet Sèvre et Maine, known for the fullest and ripest styles

The Muscadet Sèvre et Maine appellation achieves its fuller style from better sun exposure on the hilly slopes of the region and from clay, granite, and volcanic soils. Even so, most of the wines are considered light- to medium-bodied, with a delicacy that makes them the perfect accompaniment to the fresh shellfish that abound in the region. Winemakers in all the appellations have embraced stainless steel as the preferred vessel for fermentation, conducting a long, slow, cool fermentation to maintain the freshness of the grape. After the fermentation is over, many winemakers also choose to leave the wine **SUR LIE** (on its lees) until it is ready to be bottled. This process is often used in other wine regions to provide an extra level of smoothness and creaminess, a result of the breakdown of the yeast cells. The decaying yeast cells are also a powerful antioxidant, preventing any oxidation and keeping the wine fresh, even retaining a degree of spritz or *pétillance* that is noticeable when the wine is poured. Good producers of Muscadet include Domaine de la Chauvènière, Goulaine, Les Vergers, Domaine Sauvion, Château de Chasseloir, and Château de la Ragotière.

Assiduous attention in the vineyards, especially by growers who have adopted biodynamic or organic methods, have resulted in some very impressive versions of Muscadet that show depth and complexity of flavors with smooth, creamy texture, yet still defined by clean, electrifying acidity. With the image of Muscadet as the ideal simple seafood white, it is hard to picture wines of depth and complexity that age extremely well. Particularly impressive producers of this style include Domaine de l'Ecu, Bréjeon, and Bonnet Huteau. These producers go to great lengths to ensure that their wines are reflective of their origin, showing noticeable differences between wines from gneiss soils as compared with wines from granitic soils or wines from gabbro soils.

The village of Gorges in the Muscadet region boasts unique pockets of gabbro soils, which are rocky and rich in iron and magnesium.

In addition to the Muscadet grape, the Gros Plant (known elsewhere as Folle Blanche) is widely planted in the Atlantic region, producing light, simple, fresh wines in the old VDQS category, labeled as Gros Plant du Pays Nantais. Presumably, these wines will now be classified as IGP, as will the old VDQS wines of Coteaux d'Ancenis that include varietally labeled versions of Chenin Blanc or Pinot Gris, plus a lot of rosé from Gamay and Cabernet Sauvignon. Lastly, the old VDQS wines of Fiefs Vendéens offer whites from Chenin Blanc or Sauvignon Blanc, and reds from Gamay or Cabernet Sauvignon.

WINE REGIONS OF THE CENTRAL LOIRE

The Central Loire can be split into three provinces: Anjou, Saumur, and Touraine. The Atlantic region and the Upper Loire region are relatively focused in wine styles and grape types used, but the Central Loire offers the broadest selection of types and styles of wine made from several different grape types, including Chenin Blanc, Chardonnay, and Sauvignon Blanc as whites, and Cabernet Franc, Cabernet Sauvignon, Gamay, Pinot Noir, Cot (Malbec), and Grolleau as reds. The following terms are used widely throughout the region and on labels to indicate dryness/sweetness levels of wines produced: SEC (dry); *sec-tendre* (off-dry); DEMI-SEC (semisweet); MOËLLEUX (sweet). POURRITURE NOBLE *(Botrytis cinerea)* is not common in the area, but those vintages when it is widespread, such as 1990, 1995, 1997, 2002, and 2006, produce the most luscious, long-lived examples.

ANJOU

Historically, the area of Anjou was synonymous with *moëlleux* (sweet) wines of outstanding quality. More recently, Anjou fulfilled the role of producing huge quantities of innocuous but economically important semisweet rosé wines that are present in any wine market at any point in time. Today the appellation name Anjou is used to label many wines, from dry whites to rosés, reds, and sparkling wines. The best dry whites (Anjou Blanc) are produced from 100 percent Chenin Blanc, though the current laws permit the addition of up to 20 percent of Chardonnay or Sauvignon Blanc. They are fresh, lively wines, full of bracing character, sometimes softened by the Chardonnay or Sauvignon Blanc element.

The names Rosé d'Anjou and Cabernet d'Anjou are used

for semisweet rosés, the first made from Gamay, Grolleau, Cot, or Cabernet Franc, the second allowing only Cabernet Franc or Cabernet Sauvignon. Rosé de la Loire is a dry rosé made from at least 30 percent Cabernet Franc with the addition of Gamay, Grolleau, or Pinot Noir permitted.

The production of red wines has increased dramatically in the past decade as producers have adjusted their production to match the decline in consumption of rosés and the increased interest in red wines. Anjou Rouge, Anjou-Villages, and Anjou Gamay are the three major appellations, with the first two concentrating on Cabernet Franc while Anjou Gamay is made from Gamay. The Anjou-Villages appellation comprises forty-six COMMUNES recognized for the excellence of their vineyards. A fourth smaller red-only appellation is Anjou-Villages-Brissac. The reds from these appellations are light, simple, fruity reds, designed and consumed as bistro quaffing wines, not to be taken too seriously.

In addition to these basic Anjou appellations, there are several smaller appellations, some of which are very special.

SAVENNIÈRES The Savennières appellation is situated to the north of the Loire River, just to the east of the town of Angers. The high quality of Savennières is due to Chenin Blanc grown on schistose slate soil, with some volcanic rocks, giving the wines a marked concentration of mineral flavors in addition to the beguiling nuances of Chenin at its best. Two *grand cru* sites, Château de la Roche-aux-Moines and Coulée de Serrant, are the pride of the area. Savennières wines need time to develop balance between the aggressive acids and the fruit flavors. After a half dozen years the wines begin to display floral, honey, mineral, and spicy qualities in the bouquet and complex and intense herbal and earthy flavors on the palate. The wines are certainly idiosyncratic, a true reflection of their place and en-

Château de la Roche-aux-Moines in Savennières

vironment, and one of the best arguments in France for that philosophy of winemaking to be continued. The best Savennières can improve for decades and are the finest examples of dry Chenin Blanc made.

COTEAUX DU LAYON These are Chenin Blanc–based semisweet to sweet wines. The name of the best communes may be added to Coteaux du Layon wines. They are Beaulieu sur Layon, Faye-D'Anjou, Rablay du Layon, Rochefort sur Loire, St-Aubin de Luigné, and St-Lambert du Lattay. Moulin Touchais is a company that bottles its wines under the Coteaux du Layon appellation for domestic use and as Anjou for export. These wines are very rich in flavor and can live for decades. Baumard is another fine producer here. The Coteaux du Layon produces some of the finest dessert wines in France. Their high acidity balances their sweetness, and the bouquets and flavors evolve over ten or twenty years.

BONNEZEAUX AND QUARTS DE CHAUME These are two *grand cru* appellations within the Coteaux du Layon, their superiority based on the combination of schist and limestone soils that are found on the northern banks of the Layon river. They are the finest examples of the floral-honeyed nose and luscious sweetness balanced with acidity that the Chenin Blanc can produce with the right soil, climate, and low yields. Both are more than 13 percent alcohol and may be consumed young but will repay cellaring for over a decade. The Quarts de Chaume appellation has the lowest permitted yield in the nation, set at 580 gallons/22.3 hectoliters per 2.47 acres/1 hectare.

The sweet wines of the Loire rival those of Sauternes in the Bordeaux region, although the **NOBLE ROT** forms more regularly in the warmer region of Sauternes than in the cooler, more northerly Loire. The sweet wines of the Loire are most often bottled young and allowed to mature in the bottle, while Sauternes are matured in cask.

COTEAUX DE L'AUBANCE Semisweet and sweet wines are produced from the Chenin Blanc grown on the banks of the Aubance River. The dry still whites are sold under the broad Anjou Blanc appellation, while the dry reds carry the Anjou-Villages-Brissac designation.

SPARKLING WINES In the Anjou region, two appellations are used to label sparkling wine: Crémant de la Loire and Anjou Mousseux. Both rely mostly on the Chenin Blanc grape variety, though the use of Cabernet Franc and other red grapes is permitted. The laws for Crémant de la Loire are far more stringent than for ordinary *mousseux* wines, theoretically requiring lower yields, specifying lower pressure during the pressing of the grapes, and mandating a longer time (12 months) for lees contact in the bottle after the second fermentation. The reliance on Chenin Blanc as the principal grape variety give the wines a thrilling, racy acidity, while the insistence on the *méthode champenoise* brings a balancing smoothness and depth of yeast character.

SAUMUR

Like Anjou, Saumur produces the full range of wines from a wide variety of grapes. The Saumur Blanc appellation has almost identical requirements to Anjou Blanc, using mostly Chenin Blanc to make simple, attractive, lively white wines. Similarly, there has been a greater concentration on red wine production in recent years, with Cabernet Franc or Cabernet Sauvignon making fresh, easy reds under the Saumur Rouge appellation. The two Cabernet grape varieties are also used to make Cabernet de Saumur, a semisweet rosé.

LEFT: *Terraced vineyards in the village of Bonnezeaux* RIGHT: *The stately grounds at Château de Fesles*

SAUMUR-CHAMPIGNY This is Saumur's specialty red, produced from mostly Cabernet Franc with some Cabernet Sauvignon permitted. The chalky soil of the slopes to the south of the Loire River seem to create a lightness and gaiety in a wine that is full of summer raspberries and strawberries. They are generally best consumed young.

COTEAUX DE SAUMUR This appellation is Saumur's answer to Anjou's Coteaux du Layon, made from the Chenin Blanc to produce *moëlleux* wines, though the Coteaux de Saumur never quite reach the pinnacle of elegance and the depth of complex flavors the best Layon wines do.

SPARKLING WINES Not to be outdone, Saumur also produces sparkling wines under the Saumur Mousseux appellation and as Crémant de la Loire (see page 269). Second in production levels only to the Champagne region in France (but a long way behind that region), Saumur uses the *méthode champenoise* for its sparkling wines and takes advan-

tage of the naturally occurring chalk cellars to age its wines in bottle for at least nine months after the second fermentation. It is mostly Chenin Blanc that is used for the Saumur Mousseux, though Chardonnay, Sauvignon Blanc, Cabernet Franc, and other red grapes may be included. The character of the wines is very similar to Anjou Mousseux.

OLD VDQS WINES To the south of the Coteaux de Saumur, around the town of Thouars, lies the old VDQS region producing Vins du Thouarsais, white wines made from Chenin Blanc with some Chardonnay permitted, and the reds and rosés made from the two Cabernets and Gamay. These wines are likely to be classified as IGP in the future.

TOURAINE

Like its partners in the Central Loire Valley, Touraine produces a complete range of wines that carry the Touraine appellation name on the label. The best dry whites are made with the Sauvignon Blanc variety, though Chenin Blanc is also used for both still and sparkling white wines. Gamay is the most important grape for Touraine red wines, followed by the Cabernet Franc and Cot (Malbec). Still wines with the regional Touraine appellation sometimes bear the name of the grape as well, such as the Sauvignon de Touraine wines that have made enormous inroads into international markets. They are fresh, fruity wines with immediate appeal. Touraine Mousseux sparkling wine, made by the Champagne method using Chenin Blanc as the base grape, and Crémant de la Loire are also produced within the Touraine region.

There are four important subappellations to the overall Touraine appellation. They are, from west to east: Azay-le-Rideau, Amboise, Mesland, and Noble-Joué. All four produce fresh white wines from the Chenin Blanc grape, though the Mesland subappellation may add significant quantities of Chardonnay and Sauvignon Blanc to the blend. The reds and rosés from these subappellations are based mostly on the usual mixture (in varying proportions) of the two Cabernets, Gamay, Cot, and Grolleau, though the Azay-le-Rideau subappellation makes no red wine.

BOURGUEIL AND CHINON These are the two best reds of the region and are made from Cabernet Franc with some Cabernet Sauvignon. The most powerful versions are medium- to full-bodied and are produced from south-facing slopes on volcanic clay limestone tuffeau (travertine) subsoil with some gravel and clay on top. Where gravel is more abundant in the soil, the wines tend to be lighter, whereas the tuffeau soil creates a chunkier wine.

TOP: *The vineyards at Château de Villeneuve, Saumur-Champigny* BOTTOM: *The dramatic tuffeau soil around Saumur*

A Chinon from a top producer, such as Charles Joguet, will improve over a decade. Or, like Saumur-Champigny, these Loire reds offer bright red berry fruit and wild flowers in the aroma along with good fruit and acidity on the palate when drunk young. Both appellations also produce rosé wines from the two Cabernet grapes, and Chinon makes a white from Chenin Blanc

SAINT-NICOLAS-DE-BOURGUEIL   This is a similar-style red wine appellation to the northwest of Bourgueil, with a small quantity of rosé also produced.

VOUVRAY   The Vouvray appellation is situated on the north bank of the Loire, using Chenin Blanc to produce still white wines in a range of sweetness that depends on how long and warm the growing season was. Given the unreliable climate, a large quantity of Vouvray Mousseux is produced from grapes harvested relatively early and using the *méthode champenoise*. When the weather is more reliable and a warm fall can be predicted, grape growers here are more likely to leave the grapes to ripen more fully in the hopes of making at least some *moëlleux* wines. Vouvray producers also specialize in a style called *sec-tendre*, usually translated as off-dry, somewhere between dry and semisweet. Whatever the style, the better vineyards line the river, producing finer, more elegant and complex wines from the chalky tuffeau subsoils, as compared with the fuller, more foursquare wines inland from the river.

MONTLOUIS   This area is across the river from Vouvray and was granted its own appellation in 1938. Before that, the wines were sold as Vouvray. The wines are similar, but slightly lighter and may be drunk younger. The appellation also produces some sparkling wine as Montlouis Mousseux.

JASNIÈRES   The town of Jasnières is located close to the Loir River, a tributary of the Loire River, adjacent to the Coteaux du Loir appellation. Less than 200,000 bottles of dry and off-dry white wines, with high acidity produced from low yields, are made annually. These Chenin Blanc wines offer a range of smells from floral, quince, and melon to a mineral flintiness that are part of their appeal.

COTEAUX DU LOIR   Coteaux du Loir produces about the same amount as Jasnières but makes more reds and rosés than white wines. The red grapes used include Pineau D'Aunis (which is a Chenin Noir), Cabernet Franc, Gamay, and Cot (Malbec). All of the wines are best drunk young, and the reds can be enjoyed chilled. To the east of Coteaux du Loir lie the relatively new AOP vineyards Coteaux du Vendômois, producing simple whites (Chenin Blanc with a small addition of Chardonnay permitted) and firm but light, light rosés, mostly from Pinot d'Aunis (the pinkish red version of Chenin), and reds from mostly Gamay and Pinot Noir.

CHEVERNY   An appellation since 1993, Cheverny produces sparkling, rosés, reds, and whites best consumed soon after bottling. These crisp wines may include a varietal name on the label. The white wines are made mostly from Sauvignon Blanc grapes, with Chenin Blanc and Chardonnay allowed in the blend. The local variety Romorantin is used to produce the unique subappellation white wine Cour-Cheverny. The reds and rosés are made mostly from Gamay, with Cabernet Franc, Cot, and Pinot Noir also permitted. About fifteen miles directly south of Cheverny are the recently promoted AOP vineyards of Valençay, boasting some presence of flint in the soils that gives the wines an interesting mineral note, though they lack fleshiness and structure. The whites are mostly Sauvignon Blanc with the possible addition of Chardonnay, Chenin Blanc, or the rare Romorantin, while the reds are mostly Cabernet Franc, Gamay, Pinot Noir, and Gamay.

OLD VDQS WINES   The few remaining VDQS wines include Haut-Poitou, south of Chinon, and Vins du Thouarsais, presumably destined for IGP status.

WINE REGIONS OF THE UPPER LOIRE

The wines of the Upper Loire are dominated by Sauvignon Blanc. Many restaurateurs and chefs believe Sauvignon Blanc is a better match for a wider variety of foods than Chardonnay. Sauvignon Blancs are typically more tart than Chardonnay wines and their higher acidity cleanses the palate. (For more on pairing, see Chapter 14, page 555.) These wines have mineral, herbal, and gooseberry aromas, medium weight on the palate, and explosive acidity. The vivacity and complexity of the region's finest wines are due to an unusual combination of Kimmeridgian (chalky marl) and Portlandian (hard limestone) soils that promotes finesse, length of flavors, and a distinct mineral quality. This is made even more complex by pockets of flint in the soil structure. In addition, there are outcroppings of calcareous tufa, a volcanic soil that produces a softer, somewhat flatter, but distinctly fruitier wine. While offering distinct weight in the finest years, the flavors and aromas of the wines of the Upper Loire will dance tantalizingly around your mouth for several minutes even after the wine has been swallowed.

POUILLY-FUMÉ

The appellation's 1,500 acres/600 hectares of Sauvignon Blanc vines are planted in mostly limestone-based soils. Higher levels of clay in the soil make for slightly fuller, heavier wines than from the neighboring appellation of Sancerre. The grape musts are fermented in stainless steel or old oak barrels. Malolactic fermentation is allowed to occur on a piecemeal, haphazard basis, leaving the wines with obvious, sometimes searing acidity tempered by a noticeable softness on the middle palate. The largest estate is the 128-acre/51.2-hectare Château de Nozet, which, in the best vintages, also produces a high-quality, more-expensive product labeled as "Baron L." The estate of Didier Dagueneau, whose namesake founder died in a plane crash in 2008, also produces fine wines, which, like the Baron L, may improve with some cellaring but are not as ageworthy as Savennières. Most wines of the region should be drunk from two to five years from the vintage. The Sauvignon Blanc grape is known as Blanc Fumé because of its smoky or flint-like aromas when grown in the area. This inspired Robert Mondavi to begin labeling his Napa Valley Sauvignon Blanc wines as Fumé Blanc, and many other American wineries have adopted the name.

Some producers have branched out into specialty Pouilly wines, adopting small barrel fermentation and aging and full malolactic treatment to produce a wine resembling a rich white Burgundy rather than the standard acidic style that is most prevalent here. On occasion, sweet *moëlleux* styles are even produced. In addition to Château de Nozet, Château de Tracy, Les Loges, and Les Bascoins are important individual vineyard sites.

POUILLY-SUR-LOIRE

Wines produced under this appellation are made from the white Chasselas grape variety grown on the less mineral, sandier soils of the region. They are generally considered to be less characterful than the Fumés, but they have their devotees locally.

SANCERRE

Sancerre is a larger area than Pouilly-Fumé, with 4,000 acres/1,600 hectares in fourteen communes and more variations in its soil types, producing Sauvignon Blanc white wines that are leaner and more bracing than Pouilly-Fumé, as well as some reds and rosés from the Pinot Noir grape. Some producers follow a philosophy of blending wines from the marly Kimmeridgian soils with wines from the calcareous and flint soils to produce the best of three soil types: enough weight to suggest something serious; ripe soft fruit to please; and fine, bracing acidity to refresh and balance. Alternatively, producers may prefer to create individual wines from each of the soil types, showing the effect of *terroir* to the fullest. Occasionally a sweet *vendange tardive* (late harvest) white is made. Most Sancerre wines are best drunk young, within three years, while the fruit and acidity are still lively. Some of the finer vineyard sites

LEFT: *Around Pouilly and Sancerre, flint is clearly visible in the soil.* RIGHT: *Château de Tracy, part of the Pouilly-Fumé appellation*

are Le Chêne Marchand, Les Monts Damnés, Château du Nozay, La Poussie, and Le Clos du Roy.

QUINCY

Quincy is a dry Sauvignon Blanc with herbaceous and gooseberry aromas, but softer than its neighbors to the east, probably due to higher clay content in the soils, with fewer mineral notes in the wines. The vineyards are on the banks of the Cher, a tributary of the Loire.

MÉNÉTOU-SALON

Situated between Sancerre to the east and Quincy to the west, Ménétou-Salon offers dry whites, rosés, and reds from Sauvignon Blanc and Pinot Noir. The wines are similar in style to Sancerre, less steely perhaps, and may be found at a lower price as they are not as well-known.

REUILLY

Although Reuilly is located at the southwestern corner of this whole region, far away from the bright lights of

The impressive vineyards of La Poussie in Sancerre

Sancerre and Pouilly, it has a small outcropping of limestone soil that gives some of its vineyards the ability to produce clean, scented white wines with typical Sauvignon Blanc flavors and aromas. Pinot Noir is used to produce light, dry reds, and a small amount of Pinot Gris is used to produce rosé wines. (Pinot Gris has a slightly rose hue in its skin color, though Pinot Noir may also be used to attain sufficient pinkness.)

NEW APPELLATIONS

Most of the outlying wine regions that used to have a VDQS designation have since attained AOP status. They have not taken the world by storm. In fact they have likely added to the average consumer's confusion about what the French mean by "quality wine" and what guarantees the AOP notation provides. Included in the newcomers are Coteaux du Giennois (Sauvignon Blanc whites and lighter styles of red from Gamay or Pinot Noir), Côte Roannaise (snappy, light reds from carbonic maceration Gamay), Côtes du Forez (Gamay), Orléans (Pinot Noir and Chardonnay), Orléans-Cléry (Cabernet Franc), and St-Pourçain (Gamay, Pinot Noir, Chardonnay, Tressalier, aka Sacy).

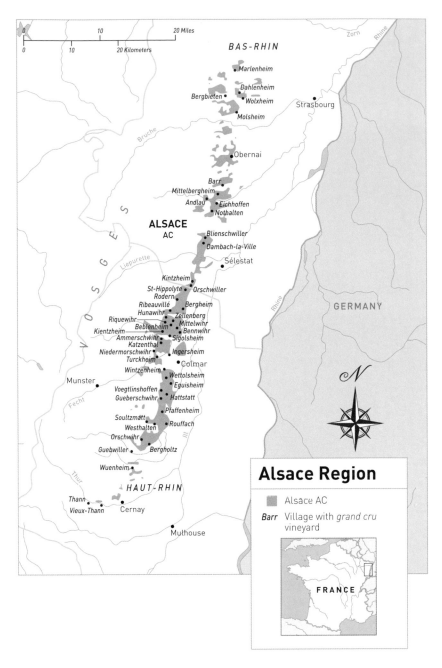

Alsace Region

	Alsace AC
Barr	Village with *grand cru* vineyard

FRANCE

Alsace

• •

The most striking thing about Alsace is that such broad diversity can exist within such a small area. Its history and culture are extremely rich, though that history has too often been marred by German-French antagonism. Perhaps this has made the Alsatians resilient, willing to work hard to make the best of a bad situation. Certainly when it comes to growing grapes, their diligence and per-

severance have helped create one of the most fascinating quilts of vineyard usage anywhere.

The vineyards of Alsace cover approximately 35,000 acres/14,000 hectares in a narrow, sunny, but cold valley of about 60 miles/100 kilometers long and 2.5 miles/4 kilometers at its widest (see map at left). The Vosges Mountains create a rain shadow that protects the vineyards from the winds and moisture from the west, and the Rhine River provides a moderating influence to the east. The result is a semi-Continental climate providing a long, dry growing season that allows the grapes to ripen slowly and develop the aromatic qualities that have become the signature of the region's wines. The foothills of the Vosges provide some steeply angled slopes with a rich variety of soil types and structures, as well as unique pockets of microclimatic influences.

Over several generations of grape growers and winemakers, the Alsatians have planted nine different grape types in their small region, with careful consideration given to matching the most suitable variety to the unique combination of geologic and climatic conditions in each vineyard site. The richest combinations of schist and limestone content in a fine-particle clay base are clustered around the town of Colmar in a north-south line from St-Hippolyte to Eguisheim that boasts 60 percent of all the region's *grand cru* vineyards. That line follows a fault line, with the result that there are uniquely localized outcroppings of granite and gneiss in addition to the limestone and schist. The best vineyard sites face south, where grapes benefit from the heat of the morning and afternoon sunshine.

Although Alsace was officially part of France in 1918, the area's viticulture was not regulated by INAO until 1945, and further regulations regarding yield, ripeness levels, and label terms continue to be updated.

Alsace is the only AOP region to label wines by their grape name. Exceptions to this are **EDELZWICKER** or "noble blend" (any combination of Riesling, Gewürztraminer, Muscat, Pinot Gris, Pinot Blanc, or Chasselas) and sparkling wines, which are labeled Crémant d'Alsace. A recent proposal by one prominent producer to remove varietal names from Alsace labels and to concentrate on place names has met with major opposition from other producers, and the recent EU reforms that allow, even promote, the presence of a grape variety name on the label of all EU wines suggest that the varietal name will remain a prominent feature on Alsace labels.

The numerous small holdings that make up the vineyards in Alsace are owned by over five thousand farmers. Cooperatives and *négociants* buy grapes and market about 80 percent of the wine; the balance is estate bottled.

The local wine board determines harvest dates and, as in Champagne, all wines must be bottled within the region, generally using the distinctive tall, thin "flute" bottle. Wines are usually fermented in neutral containers, either stainless steel vats or *fûts*—large, old oak casks.

Production is around 120 million bottles annually, 95 percent of which is white. Pinot Noir is used for reds and rosés and it has increased to about 6.5 percent of acreage, giving wines with fruity aroma and taste along with good acidity. Some oak-aged reds are being made with more weight on the palate to handle stronger food preparations. The wines of Alsace have historically been fermented dry, with good structure. A modern trend has been to leave some of the varietals with higher levels of residual sugar. This has been especially noticeable with Gewürztraminer and Pinot Gris wines. They remain the most full-bodied examples of these varietals in the world, and their style has developed along with the rich and flavorful cuisine of the region. Malolactic fermentation is avoided to maintain high acid levels to balance the wines.

In 1975 the INAO introduced the designation of *grand cru* vineyard to Alsace. Growers and producers were slow to respond to the invitation to apply for the honor, and some producers still refuse to do so. They maintain that the conditions for *grand cru* status are too lenient, and certainly the regulated maximum yield of 70 hectoliters per hectare (more than 5 tons per acre) for an Alsatian *grand cru* site is far above the yields for *grand cru* vineyards elsewhere in France. The size of the individual *grand cru* sites ranges from 7.5 to 197.5 acres/3 to 80 hectares, and some producers claim that many of the sites are too large to show unique, homogeneous characteristics.

About 5 percent of the vineyard acreage in Alsace has been awarded *grand cru* status and currently fifty-one sites produce single-varietal wines from individual *grand cru*; the name of the *cru* will be on the label along with the grape name and the phrase *grand cru*. Only the grape types that are considered the most noble are permitted to bear the highest-quality designation of *grand cru*: They are the Gewürztraminer, Pinot Gris, Muscat, and Riesling. Two of the *grand cru* sites (Altenberg de Bergheim and Kaefferkopf) are allowed to produce wines from a blend of the grape types, and the Zotzenberg *grand cru* can be made from Sylvaner.

LEFT: *A typical Alsace sign outside the restaurant Winstub au Sommelier* RIGHT: *Almost all wines from Alsace are labeled as varietal wines.*

THE GRAND CRU SITES IN ALSACE

Altenberg de Bergbieten	Moenchberg
Altenberg de Bergheim	Muenchberg
Altenberg de Wolxheim	Ollwiller
Brand	Osterberg
Bruderthal	Pfersigberg
Eichberg	Pfingstberg
Engelberg	Praelatenberg
Florimont	Rangen
Frankstein	Rosacker
Froehn	Saering
Furstentum	Schlossberg
Geisberg	Schoenenbourg
Gloeckelberg	Sommerberg
Goldert	Sonnenglanz
Hatschbourg	Spiegel
Hengst	Sporen
Kaefferkopf	Steinert
Kanzlerberg	Steingrubler
Kastelberg	Steinklotz
Kessler	Vorbourg
Kirchberg de Barr	Wiebelsberg
Kirchberg de Ribeauvillé	Wineck-Schlossberg
Kitterlé	Winzenberg
Mambourg	Zinnklpflé
Mandelberg	Zotzenberg

Those producers who choose not to label their eligible wine as *grand cru* usually use other distinctive label terms to indicate a special wine, such as *réserve, réserve personelle,* or some proprietary or historic name. Examples include Cuvée Jubilee from Hugel and Cuvée Frédéric Emile from Trimbach. As in Burgundy, the name of an unclassified site sometimes appears on a label.

Another similarity to Burgundy is the use of the term **CLOS** for vineyards that have been enclosed by walls. These wines may be equal to or superior to wines labeled as *grand cru* even if not classified as such. Some of the famous clos are the Clos des Capucins, Clos Gaensbroennel, Clos Saint Hune, Clos Saint Immer, Clos Saint Landelin, Clos Rebgarten, Clos de Schlossberg, Clos Saint Urbain, Clos Windsbuhl, and Clos Zissel.

Warmer vintages with sunny days that extend ripening produce two distinctly sweet categories of wine that, by law, are never chaptalized. *Vendange tardive* indicates late harvest, while *sélection de grains nobles* ("selection of noble grapes") means that the grapes must have been affected by *pourriture noble* (*Botrytis cinerea*). The wines must be made as single-varietal wines from one of the following varieties: Riesling, Pinot Gris, Gewürztraminer, or Muscat. Although these are higher-alcohol, sweeter wines, the northern climate provides good acidity for balance.

GRAPE VARIETIES

The varieties important in wine production in Alsace are all white grapes.

RIESLING

This is the finest and the most-planted variety in the region, with 20 percent of the acreage. The varied soils produce wines with aromas from mineral to floral and fruity. Vines planted on lighter, sandy soils yield wines that are faster-maturing and lighter in body than those planted on heavier, limestone soils. In Alsace's long, cool growing seasons, Riesling is known for its balance of fruit and acidity. The current trend is to produce Riesling in a style that emphasizes its elegance in contrast to the power that is a feature of some of the other grape types.

GEWÜRZTRAMINER

Some prefer the distinctive spicy, floral, fruity, powerful nose and taste of this grape to that of Riesling. It occupies almost as much total acreage as Riesling, even though its

Riesling vineyards around Ribeauvillé

yield is less. Gewürztraminer seems to prefer richer, deeper soils than Riesling. This pinkish-hued grape produces wines with more power and color than most white grapes, with the distinct notes of spiciness for which it is named.

PINOT GRIS

Less fruity and floral than the preceding two grapes, with a nuttier nose, the finest examples of Pinot Gris from Alsace have a scent of violets but a distinct fleshiness or oiliness. Pinot Gris accounts for about 5 percent of total plantings. Its richness, power, and intensity make it one of the region's best accompaniments to the full-flavored local cuisine.

MUSCAT

The musky floral fruit aromatics of this wine are more powerful than the body, which is often light to medium when vinified dry, but with explosive grapey ripeness. The late-harvest versions, though, will be heavier in body. The Muscat accounts for only 3 percent of plantings.

SYLVANER

Sylvaner grapes yield light-bodied fresh wines for early consumption without the intensity or elegance of their noble cousins. Second only to Riesling for acidity, Sylvaner accounts for about 20 percent of plantings.

PINOT BLANC

Pinot Blanc makes dry wines with more body than Sylvaner. Pinot Auxerrois, even though it is a different grape, may be labeled Pinot Blanc or Klevner. In either case, both ripen early and combined account for 19 percent of plantings.

CHASSELAS

Chasselas, often blended into Edelzwicker, is being replaced by the above varieties that have more acidity, structure, and flavor.

SPARKLING WINES

White sparkling wines produced by the *méthode champenoise* are labeled as Crémant d'Alsace. Like other CRÉMANT wines produced in France, the wines must age for at least nine months in the bottles with the yeast cells after the second fermentation. The grapes used include mostly Pinot Blanc, Riesling, Pinot Gris, or Pinot Noir, using the *méthode champenoise*; they account for about thirty million bottles, or 20 percent of annual production. A small amount of rosé sparkling wine is made using Pinot Noir only. They are good quality, less expensive alternatives to Champagne.

The noteworthy wine producers of Alsace include L. Beyer, A. Boxler, M. Deiss, Dopff au Moulin, Dopff et Irion, L. Albrecht, Hugel, Domaine Klipfel, M. Kreydenweiss, Kuentz Bas, M. Laugel, Jos Meyer, Meyer-Fonne, Muré-Clos St Landelin, C. Schleret, Domaine Schlumberger, P. Sparr, F. E. Trimbach, P. Blanck, Domaine Weinbach, and Domaine Zind Humbrecht.

Champagne

The word "Champagne" brings to mind notions of success, glamour, and celebration. No other beverage is so universally identified with joy and festivity.

The Champagne region is an *appellation d'origine protégée* located ninety miles northeast of Paris, making it France's northernmost wine region. The Champagne method (*méthode champenoise*) is used worldwide for the production of the finest sparkling wines, but true Champagne comes only from this one area. Champagne producers have gone to great lengths to protect the use of the word Champagne outside of their region and have even prohibited other sparkling wine producers from using the phrase "*méthode champenoise*" on labels.

Ostensibly, there are solid grounds for this protectionism, and the ground, or at least the soil, has a lot to do with it. In a nutshell, the argument is this: Champagne producers believe that their region is composed of a unique combination of influences, including soil types, soil structures, climate, grape types, and history. Whereas it is true that many other places in the world could grow the requisite grape types or boast a climate as cold as Champagne, nowhere other than Champagne has that particular combination. And, therefore, only Champagne should be allowed to use labeling terms like "Champagne" or "*méthode champenoise*."

As noted in the introduction to this section (see page 262), the recent decision to allow forty more villages to be included in the Champagne appellation has raised eyebrows and ruffled feathers. The full impact of the decision is decades away, but there are already fears that Champagne has somehow been diluted, and that the expansion is primarily good for the large Champagne houses. It's a bit like the globalization argument on a small scale! One defense of the decision is that all but one of the forty new villages fall within the existing boundaries of the appellation.

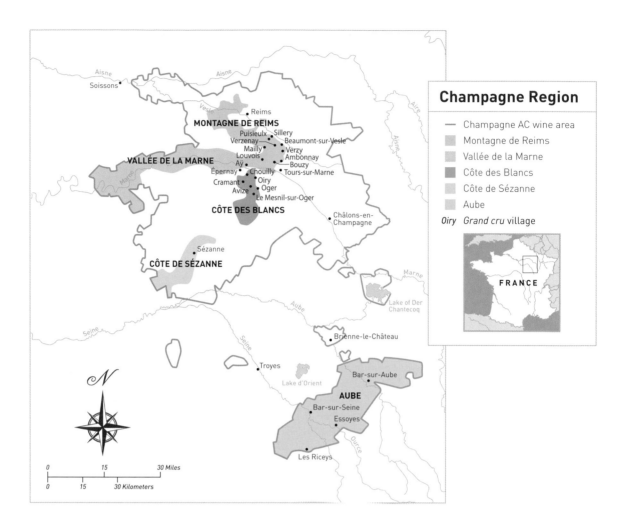

Even so, questions remain about why these forty villages were excluded in the first place and why the decision to expand coincides with the possibility of establishing new export markets in newly rich nations. Part of the justification to expand was the projected increase in demand in developed and developing nations, particularly in China and India, with a new, affluent middle class. However, those prospects were dashed by the impact of the global economic and credit crisis, and Champagne sales plummeted. Unexpectedly, Champagne producers found themselves pressing for a reduction in production rather than an expansion, yet the expansion of the appellation will go ahead. The 2009 agreement between Champagne growers and producers about how much wine can be produced from a hectare led to an unprecedented 40 percent cut in total production for that year.

France is divided into many politico-geographic units called *départements*, and the wine regions of the nation often encompass numerous *départements*. Almost 70 percent of the Champagne appellation vineyards are in the Marne *département*. The three major subregions of Champagne within the Marne are the Côte des Blancs, the Montagne de Reims, and the Vallée de la Marne. The Champagne appellation vineyards also include areas called the Côte de Sézanne and the Côte des Bar. The total acreage of the expanded Champagne vineyards is approximately 99,000 acres/40,000 hectares, spread across 359 villages. The authorized grape types are Chardonnay (planted on 27 percent of the total acreage) and two red varieties, Pinot Noir (38 percent of total acreage) and Pinot Meunier (35 percent of total acreage). These figures do not reflect the extra vineyard area that will be developed as a result of the addition of the forty villages.

In deference to the claims that the soil, climate, and regional microclimates are still at the heart of what Champagne is all about, this section will deal first with those issues, including comments on the grape types. Then will come a look at qualitative issues such as the human element in vineyard practices, winemaking, and the structure of the Champagne trade.

THE SOIL AND CLIMATE OF CHAMPAGNE

Champagne is a cold place, at the northern climatic limit of grape growing, a factor that leaves the grapes with low tannins but a particularly fine varietal aroma. Sometimes July and August will be hot, and occasionally September and October will be warm. But such weather patterns are unreliable. It is arguably for this reason that the bulk of Champagne is bottled as a nonvintage product. Producers realized early on that the adoption of a nonvintage philosophy in winemaking would eliminate the peaks and valleys of vintage variation associated with a generally cold climate and infrequent warm spells. By keeping wines on reserve from good years, the weak spots in the cooler years could be overcome. This has evolved into the notion that there is a "house style" followed by each producer, and any nonvintage Champagne released by that producer will be identical to all other nonvintage releases, or at least so very nearly the same that nobody can tell.

In those years when Champagne is blessed with a favorably warm weather pattern, most houses (producers) will offer a vintage version of wine from that one single year, with 100 percent of the wine coming from grapes harvested in the year indicated on the label. Vintage champagne is an opportunity for the winemaker to take the excellence that nature has created and to craft a wine that is representative of the Champagne region in that particular year. As such, vintage champagne is a truly extraordinary product: It is not the same as regular bottlings of nonvintage wine. Even so, a vintage-dated Champagne will usually still be a blend of different grape types and grapes from different villages and vineyards.

Champagne's northern position offers a number of other challenges to the grape grower and wine producer. Spring frosts are frequent and can severely reduce the potential crop in any year when they affect the tender young buds as they begin to open. Similarly, the uncertainty of favorable weather around flowering time may result in poor berry set and a reduced crop, as can thunderstorms and hailstorms during flowering or anytime thereafter.

The generally cold climate makes Champagne a highly

Glimpses of the chalk soil are evident throughout the vineyards in Champagne.

acidic wine, an important factor when one considers the number of years involved in producing the region's highest-quality wines. Through the long production process, and for any aging subsequent to bottling, the high acid levels keep the wine tasting fresh and lively even as the wines evolve their rich and intricate flavors and textures.

There also appears to be a link between the soil and the high acid levels of the wines. The prominent soil type is chalk, though this is not always visible on the surface. In fact, the prime sites appear to be the areas where the thick chalk bedrock (sometimes up to 1,000 feet/300 meters deep) has been covered with later soils containing clay, marl, and lignite, itself containing important traces of iron. As yet there is no substantiated proof, but there seems to be an inverse relationship between high pH soil and higher acid levels in the grapes. Certainly, from a textural perspective, there is a lean mineral quality to the grapes grown in the chalk-based vineyards, whereas the areas with heavier clay and marl deposits tend to create fuller, fleshier wines.

Additional soil considerations are that the chalk contributes heat retention and allows both surface water drainage and subterranean water storage. Many vineyard areas in Champagne claim to have root penetration to 30 or 40 feet/10 to 13 meters, promoting a healthy vine whose root system will be well protected from severe cold and access to water stored in the different porosity levels of the chalk at different depths. This is particularly important in a region that has low annual rainfall and where irrigation is illegal. The low fertility of chalk soils also produces fewer leaves on a vine canopy. This allows more sun exposure of the fruit and better air circulation than a dense canopy. The variations in soil composition and the minerals they provide to the vines is one of the factors that determine the taste of Champagne.

VINEYARD RATINGS

During World War II, a local control board named the **COMITÉ INTERPROFESSIONEL DU VIN DE CHAMPAGNE (CIVC)** was created, consisting of producers, growers, and INAO officials. One of its important functions was to set the *échelle des crus*, or rating, of all the Champagne villages, which assigns a percentage value to all vineyards within a village or commune. All vineyards within a single village are presumed to have the same rating. Updated in 1985, this scale ranks the lowest level *cru* villages from 80 to 89 percent; the forty-one *premier cru* communes are ranked from 90 to 99 percent; and seventeen *grands crus* are rated at 100 percent. Given the emphasis on the importance of the soil/climate relationship, it is not surprising that some villages specialize in growing only white or red grapes. If a village grows red and white grapes, the ranking usually applies to both, though there are a few examples where red and white grapes are ranked differently in the same commune: For example, Tours-sur-Marne is rated as 100 percent *grand cru* for red grapes, but only 90 percent *premier cru* for white grapes. Until recently, prices for each grape varietal were legally fixed by the CIVC each year. The vineyards were then paid for grapes according to their percentage rating, so that if the price of Chardonnay grapes was fixed at $100 per ton, a vineyard in a village rated at 88 percent would be paid $88 per ton. In 1990, this collective bargaining system was abandoned, and individual growers now negotiate with producers who wish to buy their grapes; however, the percentage ranking system is still referred to as a means to agree on a price for the grapes.

There are seventeen *grands crus* in Champagne, all clustered fairly close to one another in the central part of the Marne *département*. Everybody is assuming that none of the forty new villages will be granted *premier* or *grand cru* status, but time will tell how well they perform.

REGIONS

Within the total Champagne appellation there are five important regions, each with its own unique character and each considered to produce a particular style of base wine that the producers will use in varying proportions in their blend, according to their house style.

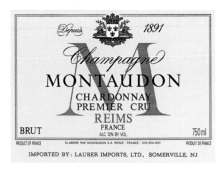

A Champagne label showing the grapes came from premier cru *villages*

MONTAGNE DE REIMS

This is the most northerly of the named regions of Champagne with just over half of the vineyards there planted with Pinot Noir, which seems to benefit from the iron-rich traces of the numerous lignite deposits in the soil. In the last decade Chardonnay has increased in acreage in this region to claim almost a third of the vineyard area, while Pinot Meunier has decreased to approximately one-sixth of total vineyard acreage in the region. Curiously, many of the Montagne's best sites, including several *grand cru* villages, are located on north-facing slopes. In this cold climate this would appear to be a contradiction. Possible explanations are that the chalk-rich soil retains heat from the daytime and continues to warm the vines after sundown, or that the descent of cold air down the northerly slope pulls in warmer southerly air from the plateau of the Montagne. Whatever the reason, the vineyards in the north produce more deeply colored, well-structured base wines with red fruit notes that are an important component in the blend for many houses.

The Montagne de Reims region has nine *grand cru* villages: Ambonnay, Bouzy, Louvois, Mailly, Verzenay, Verzy, Beaumont-sur-Vesle, Puisieulx, and Sillery.

VALLÉE DE LA MARNE

The Vallée region acts almost as a horizontal divider between the Montagne to the north and the Côte des Blancs to the south. As the Vallée region extends westward it moves farther away from the concentration of chalk deposits, and its soil is richer in clay and marl. As a river valley, it is also susceptible to both spring and fall frosts. Because of the richer soil, the decreasing concentrations of chalk, and the frost danger, the Vallée is largely planted with Pinot Meunier that, as a late budder and early ripener, produces fleshy, fruity wines that will help add on to the structure provided by Pinot Noir, which claims almost one-third of the vineyard area here. Chardonnay vineyards account for about one-tenth of total acreage in the Vallée.

Grand cru villages in the Vallée de la Marne region are Tours-sur-Marne and Aÿ.

CÔTE DES BLANCS

As its name implies, the Côte des Blancs is planted almost exclusively with Chardonnay, which is particularly well suited to the southerly continuation of the deep chalk deposits from the Montagne de Reims region, but with much less of the iron deposit. Champagne producers are eager to include Chardonnay grapes from this region for the appley citrus notes that they contribute to the blend, and for the delicacy and finesse that they overlay on the Pinot Noir and Pinot Meunier.

There are six *grand cru* villages in the Côte des Blancs region: Avize, Chouilly, Cramant, Le Mesnil-sur-Oger, Oger, and Oiry.

CÔTE DE SÉZANNE

This region is situated southeast of the Côte des Blancs and also specializes in Chardonnay plantings (70 percent of the region's vineyards), though the region contains no *grand cru* or *premier cru* vineyards, lacking the magic combination of soil, topography, and climate. Most of the region's wines mirror the lack of soil complexity, offering bright fruit characteristics, but without the lift and elegance of Chardonnay from the Côte des Blancs.

The vineyards of Salon at Le Mesnil-sur-Oger

CÔTE DES BAR

This region is some 45 miles/70 kilometers southwest of the Côte de Sézanne and was long considered the poor cousin of all the Champagne regions. It is as though the Montagne de Reims and the Côte des Blancs have turned their back on the Bars, claiming that the soils, and therefore the grapes, are different. The Bars chalky marl derives from the same Kimmeridgian soil as Pouilly and Sancerre in the Loire Valley, rather than the deeper and more ancient chalk composition of northern Champagne. Most of the plantings are Pinot Noir (85 percent of all plantings), and the grapes from this region's vineyards generally produce riper and fruitier wines.

QUALITY ISSUES

VINEYARD PRACTICES

In addition to the paramount consideration of carefully matching grape type to climatic and soil conditions in the vineyard, there are a number of other activities in the vineyard that help Champagne producers maintain their commitment to high quality. In particular, harvesting by hand is legislated in the *appellation protégée* laws for Champagne. Pickers are obliged to use small crates to collect the grapes as they pick them and to get the crop to the press house as quickly as possible. As a result, there is minimal crushing of the grapes in the bottom of the crates from the mass of grapes on top. In fact, many quality-minded producers in other regions boast about their use of Champagne crates for harvesting, even for the production of still wines. Picking by hand also allows for the continued practice of harvesting by trics, or passing through the vineyard several times in succession to pick bunches of grapes as they reach full ripeness, rather than harvesting everything at once, which runs the risk of including green, unripe grapes in the picking.

Champagne producers also insist that, despite their cool climate that keeps the grape acids high, the grapes are always left on the vine long enough to attain full physiological ripeness in terms of flavor. Even though sugar levels may be low and chaptalization may be necessary, the grapes develop true varietal flavors and characteristics.

Like other cool-climate grape-growing areas, Champagne can be hit by damaging spring frosts that might kill any buds that have begun to develop. To combat this danger, the growers use the **ASPERSION** method, spraying the vines with a fine mist of water as the temperature drops so that the buds are, ironically, protected from seriously low temperatures by the ice cover as the water spray freezes.

The annual yield for Champagne used to be set at 4.5 tons per acre/65 hectoliters per hectare; in exceptional circumstances, and only with official approval, yields were allowed to increase to 6 tons per acre/81 hectoliters per hectare. We have already alluded to the perception of duplicity surrounding the expansion of the Champagne appellation to include forty more villages to create more vineyard land to meet future global demand. In the meantime, to deal with the immediate problem of supply, the INAO authorities have been tampering with the maximum yield numbers. Producers are now allowed a maximum yield of 7.5 tons per acre/98.8 hectoliters per hectare for the total pressing. However, producers will be allowed to actually grow and harvest up to 10 tons per acre/138 hectoliters per hectare as long as they only use as much pressed juice to meet the maximum 98.8 hectoliter limit. This is a ludicrous situation. Throwing away part of the pressed juice does not improve the remaining juice. To put things in perspective, the standard table wine in France is restricted to a yield of 6.5 tons per acre/90 hectoliters per hectare.

WINEMAKING PRACTICES

Notwithstanding the above, the pressing of the grapes is considered one of the most important steps in the production of a fine Champagne. To get the clearest possible juice with the finest balance of varietal character to sugar to acids, the grapes have to be pressed whole and quickly but gently. Rather than follow the practice of most regions where grapes are crushed before pressing, whole bunches of grapes, including stems, are loaded into the press. Many producers stick with the traditional wooden Champagne press; others use the pneumatic press. In either case, the stems provide channels within the mass of the grapes, allowing the juice to run free and thereby avoid coloration from too much time in contact with the skins. When 8,800 pounds/4,000 kilograms of grapes are pressed, they yield 673 gallons/2,550 liters of juice, with the first pressing (**TÊTE DE CUVÉE**) yielding 541.5 gallons/2,050 liters. The second pressing (**TAILLE**) amounts to a further 132 gallons/500 liters. The first pressing produces the finest juice.

As in any area that uses different grape varieties to produce a final blend, each variety is harvested and pressed separately. In the case of Champagne, the pressings are done by grape type and by vineyard origin, and each batch of wine is kept separate and identified by grape type and vineyard.

Given the natural delicacy of the juice from a cool region like Champagne, an important quality consideration is to avoid too much handling of the juice and wine. In this regard, top producers do not use mechanical methods to clarify the juice prior to fermentation, and even fining of the wine after fermentation is avoided. The goal is to maintain all the aromas, flavors, and textures that have been obtained in the grape-growing process and from the gentle pressing.

The overall pattern in Champagne is to use stainless steel fermenters for the first fermentation, though a few producers (notably Krug and Bollinger) continue to use wooden barrels for at least part of the first fermentation, giving their wines added complexity. Even with chaptalization, the initial fermentation will ideally produce base wines of around 10.5 to 11 percent alcohol by volume. An important quality consideration is knowing what portion of the different base wines, if any, should go through malolactic fermentation: too much and the wine will taste too buttery and heavy; too little and the wine will be overly austere.

The soul of any producer's Champagne lies in the **ASSEMBLAGE** (blending). It is a highly complex task involving the careful balancing of characteristics from different varietals, vineyards, and vintages, and the Champagne winemaker's palate; the blend may comprise thirty to seventy individual base wines for a nonvintage product. Generally, a new batch of nonvintage wine will start with a large number of base wines from the most recent harvest. These will be blended together in the best possible combination consistent with the house style, and then reserve wines from previous years will be added to bring the whole *assemblage* to the correct point. Even then, this blend or **CUVÉE** might be considered an imperfect product, since the winemaker has to produce a base blend that will then change through the processes of the second fermentation and aging. In effect, the blender has to predict what those changes will be so that when the nonvintage product is finally released it will be as identical as possible to the previous bottling.

Each blender has his or her own preferences in blending. The nonvintage wine of most producers is blended

LEFT: *Vineyards near the Champagne village of Bouzy* **TOP RIGHT**: *Riddling racks at Salon* **BOTTOM RIGHT**: *The headquarters of Moët & Chandon in Epernay*

using all three grape types. Pinot Noir provides firmness and structure, almost like a skeleton; Pinot Meunier adds the flesh with its ample fruitiness, while Chardonnay makes everything look pretty with its elegance and finesse.

Many of the quality issues surrounding harvesting, pressing, and blending were pioneered by the famous Dom Pérignon, a monk who served at the Abbé d'Hautvillers from 1688 until his death in 1715. Though he did not invent sparkling wine, records of his achievements indicate that he introduced selective harvesting, rapid and gentle pressing of red grapes to get completely clear juice, and judicious blending of different grape types from different vineyards to produce more complex and more balanced wines. He is also credited with introducing the stronger English glass bottles and reintroducing the cork as a stopper, both factors that later on became essential to the development of fine Champagne as a sparkling wine. Today the Abbé d'Hautvillers is owned by Moët & Chandon, who use the name Dom Pérignon to market their top-of-the-line product.

Accuracy in the addition of the *liqueur de tirage* is important to ensure an appropriate increase in the amount of alcohol from the second fermentation and the production of an appropriate amount of carbonation. The invention of the **GLUCO-OENOMÈTRE** in 1836 by André François allowed the amount of sugar needed to produce the carbon dioxide bubbles to be more accurately measured and made the cellars less hazardous, as fewer bottles were lost to explosions. This led to a formula that would consistently produce sparkling wines of five to six **ATMOSPHERES** of pressure in a bottle, the normal pressure for all Champagnes. Following the second fermentation is the aging time, which is legally set at a minimum of fifteen months for nonvintage and thirty-six months for vintage. The fifteen-month minimum is considered necessary to develop the full character of the wine, including any contribution from yeast autolysis, and to fully integrate the carbon dioxide gas into the wine, thereby creating a fine perlage of bubbles when the wine is poured. Champagne producers are blessed with approximately 150 miles/250 kilometers of underground limestone caverns at a constant temperature of 52°F/11°C to store their wines during the mandatory aging period after the second fermentation.

The manual removal of the yeast cells after the fermentation was originally developed in the first decade of the nineteenth century by Madame Veuve Clicquot, proprietor of the Champagne house Veuve Clicquot-Ponsardin

and perfected by her cellar master Antoine Müller. The Veuve's method is highly labor intensive and is increasingly being replaced, even in Champagne, by computer-monitored riddling machines known as *gyropalettes*.

THE CHAMPAGNE TRADE

Just as in any wine region, the major players in the whole production process are growers and producers. A few growers make their own wine, some group together in grower cooperatives to make wine, and others sell to the large houses. In Champagne, a grower who also makes,

TOP: *Large houses like Veuve Clicquot are becoming major owners of vineyard land.* BOTTOM: *Smaller producers like this one are also an important component of the Champagne trade.*

bottles, and sells wine is called a *récoltant-manipulant;* these growers sell their own wines mostly to the domestic market and have only 7 percent of exports. Throughout the entire Champagne region, there are approximately fifteen thousand growers who grow grapes to sell to others or to make their own wine. They farm approximately 90 percent of the land, and the bulk of their harvest is used by cooperatives or the large Champagne houses. The large houses, known as **NÉGOCIANTS-MANIPULANTS**, may own some vineyards but they buy most of their grapes from small growers: The best houses have developed long-term contracts with many growers to ensure a consistent supply of high-quality grapes.

There are over two hundred *négociants-manipulants,* most of whom have their headquarters located in the towns of Reims, Aÿ, and Epernay; together they account for over two-thirds of all Champagne sales. The most powerful company of the region is Louis Vuitton Moët Hennessey. This consortium owns the firms Moët & Chandon, Veuve Clicquot, Ruinart, Mercier, Krug, and Pommery. Champagne sales have a profound effect on the French economy, because, although the vineyards amount to only 3 percent of national plantings, they represent about one-quarter of all wine and spirit exports, one-third of AOP output, and 0.6 percent of the nation's export business: About 250 to 285 million bottles are sold annually. The United States and Great Britain, the top export markets, each consume about 15 million bottles of Champagne per year.

One very welcome development over the last decade has been the emergence of more and more small, independent producers onto the world export market, offering extremely well-crafted champagnes in an array of styles, from full and biscuity to delicate and subtle.

THE STYLES OF CHAMPAGNE

Although there is arguably a general Champagne style, it is important to remember that each producer brings different nuances and emphases to their wines. Some producers use more Pinot Noir in the blend, others prefer more Pinot Meunier or Chardonnay. Some winemakers have a preference for a particular grape variety from a specific village or *cru.* Some age their wines longer than others after the second fermentation in bottle, and all producers have the choice of exactly how much sugar, if any, to add in the final *dosage,* so that for any wine labeled *"brut"* there is in fact a range of possible sweetness levels.

Variations in the aroma of the wine, the weight on the palate, and the flavors showcased by each producer are part of the intrigue of exploring wines made by different producers. A tasting of the most popular dry or *brut* style made by a half dozen houses is a good way to reveal the wines' similarities and differences. Just as a conductor brings a personal interpretation to a classical piece regardless of the orchestra and location, so must the **CHEF DE CAVES** (cellar master and winemaker) reflect the style of the house using different grape types from different sources or vintages.

The following are the Champagne styles as determined by sugar content:

EXTRA BRUT These products are bone dry with under 0.6 percent of sugar. Brut Sauvage is a proprietary name used by Piper Heidsieck for this style, while Ultra Brut is a proprietary name used by Laurent-Perrier.

BRUT *Brut* is by far the most popular style of Champagne and has less than 1.5 percent sugar. *Brut* nonvintage wines are the mainstays of the Champagne business.

EXTRA DRY Extra-dry wines range from semidry to semisweet, containing between 1.2 and 2 percent sugar.

SEC The range is from 1.7 percent sugar to the sweeter 3.5 percent sugar.

DEMI-SEC Sweeter still, this style contains between 3.3 and 5 percent sugar.

DOUX The sweetest style of Champagne has a minimum of 5 percent of sugar.

Following is a summary of the types of Champagne, which are usually made in a brut style even when not indicated on the label.

NONVINTAGE A nonvintage Champagne must be aged at least fifteen months after the second fermentation in the bottle. A majority of Champagne is made as nonvintage, blended from varietals, vineyards, and vintages. Quality producers often age their nonvintage Champagnes for thirty to thirty-six months.

VINTAGE A vintage-dated wine must be aged a minimum of three years before being disgorged. Conscientious producers age their vintage products for four or five years. Vintage wines are not made every year, and even when a producer decides to make a vintage, there are still nonvintage bottles made. In a year a producer makes a vintage, a maximum of 80 percent can be declared as such. This is to ensure that sufficient amounts will be reserved for future blending into nonvintage wines.

Vintage wines must contain 100 percent grapes of the declared year.

BLANC DE BLANCS A Blanc de Blancs is a Champagne made exclusively from Chardonnay grapes, which results in the most delicate of Champagnes. As only 27 percent of the region is planted with Chardonnay, these wines will be more expensive than nonvintage products blended with red grapes. The wines repay their cost with a green apple and citrusy aroma in youth that evolves into nuttier, butterscotch tones with age.

BLANC DE NOIRS Blanc de Noirs ("white of blacks") refers to wines made from only the red grapes. Bollinger's Vieilles Vignes is a Blanc de Noirs from Pinot Noir vines planted on their own roots and never affected by phylloxera. Blanc de Noirs will generally be fuller in body than those wines that contain Chardonnay in a blend. The red berry scents and flavors are accompanied by a rich finish as a counterpoint to the region's traditional high acidity.

ROSÉ Rosé Champagnes are most often made by blending red wine into a cuvée (blend) of white wines. Some producers may use a brief skin-contact time to release pigments, a method commonly practiced for still rosé table wines. Rosé Champagnes are *brut,* not semisweet as many "blush" wines are. They are full-bodied, elegant, and expensive wines that vary in color from pale salmon to cherry. The color of rosé Champagne is one of its attractions, but a blindfolded taster might have a hard time discerning a rosé from a classic *brut.* Again, it is house style that will determine how much red wine is added during the *assemblage* and the balance of components in the wine.

RECENTLY DISGORGED Wines in this category are aged far longer in the bottle with the yeast sediment, which contributes richer flavors and results in a fuller-bodied wine. Bollinger has trademarked the term "RD" for their **RECENTLY DISGORGED** wine, which spends about eight years on the lees. The extra aging contributes to a greater complexity of the wine, and the Bollinger firm's practice of fermenting in oak also gives this wine an extra dimension of power and interest.

CUVÉE DE PRESTIGE Cuvée de Prestige or Prestige Cuvée are the top-of-the-line wines from each house, produced from the finest quality juice from different grape types from the best vineyards. Most are single-vintage wines, though Krug's Grande Cuvée is an example of a Prestige Cuvée that is a multi-vintage wine.

COTEAUX CHAMPENOIS Coteaux Champenois are the still white wines of the region and amount to only 0.1 percent of annual production. The wines may be labeled with a name of a single vineyard. Rosé des Riceys is a dry, still blush wine and is even rarer than Coteaux Champenois.

Some of the major houses are listed here; if applicable, the name of their Prestige Cuvée follows.

A. Charbaut — Certificate Blanc de Blancs
Alain Thiénot — Grande Cuvée
Alfred Gratien — Cuvée Paradis
André Jacquart — Blanc de Blancs Spécial Club Brut
Ayala — Grande Cuvée
Barancourt — Cuvée des Fondateurs
Beaumont des Crayères — Nostalgie
Besserat de Bellefon — Grande Cuvée Blanc de Blancs
Billecart-Salmon — Nicolas-François Billecart, Elizabeth Salmon Rosé
Bollinger — Année Rare RD, Vieilles Vignes Française Blanc de Noirs
Bruno Paillard — "NPU" Nec Plus Ultra
Canard Duchène — Grande Cuvée Charles VII Brut
Charles Heidsieck — La Royale, Charlie, Blanc des Millénaires
De Castellane — Cuvée Florens de Castellane
Delamotte — Nicolas Louis Delamotte
Deutz — Cuvée William Deutz Rosé, Cuvée William Deutz
Devaux — Cuvée Distinction
Drappier — Grande Sendrée
Duval-Leroy — Authentis Cumières
Egly Ouriet — Les Crayères
G. H. Mumm — Mumm de Cramant, René Lalou, and Grand Cordon
Gosset — Grand Millésimé, Célébris
Heidsieck Monopole, GM — Diamant Bleu
Henri Abelé — Soirées Parisiennes, Le Sourire de Reims
Henriot — Cuvée des Enchanteleurs
Jacquart — Blanc de Blancs Cuvée Mosaique, Cuvée Nominée
Jacques Selosse — Blanc de Blancs Grand Cru
Joseph Perrier — Cuvée Josephine
Krug — Grande Cuvée, Clos du Mesnil Blanc de Blancs
Lanson — Noble Cuvée
Larmandier Bernier — Cramant Vielles Vignes
Laurent Perrier — Grand Siècle, Grand Siècle Alexandra Rosé

Louis Roederer — Cristal

Mercier — Cuvée Eugene

Moët & Chandon — Dom Pérignon, Dom Pérignon Rosé

Nicolas Feuillatte — Palm d'Or Rosé

Pannier — Egèrie

Perrier Jouet — Belle Epoque Brut and Belle Epoque Rosé

Philliponnat — Clos des Goisses

Pierre Gimonnet — Gastronome, Blanc de Blancs

Pierre Peters — Blanc de Blancs Grand Cru

Piper Heidsieck — Rare

Pol Roger — Cuvée Sir Winston Churchill, Réserve Spéciale Pol Roger Brut

Pommery — Cuvée Louise, Cuvée Louise Rosé

René Geoffrey — Premier Cru à Cumières

Ruinart Père et Fils — Dom Ruinart Blanc de Blancs

Salon — Le Mesnil (the only wine made)

Taittinger — Comtes de Champagne Blanc de Blancs and Rosé

Union Champagne (De Saint Gall) — Cuvée Orpale Blanc de Blancs

Veuve Clicquot Ponsardin — La Grande Dame, La Grande Dame Rosé

Vilmart — Coeur de Cuvée, Grand Cellier d'Or

Bordeaux

Throughout the twentieth century, the region of Bordeaux consolidated its reputation as the world's largest area of fine wine production. This has nothing to do with any romantic notions of the peaceful, pastoral pastime of growing grapes or any passion for the wines themselves. The prominent position of Bordeaux has much more to do with the systematic and businesslike approach that the Bordelais (the people of Bordeaux) have developed toward winemaking. This is not to say that they are out of touch with the sensual glories of the wines they produce, or that they do not understand their social responsibilities as wardens of the earth and environment from which their product springs. Indeed, the Bordelais enjoy their lifestyle and their wines as much as anybody else in the wine business. But the history of the Bordeaux region reveals an early grasp of the need to develop an infrastructure that would handle the marketing and shipping of the wines, and a philosophy of winemaking that would assure a reasonably well-made wine in even the poorest of growing seasons.

From that basis the Bordeaux region has become recognized as a leading producer of some of the world's finest red wines from famous estates such as Château Latour and Château Margaux. But although the international wine

The Quai des Chartrons, where much of the business of Bordeaux wine is conducted

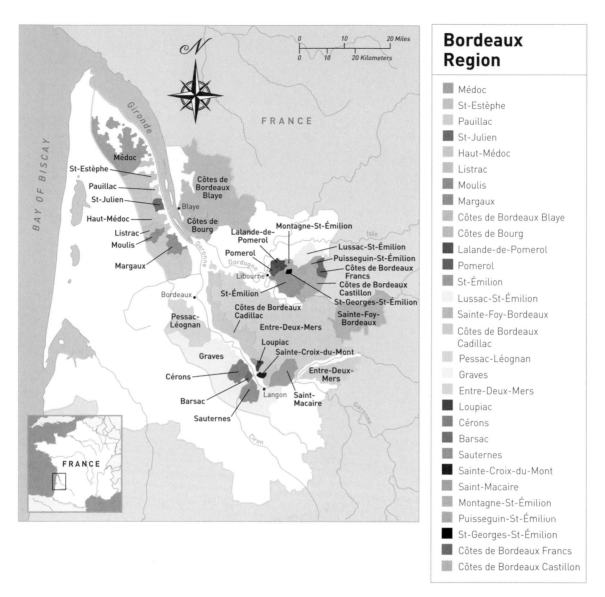

Bordeaux Region

- Médoc
- St-Estèphe
- Pauillac
- St-Julien
- Haut-Médoc
- Listrac
- Moulis
- Margaux
- Côtes de Bordeaux Blaye
- Côtes de Bourg
- Lalande-de-Pomerol
- Pomerol
- St-Émilion
- Lussac-St-Émilion
- Sainte-Foy-Bordeaux
- Côtes de Bordeaux Cadillac
- Pessac-Léognan
- Graves
- Entre-Deux-Mers
- Loupiac
- Cérons
- Barsac
- Sauternes
- Sainte-Croix-du-Mont
- Saint-Macaire
- Montagne-St-Émilion
- Puisseguin-St-Émilion
- St-Georges-St-Émilion
- Côtes de Bordeaux Francs
- Côtes de Bordeaux Castillon

press concentrates on the superb red wines from those estates, they represent only a tiny proportion of the region's total output, which also includes fresh, fruity dry whites; more complex, barrel-treated whites; some of the world's finest sweet white wines; and a broad array of dry reds, from fine, complex, intricate château bottlings at $100 and up, to more simple but honest $18 wines from lesser-known châteaux. In addition, the business structure of Bordeaux assures the availability of $12 to $15 regional wines, a small selection of rosés and sparkling wines, and even some brandies.

The region's recognized ability to produce and, more importantly, sell such a dazzling array of wines is largely based on a simple winemaking philosophy—blending. Almost all of the wine estates of Bordeaux are composite

quilts of different plots of land bearing different grape types, for red and white wines. This is not an accident. It was a business decision premised on the knowledge that individual grape types respond differently to variations in weather patterns in any growing season. Thus, if one grape type does not ripen very well one year, there are always other grape varieties that can help cover up any deficiencies or simply replace what is unusable. In many ways, growing different grape types and producing blended wines is an insurance policy that allows the Bordeaux producers to put out good wine in years when the weather is not completely cooperative. As a reference point, many Burgundy producers do not have this luxury since they rely on one grape variety. If the weather does not provide good ripening conditions for that variety, the chances of Burgundy producers making great wine that year are slim.

Thus, Bordeaux has become, and remains, a benchmark for certain types of wine. It is not an exaggeration to suggest that the current preoccupation with Merlot around the world stems from Bordeaux's success with that grape. Undoubtedly, the great Cabernet Sauvignon–Merlot blended wines of California have Bordeaux as a model, and the love affair that many other regions in the world share with those grapes and with Sauvignon Blanc–Sémillon blends is a recognition of Bordeaux's achievement.

The following sections of this chapter will deal with the business infrastructure of the Bordeaux wine market, the grape types used, approaches to winemaking, and the classification systems that have been used to rank the wine estates. Lastly, we will introduce each of the major districts of Bordeaux and highlight the finest wine styles from those locations.

THE BUSINESS SIDE OF BORDEAUX

The Bordeaux wine region covers a total of 284,000 acres/115,000 hectares, of which over 280,000 acres/ 113,000 hectares are dedicated to the production of *appellation protégée* wines, with the remainder producing lower-quality basic wines. Within the region there are fifty-seven separate appellations covering the broad array of wines outlined above, from several different districts and villages. A total of over twelve thousand VIGNERONS (wine growers) produce approximately 850 million bottles of wine (6.375 million hectoliters/68.3 million gallons) every year. These are just numbers: What they add up to is that Bordeaux is, and will remain, the world's largest contiguous area of designated appellations producing protected name fine wines as defined by the European Union.

Of the twelve thousand growers, 60 percent of them crush their own grapes and produce and bottle their own wine on site. In such cases, the words MIS EN BOUTEILLES AU CHÂTEAU assure the consumer that all facets of the wine's production were overseen by the same company or individual, roughly equivalent to the term "Estate Bottled" in the United States. For those growers who do not have their own wine production equipment, their grapes are processed by any one of the fifty-seven cooperatives in the Bordeaux region.

In addition to the growers and cooperatives, there are four hundred *négociants* (trading companies) that are re-

sponsible for marketing 75 percent of all Bordeaux wines around the world. The *négociants* merchandise the wines from the various châteaux, and they also buy surplus wines from individual growers and from cooperatives. These surplus wines are then held by the *négociants* and later blended to be sold as brand-name wines or under regional or village appellations. An example of a brand-name wine of this type would be the Rothschild company's Mouton-Cadet.

All of the growers, cooperatives, and *négociants* are represented by the Conseil Interprofessionel du Vin de Bordeaux (the CIVB, or the Bordeaux Wine Council), which helps in research, marketing, and promotion of all Bordeaux wines.

SOIL AND CLIMATE

Bordeaux's coastal and latitudinal position provides it with a gentle, mild, and temperate climate, and pine forests to the west of the vineyard area protect the region from the Atlantic Ocean winds. A relatively high average annual rainfall of 33 inches/83 centimeters is considered useful since irrigation is forbidden under current laws. Even so, the best vineyards are those on well-drained soils that allow the vines' roots to not get waterlogged but to dig deeply to the substrata where water is stored in pockets and the porosity and water retention of the soil type

A newly prepared piece of vineyard land in Haut-Médoc, showing the gravelly soils

CABERNET FRANC AND OTHER GRAPES

Covering 13,000 hectares/32,000 acres, the Cabernet Franc is found in small quantities throughout the red wine–producing districts. It is most appreciated for the mineral, floral, and red berry notes that it contributes to any blend.

The Petit Verdot, Malbec, and Carmenère are also authorized for red wine production, but are used very sparingly. The Petit Verdot is almost exclusively planted in the Graves, Médoc, and Haut-Médoc districts, but only at the top châteaux that can afford to oblige this very finicky grape type. The Malbec is more likely to be found in the St-Émilion and Pomerol districts, while the Carmenère is very rarely used anywhere in Bordeaux these days.

Under pressure from adventurous winemakers and with a nod to the possible effects of climate change, the French wine authorities agreed in 2009 to permit the testing of previously illegal grapes in Bordeaux vineyards. The testing is to last eight years, including five years of harvest, production, and test-marketing. The intent seems to be to determine if any of the current minor but allowed grape types could beneficially be replaced or supplemented by other, more suitable varieties. The varieties to be tested include Syrah, Zinfandel, Chardonnay, Chenin Blanc, and Petit Manseng Blanc. Does this mean the advent of a 100 percent Chardonnay from Bordeaux? Probably not, but it might be allowed in the future as a component in a blend.

WINEMAKING IN BORDEAUX

OLD MEETS NEW

There continues to be a reverence in Bordeaux for time-honored traditions, such as the use of oak barrels for fermentation or aging, and the use of hand-whisked egg whites to fine (clarify) a wine. At the same time, the wine producers of Bordeaux are just as innovative and technology-minded as other winemakers in any of the world's fine wine regions, and the majority of estates have embraced the technology of stainless steel vats, both for the greater convenience and controlled sanitation that these vessels provide. It is also increasingly common to find centrifuges and high-tech filtration systems in any of the region's appellations. Not only can many of the Bordeaux estates be considered on the cutting edge of wine technology, but there are also examples of experimentation at a few of the estates that can afford the machinery needed for some of these practices.

Such an example is the practice of **SAIGNAGE**, in which a more concentrated wine can be produced by drawing off clear juice from red grapes, thereby leaving a smaller quantity of juice to extract coloration, pigments, and flavor from the skins. Some estates have used a vacuum-like machine called a *concentrateur* to concentrate the juice, while others have used the process of *cryoextraction* for sweet white wine production, freezing the grapes and discarding some of the frozen water content, leaving a more concentrated juice.

But it should be stressed that these practices are experimental and limited to only the very few estates that have sufficient money to try them. It is also important to note that these processes are seen as a last resort in the quest to make a more substantial wine in those years when the growing season has produced a relatively weak crop. All wine producers in Bordeaux recognize that the best and simplest way to assure the production of a fine wine is to start with healthy, ripe grapes in the vineyard, and no amount of manipulation in the winemaking process will ever change that fact.

BLENDING

Regardless of whether or not Bordeaux winemakers have access to optimally ripe grapes from a superior vintage, the most critical factors in the production process are the skill and art of blending. The philosophy of blending in Bordeaux winemaking means that each estate makes several different batches of wine from each grape variety planted in different vineyard plots. Thus, a Médoc estate might end up with three or four different lots of Cabernet Sauvignon wine, two or three lots of Merlot, and some lots of other grapes.

After each lot of wine has completed its alcohol and malolactic fermentations, it is assessed for the contribution it might make to a final blend. But the key to blending in Bordeaux is to understand that the growing season is never the same from one year to the next, and therefore the dominant characteristics in each of the wines will vary from year to year. Bordeaux wines are not made according to a standard recipe; they are made to be the finest wine that any given estate can produce that year based on the development of each different grape type in its own vineyard setting.

In general, it is true that the majority of the red wine châteaux on the Left Bank have Cabernet Sauvignon as the highest percentage of plantings in the entire vineyard, followed by Merlot and Cabernet Franc, and in most years the wine from any Left Bank estate will reflect that general composition. By contrast, the châteaux on the Right Bank

However, when the growing season does not proceed in a "normal" manner, exceptions to these general rules do occur, leaving Left Bank wines with relatively unripe Cabernet Sauvignon but optimally ripe Merlot. In such a situation, any Left Bank estate would be foolish to try to stick with a standard recipe, so they use as much of the ripe Merlot as possible, making what could easily be described as an atypical wine. Such was the case in 1982 and 1997, when most Left Bank châteaux produced wines dominated by Merlot; as might be expected, Médoc and Graves wines from those vintages would be less astringent, with more immediate appeal than a wine made from the classic blend.

Similarly, there are generalizations to be made about the blending of wines for white wine production, with Sémillon being the favored grape for sweet white wines, while Sauvignon Blanc is the more likely leading contender in dry whites. The main exception to this is in the southern portion of the Graves appellation, where soil conditions favor the Sémillon grape so heavily that it is the majority grape in sweet and dry white wines from that area.

In sweet white wines in particular, Sémillon brings its typically peach

are more likely to have Merlot as the dominant grape type in the vineyard and in the final blend, with Cabernet Franc and Cabernet Sauvignon playing second and third fiddle. The exact percentages of each grape type in Left or Right Bank blends might vary from year to year, but the general proportionate relationships can usually be relied on. In any "average" year, given the characteristics of the grape types involved, Right Bank wines will mature faster than Left Bank wines because the greater percentage of Merlot in Right Bank wines means that they have softer fruit characteristics and lower tannin levels.

and apricot ripeness, while the Sauvignon Blanc provides some tingling, fresh acidity. These are likely to be the only two white grapes used in the finer sweet white appellations of Sauternes and Barsac, and to a lesser extent in Sainte-Croix-du-Mont and Loupiac. In the more pedestrian sweet and semisweet wines produced in small subappellations in the southern portion of the Entre-Deux-Mers region, Muscadelle is still the minority grape but is used in higher percentages to provide its signature grapey qualities and slightly tropical fruit notes, thereby compensating for the lack of botrytis in these appellations.

Sémillon grapes ripening near the village of Bommes

SECOND LABELS, REGIONAL AND VILLAGE WINES

The practice of blending has broader ramifications beyond the idiosyncratic characteristics of any wine from an individual château: It also has a major impact on the production, marketing, and pricing of other wines throughout the whole Bordeaux region. Because the exact blend for any château might vary from year to year, it follows that many estates have surplus wine every year.

As might be assumed, all of the top Bordeaux estates use their very finest wines to create a blend that will be sold as their top wine, usually under the name of the château itself, such as Château Latour. However, it is very common for individual estates to market more than one label, and most châteaux have a second label that will be used for wines blended from the remainder of the harvest after the first label blend has been finalized. In a way, second labels are useful in protecting the high quality reputation of the first label, since they provide an economic way of marketing wines that do not make the first cut in the selection process. For the consumer, second labels offer wines of integrity from first-class châteaux, at a fraction of the cost of the first label.

Whether a château makes use of a second label or not, individual growers and estates also have the option of selling surplus wines to *négociants* who will eventually blend them with other wines and subsequently market them as regional wines (labeled, for example, as "Bordeaux" or as "Médoc") or as village wines (such as "St-Émilion" or "Pauillac"). Many *négociants* also choose to sell regional blended wines under a proprietary name. The insistence on careful selection of the finest wines at the top level makes available wines of lesser quality that can subsequently be marketed under broader appellations at much more competitive prices.

Thus, the wines of Bordeaux can be grouped into a hierarchy of three appellation levels:
- The regional level, labeled after the region, such as Bordeaux or Bordeaux Supérieur, or labeled under a proprietary name, such as Sirius or Numéro Un
- The district level, named after the district where the grapes were grown, such as Entre-Deux-Mers, Médoc, or Haut-Médoc
- The village level, named after the village where the vineyards are located, such as Pomerol, Pauillac, or Pessac-Léognan

Wines produced by individual estates usually carry the name of the château on the label as the name of the wine and as the name of the producer, but individual châteaux do not have their own appellation; each château falls within a village, district, or regional appellation. Regardless of appellation, a classification or categorization of many of the finest châteaux in Bordeaux has evolved over more than two centuries, and these classifications are still used to identify those estates that have consistently produced high-quality wines that command a higher price on the market.

CLASSIFICATIONS

For more than two hundred years, people have been drawing up lists that attempt to rank the wines of some of the districts of Bordeaux, particularly Médoc. For example, in 1786 an English trade ambassador by the name of William Eden developed a list of forty-one Médoc wines deemed to be of high quality and of importance in the English trade. In the following year, while serving as the United States Ambassador to France, Thomas Jefferson wrote several pages of notes on Bordeaux wines, including a list of sixteen wines of the highest quality.

In 1815 and 1816 respectively, a Bordeaux wine merchant named Guillaume Lawton and André Jullien of Paris wrote more extensive rankings of the Médoc wines, referring to the different quality levels as *crus*. The extraordinary thing about these and other rankings is that there was and continues to be unanimous agreement on the finest quality wines of the time: Château Latour, Château Lafite, Château

Château Cantenac-Brown's wines fall under the village appellation of Margaux.

Margaux, and Château Haut-Brion. It should be noted that Château Haut-Brion, in the Graves district, is the only non-Médoc wine to be included in any of the rankings.

Since 1855, four official CLASSIFICATIONS of Bordeaux have emerged, one each for the red wines of Médoc (1855), the sweet white wines of Sauternes and Barsac (1855), the red wines of St-Émilion (1955, revised in 1969, 1986, 1996, and 2006, but then suspended), and the white and red wines of Graves (1959). The district of Pomerol has never been classified. Not surprisingly, wine merchants and consumers alike often complain that the classifications are outdated and confusing since they do not use the same descriptive terms in each district to label the different levels of quality. There are frequent calls for the older classifications to be revised, or for a single classification to be created covering all districts of Bordeaux, but the chances of such changes are extremely remote: It is a political and economic minefield, as demonstrated by the outright rejection of the revised 2006 St-Émilion classification.

Despite the opposition from some quarters, there is also solid support for the classifications, and it is generally true to say that even the 1855 classifications are broadly representative, listing most, if not all, of the finest estates in those districts. The individual classifications are listed within the relevant section below. Those tables use the official terminology for the 1855 Médoc classification. All of the wines can use the umbrella term GRAND CRU CLASSÉ, but the official table identifies each group as simply *premier cru, deuxième cru*, etc. The labels of these wines are more likely to show the aggrandized phrase *deuxième grand cru classé*. Similarly, in the Sauternes classification, Château

d'Yquem is officially titled *premier cru supérieure,* but the wine is talked about as the *premier grand cru supérieure.*

In addition to the formal, government-approved classifications, there are also looser but important associations of châteaux such as the Union des Grands Crus, which promotes and represents *grand cru* châteaux wines from all appellations. There has also been a revival of important groups of unclassified châteaux, such as the Alliance Crus Bourgeois. Although terms like *cru bourgeois* have been in use for more than a century, they have variously fallen into disuse or have deemed inadequately defined. In 2009, the use of the term *cru bourgeois* was reintroduced in a system where producers were invited to submit their 2008 vintage to a blind tasting. If the wine was approved as typical and of sound quality, the producer will be able to include the term *cru bourgeois* on the label. The Alliance Crus Bourgeois expects this system to be reviewed on a yearly basis.

DRY WHITE WINES

The widespread introduction of stainless steel fermentation vats has created a major revitalization of dry white wine production in Bordeaux, exemplified by a whole new generation of crisp, clean, fruity white wines, pleasantly simple, but always honest and well-made. Alongside these are the more traditional wines of fuller body and greater complexity, as charming as they have always been, but somehow cleaner and more stylish thanks to more careful handling in the vineyard and cellar. For blended wines, the practice, as always, is to make separate lots of each grape variety from different vineyard plots and to blend the wines once they have begun to show their own unique character.

The general approach is to destem, crush, and press the grapes as quickly as possible after harvest to obtain clean fruit characteristics and to avoid any oxidation of the juice. Some estates like to impart more complexity into the wine by leaving the juice to macerate with the skins for a short period of time, extracting more color, flavor, and phenolic compounds. Chilling the juice allows any solids to precipitate out, and the clear juice is then fermented at low temperatures for about two weeks, usually in stainless steel (but some estates will use small oak barrels to produce a much more complex wine). Malolactic fermentation is always an option for the fuller styles of dry white wine, as are blending of different grape types and different vineyard plots, and maturation in oak.

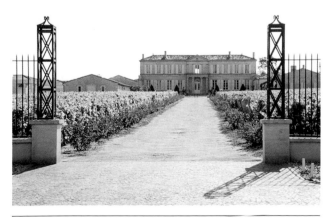

Château Branaire-Ducru was classified in the 1855 classification of Médoc red wines.

in lesser appellations also use Sémillon and Sauvignon Blanc, but rely on higher percentages of Muscadelle in the blend to provide obvious grape aromas and flavors.

Whether the grapes are late harvest or botrytis-affected, one of the most distinctive features about the vineyard work in these fine appellations is that all grapes must be hand-harvested, and most of the finest estates require that the picking be done by *tries*, with the pickers returning to the same row day after day over a three- to four-week period to harvest only those grapes that are fully ripe or botrytis-affected. Since the grapes themselves are shriveled, either by raisination or by botrytis, the quantity of juice obtained from the harvest is very small. Such numeric examples can only be general, but a fine dry white wine vineyard can usually expect each vine to produce three to four bottles of wine; at a fine Sauternes estate, it will take eight vines to produce one bottle. Understandably, Sauternes is expensive!

Despite the high levels of sugar in the grapes, fermentation is slow to start and hard to keep going, and the cellar master needs to be especially vigilant to avoid any "stuck" fermentations. Most châteaux use stainless steel vats to emphasize the fresh, clean quality underlying their rich, opulent wines; a few continue to work with small oak barrels for fermentation.

SAUTERNES AND BARSAC

Five villages and their vineyards are encompassed by the Sauternes appellation: the village of Sauternes itself, along with Barsac, Bommes, Fargues, and Preignac.

Wines from the vineyards of Barsac may be marketed under either the Sauternes appellation or the smaller Barsac appellation; most châteaux in Barsac prefer to use the Sauternes designation.

Although the Sauternes district has not always produced sweet wines, it is one of the areas in the world most naturally suited to sweet wine production. Most of the subappellation consists of a rounded hill that slopes gently downward in a northerly direction to the confluence of the Ciron and Garonne rivers. On the north side of the Garonne River, the land rises in a sharp escarpment toward the Entre-Deux-Mers region, and it is this geographic oddity that creates perfect conditions for the onset of botrytis at the end of almost every growing season. As cold air falls off the escarpment onto the warmer river, mist is formed, encouraging the development and spread of botrytis in the vineyards.

Much of the hill has a clay base, but there are pockets of gravel that define the more prestigious estates, the most famous of which is Château d'Yquem. This estate is the epitome of quality in the Sauternes appellation, taking great pains in the vineyard to harvest only the finest botrytis-affected grapes. The commitment to quality is so high that the château refuses to release any wine under the Yquem label in those years that the grapes do not develop enough botrytis character. In such years, the château has the option to produce a dry white wine, released under the name "Château Y" (a clever play on French phonetics, since the letter *Y* in French is pronounced *ee GREC*). Since Château d'Yquem established this practice decades ago, other top-

LEFT: *Château d'Yquem is Sauternes' undisputed star.* RIGHT: *Vineyards ascend to Sauternes' Château de Rayne-Vigneau.*

class châteaux have followed suit, some of them adopting the same concept of using the initial letter of the château name to label the dry wine. Whenever a Sauternes château produces a dry wine, the appellation laws require that the wine be identified as Appellation Bordeaux Blanc Sec, not as Appellation Sauternes.

However, dry wine from a Sauternes château is an oddity. The rich, enticing nectar of botrytis-affected grapes is what Sauternes is really all about. The resulting wine is a viscous ambrosia with a roasted nut–honey, citrus, tropical fruit, and floral bouquet, and luscious texture in the vintages most affected by botrytis. Although they are delicious while young, the best can last for decades.

Such wines are intensely satisfying, even in small quantities, and are most often thought of as wines to enjoy at the end of a meal, even as dessert, rather than with it. There is also the combination of Sauternes and Roquefort (sweet, extra ripe fruit contrasting with salty, pungent, blue cheese), or, for the truly adventurous and indulgent, Sauternes and foie gras (a hedonistic complementing of richness on richness).

The great sweet white wines of Sauternes were classified in 1855, with Château d'Yquem taking top honors as the only *premier cru supérieur*, followed by eleven *premiers crus classés* and fourteen *deuxièmes crus classés*. The complete classification, showing the commune for each château, is listed in the table at right.

CÉRONS

In the southern section of Graves, to the west of Sauternes and Barsac, lies the small appellation of Cérons, covering the villages of Illat, Podensac, and Cérons itself. Once again, a concentration of gravel over limestone creates good growing conditions for Sémillon, with Sauvignon Blanc providing the balancing acidity. These wines are lighter than their prestigious neighbors, without as much intensity and depth of flavor.

SAINTE-CROIX-DU-MONT AND LOUPIAC

These two appellations lie on the northern bank of the Garonne river, opposite the famed enclaves of Sauternes and Barsac. The soil varies on the steep northern bank, but pockets of gravel in the clay and limestone base favor the Sémillon grape, and the vineyards nearer the river can usually count on at least some botrytis at the end of the growing season. Sauvignon Blanc is once again the junior partner in the blend. Each appellation produces approx-

imately 13,500 hectoliters/356,400 gallons, though the lower yields practiced in Sainte-Croix-du-Mont generally make it a slightly fuller, riper wine than Loupiac.

Both appellations can be considered as medium-rich sweet white wines, not as concentrated and stylish as their more refined cousins across the river, but certainly the best of the bunch of the sweet wines from the north bank of the Garonne.

SAUTERNES-BARSAC: THE OFFICIAL CLASSIFICATION OF 1855

FIRST GREAT GROWTH (*Premier cru supérieur*)	COMMUNE
Château d'Yquem	Sauternes

FIRST GROWTHS (*Premiers crus*)	COMMUNE
Château La Tour-Blanche	Bommes
Château Lafaurie-Peyraguey	Bommes
Château Clos Haut-Peyraguey	Bommes
Château de Rayne-Vigneau	Bommes
Château Suduiraut	Preignac
Château Coutet	Barsac
Château Climens	Barsac
Château Guiraud	Sauternes
Château Rieussec	Fargues
Château Rabaud-Promis	Bommes
Sigalas-Rabaud	Bommes

SECOND GROWTHS (*Deuxièmes crus*)	COMMUNE
Château de Myrat	Barsac
Château Doisy-Daëne	Barsac
Château Doisy-Dubroca	Barsac
Château Doisy-Védrines	Barsac
Château d'Arche	Sauternes
Château Filhot	Sauternes
Château Broustet	Barsac
Château Nairac	Barsac
Château Caillou	Barsac
Château Suau	Barsac
Château de Malle	Preignac
Château Romer-du-Hayot	Fargues
Château Lamothe-Despujols	Sauternes
Château Lamothe-Guignard	Sauternes

in Graves (Château Haut-Brion) were granted the designation *grand cru classé* (classified great growth), a phrase that is usually printed on the label of those sixty-one châteaux. In addition, the sixty-one estates were subdivided into five divisions: *premier grand cru classé* (first great growth), *deuxième grand cru classé* (second great growth), etc. The number of châteaux in each division differs, and there is no ranking within the divisions. In 1855, four châteaux were designated as *premier grand cru classé*: Château Haut-Brion (from Graves); Château Margaux; Château Latour; and Château Lafite (today called Château Lafite Rothschild). Since 1855, the only change in ranking occurred in 1973, when Château Mouton Rothschild was elevated from second to first, so that today there are five first-growth châteaux.

The overall Médoc region stretches from the mouth of the Gironde estuary southward to the city of Bordeaux, but it contains two formal appellations, Médoc in the northern section and Haut-Médoc toward the south. It is the Haut-Médoc section that is home to all of the famous estates, most of them originating from one of the six villages of St-Estèphe, Pauillac, St-Julien, Margaux, Moulis, or Listrac. The first four villages are situated within sight of the Gironde estuary, giving substance to the adage that the best vineyards see the river, for these villages contain most of the top classified châteaux. The saying has less to do with the view than it does with the gentle slopes toward the river that provide good drainage and prime pockets of gravel at various depths that define the best estates.

ST-ESTÈPHE This is the most northerly and second largest of the six village appellations in Haut-Médoc, though only five of its seventy or so châteaux were included in the 1855 classification. Here the soil contains gravel, rocks, some chalk, and sand on the surface, over a deep gravel and clay subsoil. There are also fossilized oysters and limestone subsoils that, being friable, allow deep penetration of the vines' roots.

St-Estèphe used to be known for sturdy or meaty wines that took a very long time to soften and allow the fruit to show. Today however, because of increased plantings of Merlot and updated winery techniques, the wines display softer tannins and richer fruit flavors while still retaining the longevity and weight expected of a St-Estèphe. All share the characteristic dark color, earthy cedar and cassis nose, and full body. The finest of these wines are the second growths Château Cos d'Estournel (60 per-

cent Cabernet Sauvignon, 38 percent Merlot, and 2 percent Cabernet Franc) and Château Montrose (65 percent Cabernet Sauvignon, 25 percent Merlot, and 10 percent Cabernet Franc), which produce about 35,000 cases and 25,000 cases per year respectively. Château Calon-Ségur, a third growth and the most northerly *grand cru* in the Médoc, is made with 65 percent Cabernet Sauvignon, 20 percent Merlot, and 15 percent Cabernet Franc, while the only fifth-growth château is Cos Labory. Impressive unclassified châteaux include Château Meyney, Château Les Ormes-de-Pez, Château Phélan-Ségur, Château de Pez, and Château Marbuzet.

PAUILLAC The soil around Pauillac consists mostly of iron-rich gravel over a clay and limestone plateau providing good drainage. The wines are firm in structure, with a muscular power on the palate and the traditional cassis aroma.

Pauillac boasts three of the five *premier grand cru classé* châteaux. Of these, Château Lafite Rothschild is considered to be the most aromatic, offering violets as part of the Pauillac panoply of smells. The Lafite vineyards total 222 acres/90 hectares, making it one of the largest estates, comprising 70 percent Cabernet Sauvignon, 20 percent

Château Cos d'Estournel in St-Estèphe

Merlot, and 10 percent Cabernet Franc and producing up to 35,000 cases annually.

Recognized as the top of the second growths in the 1855 classification, Château Mouton Rothschild, which always fetched higher prices than the other "seconds," was elevated to *premier grand cru* in 1973. This feat was achieved by Baron Philippe de Rothschild, who brought many innovations and upgrades to the vineyards and the winemaking process over several decades. He was the first proprietor to château bottle the entire harvest. He created a magnificent wine museum at the property, and, starting in 1945, he commissioned different artists to design a new wine label each year. Mouton is planted with 76 percent Cabernet Sauvignon, 13 percent Merlot, 9 percent Cabernet Franc, and 2 percent Petit Verdot.

The other member of the trio of *premiers grands crus classés* in Pauillac is Château Latour, made from 80 percent Cabernet Sauvignon, 15 percent Merlot, 4 percent Cabernet Franc, and 1 percent Petit Verdot. Latour is con-sidered the most consistent and heaviest of the Pauillac *premiers grands crus*. Latour is fermented in temperature-controlled stainless steel vats, then aged in new oak for about two years, after which it is bottled without filtration. These three *premiers grands crus* are superlative wines in great vintages, capable of lasting for decades.

Château Pichon Longueville Comtesse de Lalande and Château Pichon Longueville Baron are highly respected *deuxièmes grands crus*. Despite the similarity of name, the wines differ dramatically in style. The "Comtesse" has lighter soil in the vineyards, and an unusual grape mix comprised of 45 percent Cabernet Sauvignon, 35 percent Merlot, 12 percent Cabernet Franc, and 8 percent Petit Verdot combining to produce a very elegantly styled wine. The "Baron" is situated slightly to the north on heavier soils with a more classic grape mix of 75 percent Cabernet Sauvignon and 25 percent Merlot, making a fuller-bodied style of wine. In the late 1990s, the second of these two châteaux dropped the "Baron" from its name to become simply Château Pichon Longueville.

Pauillac has no *troisième grand cru*, but its single fourth great growth, Château Duhart-Milon, is well worth looking at, as are any of the twelve *cinquièmes grands crus* in the village, most notably the châteaux of Lynch-Bages, Haut-Batailley, Grand-Puy-Lacoste, Grand-Puy-Ducasse, and d'Armailhac.

ST-JULIEN The gravelly soils of St-Julien, with substrata of clay and limestone, offer good drainage and allow vine roots to go deep for nourishment. *Grand cru* wines make up 75 percent of all the wines from this village, and they are of deep color, in an elegant style balanced with sumptuous fruit. One of the most prized wines is the *deuxième grand cru* Château Léoville Barton, which is planted with 72 percent Cabernet Sauvignon, 20 percent Merlot, and 8 percent Cabernet Franc. Like its second-growth namesakes Château Léoville Las Cases and Château Léoville Poyferré, this is a wine of great complexity, depth, and power, capable of aging for many years, whereas the third-growth Langoa Barton is much more delicate and graceful in its youth.

Other important *grands crus* are the châteaux of Ducru-Beaucaillou, Gruaud-Larose (second growths), Lagrange (third growth), Beychevelle, Branaire, and Talbot (fourth growths). Château Gloria, Château Hortevie, and Château Moulin de la Rose are very good examples of unclassified wines.

MARGAUX This is the only Médoc appellation with châteaux included in all five levels of *grand cru*. The gravelly

TOP: *Château Pichon-Longueville, in the Pauillac appellation*
BOTTOM: *The typically gravelly soils of St-Julien*

invalid, the French government has decreed that the provisions of the 1996 classification will remain in place alongside the promotions given in 2006 until a new classification can be undertaken. However, we have included information here on how the 2006 revision differed from the previous version, and we have included the now-defunct revision.

There are two categories in the classification: *premier grand cru classé,* of which there were thirteen châteaux in 1996 (subdivided into A and B levels); and *grand cru classé,* of which there were fifty-four châteaux. The revised but disallowed classification promoted two châteaux from *grand cru classé* to *premier grand cru classé,* promoted six unclassified châteaux to *grand cru classé* level, and removed eleven châteaux from the classification. The eleven demoted châteaux have been reinstated, and the eight promoted châteaux have been allowed to keep their promotion.

The legal battles over reclassification have left a deep wound and a political oddity behind. Behind the promotions and demotions, there are hundreds of other estates that annually apply for, and are awarded, the approved appellation of St-Émilion *grand cru.* These wines are good, but they do not exhibit the finesse and concentration shown by those wines that were included in the 2006 reclassification.

On the western gravelly slopes near Pomerol, there are two outstanding estates: Château Cheval Blanc and Château Figeac. Cheval Blanc is one of the two "A" *grands crus* and is made from almost 60 percent Cabernet Franc and 40 percent Merlot, though there is a small amount of Malbec and Cabernet Sauvignon available for blending if necessary. It is aged in new oak barrels each year, and the high percentage of Cabernet Franc makes this one of the most exotic of the *crus* of Bordeaux. Its richness can also be attributed to its proximity to Pomerol, whose best wines are typically deeply colored and intensely ripe. The wine is approachable in its youth because of its rich fruit flavors, but it may be cellared for decades. In contrast, Château Figeac, a "B" level *grand cru* estate, uses about equal parts of Cabernet Franc and Cabernet Sauvignon plus a slightly smaller percentage of Merlot.

The other "A" *grand cru,* Château Ausone, is located just south of the village proper of St-Émilion and right on the edge of the plateau, taking full advantage of the various strata of limestone and other calcareous deposits as the vineyards spill down the steep escarpment that defines the plateau. It is planted to 60 percent Merlot and 40 percent Cabernet Franc and is aged in new oak each year. Its wines are known for their aroma, concentration, and finesse. The vineyard boasts many older vines, since its altitude and exposure allowed it to survive the 1956 frost without the damage that destroyed most of Cheval Blanc's and Figeac's vines.

Other impressive *premier grand cru Classé* "B" wines come from the châteaux of Pavie, l'Angélus, Canon, and Trotte Vieille. Most of the *grand cru classé* wines offer good value, any variations in intensity and depth of flavor resulting from soil differences, with higher sand content generally giving lighter wines.

To the north of the St-Émilion appellation there are four satellite appellations—Montagne-St-Émilion, Lussac-St-Émilion, St-Georges-St-Émilion, and Puisseguin-St-Émilion. These regional wines of St-Émilion are generally competitively priced, medium-weight wines that can be

TOP: *Vineyards in the St-Émilion appellation* RIGHT: *A typical limestone outcropping in St-Émilion*

drunk within five years before their fruity quality diminishes. Among the sturdier wines, Château St-Georges (60 percent Merlot and 20 percent of each Cabernet) and Château de Musset (70 percent Merlot, 20 percent Cabernet Sauvignon, and 10 percent Cabernet Franc) are fine examples.

ST-ÉMILION:
2006 suspended classification

PREMIERS GRANDS CRUS CLASSÉS

A

Château Ausone

Château Cheval Blanc

B

Château Beauséjour
   (Duffau-Lagarrosse)

Château Beau-Séjour Bécot

Château Belair

Château Canon

Château Figeac

Château La Gaffelière

Château l'Angelus

Château Magdelaine

Château Pavie

Château Pavie-Maquin

Château Troplong-Mondot

Château Trotte Vieille

Clos Fourtet

GRANDS CRUS CLASSÉS

Château Balestard-la-Tonnelle

Château Bellefont-Belcier

Château Bergat

Château Berliquet

Château Cadet-Piola

Château Canon la Gaffelière

Château Cap de Mourlin

Château Chauvin

Château Corbin

Château Corbin-Michotte

Château Dassault

Châteaux Destieux

Château Fleur Cardinale

Château Fonplégade

Château Fonroque

Château Franc-Mayne

Château Grand Corbin

Château Grand Corbin Despagne

Château Grand Mayne

Château Grand Pontet

Château Haut-Corbin

Château Haut Sarpe

Château La Clotte

Château Laniote

Château La Couspaude

Château La Dominque

Château Larcis-Ducasse

Château Larmande

Château Laroque

Château Laroze

Château L' Arrosée

Château la Serre

Château La Tour Figeac

Château le Prieuré

Château les Grandes Murailles

Château Matras

Château Monbousquet

Château Moulin-du-Cadet

Château Pavie Decesse

Château Ripeau

Château Soutard

Château St-Georges-Côte-Pavie

Clos des Jacobins

Clos l'Oratoire

Clos St-Martin

Couvent des Jacobins

POMEROL

The appellation of Pomerol has only about 2,000 acres/800 hectares of vines, a very small area when compared with its neighbor, St-Émilion, and miniscule next to Médoc. Like St-Émilion, the vineyard landscape is one of small farms rather than large estates, and yet there is nothing unsophisticated about some of the wines from this area. Although Pomerol has never been officially classified, the limited production, compared with other fine areas, and the quality attained by the best producers has resulted in price levels often exceeding the classified growths of the Médoc. However, such gems are relatively few in number, and there are many ordinary wines that can be pleasing but not exquisite.

The most attractive characteristics of Pomerol wines are their fullness, smoothness, and ripe fruit quality, emphasized by a concentration on the Merlot grape type that occupies three-quarters of the vineyards. Cabernet Franc (called Bouchet here) is second in importance, and the Cabernet Sauvignon and Malbec (Pressac) play minor roles. Merlot yields fruity, lower-acid wines that can be drunk within four years or aged a couple of decades, depending on vintage and property. The soils vary, with clay, sand, and thin layers of gravel in pockets. Iron content in the sand is said to be one of the reasons for the richness of the wines produced.

Château de Sales, largest of the properties, yielding 20,000 cases per year, makes wine in a lighter style that is often associated with the lighter sandy soils in the western section of Pomerol. It is made from 70 percent Merlot with the balance divided equally among the Cabernets.

In contrast, the undisputed star of Pomerol, and of the Merlot grape worldwide, is the 28-acre/11.5-hectare

Vineyards on the outskirts of the village of Pomerol

two making the wine much lighter in flavor and structure. The best vineyard sites are on hilltops and south-facing slopes with clay or calcareous clay soils. The white wines offer good value, most often leaning toward the fresh, bright fruit style of Sauvignon Blanc–dominated blends. Sémillon, Mauzac, Chenin Blanc, and Muscadelle are also used for sweet whites in the Côtes de Duras appellation.

CAHORS

The most common commentary on this appellation is that its red wines have been dubbed "black wine" for their opaque, dark purple hue, even though several other appellations in southern France could make the same claim. In fact, that myth has largely been exploded with modern approaches to winemaking producing much lighter-colored but just as flavorful wines. Cahors red wine must be made from a minimum of 70 percent Malbec (Auxerrois here), with Merlot and Tannat in supporting roles, all coming together to provide a richness of plums and dried fruit, both in the nose and flavor of the wine, a full body, and a good measure of tannins. The lighter styles generally come from grapes grown on the limestone plateau and can be enjoyed within a few years; the fuller, more traditional styles derive their complexity and depth of flavor from the gravel ridges formed within the bends of the river Lot, or from the limestone foothills, and can improve over a decade. Château de Chambert, Château du Cèdre, Château Lagrézette, Château Eugénie, and Domaine la Berangeraie are worth seeking out.

Further east lie the equally intense, even impressive red wines of Marcillac, based mostly (at least 90 percent) on the spicy, sometimes overly tannic Fer variety, with Merlot offering some softer fruit and the two Cabernets providing acidic balance.

BUZET

Although this appellation can officially produce whites and rosés, it is the red wines that have gained acclaim as good value alternatives to the more expensive, sometimes less worthy reds of lesser châteaux in Bordeaux. Where gravelly marl complements any limestone content in the soil, the Bordeaux trio of red grapes produce particularly fine wines, with ripe fruit, depth, and balance, most of them produced by the very capable and efficient local cooperative. Further east lies the old VDQS designation of Côtes du Brulhois, offering lighter regional wines.

GAILLAC

Attracted by cheaper land and the excitement of local grape varieties, a number of new producers have revitalized the Gaillac appellation. Château de Vayssette, Mas d'Aurel, and Château de Gineste continue to prove that they can make fresh, perfumed, appealing white wines; bright, solid, fruity reds and rosés; and even sweet and sparkling wines. The limestone base in the north of the appellation is particularly suited to the high-acid Mauzac grape, which helps lift dry white wines and is almost ideal for the sparkling versions made by *méthode champenoise* or the fast-disappearing *méthode Gaillaçoise* (the initial fermentation is gradually slowed down and then finished in bottle).

Further south in the appellation, the limestone becomes less prevalent and is replaced by sandy, gravelly marl that seems to suit the local Len de l'El, a white grape variety that can be perfumed and fruity but flat. Blending with some Mauzac and Sauvignon Blanc has helped give some extra dimension to Gaillac whites. Also in the south, a limestone gravel mix brings out the solid fruit of the local red varieties Fer and Duras, though experience has shown that the wines benefit greatly from the extra depth of additional varieties such as Syrah, Gamay, and Merlot.

A hot, dry growing season, fine gravelly, sandy soils, and the local Négrette red grape all combine to bring a level of uniqueness to the red wines of Côtes du Frontonnais, just to the east of Gaillac. There is something silky smooth but deeply fruity about these wines, and good producers such as Château Bellevue-la-Forêt have also added some structure by including Cabernet Franc and Cabernet Sauvignon.

MADIRAN

South of the brandy region of Armagnac, this appellation is another heavyweight contender for a southwest red wine with an opaque dark color, rich fruit smell, and lots of power on the palate. A measure of the ferocity of the local Tannat grape is that Cabernet Sauvignon is used to soften it! Even so, Tannat must be at least 40 percent of the blend, with Cabernet Sauvignon, Cabernet Franc, and Fer making up the balance. New oak barrels for aging can reinforce their firmness, but long aging will bring rewards of full plummy and spicy qualities backed by leather and licorice. Château Montus and Domaine Pichard are good examples.

Just to the south of Madiran, the subappellation Pacherenc du Vic-Bihl is used for dry, medium sweet, and sweet white wines made from the local oddities of Gros Manseng, Petit Manseng, Ruffiac, and Petit Courbu. They offer full ripeness and some fullness, helped along by Sauvignon Blanc and Sémillon.

Local grapes also play important roles in the newly promoted wines of Tursan, adjacent to the northwest segment of the Madiran appellation. The white Baroque variety makes full, perfumed, aromatic wines with a little help from Sauvignon Blanc, while the Tannat and two Cabernets grown in Tursan produce reds of full fruit character. The same could be said for the reds of the also new St-Mont appellation, produced from the same grapes, but the whites need some work; maybe higher percentages of Sauvignon Blanc added to the staple blend would help.

JURANÇON

In the foothills of the Pyrenees mountains, this appellation rejoices in a mix of soils from limestone to sandy marl and stony clay, all of which seem to bring the Gros and Petit Manseng grapes to a delicate ripeness in the high-altitude vineyards (1000 feet/300 meters). Jurançon has a fine historical reputation as the producer of wonderfully exotic sweet white wines that offer that rare combination of honey-coated nuts, with fully ripe dried fruit and pure refreshing acidity. Wisely, however, many local producers have realized that the wine world is currently obsessed with dry white wines, and they have accordingly increased their production of that style. Using the same grapes, the dry whites have the tantalizing feel of smooth, ripe tropical fruit, countered by mouthwatering citric acidity.

IROULÉGUY

Once a tiny enclave of Basque culture and now a proud ambassador of its noble heritage, the Irouléguy appellation remains committed to its traditional grape varieties for red, white, and rosé wines. The stubbornly tannic Tannat seems to belong in the rugged foothills of the Pyrenees, planted at 1300 feet/400 meters, making relentlessly fruity but spicy wines with a little help from the two Cabernets. All in all they are interesting wines, but not world class. The whites (mostly Manseng grapes) and rosés are less interesting.

Scattered between and around the Irouléguy and Jurançon appellations are various patches of vineyard that make up the Béarn appellation, which makes lighter but more aromatic versions of red white and rosé from the same grapes used in the neighboring appellations. Béarn-Bellocq is a subappellation making similar wines.

LIMOUX

Way over in the southeast corner of this whole region is the appellation of Limoux. In fact, it is so far to the south and east that it could easily be considered part of Mediterranean France. What brings Limoux into the more temperate southwest zone is its reliance on temperate climate grapes such as the highly acidic Mauzac, known locally as the Blanquette; there have even been great strides made with Chardonnay and Pinot Noir, undoubtedly aided by plenty of gravelly marl and limestone in the soil. The most famous wines of Limoux have always been sparkling, building a solid reputation based on quality and freshness. Today there are three versions offered: Blanquette de Limoux, made by *méthode champenoise* from at least 90 percent Mauzac, plus Chardonnay and Chenin Blanc; Crémant de Limoux, using the same method and grapes but allowing up to 30 percent of Chardonnay and Chenin Blanc combined; and Blanquette Méthode Ancestrale, made from 100 percent Mauzac by the same *méthode rurale* used for Gaillac sparkling wines.

Now that Chardonnay has been shown to grow in the area, some producers have made some very impressive oak-fermented dry, still versions, so much so that the *appellation protégée* authorities have approved a new appellation for these wines. Where Chardonnay goes, Pinot Noir will often follow, and there have already been some impressive, if light, Pinot Noirs made here, offering fresh berry flavors and good acidity.

To the north of Limoux are the new appellations of Cabardès, Côtes de la Malepère, and Côtes de Millau. While each of these uses typical Rhône varieties such as Grenache, Syrah, and Cinsaut, there are also considerable plantings of Merlot, Malbec, and Cabernet (both types) and the typically southwestern Fer, all giving the reds a little more depth of fruit and structure, and some vivacious, refreshing acidity to emerge as a sort of hybrid Rhône-Bordeaux.

Burgundy

Like Bordeaux, Burgundy shares the honor of producing some of the world's finest and most expensive dry white and red wines, rare gems of hedonistic pleasure that seduce the lucky drinker, but defy theoretical analysis. But in all other respects, Burgundy is as different from Bordeaux as night from day. Bordeaux's generally larger estates comprise an area that is two-and-one-half times the size of Burgundy, but the Burgundy appellation is a glorious quilt of small vineyard parcels that are subdivided into ridiculously tiny holdings by individual owners, sometimes only one-third of an acre/one-tenth of an hectare in size. The differences are also apparent in the use of grape types and in the business structure of the regions. Bordeaux has long had the comfort of using multiple grape types to blend together in varying percentages, whereas Burgundy most often relies on one single variety for its wines, leaving the various appellations at the mercy of the weather to ripen that variety to the point where fine wines can be made. In Bordeaux, the single estates drive the wine business, while in Burgundy large *négociant* companies control the majority of all wines produced, even from the smallest vineyard plots.

The following sections will provide a general description of the soil and climate of Burgundy, a commentary on the grape types used, an explanation of the role of the *négociant*, and an analysis of the appellation system in Burgundy, before we give more specific descriptions of each of the major subregions and districts. The principal subregions of Burgundy are:

- Chablis
- Côte d'Or, subdivided into the Côte de Nuits and the Côte de Beaune
- Côte Chalonnaise
- Mâconnais

Given the distinctive nature of Beaujolais, we will deal with that region in a separate section, even though it is considered a subregion of Burgundy by the *appellation protégée* authorities.

SOIL AND CLIMATE

It has often been claimed that it is Burgundy's marginal climate that makes it capable of producing such stylish, even superb wines. But in many ways, Burgundy's generally continental, temperate climate is often too unreliable, and it is only the presence of seemingly mystical microclimates, a magical combination of soil and climate, that has earned Burgundy its fabled reputation. This alchemy occurs most often in the form of limestone in the middle of south- and southeast-facing slopes, which offer plenty of light and heat from direct sunlight, as well as heat retention in the soil for radiation after sunset, excellent water drainage and storage, and minimal danger from frosts. Thus it is possible for one small plot of vineyard to consistently produce exciting wine, while just ten feet away on the same hillside, the wines seem to be far less interesting. It is for this reason that the wine

Burgundy Region

Chablis
Irancy
Sauvignon-St-Bris

Côte d'Or
Côte de Nuits
Côte de Beaune

Côte Chalonnaise
Mâconnais
Beaujolais
Beaujolais Crus

jargon of Burgundy continues to refer to small, individual vineyard plots as *climats*.

Over and above the specific considerations of what makes some plots of land great, the Burgundy grape grower is faced with climatic threats every year, ranging from hail and frost to wind and torrential rains, a fact that often translates into wines that seem dilute, overly acidic, and lacking fruit. Despite such disappointing wines in some years, Burgundy continues to produce the occasional masterpiece that fascinates and leads us into the temptation of believing that such wonders will always be possible.

GRAPE TYPES

The little white lie about Burgundy grapes is generally useful and often accurate: White Burgundy is Chardonnay and red Burgundy is Pinot Noir, but that is not quite the whole truth, particularly with respect to white grapes. The use of small quantities of Pinot Blanc persists in some appellations for white wine, and Pinot Gris (called Pinot Beurot locally) is still listed as an approved variety for Corton Charlemagne. The reality though is that it is Chardonnay that is the preferred variety and Chardonnay that gives great white Burgundy its character. What is an important consideration, however, is the presence of the white grape Aligoté, used to produce regional wines and always identified on the label, as well as the presence of the Melon de Bourgogne variety used in some obscure regional wines. In the northern section of Burgundy, there are also some small pockets of Sauvignon Blanc.

What we can be sure of is that fine red Burgundy is Pinot Noir! However, there is still plenty of Gamay grown in Burgundy, especially in the southern districts, as well as a small amount of the little known César, grown in the more northern stretches of Burgundy and used for wines that are rarely seen on the export market.

THE BURGUNDY WINE BUSINESS

Throughout history, the Burgundian vineyards have been parceled into smaller and smaller plots of ownership. The two most dramatic influences in this regard have been the Napoleonic Code, which insisted that all surviving children share any bequeathed wealth and property, and the state's frequent forced acquisition of Church lands and their subsequent redistribution or sale to individuals. As a result, vineyards have gone from having one single owner

to being owned by several different individuals. And yet any one vineyard remains intact as a single, named entity, often enclosed by a stone wall. The best and most famous example to illustrate this phenomenon is the Clos de Vougeot vineyard, which grows Pinot Noir grapes in the village of Vougeot. The vineyard itself is remarkably large by Burgundian standards, covering 124 acres/50 hectares, but ownership is split among eighty different owners!

Most of these owners tend two or three rows of vines and do not have the means to produce wine from their grapes, or even if they make wine, they do not produce enough to bottle and market it themselves. So, the wine labeled as Clos de Vougeot is usually produced by *négociants* who purchase grapes or wines from individual growers and then put together a finished wine. The picture is made more complex by the fact that more than one *négociant* may purchase grapes from the Clos de Vougeot vineyard and produce their own version of the wine from that vineyard, so that in any one vintage there may be four or five different versions of Clos de Vougeot available from different *négociants*.

The *négociants* also control the production of wines from the broader regional and village appellations as well as the single vineyards. Today, the whole region covers approximately 55,000 acres/22,000 hectares, farmed by over 10,000 growers.

Each *négociant* company has its own particular style and reputation, and when purchasing Burgundy wines an understanding of those factors will help ensure that the wine offers integrity and quality. The different styles of the *négociants* are usually a reflection of the different choices made in finishing the wine. The less expensive white wines are fermented in stainless steel or large oak *foudres* that provide little to no oak character. By contrast, the most powerful, complex, and long-lived dry whites in the world are produced in the Côtes d'Or from Chardonnay

Labouré-Roi is a large Burgundy négociant.

fermented in small new oak barrels. New oak contributes tannins, and the wines acquire rich, creamy flavors both from malolactic fermentation and from the practice of *bâtonnage,* or stirring the yeast lees back into the wine while it is aging in a barrel. Simple white wines are usually bottled within six to nine months from the harvest, while the more structured, aged whites may not be bottled until twelve to eighteen months after the harvest.

There is no one recipe used by all Burgundian *négociants* to produce red wine. Fuller-bodied, more structured and tannic reds can be achieved by whole berry fermentation (not crushing the grapes beforehand) or by whole bunch fermentation (including the stems in fermentation). Another technique used is *saignage,* removing some of the clear juice and leaving no more than twice the amount of solids so that the lesser amount of juice benefits from more color and tannin extraction from the skins. Other choices for increased extraction of color, flavors, and tannins include a warmer fermentation temperature, pumping over, and the use of a rotofermenter.

As for wood treatment, some *négociants* believe that Pinot Noir is too delicate a varietal for new oak barrel aging and will therefore use only one- or two-year-old wood. The wines spend a year to two in oak before bottling. Some *négociants* believe in fining and filtering the wine before bottling, while others avoid these practices with the hope of retaining more flavors. Like white wines, simple Burgundy reds are bottled fairly soon after production, while the more complex versions may not be bottled until two years after the harvest.

It should be stressed that over the previous decade there have been substantial changes in the business framework of Burgundy, with many of the large *négociants* finding themselves in a position where they have been able to purchase more and more plots within individual *climats,* thereby exercising greater control over the grape-growing process and having a continuity of supply. There are also many more individual *climats* that are owned outright by one single *négociant,* making that property a *monopole,* with the wine from that property produced only by that *négociant.*

There has also been a dramatic increase in the number of *propriétaires-recoltants,* individual growers who make their own wines, as well as a significant increase in the number of wines that are "**DOMAINE** bottled" (**MIS EN BOUTEILLES AU DOMAINE**). Even so, the role of the *négociant* in Burgundy is still of tremendous importance, and an as-sessment of the reputation of the *négociant* is often more important than knowledge of the specifics of any individual vineyard site.

THE APPELLATION CATEGORIES IN BURGUNDY

Starting with the larger regions in Burgundy and peaking in quality with the highest rated *climats,* the *appellation protégée* laws provide four different levels of appellation. These levels are regional, village, *premier cru* vineyard, and *grand cru* vineyard.

REGIONAL

There are more than fifteen regional appellations for Burgundy still white and red wines, though only a handful of these have any major presence on export markets. The vineyards designated as the various regional appellations tend to be the peripheral areas, at higher elevations too cold for full ripening of the grapes or on the flatter lands where soils and temperatures are not conducive to the elegance that shows Pinot Noir at its best.

The most common regional appellations are:
· Bourgogne (sometimes followed by the subregion name of Hautes-Côtes de Beaune or Hautes-Côtes de Nuits): red and white wines
· Côte de Beaune: red wines
· Côte de Beaune–Villages: red wines
· Côtes de Nuits–Villages: almost all red wines
· Macon: mostly white wines
· Macon-Villages: mostly white wines
· Crémant de Bourgogne: sparkling white and rosé wines

Generally these regional appellations produce fairly ordinary wine, with little distinction. The use of the hyphenated term "Villages" indicates that within a broader appellation some villages have been identified as having "better" vineyard sites (by virtue of soil, exposure, drainage, etc.), and the wines produced from those vineyards should exhibit fuller flavor and firmer structure. The use of the term "Villages" is also found in Beaujolais and in the Côtes du Rhône.

VILLAGE

Within any region or subregion there are frequently individual villages that have been granted the right to name the wine after the village name, as long as all of the grapes used to make the wine came from vineyards within the boundaries of that village. Village appellations have stricter regulations than the region they fall within, particularly with regard to lower yields and higher alcohol requirements that should ensure fully ripe grapes and more concentrated flavors. Beaune, Meursault, Vosne-Romanée, and Gevrey-Chambertin are examples of village names that are used to name the wines made from those places. A fuller discussion of other villages will be found in the following sections on each subregion.

Over the centuries, growers and winemakers in Burgundy have established a hierarchy of individual vineyard sites, resulting in the recognition of three levels of vineyard—untitled vineyard, *premier cru* vineyard, and *grand cru* vineyard. Any wine produced from grapes harvested from one single untitled vineyard still falls under the more general Village appellation: The principal name of the wine will be the name of the village itself, though the producer has the right to add the name of the individual vineyard to the label.

PREMIER CRU VINEYARD

If the grapes were grown in a single Côte d'Or vineyard designated as *premier cru,* then the name that appears on the label will be a combination of the village name and the individual vineyard name. For example, a wine made from grapes grown in the *premier cru* vineyard named Clos-St. Jacques in the village of Gevrey-

Chambertin will be labeled "Gevrey-Chambertin Clos-St. Jacques." Underneath the name of the wine the consumer will find the phrase "Appellation Gevrey-Chambertin premier cru protégée." (Sometimes the *premier* is abbreviated to 1er, the equivalent of the English 1st.)

A *négociant* can also blend grapes or wines from two or more *premier cru* vineyards, in which case the wine will be labeled as the name of the village plus the phrase "premier cru," such as "Gevrey-Chambertin premier cru." Whether the wine is sourced from one or more vineyards of *premier*

TOP: A premier cru *label showing that the grapes came from the vineyard called Charmes in the village of Meursault* BOTTOM: *The village of Chassagne-Montrachet in the Côte de Beaune*

cru status, *premier cru* wines should represent a distinct improvement over village-level wines, showing greater intensity of flavor, more complexity, and more structure and body.

In Chablis, the labeling practices are slightly different, with wines from a single *premier cru* vineyard labeled as "Chablis premier cru," plus the name of the single vineyard. Again, if the grapes came from more than one *premier cru* vineyard, no vineyard name will appear on the label.

GRAND CRU VINEYARDS

The apex of the hierarchical pyramid in Burgundy appellations is represented by the *grand cru* vineyards, of which there are thirty in the Côte d'Or region, and seven in Chablis. There are no *grand cru* vineyards in the Côte Chalonnaise or in Macon.

The individual sites are considered to be so superlative in the Côte d'Or that they have their own appellation, and the name of the vineyard alone is considered sufficient information on the label. To continue our examples based on the village of Gevrey-Chambertin, that village has nine *grand cru* vineyards within its boundaries, so one example from that village might be a wine labeled simply as "Chambertin." In that instance, all of the grapes used to make the wine came from the single *grand cru* vineyard known as Chambertin.

Grand cru wines from the Côte d'Or are not required to put that phrase on the label, though in recent years it has become an increasingly common practice.

Again, in Chablis the labeling practices are different, with *grand cru* wines labeled as "Chablis grand cru," plus the name of the single vineyard.

A word of warning and encouragement: Over the centuries, there have been slight variations of *cru* vineyard names recorded, and a certain amount of presumption is expected in identifying specific vineyards. For example, *grand cru* vineyards sometimes are written with "Le" in front of the name, sometimes they are not—good examples of this would be Corton, Chambertin, and Musigny. Sometimes a *premier cru* or *grand cru* site is referred to as "les" such-and-such, other times the vineyard name is preceded by "aux." Further, it is almost impossible now to know whether the proper spelling of a vineyard name includes a hyphen or not. We have generally included hyphens.

THE SUBREGIONS OF BURGUNDY

CHABLIS

This subregion is physically separated from the rest of Burgundy, being located approximately 30 miles/50 kilometers northwest of the other regions. As an isolated unit, it is a study in traditionalism versus modernism in winemaking and grape growing. The first appellation law in the area was promulgated in 1919. At that time the accepted truth was that the wine named Chablis was more or less synonymous with Chardonnay grapes grown on Kimmeridgian soil, which consists of chalk, clay, limestone, and fossilized oyster shells. Today, the permitted

LEFT: *The* grand cru *vineyard of Montrachet is shared by the villages of Puligny and Chassagne, which both added the name of the famous vineyard to their village name in the nineteenth century.* **RIGHT**: *This label shows that the grapes were grown in the* grand cru *vineyard called Montrachet.*

boundaries of the appellation have been expanded to increase production, and vines are planted on less fine, hard Portlandian limestone soils as well. The debate continues to rage among winemakers and wine connoisseurs as to whether the integrity and authenticity of Chablis has been diluted by this expansion of the vineyards.

In winemaking too there are ongoing questions as to the authentic way to make Chablis, especially concerning the use of wood. The traditional way to ferment and age the wines of Chablis is in a **FEUILLETTE**, a 132-liter/34.8 gallon cask, or the larger *foudres*. Although some *négociants* still vinify and age in wood, others are using stainless steel. The sense of oak should not diminish the smell and taste of fruit, and oak does not play as large a role here as it does elsewhere in Burgundy. Experiments continue on the effect of oak for the higher-quality wines, with some *négociants* convinced it enhances fine wines and others definitely opposed to using oak. J. Moreau, A Régnard, J. Durup, and Louis Michel are producers who avoid oak, while W. Fèvre, J. P. Droin, Raveneau, and R. Dauvissat are proponents of using oak. Those using oak are doing so in varying degrees of influence. La Chablisienne, the large cooperative of the region, uses oak for some of its *cru* wines.

Basic Chablis is the perfect Chardonnay for wine consumers who appreciate high acidity in a wine. The cold climate and chalk soil provide the high acidity and the lean, green apple flavors for the Chardonnay grapes grown here. In fact, the Chablis region can often be so cold that frost presents a serious problem, requiring preventive measures such as heat stoves in the vineyards, or spraying young buds with water, providing an insulating coat of ice that ironically prevents the bud itself from freezing. The issue of cold climate certainly does underscore the importance of vineyard location, with the best sites facing south, southeast, or southwest, between 350 and 750 feet/120 and 250 meters in elevation. The finer examples from such sites usually exhibit aromas of spring flowers, green apples, or lemons, but everything is made more bracing by a steely, mineral aroma, something akin to the smell of wet rocks. On the palate, a good Chablis will offer a completeness offset by a tart fruit character and sharp lingering acidity, a beautiful example of what the Chardonnay grape can achieve when it is not overly alcoholic and not made to smell and taste like buttered popcorn from too much oak treatment.

As in any wine region, there is good wine and less good wine produced here, again emphasizing the im-

portance of a reputable producer, with the traditionalists blaming the redrawing of the boundaries for any perceived drop in quality. Where one could hope to be assured of a fine wine is from the classified *premier cru* and *grand cru* vineyards.

PREMIER CRU   There are forty *climats* judged to have better exposure and soils than plain Chablis, and these are referred to as *premier cru* Chablis. To simplify recognition, wines from any one of the forty named sites are often labeled under the names of the twelve most renowned sites. Of these dozen, better exposure and more mineral rock content in the soil make five particular sites stand out, namely:

- Fourchaume
- Mont de Milieu
- Montmains
- Montée de Tonnerre
- Vaillons

Any of these *premier cru* sites should offer slightly firmer structure and riper fruit qualities than a basic Chablis, but will still finish with piercing, refreshing acidity. Because of their slightly fuller intensity, these wines can (some would say should) age three to four years, after which time all of the fruit and mineral components will have harmonized into a truly exciting mouthful of wine.

GRAND CRU   Seven sites were granted the highest classification of *grand cru* Chablis in 1938, and standing in the old town of Chablis, looking across the river at the expanse of vines on the opposite side, it is easy to understand why. These vineyards constitute a solid block of mineral-based, well-drained, south- and southwest-facing hillside, preferred sites in a prime area. Wines from here

This label shows that the grapes were grown in the grand cru *vineyard called Les Clos in Chablis.*

made by the best producers can be enjoyed after four or five years, or cellared and then savored after one or two decades. The nose of these wines may be of ACACIA, hay, grapefruit, green apple, or pears, a delicious complex of ripe, sometimes even tropical fruit notes in a sort of lemon-honey base and the ever-present mineral acidity to finish. Each author or critic may champion a favorite site, attracted to the honey-apple nose, depth, and structure of Les Clos, the ripe fullness of Les Preuses, or the finesse of Vaudésir. The wines of Bougros come from a very steep incline and are firm and expansive on the palate. The fragrant nose of Valmur is part of its appeal, and its balance another. The wines from Grenouilles are fuller than those from Blanchot, yet both offer ripe, accented aromas.

Notable producers in the Chablis region include Brocard, La Chablisienne, Dauvissat, Droin, Drouhin, Duplessis, Durup, Michel, Moreau, Pinson, Raveneau, Verget, and Vocoret.

Also found in the surrounding region are two relative oddities—the red wine of Irancy, made from Pinot Noir with the lesser known César and Tressot grapes, plus the white Sauvignon de St-Bris, a crisp, acidic version of Sauvignon Blanc.

CÔTE D'OR

The Côte d'Or is the world's finest growing area for Chardonnay and Pinot Noir. Thirty miles/50 kilometers long and under 2 miles/3 kilometers at its widest, the area offers a myriad of nuances in style that depend on the soil, rainfall, exposure to sun and wind, drainage, and the grower's and winemaker's approach. If proof were needed that location in grape growing makes a difference, the Côte d'Or is that proof. Within those thirty miles, there are two subsections, the Côte de Nuits to the north and the Côte de Beaune in the south. The Côte de Nuits section produces mostly red wines, while the Côte de Beaune is celebrated for both white and red wines.

As in Chablis, soil is at the heart of what makes Côte d'Or wines potentially great, with microclimates playing an essential partnership role. Soil types are varied, but the important players are limestone, chalk, marlstone, and clay. Where there is a greater presence of limestone in the soil mix, Pinot Noir will shine. When marly soils dominate, Chardonnay is usually the choice. The whole question of soil types and microclimates is integral to understanding why this relatively small growing region has developed such an intricate web of sites or CLIMATS.

Both the Côte de Nuits and the Côte de Beaune have *grand cru* vineyards, and the general pattern is that the Côte de Nuits *grand cru* sites produce red wines, while those in the Côte de Beaune are white wine vineyards. With such greatness in the midst, it is perhaps not surprising that many of the villages in the Côte have officially added the name of their greatest *grand cru* vineyard to the name of the village, thereby bringing instant prestige to the village. In almost every instance, a hyphenated village name in the Côte d'Or indicates that the second part of the name is the name of a *grand cru* vineyard in the village. For example, in the village Gevrey-Chambertin, Chambertin is the name of a *grand cru* vineyard in the village.

On a pleasant upbeat note, we are excited to confirm that as of the 2005 vintage, vineyards in the Côte d'Or have eliminated the PLC (*plafond limité de classement*) that regularly allowed producers to request permission to produce more than the "permitted" yield. This is a very welcome development at a time when the entire French wine industry is under attack for duplicity and a lack of concentration on quality.

CÔTE DE NUITS

The Côte de Nuits produces very little white or rosé wine but is revered for its red wines, as demonstrated by its twenty-four *grand cru* red wine vineyards. There is one regional appellation here: Côte de Nuits–Villages. This appellation is used to market wines from villages that are relatively unknown; in particular, the appellation covers wines from the villages of Comblanchien, Corgoloin, Prémeaux-Prissey, Fixin, and Brochon. They usually present good, solid red berry, cherry characteristics in a light- to medium-weight wine.

Much higher up on the slopes are the vineyards that constitute the Hautes-Côtes de Nuits appellation. The cooler climate here usually results in wines that are noticeably lean, though the reds can have clean cherry characteristics that seem to be typical of really cold climate Pinot Noir, and the whites sometimes show attractive flinty, mineral character in solid, green apple fruit.

The major Côte de Nuits villages from north to south are Marsannay, Fixin, Gevrey-Chambertin, Morey-St-Denis, Chambolle-Musigny, Vougeot, Flagey-Echézeaux, Vosne-Romanée, and Nuits-St-Georges. We discuss each of these here.

MARSANNAY The commune of Marsannay is most famous for rosé wines, which may be labeled as Marsannay or as Bourgogne-Marsannay. The rosés tend to have an orange tinge with bright raspberry aromas. To enjoy their fruit and power, they are best drunk within three years. Domaine Clair Dau, which started the rosé style in 1919, still produces fine examples today. A 1987 decree allowed the Marsannay appellation to be applied to red and white wines as well. Compared with the rosés, the reds offer darker cherry or cranberry characteristics, while the whites can show impressive mineral and ripe apple notes.

FIXIN   Fixin consists of 488 acres/198 hectares of vineyards that more often sell their products under the more general appellation of Côte de Nuits–Villages. Higher clay content in the soil and a cooler climate than the more revered villages to the south result in wines that are often underripe and overly tannic. The application of technology in the vineyard and in the winemaking may result in more attractive wines, particularly from the *premier cru* vineyards of Clos du Chapitre and Clos de la Perrière. A little white wine is produced from Chardonnay and Pinot Blanc grapes.

GEVREY-CHAMBERTIN   The historic town of Gevrey-Chambertin is known for producing the most powerful Burgundies from its variety of soils and exposures. The simple village appellation wines tend to come from flat land or from the base of the hills, while the *premier* and *grand cru* vineyards are on slopes with the best sun exposure and drainage. There are more than 1,200 acres/500 hectares of land entitled to the village appellation, and about a fifth of the acreage has *premier cru* or *grand cru* status. This is not only the largest village appellation in the Côte de Nuits, it also boasts twenty-five *premier cru* sites and the largest number of *grand cru* vineyards (nine) in Burgundy. All the wines produced are reds from the Pinot Noir, and depending on site, yield, and methods of vinification they range from lightweight to the most powerful and rich examples with bright fruit flavors, firm structure, and an almost sinful, silken texture.

Of the *premier cru* vineyards, Combottes, Clos St-Jacques, Varoilles, Les Cazetiers, and Combe au Moine are considered the finest examples. The *grand cru* vineyard Chambertin stands out as quintessential Gevrey, with Chambertin Clos de Bèze not far behind. The other *grand cru* vineyards that may suffix the name Chambertin to their own are Charmes, Chapelle, Griotte, Mazis, Mazoyères, Latricières, and Ruchottes.

MOREY-ST-DENIS   Morey-St-Denis produces wines that may seem less generous or voluptuous than those from its more famous neighboring villages to the north and south.

But Morey-St-Denis should not be dismissed, for its wines have tenacity and an innate but fine power. They may need time to show their bright, deep currant flavors, but the wait is worth it, and will reveal some intriguing coffee or chocolate character along the way. As usual, the village appellation wines can be overly light, but the *premier cru* and *grand cru* versions are more forceful.

The village is rightfully proud of its twenty-five *premier cru* vineyards, including Clos de la Bussière, a monopole owned by Domaine Georges Roumier, as well as Clos des Ormes, Les Sorbés, Clos Sorbé, Aux Charmes, and Les Monts Luisants. The latter produces a rarity: a fine full-bodied white wine from Chardonnay blended with a white mutation of the (usually red) Pinot Noir grape.

The *grand cru* vineyards are Clos de Tart (a monopole owned by the *négociant* Mommessin), Clos de la Roche, Clos St-Denis, Clos des Lambrays, and a tiny strip of the Bonnes Mares vineyard, the greater majority of which lies in the Chambolle-Musigny commune to the south. Of these, Clos de la Roche is undoubtedly the unsung hero, providing dense, ripe fruit and sinewy power over decades of aging. The Clos de Tart can sometimes appear unbalanced, but in fine vintages it matures handsomely, whereas the Clos St-Denis will always appear somewhat reserved, but no less elegant.

CHAMBOLLE-MUSIGNY   If Gevrey-Chambertin is known for the weight and power of its wines, then Chambolle-Musigny provides wonders of sheer grace and elegance, yet still supple and taut, probably the effect of a higher limestone content in the soil. The seductive bouquet of the finest examples offers violets, cherries, raspberries, and a distinctive steely but attractive GOÛT DE TERROIR. Of the *premier cru* vineyards, Les Amoureuses and Les Charmes are the finest, offering everything that their name implies. The elegant aspects of the wines from the *grand cru* vineyards Bonnes Mares and Musigny are enhanced by great intensity and depth of wild berry flavor, with almost a perfumed essence of berry aroma. The fine producer Domaine Comte Georges de Vogüé owns about 18 of the 26 acres/7 of the 10.5 hectares of Musigny and also produces a complex, full-bodied white wine from less than three-quarters of an acre of Chardonnay. The wine of Bonnes Mares is firmer and fleshier, needing a decade to begin to show its best qualities.

VOUGEOT   The village of Vougeot is dominated by the walled *grand cru* vineyard of Clos de Vougeot, established by Cistercian monks about 1100. Likewise, the wines of

Vougeot are dominated by the *grand cru* wine, which is much more famous than the village appellation wines or the *premier cru* wines that are made there. Outside of the Clos de Vougeot's sprawling 124 acres/50 hectares there are a further 40 acres/16 hectares producing reliable, even good, village-level wine, though it is a relative rarity on the export market. Even less likely to be seen are the wines from the *premier cru* vineyards such as Les Petits Vougeots or Les Cras, even though they often offer better value than the *grand cru* wine from the Clos.

By 1336, the 124 acres/50 hectares of the Clos de Vougeot had been enclosed by stone walls, ensuring its continued existence as a single *climat*. But various episodes of property confiscation, sale, and split inheritances have resulted today in those 124 acres being split among more than eighty owners. As might be expected, there are enormous variations in soil and microclimate from one end of the vineyard to the other, particularly given that the vineyard extends from the higher slopes all the way down to the flat valley floor. Such a situation flies directly in the face of the very basis of the appellation concept— that small pockets of land exist capable of producing fine wine, like islands in a sea of mediocrity. As a result, different bottlings of Clos de Vougeot can be unreliable. The age-old advice rings particularly true for Clos de Vougeot: A reputable, reliable *négociant* can be more important than the vineyard name. Apart from the *grand cru* there are another 44 acres/17.8 hectares of *premier cru* and commune wines. When better examples are encountered, they will have a raspberry, floral, and truffle nose; good weight on the palate; and a lengthy, smooth finish.

FLAGEY-ECHÉZEAUX   There are no village-level wines bearing the name Flagey-Echézeaux, since they are sold under the name of the neighboring village, Vosne-Romanée. However, the 92-acre/37-hectare Echézeaux vineyard and the 22-acre/8.9-hectare Grands Echézeaux vineyard are both rated *grand cru*. As might be expected, the larger Echézeaux vineyard has developed a similar reputation to Clos de Vougeot: It is simply too large to provide consistently *grand cru* level wines. The "grand" in Grands Echézeaux is no mistake: The wines are big, with rich, layered fruit in a fine vintage.

VOSNE-ROMANÉE   For some wine lovers, this village contains the holy grail of Pinot Noir in the form of some of the finest single *grand cru* vineyards in the whole of the Côte de Nuits, and certainly the best Pinot Noir in the world. Even the village-level wines can be more reliable

than many other of the surrounding communes, with almost all of the vineyard land on the slopes above the village, rather than spilling into the flat, uninspiring land on the valley floor.

What is most striking about Vosne-Romanée wines perhaps is their completeness or their integrity: All of the finest attributes of Pinot Noir seem to be reflected here, from ripe berry fruit, to woodsy, leafy qualities, to meaty and spicy, all wrapped up in a sensually smooth envelope. The sixteen *premier cru* vineyards cover a total of only 140 acres/57 hectares, making wines of predictably greater intensity and yet gentle harmony. The more revered *premier cru* sites include Aux Malconsorts, Les Chaumes, Clos de Réas (monopole of Jean Gros), Les Suchots, and Les Beaux Monts.

However, these fine sites are too often overshadowed by Vosne-Romanée's six *grand cru* vineyards, which cover a mere 65 acres/26 hectares. These sites and their wines represent the epitome of fine Burgundy and deserve some individual attention.

RICHEBOURG   The most northerly of the *grand cru* vineyards is famous for rich, fleshy wines, almost indiscreetly opulent and perfumed with exotic spices (20 acres/2 hectares).

LA ROMANÉE   The smallest single appellation in France, producing leaner wines suggesting slightly unfulfilled promise, but still head and shoulders above some other *grand cru* wines (2 acres/0.8 hectares).

ROMANÉE-CONTI   For some Burgundy lovers, this is the definition of smooth, and Romanée-Conti should be in any thesaurus, right along with satiny and velvety (4 acres/1.6 hectares).

ROMANÉE-ST-VIVANT   Less powerful than Richebourg, gentler and sometimes weak—but, again, everything's relative—still an exceptional wine (25 acres/10 hectares).

LA GRANDE RUE   Promoted in 1991 from *premier cru* to *grand cru,* this vineyard certainly faces stiff competition from its more illustrious neighbors and is more renowned for refined elegance than its fuller counterparts (3.7 acres/1.5 hectares).

LA TÂCHE   If Vosne-Romanée is the quintessential Côte de Nuits, then La Tâche is, for some, the most complete and satisfying Vosne-Romanée, effortlessly combining all the finest elements and providing pure hedonistic pleasure along with intellectual stimulation (15 acres/6 hectares).

GRANDS CRUS OF BURGUNDY

The following is a list of the major villages in the Côte d'Or and the names of their *grand cru* vineyards.

CÔTE DE NUITS* VILLAGE	GRAND CRU VINEYARD
Gevrey-Chambertin	Chambertin
	Chambertin Clos de Bèze
	Charmes-Chambertin
	Chapelle-Chambertin
	Griotte-Chambertin
	Latricières-Chambertin
	Mazis-Chambertin
	Mazoyères-Chambertin
	Ruchottes-Chambertin
Morey-St-Denis	Clos des Lambrays
	Clos de Tart
	Clos St-Denis
	Clos de la Roche
	Small part of Bonnes Mares
Chambolle-Musignv	Most of Bonnes Mares
	Le Musigny (mostly red; a little white wine)
Vougeot	Clos de Vougeot
Flagey-Echézeaux	Grands Echézeaux
	Echézeaux
Vosne-Romanée	Richebourg
	Romanée-Conti
	Romanée-St-Vivant
	La Romanée
	La Grande Rue
	La Tâche

All red wine vineyards unless otherwise noted

CÔTE DE BEAUNE* VILLAGE	GRAND CRU VINEYARD
Aloxe-Corton	Corton-Charlemagne and Corton (mostly red)
Pernand-Vergelesses	Shared by first three villages at left
Ladoix-Serrigny	
Puligny-Montrachet	Chevalier Montrachet
	Part of Montrachet
	Part of Bâtard-Montrachet
Chassagne-Montrachet	Criots-Bâtard-Montrachet
	Part of Montrachet
	Part of Bâtard-Montrachet

All white wine vineyards unless otherwise noted

CHABLIS*	
	Blanchots
	Bougros
	Les Clos
	Grenouilles
	Les Preuses
	Valmur
	Vaudésir

All white wine vineyards

NUITS-ST-GEORGES This village appellation is relatively large, covering 925 acres/375 hectares in a long thin strip that covers 3.5 miles/6 kilometers. Included in this are the vineyards in the village of Prémeaux-Prissey to the south, whose wines are all marketed under the Nuits-St-Georges appellation. Because the appellation is so large there is the recurring problem of less scrupulous *négociants* making wines that are not truly representative of Nuits at its best. Thankfully, there are plenty of more reliable producers whose wines reveal the village's true character of sturdy, even muscular wines that can appear somewhat burly in their youth but age into forceful but coordinated gems of dark, plummy, spiced fruit.

Though there are no *grand cru* vineyards in the appellation, there are thirty-eight *premier cru* sites, all of which offer very fine wines, with a few aspiring to and often reaching *premier cru* quality in all but name. The *premier cru* vineyards in the north of the appellation tend to have richer, less mineral soils, and produce fleshier wines closer to the Vosne-Romanée model; some of the better examples are Aux Murgers, Aux Chaignots, Les Damodes, and Aux Boudots. To the south the soils have a higher mineral content, and the wines are correspondingly less rich with a stronger sense of mineral *goût de terroir* on the palate. Good examples of such wines come from the *premier cru* vineyards of Les Cailles, Les Vaucrains, Clos Arlot, Clos de la Maréchale, and Les St-Georges (which shares the privilege with some *grand cru* vineyards of having its name co-opted to the name of the village).

Some of the most respected growers and *négociants* in the Côte de Nuits include Amiot, Antonin Guyon, Antonin Rodet, Armand Rousseau, Barthod-Noëllat, Bertagna, Bouchard Père et Fils, Bruno Clair, Daniel Rion, Domaine de la Romanée-Conti, Doudet-Naudin, Dujac, Jaffelin, Jean Grivot, Joseph Drouhin, Joseph Faiveley, Leroy, Lignier, Louis Jadot, Louis Latour, Marquis d'Angerville, Mongeard-Mugneret, Mugnier, Mugneret-Gibourg, Roumier, Tollot-Beaut, Voarick.

CÔTE DE BEAUNE

The Côte de Beaune area is twice as large as the Côte de Nuits and is known for its great white wines as well as for some very fine reds. The area contains two regional appellations, Côte de Beaune and Côte de Beaune–Villages. Surprisingly, the Côte de Beaune appellation does not cover the whole geographic area, but only a small section of vineyards close to the town of Beaune, whereas the Côte de Beaune–Villages appellation, for red wines only, is more widespread and can be used by any of the sixteen villages that also have the right to market their wine under their own village name. Typically, the lesser-known villages have opted for this more general appellation, but there has been an increasing trend for even these villages to establish their own individuality in the wine world and to bottle their finer wines under their village name. The reputation of the Côte de Beaune–Villages appellation has suffered, and the wines are often too lightweight to be of much interest.

At the very top of the slopes is the Hautes-Côtes de Beaune appellation. As in its namesake appellation farther north, the climate here is generally too cold, and the wines suffer from a lack of body and fruit. In good years there are some stylish fruity reds and the occasional crisp, fruity white.

In the southern part of the Côte, several producers turn out very pleasant, enjoyable Bourgogne **PASSE-TOUT-GRAINS**, usually a red (there is a little rosé) blend of Gamay with at least one-third Pinot Noir. Some is also produced in the Côte Chalonnaise.

From north to south the major single village appellations in the Côte de Beaune are Ladoix, Pernand-Vergelesses, Aloxe-Corton, Savigny-lès-Beaune, Chorey-lès-Beaune, Beaune, Pommard, Volnay, St-Romain, Monthélie, Auxey-Duresses, Meursault, St-Aubin, Puligny-Montrachet, Chassagne-Montrachet, and Santenay. We discuss the principal communes here.

LADOIX The mostly red-wine appellation Ladoix is part of the village called Ladoix-Serrigny, but facts like that have become linguistic technicalities, for the truth is that, viticulturally speaking, Ladoix has been subsumed by its large and impressive neighbor Aloxe-Corton and its even more impressive cohort of *grand cru* vineyards. Theoretically, Ladoix boasts some six *grand cru* sites, but these have all been swallowed up by the *grand cru* vineyards of Corton and Corton-Charlemagne. There are six *premier cru* vineyard sites in Ladoix, but these can also use the greater marketing clout of the Aloxe-Corton name. Wines from the unclassified vineyards are usually sold under the broad, nonspecific Côte de Beaune–Villages appellation. Hence, one rarely sees the name Ladoix on a label outside of France.

PERNAND-VERGELESSES Like the Ladoix appellation, Pernand-Vergelesses has the honor of having some of its better vineyards included in the Corton and Corton-Charlemagne *grand cru* wines associated with Aloxe-Corton. In some ways this is a shame because it means that the other good vineyards of Pernand do not have the recognition of being in the same village as *grand cru* vineyards. Chardonnay and Aligoté grapes produce crisp, attractive white wines with forward fruit qualities, especially from vineyards high in chalk content. But most of the wines are red, from vineyards where the clay soil is enriched by iron, making for a good degree of sturdiness and a hard edge in addition to the familiar raspberry aroma. Particularly impressive are the *premier cru* vineyards of Les Fichots, Les Vergelesses, and Ile des Vergelesses, all of which need at least five years to show well.

ALOXE-CORTON Aloxe-Corton produces primarily red wines that seem to combine the power of the finest Nuits-St-Georges wines with the more graceful style of Beaune reds. The village-level wines and *premier cru* vineyard wines all come from the lower elevations, offering hints of gamey richness but without the layered complexity that makes for great Pinot Noir. However, they can be wines of excellent value. But Aloxe-Corton is really about *grand cru* wine, some of it extraordinary and some of it very ordinary, with the size of the *grand cru* designation again being so large as to be bound to include some lesser parcels of land.

There are two principal *grand cru* names attached to the village of Aloxe-Corton covering an astounding total of 445 contiguous acres/180 hectares: These are Corton for red wine and Corton-Charlemagne and Corton Blanc for whites. Within each of these umbrella appellations there are individually named *climats*, and, in the case of the red Corton wines, any of the *climat* names can be appended to the name of Corton on the label.

All of these *grand cru* climats stretch across the majestic and impressive hill of Corton that stands apart from the general slope of the Côte. It is not only variations in gradient and soil composition that suggest greater and lesser individual sites, but the fact that the vines are planted on almost 270 degrees of the hill indicates that, at one extreme, some vineyards face northeast and continue all the way around through south to northwest. Differences in climate, and thereby ripeness levels, abound. There is some general recognition of these differences inasmuch as the red Pinot Noir grapes are grown chiefly in the middle band around the hill where there are more ferrous and limestone elements, whereas the white grapes of Chardonnay, Pinot Blanc, and Pinot Gris are restricted largely to the top portions of the slope where outcroppings of calcareous chalk soils are visible. But the sheer expanse of the hill allows the less scrupulous *négociant* to blend grapes from lesser segments and to still label the wine as "Grand Cru Corton."

Despite this there are worthy distinctions. Corton, which consists of 300 acres/121 hectares, is the largest *grand cru* in Burgundy and the only red *grand cru* site in the Côte de Beaune. A fine red Corton should be generous in berry fruit with savory, almost gamey overtones, and the touch of velvet that is almost tranquilizing, though these qualities may take a decade to develop in the bottle. Corton Blanc is quite rare and is overshadowed anyway by the more dramatic and regal Corton-Charlemagne, which is one of the more assertive and fuller white Burgundy wines but tempered, like steel, with a taut edge in youth that finally succumbs with age to honeyed textured with nutty, rich flavors.

SAVIGNY-LÈS-BEAUNE   Approximately 90 percent of this village's wines are red, with the standard village appellation wines coming from the lower, flatter vineyards and offering acceptable but light versions, while the *premier cru* vineyards on the slopes can impress with denser fruit, some depth, and an agreeable finish. The wines from the northern section, closer to Pernand, are generally softer and friendlier, typified by the *premier cru* sites Les Vergelesses, Les Serpentières, Les Lavières, and Les Guettes. By contrast, the *premier cru* vineyards nearer to Beaune produce firmer, more concentrated but somewhat angular versions that soften attractively with age. Good examples are Les Marconnets and Les Jarrons.

CHOREY-LÈS-BEAUNE   The soft, ripe, almost raspberry preserve character of the reds from this village can be very attractive, though they are always lighter-style wines, coming from the generally flat land away from the slope and thereby showing less depth and expression. They are, however, wines of good value.

BEAUNE   Beaune, the largest town in the Côte de Beaune, is also the center of the Côte d'Or wine trade. There are over 13,000 acres/5,250 hectares of vines, but only 5 percent of the vineyards produce white wines that can display a distinctive nutty, acacia aroma enhanced by elegant but lengthy fruit. Beaune reds are about sweetly perfumed floral rose character and berry fruitiness. Village-level appellation wines are essentially open expressions of Pinot Noir; there is very little variation from site to site. But the classified vineyards are a different story. Depending on exactly how the boundaries are drawn, there are anywhere between thirty-nine and forty-five *premier cru* sites, but no *grand cru* vineyards. The *premier cru* wines from the northern section tend to be sturdier, fuller, and longer lived than those from the south, except for the Grèves vineyard whose gravel soils make for a lighter wine. Typical firmer wines from the northern section come from the *premier cru* sites of Les Bressandes, Clos du Roi, Les Marconnets, and Cent Vignes. The *négociant* Bouchard Père makes a tightly knit wine from the subplot named Vigne de l'Enfant Jésus within the Grèves vineyard.

Softer, fruitier, more accessible wines from the southern section are well represented by the *premier cru* vineyards of Clos des Mouches, Vignes Franches (including Louis Jadot's subplot called Clos des Ursules), and Les Chouacheux.

POMMARD   This village has 840 acres/340 hectares of vines, making it the second largest wine-producing area in the Côte de Beaune. In the past the area was maligned for overproduction, falsified labels, or heavy, dull wines. Today's conscientious *négociants* produce better-balanced wines, though more earthy and denser than the scented reds of Beaune. Only red wine carries the Pommard name, the best showing in their youth a typical but unattractive tannic structure that can mask the dark fruit and meaty, gamey nuances that are waiting to evolve. The density of the wines and their astringency in youth can be attributed to the deep red soils enriched by iron oxides. Les Rugiens is one *premier cru* example in such soil and is known for its depth of flavor, deep red color, and power. Of the twenty-eight *premier cru* vineyards, Les Epenots is in a softer style but will still benefit from cellaring for over a decade.

Other fine *premier cru* sites are Clos de la Commaraine (a monopole of Jaboulet Vercherre), Les Arvelets, Le Clos Blanc, Les Bertins, and en Largillière.

VOLNAY For those searching for elegance and charm in the Côte de Beaune, Volnay is the commune to choose. The wines are known for a violet and raspberry nose, silky texture, and harmonious flavors. The relative delicacy of the wines is possibly due to a higher chalk content in the soil. This would normally point to white grape plantings, but any wine carrying the Volnay name will be red. The reliability and consistently high quality of the wines is reflected in the vineyards, where over half of the 527 acres/215 hectares planted have *premier cru* status. The *premier cru* site Les Caillerets is considered the benchmark style for Volnay, particularly prized for its finesse. The chief contenders for top site are the Clos des Ducs (a monopole of Domaine Marquis d'Angerville) and Clos de la Bousse d'Or (monopole of Domaine de la Pousse d'Or), Clos des Chênes, the largest *premier cru* site, Champans, and Frémiets. Wines from a half dozen vineyards of the bordering commune Meursault may sell their reds as Volnay-Santenots. Whites from these vineyards are labeled as "Meursault *premier cru*" or "Meursault-Santenots."

MONTHÉLIE This village produces almost all red wine, with most of the village appellation vineyards lacking distinction and finesse, but the *premier cru* vineyards, especially Les Champs Fuillot and Sur La Velle, are blessed with substantial limestone content and southern or southeastern exposure that produce eloquent and expressive Pinot Noir wines.

AUXEY-DURESSES This is one of the villages that previously used the Côte de Beaune appellation for many of its wines, but now proudly puts its own name on the label. Red wines outnumber whites at the rate of two to one, but the whites are generally better, with a lack of polish in too many of the reds, but a welcome, nutty creaminess in the whites. There are seven *premier cru* vineyards in the village, of which Les Duresses, Clos Du Val, and Climat du Val are especially favored for both red and white wines.

MEURSAULT Meursault produces mostly white wines from calcareous soil rich in iron and magnesium. Standard village appellation Meursault can be so-so, but conscientious *négociants* make very pleasant peaches and cream Chardonnay wines—smooth, fruity, and just kissed with wood. When yields are kept low and the wines are given a few years to develop, they offer a wonderful hazelnut, cin-

namon, and toffee apple smell and a rich mouthful of flavor. Les Gouttes d'Or is a *premier cru* vineyard that produces a typically full, rich style, while the *premier cru* sites of Les Perrières and Les Genevières demonstrate a finer balance and persistence of flavors. Wines from the *premier cru* vineyard Les Charmes are everything that the name suggests, while the Poruzots *premier cru* site makes wines with surprising strength behind an apparently delicate frame.

ST-ROMAIN This village has some of the highest-elevation vineyards in the Côte d'Or, giving the red and white wines from here a distinctively high acidity. The chalky soil and cool climate bring out a noticeable cherry and mineral character in the reds, while a preference for no oak in the white wines produces minerally, high-acid whites similar to a good Chablis. There are no *premier cru* sites here.

BLAGNY Located between Meursault and Puligny-Montrachet, this village makes earthy red wines that are labeled simply "Blagny" or, if appropriate, "Blagny *premier cru*." White wines from Blagny vineyards are sold as either Meursault or Meursault-Blagny.

PULIGNY-MONTRACHET Puligny-Montrachet produces a tiny proportion of red wine, but is known worldwide for steely, powerful white wines in a leaner, more focused style than those of Meursault. The aromas tend to be more floral, fruity, and almond rather than the pronounced honey and hazelnut nose of Meursault. Moving up a notch from the village appellation to *premier cru* status, one begins to see the finesse, breeding, and distinction that come from individual sites such as Le Cailleret, Les Folatières, Les Perrières, and Les Pucelles. In contrast, the *premier cru* sites of Les Combettes and Les Referts, situated near Meursault, show some of the softness associated with that village.

In 1879, the village known then as Puligny added the name of the Montrachet vineyard to its own, even though

Vineyards surround the village of Puligny-Montrachet.

about half of that famous vineyard lies within the parish of Chassagne to the south. Wines from the *grand cru* vineyard Le Montrachet are considered to be the finest of all white Burgundies, suggesting the artistry of finely sculpted marble statuary—powerful, flowing, finely detailed, and completely harmonious. The neighboring *grand cru* sites of Bâtard-Montrachet, Chevalier-Montrachet, and Bienvenues-Bâtard-Montrachet can produce wines that are equally exquisite.

ST-AUBIN St-Aubin is prized for lighter-weight white wines with finesse, an expected effect of the village's high elevation in the hills above and behind the famous villages of Puligny and Chassagne. The *premier cru* vineyards named En Remilly and Les Murgers des Dents de Chien are physically the closest to Puligny, and high marl content in the soil creates a fuller white wine with typical nutty scents. Farther up the hill, the higher elevation and more limestone content combine to offer more minerally wines, especially from the *premier cru* sites of Les Frionnes and Les Perrières. The commune also makes fresh reds, with strawberry aromas and flavors. The richer *premiers crus* repay some aging, but they never quite lose their simplicity.

CHASSAGNE-MONTRACHET Given the fame of the *grand cru* vineyard for great white wine, it is not surprising that the village of Chassagne, which also co-opted the famous vineyard name, is usually associated with white wine production. In fact, Chassagne-Montrachet produces more red wine than white; something in the order of 60 percent of the wine is red. This is a reflection of the fact that many of the vineyards contain high levels of marly limestone soils that are better suited to the Pinot Noir grape. Basic village-level Chassagne-Montrachet whites share some of the mineral and fruit qualities of Puligny whites, but they seem softer, less tenacious. As in too many places, some *négociants* are too tempted by the opportunity to market poor wines under the Chassagne-Montrachet name knowing that they will sell by association with the great Montrachet name. As a result, some of the whites can be dull and thin.

The *premier cru* vineyard white wines usually provide more integrity, the best most often coming from Morgeot, Champs Gain, Les Caillerets, and Les Grandes Ruchottes. All of this is too often overshadowed by Chassagne's own portion of the great Montrachet and Batârd-Montrachet *grand cru* wines. In addition, the entire *grand cru* vineyard named Criots-Batârd-Montrachet lies completely within the village of Chassagne. This is the smallest of the white *grand cru* vineyards, and its wines seem never to scale the heights of excellence achieved by its grand neighbors, though it is a very fine wine in its own right.

The red wines of Chassagne-Montrachet can be very interesting, displaying a certain earthy spiciness, though they are usually lighter than some of their more famous counterparts to the north. The village appellation wines can be too light, while more emphatic character will be found from the *premier cru* vineyards of Morgeot, La Boudriotte, and Clos St-Jean.

SANTENAY Almost all of Santenay's wine is red, best described as earthy, though not necessarily generous. Basic village-level Santenay red from vineyards rich in marl can certainly be coarse, but the *premier cru* sites on the slopes produce wines of more elegance and length. Good examples are the *premier cru* vineyards of Les Gravières and La Comme, making good value wines with typical Pinot Noir fruit. When produced from a top site and vin-

LEFT: *Looking over the* premier cru *vineyard of Le Cailleret toward the arched entrance of the* grand cru *vineyard of Chevalier-Montrachet* RIGHT: *The* grand cru *Montrachet vineyard with the village of Chassagne-Montrachet in the background*

tage, the reds need a decade to soften. A small amount of white wine is produced as well.

Among the fine growers and *négociants* of the Côte de Beaune, some worth mentioning are Amiot, Ampeau, Antonin Guyon, Antonin Rodet, Bouchard Père et Fils, Bouzereau, Chartron et Trebuchet, Doudet-Naudin, Jaffelin, Joseph Drouhin, Louis Jadot, Louis Latour, Olivier Leflaive, Matrot, Morot, Rollin, Roux, Tollot-Beaut, and Verget.

CÔTE CHALONNAISE

The Côte Chalonnaise region is 25 kilometers/15 miles long and about 7 kilometers/4 miles wide. The vineyards are dispersed over clumps of hills, rather than all being concentrated on the one continuous slope of the Côte d'Or. The hills offer plenty of southeastern and southern exposure, and there is even room for expansion. The soils are similar to the Côte d'Or, based on limestone with some clay and sand. About two thirds is planted to Pinot Noir, with Chardonnay, Aligoté, and Gamay providing the balance. The wines have recently been acknowledged in the export market, where they offer reasonably priced alternatives to some of the excessively expensive Côte d'Or wines. Modern vinification techniques coupled with a traditional commitment to making the best wine by the conscientious producers has helped this area's wines appear on more dinner tables and wine lists around the world. Standard village-level wines are usually best drunk young, but wines from select sites in good vintages can mature very well. Note that the number of *premier cru* vineyards in these villages is relatively high compared with a Côte d'Or village of the same size.

Bourgogne Côte Chalonnaise was approved as an appellation in 1990, producing red wines from Pinot Noir

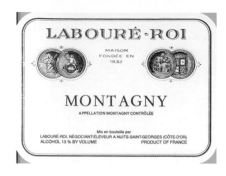

or Gamay, and white wines from Chardonnay or Aligoté. They are generally ordinary but affordable. There are five villages with the right to use their own name as an appellation on the label. From north to south they are Bouzeron, Givry, Montagny, Rully, and Mercurey.

BOUZERON This village traditionally uses all Aligoté grapes to produce crisp but fruity white wines with more ripeness and depth than the standard Bourgogne Aligoté.

RULLY Rully produces 1.25 million bottles of village level wine and another 250,000 bottles of *premier cru* wines. White wines from *premier cru* vineyards have a spicy apple aroma, medium body and color, with good fruit and acidity. The *premier cru* reds have a ruby color, strawberry aroma, and medium weight on the palate. Les Cloux is the most revered *premier cru* vineyard.

MERCUREY This village's soil contains substantial pockets of limestone and iron that favor Pinot Noir plantings. Almost all of the village's wine is red, with the Pinot Noir's typical aromas of violets and strawberries. These reds are more firm than others from the Côte Chalonnaise and can be aged between four and eight years after the vintage. There is a tiny amount of white wine produced, though it is generally less thrilling than the red.

GIVRY This is a village to look out for. There have been significant investments in replanting many of the vineyards and in updating the winemaking methods, as reflected in the recent approval of *premier cru* sites where none existed previously. Red wine makes up 90 percent of the production, and it is typified by bright strawberry fruit and attractive medium weight.

MONTAGNY Although the climate in this village can occasionally get too warm for Chardonnay at its best, this village makes only white wines from that grape. In recent years there has been an attractive, rich hazelnut quality to the wines, set against a dramatic mineral backdrop. The criterion for *premier cru* status here is not the site but a slightly higher alcohol level than the basic village appella-

LEFT: *Chardonnay vines in southern Mâcon* ABOVE: *A typical label for the wine from the village of Montagny*

tion. In other words, *premier cru* really doesn't count for much here.

Some of the principal growers and *négociants* of the Côte Chalonnaise include Caves de Buxy, Delorme, Joseph Drouhin, Dury, Joseph Faiveley, Genot-Boulanger, J.-M. Joblot, Louis Latour, Moillard, Antonin Rodet, Thénard, and E. Voarick.

MÂCONNAIS

This hilly region stretches 30 miles/50 kilometers from north to south and is 9 miles/15 kilometers wide. The Saône River flows through the region and then on through Beaujolais as well. While vines dominate agriculture in the Côte d'Or, the farms of Mâcon grow other fruits and vegetables, and raise livestock as well. The area is known primarily for white wines, with over three-quarters of its acreage devoted to Chardonnay. The climate is distinctly warmer than the Côte d'Or. The topsoil varies from marly clay and sand to granite, but the subsoil is mostly limestone. The white grapes Aligoté and Chardonnay are planted where there is more marl, and Pinot Noir is reserved for locations with more limestone. Gamay is grown on heavier clay soils and granite with sand. The east-facing slopes are preferred to those of the west, which have fewer plantings. The hills provide good drainage and are protected from wind and rain by trees planted on the summit.

The general Mâcon appellation can be used to label red or white wine, as can the Mâcon Supérieur appellation (one degree higher alcohol), whereas the Mâcon-Villages appellation is, for all practical purposes, reserved for white wines only. Basic Mâcon reds and whites can be disappointingly thin and uninteresting. Mâcon-Villages from a reputable *négociant* can be a gentle, fruity wine that at least shows some personality. The Mâcon-Villages appellation allows wines to be sold as such or they can be labeled as the name Mâcon plus any one of forty-two village names. The most frequently seen, and usually better, examples are Mâcon-Lugny, Mâcon-Viré, Mâcon-Chardonnay, Mâcon-Clessé, and Mâcon-Prissé.

POUILLY-FUISSÉ This is often considered to be the appellation producing the finest white Chardonnay wine of the region, and its fame is international. The best examples of Pouilly-Fuissé wine display a medium yellow hue, a nose of flowers, apples, and nuts, with a medium-weight fruitiness on the palate. In fact, the name Pouilly-Fuissé is a catchall appellation for wines made from grapes grown in the villages of Pouilly, Fuissé, Chaintré, Vergisson, and Solutré. Given the fame of the name, there are plenty of lackluster Pouilly-Fuissé wines on the market. A good Pouilly-Fuissé, from a good site in a good year from a reliable producer, may be enjoyed between two to seven years. One of the recent stars of good wines here is Château Fuissé, owned by the *négociant* Vincent et Fils.

Lesser wines can also be found from the appellations of Pouilly-Vinzelles and Pouilly-Loché.

ST-VÉRAN This was introduced as an appellation in 1971 to cover white Chardonnay wines from any of the villages of Chanès, Chasselas, Davayé, Leynes, Prissé, St-Amour, and St-Verand. These seven villages boast some chalk elements in their vineyards and wanted to separate themselves from the sea of mediocre white wines being sold as Mâcon-Villages. There appears to be some validity to this thinking: The wines are usually made in a fresh, lighter style with no wood but with a slight richness of obviously ripe fruit on the palate. Fresh fruit is their trump card, and they are best drunk young.

Important growers and *négociants* in the Mâconnais region include Auvigue, Cave de Lugny, Caves de Buxy, Delorme, Joseph Drouhin, Georges Duboeuf, Ferret, Château de Fuissé, Guffens-Heynen, Louis Jadot, Robert-Denogent, Thevenet, Valette, and Verget.

CRÉMANT DE BOURGOGNE

Both the Côte Chalonnaise and the Mâconnais regions produce large quantities of sparkling white wine and a small amount of rosé sparkling wine under the Crémant de Bourgogne appellation. Time was when this was pretty tired stuff, usually made from the grapes that were considered unusable for still white or red wine production. However, times have changed. Producers have understood two things: There is a market for less expensive sparkling wine than Champagne; and to make high-quality sparkling wine, you need high-quality grapes grown for that purpose, not somebody else's cast-offs. The result has been a greater concentration on Chardonnay and Pinot Noir, as well as the more traditional Aligoté and Pinot Blanc, leading eventually to some finely structured sparkling wines with excellent balance of fruit, acidity, and yeast components from the *méthode champenoise*. Some of the best producers include the Domaine Deliance, the Caves de Bailly, and the Caves des Hautes-Côtes, the last underpinning the appropriateness of the Hautes-Côtes regions in the Côte d'Or for sparkling wine production as opposed to regular, still Chardonnay and Pinot Noir.

Beaujolais

Beaujolais is technically part of Burgundy, contiguous to the Mâconnais region and stretching southward to cover some 54,000 acres/22,000 hectares between Mâcon and Lyon. However, there are significant differences between Burgundy and Beaujolais in terms of climate, soils, and even grape type.

Beaujolais is warmer than Burgundy, in some ways too warm for the cool-climate-loving Pinot Noir and Chardonnay. This is especially true in northern Beaujolais, where the granitic soils retain significant heat. With the combination of warmer climate and harder, granitic soils, the principal grape of choice is the Gamay, at one time "outlawed" from Burgundy, but truly at home in Beaujolais. In fact, the region between Pouilly-Fuissé (in the Mâconnais region of Burgundy) and St-Amour (in northern Beaujolais) is really a transition zone, with plantings of Chardonnay and Gamay evident in different villages.

The grape and the region are famous for the production of an easy-drinking, fresh, fruity, lively red wine, the kind of red wine that often converts non–red wine drinkers. Many people snobbishly but mistakenly overlook Beaujolais. Admittedly, not all Beaujolais can be thought of as "serious" wine, but most of it is eminently enjoyable. Part of the attraction lies in the fact that most Beaujolais is produced using the carbonic maceration technique, a process that minimizes movement of the skins during the winemaking stage, creating a wine that is lively, very low in tannins, and so easy to drink it can be deceptive. Beaujolais is commonly chaptalized and often reaches alcohol levels of around 13 percent.

Good Beaujolais is a very versatile wine that can be enjoyed with a wide variety of foods, from cured ham to coconut shrimp to lamb kebabs, and responds well to light chilling. And there is certainly enough of it to go around, some 150 million bottles annually, an amount that surpasses the total production of all the other regions of Burgundy.

There are five official levels of red Beaujolais: Beaujolais Nouveau, Beaujolais, Beaujolais Supérieur, Beaujolais-Villages, and *Cru* Beaujolais. There is also a small amount of rosé and white wine produced. The northern section of Beaujolais has a greater presence of granitic and schist-based soils and is considered to produce the better red wines. With a higher limestone content in the south, the reds are lighter, but there is a small amount of impressive white wine made there.

BEAUJOLAIS NOUVEAU

Sometimes called Beaujolais PRIMEUR, this category constitutes about half of the yearly production. Some would say it is purely a marketing gimmick, but it has certainly brought attention to the region. Beaujolais NOUVEAU is the first red wine of the new harvest, only about nine weeks old when it is released on the third Thursday in November each year. As such, it is sprightly, even sometimes noticeably spritzy, but full of fresh, lively aromas and flavors of bubble gum, bananas, pear juice, and cherries. The hype that surrounds its release has brought disadvantages, too: A general belief has emerged that it has to be consumed quickly and that it is already too old by New Year's Day. In fact, it is a fine wine for several months after its release and can easily enliven the first outdoor meal or barbecue in the spring.

BEAUJOLAIS

This is how the general red and white wines of the appellation would be labeled. Most regular Beaujolais comes from the lesser vineyards in the southern half of Beaujolais, where the colder limestone soils dominate. The reds, made by carbonic maceration, are generally good but simple, just what ordinary Beaujolais should be!

Gamay vines in the village of St-Amour

BEAUJOLAIS SUPÉRIEUR

As elsewhere in France (and Italy for that matter), this tag simply indicates an alcohol level one degree higher than the minimum for the basic appellation wine.

BEAUJOLAIS-VILLAGES

Red wines can claim this appellation if they are made from vineyards located in any of thirty-eight specified villages in the northern section of Beaujolais. Coming from the harder, granitic soils, they usually have more depth and character than straight Beaujolais, with riper fruit and smoother texture. The wines can be labeled as simply Beaujolais-Villages, or, if the grapes all came from just one of the thirty-eight villages, the specific name of the village can be attached, as in Beaujolais-Villages-Lancié. Other good villages in this group include Blacé, Beaujeu, Lantignié, Leynes, and Quincié.

BEAUJOLAIS CRUS

This is a collective category that includes wines from an additional ten villages in the northern section of Beaujolais that have been singled out as producing wines of distinctive quality and individuality. They are more full-bodied than regular Beaujolais or Beaujolais-Villages and in some instances can improve with as much as eight to ten years of aging. In 2009, two studies were undertaken simultaneously to accurately map the soils, topography, and climate of the entire Beaujolais region, with a view to eventually creating a classification. Presumably the ten villages below will stand out as having their own unique *terroir*, but other classified *crus* may be identified as well.

ST-AMOUR

This is the northernmost of the ten *cru* villages, and the thinner limestone soils result in a lighter-bodied wine with attractive stone fruit flavors.

JULIÉNAS

The greater presence of schist and granitic rock in this village provide for a wine with greater power and depth of flavors that can be slow to evolve but rounds out nicely after three to five years of aging into an attractive fruit medley of strawberries and stone fruits.

CHÉNAS

There is generally too much sandy soil in this village to consistently produce great Beaujolais, but some producers restrict their output to wines made from grapes grown in the more granitic soils in the western part of the appellation, producing wines with some complexity of strawberry fruit and a slightly woodsy character.

MOULIN-À-VENT

This is perhaps the most famous of the *cru* villages, its name taken from an ancient windmill in the midst of the vineyards. It is also arguably the finest of the *cru* Beaujolais, with a tightly knit structure of quite dense fruit, supple tannins, and smooth texture. Its finer quality probably derives from the presence of manganese deposits in the soil along with the granite and schist. In good vintages, Moulin-à-Vent will mature well, sometimes taking twenty years to develop its full potential.

FLEURIE

As might be expected from the name, this is indeed the most flowery of the *cru* wines in Beaujolais, with floral aromas and ripe fruit abounding, like eating a perfectly ripe peach on a sunny summer day! Their light to medium body makes them tempting to drink young, but a few years of aging will reward the drinker with more complexity and a smooth, lingering finish.

CHIROUBLES

The wine from this village is always the lightest and most fragrant, with violet aromas and light strawberry and cherry flavors. Its relative lightness is due to the village's higher elevation and cooler temperatures in the vineyards.

MORGON

This village also produces a wine capable of substantial aging, up to twenty years. The weight and power of the wine is again attributed to unusual soil elements, such as manganese and iron oxides that seem to create greater complexity and layering of ripe plum flavors and a firmer structure. For those with patience, the wait will be rewarded with a mouthful of smooth cherry and plum fruit enrobed in bitter chocolate.

RÉGNIÉ

Cru status came to this village as late as 1988, and it is still playing catch-up to the other, more established names.

Most of the wines are lively, fruity wines, a notch above Beaujolais-Villages, but generally simpler than the other *cru* wines. A few producers such as Roux and Aucoeur offer fuller, more structured examples.

BROUILLY

This appellation is named after the Mont Brouilly, which dominates the landscape. The hillsides provide the primary location for the vineyards, though the Brouilly appellation is restricted to the lower, flatter segments, producing a wine that is lighter and simpler than some of the other *cru* wines, but with attractive, grapey fruit character. The lighter, more perfumed style can also be attributed to the occasional (and legal) inclusion of a few white grape varieties, including Chardonnay and Aligoté.

CÔTE DE BROUILLY

This appellation is restricted to the upper portion of the Mont Brouilly, and the greater mineral content in the soil provides for more structure and a greater depth of flavor in the wine, with some potential for aging. The firmer structure is also reflective of the fact that Pinot Noir and Pinot Gris may be used in making the wine.

Among the finer producers of Beaujolais are Beaudet, Brun, Cheysson, Joseph Drouhin, Georges DuBoeuf, Fessy, Foillard, Louis Jadot, Lapierre, Tête, and Thorin.

Jura and Savoie

The vineyards of Jura and Savoie are located on high-altitude clay and limestone foothills in the mountainous region to the east of Burgundy. Their wines are seldom exported, perhaps because they are well appreciated by the locals, perhaps because of confusion over the different grape types and styles produced. The regions produce more white and sparkling wines, with smaller quantities of rosé and red, all of which are enjoyable mostly for their fresh fruit character, giving some truth to the notion here that the best vintage is the most recent one. Historically there are two important specialty items: **VIN JAUNE** (similar to Sherry) and **VIN DE PAILLE** (similar to Recioto di Soave; see page 407).

The continental climate provides warm summer and fall months, but the winters can be very cold, a factor that places limitations on the grape varieties that will fully ripen in this region. With such cold winters, the vines often get a late start to the growing season, so grape varieties that like cooler temperatures and mature slowly in a warm fall are preferred. These include the classic cold-climate Burgundian varieties of Chardonnay and Pinot Noir, as well as the local white grape peculiarities of Savagnin, Molette, Jacquère, and Rousette, and the local red varieties, Poulsard and Trousseau.

JURA

For wines of the Jura, the main white grape is Savagnin, a late-ripening variety that can contribute a nutty nose and some body to a white wine. The red grape Poulsard is appreciated for its red berry aromatics, and its thin skin and low color pigmentation make it highly suitable for rosé production. The red Trousseau provides darker color, a touch of spicy pepperiness, and higher levels of ripeness and sugar that provide firmer fruit and more structure in a blend.

The whole Jura region is covered by the Côtes du Jura appellation, which also includes the subappellations of Château Chalon, L'Etoile, and Arbois.

CÔTES DU JURA

Since this appellation is the largest in this region, it is no surprise that it producers a wide range of wines, including light, fresh, and bracing sparkling wines; dry, nutty whites (from Savagnin and Chardonnay); and light, easy-drinking reds (from Poulsard, Trousseau, and Pinot Noir). There are also some producers who specialize in *crémant* (sparkling) wines, *vins jaunes*, and *vins de paille*.

CRÉMANT DU JURA This can be an interestingly fresh and flavorful sparkling, though somewhat expensive for what it offers. It is usually made from a blend of Savagnin, Chardonnay, Pinot Noir, and Pinot Gris, with all four varieties providing good flavor and body and a lemony, apple/nut flavor profile.

VIN JAUNE This "yellow wine" is made by fermenting the juice of Savagnin grapes and then aging the wine at least six years in oak, with air contact, before it is released. As in Jerez, Spain, a layer of *flor* yeast grows on the surface of the wine, providing a protective layer so that it does not brown (see page 440). The typically nutty smell of oxidation evident in a Sherry is also present in these wines, and their flavor has been compared with that of a dry *fino* Sherry. While *finos* are best drunk young, *vins jaunes* can last for decades.

VIN DE PAILLE The production of *vin de paille* (straw wine) requires that grapes be dried on straw mats or hung until they lose some of their water content, as in the *recioto* wines of Veneto in northeastern Italy (see page 407). Once again, the Savagnin grape is preferred, and after the drying process has concentrated the flavors and sugars, the juice is fermented and then aged for up to four years in small wooden barrels. The result is a sweet, concentrated, dark-colored, luscious dessert wine with scents of dried fruits and nuts. *Vins de paille* are rare and expensive, and mostly sold in half bottles.

CHÂTEAU CHALON

This is not a single estate, but an appellation named after one of the four villages that produce *vin jaune* under this appellation name.

L'ÉTOILE

This small appellation (175 acres/70 hectares) grows mostly Savagnin and Chardonnay to make herbal scented dry whites, delicate sparkling wines (labeled as L'Étoile Mousseux), and *vin jaune*.

ARBOIS

The Arbois appellation can produce medium-weight, almost Burgundy-style reds from Pinot Noir, or lighter, fresher versions from Poulsard or Trousseau. Chardonnay and Savagnin are used to make fresh, appley, and citric but nutty whites, as well as small quantities of *vin jaune* and *vin de paille*.

SAVOIE

Typical white grapes in Savoie include the widely planted Jacquère, a late ripener that tends to produce light-bodied dry white wines with a slightly smoky aroma. The lower-yielding Roussette, also known as Altesse, produces spicy aromas and a richer and fuller texture, while the Molette is prized for its delicate fruit and high acidity, making it ideal for sparkling wine production. The red grape Mondeuse makes an unusual appearance here, providing deep red color and structure, with a hint of bitter almond flavor. Finally, the white Chasselas grape, widely used in eastern France and Switzerland, helps provide something of the mountain-fresh alpine meadow quality to the region's wines.

The whole region of Savoie extends over a wide area, but the appellations are dispersed in much smaller and separated segments throughout the region. They include the broad Vin de Savoie appellation, as well as the smaller appellations of Seyssel, Crépy, and Vin du Bugey.

VIN DE SAVOIE

This appellation can be used for white, rosé, red, and sparkling wines. The *méthode champenoise* sparkling wines are made in an attractive light style from local grape varieties with Chardonnay and Pinot Gris. The white wine labeling system is a little complicated, even confusing: If Roussette is the grape used to make the wine, it is usually labeled as Roussette de Savoie, or the Roussette name will appear along with the village name that made the wine; if the village names of Marignan, Marin, or Ripaille appear, the wine was made from Chasselas; if there is no mention of grape type or place, the wine was probably made from Jacquère.

The general Vin de Savoie appellation is used for red and rosé wines made mostly from Pinot Noir or Gamay, with some Mondeuse to add color, weight, and peppery flavors, whereas the village names Jongieux, Cruet, St-Jean de la Porte, and Chautagne indicate that the Mondeuse was the primary grape used.

SEYSSEL

This appellation can be used for still and *mousseux* (sparkling) white wines. The scattered vineyards are on limestone slopes on the banks of the Rhône river, giving the Molette grape a particularly spritely, high-acid vivacity, making it ideal as the dominant grape for the *méthode champenoise* sparkling wines, with some Chasselas and Altesse blended in. The Seyssel dry white wines are made mostly from Chasselas, plus at least 10 percent Altesse to give the wines their distinctive alpine flower scents.

CRÉPY

Chasselas vines are planted in this appellation south of Lake Geneva to produce light-bodied, dry whites that sometimes offer a pleasant a hint of effervescence when bottled off the lees. Slightly fuller, softer versions are the result of experimentation with malolactic fermentation.

VIN DU BUGEY

All of the wines of the newly recognized Bugey appellation offer excellent value in sparkling, white, rosé, and red styles. Local grape types are carefully blended with the better-known Gamay and Pinot Noir for reds and rosés, or with Chardonnay and Pinot Gris for whites. In general, Bugey wines are well made, fresh, and clean; the Mondeuse is also used for red wines to add fuller weight and flavor dimension.

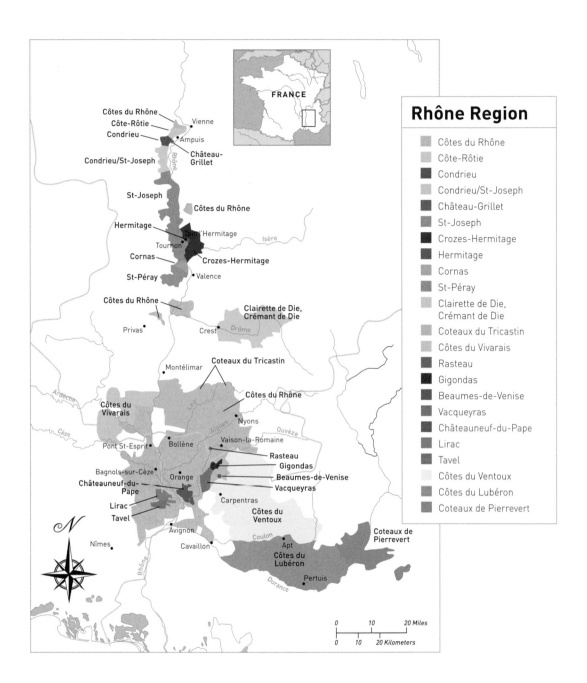

Rhône Region

- Côtes du Rhône
- Côte-Rôtie
- Condrieu
- Condrieu/St-Joseph
- Château-Grillet
- St-Joseph
- Crozes-Hermitage
- Hermitage
- Cornas
- St-Péray
- Clairette de Die, Crémant de Die
- Coteaux du Tricastin
- Côtes du Vivarais
- Rasteau
- Gigondas
- Beaumes-de-Venise
- Vacqueyras
- Châteauneuf-du-Pape
- Lirac
- Tavel
- Côtes du Ventoux
- Côtes du Lubéron
- Coteaux de Pierrevert

Rhône Valley

• •

Between the Alps to the east and the Massif Central mountains to the west, the viticultural area of the Rhône Valley stretches for 125 miles/200 kilometers between Vienne in the north and Avignon in the south, with three subsections of approximately equal length, of which only the northern and southern subsection grow vines for *appellation protégée* wines. The Rhône River begins in the Swiss

Alps and gathers force from melting snows and streams as it makes its way south to the Mediterranean. It passes through Burgundy and then on through the vineyards of the Rhône Valley. The river serves as a moderating influence, and as in other fine wine regions, the best vineyard sites are often the closest to the water.

The **MISTRAL**, the powerful wind that is particularly prevalent in the southern part of the valley, can blow hard enough to strip vines of their shoots, leaves, and fruit. As a result, many of the best vineyard sites there use cypress or poplar trees as a windbreak, and vines have traditionally been head-pruned low to the ground to diminish the effect of the winds. One positive effect of the mistral is to decrease the risk of mildew or rot by drying the plants.

The appellation known as the Côtes du Rhône is the second-largest wine-producing area after Bordeaux, producing around 87 million gallons/3.3 million hectoliters of wine, of which approximately 95 percent is red with very small production levels of sparkling, rosé, dry white, and sweet white.

The Rhône area has continued its expansion and now covers 197,000 acres/80,000 hectares, achieved mostly by upgrading lesser areas to *appellation d'origine protégée* status. In some ways this has encouraged the marketing of inferior wine under a prestigious name, but there are also signs of improvements in vineyard management and winemaking techniques that have resulted in vastly superior wine being more readily available in the worldwide market. The selection of better rootstocks, the identification of specific clones of the more noble grape varieties, and the use of cooler temperature-controlled fermentation have all contributed to an overall improvement in the quality of wines from the area. In the past, field blends of different grapes were often harvested and fermented together. Today the better producers harvest and ferment each grape variety separately, and the subsequent blend defines the producer's style.

Differences in methods of production mean that there is a wide variety of wine styles from this large region. For a simple regional appellation wine, quick pressing and fermentation without a long maceration of grape skins make for a fruity, forward wine that can be drunk young. Every kind of vessel can be found, from large stainless steel tanks to small new oak barrels, with obvious impact on the wine style. The more traditional approach has been to use large 600-liter/160-gallon wooden casks called **DEMI-MUIDS**, or the even larger **FOUDRES**. New, small oak barrels are more likely to be found in the northern section, but, as elsewhere, experimentation is widespread, allowing for stylistic differences among producers.

As in other areas in France, there are different levels of appellation within the Côtes du Rhône, generally differentiated as regional and village level; there is no official, *appellation protégée*–sanctioned *cru* system, though some producers like to use the term *cru* for the best wines from their individual vineyards, known in this region as **LIEUX-DITS**. At the regional level, the appellations are the basic Côtes du Rhône and the presumably superior Côtes du Rhône–Villages. Although the theory of *appellation protégée* provides for the production of regional wines from anywhere within the whole length of the Côtes du Rhône, the practical reality is that the vast majority of the regional appellations are within the southern section. We will describe the grapes, climate, appellations, and wines of the northern Rhône first, and then the grapes, climate, appellations, and wines of the southern Rhône, including the more general, regional appellations that abound there.

NORTHERN RHÔNE

GRAPES

The general philosophy in this region is to use one grape variety for any wine, with Viognier being the grape of choice for the small quantity of wine produced in the two white-only wine appellations, and Syrah being used for red wines. However, some of the principally red wine appellations also make a small amount of white wine from Marsanne and Roussanne, and some of the red wine appellations allow a small percentage of the white Viognier to be added to the red wines.

CLIMATE

Covering about 36 miles/58 kilometers from Vienne in the north to Valence in the south, this is an area of Continental climate, with hot summers that give way fairly early on to a cool autumn and cold winter. Rainfall is substantial but not always predictable, often at the mercy of the various winds that may or may not bring clouds and rain depending on whether they are the warm southerly winds or the colder northern version. Though the mistral is felt more to the south, there is enough of a wind problem here to require that each vine be protected with a four-stake support framework. The gradient of many of the vineyard slopes funnels the winds, making them blow more strongly, but also allows for greater exposure to the sun, an all-important element in making world-class wines. The cooler fall months mean that relatively early–ripening grapes are preferred (Syrah and Viognier), and the variability of sunshine hours and rainfall make this a more marginal climate that can result in significant differences in wine quality from vintage to vintage.

APPELLATIONS

With the exception of the sprawling St-Joseph appellation and the junior Brézème, all of the appellations here can be considered as village-level appellations. The white wine appellations, described first, are Condrieu and Château Grillet, and, from north to south, the red wine appellations are Côte Rôtie, St-Joseph, Crozes-Hermitage, Hermitage, Cornas, St-Péray, and Brézème.

CONDRIEU   Rising on steep, terraced, granitic hillsides, the Condrieu appellation is one of the wonders of the ancient and modern wine world. First, the hillsides themselves look impossible to work, and the region has certainly witnessed times of neglect and abandoned vineyards. Second, the grape growers here specialize in Viognier, a difficult grape to grow because of its susceptibility to numerous diseases and rots. And yet, not only have a few diehards persisted through the years, but the appellation is now thriving again, riding the crest of a wave of renewed interest in Rhône wines that has resulted in increased acreage both here and elsewhere in the world. Currently, the Condrieu acreage stands at about 230 acres/ 92 hectares, up from a pathetic low of 25 acres/10 hectares in the 1960s.

The reason for the persistence of those resilient growers was and is the glorious, unique wine that Viognier produces from this *terroir*. Anybody who tries it is struck immediately by the exuberant but pleasant exotic fruit-salad aroma, a bustling medley of guavas, papayas, bananas, and pears, with honey and floral scents. On the palate, the wine is deceptively dry, but with a wonderfully creamy texture; mouth-filling flavors of ripe tropical fruits; and a clean, mineral finish from the *arzelle* soil. However, Viognier wines are generally low in acidity, and these wines are best drunk within a year or two of production, before they start to "dry out" and lose the freshness that is their primary quality.

The full fruit qualities of the wine are generally enhanced by cool stainless steel fermentation, though a few producers seek more structure in their wine with new barrel fermentation. Malolactic fermentation is not usually preferred, except in any vintage when there may be too much sharp acidity left in the wine. Notable producers include Vernay, Château du Rozay, Perret, Villard, and Cuilleron.

CHÂTEAU-GRILLET   This very small single-estate appellation of only 7.5 acres/3 hectares lies completely within the Condrieu appellation and has historically been revered for its special wine. The wines are 100 percent Viognier and very similar in style to Condrieu, but a

TOP: *Typical vineyards of the northern Rhône* BOTTOM: *The terraced vineyards of Côte-Rôtie*

good deal more expensive. If there are any factors to denote it as extra special, they may be the distinction of a higher level of mica in the soil; a loose, fine, crumbled granite base soil; and a steep, south-southeast-facing incline that creates a natural sun trap for optimum ripening of the grapes. Although it is a fine wine, with a streak of steely nervosity running through it, the high price may be based on its rarity rather than anything else.

CÔTE-RÔTIE The "roasted slope" has been producing reds of great power and finesse from Syrah grapes planted on steep south -and southeast-facing slopes for at least two millennia. Despite a checkered history, including some periods when fine vineyard sites were abandoned, the area today encompasses about 500 acres/200 hectares around the village of Ampuis, planted mostly with Syrah but including some white Viognier, which by law may comprise up to 20 percent of the wine, though most producers use only 5 to 10 percent of the white grapes to add exotic aromas and grapey freshness to the blend. The original appellation was restricted to the hillsides known as the Côte Brune and Côte Blonde behind Ampuis, but the current boundaries extend northward to St-Cyr and southward to Tupin. The precipitous incline of the slopes requires that the vineyards be terraced, and must all be worked by hand.

The wines of Côte-Rôtie tend to have a perfumed violet aroma with concentrated fruit flavors, a full body, and a long finish. The best display other complex aromas and tastes such as spicy, peppery notes, smoky, toasted oak, with dense black currant, plum, and black raspberry character. The wines also display a distinctly mineral note, said to derive from the *arzelle,* the local name for the topsoil, which is comprised of broken mica schist and pebbles.

Traditionally, the original appellation has stylistically been subdivided into the Côte Brune section and the Côte Blonde, with the former having darker, heavier, iron-rich elements in the soils that make for more powerful wines than the Côte Blonde, where the vines are planted in lighter soils of limestone and granite-laced sand. Because of this, wines from the Côte Blonde section are generally approachable at a younger age. Producers have historically referred to their wines as being Côte Brune or Blonde, or, more frequently, a blend of the two. However, the use of such names can be misleading since there are individual *lieux-dits* called Côte Brune and Côte Blonde in the general slopes of the same name, and current European Union legislation states that an individual place name may be used on a label only if it is specified on the official *appella-tion* map. If Côte Brune or Côte Blonde is used on a label, all of the grapes for that wine should have come from the named site, not just from the general slope.

One of the area's leading producers, Guigal, has led the way in reducing the use of the general terms, separating out the harvest from specific *lieux-dits* such as La Landonne and La Garde. Ironically, two of the "single vineyard" wines that brought Guigal to international prominence, La Mouline and La Turque, are not official sites on the *appellation* map but are really subplots within the Côte Blonde *lieu-dit* and Côte Brune *lieu-dit* respectively. Guigal continues to use the names Mouline and Turque on his labels as trademarks.

Wines from these individual *lieux-dits* are important since they represent the epitome of the Côte Rôtie style, showing not only everything that one would expect from a great northern Rhône Syrah, but a singular identity of place that is unique to that grape in that climate. Other producers with a similar mindset include Champet, Gerin, Bernard, Gaillard, Rostaing, Jasmin, and Ogier.

ST-JOSEPH The story of the St-Joseph appellation is a sad but all too familiar one: a small, discrete appellation producing wines typical of the region, soil, and grape, inexplicably extended into areas where the soil and exposure have resulted in wines that have little in common with Rhône Valley Syrah. Intense, dark-hued, and deeply flavored wines still can be found from the original appellation area just across the river from the famous Hermitage appellation. However, the extended appellation now stretches 40 miles/65 kilometers on the west bank of the river northward to Condrieu, even overlapping that appellation. The vineyard land here is often flat, lacking the desired southern exposure and mineral soils, and producing much lighter, simpler wines, still pleasant, but without structure or longevity of Syrah from the other appellations. Red St-Joseph is allowed to include up to 10 percent of Marsanne or Roussanne, making it an even lighter, fruitier wine, best enjoyed within two to four years.

About 20 percent of total production is white wine, made mostly from Marsanne, with some Roussanne included. From some producers, there are lesser, disappointing whites that seem dull and lifeless; the best have concentrated peach, apricot, and orange marmalade flavors encased in a rich texture, with a zingy, fresh streak of acidity. To capture their freshness, they are best drunk fairly young. J. L. Grippat and J. L. Chave are two producers offering lush aromatic examples. Domaine Chèze,

Domaine Courbis, and Bernard Gripa produce fine red wines that can be enjoyed between two and eight years from the vintage.

HERMITAGE At the village of Tain l'Hermitage, the Rhône River travels in an east-southeast direction for a short way, allowing for the vineyards on the hill of Hermitage to be exposed almost directly southward. This is by far the most famous appellation of the northern Rhône, covering 360 acres/146 hectares of steep vineyards that retain the sun's warmth to bring the red Syrah and white Roussanne and Marsanne to full ripeness. More than 75 percent of the plantings are Syrah, and the red wines may include up to 15 percent white grapes; as in Côte Rôtie, most producers want their red wines to be a pure expression of Syrah, and the white varieties are usually left out of the red wine.

Hermitage red wines undergo extended maceration and usually spend a year to two in small barrels before being bottled. The opaque, densely colored wines have a range of scents that sing of dark berries, pepper, spices, cassis, smoke, tar, and an herbal mix that is reminiscent of the region's GARRIGUE, a mix of bay laurel, thyme, and lavender aromas. The great depth and variety of fruity, herbal, and earthy flavors in these full-bodied wines is followed by a rich fruit finish. However, it is generally acknowledged that a great red Hermitage needs a decade or more of bottle maturation before it even begins to show its majesty, at which stage it offers a beguiling blend of dried fruit and leather aromas with overtones of game meat and licorice on the nose and palate.

As elsewhere in the northern Rhône, the appellation has historically been divided into smaller vineyard plots referred to as *lieux-dits*, and the variations in soil across the hill account for the differences in wines that come from these individual plots. At the western end of the hill, high levels of granite with iron oxides in the soil base make it possible for the Bessards plot to produce wines of structure, depth, and substance, with deep fruit character hidden by massive tannins that will allow for great longevity. Moving eastward, more chalk in the soil base means that the wines from the Méal *lieu-dit* show softer tannins and a lighter, more delicate structure, while the southernmost MAS of Greffieux has darker, richer soils that bring out a warmer, more open fruit structure in the wines.

Understandably then, the finest Hermitage wines come from those producers who have access to grapes from several of the different *lieux-dits*, thereby allowing them to blend the product from each vineyard as the vintage dictates. For example, Gérard Chave, acknowledged as one of the master blenders and producers of Hermitage, sources grapes from such sites as Les Bessards, Méal, Beaumes, Diognières, L'Hermite, Les Roucoles, and Péléat, while Paul Jaboulet Aîné produces one of the richest, most complex wines of the area, known as Hermitage La Chappelle, named after the chapel atop the slope of

The famous chapel atop the Hermitage hill

Hermitage, blended from the finest *mas* on the hillside. In contrast, wines from lesser producers can be disappointingly light and incomplete.

Even farther east on the hill, where limestone is more present in the vineyards, the Marsanne and Roussanne dominate. Here again we see the juxtaposition of ancient and modern, with some producers making a fresh, forward, early drinking white wine, with floral, citrus peel, and golden apple character, while others stick to an older style that needs age to develop a slightly oxidized, nutty overtone, with dried fruit, marmalade, and white truffle notes. There is also a very small production of *vins de paille*, or straw wines, made by drying the grapes on straw mats to produce a sweet, oxidized wine.

For red and white Hermitage, some of the most respected producers include Chapoutier, Chave, Jaboulet Aîné, Guigal, Tardieu-Laurent, Sorrel, and Grippat.

CROZES-HERMITAGE The Crozes-Hermitage appellation covers eleven villages totaling 2,500 acres (1,000 hectares) that skirt the Hermitage appellation; 4.5 million bottles of red wine and 500,000 of white wine are produced annually. Crozes-Hermitage wines have the same authorized grapes as the more revered Hermitage wines and are therefore similar in style but not as concentrated in flavor. Some of the areas of Crozes-Hermitage that produce fine, structured wines are directly to the north of Tain l'Hermitage, closest to the river on south-facing slopes with similar granitic soils as the western end of the Hermitage appellation. In the eastern, middle section, on the plateau away from the river, the soils become progressively denser with more clay, making red wines that lack structure and balance, although in the extreme eastern section there are pockets of limestone where the white grape varieties can produce wines of fine fruit structure and elegance.

The plateau continues to the south of Tain, where the presence of large crystalline stones provides both a minerality in the soil and a heat storage system that allows the vines to continue to mature long after sunset. Here the Syrah can produce wines of extraordinary character and depth, exemplified by Jaboulet Aîné's Domaine de Thalabert, where low yields, older vines, and barrel aging combine to produce a wine with floral, fruit, and spicy notes that is rich on the palate and can be enjoyed between three to ten years after the vintage. Wines such as these can be very fine, less-expensive alternatives to Hermitage, though in general red Crozes-Hermitage is thought of as a lesser wine than its noble cousin.

Like white Hermitage, white Crozes-Hermitage is made from Marsanne and Roussanne, increasingly in a fresh, attractively fruity, early-drinking style, with the occasional exceptional vintage producing wines that age to a complex of nuts, floral perfume, and dried citrus peel in a smooth, honeyed texture.

Some producers of note include Fayolle, Jaboulet Aîné, Chapoutier, Combier, Graillot, and Pochon.

CORNAS This appellation has fully delivered on its promise of offering powerful, well-structured wines with ripe fruit character and complexity. Modern approaches, especially to tannin management, in the vineyard and in winemaking have made it possible for Cornas to throw off its "rustic" label and earn the recognition it deserves.

Currently there are approximately 200 acres/80 hectares planted with Syrah vines, although the official appellation covers an area that is seven times greater than this. The better vineyards are shielded from the mistral winds, on terraced hillsides of granite with some limestone. The word Cornas derives from the Celtic word for "scorched earth," and the heat-retentive soils and Syrah grape combine in the best sites to make a wine with deep color and chocolate, tar, prune, and black raspberry aromas, with rich fruit, earthy, spicy, and smoked-meat characteristics.

Some producers are using grapes from the lighter limestone soils and modern winemaking techniques to reduce the depth of flavor and color and to produce a simpler, lighter wine for early consumption. In contrast, August Clape and Noël Verset are traditional producers who continue to offer richly scented and flavorful wines. Jean Luc Colombo's Les Ruchets, Les Terres Brulées, and Force One are elegant examples of modern-style Cornas. Other notable producers include Delas, Jaboulet, Courbis, and Juge.

BRÉZÈME This is a curious appellation, lying physically and philosophically between two styles. Growing only Syrah grapes for red wine production, it is located about halfway between the northern and southern Rhône Valley, and represents a halfway stage between the more lowly, regional appellation of Côtes du Rhône–Villages and the more individualistic single village appellations. Labeled as Brézème–Côtes du Rhône, the wines are indicative of their halfway status.

ST-PÉRAY The rapidly diminishing St-Péray appellation consists of 150 acres/60 hectares that produce white still and sparkling wines from Marsanne and Roussanne grapes. They are not as rich or complex as their neighbors made from the same grapes in the more northerly appellations of the Rhône. The moderately priced sparkling wines are made by the *méthode champenoise,* though they generally lack vibrancy.

CLAIRETTE DE DIE   The village of Die is located on the Drôme River, 25 miles/40 kilometers to the east of the Rhône River, about halfway between the northern and southern Rhône regions. Its best and most famous appellation is the Clairette de Die, a sparkling wine made from at least 75 percent Muscat grapes with the balance being Clairette grapes. The method used is the *méthode dioise ancéstrale,* in which the wine is bottled before the fermentation is complete. The wine has no yeast added but goes through a continued fermentation in the bottle, trapping the carbon dioxide gas to make the wine sparkle. After four months or more, the wine is filtered and rebottled under pressure. The result is a delightfully fragrant, grapey, and refreshing sparkler.

There is a secondary sparkling wine called Crémant de Die, made from 100 percent Clairette grapes by the *méthode champenoise.* This is relatively dull stuff that lacks the seductive Muscat fragrance and aroma. Some dry, still, similarly dull Clairette-based wines are also made under the new Côteaux de Die appellation.

SOUTHERN RHÔNE

GRAPES

More than twenty grape varieties are allowed by current laws for the wines from the southern Rhône appellations, and, as in the northern Rhône, white grapes are often added to red wines. The signature red grape here is usually the Grenache, with Syrah and Mourvèdre providing most of the balance, and even smaller contributions from the likes of Cinsaut and Carignan. The most widely planted white grapes are the Clairette and the Grenache Blanc, both of which generally need a bit of a lift from more perfumed, aromatic varieties such as Marsanne and Roussanne and the more marginal Bourboulenc and Picpoul Gris. Almost all wines produced in the southern Rhône are blends of at least two grape varieties.

CLIMATE

Compared with the northern section of the Rhône Valley, the south is considerably warmer and drier, and can usually count on warmer temperatures in the fall to bring grapes to a level of sweet, luscious ripeness, a quality that is a characteristic of the best wines. As the Rhône River continues southward past Montélimar, moving toward its delta plain, the vineyard area becomes broader and the landscape begins to flatten out, with less dramatically steep inclines but smaller tributary river valleys. This provides for more variations in soil and wine styles, though there is generally more even consistency in wine quality from vintage to vintage.

APPELLATIONS

The southern Rhône includes most of the vineyard land that is categorized under the regional appellations of Côtes du Rhône and Côtes du Rhône–Villages, as well as the peripheral regional appellations of Coteaux du Tricastin, Côtes du Vivarais, Côtes du Ventoux, Côtes du Lubéron, and Costières de Nîmes. We will describe the wines from those areas first, followed by the village-level appellations, which, from north to south, include Vinsobres, Rasteau, Gigondas, Vacqueyras, Beaumes-de-Venise, Châteauneuf-du-Pape, Lirac, and Tavel.

CÔTES DU RHÔNE   As might be expected, this is a huge appellation with 99,000 acres/40,000 hectares planted to a broad range of red and white grape types. Theoretically, the appellation covers the northern and southern sections of the valley; indeed, there are some very fine Côtes du Rhône Syrah-driven reds from the northern section, most notably from Guigal, Colombo, and Jaboulet. But the majority of the 171 villages entitled to Côtes du Rhône status are in the south. Much of the wine is produced by large *négociants* or cooperatives using carbonic maceration to market a simple, light quaffing wine. While these may never be considered as serious, they should not be dismissed without consideration, for they are usually reliable, sound, honest red and white wines, perfect for everyday drinking. For red wines, regulations stipulate at least 40 percent of the grape mix be Grenache, except in the northern Rhône versions, where Syrah dominates.

Occasionally individual estates with a mind to quality include a simple Côtes du Rhône wine in their portfolio, applying the same parameters of grape selection and winemaking as to their more revered appellations, and thereby offering a Côtes du Rhône appellation wine that can show depth, complexity, balance, and even intrigue at a relatively low price. Good examples would include La Vieille Ferme, Coudoulet de Beaucastel, and the more recent Domaine Gramenon.

CÔTES DU RHÔNE-VILLAGES   Since the Côtes du Rhône appellation was first implemented in the late 1930s, gradual steps have been taken to identify villages capable of producing wines of superior quality on a consistent basis. The Côtes du Rhône–Villages appellation now covers some 237,000 acres/9,600 hectares scattered through ninety-five villages, of which eighteen have the right to affix their name to Côtes du Rhône–Villages to be listed as the name of the wine. Wines claiming this appellation are subject to more stringent regulations concerning grape types (a choice of nine, rather than twenty-four), lower yields, and higher levels of sugar/ripeness at harvest. All things being equal then, these should be better wines. To stress quality, regulations specify a minimum of 50 percent Grenache and 20 percent Syrah or Mourvèdre in the blend for red wines.

The same divergence of styles applies to this appellation as to Côtes du Rhône, with the more intense styles usually costing 25 percent to 30 percent more. Of the eighteen villages that can attach their name to Côtes du Rhône–Villages, the more esteemed red wine villages tend to be Cairanne, Sablet, Valréas, Séguret, and Visan, while Côtes du Rhône–Villages Chusclan and Côtes du Rhône–Villages Laudun are fine regional white wines.

COTEAUX DU TRICASTIN Located just below the town of Montélimar on the eastern banks of the Rhône, the Coteaux du Tricastin appellation produces mostly pleasant, very enjoyable, lighter-bodied red wines from a blend of the traditional Grenache, Syrah, Mourvèdre, Cinsaut, and Carignan

Typical bush-trained vines in the southern Rhône

red grapes. A small amount of fresh, dry rosé wine is made from the same grapes as for red wine, and an increasing quantity of fresh, fruity, dry whites can be found, blended from mostly Viognier, Marsanne, and Roussanne.

CÔTES DU VIVARAIS Across the river from Tricastin lies the new *appellation protégée* area of Côtes du Vivarais, where red, rosé, and white wines are produced in a fresh, clean style from the usual southern Rhône varieties. The reason for the area's elevation to *appellation protégée* status is not yet apparent.

CÔTES DU VENTOUX Directly east of the city of Avignon lie the Côtes du Ventoux. If this appellation grew apples, they would be deliciously fresh and fragrantly sweet for six to eight weeks around September and October. And then they wouldn't! And so it is with the wines: fresh, fruity, simple red wines (mostly) that are delightful when young. They owe much of their style to the limestone-based vineyards of Grenache, Syrah, Mourvèdre, and Cinsaut planted high on Mont Ventoux, which blocks the mistral and provides cooling breezes. Around 80 percent of the wines come from cooperatives that generally specialize in the lighter styles. La Vieille Ferme and Paul Jaboulet Aîné offer slightly sturdier examples of these inexpensive wines.

CÔTES DU LUBÉRON South of the Côtes du Ventoux, the Côtes du Lubéron appellation has similar limestone soils distributed throughout the valleys of the Montagne du Lubéron, and its wines are similarly fresh, fruity, and vibrant, as well as inexpensive. Red, white, and rosé wines are produced, with Grenache and Syrah being the main red grapes; Ugni Blanc, Clairette, and Bourboulenc lead the whites. All three colors are best drunk young. Some of the finer producers include La Vieille Ferme, Domaine de la Citadelle, and Château de l'Isolette.

COSTIÈRES DE NÎMES This is an extremely large but underdeveloped appellation located in the southwest corner of the Côtes du Rhône, between Nîmes and Arles. Eighty percent of the production is red wines based on Grenache, Syrah, Mourvèdre, and Cinsaut, with rosé wines accounting for around 10 percent of production. The appellation offers plenty of south-facing slopes with the same kind of pebbly soil structure found elsewhere in the Rhône. In general, the wines have been coarse, with the reds just a bit too meaty and the rosés a little too spicy.

Tellingly, perhaps, much of the land intended for *appellation protégée* planting of approved varieties has in fact been planted with the famous international varieties like Chardonnay and Sauvignon Blanc for the production of inexpensive varietally labeled wines at the IGP level, but marketed around the world.

VINSOBRES This is a new appellation making a deserved name for itself with well-crafted versions of mostly Grenache-Syrah-Mourvèdre blends.

RASTEAU There are two distinctly different styles of wine produced in the Rasteau appellation. The first is the range of red and white wines that fit into the Côtes du Rhône–Villages appellation as attractive, fruity wines with a touch of peppery Syrah in the reds; the whites are less noteworthy. What is worth seeking out, however, are the **VINS DOUX NATURELS** that are also produced in this appellation from Grenache grapes, fortified with high-alcohol grape spirit (brandy) to arrest the fermentation process before all the sugar is converted. The resulting sweet wines contain about 21 percent alcohol, and the practice of aging the wines in small oak casks in open daylight also gives some of the wines a *rancio* character, similar to Madeira or Vin Santo. One version leaves the skins in contact with the fermenting must, resulting in a darker, tawny-colored wine, or there is a white version made by separating the juice from the skins before fermentation starts.

GIGONDAS This appellation (the name is from the Latin *iocunditas,* or "happy place") is to the south of Rasteau at the foothills of the Dentelles de Montmirail, a small range of limestone-rich mountains. The soil on the lower, flatter vineyard land is rich, red clay with alluvial silts, producing full, rich, dark-colored wines, whereas gravelly, marly mix on the foothills and the limestone-influenced higher slopes produce progressively leaner wines, well-structured and tightly knit. Once again, the best wines come from those producers who have access to different grape varieties from different sites, allowing them to blend the best of each vintage. The red wines are made from a mix of Grenache, to a maximum of 80 percent, with the balance provided by Syrah, Mourvèdre, and Cinsaut, producing powerful wines with a dark plum color and a nose that can include rich aromas of fruit, spice, minerals, and smoke with jam or fruit flavors. Much of the body and power of the red wines is achieved by *saignage,* allowing some producers to put out small quantities of rosé wines that are dry, with aromas of nectarines and good weight on the palate.

Notable producers include Guigal, Jaboulet, Amadieu, Château de Montmirail, Domaine du Cayron, Château de Saint Cosme, and Domaine les Gouberts.

BEAUMES-DE-VENISE This is another area that produc-es good, reliable red wines under its own appellation as well as a sweet *vin doux naturel*, made exclusively from the Muscat grape. As in Rasteau, the wine is made by *mutage* (addition of grape brandy), producing a medium-bodied sweet white wine that has a lovely smell of peaches and orange blossoms and is best enjoyed within three years.

VACQUEYRAS The red wines of Vacqueyras are very similar to Gigondas, sharing the same grape varieties and similar soil conditions close to the Dentelles de Montmirail. Deep-colored wines offer firm but vibrant plummy fruit, indicative of the 50 percent minimum use of Grenache; occasionally, wines from lesser producers may seem rather unpolished. A small amount of white and rosé wines is also produced in the area.

CHÂTEAUNEUF-DU-PAPE This is the most famous appellation of the southern Rhône, producing deeply satisfying red wines whose rich, exuberant characteristics are primarily due to excellent exposure of vines to the sun, and soil variations that are critical in attaining the best attributes of each of the grape varieties that make up the blend. The climate is very hot, despite the effects of the strong *mistral* winds, providing fully ripe, lusciously sweet, and fruity grapes at harvest. This is aided somewhat by the presence of heat-retentive stones (*galets*), some fist-sized, others as large as boulders, that are clearly visible in many of the vineyards. Given the overall temperatures, it is likely that the grapes would reach sufficiently high sugar levels without the presence of these stones; indeed, chaptalization is illegal in this appellation. But the heat radiated from these stones can help keep down any rot associated with cool moisture, and the fruit certainly shows an intense richness that might otherwise be less formidable.

The famous stones, though, are not the only soil consideration. They often cover deposits of an iron-rich, reddish clay mixed with alluvial sand and gravel. Where the red clay dominates, the grapes produce powerfully structured, rich wines, whereas the finer, sandier soils create finely toned, less muscular versions. In the northern section of the appellation, a limestone escarpment provides good sites for white grapes. As usual in the Rhône, growers who understand all of these nuances are better situated to produce balanced, harmonious wines that take advantage of different grape types in different *terroirs*.

According to all sources, there are thirteen grape varieties (eight red and five white) that may be used to make red Châteauneuf-du-Pape; however, at least nine reds are listed in various reliable sources (Grenache, Syrah,

Mourvèdre, Cinsaut, Counoise, Muscardin, Vaccarèse, Picpoul Noir, and Terret Noir) and six white (Clairette, Grenache Blanc, Bourbelenc, Roussanne, Picpoul Gris, and Picardan)! What is certain is that the main grape for most producers' reds is Grenache, though recent planting trends favor Mourvèdre and Syrah, as well as some of the less well-known varieties that provide important elements of aroma, finesse, acidity, tannin, or color. Along with site selection, the grape mix and vinification techniques contribute strongly to style differences among producers' wines. Domaine de Mont Redon and Château de Beaucastel have traditionally been famous for using all thirteen permitted grape types, whatever they are!

There are two basic styles of red Châteauneuf-du-Pape: a lighter, fruit-forward version that is drinkable from two to six years after the vintage (often produced by mixing some traditionally fermented wine with some carbonic maceration wine) and the *vins de garde,* ageworthy wines that are darkly earthy, with deep but luscious mouth-filling fruit covering minimal tannins that begin to soften up just as the former style is fading. In a fine vintage from a good producer, such wines can age well for ten to twenty years, with colors ranging from garnet to mahogany with orange hues, and aromas of cinnamon, coffee, fig, leather, pine, bay laurel, tar, and cedar. The high alcohol level assures a generous wine whose flavors vary according to the source of the grapes as well as the blend of varieties used.

Around 5 percent of Châteauneuf-du-Pape production is white, with Clairette and white Grenache the most important varietals. There is a tendency for these wines to be uninteresting, with dull, even flabby characteristics. However, there has recently been a resurgence of interest in white wines, and careful timing of the harvest and cooler fermentation in stainless steel have shown that fresh, clean flavors can be achieved. Lack of acidity can still be a problem and, with few exceptions, the wines are best drunk young.

Larger *négociants* and cooperatives usually make the lighter style of wine, although Jaboulet would once again be a notable exception, with a very fine Châteauneuf-du-Pape subtitled "Les Cèdres." On-site domaines or estates vary enormously in size and philosophy: Some put all of their wine into one single cuvée; others have a first and second label system for the finest and less fine wines, while others still have adopted a single batch or reserve approach. Regardless of their philosophy, the most revered producers include Château de Beaucastel, Chante-Perdrix, Domaine de Beaurenard, Domaine Font de Michelle, Domaine de la Janasse, Clos du Mont-Olivet, Château Fortia, Château de la Gardine, Château la Nerthe, Le Vieux Donjon, Domaine du Vieux Télégraphe, Château de Mont-Redon, Clos de Papes, and Château Rayas.

Ruins of the Pope's summer palace in the vineyards of Châteauneuf-du-Pape

Only those estates that both grow and bottle their own wine are entitled to emboss the bottle with the coat of arms of the papal seal of crossed keys.

LIRAC   West of Châteauneuf-du-Pape and across the Rhône River is the Lirac appellation, which traditionally produced fresh, lively, medium-weight red and rosé wines from a blend of Grenache, Syrah, Mourvèdre, and Cinsaut. Since wine fashion has led to reduced consumption of rosé wine worldwide, Lirac producers have wisely shifted their attention to red and white wine production. The red wines have attractive fruit with a slight peppery bite, while the whites, based on Clairette, Bourboulenc, and Grenache Blanc are prized for their light body and perfumed bouquet. Increasing percentages of Viognier, Marsanne, and Roussanne have raised the aromatic character of the whites and given them a lift of fresh acidity when harvested in a timely manner. Most Liracs are best enjoyed within a year or two of production, though some of the reds will repay longer cellaring.

TAVEL   Just to the south of Lirac lies Tavel, a uniquely rosé wine appellation. Careful blending of Grenache and Cinsaut grapes from less fertile, low-pH soils with the same varieties from richer iron and clay soils gives the rosés of Tavel a medium to full body, with refreshing, sometimes bracing acidity. By law, these rosé wines cannot be made by blending white and red wines; they must be made directly from red grapes, either by pre-fermentation maceration or by *saignage*. Their fresh berry scents and fragrant but dry style make them wonderful spring and summer wines, though there have been too many examples on the international market that are just too old when they reach their destination, leaving the taster to guess at how fresh and fruity the wine once was. Unfortunately, Tavel is perhaps a victim of aggressively marketed rosés from other regions.

The South of France

• •

The southern crescent of France, from Spain to Italy around the Mediterranean basin, is unlike the rest of viticultural France. This area has traditionally been the wine equivalent of the bread basket to the nation, producing a full one-third of all French wine—but with almost all of it categorized as IGP or simply *vin*. There have been tremendous changes in the last decade stemming from European Union initiatives to improve quality in general and from improvements in vineyard management and winemaking

practices brought by local grape growers, *négociants* from elsewhere in France, and winemakers from as far away as California and Australia.

The whole area offered excellent opportunities for change, encumbered as it was by tradition and custom but not by regulation and law. Modern entrepreneurs have torn out whole vineyards that had been based on mixed plantings of high-yielding but lower-quality vines and replaced them with well-managed, irrigated tracts of known and marketable grape varieties. From these efforts, the whole wine world has seen an explosion of wines from this area, categorized in France as IGP wines but labeled by grape variety (since they are not from *appellation protégée* areas) to compete with the similarly labeled wines of the New World. In some instances, such as the Duboeuf line or Fortant de France, these new southern French IGP wines are well-crafted wines of substance and integrity. However, there are plenty of examples of dilute, mediocre wines where less scrupulous *négociants* simply seem to be taking advantage of a gullible consumer who will buy anything labeled as Chardonnay or Merlot.

More interesting from the perspective of *terroir* and authenticity has been the work of some truly dedicated individuals who are breathing new life into the concept of individual vineyard plots and producing wines that are a true reflection of their place of origin as well as any particular grape type. Fine examples of such commitment are the Mas de Daumas Gassac and the Domaine Richeaume.

The *appellation protégée* authorities have pressed ahead, approving promotions from one level to another. The disadvantages of this have become all too clear. Too often there is no obvious increase in quality of the wines to match the promotion to a superior category. And yet where true quality is being produced, the *appellation protégée* authorities remain reluctant to approve appellations that want to use nontraditional grapes. Experience has shown, however, that the so-called nontraditional grapes are often necessary to bring life and structure to otherwise dull wines. In at least some cases it is likely that producers will want to maintain their IGP status so that they can continue to innovate and to label their wines by grape variety and thereby continue to compete in that all-important varietal market.

Starting in the southwestern corner next to Spain, we will briefly discuss the regions of Roussillon, Corbières, Languedoc, Provence, and Corsica and their most important appellations.

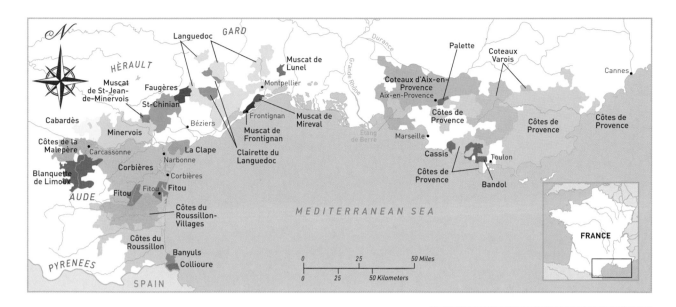

ROUSSILLON

Situated within the foothills of the French Pyrenees Mountains, which separate France from Spain, this is perhaps what one might assume to be a natural place to grow grapes and make wines: mild winters, warm summers, lots of sunshine, and a mountainous topography ringing the vineyards and protecting them from harsh wind and rain. Indeed, huge quantities of wine have been made here for thousands of years, and yet the region still struggles to compete with the neighboring regions and with the more famous northern appellations. There are two regional appellations here (Côtes du Roussillon and Côtes du Roussillon–Villages) and four smaller appellations (Collioure, Banyuls, Maury, and Rivesaltes).

CÔTES DU ROUSSILLON

White, rosé, and red wines are produced under this appellation name from a broad sweep of some 10,000 acres/4,000 hectares of vineyards that surround the city of Perpignan. The general characteristics associated with Rhône-style blends apply to these wines—fruity, slightly peppery reds, and soft, floral whites. The dominant grape in the red blends has been Carignan, a high-yielding vine generally producing dull, coarse wines, although it can be made much more appealing by carbonic maceration winemaking, as well as by generous proportions of other grapes such as Syrah and Mourvèdre, and smaller quantities of Grenache and Cinsaut. There is much pressure on the *appellation protégée* authorities to reduce or eliminate the legally required pro-

Languedoc-Roussillon Region

- Collioure
- Banyuls
- Côtes du Roussillon
- Côtes du Roussillon–Villages
- Fitou
- Blanquette de Limoux
- Côtes de la Malepère
- Corbières
- La Clape
- Minervois
- Cabardès
- Muscat de St-Jean-de-Minervois
- St-Chinian
- Languedoc
- Faugères
- Clairette du Languedoc
- Muscat de Frontignan
- Muscat de Mireval
- Muscat de Lunel

Provence Region

- Coteaux d'Aix-en-Provence
- Palette
- Côtes de Provence
- Cassis
- Bandol
- Coteaux Varois

portion of Carignan, although some producers appear to believe that such action has already been taken. Producers such as Château Mossé, Château de Caladroy, and Château La Casenove have replanted with the better vine varieties on cooler hillside sites and use a combination of cool fermentation and small barrel aging to produce wines of much more stature and depth of flavor. Côtes du Roussillon Les Aspres is a new subappellation producing similar wines in the southern part of the region.

The same situation applies to the white wines, where regulations stipulate the continued use of the traditional varieties of Macabeo and Malvoisie in preference to the more flavorful and more structured Grenache Blanc, Marsanne, and Roussanne.

CÔTES DU ROUSSILLON–VILLAGES

Lower yields and higher levels of ripeness and sugars govern the wines from some twenty-five villages spread over another 3,700 acres/1,500 hectares along the river Agly in the northern third of the Roussillon region. The appellation is for red wines only. These should be more structured wines, with greater depth of flavor, but the same concerns exist over the proportions of each variety allowed in the blend. Four villages—Caramany, Tautavel, Lesquerde, and Latour-de-France—may add their name to the label. Domaine Gauby, Domaine le Vieux Chêne, Clot de l'Oum, Mas Amiel, and Château de Jau are reliable producers.

COLLIOURE

Tucked away in a small coastal pocket is the red and rosé appellation of Collioure, though it shares exactly the same territory with the appellation Banyuls (see below). Grown on very steep hillsides that look down on the Mediterranean Sea, the Grenache, Mourvèdre, and Syrah are the principal varieties used to make a fairly sturdy, even robust red wine. Once again, as the required ingredient Carignan is reduced, the wines should become more elegant. Domaine du Mas Blanc and Domaine des Templiers produce good examples.

BANYULS AND MAURY

These two appellations at the northern (Maury) and southern (Banyuls) extremes of the Roussillon region offer the same kind of wine—*vin doux naturel*, produced from a minimum of 50 percent Grenache grapes. The fermenting juice has high-alcohol grape spirit added to it, which raises the alcohol level to around 15.5 percent,

stopping the fermentation and leaving the wine brimming over with fresh, sweet, grapey flavors. The wines are aged in oak or glass flagons (*bonbonnes*), giving them at least a hint of oxidation, and there is also the tradition of leaving some of the barrels to bask in the southern sun, giving the wines a *rancio* character of slightly sour dried fruits. Current fashion and competition from vintage Port have led many producers to concentrate on freshness of grape flavors rather than on oxidation and *rancio*. Maury is made as a red only from 75 percent Grenache or more, whereas the Banyuls appellation allows for red, rosé, and white. In the case of Banyuls, a minimum of 75 percent Grenache in the wine and thirty months' aging in oak will qualify it for the status of *grand cru*. Domaine du Mas Blanc in Banyuls and Mas Amiel in Maury are among the better producers.

RIVESALTES

Like its counterpart Beaumes-de-Venise in the southern Rhône valley, this appellation produces a red wine from Grenache grapes, as well as a *vin doux naturel* from one of the many variations of the Muscat grape. The red wine is often made by carbonic maceration, producing a light, fresh, easy-drinking wine. The white *vin doux naturel* is generally lighter and less intense than Muscat *vins doux naturels* from other appellations in southern France. The Grenache grape is also use to make Grenache-based *vin doux naturel*; again, it is less flavorful than other versions from Banyuls or Maury.

CORBIÈRES

Stretching northward from Roussillon to a line between the cities of Carcassonne and Narbonne, the appellation of Corbières is extremely varied in topography, soil types, and grape types, although the villainous Carignan still seems to dominate most vineyards and wines. Local authorities have identified eleven subregions in some attempt to distill a broad range of styles into smaller, more recognizable units, and there has already been some recognition of the subregions in the north making fuller, more flavorful wines, especially Alaric, Boutenac, and Lézignan. In recognition of vineyard and winemaking improvements, the area around Boutenac has been awarded its own appellation—Corbières-Boutenac—with the bizarre insistence that the wine contain a minimum of 30 percent Carignan.

In many ways, the large, rambling Corbières appellation summarizes the dilemma of modern winemaking in southern France. Many producers want to upgrade the vineyards and wines but feel they are hampered by narrow-sighted and narrow-minded *appellation protégée* regulations that insist on demonstrably inferior but traditional, sometimes obscure and unknown grape types. They have therefore decided to forego the presumed prestige of *appellation protégée* status for the financial comfort of Chardonnay and Merlot and Syrah as single varietal wines, labeled by grape type under the category of IGP from the Pays d'Oc region that covers the entire arc of vineyards from Spain to the southern Côtes du Rhône.

Currently the Corbières appellation includes one red wine subappellation called Fitou, which is in fact split into two small areas, one near the coast and one inland. Again, relying officially on Carignan, the wines can be uninteresting and flat, but lower yields and some judicious blending of Grenache and Syrah can sometimes create a level of complexity that includes rich, ripe fruit and a background of herbal *garrigue* character.

LANGUEDOC

North of the Corbières appellation, the topography begins to change from the hilly Roussillon region to the flatter plains of Languedoc, a factor that led to Languedoc being the largest producer in all of France of basic *vin* and IGP wines, with approximately 40 percent of the nation's vineyards but only 10 percent of the total AOP production. Again, recent investments and improvements have led to an increase in quality, with some growers taking advantage of hillside vineyard sites further inland, but the emphasis is still on IGP wines or basic *vin*.

The wine industry is based mostly on farmers with small vineyard plots who sell their grapes or wines to *négociants* or cooperatives. However, the flat plains are ideal for domestic and international investors to establish large, sprawling wineries with row upon row of gigantic stainless steel tanks for temperature-controlled fermentation and warehouses full of new oak barrels for aging. Fortant de France is the label used by the Skalli *négociants*, and Domaine de la Baume, owned by Hardy's of Australia, also produces a line of varietal IGP wines from the Hérault region. In addition, Les Salins du Midi have been innovators in the region for four decades, experimenting with organic farming and new varietals. Other important producers include Les Jamelles, Val d'Orbieu, and Réserve St. Martin.

The Languedoc area includes the very broad regional appellation of Coteaux du Languedoc, plus the smaller appellations of Minervois, St-Chinian, and Faugères. In addition, there are a couple of obscure Clairette appellations and a handful of Muscat appellations making *vins doux naturels*.

COTEAUX DU LANGUEDOC

This large appellation stretches from Narbonne to Nîmes and includes ninety-one villages producing mostly red wines that must by law contain a minimum of 20 percent Grenache, 10 percent each of Mourvèdre and Syrah, and no more than 50 percent of Cinsaut and Carignan. Rosé wines are based on the same varieties, while white wines are made mostly from Grenache Blanc, Bourboulenc, and Clairette.

In general, all of the wines are fresh, light, and excitingly clean and fruity, as much the result of technically pure winemaking as anything else. Since the appellation covers such a large area, the soils and topography are extremely varied, with the slopes farther inland offering limestone ridges as opposed to the richer alluvial soils on the plains. Some villages on the limestone ridges stand out within the Coteaux appellation as producing decidedly superior wine, with greater depth and intensity of flavor, and a more tightly knit structure. These better villages of the area are certainly worthy of their own appellation status, but for now they must content themselves with simply adding their village name to the regional Coteaux du Languedoc appellation. Some examples are La Clape (fine whites as well as reds), St. Saturnin, Pic St-Loup, Cabrières, and Montpeyroux.

Within the boundaries of this large regional appellation is one of the Midi's most expensive wines, even though it is classified only as IGP. The red wine produced at Mas de Daumas Gassac is based on Bordeaux varieties, an oddity in an otherwise sea of Rhône styles. Aimé Guibert, the proprietor, does not fine or filter the wines before bottling, and the first release in 1978 won impressive acclaim for its rich, concentrated style and fine structure, full of immediate enjoyment but capable of aging for decades. The estate also produces a remarkable white wine from the equally remarkable blend of Viognier, Chardonnay, and Petit Manseng, with Muscat, Marsanne, and Roussanne for back-up. It is this kind of conscientious, place-specific winemaking that attracts attention as the antithesis of the mass marketing of varietal mediocrity so prevalent from other parts of the region. Equally interesting can be the reds of Domaine d'Aupilhac and Domaine de la Coste.

MINERVOIS

Like the Corbières appellation in Roussillon, Minervois is a large appellation, perhaps too large for its own good since the better, more structured wines from specific villages are too often overshadowed by the more ordinary. Once again, it is a question of the appellation covering too many soils and combining flat plains with more interesting hillsides. But unlike Corbières, the Minervois appellation has seen some serious improvements in the vineyards and the cellars that result in cleaner, more elegant wines that still send a signal of ripe fruit without being flat and dull. Less reliance on Carignan and careful handling of Mourvèdre, Syrah, and Grenache have been key. Most of the wines are red, and the better ones come from the northern areas based on limestone hills. Minervois-La Lavinière has recently been awarded its own appellation, and Muscat de Saint-Jean-de-Minervois continues the tradition of *vin doux naturel.*

Estates worthy of attention for red wines include Domaine Borie de Maurel and Château Hélène. White wines vary in quality more than the reds, but some producers are making aromatic, full-bodied white wines using oak barrels.

ST-CHINIAN

Like its companion Faugères (see below), this village became the center of an appellation that now covers twenty villages, carved out of the much broader Coteaux du Languedoc in recognition of the better red and rosé wines being produced there. The wines are generally lighter, softer, early-drinking wines based on Carignan, Syrah, Mourvèdre, and Grenache, while the best show dark cherry and plum fruit with refreshing and balancing acidity, a presumed product of the juxtaposition of limestone and schist soils in the northern section around

the two new appellations of St-Chinian Berlou and St-Chinian Roquebrun. Particularly interesting and good value wines come from Château Coujan, Domaine des Jougla, and Clos Bagatelle.

FAUGÈRES

Everything about the wines of this appellation is similar to St-Chinian, although the Faugères wines are often more complex, with richer, riper fruit. Fine examples come from the Domaine Alquier and the Château des Estanilles.

MUSCAT APPELLATIONS

There are four appellations that produce Muscat *vins doux naturels* from sun-baked lusciously sweet Muscat grapes. The more obvious, immediately grapey versions tend to come from Frontignan, while there is something more reserved but, in the long run, more attractive about the wines from Mireval and Lunel, with bright peach, orange blossom, and apricot characteristics on the nose and palate. The village of St-Jean-de-Minervois offers similar fruit qualities. Each of these wines is labeled as "Muscat de" followed by the village name.

CLAIRETTE APPELLATIONS

The appellation Clairette de Bellegarde makes dry white wines from the Clairette grape, though, as has been described elsewhere, the Clairette has a dangerous tendency toward dull neutrality and oxidation. In other words, there is not much interest in these wines. The Clairette du Languedoc appellation, perhaps recognizing that something drastic was needed to give some kind of character to their wines, opted for a more openly oxidized style, closer to the manner of sherry. From that point of view, they may be interesting wines, but it is difficult not to realize that the world is turning its back on such styles.

PROVENCE

This area has a reputation as the landscape of sun, sea, and wine, fuelled by international, often overly romanticized accounts of the good life. It certainly has a history of supplying vacationers with refreshing, simple rosés made from mostly Grenache and Carignan. In reality, the Provençal landscape can be harsh and unrelenting, seared dry by sun and wind and baking the grapes to oxidative dullness. And yet, around 50 percent of all France's rosé is still made here from the same grapes; the generally more serious reds in-

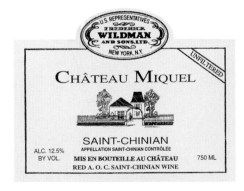

St-Chinian wines are increasingly popular.

clude higher percentages of Syrah, Mourvèdre, and even Cabernet Sauvignon. The palette of white grapes covers a wide spectrum, from Sauvignon Blanc to Sémillon, Vermentino, Rolle, and the standard Clairette.

The Mediteranean climate offers these varietals over 3,000 hours of sunshine to ripen. Rainfall is low and the various winds dry the vines of any excess humidity. The large regional appellation is the Côtes de Provence, superimposed on the smaller regional appellations of Coteaux d'Aix-en-Provence and Coteaux Varois. The highlights of the region are the small village appellations of Les Baux de Provence, Palette, Cassis, Bandol, and Bellet. Lastly, there is the new appellation of Coteaux de Pierrevert and the increasingly important IGP wines of the various departments and local zones.

CÔTES DE PROVENCE

The Côtes de Provence encompasses 45,000 acres/18,000 hectares and provides the greatest range of quality, from poor, nerveless rosé to strikingly spicy reds. Today, Syrah and Cabernet Sauvignon each may account for up to 30 percent of a blended wine, while the Carignan is held to a maximum of 40 percent. Quality-oriented producers are investing in new oak barrels and using higher proportions of Cabernet Sauvignon, Syrah, Mourvèdre, and the local reds, Tibouren and Calitor, to make finer wines. Some of the more serious producers include Domaine Ott, Domaine Richeaume, Château Vignelaure, and Domaine de la Courtade.

COTEAUX D'AIX-EN-PROVENCE

Centered on the town of Aix-en-Provence, this appellation covers about fifty villages, using the usual southern red grapes of Grenache, Cinsaut, and Mourvèdre, plus a small percentage of Cabernet Sauvignon. Although the addition of the latter has demonstrably improved many of the region's wines, the *appellation protégée* authorities have deemed that the permitted percentage should be reduced, a fact that results in more and more gifted producers opting for simple *vin* or IGP status rather than *appellation protégée*. Good, sturdy, structured reds are available from such producers as Château de Fonscolombes and Domaine les Bastides.

COTEAUX VAROIS

This appellation specializes in generally more full-bodied, plummy and peppery reds and bright, fruity rosés

from Grenache, Syrah, and Mourvèdre, and the occasional white based on the nutty, aromatic Vermentino, which is particularly well suited to the dry, hot conditions here.

LES BAUX DE PROVENCE

This appellation around the deserted medieval town of Les Baux (now a major tourist destination) successfully separates itself from the murky sea of anonymity called the Côtes de Provence based on the depth, complexity, and charm of its plummy, mocha-tinged reds and bright cranberry rosés. Here the *appellation protégée* authorities appear to have relented and permitted higher percentages of Cabernet Sauvignon to add that extra dimension to the usual Grenache-Syrah-Cinsaut blend. Anne Poniatowski at the Mas de la Dame and Peter Fischer at Château Revelette make some outstanding examples.

PALETTE

If ever there was a study in southern macro- and mesoclimates, the Palette appellation would be it. Unusually, about one-third of wines produced are white, and the remaining rosés and reds are renowned for a firm streak of acidic elegance and firm tannic structure that very few other southern wines possess. The secret is, as always, soil and climate—a north-facing though gentle slope of limestone, resulting in ripe but not baked grapes that make wine of supple strength and deep currant and berry flavors. Only two estates, Château Simone and Château Crémat, make up the appellation's tiny 56 acres/22.5 hectares.

CASSIS

A limestone gravel mixture forms the basis of the Cassis vineyards, making the white wines from Clairette, Ugni Blanc, and Marsanne more interesting than the pleasant but uninspired reds and rosés. The full-bodied, somewhat earthy but aromatic white from a single estate such as Clos Ste-Magdeleine is a fine example.

BANDOL

Limestone again shows up in Bandol, but the higher proportion of sandstones in the soil mix make this appellation's reds and rosés more sought after than its whites, which tend to revert to southern dullness. Indeed, the reds and rosés of Bandol are among the finest of southern France, with an unforgiving youthful structure derived from at least 50 percent Mourvèdre in the blend, backed up by Grenache and Cinsaut. Oak-aging for a minimum of eighteen months can help soften the wines, but their resilience can be formidable. As everywhere else, styles vary, the result of choices made in the vineyard and during the various stages of winemaking. But by and large Bandol is an impressive wine, especially from the exemplary Domaine Tempier, the Domaines Bunan, and the Château Pradeaux.

Whites are made from such local southern grapes as Ugni Blanc, Bourbelenc, and Clairette, with Sauvignon Blanc used to add acidity.

BELLET

Fashion and rarity may be part of the allure of Bellet wines, but there is also something intriguingly authentic about the white, red, and rosé wines from this small appellation on the outskirts of Nice. The cool, terraced vineyards are home to the almost inevitable Chardonnay and the ordinary Ugni Blanc and Clairette, but the relatively obscure Rolle, Pignerol, and Mayorquin bring a perfumed, fruity fullness to the whites, while the Braquet and Fuella add zesty fruitiness to the reds. The coolness of the climate helps maintain freshness in the wines.

COTEAUX DE PIERREVERT

This new appellation produces relatively light style, soft white, rosé, and red from the standard southern varieties. They are perfectly acceptable, fresh fruity wines, mostly consumed *sur place*.

CORSICA

The Mediterranean island of Corsica features a rugged, rocky topography, plenty of sunshine with temperatures moderated by the sea breezes, and enough rainfall to keep things lush and green, at least on the western side of the island, where most of the rain falls before it hits the mountainous spine that runs north-south down the island. In many ways, it is an idyllic place to grow grapes and make wine, and the IGP name for Corsican wines says it all—Ile de Beauté!

However, the average wine consumer is unlikely to be entranced by the beauty of most Corsican wines, the vast majority of which are very ordinary and are usually consumed locally anyway. But there are a few energetic souls who remain committed to the production of Corsican rarities from indigenous grape varieties or clones. Given the island's location, it is not surprising that many of the local grapes are Italianate, such as the red varieties Sciacarello (which appears to be native) and the Nielluccio (which is said to be related to Tuscany's Sangiovese), and the white varieties of Vermentino and Moscato. There are also some southern French varieties used, as well as the usual international varieties, including Cabernet Sauvignon, Syrah, Mourvèdre, Chardonnay, Pinot Noir, and Viognier. The island's producers wrestle over whether to promote their individualistic indigenous varieties or to go the international route.

Only about one-fifth of the island's total wine production falls under *appellation protégée*, with one large appellation, Vin de Corse, and eight smaller, more specific appellations.

VIN DE CORSE

Though the potential for improvement is great, much of the red, white, and rosé wine sold under this appellation is of poor quality when compared with basic regional appellation wines from other parts of France. Change has occurred, but only slowly. There seems to be a stubborn streak in many of the grape growers and wine producers that makes them resistant to change. This stubborn streak is at once a disadvantage and an advantage, since habitual overcropping, the main culprit in producing dilute, uninteresting wines, is still widespread, but there are also, thankfully, a few traditionalists who hang onto old grape types to produce wines reflective of their history and origin. Some of those special wines come from the Vin de Corse subappellations, smaller regions that affix their name to the phrase "Vin de Corse." For example, Vin de Corse Porto Vecchio can produce fuller, fruity reds and refreshing rosés, generally using the Sciacarello and Nielluccio. There are also a few worthwhile estates for similar reds and dry, perfumed whites (from the Vermentino grape) in the subappellations of Calvi, Sartène, Coteaux du Cap Corse, and Figari, all of which would add their name on the label to the general phrase "Vin de Corse." Of more interest are three singular appellations: Ajaccio, Patrimonio, and Muscat de Cap Corse.

AJACCIO

On the western side of the island around the ancient town of the same name, the vineyards of this appellation have the double benefit of granitic soils to develop a robust character and altitudes around 300 feet/100 meters to maintain fresh fruit flavors and crisp acidity in the wines. The red versions are generally better, showing full red berry fruit character mixed with a hint of peppery spice from a combination of Sciacarello backed up by a few southern French varieties. The white wines can be disappointingly dull, though a few producers, such as Clos Capitoro or Comte Peraldi, offer a fruity, herb-tinged Vermentino.

PATRIMONIO

The limestone soil content of this appellation in the north, around the town of St-Florent, immediately sets its wine apart as showing more supple and lean flavors in the reds (mostly Nielluccio, plus southern Rhône varieties) and a floral fragrance in the whites, made from 100 percent Vermentino.

MUSCAT DE CAP CORSE

This appellation was created recently to provide a separate identity for the sweet *vins doux naturels* produced from the Muscat grape on the finger-like projection at the northern end of the island. This area also enjoys limestone soils that allow the Muscat or Moscato grape to flourish to its full peachy ripeness with a filigree delicacy that distinguishes it from many other, heavier *vins doux naturels*. The dry white wines made from Vermentino in this region take the more general appellation Vin de Corse Coteaux du Cap Corse.

SUMMARY

FOR MOST OF THE PREVIOUS CENTURY, French wines dominated wine lists in fine restaurants in America, and as late as the 1970s most French restaurants in the United States continued to offer only French wines. Today, French wines must compete with wines from around the world, due in large part to the popularity of recognizable varietal grape names on labels in contrast to the place names used for most French *appellation protégée* wines. The French wine community, including national and regional wine-trade associations and their public relations firms, have responded to the challenge by upgrading wines from many areas and investing in new equipment, new technology, and new ideas. Tastings for retailers, restaurateurs, and consumers demonstrate the current versatility of French wines with a wide range of food—from Asian cuisine to American barbecue.

Wine-producing nations are crafting wines to cater to current taste preferences according to market research. The IGP wines of southern France have done the same thing, while in France's *appellation d'origine protégée* areas, an emphasis on taste characteristics derived from the *terroir* of a particular site is still evident in most wines. The mineral and gooseberry smells of a Sauvignon Blanc from Sancerre, the barnyard and raspberry bouquet of aged Pinot Noir from Chambertin, the roasted, spicy, black-fig aromas of Syrah at Côte-Rôtie, are indicative of those grapes in those soils and are welcome landmark scents of a maintained tradition. Between those two extremes, the grape growers, winemakers, and the *appellation protégée* authorities continue to try to find some balance between tradition and respect for the past, and modern innovation.

The Institut National de Recherche Agronomique continues to work with the Institut d'Oenologie de Bordeaux to improve techniques in the vineyards and wineries throughout the nation. INAO maintains quality control over French wines, and the government subsidizes the promotion and export of French wines. In every corner of France, people associated with wine are finding their own way to contend with the realities of the global market. There are those who would deal with it simply as a business and those who are artistes devoted to creating magic. Most fall somewhere in between and are finding a way to maintain the best parts of tradition, understand the taste preferences of current consumers, and prepare for the future.

NEBBIOLO

BARBERA

CHIANTI
CLASSICO

SANGIOVESE

DOLCETTO

barolo

MOSCATO

IGT · DOC · DOCG

BRUNELLO
di MONTALCINO

BOLGHERI

GAVI

VALPOLICELLA

montepulciano

SUPER
TUSCANS

ITALY

IT IS IMPOSSIBLE to speak in generalities when discussing the wines of Italy in a contemporary context. We still cannot use the blanket term "modern wines of Italy," because this would apply to a fraction of the country's tremendous wine production, some of which is made by traditional, even outmoded, methods. However, it would also be a mistake not to focus on the best wines of Italy that have found great success and an enthusiastic international audience, many made by the most innovative methods. Fine Italian wines have taken the wine world by storm, and many Italian wine producers, both traditionalists and innovators, have earned international acclaim.

Italy is the world's largest wine producer and exporter; France is a close second in both categories. Italy produces about 13.25 billion gallons/500 million hectoliters annually and exports about 25 percent of its total production, creating a market share of about 22 percent of the world market. On a per capita basis, Italian citizens consume about 50 liters/12.5 gallons (a dramatic decrease from 90 liters/22.5 gallons per person thirty-five years ago). Italy has about 2 million acres/800,000 hectares of vines under cultivation. Amazingly, France has almost exactly the same amount of vineyard acreage, give or take 20 hectares/50 acres. (This is the only significant statistic in which both countries are eclipsed by the world leader, Spain, which has about 3 million acres/1.2 million hectares under vine.)

Italy exports more than 15 percent of its total wine production to the United States—estimated at about 300 million cases of wine in 2010—and these wines includes some of the finest Italian wines ever made. At the same time, a small percentage of Italy's total production is fine wine. More than half of Italy's export wines are shipped in bulk to other countries for blending, especially Germany (35 percent of total exports) and France (20 percent of total exports). The amount of wine that is distilled into industrial alcohol—about 10 percent of total wine production—*exceeds* the entire wine production of Australia. So, while Italy produces a staggering amount of wine, the amount of wine that makes it into bottles with labels is about 40 percent, and of this, less than half is classified under Italy's DOC (see "Wine Laws," on page 354), meaning that the total of classified wines is around 20 percent of total production.

Within the relatively small amount of classified wines—if more than 2.5 billion gallons/10 billion liters of wine can be considered small—the majority are of average quality, and there are even some undistinguished, unlikable wines. However, about 15 percent of DOC and some newer DOC-equivalent wines are remarkable for their high quality. Connoisseurs look to these noble wines—some of them traditional, some new, some rediscovered, some made by solitary artisans, some by large producers with multinational wine interests—as the benchmarks to which all other Italian wines of any promise should be compared. They may be distinctive or soulful, elegant or earthy, red or white, still or sparkling, known throughout the world or known only in a hometown province.

Italy's best wines appeal to the sophisticated wine drinker as well as the novice, for they are food-friendly, appealing, and full of personality. During the last thirty-five to forty years, Italy's finest export wines have gone far to help erase their outdated image of inexpensive jug wines, a view that is still all too prevalent but these days rarely true.

Starting in 1963, when Italy's wine laws were passed, the modest stirrings of a national commitment to quality could be sensed. These laws, which have been updated and amended every few years, allow Italy to take its place on the European stage with the other premium producers of the European Union. The EU has set strict agricultural and land-use laws for its members (see page 255), and Italy, which for years played catch-up with the stars of the show, France and Germany, is now at the forefront of progressive pan-European wine legislation. The EU has provided financial help to Italy's vineyards and wineries to upgrade their properties and production methods. Italy's own DOC laws and EU oversight have helped Italian wines in their improvement process.

With hundreds of native vinifera grapes and dozens of imported ones, Italy makes an enormous array of wines. Its climate, which at its extremes can mimic North Africa in the south and Switzerland in the north, allows almost every known grape to thrive. Soils are as varied as the weather, and fine wines are made in almost every one of the twenty wine-producing regions, often from native vinifera, sometimes from French and German varietals, and increasingly from blends of both Italian and international varietals.

In considering the quality of Italian wines, the reputation of the producer is paramount, as the same grapes from the same region, even the same town, can make very different wines. In the hands of a producer committed to quality, the wine can sing a classic aria, but if a producer committed only to profit gets his or her hands on those same grapes, the wine will sing off-key, and all the notes we hear will be flat or sharp.

Until fairly recently, the portrait of Italy's wines has been unpredictable. What is clear to those who have followed the evolution of Italian wines in recent years is that the picture has unmistakably and permanently changed for the better. The overall improvement, and in some cases the rehabilitation, of the quality and image of Italian wines is a

massive undertaking, and it is exciting to witness the process unfold in the world's largest wine-producing country. It has been said before, but it bears repeating: Italy is not so much a country as it is one gigantic vineyard.

HISTORY

WHEN THE PHOENICIANS, traveling from Persia around 2000 B.C., landed in what is now Apulia in southern Italy, they found that grapes were being grown and wine was being made and sold. Later, when the Greeks conquered Sicily and a good part of southern Italy, they introduced grapes that are still being grown in modern Italy. Farmers and slaves in ancient Campania grew Greco, Aglianico, Moscato, and Malvasia—all vinifera grapes that continue to be planted in modern Italy. The Greeks embraced the wine culture of their new colonies in Magna Graecia, and what is now southern Italy came to be called *Oenotria*—"Land of the Vine."

While the Greeks began an active wine trade in the south, the Etruscans focused their energies in central Italy, especially what is now Tuscany and Umbria. Both peoples developed their own methods of viticulture, which were later synthesized and improved upon by the Romans, whose greatest poets and scholars wrote about the wonders of wine. Although they planted vines in Sicily, the central coast provinces, and the Alps, the Romans did their best work on their home turf. The area around the ancient city of Pompeii became the center for the wine trade, and it was here that new production methods originated, including primitive but successful attempts at aging the wine; making lighter, drier versions of what had been flat, alcoholic wines; and stopping fermentation by utilizing cold-water baths, a precursor to temperature-controlled cool fermentation.

The Roman wine trade spread to every part of the empire, as wines were traded across what is now Italy, France, Germany, parts of North Africa, Spain, and England. Wine traders from what is now the Piedmont region introduced wooden barrels for transport, and by extension, aging. All of this occurred before the first century A.D.

With the fall of the Roman Empire, Italy's wine culture would not surface again—except for the wines needed for sacred rites of the Catholic Church—until the end of the Middle Ages. With the coming of the Renaissance, wine enjoyed a resurgence as a subject of the arts, especially paint-

FROM TOP: *Ancient amphorae—Greek wine vessels—exhibited at the Tre Vasselle Museum in Torgiano. Greek ruins at Paestum. Roman wine plaque in ceramic relief*

ing and poetry. What little technical knowledge we have about winemaking in the sixteenth century indicates that quality generally improved, due to the desire of the richest Italians and other Europeans for good wines. However, the former *Oenotria* was still far from the days when its beloved BACCHUS was the only god of food and drink.

Beginning in the late seventeenth and early eighteenth centuries, Tuscany became the center of Italy's wine culture, and the beginnings of modern wine laws began to take root. However, the rest of the independent provinces that make up contemporary Italy, feeling the effects of war and widespread poverty, had little or no part in developing a modern wine trade. At this point, France, a culturally and politically unified country, assumed control of Europe's international wine trade.

Starting in the mid-nineteenth century, however, the provinces of a reuniting Italy began to enter the modern age. With a nod in the direction of France, the Italians began to make their red wines drier in Tuscany's Chianti region and in the Piedmont's Barolo district, where Italy's first commercially produced dry wine was made in the 1850s. Sparkling wines were produced around Asti in Piedmont, based on methods learned in the Champagne region, and the classic fortified wine Marsala was introduced to Sicily by J. Woodhouse, an Englishman with interests in the Port trade. As Italy became a more unified and somewhat more prosperous country, red, white, fortified, and sparkling wine producers developed international markets for their wines. Italy was back on the quality map, as a true rebirth of its wines had begun.

Just before the turn of the twentieth century, Italy's impressive wine industry was dealt a blow from which it seemed it might never recover. Both the vine louse phylloxera and the powdery mildew OIDIUM decimated Europe's vineyards. Italy was hit particularly hard by these dual pests for two essential reasons. First, before phylloxera, "promiscuous plantings"—the planting of grapevines alongside other crops—was the norm in Italy, so not only vines but a great deal of Italy's total agricultural output was damaged. Second, before the destruction of Italy's vineyards, two thousand different local grape varieties were used to produce wines. Since the chosen method to subdue phylloxera was to plant the vines on American rootstock, a painstaking and expensive process, marginal producers making artisanal wines were wiped out, as were many historic grape types. In place of the rare Italian vinifera, many French and German varieties were planted, along with high-yielding native vinifera that, with the help of the long growing season in southern Italy, could produce wines of high alcohol but little complexity. Italy began to develop a reputation as the world's largest supplier of inexpensive and indifferent wine, a reputation that lasted well into the 1970s.

The reputation for frivolous wines sometimes dressed up in silly bottles was hard for Italy to shake, but eventually the image and quality of Italian wines changed dramatically, and for the better. One of the important reasons for this change was the upgrading of Italy's wine laws, but the integrity, passion for quality, and increasing financial strength of Italian wine producers cannot be underestimated.

WINE LAWS

AFTER WORLD WAR II, with eventual prosperity and the attendant optimistic view of Europe as an economic and political confederacy, France and Italy, as the world's leading producers of wine, both agreed that a pan-European approach to enforceable wine laws would be necessary. Perhaps foreseeing the coming of the European Union, the two nations planned to provide equivalent laws for each wine-producing nation in Europe. Certainly, if Italy wanted to become a part of the modern wine industry, the adoption of modern wine laws was necessary. This was especially true because after World War II, in an effort to recover economically, Italy began to develop a worldwide reputation as the leading producer of inexpensive, low-quality bulk or jug wines. Producers, especially in the southern and central areas of the country, took advantage of the long growing season and warm climate to produce vapid, high-alcohol wines of little depth. Although fine wines were being produced in Italy, they were overshadowed by the cheap, one-dimensional wines that flooded the international market.

In 1963 the Italian Parliament adopted the Denominazione di Origine (denomination of origin) law, modeled after the French *appellation contrôlée* laws (see page 257). This law established the **DENOMINAZIONE DI ORIGINE CONTROLLATA** (DOC) category, guaranteeing the origin of a particular wine. The purpose of the laws was to ensure that Italy would regain its place as a producer of consistent, high-quality wines. At first, the laws did little to improve overall quality of the wines and in some ways encouraged

producers, in the name of consistency and profit, to leave the best growing districts—low-yielding hillside vineyards—for the warmer vineyard sites at lower elevations. The industrial wine producers became politically powerful, and progressive reform of the DOC laws was difficult to achieve. Intense criticism of the post-DOC Italian wines in foreign markets finally had an impact on the DOC bureaucracy and the agricultural ministry.

Although the controversial DOC legislation had been continually updated, enforcement of quality-based changes was virtually nonexistent. When Giovanni Goria, a former prime minister of Italy, was appointed agricultural minister in 1991, he promised sweeping changes in the DOC laws and miraculously pushed through his New Disciplinary Code for Denomination of Wines of Origin within three months of his government appointment. The new Law 164 has come to be known as the Goria Law, and it has made a tremendous difference in the quality profile of Italian wines.

Before Goria's overhaul of the DOC laws, the category of **DENOMINAZIONE DI ORIGINE CONTROLLATA E GARANTITA** (DOCG) became an important part of Italy's wine legislation in 1980. The DOCG regulations were part of the original 1963 law, but due to the political power of the industrial producers, not activated for seventeen years. The first DOCG zone, Brunello di Montalcino from Tuscany, was followed by Barolo and Barbaresco from Piedmont. DOCG established the tradition of a "guarantee": an even higher level of regulation for the very few wines considered to be highest in quality and reputation from a given DOC area. At present, there are a total of forty DOCG wines in Italy, with several more awaiting this highest designation.

The purpose of Italy's wine law is to uphold and improve the reputations of Italy's wines by establishing geographically delimited zones. There are roughly 350 DOC and DOCG zones spread throughout Italy's twenty regions. Each region is an independent political unit, similar to the constituent states in the United States, and the DOC-approved zones within the regions produce a total of more than 2,000 wines—white, rosé, red, sparkling, and fortified, from bone dry to overwhelmingly sweet. These zones can vary widely in size: The entire Abruzzi region contains only three DOC zones and one DOCG zone, encompassing more than 20,000 acres/8,000 hectares. The Piedmont region, about the same size as the region of Abruzzi, contains forty-one DOC zones and thirteen DOCG zones on less than 90,000 acres/36,000 hectares.

Of course, as with all members of the European Union, Italy's wine laws must adhere to the EU wine laws. Italian wines that are DOC or DOCG quality may also bear the symbol VQPRD (for sparkling wines, VSQPRD), a European Union designation. Also, Italy must recognize the import laws of other countries. For example, any Italian wine shipped to the United States must have the words "Product of Italy" on the label.

In August 2009, the European Union revamped its wine regulations and laws, affecting all member nations. So far, in Italy the impact of these changes has been minimal, especially for familiar traditional labels such as Chianti, Barolo, and Soave. (For a discussion of these EU wine law changes, see page 256.)

As in many countries, but especially in Italy, wine laws are helpful, but the reputation of the producer is the most reliable guide to quality. The following categories of Italian wines, listed here from lowest to highest quality, have been established: *vino da tarola* (VdT), *indicazione geografica tipica* (IGT), *denominazione di origine controllata* (DOC), and *denominazione di origine controllata e garantita* (DOCG).

VINO DA TAVOLA (VDT)

UNDER THE CURRENT EUROPEAN UNION wine laws, as amended in August 2009, "table wine" (*vino da tavola* in Italy) no longer exists as a quality category, as the new law proposes that all wines produced by EU member nations may list grape variety and vintage, even for those wines that do not adhere to maximum yield in the vineyard and minimum alcohol levels. As for place of origin, these wines must be labeled "Product of Italy." The idea of this new law is to enable EU wine nations to compete with New World wine producers, who have never been hampered by such restrictions. There are no formal regulations for these wines, beyond Italy's general public health and safety laws.

Before the changes in the EU wine laws, the **VINO DA TAVOLA** designation included wines that never reached bottles, much of the wine that was used for blending in inexpensive bulk wines, and most of the wine that was distilled for industrial alcohol. Even before the changes in EU regulations, VdT was a shrinking category, as wines in Italy continued to improve in quality

Before the Goria Law took effect in 1992, some of Italy's finest wines were bottled as *vino da tavola*, because many of the country's artisan producers wanted to make world-class wines that did not fit the traditional guidelines of the original DOC laws adopted in 1963. Beginning with the 1996 harvest, however, these fine wines were no longer called **VINO DA TAVOLA**, with most of the wines rolled into the **INDICAZIONE GEOGRAFICA TIPICA** (IGT) category, discussed below.

INDICAZIONE GEOGRAFICA TIPICA (IGT)

EACH IGT ZONE is regulated as to the growing area in which the grapes are grown and approved grape varieties. IGT wines may be produced within official DOC or DOCG zones (see pages 358 and 362), but IGT labels cannot lay claim to that zone, or a specific village, a recognized estate, or single vineyard. IGT zones are often larger than single DOC or DOCG zones, and will most often be named for a province (Toscana [Tuscany] is an IGT zone), part of a province, a particular valley, or a range of hills or mountains. Under the new European Union wine laws, this category will change its name to *indicazione geografica protetta* (IGP).

Until 1992, these wines were to be simply designated as "*vino tipico*." Strangely, although the *vino tipico* category had been part of the Italian wine laws since 1963, not one Italian wine was ever classified as such, and until 1996 it appeared that the IGT designation was headed for the same fate. Producers of nontraditional wines, such as Sangiovese/Cabernet blends made in the Chianti region or Chardonnay produced in Veneto, would just designate their wines as the now extinct *vino da tavola*, thereby avoiding a lot of bureaucratic hassle and also registering their protest against a law they did not respect.

In 1996, after much discussion and agreement between the Italian government and leading wine producers, applications for IGT designation poured into the agricultural ministry. Currently, there are about 120 IGT zones in Italy, and the number is increasing. Giovanni Goria's fervent, though idealistic, hope was that eventually 40 percent of Italy's wine production would fall into the IGT category. This would represent about 10 percent of the world's production of wine.

IGT includes a wide range of very fine wines, formerly elevated and refined *vinos da tavola* that rely on the reputation of the producer as a sure sign of quality. Many of these wines (such as Solaia, Tignanello, SummuS, and Tincsvil, all from Tuscany) are among the most expensive Italy offers and, at least within the confines of the Italian wine laws, some of the most nontraditional. Since these wines can be the finest expression of the winemaker's art, the IGT designation has developed a certain panache, especially since quite a few of these wines have met with astounding commercial success in the export markets. The first IGT wine to be granted DOC status—its own denomination of origin—was the historic Sassicaia, a Cabernet-based wine produced by Tenuta San Guido for the first time in 1968, using vine cuttings from Château Lafite Rothschild. Its DOC zone is Bolgheri Sassicaia, located in the coastal Maremma district of Tuscany.

Although many of Italy's IGT wines are produced in Tuscany, other wine regions, such as Veneto, Campania, Sicily, Sardinia, and Apulia are producing interesting wines made from both international varietals and Italian vinifera.

The IGT Zones of Italy

The IGT appellations consumers will find on labels include the following 122 place names, which will often be coupled with a vintage year and the name of the region. (This list is arranged by region; the regions of Piedmont and Valle d'Aosta, by choice, have no IGT zones.)

THE NORTHWEST REGIONS

LIGURIA

Colline Savonesi

LOMBARDY

Alto Mincio

Benaco Bresciano

Bergamasca

Collina del Milanese

Montenetto di Brescia

Provincia di Mantova or Mantova

Provincia di Pavia or Pavia

Quistello

Ronchi di Brescia

Sabbioneta

Sebino

Terrazze Retiche di Sondrio

Valcamonica

THE NORTHEAST REGIONS

FRIULI–VENEZIA GIULIA

Alto Livenza

Delle Venezie

Venezia Giulia

TRENTINO–ALTO ADIGE

Atesino delle Venezie

Delle Venezie

Mitterberg

Vallagarina

Vigneti delle Dolomiti

LEFT: *The Cabreo winery produces La Pietra, a Chardonnay from the Toscana IGT zone. Chardonnay is a nontraditional grape grown in a traditional place (Chianti Classico) and therefore is designated as IGT.* RIGHT: *Oreno, a blend of Sangiovese, Cabernet Sauvignon, and Merlot, is produced by Sette Ponti in Tuscany. Oreno is an example of an IGT wine that combines a traditional grape with two nontraditional grapes.*

VENETO

Alto Livenza
Colli Trevigiani
Conselvano
Delle Venezie
Marca Trevigiana
Provincia di Verona or Veronese
Vallagarina
Veneto
Veneto Orientale
Vigneti delle Dolomiti

CENTRAL ITALY

ABRUZZI

Alto Tirino
Colli Aprutini
Colli del Sangro
Colline Frentane
Colline Pescaresi
Colline Teatine
Del Vastese or Histonium
Terre di Chieti
Valle Peligna

EMILIA-ROMAGNA

Bianco di Castelfranco Emilia
Emilia or dell'Emilia
Forlì
Fortana del Taro
Modena or Provincia di Modena
Ravenna
Rubicone
Sillaro or Bianco del Sillaro
Terre di Velleja
Val Tidone

LAZIO

Civitella d'Agliano
Colli Cimini
Frusinate or del Frusinate
Lazio
Nettuno

MARCHES

Marche

MOLISE

Costa Viola
Esaro
Lipuda
Locride
Osco or Terre degli Osci
Palizzi
Pellaro
Rotae
Scilla
Val di Neto
Valdamato
Valle del Crati

TUSCANY

Alta Valle della Greve
Colli della Toscana Centrale
Maremma Toscana
Toscano or Toscana
Val di Magra

UMBRIA

Allerona
Bettona
Cannara
Narni
Spello
Umbria

SOUTHERN ITALY AND ISLANDS

APULIA

Apulia
Daunia
Murgia
Salento
Tarantino
Valle d'Itria

BASILICATA

Basilicata
Grottino di Roccanova

CALABRIA

Arghillà
Calabria
Condoleo

CAMPANIA

Beneventano
Campania
Colli di Salerno
Dugenta
Epomeo
Paestum
Pompeiano
Roccamonfina
Terre del Volturno

SARDINIA

Barbagia
Colli del Limbara
Isola dei Nuraghi
Marmilla
Nurra or Nurra Algherese
Ogliastra
Parteolla
Planargia
Provincia di Nuoro or Nuoro
Romangia
Sibiola
Tharros
Trexenta
Valle del Tirso
Valli di Porto Pino

SICILY

Camarro
Colli Ericini
Fontanarossa di Cerda
Salemi
Salina
Sicilia
Valle Belice

DENOMINAZIONE DI ORIGINE CONTROLLATA (DOC)

A WINE DESIGNATED DOC—denomination of origin, the equivalent of a French AOC, a controlled appellation of origin—is made from approved grape varieties and grown in approved vineyards located in demarcated geographical zones. Production methods and aging minimums are also controlled under DOC. Each of the approximately three hundred DOC zones can be as large as an entire region or as small as part of a commune or town. Subregions, such as a *classico* district—the traditional heartland of a region, often with the best vineyards—may be demarcated. Some of the best-known *classico* districts are Chianti Classico, Valpolicella Classico, Orvieto Classico, and Soave Classico, among many others.

Aside from the broad strokes painted by the DOC laws, local consortia of growers and producers further define the qualifications for each particular DOC. For example, the growers' CONSORZIO in Valpolicella Classico meets to decide yields per hectare in each particular vintage, within the limits set forth by the national DOC criteria. Nominations for new DOC zones are made by the *consorzio* and local chambers of commerce, submitted to regional DOC representatives, and then forwarded to the federal DOC commission, a part of the Ministry of Agriculture.

Each DOC controls the following aspects of wine produced within its boundaries:

- Grape types permitted and in what percentages; for some wines, minimum and maximum elevations for planting
- Maximum yield per hectare of grapes and pruning methods to be used in the vineyard
- Total gallons/hectoliters of wine produced
- Minimum alcohol levels for wines produced within the DOC
- Vinification method for some wines
- Aging methods and minimum length of aging for *riserva* or SUPERIORE wines (each DOC zone has its own minimum aging requirements).

In addition to these regulations, chaptalization is not allowed in the production of any Italian wine. Under the revised European Union wine laws of August 2009, this prohibition may extend to all wines produced within the EU member nations.

In a practice begun in 1990 in Piedmont, each DOC is supposed to meet certain minimum standards of color, aroma, and flavor, all of which are controlled by tasting commissions. All Italian wines offered for sale are supposed to pass stringent chemical analyses for minimum alcohol percentage by volume, as well as for total acidity. In some cases, minimum and maximum residual sugar levels are set, especially for wines that are made in a particular DOC area, but in different styles. For example, Orvieto, a white DOC wine from the adjoining provinces of Umbria and Lazio, ranges from dry to semisweet to sweet, and sugar levels are set for each wine style.

In this chapter, we will examine the major DOC zones in our discussion of each of Italy's wine-producing regions. Below is a current (2009) list of the 316 DOC zones of Italy, arranged by region. Note that under the amended EU wine laws of 2009, producers in these DOC zones may elect to become part of a larger DOP (*denominazione di origine protetta*) zone. Especially in well-known DOC zones, producers are extremely unlikely to elect this option.

THE NORTHWEST REGIONS

AOSTA VALLEY

Valle d'Aosta

LIGURIA

Cinque Terre and Cinque Terre
    Sciacchetrà
Colli di Luni
Colline di Levanto
Golfo del Tigullio
Pornassio or Ormeasco di
    Pornassio
Riviera Ligure di Ponente
Rossese di Dolceacqua or
    Dolceacqua
Val Polcevera

LOMBARDY

Botticino
Capriano del Colle
Cellatica
Garda
Garda Colli Mantovani
Lambrusco Mantovano
Lugana
Moscato di Scanzo
Oltrepo Pavese
Riviera del Garda Bresciano
San Colombano al Lambro
San Martino della Battaglia
Terre di Franciacorta
Valcalepio
Valtellina Rosso or Rosso di
    Valtellina

PIEDMONT

Albugnano
Alta Langa
Barbera d'Alba
Boca
Bramaterra
Canavese
Carema
Cisterna d'Asti
Colli Tortonesi
Collina Torinese
Colline Novaresi
Colline Saluzzesi

Cortese dell'Alto Monferrato
Coste della Sesia
Dolcetto d'Acqui
Dolcetto d'Alba
Dolcetto d'Asti
Dolcetto delle Langhe Monregalesi
Dolcetto di Diano d'Alba
Dolcetto di Dogliani
Erbaluce di Caluso or Caluso
Fara
Freisa d'Asti
Freisa di Chieri
Gabiano
Grignolino d'Asti
Grignolino del Monferrato
    Casalese
Langhe
Lessona
Loazzolo
Malvasia di Casorzo d'Asti
Malvasia di Castelnuovo Don
    Bosco
Monferrato
Nebbiolo d'Alba
Piemonte
Pinerolese
Rubino di Cantavenna
Ruché di Castagnole Monferrato
Sizzano
Strevi
Valsusa
Verduno Pelaverga or Verduno

THE NORTHEAST REGIONS

FRIULI-VENEZIA GIULIA

Carso
Colli Orientali del Friuli
Collio Goriziano or Collio
Friuli Annia
Friuli Aquileia
Friuli Grave
Friuli Isonzo
Friuli Latisana
Lison-Pramaggiore

TRENTINO-ALTO ADIGE

Alto Adige

Caldaro or Lago di Caldaro
Casteller
Teroldego Rotaliano
Trentino
Trento
Valdadige
Valdadige Terradeiforti

VENETO

Arcole
Bagnoli di Sopra or Bagnoli
Bardolino
Bianco di Custoza
Breganze
Colli Berici
Colli di Conegliano
Colli Euganei
Corti Benedettine del Padovano
Gambellara
Garda
Lison-Pramaggiore
Lugana
Merlara
Montello e Colli Asolani
Monti Lessini or Lessini
Riviera del Brenta
San Martino della Battaglia
Soave
Valdadige
Valdadige Terradeiforti
Valpolicella
Vicenza
Vini del Piave or Piave

CENTRAL ITALY

ABRUZZI

Controguerra
Montepulciano d'Abruzzo
Trebbiano d'Abruzzo

EMILIA-ROMAGNA

Bosco Eliceo
Cagnina di Romagna
Colli Bolognesi
Colli Bolognesi Classico Pignoletto
Colli della Romagna Centrale
Colli di Faenza
Colli di Parma

Colli di Rimini
Colli di Scandiano e Canossa
Colli d'Imola
Colli Piacentini
Lambrusco di Sorbara
Lambrusco Grasparossa di
   Castelvetro
Lambrusco Salamino di Santa
   Croce
Pagadebit di Romagna
Reggiano
Reno
Romagna Albana Spumante
Sangiovese di Romagna
Trebbiano di Romagna

LAZIO
Aleatico di Gradoli
Aprilia
Atina
Bianco Capena
Castelli Romani
Cerveteri
Cesanese di Affile
Cesanese di Olevano Romano
Circeo
Colli Albani
Colli della Sabina
Colli Etruschi Viterbesi
Colli Lanuvini
Cori
Est! Est!! Est!!! di Montefiascone
Frascati
Genazzano
Marino
Montecompatri Colonna
Nettuno
Orvieto
Tarquinia
Velletri
Vignanello
Zagarolo

MARCHES
Bianchello del Metauro
Colli Maceratesi
Colli Pesaresi
Esino

Falerio dei Colli Ascolani or
   Falerio
Lacrima di Morro d'Alba
Offida
Pergola
Rosso Piceno
Serrapetrona
Terreni di San Severino
Verdicchio dei Castelli di Iesi
Verdicchio di Matelica

MOLISE
Biferno
Molise
Pentro di Isernia or Pentro

TUSCANY
Ansonica Costa dell'Argentario
Bianco della Valdinievole
Bianco dell'Empolese
Bianco di Pitigliano
Bianco Pisano di San Torpè
Bolgheri and Bolgheri Sassicaia
Candia dei Colli Apuani
Capalbio
Barco Reale di Carmignano
Colli dell'Etruria Centrale
Colli di Luni
Colline Lucchesi
Cortona
Elba
Montecarlo
Montecucco
Monteregio di Massa Marittima
Montescudaio
Moscadello di Montalcino
Orcia
Parrina
Pietraviva
Pomino
Rosso di Montalcino
Rosso di Montepulciano
San Gimignano
Sant'Antimo
Sovana
Terratico di Bibbona
Val d'Arbia
Val di Cornia

Valdichiana
Vin Santo del Chianti
Vin Santo del Chianti Classico
Vin Santo di Montepulciano

UMBRIA
Assisi
Colli Altotiberini
Colli Amerini
Colli del Trasimeno
Colli Martani
Colli Perugini
Lago di Corbara
Montefalco
Orvieto
Rosso Orvietano or Orvietano
   Rosso
Torgiano

SOUTHERN ITALY AND ISLANDS
APULIA
Aleatico di Apulia
Alezio
Brindisi
Cacc'e Mmitte di Lucera
Castel del Monte
Copertino
Galatina
Gioia del Colle
Gravina
Leverano
Lizzano
Locorotondo
Martina or Martina Franca
Matino
Moscato di Trani
Nardò
Orta Nova
Ostuni
Primitivo di Manduria
Rosso Barletta
Rosso Canosa or Canasium
Rosso di Cerignola
Salice Salentino
San Severo
Squinzano

BASILICATA

Aglianico del Vulture
Matera
Terre dell'Alta Val d'Agri

CALABRIA

Bivongi
Cirò
Donnici
Greco di Bianco
Lamezia
Melissa
Pollino
San Vito di Luzzi
Sant'Anna di Isola Capo Rizzuto
Savuto
Scavigna
Verbicaro

CAMPANIA

Aglianico del Taburno
Aversa
Campi Flegrei
Capri
Castel San Lorenzo
Cilento
Costa d'Amalfi
Falerno del Massico
Galluccio
Guardia Sanframondi or
　Guardiolo
Irpinia
Ischia
Penisola Sorrentina
Sannio
Sant'Agata dei Goti
Solopaca
Taburno
Vesuvio

SARDINIA

Alghero
Arborea
Campidano di Terralba or Terralba
Cannonau di Sardegna
Carignano del Sulcis
Girò di Cagliari
Malvasia di Bosa
Malvasia di Cagliari
Mandrolisai
Monica di Cagliari
Monica di Sardegna
Moscato di Cagliari
Moscato di Sardegna
Moscato di Sorso Sennori
Nasco di Cagliari
Nuragus di Cagliari
Sardegna Semidano
Vermentino di Sardegna
Vernaccia di Oristano

SICILY

Alcamo or Bianco d'Alcamo
Contea di Sclafani
Contessa Entellina
Delia Nivolelli
Eloro
Erice
Etna
Faro
Malvasia delle Lipari
Mamertino di Milazzo
Marsala
Menfi
Monreale
Moscato di Noto
Moscato di Pantelleria
Moscato di Siracusa
Moscato Passito di Pantelleria
Riesi
Salaparuta
Sambuca di Sicilia
Santa Margherita di Belice
Sciacca
Vittoria

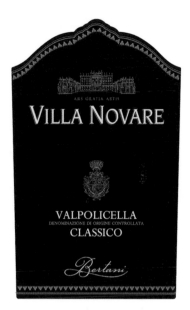

TOP: *The DOC is Valpolicella Classico, indicating that the grapes were grown in the traditional heartland (the* classico *district) of the larger DOC, Valpolicella. The wine is produced by the Bertani winery.*
BOTTOM: *A DOC label: Dolcetto d'Alba, produced by Vietti in the Piedmont region of Italy. In this case, Dolcetto is the grape name and Alba is the place name.*

CONSORZIO

Throughout Italy, the *consorzio* system is a voluntary association of wine producers and grape growers, and each *consorzio* offers technical and marketing assistance to its membership; Chianti Classico's *consorzio* is the best known and one of the best organized. Some of the Italian *consorzi* enjoy government approval and maintain standards that are higher than those set by DOC and DOCG, as demonstrated by their laboratories and tasting panels. These *consorzi* seem to work well, if for no other reason than what the possible alternative to them seems to be: lots of arguing and bickering among growers and producers.

DENOMINAZIONE DI ORIGINE CONTROLLATA E GARANTITA (DOCG)

THE HIGHEST LEVEL ATTAINABLE within the DOC laws, all DOCG wines must be sold in bottles smaller than 1.25 gallons/5 liters and an official numbered tag must be placed on the bottle across the cork's capsule or the bottle neck. It is not uncommon for the bottles to also be numbered by the producer. DOCG wines must submit to even more stringent organoleptic analysis—a serious judging of their appearance, nose, and taste—than DOC wines. Some producers from DOCG regions have had their wines publicly rejected by the tasting commissions; in such cases, the wines must be declassified.

To apply for DOCG status, the DOC zone must have at least five years, history as a recognized denomination (for an IGT wine, the process takes a minimum of ten years; it must be at least five years as part of the IGT designation and another five years as an integrated part of a DOC zone applying for DOCG status). According to Italian wine law, the proposed DOCG zone must reflect well upon itself as well as the Italian wine industry, creating a "reputation and commercial impact both at home and at an international level." There are essentially four reasons, then, for granting DOCG status to a former DOC zone. First, the potential DOCG zone has produced wines of historical importance. Second, the quality of the wines produced in the zone has been recognized and sustained on an international level. Third, the wine has improved tremendously and has attracted atten-tion. Fourth, the wines produced in the zone have contributed substantially to Italy's financial health.

According to the amended EU wine laws, producers in these DOCG zones may choose to become part of a larger DOP zone, though choosing this option is highly improbable, as DOCG status is highly coveted among Italian wine producers.

As anyone can see, DOCG designation is not an exact science. Still, many of Italy's DOCG wines represent some of the nation's best wines. The followng is an annotated list of Italy's DOCG zones, arranged by region.

DOCG ZONES FOR REDS

Currently, there are twenty-nine DOCG zones for red wines.

TUSCANY Brunello di Montalcino, Chianti, Chianti Classico, Vino Nobile di Montepulciano, Carmignano, Morellino di Scansano, and Elba Aleatico Passito.

The "backbone" grape in all but one of these wines is Sangiovese. By law, Brunello di Montalcino, the first DOCG in Italy and the most esteemed traditional wine produced in Tuscany, must be 100 percent Sangiovese. The *normale* wine must be aged for a minimum of fifty months before release, and Brunello di Montalcino Riserva must be aged a minimum of sixty-two months. Brunello di Montalcino is capable of long aging in the bottle and can be enjoyed anywhere from ten to thirty years after the wine's vintage date.

Chianti Classico is one of Tuscany's red DOCGs. Sangiovese is the most important grape in all of Tuscany's red DOCG wines.

As of 1999, Chianti may be anywhere from 75 percent to 100 percent Sangiovese, and Chianti Classico anywhere from 80 percent to 100 percent Sangiovese, with other legal grape types allowed in the blend. The Chianti DOCG actually contains seven subregions or districts, whose names may or may not appear on Chianti labels. The seven districts of the Chianti DOCG are Colli Arentini, Colli Fiorentini, Colli Senesi, Colline Pisane, Montalbano, Montespertoli, and Rufina. Chianti Classico, from the oldest and most prized district of the region, is a separate DOCG, with somewhat more restrictive standards for production.

Surprisingly, Carmignano, originally a subregion of Chianti, allows only 50 percent Sangiovese. The wine requires 20 percent Canaiolo, a local red grape, but may be made from as much as 20 percent Cabernet Sauvignon and Cabernet Franc, because that blend is consistent with its long history, going back hundreds of years.

Vino Nobile di Montepulciano also has a long and poetic history as one of Tuscany's great wines. It is a superb wine that must contain at least 70 percent Sangiovese.

Morellino di Scansano received its DOCG designation in 2006. The wine must be at least 85 percent Sangiovese.

The DOCG Sangiovese-based wines of Tuscany are all full-bodied and tannic when young, with the exception of Chianti, which, depending on its district and its age, can be a light- to medium-bodied red, labeled simply "Chianti," or a full-bodied powerhouse when produced as Chianti Classico Riserva.

Elba Aleatico Passito was awarded DOCG status in 2009. Produced on the Tuscan island of Elba, the wine is made from Aleatico grapes that, after harvest, are dried for a minimum of ten days. This intensely sweet red wine is full-bodied.

PIEDMONT   Barbaresco, Barolo, Gattinara, Ghemme, Roero, Dolcetto di Dogliani Superiore, Dolcetto di Ovada, Barbera d'Asti, Barbera del Monferrato Superiore, and Acqui/Brachetto d'Acqui

The Nebbiolo grape produces some of the finest and world-renowned full-bodied red wines of this region, especially Barbaresco and Barolo, produced in the southern Langhe area of the Piedmont. Both of these extraordinary wines must be 100 percent Nebbiolo. The age-worthy wines are full-bodied, with good tannic structure and harmonious, balanced acidity. Barbaresco must be aged a minimum of twenty-six months before release; *riserva* wines must be aged a minimum of fifty months.

Barolo must be aged at least thirty-eight months; *riserva* wines must be aged at least sixty months.

Roero, produced in the sandy soils of the hills of the Langhe region near the communes of Barolo and Barbaresco, must be 95 to 100 percent Nebbiolo. Roero is assertive, but needs less aging to achieve balance than Barolo or Barbaresco.

Gattinara and Ghemme, both produced further north, are not quite as opulent and powerful as the DOCG wines of the Langhe. Gattinara must be 90 percent Nebbiolo and may include some Bonarda and/or Vespolina grapes. The wine must be aged a minimum of three years before release, four years for Gattinara Riserva.

Ghemme can be made with between 65 percent and 85 percent Nebbiolo and includes both Vespolina and Bonarda in the blend. Aging requirements are the same as for Gattinara.

Acqui/Brachetto d'Acqui is a berry-sweet red wine, either **SPUMANTE** (sparkling) or **FRIZZANTE** (semi-sparkling), made only from the Brachetto grape. It is a fun wine and a great match with dark chocolates.

Dolcetto di Dogliani Superiore bestows recognition on the Dolcetto grape, which produces a wine that is normally—and happily—enjoyed within a year or two of its vintage date. But this wine is a bit different, because when aged a legal minimum of eighteen months (*superiore*), most of it in small oak barrels, it takes on a measure of complexity that is unusual for Dolcetto. Dolcetto di Dogliani Superiore was elevated to DOCG status in 2007.

Barbera d'Asti and Barbera del Monferrato Superiore were elevated from DOC to DOCG in 2008. Barbera is the most-planted grape in the Piedmont region, and these two DOCG zones produce some superb wines. Barbera is usually a medium-bodied wine, with searingly dramatic but pleasant acidity, enjoyable in its youth or with some age.

Both Barbera d'Asti and Barbera del Monferrato

Barolo is an esteemed DOCG wine from Italy's Piedmont region. The wine is produced solely from Nebbiolo grapes.

must be made from a minimum of 85 percent Barbera grapes, with up to 15 percent Dolcetto and/or Grignolino allowed in the blend. *Superiore* versions must be aged at least twelve months. Barbera d'Asti Superiore produced in the specific communes of Colli Astiani, Nizza, and Tinella must be aged between twenty-one months and twenty-four months.

In 2009, Dolcetto di Ovada was awarded DOCG status. Grown in and around the town of Ovada, this medium-bodied dry red wine must age for at least one year, from the first of January following the year of harvest. Dolcetto di Ovada must attain an alcohol level of at least 12.5 percent.

UMBRIA Torgiano Rosso Riserva and Sagrantino di Montefalco

Torgiano Rosso Riserva is a fine, powerful red wine made by a single producer, Lungarotti, mostly from Sangiovese grapes (50 to 70 percent, with 15 to 30 percent Canaiolo and up to 10 percent other legal varieties). The wine must be aged a minimum of thirty-six months before release.

Sagrantino di Montefalco (also known as Montefalco Sagrantino), rich and powerful, is made from the local Sagrantino varietal, a historic varietal that was close to extinction prior to its DOCG designation in 1993. The wine, in both its dry and somewhat sweeter PASSITO versions, must be aged at least twenty-nine months before release.

LOMBARDY Valtellina Superiore and Sforzato/Sfurzat di Valtellina and Moscato de Scanzo.

Since late 1998, the Valtellina Superiore DOCG designation has applied to six famous red wines made in this region and named for their subregion: Sassella, Grumello, Inferno, Maroggia, Staggafassli, and Valgella. Most of these Nebbiolo-based wines (90 to 100 percent Nebbiolo; here the grape is known as Chiavennasca) produced from vineyards bordering Switzerland are little-known outside northwest Italy and the countries bordering the region, but they can be quite elegant and ageworthy. Sasella is considered the finest of the six wines, Grumello the

lightest, Inferno the most powerful, and Valgella the simplest and most accessible. The wines must be aged for twenty-four months, the *riserva* wines for thirty-six months (thirty-five months for Valgella Riserva).

Another red DOCG of Lombardy is Sforzato di Valtellina/Sfurzat di Valtellina, produced from Nebbiolo grapes that are left to wither on the vine and are late-picked, producing a dry red wine, but with much power. The wine must be aged eighteen months before release.

In 2009, Moscato di Scanzo was elevated from DOC to DOCG. A rare red Moscato, this cherry-sweet wine is produced from partially dried grapes grown in the province of Bergamo. Moscato di Scanzo must be aged for a minimum of two years, beginning the process on November 1.

CAMPANIA Taurasi

The first red wine from Italy's southern provinces to be deemed DOCG, Taurasi is made mostly from the ancient Aglianico grape (85 percent), introduced to southern Italy by the Greeks. Taurasi is quite tannic in its youth, and when mature, it is a wonderful powerhouse of a wine. Taurasi must be aged for thirty-six months before release, the *riserva* wines for forty-eight months.

VENETO Bardolino Superiore, Amarone, and Recioto della Valpolicella

Bardolino Superiore received its DOCG designation because of improvements in the region's vineyards—yields were cut by 40 percent—and in the wineries. Bardolino Superiore must age at least a year before release. Produced mostly from Corvina grapes, sometimes blended with Rondinella and Molinara, with as much as a combined 20 percent of Sangiovese, Barbera, Merlot, and Cabernet Sauvignon allowed in the blend, Bardolino Superiore is a dependable, medium-bodied dry red wine.

Amarone and Recioto della Valpolicella received DOCG status in 2009. Made from dried (*passito*) grapes grown in the Valpolicella DOC, Amarone is dry and powerful—

LEFT: *A passito* version of the DOCG wine Montefalco Sagrantino. Passito *wine is made from dried or semi-dried grapes, resulting in a complex, sweet wine.* RIGHT: *Taurasi, made from the ancient Greek grape Aglianico, is a powerful red DOCG wine from Campania.*

about 16 percent alcohol—while Recioto della Valpolicella is sweeter, but still full-bodied.

SICILY Cerasuolo di Vittoria

Sicily's first, and so far only, DOCG zone (awarded in 2005), Cerasuolo di Vittoria is produced from Nero d'Avola and Frappato grapes. The wine is medium- to full-bodied and age-worthy, becoming noticeably more delicate with the passage of time. *Normale* must age for at least eight months before release. Cerasuolo di Vittoria Classico must age at least eighteen months.

MARCHE Cònero and Vernaccia di Serrapetrona

Cònero, formerly referred to as Rosso Cònero, is produced from mostly Montepulciano grapes (at least 85 percent, with the remainder, if any, being Sangiovese) along the seacoast of Marche, in and around the city of Ancona. The best vines grow on the slopes of Monte Cònero, which reaches altitudes of about 1,700 feet/570 meters. Cònero, a medium- to full-bodied wine, must be aged at least twenty-four months before release, therefore making the wine a *riserva*.

Vernaccia di Serrapetrona is a unique wine made in very small quantitites, from the rare red Vernaccia Nera

grape. This is a sparkling wine made in both dry and sweet styles from semi-dried grapes. Dry or sweet, the wine must be aged eight months prior to release.

ABRUZZI Montepulciano d'Abruzzo Colline Teramane

Montepulciano d'Abruzzo, a medium-bodied red wine, is produced throughout the Abruzzi region as a well-known, dependable DOC wine, but it is in the vineyards of the hills of the Teramo province—the Colline Teramane—that the wine has shown at its best. Montepulciano d'Abruzzo Colline Teramane, awarded DOCG status in 2003, is made from at least 90 percent Montepulciano grapes; *normale* must age at least twenty-four months before release, *riserva* at least thirty-six months.

LAZIO Cesanese del Piglio

In 2009, Cesanese del Piglio became Lazio's first DOCG zone. This delicate and dry red wine must be made from at least 90 percent Cesanese, an indigenous variety, and the remainder must be produced from other approved local red grape types. The *riserva* designation is assigned to wines that have aged a minimum of eighteen months.

DOCG ZONES FOR WHITE AND SPARKLING

Currently, there are sixteen DOCG zones for white and sparkling wines.

EMILIA-ROMAGNA Albana di Romagna

In 1987, this was the first white wine granted DOCG status, based on its long and fabled history and perhaps because the Emilia-Romagna region is also well-known and respected worldwide for some magnificent foods, including ham (Prosciutto di Parma), cheese (Parmigiano Reggiano), and vinegar (Aceto Balsamico). Albana di Romagna is produced in both dry and sweet *passito* versions and is made from 100 percent Albana grapes.

TUSCANY Vernaccia di San Gimignano

This was Italy's very first DOC (1966), so for historic reasons, it almost had to become DOCG in 1993. Most of the wines are perfectly drinkable, but only a

LEFT, TOP: *Made from Nero d'Avola and Frappato grapes, Cerasuolo di Vittoria is Sicily's first DOCG wine.* LEFT, BOTTOM: *Cònero, a DOCG dry red wine from Marche, is medium- to full-bodied with intense aromatics and made mostly from Montepulciano grapes.* RIGHT, TOP: *While Montepulciano d'Abruzzo is produced throughout the region as a DOC wine, the hillsides of the Colline Teramane subzone contain the best vineyards for the DOCG version.* RIGHT, BOTTOM: *Vernaccia di San Gimignano, a dry white from Tuscany, was Italy's first DOC wine; it has been DOCG since 1993.*

few stand out for their quality—a perfect example of the importance of knowing the reputation of the producer of Italian wines. Made from the Vernaccia grape (at least 90 percent), the *riserva* must age at least twelve months, but this is a wine to enjoy young and fresh; additional aging is really beside the point.

PIEDMONT Asti/Moscato d'Asti, Gavi/Cortese di Gavi, Roero, and Roero Arneis

Asti/Moscato d'Asti is a shared DOCG, which includes both the world-renowned sparkler Asti (before 1994, when it became DOCG, known as Asti Spumante) and the half-sparkling (*frizzante*) wine Moscato d'Asti, made with just a prickle of bubbles. Both are made solely from the Moscato grape, and both can be engaging sweet wines, with low alcohol of 5 to 7 percent. A perfect match with the Italian cheesecake *pizza dolce*. Enjoy the wines when they are young and fresh.

Gavi/Cortese di Gavi DOCG is located in the Alessandria province of southern Piedmont, close by the border with Liguria; the wine is dry and light- to medium-bodied. A wine labeled "Gavi di Gavi" is a wine made from grapes grown in and around the namesake town. The wine must be made from 100 percent Cortese grapes and is usually a still wine, but it may also be made as a dry *frizzante* or *spumante* wine.

Roero Arneis must be made from 100 percent Arneis, a grape that has grown in the Piedmont region for at least six hundred years. Arneis, which means "rascal" in the Piedmontese dialect, is difficult to grow, but is certainly worth the effort. The wine is medium-bodied and dry, and at its best displays a nose reminiscent of hazelnuts. Most often produced as a still wine, dry *spumante* versions are also allowed.

LOMBARDY Franciacorta and Oltrepò Pavese Spumante Metodo Classico

A fine *méthode champenoise* sparkler, Franciacorta was granted DOCG status in 1998, and deservedly so. The wine must age twenty-five months on its lees (thirty-seven for vintage-dated wines) and makes brilliant *brut* and creamy rosé bubbly. Pinot Nero (Pinot Noir), Pinot Bianco (Pinot Blanc), and Chardonnay are the permitted grapes for Franciacorta.

There is a river of wine produced in the Oltrepò Pavese DOC, but only Oltrepò Pavese Spumante Metodo Classico, made mostly from the Pinot Nero (Pinot Noir) grape—at least 70 percent, with up to 30 percent of Chardonnay, Pinot Bianco, or Pinot Grigio—was granted DOCG status in 2008. *Normale* is aged for a minimum of eighteen months, vintage wines for at least twenty-four months.

VENETO Recioto di Soave, Soave Superiore, Recioto di Gambellara, Conegliano-Valdobbiadene Prosecco Superiore, and Colli Asolani Prosecco Bianco, Bianco Spumante, and Bianco Frizzante

Recioto di Soave is a sweet white wine made from *passito* (semi-dried) grapes and has always been considered something of a rich, syrupy delicacy. Still, its elevation to DOCG has not had tremendous impact on the international wine market. Traditionally, the wine is made mostly from Garganega and Trebbiano grapes, but currently as much as 30 percent Chardonnay or Pinot Bianco may be used in the blend.

Soave Superiore is a dry white wine made from the same grapes as Recioto di Soave, but from a normal harvest; the grapes are not dried. In 2001, Soave Superiore (or Soave Classico Superiore), which must be aged ten months before release (twenty-four months for *riserva*), was awarded DOCG status, separating it from the Soave and Soave Classico DOC regions. The wines, whether DOC or DOCG, are medium-bodied, and in the hands of a great winemaker, Soave, Soave Classico, or Soave Superiore can become a memorable wine.

In 2009, three of Veneto's DOC wine regions became DOCG, including two that produce the wildly popular

---

LEFT, TOP: *Gavi, produced from 100 percent Cortese grapes in the Piedmont region, is a light- to medium-bodied dry DOCG white wine.* **LEFT, BOTTOM**: *Franciacorta is an elegant sparkling DOCG wine from Lombardy, made by the* metodo classico. *The* brut *and rosé versions are superb.* **RIGHT**: *Recioto di Soave is a rich, syrupy, sweet white DOCG wine from Veneto, produced from* passito *grapes.*

(mostly) sparkling wine Prosecco. As Prosecco is a grape, it can be produced anywhere in the world, sporting a varietal label. Brazil and Austria, for example, produce quite a bit of Prosecco. With the two major Prosecco-producing wine regions in Veneto gaining DOCG status, producers believe that their enhanced designation would distinguish their wines from the river of mostly inferior Prosecco produced in other countries and other Italian wine regions.

Conegliano-Valdobbiadene Prosecco Superiore must be produced from a minimum of 85 percent Prosecco grapes (locally sometimes called Glera). Other grapes include both native vinifera and international varieties. However, Prosecco Bianco produced in this DOCG must contain only traditional local grapes. If vintage Prosecco is produced here, the wine must be at least 85 percent from the vintage year. If the grapes are harvested in the Cartizze subzone—reputed by many to have the best vineyards—the name of the subzone may appear on the label.

The Colli Asolani Prosecco Bianco, Bianco Spumante, and Bianco Frizzante DOCG must also be produced from a minimum of 85 percent Prosecco (Glera) grapes, with the remainder made up of local vinifera. Both dry (*secco*) and sweet (**AMABILE**) wines may be produced.

The other new DOCG in Veneto is Recioto di Gambellara. This is a sweet wine made from at least 80 percent Garganega grapes, with the rest of the wine made from local varieties. All of the grapes must be grown in and around the town of Gambellara. Grapes are harvested by hand and partially dried until December for a sparkling wine, and until February for the still version.

FRIULI-VENEZIA GIULIA Ramandolo and Colli Orientali del Friuli Picolit

Both of these DOCG wines are rarely found in the American market, especially Ramandolo. A sweet dessert wine, Ramandolo is made from the *giallo* (yellow) clone of the Verduzzo Friulano grape, which grows on the steep slopes of the Ramandolo growing region.

Colli Orientali del Friuli Picolit is made from dried Picolit grapes, creating a complex, sweet wine. Picolit grapes yield only about a dozen grapes to a bunch (this natural selection is known as *acinellatura*), so production of Picolit is severely limited. Tasting fine Picolit is a singular experience.

CAMPANIA Greco di Tufo and Fiano di Avellino

Greco di Tufo is made from one of the oldest grapes grown in Italy. As its name indicates, the grape was introduced by the Greeks, and evidence of wine made from the grape can be traced back more than two thousand years.

Greco di Tufo is a medium- to full-bodied dry wine, an elegant wine that is a perfect accompaniment to seafood.

Fiano di Avellino, made from the ancient Fiano grape, can be a touch lighter in body than Greco di Tufo but is always at least medium-bodied. This dry wine is also a wonderful foil for seafood, especially seafood stews.

SARDINIA Vermentino di Gallura

In 1997, this wine became the first DOC wine from Sardinia to be promoted to DOCG. Combining the terroir of the ancient hills of Gallura with high-tech cool fermentation, this dry, crisp wine, made from Vermentino grapes, is the perfect accompaniment to simple shellfish and seafood stews.

NAMING ITALIAN WINES

IN ITALY, there are three basic ways to name a wine: by the name of the place the grapes are grown (e.g., Chianti); by a combination of the name of the grape *and* the place (e.g., Barbera d'Alba); by proprietary or fantasy name (e.g., Tignanello or SummuS). In addition, descriptive terms like *classico, riserva, vecchio,* **NOVELLO**, *secco, amabile,* **ABBOCCATO**, **DOLCE**, *superiore, frizzante, spumante, passito,* **RECIOTO**, *amarone,* and *liquoroso* may appear. The names

LEFT: *Greco di Tufo, made from an ancient grape introduced to Italy by the Greeks, is an elegant dry white DOCG wine from Campania.* RIGHT: *Vermentino di Gallura from Sardinia has been a DOCG wine since 1997. This dry white is a perfect accompaniment to seafood dishes.*

PLACE NAMES

Chianti (the general name of the DOCG zone)

Chianti Classico (the name of the subregion, the area between Siena and Florence; *classico* indicates the traditional heartland of a DOC or DOCG region, usually with the best vineyard sites)

Chianti Rufina (another of Chianti's better subregions, northeast of Florence; Chianti has a total of seven subregions and most use the general Chianti denomination)

Chianti Classico Riserva (from the traditional heartland and aged for a minimum number of months to be called *riserva*; each DOC or DOCG has its own minimum aging span for its *riserva* wines; in the case of Chianti Classico, it's twenty-four months)

Orvieto/Orvieto Classico (name of the DOC zone, its heartland)

Orvieto Secco (a dry version)

Orvieto Abbocato (a slightly sweet version of Orvieto)

Orvieto Amabile (a sweeter version than *abbocato*)

Frascati (name of the DOC zone)

Frascati Superiore (DOC wines with more aging and possibly higher alcohol)

Valpolicella (name of the DOC zone)

Valpolicella Classico Superiore (from the heartland, with more age and possibly higher alcohol)

Recioto della Valpolicella (strong, sweet wine made from semi-dried *passito* grapes)

Amarone della Valpolicella (made from *passito* grapes, as in a *recioto* wine, but the wine is produced dry; very high in alcohol, full-bodied, long-lived)

Valpolicella Chiaretto (a very light red or rosé wine, with very fresh flavors)

Barbaresco/Barbaresco Riserva (DOCG zone, aged wine)

Asti (DOCG zone that makes sparkling wine from Moscato grapes)

PROPRIETARY NAMES

Le Pergole Torte (Sangiovese, from Montevertine)

Luce (Merlot and Sangiovese, from Frescobaldi)

Tignanello (Sangiovese and Cabernet Sauvignon, from Marchesi Antinori)

La Pietra (Chardonnay, from Cabreo)

Ornellaia (mostly Cabernet Sauvignon and Merlot, from Tenuta dell'Ornellaia)

Serena (Sauvignon Blanc, from Castello Banfi)

COMBINATION GRAPE NAMES AND PLACE NAMES

Moscato d'Asti

Nebbiolo d'Alba

Sangiovese di Romagna

Vernaccia di San Gimignano

Cortese di Gavi

Barbera d'Asti

Dolcetto d'Alba

Brunello di Montalcino ("Brunello" is the local name for the Sangioveto Grosso clone of Sangiovese)

Montepulciano d'Abruzzo

Note: On this kind of label, the grape name is almost always first; Italy has hundreds of vinifera grapes. In the case of, for example, Vernaccia di San Gimignano, the dry white wine from Tuscany, the grape is Vernaccia and the place is San Gimignano. Remember: grape name first, place name second.

of significant single vineyards are increasingly found on Italian DOC and DOCG labels, but there are no legal vineyard rankings or classifications under law. Assigning *cru* status to some of these vineyards is finding some favor in the Piedmont region, in Tuscany, and in Veneto.

The EU also requires that the percentage of alcohol by volume appear on the label (e.g., 12.5 percent) and that if the bottle is the standard 750 ml (75 cl) size, this number appear on the label, followed by the letter *e* if the wine is to be sold in the EU. This quirk is due to the fact that prior to EU standardization some Italian bottles contained 720 ml (72 cl).

If the wine is estate bottled, an approved phrase, such as *imbottigliato dal produttore all'origine* ("bottled by the producer at the source"), often followed by the name of the producer, appears on the label. This is the equivalent of the phrase *mis en bouteilles au château* from Bordeaux (see page 289). If the wine is produced and bottled by a cooperative or a group of cooperatives, the phrases *imbottigliato dalla cantina sociale* or *imbottigliato dai produttori riuniti* may appear. *Imbottigliato nella zona di produzione* ("bottled in the production zone") lets the buyer know that the wine is not estate bottled, but simply bottled within the legal limits of the particular DOC or DOCG zone.

ITALY'S WINE REGIONS

ITALY IS DIVIDED into twenty regions, each a political unit with provincial subregions that bear the name of the province's major city (e.g., in the province of Rome, the eponymous subregion and city are both named Rome). Each region contains anywhere from one (in Valle d'Aosta) to fifty-six (in Piedmont) DOC or DOCG zones. Taking a look at the map of Italy, we can readily divide the country into four parts, each containing smaller constituent regions.

SOUTHERN ITALY AND ISLANDS Sicily, Sardinia, Calabria, Basilicata, Apulia, and Campania

CENTRAL ITALY Emilia-Romagna, Abruzzi, Molise, Marche, Lazio, Umbria, Tuscany

NORTHWEST ITALY Liguria, Lombardy, Piedmont, Valle d'Aosta

NORTHEAST ITALY Veneto, Friuli–Venezia Giulia, and Trentino–Alto Adige

SOUTHERN ITALY

THE VINEYARDS OF SOUTHERN ITALY prompted the ancient Greeks to call their colonized area *Oenotria*, or "Land of the Vine," and the Roman poets Virgil and Horace sang the praises of the intoxicating Falernum, which is still produced in Campania. Today, southern Italy is known for both its huge production of indifferent wine as well as a much smaller production of fine wines. The "wine lake" continues to flow, though somewhat abated in recent years. Indeed, southern Italy accounts for about 30 percent of Italy's total wine production, with Apulia producing more than 10 percent of the nation's total, more than any other single region—the equivalent of 100 million cases of wine—and Sicily a close second, with the equivalent of 90 million cases produced annually, or 8 percent of national production. Because much of this wine is being used for local drinking, blending bulk wines, or for distilling into industrial alcohol, the whole of southern Italy accounts for only about 10 percent of DOC production.

A significant portion of the DOC wines of the south can be accounted for by one justly famous fortified wine, Marsala, which produces well in excess of 5,000,000 gallons/ 190,000 hectoliters each year, accounting for about 65 percent of Sicily's DOC production. On the other hand, Sicily's best dessert wine, Malvasia delle Lipari (DOC), accounts for only 6,600 gallons/250 hectoliters total production. This is a mere drop in the ocean, when one realizes that the total production of wine from the south now exceeds 400 million gallons/15 million hectoliters per year. However, this astounding number represents a 15 to 20 percent drop in total production during the last ten years and speaks volumes about the "wine lake" just beginning to run dry.

Often we hear that because the climate of southern Italy and its islands is so hot, so sunny, it can never become a premium viticultural area. This is just not true. While much of the south is drenched in sunlight, the coastal and mountain regions can be quite cool, allowing for the production of good wines. In the not-too-distant past, climate was really not the problem in southern Italy; it was human nature, customs, and bad habits. While the EU and the Italian government provided funds to improve the wines in the south, and the EU paid a premium to growers who decreased their acreage in vines, mismanagement and corruption were commonplace. Add to this a tradition of making high-alcohol, full-bodied, one-dimensional wines designed to boost the

Italy
Main DOC/DOCG Wine Regions

Valle d'Aosta

Piedmont
1 Gattinara DOCG, Ghemme DOCG
2 Barbera d'Asti DOCG
3 Roero DOCG
4 Barbaresco DOCG
5 Dolcetto d'Alba, Barbera d'Alba
6 Barolo DOCG
7 Asti DOCG, Moscato d'Asti DOCG
8 Gavi or Cortese di Gavi DOCG

Liguria

Lombardy
9 Oltrepò Pavese, Oltrepò Pavese Metodo Classico Spumante DOCG
10 Franciacorta DOCG
11 Lugana
12 Valtellina Superiore DOCG, Sforzato DOCG

Veneto
13 Bardolino, Bardolino Superiore DOCG
14 Bianco di Custoza
15 Valpolocella, Amarone DOCG
16 Soave, Soave Superiore DOCG, Recioto di Soave DOCG
17 Conegliano-Valdobbiadene Prosecco Superiore DOCG, Colli Asolani DOCG
18 Piave

Trentino–Alto Adige
19 Alto Adige
20 Lago di Caldaro
21 Santa Maddalena

Friuli–Venezia Giulia
22 Colli Orientali del Friuli
23 Collio

Emilia-Romagna
24 Lambrusco DOCs (4)
25 Albana di Romagna DOCG

Tuscany
26 Vernaccia di San Gimignano DOCG
27 Chianti DOCG, Chianti Classico DOCG
28 Brunello di Montalcino DOCG
29 Vino Nobile di Montepulciano DOCG

Umbria
30 Orvieto
31 Torgiano Rosso Riserva DOCG
32 Sagrantino di Montefalco DOC

Marche
33 Verdicchio dei Castellli di Jesi
34 Cònero DOCG

Abruzzi
35 Montepulciano d'Abruzzo, Montepulciano d'Abruzzo Colline Termane DOCG

Lazio
36 Frascati

Molise

Campania
37 Taurasi, Greco di Tufo, Fiano di Avellino DOCG

Basilicata
38 Aglianico del Vulture

Apulia
39 Locorotondo

Calabria

Sicily
40 Alcamo, Bianco d'Alcamo
41 Marsala
42 Cerasuolo di Vittorio DOCG

Sardinia
43 Cannonau di Sardegna, Vermentino di Sardegna
44 Vermentino di Gallura DOCG

thinner wines of the northerly regions, and a certain geographical isolation (particularly in Sicily and Sardinia), and you have a situation that did not readily welcome change, including an attempt to make wines of higher quality.

Today, however, the dismal portrait of southern Italy and its islands as a region known for making dismal wines has dramatically changed, and for the better. There are many shining stars: winemakers and producers whose commitment to quality is high and whose product is glorious. While some of these producers hardly represent a revolution in the wines of southern Italy—they have been making quality wines for many generations—they have been joined by younger wine producers who want to establish southern Italy and its islands as a bastion of high-quality Italian wines that can compete on the world stage. Many people who have followed the evolution of Italy as a wine-producing nation now believe, and with good reason, that southern Italy and its islands, overall, the most exciting wine region in the entire country.

Sicily

It is no exaggeration to say that for a very long time the Italian DOC laws just did not catch on in Sicily (*Sicilia*), since there was so little DOC production in this region. Instead, Sicily battled with Apulia for the title of Italy's largest—but certainly not best—wine producer. In fact, DOC was so unimportant to much of Sicily's wine industry that the quality designation for much locally consumed Sicilian wine was a simple *Q* printed on the bottle label, but it was not by any means an objective guarantee of quality.

The situation on the ground in Sicily's vineyards and wineries has truly changed, in positive and dramatic fashion, over the last twenty to thirty years. In the mid-1980s, Diego Planeta, who owned several fine vineyard sites, supervised a project for Sicily's regional wine institute to identify the best possible varietals and clones to plant in Sicily's vineyards. Because of this pioneering research, the Sicilian wine industry was reborn, with a focus on quality aimed to guarantee its survival and expansion.

Today, there are more than two hundred wine producers in Sicily, and overall they are producing the best wines that the island has ever offered to Italy and the world. Many of the finest wines are DOC, but just as many high-quality wines are IGT, especially those made from international varietals, blends of international and local vinifera, or nontraditional blends of traditional grape types.

DOCG WINES

Cerasuolo di Vittoria, produced on the southeast section of the island in the Ragusa province, is a local red wine made from a blend of no more than 60 percent Nero d'Avola (often referred to in Sicily as Calabrese) and no less than 40 percent Frappato grapes.

DOC WINES

Of Sicily's twenty-three DOC zones (see page 361), one, Moscato di Siracusa, contains about one acre/half a hectare of land and produces no wine (a good reason to review the granting of DOC zones, none of which have ever been withdrawn). Two (Faro and Moscato di Noto) produce only a few thousand bottles annually. Faro contains little more than 15 acres/6 hectares in the entire DOC. Palari and Geraci are two dedicated producers of this historic but little-known red wine. Most of the scant production of Moscato di Noto is supervised by a state-run experimental station.

A fairly small amount of Moscato di Pantelleria is made as a fresh, sweet white wine, a sun-dried Moscato di Pantelleria Passito, and a lively *spumante*. These are probably among Sicily's best Moscato wines, highlighted by the fact that Moscato di Pantelleria was only the third Italian DOC, awarded in 1971. The grapes are grown on the tiny island community of Pantelleria, which is actually closer to Tunisia than Sicily, from the Zibibbo varietal, the colloquial name for the large Moscato grape that produces Italy's best raisins.

Another tiny island, Lipari, northeast of Sicily, is home to the Malvasia delle Lipari DOC, where the descendants of winemaker Carlo Hauner produce the wine under his name. Also made in *passito* (sun-dried, raisinated grapes) or *liquoroso* (sweet and fortified) style, the standard sweet Malvasia delle Lipari is rare but is imported to the United States, where it has many admirers.

FERRANDES

Dammuso del 160...

PASSITO DI PANTELLERIA
DENOMINAZIONE DI ORIGINE CONTROLLATA

Prodotto da Salvatore Ferrandes - c.da Tracino Pantelleria - Italia
imbottigliato da "Nuova Agricoltura" scarl Pantelleria - Italia

℮ 375 ml   V.Q.P.R.D   ITALIA   14,5% vol
NON DISPERDERE IL VETRO NELL'AMBIENTE

On the northeastern part of the main island, in the province of Catania, about 212,000 gallons/8,000 hectoliters of Etna (the wine that, according to the epic poet

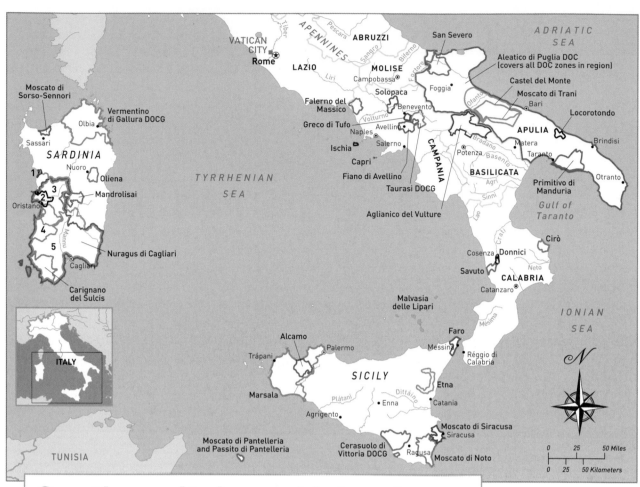

Southern Italy and Islands

Main DOC/DOCG Wine Regions

Campania
— Falerno del Massico
— Solopaca
— Greco di Tufo DOCG
— Taurasi DOCG
— Fiano di Avellino DOCG
— Ischia
— Capri

Apulia
— Aleatico di Puglia DOC (covers all DOC zones in the region)
— San Severo
— Moscato di Trani
— Castel del Monte
— Locorotondo
— Primitivo di Manduria

Basilicata
— Aglianico del Vulture

Calabria
— Cirò
— Donnici
— Savuto

Sicily
— Faro
— Etna
— Moscato di Siracusa
— Moscato di Noto
— Cerasuolo di Vittoria DOCG
— Alcamo
— Marsala
— Malvasia delle Lipari
— Moscato di Pantelleria and Passito di Pantelleria

Sardinia
— Vermentino di Gallura DOCG
— Moscato di Sorso-Sennori
— Oliena
1 Malvasia di Bosa
2 Vernaccia di Oristano
3 Arborea
— Mandrolisai
4 Campidano di Terralba
— Nuragus di Cagliari
5 Giro di Cagliari
5 Malvasia di Cagliari
5 Monica di Cagliari
5 Moscato di Cagliari
5 Nasco di Cagliari
— Carignano del Sulcis

Homer, was used by Ulysses to make the Cyclops drunk) is produced yearly as *bianco*, *bianco superiore* (said to be the best example of the wine from this picturesque town), *rosso*, and *rosato*, all made from native grapes grown in the volcanic, rocky soil created by the eruptions of Mt. Etna. There is some experimentation with Pinot Noir here, due in large part to the encouragement of the varietal by esteemed enologist Giacomo Tachis.

In western Sicily, the Alcamo DOC produces the white wine Bianco d'Alcamo from 210,00 acres/83,750 hectares, the largest vineyard expanse in all of Italy. Quality here is strictly dependent on the producer; most Alcamo wines are quite ordinary. It is a white wine made to accompany local fresh fish, made mostly from the native vinifera Catarratto—at least 80 percent. Traditionally, the best producer is Rincione.

MARSALA DOC

Far western Sicily is home to Marsala, the fortified wine with so much history, a wine that at one time was the equal of Sherry and Madeira. Since the key to the production of a great Marsala is aging of the wine in local oak barrels, the finest Marsala is the dry *vergine* or *soleras*, which is made by blending wines from various vintages, much like the *solera* method for making Sherry (see Chapter 9, page 440). Marsala Vergine ranks among the finest fortified wines in the world. During the last century, however, Marsala, which is made in a variety of styles—*secco*, *semisecco*, and *dolce*, along with *superiore* and *riserva* designations—has been largely relegated to the kitchen as an important ingredient in egg- and coffee-based dishes, as well as desserts and pastry (zabaglione and marzipan), due to its assertive flavor and lack of nuance. Also, Marsala has many imitators, and inferior fortified wines in the Marsala style have been made in other countries for many years. In 1984, the DOC laws for Marsala were rewritten, with far more restrictive regulations, so that it may one day regain its place as one of the fine fortified wines of the world. So far, the world is waiting.

Quality levels of Marsala are *fine* (aged one year), *superiore* (aged two years), *superiore riserva* (aged four years), *vergine* or *soleras* (no sweetened musts are allowed, and must be aged five years), and *vergine stravecchia* or *vergine riserva* (aged at least ten years).

Other DOC zones of Sicily that emphasize only local varietals include Eloro, Mamertino di Milazzo, Santa Margherita di Belice, and Vittoria.

DOC zones of Sicily that emphasize both local and international varietals (especially Chardonnay, Sauvignon Blanc, Cabernet Sauvignon, Merlot, and Syrah) include Contea di Sclafani, Contessa Entellina, Delia Nivolelli, Erice, Menfi, Monreale, Riesi, Salaparuta, Sambuca di Sicilia, and Sciacca.

Clearly, Sicily's vineyards and wines have undergone a renaissance. Thanks to hard work, research, and a stalwart commitment to quality, Sicily has gone from being a backwater for quality wine to being a leader. In doing so, the region has embraced the idea that local varietals can live in harmony with international grape types, so that Sicily can produce wines of high quality for both domestic consumption and export markets.

Credit for this sea change must be given to, among others, the Casa Vinicola Duca di Salaparuta, better known as Corvo, the largest winery in Sicily. Producing about 800,000 cases of wine and formerly owned by the Sicilian government, Corvo was sold to a private company in the year 2000. The Corvo group led the way in winemaking technology and export marketing with their well-made, reasonably priced white and red table wines. Their Duca Enrico, however, a red wine first produced from the 1984 vintage and made from 100 percent local grapes (Nero d'Avola) grown on fifty-year-old vines, is aged in French oak *barriques* for eighteen months. While quite expensive, the wine has met with great critical success and consumer response, proving that great wines can be made in Sicily. Corvo/Duca di Salaparuta also produces the more moderately priced Terre d'Agala, also made from local varietals and also a major success in export markets.

Another important pioneering wine producer, and one of Sicily's finest, is Regaleali, owned by the noble Tasca d'Almerita family, who produce fine wines from local varietals: Bianco is a blend of Inzolia, Cataratto, and Grecanico; Rosso del Conte is an outstanding red wine made primarily from Nero d'Avola. Regaleali produces outstanding Chardonnay and Cabernet Sauvignon, a delightful rosé, and a *méthode champenoise brut* sparkler, Almerita—made from 100 percent Chardonnay. At about 250,000 cases of wine produced each year, Regaleali is Sicily's largest wine producer.

Some of the "new" and influential quality-minded wine producers of Sicily include the following.

PLANETA

Francesca Planeta (daughter of Diego Planeta) and her cousins Allessio and Santi Planeta began their venture in the mid-1980s with a vineyard estate in the Sambuca di Sicilia DOC that has been owned by the Planeta family since the seventeenth century. Planeta wines have made a strong impact in the American market, and the winery now produces at least twelve wines, some of them from Sicilian vinifera, some from international varieties such as Chardonnay, Syrah, and Merlot. Over the past twenty years, the Planeta family has established three different wineries in Sicily to produce wines from their etstate vineyards. White wines include Cometa (made from the Fiano grape), La Segreta Bianco (Grecanico, Chardonnay, Viognier, and Fiano), and Chardonnay. Reds include Burdese (a Bordeaux blend of Cabernet Sauvignon and Cabernet Franc), a fine Merlot, La Segreta Rosso (Nero d'Avola, Merlot, Syrah, Cabernet Franc), Santa Cecilia (100 percent Nero d'Avola), and Sicily's only DOCG, Cerasuolo di Vittoria, produced from Nero d'Avola and Frappato grapes. As befits a contemporary, quality-driven, artisinal winery, each Planeta wine label is a distinctive work of modern art.

DONNAFUGATA

Speaking of beautiful wine labels, in 1983, the Rallo family founded Donnafugata winery, and since that time have made wonderful whites and reds from Sicilian and international varietals. The quality of each wine is distinctive, and the Rallos are dedicated to growing their grapes and making their wines utilizing the most sustainable methods; their winery is powered by the sun. White wines include Anthìlia (a blend of Ansonica and Catarratto), Polena (Catarratto and Viognier), Lighea (Zibibbo and Catarratto), La Fuga (Chardonnay), Vigna di Gabri (Ansonica), and Chiarandà (Chardonnay and Ansonica). Reds include Sedàra and Mille e Una Notte (both 100 percent Nero d'Avola), Sherazade (Nero d'Avola and Syrah), and Tancredi (Nero d'Avola and Cabernet Sauvignon).

FEUDO MACCARI

Founded in 2000 and owned by the Moretti family of Tuscany (the Tenuta Sette Ponti estate), Feudo Maccari produces several wines, the most important being ReNoto, a blend of 85 percent Nero d'Avola and 15 percent Syrah, and the more expensive Saia, which is 100 percent old-vine Nero d'Avola.

SPADAFORA

This producer makes very fine wines from both local and international varietals from several different vineyards. The oldest plantings go back to 1970, and the most recent vines were planted in the late 1990s. Incanto is an unusual dry white wine made from old-vine Catarratto grapes dried in the Sicilian sun. Don Pietro is a dry white, a blend of Inzolia, Grillo, and Catarratto grapes. Alhambra is fresh, fruity, and dry, and is made from a blend of Catarratto and Inzolia. Schietto Chardonnay is an oaky white in the international style. Red wines include Sole dei Padri (Syrah), Monreale Syrah (Syrah and Nero d'Avola), Don Pietro Rosso (Cabernet Sauvignon, Merlot, and Nero d'Avola), Schietto Cabernet Sauvignon, and Schietto Syrah.

Other high-quality Sicilian wine producers include Firriato, Ajello, Morgato, Cusumano, Milazzo, Feudo Principi di Butara, Rapitalà, Feudo Arancio, Caleo, Case Ibidini, Terre Nere, La Spigola, Fratelli Cambria, Valle

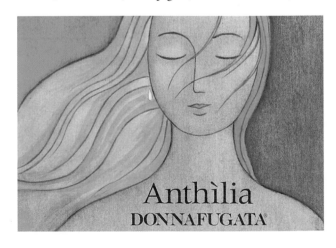

dell'Acate, Ceuso, Fourplay, COS, Calatrasi, Gulfi, Feudo Maccari, Benanti, Abbazia Santa Anastasia, Morgante, Terra, Bibo, Murana, Colosi, Biondi, MandraRossa (from the Settesoli cooperative, managed by Diego Planeta), Ferrandes, and Zisola.

Sardinia

Sardinia (*Sardegna*) is the most isolated area of Italy, an island of about one million inhabitants, about 150 miles from the mainland. Spanish, Basque, Corsican, and Arabic influences abound, reflected in several different dialects and a unique island lifestyle. Although the island is surrounded by Italy's longest coastline (a total of about 1,500 miles), farmers still tend their sheep, pastures, and farms in the hills.

Sardinia is home to nineteen DOC zones and one DOCG zone (see page 361), and much like Sicily, Sardinia has had to transform its wine quality from largely undistinguished mass-produced wines to a small production of fine wines. Of the 2.5 million hectoliters/66 million gallons produced in Sardinia, only about 15 percent is DOC, the same percentage, more or less, as Sicily. In a country with so many fine wines, hunting for a good Sardinian wine used to not be worth the effort for most people, but today it is relatively easy to find great Sardinian wines in shops and restaurants.

The most highly regarded white wine of Sardinia is Vermentino di Gallura, a dry wine from the far north, which was awarded DOCG status in 1997 (see page 367) and is the perfect accompaniment to the local *pesce alla griglia*, grilled fish in olive oil and fresh herbs. Vermentino

di Sardegna is less expensive, easier to find, and still a wonderful dry white, slightly more rustic than the more refined and *terroir*-driven Vermentino di Gallura.

Many of the best Sardinian red wines are based on the Cannonau grape, which is actually Grenache, native to the southern Rhône Valley in France (see page 338) and known as Garnacha in Spain (see page 421). The export market has been enjoying some Cannonau-based Sardinian reds, sometimes blended with about 15 to 20 percent Merlot or Cabernet Sauvignon. The Cannonau di Sardegna DOC zone takes in most of the island and produces wines in dry, sweet, and fortified styles, with both *riserva* and *superiore* designations. In the North American market, the dry, medium- to full-bodied, earthy style dominates.

Also showing promise are the red and rosé wines from the Carignano del Sulcis DOC zone. These wines are produced from the Carignan grape, one of the most widely planted red grapes in the warmer Mediterranean regions of France.

In the year 2000, Sardinia had no IGT wine zones; today, the island has fifteen (see page 357). In the North American market, we can find Cannonau-based reds from the Isola dei Nuraghi IGT. Costera, produced by Argiolas, is a wine from this IGT zone worth seeking out.

Just ten to fifteen years ago, the future of Sardinia's wine industry was unexciting and predictable, but with the ascent of the previously humble Vermentino di Gallura to DOCG status and the steady improvement in whites and reds for the export market, Sardinia is on the wine world's map as a region to watch.

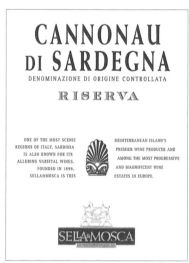

The beauty of Sardinia

Some of the best wine producers in Sardinia include Argiolas, Sella & Mosca, Santadi, Pala, Dettòri, Funtanalirus, Biondi, Contini, Capichera, Feudi della Medusa, Cantina Gallura, Cantina del Vermentino, Perda Rubia, Dolianova, Shardana, Pedra Majore, and Mancini.

Calabria

While the Greeks had Calabria in mind when they called this part of the world *Oenotria*, modern Calabria bears little resemblance to that ancient land of wine. Wine takes a backseat in Calabria's struggling economy to olive oil, grains, citrus, and vegetables. This province produces about 1.5 percent of Italy's wine, and an infinitesimal amount of that wine is DOC. However, while the wines of Calabria are for the most part undistinguished, production does not meet the demand of the citizens and tourists, who seem to enjoy drinking the local wines from the utilitarian demijohns, oversize glass bottles that hold 5 gallons/19 liters of wine and get refilled from casks and tanks on a regular basis.

The vast majority, 90 percent, of Calabria's wine is red, and a lot of that wine is based on the Gaglioppo grape. Gaglioppo, introduced to Calabria by the ancient Greeks, produces mostly high-alcohol, high-tannin wines, sometimes softened by white grapes, especially Greco Bianco and Trebbiano. Calabria is home to twelve DOC zones and three IGT zones (see pages 361 and 357). The best-known DOC is the small coastal zone of Cirò, which produces dry whites, rosés, and reds, some with *riserva* status. Cirò is the stuff of legend; it, or rather its progenitor, Krimisa, was drunk by the athletes celebrating their victorious performances in the ancient Olympics. Cirò whites, made from the Greco grape, are dry, quite fresh, and appealing. The reds and rosés, made from the ancient Gaglioppo grape, tend to be strong and alcoholic.

Adjoining Cirò is the Melissa DOC, making similar wines from more or less the same grapes. Perhaps Calabria's finest wine is Greco di Bianco, a rare, sweet wine produced on the southern coast from Grechetto grapes.

There are a small number of fine wine producers in Calabria, including Ceratti, Lento, Librandi, Linardi, Odoardi, and Senatore.

Basilicata

Basilicata produces less than 2 percent of Italy's wines. Bordered by Calabria, Campania, and Apulia on three sides, with a small outlet to the Ionian Sea on the fourth side, Basilicata (sometimes known by its ancient Roman name, Lucania) produces about 900,000 gallons/34,000 hectoliters of the DOC wine Aglianico del Vulture, which accounts for less than 10 percent of Basilicata's total wine production.

Basilicata can point to Aglianico del Vulture, grown on the high slopes of Monte Vulture in the northeast, with justifiable pride, producing wines from more than a thousand small DOC-registered plots. Aglianico del Vulture in its best *riserva* style is full-flavored and shows very deep extract of color, allowing it to age for easily five and perhaps as much as ten years. Simpler, lighter, less complex but very pleasant wines are also available and are real bargains. Aglianico del Vulture is one of only three DOC zones in Basilicata (the other two are Matera and Terre Alta Val d'Agri).

Leading wine producers in Basilicata include Paternoster, Tenuta La Querce, Terra del Re, Alovini, Cantina di Venosa, Bonifacio, D'Angelo, Tenuta del Portale, Notaio, Elena Fucci, Basilisco, Re Manfredi, Fucci, and Maschito.

Apulia

Apulia (*Puglia*) produces more wine than any other Italian region, vying with Sicily for this dubious honor. Until fairly recently, however, quality was not the focus of this region. Starting in the late 1980s, Apulia began to upgrade its wines, while at the same time, and paradoxically, Apulia eclipsed Sicily's total wine production.

Surprisingly, Apulia has been granted twenty-five DOC zones (see page 360) as well as six IGT zones (see page 357), but less than 10 percent of the region's total wine production is classified. In fact, a substantial amount of the more than 200 million gallons/800 million liters of wine pro-

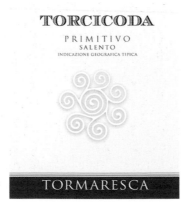

duced annually from this region is actually produced not as wine per se, but as concentrated grape musts, used for blending and *governo*—increasing alcohol and flavor levels, with the potent musts taking the place of illegal sugar. A bit more than 25 percent of Apulia's wine finds its way into bottles, and overproduction was a problem in this province even before phylloxera struck Italy.

So it comes as good news that the outlook for the wines of Apulia has brightened considerably over the last ten to fifteen years. There are at least two shining stars on the "heel of the boot." On the Salento peninsula in the southeast is the prominent DOC zone Salice Salentino. This red wine has maintained a strong presence in the export market, and Salice Salentino, made mostly from Negroamaro grapes, can be a lovely, balanced wine, medium- to full-bodied, and fruit-driven. The *bianco* and *rosato* versions of Salice Salentino are almost never seen, but the red *riservas* have made a minor splash as best-buy wines for daily enjoyment. Salice Salentino is, at its best, an ageworthy red of consistent quality that mellows nicely for five to six years.

Even more popular in the export market is Primitivo. One of the reasons that the red varietal Primitivo has caught on in the United States is that the grape is, in fact, Zinfandel, one of the major stars of California wines. Primitivo di Manduria is a DOC zone located in southern Apulia. The wine produced here is luscious, medium- to full-bodied, with moderate tannins and forward fruit. Primitivo is produced not only in the Manduria province, but in the nearby Apulian provinces of Lecce, Brindisi, and Bari, often as IGT wines.

The promise of Apulia has caught the attention of wine producers from other parts of Italy, most notably Piero Antinori of Tuscany, whose Vigneti del Sud company produces wines from his 600-hectare/1,500-acre estate in Apulia under the Tormaresca label, and Pasqua, a well-known producer in Veneto, producing wine under the Agricola Surani label. Pasqua owns 100 hectares/250 acres in Apulia.

Some of the best producers in Apulia include Taurino, the pioneering winery for quality and the export market, as well as A Mano, Appolonio, Botromagno, Caleo, Candido, Cantele, Castello Monaci, Castris, Conti Zecca, Coppadoro, La Corte, Es, Li Veli, Masseria, Matané, Mille Una, Ognissole, Perrini, Rivera, Rubino, San Marzano, Santa Lucia, Stella, Surani, Terre, Tormaresca, Vallone, and Villa Fanelli.

Campania

While rich in wine history—the ancient Romans and Greeks greatly prized the vineyards of this region—contemporary Campania (*Campagna*) has become a haven for a small quantity of quality wines. Although grapes grow easily and well in the volcanic soils of Campania, less than 10 percent of the agricultural output of the region is attributable to grapevines. With just under six million people, this is Italy's second most highly populated region. Commercial activity is centered around the coastal city of Naples, and tourists flock to Mount Vesuvius at Pompeii, as well as the beautiful island of Capri.

Campania actually imports more wine than it exports to quench the thirst of tourists and residents alike, but over the last twenty years, wine producers in Campania have made a commitment to wine quality and to fine wine exports. This is good news, because it was not so long ago that there was no concerted regional effort to improve the wines from this physically beautiful and agriculturally lush area.

About 60 percent of wines produced within Campania's three DOCG zones, eighteen DOC zones, and ten IGT appellations are white. The most important white grapes in Campania are Fiano, Falanghina, and Greco di Tufo.

Fiano can be traced to the ancient Romans, who called the grape "*apiano*," because it attracted bees (*api*). Falanghina is also of ancient Roman heritage and is said to be the main grape for the heralded and historic wine

A Campania vineyard

Falernum, the most famous wine in Caesar's empire. Greco di Tufo is as its name indicates, an ancient Greek grape.

Fiano di Avellino DOCG is a dry, medium-bodied white, best consumed young, although after a few years of bottle age, a bit of oxidation takes place, making the wine somewhat more complex, and this quality, common to many whites from Campania, is attractive to some wine drinkers.

Greco di Tufo DOCG, also from the Avellino district of Campania, is often a bit more full-bodied than Fiano di Avellino. Both wines work their magic when served with complex fish dishes, such as seafood stews.

Falanghina, especially from the Sannio, Irpinia, and Taburno DOC zones, enjoys a reputation in the American market as a very good, light- to medium-bodied, dry but refreshing wine, so good with seafood such as mussels and clams. Falanghina is about half the price of Fiano di Avellino or Greco di Tufo.

The major red grape in Campania is Aglianico (meaning

"Hellenic"), another ancient Greek variety. The basis for so many red wines of Campania and grown extensively throughout Italy's southern provinces, it is most famous as the grape of Taurasi, the first DOCG granted in southern Italy. The commune of Taurasi is located in the Avellino district, and it is here that the grapes produce a wine that is full-bodied and tannic, a wine that needs to age. Tasting a fine, mature Taurasi can be a singular experience, as the wine maintains its power while developing subtle grace notes, leading to a lovely balance of fruit and earth aromatics and flavors.

The best wine producers in Campania owe a debt of gratitude to the legendary Mastroberardino family, who redefined the vines and wines of Campania as quality-driven products. Other fine producers include Antica Masseria Venditti, Caggiano, Cantina del Taburno, Caputo, Cicala, De Conciliis, Di Prisco, Felicia, Feudi di San Gregorio, Fratelli Urciuolo, Galardi, Gelsonero, Imparato, Moio, Molettieri, Montevetrano, Mustilli, Ocone, Pietracupa, Romano, Terredora, Vesevo, Vigne Irpine, Villa Carafa, and Villa Matilde.

CENTRAL ITALY

THE SEVEN REGIONS OF CENTRAL ITALY produce a great deal of wine—25 percent of the country's total production and more than one-third of Italy's DOC and DOCG wines. This is an exciting time for winemaking in central Italy, as the area finds itself at a point in time that allows for both the best practices of tradition and the highest forms of innovation. Happily, many producers in central Italy are following the dynamic lead of Tuscany and are committed to enhancing the quality of their wines, whether those wines are traditional classics utilizing regional varietals, or modern wines showcasing international grape types. While the DOCG red wines of Tuscany—Chianti, Chianti Classico, Brunello di Montalcino, Vino Nobile di Montepulciano, Carmignano, and Morellino di Scansano—may be well-known to lovers of Italian wines, there are many other treasures to taste in these regions.

Central Italy is divided by the Apennine mountain range into two distinct subsections, geographically, culturally, and viticulturally. The west, or the area that borders the Tyrrhenian Sea, includes Emilia-Romagna, Tuscany, Lazio, and Umbria. The east, defined by its proximity to the Adriatic Sea, is made up of the Marches, Abruzzi, and Molise. The wines produced in the east and west are quite different in style, quality, and constituent grape varieties.

Tuscany is thought of as a center of Italian red wine production—Sangiovese is the undisputed varietal star—but high-quality white wines are also produced here. The Vernaccia di San Gimignano grape, for example, produces a very good white wine. As a matter of fact, Vernaccia di San Gimignano was named the first DOC of Italy in 1963 and was awarded DOCG status in 1993. Also, Trebbiano and Malvasia grapes, sometimes on their own and sometimes blended, can produce good to very fine wines. These same workhorse grapes appear in the classic DOC wines of Lazio, home to Italy's capital city of Rome. Regional favorites such as Frascati and Est! Est!! Est!!! di Montefiascone, both popular with the millions of tourists who flock to Rome, are made primarily from blends of local clones of Malvasia and Trebbiano.

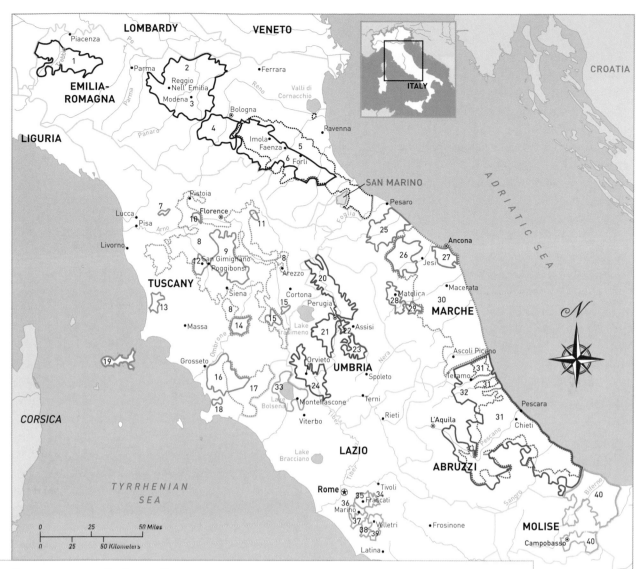

Central Italy
Main DOC/DOCG Wine Regions

— **Emilia-Romagna**
  1 Colli Piacentini
  2 Reggiano
  3 Lambrusco Salamino di Santa Croce, Lambrusco di Sorbara, Lambrusco Grasparossa di Castelvetro
  4 Colli Bolognesi
  5 Trebbiano di Romagna
  6 Albana di Romagna DOCG

— **Tuscany**
  7 Montecarlo
  8 Chianti DOCG
  9 Chianti Classico DOCG
  10 Carmignano DOCG
  11 Pomino
  12 Vernaccia di San Gimignano DOCG
  13 Bolgheri, Bolgheri Sassicaia
  14 Brunello di Montalcino DOCG, Rosso di Montalcino
  15 Vino Nobile di Montepulciano DOCG, Rosso di Montepulciano
  16 Morellino di Scansano DOCG
  17 Bianco de Pitigliano
  18 Parrina
  19 Elba Aleatico Passito DOCG, Elba DOC

— **Umbria**
  20 Colli Altotiberini
  21 Colli Perugini
  22 Torgiano Rosso Riserva DOCG, Torgiano
  23 Sagrantino di Montefalco DOCG, Montefalco
  24 Orvieto

— **Marche**
  25 Bianchello del Metauro
  26 Verdicchio dei Castelli di Jesi
  27 Cònero DOCG, Rosso Cònero
  28 Verdicchio di Matelica
  29 Vernaccia di Serrapetrona DOCG, Serrapetrona
  30 Rosso Piceno

— **Abruzzi**
  31 Montepulciano d'Abruzzo Colline Teramane DOCG, Montepulciano d'Abruzzo
  32 Trebbiano d'Abruzzo

— **Lazio**
  33 Est! Est!! Est!!! di Montefiascone
  34 Montecompatri
  35 Frascati
  36 Marino
  37 Colli Albani
  38 Colli Lanuvini
  39 Velletri

— **Molise**
  40 Riferno

In Umbria, Ovieto is the dominant white wine. Orvieto is made from Malvasia and Trebbiano, along with other local varieties. The most exciting red wines of Umbria—Sangiovese-based Torgiano Rosso Riserva and Sagrantino di Montefalco, made from the elegant and historic local varietal Sagrantino—have both been granted DOCG status.

The wines of Emilia-Romagna are mostly *frizzante*, and Emilia is best known for its sweet versions of the popular Lambrusco; in the United States the most widely known brand is Riunite. Romagna has its own very fine Sangiovese-based wines, as well as some fizzies. Unlike the serious wines of Piedmont, most of the wines from Emilia-Romagna are simple, fun to drink, and a perfect match with the food of the region. Lambrusco is especially coveted as an aid to digesting two rich staples of the local diet, prosciutto di Parma and Parmigiano Reggiano, and is said to cut the cholesterol of these items. Sangiovese di Romagna is a DOC wine quite different from Tuscan reds and is beginning to develop a small following in the wine world. Italy's first white DOCG, Albana di Romagna (see below), produces wines that, despite their lofty status, are usually nothing special, at least in their dry export versions.

Along the Adriatic coast, the two most important local varietals are the red Montepulciano from Abruzzi (not to be confused with the town Montepulciano in Tuscany) and the white Verdicchio from the Marches region. Sangiovese and Trebbiano, which are used to make wines on their own as well as blended wines, fill out the picture in the central and eastern regions. Until recently, Molise has not been an important wine area, often growing Montepulciano and Trebbiano grapes for the blended wines of Abruzzi. However, there is now growing interest by Italian and foreign producers in the coastal areas (represented by the relatively new Molise DOC) as a place to grow international varieties.

Emilia-Romagna

A compelling argument can be made that Emilia-Romagna is the culinary capital of Italy. The cheeses and dairy products, pasta, hams, and sausages produced in this region are some of the best in the world. Prosciutto di Parma and Parmigiano Reggiano both enjoy DOP (*protected denomination of origin*) status, as does Emilia-Romagna's vinegar, *aceto balsamico*, which by law must be made from cooked grape musts and aged for a minimum of twelve years in

small wooden barrels. While the foods of this region are superb, no one would ever argue that Emilia-Romagna is the viticultural center of Italy.

Emilia-Romagna produces more wine than any other region except for Sicily and Apulia, but little of it is distinguished or exciting. Of the nearly 238.5 million gallons/ 9 million hectoliters of wine produced here, only about 1,855,000 gallons/70,200 hectoliters have DOC or DOCG status, and various Lambrusco DOC zones account for about half of that production. This *frizzante*, happy wine, made in white, red, and rosé, dry or sweet, is produced from grapes grown mostly in the plains of Emilia. The locals prefer the drier versions of the bubbly Lambrusco, but the myth that the sweeter types were created solely for the American market is not true, even though Riunite Lambrusco (Emilia IGT), the original screwcap wine, is among the most popular Italian wines in the United States.

Both sweet and dry Lambrusco have been around for a long time, and both are produced from local clones of the Lambrusco grape. There are three Lambrusco-based DOC zones in Emilia-Romagna: Lambrusco di Sorbara, Lambrusca Grasparossa di Castelvetro, and Lambrusco Salamino di Santa Croce.

The hill country of Romagna is home to Italy's first white DOCG, Albana di Romagna. We wish that we could wax more rhapsodic about this wine, but the fact is that Albana di Romagna is pleasantly fruity with some overtones of nuttiness, and that's about it. The DOCG area is large, taking in almost all of the Emilia-Romagna region. Locally, there are some good *frizzante* (DOC), *amabile*, *dolce*, and *passito* versions (DOCG) of the wine,

Lambrusco is the mainstay of Emilia-Romagna's wine industry. The United States sees mostly sweeter styles. Riunite, a cooperative of twelve hundred growers, is the category's brand leader.

but the export market is exposed mostly to the dry, still Albana. The other prominent DOC white from this area is Trebbiano di Romagna.

A success story in Romagna's hills is its Sangiovese di Romagna (DOC). This wine is overshadowed by the Sangiovese-based wines of Tuscany, but it deserves more exposure, especially the wines in the *riserva* style. Always a good value, this red wine can be truly elegant: a delicate balance between generous fruit and soft tannins. The medium- to full-bodied *riserva* from Umberto Cesari, a perfect food wine, is often available in a dramatically oversized three-liter bottle—just the thing for an informal, festive dinner party.

Abruzzi

Abruzzi (*Abruzzo*) comprises one DOCG zone (see page 365), three DOC zones—Montepulciano d'Abruzzo, Trebbiano d'Abruzzo, and Controguerra—and nine IGT zones. The red Montepulciano d'Abruzzo, which may le-

gally contain up to 15 percent Sangiovese, is consistently underrated, probably because it is so little known. The wine is consistently good, with mouth-filling fruit and full-bodied character.

Montepulciano d'Abruzzo Colline Teramane was named a DOCG in 2003, based on the fact that the hills in the Teramo district of Abruzzi contain the best vineyards that produce the best wines.

When grown in the mountainous inland areas, Montepulciano yields grapes with less extract and tannin, and so a good DOC light red wine, Cerasuolo di Montepulciano d'Abruzzo, is often made from these grapes.

Approachable when young, the best examples of Montepulciano d'Abruzzo, whether DOC or DOCG, can age quite nicely over the course of five or six years. The wine is a solid bargain.

In 1996, the Controguerra DOC was established. Although at that time there were fewer than 100 acres/40 hectares of vines in the *denominazione*, Contraguerra, with an eye on the international market, has become Abruzzi's center for production of international varietals, with varietal-labeled Chardonnay, Riesling, Pinot Noir, Merlot, and Cabernet Sauvignon produced in the DOC.

In Abruzzi, the local version of the Trebbiano grape most often makes a simple, straightforward wine that should be drunk fresh, usually with fish.

Prominent producers of Abruzzi wines include the well-known cooperative Casal Thaulero, as well as Ca' Donini, Caldora, Carosso, Casal Bordino, Castelluccio, Citra, Farnese, Il Feduccio, Florentino, Illuminati, Masciarelli, Monti, Nicodemi, Pasqua, Pepe, Posis, Santangelo, Scarlata, Stella, Symposium, Umani Ronchi, La Valentina, Valle Reale, Villa Cieri, Villadoro, Villa Gemma, Zaccagnini, and Zonin.

TOP: Aceto balsamico, *balsamic vinegar, aging in oak casks in Modena, Emilia-Romagna* BOTTOM: *Wheels of Parmigiano Reggiano cheese aging in Emilia-Romagna.*

Molise

Not known for its wines, Molise makes some wines in the style of Abruzzi, from similar grape varieties. In the mid-1980s the two large production zones of Biferno and Pentro di Isernia were granted DOC status, but a total of only about 700 acres/300 hectares of vines have been planted in these two DOC zones. In 1998, the Molise DOC was established to encourage both traditional and international varietals, meeting with limited success. As a region, Molise produces less DOC wine than any other province in Italy, even though potentially favorable hillside vineyard sites and a mild Adriatic climate promise good growing conditions for a multitude of red varietals, including Aglianico.

Marche

The citizens of the Marches (*Marche*) consume more wine per capita than those of any other region of Italy, no mean feat in a country whose national consumption per person is among highest in the world. The most famous wine produced by these happy, healthy folks is Verdicchio, a wine that can achieve stellar quality, sometimes overlooked due to its easy availability. Like the Loire Valley's Muscadet (see Chapter 7, page 267), Verdicchio is the ideal accompaniment to a great variety of seafood. There are two DOC Verdicchio zones, Matelica and Castelli di Jesi. The Verdicchio dei Castelli di Jesi DOC zone encompasses Fazi Battaglia's 86.5-acre/35-hectare single vineyard, Le Moie, which produces a Verdicchio of unparalleled quality. The wine from both DOC zones is enjoying a resurgence in popularity, due largely to improved fermentation techniques—the increased use of temperature-controlled stainless steel has increased the wine's freshness and acidity—and smaller yields per hectare.

While about 25 million bottles of still Verdicchio are produced each year in the Marches (Soave from the Veneto region is the only still white DOC wine exported in greater quantity to the United States), sparkling Verdicchio is a local favorite. This is most often made by the *charmat* process, but small amounts are produced by the *metodo classico* (see "méthode champenoise," page 80).

Despite the popularity of Verdicchio, the two DOCG zones of the Marches are dedicated to red wines, and one of those—Vernaccia di Serrapetrona—is an obscure, naturally sparkling red wine made from a grape that most people think of as always white (Vernaccia Nera is the red version of the grape). Vernaccia di Serrapetrona is rarely seen in the American export market.

Cònero is the other DOCG zone of the Marches and is a fine wine made mostly from the Montepulciano grape. Under its former DOC name, Rosso Cònero, the wine created a stir of interest in both Italy and the export markets, and continues to do so as a DOCG wine. Dry, medium- to full-bodied, and reasonably complex, Cònero, which is aged at least twenty-four months and is always a *riserva*, is an enjoyable wine with a wide variety of hearty dishes.

The DOC red from the Marches that has garnered attention in the export market is Rosso Piceno, most often produced as a blend of Montepulciano and Sangiovese. This is a medium-bodied red that is a great accompaniment to hearty pasta dishes or a crusty pizza.

Some of the best wine producers in the Marches include Fazi Battaglia and Umani Ronchi, as well as Bisci, Boccadigabbia, Bucci, Le Caniette, Casalfarneto, Maria Pia Castelli, Cocci Grifone, Colonnara, Conte Leopardi, Fausti, Garofali, Giusti, Landi, Malacari, Marchetti, Mecella, Moncaro, Moroder, Saladini Pilastri, Le Terazze (whose "Planet Waves" is produced with the participation of Bob Dylan), and Velenose Ercole.

Lazio

It may come as a surprise to the world's urban dwellers that the city of Rome, which contains four DOC zones, including the famous Frascati, produces more than 10.6 million gallons/400,000 hectoliters of delimited white wine. With the Roman metropolis as its anchor, Latium (*Lazio*), where tremendous yields were once commonplace, produces about 75 percent of all the white wine of central Italy. With regional and local clones of Malvasia

THE BISHOP'S WINE

Although Est! Est!! Est!!! di Montefiascone will probably never be one of Italy's great white wines, it is the subject of one of Italy's great wine legends. The name of the wine was derived from the activities of a twelfth-century German bishop, Johann Fugger, who was traveling from Germany to Rome for the coronation of Henry V. The fat Fugger loved to eat and drink well, and had his chief of staff travel ahead of him so that the underling would mark the door of the best establishment in each town with the word *est*, short for *"Vinum est bonum"* ("The wine is good"). When Fugger's advance man got to the village of Montefiascone, he really must have enjoyed the local wine, because he wrote "Est! Est!! Est!!!" on the door of the local inn. Bishop Fugger, also taken with the local wine, cancelled the rest of his trip and lived in Montefiascone the rest of his life. Fugger's eight-hundred-year-old tomb is on display in the old village church.

and Trebbiano grapes accounting for most of Lazio's whites, the wines used to range from the simple to the undistinguished, bordering on the miserable. High yields produced wines so fragile that they could hardly travel less than twenty miles from the vineyards into the center of Rome without being bruised and shocked. The Frascati wines that were exported bore little resemblance to the frothy, tangy quaffing beverage consumed locally. Est! Est!! Est!!! di Montefiascone was also popular, but was a wine with no real distinction, especially in questionable export versions.

Frascati has greatly improved as a conscientious effort by producers to utilize the twin technologies of cool fermentation and sterile filtration has taken hold in the region. Frascati is still fruity and fairly simple, but in its usual export version—Frascati Superiore—it is also a crisp, light, and dry wine that is now able to travel well in the modern wine world. The stuff of local legend, Est! Est!! Est!!! di Montefiascone is still a work in progress.

Part of the large Orvieto DOC is located within Lazio. The Orvieto Classico district, however, is located in Umbria. Made mostly from Trebbiano and Verdello grapes, Orvieto's reputation for a simple dry (or sometimes sweet) has been ceded to Umbria.

Some of the best red DOC wines of Lazio come from only two of its twenty-five DOC zones. Aprilia, which makes white wines from the Trebbiano grape, can also produce some good red wines from Merlot grapes and red and rosé wines from Sangiovese. In the Cerveteri DOC zone, rustic red wine is made from a blend of Sangiovese, Montepulciano, and the local Cesanese grapes.

Speaking of Cesanese, Lazio's new (2009) DOCG is Cesanese del Piglio, a dry red that must be produced from at least 90 percent Cesanese grapes (see DOCG red wines, page 362).

Aside from Frascati Superiore and Est! Est!! Est!!! di Montefiascone, very little Lazio wine is imported into North America. However, one producer has made a reputation for itself—Falesco. Many wine lovers believe that Falesco's "Montiano," a single-vineyard IGT Merlot, is Lazio's best; it is certainly its most sought-after wine.

Leading producers in Lazio include Casale del Giglio, Cistercensi, Constantini, Falesco, Fiorano, Grillo, Poggio Le Volpi, Sant'Andrea, Suore San Marco, and Tenuta l'Olivella.

Umbria

Landlocked and surrounded by Tuscany, Lazio, Abruzzi, the Marches, and Emilia-Romagna, Umbria has managed to make wines with its own regional personality. Lush vineyards are planted in Umbria's magnificent green hills and watched over by the spirit of its own Assisi native, Saint Francis. Wine and the region's heady olive oil account for only a small percentage of Umbria's agricultural output, with tobacco, grains, and dairy products far more important to the Umbrian economy.

Umbria is best known for its white Orvieto, produced along the Tuscan border, sometimes by Tuscan producers (for example, Antinori, Ruffino, Cecchi, Barone Ricasoli, and Melini). A DOC since 1971, Orvieto accounts for about 60 to 70 percent of Umbria's classified wines. Very popular in export markets, Orvieto can be produced in *secco* (dry), *abboccato* (semidry), *amabile* (semidry to semisweet), and *dolce* (sweet) styles. There is also an Orvieto Classico district, where the best wines are produced, especially the dry and semisweet versions.

Today, most Orvieto destined for the export market is produced as a dry wine, the product of cool fermentation of the free-run juices of the Trebbiano grape. The Florentine producer Antinori is also producing high-quality IGT wines made from Chardonnay, Sauvignon Blanc, and Pinot Noir at Castello della Sala, within the Orvieto Classico zone. Antinori also produces two fine examples of Orvieto Classico: Campogrande and Casasole.

Among the reds of Umbria, the area around the regional capital, Perugia, boasts two DOCG wines: Torgiano Rosso Riserva, a Sangiovese/Canaiolo blend, and Sagrantino di Montefalco, also known as Montefalco Sagrantino. The most prominent producer of the Torgiano Rosso Riserva is Lungarotti. Dr. Giorgio Lungarotti died in 1999, and the winery continues to be run by his stepdaughter, the highly capable and accomplished Teresa Severini, the first female enologist in Italy, and her sister, Chiara Lungarotti. Teresa, with her mother, Maria Grazia Marchetti Lungarotti, established an elegant inn and lovely wine museum, Le Tre Vasselle ("The Three Wine Jugs"), in the town of Torgiano.

Producing both DOCG Torgiano Rosso Riserva and DOC Rosso di Torgiano under the proprietary name Rubesco, Lungarotti has brought international attention to the red wines of Umbria. Lungarotti's Rubesco Vigna Monticchio Torgiano Rosso Riserva, made from grapes grown at the Monticchio vineyard of about 27 acres/

11 hectares, is one of Italy's finest wines, aged for between four and five years before release and certainly worthy of its DOCG designation.

Though it may be made as a sweet *passito* wine from sun-dried, raisinated grapes, the dry Sagrantino di Montefalco, with its nose of blackberries and its full body, is getting international attention. Sagrantino di Montefalco must contain at least 95 percent Sagrantino grapes. In contrast, three times as much DOC Montefalco is produced, which may contain up to 75 percent Sangiovese and as little as 10 percent Sagrantino grapes. A leading producer of DOCG Sagrantino di Montefalco and DOC Montefalco is Arnaldo Caprai, whose extraordinary wines are widely available in the North American wine market.

Merlot and Barbera grapes have been planted in Umbria for more than a century and are used for blending as well as for the production of varietal wines. Over the last thirty years, both Cabernet Sauvignon and Pinot Noir have been introduced to the region, with mostly positive results.

Leading producers in Umbria include Lungarotti and Caprai, as well as Adanti, Antano, Antonelli, Bea, La Carraia, Castello della Sala, Colpetrone, Colsanto, Fongoli, Martinelli, La Palazzola, Palazzone, Pieve del Vescovo, Salviano, Scacciadiavoli, Sportoletti, Stella, Tabarrini, and Tiburzi.

LEFT: *Sangiovese and Canaiolo grapes are grown to make the wine Rubesco, a DOC Rosso di Torgiano.* RIGHT: *Lungarotti's famous Rubesco vineyard in Umbria*

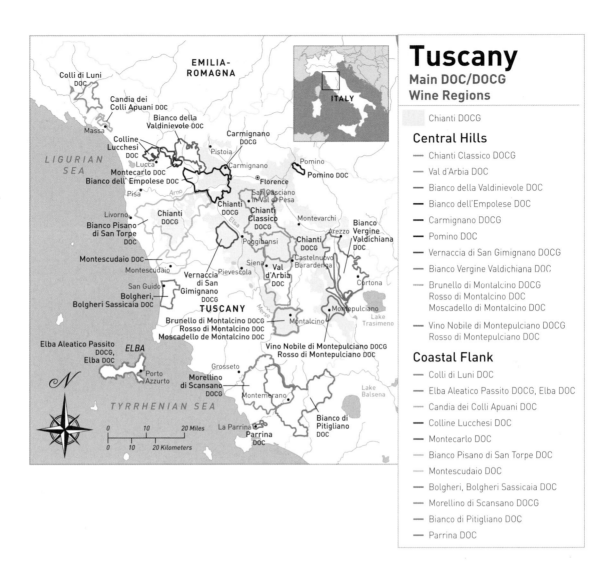

Tuscany
Main DOC/DOCG
Wine Regions

Chianti DOCG

Central Hills
— Chianti Classico DOCG
— Val d'Arbia DOC
— Bianco della Valdinievole DOC
— Bianco dell'Empolese DOC
— Carmignano DOCG
— Pomino DOC
— Vernaccia di San Gimignano DOCG
— Bianco Vergine Valdichiana DOC
— Brunello di Montalcino DOCG
  Rosso di Montalcino DOC
  Moscadello di Montalcino DOC
— Vino Nobile di Montepulciano DOCG
  Rosso di Montepulciano DOC

Coastal Flank
— Colli di Luni DOC
— Elba Aleatico Passito DOCG, Elba DOC
— Candia dei Colli Apuani DOC
— Colline Lucchesi DOC
— Montecarlo DOC
— Bianco Pisano di San Torpe DOC
— Montescudaio DOC
— Bolgheri, Bolgheri Sassicaia DOC
— Morellino di Scansano DOCG
— Bianco di Pitigliano DOC
— Parrina DOC

Tuscany

Tuscany (*Toscana*) is Italy's best-known wine region and, with Piedmont, its most important. Tuscany is home to seven red DOCG zones: Brunello di Montalcino, Vino Nobile di Montepulciano, Carmignano, Morellino di Scansano, Chianti Classico, Chianti, and Elba Aleatico Passito, which received DOCG status in 2009. With the exception of the newest DOCG, all of these wines are based on the Sangiovese grape. Sometimes Sangiovese is the only grape in the wine, and sometimes it is blended with other varietals. Tuscany also produces two white wines of note, the dry Vernaccia di San Gimignano (DOCG as of 1993) and the luscious, sweet **VIN SANTO** (sometimes DOC, sometimes IGT, depending on where and how it's produced). Add to this equation some of Italy's finest, fanciest, and most expensive, mostly-IGT, mostly red wines—Super

Tuscans—many with exotic, evocative names, and you have a region that prides itself on quality; it's a leader in the renaissance of Italian wines on the world stage.

Sangiovese is the most-planted grape in all of Italy. It accounts for about 10 percent of the country's vineyards: 215,000 acres/86,000 hectares. The fact that Sangiovese is the most-planted grape in Tuscany is an oversimplification of the situation in the region's vineyards. There are more than twenty approved and certified clones of Sangiovese, and one clone can do stupendously well in one vineyard while that same clone may be an utter failure in another vineyard. Sangiovese is known for uneven ripening even under the best circumstances, and it is highly *terroir*-sensitive. The grape grows best in limestone soils with only a moderate amount of clay and schist rocks. Sangiovese needs lots of sunlight but withers in the heat; cool nights

are important to the health of the vine. A lot of vineyard land in Tuscany does not provide the best environment for the grape, whatever the clone.

Over the last ten to twenty years, there has been a growing recognition among quality wine producers of Sangiovese's fickle nature. Much replanting of vineyards,

in an effort to match the right clone to the right environment, was undertaken by growers and producers. Many have decided that the classic approach to many Sangiovese-based wines—blending with Canaiolo, Mammolo, Malvasia Nera, Colorino, and some other local red varietals—will produce the best wine. Others believe that Sangiovese makes a great wine when blended with international varietals, such as Cabernet Sauvignon, Merlot, Cabernet Franc, and Syrah. Still others believe that to make a fine Sangiovese-only wine, it must be produced from the right clone planted in the right place, and the cellar regimen must change to favor more modern methods of vinification and aging.

In Tuscany, Sangiovese has evolved from a grape that filled a need for mass-produced, often poor-quality wines to the most important grape in harmonious, high-quality wines, sometimes as a solo performer, sometimes as a member of a duet, trio, or quartet. Many of these wines have been produced under the aegis of DOC and DOCG zones, many of them produced under IGT designations.

CHIANTI

Chianti, a very large DOCG zone that begins south of Siena on the border with Umbria and stretches north to beyond the hills of Florence (*Firenze*), is bordered to the west by Pisa and to the east by Arezzo. Chianti is Italy's most famous wine, and perhaps its most controversial. Depending on the precise area where it is produced as well as the reputation of the producer and grapes, soil, climate, and elevation of the vineyards, Chianti can be thin and insipid, or elegant and rich; ageworthy, or ready to drink when bottled; light and delicate, or a virtual powerhouse of a wine. With about 20 million gallons/757,000 hectoliters of wine produced annually, there is still plenty of simple Chianti to go around. However, DOCG status has contributed to lower yields on the vine and better wine in the bottle. Almost gone are the days of the decorative wicker basket (**FIASCO**) that enveloped a demi-**AMPHORA** of bitter, thin red wine. Today, the best Chianti is shipped in Bordeaux-shaped bottles. The wines, especially the *riserva* wines from the Chianti Classico district, with black cherry and raspberry flavors and a bouquet of wildflowers and smoke, can be world-class.

The Chianti DOCG covers five provinces within Tuscany: Arezzo, Firenze, Pisa, Pistoia, and Siena. Within these provinces are the seven official subregions of Chianti, all named with the prefix *Chianti*: Colli Aretini,

---

CLOCKWISE, FROM TOP LEFT: *Hills in the Chianti region of Tuscany. Freshly picked Sangiovese grapes, the backbone of virtually all Tuscan red wines. Although Chianti is still bottled in jugs sitting in wicker baskets (*fiasco*), the best Chianti is often produced in Bordeaux-shaped bottles.*

Colli Fiorentini, Colli Senesi, Colline Pisane, Montalbano, Montespertoli, and Rufina. The Chianti Classico subregion—the traditional heartland of Chianti—has its own DOCG with somewhat different regulations and so is not included in the general Chianti DOCG.

Chianti's primary grape is Sangiovese. As of 1999, Chianti from any of seven districts may be between 75 and 100 percent Sangiovese (Chianti Classico starts at 80 percent). The wine may include up to 10 percent Canaiolo Nero and up to a total of 10 percent of Colorino, Malvasia Nera, or Mammolo. It may also include up to 10 percent white grapes—Trebbiano or Malvasia. Most of the modern producers disregard antiquated parts of the production laws, especially when the quality of the wine is negatively affected. For example, many have long eschewed the use of white grapes in the blend, even though, until 1999, they were legally obligated to use them.

GOVERNO

While chaptalization is currently illegal in Italy, the closest thing to it is practiced in Chianti, though not by all producers. *Governo alla Toscana*, which started in the fourteenth century, introduces a secondary fermentation to the wine. When the wine has almost stopped its initial fermentation, a small percentage—between 10 and 15 percent—of legal grapes, often the Colorino varietal, which have been partially dried in the sun after early picking, are added to slowly fermenting must, creating a reinvigoration of the fermentation.

The **GOVERNO** process produces a Chianti that is softer and lower in acid; *governo* encourages malolactic fermentation. When bottled young to be drunk fresh, the Chianti is sweeter, and a bit of the carbon dioxide produced by the *governo* process can give the wine a slight but pleasant spritz, creating *Chianti di pronta beva*.

The *governo* process is used not only for young Chianti but also sometimes for *riserva* wines that will age for a minimum of twenty-four months and produce at least 12.5 percent alcohol. As these wines mature, they develop more aromas and a rich, toasted character, with none of the youthful fizz.

The *governo* process has enjoyed a resurgence in Chianti and the separate Chianti Classico DOCG, and many fine producers utilize *governo* in the production of their wines.

Other producers, who utilize stainless steel temperature-controlled fermentation tanks, have ushered *governo* into the dustbin of history.

CHIANTI CLASSICO

While Chianti is legally subdivided into seven delimited districts, it is most often Chianti Classico that includes the name of the district on the bottle label. Increasingly, we see producers in Chianti Rufina, Chianti Colli Fiorentini, and Chianti Colli Senesi proudly displaying district names on their labels. All of the seven districts are capable of producing fine wines, and just about all of them have decreased yields and improved technology since 1984, when DOCG status was first granted to the Chianti zone. It is Classico, however, which lies mostly between Siena and Florence, that enjoys the greatest international reputation.

The largest subregion of Chianti, Classico originally applied for its own DOCG, apart from and to the exclusion of the rest of Chianti. Many would argue that Chianti Classico, the traditional and historical heartland of the Chianti zone, deserved the separate and unique designation. Naturally, this move was opposed by Chianti producers outside the Classico district, some of them politically and economically powerful. As a compromise, all

TOP: *Several Tuscan producers in the DOCG zones feature their family coat of arms on their labels. The Gabbiano label creates a particularly evocative image of regional history and culture.* BOTTOM: *A dramatic view of the Chianti Classico region*

SOME OF THE BEST-KNOWN SUPER TUSCANS*

NAME OF THE WINE	COMPOSITION/BLEND
WHITE WINES	
Aglaia	Chardonnay
Batar	Chardonnay
Bonfiglio	Viognier
Canonico	Chardonnay
Castellacio	Chadonnay/Malvasia
La Faina	Trebbiano
Farnito	Chardonnay
Fontanelle	Chardonnay
Ghiaie Bianche	Chardonnay
Il Marzocco	Chardonnay
Pepestrino	Trebbiano/Chardonnay
La Pietra	Chardonnay
Al Poggio	Chardonnay/Pinot Grigio
Serena	Sauvignon Blanc
La Suvera	Chardonnay/Trebbiano
Terre di Tuffi	Primarily Vernaccia
Torniella	Sauvignon Blanc/Sémillon
Torricella	Chardonnay
Trappoline	Pinot Bianco/Chardonnay/Malvasia
Vigna Campo al Moro	Chardonnay/Trebbiano Toscano

RED WINES	
Accaiolo	Sangiovese/Cabernet Sauvignon
Alte d'Altesi	Sangiovese/Cabernet Sauvignon
Altrovino	Cabernet Franc/Merlot
Aprelis	Sangiovese/Cabernet Sauvignon
Aragone	Sangiovese/Alicante/Syrah/Carignan
Avignonesi Rosso	Sangiovese/Cabernet Sauvignon/Merlot
Balifico	Sangiovese/Cabernet Sauvignon/ Cabernet Franc
Belnero	Sangiovese/Cabernet Sauvignon/Merlot
Il Borgo	Sangiovese/Cabernet Sauvignon
Borgoforte	Cabernet Sauvignon/Merlot /Cabernet Franc
Il Bosco	Syrah
Brancaia	Sangiovese/ Cabernet Sauvignon/ Merlot
Brigante	Sangiovese/Merlot
Brusco dei Barbi	Sangiovese/Canaiolo
Camarcanda	Merlot/Cabernet Sauvignon/Cabernet Franc

RED WINES, continued	
Camartina	Sangiovese/Cabernet Sauvignon
I Campacci	Sangiovese/Merlot
Camposilio	Sangiovese/Cabernet Sauvignon
Casalferro	Sangiovese
Castruccio Rosso	Sangiovese/Canaiolo/Colorino/Ciliegiolo
Cepparello	Sangiovese
Coltassala	Sangiovese
Colvecchio	Syrah
Concerto	Sangiovese/Cabernet Sauvignon/Merlot/ Syrah
Corbaia	Sangiovese/Cabernet Sauvignon
Cum Laude	Cabernet Sauvignon /Merlot/ Sangiovese/Syrah
Desiderio	Merlot
Dogajolo	Cabernet Sauvignon/Merlot
Duemani	Cabernet Franc
Eneo	Sangiovese/Colorino/Merlot
L'Eremo	Syrah
Excelsus	Cabernet Sauvignon/Merlot
Farnito	Cabernet Sauvignon
Geografico	Cabernet Sauvignon/Sangiovese
Ghiaie delle Furba	Cabernet Sauvignon/Cabernet Franc/Merlot
Giorgio Primo	Sangiovese/Merlot
Gratius	Sangiovese
Grifi	Sangiovese/Cabernet Sauvignon
Guado al Tasso	Cabernet Sauvignon/Merlot/Syrah
Insoglio del Cinghiale	Cabernet Franc/Merlot/Syrah
Luce	Sangiovese/Merlot
Lucente	Sangiovese
Lupicaia	Cabernet Sauvignon/Merlot
Magari	Merlot/Cabernet Sauvignon/Cabernet Franc
Masseto	Merlot
Messorio	Merlot
Mormoreto	Cabernet Sauvignon/Merlot/Cabernet Franc
Nambrot	Merlot
Nardo	Sangiovese/Montepulciano/ Cabernet Sauvignon
Nemo	Cabernet Sauvignon
Olmaia	Cabernet Sauvignon
Ornellaia	Cabernet Sauvignon/Merlot/Cabernet Franc

Paleo	Cabernet Sauvignon/Cabernet Franc
Il Pareto	Cabernet Sauvignon
Le Pergole Torte	Sangiovese
Pietraforte del Carobbio	Cabernet Sauvignon
Poggio alla Badiola	Sangiovese
Poggio Granoni	Sangiovese/Cabernet Sauvignon/Merlot/ Syrah
Il Principe	Pinot Noir
Promis	Merlot/Syrah/Sangiovese
Rapace	Sangiovese/Cabernet Sauvignon/Merlot
Riccionero	Pinot Noir
Rinascimento	Sangiovese/Cabernet Sauvignon
Ripa delle Mandore	Sangiovese/Cabernet Sauvignon
Rosso dei Barbi	Sangiovese
Rovo	Sangiovese/Colorino/Malvasia Nera/ Ciliegiolo
San Leonardo	Cabernet Sauvignon/Merlot
San Leopoldo	Sangiovese/Cabernet Sauvignon
San Luigi	Sangiovese/Cabernet Sauvignon
Sangioveto	Sangiovese
Sassicaia	Cabernet Sauvignon/Cabernet Franc
Sassoalloro	Sangiovese
Schidione	Sangiovese/Cabernet Sauvignon/Merlot
Scrio	Syrah
Seraselva	Merlot/Cabernet Sauvignon
Le Serre Nuovo	Cabernet Sauvignon/Merlot/Cabernet Franc/Petit Verdot
Siepi	Sangiovese/Merlot
Il Sodaccio	Sangiovese/Canaiolo
Solaia	Cabernet Sauvignon/Sangiovese
Spargolo	Sangiovese
SummuS	Sangiovese/Cabernet Sauvignon/Syrah
Tassinaia	Cabernet Sauvignon/ Merlot/Sangiovese
Tavernelle	Merlot
La Terrine	Sangiovese/Cabernet Sauvignon
Tignanello	Sangiovese/Cabernet Sauvignon/Cabernet Franc
Tinscvil	Sangiovese/Cabernet Sauvignon
Vigna Alta	Sangiovese
Vigna l'Apparita	Merlot
Villa Pillo	Syrah
Le Volte	Sangiovese/Cabernet Sauvignon

See text on pages 390–391.

of Chianti was awarded DOCG status, but Chianti Classico was granted its own separate DOCG zone.

Another special feature of the Chianti Classico DOCG designation has been the recognition of the region's own system of appellations, which divides Chianti Classico into its nine constituent communes of Barberino Val d'Elsa, Castellina, Castelnuovo Berardenga, Gaiole, Greve, Poggibonsi, Radda, San Casciano Val di Pesa, and Tavarnelle di Pesa. Each of these communes is said to exhibit a unique *terroir* and so produce different styles of wine. Wines from the southern communes, closer to Siena, tend to be earthier and more full-bodied, while the northern communes, closer to Florence, produce wines that are lighter and more delicate.

About 95 percent of all Chianti Classico producers are members of the regional nongovernmental consortium, or *consorzio*. In Italy, the Chianti Classico Consorzio is called Gallo Nero, in honor of its centuries-old symbol, the black rooster, which appears on the neck label of each bottle of member wines. The *consorzio* maintains an important laboratory for analysis of member wines and for wine research. Since 1992, the *consorzio* has been known as the Chianti Classico Consorzio del Marchio Storico in most export markets, including North America.

Some of the leading producers in the Chianti Classico DOCG zone, most of whom also produce wine labeled simply as "Chianti," include:

Antinori, Badia a Coltibuono, Badia a Passignano, Banfi, Barbi, Barone Ricasoli/Brolio, Bibbiano, Le Bocce, Borgo Salcetino, Brancaia, Capraia, Carpineto, Casa Emma, Casalvento, Castellare, La Castellina, Castell' in Villa, Castello d'Albola, Castello di Ama, Castello di Bossi, Castello di Farnetella, Castello di Fonterutoli, Castello di Gabbiano, Castello di Nippozzano, Castello di Querceto, Castello dei Rampolla, Castello di San Donato in Perano, Castello di Verrazzano, Castello di Volpaia, Castello Vicchiomaggio, Cecchi, Cennatoio, La Cincole, Da Vinci, Dievole, Felsina, Fontodi, Isole e Olena, Lamole di Lamole, Le Fonti, Livemano, La Marcellina, La Massa, Melini, Il Molino di Grace, Monsanto, Monterinaldi, Montesodi, Montevertine, Nittardi, Nozzole, Il Palazzino, Piccini, Pieve di Spaltenna, Poggio al Sole, Querceto, Quercia al Poggio, Renzo Marinai, Rocca delle Macie, Rocca di Castagnole, Rodáno, Ruffino, La Sala, San Felice, San Giusto, San Leonino, San Michele a Torri, Savignola Paolina, Stracalli, Vignavecchia, Villa Buonasera, Villa Cafaggio, Villa Mangiacane, Villa Vignamaggio, and Viticcio.

Also look for the very fine Chianti Rufina Riserva wines from Frescobaldi and Spalletti, the excellent wines made by Diletta Malenchini in Chianti Colli Fiorentino, and the bottlings of Capezzana, Falchini, and Geografico from Chianti Colli Senesi.

THE SUPER TUSCANS

In 1948, the Marchese Mario Incisa della Rocchetta began a revolution in Tuscan winemaking—and not in a traditional wine region of Tuscany, such as Chianti Classico, but at a large farm in the village of Bolgheri, which is located close to Tuscany's Mediterranean coastline in the southwestern part of the region. It was here, at Tenuta San Guido, that Incisa decided to plant Cabernet Sauvignon and Cabernet Franc vine cuttings that he had received from Château Lafite Rothschild in Bordeaux. The Marchese made a nontraditional wine from these nontraditional grapes planted on a nontraditional site. The wine, Sassicaia, which Incisa made for his family and friends, was aged in nontraditional French *barriques*—small French oak barrels—not the classic old Slavonian oak casks preferred by Tuscan producers.

In the late 1960s, Incisa's cousin, Marchese Niccolò Antinori and his son, Piero, realized the commercial potential of Sassicaia. Working with Mario Incisa's son,

Niccolò, Antinori winemaker Giacomo Tachis, and Bordeaux-based enologist Emile Peynaud, the Antinori family brought Sassicaia to market in 1968. It was wildly successful, and the Super Tuscan era had begun. (See Super Tuscan chart on pages 388–389.)

In the mid-1970s, Piero Antinori and winemaker Tachis began to produce Tignanello, which would eventually become an 80 percent Sangiovese and 20 percent Cabernet blend, also aged in *barrique,* but produced in the Chianti Classico region. Antinori followed Tignanello

with Solaia, in which Cabernet dominated the blend. Other producers then began to produce wines blended with Bordelais grapes. Some forward-thinking traditionalists traveled a different path by producing pure Sangiovese wines, beginning with Le Pergole Torte, first produced in 1977, by the well-respected Chianti Classico producer Sergio Manetti of Montevertine. At about the same time, Roberto Stucchi-Prunetti, whose family owns Badia a Coltibuono in the Chianti Classico region, also produced a 100 percent Sangiovese wine and chose to call it simply Sangioveto, the older name for the grape.

At the time these red wines were made, there was no way for DOC law to accommodate them. The wines were either made from nontraditional grapes (e.g., Cabernet Sauvignon) nontraditional blends (e.g., Cabernet-Sangiovese), or from traditional grapes but in the wrong percentages to satisfy the tradition-bound wine laws, or the wines were aged in a nontraditional, proscribed manner (using French oak *barriques*, for example). Nontraditional white wines, usually made from Chardonnay or Sauvignon Blanc, followed the success of the reds. The producers of these new Super Tuscans had no choice but to declare their wines *vino da tavola*, even if the wines quickly became the most expensive class of wines made in Italy.

During the 1980s and 1990s these new international-style wines really caught on with the wine press and the wine-loving public, and much attention was especially focused on the Chianti Classico region, home to the great majority of the new Super Tuscans. Attempts were made to bring

---

LEFT: *Sassicaia, produced commercially by Tenuta San Guido since 1968, is a blend of Cabernet Sauvignon and Cabernet Franc, and was the first Super Tuscan.* TOP, LEFT: *Tignanello, produced by Antinori since the mid-1970s, is a Sangiovese/ Cabernet Sauvignon blend.* TOP, RIGHT: *Badia a Coltibuono, located in the Chianti Classico region, makes a Super Tuscan from 100 percent Sangiovese grapes. The wine is labeled simply as Sangioveto di Toscana. Sangioveto is an older name for Sangiovese.*

some order to these new unclassified wines, with an eye to DOC or DOCG recognition. Some of the better-known producers, led by Ruffino and Frescobaldi, formed a voluntary group, first called *Predicato*, then *Capitolare*, to broadly define the types of new wine.

Terms such as "*Capitolare di Cardisco*" might appear on an older wine label, indicating that the wine was Sangiovese-based with up to 10 percent other red grapes, but no Cabernet or Merlot. With the 1998 vintage, the *Capitolare consorzio* and its definitions were scrapped, and so far no group has taken its place.

Until the 1996 vintage, the vast majority of the Super Tuscans remained as "ultra–*vino da tavola*," and then, as the rules loosened and eventual DOC recognition was held out as a carrot on a stick, the rush to *indicazione geografica tipica* (IGT) designation began. Today, a handful of the hundreds of Super Tuscans are DOC. The wine that fired the first shot in this wine revolution, Sassicaia, was the first DOC Super Tuscan and has been since 1998. The DOC zone is Bolgheri Sassicaia.

And the great winemakers of Tuscany have not forgotten *where* the Super Tuscan revolution started. Producers such as Antinori, Cecchi, Baroncini, Frescobaldi, and Biondi-Santi have invested heavily in land in and around Bolgheri.

Even Angelo Gaja (see page 402), who made his reputation in the Langhe province of Italy's Piedmont region, purchased the Ca'Marcanda estate just south of Bolgheri, in the Maremma area. Gaja produces three much sought-

after reds under the blanket IGT Toscana: Promis, Camarcanda, and Magari.

While the Bolgheri area is getting its share of attention, much of the international wine trade is focused on the Chianti Classico area as its Super Tuscan frame of reference. These wines, many of them quite extraordinary, some of them quite disappointing, have provoked much discussion and controversy in the wine world. Controversial and even as misunderstood as the Super Tuscans have been, they had one unmistakably positive impact: Their success and reputation have helped upgrade the image and quality of their original, modest parents and grandparents—Chianti in general, Chianti Classico in particular.

(See page 388 for a partial list of Super Tuscan wines. Many, but not all, of these wines are expensive to very expensive.)

OTHER RED WINE DOCG ZONES OF TUSCANY

Brunello di Montalcino can be one of Italy's most expensive wines; sometimes it is also its best. The wine was created just after the phylloxera disaster, in 1888, by Fernuccio Biondi-Santi. His grandson, Franco, has continued the family tradition of making wine exclusively from Brunello—a local name for the Sangioveto Grosso, a grape with a rusty brown skin and medium-large berries. Brunello di Montalcino *normale* must be aged for a minimum of fifty months in cask and bottle. *Riserva* wines must be aged a minimum of sixty-two months.

While older vintages of Biondi-Santi *riservas* can match and often exceed the prices brought by old first-growth Bordeaux wines, even young Brunellos from the best producers can sell for well over $100 per bottle at retail and

A dramatic view of the Castello Banfi wine estate in Montalcino

a lot more on wine lists. Of the seven million bottles of Brunello di Montalcino sold worldwide, the United States imports about 25 percent, with a retail value of close to $80 million.

In 2008, Brunello di Montlacino became enmeshed in controversy, as producers were accused of blending small amounts—as little as 5 percent—of international varietals, especially Merlot, into their wines. Other producers were accused of exceeding the legal maximum yield of grapes per hectare. The United States refused to accept shipments of Brunello di Montalcino until the controversy was resolved and each of the producers, as well as Italian authorities, proved that they upheld the wine laws. Obviously, the impact on the citizens and workers in Montalcino and the Brunello producers was devastating.

The small hill town of Montalcino also encompasses part of the Rosso di Montalcino DOC, which is more or less geographically identical to Brunello di Montalcino. With only ten months of aging required as opposed to more than four years for Brunello, this younger sibling, which must also be made from 100 percent Sangiovese grapes, delivers consistently high quality and fantastic value at about the same price as a mid-range Chianti Classico Riserva. The wines are most often made from younger vines with slightly higher maximum yields in the vineyards that sit within the Brunello di Montalcino DOCG zone. The best producers of Brunello di Montalcino DOCG are also the best producers of Rosso di Montalcino DOC. It's a really good wine at a really reasonable price.

Moscadello di Montalcino, a DOC wine based on the Moscato Bianco grape, is a subtly sweet white wine, sometimes lightly *frizzante*, which should be consumed within a year or so of harvest.

Leading producers of Brunello di Montalcino (DOCG), Rosso di Montalcino (DOC), and Moscadello di Montalcino (DOC) include:

Altesino, Argiano, Barbi, Biondi-Santi, Camigliano, Campogiovanni, Canalicchio, Canalicchio di Sopra,

Caparzo, Cappano, Carpineto, Casanova di Neri, Case Basse-Soldera, Casisano-Colombiao, Castelgiocondo di Frescobaldi, Castello Banfi, Castello Romitorio, Castiglion del Bosco, Centolani, La Cerbaiola, Ciacci Piccolomoni, Col d'Orcia, Il Colle, Collemattoni, Collosorbo, La Colombina, Corte Pavone, Costanti, Fanti, La Fiorita, Fornacina, La Fortuna, Fossacolle, Frigaiali, La Fuga, Fuligni, Lambardi, Lisini, Le Machioche, Mastrojanni, Mocali, Nardi, Olga, Pacenti, Paganico, Palladio, Pallazzo, Il Pallazzone, Pertimali, Pian dell'Orino, Pian delle Vigne, Pieve di Santa Restituta/Gaja, La Poderina, Poggio Antico, Poggio Salvi, Il Poggiolo, Il Poggione, Le Potazzine, Le Presi, Quercecchio, La Rasina, Reiniero, Salicutti, Salvi, San Polo, Scopetone, Soldera, Tiezzi, La Togata, Uccelliera, Valdicava, Val di Suga, and Villa Le Prata.

Vino Nobile di Montepulciano is made mostly from yet another Sangioveto clone, Prugnolo Gentile (at least 50 percent, no more than 70 percent). Other grapes likely to be found in the blend include Canaiolo (up to 20 percent) and up to 20 percent of two white grapes—Malvasia and Trebbiano. The wine is produced from 1,645 acres/ 670 hectares in Montepulciano, a hilly commune due east of Montalcino. This wine suffers from an identity crisis, always compared favorably with Chianti Classico, but almost never considered a match for Brunello di Montalcino. Many of the producers of this wine have upgraded their vineyard practices and production methods, trading in their old chestnut barrels for French *barriques*.

Vino Nobile di Montepulciano must be aged for a minimum of two years in wood casks, and three years to

A vertical tasting of Biondi-Santi Brunello di Montalcino, whose older vintages are legendary. Ferruccio Biondi-Santi isolated the Brunello clone of Sangioveto Grosso in 1888.

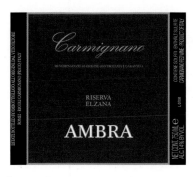

be classified as a *riserva*. DOCG since 1980, Vino Nobile di Montepulciano has been rebuilding its reputation, and the wines can be quite good. Following the lead of Brunello di Montalcino, Vino Nobile di Montepulciano producers are also making a reliable DOC wine, Rosso di Montepulciano.

Leading producers of DOCG Vino Nobile di Montepulciano and DOC Rosso di Montepulciano include Avignonesi, La Berne, Boscarelli, La Braccesca, Canneto, Carletti, Carpineto, Casanova, Cecchi, Contucci, Crociani, Dei, Fassati, Fattoria del Cerro, Lodola Nuova, Il Macchione, Nottola, Palazzo Vecchio, Paterno, Poliziano, Romeo, Saiagricola, Salcheto, Tenuta Trerose, Valdipiatta, and Villa Sant'Anna.

Carmignano is another DOCG wine. Produced within the Florentine hills of the Chianti Montalbano district, about 12 miles/20 kilometers west of Florence, Carmignano has long symbolized a commitment to quality. With a maximum production of 500,000 bottles annually (about 350,000 is the norm), true Carmignano is produced on eleven estates, most of them formerly controlled by the Medici family.

By law, Carmignano must be made from 50 percent Sangiovese, 20 percent Canaiolo, 10 to 20 percent Cabernet Sauvignon or Cabernet Franc, and up to a total of 20 percent of other local grapes. While it may be surprising that French varietals are required as part of the blend in a historic DOCG wine, the interloper grapes are part of that history, having been formally recognized at least as early as 1716 by the Grand Duke of Tuscany.

Carmignano, which must age a minimum of nineteen months before release (thirty-five months for the *riserva* versions) is worthy of long aging, yet approachable when young. Carmignano also produces a small amount of rosé and Vin Santo, both DOC wines.

Capezzana, a producer whose vineyards are located in the hills overlooking the city of Prato, has been instrumental in bringing attention to this wine and securing its DOCG status. Other producers whose wines are avail-

able in North America include Ambra, Fattoria Artimino, Piaggia, and Mauro Vannucci.

Morellino di Scansano, elevated to DOCG from DOC in 2007, is produced in the Grosseto province, close by the region's southern Maremma seacoast and not far from the border with Lazio. In the commune of Scansano, "Morellino" is the local nickname for the Sangiovese grape, and the wine must be made from at least 85 percent Sangiovese, with up to 15 percent of other local varietals allowed.

Morellino di Scansano *normale* can be released as early as the January following harvest and does not by law have to age in wood. The wine is fresh and crisp, with soft tannins. *Riserva* versions must age a minimum of two years and are somewhat more substantial and elegant. Both *normale* and *riserva* wines represent good value at retail and on a wine list.

Leading producers of Morellino di Scansano DOCG include Castello Romitorio, Fattoria dei Barbi, Fattoria di Magliano, Fattoria Mantellassi, Mocali, Moris Farms, La Mozza, Poggio Nibbiale, Le Pupille, Sellari Franceschini, Terre di Talamo, and Val delle Rose/Cecchi.

The town of San Gimignano

VIN SANTO

Vin Santo is the "holy wine" of Tuscany, made by producers large and small. Originally a dry wine, legend has it that Vin Santo was made into a sweet nectar so that children could sip it during mass. True Vin Santo, which is still made in dry and sweet versions, is made in small batches and by a painstaking process that includes carefully selected *passito* grapes, long fermentation, and maturing in chestnut or oak barrels called *caratelli* for perhaps five years, mostly in attics with cross-ventilation. Dry Vin Santo is traditionally served as an aperitif, and the sweet version is served with biscotti for dessert. These nut-studded biscuits are dipped into the wine; the wine-soaked crumbs are happily consumed.

The Vin Santo DOC zones of Tuscany are:

Bianco della Valdinievole

Bianco Pisano di San Torpé

Bolgheri Occhio di Pernice

Carmignano

Colli dell'Ètruria Centrale

Elba

Pomino

San Gimignano

Sant'Antimo

Val d'Arbia

Vin Santo del Chianti

Vin Santo del Chianti Classico

Vin Santo di Montepulciano

The white versions of Vin Santo are made primarily from Trebbiano Toscano and Malvasia grapes blended with other Tuscan vinifera. A popular style of Vin Santo rosé is *occhio di pernice*—eye of the partridge. In the Pomino Vin Santo DOC, a *rosso* version is made.

The best Vin Santo is truly sainted wine—luscious, most often sweet, and sometimes quite expensive. It is most often produced in 12.5-ounce/375-milliliter half-bottles.

Altesino, Antinori, Avignonesi (very famous and very expensive), Badia a Coltibuono, Baroncini, Capezzana, Castellare, Castello di Ama, Castello di Meleto, d'Albola, Dievole, Falchini, Fanti, Fontodi, Frescobaldi, Geografico, Isole e Olena, Pancole, Poggio Bonelli, La Sala, San Felice, Selvapiana, Sonnino, Spalletti, Tenuta Trerose, Villa Pillo, and Volpaia make excellent Vin Santo.

THE DOCG WHITE WINE OF TUSCANY

Vernaccia di San Gimignano, produced from a vine that can trace its ancestry back to at least the thirteenth century and was mentioned by Dante in his *Divine Comedy*, was named Italy's first DOC white wine in 1966 and in 1993 was awarded DOCG status. Located in the heart of Chianti country, it was the first white wine zone of Tuscany to become DOCG.

In 1966, annual production of Vernaccia di San Gimignano was about 18,550 gallons/700 hectoliters, but since then has grown to well over 1 million gallons/37,850 hectoliters. While Vernaccia enjoys a pretty good reputation, it is only recently that producers have sacrificed higher yields for higher quality. Much of the inferior-to-passable wine is still sold to thirsty tourists who descend on the beautiful hill town of San Gimignano, with its many towers overlooking the breathtaking countryside.

The best producers of Vernaccia di San Gimignano produce two or three styles of the wine. The *tradizionale* style is made from extended maceration on the skins, producing a wine that is golden in color and medium- to full-bodied. *Fiore* is produced from the free-run juice of the grapes. *Fiore* is the opposite of *tradizionale*; light in color and body, a simple quaffing wine that provides a good accompaniment to lighter foods, such as poached or steamed fish. *Carato* is barrel-fermented and creates a wine that is pleasing to the international palate, rich and a bit oaky, but restrained enough to allow the fruity character of the Vernaccia to shine through. Most good *riserva* wines, which must be aged at least a year, are produced in the *carato* style.

Vernaccia di San Gimignano, which must be made

from at least 90 percent of its namesake grape, is, when made by the best producers, complex and a bit peppery, but with refreshing acidity and a slight bitterness in the finish.

Leading producers of DOCG Vernaccia di San Gimignano include Le Calcinaie, Carpineto, Cecchi, Falchini, Fontaleoni, Montenidoli, Mormoraia, Il Palagetto, Pietrafitta, Rocca delle Macie, San Quirico, Sovestro, Spalletti, Strozzi, Terruzi & Puthod, and Vagnoni.

NORTHWEST ITALY

THE FOUR REGIONS of Liguria, Lombardy, Piedmont, and Valle d'Aosta make up the northwest sector of Italy. While these Alpine regions have a common geography, their culture and their wines are quite different from each other. Because the region is so close to France and Switzerland, French and Germanic influences can be felt throughout the Northwest, especially in Lombardy's capital, Milan. In the Valle d'Aosta, where the language is, depending on loyalties, either an Italian-peppered dialect of French or a spicy French dialect of Italian, wine labels might be written in either language, along with some in German, just for good measure.

Lombardy produces some very good wines, many of which are appreciated outside their home region. There has been a real change for the better in the wines of Lombardy. The Valtellina Superiore DOCG produces better than 500,000 cases of Grumello, Inferno, Sasella, and Valgella

Nebbiolo is the most important grape for the ageworthy wines of Piedmont and some of the best red wines of Lombardy.

wines each year, all made from the Nebbiolo grape. The neighboring Swiss, who love good wine, import almost all of this production, with most of what is left finding its way to the United States. The Franciacorta DOCG produces some of the best *metodo tradizionale* sparkling wines in Italy. Oltrepò Pavese, in the south of Lombardy, produces fifteen different types of DOC wines, and one DOCG, Oltrepò Pavese Metodo Classico—from forty-two separate communes, from still to sparkling, from dry to sweet, from white to red, from miserable to excellent quality.

Liguria and Valle d'Aosta produce little wine. In Liguria, because of the mountainous terrain, there are only about 720 acres/300 hectares of DOC vineyard. What local wine there is to enjoy is fine, but not much is seen beyond the French and Italian Alps. In Valle d'Aosta the small amounts of DOC wine produced—only 35 acres/14 hectares have DOC designation—used to dictate that to taste the wine you must visit this small but beautiful region. Today, however, a minuscule amount of Valle d'Aosta wine is exported to North America.

Lombardy

Due largely to the influence of its cosmopolitan industrial capital, Milan, the Lombardy (*Lombardia*) region is not immediately identified with fine wines, especially by the Lombardians themselves. Although the residents of the region look to neighboring Piedmont, Veneto, and (sacrilegiously) to France for their best wines, they are missing some very good ones in their own backyard. While only about 20 percent of Lombardy's total wine production is DOC or DOCG, the DOCG zones of Valtellina Superiore, Sforzato/Sfurzat, Franciacorta, and the DOC areas of Terre di Franciacorta and mostly-DOC Oltrepò Pavese can produce some very good wines.

The DOCG zone of Valtellina Superiore, with its subzones of Inferno, Grumello, Valgella, Sassella, Maroggia, and Stagafassli, produces high-quality wines based on the esteemed Nebbiolo grape (at least 90 percent), whose colloquial name in Lombardy is Chiavennasca. Inferno, Sasella, and especially Grumello are worth searching for in the United States, but the best bottlings go over the border to Switzerland. Indeed, the Swiss have invested heavily in the vineyards of Valtellina and have come to almost think of the wine as their own. While the Nebbiolo has a reputation as a powerhouse grape in its native Piedmont, in Valtellina it shows its delicate, lighter side, making a

Northwest Italy

Valle d'Aosta
- Valle d'Aosta

Liguria
- Rossese di Dolceacqua
- Cinque Terre

Lombardy
- Valtellina Superiore DOCG, Sforzato (Sfurzat) di Valtellina DOCG
- Franciacorta DOCG, Terre di Franciacorta DOC
- Riviera del Garda Bresciano
- Lugana
- Oltrepò Pavese DOC, Oltrepò Pavese Metodo Classico Spumante DOCG

Piedmont
- Carema
- Gattinara DOCG
- Ghemme DOCG
- Erbaluce di Caluso, Caluso Passito
- Barbera d'Asti DOCG
- Roero DOCG
- Barolo DOCG
- Dolcetto d'Alba
- Dolcetto di Dogliani Superiore DOCG
- Moscato d'Asti, Asti DOCG
- Barbaresco DOCG
- Brachetto d'Acqui DOCG
- Dolcetto di Ovada DOCG
- Gavi, Cortese di Gavi DOCG

wine with less concentration of tannins and a far leaner structure than Barbaresco or Barolo.

Sforzato/Sfurzat di Valtellina is a separate DOCG, made from mostly late-harvest Nebbiolo grapes, producing a wine with a minimum of 14.5 percent alcohol.

The best of these Valtellina wines, whatever the style, can age, and tasting an older Valtellina Superiore *riserva* is quite a lovely experience.

From the Franciacorta DOCG zone, centered around the city of Brescia, Lake Garda, and Lake Iseo, comes some of the finest *metodo classico* (*méthode champenoise*) sparkling wines Italy has to offer. Made from a blend of Pinot Bianco, Chardonnay, and Pinot Noir, sparkling Franciacorta from Berlucchi, Ca' del Bosco, Bellavista, or other excellent producers are a marketable match for their progenitor, Champagne. The still wines from Terre di Franciacorta (DOC) are also of the highest quality, with whites made from the Pinot Bianco and Chardonnay grapes, and reds made from a curious but successful blend of Cabernet Franc, Barbera, Nebbiolo, and Merlot.

Oltrepò Pavese, located in the southwest sector of Lombardy, produces more than 26.5 million gallons/ 1 million hectoliters of wine each year, or about half of Lombardy's total production. The wines of this area are not held in the highest regard, but some fair to good examples of Barbera, Pinot Bianco, Riesling, Chardonnay, and Moscato, among several other varietals, are produced. Oltrepò Pavese, centered around the city of Pavia and just south of the Po River, has an image problem that will not improve overnight. Some producers are striving for quality and are using modern techniques in the production of French white and red varietals. Oltrepò Pavese Buttafuoco (meaning "sparks of fire") and Oltrepò Pavese Sangue di Giuda ("blood of Judas") are two interesting *frizzante* and *spumante* red wines, in *secco* (dry), *semi-dolce* (semisweet), and *dolce* styles. Some of the varietal-labeled Barbera produced here can also be quite good. The wines of this area are little known in the United States.

Another and relatively new DOCG for sparkling wines in Lombardy, apart from Franciacorta, is Oltrepò Pavese Spumante Metodo Classico, which must be made from at least 70 percent Pinot Nero (Pinot Noir). This wine, so far at least, has almost no presence in the North American market.

Leading producers of Valtellina Superiore, Sforzato/ Sfurzat, Franciacorta, Terre di Franciacorta, and Oltrepò Pavese wines include Albani, Balgera, Barrone Pizzini, Bellavista, Berlucchi, Bersi Serlini, Bredasole, Cà dei Frati, Ca' del Bosco, Cavalleri, Contadi Castaldi, Costaripa, Curbastro, Doria, Fay, Ferghettina, Lantieri, La Montina, Il Mosnel, Negri, and Rainoldi.

Piemont

As Italian wine lovers will attest, the red wines of Piedmont (*Piemonte*), especially the "king and queen" of Italian reds—Barolo DOCG and Barbaresco DOCG—speak to a simultaneous sense of tradition and quality that is hard to find in modern Italian wines. These were among the very first DOCGs in Italy and are made only from the revered Nebbiolo grape. Both Barolo and Barbaresco, full-bodied, long-lived wines, represent a level of excellence to which other Italian wines, including other DOCGs, can only aspire. Piedmont is known by wine lovers as the quintessential premium red wine region of Italy.

The more recent DOCG zone, Roero, across the Tanaro river from the Langhe, to the north of Alba, which must be at least 95 percent Nebbiolo in its red version, joins Gattinara DOCG (comprised of Nebbiolo 90 percent,

Vineyards in the hills of Barbaresco in the Langhe region

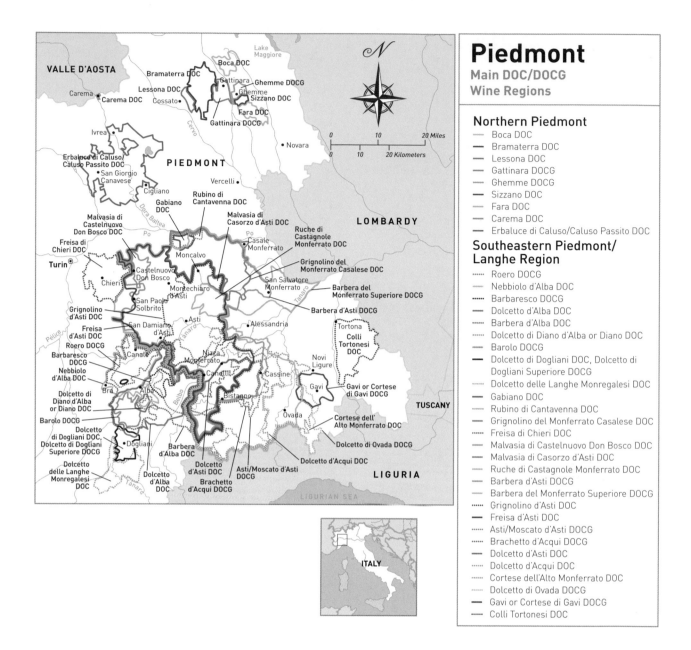

Piedmont
Main DOC/DOCG Wine Regions

Northern Piedmont
— Boca DOC
— Bramaterra DOC
— Lessona DOC
— Gattinara DOCG
— Ghemme DOCG
— Sizzano DOC
— Fara DOC
— Carema DOC
— Erbaluce di Caluso/Caluso Passito DOC

Southeastern Piedmont/ Langhe Region
···· Roero DOCG
— Nebbiolo d'Alba DOC
···· Barbaresco DOCG
— Dolcetto d'Alba DOC
— Barbera d'Alba DOC
— Dolcetto di Diano d'Alba or Diano DOC
— Barolo DOCG
— Dolcetto di Dogliani DOC, Dolcetto di Dogliani Superiore DOCG
···· Dolcetto delle Langhe Monregalesi DOC
— Gabiano DOC
···· Rubino di Cantavenna DOC
— Grignolino del Monferrato Casalese DOC
···· Freisa di Chieri DOC
— Malvasia di Castelnuovo Don Bosco DOC
— Malvasia di Casorzo d'Asti DOC
— Ruche di Castagnole Monferrato DOC
— Barbera d'Asti DOCG
···· Barbera del Monferrato Superiore DOCG
···· Grignolino d'Asti DOC
— Freisa d'Asti DOC
···· Asti/Moscato d'Asti DOCG
···· Brachetto d'Acqui DOCG
— Dolcetto d'Asti DOC
···· Dolcetto d'Acqui DOC
— Cortese dell'Alto Monferrato DOC
···· Dolcetto di Ovada DOCG
— Gavi or Cortese di Gavi DOCG
···· Colli Tortonesi DOC

Bonarda up to 10 percent, Vespolina up to 4 percent) and Ghemme DOCG (comprised of Nebbiolo, here often called Spanna, 65 to 85 percent; Vespolina, 10 to 30 percent; and Bonarda, 15 percent).

Two of the newest DOCG zones in Piedmont are Barbera d'Asti and Barbera del Monferrato Superiore. The red Barbera grape is responsible for about 50 percent of Piedmont's wines, and the Asti and Monferrato DOCG zones, as well as the DOC zone Barbera d'Alba, are regarded as the best *terroirs* in the world for Barbera. Interestingly, Barbera d'Alba must be 100 percent Barbera, while the two DOCG zones of Barbera d'Asti and Barbera del Monferrato

Superiore allow up to 15 percent of three other Piedmontese red grapes: Dolcetto, Grignolino, and Freisa.

Dolcetto di Dogliani Superiore and Dolcetto di Ovada were elevated from DOC to DOCG in 2008 and 2009, respectively. Dolcetto is a wonderfully exuberant, fruit-driven red wine, dry and medium-bodied, and these two DOCG zones produce some of the more complex versions.

The other red DOCG zone of the Piedmont is known as either Acqui or Brachetto d'Acqui. This is a delightful, sweet red wine, made in both *frizzante* (semi-sparkling) and *spumante* (fully sparkling) styles. A perfect match with dark chocolates or cheesecake, Brachetto d'Acqui

A NOTE ON PIEDMONT PRODUCERS

In the Piedmont region, the same producer might make Barolo, Barbaresco, Barbera, Dolcetto, and other red wines, as well as a selection of Piedmontese whites. There are producers, of course, that specialize in only one or two wines. This list, by no means complete, is of producers mostly from the southeastern hills of *Piemonte*, the Langhe region, whose name on a label of any Piedmontese wine—red, white, or sparkling—assures quality. Producers outside of the Langhe (such as Cantalupo in the Ghemme DOCG, in the northern reaches of the Piedmont) are included in the text describing their DOC or DOCG regions and their wines.

Leading wine producers in the Piedmont include:

Abbona, Abrigo, Ada Nada, Adelaide, Adriano, Alario, Alessandria, Altare, L'Ardi, Ascheri, Azelia, Ballarin, Batasiolo, Bava, Bersano, Boffa, Boglietti, Bongiovanni, Borgogno, Boschis, Bovio, Braida, Brezza, Bussia Soprana, Busso, Ca' Bianca, Ca' del Baio, Cantina del Pino, Cantina della Porta Rossa, Ca' Romé, Cagliero, Capellano, Cascina Castl'et, Cà Viola, Castello di Neive, Cavallotto, Le Cecche, Ceretto, Chiara Boschis, Chiarlo, Chionetti, Cigliutti, Clerico, Cocito, Cogno, Colla, Aldo Conterno, Fantino Conterno, Giacomo Conterno, Paolo Conterno, Giovanni Corino, Corino, Coreggio, Giuseppe Cortese, Cortino, Contratto, Cossetta, Costamonga, Dessilani, Einaudi, Ettore, Farina, Fontanabianca, Fontanafredda, Gagliasso, Gaja, Giacomo e Figli, Bruno Giacosa, Carlo Giacosa, Fratelli Giacosa, Gigi Rosso, Elio Grasso, Silvio Grasso, Grasso, Grillo, Grimaldi, Guasti, Lequio, La Licenziana, Luisin, Malgra, Manzone, Paolo Manzone, Marcarini, Marchese di Barolo, Marchese di Gresy, Marenco, Marengo, Bartolo Mascarello, Giuseppe Mascarello, Massolino, Moccagatta, Molino, Montaribaldi, La Morandina, Nada, Negro, Oberto, Oddero, Orsolani, I Paglieri, Palladino, Parusso, Pasquera, Pavese, Pecchenino, Pelissero, Pertinace, Piazzo, Piccolo, Pio Cesare, Pira, Principano, Produttori del Barbaresco, Prunotto, Punset, Renato Ratti, Revello, Rinaldi, Rivetti, Albino Rocca, Bruno Rocca, Giancarlo Rocca, Giovanni Rocca, Rocche dei Manzoni, Sandrone, Sant' Agata, Scarpa, Scavino, Seghesio, Sottimano, La Spinetta, Terre da Vino, Trinchero, Vajra, Valdinera, Varaldo, Giovanni Viberti, Vietti, Villa Sparina, Virna, Gianni Voerzio, and Roberto Voerzio.

Bricco Rocche, a 1-hectare/2.5-acre site owned by Bruno and Marcello Ceretto, who make a much sought-after single-vineyard Barolo from this vineyard

has developed a small but dedicated following among wine consumers.

Although forty-five of the fifty-four DOC and DOCG zones in Piedmont produce red wines only, Piedmont is also home to three white DOCG zones: Asti; Gavi, also known as Cortese di Gavi; and Roero, which is the only DOCG zone to be represented by both a red and a white wine.

Asti, a frothy, softly sweet, light-bodied, low-alcohol wine produced as either a *spumante* (Asti) or a *frizzante* (Moscato d'Asti) from 100 percent Moscato grapes, has long been a popular mainstay of Italy's domestic and export markets.

Gavi, a light-bodied dry white wine made from 100 percent Cortese grapes, is most often seen as a still wine, but is also quite enjoyable in its *frizzante* and *spumante* styles, as well as the gently sparkling *perlante* style.

Roero Arneis, in its dry white version, must be made from 100 percent Arneis grapes. As we have already noted, Roero *rosso* is made mostly from Nebbiolo grapes.

RED WINES OF PIEDMONT

"Il vino è rosso" ("Wine is red") is an old Piedmontese adage that has contemporary resonance, because this region takes its red wines *very* seriously. All of Piedmont's reds, whether light and fruity or massive, complex, and tannic, strive to define what the constituent grapes are capable of producing in their native soils. Piedmontese winemakers struggle to work almost exclusively with native varietals—Nebbiolo, Barbera, Dolcetto, Grignolino, Freisa, and several others—in a market that thirsts for Chardonnay, Cabernet Sauvignon, and Pinot Noir. As if to amplify this commitment to history, tradition, and *terroir*, the Piedmont is the only wine region in Italy (apart from minuscule Valle d'Aosta) that does not contain even a single IGT zone. Just about 100 percent of the wine produced in *Piemonte* is either DOC or DOCG.

The red wines of Piedmont are as *terroir*-driven as any wines from Burgundy. The classic reds of Piedmont are all about the vineyard sites—the *vigneti*—the calcareous and clay soils, the sun, and the fog that hangs over the region. As air currents from the Alps and lowlands intermingle, Piedmontese spring and summer are filled with hot days, while the autumn welcomes foggy days and nights, allowing the classic red grapes of Piedmont—Nebbiolo, Barbera, Dolcetto—to achieve high levels of acidity, ripeness, and complexity.

Whether Piedmont wines are produced in the traditional style (big, complex wines that need much aging) or in a more contemporary version (maintaining complex character, but approachable sooner), elegance is their signature.

BAROLO AND BARBARESCO

While Piedmont is steeped in tradition, it is not standing still. Barolo and Barbaresco, in the southeastern Langhe hills, share the honor of being named Piedmont's first DOCG zones, awarded in 1980. Historically, these wines, especially Barolo, were made from very ripe grapes and fermented in contact with their skins for months, usually in large chestnut casks, where the wine aged for years before bottling. These wines, much appreciated by some connoisseurs but not accessible to the general wine-drinking public, have virtually disappeared from the Langhe.

Today, Barolo and Barbaresco are just as likely to come from select clones of Nebbiolo grapes grown in cooler areas within the delimited zone, in vineyards with much closer vine spacing than ten to twenty years ago, in order to concentrate flavors in each berry. In the winery, skin contact is limited to days, not months, as Nebbiolo is a relatively thin-skinned, pale-colored red grape. Perhaps most important, both alcoholic and malolactic fermentations take place in stainless steel temperature-controlled vats, producing wines of fine structure and balance, without unnecessarily hard tannins. Some producers have also chosen to age their wines in French *barriques*, following the lead of Angelo Gaja, the region's best-known producer of fine wines, who began the practice in the mid-1980s.

The "old" style of Barolo emphasized tannins extracted over time, but today most producers strive to capture the searing acidity of the Nebbiolo grape and look for elegance, not drama, in the finished wine. Even as modern Barolo and Barbaresco are accessible at an earlier age, the best of these

LEFT: *Vineyards in the rolling hills of the beautiful village of Castiglione Falletto* RIGHT: *Pietro Ratti, the son of Piedmont legend Renato Ratti, tasting component wines for his Barolo at the state-of-the-art Renato Ratti winery*

wines, and there are many, can still improve in the bottle for ten to twenty years and beyond, depending on the vintage.

Renato Ratti, a wine producer, writer, and man of great intellectual depth, developed the maps that define the best Barolo and Barbaresco vineyards in 1979. He carefully pointed out those growing areas whose quality or historical significance needed to be recorded for posterity. Ratti's maps remain virtually unchanged, the reference points for some of the great wines of the Langhe. Ratti believed that, much as the *grand crus* of Burgundy define the best properties in that region, it was important for historical and commercial reasons to recognize the superior vineyards of Barolo and Barbaresco. Essentially, Ratti was arguing for the equivalent of the *grand cru* system in France (see page 265) in the superior vineyards of the two DOCG zones. Since the creation of his maps, the very finest Barolo and Barbaresco wines, which previously had been mostly blends of wines produced from vineyards throughout the two wine regions, are single-vineyard wines. Ratti died in 1988 at age 53; his son, Pietro, is in charge of the Renato Ratti winery.

Italy does not have a legal mechanism to rate its best vineyards, and so there is informal recognition by producers and wine lovers of the *crus* of both Barolo and Barbaresco. The names of these esteemed single vineyards will appear on the labels of wines sourced from them. The single-vineyard *crus* of Barolo and Barbaresco follow.

Barolo: Arborina, Briccho Fiasco, Bricco Rocche, Bricco Viole, Brunate, Bussia, Cannubi, Cannubi Boschis, Cerequio, Falletto, Francia, Gattera, Giachini, Ginestra, Lazzarito, Marcenasco, Marenca, Marenca-Rivette, Margheria, Mariondino, Monfalletto, Monfortino, Monprivato, Ornato, Parafada, Pira, Prapò, Rivera, Rocche dell'Annunziata, Rue, San Lorenzo, Santo Stefano di Perna, Sarmassa, La Serra, Sperss, Via Nuova, Vigna Rionda, and Villero.

Barbaresco: Asili, Basarin, Berbardot, Il Bricco, Costa Russi, Gallina, Martinenga, Moccagatta, Montefico, Montestefano, Nervo, Ovello, Pajè, Pora, Rabajà, Rio Sordo, Sori San Lorenzo, Sori Tildin, Serraboella, and Stardetti.

BAROLO This is considered to be one of the most assertive and complex DOCG wines in Italy, though Barolo's profile is moderating as modern winemaking methods take hold in the zone. With softer tannins, the "king" of wines, made from 100 percent Nebbiolo grapes, has become more benevolent and is no longer reserved for the most exaggerated styles of cooking and the oldest cheeses.

Contemporary Barolo, which comes from its namesake town located south of Alba, as well as the neighboring communes of La Morra, Serralunga, Monforte, and Castiglione Falletto, is likely to be a well-balanced wine, redolent of violets, spices, tobacco, and the heady white truffles for which the region around Alba is so well-known. With a medium black cherry color and intense structure, its balance of acid, fruit, and tannin give the wine an edge that makes it an ideal accompaniment to rich foods and sauces. Barolo is an ideal wine for a great meal's cheese course, but also is wonderful with game, braised stews, and roasts.

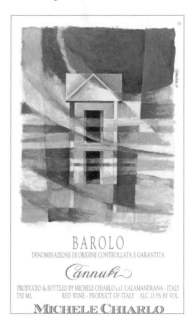

Barolo, especially single-vineyard *cru,* can be very expensive, but the pleasure in drinking a fine glass of Barolo is worth it.

BARBARESCO It was not that long ago that Barbaresco had to be content to live in the shadow of its regal neighbor, Barolo, but those days are over. The wine is, like Barolo, pure Nebbiolo, but planted to the north and west of Alba. In the Barbaresco DOCG zone, the grapes ripen sooner

TOP: *A signpost marking some of the best* terroir-*driven single-vineyard sites in Barbaresco* RIGHT: *A Barolo produced by Michele Chiarlo. Note that this wine is produced from one of the* crus *of the Barolo DOCG zone, the Cannubi vineyard.*

CHAPTER 8 ITALY

401

and maintain a bit more acidity than the more ponderous Barolo. While by no means a light wine, classic Barbaresco seems not as intense on the palate as "the king" and is, in the best Italian tradition, one of the great food-friendly wines. However, depending on the practices utlized by wine producers in the vineyard and the winery, Barbaresco can be fuller-bodied, though often more graceful, than some Barolo. Barbaresco, Treiso, and Neive are the three communes that comprise the DOCG zone, with the best single vineyard *cru* sites located in Barbaresco itself.

Two producers, each of them taking a different approach, each of them producing very fine wines, are largely responsible for the reputation that Barbaresco wines now enjoy in the export market. Angelo Gaja is one of the most famous Italian wine producers and one of the most progressive. His wines can sell for hundreds of dollars, and even at that price are severely allocated to export markets around the world. Gaja has focused on three *cru* vineyard sites that he owns in Babaresco—Sorí Tildin, Sorí San Lorenzo, and Costa Russi—and the world has taken notice, so much so that Gaja has chosen to market and label them strictly by the name of each vineyard (as *grand cru* wines are labeled in Burgundy, see page 316), removing the Barbaresco DOCG from the label and choosing instead the Langhe DOC. In so doing, Gaja is declaring these three wines to be his personal *grands crus*, because Italian wine law does not recognize such a category. He still produces a very fine and very expensive DOCG Barbaresco, which is not a single-vineyard wine. Gaja also produces a wine in Barolo, Sperss, but has removed that DOCG as well, producing yet another *cru*. Gaja also has vineyards in Tuscany, where he produces Brunello di Montalcino and Super Tuscan wines.

TOP: *Aldo Vacca, director of the Produttori del Barbaresco, pointing out the best vineyard sites—the* crus *of the Barbaresco DOCG zone* BOTTOM: *Barbaresco Riserva from the excellent 1999 vintage, each produced by the Produttori del Barbaresco cooperative from a single vineyard—in this case, Pajè and Asili. Each bottle of the small production is individually numbered.*

Just as important, but on the other end of the tradition and marketing spectra, is the Produttori del Barbaresco, overseen by Aldo Vacca, who early in his career worked for Angelo Gaja. Founded in 1958, the Produttori is a cooperative with fifty-six members who own about 250 acres/ 100 hectares of land, a considerable percentage of the Barbaresco DOCG, which is only about 1,400 acres/560 hectares in its entirety. Because all the wine produced from the Nebbiolo grapes grown by its members is made by the Produttori, the growers can focus on true quality in the vineyard, and that focus has helped set a very high standard for the finished wines. About 40 percent of the production of the Produttori is DOCG Barbaresco, made from a collection of member vineyards, but another 40 percent is single-vineyard *cru* Barbaresco, produced from nine vineyard sites, with the name of each site appearing on the label. At their best, the single-vineyard bottlings rival Angelo Gaja (and other well-known producers) for quality, but at less than one-third the price of Gaja's wines.

Wine produced from the Nebbiolo grape, but not necessarily under the rules of the Barolo or Barbaresco DOCG zones, may be classified as Nebbiolo d'Alba, a DOC zone that encompasses ten communes in the Langhe, or as DOC Langhe Nebbiolo. These wines are 100 percent Nebbiolo, medium-bodied, and with only moderate aging potential.

Often showing the best traits of their DOCG progenitors, Nebbiolo d'Alba and Langhe Nebbiolo (with the exception of Gaja's single-vineyard *crus* as a special case) are always good values. About 20 percent of the Produttori del Barbaresco's production is Langhe Nebbiolo.

GATTINARA AND GHEMME

It seems likely that Gattinara and Ghemme must have been awarded their DOCG status based on the fact that both of these wines are historically important and because of the tireless work of Gattinara's best producers, such as Mario Antoniolo and the Arlunno brothers, and Le Colline in Ghemme.

The entire Gattinara DOCG includes only 216 acres/90 hectares of vineyard. Gattinara, which encompasses the northernmost growing area in Piedmont for the Nebbiolo grape, can be an excellent wine, and because of its location in the Novarra hills hard by the eastern bank of the Sesia River, a wine with good acidity.

In the past, there was quite a bit of illegal overcropping and improper labeling in Gattinara, with not much attention being paid to the delimited zone and its laws. However, with DOCG status awarded in 1990, the zone had to withstand a lot more supervision, and all Gattinara wines now must pass a stringent tasting and chemical analysis. At its best, Gattinara, which must be at least 90 percent Nebbiolo (which has the local name Spanna), can be highly attractive, usually higher in acid and often a bit lighter than many Piedmontese Nebbiolo-based wines, and worthy of its DOCG status.

Leading Gattinara producers include Antoniolo, Bianchi, Dessilani, and Traviglini.

On the east bank of the Sesia River lies Ghemme (DOCG awarded in 1995), a wine that has been made from 125 acres/50 hectares of vineyard in the Novarra hills for hundreds of years. There is no doubt that Ghemme received its DOCG status for past glories and historical importance. In the latter part of the nineteenth century, it was Ghemme and Gattinara that were getting the attention of wine experts, not Barolo and

Barbaresco. Today, that picture has turned upside down and inside out.

The best Ghemme wines are powerful but balanced. Ghemme must be at least 65 percent but no more than 85 percent Nebbiolo, with Vespolina and Bonarda filling in the rest of the blend. These blending grapes seem to control the high acidity of the Nebbiolo grape, making for a lovely wine.

Some Gattinara producers also produce Ghemme, but the leading producer of Ghemme is Cantalupo, especially the wines made from the single vineyards, Collis Breclemae and Collis Carellae.

DOLCETTO

Dolcetto grapes, the "little sweet things," produce a dry red wine, usually medium-bodied and fruity, although some Dolcetto d'Alba and especially Dolcetto di Diano d'Alba can be mouthfilling and complex and may benefit from some aging. Dolcetto is often, but erroneously, compared to Beaujolais (see page 328), which is a lighter and simpler wine. There are actually six Dolcetto DOC zones—Dolcetto d'Acqui, Dolcetto d'Alba, Dolcetto d'Asti, Dolcetto delle Langhe Monregalesi, Dolcetto di Diano d'Alba, Dolcetto di Dogliani—and two new DOCG zones: Dolcetto di Dogliani Superiore and Dolcetto di Ovada, both of which must age a minimum of one year starting January 1 after the harvest. Both must achieve a minimum alcohol of 12.5 percent. Dolcetto, whose tannins are usually very light to moderate, is a "crossover" wine, an appropriate match for lighter meats, poultry, fatty fishes, vegetarian dishes, and various pastas, like ravioli filled with veal in a light cream sauce, or pasta primavera. Lighter Dolcetto wines may benefit from a bit of chilling.

BARBERA

The villages of Alba, Asti, and Monferrato are the three touchstones for Piedmontese wines made from Barbera grapes. Barbera d'Alba is a DOC, while both Barbera d'Asti and Barbera del Monferrato Superiore received the

DOCG designation in 2007. All three appellations make wonderful wine: Barbera is a fruit-driven wine with extremely high acidity, and depending on the style, can be a wine that is ready for immediate drinking or a wine that can age for up to ten years. Most of the Barbera wines we see in the North American market tend to be medium-bodied and give immediate pleasure, while a small number of special bottlings are made for the long term.

Ironically, Barbera d'Alba, a DOC wine, must be made from 100 percent Barbera grapes, while Barbera d'Asti (DOCG) may be made from 85 percent to 100 percent Barbera, and Barbera del Monferrato (a DOC, but DOCG in its *superiore* version) is made from 85 percent Barbera, with Dolcetto, Freisa, or Grignolino grapes rounding out the blend. Blending helps tame the high acidity of the Barbera grape.

After generations of poorly made, oxidized wines, contemporary Barbera is a refreshing, sometimes lighter wine with good acidity and balance. The quality of Piedmontese Barbera is much improved, due to stainless steel cool fermentations and controlled malolactic fermentation. Several producers make wines of real elegance. The best Barbera wines are produced from single vineyards.

Perhaps the man most responsible for the new respect afforded Barbera is the late Giacomo Bologna, who died in 1991 and whose wines are produced by his daughter, Raffaella, and his son, Giuseppe, under their father's nickname, "Braida." Bologna's Bricco dell'Uccellone (named for the loon, a bird who is said to have nested in the hilltop vineyard), aged in French oak, established Bologna as the master of Barbera; his Bricco della Bigotta

(named for the gossips who sit in their chairs on the streets of Rocchetta Tanaro) and a *frizzante* Barbera ("La Monella") are wines that put Barbera on the map.

GRIGNOLINO

With DOC zones in both Asti and its native Monferrato, the Grignolino grape produces purplish-red wines with refined aromas and light body, but astringent, hard tannins. Grignolino is said to be named for a word in the Piedmontese dialect, *grignole*, which speaks to the great many seeds in the grape, doubtless a source of the tannins in the wine. Due to its light fruitiness and tannic structure, Grignolino is often served cool, which brings out the wine's sparse acidity. Drink this wine as young as possible.

OTHER RED WINES

FREISA, BRACHETTO, AND RUCHÉ

Two unusual red wines are Freisa and Brachetto, made mostly in areas surrounding the towns of Asti and Acqui, respectively. Freisa d'Asti (DOC) may be a dry red, but the *frizzante*, sweet and fruity version, with a light cherry color and a raspberry flavor, is the more popular style. Freisa is charming and simple, and its froth makes it fun to drink.

Fun also is the bubbly Brachetto d'Acqui DOCG, a sweet red *frizzante* or *spumante*. Brachetto is the red answer to Asti. Unlike the white sparkler, however, Brachetto can be a bit hard to find, and a relatively small amount—less than 60,000 gallons/2,270 hectoliters—is produced annually from this small growing area. Banfi's Vigne Regali Brachetto d'Acqui, "Rosa Regale," is a very popular, very good, refreshing, fully sparkling wine. Braida makes a *frizzante* wine of fine quality. Baravalle, Bersano, Ca' dei Mandorli, Castelluci, La Dogiola, Gancia, Garitina, and Marenco also produce some lovely Brachetto wines.

Ruché is a rare red grape that produces a wine with a nose of white fruits: quince, orange blossom, peaches, figs, and apricots, as well as violets and black cherry. The wine has a good fruit-acid balance, with just a hint of bitterness. Very little of this exciting, medium-bodied, dry wine is produced, and it is meant for early consumption. Bava, Ca de Bò, Cascina Tavijn, and Sant' Agata are well-known

---

TOP: *Vietti is a quality-driven producer, well-known for its Barbera d'Alba "Tre Vigne," made from the grapes of three vineyard sites.*
BOTTOM: *The label of a Barbera d'Asti (DOCG) produced by Cascina Castlet, depicting winemaker and owner Marriuccia Borio and her three sisters on a 1950s Italian icon: a Vespa motor scooter*

producers of fine Ruché di Castagnole Monferrato DOC, an area of only about 100 acres/40 hectares.

WHITE WINES OF PIEDMONT

GAVI

Gavi (DOCG) is a dry, light- to medium-bodied white wine made from 100 percent Cortese grapes. Gavi is a testament to the winemakers of the southeastern Piedmont, because whether the wine is *barrique* aged or the product of cool fermentation in stainless steel, it is almost always well made and a fine accompaniment to fish. The wine may be labeled as Gavi, Cortese di Gavi, or Gavi di Gavi, with the latter label reserved for those wines actually produced in the namesake village. The most famous producer of Gavi is La Scolca. In addition to the major Piedmontese wine producers (see page 399), producers who specialize in Gavi include Banfi's Principessa Gavia (including a lightly-sparkling *perlante* style), Bergaglio, Ca' Bianca, La Chiara, Figini, Giribaldi, La Giustiniana, La Merlina, I Moncalvi, Morgassi Superiore, Neirano, Picollo, Saulino, La Smilla, Spinola, Valditerra, Il Vignale, and Villa Sparina.

ARNEIS ROERO

Arneis is a white wine made from an ancient grape, but Arneis Roero is actually a fairly new DOCG. The Arneis grape is grown mostly in Alba's Roero hills; its name in Piedmontese dialect translates as "rascal," because Arneis has a centuries-old reputation of unpredictability. With its energies harnessed by modern winemaking methods, Arneis, which surprisingly for Italy is a white wine of singular character, can be a fruity pleasure, medium-bodied, floral, and with a touch of almonds in the finish.

PIEDMONT'S FAMOUS SPARKLER

ASTI

While wine connoisseurs pine for the red wines from the hills of the Langhe and applaud the Gavi from Monferratto and the Arneis from Roero, one of the Piedmont's best-known wines is sparkling Asti DOCG. Informally known worldwide by the phrase "Asti Spumante," Asti is made from the Moscato grape and grown in the areas surrounding the towns of Asti and Cuneo. This bubbly, softly sweet wine is a frothy, refreshing wine that is fun to drink, low in alcohol (6 to 9 percent), and moderately priced. Asti, along with its mildly sparkling counterpart, Moscato

d'Asti, is fun to drink and a great match with cookies or cheesecake.

Sparkling Asti, with a minimum pressure of five atmospheres, is not produced by the *méthode champenoise*, and unlike sparklers made by the *charmat* process or transfer method (see Chapter 2, page 85), most often does not go through a secondary fermentation at all. The grapes are harvested early to emphasize acidity in the wine and then quickly crushed, so that minimal oxidation can occur. The must is then filtered several times to keep it clean and pure, and stored in stainless steel tanks at temperatures just shy of freezing to prevent fermentation. Because Asti is very delicate and largely a nonvintage product, it is fermented in batches, so that it is fresh when purchased. In a fermentation process that takes a little more than a month, the must is introduced to the winemaker's yeasts and fermented in anaerobic stainless steel vats (to create carbon dioxide naturally), which are quickly chilled when the must produces the requisite alcohol and residual sugar. The wine is filtered, bottled, finished with a champagne cork and cage, and shipped almost immediately.

Moscato d'Asti is a *frizzante* (lightly sparkling) version of Asti and is made by a slightly different process. The finished wine has a light, well-defined spritz but is usually somewhat lower in alcohol and slightly higher in residual sugar than Asti.

LEFT: *Every DOCG wine in Italy must display its neck label, which includes the number of each bottle produced in the DOCG zone.* CENTER: *The neck label on this Asti bottle covers the cork and foil.* RIGHT: *Ceretto produces the elegant "Santo Stefano" Moscato d'Asti, a lightly sparkling (frizzante) DOCG wine.*

The best Moscato d'Asti comes from small producers and can be quite expensive, while the most reliable—and affordable—sparkling Asti usually comes from those shippers with an active international market to ensure that the wine has not been sitting in a warm warehouse for too long. Perhaps the most acclaimed producer of Moscato d'Asti is Paolo Saracco, whose wine is truly delicious. Other fine producers include Bosio, Braida, Cascinetta, La Caudrina, Ceretto/Santo Stefano, Chiarlo, Contratto, Coppo, Gallina, Giribaldi, Icardi, Mondoro, Neirano, Perrone, and La Spinetta.

NORTHEAST ITALY

COMPRISING THREE REGIONS, Veneto, Friuli–Venezia Giulia, and Trentino–Alto Adige, northeast Italy is, by any measure, among the most technologically advanced and the most quality-conscious winemaking areas of all of Italy. The white, red, and sparkling wines made in these regions are impressive and might be considered the most cosmopolitan and least "Italian" of any Italy has to offer. The wines of the *Tre Venezie* are worldly, because the winemakers toil to make wines that will please the thirsty palate of the wine world, especially outside Italy. (The three regions are sometimes called Tre Venezie, because of their ancient historical links to Venice.) Perhaps this bow to foreign markets accounts for the surprising fact that there are only seven DOCG zones in the three regions of the northeast: Bardolino Superiore, Soave Superiore, Recioto di Soave, Amarone, and Recioto della Valpolicella in Veneto, and the internationally obscure Ramandolo and Colli Orientali del Friuli Picolit in Friuli–Venezia Giulia.

Veneto

Veneto is Italy's largest producer of DOC wines, with about 54 million gallons/2 million hectoliters of classified wine produced yearly. Although the region contains five DOCG zones

A Soave Classico made from grapes grown in a single vigneto (vineyard). Inama is a fine producer.

and twenty-five DOC zones, just three DOC zones account for half of the classified wine produced in Veneto, all centered around the city of Verona in the southwestern Veneto. Soave, one of the most popular wines in the United States, and two popular DOC reds, Valpolicella and Bardolino, account for a total of more than 27 million gallons/1 million hectoliters each year. Near the center of Veneto to the north of Venice and Treviso, about 700,000 gallons/27,000 hectoliters of Prosecco is produced. Prosecco, the refreshing dry to semidry, mostly *spumante* wine, has found an enthusiastic audience outside of Italy, especially in the United States. Veneto also produces a great deal of DOC wine from an international array of varietals, both red and white. For example, the DOC zone Lison-Pramaggiore lists thirteen types of legal grapes, including Cabernet Franc, Cabernet Sauvignon, Malbec, Merlot, Chardonnay, Sauvignon Blanc, Riesling, and several local varietals.

Veneto produces a vast amount of quality wine from delimited zones. Soave, Valpolicella, and Bardolino, along with Tuscany's Chianti, are among Italy's main representatives in international markets, especially the United States. Veneto makes a lot of wine.

SOAVE

There are more than a thousand growers in the Soave DOC and Soave Superiore DOCG under contract to provide Garganega, Trebbiano, Pinot Bianco, and Chardonnay grapes for this wine. Soave must be at least 70 percent Garganega, with up to 30 percent of the other legal white grapes in the blend. Successful in export markets, Soave, precisely because of its popularity, is also sometimes misunderstood. Many people dismiss Soave as predictable and bland, pleasant but without much character. In many cases this profile is correct, but there are several Soave producers working successfully to upgrade the wine's image.

It is a shame that the world of thirsty Soave drinkers rarely gets to taste a fine Soave Classico. Soave's best wines come from its *classico* area, where yields are traditionally lower and there is generally far more Garganega in the blend (usually at least 80 percent). Soave Classico, when made by a producer like Pieropan, Inama, Allegrini, Gini, Pra, Masi, Ca' Rugate, Tamellini, or Suavia, can be everything people who enjoy medium-bodied white wines look for: balanced, fresh, and fruity, with some minerality and bracing acidity. On the other hand, Soave Superiore, with

a minimum aging of ten months (twenty-four months for *riserva*), can miss the point of Soave at its best. While the additional aging of the wine may provide more complexity, it may also work against Soave Classico's true character, which emphasizes freshness and delicacy.

There is no doubt that knowing the best producers of Soave, and in particular, Soave Classico, will separate and change the experience of drinking Soave from the predictable and banal to the exciting and illuminating.

Perhaps the best wine producer in Soave does not produce Soave. Roberto Anselmi produces dry white wines in the Soave DOC, but chooses to use the Veneto IGT for his artisanal wines in order to exercise creative freedom and to never compromise integrity. His Capitel Croce, Capitel Foscarino, I Capatelli, and San Vincenzo wines are all dominated by the heritage white grape of Soave, Garganega. Capitel Croce and I Capatelli are both 100 percent Garganega; Capitel Foscarino is 90 percent Garganega, 10 percent Chardonnay; and San Vincenzo is 80 percent Garganega, 15 percent Chardonnay, 5 percent Trebbiano. All of the wines are outstanding examples of the *terroir* that defines the Soave region and the Garganega grape.

RECIOTO WINES OF VENETO

Recioto di Soave DOCG is a sweet white wine made mostly from semi-dried Garganega and Trebbiano grapes; Pinot Bianco and Chardonnay are allowed in the blend. The topmost grape bunches, the ones that have gotten the most sun, are dried on wicker racks before pressing. The sun-shriveled grapes produce a wine of 14 percent alcohol and 2.5 percent residual sugar. *Spumante* versions are also produced.

In the Valpolicella DOC zone, which we will discuss next, a sweet Recioto della Valpolicella is produced. An ageworthy, full-bodied, sweet red wine made mostly from dried Corvina, Rondinella, and Molinara grapes, the finished wines are the same style as Recioto di Soave, but far

---

Roberto Anselmi's San Vincenzo is 80 percent Garganega, the traditional white grape in the Soave district of Veneto. Other grapes in the wine include Chardonnay and Trebbiano.

more powerful. We will also discuss Amarone, a *dry* recioto red wine.

VALPOLICELLA

Valpolicella is an unsung member of the Italian pantheon of fine wines. Like its neighbors, Soave and Bardolino, Valpolicella can be overlooked because it is so readily available. The charm of this wine is its modesty; Valpolicella does not overwhelm the palate, but sings a soft tune as background music to good food. The Corvina and Rondinella grapes in the classic blend create a wine that is light- to medium-bodied and eminently drinkable, with the resonance of cherries. A third grape, Molinara, high in acidity, is losing its place in the blend to other local grapes and sometimes Merlot and Cabernet Sauvignon. Valpolicella is a good crossover wine, because its tannins are quite soft, almost imperceptible. As with Soave, some of the best wines are made from grapes grown in the *classico* district, and here the best wines can often be those labeled as Valpolicella Classico Superiore, with a minimum of fourteen months of aging.

The best examples of Valpolicella are the small vineyard wines from the *classico* area and the areas to the east of *classico*—especially the Valpantena and Messane valleys. These wines are among the greatest red wine values in the American market, and when the inevitable price to quality comparison is made, a good Valpolicella or Valpolicella Classico Superiore stands tall.

Sweet Recioto della Valpolicella and dry Amarone della Valpolicella (both DOCG as of 2009) are made from the same process as Recioto di Soave, but the grapes are pressed somewhat earlier than for the sweet Recioto della Valpolicella. Amarone is vinified dry, reaching about 15 to 16 percent alcohol, and is a powerhouse, full of fruit and a pleasantly bitter (*amaro*) finish. Amarone is best with heavy meat and game dishes and fine cheeses, or appreciated in place of Port after dinner.

In the old days, Amarone wines had to be aged at least ten to twenty years before we could enjoy them. Today, the new styles of Amarone make them far more enjoyable at an earlier age, while maintaining their dark and brooding core, and their ability to age. Look for Amarone Classico, produced from the grapes grown in the Valpolicella Classico district. A true *vino da meditazione* ("meditation wine"), Amarone is, by virtue of the way it is produced, an extraordinary example of the sensuality of Italian red wines.

In addition to Valpolicella and Amarone, a third style of Valpolicella has become popular, and that is Valpolicella *ripasso*, which was developed by Sandro Boscaini for his Masi winery. Essentially, the lees of Amarone grapes, must, and pomace are added to the fermentation of the basic Valpolicella, producing an extraordinary hybrid that tastes like a cross between a fruity Valpolicella and the earthy, sensual Amarone. One of the best examples of the effect *ripasso* has on the wine lover's palate is Masi Campofiorin.

BARDOLINO

Located along Lake Garda, close to the border with Lombardy, Bardolino (DOC) can be *rosso* (dry, light red), *chiaretto* (a charming dry rosé), or *novello* (fruity, young red made in the Beaujolais style, and Italy's first DOC-approved novello). The *chiaretto* Bardolino can also be made in sparkling versions.

An older style, Bardolino Classico Superiore, is not often seen in the United States, but that may change, as Bardolino Superiore has been granted DOCG status. Also comprising mostly Corvina, Rondinella, and sometimes Molinara grapes, Bardolino is often a bit lighter than Valpolicella, even though the grapes, soil, and climate are quite similar.

In the last ten to fifteen years, quite a bit of Merlot  and Cabernet Sauvignon wines have been produced in Veneto and distributed to the international market. Most of the wines have been drinkable if not exceptional. There is, however, a small group of producers working hard to produce fine wines from these varietals in two little-known DOC zones: Colli Euganei and Colli Berici, located in the hills of Padua and Vicenza. Volcanic soils in these regions seem ideal for both Merlot and Cabernet Sauvignon. Chardonnay and Sauvignon Blanc also grow here, along with native varietals.

A producer of fine wines in the Alpine commune

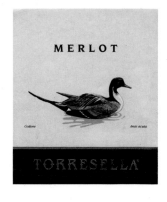

of Breganze is Fausto Maculan, whose sweet Torcolato is one of Italy's best. Torcolato is made from the Vespaiolo grape, and with a nose of honey, ginger, dried pineapple, and papaya and a viscous but clean taste, Torcolato has developed an international following. Maculan also produces good Chardonnay and a much sought-after red wine, Fratta, his Cabernet Sauvignon/Merlot blend.

No discussion of Veneto would be complete without at least a mention of Prosecco, one of the most pleasant sparkling wines in the world, made from an ancient white grape of the same name. Produced by the *charmat* (bulk) sparkling wine process, this crisp, vital sparkler is the perfect summer aperitif to enjoy while people-watching along the canals of Venice, or when you wish you were. Officially, DOCG Prosecco from Veneto must be labeled as Conegliano-Valdobbiadene Prosecco Superiore or as Colli Asolani Prosecco; more than 270 million bottles of Prosecco are produced in these DOCG zones annually. The hilly terrain in the DOCGs provide well-drained soils, and Alpine breezes allow the grapes to develop a high level of acidity. The finest examples of Prosecco are often from the Prosecco di Valdobbiadene Superiore di Cartizze DOCG, a 250-acre/100-hectare hillside vineyard area.

Leading producers of still wines from Veneto, including, but not limited to Soave, Valpolicella (as well as Amarone), and Bardolino include Accordini, Allegrini, Anselmi, Baltieri, Begali, Bertani, La Biancara, Bolla, Boscaini, Brigaldara, Buglioni, Bussola, Ca del Monte, Ca La Bionda, Ca' Montini, Ca' Rugate, Canella, Castellani, Cavalchina, Cavazza, Contrà Borda, Corte Campagnola, Corte Rugolin, Corte Sant'Alda, Dal Maso, Gini, Guerrieri Rizzardi, Inama, Lamberti, Lonardi, Maculan, Le Mandolare, Marion, Masi, Mazzi, Pieropan, Piona, Piovene, Portinari, Pra, Quintarelli, Le Ragose, Righetti, Romano Dal Forno, La Salette, San Rustico, Sant'Antonio, Santa Margherita, Santa Maria, Sartori, Speri, Suavia, Tamellini, Tedeschi, Tommasi, Valetti, Venturini, Vignalta, Villabella, Villa Bellini, Zenato, Zeni, and Zonin.

Leading producers of *frizzante* or *spumante* Prosecco di Conegliano-Valdobbiadene include Adami, Althea, Aneri, Bellenda, Bellussi, Bisol, Bortolomiol, Bortolotti,

LEFT: *A single-vineyard (Tacchetto) Bardolino Classico, produced by Guerrieri Rizzardi* TOP RIGHT: *Merlot is produced widely in Veneto. This bottling by Torresella uses the region-wide Veneto IGT.*

Ca' Montini, Canella, Canevel, Cantina Produttori di Valdobbiadene (Val D'Oca), Carpene Malvolti, Casalnova, Le Case Bianche, Cima di Conegliano, Col Saliz, Le Contessa, Costa Re, Col Vetoraz, Domenico de Bertiol, Drusian, Il Faé, Nino Franco, Frozza, La Marca, Martellozzo, Martini & Rossi, Maschio, Mionetto, Montesel, Oriel, Il Prosecco, Riondo, Rocchat, Ruggeri, Santa Eurosia, Santa Margherita, Serre, La Selva, Sorelle Bronca, Toffoli, Trevisiol, Valdo, Vettori, Villa Sandi, Zardetto, Zefiro, and Zucchetto.

Friuli–Venezia Giulia

Friuli–Venezia Giulia, more commonly known as "Friuli," which borders Austria and Slovenia, is home to Italy's most technologically advanced wines. Under Austrian control until after World War I, Friuli's vineyards were decimated during the battles of World War I. Its capital, Trieste, a port city, was ceded to Italy, but much of the rest of the former region of Istria was eventually awarded to (then) Yugoslavia in the early 1950s. Culturally, however, Friuli is influenced more by Italy than by Austria and the former Yugoslavia, and both its white and red wines are, much like Italian design, a testament to modernism in the wineries and the vineyards. Friuli produces about 65 million cases of DOC wine per year.

Friuli plants French and German varieties—Chardonnay, Sauvignon Blanc, Riesling, and Gewürztraminer—alongside the native grapes such as Friulano (formerly Tocai Friulano), Riesling Italico, Ribolla Gialla, and Verduzzo Friulano. Pinot Grigio and Pinot Bianco, which are produced throughout the region, are the same as the French grapes Pinot Gris and Pinot Blanc. Still known primarily for white wines, Friuli winemakers have made a concerted and successful effort to serve the world wine market with high-quality red wines. Most of the reds are made from Cabernet Sauvignon, Merlot, Cabernet Franc, and Pinot Noir. Refosco dal Peduncolo Rosso is an important red here and is believed to be a clone of the French grape Mondeuse Noir.

The DOC red wines of Friuli made from Cabernet Sauvignon, Cabernet Franc, and Merlot (all of which have been planted in the region for more than 150 years) are not as full-bodied as their Bordeaux counterparts, nor as tannic and complex as the Super Tuscans made from these same varietals. Taking advantage of its cool climate and high-tech production methods, Friuli focuses on fresh, fruit-driven red wines, with mostly medium body. Pinot Noir is also produced in a light style. Locally, Friulians enjoy the fruity red wine made from Refosco dal Peduncolo Rosso, which they drink in copious amounts with their celebrated Prosciutto di San Daniele.

In their white wines, Friuli producers emphasize freshness and, unusual for Italian dry whites, fruitiness. Starting in the 1970s, Friuli winemakers, led by Mario Schiopetto, began a white wine revolution, by eschewing tradition and embracing high-tech methods of wine production. Cool, temperature-controlled fermentation in stainless steel vats and soft-pressing the grapes in a scrupulously clean environment became the rule in Friuli. In the 1980s, the Friuli producers focused on lowering yields in their vineyards and improving the quality of the grapes harvested for winemaking. By the beginning of the 1990s, the reputation of Friuli's wines began to spread slowly, first in Italy, and now, in the twenty-first century, to the world market.

In terms of success in the marketplace, Friuli has done very well with Friulano (named Tocai Friulano until the 2007 vintage), a medium-bodied white. Sauvignon Vert and Sauvignon Blanc wines, here most often labeled simply as "Sauvignon," have attracted attention, as have many Chardonnay bottlings. Pinot Bianco and Sauvignon may just be Friuli's best quality-driven, affordable white wines, but it is the region's Pinot Grigio that brings in the money that keeps the engine of the Friuli wine trade humming.

Over the last decade or so, there has been a serious shift to producing DOC wines in Friuli. There are two DOCG zones, Ramandolo and Colli Orientali del Friuli Picolit, both sweet whites and both fairly obscure in the American market, especially Ramandolo. Picolit has a small, dedicated following. The region still has its share of very fine IGT wines, mostly represented by nontraditional blends.

Refosco dal Peduncolo Rosso is a fruity red that is popular in Friuli.

Of the nine DOC zones of Friuli–Venezia Giulia, the most important are Collio, Collio Orientali del Friuli, and Friuli Grave. The hills bordering Slovenia contain the vast Collio DOC zone, sometimes called Collio Goriziano for the border town of Gorizia in the southeast. Most of the

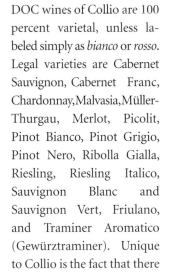

DOC wines of Collio are 100 percent varietal, unless labeled simply as *bianco* or *rosso*. Legal varieties are Cabernet Sauvignon, Cabernet Franc, Chardonnay, Malvasia, Müller-Thurgau, Merlot, Picolit, Pinot Bianco, Pinot Grigio, Pinot Nero, Ribolla Gialla, Riesling, Riesling Italico, Sauvignon Blanc and Sauvignon Vert, Friulano, and Traminer Aromatico (Gewürztraminer). Unique to Collio is the fact that there can be no DOC wines produced in the lowlands or plains of Collio, only hillside and mountain vineyards (*collio* means "hillside" in Italian).

The Collio Orientali del Friuli region is a geographic continuation of Collio, but the winemakers insist that their wines are different from those of their neighbors. To qualify for varietal labeling, the wines must be a minimum of 85 percent of the stated grape, with the other 15 percent made up by a complementary grape of the same color. Permitted grape types include those permitted in Collio, as well as the local red grapes Pignolo, Schioppettino, and Tazzelenghe. The region is best-known for its Friulano white wine; Merlot and Cabernet Sauvignon are the best-known reds.

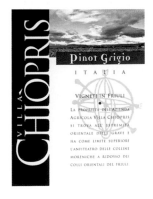

Friuli Grave (formerly Grave del Friuli) is Friuli's largest DOC, located on elevated plains. More than half of the Friuli's DOC wines come from Grave, which, like the Graves appellation in Bordeaux, is named for its gravely soil. Quite a bit of Friulano is produced in this zone, but more Merlot is produced than any other varietal wine. Pinot Grigio and

---

TOP: *Vineyards in Collio, Friuli* LEFT, TOP: *The white variety on this label, Tocai Friulano, has been renamed: Today, it is Friulano.* LEFT, BOTTOM: *Marco Felluga produces classic wines in Collio.* RIGHT: *Pinot Grigio from Friuli is highly successful in export markets. Friuli Grave is Friuli's largest DOC, and along with Collio, its most important.*

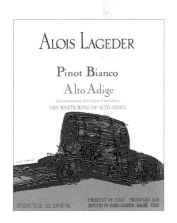

Jermann, Keber, Lis Neris, Livon, Meroi, Miani, La Montecchia, Moschioni, Movia (one of several producers whose vineyards are on the Slovenia side of the border), Muzic, Parovel, Pighin, Polencic, Primosic, Prinsic, Raccaro, Radikon, Rocca Bernarda, Ronc del Gnemiz, Ronchi di Cialla, Ronco del Gelso, Russiz Superiore, Sant' Elena, Schiopetto, Terpin, Toros, Torre Rosazza, Venica, Vie di Romans, Vigneti Le Monde, Villa Russiz, Vodopivec, Volpe Passini, Zamò, Zidarich, and Bastianich, owned by renowned Friulian-American restaurateurs Joseph and Lidia Bastianich, whose wines are superb, especially the Vespa Bianco (IGT), a dry white blend of Chardonnay, Sauvignon Blanc, and Picolit.

Trentino–Alto Adige

Bordering Austria and Switzerland, Trentino–Alto Adige may have been created as a region only for the sake of convenience. While Trentino's culture is undoubtedly Italian, officially bilingual Alto Adige (Südtirol in German) has a predominantly Austrian culture, as Austria ruled this area from 1363 to 1920. Trentino has been linked to Alto Adige as a political unit so that Italy can exercise some control over the region. Whatever the practical difficulties of folding a Germanic culture into a Latin country, the wines of this Alpine region are phenomenal. About 40 percent of DOC wine production finds its way to export markets.

Practically all of the wine produced here is DOC. The eight DOC zones of Trentino–Alto Adige are not terribly significant, for here it is the grapes— and often how those grapes are made into single-varietal and blended wines—that differen-

Pinot Bianco take precedence in the export markets, with Sauvignon Blanc and Chardonnay making inroads. Few well-known producers sell to the U. S. market, as so much of Grave's production is consumed in the EU countries. Varietal labels must be 100 percent of the grape cited on the label. Permitted grape types are similar to those permitted in the Collio DOC.

The most important producers in Friuli–Venezia Giulia include Antico Brolio, Attems, Borgo del Tiglio, Borgo Magredo, Borgo San Daniele, Le Castellada, I Clivi, Collavini, Conte Brandolini, Dal Fari, Dorigo, Le Due Terre, Livio Felluga, Marco Felluga, Gravner, Grion,

LEFT, TOP: *Silvio Jermann continues to be a leader in making the wines of Friuli famous. Note Jermann's passion for screwcaps.* LEFT, BOTTOM: *Vineyards in Friuli Grave* RIGHT, TOP: *Alois Lageder produces some of the finest white and red wines in Alto Adige/Südtirol.* RIGHT, BOTTOM: *Köfererhof is a relatively small producer in Alto Adige/Südtirol. The wines are excellent.*

tiate one well-made wine from the other. The Alto Adige (Südtiroler) DOC designation allows at least twenty varietals, and so does the Trentino DOC. Trentino–Alto Adige's wines, including some fine, expensive sparklers and its ubiquitous Pinot Grigio, are among the best made in Italy.

Of the eight DOC zones in Trentino–Alto Adige (most of which have both Italian and German names), four are of significance in the world market: Alto Adige (Südtiroler), Trento, Teroldego Rotaliano, and Valdadige. Important native red grapes are Schiava (Vernatsch), Lagrein, and Teroldego. Significant red and white foreign grapes include the Bordeaux and Burgundy varietals, and Müller-Thurgau, a grape widely planted in Germany (see page 492).

ALTO ADIGE (SÜDTIROL)
....

This is a large DOC zone, with the Teutonic town of Bolzano (Bozen) as its northernmost anchor. The winemakers of Südtirol are known for their ability to work with a wide variety of grapes, turning them into fine wines. When DOC wines are labeled by varietal, the wine must be at least 85 percent of the named varietal. Wines made from two varietals—both varietal names appear on the label—must be

51 to 84 percent of the first named varietal and 16 to 49 percent of the second. *Spumante* wines may include Pinot Bianco or Pinot Nero or Chardonnay; most are made in the *metodo tradizionale* (*méthode champenoise*).

Red varietals include Cabernet Sauvignon, Cabernet Franc, Lagrein, Merlot, Pinot Nero (Blauburgunder), and Schiava (Vernatsch). Whites include Pinot Bianco (Weissburgunder), Pinot Grigio (Ruländer), Chardonnay, Moscato (Muskateller), Müller-Thurgau, Kerner, Riesling Italico and Riesling Renano (Welschriesling, Rheinriesling), Sauvignon Blanc, Silvaner, and Traminer Aromatico (Gewürztraminer).

There are many single-varietal DOC wines produced in Alto Adige, but they are far outnumbered by the dozens of approved blends. Most of the wines are dry, but there are several DOC-approved sweet wines made here, also.

Santa Maddalena (St. Magdalener) is considered to be one of the finest red wines of northeastern Italy. It is made in the Southern Tyrol from the Schiava (Vernatsch) grape. Schiava means "slave girl," reflecting the grape's ability to bend to the will of the winemaker while always maintaining a certain delicacy. Santa Maddalena—a wine

The Alpine vineyards of Alto Adige

of medium body, good ruby color, and moderate aging potential—is considered to be the best example of the Schiava grape. We see very little Santa Maddelena in the United States, because most of the wine is consumed by the Swiss, Austrians, and Germans.

TRENTINO

A blanket DOC for wines produced from the vineyards of the Trentino section of Trentino–Alto Adige, Trentino produces fine white and red wines from a wide variety of grapes. With Pinot Grigio as the export leader, several other single-varietal wines and blends are produced here. In the smaller DOC Trento, wholly contained by Trentino, *metodo classico* sparkling wines are produced from Chardonnay, Pinot Bianco, Pinot Nero, and Pinot Meunier.

There are sixteen DOC-approved single-varietal wines produced in the Trentino DOC, all made from 85 to 100 percent of the named grape. In addition, there are fifteen DOC-approved white and red blends.

TEROLDEGO ROTALIANO

A single-varietal DOC, the region produces wines from grapes grown near the city of Trento. Teroldego is often considered to be Trentino's finest red wine, with a full body and flavor, and ageworthy character. Recent versions of Teroldego have emphasized a lighter style to make the wine more accessible in its youth. Teroldego rosé has begun to develop a following.

VALDADIGE

This DOC encompasses land that is shared by the provinces of Bolzano and Trento in Trentino–Alto Adige and Verona in Veneto. Here, large wine producers make a lot of drinkable varietal wine, especially Pinot Grigio, but also

---

Teroldego Rotaliano is a single-varietal DOC in Trentino. Depending on the producer, Teroldego Rotaliano can be a simple wine made for early drinking, or a complex, ageworthy red.

Chardonnay, Pinot Bianco, and Schiava. You will often find the Valdadige DOC on well-known brands, such as Santa Margherita.

For those large producers who really need to source their grapes from wide-ranging vineyards, there is the Delle Venezie IGT zone, which takes in vineyard areas of Veneto, Friuli–Venezia Giulia, and Trentino–Alto Adige. Delle Venezie appears on well-made, mass-produced wines, such as Pinot Grigio made by the very large cooperative winery Ca'vit.

Some of the most notable producers in the various DOC zones of Trentino-Alto Adige include Abbazia di Novacella, Barone Fini, Bollini, Cantina Rotaliano, Casata Monfort, Ca'vit, De Vescovi Ulzbach, Ferrari, Foradori, Garlider, Gottardi, Guerrieri Gonzanga, Hofstatter, Kettmeir, Kuenhof, Lageder, Laimburg, Manincor, Mayr, Mezzacorona, Niedermayr, Rosi, Santa Margherita, St. Michael Eppan, Terlano, Tieffenbruner, Tolloy, Elena Walch, Zemmer, and Zeni.

SUMMARY

ALTHOUGH ONCE a major tributary of the "wine lake," today Italy produces some of the finest wines in the world, and many of them are available in the American market. The quality wines of Tuscany and Piedmont are the most highly regarded Italian wines, but wines from Umbria, Trentino–Alto Adige, Veneto, Friuli–Venezia Giulia, Lombardy, Marche, Sicily, Sardinia, and Campania can also be excellent. These wines represent a small fraction of Italy's prodigious output, but the actual number of wines available to the consumer can be staggering. A good rule of thumb when buying any Italian wine is to purchase based on the strength of the reputation of the producer.

Like the food of Italy, the wines of Italy are full of regional and local personality and spirit; they speak to the soul.

TEMPRANILLO

FINO

PENEDÈS

jerez

PRIORATO

ALBARIÑO

GODELLO

RIOJA

RÍAS BAIXAS

GRAN RESERVA

MANZANILLA

CARIÑENA

CAVA

PAGO

MONASTRELL

garnacha

CHAPTER
SPAIN
9

THE IMAGE OF SPAIN and its diverse culture has never been more prominent in America and around the world. The architecture of Antoni Gaudí, the guitar playing and compositions of Segovia and Paco de Lucia, and the films of Pedro Almodóvar have inspired millions of people. The artistic achievements of Picasso, Dalí, and Miró are mirrored by a new wave of Spanish gastronomy led by the world-renowned chef Ferran Adrià. His disciples are now creating magic in kitchens all over the world. North American chefs from Vancouver to Montreal, New York to Miami and Mexico City are incorporating Spanish techniques and foodstuffs into their repertoire. From Puerto Rico to Peru, native Spanish speakers look first to the motherland for wines to pair with their foods. The authors have always been fans of Spanish wines, partially because so many of them are affordable and also because the many styles of wine allow seamless pairings with a wide range of foods.

The four principal red grapes, Tempranillo, Garnacha, Monastrell, and Mencía, and the four white grapes, Albariño, Verdejo, Viura, and Godello, produce a majority of the nation's finest table wines. Spain does not possess the array of grape types of Italy, France, or Portugal, but they do make every style of wine, including sparkling, still, and fortified in varied expressions. Even with the decline of the dollar against the euro, Spanish wines are often undervalued. Spain, however, does not promote itself solely on price. Magazines such as *Spain Gourmetour* and

government agencies such as ICEX and Wines From Spain popularize the notion that all things Spanish are chic.

Spain has the most land mass under vine, with 2,865,200 acres/1.16 million hectares. Spain ranks third in the world in terms of wine production, positioned after France and Italy. By replanting vineyards with the best grape varieties and employing the best growing methods and modes of marketing, Spain is poised to overtake France in total wine production by 2015.

A French study revealed that as France is pulling out many of its vineyards, its domestic and export sales are shrinking. In contrast, new vineyards are being planted in Spain, and the nation's exports are growing. Indeed, it seems the pupil is outperforming the teacher.

It was the French who taught the Spanish how to make modern-style fine wines in the latter half of the nineteenth century. The Marqués de Murrieta, who studied in Bordeaux, and the Marqués de Riscal refined their Rioja wines based on French techniques. The celebrated blended wines of Bordeaux became the role models for the Rioja region and soon spread their influence throughout the entire nation.

In the past, the wealthiest Spanish families often preferred to drink French wines and eat French food. However, those days are over, as the Spanish wines and cuisines, or *cocinas*, of today are competing with the gastronomy of France.

The annual per capita consumption of wine in Spain is about 20 gallons/76 liters, or about two glasses of wine per person each day. Historically, inexpensive wines were part of the daily diet. However, during the late 1970s, in the waning years of the totalitarian Franco regime, Spain experienced a rise in its middle class and with it came a more sophisticated approach to wine. Today, locally produced fine wines are enjoyed by all classes of Spaniards.

When Spain joined the European Union in 1986, there was a great shift from the production of simple table wines (produced mostly for local consumption) to fine wines that could appeal to both local and export markets. A virtual lake of unsold wine in Western Europe prompted member nations to urge Spain to reduce its total vineyard acreage. Under this pressure, the La Mancha region, located in the belly of the country, experienced the greatest loss of vineyards because it mostly produced inexpensive wines.

In the past two decades, many investors have seized the opportunity to plant new vineyards, reclaim old vineyards, and build modern wineries in areas of varying climate: in the cooler northern regions, at higher elevations, or along the coastal regions where water moderates the climate.

Farmers working vineyards in coastal and northern areas are not faced with the same challenges as those in the Meseta Central. The huge arid plain that takes up most of central Spain can stress not only the vines but also the growers who seek to create fine wines. When conditions are too hot and dry, the vines shut down. Since 2003, drip irrigation has sometimes been permitted in such situations and is used to resuscitate the vines. Planting vineyards at high elevations allows grapes to maintain a good balance of acid and sugar. During the day, sunshine raises sugar levels, while at night, sugar levels fall and acidity increases. Many of Spain's vineyards are situated at high elevations, and the shifts in diurnal temperature result in extended "hang time" and fully ripened grapes.

Wind also plays a major role in Spain's vineyards. Wind can bring needed humidity to vines or remove excess moisture that may otherwise cause rot. However, wind stress can also interrupt the vine cycle or cause physical harm to the plant. This chapter includes information about wind, water, elevation, and mountains that are pertinent to understanding Spain's wine regions. Soil types such as the **ALBARIZA** chalk in Jerez and the *licorella* slate in Priorato also play a role in the styles of wines produced in each wine-growing region.

Ten to fifteen years ago, most of the finest and best-known wines came from the northern regions of Catalonia,

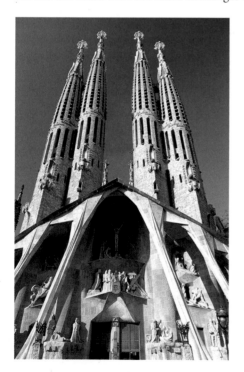 

The revolutionary architecture of Antoni Gaudí and creative dishes of Chef Ferran Adrià are just two facets of Spanish culture that have affected the world. Art, music, and wine also play a major role in the international image of Spain.

Ribera del Duero, and Rioja. Wine connoisseurs were able to recognize Spanish wines by the identifiable smell of the native grape varieties and use of American oak. Today, the wine scene is much more complex and exciting because of the many new regions producing delicious wines.

There are traditional wines and experimental or new-wave wines. The latter are often made with international varieties, such as the ubiquitous Cabernet Sauvignon, and are characterized by a heavy-handed use of new French oak barrels. Good wine is good wine, regardless of formulas, but many classic Spanish wines are based on native grape types and are not shrouded by excessive use of oak.

Today, both wine shops and restaurants offer a broad selection of Spanish wines, including a wealth of styles and choice of price points. Fine wines are being produced in almost all of Spain's more than sixty **DENOMINACIÓNES DE ORIGEN** (DO), as well as in some regions outside the DO system. From Montsant in the east to Bierzo in the west, and from Chacolí in the north to Jerez in the south, there has never been a more exciting time for Spanish winemakers and consumers.

Sparkling **CAVAS**, dry whites, rosés, and Sherries are wines that can be sipped on their own, mixed in a cocktail or *sangría*, or easily paired with either native or international fare, but it is Spain's red wines that are most rewarding for connoisseurs. For $10 to $15 retail, there are many interesting wines from up-and-coming DOs such as Campo de Borja, Jumilla, Calatayud, and Yecla. Penedès red wines have been a source of good value for decades. Today, however, Spain offers wines priced from $100 to over $300 for those who can afford them.

Perhaps the greatest stylistic change has been the transformation of Spain's white wines. In the past, many were flabby, oxidized, heavy wines with more scents of sulfur and oak than fruit. The modern white wines are mostly pale straw in color, light in body, and have crisp, fresh fruit flavors (not to mention being affordable). Indeed, the finest white wines from the New World or France may cost hundreds of dollars retail, while fine Spanish whites are usually priced under $25 retail.

In this chapter, we will discuss wine labels, grape varieties, wine-producing regions, and include an occasional reference to wine and food pairing. Readers who are eager to learn about Spanish wines should be equally enthusiastic to experience them with the groundbreaking new *cocina* of Spain.

WINE LAWS

SPANISH WINEMAKING LAWS date back as far as the Middle Ages, but it was not until 1926, when Rioja was proclaimed a demarcated region—a *denominación*—that modern regulations took hold in Spain. Today, there are many official *denominaciónes*, each governed by its own **CONSEJO REGULADOR**. These regulatory councils are joint regional-federal bodies with strong local ties that regulate the growing, making, and shipping of the regional wines.

Spanish wine laws entered the modern era in 1970 with the adoption of the Estatuto de la Viña, del Vino, y de los Alcoholes, a complex set of federal wine regulations requiring that all Spanish wines adhere to certain quality standards and winemaking procedures, methods of viticulture, transport, distribution, sale, and export. This government decree was followed two years later by the formation of the Instituto Nacional Denominación de Origen (INDO) to oversee and coordinate the activities of the various *consejos reguladores*.

In addition to the general regulations specified in the *estatuto* document of 1970, the INDO, in concert with the regional regulators, governs boundaries of the wine regions, grape varieties, yields per hectare, pruning methods, vinification and aging methods, and minimum alcohol content. Some laws are specific to each growing region, while others apply to all of Spain (e.g., the sparkling wine laws). In Catalonia, which includes four autonomous provinces (Barcelona, Gerona, Lérida, and Tarragona), the Instituto Catalan de Vino (INCAVI) is the equivalent of INDO. (Catalan spelling is different from the Castilian used in most of Spain. Most of this chapter will use the standard Castilian Spanish terms.)

Spain's fine wine–producing regions are entitled to the **DENOMINACIÓN DE ORIGEN (DO)** designation, and as of 1986, the category *denominación de origen calificada* DOC (DOQ in Catalan) was added to Spain's wine laws to recognize truly superior wine regions. So far, the only DOC regions are Rioja and Priorato.

The *denominación de origen de pago* designation was introduced by the Castilla y León regional government in 2000 and adopted on a national scale in 2004. *DO de pago* gives wineries the opportunity to create any style of wine they wish to produce. The stipulation for **PAGO** is that the grapes must be grown and fermented at a single estate and a petition must be filed to approve the estate. A *DO de pago* may exist in a traditional or new winemaking area. The wines originate as **VINOS DE CALIDAD**, and if the quality of the wines is high enough during the five-year probation period, the wines are granted the official *DO de pago* designation.

As of 2009, there are seven *DO de pago* estates—from the province of Castilla-La Mancha: Finca Élez (the first *DO de pago*, awarded in 2002), Dominio de Valdepusa, El Guijoso, and Dehesa del Carrizal; from the province of Navarra: Otazu, Prado de Irache, and Señorio de Arinzano.

INDO QUALITY DESIGNATIONS AND LABEL TERMS

INDO HAS ESTABLISHED the following quality designations for Spanish wines, listed in order of increasing quality. We cover the five traditional quality levels, but current European Union legislation (see page 256) promotes the use of just two categories: *indicación geográfica protegida* (IGP) and *denominación de origen protegida* (DOP).

Table Wines

VINO DE MESA (VDM)

Vino de mesa was the term used for basic table wine or used by maverick winemakers who produce wines with grapes unauthorized for the traditional designations and employing methods that some might perceive as unorthodox, yet still produce them in a registered *denominación de origen* (see below). The new EU category, *viño*, replaces the *vino de mesa* category.

VINO DE LA TIERRA (VDT)

Wine labels from vintages prior to August 2009 may carry this term, but more recent versions may be labeled as *indicación geográfica protegida* (IGP). Much like the former French *vins du pays*, these are wines from a specified place but with a much broader list of permitted grapes and less stringent regulations on yields or aging compared with DO and DOC wines.

One of the most important *vino de la tierra* wine regions is Castilla y León, which includes a huge swath of northern vineyards inland from the coasts. The other is Castilla-La Mancha, which accounts for more than half of all Spain's vineyards and about 6 percent of the world's total vineyard acreage.

VINO DE CALIDAD CON INDICACIÓN GEOGRAFICA (VCIG)

This is another potential IGP category that is similar to the French **VIN DELIMITÉ DE QUALITÉ SUPÉRIEUR** (VDQS) category (see page 274) and a possible stepping stone toward *denominación de origen* status. There is a five-year waiting period to receive approval of VCIG status.

DENOMINACIÓN DE ORIGEN (DO)

This category is equivalent to the AOC wine regions of France (see page 264), with similar rules governing production. Wines in this category are generally of a high standard but will vary in quality according to the dedication of the wine producer, the vintage, and locations the grapes are sourced from within the DO. For example, a winery may treat a single-vineyard wine differently from a wine with scattered vineyard sources within a DO. The

TOP: *A varietal label with the name of the white grape Albariño and the region Rías Baixas* BOTTOM: *The wine Dehesa la Granja was promoted from* vino de mesa *to* vino de la tierra *in 2002.*

Spanish also invest a lot of time and money in aging their wines, ensuring that a DO *gran reserva* red wine aged for five years before release will cost more than a *joven*, or young wine, from the same DO.

Wineries have the option to use the more recent *denominación de origen protegida* (DOP) designation on labels rather than using the name of the traditional DO.

DENOMINACIÓN DE ORIGEN CALIFICADA (DOC)

For wines to attain DOC status, they must be bottled within the region and follow laws similar to those for DO wines in terms of permitted grape varieties, vineyard, and winery practices.

This is the highest category in the Spanish wine laws, but why government agencies have been hesitant to award it to many deserving DO areas is a mystery. To date, only Rioja (in 1988) and Priorato (in 2003) have been awarded DOC status.

DOC wines must be bottled at the original *bodega* within the wine region. More than 90 percent of the wine's production must take place within the DOC zone, and over 90 percent of the grapes for the wines must be sourced from

---

TOP: *A wine label with the region of Rioja, which is a* denominación de origen calificada BOTTOM: *A label with the proprietary name "Coronas"*

approved vineyards within that DOC. The local *consejo regulador* must check the quality of each batch of wine for approval, and the amount submitted each time may not exceed 26,400 gallons/1,000 hectoliters. Therefore, a winery with large capacity may have to submit several batches of wine to have their entire production run approved.

Current European Union legislation allows the use of the term DOP for both the DO and DOC wines, but it is unlikely that DOC regions now or in the foreseeable future will relinquish their coveted and rare status.

OAK AND GLASS: SPANISH AGING OF WINE

Oxygen enters the wine through the oak staves, and the wine develops some of its complexity during this oxidative period. In bottle aging, there is a reductive period during which the wine continues to evolve. The following categories of wine are organized from youngest to oldest.

VINO DE COSECHA

This is vintage wine, with at least 85 percent of the wine made from grapes harvested in the stated vintage. Some *joven* (young) wine is offered for sale almost immediately, usually in the spring following the vintage. In Rioja, Ribera del Duero, and Navarra, wine may not be sold until a year after the harvest.

ROBLE

These wines spend just a few months in oak barrels.

VINO DE CRIANZA

This wine is released to the market in its third year, having spent at least six months in small oak barrels and eighteen months in the bottle. In Rioja, Ribera del Duero, and Navarra, CRIANZA wines must have at least one year of barrel aging plus one year bottle aging.

RESERVA

These red wines are aged at least three years, with one year of the three in BARRICA, or in barrel. American oak is most often used throughout Spain. For RESERVA wines, producers can choose to exceed the minimum aging requirements. White and rosé wines are aged at least two years, including six months in oak barrels, but white *reserva* wines are rare in the export market, where they have generally not been well received because of an oxidized flavor (RANCIO) that many Spanish wine drinkers love.

GRAN RESERVA

Made only in exceptional vintages, the production of **GRAN RESERVA** wines must meet with the approval of the *consejo regulador*. The red wines must be aged a minimum of two years in the barrel and three in the bottle. *Gran reserva* red wines may not reach the market until six years after the vintage. The finest of these wines may not appear on the market for eight to ten years after harvest. White and rosé *gran reserva* wines are extremely rare and must be aged four years, including six months in oak barrels.

Gran reserva is a category of wine that is losing ground, due to the market's preference for wines with more fruit character and less oxidized, earthy flavors. On the other hand, some wineries go beyond the minimum aging period.

Sparkling Wines

Espumosos refers to sparkling wines in general. Cava wines must be made by the traditional Champagne method.

The approved grape types for Cava include the native white trio of Parellada, Macabeo, and Xarel-lo. The local red grape Trepat is also used to make Cava. Some producers opt to use the international varieties of Chardonnay and Pinot Noir.

As in Champagne, Cavas are labeled by their level of sweetness. From bone dry to sweet, they are *extra brut, brut, extra dry, seco, semiseco, semidulce,* and **DULCE**. Over 90 percent of Cava comes from the province of Catalonia, with the Penedès DO bearing the most fruit. Some Cava is made in areas as distant from Catalonia as Rioja, Navarra, Valencia, and Cariñena.

Reserva wines must be aged at least fifteen months before release, while *gran reserva* wines benefit from a mini-

Sparkling wines made by the Champagne method are known as Cava in Spain. The minimum aging period is nine months before they may be sold.

mum of thirty months' aging before they are sold. There are many miles of underground cellars where Cava matures before it is riddled by machine and disgorged. (For a discussion of the Champagne method, see page 78.)

OTHER SPANISH WINE TERMS

EMBOTELLADO DE ORIGEN Estate bottled

BODEGA Winery

VIÑA, VIÑEDO Vineyard

BLANCO White

ROSADO Rosé

TINTO Red

DOBLE PASTA The maceration of red wine with twice the amount of skins for extra color and tannins. Can be used as a blended ingredient to increase the color and weight of a lighter wine.

RANCIO A term used to describe wines that are affected by oxygen, heat, or a combination of the two. These wines may smell of overripe cheese or fruit and may also have nut and honey notes.

SPAIN'S INDIGENOUS GRAPE VARIETIES

Red Grapes

TEMPRANILLO Tempranillo is considered to be the finest grape in Spain; it is the most-planted varietal in the country. On the plus side, its fairly thick skin can contribute tannins and color; however, its wines tend to lack acidity. This problem is remedied when Tempranillo is planted in cool climates or at high elevations with a large diurnal difference between daytime and nighttime temperatures. Tempranillo does not oxidize quickly and can therefore age very well. Trademark aromas include blackberry, licorice, red cherry, and an array of spice notes. In Ribera del Duero, the local clone of Tempranillo is known as Tinto Fino or Tinto del País. These wines are richer and more ageworthy than those of many other areas of the nation. The general agreement is that it is the grape used to make Toro red wines (Tinta de Toro is Tempranillo, for example), but it is a hotly disputed topic among some locals who prefer to think Toro's grape is entirely unique. Tempranillo is known as Ull de Llebre in Catalonia,

Tinto de Madrid in vineyards close to the capital, and Cencibel in La Mancha.

GARNACHA Garnacha Tinta is the Grenache grape and Spain is its birthplace (also known as Aragón in some regions). This is the world's second most-planted red variety after Cabernet Sauvignon. (For additional details, see page 45 in Chapter 1.)

GARNACHA TINTORERA This grape is also known as Alicante Bouschet. Unlike most red grapes whose juice is clear, this grape's juice is a dark color. Aside from its dark-color contribution, the Tintorera can add weight to a blended wine.

MONASTRELL Monastrell is the same variety as the Mourvèdre planted in many wine-producing nations of the world. It can be found as a single-variety wine or in blends, and it contributes dark color, black fruit aromas, and alcohol through its ripeness.

MAZUELO Known by this name in Rioja and as Cariñena elsewhere, except in Catalonia where it is sometimes called Samso. Mazuelo is the same grape as the Carignan variety grown in France. Its vines yield large grapes that produce a must with deep color and extract, along with high levels of tannin. Because Garnacha oxidizes easily, Mazuelo is often blended with it to preserve color in the wine and to add some freshness.

GRACIANO This grape adds freshness and a spicy aroma to blended wines and is also found as a varietal wine that reaches only about 11 percent alcohol. It does not add color to a wine, and if not fully ripe, it can contribute vegetal and bitter aromas. It is a low-yielding variety, but it does add some zest to wines from Rioja.

PRIETO PICUDO Inexpensive versions made from this grape are lightweight, and the finer examples are more tannic with a good degree of acidity for balance. It does well in the Tierra de León region, where it produces wines with tart red fruit flavors.

MORISTEL A grape that produces a lightweight wine with red fruit flavors.

BOBAL A grape used to make rosé and red wines that have a good level of acidity.

MENCÍA The principal grape of Bierzo, where it produces some medium-weight wines with bright red cherry flavors as well as more complex medium- to full-bodied wines. Known as the Jaen grape in Portugal.

TREPAT A variety primarily used to make light- to medium-weight rosé still and sparkling wines.

RUFETE Not a widely planted grape, but it can produce interesting spicy and herbal wines.

PARRALETA Wines from this grape mostly show aromas of red berries in a medium-weight package.

SUMOLL A variety used mostly in Catalonia in red wine blends.

White Grapes

ALBARIÑO Aromas and flavors of peach, citrus, melon, and cinnamon are attributes of the wines made from this esteemed variety. It can be bottled on its own or

LEFT: *Tempranillo red grapes* RIGHT: *Garnacha red grapes*

blended with Loureira and Treixadura for Rías Baixas wines. In Portugal, it is known as Alvarinho and often blended with the same varieties. It is mostly used in Galicia.

LOUREIRA This variety, grown in Galicia, produces wines with stone fruit aromas and flavors.

TREIXADURA This grape produces characteristic notes of apples and floral aromas and flavors, and is also grown in Galicia.

GODELLO Citrus, floral, and spice notes with a natural textural richness combine to make this one of the more exciting Spanish grape varieties. Used in Ribeiro, Valdeorras, Monterrei, and Bierzo.

LADO This is a blending grape used in Ribeiro wines for its high acidity.

VERDEJO This high-acid grape contributes earthy qualities and melon, apricot, and pear flavors to wine. It may be blended with Viura, Sauvignon Blanc, or both. Oaked and unoaked versions are available from Rueda.

HONDARRIBI Used in the Basque region to produce zingy white wines with green apple flavors known as Chacolí, or Txacoli. The grape is also known as Hondarribi Zuri.

AIRÉN About 1 million acres/400,000 hectares are planted with this grape, which is used to make inexpensive white wines as well as brandies. Yes, the irony is that Airén is the most-planted grape in the world, yet so few wine drinkers know the variety.

TORRONTÉS Its high acidity makes it useful in blended wines from Ribeiro and Rías Baixas. It is not the same variety as that which makes the floral wine that hails from Argentina.

PALOMINO FINO This variety, also known as Listán, gives a flavor of almonds to the table wines from Galicia or León. It is most famous as the base for over 90 percent of the wines of Sherry.

VIURA This grape is a component of Cava and still wines in Catalonia, where it is known as Macabeo. It is also the principal grape used for white Rioja wines and in Rueda. It is well suited for making *reserva* wines because it does not oxidize as quickly as other varieties when aged in oak barrels.

PARELLADA A component of Cava as well as still wines, this variety has citrus and floral aromas, low alcohol, and high acidity.

XAREL-LO Contributes complex aromas and structure to still and sparkling wines.

PARDINA Native to the central regions of Spain and Extremadura, this variety has the potential to make complex wines with herbal notes.

MERSEGUERA A grape used to make dry white wines; it produces herbal and nutty aromas and flavors.

PEDRO XIMÉNEZ This grape is used to make sweet Sherry as well as dry and sweet versions of Montilla-Moriles fortified wines.

SPAIN'S WINE REGIONS

SPAIN'S WINE REGIONS exist within political boundaries, and that is how most wine books organize them. However, wine-growing areas often overlap different zones. Consider the up-and-coming area of Jumilla, which is partially in the Murcia province and partially in Castilla y León. Also consider that the latter contains such different topography and climatic conditions. For students, educators, and journalists, this chapter provides a traditional map, which includes the major wine regions and their DO, DOC, and *DO de pago* wine areas as well as a reference list of all of Spain's DO and DOC wines.

For consumers and others who look to demystify wines, there is also a map organized as Wines from Spain does in its *Far from Ordinary* guide. It makes a lot of sense and is gaining ground in the way educators and wine lovers talk about Spanish wines. The six most important areas in this scheme are *Green Spain, Duero River Valley, Ebro River Valley, Mediterranean Coast, Meseta,* and *Andalucía.* Only a brief mention will be given to the grape types of the seventh area, the Islands of Spain, as their wines are seldom exported to North America.

The proximity of the Atlantic Ocean brings beneficial rain to the vineyards of the northern coastal region, an area that is often referred to as Green Spain.

The Cordillera Cantabrica mountains protect the wines of the Duero River Valley from too much wind stress from the ocean. Spain's premier red wine for a century, Vega Sicilia (located in Ribera del Duero), was founded in the latter half of the nineteenth century and inspired by the winemaking practices of Bordeaux, France.

The Duero River and Ebro River waterways moderate the heat in the vineyards surrounding them, and the

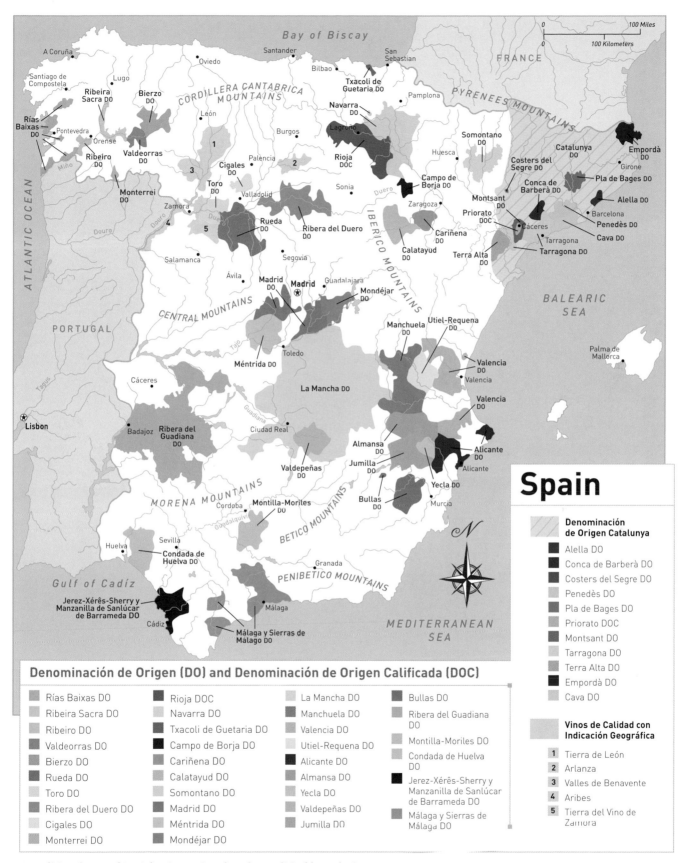

A traditional map of Spain's wine regions based on political boundaries

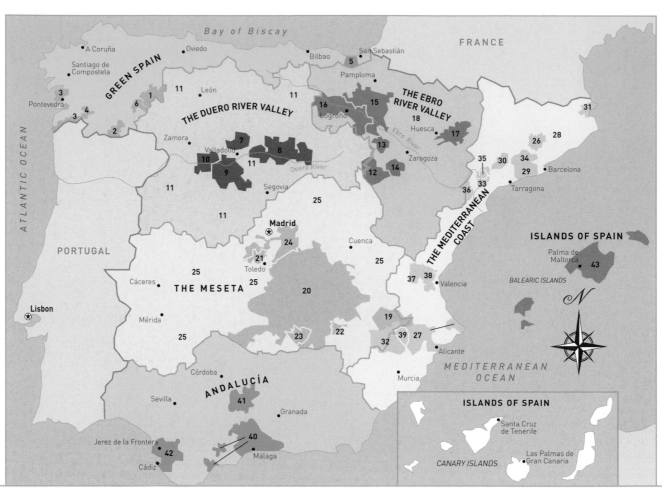

Spain Modern
Main Wine Regions

Green Spain
1 DO Bierzo
2 DO Monterrei
3 DO Rías Baixas
4 DO Ribeiro
5 DO Txacolí de Guetaria
6 DO Valdeorras

The Duero River Valley
7 DO Cigales
8 DO Ribera del Duero
9 DO Rueda
10 DO Toro
11 VT de Castilla y León

The Ebro River Valley
12 DO Calatayud
13 DO Campo de Borja
14 DO Cariñena
15 DO Navarra
16 DOC Rioja
17 DO Somontano
18 VT Ribera del Jiloca

The Meseta
19 DO Almansa
20 DO La Mancha
21 DO Méntrida
22 DO Ribera del Júcar
23 DO Valdepeñas
24 DO Vinos de Madrid
25 VT de Castilla

The Mediterranean Coast
26 DO Pla de Bages
27 DO Alicante
28 DO Cataluña
29 DO Cava
30 DO Conca de Barberà
31 DO Empordà
32 DO Jumilla
33 DO Montsant
34 DO Penedès
35 DOC Priorato
36 DO Terra Alta
37 DO Utiel-Requena
38 DO Valencia
39 DO Yecla

Andalucía
40 DO Málaga
41 DO Montilla- Moriles
42 DO Jerez-Xérès-Sherry &
DO Manzanilla de Sanlúcar
de Barrameda

Islands of Spain
43 VT Illes Balears

A contemporary map of Spain's wine regions adapted from the Far From Ordinary *guide by the Spanish wine bureau in the U.S.A.*

THE PROVINCES OF SPAIN AND THEIR DO AND DOC WINES BASED ON THE TRADITIONAL GEOGRAPHIC MAP

For a quick reference, here is a traditional listing of provinces followed by their DO wines, as well as the DOCs of Rioja and Priorato.

CATALONIA Catalunya, Alella, Penedès and Cava, Conca de Barberà, Tarragona, Priorato DOC (DOQ Priorat in Catalan), Pla de Bages, Terra Alta, Costers del Segre, Montsant, Empordà

VALENCIA Alicante, Utiel Requena

MURCIA Jumilla, Yecla

EXTREMADURA Ribera del Guadiana

ARAGÓN Somontano, Cariñena, Calatayud, Campo de Borja

LA RIOJA Rioja (DOC)

NAVARRA Rioja (DOC), Navarra

BASQUE COUNTRY, CANTABRIA Chacolí de Guetaria, Chacolí de Vizcaya, Rioja (DOC)

CASTILLA Y LÉON Ribera del Duero, Rueda, Toro, Bierzo, Cigales, Mondéjar, Manchuela, Méntrida

CASTILLA LA MANCHA La Mancha, Valdepeñas, Almansa, Finca Élez (one estate winery)

MADRID Vinos de Madrid

GALICIA Rías Baixas, Valdeorras, Ribeiro, Ribeira Sacra, Monterrei

MURCIA Yecla, Yecla Campo Arriba

ANDALUCÍA Jerez (also Xérès or Sherry), Manzanilla de Sanlúcar de Barrameda Jerez, Montilla-Moriles, Málaga, Sierra de Málaga, Condado de Huelva

The islands are not discussed in the chapter, so grape variety information is provided here.

CANARY ISLANDS Abona, Lanzarote, La Palma, Valle de Gûimar, Valle de la Orotava, Ycoden Daute-Isora. White wines are based mostly on Malvasia and Listán Blanca, and red wines are from Listán Negra and Negramoll.

MALLORCA Pla I Levant. White grapes include Moll (Prensal), Parellada and Macabeo; red grapes are Manto Negro, Callet, Monastrell, and Tempranillo.

---

vineyards are also blessed by the cooling breezes from the Pyrenees mountains. The Ebro River Valley contains Spain's first significant dry-wine region, Rioja, and is still the country's most famous name in wine.

The Mediterranean Coast and Rioja have been influenced by their proximity to France. As previously mentioned, French winemaking consultants were brought in to elevate Spanish wines and advance winemaking practices from medieval techniques to modern methods. Josép Raventós's visit to the Champagne region in France in the nineteenth century gave him the knowledge and enthusiasm to create the winery and cellars of Codorníu, a sparkling wine producer located in Penedès, Catalonia, of the Mediterranean Coast. Two of the top three brands of wine in Spain are sparkling Cavas made by the Champagne method in the Catalonia region of the Mediterranean Coast (Freixenet and Codorníu). Vineyards within the region are cultivated with both indigenous and French grape varieties.

The Meseta winemakers still satisfy the needs of the domestic market with cheap wines, but some highly regarded wines are also produced. About 60 percent of wine consumed in Spain are bottles that cost under $3, and much of it is from thc Meseta. A few gems can also be found within the Meseta, such as the *pago* wines.

Andalucía is the home of Jerez, also known as Xérès or Sherry, the oldest wine region of Spain. Andalucía is now redefining itself with a campaign that promotes its wines to a younger audience while also highlighting its ability to pair with foods. Do not scoff unless you have experienced pouring some Pedro Ximénez Sherry over vanilla ice cream or had a sip of P.X. after tasting the ice cream. It is one of the gastronomic portals to heaven!

THE SIX MAJOR AREAS OF SPAIN

Green Spain

While many vineyards in Spain are parched, these verdant areas are inundated with sufficient rainfall to thrive. Humidity can pose a threat to the vineyards, causing farmers to use grape varieties and growing techniques to avoid rot. Grapevines are often trained high and are spaced apart so there is sufficient room for wind to ventilate the vineyards.

Fishermen provide the spoils of a bountiful diversity of seafood. Some of the local specialties along the Atlantic include barnacles, spiny lobster, shrimp, oysters, clams, hake, grouper, and the prized baby eels known as *angullas*. The style of dry white wines in the area evolved to match the local fare. The climate provides conditions ideal for the production of crisp white wines that coexist wonderfully with regional dishes.

GALICIA

Granite and sandy soils dominate the landscape and are conducive to the production of aromatic white wines. Vines are often trained to grow above other crops to maximize use of the land. Vineyard holdings are small. The inlets along the coast (*Rías*) resemble the fjords of Norway and parts of the coastline of Great Britain. There is a strong Celtic presence in the area evident in the language of the people and their music, which features the *gaita*, or bagpipe. The local *Gallego* citizens have their own official language. Since the 1980s, the Albariño grape from the Rías Baixas area has been Spain's most successful white wine export.

RÍAS BAIXAS DO

Located by the Atlantic Ocean, the area benefits from having a mild Atlantic climate and from the cooling winds of the ocean. Albariño from Rías Baixas is at least 12 percent alcohol, medium to full in body, with a complex nose and flavors that often include peaches, pears, and white flowers.

Grapes are grown in small vineyards and are handpicked on steep slopes. The grapes are gently crushed in chilled pneumatic presses, and the must is fermented in temperature-controlled stainless steel vats. Although some wines see oak, its influence is rarely so heavy that it hinders the appreciation of Albariño's fruit flavors. Wines labeled Albariño are 100 percent varietal. The *denominación* also produces a dry wine labeled as Rías Baixas, which must include at least 70 percent Albariño grapes in the blend. The other authorized varieties include Loureira, Treixadura, Caiño, Godello, and Torrontés. Rías Baixas and Albariño wines shine when paired with shellfish and seafood such as red snapper, grouper, or hake (*merluza*). A small amount of red wine from Mencía, Espadeiro, Caiño Tinto, Brancellao, and Loureira Tinta is also produced but is not usually exported.

The subregions of Rías Baixas include the Val do Saines, O Rosal, Ribeira de Ulla, Condado do Tea, and Soutomaior. The latter produces only pure Albariño wines, and Val do Saines also mostly produces pure Albariños.

Good producers of Albariño include Palacio de Fefiñanes, Lusco do Miño, Morgadio, Valdamor, Terras Gauda, Santiago Ruiz, Martin Codax, Agro de Bazan, Nora, Pazo de Senorans, Pazo de Barrantes, Pazo Sanamaro, and Fillaboa.

RIBEIRO DO

For centuries, Ribeiro had relied on the Palomino grape, the grape of Sherry, to make its white wines. The high-yielding variety produced wines that tended to be heavy and oxidized; very little was actually bottled. With the help of a regional research station and the encouragement of the local Ribeiro cooperative, many Palomino Fino vines were replaced with two native varieties: Treixadura and Torrontés. When vinified with cool-fermentation techniques, these two grapes make a wine that is light- to medium-bodied and refreshing, with appealing aromas. Since the late 1980s, the Ribeiro cooperative has invested millions of dollars in stainless steel tanks and filters, with results that are nothing short of outstanding. The wines, made either by the co-op or the Caves de Ribeiro Company, are wonderful with fish and are appearing in increasing numbers on the export market. Equally exciting are the Godello-based wines made by companies such as Campante. Their Gran Reboreda offers mineral, citrus, and stone fruit flavors that showcase Godello's potential in the area. The simple Reboreda qualifies as a best-value wine. Other white grapes grown here include Macabeo, Loureira, Albariño, and Albillo.

Red wines are based on Garnacha, Caiño Tinto, Alicante, Mencía, Brancellao, Sousón, and Tempranillo grape varieties.

A view of the Miño River from a vineyard in Ribeiro

RIBEIRA SACRA DO

Located between Ribeiro and Bierzo to its east, the Ribeira Sacra region is home to some good dry whites made from Albariño, Treixadura, and Godello. The area is best known for its fruit-forward, medium-bodied Mencía-based red wines. Peza do Rei is a fine producer.

VALDEORRAS DO

The winemakers of this "golden valley" are hard at work improving their wines, especially for the export market, by replanting their vineyards with white Godello and red Mencía grapes. One of the finest white wines from Spain is made in Valdeorras by the Godeval winery, established in 1986 with a huge investment in modern winemaking equipment. Viña Godeval, made from 100 percent Godello grapes, has lovely aromas and flavors of stone fruit. Other white grapes of the region include the Palomino, Lado, and Moscatel. Adega o Casal winery produces fine white Godello and red Mencía wines.

Ricardo Perez, winemaker for Descendientes de José Palacios, sources his Mencía grapes from steep vineyards in Bierzo.

BIERZO DO

This is one of the hot new wine DOs of Spain. Actually. it is quite cool in temperature due to its elevation and the cooling breezes from the Atlantic Ocean. Less rain falls here than in Galicia, but it is still enough to maintain the vines' natural evolution. Cold nighttime temperatures result in wines with good acidity. Its steep vineyards require dedication because of the difficulties involved in the tending and harvesting of the vines.

The Mencía represents at least 70 percent of Bierzo wines: It delivers fresh red cherry, strawberry, and raspberry flavors, usually in a medium- to full-bodied package.

Suggested wines include Descendientes de José Palacios, Casar de Burbia, Dominio de Tares, Adria, Luzdivina, Martin Codax, del Abad, El Castro de Valtuilee, Estefania, Pago de Valdoneje, Paixar, Luna Beribede, and Joaquin Rebelledo.

BASQUE COUNTRY

Whether it be small plates of *pintxos* or the more refined dishes created by chefs from the local cooking schools, there are many flavors to savor in this region. The local people consider themselves Basque first, and for some, Spanish second.

CHACOLÍ/TXACOLINA DO

The local specialty is crisp, dry white wine. Chacolí or Txacolina DO wines from Vizcaya are based on the Hondarribi Zuri grape variety. There is also a red Hondarribi Beltza grape grown in the DO. The three subregions' DO wines are Chacolí de Guetaria, Chacolí de Alava, and Chacolí de Vizcaya. They are low-alcohol, crisp white wines with the malic acid flavor of green apples and may have a light effervescence. Most of the wine (90 percent) is consumed in Spain, but a few bottles may be found in North America, such as wines from Bodega Etxanis, Elzaguirre, and Ulacia.

The Duero River Valley

The Duero River, known as the Douro in Portugal, provides a moderating influence on the vineyards near it. The famous Ribera del Duero on the northern side of the river is situated at a much higher elevation than the Rueda DO to its south. The Ribera del Duero's cold nighttime temperatures allow for the slow ripening of its Tempranillo grapes. Some of Spain's most refined red wines come from this area.

The more moderate temperatures of the Rueda DO are best suited for white wines. Unlike Galicia's Atlantic climate, these areas may be classified as a mixture of Continental and Atlantic growing conditions. Two up-and-coming DO areas that are slightly warmer are Toro and Cigales.

RIBERA DEL DUERO DO

Ribera del Duero has 29,650 acres/12,000 hectares under vine on dry highlands. As mentioned earlier, many of Spain's finest growing regions are at high elevations; Ribera del Duero lies at 2,789 feet/850 meters elevation. The vines literally cling to the earth to protect themselves from bitterly cold winters and shield themselves under a lush leaf canopy during burning summers. A diurnal difference up to 40°F/4.4°C on some days allow the grapes to establish good acid balance for their ripe sugar levels. Ultimately, that acidity and the tannins imparted by the local Tinto Fino clone of Tempranillo is what will allow the wines to age for decades.

On the upper slopes, the soil is rich in chalk, while the lower slopes are alluvial clay. The former allows for good drainage and the latter for water retention.

Ribera del Duero produces a little white wine from Albillo and makes a small amount of rosé. The focus is on red wine, the best of which was and still may be Vega Sicilia. This extraordinary wine is made from a blend of local Tempranillo (here called Tinto del País or Tinto Fino) and Garnacha, as well as classic Bordeaux varieties (Cabernet Sauvignon, Merlot, and Malbec), which account for about 30 percent of the finished wine. Vega Sicilia's Unico, never released before aging ten years in oak and two more in the bottle, commands prices in excess of $300 per bottle. Vega Sicilia has been famous as perhaps Spain's greatest red wine for more than a hundred years and has only improved with time. Valbuena is the second wine of the estate, released after five years of aging, and it has many of the same flavors as Unico at half the price.

The first challenger to Vega Sicilia was Alejandro Fernandez with his Pesquera wine, based purely on the local clone of Tempranillo. In the greatest vintages, he released Janus, a wine inspired by the Roman god of beginnings and endings. True to its name, Janus wines have an impressive attack, unfaltering middle, and a very long finish. For value, try the *crianza* Pesquera wines. They are true expressions of Ribera del Duero at a moderate price.

Peter Sisseck emigrated from Denmark to produce some of the most celebrated wines of Ribera. His Hacienda de Monasterio wine uses a similar formula to Vega Sicilia by using mostly Tempranillo and balancing it out with Bordeaux varieties. His Flor de Pingus wines and Pingus wines are similar in style to Pesquera, being pure expressions of Tino Fino.

What is typical in a wine from the region? Ribera del Duero wines should have an opaque color that is darker than their rival Rioja wines. The nose should be of black fruit, such as plum, cherry, and blueberry, with notes of licorice. Over time, herbal, vegetal (mushroom and grilled peppers), and earth flavors are just some of the bouquets that may be found in these wines.

Unfortunately, in the rush to cash in on the fame of the great wineries, some new plantings of Tempranillo are not Tinto Fino or Tinto del País but other clones prized for their higher yields and quicker maturation. Cabernet Sauvignon acreage has increased. Perhaps the native Pardina and Garnacha red grapes will make a comeback and contribute to the fine wines of the region in the future.

Visiting the finest sites of Ribera del Duero, one can see the ridge of chalk at the top of the slopes. That ridge extends just beyond the official boundaries of Ribera del Duero to Sardon del Duero, home to the producer Abadia

Vega Sicilia was Spain's first super-premium wine and continues to be one of the finest red wines of the nation. Winemaker Mercedes Aussas also makes Pintia, a wine from the Toro region.

Retuerta, whose location outside the Ribera boundaries allows it the freedom to incorporate international varieties such as Syrah. This "new" state-of-the-art winery, owned by the wealthy Swiss drug company Novartus, is housed in an abbey that has produced wines since the seventeenth century. A good deal of the wine from the original winery must have gone to the nearby capital of Spain back then, the city of Valladolid. Both in the past and present, a time-honored pairing with the Duero red wines is baby lamb cooked in a wood-fired oven. The richness of the lamb reduces the tannins of the wine and allows the wine's complex flavors to be revealed.

Other producers worth exploring include Condado de Haza, Dominio de Atauta, Protos, Valduero, Montecastro, Emilio Mauro, Mauro, Diaz Bayo, Felix Callejo, Matarromera, Dominio Romano, Pago de Carraovejas, Pagos del Infante, Parxet, Real Sitio de Ventosilla, Viñedos y Bodegas Gormaz, Viña Mayor Páramo de Corcos, and Valeriz-Tomas Esteban.

RUEDA DO
....

Famous since the seventeenth century for its white wines, Rueda is located at the southwestern tip of Valladolid along the Duero River. It has a Continental climate and most of its vineyards are planted at altitudes between 1,969 and 2,625 feet/600 and 800 meters on soils of sand and clay.

Most modern Rueda white wines are fermented in stainless steel to retain their fresh fruit flavors and are fermented dry to about 12 percent alcohol. Some are aged in oak. Martinsancho by Angel Rodriguez is a fine and unusual Rueda, as the unpressed Verdejo juice is fermented in a 5,283-gallon/20,000-liter glass tank.

The dominant grape in Rueda's new styles is the native Verdejo, which occupies over half of the vineyards. A little

The Rueda region is known for its crisp white wine dominated by the Verdejo grape.

over 20 percent of the land is devoted to Viura; the balance of white grapes includes Chardonnay and Sauvignon Blanc. A wine labeled Rueda Superior must contain a minimum of 75 percent Verdejo, yet pure Verdejo wines are available as well.

In general, the flavors of Rueda may include fresh flowers, lemon, citrus, and pear, with some mineral and creamy notes. The wines are bone dry and medium-bodied. Although the region has a hot climate during the short summer growing season, the wines are still able to develop a fair degree of acidity, which suggests pairing them with acidic dishes. A Greek salad with tomatoes and feta cheese or red snapper with a *grenobloise* sauce (capers and lemon) are some pairings that work with Rueda wines.

Other suggested wines include Marqués de Riscal, Villa Narcisa Verdejo by Javier Sanz, Aura by Domecq, Nosis by Buil & Giné, Trascampas Verdejo by Maria Jesus de la Hoz Monsalve, El Hada, and Naia by Aldial.

Traditional Rueda was a blend of Verdejo and Palomino grapes, 15 percent alcohol, **AMBER** in color, with a natural **FLOR** yeast. The wine is allowed to mature in a modified **SOLERA** and tastes like a coarse Sherry. This style is not exported. Sparkling wines made by the Champagne method are also made in the region, as are some Tempranillo, Garnacha, and Cabernet Sauvignon red wines.

TORO DO
....

A local proverb, "*Tomando vino de Toro, mas que comer devoro,*" translates to, "Drinking Toro wines is more devouring than eating."

Yes, Toro is indeed a big wine, with an opaque black plum color and aromas and flavors of black fruit. The local clone of Tempranillo is Tinta de Toro, and Garnacha may comprise up to a quarter of a blended wine. A higher percentage of Garnacha in the wine may result in a slightly lighter-color Toro, as the grape is known for its tendency to oxidize. But a positive result of using Garnacha is the red fruit notes that it can add to a blend.

Toro wines range from inexpensive to expensive and are best appreciated with food. Lamb is a traditional pairing, but try pairing the inexpensive versions with a cheeseburger and steak fries, or for vegetarians, thick slices of grilled eggplant, onion, and red pepper over buckwheat pasta or kasha. Wineries to look for include Farina, Alejandro Fernandez, Numanthia Termes, Maurodos, Pintia, Rejadorada, Telmo Rodriguez, Vina Bajoz, and Gil Luna.

CIGALES DO

This is an area best known for rosé wines based on Tempranillo and Garnacha, but it is shifting toward more red wine production.

Rosés such as the Fuente del Conde by González Lara have fresh strawberry flavors and are dry. A *crianza* rosé spends half a year in the barrel and one year in bottle before it is released. The inexpensive reds of the Cigales DO are light- to medium-bodied and are based on the Garnacha, Tinta, and Tinto del País (Tempanillo) grapes. Other suggested wineries include Frutos Villar, Telmo Rodriguez, and El Coto.

The Ebro River Valley

CAMPO DE BORJA DO

An arid area with soils containing limestone and iron-rich clay, Campo de Borja's vineyards are at 1,148 to 2,296 feet/350 to 700 meters altitude and planted mostly with the traditional Garnacha grape. Modern-style wines often include some Tempranillo or Cabernet Sauvignon in a blend.

An example of this style is Borsao, which is a blend of three-quarters Garnacha and one-quarter Tempranillo. This appealing medium-weight wine with black fruit flavors is produced by the local cooperative and is a best-value wine at under $10. The pure Garnacha Tres Picos by the same winery is well worth the extra few dollars. Another major winery to seek out is Bodegas Aragonesas. Try their inexpensive pure Garnacha Coto de Hayas.

CALATAYUD DO

As do many other arid growing regions, this one specializes in Garnacha, with Tempranillo as a partner. Clay-based soils with rocks and limestone are planted with vines at elevations of 1,804 to 2,624 feet/550 to 800 meters.

The Los Rocas de San Angelo, a Garnacha-based wine by the San Alejandro cooperative, is another wine that qualifies as a best value. Some fresh dry whites based on Viura are also available from this up-and-coming area.

Other wineries to try include Zabrin, Réal de Aragon, and Bodegas Ateca.

CARIÑENA DO

The area has a Continental climate with hot summers, but the vineyards are planted at elevations between 1,312 and 2,624 feet/400 and 800 meters, which keeps the acids in balance with the sugar in the grapes. The grape Cariñena used to dominate the vineyards of this area. Garnacha may be better suited to the arid conditions than Cariñena and may increase its presence, but most of the vineyards are still planted with Cariñena. However, as in other areas of the Ebro, Tempranillo and Cabernet Sauvignon are increasing in importance. The area was once known for its high-alcohol wines, but recent legislation has reduced the minimum alcohol level requirements and some wineries are now using temperature-control methods to produce lighter wines. There are also some traditionalists who continue to make *rancio*-style wines. Dry white wines are based on Viura, Garnacha Blanca, and Parellada.

SOMONTANO DO

The name is derived from the fact that the region is under the shadow of mountains—the Pyrenees Mountains, in this case. A different landscape and climatic condition exist here compared with the previous three DOs discussed. There is sufficient rainfall and moderating influences from rivers and streams to make this area more verdant than the Cariñena, Calatayud, or Campo de Borja. The climate is Continental with hot summers and cold winters, and the vineyards are planted at elevations of 1,804 to 2,624 feet/550 to 850 meters. Soils are limestone, with some clay and sand as well.

The Moristel grape is a more important native variety than the better-known Tempranillo. Moristel wines tend to be light- to medium-weight with flavors of red and black fruit such as cherries. The inexpensive Alquézar by Bodegas Pirineos is a great value wine. For Bordeaux and Cabernet fans, try the Enate or the Viñas del Vero *gran reserva* wines.

The native white Viura is known as Macabeo here, perhaps due to the proximity to France. The international cool-climate-loving Chardonnay and Gewürztraminer are also grown in Somontano.

NAVARRA DO

Navarra's calling card has been rosé wines for a long time. Although a good deal of Grenache-based rosé is still being made, the local entrepreneurs realize the added value red wines can bring. The Tempranillo grape does well in the cooler northern parts of the DO, while the Garnacha is more easily grown in the warmer subregions of Navarra. The international varieties Cabernet Sauvignon, Syrah, Merlot, and Chardonnay are an increasing presence in this region, which is experiencing a transition.

The lovely, crisp rosé wine Gran Feudo by Chivite is a good choice for "N'Awlins" foods such as jambalaya, seafood gumbo, and crawfish étoufée.

For Cabernet-Merlot fans, try the wines of Bodegas Inurrieta, Aroa, or Señorío de Sarría. Once again, the effects of the Continental climate are balanced by the vineyards' elevations, ranging from 1,148 to 2,460 feet/350 meters to 750 meters in the coolest Baja Montana subregion.

The three *DO de pago* wines of the region are the Prado de Irache from Bodegas Irache, Señorio de Arinzano from Bodegas Julián Chivite, and Bodega Otazu. All of these wines are blends of Tempranillo, Cabernet Sauvignon, and Merlot in varying percentages.

RIOJA DOC

There are 156,835 acres/63,496 hectares of vineyards in Rioja, which produce about 33 million bottles of wine a year. The name is sourced from the Oja River, which joins forces with the Tiron and flows into the Ebro River.

Rioja's climate is regulated by its position, halfway between the Atlantic Ocean and the Mediterranean. The Atlantic provides cool breezes in a generally temperate zone, lending a touch of acidity to the wines. The Mediterranean's breezes are warmer, providing strength and body to the wines. The three subregions of Rioja—Alavesa, Alta, and Baja—are planted at elevations from 1,312 to 2,624 feet/400 to 800 meters, with the Baja being the lowest and warmest of the three. There are a variety of different soils,

yet most are of iron-rich clay and alluvial with some sand, and there is more chalk and clay in the Rioja Alavesa. The region is surrounded by 121,000 acres/49,000 hectares of mountains that protect it from the elements.

Rioja is best known throughout the world for the quality of its red wines, made primarily from the Tempranillo and Garnacha, with some Graciano and Mazuelo to add complexity. Tempranillo comprises about 85 percent of a typical red Rioja blend. Wineries such as Marqués de Riscal (established 1860) and Marqués de Murrieta (established 1852) that imported Cabernet Sauvignon vine cuttings are grandfathered into the more recently written regulations on grape types and may include it in their wines. Other Rioja firms are experimenting with Cabernet Sauvignon, even though it is not one of the legally prescribed grapes of the region.

The Viura, Malvasía, and Garnacha Blanca are the approved white grapes in Rioja. Viura tends to dominate white blends and there are some full-bodied *reserva* examples with oak influence.

Gran reserva is the most revered category of Rioja wines, but tastes of consumers prove more favorable toward the *reserva* category, which sees less time in oak. Responses are much more mixed in reaction to a new style of Rioja known as *alta expresión* or *vinos de autor*. Detractors feel the wines lack a sense of origin, while supporters feel people should lighten up and enjoy the amplitude of these beefed-up versions of the area's wine style.

Roble, crianza, or *reserva* Rioja are wines to be appreciated for their charming red fruit and spice flavors, soft tannins, and medium weight.

In 1992, it was made mandatory that all Rioja wines be bottled, thereby prohibiting the sale of bulk wine under law. This was a giant leap forward in quality for Rioja, and it is consistent with its distinction as the first wine region granted DOC status by the Spanish government.

Conde de Valdemar, owned by the Martinez Bujanda family, is one of the most popular red Rioja wines sold in America. Whereas 86 percent of Rioja wineries own under 10 acres/24.7 hectares, the Martinez Bujandas own 740 acres/300 hectares, and all of their wines are estate bottled. Although the legal minimum for a gran reserva is sixty months of aging, their gran reserva spends thirty-six months in oak and forty-four in bottle before release. While some wineries in Rioja are shortening the time the wine spends in bottle, others go beyond the minimum period of aging. In the cellar, the harsh tannins of youth are softened and incorporated with fruit, acid, alcohol, and other flavors.

Some of the red wines of Rioja consumed in the region's restaurants, bars, and homes are quite different from the export versions, though the quality remains high. These wines are produced by what can best be described as a modified carbonic maceration technique (see page 66), but held in uncovered concrete vats. *Vino de cosechero* is fruity and fragrant, and it is meant to be drunk young.

In general, the character of most red Rioja wines can be described as a light cherry color, aromas of black cherry and spices, and with time, a bouquet of earth, leather, game, tobacco, and mushroom develops. The majority are medium- to full-bodied wines and are produced in numerous styles. *Gran reserva* wines aged a couple of decades or more often exhibit notes of aged fine balsamic vinegar, dried fig, walnut, date, leather, licorice, and mushroom in their bouquet. On the palate, they remain fresh, with flavors of baked apple, black fruits, nuts, spices, and fine aged balsamic vinegar.

It is well worth exploring the vibrant wines of this region to discover the many variations of flavor these wines can offer.

Some of the greatest vintages of Rioja are 1964, 1981, 1982, 1994, 1995, 2001, 2004, 2005, and 2007.

Some of the most important producers in the Rioja DOC include Marqués de Cáceres, Marqués de Riscal, Primicia, Altanza, Beronia, Ramón Bilbao, Bodegas Bréton Criadores, Vivanco, Covila, Kefrén, Riojanas, Faustino, Finca Allende, Finca Valpiedra, Ijalba, Bodegas Lan, Montecillo, Marqués de Arienzo, Artadi, Marqués de Griñón, Marqués de Vargas, Valserrano–De la Marquesa, Labastida, Ramirez de la Piscina, La Rioja Alta, Campo Viejo, Muga, Marqués de Murrieta, Telmo Rodríguez, El Coto, Remelluri, Contino, Sierra Cantabria, CVNE, Benjamin Romeo, Paganos, Valenciso, Palacios Remondo, Viña Izadi, Viña Valoria, and Conde de Valdemar–Martínez Bujanda.

Mediterranean Coast, including Catalonia

The climate along the coast of the Mediterranean is a warm one. Further inland however, the vineyards experience a dramatic shift to cooler climates at higher altitudes.

The subregions are known as the Baja, which is the warmest of the three, the Medio, and Superior. The vineyards of the latter two are found at altitudes up to 2,624 feet/800 meters.

Soil types are also varied. Within the Penedès DO, for example, the soil of eastern vineyards is composed of a mix of sand, clay, and chalk, while limestone dominates in the higher-altitude vineyards inland. Below the Pyrenees are the Sierra de Montsec, Sierra de Cadi, Sierra de Port del Comte, and Sierra de Cani, which form the Catalunya Range.

The unification of Spanish states began when Isabel of Castilla was betrothed to Fernando of Aragon in 1464. The Catalans, with their unique language and culture, began their battle for independence at that time. Today, as an autonomous state within Spain, the local people identify themselves as Catalans first and Spanish second.

Catalonia's financial strength benefits from the wine industry: 17,721 growers supply 547 wineries to produce about 92.5 million gallons/3.5 million hectoliters of wine. A little over half of that is the Champagne method sparkling wine known as Cava. Wine lovers can find inexpensive to expensive sparkling, still, and fortified wines within Catalonia. Cavas are labeled by their level of sweetness (*brut*), while still wines may be labeled by grape name, place name, or a fantasy or proprietary name.

Further south along the coast of the Levante are the up-and-coming DO areas of Yecla and Jumilla, where the warmer climate favors the production of red wines.

CATALUNYA DO

White grapes cover over three-quarters of the region. There are simply not enough red grapes to meet increased demand (although many wine regions would love to have this problem). Rather than importing grapes from other parts of Spain, some of the major wineries of the region came up with the idea of developing a regional DO, which could be a blend from different smaller DOs within it. Another benefit of this broad DO is that the rules of accepted grapes and styles are more lax than within one of the specific DOs. A couple of producers who are presently using this particular DO include Mas Gil and Catalan de Vins Artesans. Only time will tell how important this generalized DO will be.

CAVA DO

Cava has been an incredible success. While it is enjoyed in its producing region, over half of all Cava is exported.

The majority of Cava is based on the native white grapes Parellada, Xarel-lo, Macabeo, and Subirat (Malvasia), yet some Chardonnay is also used. The native red varieties are Garnacha, Trepat, and Monastrell, with some Pinot Noir as well.

An incredible 95 percent of all Cava is produced in the region Catalunya, most of which comes from Penedès. However, some is also produced in areas as far away as Navarra and Rioja. The wines are labeled according to their level of sweetness. From the driest to sweetest, the terms are *extra brut, brut, extra seco, seco, semiseco, semidulce,* and *dulce.*

The two largest Champagne method–producing companies are Codorníu and Freixenet. Their wines are dependable and range from good values to more substantial wines. There are also smaller wineries with most sophisticated, aged wines worth seeking out. Presently, there are about 168 million bottles produced each year, but the amount varies according to vintage conditions.

Other good Cava producers include Juvé Camps, Cristalino, Huguet de Can Feixes, Gramona, Llopart, Ferret i Mateu, Parés Baltà, Roger Goulart, Mont Ferrant, Raventós i Blanc, Albet I Noya, Mont Marcal, Montsarra, Naveran, Parxet, Giró Ribot, Segura Viudas, Paul Cheneau, Castell Roig, Agusti Torello, Castellblanch, Sarda, Cavas Masachs, Masia Vallformosa, and Marqués de Monistrol.

PENEDÈS

The Cava industry in Penedès dates back to the nineteenth century, yet the region's reputation and success with its still wines is a far more recent phenomenon. There are over a hundred wineries producing fine still wines today, but just a couple of decades ago, there were only twenty.

In 1970, the leaders of the revolution to produce quality table wines were members of the Torres family. Miguel Agustín Torres learned his craft studying in Montpellier, Madrid, and Dijon. His exemplary work began in upgrading methods in the vineyards by introducing nontraditional trellising and spacing. He expanded his influence by establishing French grape varieties to plant alongside native grapes.

The use of controlled fermentation in stainless steel vats and treatment of the wines during aging resulted in fine world-class wines. The marketing genius of describing the wine in detail on the back label of Torres wines is something winemakers around the world should adopt. Rather than some vague statement about the wine, Torres wine labels go into detail on the nature of the wine and some possible food choices. The entry-level Sangre de Toro red and Viña Sol white wines make for enjoyable picnics. While these wines are fundamentally simple, they are nonetheless a part of a portfolio that also includes some very complex wines. The premier Torres wine is the Mas de Plana Cabernet Sauvignon, once called Gran Coronas black label. Its success in blind tastings against the finest red wines of the world has been a great source of pride not only for the Torres family, but to all the producers of Penedès. The legacy of the Torres family has spread to the New World as they have established vineyards in Chile, all producing very fine wines. Miguel's sister, Marimar, produces delicious Chardonnay and Pinot Noir in the Green Valley of California's Sonoma County. Torres was undoubtedly an influential pioneer in the world of winemaking. Yet we must not forget to tip our hats to Jean Léon, who in 1963 was the first to label international varieties such as Chardonnay and Cabernet Sauvignon from this region.

Though acknowledging the accomplishments of these two modern-era wineries, one must also give credit to two historic producers who have consistently made fine wines. The first, Can Feixes-Huguet, was established in 1768. Can Feixes Seleccio white is a great value blend of Parellada, Macabeo, and Chardonnay,

The Can Feixes and Parés Baltà wineries, founded in the eighteenth century, make some of Spain's best wines. This Can Feixes is a crisp white that can be enjoyed young, while the Absis by Parés Baltà is an ageworthy, complex red wine.

with just a bit of Malvasia. The Reserva Especial red is a complex, full-bodied blend of Cabernet Sauvignon and Merlot.

Twenty-two years later, in 1790, Parés Baltà was established, creator of the Dominio Cusiné wines, named for the founder's family. For an elegant expression of Xarello, try the Parés Baltà Calcari or Electio. The proprietary-labeled Absis is a blend of Tempranillo, Cabernet Sauvignon, Syrah, and Merlot. They also produce estate-grown Garnatxa (Garnacha), and Marta de Baltà Syrah.

The fine red wines of Penedès such as those from Can Feixes and Parés Baltà will show best after at least a few years of cellar time and can age for a couple of decades. With the wealth of blends and use of both indigenous and international grape varieties, it is hard to generalize about the flavor of Penedès DO wines. The finest will repay cellaring with bouquets that speak of fine balsamic vinegar, mushrooms, and earth, while the inexpensive wines will have fresh red and black fruit character.

White wine grapes include the native Parellada, Macabeo, Xarel-lo, and the international varieties Chardonnay, Sauvignon Blanc, Gewürztraminer, Chenin Blanc, Riesling, Moscatel, and Malvasia.

Other Penedès producers to try are Rene Barbier, Jaume Serra, Gramona, Albert y Noya, Sumarroca, Caves Ferret, Caves Naveran, Cellars Puig i Roca, Jané Ventura, Juvé Camps, Masia Bach, Masia Vallformosa, Marqués de Monistrol, Mont Marçal, and Can Rafolsdel Caus.

PRIORATO DOC (PRIORAT IN CATALAN)

Priorato is one of Spain's two DOC (also known as DOCa) regions. Its esteemed status is based on the very high quality of all its wines. In a region as large as the other DOC, Rioja, there are some "clunkers," fine wines, and extraordinary wines. A couple of unique label terms are used here: *Clos* is a French term for a walled vineyard, and *finca* is a Spanish term for a farm or estate.

Here there are only about 1,700 acres/688 hectares of vineyards farmed by about 620 growers. The climate is mild, and the most discerning feature of the region is its steep-sloped and terraced vineyards of slate, with some volcanic granite. The slate, referred to locally as *licorella*, imparts a mineral nose and flavor to the wines. Another distinguishing feature of Priorato wines is the Garnacha Peluda ("Hairy Garnacha"), which gives much more color and depth of flavor than other clones of the variety. The Garnacha Peluda, Garnacha Tinta, and Cariñena vines used are often very old, fifty to seventy years of age. These older vines, planted in well-drained soils, have roots that go deep into the substrata to seek nourishment. More re-

LEFT: *A dramatic example of slate soil in the vineyards of Priorato* RIGHT: *Priorato is one of Spain's two DOC regions. Old vineyards of Garnacha and Cariñena share the spotlight with newer plantings of international varieties, such as Syrah and Cabernet Sauvignon.*

cent plantings are of the international varieties Cabernet Sauvignon, Merlot, Pinot Noir, and Syrah. The Portuguese Touriga Nacional is also found here. Over 90 percent of production is red wine. Native white grapes in this region include the Macabeo, Garnacha Blanca, Parellada, and Pedro Ximénez; Viognier and Chenin Blanc are among the international white grapes grown.

The pioneers who rediscovered this region and brought the wines to international acclaim are René Barbier with the Clos Mogador winery; Alvaro Palacios (L'Ermita and Finca Dofi wines); Dafne Glorian, Carlos Pastrana, José Luis Pérez of Mas Martinet winery; and the owners of Scala Dei winery. The Scala dei Negre and Cartoixa Reserva wines are pure expressions of Garnacha.

For those who have long been ardent fans of Garnacha, or Grenache elsewhere in the world, there is cause for celebration with the success of these wines. With complex bouquets of minerals, spices, wildflowers, and red and black fruits, they are very generous on the palate without being harshly tannic.

The estate bottled wines by Alvaro Palacios include the L'Ermita (Garnacha, Cariñena, and Cabernet Sauvignon) and Finca Dofi (Cabernet Sauvignon, Syrah, Merlot, Garnacha Tinta, and Cariñena). He also purchases grapes to make Les Terraces, which is primarily Garnacha. René Barbier's signature wine is Clos Mogador, a blend of Garnacha, Cabernet Sauvignon, and Syrah. Carlos Pastrana's Costers del Siurana winery produces Clos de L'Obac, a blend of Garnacha, Cabernet Sauvignon, Merlot, Syrah, and Cariñena. Miserere is a similar blend but replaces the Syrah component with Tempranillo. Another superb wine is the Mas Reserva blend of Garnacha and Cariñena by Mas Igneus.

Pasanau German's line of wines include the Finca la Planeta wine, based on 80 percent Cabernet Sauvignon and 20 percent Garnacha. Another great value of his is Cep Nous, which is 40 percent Garnacha, the balance sourced from Merlot, Mazuelo, and Syrah grapes.

Mas Martinet makes the very fine Clos Martinet from Garnacha, Cabernet Sauvignon, Merlot, and Syrah grapes.

Buil & Giné make a relatively inexpensive Giné Giné, a moderately priced Joan Giné, and Pleret, based mostly on old-vine Garnacha and Cariñena.

Laurent Combier, Peter Fischer, and Jean Michel Gérin are three great winemakers from southern France who created the Trio Infernal winery in Priorato. Their Trio Infernal No. 2/3 is pure Cariñena from ancient vines, while their No. 1/3 is 60 percent old-vine Garnacha and the balance Cariñena.

Gratavinum's delicious 2πR is dominated by Garnacha while their elegant GV5 features Cariñena, with support from Garnacha, Cabernet Sauvignon, and Merlot.

Vall Llach winery uses a similar formula for their exquisite Embruix and Idus wines, while the estate version is made from Cariñena, Merlot, and Cabernet Sauvignon.

MONTSANT DO

The Monsant DO is a subregion of the Tarragona DO and was created in 2001. Prior to that, the zone used to be known as the "Baix" or lower Priorato and was also part of the Falset subregion of Tarragona.

The region receives some humidity from Mediterranean winds, but mountains provide both shelter and elevation resulting in a Continental climate. Warm days and cool nights promote easy ripening of the grapes and good acid balance. The region is composed of a variety of soil types including the same slate soils as Priorato, as well as some granitic soils in Falset.

The most important black grapes are the Garnacha Peluda, Garnacha Tinta, Cariñena, and Monastrell. Other grapes permitted include the Tempranillo, Mazuela, Picapoll, Merlot, Syrah, and Cabernet Sauvignon. Wines with a similar character and a lower price tag are available from this area. They may not be quite as concentrated as the wines of Priorato, but they are approachable at a younger age and seem to coexist rather than compete with a wide range of foods. About 75 percent of the region's production is exported.

Fra Guerau is a great value in a blended red wine. Another affordable and delicious wine is the Celler Acustic Vinhas Velhas Nobles ("noble old vines"), a blend of Samso (Cariñena) and Garnatxa (Garnacha).

Also recommended is the Celler de Capçanes Cabrida, which is pure Garnacha, or the winery's Flor de Primavera Peraj Ha'Abib (dry, kosher), which is a blend of Garnacha, Cabernet Sauvignon, Tempranillo, and Cariñena. Cap de Capçanes, a village cooperative, makes a range of fine wines. White grapes include the native Garnacha Blanca, Macabeo, Pansal, Parellada, Moscatel, and Chardonnay. The Garnacha Blanca is used to make full-bodied dry white wines, as well as sweet wines.

VINO DE LA TIERRA DE CASTILLA: THE WORLD'S LARGEST VINEYARD AREA

The Vino de la Tierra de Castilla was created in 1999. The European Union and Spanish federal government gave financial incentives to growers and wineries to improve the vineyards by using trellising systems and drip irrigation in the most parched sites and to replant with better grape varieties. A lot of Airén has been and will continue to be replaced with grape varieties such as Cencibel (Tempranillo), Chardonnay, and Cabernet Sauvignon. A whopping 3.498 million gallons/13.25 million hectoliters of wine from 865,404 acres/350,366 hectares are produced as Vino de la Tierra de Castilla. A comparison of yields from the Vino de la Tierra versus the DO wines within it is about 2.9 tons per acre/37.87 hectoliters per hectare versus 2 tons per acre /26.66 hectoliters per hectare.

Including the seven DO areas of La Mancha, Manchuela, Méntrida, Mondéjar, Almansa, Ribera del Júcar, Valdepeñas, and part of Jumilla that can also be called Vino de la Tierra, the total area increases from the 865,404 acres/350,366 hectares of non-DO vineyards to a total of 1,482,000 acres/600,000 hectares. These numbers not only represent 50 percent of Spain's vineyard area but are equal to 6 percent of the entire world's vineyard land.

In an area this large, there are a variety of soils, most are part clay, sand, and chalk. The altitude of the vineyards is 1,968 to 2,624 feet/600 to 900 meters.

For now, we mostly look to these wines for value. There are some wineries within the DOs of the Meseta that can declassify their wines to the Vino de la Tierra designation in order to make wines outside the DO guidelines.

Some best-value Vino de la Tierra de Castilla include the Shiraz-Tempranillo #1 by Beberana, Protocolo and Codice by Dominio de Eguren (both pure Tempranillo, the latter aged six months in oak), Garnacha by Tapen, and Solaz Tempranillo-Cabernet Sauvignon by Osborne.

of Tempranillo leads the way in that category. A word of caution: Tempranillo's clones and styles are a mixed bag. The Cencibel does not produce wines with the color and depth of flavor of the Tinto Fino or Tinto del País, the Tempranillo clone most often used in Ribera del Duero.

Other white grapes of the Meseta include the Chardonnay, Sauvignon Blanc, Macabeo, and Pardilla. For red grapes, there are increasing plantings of the international varieties Cabernet Sauvignon, Merlot, and Syrah. The native Garnacha, well suited to arid conditions, is at home in this area, where the native varieties Bobal, Monastrell, and Moravia are also grown.

A great deal of inexpensive wine is consumed within Spain, but its export market continues to grow.

Bargain shoppers can find decent wines here, but for those seeking something more complex, the first four approved DO de pago areas are all found within the Meseta. Dominio de Valdepusa, owned by Marqués de Grinon, is planted with Cabernet Sauvignon, Petit Verdot, and Syrah. The vineyards of Finca Élez, owned by Manuel Manaeque, are planted with Chardonnay, Cabernet Sauvignon,

Tempranillo, and Syrah. Deheza de Carrizal make wines from Chardonnay, Cabernet Sauvignon, Tempranillo, Merlot, and Syrah. El Guijoso, owned by Sánchez Muliterno, offers pure Chardonnay wines.

The DOs of La Meseta include Vinos de Madrid, Valdepeñas, Ucles, Ribera del Júcar, Méntrida, Almansa, Ribera del Guadiana, Manchuela, Mondéjar, a portion of Jumilla, and the enormous La Mancha.

LA MANCHA DO

This is Spain's largest DO, with 472,078 acres/191,125 hectares of vineyards that produce about 85 million bottles of wine a year. Over 21,000 farmers supply almost 300 bodegas with fruit. The soils are similar to the Vino de la Tierra de Castilla, and the Continental climate means hot summers and cold winters. Elevation of the vineyards ranges from 1,970 to 2,625 feet/600 to 800 meters.

Airén is by far the most important white grape, followed by the Macadeo, Chardonnay, Sauvignon Blanc, and native Pardilla. White wines are mostly dry, clean, and simple. An aggressive campaign to decrease the white grape vineyards and plant red grapes in the past years has resulted in the current mix of about one-third white grapes and two-thirds red. The Cencibel clone of Tempranillo rules the red grape roost and is followed by Cabernet Sauvignon, Merlot, Syrah, and the native grapes Garnacha and Moravia.

The fresh red fruit flavors of Cencibel (Tempranillo) are evident in the light- to medium-weight *joven* wines. They account for over two-thirds of production.

The balance of wines are aged in wood, with *crianza* being the largest category, followed closely by *reserva* wines. Less than 2 percent of La Mancha DO are *gran reserva* wines. Campos Reales is one of the top local wineries, and its entire line of wines is good. The inexpensive Tempranillo-based *crianza* by Condesa de Leganza has attractive red and black fruit character. Often, the most important piece of information on a label is the name of the people who make the wine. Two producers who deserve respect are Alejandro Fernandez and Martinez Bujanda. From the former, try the pure Tempranillo *crianza* El Vinicola, and from the latter, try the *crianza* Finca Antigua: It is a blend of Tempranillo, Cabernet Sauvignon, Merlot, Syrah, and Petit Verdot. Another affordable La Mancha wine is Volver.

EXTREMADURA

The Extremadura region lies to the west of the Meseta by the Portuguese border and includes the DO Ribera del Guadiana. That DO of 9,311 acres/23,000 hectares of vineyards is spread over the 56,810 acres/87,000 hectares of the Extremadura. Over half of the vineyard acreage is devoted to the Tempranillo grape, and a good deal of Garnacha is planted as well. Both native and international white and red grapes combine to produce over 1,849,204 gallons/7 million liters of dry white, rosé, and red wines annually. Three-quarters of the wines are exported.

Andalucía

This is one of those wine regions that must be experienced firsthand to best appreciate its wines. To smell the sea, listen to the flamenco music, see the flamenco dancers and the amazing architecture, and taste the local foods with local wines is a true revelation of the senses. Africa is very close by, and its influence permeates the Andalusian culture.

The hot temperature of southern Spain is best suited to fortified wines. There are five fortified DO wines. Jerez (or Xérès or Sherry) and its subregion Manzanilla de Sanlúcar de Barrameda are the most important and will be covered in depth in this section. Throughout this section, the term *Jerez* will refer to the region and *Sherry* will refer to the wine. A brief overview of Málaga, Montilla–Moriles, and Condado de Huelva will also be provided. There are some still wines also produced in Andalucía under the DO Sierras de Málaga, but so far none have been great.

JEREZ DO AND ITS SUBREGION MANZANILLA DE SANLÚCAR DE BARRAMEDA DO

Referred to by the Spanish as Jerez, and **SACK** or Sherry by the British, the term will be Sherry for the rest of this section. The English word is derived from *sacar,* which means "to take out." Sherry exports paid to England were not taxed, and it became a popular alternative to claret, the red wine from Bordeaux. By the latter half of the sixteenth century, England and the Netherlands imported two-thirds of the annual production of Sherry. Many of the vineyards and wineries were destroyed during the Peninsular wars at the beginning of the nineteenth century, and after a period of growth, phylloxera wiped out many of the vineyards. In 1933, the local *consejo regulador* was formed, and Jerez became a DO in 1935. Today, there is increased interest in Sherry wines in America. Sherries can be superb wines on their own or with food.

The finest Sherry soils are known as albariza.

The wines of Jerez are exciting. There is a need to dispel some myths about Sherry being too "old-fashioned" or "too complicated" to figure out. True, the first sip of a dry **FINO** or **MANZANILLA** may not be every person's cup of tea. Once partnered with the proper food, however, Sherry can be quite addictive.

The region is located at the southwestern tip of Europe. Beneficial breezes from the Atlantic Ocean moderate the heat in the vineyards of this hot growing region and provide humidity. The *levante* wind from the southeast is hot and dry, while the *poniente* wind from the west is cooler and more humid. The moisture from humidity as well as rainfall is retained by the *albariza* soil, which is a composite of chalk, silica, and clay. It is the dominant soil of the Jerez Superior. The soil is also excellent in reflecting sunshine to the grapes. The *zona*, a less-prized soil type, has less chalk and more sand and clay. The landscape of rolling hills results in a drainage system from the higher to lower levels of the vineyards.

More than 90 percent of the vineyard area in Jerez is devoted to the Palomino Fino grape. The other white varieties include Moscatel and Pedro Ximénez, which are used to make varietal sweet wines or added to blended dry wines to increase their sugar content.

In the process of making most Sherry, the grapes are crushed and then the pH of the must is lowered from 3.7 to 4 by the addition of tartaric acid and sometimes gypsum to a range of 3.1 to 3.4. After clarification, *pie de cuba*, fermenting musts with selected yeast strains, are added to the must or grape juice to start fermentation. The native yeast strains chosen are an important component of the character of Sherry. Traditionally the wines were fermented in *botas*—132-gallon/500-liter oak barrels ("butts")—but today, temperature-controlled stainless steel vats are used. The yeast consumes the sugars in the must of the Palomino grape to produce a dry wine that is about 11 to 12 percent alcohol until it is fortified with clear brandy, elevating that percentage. The wine is then transferred to Sherry **BUTTS**.

The wines are analyzed and separated into two categories. The lighter-weight *fino* and *manzanilla* wines are destined for biological (oxidative) aging in a *solera* system (see below), while the fuller-bodied *oloroso* wines undergo physiochemical aging. The former are fortified with clear brandy to 15.5 percent alcohol, and the *olorosos* to 17 or 18 percent. After fortification, the wines are clarified and transferred to wooden casks. At this point, the young wines

that will become *fino* or *manzanilla* are referred to as *añada* and the future *oloroso* wines are called *sobretabla*.

The famous velo de flor (meaning " veil of flower") yeast will form if the wine is kept under 15.5 percent alcohol. The *flor* is maintained by feeding it fresh wine and yeast nutrients over time. The dominant strain of *flor* yeast is the *Saccharomyces beticus*, and the other strains include *Saccharomyces montuliensis*, *Saccharomyces cheresientis*, and *Saccharomyses rouxi*.

Within the regions of Jerez, there are slight differences in humidity and temperature—two factors that can increase or decrease the presence of *flor*. The result is the pale color of dry *fino* and *manzanilla* wines that are protected from oxidation by the layer of *flor* yeast that forms on top of the wine. The yeast consumes alcohol, sugar, and glycerin, which results in bone-dry wines.

Oloroso wines have an alcohol level of about 17 to 18 percent. They have a darker color, as they are not protected from oxidation by the *flor*.

Amphorae used to be the vessels for the *crianza*, or aging, of Sherry wines. Today, older American oak casks of 158 gallons/600 liters are preferred. *Fino* and *manzanilla* wines are affected by the biological influences of the *flor*. The *oloroso* wines develop their character by *envejecimiento* (concentration)—affected by the location where they are matured.

Barrels in a *bodega* with more humidity will lose less to evaporation than those in a drier environment. The range of loss annually is 3 to 4 percent of the wine, which serves to concentrate the flavors in the wine. From one-sixth to

The flor *yeast protects the wine from oxidation. It forms a protective layer over* fino *and* manzanilla *wines, which explains their pale straw color.*

one-eighth of the barrel is left empty to ensure that there is enough room for the *flor* to develop and be maintained. The earthen floors of the *bodegas* are often sprayed with water to maintain sufficient humidity in the cellars.

Another criterion for the presence of *flor* is a temperature range from 64.4° to 68°F/18° to 20°C in the *bodega*.

AMONTILLADO refers to a style of wine that has evolved from a pale-colored *fino* to an amber-colored wine because the *flor* yeast dies off and can no longer protect the wine. The *flor* feeds on fresh wine to survive. If the winemaker decides a wine has the potential to be a fine *amontillado*, they either stop adding fresh wine to the barrel or fortify the wine from 15.5 to 17 percent alcohol. Many of the most noble wines of Jerez are aged *amontillado* wines. Their rivals are the aged *oloroso* wines. We will continue our discussion of Jerez styles further in this section.

Next in the process of making Sherry is the *solera* system, named for the *suelo*, or row of barrels closest to the floor. The most important thing to understand about the system is that it is a fractional blending system that is intended to marry the freshness of youthful wines with the more complex personality of older wines.

A *bodega* may have three to four rows of Sherry butts stored on top of each other in a stack of barrels. There may be numerous stacks located in a particular *solera*. In these stacks, there could be up to fifteen rows of barrels, which will travel from the youngest row to the oldest row in the *solera*. Each time a *bodega* wishes to remove some wine for sale, from a *fino solera*, for example, they must notify the local *consejo regulador* to witness the operation. It is common to go through this process three or four times a year for *fino* wines. Each time it is done, they can only remove up to 30 percent of the wine from the oldest barrel and bottle it. That drained wine is replaced with wine from the barrel directly on top of it. This process is repeated through all of the rows of barrels in the *solera*. The last and youngest barrel in the *solera* is used to bring refreshing wine to the barrel beneath it. The younger barrel will then receive the new wine of the recent harvest. During each stage of transferring wine, it is always from the younger **CRIADERA**, or "nursery," to the older one below it. This labor-intensive system began at the end of the eighteenth century. It is wild to consider that some of the Sherry in the glass may be over a hundred or two hundred years old. The *solera* system gives each of the *bodegas* a consistent style.

It is interesting to visit the *bodegas* and see the thousands of barrels marked with chalk to identify them. Even

when outdoor temperatures are hot, the *bodegas* are cool inside. The thick-walled *bodegas* of Jerez and window shades of sparta grass keep the heat out in the daytime. In the evenings, those shades are pulled up and the doors of the *bodegas* are opened to welcome the cooling nighttime breezes. Some *bodegas* trap rainfall from the roofs in descending columns that drain at the bottom. The water provides humidity to the barrels stored within.

The *bodega* will train some employees to use a *venencia* (a silver cup attached to a long handle) to draw wine from a cask for sampling. It is an honor and a pleasure to taste the aged wines directly from the cask.

TOP: *The fractional* solera *system ensures consistency in the flavors of Sherries by blending young wines with older wines.* BOTTOM: *The* venencia, *a silver cup on the end of a long, flexible whalebone or bamboo handle, is used to draw small amounts of Sherry from a cask to sample the wine.*

STYLES OF SHERRY

Sherries have an alcohol level of between 15 and 22 percent and fall under the umbrella of the European Union's VLCPRD (quality liquor wines produced in specific region) category. The three subdivisions are:

VINO GENEROSO for the dry wines. *Fino, manzanilla, amontillado,* and dry *oloroso* fall under this category.

VINO DULCE for sweet wines made from sundried grapes. Pedro Ximénez and Moscatel are in this category.

VINO GENEROSO DE LICOR for sweet wines made by adding concentrated must or sweet wine to a dry wine. Medium cream Sherries are in this category.

FINO

Fino is by far the most popular type of Sherry. The Palomino Fino grapes are sourced from anywhere in the region. The city of Puerto de Santa Maria is a picturesque old port town. The wines are pale in color and bone dry, with an aroma of almonds and a good balance of acidity. Other flavors often found in these wines include apple, banana, and baked goods. To keep the *flor* alive, fresh wine is routinely added to *finos.* Serve 2 to 2.5 ounces/60 to 75 milliliters cold in a small wineglass or the local glass known as a **COPITA**.

MANZANILLA

Manzanilla is basically a *fino* Sherry that comes from the Sanlúcar de Barrameda subregion. The area is cooler and more humid than the other subregions of Sherry. Many tasters feel that this region's wines have the most briny flavors because the *bodegas* are situated close to the ocean and the vineyards close to salt marshes. These wines, as well as other *finos,* offer a whiff of sea air. *Manzanilla* and *fino* are most-

ly sourced from grapes grown on *albariza* soils. *Manzanilla* Pasada is a wine with extended aging, which provides a gold color and a complex bouquet. *Manzanillas* Pasadas are not refreshed with wine as often as *finos* and are bottled younger than an *amontillado.* Pastrana by Hidalgo and Jurado by Lustau are excellent examples of *manzanilla* Pasada.

Fino and *manzanilla* wines have have less than 0.03 ounces/1 gram of sugar per liter. Their briny quality makes both *fino* and *manzanilla* wines the ideal complement to salty foods such as olives, anchovies, *jamon,* and aged Manchego cheese. The nutty notes of almonds and sometimes cashews in these wines makes for an easy pairing with those nuts as well as dishes that incorporate nuts in the preparation. Kung Pao chicken, trout amandine, or a Middle Eastern rice with pine nuts are just a few other examples. Tapas such as codfish-stuffed *piquillo* peppers, chickpeas and spinach with coriander, and squid and potato salad are also excellent with these wines.

Wine antagonists such as eggs, vinegar, or certain green vegetables are often tamed by a *fino* or *manzanilla.* For many problematic pairings, underappreciated Sherry can often rescue the situation. (For further discussion of wine-and-food pairing, see page 556.) Tio Pepe, by González-Byass, is the leader in the *fino* style, and a kosher version is available. La Gitana, by Hidalgo, is a top *manzanilla.*

AMONTILLADO

These wines have an amber color and are more full-bodied than *fino* or *manzanilla* wines. Aromas and flavors include hazelnut, Brazil nut, cinnamon, clove, nutmeg, orange peel, quince paste, papaya, cocoa powder, caramel, and miso. Try experimenting with these wines. Some successful *amontillado* pairings include mushroom soup, grilled tuna with snails, Chinese eggplant with garlic sauce, and

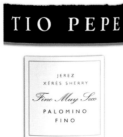

A variety of Sherry labels

fried tempeh in a salad with sesame-based dressing. These wines may be served slightly chilled in the summer and at room temperature during the winter.

OLOROSO

A mahogany color and medium to full body are typical of *oloroso* wines, which are mostly sourced from the *zona* soils. *Olorosos* offer a range of styles from dry to sweet and from simple young wines to very complex matured wines. Finer *oloroso* wines are usually served at room temperature, while lesser qualities may be served slightly chilled. Some of the aromas and flavors of the dry wines include ginger, clove, orange, mocha, and salted pecans. Sweet wines offer dried fruit, molasses, coffee, mushrooms, beef consommé, pecans, tamarind, and Christmas fruitcake flavors.

Emilio Lustau makes fine *amontillado* wines, as well as an "East India" style that is a blend of Palomino and Pedro Ximénez that has been aged for a dozen years. East India is a complex wine with flavors of dried and fresh fruits, nuts, and chocolate. It is a dessert unto itself or a suitable partner to many desserts. Greek baklava, Hungarian *palacsinta* pancakes drizzled with dark chocolate, and American Fig Newton cookies are just a few excellent pairings.

PALO CORTADO

This is a quirky type of Sherry that is sometimes referred to as having the nose of an *amontillado* and the color of an *oloroso*. Another way to describe these rare wines, which are under 2 percent of total Sherry production, is that they have the delicacy of an *amontillado* paired with the generosity of an *oloroso*. **PALO CORTADO**, *amontillado*, and *oloroso* wines all have less than 0.17 ounces/5 grams of residual sugar per liter.

PEDRO XIMÉNEZ AND MOSCATEL

The grapes for these single-variety wines are usually dried on outdoor mats to draw out moisture and increase their sweetness. The high humidity of Jerez can ruin the grapes, so a special allowance was made authorizing the importation of Pedro Ximénez grapes from the nearby Montilla-Moriles DO, where the climate is much drier.

Aside from the production of varietal-labeled wines, Pedro Ximénez and Moscatel are also used to make another category, cream Sherries.

The pH of these moderately acidic Sherries is 4 to 5 compared with dry Sherries such as *fino, manzanilla, amontillado, palo cortado,* and dry *oloroso,* all of which have higher acidity of 3 to 3.5 pH.

Moscatels have 7 ounces/200 grams to 10.5 ounces/300 grams of sugar per liter, while Pedro Ximémez wines have 14 ounces/400 grams to 17.5 ounces/500 grams of sugar per liter.

"Noé" Pedro Ximénez by González-Byass is one of the world's great dessert wines. Enjoy it at room temperature in the winter and with a light chill in summer.

CREAM SHERRIES

These inexpensive sweet wines may be blended with soda or drunk on their own and are labeled dry, pale, medium, rich, or simply cream. They are made by various techniques that add sweetness to a base wine.

AGED SHERRY

There are twelve- and fifteen-year-old Sherries available that are quite good. Dry Sack 15 Years by Williams & Humbert is a very good example. However, the finest Sherries are the *vinum optimum signatum (VOS)*, also known as Very Old Sherry, which is aged a minimum average of twenty years before it is sold, and the *vinum optimum rare signatum (VORS)*, or Very Old Reserve Sherry, which must be aged a minimum average of thirty years before release. These VOS and VORS wines are generous and remarkably complex wines that every wine lover should experience.

The **PALO CORTADO** VORS, wine Sibarita by Pedro Domecq (98 percent Palomino, 2 percent Pedro Ximénez),

Cocinella, *roast suckling young pig, served in Segovia in northern Spain*

Apôstoles Palo Cortado by Gonzalez-Byass (80 percent Palomino, 20 percent Pedro Ximénez), and Jalifa VORS Amontillado by Williams & Humbert (100 percent Palomino) are three of the greatest wines of the region.

RECOMMENDED SHERRY BODEGAS

The Sherry trade has over a hundred *bodegas*, or wineries. Some are used just for fermentation and do not age wine on-premise. The major wineries do everything from fermentation to the aging of wines, which sometimes requires decades.

The term **ALMACENISTA** refers to a wine from a grower-winemaker that is sold by another winery. A farmer may sell must or wine to an individual who can age the wine but is not licensed by the *consejo regulador* control board to bottle the wine. Emilio Lustau is one of the top wineries of the region, and one of their specializations is the *almacenista* wines. They may purchase just a barrel or two of fine wine and consider it a great discovery and addition to their portfolio of wines. Some *bodegas* are now releasing single-vintage wines that do not go through the *solera* system. An example is the 1989 Oloroso by Emilio Lustau. This semisweet wine was aged fourteen years in cask before bottling in 2003. Expect to see more *bodegas* release limited amounts of vintage Sherry.

Sherry producers worth recommending include Hidalgo (Manzanilla), Delgado Zuleta (Manzanilla), Antonio Barbadillo (Manzanilla), Hijos de Rainera Perez Marín (Manzanilla), Emilio Lustau, Gónzalez-Byass, Williams & Humbert, Sanchez Romate, Pedro Domecq, Dios Baco, Sandeman, Osborne, and Marqués de Real Tesoro.

MONTILLA–MORILES DO

The best vineyards of the region are found in the Moriles Alto, or higher section of the region. *Albariza* chalky soils dominate there. In the lower-lying Sierra de Montilla, there are more sandy soils with some limestone.

These fortified wines are made in a manner similar to Sherry with the use of a *solera* system. The Pedro Ximénez is the main grape type and is not only used for these wines but also sent to nearby Jerez for Sherry. Because this region is drier than Málaga or Jerez, the Andalusian authorities allow the export of grapes to the other DOs where moisture can ruin the grapes while they are set to dry outdoors.

The Pedro Ximénez is harvested earlier, and the level of fortification is lower than in Jerez. Dry *fino, amontillado,* and *oloroso* wines can be very fine and complex. It is the sweet Pedro Ximénez wines that get the most attention as the finest wines of the region.

The wines of Alvear and Toro Albala, which are avail-

El Rincocillo restaurant in Seville has been dishing up tapas *since 1670.*

able in North America, can be recommended. They can be very complex wines and because they are off the beaten path, they are undervalued for their level of quality. The dry nonfortified Viejissimo Amontillado Solera 1922 and the sweet fortified Don Pedro Ximénez Gran Reserva by Toro Albala (aged for twenty-five years before release) sell for under $40 and under $50, respectively.

The Alvear winery has the distinction of selling its wines in bottles since 1729, making it the oldest winery in Spain. It produces wines that range from a dry *fino* to sweet Pedro Ximénez wines, with both a vintage (de **AÑADA**) and Solera (traditional version) available.

As previously mentioned in this section, this region is less humid than Jerez. The conditions allow some of the *amontillado viejisimo* wine to naturally evaporate, which brings its alcohol level up to 21 percent without fortification.

MÁLAGA DO

Málaga wine is made in a *solera* system similar to that for Sherry. Most of it is sweet, by the addition of sweetening additives. Both the natural sweet wines and the liqueur wines range from 15 to 22 percent in alcohol content and are labeled as either Moscatel or Pedro Ximénez. There is a dry wine based on Pedro Ximénez labeled *seco*, but it is not as popular as those labeled *dulce,* the sweet wines of the area.

Málaga wines are also labeled by age. Unaged wines are labeled *joven*. Wines with half a year to two years of age are called *Málaga*. *Málaga noble* are aged for two to three years, *Málaga añejo* are aged for three to five years, and the *Málaga trasañejo* are aged over five years. The largest company in Málaga is Lopez Hermanos.

Jorge Ordóñez is one of the leading Spanish wine importers in the United States. Among his many offerings are wines from his birthplace of Málaga. The Selección Especial, Victoria, and Vinas Viejas "Old Vines" offer the seductive floral and honeyed flavors of pure Moscatel and much more.

CONDADO DE HUELVA DO

This DO is best known for its fortified wines such as the Palido, which is similar to a *fino*-style Sherry and is also based on the Palomino Fino grape. Zalema is the local white grape for dry still wines, yet there is a move toward planting red varieties in the region. The presence of Tempranillo, Cabernet Sauvignon, Cabernet Franc, Merlot, and Syrah are increasing in the region.

SUMMARY

BOTH CLASSICAL and the new Spanish gastronomy have captured the attention of epicures around the globe. Wine producers, fueled by their own increasing sales and international success, are keeping pace with chefs and producers of artisan delicacies.

Spanish winemakers have the confidence to experiment in their vineyards and wineries. The creation of the single-vineyard *DO de pago* category, the increased use of French oak barrels, and the embrace of non-native grapes represent just some of the new wave of wines available to consumers. Many of the new-style Spanish red wines are full-bodied with rich, youthful flavors. Spain's strong suit has always been the production of mature red wines that by law had to spend a set minimum aging period in cask and bottle. The bouquet, harmony of flavors, and softer tannins of the *crianza* and *reserva* wines still attract a large audience, while the appeal of *gran reserva* wines that have the longest minimum aging requirements (five years) before they are sold may be diminishing.

Spain's great success in the wine world is partially due to its complex red wines. Rioja and Ribera del Duero have been the benchmark for fine Spanish red wines, but today, wines from regions such as Priorato, Bierzo, Toro, and Penedès are equally exciting. Albariño is the nation's most important grape for dry white wines, but wines made from the Godello, Verdejo, or Xarel-lo grapes can also be delightful.

There are lots of dry rosé, white, and red wines from Spain available for under $15 a bottle. Sparkling Cava may just be the best value for *méthode champenoise* wines in the world. Undervalued and often misunderstood fortified Sherry wines provide unique food pairing possibilities.

For those who drink wine daily, it is the value, diversity, and charm of Spanish wines that makes them irresistible.

CASTELÃO

DÃO

touriga nacional

VERDELHO

COLHEITA

ALVARINHO

ALENTEJO

MALMSEY

TAWNY

QUINTA

LATE-BOTTLED
VINTAGE PORTO

GARRAFEIRA

MOSCATEL
DE SETÚBAL

DOURO

SERCIAL

PORTUGAL

PORTUGAL IS ONLY 575 miles/925 kilometers long and 140 miles/225 kilometers wide. As small a country as it is, Portugal in fact has a great variety of landscapes and growing conditions for viticulture. Such variety allows Portuguese wineries to produce an equally diverse range of wines.

Water and sunshine are the lifeblood of the vine. With almost 1,800 miles/1,118 kilometers of coastline, proximity to the Atlantic Ocean and surrounding rivers has guided the selection of vineyard sites and grape types best suited for those areas. Multiple waterways also allowed for easier transport of wine barrels to markets. The four major rivers that traverse the nation include the Douro, Tagus, Sado, and Guadiana. Rainfall is another factor that greatly influences the health of vineyards. While there is ample rainfall along the coastal regions, the interior regions of Portugal suffer a much drier and hotter climate. Along the border with Spain, red grapes dominate the vineyards.

The verdant Minho coastal region is home to the nation's most famous white wines, known as Vinho Verde, while the parched vineyards of the interior Douro Superior region is where thick-skinned red grapes thrive and produce some of the nation's finest red wines.

Mountains also play a major role in viticulture by protecting vineyards from excessive rainfall and stressful winds. Vineyards planted at high elevations experience cooler growing conditions than those planted at sea level, keeping the acidity of the grapes in balance with their sugars and tannins, and also allowing for an extended ripening period. Factors such as a vineyard's location, the amount of sun it receives, and the ability of its soils to reflect or retain heat are all taken into account by farmers. Soil permeability and composition also contribute to the character of Portuguese wine.

In this chapter, many of these scientific considerations will be discussed for those who may be interested in such technical information.

The styles of wines available in each of Portugal's wine regions have been strongly influenced by the local fare, just as the styles of other wine-producing regions have evolved to be well suited to the classic dishes of their respective areas. For example, Portugal's role in the spice trade and its explorations have certainly impacted its cuisine. Piri Piri hot sauce, *caldo verde* (kale soup); seafood *açorda* soup with fresh coriander; *amêijoas* (clams) cooked in a *cataplana*; *alheira, morcela, linguiça,* and *chouriço* sausages; *perdiz* (partridge); *cabrito*; and *Leitâo assado* (spit-roasted baby suckling pig) provide just a few examples of Portuguese fare.

It should also be mentioned that the Portuguese claim to have 365 ways to prepare *bacalhau* (codfish). It is when these foods are paired with the local wines that "the light comes on" and Portuguese wines really begin to make sense and give the most pleasure. This chapter and Chapter 14, "Wine and Food," will cover some typical pairings along with a few more adventurous ones.

Portugal's 864,500 acres/350,000 hectares of vineyards place it fifth in the world in acreage devoted to grapes. Over 190,000 farmers grow vinifera in Portugal, bringing its annual output to 23.7 million gallons/9 million hectoliters of wine (about 10 million cases annually), making the country the tenth-largest producer in the world.

Although the fortified wines of Oporto have a storied success, respect for the nation's fine dry wines is fairly recent.

The first elegant dry red wine, Barca Velha, was introduced in 1952 by the Ferreira winery. Back then, it was so hot in the Douro Valley that ice was brought up from the city of Oporto to cool the fermentation casks. Thank air-conditioning for allowing the wineries of the Douro and other hot regions of Portugal to make fresh wines that no longer exhibit a "baked" characteristic. Barca Velha's reign as the finest wine of the country went unchallenged for about thirty years.

By the 1960s and 1970s, inexpensive semisweet rosés such as Lancers and Mateus as well as dry whites and reds from larger corporate wineries were the norm. Today, the Portuguese wine trade is savvy enough to realize it must count on exports to grow. The large companies with wineries in multiple locations throughout the country, the small single QUINTAS (estates), and *herdades* (farms) combine to produce enough wine to slake the thirst of the local market while supplying the rest of the world with some very unique wines.

Many new wineries focused on the production of fine wines arrived on the scene in the early 1980s. In 1986, entry into the European Union spurred research and financial investments toward upgrading vineyards and building state-of-the-art wineries. For example, in 1986 the World Bank financed the planting of 6,175 acres/2,500 hectares in the Douro. One of the conditions, however, stated that only the top five grape varieties of the region were to be planted. The fruits of that investment have since paid off, and the Douro, which has always experienced success with its fortified Porto wines, is now also the leading region in the production of fine still wines.

TOP: *The beauty of the Douro Valley* BOTTOM: *Barca Velha, made from grapes grown in the Douro Valley, was the nation's first super-premium dry red wine.*

Portugal

Denominação de Origem Controlada within Vinho Regional (DOC)

Minho VR
Vinho Verde DOC

Trasmontano VR
Trás-os-Montes DOC

Duriense VR
Porto and Douro DOC

Beiras VR
Bairrada DOC
Dão DOC

Lisboa VR
Lourinhã DOC
Torres Vedras DOC
Colares DOC
Carcavelos DOC
Bucelas DOC
Arruda DOC
Alenquer DOC

Ribatejo VR
Tejo DOC

Terras do Sado VR
Palmela DOC
Setúhal (Moscatel) DOC

Alentejano VR
Alentejo DOC

Algarve VR

Madeira DOC

DÃO Denominação de Origem Controlada
MINHO Vinho Regional

Encouraged by higher prices for their grapes, farmers and investors throughout the nation are planting new vineyards with the best clones of the finest grape varieties. Using information from prosperous wine-producing regions of the New World, they are implementing new approaches to trellising, vine spacing, and coordinating the density of plantings. (See discussions of vineyard management on pages 13 and 15.) In response to Portugal's efforts, the EU continues to support growers and wineries by providing financial assistance to those who are willing to plant premium varieties in superior locations.

One of the romantic things about Portugal's wines is that their winemaking may involve historical techniques such as the use of the *lagar* (stone trough) to tread the grapes or *talha* (amphora) to ferment the wine. Indeed, many wineries today take advantage of both traditional and state-of-the-art equipment to create their wines. The elaboration of these grapes whether by traditional or modern techniques has resulted in a gamut of styles, ranging from refreshing light-bodied, low-alcohol whites to complex, powerhouse reds.

The annual wine consumption of a Portuguese wine drinker dropped from 21.1 gallons/80 liters in the 1970s to 13.2 gallons/50 liters today. Those figures are motivating wineries to produce the styles of wines and labels that will appeal to the export market. Traditional Portuguese wines were labeled mostly by place name, but there has been a significant increase in varietal-labeled wines. Labels bearing the name of the grape are meant to appeal to the export market, especially North America. In the dessert and fortified category, Portugal ranks first in U.S. imports, with over a third of the market share. In 2007, Portugal exported $70 million worth of wine to the United States, 80 percent of which was Porto wine. Its other unique fortified wines are Madeira and Moscatel de Setúbal. Sweet Porto, crisp dry Vinho Verde, and red Douro wines are Portugal's best-known wines today. Hopefully, their success will be a springboard for the exploration of other regions' distinct wines.

In each area of this small nation, there are many dedicated growers and winemakers producing world-class wines. The fairly recent success story of fine still wines led by the producers of the Douro should not overshadow the visionary winemakers of other regions of Portugal. Whether it be a major company producing wine from numerous regions, or a single-*quinta* estate, the most important piece of information on a wine label is the name of the producer.

Today there are quality white, rosé, and red wines available at all price points. The simple, refreshing, low-alcohol Vinho Verde white wines as well as inexpensive rosés and fruity reds under $10 are some of the world's best-value wines. Wines with more pronounced expressions of a particular region or with the singular characteristics of a grape type may be found from $15 to $150. If a Portuguese red wine at $45 to $100 can compete with some of the best wines from other countries at double or triple the price, those Portuguese wines are still of great value.

With so much wine available from so many countries, a wine consumer may wonder why they should choose Portuguese wines. Most of all, there are the unique flavors of Portugal's three hundred-plus indigenous grape varieties. Savored as single-variety wines or as blends, Portugal provides an opportunity to break out of the rut of Pinot Grigio, Chardonnay, Shiraz, and Cabernet that is so easy to fall into. Exploring new wines can be unpredictable and intimidating; however, this chapter's explanations will hopefully lend confidence and inspire readers to take the leap and explore the wines of Portugal.

PORTUGUESE GRAPE VARIETIES

PORTUGAL'S UNIQUE OFFERINGS of over three hundred grapes varieties can truly be a turn-on. They are available as pure expressions of the grape variety and in blended wines, often bearing the name of their birthplace on the label. Helpful information about the grape or grapes used is sometimes found on the back label of a Portuguese wine bottle.

RED GRAPES

TOURIGA NACIONAL This small- to medium-size grape (pronounced *Too ree gah Nahz yo nahl*) with a high skin-to-juice ratio produces dark-colored tannic wines with good acidity. A challenge for farmers is that the grape is prone to *coulure* (floral abortion) and must be planted in locations that receive plenty of sunshine. A positive attribute of the Touriga Nacional is that it excels at finding sufficient water to thrive, even in the most arid conditions. In such conditions, it may drop some of its leaves, but its thick skin helps defend the plant against dehydration. To avoid overly moist conditions, Touriga Nacional is usually planted at higher elevations due to the danger of excess moisture from fog. Nevertheless, this early-ripening variety typically produces lower yields. Characteristic aromas include mulberry, black cherry, violets, rose petal, strawberry, cardamom, bergamot, and gamy scents reminiscent of smoked meat. Varietal wines based exclusively on Touriga Nacional are seductive with their floral spicy notes and silky texture. They often possess a good vein of acidity even when grown in warmer sites. We hope *Exploring Wine* readers will do their own research and discover the diversity of flavors Touriga Nacional can offer in a still wine or a fortified Port.

TINTA RORIZ This high-quality Iberian variety, known as Tempranillo in Spain, produces wine with lots of sugar (ripeness), body, astringency, and potential for longevity. The nose is often floral, herbal, and spicy, while on the palate, berry and licorice flavors may be sensed. An early ripener with a thick skin, the Tinta Roriz can be grown in warmer locales, and it prefers soils rich in minerals. While its yield per vine can be twice that of Touriga Nacional, Tinta Roriz is sold as a single-variety wine or may be blended with other grapes to compensate for its low acidity. Roriz is an essential part of many Douro and Porto DOC wines and is also grown in the south, where it is known as Aragones. It is the one non-indigenous red grape discussed in this section because it is so widely used in Portugal. Both the Aragones and Aragonez spellings can be found on labels.

TINTA BARROCA This thin-skinned grape grows best in cooler sites along the Douro where it is a component of blended dry wines and sweet Portos. Tinta Barroca produces wine with softer tannins and lower acidity than Touriga Nacional, yet bears higher yields. It adds good, deep, rich color and a floral, fruity nose to blends but is not particularly assertive on its own.

TINTA CÃO This component of Douro and Porto blends prefers cooler climates. While Tinta Cão (cow) takes a long time to develop and show its qualities, it lends longevity and complexity to blended wines. Like the Touriga Nacional, the Tinta Cão is a low-yielding grape. Tinta Cão produces a wine with fine floral and fruit flavors and a hint of spiciness as well. Although it is thick-skinned, it contributes the least color of the five top Porto varieties, as its juice is prone to oxidizing quickly.

TOURIGA FRANCA The final variety in our list of the top five grapes of the Douro, this is the most floral in aroma, particularly pungent of the scent of the herb *esteva* (rockrose). This grape contributes good sugar, acid, and fruit qualities such as strawberry and orange to Douro and Porto blends yet tastes earthy on the palate. This particular variety is best suited to hot soils but would also fare well in moderate-temperature zones.

TRINCADEIRA Although it is not one of the top five varieties for production of Porto, this remains a popular grape. The Ferreira Company uses the variety, which is called Tinta Amarela in Douro, for its Portos and table wines. Trincadeira (*Trink as die rah*) is used for table wines in other parts of the nation, and it produces medium- to full-bodied wines. Some of the flavors associated with

The Touriga Nacional is Portugal's most important red grape and may be enjoyed as a single-variety wine or in a blend. Impressive wines are found in its birthplace, the Douro region of the north, as well as in central and southern Portugal.

Trincadeira are red plum, black fruits, herbs, spices such as clove, and some vegetal earthiness. It is bottled as a single variety and also used to make blended wines. Known as Espadeiro in the Minho, Tinta Amarela does well in the warmest areas of the Douro and is similar to the Tinta Barroca, but is notably spicier.

SOUSÃO Sousão exhibits a deep color, strong body, tart black fruit flavors, and vinosity on the nose. Though excluded from top five, many Douro wineries love to use Sousão in their blends. Sousão grown farther south can be found in blends and also as single-varietal wine.

BAGA The Baga grape reigns supreme in the Beiras and Bairrada regions and can be found as a single variety or in a blend of Baga and Touriga Nacional. High acidity and tannins allow Baga wines to pack quite a wallop on the palate when young. Elegant and rustic red wines are based on the grape and by "bleeding" (see Chapter 2, page 68). Some typical Baga aromas and flavors include black currant, black fig, black plum, *goudron* (tar), and anise seed or fennel. Some fun rosé, still, and sparkling wines are made using this grape.

CASTELÃO The grape is formerly known as Periquita and is a mainstay of central and southern Portuguese wines. It is the most-planted red grape variety in Portugal. Red fruit aromas and flavors play a large part in Castelão's character.

ALFROCHEIRO PRETO This produces spicy and floral wines of medium body. It is used in blends and made as a single-variety wine, especially in the Dão region.

JAEN Black fruits and black pepper are common descriptors for Jaen-based wines. It is used as a blending grape and also makes single-variety wines, especially in the Dão region. Jaen is the Portuguese name for the Mencía grape of Bierzo, Spain.

RAMISCO Ramisco is the principal red grape of the Colares region, where it grows in sandy soils ungrafted to new rootstock. Aged, complex wines made from this grape are rare treats, yet sadly, the vineyard acreage is shrinking.

BASTARDO Bastardo may compose up to 60 percent of a Porto blend but is no longer planted in new vineyards because of its high yield and high sugar levels. Bastardo is known as Trousseau in the Jura region of France.

TINTA PINHEIRA Red fruit flavors and medium body are the characteristics of this variety, which is also known as Rufete.

ALVARELHÃO Alvarelhão is a component in red-wine blends from central and northern Portugal. It provides a good level of acidity but only adds light body to wines from the Douro and the Dão regions. It is known as the Brancelho in the Minho, and the Brancellao in nearby Galicia, Spain.

WHITE GRAPES

ALVARINHO This is the most important white grape of Portugal and is the same variety as the Albariño of Spain. Alvarinho (*Al vah reen yo*) wines from the Vinho Verde region are usually medium- to full-bodied and some may in fact have just a kiss of oak. Winemakers do not want the wood to overwhelm the aromas and flavors of white flowers, peaches, and mango of dry white wines sourced from this grape.

ARINTO Like Azal, this white grape is prized for its natural high acidity. Often used in Vinho Verde blends, and the unoaked versions of this wine are generally better examples. Arinto is also called Pederna and is also widely used in regions such as Bucelas, Bairrada, and the Alentejo.

ENCRUZADO Many Encruzado wines of the Dão region have the "wow" factor. Big and bold, they can handle some oak

Castelão is the most planted red grape of Portugal.

treatment and still shout out yellow plum, nuttiness, and mineral flavors. Search out the single-variety wines or enjoy Encruzado's contribution to white blends.

FERNÃO PIRES, OR MARIA GOMES This is a grape with a serious identity crisis. Masculine Fernão Pires in northern Portugal becomes feminine Maria Gomes in the central and southern regions of the nation. Either way you squish it, there are plenty of citrus and white pepper notes contributed by this ubiquitous grape.

AVESSO Avesso can add structure to white blends or shine on its own. Single-variety wines from Vinho Verde DOC are worth seeking out, as some of their interesting aromas and flavors include mango, grapefruit, and kumquat.

LOUREIRO Bay laurel, orange blossom, and quince aromas are part of Loureiro's charm. An important component of Vinho Verde DOC blends, it is also made into single-variety wines.

TRAJADURA Lemon and lime flavors dominate the profile of this grape, used in the Vinho Verde DOC. It is available as a single-variety wine.

AZAL The Azal grape is prized for its high levels of acidity and is often used in Vinho Verde blended wines.

ASSARIO Assario is a component of dry white wines in the Dão DOC and makes sweet fortified wines known as Malmsey in the Madeira DOC. It is also called Malvasia Fina.

BICAL This grape can make high-acid white and sparkling wines. It ripens well and produces wine of substantial alcohol. It is also known as the Borrado dos Moscas, or "fly droppings," a reference to the brown spots found on the grape skin.

ESGANA CÃO Esgana Cão means the "dog strangler," because of its very high levels of acidity. It is called **SERCIAL** in Madeira.

CERCIAL This grape is used to make tart dry white wines in the Bairrada region.

CERCEAL BRANCA The Cerceal Branca is used to make tart, dry white wines in the Dão region. (Notice that there are three different grape varieties with similar names: Sercial, Cercial, and Cerceal Branca.)

VERDELHO Verdelho is one of the top five grapes used in Madeira for the production of dry to off-dry fortified wines.

GOUVEIO Used to make dry wines in the Douro, Dão, and Alentejo regions, this is the same variety as the Godello of Spain, though not the same grape as the Verdelho, as some books suggest.

ANTÃO VAZ An important grape in the Alentejo, where it can withstand hot temperatures and make a balanced wine with spice and mineral notes. Lighter versions are made in stainless steel, while oak-influenced wines are medium- to full-bodied.

ROUPEIRO Also known as Siria, Códega, or Alva, this is used in blends in the Alentejo and central Portugal.

RABIGATO Old-vine Rabigato grapes are being used to make some very fine dry wine in the Douro. It is known as Rabo de Ovelha, meaning "ewe's tail," in the Alentejo, where it is used to make blended still wines.

MOSCATEL The seductive orange blossom–honey aromas and flavors of Moscatel are enticing as a single-variety or blended dry table wine from the Terras do Sado region, or as a sweet fortified Moscatel de Setúbal DOC wine. Originally from Greece and known elsewhere as the Muscat of Alexandria, it is the one nonindigenous white grape discussed here.

LAWS, LABELS, AND KEY TERMS

THIS CHAPTER WILL EXPLAIN the wine laws and labels and will highlight some of the top wineries in each region. However, who can help but have a soft spot for family-owned wineries whose responsibilities to their ancestors and progeny trump those of purely financial motivation. Additionally, the chapter will cover flavor profiles for the most important grape varieties and explain the traits of wine produced in the major **VINHO REGIONAL** (VR) and **DENOMINAÇÃO DE ORIGEM CONTROLADA (DOC)** grape-growing areas. DOC may sound familiar; Italy and Spain use similar terms. DOP (explained below) is a recently introduced alternative to DOC in the member countries of the European Union.

As mentioned in the introduction to this chapter, today there are many Portuguese wines labeled by the name of the grape variety, for example Touriga Nacional. Proprietary or fantasy names such as Chryseia usually also carry the name of the area where the grapes were grown. Portuguese wines labeled by place name may be produced in a *vinho regional* (a large region, Beiras for example), or in a smaller *denominação de origem controlada* (DOC) zone within the *vinho regional* (such as Dão). Today, only a dozen major DOC wine-producing regions and a few *vinho regional* zones dominate the Portuguese wine scene.

Another type of labeling by place is by the name of a farm or an estate (for example, Herdade do Esporão or Quinta do Crasto) in the fashion of châteaux in Bordeaux, France. Their single-vineyard wines are prized for their distinctive personality and are also sought after because of their limited production.

Portugal had a four-tier system similar to other European nations, but there has been a lot of consolidation in the past decade. Some subzones of DOC regions have been absorbed into the larger DOC. For example, Borba DOC is now part of the larger Alentejo DOC. By law, each region and its subregions grow *castas recomendadas* (recommended grape types), and those grapes must meet requirements of a maximum yield and a minimum alcohol level. Several regions also require a minimum period of aging the wine before it may be sold. Finally, all of these wines must pass a tasting test to ensure they are not flawed and that their flavors are representative of the grape or place name used on the label.

The four levels of the Portuguese wine-quality pyramid are similar to those of France, Italy, and Spain:

VINHO DE MESA These table wines were the lowest level of domestic wines, and since August 2009 the term has been discontinued on labels. **VINHO DE MESA** and Vinho Regional wines will be labeled as *indicação geográfica protegida* (IGP).

INDICAÇÃO DE PROVENIÉNCIA REGULAMENTADA (IPR) This category is being phased out. For example, the former IPR growing regions Chaves, Planalto Mirandés, and Valpaços are now subregions of the Trás-os-Montes DOC within the Transmontano Vinho Regional.

VINHO REGIONAL (VR) The major regional wine areas are Minho, Beiras, Ribatejo, Lisboa, Alentejano, Terras do Sado, Trasmontano, and Duriense. Minor VR zones include Algarve, Terras Madeirenses, and Açores (see map on page 449). Older wines will feature the phrase *vinho regional* on a label, while more current releases may use the *indicação geográfica protegida* designation.

DENOMINAÇÃO DE ORIGEM CONTROLADA (DOC) Portugal's highest echelon of wine is equivalent to the French *appellation d'origine contrôlée,* Italy's *denominazione di origine controllata,* or Spain's *denominación de origen.* Currently, Portuguese wine producers have the option of using either the traditional *denominação de origem controlada* or *denominação de origem protegida* designations on their labels, due to changes in European Union wine regulations that were approved in 2009 (see page 256).

As of 2009, there were twenty-nine DOC wine regions in Portugal. The most important regions are Vinho Verde, Douro, Dão, Bairrada, Tejo, Bucelas, Palmela, and Alentejo. Best-known for Portugal's unique fortified wines are Madeira, Setúbal, and Porto.

Portugal's higher-quality wines are subject to stringent controls on production, labeling, and taste, just as their counterparts are in other European countries. (See "Portuguese Regulation and Promotional Agencies," opposite.) Some producers opt to declassify and market their high-quality wines in the *vinho regional* category, because

LEFT TO RIGHT: *Touriga Nacional by Quinta do Crasto is a single-varietal label from a single estate in the Douro DOC. Quinta da Leda by Ferreira is made from a blend of red grapes in the Douro DOC. A proprietary or fantasy-named wine "Meandro" from Quinta do Vale do Meão in the Douro DOC. An aged reserva wine from Marquês de Borba in the Alentejo.*

PORTUGUESE REGULATION AND PROMOTIONAL AGENCIES

Today, the Instituto da Vinha e do Vinho (IVV) is the federal governing body responsible for granting demarcated areas and establishing production and exportation laws within production zones. Official agencies that report to the IVV are set up in each region to control the growing of grapes and the making of wine. The Associação dos Produtores dos Engarrafadores de Vinho Verde is an example of a regional organization controlling and promoting local wines while working under the aegis of the IVV.

The still wines Douro and Duriense and fortified Porto are the only independently controlled DOCs, under the aegis of the Instituto do Vinho do Porto (IVP, Port Wine Institute). Each of the wines approved by them carries a "selo"/seal of approval on the neck of the bottle.

Determined to sell more wine, provincial wine associations throughout Portugal are working with the VINI PORTUGAL and Investimentos, Comércio e Turismo de Portugal (ICEP) government agencies to maintain quality control and to promote their wines abroad.

the rules are less restrictive than those of a DOC. For example, a winery labeling its wine as Beiras—a *vinho regional*—can include grape types not traditionally used in its DOC subregions such as Dão or Bairrada, or the wine may be a blend of grapes from those two DOC wine-producing areas. Again, current vintages of Beiras wines may be labeled as *indicação origem protegida* rather than *vinho regional*.

SPARKLING WINES These wines are under the QSWPSR or Quality Sparkling Wines Produced in a Specified Wine Region category (semi-sparkling wines are QSSWPSR).

LIQUOR WINES This category is under the same rules as those of other EU nations and are QLWPSR or Quality Liquor Wines Produced in a Specified Region.

GRAPE VARIETY To use a grape name such as Touriga Nacional, a minimum of 85 percent of grapes recommended or authorized for the specified region must be used. Such is the law as in all wine-producing European Union countries.

GARRAFEIRA This term usually denotes red wines that are aged a minimum of two and a half years, including a year in the bottle before release. Whites and rosés are aged a minimum of one year, including six months in the bottle. In the Dão DOC, it is a minimum of thirty-six months aging, including twelve months in the bottle, for red wines. A minimum alcohol content of 11.5 percent for all styles must be achieved. Although *garrafeira* is officially the highest quality level in respect to a minimum aging period, some wineries believe the term is too obscure or difficult to pronounce and opt to use the term *reserva* or *grande escolha* (great selection) instead.

RESERVA These wines must have an alcohol content that is 0.05 percent *higher* than the minimum for their respective region. In some regions, the wines must achieve a score higher on a ten-point scale than non-*reserva* wines from the region and may have a minimum aging period before they can be sold. Dão reserva red wines, for example, must be aged a minimum of twenty-four months before they are sold. The term is used for better products from better vintages and may be used in conjunction with the term *garrafeira*. For sparkling wines, *reserva espumante* requires a minimum of twelve months in the bottle, and for *velha reserva* bubbly, thirty-six months.

VELHO These "old" wines must be aged a minimum of three years for the red wines and two for the whites before they may be sold.

COLHEITA SELECIONADA These are high-quality vintage-labeled wines with an alcohol content at least 1 percent higher than the minimum for the region, not to exceed 12 percent.

SUPERIOR As with *colheita selecionada*, these wines have a higher minimum alcohol by at least 1 percent but do not have to be vintage-labeled.

ESCOLHA, OR GRANDE ESCOLHA Sometimes used for a producer's top selected wine. The IVP governing body of the Douro imposes a minimum score by a tasting panel before permission is granted to use the term on labels from that DOC.

An aged Garrafeira wine from Esporão in the Alentejo

ENGARRAFADO NA ORIGEM Wine bottled at the estate.

ENGARRAFADO NA REGIÃO Bottled in the region where the grapes were grown.

ADEGA A cellar or winery.

ARMAZÉM A warehouse where fortified wines are stored. Historically, the grapes for Porto were grown in the Douro Valley, transported downriver to the city of Vila Nova de Gaia, fermented, and stored in *armazéms* or lodges. In Madeira, the *armazéms* are in the city of Funchal.

QUINTA, OR HERDADE An estate, farm, or vineyard; sometimes used as part of the name of a particular producer.

SOLAR, OR PALACIO A vineyard with a magnificent house. Similar to a château in Bordeaux, France.

CALÇO A walled section of a vineyard in the Douro. Similar to *clos* in Burgundy, France.

CASTA Grape variety.

ÂNFORA, OR TALHAS Clay pots used to ferment and store wine.

LAGARES Stone troughs used to trod or press grapes.

SECO Dry, with residual sugar under 4 grams per liter.

DOCE Sweet.

COLHEITA Vintage.

VINHO Wine.

BRANCO White.

TINTO Red.

ESPUMANTE Sparkling. *Bruto* is dry and *extra seco* is semidry.

WINE REGIONS

PORTUGAL'S VARIED TERRAIN and climatic conditions allow for the production of a diversity of wine styles. As in France and other countries, certain grape varieties or blends have proven to be more successful in specific appellations over time. Briefly mentioned in the opening remarks of this chapter, the coastal northwest has more rain, fewer cold winters, and shorter summers than the northeast. Farther south, the winters are milder, the summers hotter, and as in the north, there is more precipitation along the coastal areas than inland. Rainfall varies from 78 inches/2,000 millimeters in some coastal areas to under 19 inches/487 millimeters in some inland vineyards. The more temperate areas produce a variety of styles, while in the hottest areas, thick-skinned red grapes do best.

Arguably Portugal's finest grape, the Touriga Nacional, is now planted in most of the red wine–producing regions within the nation. It has not only adapted to different growing conditions but has also formed some interesting new relationships. Partnered with Baga in Beiras, Alfrocheiro Preto and Jaen in the Dão, Trincadeira in the Alentejo and Castelão in the Ribatejo, the floral and fruit flavors it contributes vary. On its own in the Douro or within a traditional blend, Touriga Nacional is always sumptuous. It is worth having a Touriga tasting of a half dozen wines, including pure examples and blends from different regions.

Refer to the grape profile section at the beginning of this chapter to better understand what each grape contributes to a blend, as well as the flavor profiles of single-variety wines. There are descriptions of the general style of wine in each region. Vinho Verde blends for example, are relatively homogenous in style, but with over three hundred indigenous varieties and international grapes thrown in the mix, it is not always practical to generalize about the wines. Another factor is that the inexpensive wines of an area (under $10) will not have the structure, complexity, or concentration of wines sold at $25 or more.

The best way to explore the wines of Portugal is to taste them, share opinions, and drink them with food.

DURIENSE VINHO REGIONAL

Douro DOC, Porto DOC

Within the Terras Duriense Vinho Regional (see map on page 449) the fortified wines are known as Porto DOC, traditional dry still wines from a demarcated region in the southern portion as Douro DOC, and still wines not within the subregion or not meeting the criteria of Douro DOC are labeled as Vinho Regional Duriense.

The Douro is named for the 497-mile/800-kilometer river that runs through it and is shared with Spain, where it is known as Duero. There are 685,000 acres/277,323 hectares of land and about 18 percent is devoted to vineyards. Over thirty-three thousand farmers grow grapes here, and holdings are small. Most are small farms, with about 2.47

acres/1 hectare of vines. Annual wine production for the region is about 23.7 million gallons/90 million liters.

The Serra do Marão and Serra do Montemuro mountains are at elevations of about 4,600 feet/1,402 meters, and they provide protection from wind, hailstorms, and excessive rainfall from the west.

The Douro River and the smaller rivers that feed into it help moderate the climate as well. Vineyards on the north bank of the river are considered the best because they get sunshine throughout the day and are affected by dry winds from the south. Vineyards on the southern slopes are affected by cool winds and humidity from the north, and they receive mostly hot afternoon sunshine.

Vineyards on the bottom of slopes are more fertile and vigorous than on the higher sites. At higher elevations, the best vineyards sites start cooling at 2 P.M., resulting in an increase of acidity within the grapes. It is that freshness of the acids that will ultimately balance the rich fruits and tannins of the wines.

The varieties grown here have been chosen not only for the characteristic aromas and flavors they provide the wines, but also for their ability to withstand the extremes of temperatures and rainfall in the subregions of the Douro. Although schist soil (crystalline metamorphic rock with minerals arranged in even layers) dominates the region, slate and granite-based soils may also be found.

If chalk is the defining element that makes the soil composition of the Champagne region unique, here it is the heat-retentive schist. Vines, olive trees, and *esteva*—the rockrose gum tree, the sticky residue of which blows onto the vines, imparting a unique perfume detectable in the wines—are the major plants hardy enough to thrive in the Douro. Schist must be broken to a depth of 5 feet/1.5 meters to plant vines. After five years of growth, vine roots are able to penetrate the fissures in the rocky soil and may go as deep as 65.6 feet/20 meters in search of water stored in the subsoils of volcanic rock and granite. Older vines are prized not only for their ability to access water, but

The views from Quinta do Crasto are breathtaking. The estate is recognized as one of the finest wineries of Portugal. The name Crasto is derived from the Roman crastum for fort, and there are stone markers that date to the Roman presence on the property. The estate owners have grown grapes and produced wine since 1615. Jorge Roquette and his sons Tomas and Miguel are the current proprietors.

also for their ability to extract a greater amount of essential minerals from the soil, such as potassium, resulting in wines of more complexity and depth. Because schist-based soils are low in organic materials and do not produce large yields of grapes, experimenting continues in

the hope of finding ways to increase production without sacrificing quality.

Erosion is a major problem in the Douro, thereby warranting the stone walls found in most vineyards. Before the phylloxera attacked, rows of vines alternated with walls. Subsequent replanting placed five to ten rows of vines between walls. Today, growers continue to experiment with the number of rows between walls, as well as the density of those rows. One concern in more densely planted vineyards is the lack of water. To counter this problem, many sites have chosen to use drip irrigation within their vineyards.

The cost of maintaining the stone walls ultimately led to the development of a system called *patamares*, in which terraces were bulldozed out of the slopes. One disadvantage to the *patamares* is that the traditional 2,400 vines per acre/5,928 vines per hectare are now limited to half that number, requiring each vine to yield double the fruit. A third system is *vinha ao alto*, in which rows are

Schist is the dominant soil type in the Douro region.

planted up and down the slopes rather than laterally. A major advantage of this system is that many of the arduous tasks once performed by hand in the vineyards are now given over to machines. When and where possible, tractors can be used up to an incline of 30 degrees, but not on the precipitous slopes of 45 degrees or more.

Originally the subregion Lower Douro (or Baixo Corgo) was the most densely planted. As a result, the wines of this area were more plentiful and lighter in color and body, yet still offered appealing aromas of fruit. As the British (Portugal's largest importer at the time) demanded richer wines, the vineyards expanded eastward, and in 1907, the warmer, drier Upper Douro (or Cima Corgo) was officially demarcated. These wines smell and taste of bright red fruit, flowers, and spices. Not too long afterward, the Douro Superior, farther inland, was demarcated. This area of even less rainfall, hotter summers, and colder winters produces riper grapes with lower acidity.

Wines made from these vines smell of black currant and exhibit more complexity. Today, a comparison of average yields reveals that 1,000 vines in the Lower Douro yield 528.4 gallons/2,000 liters of juice, while the same number of Upper Douro vines yield only 145 gallons/550 liters.

There are some high-quality producers in the Lower Douro, such as Alves de Sousa's Quinta da Gaivosa and Quinta do Raposa, which keep yields down to produce concentrated fine wines. Abandonado is a single-vineyard wine worth seeking out.

Today, the Lower Douro provides about 18 percent, the Upper Douro 38 percent, and the Superior 44 percent of the grapes used to make wines in the region.

Piggybacking on the success of Porto, the wineries of the Douro have led the way in the quality revolution for still wines. In the past, the production of still wines was mostly an inescapable responsibility imposed by production limits set for Porto by the Instituto do Vinho do Porto. Today, some wineries place still wines first and fortified second.

The IVP controls and promotes all the wines from the Duriense, Douro, and Porto, and it forecasts continued growth in table wine sales. The success of its table wines and Porto, whether bargain-priced, moderate, or expensive, is a source of great pride for most Portuguese and perhaps a little jealousy for some other regions' producers.

Since its original demarcation in 1756, the Douro's wine laws have changed many times, and the current **BENEFÍCIO** system of licensing and scoring each vineyard began in 1945.

About 20 million cases of wine from the Douro are made each year, and Porto production is controlled by the *benefício* system and changes annually. The production volume is set by PIPES of wine, barrels that contain 550 liters/145 gallons. In 2008 a total of 123,500 pipes was permitted, and in 2009 it was lowered to 110,000 pipes.

The permitted amount of Porto production is restricted to maintain price levels for the wines. For example, in 2000 an owner of an "A" vineyard could make 343.3 gallons per acre/3,210 liters per hectare into Porto wine and the rest into table wine. In 2008, the same vineyard was only permitted to produce a total of 251.4 gallons per acre/2,351 liters per hectare into Porto, and the rest into still and sparkling wine.

Table and Sparkling Wines of the Douro

The table wines of the Douro were often produced in locations that were not highly rated in the *benefício* system, created in 1945—a time when Port production was the main consideration. Table wine–producing vineyard areas tend to have more temperate climates and are at higher elevations, resulting in grapes with high acidity to balance the ripe sugar levels in the grapes.

As noted earlier, many producers considered the production of table wines as an obligation and made inexpensive still wines. The average price paid to a farmer for Port grapes is much higher than for table wine grapes. Today, some wineries specialize in still wines and promote them more aggressively than their fortified Porto wines.

Touriga Nacional and Tinta Roriz are the primary grapes used in the region's blended red table wines. Today, consumers have a choice of single-varietal wines or blends. We certainly can recommend both. A pure Touriga Nacional or Tinta Roriz wine's flavor profile should express its birthplace, especially if it is sourced from a single vineyard or *quinta*.

Although we enjoy the pure expression of these noble varieties, we also enjoy the complexity of blends grown separately, as well as field blends. For example, the organic Vinha Da Ponte and Maria Theresa are seventy-year-old single-vineyard wines by Quinta do Crasto and are field blends of about one hundred native varieties. Vinha da Ponte is sourced from twenty-two native varieties and has spicy flavors such as black pepper, cardamom, and licorice. Vinha Maria Theresa is silky on the palate with lush fruit flavors of blackberry, raspberry, red cherry, and a scent of violets.

The flavors of their proprietary label Quinta do Crasto Reserva red wine include black cherry, blueberry, fig, and cassis fruits as well as spice, chocolate, tobacco, leather, and game. Their Touriga Nacional has enticing floral, spice, and fruit aromas and flavors such as black cherry and violets.

These wines were first released in 1998, stunning wine enthusiasts and professionals by besting some of the world's most esteemed and expensive wines in blind tasting competitions. There is an extensive list of other recommended blended wines on page 460.

As with Porto, red wines were the source of pride while white wines were perceived as simply affordable wines used to round out a producer's portfolio. Reds are the strong suit because their thick skins can handle the heat better than white varietals. However, as with many wine regions around the world, there are certain "sweet spots" where white grapes can grow well, and with guidance in the wineries, some superb whites are now available from the Douro. Dirk Niepoort has elevated the image of white

THE BENEFÍCIO RATING SYSTEM

There are thirty-three thousand farmers who manage eighty-three thousand individual vineyards in the Douro. The *benefício* system ranks these vineyards from A for the finest to F for the lowest level.

The Casa do Douro in the town of Régua has controlled the *benefício* rating system since 1947. Points are awarded based on factors such as geographic position (up to 600 points), position in relation to climate (210), soil (180), altitude (150), grape quality (150), production (120), gradient (100), upkeep and maintenance (100), and age of the vines (70). The maximum score is 1,680 points, but 1,200 earns an A rating, which allows the highest percentage of wine that can be produced as Porto (185 gallons/700 liters per 1,000 plants). The vineyards below the A ranking gradually make less Porto and more table wine. Investors wishing to plant new vineyards in the Douro gain government assistance when they destroy a lesser-ranked vineyard to replant one that will qualify for a higher letter grade and use the top-rated grape types.

wines in the Douro with his Tiara, Batuta, Charme, and Redoma wines. They are elegant and full-bodied wines with a lovely attack of fruit and a fine mid palate that extends flavors to a long finish

Although the Niepoort Port lodge was established in 1842, it was not until 1987 when Dirk Niepoort joined the company that vineyards were purchased in the Upper Douro. The Redoma Reserva is based primarily on Rabigato with a complement of Donzelinho, Viosinho, Cógega, and Arinto. The ancient vines are planted at altitudes of 450 to 800 feet/137 to 244 meters, which accounts for the wine's high acidity. His red wines and Port wines are also delicious. Another excellent dry white is

Guru made by Wine and Soul from old-vine Gouveio, Vioshinho, Rabigato, and Códega do Larinho grapes.

Raposeira and Vertice are two local *méthode champenoise* sparklers (the late Jack Davies, founder of the Schramsberg winery in Napa Valley, California, started Vertice in 1988). The wines are made from Chardonnay, Pinot Noir, Pinot Blanc, Malvasia Fina, and local grapes such as Gouveio, Cerceal, Códega, Rabigato, Viosinho, and Touriga Franca. Served well chilled, they are a refreshing way to cool down from the heat of the Douro, especially when consumed in one of the many swimming pools at *quintas* in the Douro.

Douro wines range in price from under $10 retail to over $100. The best red wines may be enjoyed a couple of years after the vintage or cellared for twenty to thirty years. The lush wines of the Douro develop seductive fruit and floral flavors with an exotic bouquet of mushroom, earth, leather, and spice notes over time.

For inexpensive reds (under $15), try Adriano by Ramos Pinto, Altano by Symington, Charamba by Aveleda, Caldas by Alves de Sousa, Quinta do Portal, Cister de Lagar by Quinta do Ventezolo, Foral by Alianca, and Callabriga by Sogrape. These light- to medium-weight wines can be served with a slight chill to emphasize their fruit flavors. They are perfectly suited for an outdoor picnic with cold cuts, grilled sausage and peppers, or burgers. The more noble and expensive red wines are paired locally with *cabrito* (baby lamb

Niepoort produces some of the Douro's tastiest dry white wines as well as fine reds and Ports.

cooked in a wood-fire oven) or partridge. Try pairing powerful and noble Douro red wines with grilled steak or eggplant, wild mushroom ravioli, or tandoori lamb.

Some of the region's finest wines include:

Duas Quintas Reserva and Collecion by Adriano Ramos Pinto, the estate wine and Fransisco by Quinta do Vale do Meão and their second label Meandro, Prazo de Roriz and Post Scriptum by Symington, Chryseia by Prats and Symington, Xisto by Roquette e Cazes, Pintas and Pintas Character by Wine and Soul, Redoma, Tiara, Vertente, and Batuta by Niepoort, Lagar de Sá by Cálem Grande Reserva and Quinta da Coa by CARM (Casa Agricola Roboreda Madeira), Quinta da Cotto, Quinta de la Rosa, Fogo by Borges's, Quinta das Murças, Reserva by Manoel Poças Junior, Quatro Ventos by Caves Aliança, Villar de Galeira by Barros, Quinta da Gaivosa, Vale da Raposa, and Incognito by Alves de Sousa, Quinta do Vallado, Quinta de la Rosa, Quinta do Ventozelo, Quinta do Cachão Grande Escolha by Caves Messias, Confradeiro by Sandeman, Grande Escolha by Quinta da Cotto, Calços de Tanha by Manuel Pinto Hespanhol, Tinta Roriz and Auru by Quinta da Portal, Poeria by Quinta da Terra Feita, Quinta da Sa, Quinta do Vale do Dona Maria, Quinta das Pias by Lavadores de Feitora, Quinta da Passadouro, Quinta das Aciprestas by Real Compania Velha, Touriga Nacional by Barros, Quinta de Macedos, the entire line of wines from Quinta do Crasto, and Douro Antonio by Quinta do Noval, which also makes a moderately priced Vinho Regional Duriense, Cedro do Noval.

Porto: The Fortified Wine of the Douro

No discussion of the Douro can omit its famous *denominação de origem controlada* Porto. Porto is a fortified wine made by transferring fermented wine with an alcohol content of 6 to 7 percent to *pipes* (casks) containing clear **AGUARDENTE** (grape brandy) that is 77 percent alcohol/154 proof. The ratio is 116 gallons/440 liters of wine to 29 gallons/110 liters of spirit. The final Porto product ranges between 18 and 20 percent alcohol.

The chief concern when grapes arrive at a winery is to achieve the maximum amount of color extraction from the skins before the addition of *aguardente*. The grapes are usually destemmed to reduce bitterness. At the winery, a portion of the grapes (if not all) may be crushed in rollers.

However, some of the best Porto wines are made in the traditional manner—in *lagares,* or stone troughs. (See photo below.) They may be made of granite or slate and can hold a couple dozen people. Once feet are inspected for cleanliness, crushers are set to the task of the *corte,* a controlled treading of the grapes by foot, for several hours. The idea is to get the most extract from the *manta,* or cap, and not to crush the grape pips, which, like stems, contribute overly bitter tannins. The *manta,* which consists of the skins (and other matter), contains the pigments so vital to maintaining the dark color of Porto. Once the fermentation is under way, wooden planks are put over the top of the *lagar.* Workers stand on the planks and continue to push the cap down with wooden plungers into the wine until the proper color and tannins are extracted. The Symington family uses robotic treading machines at Quinta da Sol, which apply 0.264 pounds per square inch/120 grams per square

centimeter of pressure, similar to the human foot. The robot "feet" are also warmed to simulate the warmth of human feet.

Similar results can be obtained mechanically by using an autovinifier. The autovinification method (known as the Ducellier system in Algeria, where it began) uses large closed vats. Pressure builds up from carbon dioxide and forces juice up and over the *manta,* extracting color and tannins. Autovinification is obviously less labor-intensive than the system using *lagares,* does not require electricity, and allows for a great deal of color and tannin extraction in a short, hot fermentation (84°–88°F/29°–31°C) before fortification. The first containers used were concrete, but stainless steel is preferred today. Some producers are now using a combination of *remontage* (pumping over) followed by autovinification. Another method for obtaining the dark color and tannins desired is to add back the press wine to the final product (see Chapter 2, page 66).

STYLES OF PORTO

Porto may be made from one harvest or a blend of years. It is the aging period that determines the wine's style and how it may be labeled. The two main types are the ruby or vintage style, which is bottled young, and the wood or tawny style, which is aged longer in a cask prior to bottling.

The wines in casks are racked (see Chapter 2, page 72) at least once a year, and over time the precipitation of the sediments and the slight oxidation that takes place in the cask result in lighter-colored, softer, aged **TAWNY PORTOS** that may be consumed when released. Wines must be submitted to the IVP for a tasting and chemical analysis before being approved.

Various styles of Porto exist, each with its own loyal following. The IVP uses thirty-one parameters to judge Porto quality, and the superior Portos (beyond basic white, ruby, and tawny) must score 7 out of 10 to receive the seal, while crusted and vintage must score 9 out of 10. The IVP also checks the authenticity of product and ensures that *no more than a third of stock is sold each year.* Also, only a portion of the Douro's wines may be made into Porto; the balance must be used for table wines.

Foot-trodding in lagar *for the crush at Quinta do Vesùvio. The Symington family uses this technique for some wines, while others are made using "robots."*

PLEASURES OF YOUTH

RUBY

RUBY PORTO is a youthful blend that spends up to three years in stainless steel or wood before it is bottled. Red and black fruit flavors are present in both the nose and taste of this sweet wine. This category of inexpensive Porto is much appreciated in northern Europe. Historically, natives coming indoors from the cold weather would make a cocktail of this high-alcohol wine to warm them up before dining.

RUBY RESERVE

These higher-quality ruby blended Porto wines are aged four to six years. They are usually made with less maceration time than vintage Portos, resulting in wines with less concentration and complexity than vintage Portos. These wines are a good value for those not prepared to invest in vintage or **INDICATED-AGE TAWNIES**. They are from finer sources than regular ruby and make up about 12 percent of total annual production. Warre's Warrior, Graham's 6 Grapes, Sandeman's Founder's Reserve, and Fonseca Bin 27 are some recommended examples of this style of Porto. They do not have to include the term "Super Ruby" or "Vintage Character" on their labels.

SINGLE QUINTA

True single-*quinta* Porto is made from the grapes of one vineyard and may be vintage or nonvintage. New legislation under consideration will require single-*quinta* wines to be not only made from grapes grown on the estate, but also *bottled* on the estate. As it now stands, single-*quinta* Porto can be made at one of the Port lodges in the city of Vila Nova de Gaia or can be just a *quinta* brand name.

The 1986 law allowing Porto to be made and exported by grower-producers from the Douro without lodges in Vila Nova de Gaia has opened the door for many wonderful single-*quinta* bottled wines. Single-*quinta* producers often elect to wait a few years after bottling to release these wines so they are immediately ready for consumption.

Controversy about single-*quinta* wines exists because some producers label their wines from an "off" or nonvintage year with the name of a single vineyard, while others are truly fine expressions of a single site. An example of the former is Guimaraens by Fonseca and an example of the latter is Quinta de Vargellas by Taylor Fladgate—two wines sourced from the Douro and made by the same firm in Oporto. Another example would be from the Symington family, who declare a Vintage Graham's Port only in the finest years and in other years sell the wine as Quinta do Bonfim.

Quinta do Vesùvio, Quinta do Noval (they also make a very expensive Quinta do Noval Nacional), Quinta do Portal, Quinta do Vale do Meão, and Quinta do Crasto are single estates who source their grapes, ferment, age, and bottle all their wines in the Douro.

A sampling of Port labels: The Fonseca Bin 27 Ruby Reserve, the Taylor Fladgate Single-Vineyard Vintage, the Dow's Late-Bottled Vintage, the Graham's 1980 Vintage, and the 20 Year Tawny Port from Ramos Pinto

CRUSTED

Crusted Portos are blended wines bottled early. Dark and powerful in their youth, they share some of the characteristics of vintage Porto and, similarly, should always be decanted when served. These Portos are not produced by all wineries; Dow's makes a great Crusted Port.

LATE-BOTTLED VINTAGE (LBV)

This type of Porto is made from a single vintage and bottled, from oak cask or stainless steel tank, between July 1 of the fourth year and December 31 of the sixth year after the harvest. LBV wines labeled "Bottle Matured" (*Envelhecido em Garrafa*) may be released after a minimum of three years of aging. Warre's make wonderful Bottle Matured wines that are aged four years in cask and four in bottle before release. Quinta do Noval, Niepoort, and Fonseca offer delicious "Unfiltered" wines. Wines labeled as Bottle Matured or Unfiltered are longer lived, richer, and more complex than LBV wines that have been fined, filtered, and cold stabilized.

The wines that do merit aging are sealed with a traditional driven cork, while those meant for consumption on release have a screwcap.

The former must be decanted, while the latter do not require decanting. Similar to the different styles of French Champagne houses, the producers of late-bottled vintage and vintage Portos each offer a unique house style. It is more affordable to experiment with the LBVs, which usually cost under $30 retail, than the true vintage and single-*quinta* vintage wines. This style of Port has a lot of variation in flavor, body, tannins, sweetness to some degree, and longevity.

VINTAGE

Vintage Porto is the rarest and most expensive style made. Only the finest vineyard sites and grapes are used. The best producers use a selection of the superior grape varieties from the best *quintas* for their high-end wines. The wines must be bottled between July 1 of the second year and July 30 of the third year after the harvest.

Vintage Porto is bottled young, when the wine is an opaque, dark purple in color with very high tannin and fruit concentration. This is an appropriate generalization, but take the opportunity to smell and taste a variety of vintage wines to discover the consistent style each Port firm maintains. For example, from the Symington families products, the Dow's wines generally have more black fruit and chocolate flavors and are drier and more muscular than those from Warre's, which have more bright red fruit, floral and menthol flavors, and a little more sweetness.

Over years in the bottle, pigment matter and tannins form sediments, making it necessary to decant these wines before serving (see Chapter 16, page 659). The wines should project a sense of harmony or balance, allowing the complexities of bouquet and taste to be fully enjoyed. For some, a vintage Porto is best after twenty years of aging, while others jump on the wine as soon as it is released. Decanting a young vintage wine for a couple of hours will allow it to open up and reveal more of its personality than just pouring it straightaway.

The more companies that declare a vintage, the more likely it is that a given year will be accepted as superior by collectors and the trade. For example, in 1970, thirty-nine companies declared vintages; in 1952, only two companies did. Outstanding vintages from this and the last century include 2007, 2003, 2000, 1997, 1995, 1994, 1992, 1991, 1985, 1983 (though more tannic and robust, they will be longer-lived than the early-harvested 1982s), 1982 (as many producers declared a vintage in 1982, they declined to do so in 1983), 1977, 1975 (first vintage bottled entirely in Portugal), 1970, 1966, 1963, 1960, 1955, 1948, 1945, 1935, 1931, 1927, 1924, 1922, 1920, 1917, 1912, and 1908.

GRACE AND ELEGANCE WITH AGE

TAWNY

True, high-quality tawny Porto is aged at least six years in the cask before release. When the bottling date is provided, the consumer should enjoy the product within a couple of years from the date. These wines, served slightly cooler than vintage styles at 44.6°F/7°C, have a nose of dried fruits and nuts. The taste is not as rich and sweet nor as tannic as the ruby and vintage styles.

The majority of tawnies are only three years old and are produced by the lighter-style techniques to give the trade a less expensive, high-volume product. Less expensive commercial tawnies are made by using red wines with less color extraction or by blending white and red Porto together to achieve a tawny color. Delaforce, for example, makes an affordable version.

INDICATED-AGE TAWNIES

The four products available are the 10 Year, 20 Year, 30 Year, and 40 Year versions. The wines are made from a blend of vintages. The indicated age is the average age of

the wines used for each type. Average age is a quality indicator set by the Instituto do Vinho do Porto. If the wine does not pass taste tests, it will not receive the IVP's seal. The complexities of a 30 Year Old or a 40 Year Old compared with a younger wine have made the indicated-age category a favorite of many wine lovers.

Flavors of dried fruits, honey, and spice are common in these wines, and they usually have a good degree of acidity to balance their sweetness. They can be the most elegant of all the Porto styles. Predictably, price increases with age. The retail price for a 10 Year Tawny should be about $30, 20 Year about $50 (a superb value), while a 30 Year or a 40 Year wine will cost from $65 to $150. Indicated-age tawnies must carry the date of bottling on the label. The 40 Year tawnies and **COLHEITA** Portos (see below) are aged longer before release than any other wines in the world. The amber color of younger tawnies evolves into a wine with green highlights for the 30 or 40 Year indicated-age wines.

House styles vary among producers, just as several methods of ensuring consistency in those house styles exist. Winemaker David Guimarens sets aside selected wine lots after four or five years for blending into their Fonseca or Taylor Fladgate & Yeatman wines of this style. João Nicolau de Almeida of Adriano Ramos Pintos keeps a *madre,* or mother blend, of each of the 10s, 20s, 30s, and 40s. When he draws a portion from a *madre* to bottle, he then replenishes it, thus never depleting the entire stock of his *madre.*

COLHEITA

Colheita is an aged tawny from a single vintage. The wines are legally cask-aged for a minimum of seven years yet can be aged for up to fifty. They vary in style by both vintage and house but, like indicated-age tawnies, while aging they develop a softer fruit and lower tannin profile with an intriguing bouquet. Some of the firms specializing in *colheitas* include Niepoort, Cálem, Poças, Kopke, and Burmester. These wines are not as easy to find as the indicated-age blends. They are ready to enjoy upon release.

A view of the Douro vineyards

PLEASANT PORTS

WHITE

White Portos are made in both semidry and sweeter styles, with the sweetest labeled *lagrima*. Most often served as an aperitif, these wines are best when chilled. A popular cocktail in Port houses is a mixture of white Port and tonic. Grapes used include the Malvasia for its floral nose, the Viosinho for its sweet nose, and both the Rabigato and the Gouveio for acidity. Some producers use skin contact for the fermentation of their white grapes. The wines aged in oak have a nutty character.

ROSÉ

In 2008, Croft introduced this new category of Porto. Short skin contact creates a low-tannin wine with lots of red cherry and strawberry flavors. Serve chilled, alfresco for a summer picnic.

DOURO VALLEY SUMMARY

True Porto wine is only produced in the Douro Valley of Portugal, the oldest demarcated wine region in the world; or one of the two oldest. Hungarians, who believe Tokaji Aszú is the oldest, challenge this distinction. Regardless of seniority, the ultimate Porto experience is in tasting the vintage wines (including single-*quintas*) and indicated-age tawnies (including *colheita*). They are unparalleled, delicious wines with sweetness as only one part of their charm.

North America leads in consumption of premium Portos. The biggest markets in volume sales of all styles of Porto are, in order, France, Holland, Portugal, Belgium, and Britain. Though many northern European countries serve Porto as an aperitif, it is traditionally consumed at the end of a meal with aged (Cheddar, Jack) or blue cheeses (Stilton, Maytag), nuts, or dried fruits, or as a dessert unto itself. Panna cotta, *crème de marron* (chestnut cream) over vanilla ice cream, and carrot cake (not too sweet) are excellent with 10 Year Tawny. For a more adventurous pairing, try tawny with sautéed foie gras and quince.

White and rosé Porto wines are a minor part of a Porto producer's portfolio and are not as complex as some of the previously discussed styles.

The commercial-grade tawnies and simple rubies make up over 80 percent of each year's production. The finer ruby and tawny wines are known as premium Ports. Inexpensive wines may be served chilled or in a drink with club soda. Tawnies can be served with just a slight chill or

PORTO PRODUCERS

The firms of Porto include Adriano Ramos Pinto, Quinta da Amarela, J. H. Andresen, Barros Almeida, Borges and Irmão, Burmester, Cálem, Champalimaud, Churchill Graham, Cockburn Smithies, Croft, Dalva, Delaforce, Dow's, H. and C. J. Feist, Ferreira, Fonseca Guimaraens, Gould Campbell, W. and J. Graham, Gran Cruz, Hutcheson, Kopke, Martinez-Gassiot, Niepoort, Offley Forrester, Osborne, Manoel Poças Junior, Presidential, Quarles Harris, Quinta do Castelinho, Quinta da Crasto, Quinta da Pacheca, Quinta do Portal, Quinta de la Rosa, Quinta do Tedo, Quinta do Vale do Dona Maria, Quinta do Vale do Meão, Quinta do Vallado, Quinta do Ventozelo, Quinta do Infantado, Quinta do Noval, Quinta do Vesùvio, Rainha Santa, Real Companhia Velha, Robertson (also bottled as Rebello Valente), Romariz, Royal Oporto, Rozés, Sandeman, Smith Woodhouse, Souza, Taylor Fladgate & Yeatman, Van Zellers, Warre's, Wiese & Krohn, and Wine and Soul.

at cellar temperature (about 55°F / 12.75°C) while the late-bottled vintage and vintage wines are best served at about 62°–65°F/16.7°–18.3°C. Two to two and a half ounces is the proper amount to serve in a thin-lipped glass.

The fine white and red still wines of the Douro deserve a thin-lipped glass of a sufficient size to swirl, smell, and savor. Five ounces is a standard pour for still wines. The future is bright for the single-variety wines led by the native Touriga Nacional and for the blended wines.

There is also a small amount of fortified, sweet Moscatel produced in the Douro region.

MINHO VINHO REGIONAL: VINHO VERDE DOC

THE NATION OF PORTUGAL, created in 1143, is one of the oldest in Europe. Its first capital under its first king, Alfonso Henriques, was in this Minho province in the town of Guimarães.

Minho is named after the river Minho, which defines the Spanish border to the north. Though Minho comprises only 9.2 percent of the nation's landmass, over 20 percent of the population lives in this verdant area. This

HISTORY OF THE DOURO

Portos from a single, unblended year were first recognized in 1734. In the 1750s the Marquis of Pombal established a controlling agency that eventually reduced the area where Porto could be made, restricted the addition of manure to the soil (to avoid increasing the yield per plant), and ended the practice of adding elderberries to the wine (which gave it a darker color and more fruit flavor).

Shipped in bulk, lower in alcohol than it is now, and put into squat bottles with poorly fitted corks, the wines of this period would sometimes spoil. The longer, cylindrical bottle (so useful for aging vintage Porto) replaced the squatter version circa 1775. The superior bottle design, with proper corks, allowed the wines to be cellared for longer periods. Most of the vintage-dated wines, bound for Britain, were shipped in **PIPES** (casks of 145.2 gallons/550 liters, equivalent to sixty cases of wine) and subsequently bottled in England. Trade agreements with the British began with the Treaty of Windsor in 1385 and continued with the Methuen Treaty (1703), which gave Portugal preferential trade status with England. Some Portuguese natives resisted the English influence on their wine business and pushed for laws that would benefit domestically owned wineries.

By 1786, the British regained some of their influence in Portugal and established the Factory House in Oporto. This edifice was built only for British firms dealing in wine. The members of this powerful agricultural club still meet every Wednesday, as they have for over two centuries, to discuss the state of the Porto business and the actions of the farmers, producers, and governmental agencies.

James Forrester perhaps best exemplifies the British influence on the wines of Porto. One of the most influential Englishmen in the history of the Porto trade, Forrester emigrated to work for the family firm in Oporto in 1831. His contributions include very specific writings on the sites within the Douro and on growing and maintaining the grapes within those sites. His detailed maps of the region's topography and his hydraulic maps of the Douro were a boon to those in the trade. Forrester favored what he called a "return to the old system," to the making of "pure, dry wines" prepared with a lot of fermentation, fortified with little or no added *aguardente,* and aged. Because of his influence, by the mid-1800s standard practice was to fortify Porto to its current 18 to 20 percent alcohol level, leave the wine in casks for four years, then let it mature slowly in the bottle.

Though Forrester was the foreigner with the most influence historically, clearly Antónia Adelaida Ferreira, who was widowed at age thirty-three, remains a local legend in the Douro. She was a great contributor to the expansion of vineyards and roads throughout the region, while she also financed the building of schools and hospitals in the Douro. Her vision of development and quality led the firm of Ferreira to be the largest landholders of the nineteenth century. Located in the Douro Superior, Ferreira's first vineyard was planted in 1888, yet the first declared vintage of a noble dry red wine was not until 1952, when winemaker Fernando Nicolau de Almeida returned from a visit to Bordeaux, France.

Before the phylloxera pest struck in the late 1800s, farmers in the Douro made single-variety dry whites from Moscatel and Malvasia Fina and reds from Touriga Nacional and Sousão. The scourge forced many farmers to replant using American rootstock, and today the vinifera grape varieties grown have evolved from more than eighty approved varieties to new plantings focusing on about a dozen of the finest grape types.

Major changes in shipping the wines of the Douro occurred in the 1870s with the arrival of the railway. The construction of the Carrapatelo Dam signaled the demise of the traditional *barco rabelo* (flat-bottomed boat) used to transport wine down to Oporto and to the *armazéms* (lodges) across the river in Vila Nova de Gaia. Today, most wines are transported by rail or truck.

In 1914, the Portuguese and British signed a treaty officially defining Porto. A 1974 law stated that vintage Porto may only be sold in bottles and must bear the *selo de origem* (seal of origin) from the Douro. In the same year, the Port Wine Exporters Association was formed and declared that *all Porto wine must be bottled in Portugal.*

The Douro studies for the selection of the finest vinifera (begun in 1967) were led by João Nicolau de Almeida and José António Rosas, with assistance from the Associação Para o Desenvolvimento da Viticultura Durense (ADVID), the local university, and other wine professionals. Through tastings and experiments based on microvinification, they determined the top five red grapes to be Touriga Nacional, Tinta Roriz, Tinta Barroca, Tinta Cão, and Touriga Franca. In 1986, the World Bank financed the planting of 6,175 acres/2,500 hectares in the Douro on the condition that only these grape types be planted. Since then, financial assistance from the EU for new plantings has also been contingent on using these grapes.

A 1986 law eased limitations on where Porto must be stored (and therefore bottled), making it easier for growers to bottle their own wine. This law has created an exciting opportunity for some small farmers or producers to grow, ferment, and age complex estate-bottled wines in small quantities. Today some of these single-estate *quinta* wines are among the finest wines of the world, both as dry red Douro wines and as sweet fortified Portos.

The small *quinta* producers certainly merit praise, but some of the prominent leaders of the region should be recognized for their historic contributions and their continuing research in elevating the wines of the area.

A father and son head the list. The father, Fernando Nicolau de Almeida, made Portugal's benchmark fine dry red wine Barca Velha. The traditional blend was 60 percent Tinta Roriz, 10 percent Tinta Barroca, 10 percent Tinta Amarela, and 20 percent Touriga Franca. The original version was made possible by bringing huge blocks of ice up from Oporto to keep the fermentation temperature down. Today, wines undergo temperature-controlled fermentation in stainless steel and are then allowed to rest in Portuguese oak casks. The scent of Barca Velha often includes violets, blackberries, figs, Damson plums, and spice. The wine is full-bodied and rich in fruit, and it

Oporto, where the Douro runs into the sea, is the center of the Porto wine trade, and most Porto is stored at lodges in Vila Nova de Gaia.

has good acidity to support its weight. José Maria Soares-Franco is the respected winemaker at Ferreira, where he also makes the excellent wine Ferreirinha Reserva Especial as well as Quinta da Leda.

João Nicolau de Almeida, son of Fernando, may be the finest winemaker of the Douro for both still and Port wines. His research on the top five grape varieties in the Douro and their characteristics, as well as his work in vineyards and winery techniques, has benefited Adriano Ramos Pinto as well as other farmers and wineries in the Douro. All the wines of Ramos Pinto offer great value and flavor, but the aged single-vineyard tawnies, such as the 20 Year Quinta da Evormoira, are truly exceptional.

Next is Vito Olazabal, who was at the helm of the Ferreira winery (he is Antónia Adelaida's grandson) and now owns one of Portugal's most celebrated wines, Quinta do Vale do Meão. He is also the elder statesman of "The Douro Boys," an association of single *quintas* producing some of the best wines in Portugal. The other members include Quinta do Crasto, Quinta do Vale do Dona Maria, Quinta do Vallado, and Niepoort.

Also, the work of the Symington family must be acknowledged. The family owns Quinta do Vesùvio, Dow's, Quarles Harris, Smith-Woodhouse, W. and J. Graham, Warre's, and Quinta da Roriz (part owner), and all are respected producers of Porto, yet their still wines are also delicious. The Symingtons championed the expression of single-*quinta* wines in the Douro. They own over 2,470 acres/1,000 hectares of vineyards that are spread out over twenty-three *quintas*. Their tireless efforts to increase the quality of their wines has led to the use of robots to press grapes and trials with different trellising systems and plant density. Miles Edelman is the vineyard manager, and his field trials will benefit others in the region.

Lastly, a salute to the contributions of another father-and-son team. The late, larger-than-life Bruce Guimarens led the way for Taylor Fladgate and Fonseca wineries for many years, and his son David is now their winemaker. The company's Portos at every price point are dependable and among the tastiest available.

The history of the Douro is in the minds of everyone involved in the wine trade. With respect to tradition and a keen sense of adventure, they know they have the raw materials, the artistic vision, and the science to continue to produce some of the finest wines in the world.

region has a longer winemaking tradition than the Douro and has been exporting its wines for seven hundred years. Although the area was first demarcated in 1908, the *selo de garantia* control and approval system began in 1959.

Vinho Regional Minho wines can be quite good. The vineyard location, the grapes planted, or the methods of production may motivate a winery to label their wines as Minho rather than Vinho Verde. An example is the Casa de Cello, which makes fine dry Minho wines under the Quinta da Sanjoanne label. The Superior blend of Alvarinho and Malvasia is all stainless steel, while their Escolha is a barrel-aged blend of Alvarinho, Avesso, and Chardonnay grapes.

Both the popular white and less popular red DOC wines from the Minho are called Vinho Verde. Vinho Verde (green wine) gets its name not because of its color, but because it is best enjoyed when young and fresh, not **MADURO** (mature or aged).

The principal soil type in this region is granite. The area is planted with an abundance of Australian gum trees that prefer this type of soil. Harvested for paper products, these trees deplete the soil of moisture needed to grow grapes. Therefore, irrigation is permitted under extreme conditions, authorized by local boards, and practiced despite an average rainfall four times that of the Douro. Though breezes from the Atlantic moderate the temperatures somewhat, the days are hot and the nights are chilly, resulting in grapes that mature slowly on the vine.

A sixteenth-century law forcing farmers to grow grains and other food crops required that grapes be planted only on the periphery of fields, where some can still be found today. As a result, numerous ways to plant vines for Vinho Verde exist, but most involve training the vines to grow up to great heights (*enforcado*). Advantages include protection from spring frosts and rot; also, there is room for second crops of lower-bearing fruits and vegetables. Growing the vines tall also prevents excessive heat from reflecting off the soil onto the grapes. *Enforcado* is the term used for

Vines grown by the traditional enforcado *system in the Minho region. The grapes are shielded from excessive heat by the canopy of leaves and do not get much reflected heat because they are high off the ground.*

forcing the vines upward, often on tree trunks, and then stretching them across branches to other trees. Variations include the *ramada* or *latada* versions—trellises supported by posts. The *cruzeta,* or cross system, has posts over 6 feet/1.8 meters high and double rows of wires to support grapes. In cooler climates, where grapes have difficulty ripening, low-bearing systems are used where there are heat-retentive and heat-reflective soils. Lower-planted single-wire systems called *bardo,* as well as other modern trellising systems, are increasing in popularity because it allows the *quintas* to do mechanical harvesting.

Minho is known internationally for its white wines. Excellent values, these wines are light-bodied and acidic, low in alcohol, a bit spritzy, and full of fruit flavor. The minimum acidity is 0.2 ounces per gallon/6 grams per liter by law, and the minimum alcohol content is 8 percent. There are no aging requirements and they often do not carry a vintage date. The wines are usually bottled from the original container in which they were fermented in an effort to prevent oxidization. Stainless steel or epoxy-lined vats allow for cooler fermenting than wood. Malolactic fermentation is not practiced, since most producers want to retain as much acidity as possible in the wines. Adding carbon dioxide before bottling is permitted, but the amount rarely exceeds one atmosphere. Fully sparkling wines must achieve 10 percent alcohol and be aged at least nine months before they are sold.

The thicker-skinned Alvarinho produces wines with more body than the average Vinho Verde, and the scent is reminiscent of apple, peaches, and lime with some floral hints as well. The wines are rich without being heavy, and may be enjoyed young or aged for five to ten years.

The subregions are Amarante, Ave, Baiao, Basto, Cavado, Val de Lima, Palva, Sousa and the stellar Monção (which includes Melgaço). Vinho Verde wines with an alcohol level over 11.5 percent must include the name of one of these subregions on the wine label. Wines from the Moncão subregion and single-variety Alvarinho wines must achieve a minimum of 11.5 percent and maximum of 13 percent alcohol. Yields are 25 percent lower than that of other Vinho Verdes. Only Alvarinho, Loureiro, and Trajadura may be grown in Moncão.

Anselmo Mendes has dedicated his professional life to making the best white wines of Portugal. His single-variety wines and blends from the Vinho Verde region and environs are superb. He sometimes uses a technique of leaving the skins of the white grapes in contact with the

juice for 48 hours before fermenting at 59°F/15°C. His finest Alvarinho wines then spend nine months aging with the lees in oak barrels. He believes that the wines from the Melgaço subregion of the Monção have more minerality and acidity, while the Monção offers a more floral expression. Anselmo believes that the best source for Loureiro is from the Val de Lima subregion and the best Avesso comes from the border area with the Douro.

Quinta do Covela is another believer in sourcing their white grapes from the area by the border of the Douro. He also crafts wines for other wineries, such as his Douro and Dão reds for Azul Portugal.

The other Minho pioneers that deserve special mention are the Guedes family of Quinta da Aveleda. They have produced basic Vinho Verde wines in a variety of styles from off-dry and spritzy inexpensive blends to bone-dry and single-variety wines. Their green-labeled Vinho Verde blend has 15 grams of residual sugar per liter, while their white label has only 3 grams. The blend for the white label is 55 percent Loureiro, 32 percent Trajadura, and 13 percent Alvarinho.

The most famous of the Alvarinho-Monção wines and producers are Muros Antigos by Anselmo Mendes, Palácio da Brejoeira, Muralhas de Monção by the Adega

Inexpensive blends from Vinho Verde are the most popular whites of Portugal and should be drunk in their youth. The more complex Alvarinho wines are fuller in body and may be cellared for five years or more. Vinho Verde blends are our go-to wine for summertime sipping, as they are light, low-alcohol, and go with a wide range of foods, including spicy hot dishes.

Cooperative Regional de Moncão, Quinta da Aveleda, Morgadio da Torre by Sogrape, Carapeços, and Soalheiro. The pride of Portugal's white wines can be enjoyed for $12 to $25 retail—truly a great value. The medium to full body of an Alvarinho can balance a rich codfish dish. Other fine pairings for Alvarinho include butter-poached lobster, roast chicken with tarragon, or butternut squash ravioli with toasted pumpkin seeds.

Some cooperatives in Portugal are still churning out mass-produced inexpensive wines, but the Moncão co-op is one of Portugal's finest. The Adega Cooperativo, which began in 1958 with just 25 members, now has over 1,700 farmers, and their line of wines from the basic Vinho Verde to the Deu de Deu Alvarinho are superb. A 1999 Alvarinho of theirs recently tasted exhibited aromas and flavors of orange blossom, apricot, tangerine, and petrol, with great length and acidity. Those descriptors sound similar to some aged Rieslings; more importantly, they are proof that fine Alvarinho wines can improve with age.

Quinta do Ameal makes a lovely pure Loureiro with fresh flavors of lemon and Bartlett pear that is worth seeking out, as is the Muros Antigos Loureiro by Anselmo Mendes. Mendes and José Domingues of PROVAM collaborate to make Côto de Mamoelas Bruto Reserva Alvarinho Espumante. They use the *méthode champenoise,* and this fine wine is aged a year before release.

Often under $10 a bottle and less than 10 percent alcohol, Vinho Verde blends are about the most important summertime wines. These spritzy and tart wines are not intimidated by spicy fare such as seafood or chicken prepared in a Thai curry, Cajun blackened, or Indian vindaloo style. Shrimp, chicken, or vegetable fajitas with spicy jalapeño salsa are another option for versatile Vinho Verde wines.

A few of the leading brands of Vinho Verde are the wines of Quinta da Aveleda, Gatão by Borges and Irmão, Casa de Sezim, Tâmega, Famega, Fuzelo, Casa de Vila Verde, Broadbent, and Gazela made by Sogrape. Five million liters of Gazela are consumed each year. The wine is made from a blend of Loureiro, Pedernã, and Trajadura grapes. The base wines are kept stable with sulfur until they are needed. A special machine is used to remove the sulfur so the fermentation can begin. A similar process is used to produce some Lambrusco wines from Italy.

Other Vinho Verde wines we suggest include Alvarinho Portal do Fidalgo by Provam, Alvarinho by Qunita do Feital, Alvarinho by Quinta do Carapeços, Alvarinho

Quinta da Pedra by Vinompor, a Pedernã-based white by Borges, and blended whites from Quinta do Minho and Capeçanes.

The tart and spritzy red wines are mostly consumed within the region. They are best served cool, and when poured from a few inches above the traditional ceramic cups used for drinking, the wines froth up! Vinho Verde red wines are under 10 percent alcohol and, like Beaujolais Nouveau, are ready to drink within several months of the harvest. Reds are made from indigenous grapes such as Espadeiro (also known as Tinta Amarela), Vinhão (also called Sousão), Borraçal, and Tinto Azal.

As in many of the world's wine regions, local wine with local fare and good company can make a memorable experience. Especially well-suited for summer quaffing, white Vinho Verde works well as an aperitif, and its cleansing qualities also make it a useful companion to a wide range of foods. A chilled red Vinho Verde with its red berry flavors, high acidity, low alcohol, and slight effervescence complements a broad variety of dishes beyond the regional foods such as *bacalhau* (codfish).

BEIRAS VINHO REGIONAL: BAIRRADA DOC, DÃO DOC

THE LARGE BEIRAS REGION is split into the Littoral near the Atlantic Ocean, and the Alta (upper) and Terras de Sicó (lower) inland areas. The area is mountainous and has many steep-sloped vineyards. High altitude results in wines with a good vein of acidity, as the slopes allow for both water and air drainage.

The trend today is to declassify wines from the DOCs of Bairrada and Dão to the more broad Beiras Vinho Regional classification in order to have the freedom to make wines that challenge the traditional "recipes" of those DOCs.

Luis Pato is the best-known producer of Bairrada DOC wines internationally. He now labels all his wines as Beiras to allow him the creative freedom of expression in the composition of his wines. We highlight his wines in this section, as he is acknowledged domestically and internationally as one of the nation's finest winemakers.

Luis Pato's tireless travels around the globe to promote his beloved Baga grape and Bairrada brought much respect to Portuguese wines in general. Today, he continues to experiment with Baga by blending it with Touriga Nacional, planting it without grafted rootstocks in sandy soils (his Pé Franco wine), and making different styles of wines that express their birthplace. Pato believes the Baga grape is best when grown on clay soils with some chalk. He cites that the climatic influences of the Atlantic Ocean is similar to Bordeaux (and perhaps better), since more sunshine in Bairrada's vineyards allows for natural ripeness of the grapes without the need for chaptalization. Another physical advantage of his vineyard sources is that some are surrounded by eucalyptus trees, which impart their flavor to his wines.

Pato's entry-level dry red wines are the pure Baga Vinhas Velhas (the name means "old vines") and a Baga–Touriga Nacional blend. Both are excellent values. His dry red, Vigna Pan (an abbreviation of the Portuguese for "vineyard Penascera"), offers bright red plum and rosehip flavors and is medium- to full-bodied.

For a weightier expression of Baga, try his Vinha Barossa or Pé Franco wines. The seventy-year-old Barossa section of the vineyard is naturally low yielding. Young Barossa red wines are full-bodied and have high acidity to balance the tannic grip of the wine. Flavors of young Barossa include black plum, black cherry, and licorice. With a decade or more of aging, some intriguing secondary and tertiary flavors such as walnut, violet, dried fig, coriander, and eucalyptus develop. Perhaps Pato's most elegant wine is the Pé Franco. It is 100 percent Baga grown on ungrafted wines in sandy soil. Pé Franco is full-bodied and offers violet, rose, raspberry, and spice flavors in youth. Pato's red wines can be cellared for over a decade.

Pato also produces two bargain-priced bubblies. His Bruto rosé sparkler is made by drawing off some of the juice from the red wine. It is garnet-colored with firm structure, bright acidity, and flavors of persimmon, rhubarb, and raspberry. The Foral white sparkler is based on Arinto and Bical grapes and has bright melon flavors. His crisp white Vinha Velhas wines are based on Bical, Cercealinho, and there is also a Maria Gomes dry white.

Filipa Pato, Luis's daughter, makes a Lokal Silex wine from Touriga Nacional and Alfrocheiro Preto grapes grown in the Dão, but because the wine is fermented outside of the DOC in Bairrada, it carries a Beiras Vinho Regional designation. The wine is full-bodied with black currant, dark chocolate, and earthy flavors.

Another top wine from the region is the Baga and Touriga Nacional blend Vinhas Velhas de Santa Maria by Quinta da Fonte de Arouce. The Reserva by Rogenda and Tinta Roriz Varosa by Murganheira are other fine reds bottled as Beiras. We also suggest the Murganheira dry white labeled Abadia Velha and the dry rosé Santola based on Baga and Tinta Roriz by Messias.

Bairrada DOC

The Bairrada region is mostly a coastal plain. Barro (clay) soil dominates the area, but there are also sandy, marl, and limestone areas. The region stretches from the city of Aveiro in the north to Coimbra in the south. There are over twenty thousand farmers growing grapes in the region. Farmers sell primarily to cooperatives or other large producers. Bairrada produces over 6.5 million cases of wine a year.

The Estacão Vitivinicola, a research station for viticulture founded in 1887, has provided guidance for many Bairrada growers. After the devastation of phylloxera in the late nineteenth century, the region exported a lot of their still and sparkling wines to Bordeaux, France. When Bordeaux's vineyards were restored, there was no more need for the still wines; however, sparkling exports continued.

Bairrada sparkling wines are made by the Champagne method and must be aged at least nine months before they are sold. They have a VEQPRD quality seal affixed to the neck of the bottle. About 60 percent of Portugal's sparkling wines are made in the region. Most are *bruto* or *seco* (dry), and some *meio seco* (semidry) wines are made as well. These inexpensive wines by producers such as Alianca and Messias may be enjoyed at a cocktail reception with a variety of foods, such as codfish fritters, codfish cakes, or *presunto* (the best cured ham of Portugal).

Luis Pato is one of the nation's finest winemakers. His old-vines Vinhas Velhas is a fine example of a Baga-based wine.

The Maria Gomes grape (also known as Fernão Pires) is used in both sparklers and still whites and accounts for over half the vineyard acreage devoted to white grapes in Bairrada. Wines made with this grape emit aromas of orange zest and pepper. The Bical (also called Borrado dos Moscas), second to Maria Gomes in plantings, lends structure to blends and is most often used in sparklers. The high-acid Cerceal provides a lanolin-type aroma. The Rabo de Ovelha (also called Rabigato) is an early ripener that makes a light-style wine. International varieties such as Chardonnay and Sauvignon Blanc are also grown in Bairrada.

We have saved the best for last in this section, for it is the red wines of the region that garner the most praise and generate the most excitement.

Over 80 percent of the wine in Bairrada is made from the high-acid, thin-skinned, tannic red Baga grape. Baga grapes are usually destemmed to avoid the harshest tannins. Other methods used to make the wines less tannic include carbonic maceration, less skin maceration time, and cooler fermentation temperatures. The results are wines rich with scents and flavors of berries and plums. Baga has been the heart and soul of Bairrada wines for a long time, but today, other red grapes are being used as well.

Current laws dictate that Bairrada *classico* wines must be made from at least 50 percent Baga and another 35 percent may come from Touriga Nacional, Castelão, Alfrocheiro Preto, Jaen, or Camarate. The balance of 15 percent can be from Aragonez, Bastardo, Cabernet Sauvignon, Merlot, Pinot Noir, Rufete, Syrah, Tinta Barroca, Tinto Cão, or Touriga Franca. Considering that only one winery has opted to use the term *classico* in the past few years, we believe that the current crop of Bairrada wines are made with whatever grape type or grape blends the wineries want to use.

For a pure expression of traditional Baga, try the Quinta da Bageiras Garrafeira wine by Sergio Alves Nuno. Eighty-year-old vineyards are the source of the grapes, which are stomped in *lagares*. The wine has a great attack of black fruits and acidity, followed by flavors of dark chocolate, black pepper, and black mission fig. This wine is textbook Bairrada.

Based in Bairrada and inspired by the use of grape varieties beyond Baga is Campolargo. Their Campolargo wine is a pure Pinot Noir. Other Campolargo wines we suggest include the Termão blend of Touriga Nacional, Castelão, and Cabernet Sauvignon and the Roi de Coisas Antigas blend of indigenous grapes including Touriga Nacional, Alfrocheiro Preto, Sousão, and of course Baga. The winery also produces enjoyable white and sparkling wines.

Luis Pato's daughter Filipa also makes Lokal Calcario, an ageworthy, full-bodied, dry red Bairrada. It is pure Baga and has an opaque deep purple color with aromas of violets and black plums, black cherry and dark chocolate, and flavors of black figs and pine needles with an acidity that builds with time on the palate. Luis and Filipa Pato make a sweet dessert wine by cryoextraction (post-harvest frozen grapes) from Sercealinho, Bical, and Maria Gomes grapes that they refer to as their "molecular" wine.

Quinta da Aveleda, best known for its white Vinho Verde wines, makes some good value Bairrada Follies wines. Try the Touriga Nacional (80 percent) and Cabernet Sauvignon (20 percent) blend, which has flavors of black currant and licorice, or their pure Touriga Nacional, which offers rose petal and eucalyptus scents. Quinta do Encontro makes a bargain-priced red Bairrada.

Travelers to the region should experience the delicious local dish: pork roasted in a wood oven, known as *leitão*. The succulent *leitão* pork dish is a specialty of the Bairrada region. Locals can cleanse their palate from the richness of the dish with sparkling *espumante* or crisp whites in the daytime. In the evening, the native Baga grape is the foundation for wines with the high tannins necessary to balance the dish.

Once satiated with a "dose" or two of *leitão* sold at roadside restaurants, we entreat our readers to travel back in time and visit the gardens of the royal hunting palace known as Bussaco. The hotel not only has lovely gardens, but also makes an ageworthy red wine worth trying. Other tourist highlights include the local art museum and nearby city of Coimbra, home to Europe's second-oldest university. Coimbra is a city with a unique personality. Many students don the traditional black cape and cap even when they are carousing. Other tourist attractions in Bairrada we recommend include the wine museum and the school for winemaking.

Recommended Bairrada producers include Aliança, Casa de Saima, Campolargo, Messias, Quinta do Encontro, Quinta de Foz de Arouce, Filipa Pato, Quinta da Poco de Lobo, Quinta de Baixo, Sogrape, Marques de Marialva, and the wines of the Hotel Palace do Bussaco.

Dão DOC

The Dão area, located to the east of Bairrada, is warmer and drier than the Bairrada region located to its west. Vineyards benefit from the moderating influence of the

Dão and Mondego rivers. A *meseta* (plateau) of mostly granite with some clay, schist, and sandy soils is host to vineyards planted at 1,312 to 2,624 feet/400 to 800 meters. The mountainous terrain of the Serra da Estrella protects the vineyards in the southeast from warm southern winds, and the Serra do Caramulo to the west from rain and wind from the Atlantic Ocean. Forests of pine and eucalyptus also offer protection from wind. The best vineyards are commonly planted at high elevations, with the steepest laid out in labor-intensive terraces. Some lighter wines are made from the flatter, sandier sections in the west.

About 75 percent of the region's production is red wine, but whites are also planted, mostly on the fertile schist-based or sandy soils.

Dão wines are aged longer than the national minimum amount of time. *Reserva* red wines must be aged a minimum of twenty-four months and Garrafeira reds a minimum of thirty-six months (twelve in bottle) from the harvest before they may be sold.

Dão red wines are available from $8 to $80. The medium- and higher-priced wines have a spicy, earthy character and a good balance of acids to tannins in a medium- to medium-full-bodied style. The red wines are certainly food friendly. Most wines have high acidity to balance bitter tannins and refresh the palate. Red fruit and spices offer possibilities to complement similar flavors in dishes they are paired with. Grilled meats, coriander soup, and jugged hare are some of the local dishes that pair well with the red wines.

Legislation requires that blended red wines include at least 20 percent Touriga Nacional. There has been an increase in single-varietal wines based on the Touriga Nacional and Tinta Roriz (described earlier in this chapter) as well as the Jaen (black cherry, white pepper, and

Quinta dos Roques produces excellent monovarietal wines and blends from the Dão. The Encruzado has the richness to pair with lobster, grilled swordfish, or the sheep cheese Queijo da Serra.

fennel flavors; known as Mencía in Spain) or Alfrochiero Preta (spice, strawberry, and floral scents and high acidity but not a lot of structure, so it is best in a blend). The Tinta Pinheira (also known as Rufete) and Bastardo are used for blends.

Encruzado is the top white grape for quality yet, like Touriga Nacional, does not produce a large yield. Single-variety wine made from this grape has a nutty aroma and when aged in oak, has the structure to stand up to rich seafood or chicken dishes. Other white grapes include Assario Branco, Cerceal, and Borrado das Moscas. The latter name means "fly droppings"; in Bairrada this grape is known by the less-whimsical name Bical. Malvasia Fina is known as Arinto do Dão in this region.

Until the 1980s, more than a hundred thousand farmers worked the 50,000 acres/20,000 hectares of land. In an effort to control quality, the government stepped in and insisted that wines be made at cooperatives. In the 1990s, the European Union interceded and stopped the practice of shipping grapes to cooperatives. Since then, there has been a dramatic shift from mostly inexpensive wines to wines of higher quality.

An exception to the cooperative rule was the Casa de Santar estate, founded in 1640 and once the leader in the production of fine wines. Its gardens, museum, and the house itself are truly beautiful. Today, there are many competitors for the crown of finest Dão producer, but Casa de Santar has maintained its focus on quality. Its red Reserva, Conde de Santar, and Touriga Nacional are complex wines that are best appreciated after three to ten years from the vintage.

Quinta dos Roques is another winery attracting attention for its quality wines. A new winery was built in 1990 and is used by their enologist and friend Virgilio Loureiro to make wines for them as well as a separate brand, Quinta das Maias. Grapes used at Quinta dos Roques are sourced from vineyards that are granite-based with some clay, while the Maias grapes are strictly grown in granite. Both wineries use grapes that come from a plot in which only one variety is grown. In contrast, many farmers still promiscuously mix varieties in the same vineyard. In the best vintages, the estate makes *reserva*, complex reds from older vines. Their basic red blend has 40 percent Touriga Nacional, with the balance coming from Jaen, Alfrochiero Preto, Tinta Roriz, and Tinta Cão. The Quinta das Maias red has a high percentage of Jaen, with Touriga Nacional and a little Roriz and Cão. For white wine, Encruzado is the preferred grape for both wineries in blends that also utilize Bical, Cerceal, and Malvasia. They also make delicious pure Encruzado and Touriga Nacional wines. The pure Encruzado wine has flavors of golden delicious apples, mango, and banana. The full body and richness is reminiscent of a Meursault white Burgundy wine.

Another respected winemaker in the Dão is Alvaro Castro. He makes fine wines at Quinta da Saes and Quinta da Pellada. The Pellada white is based on Encruzado, Bical, Terrantez, and Cerceal. It is a full-bodied tart wine with citrus and nut aromas and flavors. The Quinta da Saes and Quinta da Pellada red *reserva* wines are both worth seeking out. The Pellada is a field blend of old vines, and it offers flavors of coriander, violets, and red berries. His Pape is an elegant wine based on Touriga Nacional and Baga. There is also an interesting wine made from a blend of Dão and Douro grapes. Alvaro Castro and Dirk Niepoort of the Douro collaborate to make Dado. Alvaro says he is pleased with his wines, but he dreams of refrigerating his vineyards—then his life would be perfect!

Cooler climates are part of the attraction of mountain vineyards, and the Alianca Particular is sourced from vineyards planted at 3,280 feet/1,000 meters. The wine is a traditional Dão blend and one of the best-value wines from the Dão.

Other Dão red blended wines with typical earth, red fruit, and tart flavors that we suggest include the Reserva Cabriz by Dão Sul, Duque de Viseu by Sogrape, Quinta dos Grilos, and Quinta da Falorca. Some other pure Touriga Nacional wines include the Quinta da Carvalhais by Sogrape, Quinta da Vegia, and Quinta do Cerrado.

PENÍNSULA DE SETÚBAL: TERRAS DO SADO VINHO REGIONAL, PALMELA DOC, SETÚBAL DOC

THE SETÚBAL PROVINCE is located south of Lisbon. The Atlantic Ocean, as well as the Tagus, Sorraia, and Sado rivers, provides a moderating influence on the climate. Setúbal proper, a port town, is on the Sado, and Terras do Sado is the designation used for regional still wines from within the Setúbal Peninsula.

The Serra da Arrábida mountain region to the west has more limestone- and clay-based soils, which give vibrant fruity qualities to its wines, while the warmer sand- and gravel-based soils of the inland Palmela plains give structure and depth to its DOC wines. Both traditional and modern wines are produced in these regions.

The pioneer of traditional wines was the Fonseca family. Vineyards had existed in the area for centuries, but it wasn't until the 1830s that casks of wines were first exported. José Maria da Fonseca first came to the area in 1834, and by 1849 bottled wines from Setúbal were sold in the Americas, Asia, Africa, and Europe. He was the first producer to commercialize and export the region's wines in bottle instead of bulk. He improved vineyard quality, mechanized winery production, and founded organizations to coordinate exporting of wines and spirits from the mainland and Madeira. His legacy continues with Domingo Soares Franco. He maintains a portfolio of traditional wines, which include the easy-drinking dry red Periquita and semidry rosé Lancers wines, as well as the complex, sweet Moscatel de Setúbal DOC. *Periquita* (meaning "parakeet") was the nickname given to the most important red varietals in the region. Officially known as the Castelão, it was brought from the Ribatejo region by José Maria da Fonseca to be planted at a vineyard he purchased in 1846 called Cova de Periquita. The wine made from this grape was labeled Periquita, and it was so popular that it lent its name to the grape. Other grapes included in the Periquita blend are Trincadeira and Aragonez. The wine exibits bright red berry flavors that contrast well with the saltiness of cured meat—for example, pepperoni pizza. For a complement, try Periquita with a turkey sandwich with a little cranberry sauce.

Periquita was the first dry red wine exported from Portugal. It is light- to medium-bodied and has bright red fruit flavors.

Periquita Reserva is made from Touriga Nacional, Touriga Franca, and Tinta Roriz. "Domingos" is a floral and spicy blend of Touriga Nacional and Syrah.

Domingo's creative nature and talent is expressed by his innovative blended wines from both indigenous and international grape varieties. Terras do Sado has a much broader list of permitted grapes types compared to other Portuguese DOCs, and as a result, native and indigenous grape varieties are often blended in this area.

Bacalhôa is another major producer of fine table wines in the Setúbal and makes wine in other regions as well. Fans of Bordeaux-style wines will appreciate their Quinta da Bacalhôa blend of Cabernet Sauvignon and Merlot. We suggest their Touriga Nacional, Moscatel de Setúbal, and the "J.P. Azeitão" blend of Muscatel and Fernão Pires. This white wine has a seductive aroma of honeysuckle and is semidry. Its hint of sweetness allows for some fun pairing possibilities. For a contrast of flavors, try this Muscat blend with spicy seafood curries from Malaysia, India, or Thailand.

The local red grape, Tinta Miúda, is known as Graciano in Spain and Morastell in France. Other red grapes grown in the region include Touriga Nacional, Tinta Francesa, Alfrocheiro Preto, Moreto, and Syrah.

Moscatel de Setúbal has lovely honey and floral flavors. It may be enjoyed as an after-dinner drink or paired with desserts. The Portuguese have many sweet egg desserts with cinnamon that are delicious with Moscatel. We also enjoy Moscatel de Setúbal with ice cream and dried figs or dates.

The principal local white grapes for dry wines are Fernão Pires, Arinto, and Esgana Cão (the last of which translates as "dog strangler" because it is so tart). Both Arinto and Esgana Cão are prized for their refreshing acidity.

Setúbal DOC

Moscatel de Setúbal, a fortified-wine-producing DOC region, was demarcated in 1907 and exported soon afterwards.

Southern exposures with more sunshine are often preferred in other parts of Europe, but here the northern-exposed hillside vineyards yield the finest grapes. The Muscat of Alexandria grapes that grow here are crushed and fermented and then spirits are added to arrest fermentation, resulting in a final alcohol level of about 18 percent. What makes these products special is the five to six months they spend in contact with the grape skins (which develops aromatics and flavors), followed by wood aging. The minimum aging period for both the more popular white and the rarer Roxo (red) Muscat is twenty-four months. Wines tasted from casks at fifty and even eighty years of age were incredible nectars, with flavors ranging from clove, quince, and apricot in younger wines to toffee, apple, walnut, chestnuts in syrup, and buttery French toast with cinnamon in older examples. Each wine, however, maintained the proper level of acidity to balance their rich sweetness. Once shipped beyond the equator and then returned (it was believed the voyage would enhance the wine's quality), old treasures like these were dubbed *torna viagem*, meaning "world traveler."

The hue of these wines ranges from orange-red to walnut for the oldest versions. Another clone of Muscat, called Roxo ("purple"), is also vinified in small amounts and its varietal is identified on the label and by its dark color. Up to 30 percent of Arinto, Esgana Cão, Rabo de Ovelha, Tamarês, or Roupeiro may be legally included in the blend if the label omits the grape type Moscatel.

The Trilogia by J. M. Fonseca is a complex and luscious wine made from a blend of the 1965, 1934, and 1900 vintages.

When age is indicated, such as five or twenty years, the wine is often a blend, and the given age indicates the youngest wine included in the blend, as in Madeira. These wines are definitely worth seeking out both for their value and for their complexity. Simple desserts such as not-too-sweet apple pie or almond cake are best to show off the wine.

LISBOA VINHO REGIONAL

LISBOA IS ON THE WEST COAST of the country. Its vineyards closer to the Atlantic Ocean experience a high level of rainfall and humidity. Further inland, its landscape of rolling hills receives much less rain. Soils are mostly based on clay and sand, but there are some areas with limestone.

The Lisboa region produces the largest volume of wine in the nation, the majority of which is red. Land holdings are small and a lot of jug wine is made at cooperatives. Native red grape varieties grown here include the Alfrocheiro Preto, Alicante Bouschet, Amonstrina, Aragonez (Tinta Roriz), Baga, Bastardo, Camarate, Castelão, Jaen, Monvedro, Moreto, Negra Mole, Parreira Matias, Preto Martinho, Rufete, Tinta Barroca, Tinto Caiada, Tinta Cão, Tinta Carvalha, Tinta Grossa, Tinta Miúda, Tintinha, Touriga Franca, Trincadeira, and Touriga Nacional. As previously discussed in this chapter, there are over three hundred native varieties, and a good number of them are planted in the Lisboa region. International varieties such as Cabernet Sauvignon and Syrah are also planted in the region. The most important white grapes are the Arinto, Fernão Pires, and Vital.

DOC Zones of Lisboa

The region includes the DOC zones Alenquer, Bucelas, Colares, and Carcavelos as well as Encostas de Aire, Lourinhã, Óbidos, Torres Vedras, and Arruda. The most famous area historically was Colares, but today the Alenquer and Bucelas are the best-known DOCs.

BUCELAS DOC

Located just 10 miles/16 kilometers north of Lisbon, Bucelas produces exclusively white wines on mostly chalk-based soils. The vines are sheltered from ocean winds by hills surrounding the valley of the Trancão River. This region produces crisp whites, mostly from Arinto, with Esgana Cão, Rabo de Ovelha, and Cerceal permitted up to 25 percent of the blend. All Bucelas wines must achieve a minimum alcohol content of 10.5 percent and be aged for eight months, two of which are in the bottle.

The Quinta da Romeira was restored in 1987, and a modern winery was built to craft fresh, balanced wines from a blend of 85 percent Arinto (the finest grape of the region), 10 percent Esgana Cão for acidity, and 5 percent Rabo de Ovelha for more alcohol. Arinto produces only up to 4.4 pounds/2 kilograms of grapes per vine, but its thick skin is quite resistant to humidity and disease. A crisp best-value wine made exclusively from Arinto is labeled as Prova Regia.

COLARES DOC

Lisbon has taken over much of the vineyards of Colares, and production is small. This historic site produced wines even in the times of phylloxera, as the louse could not attack vines grown on sand dunes over clay soils. Ramisco is the main red grape used, at a minimum of 80 percent, and the low yields can result in an extraordinary wine that has the potential to improve over twenty years. The rich fruit and floral bouquet evolves with time, as does the softening of tannins. Other red grapes used in this zone are João Santarém, Perreira Matias, and Molar.

ALENQUER DOC

The Alenquer is protected from excessive rainfall by its position east of the Montejunto Mountains and from extremes of temperature by the Tagus River. Quinta das Setencostas is a medium-weight red based on Castelão, Camarate, Tinto Miúda, and Preto Martinho. Some Alenquer wineries we recommend for their red wines include Quinta da Abrigada, Quinta da Carneiro, Quinta de Pancas, and Quinta da Boavista.

Lisboa Vinho Regional Wines

The aforementioned Quinta da Boavista is owned by José Luis Oliveira da Silva, who also makes Vinho Regional wines at Casa Santos Lima. Their inexpensive dry white and red Palha Canas wines are meant for quaffing, but the single-variety Touriga Nacional and Sousão, as well as the Touriz blend of Touriga Nacional, Touriga Franca, and Tinta Roriz, are more complex wines and some of the best-value wines of the nation.

Quinta do Monte d'Oiro may be the finest winery of the Lisboa region. Their Syrah blended with a little Viognier is a powerful wine that does honor to the Rhône red wines it was inspired by. They also make an Aurius blend of

Touriga Nacional, Syrah, Touriga Franca, and Petit Verdot. The pricy Homenagum a Antonio Carqueijeiro can compete with the finest red wines of the world. The wines of Quinta do Monte d'Oiro are grown on chalky clay soils. The grapes used are Touriga Nacional, Tinta Roriz, Tinta Franca, Cinsaut, Petit Verdot, Syrah, and Viognier.

Another Lisboa wine we suggest trying is the Touriga Nacional wine by Quinta da Cortezia.

RIBATEJO VINHO REGIONAL: TEJO DOC

THE TEJO DOC is named for its vineyards situated on the banks of the Tagus River, known locally as the Tejo.

The landscape of the Leziria, or Campo, area has fertile alluvial soils on the marshy flatlands by the Tagus River. On the right side of the river, there are soils with iron-rich clays, limestone, and sandstone. These vineyard areas are known as the *bairro*. The *charneca* is on the left bank of the Tagus, where vines receive reflected sunshine from white sandy soils. The grapes' greater degree of ripeness translates to wines with a potential for high alcohol. The Tagus and the Atlantic Ocean mitigate the hot temperature in this Mediterranean climate.

The Ribatejo Vinho Regional and Tejo DOC produce the second-largest volume of wine in Portugal. The

The Touriz red blend from Lisboa may be served with burgers, grilled red meats, or hearty bean soups.

Trebbiano of Italy or Ugni Blanc of France is called Tália here. It is widely planted due to its ability to maintain its high acidity despite the heat. Vital and Fernão Pires are the most-planted indigenous grapes.

Because of the warm climate, two harvests of the white grapes may occur. The early picking in August provides a good balance of acidity, while the regular harvest provides riper flavors and more sugar to convert to alcohol.

Red grapes in this region include João de Santarém (the local name for Castelão) and the Poerinha (the local name for Baga). They are the principal reds along with Touriga Nacional, Touriga Franca, Trincadeira Preta, Tinta Miúda, Tinta Roriz, and Camarate. International varieties such as Chardonnay, Cabernet Sauvignon, and Syrah are an increasing presence.

Casa Cadaval, in the Almeirim DOC subregion, is a historic estate owned by Theresa von Schönbrun. Because sandy soils on her property are subjected to lots of rain, deeply planted rootstocks are used to reduce the effect of the damp topsoil. Here, old-vine Pinot Noir is ungrafted (since phylloxera is not a problem in sandy soil) and has an attractive strawberry-cherry yogurt nose with good acidity. The soft Cabernet Sauvignon has the traditional smell of cassis with floral notes of violets and roses. The intriguing Trincadeira Preta offers smells of black fig, boysenberry, and spices such as coriander and cardamom. The top-of- the-line red wine is the complex, full-bodied Marquesa de Cadaval. It is composed of 60 percent Touriga Nacional, 30 percent Trincadeira, and 10 percent Alicante Bouschet and has flavors of black plum, licorice, blueberry, and earth. It may very well be the best red wine of the Tejo.

Quinta da Casal Branco is a family-owned vineyard that started as a hunting lodge for the king. That was the inspiration for the proprietary label Falcoaria. Since 1997, *lagares* have been used to extract more color, tannins, and flavors from the best lots of Castelão, Cabernet Sauvignon, and Trincadeira. The Reserva remains their finest red wine.

Other red wines we suggest are the Reserva by Conde de Vimiosa winery and the Quinta da Lagoalva de Cima's full-bodied red wine based on Cabernet Sauvignon and Syrah. The wine has aromas of black pepper and roses and has a long, rich finish. A sweet white we suggest is their botrytised Colheita Tardis.

A dry white wine we enjoy is Quinta da Alorna's pristine expression of the acidic Arinto grape. The wine has crisp citrus, apple, and pear flavors and is a great value at under $10 retail. Winemaker Nuno Cancella de Abreu also makes complex red wines at the historic estate. Their pure Touriga Nacional and Colheita Seleccionado are worth seeking out for their rich texture and complex flavors.

ALENTEJANO VINHO REGIONAL ALENTEJO DOC

THIS VAST AGRICULTURAL AREA, which encompasses about one-third of the nation's landmass, stretches from the river Tagus east to the border with Spain. The plains are planted with grapes, olives, grains, fruits, and vegetables and are the largest source of cork trees in the world. Even though the area is large, fewer than 5 percent of the nation's wines are produced here.

In general, the soil types are schist and granite with some loam. Summer temperatures can exceed 100°F/38°C, which prompts some growers to harvest their white grapes early in order to maintain acidity.

Unlike the Minho and Lisboa, where landholdings are small and there is ample rainfall, this region has many large estates and very low rainfall. Irrigation is commonly used to keep the vines satisfied, and there are various trellising systems used to adjust to the climate. An example is the Smart-Dyson trellising system—found in the Alentejo at modern wineries such as Cortes de Cima. The high-elevation vineyards on Serra de São Mamede, Serra de Ossa, Monfurado and hillsides are the source of grapes that produce wines with higher acidity than those from the flat plain lands.

Alentejano is the Vinho Regional that contains the DOC Alentejo. Wineries using the *regional* designation can utilize grape varieties that are not approved for the DOC Alentejo. Within the Alentejo DOC are subregions that may use their names on labels. The subregions are Reguengos, Borba, Granja-Amarejela, Redondo, Vidiguera, Évora, Moura, and Portalegre. It is an interesting comparison to taste a blended red wine from Portalegre, the northernmost sub-

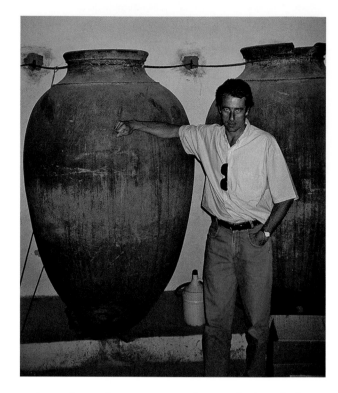

region, where vines grow on the granite-based slopes, alongside one from Borba further south, where the soils are chalky clay.

The Alentejo is a region that offers dry white, rosé, and red wines at bargain to expensive prices. Some traditional wineries offer only wines based on traditional grapes and traditional vinification methods: Grapes may be trod by foot in *lagares*, sometimes fermented in **TALHAS** (clay pots), and may be aged in either chestnut or Portuguese oak casks. Some Alentejo wineries mix traditional methods with modern techniques, just as they may blend indigenous and international grape types using stainless steel, American, or French oak barrels.

The principal red grapes used in Alentejo are Trincadeira for aroma, body, and black fruit flavors; Aragonez (Tinta Roriz) for elegance and spice; Castelão for blackberry and anise scents and red berry tastes; Alicante Bouschet for structure and color; and a hybrid, Grand Noir, for color. Each of the subregions of the Alentejo has a specific list of approved grape varieties.

TOP RIGHT: *Celebrated winemaker João Portugal Ramos with* talhas, *traditional clay amphorae* MIDDLE: *This blend of Trincadeira and Aragonez exhibits black fruits such as figs, licorice, black olive, and earth, and would pair well with steak or wild game.*

Some other permitted red grapes of the subregions of the Alentejo include Moreto, Carignan, Corropio, Cabernet Sauvignon, Cinsault, Tinta Caiada, and Tinta Carvalha. As for whites, Alva (Roupeiro) provides structure, Arinto its high acidity, and Fernão Pires its higher alcohol and high yields. Perrum, Manteúdo, Diagalves, Siria, Antão Vaz, Tamarez, Chardonnay, and Assario are also used.

The first celebrity local winemaker of the region was João Portugal Ramos. Here in Alentejo, as elsewhere in Portugal as a consultant, Ramos experimented with different rootstocks as well as various growing and vinification techniques. His Marquês de Borba winery utilizes both traditional and modern techniques. Traditional stone troughs, or *lagares*, are used to extract maximum flavor from red grapes for his finest wines such as his Reserva. He also produces a very fine pure Trincadeira wine.

Another winemaker we respect is the Australian transplant David Baverstock. He helped craft the acclaimed wines at Quinta do Crasto in the Douro before joining Herdade do Esporão; the owners of these properties are cousins. At Esporão he oversees an enormous estate of almost 5,000 acres/2,000 hectares. Inexpensive Monte Velho and Defesa white, rosé, and red wines are all best-value wines. The Garrafeira based on Aragonez and Alicante Bouschet; the Reserva based on Trincadeira, Aragonez, and Cabernet Sauvignon; and the pure Touriga Nacional are three of the greatest reds of the region.

A third respected Portuguese winemaker and consultant is Luis Duarte. He worked with David Baverstock for many years at Esporão. We can recommend his entire line of Herdade dos Grous wines. Their basic white based on Antão Vaz, Arinto, and Roupeiro offers lemon, apple, and pear flavors, has a medium weight, and is moderately priced. The "moon-harvested" pure Alicante Bouschet is testimony to the importance of that grape in the Alentejo: lots of black fruit flavors in a big package. The Reserva is a fine red based on a blend of Alicante Bouschet, Syrah, and Touriga Nacional. This silky wine has rich red and black fruit flavors balanced by acidity. Luis Duarte is also the winemaker for the well-respected Maladinha and Quinta do Mouro wineries.

Adega Cartuxa is a 593-acre/240-hectare estate owned by Fundação Eugénio do Almeida, which produces traditional-style wines, approximately two-thirds red with the balance white. Coffee and spicy notes as well as dark fruit flavors are found in the red *reserva*, made with Castelão, Aragonês, Trincadeira Moreto, Tinta Caiada, a little

Cabernet Sauvignon, and Alicante Bouschet. Pera Manca is the estate's elegant expression of Trincadeira. An interesting contrast in styles can be made by tasting the traditional wines of Adega de Cartuxa winery next to the modern wines of the Cortes de Cima winery.

Cortes de Cima has utilized consultants for the vineyards and "flying winemakers" for their winery. As previously mentioned in this section, Dr. Richard Smart of New Zealand set up the Dyson trellising system here while a team of French oenologists apply modern techniques to create some very interesting and tasty wines. We are partial to the Syrah labeled Incógnito, as its name was a poke at local authorities who were hesitant to allow the non-indigenous Syrah to be grown in the Alentejo.

Château Lafite Rothschild of France has a controlling interest in Quinta do Carmo. The fine blended red wines from the estate are made mainly from Alicante Bouschet, a grape type that in other nations is usually associated with high alcohol and high yields but not necessarily high quality. The second label is Dom Martinho. The reds are all estate-bottled from 173 acres/70 hectares, with more plantings under way. Unfortunately, the best soils are where the cork trees are planted on the 2,470-acre/1,000-hectare property. By law, cork trees cannot be uprooted.

Another fine producer of Alicante Bouschet is J. B. Bastos. The grapes are foot-trod in *lagares* for his fine Garrafeira, which is aged in French oak barrels.

Herdade dos Coelheiros is a winery that also produces a fine Garrafeira based on Cabernet Sauvignon and Aragones, as well as a white blend of Chardonnay, Arinto, and Roupeiro. Additionally, their pure Chardonnay is very impressive.

The 74-acre/30-hectare Tapada do Chaves in Portalegre has a national reputation for its reds, made with 90 percent Trincadeira. **TAPADA** means "walled vineyard," as *clos* does in Burgundy, France. Although the winery dates from 1900, its first commercial bottling was in 1965, when J. P. Ramos joined the winery and switched from 1,320-gallon/5,000-liter barrels to 132-gallon/500-liter barrels to gain more intensity in the aging process. Furthermore, he prefers temperature-controlled fermentation in stainless steel and only occasionally uses *talhas*. The reds have a raspberry-cherry, spicy nose and good fruit on the palate, with a silky feel after aging.

Also in Portalegre, Morgado de Reguengo is a 111-acre/45-hectare vineyard that grows Trincadeira, Castelão, and Aragonez. Spicy red-fruit flavors are found

in this wine, made by Domingo Soares Franco of Fonseca Successores for his cousin. He also makes Tinto Velho in amphorae from a blend of mostly Trincadeira and Castelão as José de Sousa in Reguengos. The wine has rich fruit flavors and is medium to full in body.

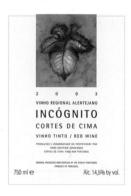

The historic 360-acre/900-hectare Herdade do Mouchão estate may have been the first to plant Alicante Bouschet in the Alentejo. Their red wine is based on 70 percent Alicante Bouschet and 30 percent Trincadeira. The grapes are foot-trod in *lagares* and the wine is aged four years before it is released. It is a fine expression of the Alentejo, but in the best years they make an expensive Tonel 3-4, which is one of the top wines of the Alentejo.

Some of Portugal's major wineries such as Sogrape, Alianca, and Bacalhoa make wine in other regions as well as the Alentejo. Quinta da Terrugem by Alianca, Callabriga by Sogrape, and Grande Escolha Tinta da Anfora are fine wines made from native grape varieties.

Other recommended wines include the Marias de Maladinha by Herdade de Maladinha, Terras de Baco by Adega Cooperativa de Portalegre, Herdade de Perdigão, and the Reserva by Monte de Penha Geraçoes.

ALGARVE VINHO REGIONAL: LAGOA DOC, PORTIMÃO DOC, LAGOS DOC, TAVIRA DOC

THE ALGARVE AREA is better known for its beaches than for the quality of its wines. The region has been assigned four separate DOC designations.. The area produces 97 percent red wine from grapes that are able to withstand the heat and produce a high-alcohol product.

TOP: *The island of Madeira.* LEFT: *Cortes de Cima is a modern winery that produces wines from both native and international grape varieties. Their Syrah is labeled "Incógnito," as it was not an approved variety for the region.*

MADEIRA DOC

THE VIEW FLYING toward the majestic isle of Madeira is breathtaking. The island is 35.5 miles/57 kilometers long and about 14.7 miles/23 kilometers wide and is made up primarily of mineral-rich clay atop volcanic soil. Ocean and sky offset peaks and valleys adorned with plantings of silver bananas and the grapevines that produce one of the most complex, satisfying, and longest-lived of all wines.

To facilitate the tending and harvesting of the vines and to reduce the loss of topsoil on the steep slopes, dramatic terraces separated by *poios* (stone walls) rise up to 2,625 feet/800 meters above sea level. In superior growing regions, soil laced with gravel or stone retains warmth and assists drainage. Most vineyards are planted on mineral-rich clay topsoils over volcanic subsoils. Hot growing conditions dictate that the vines be trained high, forming cooling canopies, to reduce the risk of rot or heat reflection from below. Despite heavy rainfall, an elaborate irrigation system is necessary because of the heat and porous soil.

The Symington family, the largest producer of Porto wines, became majority owner of the Madeira Wine Company in the 1980s, and they now make over 25 percent of the island's wine

AZORES VINHO REGIONAL: BISCOITOS IPR, GRACIOSA IPR, AND PICOS IPR

NINE ISLANDS COMPOSE the Azores region (also known as Açores), which is located 1,000 miles/1,600 kilometers west of mainland Portugal. The island of Terceira produces a fortified liquor wine called Biscoitos, from Verdelho, Arinto, and Terrantez grapes. Picos is also a liquor wine based on the same grapes as Biscoitos, and both must have a minimum alcohol level of 16 percent. Portuguese sailors depended on their *biscoitos,* or biscuits, to survive during their long sea voyages. Biscuits were their substitute for bread, which spoiled too quickly. The strength of the liquor wines also allowed for their longevity.

Graciosa is a dry, light-bodied white based on Verdelho, Arinto, Terrantez, Fernão Pires, and Malvasia Fina. It is well suited to the local seafood dishes.

LEFT: *Vines are shielded from direct sunlight by leaves.* TOP RIGHT: *Sercial wines are dry with high acidity and work well with a wide range of savory appetizers. Codfish fritters and Sercial are a typical pairing served on the island.* MIDDLE RIGHT: *The Bual grape (known as Sémillon in other nations) produces sweet wines in Madeira. The* colheita *is a younger version of* vintage *Madeira, bottled after five years of aging.* BOTTOM RIGHT: Vintage *Madeira wines are very complex and long lived. The Bual style may be served with sweets or enjoyed on its own as a sublime drink.*

production. They have wines under the labels Blandy's (established 1811), Cossart Gordon (established 1745), and Leacock (established 1760).

Membership in the European Union in 1986 brought new controls (such as sweetening wine only with concentrated must that contains 20 percent alcohol) and new labeling laws. The EU has also been a source for funding for new vineyards established with recommended varieties on modern trellising systems.

Like Porto, Madeira production and exportation is governed by its own agency, the Instituto do Vinho da Madeira, located in the city of Funchal. Production is 924,000 to 1,188,000 gallons/35,000,000 to 45,000,000 hectoliters annually.

Grape Types, Production Methods, and Label Terms

Today, eight thousand local pickers begin the harvest season by picking the lesser red grape variety Tinta Negra Mole and then proceed to the premium white grapes Bual, Malvasia Fina, Malvasia Candida, Verdelho, and finally Sercial. The adaptable Tinta Negra Mole represents 85 percent of vinifera acreage, yet producers are not allowed to label their wines as such. It is used for younger-style wines whose labels carry an indication of sweetness—*seco* (dry) or *doce* (sweet).

Some other authorized grape varieties include the whites Terrantez, Malvasia Babosa, Caracol, Carão de Moça, Listrão, Moscatel, Rio Grande, and Valveirinho. The authorized red grapes are the Malvasia Candida Roxa, Verdelho Tinto, Bastardo, Tinta da Madeira, Complexa, Triunfo, and Deliciosa.

The name of the grape type appears on labels of the best Madeira wines. The Tinta Negra Mole grape variety is not found on labels.

The four most important *castas nobres* (noble grapes) are Sercial, Verdelho, Bual, and Malvasia Candida (used for Malmsey):

SERCIAL Naturally high in acidity and resistant to powdery mildew or rot, it produces the driest and most delicate style of Madeira. Permitted residual sugar is 0.6 to 2.3 ounces/18.6 to 65 grams per liter. The grape is also known as Esgana Cão on mainland Portugal. Its texture, flavor profile of dried fruit and nuts, and high acidity make it an ideal foil for appetizers as diverse as

uni (sea urchin roe) and duck pâté with pistachios and orange zest.

VERDELHO Wines made from this grape are semidry, smoky, and have high acidity. Permitted residual sugar is 1.7 to 2.7 ounces/49 to 78 grams per liter.

BUAL Usually made into a semisweet to sweet style of Madeira, it is the vinifera Sémillon. Also sometimes spelled Boal. Permitted residual sugar is 2.7 to 3.3 ounces/78 to 96 grams per liter.

MALVASIA CANDIDA The opposite end of the spectrum from Sercial, this grape is quite sensitive to mildew and rot, and it makes the sweetest style of Madeira, Malmsey. Permitted residual sugar is 3.3 to 4.7 ounces/96 to 135 grams per liter. A similar variety, Malvasia de São Jorge, is also used to produce Malmsey.

TERRANTEZ More difficult to find but worth seeking out, the grape has higher sugar levels and lower acidity than Sercial, and the wine is usually made in an off-dry style with a bitter finish. It is also known as Folgasão.

BASTARDO Made into dry sweet styles of wines, but its availability is limited.

MOSCATEL This variety is authorized for Madeira production, but its low acidity and very sweet nature allow farmers to get higher prices as a table grape than for winemaking. Some old Moscatel Madeiras can be found, tending to be rich in texture and sugar.

Wineries used to purchase the must after the grapes were trod in *lagares*, but today it is commonplace to purchase whole grapes. After the grapes arrive at the winery, they are destemmed and placed in a receptacle; a small amount of sulfur dioxide or potassium bisulfate may be added to hinder the growth of bacteria. Fewer than 10 percent of the year's crop can be ameliorated, when necessary, by the addition of must concentrate to boost alcohol. Tartaric acid or gypsum may be added to enhance acidity. Madeira wines do not go through malolactic fermentation (sometimes referred to as malolactic degradation).

The red grape Tinta Negra Mole is often fermented on its skins for the semisweet and sweet styles, and producers use a variety of practices for the dry and semidry styles. Henriques and Henriques macerate all of their reds, just as Justino Henriques eschews maceration for all of its products. The Madeira Wine Company, however, does not do so for any of its dry or semidry wines.

The temperature of fermentation is usually controlled, between 77° and 104°F/25° and 40°C. Cooler tempera-

tures tend to be used these days to reduce levels of volatile acidity. A variety of containers are used with autovinifiers, which require the shortest amount of time. After fermentation, the lees are pressed from the tank and used for inexpensive *granel* (bulk wine) by some producers or added back into the base wine by others.

The vast majority are made by the *estufagem* method. The wine is heated to a maximum temperature of 122°F/50°C for three months in a stainless steel or concrete tank. This method can approximate the nutty character that would take many years to develop in the cask.

For the *canteiro* method (natural warming in cask), the preferred location to store the casks of wine is in dry areas, as humid locations would promote a greater loss of alcohol than water in the wine. Between 3 and 4 percent of wine is lost yearly through evaporation, and because very old cask-aged wines increase in acidity, alcohol, and texture, they may be "refreshed" with a small amount of young wine to balance them out.

Two procedures are involved in the production of

The José Maria da Fonseca winery in the Setúbal is a historic estate that produces fine table and fortified wines.

Madeira (which are similar to those used with Porto). First, there is the enforced maintenance of a minimum level of wine stock for each producer, and second, once the wine passes the criteria enforced by the Instituto do Vinho da Madeira, it receives a *selo de garantia* (seal of guarantee), which is attached to the neck of the bottle.

Current legislation states that only after a minimum of five years of aging can a tenth of each cask be drawn off for "Solera" wines. If a vintage appears on the bottle, it is the year of the base wine used.

The laws for sugar levels are expressed in terms of the Baumé scale (see Chapter 2, page 55):

VERY DRY: 0 to 0.5 Baumé
DRY: 0 to 1.5 Baumé
MEDIUM DRY: 1 to 1.25 Baumé
MEDIUM SWEET: 2.5 to 3 Baumé
SWEET: Minimum of 3.5 Baumé

By law, alcohol content should be between 17 and 22 percent, volatile acidity up to 0.1 ounce per gallon/1.2 to 1.5 grams per liter, and the pH level 3.3 to 3.5. Older wines, however, may have higher volatile acidity levels. Some countries request lower-alcohol versions, so exceptions do occur.

STYLES OF MADEIRA

The types of Madeira produced are:

GRANEL

Over a third of the total production of Madeira is this bulk wine, which is adjusted by caramel and sold after a year and a half. *Granels* are heated in the large epoxy-lined concrete tanks called **ESTUFAS**; the term *granel* can also be used for large wooden casks that are warmed by hot-water pipes for up to a year.

SELECCIONADO

This Madeira is aged three years before release, and it may also be labeled Finest, Choice, Select, or Three Year Old. A combination of *estufas* and wooden casks is used for three-year-old wines, and the Tinta Negra Mole is the dominant grape variety.

RESERVA

This category of wine is aged five years before release and is made by a combination of the *estufagem* and *canteiro* processes. They can be made from lesser grape varieties such as Tinta Negra Mole or one of the better grape varieties such as Sercial or Verdelho. The label terms may also be Old, Reserve, or Five Year Old. Wines sourced from the superior grapes will bear their name on the label.

RESERVA VELHA

This type of Madeira is a blend of harvests, with the youngest wine aged ten years before it can be used. This is also labeled Old Reserve, Special Reserve, or Ten Year Old. The wines are made in wooden cask, usually from one of the top grape varieties.

EXTRA RESERVE

The wines for these blends are aged at least fifteen years before release, and they are made in wooden cask.

SOLERA

A system used for wines aged a minimum of five years in cask, and only 10 percent can be drawn off each year. The term *solera* may appear on labels of older wines, but as verifying the true origin of the wine is difficult, such labeling is being phased out.

COLHEITA

A *colheita* wine is made from a single vintage and must be aged at least five years in cask before it is bottled.

VINTAGE FRASQUERIA OR GARRAFEIRA

The finest style of Madeira is sourced from a single year's harvest and aged a minimum of twenty years in *canteiros*, after which it may be transferred to bottles or to glass *garrafoes* (known in France as *bonbonnes*), containing 6.6 gallons/25 liters.

HISTORY OF MADEIRA

Captains working under Prince Henry the Navigator of Portugal claimed the islands of Porto Santo in 1418 and Madeira in 1420. With the arrival of settlers, forests were burned to provide arable land to grow crops such as grain and sugar cane that were exported to mainland Europe and Africa. The Malvasia grape was imported from Greece to establish vineyards on the island. Other grape varieties from mainland Portugal followed.

With trade flourishing, British merchants established their presence in Madeira as they had in other parts of Portugal, and by the late 1700s their ships had the exclusive right to transport Madeira to the Americas, West Indies, and England in exchange for imported goods.

Worldwide demand became so great that in 1768, the area was demarcated and quality controls were established to prevent, among other things, the blending of inferior, less ripe grapes from the northern portion of the island and to ensure the export of better wines.

During the mid-eighteenth century, the technique of fortifying the wines to better withstand travel began, and by the end of the century, the beneficial effects of sun and heat on aging were recognized. *Estufas* (heated vats) began to be used. During the same period, a blended lighter style of Madeira diluted by water and filtered through charcoal, called **RAINWATER**, was produced for the American market.

As elsewhere in Portugal, the nineteenth century witnessed the destructive forces of powdery mildew and phylloxera as well as a decline in demand, due in part to the lesser-quality fraudulent Madeira being produced and sold. John Blandy, a British producer, led the legal battle to protect and define the genuine product as coming solely from Madeira. The law was established after a Portuguese-British treaty in 1914.

To best appreciate these exquisite treasures, the wine should be opened or decanted a few hours (some say a day) before service. Vintage wines are never made by the *estufagem* method, only by the *canteiro* method. The slow absorption of oxygen in these high-alcohol and high-acid wines develops the sophisticated *rancio* bouquet associated with vintage Madeira. *Rancio* smells include dried fruits, nuts, and dairy notes of cheese and butter. After a decade or two of aging, they are capable of resisting damage by oxygen for a longer period than any other wine. Unopened wine can last a century, and an opened bottle of vintage Madeira can be enjoyed for months.

As with Porto, the wine's fermentation is halted by the addition of *aguardente* (clear brandy), usually by transferring the fermenting wines to casks containing the brandy. The percentage of *aguardente* varies depending on the style of Madeira—from 9 percent for the driest style to about 20 percent for the sweetest styles. The wine can also be sweetened later in the process by the addition of products called *abafado*, or *surdo* (caramel).

RAINWATER

This is a category that indicates a wine that is semidry to semisweet and based on the lesser grape varieties. The name Rainwater derives either from a parched vineyard that depended on rain for survival or from the idea that some casks of wine bound for America were adulterated by rain. Less expensive styles such as Rainwater are useful in the kitchen.

OTHER NOTES ON MADEIRA

Madeira is best appreciated when served in a small glass (2 to 3 ounces/59 to 88.7 milliliters), the drier versions chilled and the sweeter and vintage wines served at room temperature. The finest examples should be served as an aperitif, with a soup, appetizer, or dessert course, or alone at the end of a meal.

The Latadas Verdelho-based still wine by Seical is an example of the Madeirense DOC used for nonfortified wines from Madeira. It is a crisp dry white wine.

SUMMARY

THE FIRST WINE that comes to mind in Portugal is Porto, or Port. The boundaries for the production of these sweet fortified wines were established in 1756. Today, dry wines from the same area are labeled as Douro. *Awesome* is an adjective that is overused in America, but it is quite appropriate for both the landscape and the still wines of the Douro. The finest dry red wines are as complex and rewarding as their sweet cousins. In both the fortified wines of Porto and the dry red wines of the nation, Touriga Nacional is the most important grape for high quality, on its own and in blended wines. Wines from the Beiras Vinho Regional and the DOCs within it, Dão and Bairrada, as well as the Alentejo DOC and Tejo DOC, also feature the Touriga Nacional grape.

Red wines from indigenous and international grape varieties range from lightweight, easy-quaffing wines to complex, ageworthy, full-bodied examples. Baga-based Bairrada and Beiras wines are among the most powerful and satisfying red wines in the world.

Seafood is a big part of the Portuguese diet, and Vinho Verde from the Minho region of Portugal is one of the best white wine values in the world and can accompany native or international seafood dishes. Single-varietal Vinho Verde wines, produced from the Alvarinho grape, are medium-bodied and a bit more complex, yet still affordable. Arinto, Encruzado, Avesso, Cercial, Antão Vaz, and Fernão Pires (also known as Maria Gomes) are just some of the local white grapes whose unique flavors contribute to the diversity of Portuguese white wines.

The fortified wines Moscatel de Setúbal and Madeira are both undervalued and underappreciated in the American market. Madeira is available in both dry (Sercial and Verdelho) and sweet (Bual and Malmsey) versions. Sweet Moscatel de Setúbal and Madeira wines may improve in cask and bottle over decades.

Portuguese *espumante* (sparkling), white, rosé, red, and fortified wines are available at bargain prices for everyday drinking and at higher prices for special dinners and celebrations.

Our passion for the wines of Portugal is inspired by the unique flavors of the wines sourced from the more than three hundred indigenous grapes grown throughout the country, as well as some interesting blended wines that include international varieties. Whether it is a refreshing young Vinho Verde or an aged vintage Porto that "grips" the palate with its power, the small nation of Portugal is producing wines of distinction.

ERSTE LAGE

mosel

EINZELLAGE

CHARTA

PFALZ

GROSSES GEWÄCHS

AUSLESE

EISWEIN

PRÄDIKATSWEIN

RHEIN

QUALITÄTSWEIN

SEKT

SCHLOSS

RUWER

NACKENHEIM

GERMANY, AUSTRIA, SWITZERLAND

GERMANY, AUSTRIA, AND SWITZERLAND are in the same chapter simply because they represent a cluster of nations in central Western Europe with a long tradition of cool-climate winemaking. There are also a number of similarities in wine styles and labeling practices between the countries. Both Germany and Austria are experiencing a resurgence of interest in their wines, and producers in both those nations continue to confront the problem of clear label language in a global market.

GERMANY

TWO STATISTICS will immediately convey how much has changed about German wine in the past decade. Consumption of German wines in the reunited Germany (since 1990) is at an all-time high of 5.4 gallons/20.6 liters per person per year, and exports of German wines have been rising by approximately 8 percent per year. While other European nations like France and Italy have lost ground in consumption and exports, German wine producers have enjoyed growth. Much of this has to do with three factors: German wine drinkers, especially younger ones, have come to recognize the great value and quality of their homegrown wines; international consumers have accepted that German wine producers offer a full range of styles, from dry to ex-

tremely sweet, all concentrating on clean fruit flavors; and some producers have taken to simplicity in labeling, offering brands rather than the old style of German labels.

What has not changed is the ongoing set of disputes about how German wines should be categorized, a major consideration since decisions about categories impact how the wine will be labeled and marketed. The basis for the German wine categories has been the amount of sugar in the grapes at harvest, and to a certain extent this remains true. Higher sugar levels permit winemakers to claim a higher category for their wine. This system has been attacked on several fronts, and, ironically, it may be that the new EU wine laws of August 2009 have opened

A typically cool day in the vineyards near Nierstein

the door to an acceptable solution to address the critiques. The new emphasis on "protected name" categories reduces the importance of sugar-at-harvest nomenclature, and the continued move toward a classification of vineyard sites similar to the system of *crus* in France reinforces that idea. (This topic will be covered in detail later in this chapter.)

Because Germany sits on the northernmost boundary for grape growing (the 50th parallel runs right through the vineyards at the famous Schloss Johannisberg), it occasionally experiences unreliable weather patterns, resulting in inconsistent levels of ripeness and sugar from year to year. Germany's climatic conditions emphasize the immensely important role that vineyard location plays, with the optimally sited vineyards usually capable of producing fine wine even in years when the weather is uncooperative.

The 50th parallel marker is visible here in the vineyards at Schloss Johannisberg.

CLIMATE

GERMANY'S WINE-PRODUCING REGIONS are some of the coolest in the world because of their location in high northern latitudes, but summer daylight hours are long, compensating for the relatively cool temperatures. As a result, careful site selection is needed to grow grapes that will provide full, ripe flavors. Rivers, which moderate climate by heat retention and light reflection, play a fundamental role in the most northerly regions, where steep riverbanks provide elevation and angling of the vineyards into the sun's light and heat.

All of these factors provide for a long, slow maturation period, resulting in fully developed yet delicate fruit aromas and flavors in grapes that are often picked when the grapes of southern Europe are already fermenting, even for dry wines. The lack of extreme heat and the continued presence of cool night temperatures leave the ripe grapes with good to excellent sugar levels but high acid levels.

WINE STYLES

BECAUSE OF GERMANY'S COOL CLIMATE, the majority of Germany's wines are white (75 percent), with most of the white wines produced from cool climate grape varieties (see page 25). These include Riesling, all of its cousins, and subsequent biological crosses (to be discussed later in this chapter). In addition, most of the wines show fresh, lively acidity, and the coolest areas produce wines with relatively low alcohol levels.

Despite the revitalized attention given to dry wines, Germany remains famous as a producer of some of the world's finest sweet wines, and it is somewhat ironic that the generally cool climate is what makes this possible. Cool, misty conditions toward the end of the growing season often promote the development of botrytis (see page 74), allowing the production of rich, concentrated,

Steeply inclined vineyards on the banks of the Mosel River

very sweet wines. In addition, hard frosts in November or December have provided the opportunity to make the magical, sweet *Eiswein*. However, there is widespread concern that climate change will make *Eiswein* production less and less likely, since the required freezing temperature of 17.6°F/8°C is being seen less frequently.

However, the relatively cool climate still makes Germany a natural site for the production of sparkling wines, the best of which are labeled SEKT, or Deutscher Sekt if all of the wine's grapes are grown in Germany. Sekt (the *S* is pronounced more like a *Z* in English) has been in use as a term to identify German sparkling wine since the Treaty of Versailles in 1918 restricted the use of the term *Champagne* to France, at least within Europe.

Like many nations, Germany makes both low-end and high-end sparklers. The bulk of Sekt is in fact produced by using surplus French and Italian wines as a base, with the addition of approximately 20 percent German wines. However, some producers do make Deutscher Sekt using 100 percent domestic wines. In addition, if a label states a grape variety or a vintage year, the wine must be made from at least 85 percent grapes of the stated variety or year.

Most Sekt is produced using the *charmat* method, and some is produced by the transfer method (see page 84). However, a number of quality-minded producers are now marketing *méthode champenoise* wines using high-quality Riesling, Chardonnay, Pinot Noir, Pinot Blanc, or Pinot Gris. These individually crafted sparkling wines are well worth seeking out (while most other German Sekt is worth avoiding).

WINEMAKING

THE CLEAN, FRESH, CRISP, AROMATIC STYLE of many of Germany's wines is achieved by long, cool, slow fermentation in inert containers. Stainless steel fermenters are now commonplace in Germany, though many of the older wineries still use very old large oak casks. These are generally not being used to give oak character; they have been used many times and have very little oak character left, and many of them are lined with a layer of epoxy. However, some of the new generation of German winemakers have been experimenting with the use of newer oak barrels of different sizes for fermentation and for aging. So far, results are inconsistent, but some wines show great promise, especially when made from fuller-bodied varieties, such as Pinot Gris. The

newly fashionable Pinot Noir also benefits from the extra structure that small-barrel treatment can provide.

In addition to the advanced technology of refrigerated, temperature-controlled stainless steel fermentation tanks, German winemakers take full advantage of German technology, using precision-engineered centrifuges, especially for the production of bulk and middle-market wines. Refrigerated stainless steel containers can chill the fermenting wine to around 33°F/0.5°C, allowing the winemaker to stop the fermentation at exactly the point when the desired level of residual sugar is left in the wine. The wine can then be placed in a centrifuge, which spins the wine at high speed and expels the solid yeast particles from the liquid but leaves the dissolved sugars. If a centrifuge is not used, winemakers can achieve the same effect by passing the wine through a micropore filter that extracts all of the yeast cells from the wine. In either scenario, since the yeast cells have been removed, the wine will not referment as it warms up, even though there is residual sugar present.

Again, it is important to point out that quality-minded producers do not use such methods to "engineer" a wine.

LEFT: *These miniature high-tech stainless steel fermentation tanks make it possible to ferment individual batches of grapes harvested from a small parcel of vineyard land.* MIDDLE: *A modern high-tech version of the old-fashioned basket press* RIGHT: *Some German wine producers have incorporated new oak barrels into their aging program.*

Such producers view their role as caretaker who should provide an environment in which the wine will reach its natural outcome. For these producers, the wine is complete when the fermentation stops naturally, and sometimes it will stop even though there is sugar left in the wine. As a result, regardless of the amount of sugar at harvest, some wines end up as dry, while others retain higher levels of residual sugar. This has resulted in the introduction of the terms TROCKEN, Classic, or Selection on many German wine labels to indicate dry wines. German winemakers insist that many of Germany's wines have always been produced dry and that the phenomenon of sweet, fruity, soda-pop wines was simply an aberration. Whatever the historical truth may be, Germany's finest winemakers are now making waves, and a name for themselves, with their distinctly dry white (and increasingly red) wines.

Because of the challenges presented by Germany's climate and the occasionally low sugar levels in nonpremium sites, chaptalization is a regular practice for bulk and mid-level German wines. Chaptalization is forbidden in wines that fall into the highest quality category, and prestigious producers scorn the practice.

Also permitted, at all levels, is the addition of SÜSSRESERVE (sweet reserve) to the finished wine. *Süssreserve* is unfermented sterile grape juice, equal in quality to the wine. In other words, before fermentation of the grape juice begins, a winemaker can separate out a small quantity of juice and render it sterile so as to prevent fermentation. The remainder of the juice is allowed to ferment

CLASSIC AND SELECTION

As part of a commendable attempt to simplify labels and attract new consumers, the German wine authorities introduced two new label terms in 2000: Classic and Selection. The overriding emphasis is that only dry wines can be labeled with these new terms, a welcome innovation and an obvious reaction to the general perception that all German wines are sweet.

For Classic wines, the parameters are:

- The term is available to any producer in any of the thirteen quality wine regions.
- The wine must be "harmoniously dry" (the exact relationship of sugars to acidity varies by grape variety and by region—a slight sweetness might be detectable).
- The wine must be a single-varietal wine made from one of the classic varieties such as Riesling, Silvaner, Grauburgunder (Pinot Gris), Weissburgunder (Pinot Blanc), Spätburgunder (Pinot Noir); each of the regions can specify which grapes may be used.
- The grape variety must appear on the label along with the term *Classic*.
- The grape-growing region must appear on the label, but there can be no mention of a vineyard.
- The wine must be vintage dated.

For Selection wines, these additional criteria must be met:

- The grapes must be harvested by hand from a single vineyard.
- The wine must be measurably "dry" (less than nine grams of residual sugar per liter).
- The maximum yield is 60 hectoliters per hectare/ 4.5 tons per acre.
- The minimum potential alcohol is 12.2 percent, roughly equivalent to harvesting grapes at Auslese level (see page 495).
- The individual vineyard name will appear on the label along with the term *Selection*.

While these measures might make choosing a German wine easier for the average consumer, they have not been enthusiastically embraced.

completely dry, and at the end of the fermentation process, the *Süssreserve* juice can be blended in, giving the wine a fruitier, even sweeter character. The addition of *Süssreserve* is widely practiced in low- to middle-quality German wine-making but is frowned on by top-quality producers.

GRAPE VARIETIES

GERMANY'S CLIMATE is best suited to the recognized cool-climate grapes. Most of the vineyards are planted with white Region 1 varieties, and approximately 25 percent of plantings is given to the lighter red varieties, such as Pinot Noir. Germany has long been famous as the originator of numerous vinifera crosses, such as Müller-Thurgau, but interest in these varieties has decreased as growers and winemakers have reverted to the old classics Riesling and Pinot Noir. There has also been a surge of interest in the ancient varieties Pinot Blanc and Pinot Gris. In order of numbers of acres planted, the following are the most important grape varieties.

Riesling

The noble Riesling grape has maintained its place as Germany's most widely planted grape, with 22 percent of total acreage. It is highly revered by all German grape growers and winemakers for its ability to produce wines of outstanding beauty and delicacy, tasting incredibly fresh when first made, but capable of extensive aging and development.

Riesling in the Rothenberg vineyard near Nackenheim

Despite its glowing reputation, Riesling faces a major problem, especially in Germany's cold climate. To fully ripen, Riesling needs a long, slow growing season because the grape is a late ripener. Riesling's internal clock leaves it quite susceptible to fall frosts, and it is therefore not the most practical grape to grow in Germany's colder vineyards. Surprisingly, Riesling is the dominant grape in the cold northern region of Mosel and is the most-planted grape in six more of the thirteen wine-producing regions.

Müller-Thurgau

In what turned out to be a successful attempt to capture the delicacy and ripeness of Riesling in a shorter growing season, Professor Hermann Müller in 1882 created a cross of Riesling and Gutedel (known as Chasselas in France and Fendant in Switzerland, Professor Müller's home country). The resulting new grape variety, called Müller-Thurgau, has many of the fruit-and-acid-balance characteristics of Riesling but does not need such a long growing season, meaning that it is less likely to be exposed to early or late frosts. Given the grape's practicality from the growers' point of view, and its attractive flavors and balance from the winemakers' point of view, it is not surprising that Müller-Thurgau is now the second most widely planted grape in Germany, with 20 percent of all acreage. Its floral character and fresh fruit mean that it makes attractive everyday wines, and it is particularly useful in simple, fruity blends.

Harvested Müller-Thurgau grapes ready for pressing

Pinot Noir

The Pinot Noir grape (traditionally called Spätburgunder) now occupies a surprising 8 percent of total acreage. It is used to produce Blanc de Noirs white wines, some rosé (*Weissherbst*), and red wines, though the majority of the red wines are very light and have little fruit character on the middle palate, mostly because of ridiculously high yields in the vineyards. A few producers have made stunning wines, achieving higher concentration through lower yields and by aging in small wooden barrels, providing structural tannins. Perhaps in the future there will be other winemaking techniques, such as whole-cluster or whole-berry fermentation, bleeding off excess clear juice, or the use of rotofermenters, but the most important thing is to reduce the yields in the vineyards.

Silvaner

Plantings of the Silvaner (Sylvaner in Alsace) grape have decreased in total acreage over the past five years, but it still holds at 7 percent. It has been popular as a workhorse grape that made ordinary to good wines but rarely exceptional ones. The advantage of the Silvaner grape, and what made it so popular with growers, is that it is late-budding and early-ripening. This makes it a vine type that is well suited to Germany's climate. Silvaner has been revived by some producers in Rheinhessen, Nahe, and Franken. With careful vineyard practices, it can produce attractive, fruity wines, especially if enhanced by some minerality.

Other Grapes

Since the landmark cross of Müller-Thurgau in 1882, many more crosses have been developed from various grape varieties and clones, all specifically engineered for the cold northern climate. Crosses such as Kerner, Bacchus, and Scheurebe abound, but they have all been losing acreage recently as growers and winemakers show more interest in Pinot Gris (called Grauburgunder or Ruländer in Germany) and Pinot Blanc (known as Weissburgunder). Both of these grapes are now becoming widely used by winemakers who want to produce firm, dry white wines with higher alcohol levels and fuller flavors.

Despite its German-sounding name, Gewürztraminer is not widely grown in Germany, and it is probably not a native German grape anyway. The markedly pungent aroma and flavors of Gewürz tend to be too strong for many German winemakers, who prefer to concentrate on the delicacy and finesse of Riesling or Müller-Thurgau.

Two red grapes that have shown increases in acreage are Portugieser and Dornfelder (the latter is a cross that was developed in 1955). So far, the wines from Portugieser remain very light in style, or they are used for *Weissherbst*. In contrast, the Dornfelder was bred to provide color, and some producers in Pfalz and Rheinhessen see the potential of barrel fermentation or barrel aging to create complex, full-bodied wines with this grape.

Lastly, the seemingly ubiquitous Chardonnay was approved by the German wine authorities in 1991 as a grape variety permitted in most regions, though it has already decreased in acreage. Even Cabernet Sauvignon has been approved, but it will take several decades before it finds a place in the German wine landscape.

WINE LAWS

IN MANY WAYS, the practical embodiment of any nation's wine laws, from the consumer's point of view, is the label on the bottle, which also acts as the primary selling agent for any bottle of wine. Germany's wine labels are a fine example of a curious paradox: Historically, they were the worst-selling agents of any wine from anywhere, but they were also the most accurate and most informative reflection of the wine laws and culture that govern wine production in the country. For most people, however, especially Americans used to simple varietal labels, German wine labels were all but impossible to understand.

Vertical-shoot positioning is typical in Germany's cooler regions.

Like other European wine-producing countries, Germany has been active in accepting the need for laws to govern grape growing, winemaking, and labeling and the need to review and, if necessary, change those laws. However, keeping pace with trends and satisfying everybody is next to impossible, and there are certainly groups in Germany who have been critical of the laws.

The principal reason for this discontent is that the categorization within the wine laws was based solely on the natural sugar content of the grapes at harvest. The grape sugar content must be measured and recorded, and there are specified levels of sugar that must be achieved if a producer wants to classify his or her wine in any of the traditional legal categories. In addition, certain descriptive words are allowed to be used on the labels only if a predetermined sugar level was reached at harvest time.

Defenders emphasize that the sugar-at-harvest system is much more democratic—it means that any vineyard in any region in Germany, assuming that the climatic conditions are right, can achieve the highest category of wine classification. Critics argue that the system encouraged the production of sweet wines and that it flies in the face of the accepted and conventional winemaking experience that the precise geographical origin (*terroir*) of the grapes is the overriding factor in determining quality. This *terroir* argument has been reinforced by Austria's development of a place-oriented labeling system that overrides that nation's sugar-at-harvest system, and now Germany is adopting labeling terms that give more importance to the place name.

WINE CATEGORIES

LIKE ALL MEMBER NATIONS of the European Union, Germany recognizes three broad types of wine outlined in the August 2009 reforms:
- Wine, what Germans used to call **TAFELWEIN**
- Two protected place-name categories (PDO and PGI)

The German categories parallel the systems used to classify wines in all other EU countries. In ascending order, Germany's main categories are:
- *Wein*
- *Geschützte geographische Angabe (ggA)*, previously referred to as *Landwein* (PGI wine with at least 85 percent of the grapes grown in one of the twenty *Landwein* regions of Germany)

- *Geschützte Ursprungsbezeichnung* (gU), previously covered by the *Qualitätswein* and *Prädikatswein* categories (quality wines produced from 100 percent of the grapes grown in one of the thirteen designated quality regions)

Geschützte Geographische Angabe

These regional wines are assumed to be quality wines with regional distinction. At least 85 percent of the grapes used to make the wines must come from one of twenty designated *Landwein* regions. The particular region will be specified on the label.

LANDWEIN REGIONS

Ahrtaler Landwein	Starkenburger Landwein
Rheinburgen Landwein	Landwein der Mosel
Landwein der Saar	Landwein der Ruwer
Nahegauer Landwein	Rheingauer Landwein
Rheinischer Landwein	Pfälzer Landwein
Fränkischer Landwein	Regensburger Landwein
Schwäbischer Landwein	Saarländischer Landwein der Mosel
Badischer Landwein	Taubertaler Landwein
Bayerischer-Bodensee Landwein	Sächsischer Landwein
Mitteldeutscher Landwein	Schleswig-Holstein

Some producers claim that wine categorization should be based on the terroir *of a vineyard. This soil is one of the elements of terroir in the Kloster Eberbach vineyard in the Rheingau region.*

Geschützte Ursprungsbezeichnung

This new category introduced by the EU reforms covers the old German categories of *Qualitätswein* and *Prädikatswein*. Until 2011, German producers will continue to use the old terms alone or in conjunction with the new category. All the wines in this group are Protected Designation of Origin wines. They must carry a place name on the label, and 100 percent of the grapes used to make the wine must come from the smallest named place on the label.

Since the *Qualitätswein* and *Prädikatswein* categories continue to be used, the following sections discuss the regulations that apply to these traditional categories.

QUALITÄTSWEIN

The grapes for **QUALITÄTSWEIN** must be varieties approved by German wine authorities and must be sufficiently ripe at harvest to reflect the natural flavor characteristics of the grape and the region. The German wine laws allow *Qualitätswein* to be "enhanced" by chaptalization or the addition of *Süssreserve* (see page 490).

The grapes used to produce the *Qualitätswein* wines must be grown in one of thirteen *Anbaugebiete*, or specified regions. These regions are then subdivided, as shown in the table below. In order of increasing specificity, the subdivisions are region, district, village, collective vineyard site, and individual vineyard site.

STRUCTURE OF GERMAN WINE REGIONS AND THEIR SUBDIVISIONS

LAND UNITS

13 ANBAUGEBIETE
Specified wine regions, each with its own name, e.g., Mosel

40 BEREICHE
Small districts within a region, each with its own name, e.g., Bernkastel

APPROXIMATELY 1,400 VILLAGES
In this case, the *Bereich* and the village just happen to have the same name, e.g., Bernkastel

163 GROSSLAGEN
Within a district there are collective vineyard sites, each with its own name, that group together several smaller vineyard sites, e.g., Bernkasteler Badstube

2,715 EINZELLAGEN
Very small plots of land that are individual vineyard sites, each with its own name, e.g., Bernkasteler Doktor

PRÄDIKATSWEIN

Wines that are labeled as *Prädikatswein* cannot be chaptalized. At this level it becomes glaringly obvious that Germany's wine laws and label terminology are not based on historical perspective, soil considerations, or vineyard classifications, but simply on the degree of ripeness of the grapes at harvest and the measurable sugar in the juice of those grapes. In theory at least, any vineyard in any of Germany's thirteen *Anbaugebiete*, given suitable weather during the growing season, could garner enough sugar in the grapes to qualify for the status of *Trockenbeerenauslese*, the highest rung on the old ladder of German wine classification (see page 496).

It is also theoretically possible (and it happens in practice) for one vineyard to go through several successive pickings during one harvest period, with each subsequent picking yielding grapes that are higher in sugar than the grapes from the previous picking. Alternatively, grapes may be harvested at the same time but sorted according to sugar levels into different categories in the vineyard or at the winery. By these methods it is possible for one vineyard to produce two or (rarely) three classifications of the same wine within the same harvest year.

The *Prädikatswein* category is subdivided into six classifications or distinctions. Again, to qualify for any of these distinctions, the winemaker or grape grower must be able to show that the original grape sugar levels at harvest were sufficiently high to meet the predetermined standard. Remember that in achieving higher sugar levels, the grape growers also achieve fuller ripeness of the natural grape flavors. Thus the objective is to produce clean, natural varietal character within the balancing parameters of acidity, alcohol, and sweetness. Again, top producers do not manipulate their wines or use technology to arrive at precise alcohol or sweetness levels. For these finer producers, the fermentation must stop naturally, so wines at many of the different levels within *Prädikatswein* may be dry or sweet, and they may have alcohol as low as 9 percent or as high as 14 percent by volume. For any wine deemed *Prädikatswein*, one of the six classifications described below must be printed on the label.

It is important to remember that a wine in some of these categories may additionally carry the notation *trocken* or **HALBTROCKEN**, indicating that it is dry or off-dry, with lower levels of residual sugar.

KABINETT

KABINETT wines are usually fine, relatively light wines, made from fully ripe grapes. Remember that "fully ripe" in the context of the cold German climate is not the same as it is in, say, the context of California or another more temperate climate. Here it means very fresh, just-ripe flavors, with plenty of acidity still present.

SPÄTLESE

The word **SPÄTLESE** literally means "late-picked" or "late-harvest," but again, this should not be equated with a California late-harvest designation. To make this wine, the grapes are left on the vine slightly longer than for *Kabinett*, allowing them to reach higher sugar levels. The wines show fuller flavor and more concentration but are not necessarily sweeter, since the greater amount of sugars at harvest may all have been converted into alcohol.

AUSLESE

AUSLESE translates as "selected," indicating that, at harvest, some bunches of grapes were selected as showing very full ripeness or obvious signs of botrytis. The resulting wines are usually intense in aroma and taste. They are usually sweet, but some producers ferment them dry.

BEERENAUSLESE

The term *Beerenauslese* is often abbreviated to BA when spoken, though not on the label. The literal translation is "selected berries," suggesting that at harvest the pickers select from the grape bunches those individual grapes that are considered overripe or that show signs of extensive botrytis rot. The wines made from these grapes are very

Riesling grapes affected by the botrytis mold

rich and luscious. Only a small number of wines in very small quantity are made in this style, and they are relatively expensive.

EISWEIN

Eiswein, or Icewine, is a separate distinction within the *Prädikatswein* category, although the measured sugar content at harvest must be at least equal to *Beerenauslese* standards. *Eiswein* from Germany is rare and expensive, and it represents one of the purest renditions of the essence of grape varietal character, unblemished by botrytis.

To qualify as *Eiswein*, the grapes are left on the vine, often into December, until a sudden drop in temperature freezes the water content of the grapes. Legally, the grapes must be exposed to a temperature of at least 17.5°F/–8°C for a minimum of six hours. The attendant risks involved are as great as, if not greater than, with **TROCKENBEERENAUSLESE**, the next rung up, since the grapes used to make *Eiswein* cannot show any sign of botrytis or any other kind of rot and should have no breaks in their skin. The objective is to allow the varietal characteristics of the grape to develop to their maximum. Because the grapes are not affected by rot, they maintain an optimal balance of sugars and acids.

Riesling grapes frozen on the vine for Eiswein *production*

That balance can then be shown off to the highest degree by harvesting the frozen grapes and pressing them so gently that the frozen water content is left untouched. Thus all that drips from the press is pure, concentrated liquid grape character. The resulting wines are sweet, though not excessively so, but they are very concentrated renditions of the sugar-acid balance of the grapes.

As mentioned above, climate change and milder winters are threatening the continued production of *Eiswein* in some parts of Germany.

TROCKENBEERENAUSLESE

By now it should be clear that many German words are compounds of several shorter words—three, in this case. Pieced together, this tongue-twister simply means "dried berries picked out," or selected raisins. That is to say, the grapes used to make this wine are selected at harvest for the fact that they are probably covered with botrytis and have also shriveled to raisins while still on the vine. Many winemakers and grape growers take enormous risks (the grapes are exposed to frosts, high winds, hail, rainstorms, and natural predators, such as birds, deer, and appreciative children) to leave the grapes on the vines as late as November or December in order to get these prized grapes. Since they are raisins, they contain very little juice, but that juice is extremely rich and concentrated in natural grape sugars. It makes a wine that comes close to pure nectar, an incredibly concentrated essence of the grape variety. Fine **TROCKENBEERENAUSLESE** wines are rare and very expensive. (The word *Trockenbeerenauslese* is usually abbreviated to TBA in speech.)

THE QUALITY-CONTROL PROCESS

···

AS DO ALL EUROPEAN WINE-PRODUCING COUNTRIES, Germany operates a system of checks on quality wines. At the vineyard level, the German wine laws do the following:

- Stipulate which permitted grape varieties can be grown.
- Define the growing regions (appellations of origin).
- Set the minimum sugar levels that grapes must reach in order to qualify for the various label designations of *Kabinett*, *Spätlese*, and so on. The required sugar levels vary from region to region and from grape type to grape type.

At the postproduction level, the laws require that any quality wine go through an analysis and a tasting test. The analysis measures the wine's content of alcohol, residual sugar, and acidity and also tests for any fraudulent additions to the wine. The tasting test is done by experts familiar with the region where the grapes were grown. The tasters expect to be able to identify the "correct" characteristics derived from the grape, the region, and the vintage.

If a wine passes these tests, it is given its **AMTLICHE PRÜFUNGSNUMMER** (usually abbreviated to A.P. No.), which must be printed on the label and can be used in the future to identify the exact origin of the wine (see the breakdown below). Two bottles of each wine are kept sealed by the wine authorities for at least two years, in case complaints are leveled against the wine.

If a wine is judged not to meet the panel's standards, the panel may approve a lower status for the wine than the one requested by the producer, or it may refuse the wine outright. If a wine is rejected, the producer can blend it in with another wine or initiate legal proceedings against the decision.

WHAT THE A.P. NO. MEANS

On a label, the A.P. No. might be 4 382 123 9 10.
Each set of numerals has a meaning. In this case:
- 4 is the number assigned to the examination board.
- 382 is the number of the community where the vineyard is located.
- 123 is the assigned number of the bottler or producer.
- 9 is the bottler or producer's lot or current number.
- 10 is the year of the examination (not the vintage year).

LABELS

EVEN THE MOST PROTECTIVE German winemakers would, or should, admit that one of the biggest barriers to increased sales of German wines has been the German wine label. To the average wine consumer around the world, German wine labels have been daunting and intimidating.

The irony is that the laws that control the German wine categories require that certain pieces of information be printed on the label. If the producer claims that the wine is *Qualitätswein*, it must, by definition, come from a designated *Anbaugebiet* or quality wine region, and the produc-

er must state the region on the label. Therefore, a consumer who knows anything about the style of the wines from the Mosel area or from the Rhine area will have a pretty good idea of the style of the wine in the bottle. Furthermore, if the producer claims that the wine is *Prädikatswein*, the label must show what *Prädikat* level was reached. Again, the consumer is given key information about the ripeness of the grapes at harvest and can make some reasonable assumptions about the style of the wine in the bottle. This is especially true if the producer includes an indication of *trocken* or *halbtrocken*.

However, there have been some significant changes in labeling by some producers, most of them for the better. Most obviously, there have been a number of attempts to simplify, even to create brand identities for German wines, providing for the simplest kind of label. Examples of this include Saint M, Twisted River, and Clean Slate.

Even among more traditional producers, the trend is toward cleaner, less cluttered labels, with fewer words and less Gothic script. The traditional naming system for quality wines in Germany is very similar to the categories used in Burgundy, as the following examples illustrate.

- Regional wines are named after the region (*Anbaugebiet*) if the grapes used to make the wine came from several nonspecific sites within that region. If a grape variety is named, the wine must contain at least 85 percent of that variety. An example would be Mosel Riesling.

A new generation of simplified German labels: Clean Slate refers to a new beginning and the principal soil type along the Mosel River.

- If a wine is made from grapes gathered from several vineyards within a subdistrict (**BEREICH**) of any region, then the wine can take the name of the district. The same percentage minimum applies to any named grape variety. An example would be Bereich Bernkastel Riesling, where Bernkastel is a district (*Bereich*) in Mosel region.
- Wines made from grapes from two or more vineyards within the same village can take the village name, so that Riesling wine from several vineyards in the village of Wehlen could be labeled as Wehlener Riesling.
- Alternatively, the producer may choose to use a name that groups together several vineyards within one village. For example, the collective vineyard name that covers all of the single vineyards in Wehlen is Münzlay. The wine name therefore could be Wehlener Münzlay.
- If a wine is made from grapes from one single vineyard, the label will most often carry the name of the village and the name of the vineyard, as in Wehlener Sonnenuhr, where the grapes came only from the Sonnenuhr vineyard in the village of Wehlen.
- There are a few historical cases where single-vineyard wines are identified on the label by the vineyard name only, with no mention of the village. Examples of such vineyards include Scharzhof in the Mosel region and Schloss Johannisberg and Schloss Vollrads in Rheingau.

VINEYARD CLASSIFICATION

THERE IS A MAVERICK GROUP of producers who continue their quiet revolution in making, labeling, and marketing German wines. The group is represented by the likes of Weingut Georg Breuer and Weingut Robert Weil in the Rheingau region. In Mosel, Weingut von Othegraven, Weingut Selbach-Oster, and Weingut Schloss Lieser are key players, just as Weingut Bürklin-Wolf and Weingut Pfeffingen-Fuhrmann-Eymael are in Pfalz. Weingut Freiherr Heyl zu Herrnsheim is among the leaders in the Rheinhessen region. What characterizes these wine estates is an unerring commitment to quality and the recognition that the quality of a wine is first and foremost a reflection of its provenance.

Most important, all of these producers are stressing the quality level of wines produced in a dry style. They have therefore turned their back on the traditional labeling practices that indicate sugar level at harvest, and they have begun concentrating more and more on the vineyard site as the most important piece of information on the label, the true arbiter of quality. This parallels the official route taken by some Austrian regions, where the geographic name will preempt any mention of the grape variety on the front label. Many German producers belong to groups that promote the theory of *Erste Lage* (literally, first site) or first growths, just like the *premier cru–grand cru* system of France. Their claims are similar to the age-old Burgundy practice that identifies certain vineyard sites as being of superlative quality and deserving of such recognition.

The main lobby group that favors vineyard classification is the **VERBAND DEUTSCHER PRÄDIKATSWEINGÜTER (VDP).** Its members are all single-estate wine producers who are committed to producing high-quality wines that exhibit the distinctiveness of their geographic and varietal origin. To achieve this, they follow self-imposed guidelines that go beyond the standards set by the German wine laws, using no chaptalization, decreasing yields in the vineyards, concentrating on Riesling and other classic varietals from premium sites, and insisting on higher ripeness levels at harvest. Wines made by VDP members can be identified by the association logo (an eagle with a cluster of grapes) printed on the bottle capsule.

To move even further away from the image that grape sugar levels at harvest are all-important, some producers are even declassifying their finest wine down from *Prädikatswein* level to simple *Qualitätswein* level. By doing this, they are no longer required to indicate the sugar level at harvest by a descriptive term (such as *Spätlese* or *Auslese*) on the label, even though the wine would easily qualify for that category under the existing wine laws. Their perspective is that any inclusion of words like *Spätlese* leads too many consumers to assume that the wine will be sweet.

The VDP has worked long and hard to establish a set of guidelines that would allow members to use vaunted phrases like *Erste Lage* (first-class site) or *Grosses Gewächs* (great growth, or *grand cru*) to identify their premium wines from specific high-quality vineyards.

To claim the VDP's *Erste Lage* designation, the grapes must be an approved variety (decided by regional VDP associations) from a high-quality single vineyard (approved by the VDP), with a maximum yield of 3.5 tons per acre/50 hectoliters per hectare. Dry versions of such wines would be referred to as *Grosses Gewächs*, but the name of the wine on the label would be the vineyard name. "Fruity versions with natural sweetness" would revert to the standard German labeling practices, with village and/or vineyard name and the standard phrases like *Prädikatswein Auslese*. To identify these top-echelon wines, the *Erste Lage* logo will be embossed on the bottle or printed on the label.

Predictably perhaps, initial enthusiasm has been tempered by resistance to what amounts to another set of rules and regulations about which vineyards and wines qualify for these exalted titles.

Despite any setbacks, these top producers are proud to lead by example—high-quality wines from high-quality vineyards, without reference to sugar at harvest. And their work has already born fruit. There have been notable improvements in many of the mediocre wines that used to be standard in parts of Rheinhessen and Pfalz. More and more producers are paying more and more attention to the importance of site and to the selection of quality grape varieties, rather than simply opting for the highest-yielding varieties.

WINE REGIONS

GERMANY HAS THIRTEEN RECOGNIZED *Anbaugebiete* (wine regions) producing wines at the *Qualitätswein* and *Prädikatswein* levels, including two new regions from the former East Germany. The total area under vine in these thirteen regions is just shy of 252,000 acres/102,000 hectares, producing approximately 277 million gallons/10.5 million hectoliters of wine. Not all of Germany's wine regions are represented on the export market. The five most important regions are Mosel (formerly Mosel-Saar-Ruwer), Rheingau, Pfalz, Rheinhessen, and Nahe. These five regions will be covered in some depth, and the chapter will offer a summary of the salient facts of the other eight wine-producing regions in Germany. Remember that each *Anbaugebiet* consists of anywhere from one to eight *Bereiche* (smaller districts within the region), each of which contains from one to twenty-five GROSSLAGEN (collective vineyards) and from 17 to 525 EINZELLAGEN (single vineyards).

Mosel

This highly regarded region concentrates on white wine production (92 percent), with a large percentage of Riesling (56 percent) in the vineyards. It is famed for its very elegant wines that display an attractive mix of pure fruit, delicacy, and minerality. The slate soil is a major factor in the total *terroir*. With 23,500 acres/9,500 hectares of vineyard, the six *Bereiche* of the region are Zell/Mosel, Bernkastel, Obermosel, Saar, Ruwertal, and Moseltor. They are subdivided into nineteen *Grosslagen* and 525 *Einzellagen*. Visitors

The highly regarded Hipping vineyard near Nierstein

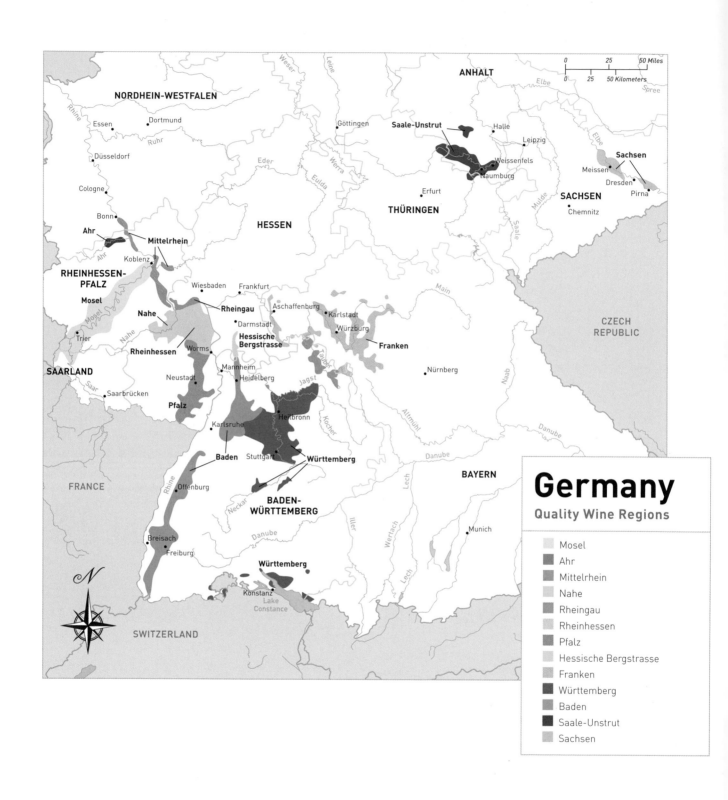

Germany
Quality Wine Regions

- Mosel
- Ahr
- Mittelrhein
- Nahe
- Rheingau
- Rheinhessen
- Pfalz
- Hessische Bergstrasse
- Franken
- Württemberg
- Baden
- Saale-Unstrut
- Sachsen

0   25   50 Miles
0   25   50 Kilometers

NORDHEIN-WESTFALEN

ANHALT

Saale-Unstrut

SACHSEN

Sachsen

THÜRINGEN

HESSEN

CZECH
REPUBLIC

Ahr

Mittelrhein

RHEINHESSEN-
PFALZ

Mosel

Nahe

Rheingau

Rheinhessen

Hessische
Bergstrasse

Franken

SAARLAND

Pfalz

Baden

Württemberg

FRANCE

BAYERN

BADEN-
WÜRTTEMBERG

Württemberg

SWITZERLAND

Essen · Dortmund · Göttingen · Halle · Leipzig · Meissen · Dresden · Pirna
Düsseldorf · Weissenfels · Naumburg · Erfurt · Chemnitz
Cologne · Bonn · Koblenz · Wiesbaden · Frankfurt · Aschaffenburg · Karlstadt · Würzburg · Nürnberg
Trier · Worms · Darmstadt · Mannheim · Heidelberg · Neustadt · Saarbrücken · Karlsruhe · Heilbronn · Stuttgart · Offenburg · Munich · Breisach · Freiburg · Konstanz

Rhine · Ruhr · Weser · Leine · Werra · Elbe · Spree · Eder · Fulda · Mulde · Saale · Main · Naab · Mosel · Nahe · Saar · Tauber · Jagst · Kocher · Altmühl · Danube · Lech · Neckar · Iller · Wertach · Lake Constance

The product of all this care and attention is wines that are always acceptable and occasionally superb.

It is hard to talk about quality in the Mosel without certain producers' names cropping up. In many ways, the region is dominated by the Haag family, with Wilhelm Haag still in control at Weingut Fritz Haag and his son Thomas bringing new brilliance to the wines of Weingut Schloss Lieser, while Marcus Haag continues to impress at Weingut Willi Haag. There are others: Dr. Loosen, Egon Müller, and Johann Josef Prüm all make outstanding wines; Dr. Peter Pauly continues the tradition of excellence of his own family's estate and that of his wife's family; and there are rising stars like Johannes Selbach of Selbach-Oster.

With the effects of climate change becoming more noticeable, this northerly growing region generally produces good-to-excellent growing conditions on a fairly regular basis. Even so, top-quality producers continue to concentrate on grapes from prime vineyard sites to take full advantage of exposure to sunlight and heat to guarantee fully ripe grapes.

The rivers play an important role in this regard. The riverbanks are very steep, sometimes impossibly so, but they provide an elevated and angled piece of land that in effect lifts the vineyards up into more-direct sunlight, providing the essential elements of light and heat. In addition, the mirror-like surface of the rivers provides reflected light, and the bodies of water act as temperature-moderating influences, maintaining warmer air temperatures in October and November as the grapes reach the end of their growing season. This reliance on rivers is common in all grape-growing areas of the world, but it is especially important here, where the rivers provide enough extra heat to allow the mercurial Riesling grape to ripen fully and develop all of its delicious varietal characteristics. Grape growers also know that the rivers are slower to warm up in springtime, and this holds back the air temperatures on the hillsides, maintaining colder temperatures in the vineyards and delaying budding until most of the danger of frost is past.

Of all the steep vineyard terraces, it is, understandably, the south-facing hillsides of the Mosel that are most prized. Such vineyards would fetch enormous amounts of money if any grape grower wanted to sell such a parcel of land.

The entire Mosel region includes the smaller subregions of Saar, Ruwer, Upper Mosel (from the southern-

to Mosel usually come away with two lasting impressions, vines and rivers, for they are the heart and soul of the region. The Saar and the Ruwer, two small tributaries of the Mosel River, flow in a generally northerly direction into the Mosel as it winds its tortuously meandering way from France to Koblenz, where it empties into the Rhine.

The rivers play a vital part in making grape growing and winemaking possible in an otherwise difficult climate. Everywhere the visitor looks, every available riverbank hillside, including the smallest, seemingly inaccessible ledges, is planted with vines. And the reason is simple: Nothing else will grow in the predominantly slate soil, and no other crop warrants the care and devotion expended on the vines. Each vine is individually tended; indeed, the Mosel tradition is to train each vine on its own stake rather than on a trellis system with wires. This is because the slopes are so steep in places that trellis wire systems simply do not work.

TOP: *The hillsides of the Mosel region are so steep that normal trellising is impractical. Instead, each plant is supported by a single pole.* BOTTOM: *Slate is common in the Mosel vineyards.*

most village of Perl to where the Ruwer River enters the Mosel), Middle Mosel (from the village of Kenn to the village of Bullay), and Lower Mosel (from Bullay to Koblenz, where the Mosel joins the Rhine). There are subtle nuances of style from one region to another.

Saar wines have a very high, bracing acidity from its relatively unsheltered geography, which allows brisk, cold winds to cool the vineyards. Although Saar wines may not have high natural sugar levels at harvest, they always have high fruit aromatics, and the best vineyards produce wines of outstanding body and concentration, all couched in an elegant, subtle structure.

In Ruwer, in contrast, a more protected topography means that the vineyards are more sheltered than in Saar. In addition, there is a higher humus content in Ruwer's red-slate soils, making for a more evident sense of ripe fruit in the wine's youth.

In Upper Mosel, limestone is the more dominant soil type, giving the wines a crisp, steely quality, while Middle and Lower Mosel display more of the flinty, mineral qualities associated with the higher slate content there.

Despite the region's notoriously difficult climate, it is still the Riesling grape that is preferred by most growers and winemakers, accounting for about 56 percent of total acreage. The next most common grape in this region is Müller-Thurgau, with very small percentages of Elbling, Bacchus, Optima, and Kerner. The great advantage of new biological crosses such as Bacchus and Optima is that they can ripen enough for decent *Qualitätswein* wine to be made even in years when the weather at harvest time is not too cooperative. These wines can either be sold under their own varietal name or blended with Riesling to provide the extra ripeness that Riesling wines lack in poor years.

The Mosel, then, is not the most consistent region for producing fine wines. There are some years when the grapes lack fruit development, and many producers will not even offer the wines for sale under their name. Plenty of Sekt producers are happy to buy the immature, high-acid grapes, or the finished wines, for their sparkling-wine production.

But when all of the planets are aligned and all of the omens are right, Mosel wines can be some of the finest on earth. As *Qualitätswein* and *Prädikatswein* wines, they always show an astounding elegance, finesse, and balance of fruit and acidity. Even experienced tasters can be

---

TOP: *The Sonnenuhr (sundial) vineyard near the village of Wehlen*   MIDDLE: *A typical Mosel scene, with steep hillside vineyards among the rocky ledges near the village of Wehlen* BOTTOM: *Riesling vineyards cover the hillsides above the village of Zeltingen.*

SAAR VILLAGES AND VINEYARDS

Wiltingen, with the famous *Einzellagen* Braune Kupp, Rosenberg, Schlossberg, Kupp, Hölle, and Klosterberg. The most renowned *Einzellage* is Scharzhofberger, whose name appears on labels without the town name of Wiltingen.

Ockfen, whose three best-known *Einzellagen* are Kupp, Herrenberg, and Bockstein.

Ayl, with the famous *Einzellagen* of Kupp and Herrenberger.

Oberemmel, where Karlsberg, Rosenberg, and Altenberg are the three most significant *Einzellagen.*

Kanzem, with its famous *Einzellage* Altenberg.

RUWER VILLAGES AND VINEYARDS

Kasel, Metersdorf, Waldrach, and Maximin Grünhaus are all famous villages in the *Grosslage* Römerlay.

Herrenberg and Nieschen are the best *Einzellagen* in the villages of Kasel and Maximin Grünhaus.

MIDDLE MOSEL VILLAGES AND VINEYARDS

Bernkastel, which produces wines with *Bereich* labeling but also contains the great *Einzellagen* Doktor and Graben.

Piesport, where the large *Grosslage* Michelsberg and the *Einzellage* Goldtröpfchen are the most famous.

Graach, whose perfect location on the river makes it famous for the *Einzellage* Himmelreich.

Wehlen, which is world famous for the *Einzellage* Sonnenuhr.

Zeltingen, which is best known for its largest *Einzellage*, Schlossberg, as well as its share of the Sonnenuhr *Einzellage.*

Brauneberg, where the finest *Einzellage* is Juffer.

MAJOR PRODUCERS OF THE MOSEL

Deinhard	Egon Müller
Pauly-Bergweiler	Schloss Lieser
Dr. Fischer	Fritz Haag
Dr. Thanisch-Müller	von Schubert
Dr. Loosen	Selbach-Oster
Rudolf Müller	Willi Haag
J. J. Prüm	Reichsgraf von Kesselstatt

stopped in their tracks by the seemingly impossible high-wire balancing act that the wines represent, treading a very fine line between the fresh but mouth-filling Riesling fruit flavors and latent sweetness. At the same time, the lively, crisp citrus character cleanses the palate and allows the delicate flavors to linger for an incredibly long time in the mouth. These characteristics are visually apparent in the lively tinge of green color of all Mosel wines. According to tradition, Mosel wines are bottled in a tall, narrow green bottle, called a flute. Plenty of Mosel producers have shaken off that tradition, however, and it is not unusual to find blue or even red bottles today.

Even in those rare years when *Auslese* or *Beerenauslese* wines are produced, the wines still maintain the alluring freshness and lightness that make them so appealing. Whatever style the wines are made in, they rarely exceed 12 percent alcohol by volume and more often contain between 8 and 12 percent.

The steeply inclined Altenberg vineyard rises above the von Othegraven winery in the village of Kanzem in Saar.

As with all fine wine-producing regions where the wines are named for their place of origin, the name of the producer is an equally important consideration. Listed on the opposite page is a selection of some of the most important villages, with some of the well-known *Grosslagen* and *Einzellagen* in those villages, plus a number of the major producers' names.

Rheingau

For most of its journey to the sea, the Rhine River heads in a northerly and northwesterly direction. But at Mainz it turns in a west-southwesterly direction for about 18 miles/30 kilometers until it reaches Rüdesheim, where it heads north again. This provides an uninterrupted strip of hillside running up from the river with an almost perfect exposure to the summer sun during the daytime. In addition, the top of the hillside is heavily forested, providing a useful barrier to colder air from the north. Of course, the Rhine itself helps maintain advantageous temperatures in the spring and autumn.

Even more than the Mosel, Rheingau is heavily planted with Riesling vines. There has been a dramatic increase in recent years in the plantings of Spätburgunder (Pinot Noir), which accounts for almost 13 percent of all plantings in the region.

As a group, Rheingau wines are considerably fuller in body and flavor than those of the Mosel, reflecting the higher red slate content of the soil, with quartzite as an additional component. The best of the wines maintain the elegance and distinction of the Riesling grape grown in a cool climate, but they are generally firmer, riper, richer wines in color, aroma, and taste. The very finest are the single-vineyard wines of the best producers, such as the traditional and long-standing estates of Schloss Johannisberg and Schloss Vollrads, as well as the more modern Weingut Robert Weil and Weingut Georg Breuer. Their total commitment to maintaining the integrity and quality of their premium vineyard sites results in wines that have amazing structure and longevity and could easily stand shoulder to shoulder with the finest Savennières from the Loire Valley or a lean Puligny-Montrachet from Burgundy. Such wines are likely to be at least off-dry, if not completely dry, with alcohol levels around 12 or even 13 percent.

In the past, tradition dictated that wines from Rheingau and other Rhine areas would be bottled in tall, slim brown bottles. Count Erwein Graf Matuschka-Greiffenclau pioneered the introduction of a more distinctive antique blue bottle for Rheingau Riesling producers, but not everybody has followed suit, and individualism seems to be more prevalent than ever in the color of bottles chosen by various producers.

Pfalz

Pfalz is Germany's second-largest region, with 57,800 acres/23,400 hectares under vine, producing 62 percent white wine and 20 percent of the acreage planted with Riesling and a further 12 percent planted with Müller-Thurgau. Remarkably, plantings of red varieties have increased dramatically, with Dornfelder and Portugieser occupying 13 percent and 11 percent of vineyard land, respectively.

The *Bereiche* are Mittelhardt/Deutsche Weinstrasse and Südliche Weinstrasse. These comprise twenty-five *Grosslagen* and 333 *Einzellagen*. The recent history of Pfalz is a very good example of how rapidly a region can change its identity, and how that rapid change mirrors many of the slower changes in grape growing and winemaking that have been taking place in Germany and the rest of Europe over the past two decades. Not too long ago, it was easy to make generalizations: The best Pfalz wines came from the Riesling vineyards in the northern half of the region, with a very large quantity of lesser, ordinary wines produced from Silvaner in the southern half of the region. In fact, so much ordinary wine was produced here that the Pfalz once had a reputation as the region that produced

The forests of the Haardt Mountains play an important protective role in allowing the Pfalz vineyards to produce Riesling grapes of exceptional ripeness.

the largest quantity of wine, even though it is only second-largest in acreage.

While it is still true that the most elegant and finest wines continue to be Rieslings from the northern section, southern grape growers have revolutionized their vineyard practices, spurred on by the commitment to quality and use of specific vineyard sites demonstrated by wine estates such as Bürklin-Wolf, Müller-Catoir, Pfeffingen-Fuhrmann-Eymael, and Reichsrat von Buhl. The revival in the south means that there is a greater concentration on site-specific grape varieties, such as more Riesling, Müller-Thurgau, Scheurebe, and Morio-Muskat. There has also been an increase in red grape acreage, concentrating particularly on Portugieser, Dornfelder, and Spätburgunder. The result is that some fine wines from southern vineyards now compete for attention with the northern Rieslings.

Overall, Pfalz wines are recognized as being sturdier, higher-alcohol, rounder styles of German wine, with slightly lower acidity levels because of the warmer climate and the larger amounts of sandstone, gravel, and granite in the soil. The wines often show a light earthiness or spiciness. These characteristics make these some of Germany's most food-compatible wines, since they have the structure and authority to match even the strong flavors of game, fish, and meats.

Rheinhessen

Rheinhessen is Germany's largest viticultural region, at 64,250 acres/26,000 hectares, and it produces the largest volume of German wine. A wide variety of grape types is planted, but Müller-Thurgau dominates, at 18 percent of all plantings, with Silvaner and Riesling following suit at

10 percent each. Red grapes are gaining ground, especially Portugieser (10 percent) and Dornfelder (13 percent). The *Bereiche* are Bingen, Nierstein, and Wonnegau, subdivided into twenty-four *Grosslagen* and 434 *Einzellagen.*

Most of Rheinhessen is a fertile, flat plain on a plateau located within the broad sweep of the Rhine where it changes direction at Mainz, and many of the plateau vineyards are planted with high percentages of the newer crosses of Scheurebe, Kerner, and Bacchus in addition to the reliable Müller-Thurgau. Each of these varieties can produce more than the average Riesling vine, especially when planted on the loess, marl, and clay soils of the *Hügelland*, or hill country, that makes up most of the plateau. The wines from these grape types and vineyards are most appreciated for their soft, mild, flowery aromas and flavors, which show many of the newer grape crossings in their best light. They are straightforward, unpretentious wines, enjoyable as a chilled drink on their own or with simple food.

But a revolution is afoot in the better-known areas for quality wine production in Rheinhessen, especially around the villages of Nierstein and Nackenheim and south to the northern limits of Oppenheim. In this district, known as Rheinfront, impressive producers are creating some superb wines based on the same premise as in the neighboring regions: the most suitable grape types (preferably Riesling) from the finest sites. Here, the red slate soils give Riesling a chance to show its more elegant side, even within the generally lower acid structure that Rheinhessen provides. Of note in this area are producers such as Freiherr Heyl zu Herrnsheim, St. Anthony, and Gunderloch.

In the rest of this very large region, it is by sheer determination that the new mavericks have turned their back on the ubiquitous and easy Müller-Thurgau and have sought out special pockets of vineyard land suited to particular grapes. In addition, they are farming the vineyards completely with an eye to quality, restricting the yield per

The Nahe River, in the background, separates the Rheinhessen region (left) from the Nahe region (right). The Nahe River joins the much larger Rhine River at Bingen.

vine. The results, in some cases, have been nothing short of astounding, with Riesling to be sure, but also with the unheralded Silvaner grape and the previously untried Sauvignon Blanc.

Whatever the variety, the wines show a depth of flavor and concentration that was previously unknown in this region. Notable producers in this group include Keller, Wagner-Stempel, Winter, and Wittman.

Nahe

A wide variety of soil types throughout the Nahe region allow for many different grape types, mostly white, with 25 percent Riesling and 15 percent Müller-Thurgau planted on 10,400 acres/4,200 hectares. Dornfelder now makes up 10 percent of all vineyard plantings. The wines are said to resemble those from the surrounding regions of Mosel, Rheingau, and Rheinhessen. An important *Anbaugebiet* for trade within Europe, its sole *Bereich* is Nahetal, with seven *Grosslagen* and 323 *Einzellagen*.

Until recently, Nahe wines have not been much admired in the United States, perhaps because the Mosel, Pfalz, and Rheingau are so much more famous and more marketable. But there are gems to be had here, especially if you can find some Riesling from the villages of Bad Kreuznach or Schlossbockelheim or their nearby neighbors. These villages lie about midpoint on the Nahe River as it winds its way in a particularly snaky slither northeastward to Bad Kreuznach. Here, the volcanic soils give Riesling from the best (south-facing) vineyards a healthy dose of hard minerality that seems to perfectly set off the riper apricot and peach notes of this noble grape.

Further north, as the Nahe River valley flattens out heading toward Bingen, some growers are experimenting with Spätburgunder, Grauburgunder, and Weissburgunder. Notable Nahe producers include Crusius, Diel, Emrich-Schonleber, Dönnhoff, and Tesch.

Ahr

The majority of the vineyards (88 percent) in the Ahr region are planted with red grapes, especially Spätburgunder and Portugieser, and most of the region's wine is consumed locally. Ahr, which contains 1,300 acres/530 hectares of vineyard, has one *Bereich*: Walporzheim/Ahrtal. The region also contains one *Grosslage* and forty-three *Einzellagen*. Red wines span several styles, from fiery to vel-

vety smooth. The Riesling is the most important white variety, and its wines are crisp and fresh, with good acidity.

Mittelrhein

Mittelrhein's northerly climate produces white wines of high acidity; most of the region's wine is consumed locally. With close to 70 percent of Mittelrhein planted with Riesling, its 1,235 acres/500 hectares under vine include two *Bereiche*, Loreley and Siebengbirge, subdivided into eleven *Grosslagen* and 112 *Einzellagen*. The wines are robust, but with pronounced acidity.

Baden

Baden, Germany's third-largest (40,000 acres/16,000 hectares) and most southerly region, is located in the Upper Rhine Valley along the Black Forest. It is very diverse in its vine plantings, with over 40 percent of its acreage given over to red varieties, especially Spätburgunder. Possibly the large production and variety of wines account for the fact that the average Baden citizen drinks about 50 percent more wine per year than the average German. The nine *Bereiche* are Badisches Frankenland, Badische Bergstrasse-Kraichgau, Remstal-Stuttgart, Bodensee, Bayerischer-Bodensee, Markgräflerland, Kaiserstuhl-Tuniberg, Breisgau, and Ortenau; there are sixteen *Grosslagen* and 351 *Einzellagen*.

Franken

Franken is planted mostly with white grape varieties. Silvaner and many of the new crosses, planted on 14,800 acres/6,000 hectares east of Frankfurt, make wines with fuller, earthier characteristics than those of other regions. Top-quality wines are often bottled in the region's traditional short, flagon-shaped bottle, the **BOCKSBEUTEL**, a squat, flattened round bottle with a short neck. Franken's three *Bereiche* are Mainviereck, Maindreieck, and Steigerwald, and the region contains twenty-three *Grosslagen* and 212 *Einzellagen*.

Württemberg

This region is set in a broad valley, and with its relatively warmer southern climate, is Germany's largest producer of red wines, and its white wines are generally full and hearty.

Most of the region's wines, very few of which are grown on plots larger than 12.5 acres/5 hectares, are consumed locally. The six *Bereiche* are Remstal-Stuttgart, Württembergisch Unterland, Kocher-Jagst-Tauber, Bayrischer-Bodensee, Württembergischer Bodensee, and Oberer Neckar; there are sixteen *Grosslagen* and 205 *Einzellagen*.

Hessische Bergstrasse

This region produces mostly full-bodied and lower-acid white wines. Most of the region's wines are consumed locally. There are two *Bereiche*, Starkenburg and Umstadt, and only 1,000 acres/405 hectares under vine, encompassing three *Grosslagen* and twenty-three *Einzellagen*.

Saale-Unstrut

In what was formerly East Germany, this region is now Germany's most northerly, growing 75 percent white grapes, which produce some very good *Qualitätswein* and *Prädikatswein Kabinett*-level wines. The two *Bereiche* are Meissen and Elstertal, with four *Grosslagen* and seventeen *Einzellagen*.

Sachsen

Sachsen, also referred to as Elbtal, is also in former East German territory. This region is now Germany's most easterly wine region, producing 85 percent dry, medium-bodied white wines. Most are consumed locally. The two *Bereiche* are Thüringen and Schloss Neuenburg, with four *Grosslagen* and eighteen *Einzellagen*.

AUSTRIA

THE WINES OF AUSTRIA are enjoying a renaissance, thanks to the attractive, bright flavors of their rare and elegant Rieslings, but also because of increased interest in Austria's very own white grape, Grüner Veltliner, and a couple of indigenous red grapes, Blaufränkisch and Zweigelt. Historically, Austria is home to the world's oldest enology school at Klosterneuburg, founded in 1860, about the same time Chardonnay (here called Morillon) grapes were introduced. In the nineteenth century, serious production of Sekt sparkling wines began. In 1866, a killing frost destroyed many of Austria's best vineyards, and as in the rest of Europe, Austria's vineyards fell victim to phylloxera shortly before the turn of the century. A painful process of rebuilding began, including the adoption of American rootstock and the development of new, more frost-resistant grape types, such as Grüner Veltliner, Neuburger, and Zierfandler. These and other new varieties were developed in the laboratories of the Klosterneuburg academy, starting in the early twentieth century.

Austria's wine producers use the Klosterneuburger Mostwaage (KMW) scale. Developed in 1861 at the heralded enology school by August Wilhelm von Babo, the first director of the Klosterneuburg institute, this scale is expressed in degrees, such that 1° KMW is roughly equivalent to 1 percent sugar in the grape must.

WINE LAWS

AUSTRIAN WINES are labeled and marketed chiefly by grape variety and geographic origin. However, like Germany, the official quality categories of Austrian wines have been based on the amount of sugar in the grape at harvest. Whenever a grape type is indicated on a bottle of Austrian wine, no matter the quality level, the wine must contain at least 85 percent of that variety. The same percentage requirement applies to the label's vintage year. If a growing area is indicated on the label, 100 percent of the grapes must come from that area. If the wine is labeled simply as Austrian wine, all grapes must have been grown in the country.

Austria uses wine category names that are very similar to the classic, pre-2011 German wine categories. The lower-level Austrian wines are identified as *Tafelwein* and *Landwein*, which must measure minimum must weights of 10.6° and 14° KMW, respectively.

Austria's *Qualitätswein* (minimum 15° KMW) may be lightly chaptalized, but chaptalization is forbidden at the higher levels.

Kabinett wines have their own category in Austria, between *Qualitätswein* and *Prädikatswein*. Wines in this category must reach a minimum of 17° KMW.

Prädikatswein

There are some special considerations about this Austrian category, with some notable differences from the German system.

In order to attain *Prädikatswein* status, the wine must:

- Be made with grapes from one growing area.
- Be certified by Austria's must-weighing panel, the Mostwaager.
- Show an official examination number and vintage on the label.
- Not be chaptalized nor use *Süssreserve* in the production of the wine.

All *Prädikatswein* must also fall into one of the following quality categories.

SPÄTLESE The grapes must be completely ripe at harvest, with a minimum 19° KMW.

AUSLESE Ripe grapes only, with any unripe grapes removed from the bunch, at a minimum 21° KMW.

STROHWEIN OR SCHILFWEIN Grapes must be a minimum of 25° KMW, overripe, and stored on straw mats for at least three months, or a minimum of 30° KMW if stored for only two months.

EISWEIN Produced from grapes that must be frozen when picked and pressed at a minimum of 25° KMW.

BEERENAUSLESE Grapes must be overripe or botrytis-affected, and at a minimum of 25° KMW.

AUSBRUCH Grapes must exhibit noble rot and reach a minimum of 27° KMW.

TROCKENBEERENAUSLESE The great majority of the grapes must show botrytis, with a minimum of 30° KMW.

The wines of Austria range from quite dry to very sweet, and legal guidelines describe the style of the wines. *Trocken* (dry) wines must contain less than 4 grams of sugar per liter, and *Halbtrocken* (semidry) must contain at least 5 grams but less than 9. *Halbsüss* (semisweet) wines must contain a minimum of 10 grams of sugar per liter but less than 18 grams, while *Süss* (sweet) wines must contain over 18 grams sugar per liter.

APPELLATIONS (DACS)

IN 2001, THE AUSTRIAN WINE AUTHORITIES formally approved the use of already-existing geographic terms on labels as the primary name of a wine, with the underlying intent of linking that geographic area with a specific grape type. This is basically the same concept as the term Chablis (in France) indicating that the wine is made from Chardonnay.

The areas that are granted this new status will label their wines with the place name, plus the acronym DAC (*districtus austriae controllatus*), as long as the wine that bears the place name is made from the approved grape variety or varieties. This does not stop producers in that region from making wines from other grape varieties. However, if they do use other grape varieties, they will not be allowed to use the DAC logo on the label. They will simply use the old style of labeling that usually includes grape variety and a place name.

Regional wine committees decide which grape variety or varieties win the honor of representing the wine area. The committee also determines any special considerations such as maximum yield, minimum alcohol, aging specifications, and typical flavor profile. Four wine areas have so far been granted DAC status.

MAJOR GRAPE VARIETIES

Riesling

The Riesling grape is the source of Austria's most elegant wines, from bone dry to very sweet, but there is very little Riesling planted in Austria. Each year, more and more vineyards are being dedicated to this noble grape, but Riesling from Austria, somewhat similar in style to the fine Rieslings of Alsace, is a rare and expensive prize to be savored.

Grüner Veltliner

Grüner Veltliner has made major inroads to the international wine market. The 47,000 acres/19,000 hectares planted in Austria account for more than a third of the nation's vines. This grape ripens late and usually gives a wine with a pale color and a green tint. Muskiness, smokiness, or white pepper

Grüner Veltliner has led the way in introducing Austrian wines to consumers.

may be found in the nose, while the taste is reminiscent of pears. The wine may be prickly with a light to medium body, and most of it is made without aging in oak. Most Grüner Veltliner is relatively light and simple, and is best consumed within a couple of years, but the more full-bodied styles age fabulously.

Welschriesling

Planted in 9 percent of Austria's vineyards, the Welschriesling is a late-ripening grape that produces light-bodied, tart wines with a spicy nose. This grape, sometimes called Riesling Italico, should not be confused with the true White Riesling. Burgenland produces botrytis-affected examples of wines from this grape that are fuller in body and richness than the standard dry style.

Other White Varieties

Rotgipfler and Zierfandler are the two white grapes that are blended to produce the famous Gumpoldskirchener wine. This dry wine has a spicy perfumed nose and is full-bodied. These grapes conspire to make lovely sweet wines as well.

Grauburgunder (Pinot Gris) and Weissburgunder (Pinot Blanc) produce good dry wines, but without the rich character of the examples from Alsace. Morillon (Chardonnay) from Austria can be pretty good, but does the world need another pretty-good Chardonnay?

Zweigelt

With 9 percent of the nation's plantings, Blau Zweigelt has become the most important Austrian red variety. It produces fresh, grapey wines with bright purple hues.

MAJOR AUSTRIAN WINE PRODUCERS

Major Austrian wine producers include Lenz Moser, Pichler, Freie Weingärtner, Hirtzberger, Stiegelmar, Kracher, Jamek, Brundlmayer, Prager, Jurtschitsch, Holler, Schandl, Nigl, Sonnhof, Mantlerhof, Knoll, Nikolaihof, Salomon, Tement, and Polz. Two large wine cooperatives are Burgenlandische Winzverband and Winzergegenossenschaft St. Martinus.

Other Red Varieties

Blaufränkisch (thought to be Lemberger) and Blauer Portugieser account for about 10 percent of the nation's wines, producing light-bodied, fruity, dry reds. Pinot Noir (Spätburgunder) is also grown. As climate change becomes more noticeable, more well-made red wines may be coming from Austria.

REGIONS

Austria has just over 123,500 acres/50,000 hectares under vine, mostly in the eastern half of the country. The vineyards are spread throughout four major regions: Weinland Österreich, Steierland, Vienna, and Bergland Österreich. Within these large regions, there are eighteen wine areas, some very small and others quite large. The region of Bergland Österreich comprises less than 0.5 percent of the nation's vineyards and will not be discussed here.

Weinland Österreich

This region comprises two federal Austrian states: Niederösterreich (77,500 acres/31,350 hectares) and Burgenland (38,650 acres/15,650 hectares). The two states are defined as wine areas, and wines produced from vineyards spread throughout either state could carry the state name on the label as the area of origin. In addition, Niederösterreich contains eight official wine areas, three of which have DAC status, and Burgenland covers four official wine areas, including one DAC area.

NIEDERÖSTERREICH

The eight wine areas in Niederösterreich are Wachau, Kremstal DAC, Kamptal, Traisenstal DAC, Weinviertel DAC, Wagram, Carnuntum, and Thermenregion. The more important areas are discussed below.

WACHAU

This narrow valley area, with vineyards on both sides of the Danube, is characterized by steep terraced hillsides based mostly on loess and gneiss soils. The area concentrates on white wines, with Riesling and Grüner Veltliner leading the way.

The Wachau area has some different labeling nomenclature, but the quality of its wine must meet the same federal standards as any other wine-producing area. In Wachau, variants in label terminology are:

- *Steinfeder* is the equivalent term for *Qualitätswein*.
- *Federspiel* is the equivalent term for *Kabinett*.
- *Smaragd* is the equivalent term for *Spätlese*.

KREMSTAL DAC

Situated to the east of Wachau, again with vineyards on both sides of the Danube, this area also excels in Riesling and Grüner Veltliner, the two grapes that have been approved to make Kremstal DAC wines. As in many other areas, Kremstal benefits from the effects of the Danube, providing a long growing season to allow the grapes to reach their fullest expression of ripeness and maturity.

KAMPTAL

To the north of Kremstal and away from the Danube River, this area is centered on the much smaller Kamp River. In the north and center of the region, deep sandstone and volcanic deposits provide white wines of great depth, structure, and minerality, best exemplified by the styles of wines from individual vineyards such as Heiligenstein. Further south, where the wine area just touches the Danube, the soils and the wines become more varied, and the region offers both whites and reds.

TRAISENTAL DAC

Covering only 1,700 acres/700 hectares, the Traisental vineyards lie to the southeast of Kremstal and concentrate on fine aromatic versions of Riesling and Grüner Veltliner. Not surprisingly, it is these two grape varieties that have been approved for use in Traisental DAC wines.

WEINVIERTEL DAC

This was Austria's first DAC, a curious fact in that it is a relatively large wine area growing a broad variety of grapes. Nevertheless, the regional wine committee reached consensus that the most typical wine of the area is Grüner Veltliner, so that variety is now the designated grape for Weinviertel DAC.

BURGENLAND

As a much warmer region, with rolling hillsides and flatter land rather than steep valley slopes, Burgenland concentrates more on red wines and white dessert wines—indeed, many authorities would cite the village of Rust in Burgenland as the mecca for sweet dessert white wine. The vineyards here seem to have no problem producing fully ripe grapes with elevated sugar levels while retaining high levels of acidity to provide balance in the finished wines.

For reds, the plantings include the indigenous varieties Zweigelt and Blaufränkisch as well as the international varieties Cabernet Sauvignon, Merlot, and Syrah. Of the two native varieties, the Blaufränkisch produces a fuller, darker wine with firm tannins and high acidity, a bit like

Austria
Wine Zones and Regions

— **Niederösterreich**
- Wachau
- Kremstal
- Kamptal
- Traisental
- Weinviertel
- Wagram
- Carnuntum
- Thermenregion

— **Wien**
- Wien

— **Burgenland**
- Neusiedlersee
- Neusiedlersee-Hügelland
- Mittelburgenland
- Südburgenland

— **Steierland**
- Süd-Oststeiermark
- Südsteiermark
- Weststeiermark

Switzerland
Wine Cantons and Regions

- ◼ Jura
- ◼ Neuchâtel
- ◼ Vaud
  1 Bonvillars
  2 Côtes-de-l'Orbe
  3 Vully
  4 La Côte
  5 Lavaux
  6 Chablais
- ◼ Geneva
  7 Mandement
  8 Arve-et-Rhône
  9 Arve-et-Lac
- ◼ Valais
- ◼ Ticino
  10 Sottoceneri
  11 Sopraceneri
- ◼ Graubünden (Grisons)
  12 Misox
  13 Herrschaft
- ◼ Aargau

- ◼ St. Gallen
  14 Oberland
  15 Rheintal
- ◼ Thurgau
  16 Thurtal
  17 Untersee
- ◼ Zürich
  18 Weinland
  19 Lake Zürich
  20 Limmattal
  21 Unterland
- ◼ Schaffhausen
  22 Klettgau
- ◼ Basel
- ◼ Bern
  23 Lake Thun
  24 Bielersee
- ◼ Fribourg
  25 Vully
  26 Broye

Chasselas

This white grape is planted in 45 percent of Switzerland's vineyards, virtually all of it in the French-speaking parts of the country, along the banks of Lake Geneva. Chasselas is an early ripener and produces a refreshing but largely neutral white wine.

Sylvaner

Found mostly in the Valais canton, Sylvaner produces a white wine with distinct flavors, full body, rich texture, and high acidity. Sylvaner from Valais is most often marketed under the name Johannisberg.

Riesling x Sylvaner

Although very little true Riesling is grown in Switzerland, this biological cross of two vinifera parents grows widely in the German-speaking areas of the country, where it makes a fairly delicate, exotically fragrant white wine.

Pinot Noir

This esteemed red grape is grown throughout Switzerland and has often been blended with Gamay to produce Switzerland's best-known red wine, Dôle, in the Valais canton, as well as Salvagnin in Vaud. Pinot Noir is the only red wine grape allowed in the German-speaking canton Neuchâtel.

Gamay

This is a highly productive grape that ripens later than Pinot Noir. Dôle may contain as much as 49 percent Gamay. The grape is the premier red variety in the vineyards of Geneva and is also an important grape in Valais and in Vaud, mostly for blending with Pinot Noir.

Merlot

Cultivated almost exclusively in the Italian-speaking Ticino canton, the wine made from Merlot almost never leaves the country, as the Swiss enjoy it very much.

Other white grape types grown in various cantons include Aligoté, Arvine, Chardonnay, Gewürztraminer, Marsanne, Muscat, Pinot Blanc, Pinot Gris, and Sauvignon Blanc. Growers farm a handful of other red grapes, including sparse plantings of Syrah and Cabernet Sauvignon. Along with about a dozen other grape types, these white and red varieties account for less than 5 percent of Swiss wine production.

MAJOR WINE REGIONS AND WINES

THE MOST IMPORTANT WINE REGIONS of Switzerland are all named after their home cantons. They include Valais, Vaud, Geneva, Neuchâtel, and Ticino.

Valais

Located in the south of Switzerland, with many of its vineyards planted on the right bank of the Rhône River, Valais is quite a dry area, so the *vignerons* here depend on irrigation. Fully one-third of the nation's vineyards are planted in this canton, and holdings can be tiny. There are twenty thousand growers in Valais but only 13,000 acres/5,136 hectares, with vines planted at altitudes as high as about 3,700 feet/1,100 meters.

The most widely planted white grape in Valais is Chasselas, which produces the light, crisp, fruity wine Fendant. Best drunk young, Fendant's label often includes

Aging Blauburgunder (Pinot Noir) in bottles at the Nussbaumer winery outside of Basel, Switzerland

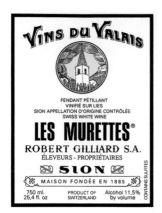

the name of the town in which it was produced (e.g., Fendant de Sion). Another important white wine from Valais is Johannisberg, produced from Sylvaner grapes.

Other white wines from Valais include the high-alcohol Malvoisie, made from the Pinot Gris variety, and Ermitage, made from the Marsanne grape. The native Armigne and Petite Arvigne grapes produce white wines that are dry and spicy. The best of these wines can age gracefully, and the wines made from Petite Arvigne can resemble Viognier-based white wines from the Rhône Valley.

Switzerland's most famous red wine, Dôle, also originates in the Valais region. It is a blend of at least 51 percent Pinot Noir, with the balance being Gamay grapes. Dôle Blanche and Rosé du Valais are also made from the same grape varieties.

Vaud

Located in the southwest, close by lakes Leman and Morat, fully 80 percent of plantings in Vaud are Chasselas. The wines produced here may bear the name of the canton (Vaud), district (e.g., Lavaux), or smaller *cru* appellation (e.g., Dézaley). The major wine districts of the Vaud region are La Côte, Lavaux, Le Chablais, Le Vully, Côte de l'Orbes, and Bonvillars. Dézaley and Calamin are *crus* that produce red wines made from Pinot Noir and Gamay and white wines made from the ubiquitous Chasselas.

Vaud is the second-largest wine region in Switzerland and produces about 25 percent of the nation's wines.

CLOCKWISE, FROM TOP LEFT: *Fendant de Sion, a wine from the Valais region, is made from the Chasselas grape. A white wine from Henri Badoux, a major wine producer in the Vaud canton. Dezaley, from Vaud, is a* cru *label; Dezaley's white wines are made from Chasselas, its reds from Pinot Noir and Gamay. Aigle is an important wine village on the Vaudois River; Neuchâtel is an important wine-growing region in Switzerland. It is not unusual to find a Riesling-Sylvaner blend labeled this way in Switzerland.*

Geneva

There are only 2,400 acres/1,000 hectares under vine in and around the Geneva canton, but it was the first to apply for Swiss *appellation contrôlée* status. Chasselas, here sometimes called Perlan, accounts for 50 percent of vines planted. Red grapes are dominated by Gamay, with 30 percent of the vineyards in Geneva planted with this variety. Recently, Geneva has begun to grow and produce some good Chardonnay.

Neuchâtel

At the foot of the Jura Mountains, there are 5,280 acres/2,200 hectares under vine in the northwestern canton of Neuchâtel, with vineyards on the banks of the Neuchâtel, Bienne, and Morat lakes. This French- and German-speaking region produces mostly Blauburgunder-based (Pinot Noir) red wines, which benefit from the warm *föhn* winds from the southeast. Oeil-de-Perdrix ("Eye of the Partridge"), a fruity rosé of Pinot Noir, is produced here, as is a good Pinot Gris.

Ticino

For the train to reach the town of Ticino from almost any other town in Switzerland, the train must travel into Italy and return to Switzerland. The Italian culture and language dominate here. The region of Ticino is divided into two zones by Monte Ceneri: Sottoceneri in the south and Sopraceneri to the north. The vast majority, 90 percent, of the 2,880 acres/1,200 hectares under vine in this eastern, alpine canton bordering bucolic Lake Lugano are planted to Merlot. Most of the wine is made in a lighter, easy-to-drink style. A sign of quality on a Ticino label is the term "Viti," which means that the wine has passed a tasting analysis and is 100 percent Merlot.

SUMMARY

THERE ARE A SMALL NUMBER of fine wines to be had from Switzerland in the North American market. Switzerland is focused on making high-quality wines for the domestic market. The world wine market is still largely volume- and value-driven, and this creates a problem for the wines of Switzerland. Swiss wines are hard to find and fairly expensive. However, this appears to be more of a problem for consumers in export countries than for the Swiss themselves. Swiss wine producers will continue to focus on Switzerland itself, which, as one of the only major European countries not to join the European Union, seems consistent with national priorities.

German producers know that they can produce large volumes of inexpensive wines, but they have been down that road before and seen exports and profits plummet. German producers are now back on track with quality wines for the export market, and Austria has similarly concentrated on quality wines and specialty niche markets for its indigenous grapes.

The challenge for all three nations is to at least maintain their current market position, if not increase market share, as Germany and Austria have done. In addition, Germany is still faced with the ever-present problem of inconsistent and confusing label language. Switzerland and Austria may soon experience similar problems if grape growers and winemakers fail to reach consensus about what terms can or should be used on labels.

While the advent of the DAC designation in Austria is commendable, this has the potential to lead to dissent within the ranks of winemakers, with some already complaining that the regulations are too rigid or not inclusive enough, or too exclusive. That has been Germany's experience, and it has not been healthy for the German industry as a whole.

The Nussbaumer vineyards in the Neuchâtel wine region

TOKAJI
ASZÚ

SZAMORODNI

essencia

ROMANIA

GEORGIA

BULL'S
BLOOD

PUTTONYOS

RKATSITELI

HUNGARY

BULGARIA

FURMINT

kadarka

KÉKFRANKOS

UKRAINE

RUSSIA

WINES OF EASTERN EUROPE

WHERE DO EASTERN EUROPEAN WINES fit in the wine world? Many of the indigenous grapes of these nations have been abandoned in order to produce more in the "international" style, wine from French and German vinifera. This is a direction that will definitely continue to ensure survival in the marketplace, but it is an unfortunate historical and cultural trend. Regional wines made from native vinifera were an integral part of the indigenous cuisine of Eastern Europe, and now some of those wines and foods may all but disappear. Eastern European nations are part of the global wine trade, mostly at the inexpensive varietal level, with wines made largely from Chardonnay, Merlot, and Cabernet Sauvignon. The wines are priced aggressively and feature varietal labels in order to compete against wines from the New World—the Americas, Australia and New Zealand, and South Africa—and the inexpensive wines from the south of France.

Historically, wine's place in Eastern Europe has gone through periods of expansion and contraction. During the sixteenth and seventeenth centuries, many nations were under the rule of the Muslim Ottomans, whose faith forbids wine consumption. The devastation wrought by phylloxera in the late nineteenth century was followed by the world wars, Communist control, and a period of political uncertainty, as different groups sought to establish their political autonomy. After World War II, many small farms were reorganized into large cooperatives in which

quantity was stressed over quality. The majority of wines were meant for consumption within the Communist bloc, and prices had to be low. The Russian penchant for some residual sugar in both still and sparkling wines was not shared by most of the international market, which preferred drier wines.

During the 1980s, General Secretary Mikhail Gorbachev attempted to curb alcoholism in the Soviet Union by limiting the amount of alcohol available. He ordered the plowing under of many vineyards and replaced vines with other crops. Another problem was, and continues to be, less than total cleanliness of winemaking facilities and storage containers, such as vats, corks, and bottles. Neglect in these areas leads to inconsistent or flawed wines, some with unpleasant smells and tastes. Today, these problems are being addressed, as international funds and wine advisers are working to map out a new direction for these wines. Wine laws are being updated, and so are vineyards and wineries.

In this chapter, we will survey the wines of Eastern Europe's most important wine-producing nation—Hungary—as well as the current status of wine in Romania, Bulgaria, Georgia, Moldova, Ukraine, and Russia.

Currently, most Eastern European wine-producing nations must compete in a more-or-less free market, both domestically and at the international level. Some nations are succeeding, some are improving, some are falling behind.

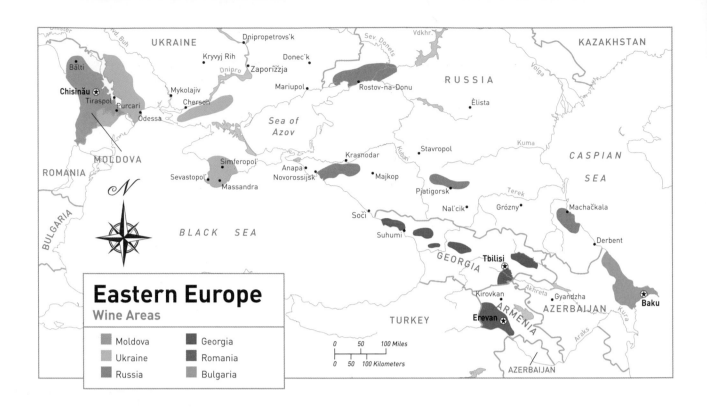

Eastern Europe
Wine Areas

- Moldova
- Ukraine
- Russia
- Georgia
- Romania
- Bulgaria

HUNGARY

HUNGARY, the world's eighteenth-largest wine-producing nation, with a per capita consumption of about 9 gallons/35 liters per year, exports more than half of its annual production of 80 to 160 million gallons/3 to 6 million hectoliters. The Federation and the Product Council of Hungarian Growers is involved with wine production and market research. The Association of Wine Merchants, a group of independent private firms, has replaced the federal monopoly, MONIMPEX, to promote export efforts.

Hungary's National Wine Qualifying Institute has established four designations for wine quality: table wine (*asztali bor*), regional wine (*táj bor*), quality wine (*minőségi bor*), and extra-quality wine (*különleges minőségű bor*). Quality and extra-quality wines are mainly found in the export market. A red-white-and-green numbered ribbon is found on the neck of every approved *különleges minőségű bor* wine.

Under Communist rule, some of Hungary's best vineyard sites were destroyed. The vines were pulled out because the vineyards, many planted on desirable steep slopes, were not accessible to tractors—the symbol of collective farming. For those vineyards that remained, the emphasis was on high yields and mass production. Yields in the vineyard were as high as 10 tons per acre/25 tons per hectare. Vine density dropped from about 4,000 vines per acre/10,000 vines per hectare to little more than 800 vines per acre/2,000 vines per hectare, so that tractors could get to the vines. Several grape varieties that needed care and attention were literally destroyed.

When Communist rule ended in 1989, Hungarian wine producers, many of them young and idealistic, began to reclaim the nation's best vineyards and plant grape types that were suitable to the soils. Compared with the rest of Eastern Europe, Hungary has worked harder and been more successful in expanding its wine industry.

One winemaker in particular, Tibor Gál, helped attract worldwide attention to his native Hungary. Gál gained international prominence not in Hungary but in Italy, as the winemaker for Ornellaia, the famous Super Tuscan red wine. Gál turned his attention to his homeland and encouraged young Hungarian winemakers in their craft. In 2005, Gál died in a car accident in South Africa, where he was consulting during harvest, at the age of 46. Today, Tibor Gál's message about the potential of Hungarian wine remains alive.

As with other Eastern European nations, the 1990s were a period of change for Hungary, as it attracted international investment to upgrade and expand production. A wide range of Western investors led by Italy, Great Britain, Spain, Germany, France, and the United States has been working with the best Hungarian winemakers to make dry wines from international varieties, such as Chardonnay and Cabernet Sauvignon, as well as Hungary's traditional wines, especially the sweet Tokaji Aszú. Today, about 50 percent of Hungary's wine industry is foreign-owned, which has caused a bit of controversy among Hungarians. This controversy has led to restrictions on foreign ownership of vineyard land (but not wineries) in Hungary.

GRAPE TYPES

MORE THAN TWO-THIRDS of Hungary's production is white wine. The principal grape is Olaszrizling (known elsewhere as Welschriesling), utilized for its high acid content and spicy, almondlike flavors. Furmint, the principal grape for Tokaji, an internationally acclaimed sweet wine, is also used throughout the nation for dry wines. Another grape used in Tokaji is Hárslevelű, or "lime leaf," which can be less acidic and fail to reach the sugar levels of Furmint, but contributes powerful, spicy aromatics. A third grape found in the Tokaj region and elsewhere is Muskotály, also known as Muscat Lunel, which is used for semisweet and sweet wines. Ezerjó is widely planted and can make light-bodied, crisp whites, such as those from the Mór area. Other Eastern European varieties include the white

Tramini, used for making semidry to semisweet wines, all of them spicy and aromatic. Chardonnay, Pinot Blanc, Sauvignon Blanc, and other internationally known varieties are planted in Hungary for domestic and export wines.

Kadarka was for centuries the most-planted grape in Hungary because of its ability to make full-bodied, spicy reds with the power to match the heavy dishes of traditional Hungarian cuisine. However, eating habits have changed in Hungary, and the Kadarka grape has been superseded by Kékfrankos, which produces a full-bodied wine with high acidity. Other popular red varieties include Cabernet Sauvignon, known in Hungary for its paprika and blackberry flavors; Cabernet Franc, which makes a lighter red and is often used for blending; Merlot, which makes a full-bodied, spicy red wine with marked tannins; and Zweigelt, known for making wines that are well balanced, full of character, and at their best after three years of age.

REGIONS

THE NATION IS BISECTED by the Danube River, which is known as the Duna in Hungary. Lake Balaton, Europe's largest lake, provides a moderating influence on the vineyards of the Transdanubia region surrounding it. Traditional grape types (Szürkebarát, Kéknyelű, Juhfark) are planted in the volcanic-based soils of Badascony to the north of the lake, while international varieties such as Chardonnay and Cabernet Sauvignon are found on the fertile southern shores. South of the lake are the warmer

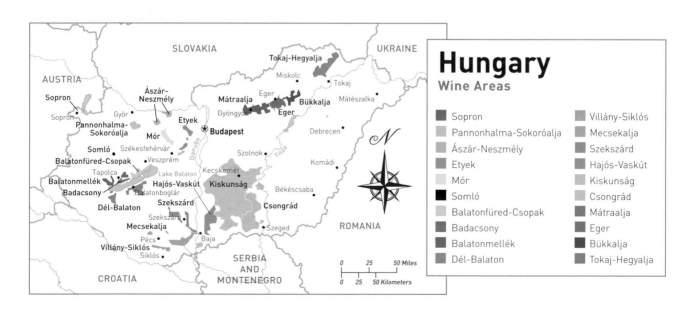

"BULL'S BLOOD" WINE

In the Northern Massif region, the famous Egri Bikavér, or "Bull's Blood" wine, is made in the area around the beautiful town of Eger. The name dates back to a battle with the Ottomans in 1552, when the largely outnumbered Hungarians, led by Captain István Dobó, were able to defend the fortress on Eger's Castle Hill because of the powers of the wine.

According to one legend, the enemy was frightened by the beards of the soldiers, which were stained red from the wine; another states that the swords of the enemy could not cut through Magyar (Hungarian) blood thickened by the wine. The heroic struggle to defend Eger was crowned with success, as the Turkish Ottoman army was forced to withdraw. Ottoman westward expansion was delayed for forty years after this battle.

The wine is still produced in a full-bodied, rich-fruit style, although its popularity on the domestic and international market has diminished. Formerly based on the Kadarka grape, today the blend is often 40 percent Kékfrankos and 30 percent Kékoportó, with the balance equally divided between Merlot and Cabernet Sauvignon. These are grown on the black-clay-and-lime foothills of the Bükk Mountains.

The wine may also be produced in the Szekszárd region, where it is known as Szekszárdi Bikavér.

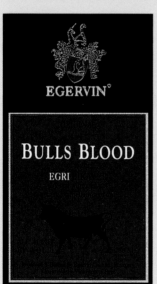

An export label for the legendary Hungarian red wine Egri Bikavér, or "Bull's Blood"

Szekszárd and Villány-Siklós areas, which produce mostly reds from the local Kékfrankos and Kékoportó, as well as international varieties. The Siklós subregion of Villány-Siklós specializes in whites, while the nation's warmest region, the Mecsek Hills, produces both white and red wines from local and international grape types.

Great Plain

East of the Danube is the Great Plain region, where more than half of Hungary's wines are produced. The area was heavily planted after the late-nineteenth-century phylloxera epidemic, when research showed that its sandier soils would be inhospitable to the deadly pest. Here, flat lands make mechanized harvesting easy, but the area suffers from dry, hot summers and possible frost damage in colder seasons.

Mátra

In the foothills of the Mátra Mountains, grape growers specialize in whites, such as the local Debrői Hárslevelű, a variety that attains an average sugar level of 14.5 grams per liter. The Gyöngyös and Nagyréde wineries concentrate on making dry wines from popular varieties such as Sauvignon Blanc and Chardonnay.

Tokaj-Hegyalja

Farthest east of the Massif mountainside areas is Tokaj-Hegyalja, the eponymous region of Hungary's most famous wine, Tokaji Aszú. Here, the principal grape is Furmint, supported by Hárslevelű and Muskotály. The Carpathian Mountains provide protection from winds and cold, while the Bodrog and Tisza rivers, along with the warmth of the area, combine to facilitate the appearance of botrytis (*aszú*). Hungarians claim that the world's first botrytis-affected wine was made here in 1647. That year, the harvest was delayed so that the Ottoman Turks would not steal the juice. The late-harvest botrytis-affected grapes were then added to the regular must, and the resulting wine was greatly appreciated as Tokaji Aszú.

Tokaji Aszú is made from a paste composed of late-harvest botrytis-affected grapes. Unaffected must or wine is added to this paste in controlled quantities. A *puttony* is a small barrel of 10 gallons/36 liters, which is the measure for the paste that is blended into the larger cask (35 gallons/136 liters), called a *gönci*. Wine labels indicate three, four, five, or six **PUTTONYOS**, indicating increasing portions of paste to wine, with correspondingly higher sugar levels. A three-*puttonyos* wine must be aged three years before release and contain a minimum of 2 ounces/60 grams of residual sugar per liter; four-*puttonyos* wine must age four

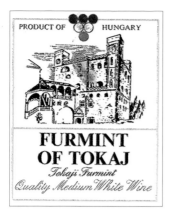

years and must have a minimum of 3 ounces/90 grams per liter; five-*puttonyos* wine must age five years and must have a minimum of 4 ounces/120 grams per liter; and six-*puttonyos* wine must have a minimum of 5 ounces/150 grams of sugar per liter and be aged for five years. Tokaji Aszúescenzia must contain a minimum of 6 ounces/180 grams of residual sugar per liter.

Tokaji Eszencia (not to be confused with Aszúescenzia, and often referred to by its English name, "Essencia"), an "essence," is made the same way as six-*puttonyos* Aszú, but the sugar content of the wine must be at least 15 ounces/450 grams per liter; it is aged a minimum of five years. An essence is made from the free-run juice and is used for blending special-quality Aszú wines. Essencia is described by Michael Broadbent in his *Great Vintage Wine Book* as "the world's longest-living wine." He suggests storing it straight up, rather than on its side, to allow the wine to settle. The wines have high acidity to balance the rich sweetness. Essencia is the rarest, most complex, and most expensive of all Eastern European wines still produced and can still be delicious after a century of aging.

The Tokaji wines, ranging from three-*puttonyos* to Essencia, display the color, nose, and taste of apricots, as well as a rich sweetness. They are bottled in 500 ml bottles, rather than the standard 750 ml size used for Tokaji-Furmint wines in the dry style. This dry wine results from a separate batch of grapes—lower-sugar berries are separated from the sweet *aszú* berries during picking. A *szamorodni* style is semidry to semisweet; less than half the grapes used are affected by botrytis. A *szamorodni* may be labeled "sweet" if the unfermented juice or must is at least 25 percent sugar, resulting in a wine with about 2 ounces/56 grams of residual sugar per liter. *Szamorodni* means "as it grows," and it is a useful method of harvesting *aszú* and regular grapes together when there is not enough *aszú* available to pick separately. The dry wines are served well chilled, and the sweet wines may be served between 50° and 60°F/10° and 16°C. A fine producer of the *szamorodni* style is Erzsébet Pince.

ROMANIA AND BULGARIA

ROMANIA

THE TWELFTH-LARGEST wine-producing nation in the world, Romania has about 620,000 acres/250,000 hectares that produce an average of 132 million gallons/5 million hectoliters annually. The bulk of Romania's wine production is consumed within the country, where per capita consumption is about 7 gallons/27 liters per year. Historically, vineyard practices and winemaking were based more on quantity than quality production, but today there is a desire to increase exports, and so different trellising systems and a greater number of stainless steel vats for controlled fermentation are used.

Romania plants many international varieties, and the wines are, if not distinctive, usually quite drinkable and affordable. Indigenous grape varieties in Romania include many that are unknown outside the country, such as Feteasca Alba, Feteasca Regala, Feteasca Neagra, Grasa de Cotnari, and Tamaiosa Romaneasca.

TOP, FROM LEFT: *A label from a dry Tokaji wine, made, like all Tokaji styles, mostly from the Furmint grape. Tokaji Szamorodni can be semidry, semisweet, or sweet; for the label to read "sweet," or "doux," the unfermented juice of the Furmint grape must be at least 25 percent sugar. Essencia is the rarest and most expensive wine made in Eastern Europe; aged at least five years before release, its character can develop for decades. The famous Tokaji Aszú from Hungary, a sweet wine made from botrytis-affected grapes.*

Romanian wine is popular in some European export markets, such as Great Britain, but after some popularity in the 1980s and early 1990s, there is little Romanian wine to be found in the United States. The wines are available through Internet sources, though.

BULGARIA

WINEMAKING HERE dates back more than two thousand years, to when the area was known as Thrace. Bulgaria has been a nation since 1908, and state control of its wine industry ended in 1989. Today, it is the seventeenth-largest wine producer in the world. Mosat wines are labeled as varietal, and the best wines bear the term "Reserve" or "Special Reserve" on the label, along with a legal appellation.

The wine landscape of Bulgaria has been shifting from focus on wine made from indigenous varieties to the internationals: Merlot, Cabernet Sauvignon, Chardonnay, Riesling, and Sauvignon Blanc, among others. The University of California, Davis has influenced the Bulgarian wine industry by sharing its knowledge with local vineyard managers and winemakers.

Indigenous grape varieties include Gamza (known as Kadarka in Hungary), which produces light-bodied reds; Mavrud, which produces more full-bodied reds; and Melnik, which is grown in the south of Bulgaria and produces rustic, full-bodied reds.

Much like Romania, Bulgaria is a major exporter of bargain-priced wines, but maintains a limited presence in the U.S. market. The wines are available through Internet sales.

GEORGIA, MOLDOVA, UKRAINE, RUSSIA

THE UNION OF SOVIET SOCIALIST REPUBLICS was the fourth-largest producer of wine in the world until its dissolution. The former Soviet Union has evolved into the broad Commonwealth of Independent States (CIS) consortium, with each of the member republics setting its own course for wine production.

Selling wines in the international market is a huge challenge for the CIS member states, as many vineyards and winemaking facilities have not kept up with the standards of the world's major winemaking regions. Investment in vineyards and modern winemaking equipment, as well as guidance from international consultants, may give these states a chance to compete in the international arena.

Georgia, Moldova, Ukraine, and Russia are the major wine-producing member states of the CIS.

GEORGIA

MANY ARCHEOLOGISTS BELIEVE that present-day Georgia, in the south Caucusus region of Eurasia, is the site of the world's first cultivated grapevines, going back more than 7,000 years. Whether or not Georgia was first in the world, it certainly is the oldest wine region in Europe. Because of its long history, wine is an indelible part of Georgian culture.

Today Georgia, with 154,000 acres/62,500 hectares of vineyards, is the twenty-sixth-largest wine producer in the world, and some of the wines can be excellent. Georgia's good reputation has a downside; quite a bit of counterfeit wine has entered the export pipeline. In 2006, Russia declared an embargo on Georgian wines because of this problem. In 2007, many wineries were closed by the government for collusion in this counterfeiting. Russia lifted this embargo in 2008, the same year that Russia invaded Georgia to "liberate" the breakaway Georgian province of South Ossetia.

Politics, counterfeiting, and wars aside, Georgia is poised to become the most quality-focused of the former Soviet republics, and it has engaged in quite a bit of wine export to Western Europe, particularly trading with Switzerland. Georgia has focused on a stylistic change in its wines, from sweet to dry, and although it grows some international grape varieties, Georgia is coming into the world's export markets with its own traditional varietals. Georgian wines are available in the North American market, but sporadically, and it is often hard to find the wines, except through the Internet.

The most important white wine grape in Georgia is Rkatsiteli, the third-most-planted white grape in the world (first in Eastern Europe), which can make a delightfully floral, crisp white wine. Mtsvani, often blended with

Rkatsiteli, is also an important white grape. The most important red grape is Saperavi, which at its best produces balanced, full-bodied wines capable of long aging.

The best Georgian wines carry place-name labels. The most important wine region in the country is Kakheti, in eastern Georgia, which is the source of 70 percent of the nation's wine. The climate features warm but not overly hot summers, with air cooled by the Black Sea, and mild winters. Two subregions of Kakheti that may appear on a label are Telavi and Kvareli.

MOLDOVA

THE SIXTEENTH-LARGEST wine producer in the world, this independent republic, created in 1991, is situated between Ukraine and Romania. Unlike those of most of its fellow CIS members, most of Moldova's vineyards are situated in temperate zones; its moderate rainfall is not a threat to grape quality. Grafted vineyards are already planted with the popular international varieties, including Cabernet Sauvignon and Chardonnay. Most of the 371,000 acres/150,000 hectares of vines are harvested by machine.

Foreign investment by such firms as Penfolds of Australia means access to working capital and technical assistance in the vineyards and wineries of Moldova. Exports will most likely concentrate on moderately priced varietal-labeled dry table wines.

Russia is Moldova's largest export market, but in 2006, Russia declared that it would not accept any imports of Moldovan (or Georgian) wines "for reasons of quality," although many accused Russia of playing politics. The ban was eventually lifted, but the initial action emphasized how dependent Moldova's wine industry is on Russia and how damaging that dependence can be.

UKRAINE

WITH ABOUT 250,000 ACRES/100,000 HECTARES of vines split between the Crimea and Odessa regions, Ukraine is the nineteenth-largest wine producer in the world, and plants more than a hundred different grape types in its vineyards, but with a current emphasis on popular international varietals. Lower yields from mechanized vineyards have been the recent practice, resulting in about 12 million gallons/460,000 hectoliters of mostly red wine annually.

In 1986, under the direction of Mikhail Gorbachev and as part of his campaign to lower alcohol consumption in the USSR, tens of thousands of acres of vineyards in the Soviet Union were ripped out of the soil. Among all of the republics, Ukraine was Russia's largest supplier of wine and was hit hardest, losing about 310 square miles/800 square kilometers of vineyard.

Since the end of Soviet rule, the Ukrainian wine industry has been rebuilding, exporting much of its wine to Russia and to markets in Europe. A tiny amount of Ukrainian wine shows up in the American market.

RUSSIA

WITH ABOUT 175,000 ACRES/70,000 HECTARES of mostly cold-hardy, disease-resistant, prolific grapes under vine, Russia plants both international varieties and climate-appropriate biological crosses, such as Cabernet Saperavi. The vast majority of vineyards are in the northern Caucasus; farmers often protect their grapes by covering them with soil so that the typically cold winters do not destroy the vines.

Russia plants about a hundred different grape types, but leading all plantings is Rkatsiteli. Although it ranks only fourth among the CIS member nations in vine plantings, Russia remains the largest producer of sparkling wines, still wines, and brandies within the confederation by bringing in fruit from other republics, such as Azerbaijan, to Russian wineries and distilleries.

SUMMARY

THE WINES OF EASTERN EUROPE must improve dramatically to attract and sustain an international audience, today and in the future. There may always be a market for inexpensive Eastern European wines, but perhaps the more important question is: Who, if anybody, in this politically and economically unstable region will elevate the image of these wines? Odds are it will be a syndicate of foreign investors and a new generation of more optimistic, more individualistic native winemakers and entrepreneurs. Raising the quality of Eastern European wines will ensure growth and prosperity in what is now, with a few exceptions that prove the rule, an industry focused on the lowest prices in the world.

COMMANDARIA

THRACE

NASHIK

GALILEE

NAOUSSA

SANTORINI

XINJIANG

TIANJIN

ASSYRTIKO

BEKAA VALLEY

XINOMAVRO

AGIORGITIKO

MALAGOUSIA

NEMEA

CHAPTER 13

THE EASTERN MEDITERRANEAN AND ASIA

WHILE FEW WINE DRINKERS THINK OF THE LEVANT (the eastern Mediterranean countries of Europe, Asia Minor, and North Africa) as important wine regions, this part of the world is the cradle of ancient wine history, commerce, and culture. The ancient Greeks, Syrians, and Egyptians were among the first peoples to recognize the economic value of wine as an agricultural product and commodity.

Greece in particular was able to spread its dominion throughout the Mediterranean and the Black seas, exporting wine in exchange for grain from Egypt and precious metals from Spain. The power of the god of wine, Dionysus (the Romans called him Bacchus), was celebrated, revered, and feared by the ancient cultivators of the vine. The epic poet Homer, as well as Aristotle, Plato, and the entire pantheon of classical Greek philosophers, all had something good to say about wine.

We know from the artifacts of antiquity that early societies grew vines and made wine in Greece and what is now Turkey at least four thousand years ago, and the Talmud and Old Testament imply that one of the first things Noah did after the Great Flood was to plant a vineyard to celebrate life and fertility. So there is little doubt that the eastern Mediterranean is where the story of wine began.

The same area is also the historical home of the Ottoman Empire and the spread of the Islamic faith. Although the Ottomans in Greece and Turkey, and other Muslim rulers throughout the region, realized the financial importance of growing grapes and exporting wine, wine drinking was proscribed by Muhammad. Therefore, pious Muslims ripped out vineyards and instead planted grain or raised sheep and goats.

While the Ottoman Empire flourished, the Levant lost its identity as a wine culture, only to regain it briefly when countries such as Algeria and Morocco became colonies of France. French Algeria was, until 1960, the fourth-largest producer of wine in the world, much of it anonymously blended into wines of Burgundy and the Rhône. Independence came to Algeria in 1962, and the country is now only the twenty-ninth-largest producer of wine in the world. After gaining independence in the 1950s and 1960s, other former French colonies also quickly returned to their Muslim heritage. Today, while wine production is small by worldwide standards, there are pockets of quality wine production in the Eastern Mediterranean and a healthy, expanding wine industry in Greece, the world's thirteenth-largest producer of wine.

This chapter will briefly discuss the contemporary wines of Lebanon, Algeria, Tunisia, and Morocco, but today, the most prominent wine-producing countries in the Levant are Greece, followed by Cyprus, parts of Turkey, and—coming on strong for quality—Israel, one of the world's smallest wine producers (ranked only fiftieth in the world in production volume). Finally, moving away from historical wine-producing lands, the chapter ends with a look at the state of the wine industries of China and India; both countries are producing wine and, just as important, have become major import markets for wine made in other parts of the world.

GREECE: A WINE RENAISSANCE

WINES OF ANTIQUITY AND WINES FOR TODAY

GREECE IS KNOWN as the cradle of western civilization. Viticulture references in Greek literature date back to 7000 B.C. The methods of vineyard management, aging, and fermentation recorded by the Greeks were adopted by the Romans and then spread throughout much of Europe. Though Greece has known its share of glory through its historic achievements, the production of fine modern wines dates back less than thirty years. Prior to this, Greek wine production experienced a significant decline during the years of Turkish occupation that began in the mid-1400s because of the high taxes imposed by the Turks. (Some islands such as Cephalonia and Crete were not under Turkish rule and were able to export during this period.) After the Greeks declared independence from the Turks in 1821, it took until the early 1900s before the country was finally liberated; then came the two World Wars and the civil war that ended in 1951, which left the country devastated. Wine production was limited to providing for the basic needs of the local population. Phylloxera also made an appearance in 1898, wreaking further havoc. It was not until 1981, when Greece joined the European Union, that things started to change for the better. It was after this event that the Greek wine industry began to transform itself with a tremendous investment in modern winemaking technology and upgrading the vineyards. The new generation of winemakers left Greece to train at the best schools around the world, in France, Italy, Australia, and the United States. Once they returned to Greece, they put their passion and efforts into exploring the potential of their native Greek varieties.

Initially, as with many other European nations, wine production was focused mainly on providing inexpensive wines for daily consumption. Wineries did not have the good fortune of other historically successful vineyard sites, such as the *crus* of France, which could produce very expensive wines. This makes the current wine renaissance in Greece all the more exciting. New areas are being planted with traditional regional grape varieties as well as grape varieties native to other parts of the country and international varieties. In some areas of Greece, the most current vineyard and winery techniques are being practiced alongside traditional methods. The machinery and cooperages are in place to allow winemakers to fulfill their ambitions. While some producers have gained experience studying and working in both the Old World and the New World, others still opt for traditional local training.

Greek winemakers are now experimenting, and some wines made from blends of international and indigenous grapes are truly impressive, emotionally and intellectually. These unique wines, such as an Assyrtiko and Sauvignon Blanc blend or a Syrah, Xinomavro, and Merlot blend, can only be found in Greece.

Although Greek wines are a very small piece of the import pie in the United States, American wine consumers and professionals are enamored with the new wave of Greek wines and are enjoying them with a wide range of foods. Greek wines will never dominate the American market, yet it's still an exciting time to discover and drink the unique wines of Greece.

THE LANGUAGE OF THE LABEL

GREEK TABLE WINES may be labeled in a variety of ways:
- By grape name, such as Moschofilero (a dry white). European law stipulates that the wine must contain at least 85 percent of the grape named on the label.
- By place name, such as Nemea (in this case, a dry red).
- By grape and place, such as Muscat of Samos (in this case, a sweet white).
- By fantasy or proprietary name, such as Avaton by Gerovassiliou (a dry red).

Sparkling wines use the usual terms to denote dryness or sweetness, such as *brut*. Some wineries label their sparkling wines with a fantasy or proprietary name, such as

Ode Panos (produced by Domaine Spiropoulos), Poême (Glinavos), or Amalia (Domaine Tselepos).

The quality pyramid for Greek wines, in order of increasing quality, starts with *oenos epitrapezios*, or table wines. These may have just a brand name or may simply be a traditional wine such as retsina. *Vins de pays*, a French term for country wines but also used in Greece, is known locally as *topikos oinos* (TO).

The highest echelon in Greek wines is *appellation of origin* (AOC), which is modeled on the French system and meant to guarantee authenticity and maintain traditional "recipes" of grape content for the wines. It is also similar to the Italian DOC system because in some areas, such as Cephalonia, a minimum altitude for vineyards is enforced. The two AOC designations are *onomasias proelefseos anoteras poiotitas* (OPAP) for appellations of superior quality and *onomasias proelefseos eleghomeni* (OPE) for appellations of controlled quality. Greek wine bottles will have either an OPAP pink seal for dry wines or an OPE blue seal for sweet wines.

Due to the restrictions on the AOC designation and the less-than-speedy response of official agencies to allow new varieties or vinification methods to be used, the wineries will sometimes declassify and sell their best wines with a TO label to allow them the freedom to innovate. Inspired by successful declassification programs in Italy (IGT), Spain (Vino de la Tierra), and Portugal (Vinho Regional), the Greeks use the *topikos oinos* or TO category to break from tradition and create wines that they believe have merit. Although these wines are officially rated lower than the AOC wines, some of them may actually be superior to many AOC wines. They are placed under the TO or *Vin de Pays* category to take advantage of the looser rules that allow using both native and international grape varieties and more freedom with vinification methods. Some wineries that work with varieties such as Merlot, Chardonnay, or Gewürztraminer declassify their wines to the TO or regional level.

In this chapter, we will refer to the OPAP and OPE wines as AOC and the *topikos oinos* wines as *Vin de Pays*. As in France, the *Vin de Pays* term may be replaced with the phrase *indication géographique protégée* (IGP) and AOC may be replaced with the phrase *appellation d'origine protégée* (AOP). The labels of older wines will feature the traditional phrases and more recent releases may display the IGP and AOP terms. (For more on the evolution of wine label laws and regulations adopted by member countries of the European Union, see page 256.)

Aging Terms: Reserve, Grand Reserve, and Cava

Only the wines carrying an appellation of origin (OPAP or OPE) are allowed to use the terms *reserve* and *grande reserve*. The wineries that produce the best wines limit their yields in the vineyards, producing well under the permitted 5 tons per acre/12.5 tons per hectare.

RESERVE (EPILEGMENOS) AND GRAND RESERVE (EIDIKA EPILEGMENOS)

For white wines to be allowed the use the term *reserve* or *epilegmenos* requires the wine to be aged one year, of which at least six months are spent in barrel and a minimum of three months in bottle. The requirement for reds is two years of aging, with minimums of one year spent in barrel and six months in bottle.

To use the term *grande reserve* or *eidika epilegmenos*, whites must be aged two years, with minimums of one year in barrel and six months in bottle. Red wines require four years of aging, with at least eighteen months in barrel and eighteen months in bottle.

The labels of either Reserve or Grand Reserve wines can also include the additional terms *palaiomenos se vareli* or *palaiose se vareli* (which both mean "aged in barrel"). Labels may also include the designation for how many months or years the wine has been aged in barrel. For example, a Reserve white that has had a full twelve months of barrel-aging may be labeled *gia 12 mines*; a Grand Reserve red that has had two full years of aging in oak barrel may be labeled *gia 2 eti*.

CAVA

The term *cava* can only be used by *Vin de Pays* (TO) wines, and it describes aging in barrel and bottle. (There is no connection between this Greek term and the Spanish term *Cava* for sparkling wines.)

For white and rosé wines, *cava* means the wine was aged twelve months before release, of which six months were spent in barrel and six months in bottle. For red wines, the term means thirty-six months of aging, with a minimum of twelve months in barrel and at least twelve months in bottle. As with the *reserve* and *grand reserve* categories (see above), the labels can also use the terms indicating how long the wine was aged in barrel.

OTHER TERMS

A label may show the term *ktima*, which refers to a wine estate. Some wineries used the English term *Estate* while others maintain the Greek term (for example, *ktima pavlidis* or *ktima kir yianni*) on their labels. *Pyrgos* is a term that may be used when there is a château or fine building on a wine estate.

Ampelones or *oreinoi ampelones* are the terms for vineyard and mountain vineyard. To use these terms, the winery and vineyards must be in the same place of origin or town. Also at least half of the vineyard used and the winery itself must be owned by the producer whose name is on the label.

THE GRAPES OF GREECE

SOPHISTICATED GREEK WINE DRINKERS need no longer look to imported wines to sample acclaimed international varietals. The usual suspects that first gained fame in France—Chardonnay, Sauvignon Blanc, Cabernet Sauvignon, Merlot, and Syrah—are all planted in their homeland. The Greeks are producing wines from grapes native to Italy (Sangiovese, Refosco), Spain (Tempranillo, Garnacha), and Germany (Riesling). While some are quite good and a few rather exceptional, the most interesting and exciting Greek wines are still the ones based on the country's three hundred unique indigenous grape varieties. Luckily, you only need to know a handful of them to start exploring the wonderful world of these wines.

Agiorgitiko and Xinomavro are the two most important red grapes for dry wines; another red grape, Mavrodaphne, produces exceptional sweet wines. Black, gray, and white Moschofilero grapes are the basis for some of the finer Greek white, rosé, and sparkling wines. Finally, the premier white grapes for fine wines are Assyrtiko and Malagousia.

The Reds

AGIORGITIKO

The grape is also known as Saint George and is the most important red grape of the Peloponnese and the AOC within it, Nemea. It produces wines with garnet color and aromas and flavors of black currant, strawberry, cherry, and plum.

Both dry and sweet red versions are made, as well as dry rosé wines. Inexpensive wines meant for early consumption are medium in body with soft tannins, while the moderate to expensive wines are full-bodied and have more tannins and sufficient acidity to make them ageworthy. In the vineyard, high yields of Agiorgitiko grapes may result in wines with a shorter life span and vegetative flavors.

MAVRODAPHNE

The name means "black laurel," and the grape is used in blended dry wines to contribute dark color, tannins, and blackberry flavors. It is often partnered with Cabernet Sauvignon, Merlot, or Refosco to make full-bodied wines that can be cellared. The only red OPE sweet wines of Greece are the Mavrodaphne of Patras and Mavrodaphne of Cephalonia. Some of the flavors commonly found in these wines include raisins, honey, and walnuts.

XINOMAVRO

The finest grape of northern Greece, Xinomavro translates as "acid black," which is a good indication of the grape's character: tart and tannic. Wines based on this grape have aromas and flavors of black pepper, blackberries, black olives, and tobacco. There is always a slight scent of tomato in the wine, and the further south it is planted, the more pronounced the sun-dried tomato flavor. Just as Pinot Noir is difficult to grow, so is Xinomavro, which has a ruby color in its youth similar to Pinot Noir. When tasted blind, some people have even confused quality, aged Xinomavro-based wines either for highly regarded French Burgundy or Italian Barolo. Such comments reveal how difficult it is to blind-taste wines, and how one person's Barolo is another's Beaune. One fact is indisputable: Xinomavro makes some of the most complex and ageworthy wines of Greece.

Other Red Grapes

LIMNIO

The grape is Greece's most ancient variety, and it (or the Muscat) may very well be the oldest in the world. Its wines contribute herbal (sage) and spicy aroma, medium to high acidity, high alcohol (from ripe sugars), and tannins to blended wines. Although it originated on the island of Limnos, it is also planted in northern Greece.

MANDELARIA

This particular variety supplies lots of color and tannins as well as some acidity to blended wines. It tends to be used in blends because on its own, low sugars result in low-alcohol wines. It is often paired with the Kotsifali variety. The blackberry-scented grape is used in the rosés and reds of such regions as Rhodes and Santorini.

KOTSIFALI

The grape has a light color and low acidity, so is dependent on the Mandelaria or Syrah in blended wines for enhancing those qualities. It does, however, offer intriguing aromatics as well as ripe sugar levels, which add alcohol to a blend.

MAVROTAGANO

The name translates as "black and crunchy," referring to the deep color of the wines and its "chewy," or heavy, tannins. Those tannins give the wines aging potential and also generally provide a lot of ripe red fruit and spice flavors. Although the grape was first used on the island of Santorini, it is now also planted in northern Greece.

LIATICO

The variety is used in Crete to produce both light-colored dry reds, such as the Dafnes and Sitia AOC wines. It also has a long history of making luscious dessert wines.

The Whites

ASSYRTIKO

This is the principal grape grown on the island of Santorini, where it is used to make dry, ageworthy wines and sweet **VINSANTOS**, both of which are high in acidity. The Assyrtiko vines are trained to grow in the shape of a wreath (*ampelia*) on the island of Santorini (see the photo on page 541). They are unusual in having such high levels of acidity, considering the hot climate they are grown in. In their youth, they express aromas of white pepper, the ocean, mineral, and pear. Over time, Assyrtiko wines of Santorini develop flavors of caramelized pineapple and lemon or orange marmalade. When grown in northern Greece and Attica, the wines display less of the mineral flavors of Santorini and more diverse fruit aromas of their youth.

MOSCHOFILERO

The word *moscato* means "aromatic" in Greek, and the name of the grape variety is Fileri, which is used for Moschofilero, the wine. Of the three clones of Fileri—black, blonde-gray, and white—the white has the most acidity, the black has the strongest floral expression, and the blonde-gray has a subtle expression of the qualities of the other two. Sparkling, white, and rosé wines are made from this grape variety, all of which possess aromas and flavors of rose petal, ginger, honey, and orange blossom. DNA testing has confirmed that it is not a clone of Muscat or Gewürztraminer, even though its aromatics and flavors may be comparable to those varieties. Other positive attributes of Moschofilero wines are their crisp acidity and low alcohol, which makes them ideal candidates to pair with spicy seafood, fowl, and vegetarian dishes (for further discussion, see page 594).

MALAGOUSIA

This white grape has just a hint of the floral and citrus aromas that are similar to Moschofilero, but Malagousia also offers basil and mint aromas and peach and pineapple flavors. Malagousia has a richer texture than Moschofilero. A lot of new plantings of this variety are testament to the growers' belief that it makes some of the best wines of the nation.

Other White Grapes

AIDANI

Used in blends from islands such as Santorini, Aidani lacks acidity, but contributes floral and apricot aromas to the wines.

The idyllic isle of Santorini

ATHIRI

The grape originates from Santorini, and its ancient name was Thira. Athiri wines are light-bodied with citrus aromas and flavors, as well as some notes of pear, green melon, and stone fruit. It is used as a blending grape in Santorini and on its own in Rhodes.

LAGORTHI

This grape provides high levels of mouthwatering malic acid, as well as peach and citrus aromas and flavors.

MUSCAT

There are two varieties of Muscat used in Greece. The Muscat Alexandria is grown in Limnos, and the Muscat a Petit Grains, is the grape in Samos, Rhodes, Celphalonia, Patra, and Rio of Patras. The wines may be made sweet by drying the grapes in the sun or by fortification. The seductive smell of Muscat is always reminiscent of orange blossoms and honey.

RODITIS

This makes a popular wine in casual taverna restaurants throughout the nation, because it offers a simple background to the flavors of fish or *mezze* appetizers. It is one of the most-planted white grapes in the nation. It has flavors of lemon, peach, melon, and apple. When grown at high altitudes in the mountains, it produces wines with mouthwatering acidity.

ROBOLA

This variety produces wines with notes of lemon, green melon, and mineral flavors on the island of Cephalonia.

SAVATIANO

The most widely planted white grape in Greece and a major component of retsina wines. Savatiano is occasionally used to make good, medium-bodied wines with orange blossom aromas, but it needs a blending partner to supply acidity.

VILANA

This grape is grown in Crete, where it produces crisp, dry wines with floral aromas and green apple flavors. The dry white OPAP wines of Peza are made exclusively from Vilana.

MONEMVASIA

The famous ancient Malvasia wines were based on this variety. It is used to make single-variety wines for the Paros OPAP as well as in blends with the red variety Mandelaria to make red Paros OPAP wines. It is also planted in other areas of the Cyclades Islands.

DEBINA

Still and sparkling wines from the AOC of Zitsa are based on Debina. It has green apple and pear aromas and crisp acidity.

THE WINE REGIONS OF GREECE

VINEYARDS ARE PART OF THE LANDSCAPE throughout Greece. From the sun-soaked islands in the south to the cooler mountainous areas in the north, the nation's 28,000 acres/70,000 hectares of vineyards grow grapes for eating, producing wine, and for making Greece's version of grappa, *tsipouro*.

Two of the greatest challenges when growing grapes include insufficient rainfall and excessive heat. Lack of rain can cause stress on the vines, while perpetual heat can result in grapes with low acidity. One tactic used in Greece to maintain acidity in their grapes (and ultimately their wines) is to plant vineyards at higher elevations or by bodies of water that will moderate the climate with cooling breezes. Another tactic used by farmers to produce balanced wines is to plant vineyards facing north to reduce the intensity of the heat and the amount of sun exposure.

Rainfall varies in Greece dramatically. Irrigation is generally only permitted for the establishment of new vineyards, but proximity to water can supply needed moisture to the vines. For example, on the picturesque isle of Santorini, the unique *ampelia* system (see photo on page 541) protects the grapes from wind stress while the vines are nourished by moisture from sea breezes. In general, the eastern and southern parts of the nation receive less rain than those in the west and the north of the country, the range being from 16 inches/414 millimeters to 43 inches/1,097 millimeters annually. Most of the rain falls after the harvest in the cooler months. During the flowering, ripening period, and harvesting, the arid conditions can stress the vines.

Phylloxera destroyed many of Greece's vineyards in

Greece
Major Wine Regions

Macedonia
1 Côtes de Meliton OPAP/AOC
2 Naoussa OPAP/ AOC
3 Amyndeo OPAP/AOC
4 Goumenissa OPAP/AOC

Thessaly
5 Rapsani OPAP/AOC
6 Anhialos OPAP/AOC
7 Messenikolas OPAP/AOC

Epirus
8 Zitsa OPAP/AOC

Central Greece

Peloponnese
9 Nemea OPAP/AOC
10 Mantinia OPAP/AOC
11 Patras OPAP/AOC

Ionian Islands
12 Cephalonia OPAP/AOC

North Aegean Islands
13 Limnos OPAP/AOC
14 Samos OPE/AOC

Cyclades Islands
15 Paros OPAP/AOC
16 Santorini OPAP/AOC

Dodecanese Islands
17 Rhodes OPAP/AOC

Crete
18 Peza OPAP/AOC
19 Dafnes OPAP/AOC
20 Archanes OPAP/AOC
21 Sitia OPAP/AOC

the late nineteenth century, and today, *Vitis vinifera* vines are grafted onto resistant rootstocks. The most popular rootstocks used are those able to cope with the drought-like conditions in many of the nation's vineyards. In the colder regions of Greece, the challenge is to get the grapes to ripen. The exposures and trellising systems in the cool mountainous regions are in contrast to the warmer and drier zones of Greece.

A lot of the new vines throughout the nation have been planted at a lower density than vineyards in the past in order to lessen stress on the vines. The traditional gobelet bush vine style of planting is out of fashion, and new vineyards are shifting to vertical trellising systems such as the Cordon de Royat.

The vineyards of Greece are planted between latitudes 34 to 42 degrees north, closer to the equator than cool growing regions, such as Alsace, France, which is at 48 degrees north. However, cool-climate grapes such as Alsace's Gewürztraminer can be successfully grown at higher elevations in Greece. Gewürztraminer is one of the many international varieties found in both southern and northern parts of the nation. Yet there are also over three hundred indigenous grape varieties that offer unique flavors, on their own or in blended wines.

In general, much of Greece has a Mediterranean climate with long, hot summers and short winters. Although there may be large areas with a homogenous topography and climate, it is difficult to generalize about the flavor of wines throughout those regions. Experimentation with different blends of grape varieties and techniques in the winery allow for a diversity of styles within many of these regions. This chapter describes the style of the traditional wines and highlights some specific wines.

Macedonia

There are more rivers and lakes in this region than in any other region of Greece. Many of its growing areas are also blessed with a good amount of rainfall to supplement the water supply to the vineyards. The western part of the province has higher-altitude vineyards, where conditions are cooler than in the valleys of the other parts of the province. Because the area receives limited rainfall, the Aliakmonos Reservoir was created to ensure sufficient water for farmers. In general, Macedonia has a Continental climate.

Approved grape varieties for Macedonian *Vin de Pays* white wines include the native Athiri, Assyrtiko, Malagousia, and Roditis, and the international varieties Chardonnay and Sauvignon Blanc.

Red *Vin de Pays* wines are produced from the native Limnio and Moschomavro, as well as the internationals Syrah, Pinot Noir, Merlot, and Cabernet Sauvignon. Modern blends based on Xinomavro with international grapes such as Syrah or Merlot from AOC areas such as Naoussa or Amyndeo are declassified and sold as a *Vin de Pays* of Macedonia. The indigenous Moschomavro has an attractive floral nose and red fruit aroma and tends to produce dry, light-bodied wines.

Important AOC regions are Naoussa, Amyndeo, Goumenissa, and Côtes de Meliton. *Vin de Pays* regions include Epanomi, Drama, Mt. Athos, Macedonia, Imathia, Florina, and Pangeon.

NAOUSSA AOC

This region is the first and most famous AOC of northern Greece, gaining its status in 1971. The Xinomavro grape is grown on the foothills and southeast slopes of Mount Vermio. Here, the grape's natural acidity is heightened as it is grown at altitudes of 492 to 1,312 feet/150 to 400 meters. The best wines are sourced from vineyards on slopes facing southwest. Soils range from mostly sand and clay with some limestone and humus on the plains to rocks (in a few cases) and mostly sandy loam to clay loam on the slopes. Just as Barolo is referred to as the "king of Italian reds," Naoussa is referred to as the "king of Greek red wines." Indeed, their flavor profiles are often compared. A typical Naoussa wine has a ruby red color in its youth, flavors of sun-dried tomato, black olives, licorice, black fruits, and high acidity, as well as a firm, tannic structure.

The wines are aged a minimum of one year in oak, with the Reserves spending two or more years in oak before they are bottled and sold. After a decade or more of aging, a Naoussa will have an orange or onion-skin hue and will offer gamy, mushroom, earthy, and *goudron* (tar) flavors.

Boutari, one of the largest wine companies in Greece, urged the farmers to begin new vineyards and replant older vineyards with Xinomavro, thereby promoting Naoussa around the world. Yiannis Boutari left the family company to form the Kir-Yianni winery, and today he is assisted by his sons Stelios and Michalis. Kir-Yianni's Yianakohori vineyard is at the highest elevation in Naoussa. Kir-Yianni's vineyard practices and vinification methods take full advantage of the research provided by the best wineries of the New World. Only pure Xinomavro wines such as the winery's Ramnista are entitled to the Naoussa AOC, while blends such as its Dyo Elies (made from Xinomavro, Merlot, and Syrah) must

Kir-Yianni makes a fine Amyndeo rosé wine as well as the exceptional Xinomavro-based Ramnista from its vineyards at Yianakohori in Naoussa.

be labeled as a *Vin de Pays* of Imathia. Both wines are fine expressions of the grapes and the *terroir* of the vineyard.

The wines of Tsantali and Boutari are good examples of a traditional, medium-weight style of Naoussa. Lamb chops are standard fare with Naoussa, but any dish that uses black olives will make a fine complement to the wine. A steak with tapenade or a pizza with olives are a couple of great pairings for Naoussa wines. Inexpensive wines will be medium-bodied and fine for the pizza, while pricier wines will have more heft and are more appropriate for steak.

AMYNDEO AOC

Amyndeo produces fine dry rosé wines, crisp whites and sparklers, and some serious red wines as well. Xinomavro is the dominant red grape, offering bright red berry flavors. Growing conditions are the coolest in Greece, with many vineyards situated at altitudes of 1,870 to 2,460 feet/570 to 750 meters on the northwest slopes of Mount Vermio.

Mount Vermio protects the vineyards from the Aegean Sea's warming winds. Four lakes in the area are the source of cool winds that remove moisture from the grape clusters. Topsoils are mostly sandy and subsoils are limestone. The phylloxera louse is not a problem in sandy soils, so ungrafted vines can be planted in the region.

Alpha Estate's Angelos Iatridis is the Bordeaux-trained winemaker who produces some of the nation's finest wines from the local Xinomavro as well as international

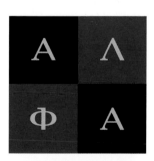

varieties. Alpha Estate uses modern techniques in the vineyards such as drip irrigation, green pruning, and leaf pulling, while *bâtonnage* is also practiced for both the white and the red wines. The pure Xinomavro wine offers mouthwatering acidity to balance the high tannins as well as complex floral, spice, and fruit aromas and flavors. Alpha's blend called Estate is mostly Syrah with some Xinomavro and Merlot, and the Alpha One wines' composition vary by vintage. Some of

---

The Xinomavro wine by Alpha Estate is among the nation's finest red wines. Simply prepared grilled red meats or a pasta with wild mushrooms are suitable partners for this complex wine.

the recent examples have been based on Montepulciano, Tannat, and a blend of those varieties. Axia is a Xinomavro and Syrah blend, and the winery also produces fine Syrah and Pinot Noir wines.

As in Naoussa, only the pure Xinomavro are entitled to the Amyndeon AOC, while the other wines are labeled as *Vin de Pays* wines of Florina or Macedonia. Another great wine from this region is the Xinomavro-based AOC rosé by Kir-Yianni. Rosé wines are always affordable, adaptable to diverse foods, and a pleasure to drink in summertime. The version from this winery is bone dry, with charming red fruit flavors.

Vin de Pays white wines from the region include dry and spicy blends of native and international grapes, crisp single-variety Sauvignon Blanc, Chardonnay, Roditis, and Gewürztraminer.

GOUMENISSA AOC

The vineyards are planted at altitudes as high as 2,100 feet/650 meters. The "acid black" Xinomavro is even more acidic when grown at these high altitudes. Local laws dictate that it be blended with at least 20 percent of the Negoska grape. The Negoska, with its softer tannins and lower acidity, provides good balance to a blend. It also adds color, and because it ripens well, adds alcohol. The Boutari winery's Filiria, a full-bodied red wine with chocolate, black fruit, and spice flavors, is a good example.

CÔTES DE MELITON AOC

This region produces medium-bodied, crisp whites from the Assyrtiko, Malagousia, Roditis, and Athiri grapes that provide an ideal backdrop to *mezze*. The medium- to full-bodied red wines are based on the local Limnio grape, partnered with French varieties such as Cabernet Sauvignon, Cabernet Franc, and Merlot.

Domaine Porto Carras, the country's largest wine estate and vineyard, is in the Côtes de Meliton. In 1967, the winery developed vineyards under the guidance of revered Bordeaux consultant Emile Peynaud. He brought on his star student, Evangelos Gerovassiliou, with the goal of producing the finest wine in Greece. This world-class winery produces wines with an international appeal; its success, in fact, kick-started the modern Greek wine renaissance. Today, the Château Carras is a dry, full-bodied blend of Limnio, Cabernet Sauvignon, Cabernet Franc, and Merlot with raspberry, plum, and bell pepper flavors.

Gerovassiliou has since established an eponymous winery within this AOC, Domaine Geravassiliou, as well as a partnership, Biblia Chora, with his protégé at Domaine Porto Carras, Vassilis Tsaktsarlis. Both wineries produce excellent wines.

EPANOMI VIN DE PAYS

The soils of the area are mostly sandy with some clay and marine fossils. The proximity of the sea moderates the climate of Epanomi and steady winds keep the grapes dry.

Domaine Gerovassiliou is one of Greece's finest wineries. Try its dry Malagousia white for its charming flavor of ripe apricots. For a fine red wine, try the winery's full-bodied Syrah, which offers characteristic aromas of black pepper combined with earthy and gamy scents, followed by lots of black fruit flavors and richness on the palate. Pair the Syrah with black peppercorn–crusted steak or black bean soup.

The winery's Avaton red wine is a full-bodied blend of Limnio, Mavrotragano, and Mavroudi that offers expressive flavors of ripe berries and sweet spices. Gerovassiliou also makes fine Viognier, Sauvignon Blanc, and Chardonnay wines at his winery.

PANGEON VIN DE PAYS

Evangelos Gerovassiliou and Vassilis Tsaktsarlis share winemaking duties for the Biblia Chora winery, located on the slopes of Mount Pangeon near the city of Kavala. The vineyards are planted at altitudes of 1,148 feet/350 meters, and there are cooling winds from the Strymmonic Gulf that provide a bracing acidity to their wines. The white wine is an elegant, crisp, and complex blend of Assyrtiko and Sauvignon Blanc grapes. Chardonnay, pure Assyrtiko, and a blend of Assyrtiko and Sémillon are their other white wines. A rosé based on Syrah, a red blend of Merlot and Cabernet Sauvignon, a pure Cabernet Sauvignon, and an Agiorgitiko round out the portfolio of wines.

DRAMA VIN DE PAYS

Drama is located in a valley about 12.5 miles/20 kilometers from the Aegean Sea. Cooling winds from the sea and cold nighttime temperatures result in refreshing acidity in the wines. Soils are mostly sand and clay with some limestone.

Assyrtiko from the island of Santorini is better known, but this grape can produce wines with similar electrifying acidity in Drama. Pavlidis winery makes fine Assyrtiko, rosé and red wines based on Tempranillo, as well as a Syrah and a Syrah-Agiorgitiko blend. Wine Art is another fairly new winery that produces crisp Assyrtiko and Assyrtiko–Sauvignon Blanc white wines, as well as complex Nebbiolo and Touriga Nacional red wines.

Château Nico Lazaridi and Domaine Costa Lazaridi are best known for international grape varieties, producing wines such as the Sauvignon Blanc–based Magic Mountain by Château Nico Lazaridi.

Thessaly

There are three AOC regions of Thessaly: Anhialos, for dry white wines based on equal parts Savatiano and Roditis; Messenikolas, for dry red wines based on the Mavro Messenikola grape and for dry red wines sourced from 70 percent Mavro Messenikola and 30 percent Syrah and Carignan; and Rapsani, for dry red wines based on equal parts Xinomavro, Krassato, and Stravroto.

RAPSANI AOC

Rapsani is the most important AOC in Thessaly. Tsantali is one of the major wineries of Greece and is primarily responsible for resurrecting this wine to its rightful place of honor on the international wine stage.

The iron and schist soils on the slopes of Mount Olympus are partially responsible for the power of the wines produced here. A typical blend balances the tannic and tart Xinomavro with the local Krassato and Stravroto grapes. The Krassato adds a dark color and ripe sugar levels to the blended wines. It is also high in dry extract, which can contribute to the wines' longevity. The Stavroto adds some tannins to the blended wines, which also can lead to longev-

LEFT: *The Malagousia grape makes some of the nation's best white wines.* RIGHT: *The powerful wines of Rapsani can be paired with hearty fare.*

ity. The Reserve by Tsantali features a deep purple color, aromas and flavors of black tobacco, black pepper, and black plums in a full-bodied package. Try it with richer foods such as a vegetarian seitan, beef Stroganoff, or a *pastisio* (a Greek version of meat lasagna). The Tsantali wines sourced from the vineyards at the monastery of Mount Athos are labeled as Metoxi and are blends of the Xinomavro, Limnio, and Cabernet Sauvignon grapes. Athina Tsoli is the talented winemaker whose youthful energy is expressed in her current wines.

Epirus

In 1963, the Katogi Averoff winery planted Greece's first Cabernet Sauvignon vines in the mountain town of Metsovo. The Averoff Estate contains 90 percent Cabernet Sauvignon, and the balance is equal parts of Merlot and Cabernet Franc. It is a *Vin de Pays* of Metsovo. Today, the Katogi-Strofilia company also makes wines from vineyards in Macedonia, Attica, and the Peloponnese regions.

ZITSA AOC

Vineyards are planted at 2,066 to 2,362 feet/630 to 720 meters on sand-and-limestone-based soils. Debina is the principal white grape used to make both still and sparkling wines in Zitsa. Glinavos is the premier winery in the region, making fine still and sparkling white wines, as well as blended red wines from native Bekari, Vlahiko, and Agiorgitiko grapes along with some Cabernet Sauvignon.

Central Greece

ATTICA VIN DE PAYS

Dionysus, the god of wine, resided in this part of central Greece. Today, both local and international grape varieties are grown here. Unfortunately, the proximity to Athens has led to urban expansion and the uprooting of some of the ancient vineyards.

The Semeli winery is named after the mother of Dionysus. Look for its floral-scented dry white blend Orinos Helios, based on Moschofilero and Roditis, as well as its Savatiano white and its Cabernet Sauvignon–Merlot red blend.

On the hillsides of Mount Gerania lie the vineyards of the Evharis winery. Its dry white blend of Chardonnay and Assyrtiko uses the extra acidity gained from the high elevation for the tartness of the Assyrtiko to balance out the richness of the Chardonnay. Evharis's finest red is a full-bodied pure Syrah containing rich black fruit flavors.

The lovely estate of Château Matsa, located at Kantza, produces a moderately priced blend of Assyrtiko and Sauvignon Blanc. The fresh mint and citrus flavors provide a wonderful accompaniment to stuffed grape leaves with a yogurt dressing. It also produces a pure Malagousia dry white wine with aromas and flavors of citrus and peach.

ATALANTI VIN DE PAYS

Although this region is quite warm, Ktima Hatzimihali successfully produces balanced wines using grapes from its own vineyards combined with those purchased from other regions. Try the inexpensive Robola-based Ambelon with its notes of citrus and flowers, or go for its Kapnias Chardonnay or Kapnias Cabernet Sauvignon, which can be found at moderate to expensive prices, respectively.

Peloponnese

Historians trace viticulture in the Peloponnese from at least 4,000 years ago, yet others argue that it is more likely 7,000 years of grape growing in the area. Homer made the first written reference to the Peloponnese vineyards in *The Iliad*, calling them *ampeloessa* or "full of vines." In an area this large, there are diverse mesoclimates and soil types. The region is mostly mountainous, with lower altitudes by the sea. The western portion is greener because it enjoys more rainfall than the eastern half.

There are fine wines available at both the AOC and *Vin de Pays* levels. While many of the region's wines are made in accordance with the AOC laws, a number of "outlaw" wines use either a Peloponnese regional label or a *Vin de Pays* designation such as Tegea or Arcadia. Some of these are easy-drinking, bargain-priced wines, while others are more complex and expensive.

Mercouri Estate, founded in 1860, is a *Vin de Pays* Pissatidos. Ktima, the affordable, medium-bodied blend of Mavrodaphne and Refosco is chock-full of fresh blackberry and raspberry flavors. This wine pairs beautifully with roast lamb crusted with sun-dried tomato pesto. Other fine reds from Mercouri include a pure Refosco dal Peduncolo and Antaris, an Avgoustiatis-Mourvèdre blend. Mercouri also makes a dry white based on the Italian variety Ribolla Gialla, and its crisp, unoaked, Roditis-based wine, Foloi, is especially enjoyable. This wine is wonderful

RETSINA

Retsina has a reputation for being a rustic wine that many tourists encounter on their travels or at home at inexpensive tavernas. Savatiano is the white grape used in retsina, while there is also a rosé version, Kokkineli, based on the grape Roditis.

There was once an abundance of pine trees in central Greece, which were used by those in the wine industry. A lot of forests have since been harvested or lost to fires. **RESIN** was used to protect the wine from oxidation, add

flavor, and seal the amphorae the wines were stored in. Today, a smaller amount of the pine resin is added to the must than in the past. The amount of resin must be between 0.15 percent and 1 percent compared with wines that were historically over 7 percent resin. Minimum and maximum alcohol levels are set between 10 percent and 13.5 percent.

Retsina is no longer the calling card for Greek wineries, but it still has a local fan base. Drunk icy cold with *mezze*, retsina can be a suitable quaff, but for a more refined version, check out the Ritinitis (Retsina) Nobilis by Gaia.

with *barbouni*, mullet served with some fresh lemon. The historic Mercouri Estate is one of the most picturesque in Greece, and its wines are some of the most interesting and unique in the nation.

The *Vin de Pays* of Laconia grows many indigenous grape varieties, often at high altitudes. The local white grape Kidonitsa is known for its aromas of quince; the Petroulianos grape offers plantain and pear aromas. The version by Vatistas winery is a medium- to full-bodied wine with balanced acidity. Athiri, Aidani, Assirtiko, Roditis, and Monemvasia are other white wines of the region. Thrapsa, Mandelaria, Mavroudi, and Agiorgitiko are the red grapes grown in this area.

The *Vin de Pays* of Messinia produces more wine than Laconia and is also known for its diversity of indigenous grapes, but there is an increasing presence of international varieties.

The vineyards of the *Vin de Pays* of Arcadia are often

planted at high elevations and are generally the last to be harvested in the Peloponnese. The low acidity and high alcohol of wines from the white grape Glikerithra (also known as Glikasprouda) provide an ideal balance in blends with the high-acid and low-alcohol attributes of Moschofilero.

MANTINIA AOC

Here the Moschofilero grape is planted at altitudes up to 2,130 feet/650 meters, where the cool temperatures and sunshine result in wines with ripe fruit flavors balanced by high acidity. There is a movement toward organic and biodynamic farming facilitated by the lack of humidity in this region.

The sparkling, white, and rosé wines produced from this grape all feature characteristic aromas and flavors of rose petals. By law, a Mantinia wine must be a minimum of 85 percent Moschofilero. The balance is usually *Asproudes*, **FIELD BLENDS** of various indigenous grapes such as Glikerithra, mentioned earlier in this section.

Two outstanding Greek sparkling wines come from the Mantinia AOC. Ode Panos is a fine dry bubbly made by Domaine Spiropoulos that has rose petal and orange zest flavors. The medium-bodied Amalia, by Domaine Tselepos, is also a standout with notes of allspice, ginger, grapefruit, and pear. Also charming are the floral and spicy notes of the Mantinia AOC and the Gewürztraminer *Vin de Pays* Tegea, by Tselepos. Mantinia is famous for its white, rosé, and sparkling wines, but Tselepos *Vin de Pays* reds are proof that fine red wines can be made there.

For a dry rosé, look no further than Meliasto by Domaine Spiropoulos, with its unusual notes of rose petal, lychee, cherry tomatoes, and paprika. Winemaker Apostolos Spiropoulos is a graduate of the University of California, Davis and has brought New World techniques to both the vineyards and the winery.

The Antonopoulos winery offers a classic example of Mantinia white wine. It offers flavors of clove, nutmeg, tangerine, and rose water. There is also a crisp blend of Lagorthi, Asproudes, and Chardonnay called Adoli Ghis, which provides a good example of the marriage of local and international varieties. Haggipavlu also produces a fine Mantinia white wine. Kourtaki winery, founded in 1895, has been renamed Greek Wine Cellars, and it produces over 3.2 million cases of wine annually. The pure Moschofilero has bright citrus flavors and floral aromas that make it ideal as an aperitif or as a partner with food. Moschofilero-based wines are well suited to the salty-sweet profile of many Asian or Caribbean seafood, vegetarian, or chicken dishes.

NEMEA AOC

Nemea has the largest AOC vineyard area in Greece, with about 15,570 acres/6,300 hectares. Just outside the AOC Nemea is the city of Nafplio, which was the first capital of modern Greece. Wine and *mezze* flow amply at the outdoor restaurants in this charming town.

The region's red wine is referred to by the locals as the "blood of Hercules" for its deep red color, as it was in this region that he killed the lion. The Agiorgitiko grape rules in this region and is used to produce dry rosés and dry reds that are medium to full in body. Vineyards are planted in the valley as well as on hillsides at elevations up to 2,640 feet/800 meters. Some locals would love to establish a *cru* system, similar to that of Burgundy, France. Because the region is so diverse, some feel that the inclusion of a subregion or vineyard name is the next step in educating and assisting fans of the wines to explore the diversities of Nemea. Some wineries will include the name of the subregion Koutsi on their label (see right). Will the Asprokambos subregion, where vineyards are planted as high as 2,953 feet/900 meters, also be featured on labels in the near future? Wines sourced from there are certainly more acidic than those sourced from the valley floor at 755 feet/230 meters.

Each location and winery philosophy can create a variation on Nemea wines, but they can generally be described as having aromas and flavors of red and black cherry, raspberry, tobacco, and black fig with soft tannins. Inexpensive Nemea wines can be light- to medium-weight and pleasant. The ageworthy, more powerful, and tannic wines available today were first introduced by the Gaia winery in 1997. Winemaker and co-owner Dr. Yiannis Paraskevopoulos's efforts were rewarded by approval from both the local and international press. The Gaia Estate red has flavors of black licorice and black plums and is medium- to full-bodied, with a good balance of acidity. It is one of the finest reds of the Peloponnese and the nation. Today, Gaia wines are faced with healthy competition.

Father Thanassis and son George Papaïoannou grow both international and indigenous grape varieties on their farm in the Xerokampos Valley subregion of Nemea. Their Palaia Klimata (old-vine) pure Agiorgitiko is a full-bodied and complex expression of Nemea. The 30-year-old-vine Palia Klimata is an impressive wine, and the Mikroklina

(microclimate) Nemea based on 70-year-old vines and aged over three years in oak and bottle before release is the finest wine of Papaïoannou and one of the best in the nation.

Georges Skouras is another local winemaker who trained in France. He makes Agiorgitiko Nemea wines—Saint George and Grand Cuvée—as well as a regional Peloponnese wine Megas Oenos, which is a blend of Agiorgitiko and Cabernet Sauvignon. The Nemea wines have bright red cherry and raspberry flavors, while the Megas Oenos is full-bodied, with a long aftertaste of currants.

Based in ancient Nemea, George Palivos has done many trials in his vineyards, making Agiorgitiko-based Nemea wines in a New World, or modern, style. Another New World–style producer is Semeli, who, after much success in the Attica region, built the Nemea winery Domaine Helios in 1999. It produces a rosé, a fresh and lightweight red called Mountain Sun, a light- to medium-weight Nemea, and a Reserve, all of which are based on Agiorgitiko. Boutari makes a nouveau-style light-bodied Nemea, a medium-bodied traditional version. Yiannis Tselepos produces a Nemea with an opaque black cherry color, flavors of black fig and black chocolate, and full body.

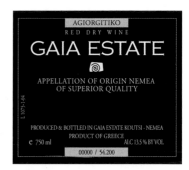

TOP: *This fine, full-bodied version of Nemea references the Koutsi subregion.* BOTTOM: *Yiannis Tselepos produces fine sparkling, white, and rosé wines from his vineyards located in Mantinia. He believes the magic begins in the vineyards.*

PATRAS AOC

This lively, culturally significant region offers both dry and sweet wines, almost all of which are inexpensively priced. Dry whites are labeled as Patras AOC; try the lemon-and-grapefruit-flavored Asprolithi by Oenoforos Winery. Sweet wines include the white Muscat of Patras AOC, Muscat of Rio Patras, and the red Mavrodaphne of Patras. Antonopoulos made the first 100 percent dry Mavrodaphne, a wine that shows great potential. There is also sweet, full-bodied Mavrodaphne. Enjoy the raisiny-sweet flavors in the bargain-priced Mavrodaphne wines by Achaia Clauss and Greek Wine Cellars. For a great value in dry white wine, try the Roditis-based Kouros by Greek Wine Cellars.

The Islands

CEPHALONIA AOC (IONIAN ISLANDS)

One of the most beautiful and hospitable islands in Greece is Cephalonia. The limestone soil, which produces many of the world's finest white wines, imparts a mineral flavor to Robola-based dry white wines. Sashimi, crab, and lobster are well suited to highlighting the lemon curd, green melon, and nectarine pit flavors of the wine.

SAMOS AOC (AEGEAN ISLANDS)

Muscats can be produced in a variety of ways, ranging from fresh white wines of moderate alcohol to sweet liqueur whites of high alcohol. The sweet Muscat of Samos wines have the seductive floral and honey nose and flavors similar to the world's best Muscats. The local cooperative makes Anthemis, which is aged five years in oak before it is released. The wine offers caramel and honeysuckle flavors and is a delightful after-dinner drink. It can also be paired with baklava, *dulce de leche* ice cream, or cheesecake. Muscat of Samos wines are undervalued and worth seeking out.

RHODES AOC (DODECANESE ISLANDS)

This island's vineyards receive lots of sunshine and enough rainfall to prevent parched vines. The best wines are made at elevations up to 2,640 feet/800 meters. In the past, the island was best known for Malvasia, but today, Athiri is the most important white grape and Mandelaria the dominant red grape, followed by Grenache. Sweet wines are sourced from Muscat grapes. CAIR is the largest winery in Rhodes.

CRETE AOC (AEGEAN ISLANDS)

The oldest wine press in the world, circa 1600 B.C., was found on the island of Crete. Today, the island is popular with tourists who can savor the local cuisine with an assortment of different wine styles.

TOP: *A Moschofilero from Mantinia by Tselepos.* BOTTOM, FROM LEFT: *A delightful Moschofilero-based sparkling wine that pairs well with Caribbean, Indian, and Thai dishes. The mineral nose of this Robola is coupled with bracing acidity on the palate; it is an ideal wine with uni, ceviche, or a Greek salad with feta cheese. The floral-scented Moschofilero grape produces some of Greece's best white wines in Mantinia; Boutari is one of Greece's largest wineries. The honey flavors of Muscat pair well with Greek yogurt with honey or sweet pastries such as baklava.*

Crete is the southernmost island in Greece, and it produces about 15 percent of the nation's wine. Vineyards are often planted at high elevations to maintain acidity in the grapes. The soils are mostly a mixture of clay and chalk.

Phylloxera is a threat to the vines, so old vines destroyed by the louse have been replaced by grafted vines. Vilana is the dominant white grape, and Mandelaria, Kotsifali, and Liatiko are the most important red grapes of Crete. International grapes are also grown on the island.

The AOC wines are Peza for dry white wines based on Vilana, Archanes for dry red wines based on Kotsifali and Mandelaria, and Daphnes for dry and sweet red wines based on Liatiko. The Sitia AOC produces dry whites based on Vilana and Thrapsathiri as well as dry red wines based on Liatiko and Mandelaria, and sweet reds produced from Liatiko grapes.

One of the finest red wines of the island is Boutari's Skalani, a blend of Kotsifali and Syrah from Archanes AOC.

SANTORINI AOC (CYCLADES ISLANDS)

Santorini is an odd mix of ancient culture combined with the demands of the tourist trade. It is said that the lost world of Atlantis was enveloped by a tsunami, burying it deep beneath the waters near Santorini. Ruins and museums of antiquity on this island speak of the Minoan culture, with evidence of wine production dating back to the second century B.C.

Santorini whites must be made from at least 70 percent Assyrtiko, which supplies lots of acidity to the blend, while the Athiri grape contributes fruit and vegetal aromas and the Aidani adds some aroma and softness. Santorini white wines often have a pH of 3 or lower, which is similar to the high acidity of the wines from the cold wine-growing region of Mosel in Germany.

Santorini wines are made from the lowest-permitted yields in the nation, at about 3.3 tons per acre/50 hectoliters per hectare. In truth, the conditions for growing are so severe that farmers rarely achieve that yield. However, while most of the world's whites are better when drunk within three years of their harvest date, these wines improve with age—a decade for the dry whites and even longer for the sweet wines.

It is amazing that the grapes can survive—and thrive—in this hot, arid climate. There is little rainfall, so the grapes receive water via the moisture brought by sea breezes. As a result, the vineyards and the wines they produce are truly unique. In Santorini there is a unique "ampelia" method of growing grapes. Vines are planted close to the ground and protected from direct sunshine by a wreath of branches and leaves. The soils are composed of mostly volcanic ash and chalk. Since there is less than 5 percent clay, phylloxera is not a problem and the vines are ungrafted.

A top producer in the region, Sigalas, makes white wine both oak-aged and in stainless steel. The clean flavors of the version made in stainless steel from the town of Oia

LEFT: *Paris Sigalas produces very fine, ageworthy dry white wines as well as the historic sweet Vinsanto on the isle of Santorini. He is holding vines grown in the unique method known as* ampelia. *Vines are planted close to the ground and protected from direct sunshine and winds by a wreath of branches and leaves.* RIGHT: *Tending the vines in Santorini*

are attractive. Aromas and flavors of lemon, cucumber, and green melon are enveloped in a medium-bodied wine with a long finish. Paris Sigalas was a pioneer in organic farming in Greece and is well respected as one of the nation's finest winemakers.

Boutari makes Kallisti, a fine oak-aged dry Santorini white wine, as well as a popular Assyrtiko called Boutari Santorini, made in stainless steel. Other fine producers in the region include Argyros, Santo, Gaia, Kourtakis, and Hatzidakis.

Seafood reins supreme in the region's restaurants and provides an ideal accompaniment to the region's wines. Fried mullet (*barbouni*) served with lemon, grilled swordfish steaks, and sea bream are some of the delicacies that pair well with these dry whites. A cool fava purée, a Santorini salad with tomatoes, capers, and feta cheese, or *horta*—steamed dandelion greens—also make delicious accompaniments.

Santorini is also home to Mavrotagano and Mandelaria grapes, which produce medium- to full-bodied reds. While not yet approved for AOC status, these wines, with their aromas and flavors of black cherries, blackberries, and violets, are certainly worthy.

Vinsanto is a luscious dessert wine made from Assyrtiko and Aidani grapes sun-dried on mats. Some producers use late-harvested grapes. By law, the Vinsanto wines must be aged a minimum of two years in barrel, but most are aged longer. Aromas and flavors typically include dried apricots, figs, and dates as well as caramel corn and tangerine. These are fabulous wines to accompany a *galaktoboureko* custard or a baklava with nuts and honey. Although they are different products, it is inevitable that people will compare the Vinsanto from Santorini with the

Vin Santo wines produced in Italy. While some Italian Vin Santo wines range from dry to sweet, all Vinsanto from Santorini is sweet, and it has a higher level of acidity than the Vin Santo wine of Italy.

In Italy, Vin Santo refers to a style of wine, whereas in Greece it refers to a place of origin. During the Byzantine age, the Aegean trade was controlled by the Venetians, who named the island after the church of Santa Irini. At first, they just exported the wines of the area, and in the fifteenth century, the process of making Vinsanto was brought to Italy.

CYPRUS

THE THIRD-LARGEST AND MOST EASTERLY ISLAND in the Mediterranean, Cyprus lies southeast of Greece and about 60 miles/96 kilometers from the coasts of Lebanon and Syria. Despite its proximity to the Muslim world, the wine traditions in Cyprus are distinctly Greek and European. While its wine is little known in the United States, Cyprus exports about 75 percent of its 25 million gallons/950,000 hectoliters of bulk wine, mostly to Britain, Russia, and the Balkan countries. The island has never been attacked by phylloxera, so until recently has depend-

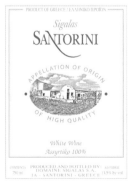

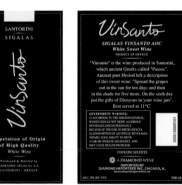

TOP: *A traditional Greek* mezze *with wine. The concept of* kerasma *reminds us to break free from fast foods and enjoy healthy foods with wine to satisfy our heart and soul.* LEFT: *Vineyards in Santorini, planted by the* ampelia *method.* MIDDLE: *Santorini is the dry white wine based on Assyrtiko, which offers citrus and briny flavors.* RIGHT: *Vinsanto is the sweet white wine from Santorini.*

ed on three native vinifera grapes: the red Mavro (meaning "black"), which accounts for 80 percent of plantings, and the two whites, Xynisteri (meaning "white") and Muscat, with 10 percent and 3 percent of acreage, respectively. In the late 1960s, new plantings of the noble varieties began, but under a very carefully monitored program. To avoid the potential for phylloxera infestations, these new varieties were originally isolated in experimental stations and have only

COMMANDARIA

Cyprus is best known for its fine fortified dessert wine Commandaria, which many historians of wine and archeologists believe is the world's oldest continuously produced wine, having first been vinified as early as 1000 B.C. The wine was often drunk during festivals honoring Aphrodite, who was, according to Greek mythology, the patron goddess of this romantic island. The love affair between Cleopatra and Marc Antony was fueled by Commandaria. In 1191, King Richard I of England gave the island of Cyprus to the Knights Templar as a reward for royal service. The royal plunderers renamed the wine Commandaria (its original name was Nama), and it has been made under that name on Cyprus ever since.

Today, Commandaria is still made in the mountain villages of Cyprus from a blend of red Mavro grapes and white Xynisteri grapes. Small producers still follow the ancient Mana system, which is similar to the *solera* system of Jerez, but the blending is done in earthenware jars instead of barrels (see page 441). The larger wine shippers in the port of Limassol, such as Keo, Sodap, Etko, and Loel, blend the wines in huge cement tanks, but they still dry the grapes in the sun, just as was done in antiquity.

Commandaria is a wine with a chestnut color and scents and flavors of candied fruit, dried figs, dried quince, walnut, caramel, and chocolate. Commandaria should be served at room temperature after dinner or with desserts such as baklava, praline ice cream, or fig and almond cake. It is not uncommon to find a Commandaria aged for a century or more that can still provide great pleasure.

Commandaria is a great bargain, often selling for less than $20 per bottle. Commandaria producers whose wines are available in North America include St. John by KEO, St. Barnabas by Sodap, St. Nicolas and Centurion by Etko, and Alasia by Loel.

slowly been integrated into Cypriot viticulture. With 10 percent of the country's arable land under vine, wine is an important part of the economy of Cyprus, accounting for close to 10 percent of its exports. Cyprus has been quite aggressive in seeking advice and counsel from European wine technologists in order to modernize and expand its wine industry.

Xynisteri is the principal white grape used for still wines, and it produces light-bodied wines with low acidity that should be drunk young. Other white grapes grown on Cyprus include Promara and Spourtiko, as well as Chardonnay, Ugni Blanc, Muscat, Palomino, Sémillon, and Malvasia.

Indigenous Mavro, Maratheftiko, Lefkada, and Opthalmo grapes produce red wines, the best of them sourced from cooler hillside vineyards at high elevations. Maratheftiko has the highest natural acidity, tannins, a deep color, and the most potential for aging. Cypriots realize that the Maratheftiko grape (also known locally as Vamvakada) is their best bet for the production of fine wines made from a local variety. International red wine grapes include Cabernet Sauvignon, Cabernet Franc, Mataro (also known elsewhere as Monastrell or Mourvèdre), Grenache, and Carignan.

There are four Controlled Appellations of Origin in Cyprus: Akamas Laona, Vouni Panayias, Pitsilia, and Lemesos. In all four appellations, white wines must be a minimum of 85 percent Xynisteri grapes and reds a minimum of 85 percent Maratheftiko or Opthalmo grapes. In three of the appellations—Vouni Panayias, Pitsilia, and Lemesos—there is an additional regulation that allows reds that are made from at least 60 percent Mavro grapes blended with other authorized grape varieties. Maratheftiko is called Pambakina or Bambakada in the Pitsilia region.

Since Cyprus is off the beaten track for most wine lovers, there are some great values to be found as well as some unique wines.

TURKEY

ALTHOUGH MODERN TURKEY ranks fourth in the world for acres under vine (1.5 million acres/600,000 hectares), only 5 percent of its grapes are made into wine. This was not always true. It is almost universally acknowledged that Turkey was the first country to produce wine, since vines

Eastern Mediterranean: Cyprus, Lebanon, Israel

■ **Cyprus**
1 Troodos West
2 Troodos North
3 Marathasa
4 Pitsilia
5 Commandaria
6 Troodos South

■ **Lebanon**
7 Bekaa Valley

■ **Golan Heights**
8 Golan Heights

■ **Israel**
9 Galilee
10 Shomron
11 Samson
12 Negev
13 Judean Hills

grew wild in the mountains of its Anatolia province at least four thousand years ago, and archeologists have discovered barrels from that era in central Anatolia. Until World War I, Turkish wines were well known and appreciated in Europe, but the war and the armed conflict between the Greeks and the Turks almost completely decimated the Turkish wine industry.

The best land in Turkey for growing wine grapes is, and always has been, in Thrace and Marmara, areas that are evenly divided between Europe and Asia. After the conflict with the Greeks in the 1920s, the vines of this area were ceded to table-grape growers. Of course, the strong Muslim tradition of the country was an important element in the weakness of the postwar wine industry. However, since 1928, when the government decreed that the Islamic faith was no longer the official religion of the country, Turkey has slowly regained some lost ground in the wine world. While the great majority of growers still do not make wine from their grapes, some sell their grapes to the government-controlled wine monopoly and to a few private concerns.

The Turkish government has invested heavily in modern winemaking equipment and has created a compulsory program to teach *vignerons* the most up-to-date approaches to viniculture and viticulture. However, Turkey still grows too many grapes, and not all of them make good wines. The current trend in the Turkish wine industry is to focus on the classic French varietals for both red and white wines. The red wines produced in Thrace, Anatolia, and the Aegean provinces are uniformly well made, and the white Izmir, made from Sémillon grapes, has developed a following among European tourists in Turkey. The country's best wine is a dry, full-bodied red with the catchy name Buzbag.

ISRAEL

THE BIBLE MENTIONS WINE OFTEN and with enthusiasm. The wine traditions of Israel, however, are really only a little more than a century old, starting with the creation of Zionist settlements in Palestine. Some of these settlements were sponsored by Baron Edmond de Rothschild, who founded wineries near Tel Aviv and Haifa in 1882 and organized a grape-growers' cooperative in 1906. The initial goal of these wineries was to make traditional **KOSHER WINES** for religious observance. The original wines were similar to the kosher wines popular in the United States forty or fifty years ago—sweet, alcoholic, and one-dimensional. Today, Israel is focused on producing dry wines in an international style. The best wines carry varietal labels, indicating that at least 85 percent of the wine in the bottle is made from a particular variety.

Israel, with much help from graduates of the University of California, Davis is making very fine wines. Merlot, Cabernet Sauvignon, and Sauvignon Blanc do especially well in the relatively cool Galilee region, and Chardonnay is finding its place as well. Although some of the Galilee's Golan wine region has been ceded to Lebanon, reports indicate that the Lebanese government will, for practical reasons, continue the progress made in Israel's wine industry. Israel has a total of about 20,000 acres/8,000 hectares of wine grapes planted in a country the size of New Jersey. Drip irrigation, first invented by Israeli farmers and engineers, controls consumption of precious water in this arid desert climate.

There are about 7.3 million people in Israel, and wine consumption is quite low, a little more than 1 gallon/4 liters per capita per year, far less than half of the per capita consumption of the United States. However, during the

WHAT MAKES A WINE KOSHER?

A majority of Conservative and Reform Jews, many of whom do not restrict themselves to kosher food and wine on a daily basis, believe that all wines—like all fruits—are kosher and do not need any further elaboration. This secular interpretation flies in the face of Orthodox Jewish law and custom. Essentially, the Orthodox approach to kosher wine includes the following rules:

- As with all kosher food products, the wine must be made under the general supervision of a rabbi who must be certified or licensed to perform such duties.
- All equipment and machinery used to make the wine must be used to produce only kosher wines. If a wine is certified as "Kosher for Passover," equipment and machinery must undergo a special cleaning and sanitizing procedure and can be used only for that purpose.
- Any yeasts, filtering agents, or clarifying agents must be certified as kosher. Since no milk or gelatin can be used for clarification, the overwhelming majority of kosher wines are clarified with bentonite clay or diatomaceous earth.

- No artificial coloring or preservatives can be used.
- Only Sabbath-observant Jews can be involved in the growing of the grapes, the winemaking process, the service of the wine, and, technically speaking, *the consumption of the wine*, unless the wine has gone through a pasteurization process known as *mevushal*.

In the modern kosher wine industry, both non-*mevushal* wines, which are produced by and for Orthodox Jews, and *mevushal* wines, which can be produced and consumed by anyone regardless of his or her religion, are available. *Mevushal*, which in Hebrew means "boiled," is actually a flash-heating and cooling process that is perhaps as much ritual as it is science and harks back to the origins of Judaism itself. The most revered rabbis insisted that all wine must be boiled so that the wines would not taste good enough to enjoy for pleasure—just barely good enough to drink to observe the sacraments of faith.

White and rosé wines that undergo *mevushal* are flash-pasteurized before the juice is fermented;

reds immediately following alcoholic fermentation, but before malolactic fermentation. The pasteurization process occurs as either the juice or the wine (depending on if the finished wine is white, rosé, or red) is heated to 185°F for a few moments and then cooled very quickly. According to researchers at the University of California, Davis, *mevushal* wines do not even come close to the time and temperature threshold at which a wine drinker can perceive any difference in color, nose, or taste of the wine. Kosher wine labels will indicate, usually in fairly small print, if the wine in the bottle is *mevushal* or non-*mevushal* wine.

Good kosher wines—both *mevushal* and non-*mevushal*—are increasingly available to the general public in wine shops and restaurants (mostly, but not exclusively *mevushal*) and via the Internet (both *mevushal* and non-*mevushal*). The wines are produced in Israel, but also in many other countries in both the Old World and New World. These wines are worth tasting by all those who enjoy good wine, no matter their religious beliefs (or beliefs about religion).

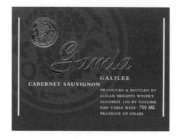

last twenty-five years, Israel has worked on developing its wine economy. Along with fine hotels, elegant restaurants, and wine-and-food magazines, wine shops and informal wine bars have opened in the major cities of Haifa, Jerusalem, Tel Aviv, and beyond.

Until the early 1990s no foreign wines were allowed to be sold in Israel because of kosher dietary laws; that is no longer the case. Israelis can now taste fine wines from all over the world, a first step in refining their palates for better Israeli wines. Several wineries now make nonkosher wines as part of a trend to make the best wines possible, kosher or not. Prior to this new viewpoint taking hold, all the wineries in Israel had to employ observant Jews in the vineyards, wineries, and cellars; even the winemaker could not draw samples from barrels without the help of an observant Jew. In order for kosher wine to be poured by anyone other than a nonobservant Jew, the wine has to go through the *mevushal* process of pasteurization, which flash-heats the wine to 185°F/94°C. Israel produces both *mevushal* and non-*mevushal* kosher wines, and now non-kosher wines as well.

By 2000, the Israeli wine industry, though infinitesimal by international standards, had matured, producing white, red, rosé, and sparkling wines in New World styles (ironic for this very old part of the Old World). Today, there are more than 150 wineries in Israel, most of them tiny enterprises. About a dozen large wineries control more than 90 percent of the domestic and export market.

Galilee (Galil in Hebrew) is Israel's most-prized wine region, due to its high altitude, cool breezes, and volcanic soil. Golan Heights is the major subregion of Galilee. The Judean Hills, situated north of Jerusalem and south of Hebron, is another important region for quality-focused wines that shows real promise with Chardonnay, due to a relatively cool climate and high-altitude vineyards. The semiarid Negev region, which grew vines in antiquity, does well with Merlot. Samaria (Shomron) is Israel's largest wine region, bounded by the Carmel Mountains and the Mediterranean. Samson (Shimshon) consists of lowlands and rolling hills. Both regions are home to the vineyards for some of Israel's most mediocre domestic wines, but are showing some improvement.

Israel is a very high-tech nation and has adopted, and in some cases developed, new and promising technologies for its wine industry, both in its vineyards and its wineries.

The best-known Israeli wines in the export market are produced at the Golan Heights Winery, a cooperative of *kibbutzim* (collective farms) and *moshav* (collective and individual farms). Founded in 1983, Golan Heights welcomes more than a hundred thousand visitors per year to its state-of-the-art winery and produces three wine labels: Yarden, their boutique line of quality wines, and the Gamla and Golan labels. The Golan Heights Winery is credited with bringing the Israeli wine industry into the twenty-first century because of its emphasis on quality and its understanding of the international market.

Other quality wine producers of Israel with a presence in the export market include Amphorae, Barkan, Bazelet ha Goaln, Ben-Ami, Benhaim, Binyamina, Bustan, Carmel, Castel, Chillag, Dalton, Flam, Galil Mountain, Gush-Etzion, Hamasrek, Margalit, Psago, Ramim, Recanati, Segal's, Shiloh, Tishbi Estate, and Yatir.

LEBANON

MOST WINE DRINKERS usually don't combine the words *Lebanon* and *wine* in the same sentence, and that's certainly understandable; it is also a mistake. Lebanon produces some very fine wines.

The Bekaa Valley, just northeast of Beirut, is the center of Lebanon's tiny wine industry. In 1857, the Jesuits of Lebanon founded Ksara, a wine estate in Bekaa. Ksara still has 47,000 acres/19,000 hectares under vine, an amazing accomplishment considering that Lebanon had been in an almost constant state of war for the last twenty years of the twentieth century; the twenty-first century has yet to bring peace to Lebanon.

The wine world would pay scant attention to Lebanon were it not for Château Musar, produced just fifteen miles from Beirut. Gaston Hochar, a Christian, started Château Musar in the mid-1930s, and in 1959, his son, Serge, who was trained in Bordeaux, became the winemaker. Ronald Hochar, Serge's younger brother, is in charge of marketing and selling the wine.

Although there have been a few missed harvests due to civil war and war with Israel, and occasionally the dry-farmed grapes have been harvested under gunfire, there is no doubt that Château Musar, made from a blend of Cabernet Sauvignon, Carignan, and Cinsaut, aged in French oak, and released six or seven years after its vintage, is considered a fine wine. Serge Hochar, who has conducted vertical tastings of Musar going back to the 1940s, also makes a fine white wine at the estate—Château Musar Blanc—produced from the indigenous varieties Obeideh and Merwah and aged for five years before release. A lighter red and white, both called Cuvée Musar, which are not aged in oak and are released one year after vintage, are both fine wines that express the *terroir* of the Bekaa Valley.

In addition to Château Musar and Château Ksara, other serious Lebanese wine producers in the export market include Clos St. Thomas, Domaine Wardy, and Massaya.

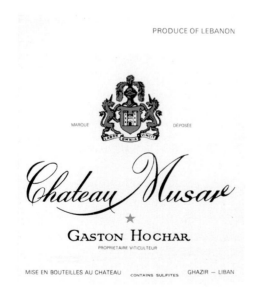

PRODUCE OF LEBANON

THE MAGREB: ALGERIA, MOROCCO, AND TUNISIA

THE MAGHREB IS MADE UP OF THREE COUNTRIES— Algeria, Morocco, and Tunisia. Common to all are the Atlas Mountains, which separate the Mediterranean coast from the Sahara Desert. The governments of the three Maghreb member states are beginning to pay attention to the potential of their wines in the export market.

Largely due to the colonial influence of France in these countries, wine laws are based on the traditional French *appellation contrôlée* system (see page 264). However, quite a bit of bulk wine is exported from the Maghreb, and the foreign bottler may often determine the name of the wine.

ALGERIA

UNDER FRENCH RULE from 1830 to 1962, Algeria had 860,000 acres/344,000 hectares of wine grapes and was the fourth-largest wine-producing nation in the world, and the largest exporter of wine in the world producing wine that was blended into the wines of the French Midi and other *vins ordinaires*. Independent Algeria, a Muslim country, now has less than 200,000 acres/80,000 hectares under vine and is the twenty-ninth-largest wine producer in the world. Despite religious prohibition, in 1970 the Algerian government began to establish seven *appellations d'origine garantie* (AOG) throughout the Oran and Alger regions on the coast of the Mediterranean Ocean.

In the Oran region, the best-known appellation is Coteaux du Mascara, which, true to its name, is almost black in color, rustic, and full-bodied. White wine is also produced in this AOG. Coteaux de Tiemcen, close to Algeria's border with Morocco, produces drinkable white, rosé, and red wines.

The Alger region features cool climate, mountainside vineyards, including Milana, the source for full-bodied reds, as well as the Medea appellation that produces balanced, subtle reds. The mountainous Dahra and Haut Dahra AOGs, close by Oran, produce good whites and reds.

Much of the best wine of Algeria is made by winemakers trained in France, using modern equipment. Medium- to full-bodied red wines account for close to 70 percent of production, and classic Rhône varietals are emphasized.

Not much Algerian wine is exported to the United States; try the Internet and look for producer ONCV-ATIMEX.

MOROCCO

WITH LESS THAN 37,000 ACRES/15,000 HECTARES of wine grapes, Morocco isn't a large producer, but it makes the finest red and rosé wines in North Africa. Of the twelve AOG areas, the best wine-growing regions in Morocco are those along the Atlantic coastline, plus the easterly areas of Fez and Meknès. The Rabat appellation produces Morocco's most popular wine, a light rosé, *Gris de Boulaouane.*

The wines range from light whites to full-bodied reds, with a special emphasis on rosé wines, and are strictly governed by Morocco's *appellation d'origine garantie* system. As with Algeria, the French influence in the winemaking of Morocco is palpable. Morocco has had a problem with phylloxera, as many vines were still planted on native roots, and wine technology spread faster to viniculture than to viticulture.

Best producers to seek out are Castel, Celliers de Meknès, Diva Sud, Domaine des Ouled Thaleb, Magrez, Thalvin/Allain Graillot, and SODIVINS.

TUNISIA

INDEPENDENT SINCE 1956 and located not far from Sicily, Tunisia has picked up both French and Italian influences in its wines. With less than 67,000 acres/26,800 hectares under vine in Tunisia, its small wine output is best known for Vin Muscat de Tunisie, a sweet dessert wine. Dry, oxidized Muscat wines, some tasty rosés, and some passable red wines are made in Tunisia as well. Vineyards are located around the capital city of Tunis and the ancient city of Carthage on the country's north coast.

Tunisia has attracted some international investment, particularly from France and Italy, and is committed to expanding its export market. Best producers include Calatrasi, Château St. Augustin, Domaine Atlas, Domaine Neferis, and Les Vignerons de Carthage.

ASIA: CHINA AND INDIA

CHINA

SEEMINGLY OVERNIGHT, China has become the world's sixth-largest wine producer and has planted close to 1 million acres/400,000 hectares of vineyards. Much like India, wine has become the drink of choice among the growing Chinese middle and business class. China has more cell phones than any other country on earth. Can a major wine boom be far behind?

China is also a major wine importer, bringing in wines from both the Old World and the New World, with a special emphasis on France's Bordeaux and Champagne regions. Italy, Australia, and California are also significant suppliers of wine to Chinese wine drinkers, who really only represent a small percentage of drinkers of alcoholic beverages. However, the number of wine drinkers has grown at a rate of at least 10 percent per year over the past decade.

There are about five hundred wineries in China, but three of them produce about 50 percent of the wine in the country: Great Wall, Changyou, and Dragon Seal. Grace Vineyard is considered to be an emerging "boutique" winery focused on quality, with production of about 40,000 cases per year. There are several multinational partnerships focused on quality wine production, too. Most Chinese wine is sold in China, but the best Chinese wines are appearing in the export markets of Europe and the United States.

Wine imports to mainland China can be problematic, as taxes can be very high on imported wines. Hong Kong, however, has eliminated a previously onerous tax on imported wines and has quickly become Asia's center for wine imports and international wine auctions. There are some tremendously wealthy people in Hong Kong, Macao,

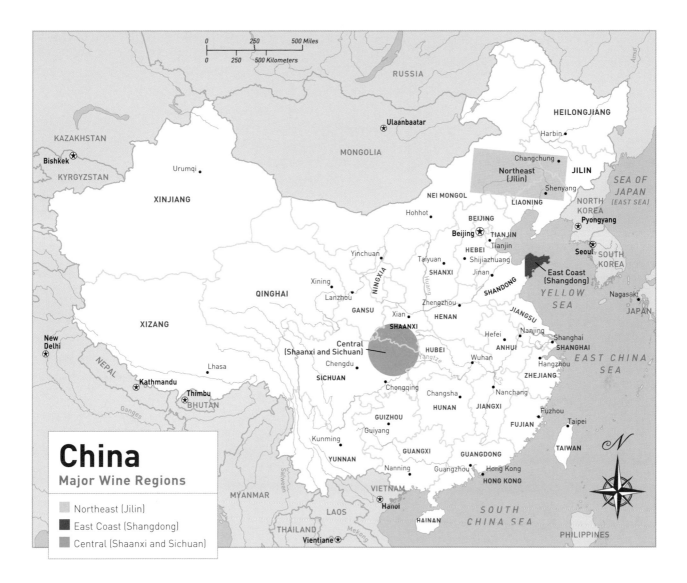

China
Major Wine Regions

- Northeast (Jilin)
- East Coast (Shangdong)
- Central (Shaanxi and Sichuan)

Singapore, and mainland China, and they are actively involved in wine commerce.

Well-known chefs, including such luminaries as Daniel Boulud and Jean-Georges Vongerichten, have established fine restaurants in China, and the mainland now boasts many extraordinary places to dine, complete with world-class wine lists. The Chinese economy supports an active food and wine industry, and many Chinese embrace wine as an important part of doing international business.

While producers such as Grace Vineyard and Huadong (both financed by Hong Kong entrepreneurs) focus on international vinifera, only about 15 to 20 percent of the wine produced in China is made from international varieties. Of these, the focus is on red wines, especially Cabernet Sauvignon and Merlot, which may come as a surprise to many who feel that Chinese food pairs much

better with white wines. At least for now, there seems to be something of a disconnect between Chinese food and Chinese wine, as the Chinese middle class has dived into a learning curve that teaches red wine as the more important wine for international commerce. Huadong winery does produce a good Chardonnay, however, and Dragon's Hollow produces sound varietal-labeled wines, which are available in the United States.

Wine Regions

Grapes are grown in several Chinese provinces, and a few stand out as the most promising.

Xinjiang, which is located in the extreme northwest of the country, has very cold winters, and vines need to be protected from frost starting in mid-autumn of each year.

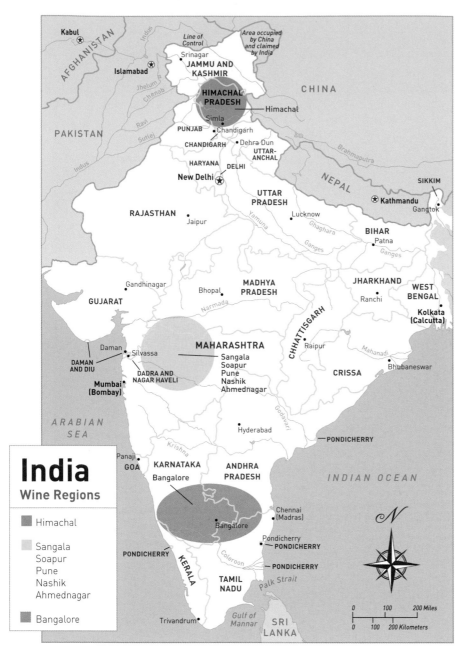

India
Wine Regions

- Himachal
- Sangala
  Soapur
  Pune
  Nashik
  Ahmednagar
- Bangalore

the maritime climate as well as well-drained soils on hillsides and mountainsides create a fine environment for vines for quality wine.

INDIA

INDIA HAS CREATED a wine industry that is growing by leaps and bounds. While per capita consumption of wine is really little more than 1 tablespoon/15 milliliters per person, that number is set to increase, and even if, in the next ten years, that becomes one glass per person, the impact will be enormous. The reason is that over the next decade, India will have approximately 300 million people who will be able to afford to drink wine, and will choose to do so.

In just one calendar year, from 2007 to 2008, investment in the Indian wine industry nearly doubled, and the source of that investment is both homegrown and foreign-based. As of 2010, there were more than one hundred wineries in India, and by the time you read these words, there will be a lot more. In addition to the wine itself, most of which is consumed in India, the society seems to be wine-conscious: Wine magazines and websites have high visibility, and Indian wineries are participating in international wine competitions and hosting their own as well, such as the annual Indian Wine Challenge. Restaurants and specialty shops feature the best Indian wines, and chefs and wineries work together to create winemakers' dinners.

For the last several years, wine consumption in India has been growing by a factor of at least 25 percent per year. As India has become one of the driving forces in the world economy, wine is increasingly perceived to be a sophisticated drink, one that is served with food and consumed in moderation. Historically, Indian women have not consumed alcohol in the form of beer and especially spirits,

About 25 percent of China's vineyards are planted in this region, including some very new vineyards.

Tianjin and Hebei, close to China's capital, Beijing, in the northeastern part of the country, are home to about 20 percent of China's vineyards. Here, local varieties, such as Dragon's Eye (Long Yan) produce sweet white wines. Still, plantings of international vinifera are increasing at a steady pace.

Shangdong, south of Beijing, forms a peninsula that shows real promise for growing vinifera grapes. About 35 percent of China's vineyards are planted here, and

but middle- and upper-class Indian women feel that it's perfectly fine to sip a glass of wine. The stars of India's Bollywood films, who are revered by the general population, are often seen at wine tastings, wine dinners, and visiting wineries. Add to this, at least 70 million people under the age of 25 in the country, and the future of wine in India seems assured.

In 2009, more than a million cases of wine—both domestic and foreign wines—were consumed in India. This figure is expected to grow exponentially over the next decade. The country has about 200,000 acres/80,000 hectares of vineyards, and that number is also growing at an astounding rate. Quite a bit of Indian wine is made for the local taste—kind of sweet and alcoholic—but there is also a considerable amount of better-than-average wine produced from international varieties.

Wine exporters see India as a potential goldmine, possibly the largest wine market in the world, and are moving aggressively to sell their wines in the country. In 2009, there were more than eighty international wine exporters in the Indian market. Wineries from France, Italy, Spain, and other nations have formed partnerships with Indian entrepreneurs to create wineries in the best wine-growing regions.

Some of the best-known wineries in India include Chateau d'Ori, Chateau Indage, Grover Vineyards, Indus, Renaissance Wines, Revello, Sankalp Wines, Sula, and Vinicola. Most of these wineries were founded in the last ten to fifteen years; Grover Vineyards was founded in 1988.

Major Wine Regions

India has four major wine-growing regions, all of them quite warm and some of them threatened by monsoons in the country's rainy season.

Nashik, in the state of Maharasta, is the country's largest wine-growing region. The vineyards are planted at about 800 meters/2,600 feet above sea level. The Nashik (also spelled Nasik) region is considered to be India's best wine region for the cultivation of international varietals. Sangala is another region in Maharasta.

Bangalore, located in the southern state of Karnataka, features vineyards in the Nandi Hills, about 28 miles/45 kilometers from the city of Bangalore. Warm days, cool nights, and well-drained soils make this one of India's best regions for wine.

Himachal is the most northern of India's vineyard regions, and the coolest. Surrounded by the states of Kashmir and Punjab, this is considered an important region for future vineyard plantings.

SUMMARY

For American wine consumers, the wines of the Eastern Mediterranean are a distinctly mixed bag. The arrival of modern winemaking methods and the influx of large investments in many of the vineyards and wineries of Greece confirm that Greek wines are undergoing nothing short of a renaissance. The finest versions of the ancient fortified wine from Cyprus, Commandaria, can be most enjoyable following a good meal. Lebanon's Château Musar is a singular wine of finesse and elegance and will always find its audience.

Israel now makes good varietal wines in a New World style, especially reds. Its white wines are improving, and with a change in international marketing strategy that stresses quality, Israel has begun to find a niche in the export market for its best wines.

Not much wine from Turkey, Algeria, Tunisia, and Morocco is imported into the United States, which is, on balance, no great loss to American wine lovers. The overwhelming majority of these wines are, with a few exceptions, curiosities.

China is now the sixth-largest wine producer in the world and a major importer of wines. India's wine industry and imports are growing exponentially. There are some good wines produced in these countries, and if recent economic and social history tells us anything, it is that wines produced in China and India will get better and better, and as their economy prospers, wine will become part of daily life for many. With support from both government and industry, the two countries, which represent the world's first- and second-largest populations, respectively, are poised to become major players in the globalization of wine.

BOG
VINEY

Immigrants imported cut
than a century ago. The f
wines of extraordinary f

Appellation of Origin Rhoa
of High Quality

Athir

OUNTAIN SLOP

DRY WHITE WINE
V.Q.P.R.D.

rtinsano

Vargele

1692

4 · QUINTA DE VARG

Gewürztraminer

EGRI

ESTATE BOTTL
FIRST GROWTH

D

OBOG

6 put

kaji a

te wine

PART 4
WINE, FOOD, AND HEALTH

PART 4 of *Exploring Wine* is divided into two chapters. First, we address the theoretical and practical issues surrounding the successful pairing of food with wine. Second, we examine the role of wine in a healthy diet and lifestyle.

Chapter 14, "Wine and Food," is a multilayered look at how we approach the ideas of taste, texture, and flavor intensity, as well as understanding complementary and contrasting flavors, all in an effort to attain a happy marriage between food and wine. This chapter is as free of dogma and jargon as possible so that you, the reader, can apply our basic wine and food guidelines successfully in a social or professional environment.

We urge our readers to create their own imaginative menus pairing food and wine, and to encourage you, we have included some of our own menus. Reflecting a "global village" approach, our menus range from classic French to pan-Mediterranean, from regional African to regional American.

Chapter 15, "Wine and Health," makes the point that wine, when consumed in moderation, plays a significant role in a healthy diet for adults. We have scanned the early work done in this field as well as some of the latest research and articles, conducted our own interviews, and attended symposia on the place of wine in the daily diet. The inescapable conclusion is that wine consumed in moderation with meals provides an overall health benefit.

While health professionals in general agree that mod-erate wine consumption can help lead to better health indices, they are not so sanguine about the public policy issues surrounding wine. Should a doctor prescribe a glass of wine with dinner for a heart patient or withhold this recommendation out of fear of alcohol abuse by even one patient? What about wine, women, and pregnancy, and the danger of fetal alcohol syndrome? In Chapter 15 we contribute to this increasingly important and controversial discussion in American society.

MARRYING

cooking methods

ETHNIC

SPICY

complement

SALTY

CONTRAST

PAIRING

GLOBAL VILLAGE

SMOKED

RAW

COOKED

INTENSITY

ANTAGONISTS

WINE AND FOOD

14

Matching food and wine to each other to enhance the quality of a meal can be both simple and difficult. The simple part is that if you bear in mind a few basic guidelines and enjoy a moderate degree of gastronomic exploration and experimentation, you cannot go too far wrong. The difficult part is this: There is no "perfect" food and wine combination that is right for everybody, but we are often called upon to come up with this elusive, even impossible, combination. Somewhere between the two extremes—the casual, spontaneous approach and the rigorous, classical approach—most people, especially food and wine lovers and professionals, find their own comfort zone.

In this chapter we will discuss why certain food and wine choices either marry well or should be divorced from each other. It is especially important to begin this discussion without a lot of preconceptions, prejudices, and pretenses. Too many of us have had to suffer through dinners, lectures, or books by "wine experts" in which some boorish, affected, snobby wine geek has laid down the law about what wine to drink with what food. We will try to steer clear of this approach, because we believe that pairing wine and food should not be intimidating; it should be educational and as free of indecipherable wine-speak as humanly possible. Above all, pairings should be fun and should serve as useful tools to enhance the enjoyment of virtually any and all meals.

Perhaps food and wine pairing boils down to the twin issues of personal taste and experience. At the same time, there are some basic suggested guidelines—*not rules*—to make the pairing of food and wine fun, exciting, and rewarding. Think of food-and-wine pairing as a journey. This journey can be local or regional, matching the foods and wines of the bioregion in which you live; it can be national, sampling the cuisine of a particular country; or it can be truly international, crossing borders, time zones, and datelines to pair foods and wines of many parts of the world, joined together by a culinary détente of ideas, memories, and taste buds.

THE BASIC TASTES AND SENSATIONS

Chapter 3, "Tasting Wine," discussed how the human nose can discern innumerable smells, but our palates can distinguish only four basic tastes: sweet, sour, bitter, and salt (and a fifth taste, *umami*, which was discovered more recently and is the taste abundant in shiitake mushrooms, seaweed, shellfish, Parmesan cheese, or any food rich in glutamic acid). Most wines are not really perceived on the

CHAPTER 14 WINE AND FOOD

palate as salty or shiitake-like, so we are left with sweet, sour, and bitter as the three basic tastes in wine. Food, of course, allows us to experience all five tastes and, perhaps just as important, the sensations of cold and heat. Heat is experienced as a temperature sensation (food served warm) or as spiciness (jalapeño peppers, spicy curries). The sensation of cold can also be experienced as a chilling contrast to heat (cold white wine with fried chicken, with its heat escaping from under the crispy batter) or as a cooling extinguisher to something spicy hot (fatty sour cream served with spicy chili).

The four basic tastes (plus *umami*) and the sensations of hot and cold are important when considering what wine to match with what food. The same wine will taste completely different when paired with various foods. Try a medium-bodied dry white wine with a grilled fish and you've got the basic building blocks for a good match. Pair that same wine with dessert and you're asking for trouble: sour wine and overly sweet food. Try that wine with a rare steak and you might as well be drinking water. In fact, you'll be better off with water; at least it won't taste like leftover grapefruit juice (if the wine has been made in stainless steel) or like a bitter hunk of wood (if the wine was made in an oak barrel).

Bear in mind that wine, like food, is composed of various flavors and textures and should be matched with the other elements of a meal based on those flavors and textures. It's as simple—and as complex—as that.

FOOD AND WINE PAIRING: A LEARNED RESPONSE

IT WOULD BE A HIGHLY UNUSUAL PERSON who upon first tasting a harsh, tannic, young red wine thinks, "Gee, this would be great with a rare red meat." He or she would be more likely to dismiss the wine as undrinkable. Equally fantastic would be a scenario where a taster experiences foie gras for the first time and says, "If only I had some Sauternes," never having tasted the luscious, sweet wine from Bordeaux. Pairing food and wine just does not work this way. Rather, people make their judgments based on experience—be it limited or broad—and personal preference.

We have noticed among the great majority of new wine drinkers that the appreciation of wine—especially dry, complex, challenging red wines—is a gradual process. It is not uncommon for Americans who enjoy wine to start tasting wines that are quite fruity, even sweet, and slowly, over time, develop an appreciation for drier whites and reds. Some people find *brut* Champagne sour, because they prefer the sweeter *spumante* Asti, but little by little, they acquire a taste for the drier wine. There is no law that people have to love dry wines, and some people are perfectly happy drinking sweet wines. On the other hand, some people never acquire a taste for the balance of razor-sharp acidity and fruitiness that some Riesling wines from Germany deliver, thinking all German Rieslings are just too sweet. Again, personal taste rules.

Some people enjoy vegetables, fruits, and grains, while others eschew those for a juicy steak. Obviously, most vegetarian dishes (with the possible exception of seitan or some *umami*-infused mushrooms that can be quite "beefy") will call for a different wine than Tournedos Rossini—filet mignon pan-fried in butter and served on a crouton with sautéed foie gras, in a Madeira demi-glace sauce garnished with black truffles. In the United States, many of us grew up as true omnivores—we ate everything. As our personal tastes developed in adulthood, and our food and cultural experiences may have broadened, many of us have refined our preferences. No meat. Meat at every meal. No dairy products. No gluten. Pasta at home, steak in a restaurant. Always have a salad. Skip the salad to save room for dessert. Have the chicken. High-protein diets. Low-carbohydrate diets. When we were kids, we hated canned tuna fish, but now we love a grilled fresh tuna steak, served rare.

The same maturation process that happens with food happens with wine. Consider a hypothetical couple. At age twenty-one, he lived for beer. At twenty-four, she drank only oaky Chardonnay from Napa Valley. At twenty-six, he tasted a classic Margaux for the first time and was hooked. At twenty-eight, she discovered the fruit and richness of red wines from the Rhône Valley. At thirty, they traveled to Spain for the first time and now search for the perfect red Rioja. At thirty-two, she attended her first serious wine tasting and discovered she loved Riesling but that all the Chardonnays tasted alike. At forty, they each had a glass of Champagne every night before dinner. At fifty, they now taste wine with their adult children, teaching them all they know, all they have learned. Their progeny do a bit of teaching, too, turning their parents on to the newest New World wines made from the oldest Old World grapes. Tastes change; our palates are conditioned by our life experiences.

TEXTURE

FOODS AND WINES both have texture, which we can loosely define as how they feel—on their own and together—in the mouth. This mouthfeel is highly subjective and is largely based on cultural and culinary experience, but we can all agree that certain foods and wines seem richer or fattier in the mouth, while others feel far more austere or lean. Foie gras—the fatty liver of ducks or geese—has a rich texture, while lightly dressed salad greens are exactly the opposite. A rare porterhouse steak is richly textured, while Dover sole poached in white wine and served with a green salad is quite a lightly textured dish. The mouthfeel or textures of these dishes will be distinct, and this creates another consideration for matching wine and food.

Wine, too, has texture. A dry Sauvignon Blanc from California fermented in stainless steel will be refreshingly tart and light in texture, evaporating on the tongue rather quickly. An oak-aged Chardonnay wine from the Côte de Beaune in Burgundy will coat the palate and create a feeling of richness in the mouth, due in large part to malolactic fermentation and wood-aging. Likewise, a Beaujolais-Villages, made from the Gamay grape, is a fruity, young, and simple red wine, suggesting a simple, light texture. However, a mature Barbaresco—made in Piedmont, Italy, from Nebbiolo grapes—will exhibit a rich, complex balance of tannin, acid, and fruit and leave an indelible, rich taste in the mouth. So, just as we must consider the texture of the food we want to marry to the wine, we must also consider the texture of the wine in the matchmaking process. In fact, one of the simplest but most important guidelines for matching food and wine is to marry "power with power"—light-tasting and light-textured dishes with lighter wines, heavier dishes with fuller-bodied wines.

INTENSITY IN FOOD AND WINE: COOKING METHODS

WHILE WE ALL HAVE TASTE PREFERENCES, not many of us insist on eating foods that are prepared only one way. Most of us can enjoy a poached salmon at lunch on Tuesday and still enjoy salmon grilled on the barbecue over the weekend. We eat roast chicken, but we also enjoy braised Coq au Vin. Sometimes zucchini is steamed, sometimes it is served à la grecque—rubbed in olive oil and then grilled. Baked potatoes are great, but other times only French fries will do. Clearly, our palates can accommodate many cooking methods, and often these cooking methods go virtually unnoticed.

When matching food and wine, cooking method is of paramount importance. Obviously, a dish that is delicately poached in white wine will call for a far different wine than a perfectly seared New York strip steak served in a rich sauce. Just as important, however, the same product—a grouper fillet, for example—might call for a crisp, fruity, light white wine when poached but could support a full-bodied dry white or even a light- to medium-bodied dry red wine when it is grilled. Why? When you taste these dishes, it is obvious that the flavor intensity changes radically, at least partially due to the chosen cooking method.

POWER WITH POWER

AS FOOD FLAVOR INTENSIFIES, so should the flavors in the accompanying wine. To put it another way, one important guideline in pairing food and wine is that you will most often achieve a happy gustatory marriage by matching equivalent levels of flavor intensity in both the food and the wine.

Consider food by its method of preparation (in rough order of increasing flavor intensity): poached, steamed, sautéed, stir-fried, pan-fried, deep-fried, braised, roasted, broiled, grilled, or blackened.

As the food's flavor intensity increases by its method of preparation, it might be matched to white wines based on (again, in rough order of increasing intensity) Chenin Blanc, Riesling, Sauvignon Blanc, Gewürztraminer, Viognier, and Chardonnay. It might be matched to red wines based on Gamay, Barbera, Pinot Noir, Dolcetto, Sangiovese, Merlot, Zinfandel, Nebbiolo, Cabernet Sauvignon, and Syrah, among a host of other varietals.

The idea here is to match the flavor intensity of the dominant ingredient or dominant flavor of a dish with the flavor intensity—the power—of the wine. We are not looking to overpower either the wine or the food, nor are we trying to mask the essential nature of good ingredients on the plate or in the glass.

INTENSITY IN FOOD AND WINE: SAUCES AND GARNISHES

IN MANY CASES, we match wines to the flavor of the main ingredient of a dish, often a protein (meat, fish, tofu, etc.). Another approach might be to match a wine to the sauce in the dish, or even a garnish. London broil, a fairly lean cut of beef, served in its own juices with matchstick potatoes and morels, would work well with a medium-bodied red wine, such as Pinot Noir or a lighter Merlot. However, if the same cut of beef—cooked the same way—is encrusted in peppercorns and served with a red wine demi-glace sauce and creamy whipped potatoes, a Cabernet Sauvignon, Syrah, or Zinfandel might better match the higher level of spicy intensity and richness in the dish.

In the first case—the simpler London broil preparation—the Pinot Noir or lighter Merlot will be a good choice because the flavors and textures of the dish are reasonably gentle. The character of the wines is similar: medium-bodied with moderate tannins and good levels of fruit, with moderate to moderately high levels of acidity. This dish is softer and lighter in texture and less intensely flavored than the same cut of meat served with a crust of peppercorns, the red wine demi-glace, and the creamy potatoes. With this preparation, the flavors of the pepper-

corns (a garnish) and the demi-glace (a sauce) dominate. At the same time, the potatoes create a rich and creamy counterpoint to the intense spiciness and meaty flavors of the sauced and encrusted London broil. Naturally, the wine that we choose for this dish—Cabernet Sauvignon, Syrah, or Zinfandel, among a myriad of possible choices—will exhibit sufficient intensity of flavor to match the intensity of the pepper and sauce. These wines, each with moderately high to high levels of tannin, will create a contrasting texture with the smooth, rich potatoes. The richness of the potatoes will cut the tannin, as the flavors and textures of the dish and the wine harmonize.

COMPLEMENTING AND CONTRASTING FLAVORS

DEPENDING ON WHAT FLAVORS and textures we wish to highlight in the marriage of food to wine, most often there are two approaches to playing gastronomic matchmaker. First, we can choose to complement the flavors and textures of the food and the wine, matching intensity with intensity, richness with richness, power with power. Second, we can contrast the flavors and the textures of the food with the wine, playing off tannin against fat, fruit against spice, complex against simple, while being careful to maintain equivalence in the intensity of flavors in the wine and the food.

Say, for example, we are preparing boiled lobster, served cold and sliced thin, accompanied by an aioli sauce, and we want to choose one white wine to match this dish. Let's ask a few questions before we make a wine choice. Do we want to emphasize the clean, medium-intensity flavor and texture of the lobster, cleanse the palate of fat, and invigorate the appetite? Or do we want to celebrate the richness of the garlicky mayonnaise that coats the lobster—and the palate—so that the dish becomes a sensual meditation from one bite to the next?

If we choose to cleanse our palates of the mayonnaise so that we can enjoy the lingering clean flavors of the shellfish, we might choose a wine that is light in body and high in acid, such as an inexpensive Muscadet from the Loire

Valley of France. This wine, with its fruity, tart flavors, will help bring out the neutral flavor and the pleasing but leaner texture of the lobster, while almost erasing the rich aioli from our palates. A sip of Muscadet, a still, light white—sometimes called the perfect shellfish wine—will leave us wanting to taste another bite of the lobster.

If we really want to deemphasize the fat in this dish but make the pairing a bit more elegant, we could also try a dry sparkling wine—a *brut* Champagne, for example—which would cleanse our palates with its dance of bubbles and its bracing acidity. The choice of either the Muscadet or the Champagne would be a classic example of contrasting the food with the wine—light, fruity wine with a good level of acidity versus the opulent richness of the lobster dipped in the sauce.

The Muscadet is light, fruity, and tart, as is the *brut* Champagne, and so contrasts with the briny (lobster) and rich (aioli) flavors of the dish, but if we want to complement this dish with a wine of similar taste and texture, how shall we proceed? We can think of the components of the dish—just lobster and aioli—and seek a wine that demonstrates a richness similar to the tastes and textures of the dish. A rich, oak-aged Chardonnay—from California, Australia, or Côte de Beaune in Burgundy, full of vanilla and cedar flavors that bear down on the palate—may be just the ticket. The net effect of this food and wine pairing will be a feeling of "weight," of fullness on the palate, honoring the sumptuous combination of shellfish and mayonnaise. For some people this combination might be too rich, especially if there are other courses to come in a multicourse dinner. However, if this classic dish is the main course for a three-course summer lunch, then pairing it with a full-bodied, classic wine will provide a sensual, luxurious highlight to the meal.

Another consideration of both contrasting and complementing flavors is the pairing of spicy, salty, or smoked foods with wines. We have found that fruity, dry to semidry wines, as well as lighter sparkling wines, work best with these types of foods. Consider prosciutto and melon, a dish that contains both salty and fruit-driven flavors, a very attractive combination. Semidry wines such as Riesling, Gewürztraminer, and Chenin Blanc, as well as sparkling wines such as Prosecco from Italy or Cava from Spain, create a tasty contrast with the prosciutto while complementing the flavor of the melon.

Consider also a dish such as a spicy shrimp curry paired with a semidry Riesling from the Finger Lakes of New York State or the Mosel region of Germany. The hint of sweetness in the wine offsets the heat of the curry, while amplifying the sweet fruit chutney. The cool serving temperature of the Riesling also serves as a physical contrast to the spicy heat of the dish, cooling your palate. The Riesling is just one example of a style of wine that will work with spicy, salty, or smoked foods.

THE DOMINANT FLAVOR

IN THE PRECEDING EXAMPLE of lobster and aioli, we had to choose between complementary and contrasting flavors in the accompanying wine. Just as important a choice in making this match is knowing or finding out what flavor dominates the dish. The lobster? The sauce? Probably in this case, a lot will depend on how much mayonnaise is eaten with the lobster. If we choose just a drop or two on each piece of lobster, then the fleshy, neutral, briny flavors of the lobster will dominate, and the Muscadet is an excellent match. However, if we slather the lobster in the sauce, the lobster—and the palate—become encased in rich fat, making the oaky Chardonay the better choice. In terms of marrying food and wine, this example is kind of diner-dependent, because there are only two major elements in the dish, and it is up to the diner to decide which element—the lobster or the sauce—he or she wishes to emphasize. In a restaurant environment or a banquet setting, this choice might be left to the chef and the sommelier.

A POWER CHART

ONE OF THE EASIER WAYS to match food and wine is to remember that certain wines are light-bodied, some medium-bodied, and some full-bodied. The relative power of a wine is based not only on the grape types that go into the wine, but also on vineyard practices—especially grape yield levels, where the grapes are grown, and how the wine is made. A Chardonnay wine fermented in stainless steel and aged in the bottle will taste entirely different from an oak-fermented and oak-aged Chardonnay. The first wine may have been made from grapes in a high-yield vineyard;

FOCUS ON SAUCES

Sauces are often intensely flavored and rich in texture, so they become an important consideration in matching food and wine. Traditional sauces are high in fat, and frequently they are the main taste element in a complex dish. If a poached fish is served with a meunière or hollandaise sauce, the richest part of the dish is found in the sauce. If a filet mignon is covered with a béarnaise sauce, the richness of the sauce deemphasizes the flavor of a cut of meat that is not densely marbled with internal fat. Sauces based on butter, cream, and fat from other dairy products tend to dominate the flavors of many protein-based dishes. In choosing a wine to marry with a richly sauced dish, we might very well choose the flavors in the sauce as dominant and match the wine with those flavors.

Increasingly, restaurant patrons are electing to enjoy sauces and other rich accompaniments on the side, in order to consume fewer calories from fat and also to taste the food relatively unadorned and unmasked. In addition, the nature of sauces is changing. A grilled salmon that in the past might have been served with a butter sauce now may be served with a spicy fruit or vegetable salsa. A poached salmon might be served in its poaching liquid of wine and herbs. Meats might just as easily be served with sauces based on vegetable juices and purées, or with a lentil ragoût, as with a rich demi-glace sauce. Grilled or steamed vegetables, or rice and pasta, once thought to be side dishes, now occupy the center of the plate and the center of the palate. Clearly, the wines chosen to match such contemporary cuisine will be quite different from those chosen to marry with rich sauces.

We use the example of sauces and their changing nature to emphasize that choosing wines for certain dishes is most often dependent on the dominant flavors of those dishes. Sauces can be dominant, but so can meat, fish, poultry, vegetables, or grains. Even a garnish—fresh horseradish, for example—can be the dominant flavor in a delicate, lighter dish, such as a classic shrimp cocktail. It follows that if you are picking wines to accompany food, you have to know what the food tastes like, and unless you are trying to show off the wines at the expense of the food, you will most often match the wine to the food, not the food to the wine. Certainly entire dinners can—and do—revolve around particular wines and their food affinities, but in most cases, wine should be seen as part of a harmonious whole—another flavor element in a successful meal.

the more grapes per acre, the less concentration of flavor. The oaky Chardonnay may have undergone malolactic fermentation and may have come from a low-yielding vineyard, with fewer grapes per acre but more flavor concentration per grape. So the same grape, in this case Chardonnay, can make wines that are light- to medium-bodied, medium- to full-bodied, and full- to extra-full-bodied. The same is true of certain red grapes, such as Sangiovese, which can make a light- or medium- to quite full-bodied wine, depending on where the wine is made, how the grapes are grown, and how the winemaker treats the wine.

While this power chart is not foolproof—tasting is the final arbiter of the power of a wine—it begins to illuminate how certain wines express their intensity of flavor, texture, and body.

Where the wines are not called by their varietal names (e.g., Barolo), the varietal name is provided (e.g., Nebbiolo). Likewise, if a wine is best-known as native to a particular region or regions, those too are listed. Since some varietals or styles of wine are found in different regions of the same country, the country name is given first, followed by the most prominent wine region. The "Power Chart" (tables on pages 561–563) is presented in *approximate* order of power, from lightest to fullest body, focusing on dry, semidry, semisweet, and sweet wines.

Based on our experiences working closely with chefs to create food-and-wine brunches, lunches, dinners, and receptions, as well as teaching thousands of aspiring chefs, we have come to realize just how vitally important cooking methods and techniques are when considering what food to match with what wine. The tables on pages 564–567 include examples of the wines listed in the power chart cross-referenced to cooking methods listed in their approximate order of "power" or intensity.

POWER CHART: WHITE WINES AND ROSÉ WINES

LIGHT- TO MEDIUM-BODIED DRY WHITE WINES

LABEL	PLACE OF ORIGIN	VARIETALS
Muscadet	France (Loire)	Melon de Bourgogne
Entre-Deux-Mers	France (Bordeaux)	Sauvignon Blanc/Sémillon
Verdelho	Portugal, Australia, others	varietal
Verdejo	Spain (Rueda)	varietal
Viura	Spain (Rioja)	varietal
Sauvignon Blanc	Various countries	varietal
Graves (and Pessac-Leognan)	France (Bordeaux)	Sauvignon Blanc/Sémillon
Orvieto	Umbria or Lazio	Trebbiano, Malvasia
Frascati	Lazio	Malvasia, Trebbiano
Soave	Italy (Veneto)	Garganega, Trebbiano, Chardonnay
Verdicchio	Italy (Marche)	varietal
Tocai Friulano (or Friulano)	Italy (Friuli-Venezia Giulia), others	varietal

LIGHT- TO MEDIUM-BODIED OFF-DRY TO SLIGHTLY SWEET WINES

LABEL	PLACE OF ORIGIN	VARIETALS
Vinho Verde	Portugal (Minho)	Loureiro, Trajadura, others
Chenin Blanc	France (Loire Valley), South Africa, U.S.A., others	varietal
Riesling	New World (U.S.A., Australia, others)	varietal
Riesling Kabinett	Germany	varietal
Saumur and Vouvray	France (Loire)	Chenin Blanc

MEDIUM- TO FULL-BODIED DRY WHITE WINES

LABEL	PLACE OF ORIGIN	VARIETALS
Muscat, Riesling, Gewürztraminer, Pinot Gris	Alsace, France	varietals
Chablis and unoaked Chardonnay	France (Burgundy), U.S.A., Australia, New Zealand, several others	Chardonnay

MEDIUM- TO FULL-BODIED DRY WHITE WINES (CONT.)

LABEL	PLACE OF ORIGIN	VARIETALS
Sancerre	France (Loire)	Sauvignon Blanc
Pouilly-Fumé	France (Loire)	Sauvignon Blanc
Falanghina	Italy (Campania)	varietal
Fumé Blanc	U.S.A.	Sauvignon Blanc
Fiano di Avellino	Italy (Campania)	varietal
Greco di Tufo	Italy (Campania)	varietal
Sémillon	Australia, U.S.A.	varietal
Assyrtiko	Greece	varietal
Albariño/Alvarinho	Spain, Portugal	varietal
Savennières	France (Loire)	Chenin Blanc
Mâcon-Villages, St-Véran, Pouilly-Fuissé	France (Mâcon, Burgundy)	Chardonnay
Viognier	U.S.A., New World	varietal
St-Joseph	France (Northern Rhône)	Marsanne, Roussanne, others
Condrieu	France (Northern Rhône)	Viognier
Meursault, Puligny-Montrachet, Chassagne-Montrachet, Premier Cru and Grand Cru White Burgundies	France (Côte de Beaune, Burgundy)	Chardonnay
Barrel-fermented or oak-aged Chardonnay	U.S.A., Australia, New World	varietal

MEDIUM- TO FULL-BODIED SWEET WHITE WINES

LABEL	PLACE OF ORIGIN	VARIETALS
Icewine	Canada, Germany, U.S.A., others	Riesling, Vidal, others
Spätlese, Auslese, Beerenauslese, Trockenbeerenauslese	Germany (Mosel/Rhine)	Riesling, others
Coteaux du Layon	France (Loire)	Chenin Blanc
Vin Santo	Italy (Tuscany, others)	Trebbiano, Malvasia
Barsac, Sauternes	France (Bordeaux)	Sémillon with Sauvignon Blanc
Tokaji Aszú	Hungary	Furmint, others

POWER CHART: WHITE WINES AND ROSÉ WINES (CONTINUED)

LIGHT- TO MEDIUM-BODIED ROSÉ WINES (DRY TO OFF-DRY)

LABEL	PLACE OF ORIGIN	VARIETALS
White Zinfandel and other blush wines	U.S.A. (California)	various
Rosado	Spain (Navarra, other regions)	Garnacha, others
Rosé of Pinot Noir	U.S.A. (California)	varietal
Rosé de Marsannay	France (Burgundy)	Pinot Noir
Rosé of Cabernet Sauvignon	U.S.A. (California)	varietal
Rosé d'Anjou	France (Loire)	Grolleau, Cabernet Franc
Tavel	France (Southern Rhône)	Grenache, Cinsaut, others
Rosé Bandol	France (Provence)	Mourvèdre, Grenache, Cinsault

POWER CHART: RED WINE

LIGHT- TO MEDIUM-BODIED DRY RED WINES

LABEL	PLACE OF ORIGIN	VARIETALS
Bardolino, Valpolicella	Italy (Veneto)	Corvina, Rondinella, others
Grignolino	Italy (Piemonte)	varietal
Gamay	U.S.A., others	varietal
Beaujolais-Villages	France (Southern Burgundy)	Gamay
Cru Beaujolais: Régnié, Chiroubles, Côte de Brouilly, Brouilly, St-Amour, Fleurie, Juliénas, Chénas, Moulin-à-Vent, Morgon	France (Southern Burgundy)	Gamay
Chianti	Italy (Tuscany)	Sangiovese, others
Dolcetto	Italy (Piemonte)	varietal
Barbera	Italy (Piemonte)	varietal
Côtes du Rhône	France (Rhône)	Grenache, Syrah, others
Corbières	France (Languedoc)	Carignan, Grenache
Rioja Robles, Joven, Cosecha, or Crianza	Spain (Rioja)	Tempranillo, others

MEDIUM- TO FULL-BODIED DRY RED WINES

LABEL	PLACE OF ORIGIN	VARIETALS
Barbera	Italy (Piemonte)	varietal
Chianti Classico	Italy (Tuscany)	Sangiovese, others
Pinot Noir	U.S.A. (California, Oregon), New World	varietal
Bourgueil, Chinon, Saumur-Champigny	France (Loire)	Cabernet Franc
Côte de Beaune-Villages, Beaune, Chambolle-Musigny, Pommard, Nuits-St-Georges, Vosne-Romanée, Gevrey-Chambertin, others	France (Côte d'Or, Burgundy)	Pinot Noir
Merlot	U.S.A., New World	varietal
Dão	Portugal	Touriga Nacional, others

MEDIUM- TO FULL-BODIED DRY RED WINES (CONT.)

LABEL	PLACE OF ORIGIN	VARIETALS
Rioja Reserva	Spain (Rioja)	Tempranillo, others
Premier Cru and Grand Cru Burgundies	France (Côte d'Or, Burgundy)	Pinot Noir
Zinfandel	U.S.A. (California)	varietal
Naoussa	Greece	Xinomavro
St-Émilion	France (St-Émilion, Bordeaux)	Merlot, Cabernet Franc
Pomerol	France (Pomerol, Bordeaux)	Merlot
Graves (and Pessac-Leognan)	France (Graves and Pessac-Leognan, Bordeaux)	Cabernet Sauvignon, Merlot
Margaux, St-Julien, Pauillac, St-Estèphe, others	France (Haut-Médoc, Bordeaux)	Cabernet Sauvignon, Merlot
Châteauneuf-du-Pape	France (Southern Rhône)	Grenache, Mourvèdre, others
Gattinara, Ghemme	Italy (Piemonte)	Nebbiolo, others
Cabernet Sauvignon	U.S.A., Australia, New World	varietal
Chianti Classico Riserva	Italy (Tuscany)	Sangiovese, others
Carmignano, Vino Nobile di Montepulciano, Morellino di Scansano	Italy (Tuscany)	Sangiovese, others
Barbaresco, Barolo	Italy (Piemonte)	Nebbiolo
Syrah	U.S.A., others	varietal
Brunello di Montalcino	Italy (Tuscany)	Sangiovese
Côte-Rôtie, Hermitage	France (Northern Rhône)	Syrah
Douro	Portugal	Touriga Nacional, others
Bairrada	Portugal (Beiras)	Baga, others
Amarone	Italy (Veneto)	Corvina, Rondinella, others

Again, this chart is just a guideline for wine-and-food pairing, but more often than not, the cooking method is overlooked when considering wine with food. And the cooking method is key! Would you serve the same wine with a poached salmon as you would with a grilled salmon served rare? The proteins and sugars of the poached salmon are released into its cooking liquid, while the grilled salmon's sugars have caramelized and its proteins are largely uncoagulated (which is true of almost all meats and fatty fish served rare).

The poached salmon, with its mild flavor profile, calls for a light- to medium-bodied dry white wine. The rare grilled salmon needs a more intense, more powerful wine: a full-bodied elegant white or a light- to medium-bodied, fruit-driven red.

CHOOSING WINE BY COOKING METHOD

FLAVOR INTENSITY = WINE INTENSITY. That's what the tables on the following pages are about.

WHITE WINE/COOKING METHODS

WHITE WINES	POACHING	STEAMING	SAUTÉING	PAN-FRYING	STIR-FRYING
LIGHT- TO MEDIUM-BODIED DRY WHITE WINES					
Muscadet	■	■	■	■	■
Entre-Deux-Mers	■	■	■	■	■
Verdelho	■	■	■	■	■
Verdejo	■	■	■	■	■
Viura	■	■	■	■	■
Sauvignon Blanc	■	■	■	■	■
Graves (and Pessac-Leognan)	■	■	■	■	■
Orvieto	■	■	■	■	■
Frascati	■	■	■	■	■
Soave	■	■	■	■	■
Verdicchio	■	■	■	■	■
Tocai Friulano (or Friulano)	■	■	■	■	■
LIGHT- TO MEDIUM-BODIED OFF-DRY TO LIGHTLY SWEET WINES					
Vinho Verde	■	■	■	■	■
Chenin Blanc	■	■	■	■	■
Riesling	■	■	■	■	■
Riesling Kabinett	■	■	■	■	■
Pinot Blanc			■	■	■
Saumur, Vouvray			■	■	■
MEDIUM- TO FULL-BODIED DRY WHITE WINES					
Muscat, Riesling, Gewürztraminer, Pinot Gris from Alsace			■	■	■
Chablis, unoaked Chardonnay			■	■	■
Savennières			■	■	■
Sémillon			■	■	■
Albariño/Alvarinho			■	■	■
Mâcon-Villages, St-Véran, Pouilly-Fuissé				■	■
Sancerre			■	■	■
Pouilly Fumé and Fumé Blanc			■	■	■
Chardonnay from U.S.A., Australia, others					
Viognier, Condrieu					
Côtes du Rhône, St.-Joseph, Hermitage					
Meursault, Puligny-Montrachet, Chassagne-Montrachet, Corton-Charlemagne, Le Montrachet					
MEDIUM- TO FULL-BODIED SWEET WHITE WINES					
Spätese, Auslese, Beerenauslese, Trockenbeerenauslese					
Barsac, Sauternes					
Tokaji Aszú					

WHITE WINES	DEEP-FRYING	ROASTING	BRAISING	BROILING	BAKING/ GRILLING	PASTRY MAKING
LIGHT- TO MEDIUM-BODIED DRY WHITE WINES						
Muscadet	■					
Entre-Deux-Mers	■					
Verdelho	■					
Verdejo	■					
Viura	■					
Sauvignon Blanc	■					
Graves (and Pessac-Leognan)	■					
Orvieto	■					
Frascati	■					
Soave	■					
Verdicchio	■					
Tocai Friulano (or Friulano)	■					
LIGHT- TO MEDIUM-BODIED OFF-DRY TO LIGHTLY SWEET WINES						
Vinho Verde	■					
Chenin Blanc	■					
Riesling	■					
Riesling Kabinett	■					
Pinot Blanc	■					
Saumur, Vouvray	■					
MEDIUM- TO FULL-BODIED DRY WHITE WINES						
Muscat, Riesling, Gewürztraminer, Pinot Gris from Alsace	■	■	■			
Chablis, unoaked Chardonnay	■	■	■			
Savennières	■	■	■			
Sémillon	■	■	■			
Albariño/Alvarinho	■					
Mâcon-Villages, St-Véran, Pouilly-Fuissé		■	■			
Sancerre		■	■			
Pouilly Fumé and Fumé Blanc		■	■			
Chardonnay from U.S.A., Australia, others		■	■	■	■	
Viognier, Condrieu		■	■	■	■	
Côtes du Rhône, St.-Joseph, Hermitage		■	■	■	■	
Meursault, Puligny-Montrachet, Chassagne-Montrachet, Corton-Charlemagne, Le Montrachet		■	■	■	■	
MEDIUM- TO FULL-BODIED SWEET WHITE WINES						
Spätese, Auslese, Beerenauslese, Trockenbeerenauslese						■
Barsac, Sauternes						■
Tokaji Aszú						■

RED WINES	POACHING	STEAMING	SAUTÉING	PAN-FRYING	STIR-FRYING
LIGHT- TO MEDIUM-BODIED DRY RED WINES					
Bardolino, Valpolicella			■	■	■
Gamay, Beaujolais-Villages			■	■	■
Régnié, Chiroubles, Côte de Brouilly, Brouilly, St-Amour			■	■	■
Fleurie, Juliénas, Chénas, Moulin-à-Vent, Morgon			■	■	■
Grignolino			■	■	■
Bourgueil, Chinon, Saumur-Champigny			■	■	■
Chianti			■	■	■
Dolcetto			■	■	■
Dão, Alentejo			■	■	■
Côtes du Rhône			■	■	■
Corbières			■	■	■
Rioja Crianza			■	■	■
MEDIUM- TO FULL-BODIED DRY RED WINES					
Barbera			■	■	
Chianti Classico			■	■	
Pinot Noir (New World)			■	■	
Merlot (New World)					
Rioja Reserva					
Côte de Beaune-Villages, Beaune, Chambolle-Musigny, Pommard					
Nuits-St-Georges, Vosne-Romanée, Gevrey-Chambertin					
Médoc, Margaux, St-Julien, Pauillac, St-Estèphe					
Graves (and Pessac-Leognan), St-Émillion, Pomerol					
Zinfandel					
Naoussa					
Châteauneuf-du-Pape					
Cabernet Sauvignon from U.S.A., Australia, New World					
Nebbiolo					
Bairrada, Douro reds					
Gattinara, Barbaresco, Barolo					
Brunello di Montalcino					
Côte-Rôtie, Hermitage					
Amarone					

RED WINE/COOKING METHODS (CONTINUED)

RED WINES	DEEP-FRYING	ROASTING	BRAISING	BROILING	BAKING/ GRILLING	PASTRY MAKING
LIGHT- TO MEDIUM-BODIED DRY RED WINES						
Bardolino, Valpolicella	■					
Gamay, Beaujolais-Villages	■					
Régnié, Chiroubles, Côte de Brouilly, Brouilly, St-Amour	■					
Fleurie, Juliénas, Chénas, Moulin-à-Vent, Morgon	■					
Grignolino	■					
Bourgueil, Chinon, Saumur-Champigny	■					
Chianti	■					
Dolcetto	■					
Dão, Alentejo	■					
Côtes du Rhône	■					
Corbières	■					
Rioja Crianza	■					
MEDIUM- TO FULL-BODIED DRY RED WINES						
Barbera		■	■	■	■	
Chianti Classico		■	■	■	■	
Pinot Noir (New World)		■	■	■	■	
Merlot (New World)		■	■	■	■	
Rioja Reserva		■	■	■	■	
Côte de Beaune-Villages, Beaune, Chambolle-Musigny, Pommard		■	■	■	■	
Nuits-St-Georges, Vosne-Romanée, Gevrey-Chambertin		■	■	■	■	
Médoc, Margaux, St-Julien, Pauillac, St-Estèphe		■	■	■	■	
Graves (and Pessac-Leognan), St-Émillion, Pomerol		■	■	■	■	
Zinfandel		■	■	■	■	
Naoussa		■	■	■	■	
Châteauneuf-du-Pape		■	■	■	■	
Cabernet Sauvignon from U.S.A., Australia, New World		■	■	■	■	
Nebbiolo		■	■	■	■	
Bairrada, Douro reds						
Gattinara, Barbaresco, Barolo		■	■	■	■	
Brunello di Montalcino		■	■	■	■	
Côte-Rôtie, Hermitage		■	■	■	■	
Amarone		■	■	■	■	

WINE AND FOOD– PAIRING CHARTS

THE SERIES OF TABLES on pages 569–576 cross-references many of the same wines listed in the previous chart of wine and cooking methods, but with foods rather than methods. This chart is quite general, painted with broad strokes. As a general rule, the lightest wines match the lightest foods, the most full-bodied wines match the richest foods, and the sweetest wines match desserts. As always, there are some exceptions. For example, sweetness and richness commingle as a rich blue cheese is paired with a sweet, rich, full-bodied Sauternes.

The purpose of this chart is to emphasize food and wine flexibility, but also to create broad categories for successful pairing. You will also notice wide gaps of empty cells in this chart indicating that, for example, virtually no light-bodied white wine is a fine accompaniment for beef (not enough body to the wine) and no full-bodied red will work well with fish (too much tannin in the wine) or with most desserts (the wine is not sweet enough).

As with cooking methods, the message of this chart is essentially the same: food intensity = wine intensity.

The charts in the tables on pages 577–591 are somewhat more anecdotal and represent a different way of looking at food and wine pairing. What we've done is to set up categories and subcategories for white, red, rosé, sparkling, and fortified wines, based on the style of the wines. We have listed a number of wines that fit each subcategory (e.g., unoaked, light-bodied, refreshingly simple dry white wines) and then paired them with well-known classic dishes or dominant flavors.

While this chart is the most specific in terms of wine and food pairing, it should not be seen as a closed system. Rather, think of this as a kind of "recipe file" that you can add to and expand with your own food and wine choices.

You may notice that some wines are listed in more than one category. There are several reasons for this. The same grape varieties can be grown in cooler or warmer climates (the best example is Chardonnay, which does best in cool climates but is planted just about everywhere), and the same grapes can be made into very different wines, depending on choices made in the vineyards (low or high yields, for example) and the winery (choosing oak barrels or stainless steel as fermentation vessels, as just one obvious example).

WHITE WINES AND FOOD CHART

WHITE WINES	LIGHT APPETIZERS	PÂTÉS/DIPS	SHELLFISH (MOLLUSKS AND CRUSTACEANS)	SEAFOOD WITH LIGHT SAUCES	SEAFOOD WITH RICHER SAUCES	SALMON/ TUNA	POULTRY
LIGHT- TO MEDIUM-BODIED DRY WHITE WINES							
Muscadet	■		■	■			
Entre-Deux-Mers	■		■	■			
Verdelho, Verdejo, Viura	■	■	■	■			■
Sauvignon Blanc, Graves (and Pessac-Leognan)	■	■	■	■			■
Orvieto, Frascati, Soave, Verdicchio, Friulano	■	■	■	■			■
LIGHT- TO MEDIUM-BODIED OFF-DRY TO LIGHTLY SWEET WINES							
Riesling	■	■	■	■			■
Chenin Blanc from U.S.A., others	■	■	■	■			■
Saumur, Vouvray	■	■	■	■			
MEDIUM- TO FULL-BODIED DRY WHITE WINES							
Verdicchio, Friulano					■		
Pinot Blanc					■	■	
Muscat					■	■	■
Pinot Gris					■	■	■
Gewürztraminer					■		■
Savennières					■	■	
Sémillon					■	■	
Albariño/Alvarinho					■	■	
Mâcon-Villages, St-Véran, Pouilly-Fuissé					■	■	■
Chardonnay from U.S.A., Australia, others					■	■	■
Viognier, Condrieu					■	■	■
Côtes du Rhône, St-Joseph					■	■	■
Meursault, Puligny-Montrachet, Chassagne-Montrachet					■	■	■
Corton-Charlemagne, Le Montrachet					■	■	■
MEDIUM- TO FULL-BODIED SWEET WHITE WINES							
Spätlese, Auslese, Beerenauslese, Trockenbeerenauslese							
Barsac, Sauternes							
Tokaji Aszú							

WHITE WINES	GAME BIRDS	LIGHT PASTA	PORK/VEAL	BEEF/ BARBECUES	LAMB	DUCK/GOOSE	GAME (VENISON, RABBIT, BOAR, ETC.)
LIGHT- TO MEDIUM-BODIED DRY WHITE WINES							
Muscadet							
Entre-Deux-Mers		■					
Verdelho, Verdejo, Viura		■					
Sauvignon Blanc, Graves (and Pessac-Leognan)		■					
Orvieto, Frascati, Soave, Verdicchio, Friulano		■					
LIGHT- TO MEDIUM-BODIED OFF-DRY TO LIGHTLY SWEET WINES							
Riesling			■				
Chenin Blanc from U.S.A., others		■	■				
Saumur, Vouvray	■		■				
MEDIUM- TO FULL-BODIED DRY WHITE WINES							
Verdicchio, Friulano		■	■				
Pinot Blanc							
Muscat			■			■	
Pinot Gris			■			■	
Gewürztraminer			■			■	
Savennières	■		■				
Sémillon	■					■	
Albariño/Alvarinho		■					
Mâcon-Villages, St-Véran, Pouilly-Fuissé	■	■	■				
Chardonnay from U.S.A., Australia, others	■		■		■	■	
Viognier, Condrieu	■		■		■	■	■
Côtes du Rhône, St-Joseph	■		■	■			■
Meursault, Puligny-Montrachet, Chassagne-Montrachet	■		■	■	■	■	■
Corton-Charlemagne, Le Montrachet	■		■	■	■	■	■
MEDIUM- TO FULL-BODIED SWEET WHITE WINES							
Spätlese, Auslese, Beerenauslese, Trockenbeerenauslese							
Barsac, Sauternes							
Tokaji Aszú							

WHITE WINES	PICNICS/ COLD CUTS	ASIAN FOODS	LATIN FOODS	MILD CHEESES	STRONG CHEESES	FRUITS/ DESSERTS	DARK CHOCOLATE DESSERTS
LIGHT- TO MEDIUM-BODIED DRY WHITE WINES							
Muscadet		■	■	■			
Entre-Deux-Mers		■	■	■			
Verdelho, Verdejo, Viura	■	■	■	■			
Sauvignon Blanc, Graves (and Pessac-Leognan)	■	■	■	■			
Orvieto, Frascati, Soave, Verdicchio, Friulano	■	■	■	■			
LIGHT- TO MEDIUM-BODIED OFF-DRY TO LIGHTLY SWEET WINES							
Riesling	■	■	■	■			
Chenin Blanc from U.S.A., others	■	■	■	■			
Saumur, Vouvray	■	■	■	■			
MEDIUM- TO FULL-BODIED DRY WHITE WINES							
Verdicchio, Friulano	■	■	■	■			
Pinot Blanc	■	■	■	■			
Muscat	■	■	■	■	■		
Pinot Gris	■	■	■	■	■		
Gewürztraminer	■	■	■	■	■		
Savennières	■	■	■	■			
Sémillon				■			
Albariño/Alvarinho	■		■	■			
Mâcon-Villages, St-Véran, Pouilly-Fuissé				■			
Chardonnay from U.S.A., Australia, others				■	■		
Viognier, Condrieu				■			
Côtes du Rhône, St-Joseph				■	■		
Meursault, Puligny-Montrachet, Chassagne-Montrachet					■		
Corton-Charlemagne, Le Montrachet					■		
MEDIUM- TO FULL-BODIED SWEET WHITE WINES							
Spätlese, Auslese, Beerenauslese, Trockenbeerenauslese						■	
Barsac, Sauternes						■	
Tokaji Aszú						■	

RED WINES AND FOOD CHART

RED WINES	LIGHT APPETIZERS	PÂTÉS/DIPS	SHELLFISH (MOLLUSKS AND CRUSTACEANS)	SEAFOOD WITH LIGHT SAUCES	SEAFOOD WITH RICHER SAUCES	SALMON/ TUNA	POULTRY
LIGHT- TO MEDIUM-BODIED DRY RED WINES							
Bardolino, Valpolicella					■	■	■
Gamay, Beaujolais-Villages					■	■	■
Cru Beaujolais: Régnié, Chiroubles, Côte de Brouilly, Brouilly, St-Amour, Fleurie, Juliénas, Chénas, Moulin-à-Vent, Morgon					■	■	■
Grignolino					■	■	
Bourgueil, Chinon, Saumur-Champigny					■		
Chianti					■	■	■
Dolcetto					■	■	■
Dão, Alentejo					■	■	
Côtes du Rhône					■	■	■
Corbières					■	■	■
Rioja Crianza					■	■	■
MEDIUM- TO FULL-BODIED DRY RED WINES							
Barbera					■	■	■
Chianti Classico					■	■	■
Pinot Noir (New World)					■	■	■
Merlot (New World)						■	■
Rioja Reserva						■	■
Côte de Beaune-Villages, Beaune, ,Chambolle-Musigny, Pommard					■	■	■
Nuits-St-Georges, Vosne-Romanée, Gevrey-Chambertin					■	■	■
Médoc, Margaux, St-Julien, Pauillac, St-Estèphe							■
Graves (and Pessac-Leognan), St-Émilion, Pomerol							■
Zinfandel							■
Naoussa							■
Châteauneuf-du-Pape							■
Cabernet Sauvignon (New World)							
Nebbiolo							
Bairrada, Douro reds							
Gattinara, Barbaresco, Barolo							
Brunello di Montalcino							
Côte-Rôtie, Hermitage							
Amarone							

RED WINES AND FOOD CHART (CONTINUED)

RED WINES	GAME BIRDS	HEARTY PASTA	PORK/VEAL	BEEF/ BARBECUES	LAMB	DUCK/GOOSE	GAME (VENISON, RABBIT, BOAR, ETC.)
LIGHT- TO MEDIUM-BODIED DRY RED WINES							
Bardolino, Valpolicella	■	■	■				
Gamay, Beaujolais-Villages	■	■	■				
Cru Beaujolais: Régnié, Chiroubles, Côte de Brouilly, Brouilly, St-Amour, Fleurie, Juliénas, Chénas, Moulin-à-Vent, Morgon	■	■	■	■			
Grignolino		■	■				
Bourgueil, Chinon, Saumur-Champigny	■	■	■		■		
Chianti	■	■	■				
Dolcetto		■	■				
Dão, Alentejo	■	■	■		■	■	■
Côtes du Rhône		■	■	■	■	■	■
Corbières		■	■	■	■	■	■
Rioja Crianza		■	■	■	■	■	■
MEDIUM- TO FULL-BODIED DRY RED WINES							
Barbera	■	■	■	■		■	■
Chianti Classico	■	■	■	■		■	■
Pinot Noir (New World)	■	■	■	■		■	■
Merlot (New World)	■	■	■	■		■	
Rioja Reserva	■	■	■	■		■	
Côte de Beaune-Villages, Beaune, Chambolle-Musigny, Pommard	■	■	■	■			■
Nuits-St-Georges, Vosne-Romanée, Gevrey-Chambertin	■	■	■	■		■	■
Médoc, Margaux, St-Julien, Pauillac, St-Estèphe	■			■	■		■
Graves (and Pessac-Leognan), St-Émilion, Pomerol	■			■			■
Zinfandel	■	■	■		■	■	■
Naoussa	■		■	■	■	■	
Châteauneuf-du-Pape	■			■	■	■	■
Cabernet Sauvignon (New World)	■			■			
Nebbiolo	■			■	■	■	■
Bairrada, Douro reds	■			■	■	■	■
Gattinara, Barbaresco, Barolo	■			■	■	■	■
Brunello di Montalcino				■	■		■
Côte-Rôtie, Hermitage				■	■	■	■
Amarone					■	■	■

RED WINES	PICNICS/ COLD CUTS	ASIAN FOODS	LATIN FOODS	MILD CHEESES	STRONG CHEESES	FRUITS/ DESSERTS	DARK CHOCOLATE DESSERTS
LIGHT- TO MEDIUM-BODIED DRY RED WINES							
Bardolino, Valpolicella	■	■	■	■			
Gamay, Beaujolais-Villages	■	■	■	■			
Cru Beaujolais: Régnié, Chiroubles, Côte de Brouilly, Brouilly, St-Amour, Fleurie, Juliénas, Chénas, Moulin-à-Vent, Morgon	■	■	■	■			
Grignolino	■	■					
Bourgueil, Chinon, Saumur-Champigny	■			■			
Chianti	■			■			
Dolcetto	■			■			
Dão, Alentejo				■			
Côtes du Rhône	■			■			
Corbières	■			■			
Rioja Crianza	■			■			
MEDIUM- TO FULL-BODIED DRY RED WINES							
Barbera	■			■			
Chianti Classico	■			■			
Pinot Noir (New World)	■			■			
Merlot (New World)	■			■			
Rioja Reserva							
Côte de Beaune-Villages, Beaune, Chambolle-Musigny, Pommard				■			
Nuits-St-Georges, Vosne-Romanée, Gevrey-Chambertin				■			
Médoc, Margaux, St-Julien, Pauillac, St-Estèphe				■			
Graves (and Pessac-Leognan), St-Émilion, Pomerol				■			
Zinfandel				■			
Naoussa				■			
Châteauneuf-du-Pape				■			
Cabernet Sauvignon (New World)				■			
Nebbiolo				■			
Bairrada, Douro reds					■		
Gattinara, Barbaresco, Barolo					■		
Brunello di Montalcino					■		
Côte-Rôtie, Hermitage					■		
Amarone					■		■

ROSÉ WINES, SPARKLING WINES, CHAMPAGNE, AND FOOD CHART

ROSÉ WINES	LIGHT APPETIZERS	PÂTÉS/DIPS	SHELLFISH (MOLLUSKS AND CRUSTACEANS)	SEAFOOD WITH LIGHT SAUCES	SEAFOOD WITH RICHER SAUCES	SALMON/ TUNA	POULTRY
LIGHT- TO MEDIUM-BODIED ROSÉ WINES (DRY TO OFF-DRY)							
Rosé de Marsannay	■	■	■	■			
White Zinfandel and other blush wines, such as Grenache Rosé, Rosé of Cabernet, Grignolino Rosé	■	■	■	■			
Rosé d'Anjou	■	■		■			
Lirac, Tavel	■	■	■	■	■	■	■
Rosé Bandol			■	■	■	■	■
STYLES OF SPARKLING WINE AND CHAMPAGNE							
Blanc de Blancs	■	■	■	■			
Blanc de Noirs					■	■	■
Extra-dry							
Brut	■	■	■	■	■	■	■
Extra-brut, Natural/Naturel	■	■	■	■	■	■	■
Rosé					■	■	■
Demi-sec							
Sec							
Doux							

ROSÉ WINES	GAME BIRDS	LIGHT PASTA	PORK/VEAL	BEEF/ BARBECUES	LAMB	DUCK/GOOSE	GAME (VENISON, RABBIT, BOAR, ECT.)
LIGHT- TO MEDIUM-BODIED ROSÉ WINES (DRY TO OFF-DRY)							
Rosé de Marsannay		■					
White Zinfandel and other blush wines, such as Grenache Rosé, Rosé of Cabernet, Grignolino Rosé		■	■				
Rosé d'Anjou							
Lirac, Tavel	■	■		■			
Rosé Bandol	■		■	■			
STYLES OF SPARKLING WINE AND CHAMPAGNE							
Blanc de Blancs		■					
Blanc de Noirs		■		■			
Extra-dry		■					
Brut	■	■	■				
Extra-brut, Natural/Naturel	■		■				
Rosé	■		■	■		■	■
Demi-sec							
Sec							
Doux							

ROSÉ WINES	PICNICS/ COLD CUTS	ASIAN FOODS	LATIN FOODS	MILD CHEESES	STRONG CHEESES	FRUITS/ DESSERTS	DARK CHOCOLATE DESSERTS
LIGHT- TO MEDIUM-BODIED ROSÉ WINES (DRY TO OFF-DRY)							
Rosé de Marsannay	■	■	■	■			
White Zinfandel and other blush wines, such as Grenache Rosé, Rosé of Cabernet, Grignolino Rosé	■	■	■	■			
Rosé d'Anjou		■	■				
Lirac, Tavel	■	■		■			
Rosé Bandol	■			■			
STYLES OF SPARKLING WINE AND CHAMPAGNE							
Blanc de Blancs	■	■	■	■			
Blanc de Noirs	■	■	■	■			
Extra-dry	■	■	■	■			
Brut	■	■	■	■			
Extra-brut, Natural/Naturel	■			■			
Rosé	■	■		■			
Demi-sec		■		■		■	
Sec						■	
Doux						■	

CATEGORY 1 CLASSIC FOOD PAIRINGS: WHITE WINE STYLES

UNOAKED, LIGHT-BODIED, REFRESHINGLY SIMPLE DRY WHITE WINES

Alella; Anjou Blanc Sec; Bianco di Custoza; Bordeaux Blanc; Bourgogne Blanc; Chenin Blanc (New World); Colli Albani; Corbières; Coteaux du Languedoc; Côtes du Ventoux; Dão; dry Riesling (New World); Entre-Deux-Mers; Est! Est!! Est!!!; Frascati; Galestro; Gros Plant; Grüner Veltliner; Lacryma Christi del Vesuvio; Moschofilero, Muscadet; Orvieto Secco; Sauvignon Blanc (New World); Soave Classico; Trebbiano d'Abruzzo; Vin de Corse; Vin de Pays; Vinho Verde, among many others

HERBS, SPICES, NUTS, SEASONINGS

Capers

Chervil

Cumin

SAUCES, SALSAS, DRESSINGS, COULIS

Aioli

Beurre Blanc

Tartar Sauce

Yogurt Dressing

SOUPS

Chicken

French Onion

Gazpacho

Hot and Sour

Tomato

SALADS

Cold Pasta

Greek

Potato

VEGETARIAN AND VEGETABLE-BASED DISHES

Avocado with Vinaigrette

Falafel

Hummus

Steamed Asparagus with Lemon and Sesame Seeds

EGGS, OMELETTES, QUICHES

Huevos Rancheros

Omelette with Smoked Salmon

GRAINS, CEREALS, PASTAS, BREADS

Fettuccine Alfredo

Gnocchi with Gorgonzola

Pasta alle Vongole (Baby Clams)

Pasta Primavera

Pizza

Risotto Milanese

FISH, SHELLFISH, AND MOLLUSKS

Bacalao

Boiled Shrimp

Brandade de Morue

Ceviche

Deep-Fried Calamari

Escabeche

Fish and Chips

Fresh Anchovies

Gefilte Fish

Grilled Fresh Sardines

Grilled Octopus

Langoustines/Crayfish

Oysters on the Half Shell

Poached Dover Sole

Poached Scallops

Shrimp Cocktail

Steamed Clams

Steamed Mussels

Sushi/Sashimi

POULTRY

Buffalo Wings

CHEESES

Caerphilly

Fresh Goat or Sheep

Mozzarella

UNOAKED, FRUITY, MEDIUM-BODIED DRY WHITE WINES

Alsace Edelzwicker; Alsace Pinot Auxerrois; Alsace Pinot Blanc; Alsace Sylvaner; Anjou Blanc Sec; Arneis; Auxey-Duresses; Bandol; Beaujolais Blanc; Bergerac Sec; Bourgogne Aligoté; Chablis; Chardonnay (New World); Châteauneuf-du-Pape Blanc; Colombard (New World); Condrieu; Coteaux d'Aix-en-Provence; Coteaux du Languedoc; Côtes de Blaye; Côtes de Bourg; Côtes de Provence; Côtes du Jura; Côtes du Rhône-Villages; Côtes du Roussillon; Crozes-Hermitage; Dezaley; Fendant; Fiano di Avellino; Gavi di Gavi; Greco di Tufo; Hermitage; Mâcon-Villages; Malagousia; Mercurey; Minervois; Montagny; Morey-St-Denis; Muscadet Sèvre-et-Maine sur lie; Oregon Riesling; Orvieto Secco Classico; Pinot Bianco; Pinot Blanc (New World); Pinot Grigio; Pomino; Pouilly-Fuissé; Pouilly-Loche; Ribeiro; Rioja; Rully; Saumur; Sauvignon Blanc (New Zealand); Sauvignon Blanc/Sémillon (Australia); Sancerre; Savennières; Sémillon (New World); Sémillon/Chardonnay (New World); Seyval Blanc; Silvaner Kabinett Trocken; Silvaner Spätlese Trocken; Soave Classico Superiore; St-Joseph; St-Véran; Verdicchio dei Castelli di Jesi; Verdicchio di Matelica; Vermentino di Gallura; Vermentino di Sardegna; Vernaccia di San Gimignano; Vin de Pays; Viognier (New World); Vouvray Sec, among many others

HERBS, SPICES, NUTS, SEASONINGS

Chili

Cumin

Mint

Parsley

Saffron

Sorrel

SAUCES, SALSAS, DRESSINGS, COULIS

Chili Sauce

Chinese Oyster Sauce

Mayonnaise

Pesto

Salsa Verde

Soy Sauce

Tartar Sauce

Tropical Fruit Salsa

Vinaigrette

Yogurt Dressing

SOUPS

Chicken

Consommé

French Onion

Gazpacho

Lobster Bisque

Manhattan Clam Chowder

Tomato

SALADS

Caesar

Chef's

Cold Pasta

Green

Niçoise

Seafood

Tomato, Basil, Mozzarella,
and Balsamic Vinegar

Waldorf

VEGETARIAN AND VEGETABLE-BASED DISHES

Avocado with Vinaigrette

Braised or Roasted Fennel

Courgette/Zucchini

Crudités

Onion Tart

Pumpkin/Winter Squash

Ratatouille

Sautéed or Stuffed Bell Peppers

Vegetable Lasagna

White Truffles

EGGS, OMELETTES, QUICHES

Cheese Soufflé

Omelette with Smoked Salmon

Quiche Lorraine

Vegetable Quiche

GRAINS, CEREALS, PASTAS, BREADS

Chicken Risotto

Dolmades

Fettuccine Alfredo

Macaroni and Cheese

Pasta alle Vongole (Baby Clams)

Pasta Primavera

Seafood Risotto

Tabbouleh

Tortellini

FISH, SHELLFISH, AND MOLLUSKS

Bacalao

Bouillabaisse

Brandade de Morue

Broiled/Grilled Scrod

Broiled/Grilled Shark

Ceviche

Cioppino

Deep-Fried Calamari

Fresh Anchovies

Freshwater Trout/Perch

Fried Catfish

Fried Shrimp/Prawns

Fritto Misto

Grilled Halibut

Grilled Red Mullet

Grilled Shrimp/Prawns

Grilled Skate

Grilled Turbot

Mussels in White Wine

Oysters Rockefeller

Sautéed Lemon Sole

Seared Scallops

Smoked Trout

Striped Bass

Sushi/Sashimi

Tempura

Trout Amandine

POULTRY

Chicken Pie

Roast Rock Cornish Hen

MEAT

Barbecued Pork Ribs

Beef Tacos or Burritos

Choucroute Garnie

Escargots

Garlic Sausage

Rillettes

Vitello Tonnato

GAME

Duck Confit

Peking Duck

CHEESES

Caerphilly

Cream Cheese/Cottage Cheese

Lancashire

Mozzarella

Pecorino

Raclette

Reblochon

Ricotta

RICH, ELEGANT, OFTEN OAKY DRY WHITE WINES

Auxey-Duresses; Beaune Blanc; Bianco di Franciacorta; California Chardonnay; California Fumé Blanc; Canadian Chardonnay; Canadian Pinot Blanc; Chablis *premier cru* and Chablis *grand cru*; Chassagne-Montrachet and Puligny-Montrachet (especially *premier cru* and *grand cru* vineyard sites); Château-Grillet; dry Chenin Blanc; Condrieu; Corton-Charlemagne; Encruzado; barrel-fermented Graves (and Pessac-Leognan); Hermitage Blanc; Long Island Chardonnay; Meursault; Montagny; Monthelie; Morey-St-Denis; New World Chardonnay (Northern and Southern hemispheres); Pernand-Vergelesses; Pouilly-Fumé; Rioja *crianza*; White Meritage, among many others

HERBS, SPICES, NUTS, SEASONINGS

Chestnut

Coconut

Ginger

Smoke

SAUCES, SALSAS, DRESSINGS, COULIS

Béarnaise Sauce

Beurre Blanc

Black Bean Sauce

Mornay (Cheese) Sauce

SOUPS

Chicken

Cream Soups

French Onion

Lentil

Lobster Bisque

Manhattan Clam Chowder

New England Clam Chowder

Tomato

Vichyssoise

VEGETARIAN AND VEGETABLE-BASED DISHES

Corn on the Cob

Crudités

Steamed Asparagus with Lemon and Sesame Seeds

EGGS, OMELETTES, QUICHES

Cheese Soufflé

Eggs Benedict

GRAINS, CEREALS, PASTAS, BREADS

Chicken Risotto

Fettuccine Alfredo

Gnocchi

Pasta Carbonara

Ricotta Cheese Ravioli

Risotto Milanese

PÂTÉS AND TERRINES

Game Pâté

Lobster Pâté

Salmon Pâté

Smoked Salmon Pâté

FISH, SHELLFISH, AND MOLLUSKS

Brandade de Morue

Broiled/Grilled Flounder

Broiled/Grilled Shark

Fritto Misto

Grilled Skate

Grilled Swordfish

Grilled Tuna

Grilled Turbot

Mussels in White Wine

Oysters Rockefeller

Smoked Trout

Sushi/Sashimi

POULTRY

Chicken Cordon Bleu

Chicken Curry

Chicken in Garlic Sauce

Chicken Kiev

Ginger Chicken

Jerk Chicken

Roast Chicken

Roast Lemon Chicken

Roast Turkey

MEAT

Chorizo

Jerk Pork

Rumaki

Saltimbocca alla Romana

Smoked Ham

Veal Piccata

Vitello Tonnato

GAME

Roast Quail

Smoked Duck

CHEESES

Abondance

Appenzeller

Emmenthal

Fontina

Gouda

Gruyère

Jarlsberg

Smoked Cheeses

Valencay

CATEGORY 1 CLASSIC FOOD PAIRINGS: WHITE WINE STYLES (CONTINUED)

HERBACEOUS, FRESH, GRASSY DRY WHITE WINES

Australian Sauvignon Blanc; Bordeaux; California Sauvignon Blanc; New World Fumé Blanc; New World Sémillon; New World Sémillon/Sauvignon Blanc; New Zealand Sauvignon Blanc; Pouilly-Fumé; Quincy; Rueda; Ruilly; Sancerre; Sauvignon de Touraine; South African Sauvignon Blanc, among many others

HERBS, SPICES, NUTS, SEASONINGS
Basil
Capers
Caraway Seeds
Chervil
Cilantro
Coriander
Dill
Fennel
Marjoram
Oregano
Parsley
Sage
Sorrel
Tarragon

SAUCES, SALSAS, DRESSINGS, COULIS
Hollandaise Sauce
Tomato Sauce

SOUPS
Chicken
Gazpacho
Lobster Bisque
Manhattan Clam Chowder
Tomato

SALADS
Caesar
Chef's

Cold Pasta
Greek
Green
Niçoise
Seafood
Tomato, Basil, Mozzarella,
and Balsamic Vinegar

VEGETARIAN AND VEGETABLE-BASED DISHES
Avocado Stuffed with Shrimp or Lobster
Courgette/Zucchini
Garden-Fresh Tomatoes
Guacamole
Sautéed Bell Peppers
Sun-Dried Tomatoes

EGGS, OMELETTES, QUICHES
Eggs Benedict
Huevos Rancheros
Omelette with Smoked Salmon

GRAINS, CEREALS, PASTAS, BREADS
Gnocchi
Pasta in Tomato Sauce
Tabbouleh

FISH, SHELLFISH, AND MOLLUSKS
Bacalao
Bouillabaisse
Ceviche

Cioppino
Deep-Fried Calamari
Freshwater Trout/Perch
Fried Catfish
Fried Shrimp/Prawns
Fritto Misto
Grilled Halibut
Grilled Shrimp/Prawns
Grilled Turbot
Mussels in White Wine
Oysters Rockefeller
Sautéed Lemon Sole
Seared Scallops
Sushi/Sashimi

POULTRY
Chicken Curry
Roast Chicken with Herbs
Roast Lemon Chicken
Traditional Southern Fried Chicken

MEAT
Kielbasa
Veal Marsala
Wiener Schnitzel/Costolletta alla Milanese

CHEESES
Cabecou
Chèvre
Feta
Fresh Goat or Sheep Cheese

DRAMATICALLY AROMATIC, SPICY, AND FLORAL DRY WHITE WINES

Alsace Edelzwicker; Alsace Gewürztraminer; Alsace Riesling; Alsace Pinot Gris; Alto Adige Gewürztraminer; Australian Riesling; Austrian Riesling; Bacchus; California Viognier; Canadian Riesling; New World dry Riesling; New World Gewürztraminer; New World Müller-Thurgau; Oregon Pinot Gris; Oregon Riesling; Petite Arvine; Rias Baixas; Riesling from Germany; especially Riesling Trocken and Halbtrocken (dry and semidry versions); Riesling x Sylvaner; Tocai Friulano; Torrontés; Trebbiano d'Abruzzo; Txakoli Txomin; Valdeorras; Viognier; among many others

HERBS, SPICES, NUTS, SEASONINGS
Cardamom
Chestnut
Ginger
Lemongrass
Saffron

SAUCES, SALSAS, DRESSINGS, COULIS
Curry
Mushroom Sauce
Mustard Sauce
Peanut Sauce
Soy Sauce

SOUPS
Borscht
Chicken
Consommé
Cream Soups
French Onion
Game
Hot and Sour
Lentil
Lobster Bisque
New England Clam Chowder
Tomato
Vichyssoise

SALADS
Caesar
Chef's
Chicken with Spiced Pecans
Niçoise
Potato
Tomato, Basil, Mozzarella, and
Balsamic Vinegar
Waldorf

VEGETARIAN AND VEGETABLE-BASED DISHES
Avocado Stuffed with Shrimp or Lobster
Black Truffles
Boston Baked Beans
Cabbage/Sauerkraut
Grilled Vegetables
Onion Tart

EGGS, OMELETTES, QUICHES
Cheese Soufflé
Omelette with Smoked Salmon
Quiche Lorraine
Vegetable Quiche

GRAINS, CEREALS, PASTAS, BREADS
Dolmades
Ricotta Cheese Ravioli

PÂTÉS AND TERRINES
Chicken Liver Pâté
Lobster Pâté
Pâté de Campagne

FISH, SHELLFISH, AND MOLLUSKS
Bouillabaisse
Brandade de Morue
Broiled Shark
Curried Shrimp/Prawns
Deep-Fried Calamari
Fried Catfish
Grilled Red Mullet
Grilled Shrimp/Prawns
Grilled Skate
Grilled Turbot
Oysters Rockefeller
Sautéed Lemon Sole
Seared Scallops

POULTRY
Chicken Curry
Chicken Satay with Peanut Sauce and
Cucumbers
Chicken Stuffed with Sausage and Sage
Ginger Chicken
Roast Chicken
Roast Lemon Chicken
Roast Turkey

MEAT
Baked Ham
Choucroute
Lamb Curry
Prosciutto, Prosciutto with Melon
Rumaki
Sautéed Sweetbreads
Veal Marsala

GAME
Duck Confit

CHEESES
Appenzeller
Emmenthal
Feta
Fontina
Gouda
Gruyère
Jarlsberg
Münster
Raclette

MEDIUM-SWEET TO DRAMATICALLY SWEET WINES

Albana di Romagna Dolce; Alsace Riesling Sélection de Grains Nobles; Chenin Blanc; late-harvest Gewürztraminer; late-harvest Riesling; Moscato d'Asti; New World Muscat Canelli; New World Riesling; Orvieto Classico Abboccato; Riesling Beerenauslese; Riesling Trockenbeerenauslese; Riesling Auslese; Riesling Beerenauslese; Riesling Trockenbeerenauslese; Tokaji Aszú; Vin Santo; Vouvray Moelleux; among many others

HERBS, SPICES, NUTS, SEASONINGS
Cardamom
Cinnamon
Coconut
Coffee
Ginger
Honey
Nutmeg
Vanilla

SAUCES, SALSAS, DRESSINGS, COULIS
Chutney
Curry
Ketchup
Sabayon Sauce

SOUPS
Chicken
Consommé
Cream Soups
French Onion
Game
Gazpacho
Hot and Sour
Lobster Bisque

EGGS, OMELETTES, QUICHES
Cheese Soufflé
Crepes
Custard
Quiche Lorraine

PÂTÉS AND TERRINES
Chicken Liver Pâté
Duck Pâté
Fish Pâté
Seafood Terrine
Terrine of Foie Gras

FISH, SHELLFISH, AND MOLLUSKS
Freshwater Trout/Perch

MEAT
Barbecued Pork
German Sausages
Prosciutto/Westphalian Ham

GAME
Peking Duck
Roast Duck

CHEESES
Boursault
Cheddar
Cheshire
Danish Blue
Dolcelatte
Gloucester
Gorgonzola
Maytag Blue
Monterey Jack
Pecorino
Reblochon
Robiola
Roquefort
Stilton

DESSERTS
Almond Tart
Apple Pie
Apple Strudel
Baked Apple
Baklava
Charlotte Russe
Cheesecake
Cherry Cobbler
Chocolate Desserts
Coffee Cake
Crème Brûlée
Crème Caramel
Fresh Blackberries
Fresh Peaches
Fresh Pears
Fresh Plums
Fresh Raspberries
Fresh Strawberries
Fruit Salad
Fruit Sorbets
Hazelnut Torte
Lemon Tart
Linzer Torte
Meringue
Mince Pie
Pear Poached in Red Wine
Pear Tart
Pecan Pie
Profiteroles
Rice Pudding
Sacher Torte
Savarin
Tarte Tatin
Tiramisu
Zabaglione

CATEGORY 2 CLASSIC FOOD PAIRINGS: RED WINE STYLES

YOUNG, FRESH, LIGHT REDS

Rioja Cosecha; Gamay Beaujolais; Valpolicella Classico; Cannonau di Sardegna; Dolcetto d'Alba; Beaujolais Nouveau, Beaujolais-Villages, and *cru* Beaujolais: Morgon, Fleurie, Chénas, Moulin-à-Vent, Chiroubles, Régnié, Juliénas, Côte de Brouilly, St-Amour, and Brouilly; Bourgogne-Côte Chalonnaise; Bardolino; Grignolino d'Asti; Bourgogne Passe-Tout-Grains; Bourgogne Pinot Noir; Rosso di Montepulciano; Dôle; Rully; New World Pinot Noir; Sancerre Rouge; Saumur-Champigny; Chianti; Santa Maddalena; Navarra; Gamay; Blauer Zweigelt; Bourgueil; Valdigué; inexpensive, lighter styles of Zinfandel, Merlot and Pinot Noir; Dolcetto d'Alba; Côtes du Ventoux; Lacryma Christi del Vesuvio; Valdeorras, among many others

SAUCES, SALSAS, DRESSINGS, COULIS

Chinese Oyster Sauce

SOUPS

Beef Barley

Black Bean

Borscht

Chicken

Cream Soups

French Onion

Game

Gazpacho

Lentil

Lobster Bisque

Minestrone

Ribolita

Tomato

VEGETARIAN AND VEGETABLE-BASED DISHES

Hummus

EGGS, OMELETTES, QUICHES

Huevos Rancheros

Omelette with Smoked Salmon

Quiche Lorraine

GRAINS, CEREALS, PASTAS, BREADS

Lasagna

Pasta with Pesto

Pizza with Seafood

FISH, SHELLFISH, AND MOLLUSKS

Bacalao

Bouillabaisse

Brandade de Morue

Broiled Shark

Cioppino

Deep-Fried Calamari

Fritto Misto

Grilled Halibut

Grilled Red Mullet

Grilled Skate

Grilled Swordfish

POULTRY

Chicken Pie

MEAT

Cold Roast Beef

Cured Meats: Bacon, Bresaola, Corned Beef, Pastrami, Salami, Tongue

Hamburger

Lamb Kebabs

Roast Pork

Steak Tartare

Wiener Schnitzel/Costolletta alla Milanese

CHEESES

Abondance

Appenzeller

Asiago

Banon

Bleu de Bresse

Emmenthal

Feta

Fontina

Gouda

Gruyère

Jarlsberg

Montasio

Münster

Raclette

Reblochon

Stracchino

DESSERTS

Fresh Strawberries

MODERATELY COOL TO MODERATELY WARM CLIMATE, MEDIUM- TO FULL-BODIED RED WINES

Barbaresco; Barbera d'Asti; Barolo; Cabernet Franc from the New World; Cabernet Franc from the Old World, including the Loire Valley; Cabernet Sauvignon from the New World; Cabernet Sauvignon from the Old World, including Bordeaux; Cabernet-Merlot blends; Chianti Classico Riserva; Dolcetto d'Alba; Meritage and Bordeaux-style blends; Merlot; Nebbiolo d'Alba; New World Rhone Rangers; Pinot Noir from the New World; Pinot Noir from the Old World, including Burgundy; red wines from the northern Rhône Valley; Rioja Reserva and Gran Reserva; Sangiovese from the New World; Sangiovese from the Old World, including Tuscany; Syrah from the New World, including Shiraz from Australia; Tempranillo and Garnacha-based wines from Spain; Zinfandel, among many others

SAUCES, SALSAS, DRESSINGS, COULIS
Cranberry Sauce
Pizzaiola Sauce

SOUPS
Beef Barley
Black Bean
Borscht
Chicken
Cream Soups
French Onion
Game
Lentil
Minestrone
Ribolita
Tomato

VEGETARIAN AND VEGETABLE-BASED DISHES
Falafel
Grilled Mushrooms
Grilled Vegetable/Grain Burgers
Mushrooms à la Grecque
White Truffles

GRAINS, CEREALS, PASTAS, BREADS
Chicken Risotto
Gnocchi with Gorgonzola
Mushroom Risotto

Pasta alle Vongole (Baby Clams)
Tagliatelle with Butter and Sage

PÂTÉS AND TERRINES
Salmon Pâté

FISH, SHELLFISH, AND MOLLUSKS
Bouillabaisse
Broiled Shark
Cioppino
Deep-Fried Calamari
Fritto Misto
Grilled Halibut
Grilled Red Mullet
Grilled Salmon
Grilled Skate
Grilled Swordfish
Grilled Tuna

POULTRY
Chicken Fricassee
Cold Roast Chicken
Coq au Vin

MEAT
Baked, Roasted, or Smoked Ham
Beef Tacos or Burritos
Cured Meats: Bacon, Bresaola, Corned Beef, Pastrami, Salami, Tongue
Grilled Calf Liver

Grilled Pork Chops
Grilled Prime Beef Steaks
Hamburger or Ground Beef
Lamb Kebabs
Pot-au-Feu
Prosciutto, Prosciutto with Melon
Roast Lamb
Sautéed Calf Liver with Sage Butter
Sautéed Sweetbreads
Serrano Ham
Steak Tartare

GAME
Grilled or Braised Rabbit
Roast Duck
Roast Guinea Hen
Roast Woodcock

CHEESES
Appenzeller
Cantal
Epoises de Bourgogne
L'Ami du Chambertin
Tomme de Savoie
Vacherin Mont d'Or

CATEGORY 2 CLASSIC FOOD PAIRINGS: RED WINE STYLES (CONTINUED)

WARMER-CLIMATE, MEDIUM- TO FULL-BODIED RED WINES

Bairrada; Dão; Douro; most fine Portuguese red wines; Rosso di Montalcino; Cabernet Sauvignon; Cabernet-Merlot blends; Carmignano; Chianti Classico; Chianti Colli Aretini; Chianti Colli Fiorentini; Chianti Colli Senesi; Chianti Colline Pisane; Chianti Montalbano; Chianti Rufina; Corbières; Côtes du Rhône and Côtes du Rhône-Villages; Crozes-Hermitage; Merlot; Minervois; Pinotage and other South African red wines; red wines from central and southern Italy; red wines from Corsica, Sardinia, and Sicily; red wines from Greece and the Eastern Mediterranean; red wines from Provence and Midi; red wines from the southern Rhône Valley; Rioja; Ribera del Duero; Vino Noble di Montepulciano; Zinfandel or Primitivo, among many others

HERBS, SPICES, NUTS, SEASONINGS

Chestnut

Chili

Coffee

Garlic

Juniper

Marjoram

Oregano

Sage

Thyme

SAUCES, SALSAS, DRESSINGS, COULIS

Barbecue Sauce

Chile Sauce

Cumberland Sauce

Mushroom Sauce

Peanut Sauce

Red Wine Sauce

Salsa Verde

Tomato Sauce

Vinaigrette

SOUPS

Beef Barley

Black Bean

French Onion

Game

Lentil

Minestrone

Ribolita

VEGETARIAN AND VEGETABLE-BASED DISHES

Courgette/Zucchini

Grilled Vegetable/Grain Burgers

Grilled Vegetables

Ratatouille

Vegetable Curry

Vegetable Lasagna

Vegetarian Chili (not searingly hot)

GRAINS, CEREALS, PASTAS, BREADS

Couscous

Gnocchi

Lasagna

Paella

Pasta Carbonara

Pizza

Putanesca (Pasta in Spicy Tomato-Based Sauce)

Spaghetti Bolognese

Tagliatelle with Butter and Sage

Tortellini

PÂTÉS AND TERRINES

Duck Pâté

Game Pâté

POULTRY

Barbecued Chicken

Chicken Cacciatore

Coq au Vin

Roast Chicken

Roasted Rock Cornish Game Hen

Roast Turkey

Traditional Southern Fried Chicken

MEAT

Andouille Sausage

Barbecued Beef

Beef Goulash

Beef Stroganoff

Boeuf à la Bourguignonne

Braised Brisket

Cassoulet

Garlic Sausage

Grilled Calf Liver

Grilled Prime Beef Steaks

Irish Stew

Kielbasa

Pot-au-Feu

Pot Roast

Rillettes

Suckling Pig

GAME

Duck Confit

Grilled or Braised Rabbit

Roast Quail

Roast Squab

CHEESES

Aged Gouda

Fontina d'Aosta

Idiazabal

Parmigiano Reggiano

Pecorino

Provolone

CATEGORY 2 **CLASSIC FOOD PAIRINGS: RED WINE STYLES (CONTINUED)**

EXTRA-FULL-BODIED, EARTHY, SPICY, PLUMMY REDS

Aglianico del Vulture; Alentejo; Amarone della Valpolicella; Argentine Malbec; Australian Shiraz/Cabernet blends; Bandol; Barbaresco; New World Barbera; Barbera d'Alba; Barolo; Brunello di Montalcino; Cabernet Sauvignon; Châteauneuf-du-Pape; Collioure; Cornas; Côte-Rôtie; Crozes-Hermitage; Douro; Gigondas; Madiran; New World Meritage blends; New World Rhone Rangers; Petite Sirah; Priorato and Penedès; Sagrantino di Montefalco; Shiraz; St-Joseph; Syrah; Vacqueyras; Valtellina Superiore; Zinfandel, among many others

HERBS, SPICES, NUTS, SEASONINGS

Rosemary

SAUCES, SALSAS, DRESSINGS, COULIS

Chile Sauce

Cumberland Sauce

Madeira Sauce

Mint Sauce

Mushroom Sauce

Mustard Sauce

Pizzaiola Sauce

Red Wine Sauce

Sauce au Poivre

SOUPS

Beef Barley

Black Bean

French Onion

Game

Lentil

Ribolita

VEGETARIAN AND VEGETABLE-BASED DISHES

Boston Baked Beans

Grilled Eggplant

Stuffed Bell Peppers

Stuffed Eggplant

GRAINS, CEREALS, PASTAS, BREADS

Gnocchi with Gorgonzola

Pasta in Tomato Sauce

PÂTÉS AND TERRINES

Pâté de Campagne

POULTRY

Chicken Cacciatore

Chicken Mole

Chicken Satay with Peanut Sauce and Cucumbers

MEAT

Beef Fajitas

Beef Stew/Daube

Braised or Roast Lamb

Cassoulet

Chili (not searingly hot)

Grilled Prime Beef Steaks

Meatloaf

Osso Buco

Pot Roast

Steak au Poivre

Steak Diane

Suckling Pig

GAME

Duck à l'Orange

Peking Duck

Roast Guinea Hen

Roast Partridge

Roast Pheasant

Roast Squab

Roast Venison

Venison Stew

CHEESES

Aged Banon

Aged Gouda

Aged Manchego

Aged Montasio

Asiago

Beaufort

Beaumont

Brie

Cabrales

Camembert

Cheddar

Cheshire

Gloucester

Gruyère

Livarot

Monterey Jack

Morbier

Parmigiano Reggiano

Pont l'Evêque

CATEGORY 2 CLASSIC FOOD PAIRINGS: RED WINE STYLES (CONTINUED)

CLASSICALLY ELEGANT, AGE-WORTHY REDS

Australian single-estate Shiraz and blends; Barolo Riserva and Barbaresco Riserva single-vineyard wines; Brunello di Montalcino Riserva, Chianti Classico Riserva, and other DOCG red wines from Tuscany; Chilean single-estate Cabernet Sauvignon and blends; Beiras, Bairrada, Dão, and Douro Valley single-vineyard reds; *grand cru* red wines from the Côte de Nuits and Côte de Beaune (Côte d'Or) of Burgundy; Super Tuscans; Bordeaux classified growths from the Haut-Médoc, Graves (and Pessac-Leognan); St-Émilion and fine Pomerol wines; Hermitage and Côte-Rôtie single-estate wines; Long Island Cabernet and blends; Mendocino old-vine single-vineyard Zinfandel and Petite Sirah; Napa Valley estate Cabernet Sauvignon and Meritage-style blends; New World Rhone Rangers; Oregon single-vineyard Willamette Valley Pinot Noir; Priorato; Ribera del Duero Gran Reserva and single-vineyard wines; Rioja Gran Reserva; Washington State estate-bottled Columbia Valley and Walla Walla Cabernet Sauvignon and Merlot, among many others

HERBS, SPICES, NUTS, SEASONINGS
Capers
Mint

SAUCES, SALSAS, DRESSINGS, COULIS
Cranberry Sauce
Mint Sauce

SOUPS
Beef Barley
Black Bean
Cream Soups
French Onion
Game

POULTRY
Coq au Vin
Roast Turkey

MEAT
Beef Goulash
Beef Wellington
Boeuf à la Bourguignonne
Braised Lamb
Carpaccio
Châteaubriand
Filet Mignon
Roast Beef
Roast Lamb

GAME
Duck à l'Orange
Roast Duck

Roast Guinea Hen
Roast Partridge
Roast Pheasant
Roast Venison

CHEESES
Beaufort
Brie
Camembert
Cantal
Coulommiers
Dolcelatte
Maytag Blue
Morbier
Pont l'Evêque
Saga Blue
Taleggio

SWEET RED WINES

Banyuls; Black Muscat; Blauburger Eiswein; Brachetto d'Acqui; late-harvest Zinfandel; Mavrodaphne; Pinot Noir Icewine; Recioto della Valpolicella; Sagrantino Passito

DESSERTS
Cheesecake
Fresh Black Cherries
Fresh Blueberries
Vanilla Ice Cream

CHEESES
Parmigiano Reggiano

CATEGORY 3 CLASSIC FOOD PAIRINGS: ROSÉ WINE STYLES

DRY ROSÉ WINES

Arbois; Bandol; Bardolino Chiaretto; Bergerac; California Rosés; Cigales Rosado; Corsica Rosés; Costières de Nimes; Coteaux d'Aix-en-Provence; Coteaux du Languedoc; Côtes de Provence; Côtes du Lubéron; Côtes du Rhône; dry Grenache Rosé; Greek rosés; Grignolino Rosé; Lacryma Christi del Vesuvio Rosato; Lirac; Navarra Rosado; Portuguese *rosados*; Rioja Rosado; Riviera del Garda Bresciano Chiaretto; Rosé de Loire; Rosé de Marsannay; Rosé des Riceys; Sancerre Rosé; Sangiovese Rosato; Tavel; among many others

SAUCES, SALSAS, DRESSINGS, COULIS
Aioli
Barbecue Sauce
Tropical Fruit Salsa

SOUPS
Black Bean
Borscht
French Onion
Game
Gazpacho
Lobster Bisque
Manhattan Clam Chowder
Minestrone
Ribolita
Tomato
Vichyssoise

SALADS
Caesar
Chef's

Greek
Green
Niçoise
Potato
Tomato, Basil, Mozzarella, and Balsamic Vinegar

VEGETARIAN AND VEGETABLE-BASED DISHES
Garden-Fresh Tomatoes
Grilled Eggplant
Grilled Vegetables
Grilled Vegetable/Grain Burgers
Ratatouille
Stuffed Eggplant
Vegetable Terrine
Vegetarian Lasagna

GRAINS, CEREALS, PASTAS, BREADS
Cold Pasta Salad
Dolmades
Paella

FISH, SHELLFISH, AND MOLLUSKS
Bouillabaisse
Brandade de Morue
Cioppino
Deep-Fried Calamari
Fried Catfish
Fritto Misto
Grilled Red Mullet
Grilled Skate
Grilled Turbot
Mussels in White Wine
Sushi/Sashimi
Zuppa di Pesce

POULTRY
Cold Grilled Chicken

CHEESES
Banon
Chèvre
Manchego

SEMISWEET TO SWEET ROSÉ WINES

Cabernet d'Anjou; Lancers Rosé; Rosé d'Anjou; White Grenache; White Merlot; White Zinfandel, among many others

SALADS
Chicken with Spiced Pecans
Cold Pasta
Niçoise
Seafood

VEGETARIAN AND VEGETABLE-BASED DISHES
Winter Squash/Pumpkin

EGGS, OMELETTES, QUICHES
Cheese Soufflé
Crêpes

Eggs Benedict
Omelette with Smoked Salmon
Quiche Lorraine

MEAT
Hamburger

CATEGORY 4 CLASSIC FOOD PAIRINGS: SPARKLING WINE STYLES

LIGHT, DRY, REFRESHING SPARKLERS

Australian *méthode champenoise* brut, Blanc de Noirs, and Blanc de Blancs; Blanc de Blancs Champagne nonvintage; brut nonvintage Champagne; California *méthode champenoise* brut, Blanc de Noirs, and Blanc de Blancs; Cap Classique; Cava; Clairette de Die; Crémant d'Alsace; Crémant de Bourgogne; Crémant de Loire; extra-dry Champagne nonvintage; Franciacorta; New Zealand *méthode champenoise* brut, Blanc de Noirs, and Blanc de Blancs; Pacific Northwest *méthode champenoise* brut, Blanc de Noirs, and Blanc de Blancs; Prosecco; Saumur Mousseux; *Sekt* from Austria and Germany; South American sparkling wines; sparkling wine made by the *charmat* process and the transfer method; Trento Classico Brut; Vouvray Mousseux, among many others

SOUPS
Chicken
Consommé
Gazpacho
Hot and Sour
Manhattan Clam Chowder
New England Clam Chowder

VEGETARIAN AND VEGETABLE-BASED DISHES
Black Truffles
Olives
Vegetable Terrine

EGGS, OMELETTES, QUICHES
Cheese Soufflé
Crepes

Eggs Benedict
Huevos Rancheros
Omelette with Smoked Salmon
Quiche Lorraine

PÂTÉS AND TERRINES
Seafood Terrine

FISH, SHELLFISH, AND MOLLUSKS
Bacalao
Brandade de Morue
Ceviche
Deep-Fried Calamari
Fried Catfish
Fried Shrimp/Prawns
Fritto Misto

Grilled Shrimp/Prawns
Mussels in White Wine
Sautéed Lemon Sole
Seared Scallops
Sushi/Sashimi

POULTRY
Cold Roast Chicken

MEAT
Wiener Schnitzel/Costolletta alla Milanese

DESSERTS
Fresh Blueberries
Fresh Raspberries
Meringue

MEDIUM-BODIED, DRY SPARKLERS

Australian *méthode champenoise* brut and Blanc de Noirs; brut nonvintage Champagne; brut vintage Champagne; brut *cuvée de prestige* Champagne; California *méthode champenoise* brut and Blanc de Noirs; Cap Classique; vintage Cava; Clairette de Die Tradition; Crémant d'Alsace; Crémant de Bourgogne; Franciacorta; New Zealand *méthode champenoise* brut and Blanc de Noirs; Pacific Northwest *méthode champenoise* brut and Blanc de Noirs; *Sekt*; Trento Classico Brut, among many others

SOUPS
French Onion
Game
Gazpacho
Hot and Sour
Lobster Bisque
Manhattan Clam Chowder
New England Clam Chowder

VEGETARIAN AND VEGETABLE-BASED DISHES
Black Truffles
Cheese Soufflé
Eggs Benedict
Omelette with Smoked Salmon
Quiche Lorraine
Winter Squash/Pumpkin

GRAINS, CEREALS, PASTAS, BREADS
Couscous
Pasta Primavera

PÂTÉS AND TERRINES
Game Pâté

FISH, SHELLFISH, AND MOLLUSKS
Bacalao
Bouillabaisse
Brandade de Morue
Broiled/Grilled Scrod
Broiled Shark
Cioppino
Fried Catfish
Fried Shrimp/Prawns
Fritto Misto
Grilled Halibut

Grilled Red Mullet
Grilled Shrimp/Prawns
Grilled Skate
Grilled Turbot
Mussels in White Wine
Oysters Rockefeller
Sautéed Lemon Sole
Sushi/Sashimi

GAME
Smoked Duck

CHEESES
Explorateur
Maytag Blue

DESSERTS
Hazelnut Torte

CATEGORY 4 CLASSIC FOOD PAIRINGS: SPARKLING WINE STYLES (CONTINUED)

MEDIUM-BODIED, DRY ROSÉ SPARKLERS

Rosé styles of Australian *méthode champenoise*; brut nonvintage Champagne; California *méthode champenoise*; Cava; Franciacorta; New Zealand *méthode champenoise*; Trento Classico Brut, among many others

SAUCES, SALSAS, DRESSINGS, COULIS
Aioli

SOUPS
Borscht
French Onion
Game
Gazpacho
Lobster Bisque

VEGETARIAN AND VEGETABLE-BASED DISHES
Garden-Fresh Tomatoes

GRAINS, CEREALS, PASTAS, BREADS
Couscous

EGGS, OMELETTES, QUICHES
Cheese Soufflé
Crêpes
Eggs Benedict
Huevos Rancheros
Omelette with Smoked Salmon

FISH, SHELLFISH, AND MOLLUSKS
Bouillabaisse
Brandade de Morue
Broiled/Grilled Scrod
Broiled Shark

Cioppino
Grilled Halibut
Grilled Red Mullet
Grilled Skate
Grilled Turbot
Mussels in White Wine
Sushi/Sashimi

DESSERTS
Baked Apple
Crème Brûlée
Fresh Peaches
Fresh Strawberries
Fresh Tropical Fruits

MODERATELY SWEET TO INTENSELY SWEET WHITE SPARKLERS

Demi-sec Champagne; Asti; Clairette di Die; sweeter styles of *Sekt* (Germany, Austria), among others

HERBS, SPICES, NUTS, SEASONINGS
Coconut
Honey

SAUCES, SALSAS, DRESSINGS, COULIS
Sabayon Sauce

SOUPS
Consommé
Cream Soups

French Onion
Game
Hot and Sour
Lobster Bisque

PÂTÉS AND TERRINES
Fish Pâté
Pâté de Campagne
Seafood Terrine
Terrine of Foie Gras

DESSERTS
Almond Tart
Charlotte Russe
Cheesecake
Crème Brûlée
Mince Pies

FULL-BODIED, DRY, RARE RED SPARKLERS

Dry Lambrusco; Brachetto d'Acqui and sparkling Shiraz, among others

GRAINS, CEREALS, PASTAS, BREADS
Pasta Carbonara
Spaghetti Bolognese

MEAT
Hamburger
Prosciutto, Prosciutto with Melon

CHEESES
Parmigiano Reggiano

Fresh Black Cherries

CATEGORY 5 CLASSIC FOOD PAIRINGS: FORTIFIED WINE STYLES

DRY, LIGHTER-BODIED FORTIFIED APERITIF WINES

Fino and Manzanilla Sherries; Sercial Madeira

SOUPS
Consommé
French Onion
Game
Lobster Bisque

VEGETARIAN AND VEGETABLE-BASED DISHES
Olives

EGGS, OMELETTES, QUICHES
Plain Omelette

FISH, SHELLFISH, AND MOLLUSKS
Brandade de Morue
Deep-Fried Calamari
Fried Shrimp/Prawns
Fritto Misto
Seared Scallops
Sushi/Sashimi

MEAT
Chorizo
Prosciutto
Serrano Ham

CHEESES
Cabrales
Manchego

SWEET, LIGHT-MEDIUM AND FULL-BODIED FORTIFIED DESSERT WINES

Black Muscat; Cap; Cream Sherry; Málaga; Marsala Superiore 20 Year Old; Moscatel de Setúbal; Muscat from Frontignan; Orange Muscat; Rivesaltes; St-Jean-de-Minervois

EGGS, OMELETTES, QUICHES
Custard

DESSERTS
Apple Strudel
Fresh Blackberries
Fresh Black Cherries
Fresh Peaches
Fresh Plums
Lemon Tart
Zabaglione

SWEET, RICH, EXTRA-FULL-BODIED FORTIFIED DESSERT WINES

Australian and New Zealand fortified Muscat; Australian vintage Port; Crusted Port; highest-quality late-bottled vintage Portos; Liqueur Muscat; Madeira 10-Year-Old Malmsey; Pedro Ximénez (P.X.) Sherry; vintage Porto

HERBS, SPICES, NUTS, SEASONINGS
Coffee
Vanilla

CHEESES
Cheddar
Cheshire
Danish Blue
Gloucester

Gorgonzola
Maytag Blue
Monterey Jack
Pecorino
Reblochon
Roquefort
Stilton

DESSERTS
Chocolate Desserts
Fresh Apples
Lemon Tart
Mince Pie
Vanilla Ice Cream
Zabaglione

THE GLOBAL VILLAGE OF FOOD AND WINE PAIRING

THROUGHOUT MUCH OF THE WORLD, more and more people are enjoying wine and food than ever before. In the past, the topic, theory, and practice of wine and food pairing was Eurocentric, because the tradition of wine with food was largely perceived to be the province of Europeans and their descendants. At one time, this generalization made sense, but today, such a parochial view of the subject is old-fashioned, limited, and ill informed about the "revolution" that is happening in world cuisines in so many homes and restaurants across the country and the world.

Just ten to twenty years ago, the idea of wine with what has been awkwardly called "ethnic" cuisines and food traditions was not on the world's wine map, or was certainly flying under the radar. Today, professionals, restaurant guests, and home cooks think that enjoying wines with the world's foods is a given. And it is.

The following are just a few ideas on pairing wines of the world with foods of the world and by no means exhaustive; they barely scratch the surface of what is possible. Hopefully this list will spur your imagination and spread the idea that enjoying wine with food crosses cultures, datelines, and international boundaries.

ASIA

China

MOO SHU PORK Semidry white such as Riesling (China, New York State, Canada, or Australia); medium-bodied reds such as Merlot (Washington State), Carmenère (Chile), or Malbec (Argentina); Amontillado Sherry (Jerez, Spain)

EGGPLANT IN BLACK BEAN SAUCE Full-bodied reds such as Ribera del Duero (Spain), Douro (Portugal), Xinomavro (Greece), or Petite Sirah (Mendocino, California)

SZECHUAN SCALLOPS Semidry white such as Riesling (New World or Germany); a low-alcohol dry white such as Vinho Verde (Minho, Portugal)

India

SAMOSA Sparkling Brut (U.S.A. or India) or Extra Dry (Champagne, France); a dry, medium to full-bodied white such as Marsanne (Australia or U.S.A.) or white Côtes du Rhône (France)

SHRIMP OR LOBSTER WITH MILD CURRY SAUCE Full-bodied dry whites with forward fruit flavors such as Chardonnay (Australia) or Encruzado (Dão, Portugal)

SHRIMP OR LOBSTER WITH SPICY CURRY SAUCE AND CHUTNEY Light-bodied, fairly low-alcohol dry white wine such as Vinho Verde (Minho, Portugal); semidry white wine such as Riesling (Germany, U.S.A., or Canada); Chenin Blanc (Loire, France, or India)

TANDOORI LAMB WITH RED LENTIL DHAL Dry full-bodied red such as Petite Sirah (California), Douro (Portugal), or Ribera del Duero (Spain)

Indonesia

CHICKEN SATAY Dry fortified wines such as Amontillado Sherry (Jerez, Spain) or Sercial Madeira (Portugal); semidry white such as Gewürztraminer (California, Washington State, or Alsace, France)

NASI GORENG Crisp whites such as Rueda (Spain) or Grüner Vetliner (Austria); a richer white such as Sémillon (Washington State or Australia)

Japan

SUSHI AND SASHIMI Sparklers: Brut (U.S.A.), Cava (Spain), or Prosecco (Veneto, Italy); dry Fino or Manzanilla Sherry (Jerez, Spain); dry light- to medium-bodied whites such as Verdelho (Australia) or Rueda (Spain); semidry whites such as Chenin Blanc or Gewürztraminer (U.S.A.)

TEMPURA Dry, tart white such as Sauvignon Blanc (Chile or New Zealand)

CHICKEN OR BEEF TERIYAKI Fruity, light-bodied reds such as Gamay (U.S.A. or Beaujolais, France) or Valpolicella (Veneto, Italy)

Korea

BEEF WITH SPICY KIMCHEE Dry rosé sparkling wines (U.S.A.) or Cava (Spain); medium-bodied reds such as Barbera (Italy), Rioja (Spain), or Dão (Portugal)

Thailand

PAD THAI NOODLES WITH SEAFOOD Light- to medium-bodied, semidry whites such as Vouvray (Loire, France) or Gewürztraminer (Alsace, France); Chenin Blanc (U.S.A. or South Africa)

COCONUT MILK–BASED SEAFOOD CURRY Dry, tart, medium-bodied whites such as Sauvignon or Fumé Blanc (Sonoma, California); Sancerre or Menetou-Salon (Loire, France)

Vietnam

SPRING ROLLS Dry, light-bodied whites such as Soave (Italy) or Sauvignon Blanc (New Zealand); light sparkling such as Blanc de Blancs (U.S.A.)

PHO SOUP WITH BEEF In the summer: full-bodied white such as Chardonnay (U.S.A.); in the winter: light- to medium-bodied reds such as Beaujolais-Villages (France) or Cabernet Franc (New York or Canada)

EUROPE

Belgium

MOULES FRITES Dry, light-bodied whites such as Muscadet (Loire, France) or Vinho Verde (Minho, Portugal); dry sparkling Crémant d'Alsace (France)

WAFFLES WITH STRAWBERRIES AND WHIPPED CREAM In the summer: sweet, sparkling (and low-alcohol) Brachetto d'Acqui (Piedmont, Italy); in the winter: sweet, higher-alcohol Ruby Reserve Porto (Douro, Portugal)

Central and Eastern Europe

BORSCHT SOUP Dry reds such as Grenache or Grenache blends (California, Australia), Cannonau di Sardegna (Sardinia), or Gigondas (Rhône Valley, France); Zinfandel or Petite Sirah (Mendocino, California)

CHICKEN SOUP WITH MATZOH BALLS Dry, full-bodied white such as Chardonnay; sparkling Brut (Israel or U.S.A.)

WIENER SCHNITZEL Dry, medium- to full-bodied whites such as Pinot Gris (Oregon or Canada), Rülander (Germany), or Pinot Grigio (Italy)

VEAL OR BEEF GOULASH (GULYAS) Dry, medium- to full-bodied reds such as Egri Bikavér (Hungary), Nemea (Greece), or Alentejo (Portugal)

CHICKEN PAPRIKA Medium- to full-bodied whites such as Marsanne (California or Australia) or a white Côtes du Rhône (France); medium-bodied reds such as Dolcetto (Italy), Pinot Noir (Santa Ynez Valley or Santa Maria Valley, California), or Egri Bikavér (Hungary)

DUCK WITH RED CABBAGE Dry, medium- to full-bodied reds such as Mourvèdre (California) or Monastrell (Spain); Zinfandel (California), Shiraz (Australia), or Salice Salentino (Puglia, Italy)

PIEROGIS Dry, full-bodied white such as Chardonnay (California); Pouilly Fuissé (Mâcon, France); Greco di Tufo (Italy); sparkling Brut (California, Spain, Italy)

France

PÂTÉ DE CAMPAGNE (COUNTRY PÂTÉ) Gewürztraminer (Alsace, France); dry, medium- to full-bodied French reds such as Gigondas, Minervois, St Chinian, or Côtes du Rhône-Villages

CHOUCROUTE ALSACIENNE (CABBAGE AND CHARCUTERIE) Dry or semidry, medium- to full-bodied whites such as Muscat, Riesling, Pinot Gris, or Gewürztraminer (Alsace, France); semidry still or sparkling cool-climate Riesling (Germany, Canada, or New York State)

CASSOULET (WHITE BEANS WITH PORK AND DUCK) Full-bodied reds from France such as Châteauneuf-du-Pape or Gigondas (Rhône Valley); Zinfandel (Paso Robles or Dry Creek, California)

SALADE NIÇOISE Dry, Grenache-based rosés from California, Bandol (France), or Navarra or Cigales (Spain); dry, crisp whites such as Sauvignon Blanc or Fumé Blanc (California)

BOUILLABAISSE Dry sparkling rosés such as Crémant de Bourgogne or Champagne (France); full-bodied whites such as Condrieu or Côtes du Roussillon (France); medium-bodied red Burgundy such as Marsannay, Pernand-Vergelesses, or Chorey les Beaune, or a regional Bourgogne (France)

DUCK CONFIT How it is served determines the choice of wine. In a salad (as an appetizer) at room temperature: medium-bodied whites such as Chardonnay-based Mâcon-Villages, St-Veran, or Pouilly-Fuissé (Burgundy, France) or a Pinot Gris (Oregon or Alsace, France). As a main course, served hot: bold French reds such as St-Estèphe or St-Émilion (Bordeaux), or Cornas or Côte-Rôtie (Rhône). Full-bodied versions of Zinfandel, Cabernet Sauvignon, or Syrah (California); Nebbiolo d'Alba (Piedmont, Italy)

Great Britain

FISH AND CHIPS Tart, dry, medium-bodied white such as Sauvignon Blanc (New Zealand); sparkling Cava (Spain) or sparkling wines from England. (Watch out for the vinegar; it can make the wine taste sour!)

ROAST BEEF WITH YORKSHIRE PUDDING Dry, full-bodied, noble reds such as château or estate wines from Pauillac or Margaux (Bordeaux, France); Cabernet Sauvignon or Shiraz (Australia)

Greece

MOUSSAKA Dry, full-bodied reds such as Naoussa (Greece)

GYRO OR SOUVLAKI SANDWICH In the summer: dry or semidry rosé wines based on Moschofilero (Greece); dry rosé (California); in the winter: medium-bodied reds such as Nemea (Greece)

SPANAKOPITA WITH TZAZIKI OR GREEK SALAD WITH FETA Dry, tart wines based on Roditis or Assyrtiko (Greece); tart Sauvignon Blanc (New Zealand, Australia, or South Africa)

GRILLED OCTOPUS, MULLET, OR SWORDFISH WITH OLIVE OIL Dry, floral whites based on Moschofilero or Malagousia (Greece)

Italy

LINGUINE WITH PESTO Dry, tart whites such as Sauvignon Blanc (South Africa) or Vermentino (Sardinia or Tuscany, Italy)

FETTUCINE ALFREDO Dry sparkling Brut (Franciacorta, Italy) to break through the richness, or Chardonnay (France or California) to complement it

SPAGHETTI WITH WHITE CLAM SAUCE Dry, medium-bodied whites such as Vernaccia di San Gimignano, Orvieto Classico, or Pinot Grigio (Italy)

SPAGHETTI WITH MEAT SAUCE Dry, medium- to full-bodied reds such as Chianti Classico (Tuscany, Italy) or Barbera d'Asti (Piedmont, Italy); Grenache blends (Australia or U.S.A.)

MEAT LASAGNA Dry, full-bodied reds such as Cabernet Sauvignon, Petite Sirah or Syrah (California); Amarone (Veneto, Italy) or Aglianico del Vulture (Basilicata, Italy)

CALZONE OR WHITE PIZZA Dry, full-bodied whites such as Chardonnay (California); Sémillon (Australia); Greco di Tufo or Fiano di Avellino (Campania, Italy)

PIZZA WITH RED SAUCE The toppings dictate the choice of wine, but Chianti (Tuscany, Italy) or Zinfandel (California) are dependable choices.

VEGETABLE PIZZA Light to medium reds such as Valpolicella (Veneto, Italy), Dolcetto (Piedmont, Italy), or Merlot (U.S.A.)

ZUPPA DI PESCE (SEAFOOD SOUP) Dry rosé (Navarra, Spain); sparkling Franciacorta rosé (Lombardy, Italy); light- to medium-bodied reds such as Chianti Classico (Tuscany), Sangiovese di Romagna (Emilia-Romagna), or Grignolino (Piedmont); Pinot Noir (New Zealand or Oregon) or inexpensive Barbera or Zinfandel (Amador County, California)

CHICKEN PICCATA Dry, light to medium-bodied whites such as Soave Classico (Veneto) or Gavi (Piedmont); Sémillon (Australia or Washington State)

OSSO BUCO (SERVED WITH A SAFFRON RISOTTO) Full-bodied Chardonnay (Tuscany or Friuli); medium-bodied Italian reds such as Merlot (Sicily) or Dolcetto (Piedmont); full-bodied Italian reds such as Carmignano (Tuscany) or Barbaresco (Piedmont)

BISTECCA FIORENTINA Full-bodied reds such as Brunello di Montalcino or Carmignano (both from Tuscany), Sagrantino di Montefalco (Umbria), Taurasi (Campania), or Amarone (Veneto)

Portugal

CALDO VERDE (KALE SOUP WITH CHORIZO SAUSAGE) Dry, medium- to full-bodied whites from the Dão, Beiras, Terras do Sado, or Bucelas regions (Portugal); light-bodied, low-alcohol dry white such as Vinho Verde (Minho, Portugal); Chenin Blanc (South Africa)

CABRITO (BABY GOAT COOKED IN A WOOD-FIRED OVEN) Dry,

full-bodied noble reds from the Douro, Beiras, or Alentejo (Portugal); Cabernet Sauvignon (Napa Valley, California, or Tuscany, Italy).

CARNE DE PORCO ALENTEJANO (PORK AND CLAMS WITH PO-TATOES) In the summer: dry, medium-bodied whites from Alentejo, Ribatejo, or Terras do Sado (Portugal); in the winter: light- to medium-bodied inexpensive reds from the same regions

Spain

CLASSIC PAELLA (WITH CHICKEN AND SEAFOOD) Dry, medi-um- to full-bodied whites such as Albariño, Ribeiro, or Rueda (Spain); Chardonnay (California).

ROAST SUCKLING PIG In the summer: a dry, medium- to full-bodied white such as Albariño (Rías Baixas, Spain); in the winter: medium- to full-bodied reds such as Rioja, Ribero del Duero, or Bierzo (Spain)

TAPAS OR PIXTOS (AN ASSORTMENT OF LITTLE PLATES OR TASTES) Sparkling Cava (Spain); dry, fortified Fino or Manzanilla Sherry (Jerez, Spain)

Sweden

GRAVLAX Semidry, light-bodied whites such as cold-climate Riesling (New York State, Canada, or Germany); dry, medium- to full-bodied rosé Champagne (France); Sauvignon Blanc (South Africa or New Zealand)

AFRICA

Ethiopia

INJERA AND WAT (TEFF GRAIN PANCAKE WITH SPICY MEAT STEW) Dry, light-bodied reds that can be served with a light chill, such as Gamay (U.S.A. or Beaujolais, France); Valpolicella (Veneto, Italy); dry and semidry rosés (U.S.A.)

Morocco and Algeria

VEGETABLE COUSCOUS Dry, medium-bodied to full-bod-ied white such as Chardonnay (California); if you prefer a lot of spicy *harissa*, then a dry, light-bodied, low-alcohol Vinho Verde (Portugal); semidry, low-alcohol Riesling (Germany).

LAMB TAGINE Dry, fruity, medium-bodied red such as an in-expensive to moderately priced Zinfandel (California); semidry rosé such as White Zinfandel; (California); dry rosé (Rioja, Spain)

MIDDLE EAST

Israel, Lebanon, and Syria

VEGETARIAN MEZZE OF TABBOULEH, FATOUCHE, BABA GHANOUSH, AND HUMMUS Dry, light-bodied whites such as Sauvignon Blanc (Israel) or a white blend such as Château Musar Blanc (Bekaa Valley, Lebanon); Brut sparkling (California, Washington State, or Oregon); or a fruity white such as Moschofilero or Malagousia (Greece)

KEFTA KEBABS OR SHUWARMA Dry rosé or sparkling wines (U.S.A. or Australia); medium- to full-bodied reds such as Cabernet Sauvignon blends (Israel, Lebanon, North Coast of California, Southeastern Australia, or Chile)

THE AMERICAS AND THE CARIBBEAN

Argentina

BEEF CHIMICHURRI Full-bodied reds such as Malbec, Bonarda, Cabernet Sauvignon, or Syrah (Argentina); Toro (Spain)

Brazil

FEIJOADO Full-bodied reds such as Cabernet Sauvignon, Carmenère, or Syrah (Chile); Tannat (Uruguay); Toro (Spain)

Jamaica

CURRY GOAT If served by itself: dry, light- to medi-um-bodied red such as an inexpensive Zinfandel (California); if served with a jicama salad or fruity slaw (as is customary): a semidry white such as Chenin Blanc (U.S.A., South Africa, or Loire Valley, France);

Riesling (New York State, Washington State, or Germany)

ACKEE Dry, floral white with some richness such as Torrontés (Argentina); Malagousia (Greece); sparkling Prosecco (Veneto, Italy)

POZOLE If green pozole: dry, tart Sauvignon Blanc or Fumé Blanc (Mexico or U.S.A.); if red pozole: light-bodied red such as Gamay (California or Beaujolais, France); Moristel (Spain)

RED SNAPPER VERACRUZ Dry, light- to medium-bodied white such as Sauvignon Blanc (Mexico or Chile)

GUACAMOLE To complement the avocado's richness: a rich, full-bodied Chardonnay (California); to offset it: a tart Sauvignon Blanc (New Zealand or South Africa); sparkling Cava (Spain)

CHILES RELLENOS Semidry white such as Riesling (Germany); dry, fruity whites such as Torrontés (Argentina) or Moschofilero (Greece)

BEEF TACOS Dry rosé or sparkling rosé wines such as Cava (Spain); light to medium-bodied reds such as Merlot (Mexico or Chile); inexpensive Tempranillo or Monastrell (Spain)

LOBSTER WITH HUITLACOCHE SAUCE Vintage Brut Champagne (France); fine white Burgundy such as Chassagne-Montrachet (France)

BEEF CHIMICHANGAS, ENCHILADAS, OR FAJITAS For mild preparations: full-bodied reds such as Cabernet Sauvignon or Mourvèdre (California); for spicy-hot versions: still rosé or sparkling wines such as Cava (Spain); a light-bodied red such as Gamay (U.S.A. or Beaujolais, France), served chilled

Puerto Rico

PERNIL OF PORK In the summer: dry, medium- to full-bodied whites such as Albariño (Rías Baixas, Spain) or Chardonnay (Chile); in the winter: medium-bodied reds such as Merlot (California), Campo de Borja, or Jumilla (Spain)

UNITED STATES

Cajun and Creole

SEAFOOD GUMBO Dry or semidry still or sparkling rosé wine, such as Cava (Spain) or Crémant de Bourgogne (France)

CRAWFISH ÉTOUFFÉE Medium- to full-bodied white such as Chardonnay (Pouilly-Fuissé, Mâcon-Villages, or Rully from Burgundy, France); sparkling Blanc de Noirs (California); Pinot Blanc (Alsace, France)

JAMBALAYA Dry or semidry rosé such as Tavel or Bandol (France) or other Grenache-based versions (Navarra, Spain, or California)

CRAWFISH BOIL Dry, light-bodied sparkling wine such as Prosecco (Italy); semidry whites such as Gewürztraminer, Riesling, or Chenin Blanc (U.S.A.)

RED BEANS AND RICE WITH SAUSAGE Medium- to full-bodied reds with ripe fruit flavors such as Zinfandel or Petite Sirah (California), Shiraz (Australia), Bierzo (Spain), or Alentejo (Portugal)

MUFFALETTA SANDWICH In the summer: dry, light- to medium-bodied whites such as Vermentino (Sicily, Italy) or Sémillon (Washington State); in the winter: medium-bodied reds such as Merlot (Chile), Nemea (Greece), or a Penedès blend (Spain)

Down-Home American Classics

HAMBURGER OR CHEESEBURGER Cabernet Sauvignon or Cabernet blend (California, Australia, or Chile); Zinfandel or Syrah blend (California)

HOT DOG With mustard: inexpensive Chardonnay (California); chili dog with onions and cheese: Zinfandel (California) or Primitivo (Italy); Gewürztraminer (Anderson Valley, California)

CHILE CON CARNE For mild versions: inexpensive Zinfandel (California); if super spicy: semidry white Zinfandel (California) or a light red served chilled, such as a Gamay (California or Beaujolais Nouveau, France); Bardolino (Veneto, Italy); sparkling rosé (California) or Cava (Spain)

PASTRAMI SANDWICH Blanc de Noirs or sparkling rosé (New Mexico, Oregon, or California); dry rosé from Cigales or Navarra (Spain); semidry Riesling (New York State or Washington State)

MACARONI AND CHEESE   To complement the richness: Chardonnay (California); to cleanse the palate: Sauvignon Blanc or Fumé Blanc (California)

FRIED CHICKEN   Dry, full-bodied white such as Viognier or Chardonnay (California); sparkling Brut (U.S.A.); Cava (Spain)

BBQ RIBS   Dry, full-bodied red such as Zinfandel (California); Shiraz or "GSM" Grenache/Shiraz/Mourvèdre blend (Australia); Amarone (Veneto, Italy). Outdoors on a hot day: a semidry white such as a Gewürztraminer (Washington State or California) or sparkling rosé (California or Loire Valley, France)

NEW ENGLAND CLAM CHOWDER   Chardonnay or Brut sparkling wine (New York State)

MANHATTAN CLAM CHOWDER OR CALIFORNIA CIOPPINO   Cool-climate Pinot Noir (New York State, Oregon, or California's Russian River Valley, Carneros, Anderson Valley, Santa Ynez Valley, Santa Rita Hills, or Santa Maria Valley); rosé of Pinot Noir

HORIZONTAL AND VERTICAL CHOICES

SOMETIMES WE WANT TO MATCH a particular dish with just one wine, and this gustatory marriage is not related to a multicourse, multiwine meal. This is called a horizontal wine choice, and we may choose to complement or contrast the wine to the food, as previously discussed. Often, however, we will match several food courses with several wines in a multicourse, progressive dinner. These pairings, by contrast or by complement, represent a series of vertical wine choices. While we are climbing a ladder of intensity for the wines, each successive food course should also reflect an increase in flavor intensity. (For examples, see the menus at the end of this chapter.)

A horizontal choice might be simply matching one wine to an entrée, such as roasted chicken studded with garlic under the skin, served in its own juices, accompanied by mushroom risotto and sautéed snap peas. The dominant flavor of the dish is the garlic-infused chicken, and so we would consider this dish to be of medium to high flavor intensity. We might choose a Chardonnay that

has been aged in oak and has undergone malolactic fermentation to complement the moderately rich flavors of the chicken's crispy skin and the creaminess of the risotto. If, on the other hand, we choose a red Pinot Noir, full of racy acidity (but still the same level of intensity of flavor as the chicken dish), the wine becomes a compelling counterpoint to the richer elements of the dish. The wine will be a fruity and refreshing accompaniment, bringing out the earthy flavors of the dish, especially the mushrooms. There are many other choices available, but the important issue here is that we are choosing one wine to match one dish, in this case a main course.

Making vertical choices is somewhat more complex than matching one dish to one wine. If we have the opportunity to choose all the wines to accompany a multicourse meal, we need to be aware of some guidelines that will help us make logical choices. These guidelines are linked closely to the idea of intensity in food and wine matching, and they apply whether you choose to complement or contrast food flavors in your wine choices. Again, these guidelines are not rules but helpful hints in successfully marrying an array of foods, their textures and flavors, with an array of wines, served in the context of a multicourse dinner.

DRY BEFORE SWEET

DRY WINES do not leave a lingering or cloying sweetness on the palate, which can interfere with the enjoyment of food, especially early in the meal. Although dry wines may be fruity, their lack of residual sugar (or added sugar in the case of sweeter sparkling wines) allows the palate to be ready to taste more food. Sweet wines, on the other hand, especially those high in alcohol and low in acidity—sweet fortified wines being the most obvious example—tend to deaden the palate, and so are more appropriate at the end of a meal.

Of course, there are exceptions to this guideline: Sweet, rich Sauternes served with a decadently rich terrine of foie gras is an obvious one. If the foie gras is served as an appetizer, it should be followed by a palate cleanser: a green salad, a clear soup such as consommé, or pleasantly acidic sorbet to purge the palate of the fat. A Champagne or sparkling wine toast will also do the job nicely. Once the palate is cleansed, the multicourse dinner can resume with the service of dry wines.

LOWER ALCOHOL BEFORE HIGHER ALCOHOL

WHILE MANY STILL AND SPARKLING WINES are between 10 and 15 percent alcohol—a tight range—it really does make a difference when they are served. If you serve a wine lower in alcohol after a higher-alcohol wine, the lower-alcohol wine could very well taste thin and watery, with unappealing flavor qualities. If all the wines served are about the same level of alcohol, say 13.5 percent, then other taste factors—acid, tannin, relative youth, production method (stainless steel or oak barrel maturation, for example)—come into play. High levels of glycerin (the "legs" or "fingers" that coat the glass) in the wine will increase the feeling of softness and fatness in the mouth. Glycerin, a by-product of fermentation, is often more pronounced in high-alcohol wines and less so in low-alcohol wines.

SPARKLING BEFORE STILL

CHAMPAGNE and other fine sparkling wines can invigorate and cleanse the palate at the beginning of a meal. They can also serve as a palate cleanser, an intermezzo, or a toast after the main course of a meal to reinvigorate the taste buds. Although they are often overlooked as dinner wines, an entire menu can be planned around sparklers, starting with the lightest Blanc de Blancs and working forward to the fullest rosé Brut Champagne. Sparkling wines work well with hors d'oeuvres at the beginning of a meal, especially high-salt and briny items such as smoked salmon and shrimp, as well as food that, though small in size, is intensely flavored and rich, such as several kinds of canapés, hors d'oeuvres, or tapas. The bubbles in the wine strip away salt and fat and stimulate the appetite.

YOUTH BEFORE AGE

YOUNGER WINES usually lack the complexity and nuance of older vintages and so should be served first. If serving two wines with a course—one younger, one older—the wines should somehow be differentiated, perhaps with

THE BEAUTY OF BUBBLES

Champagne and other high-quality sparkling wines, although much appreciated for their refreshing effervescence, are often overlooked as serious dinner wines. What a mistake. While it is true that sparkling wines are delightful **APERITIFS** and marry well with hors d'oeuvres and appetizers—Champagne and caviar is a classic—these wines also make fine matches with the rest of the menu. The bubbles in fine sparklers cleanse, refresh, and invigorate the palate, so we are able to enjoy each stage of a multicourse meal.

Fine sparkling wines contain an appealing combination of high acidity and fruitiness, and range in style from bone dry to extra sweet. Since true Champagne and many other fine sparkling wines are dominated by Pinot Noir and Chardonnay grapes, the wines tend to be medium-bodied. However, the bubbles in the wine—trapped carbon dioxide—can often give a taste impression of lightness and delicacy. The more Chardonnay in the *cuvée*, the lighter the taste, so a Blanc de Blancs Champagne—which is 100 percent Chardonnay—will usually be far lighter than a rosé sparkler, a wine that can be quite full-bodied. Likewise, different Champagne houses produce Brut bubblies in light-, medium-, and full-bodied versions, as well as Demi-sec Champagnes that are much sweeter than any of the Brut wines. Blanc de Noirs sparkling wines, the best made from mostly Pinot Noir grapes, are quite fruity and medium-bodied.

It we apply the same logic to sparkling wines as we do to still wines—light before full, dry before sweet—we see that bubbly should not be relegated only to the hors d'oeuvre plates but can also make for fine dinner wines. In fact, it is great fun to plan a dinner around sparkling wines: Blanc de Blancs with hors d'oeuvres or tapas, Brut with the appetizer, rosé with grilled fish or lighter meats, Asti with a simple dessert, maybe even Blanc de Noirs with dark, liqueur-filled chocolates. What could be more festive than a meal accompanied by a variety of fine Champagnes or sparkling wines?

a more elegant glass for the older wine. Usually the oldest wines are reserved for the main course, or sometimes the cheese course, as complex, rich, moderately tannic red wines served with aged, rich cheeses are the ultimate expression of the contrast between food and wine.

A corollary to this guideline is that as the meal progresses, the chosen wines might build in quality from one wine to the next, so that by the time the main course is served, a dramatic wine (or wines) is served with it. Of course, the best and rarest wine can be served with the cheese course or even the dessert, but if a very fine red wine is served with the main course, it is not mandatory to try to top it with the wines chosen for the cheese and dessert courses.

WINE IN THE SAUCE, WINE IN THE GLASS

FOOD PREPARED WITH WINE should be served with wine of the same type, style, or grape variety, because the wine you are drinking will reemphasize and highlight the wine in the food. This concept is known as "bridging" or "echoing." Matching the wine in the food with the wine in the glass makes for a basic complementary match, building a bridge to a successful pairing. It is normally not a good idea to taste two dramatically different wines at once, as the flavors might fight each other.

A good rule of thumb: Never cook with a wine you are unwilling to drink. Why would a wine that tastes bad in a glass taste better in a sauce? As the wine is heated, the liquid is reduced and all the flavors, but especially the off-flavors, are concentrated; the wine will likely taste worse than before it was cooked. Cooking with an unpalatable or just passable wine is a major mistake that can rob you and your guests of a lot of pleasure. On the other hand, wine used in cooking need not be of the same high quality, famous region, sought-after vintage, or high price as the wine being served. You probably will want to serve a higher-quality wine than you used to make the sauce or marinade.

LOWER INTENSITY TO HIGHER INTENSITY

THIS TRANSLATES as low-tannin wines before high-tannin wines; light whites precede full-bodied whites; light reds precede full-bodied reds. The normal progression of

wine and food calls for the white wines to be served in order of intensity—light, medium, full—and then the red wines in the same order. Obviously, the message here is that even a lighter red wine may have more intense flavors than a fairly full-bodied white wine, but this is not always the case. For example, we might choose to serve a light red, such as Beaujolais-Villages, with the sautéed wild salmon course, and in the next course serve an oaky Chardonnay as a white "crossover" wine with the grilled quail. So although the color of the wine is important, another critical issue is the level of tannin in each of the wines. The Beaujolais-Villages has negligible skin tannins, but the Chardonnay's oak tannins are palpable. The menu might also feature the oaky Chardonnay *and* the young, fruity Beaujolais with the *same* fish course, but not a medium- to full-bodied red, whose tannins will clash with the omega-3 fatty acids of the fish.

The flavors of white wines are very different from those of red wines, and the levels of intensity are also quite different. With the exception of pronounced oak flavor and richer texture provided by malolactic fermentation and high levels of alcohol, white wines are far more adaptable, meshing well with a wide variety of lighter dishes and ingredients. Red wines are not as flexible as whites; fruit and wood tannins, alcohol level, age, grape type, and vinification all enter into the flavor and texture profiles of red wines. Lighter red wines are relatively easy to match with a variety of foods, but as the wine becomes more complex, the list of culinary marriage possibilities is lessened, providing a compelling challenge. If the union is a good one, the marriage is exciting, synergistic, and sexy. If the union is less than ideal, the marriage quickly becomes awkward and fades before the palates of the guests.

DELICATE WITH DELICATE, ASSERTIVE WITH FULL-FLAVORED

IF A DISH is a delicate preparation—poached turbot in Sauvignon Blanc and fines herbes, for example—the wine should be delicate and straightforward in flavor, perhaps a Sauvignon Blanc from Chile. If the same turbot is grilled and served with a beurre blanc and more assertive herbs, a much more complex white wine, perhaps a Viognier from Napa Valley or the Rhône Valley, or a fruity red Hudson

Valley Pinot Noir or light young Valpolicella from Veneto might be in order. Notice that the red wines are distinctively flavored but low in tannins; they are red "crossover" wines. On the other hand, a peppercorn-encrusted rare Black Angus steak, served with a rich red wine sauce and sautéed portabello mushrooms, will call for a full-bodied, mature California Cabernet Sauvignon, a Syrah-based wine from the northern Rhône, or a Rioja Reserva, among many other "big" red choices.

FAT AND "BLOOD" VERSUS TANNIN, AND RED WINE WITH FISH: CROSSOVER WINES

IF TANNINS ARE PROMINENT in the flavor of any given wine, the food should be at least somewhat creamy-textured, which usually translates as fat (and sometimes collagen, as in braised lamb shanks). The creaminess of fat cuts tannin, so that the fruit and perhaps spice of a full-bodied wine will be emphasized, and the tannin will be moderated. On the opposite end of the spectrum, if we try to pair a light-bodied, simple wine with the same steak dish, the flavors and textures of the wine will be lost, and it will probably taste like water with added acid flavor—not even as pleasant as unsweetened lemonade. Even a somewhat full-bodied white wine would be unlikely to stand up to the richness of the dish, and it will taste lean and, at best, inoffensive. It will not, however, help make a happy marriage between wine and food.

A slightly more abstract concept to grasp is the idea of uncoagulated proteins, often referred to as "blood"—the juices that flow in meats and fatty fishes cooked rare—as an important issue in the matching of wine and food. As more heat is applied over time to food, the item cooks more fully and the juices that flow from the fatty part of the food will coagulate, leaving a less fleshy and very likely less tender item. This is why it is not uncommon for restaurant customers to order their tuna, salmon, swordfish, or other fatty fish cooked rare, just as patrons have ordered steaks cooked rare for many years; cooking to this point preserves moisture and flavor. The era of "flaky fish"—fish that has been overcooked and dried out—has hopefully

AGAINST THE POPULAR WISDOM: CHEESE AND WHITE WINE

A surprise to many wine drinkers, even those with years of wine and food experience, is that most cheeses marry well with white wines, and only a select few pair successfully with full-bodied red wines. While the facts seem to go against the popular wisdom, the cliché of red wine and cheese is just that: a cliché. Because the wide variety of young and rind-ripened cheeses are tangy, they work beautifully with young, acidic white wines or contrast nicely with more assertive, oak-aged whites. Cheeses that are soft and semisoft exhibit this texture because water cuts the fat in these cheeses; with less fat, the richness is less assertive. Assertive red wines actually marry well with hard cheeses (with little water content), such as Asiago and Parmigiano-Reggiano, and with cheeses that might have bitter properties (aged blue cheeses). The bitter vein of the cheese counters the bitter tannins in the wine, making the cheese taste richer and the wine taste fresher and fruitier. However, even rich, aged blue cheeses, such as Roquefort or Stilton, pair well with sweet, rich white wines (such as Sauternes from Bordeaux, France, or Muscat of Samos, Greece) or sweet fortified wines, especially vintage Portos.

In a process that is almost exactly the opposite of the learning curve that novice wine drinkers navigate, experienced wine and cheese lovers might want to slowly reverse themselves, trying some of their favorite cheeses first with lighter reds, then with full-bodied whites, then with lighter, younger, livelier whites. Try that blue Gorgonzola with Sauternes, that Camembert with apples and Chablis, Münster with dry Riesling, and that fresh goat cheese with Sauvignon Blanc.

MIXING AND MATCHING: THE OLD RULES VERSUS THE NEW REALITY

If you have been reading this chapter closely, it is clear that the old dictum "white wine with fish, red wine with meat," while serviceable in a pinch, is no longer the only way to go. As our palates have become more adventuresome and our interest in the foods of indigenous, ethnic, and foreign cultures has grown, we also want to try some new possibilities where food and wine are concerned. Today, we are interested in celebrating the pleasures of the table, and the formal notions of an earlier time, though based in logic and experience, just might not provide the excitement that our palates crave.

The old rules of food and wine pairing are now about a century old and so never took into account the possibility of enjoying wine with various ethnic and new regional cuisines. Blanc de Noirs sparkling wine with sashimi, Gewürztraminer with a mild curry, Zinfandel with chili, and semidry Riesling with pulled-pork North Carolina barbecue weren't even blips on the food and wine radar screen. Today, we relish the opportunity to try different wines with exciting, even exotic foods.

Geographical, cultural, and historical relationships among wine and food have often been taken as a given when matching regional food (e.g., risotto) to regional wine (e.g., Nebbiolo). Drinking the local wine with the local food is still a very good idea, but on a planet where authentic foods from Europe, Africa, Asia, or South America can be served in Chicago, New York, or San Francisco, or even small towns and suburbs, one of the old saws now being exploded is nationalism or regionalism in food and wine pairing. Although you will not go too far wrong by matching food from a particular region with an appropriate wine from that region, especially when it comes to wine and food from the wine regions of the Old World, there is nothing wrong with matching a wine from Oregon with a dish native to Burgundy. The classic boeuf à la Bourguignonne may have been born to marry with a regional or communal red wine from the Côte de Nuits in Burgundy, as well as bathe in it as a braising medium, but a Pinot Noir from Oregon's Willamette Valley will also do the job nicely. Bélon oysters on the half shell

from Bordeaux's Arcachon district, served with a mignonette of vinegar and shallots, make an incomparable match with a local young Entre-Deux-Mers, but a crisp Sauvignon Blanc from New Zealand may be just the ticket to palatal happiness because of its high acidity, medium body, and assertive fruit flavors.

The food and wine world is vast, and there is no doubt that when we visit the classic wine-growing regions of that world, it is always a special treat to taste the local food and wine together. That gastronomic world is also changing; instead of or in addition to our traveling to Burgundy and Bordeaux, their wine travels to us, and Oregon and New Zealand wines, among so many other New World wine regions, travel to Europe and beyond. International intermarriage is sure to become the order of the day at the table as we continue our quest for knowledge of and experience with both the classic cuisines and the innovative dishes of so many cultures.

ABOUT WINE AND SOUP

Traditionally, wine is usually not served with the soup course during a multicourse meal. Aside from the obvious temperature problem of soup and wine—soup is usually served very hot—some clear soups act as palate cleansers after the hors d'oeuvres or cold appetizers.

In warm weather, a cold soup, perhaps a gazpacho or a fruit soup, may be served. In this case, a crisp white wine with forward fruit, such as a Riesling Kabinett from the Mosel, might be just the thing to marry with the cold dish. Also, if a consommé is being served, a medium-dry Sherry or Madeira might be served alongside or actually in the soup. In general, however, unless the soup is a highlighted or featured part of the meal, a separate wine is not served. If a guest desires wine with the soup, the wine from the first course usually will do the trick.

Of course, wine is a terrific accompaniment to knife-and-fork soups, or whenever a soup or stew is the main course of the meal. Hearty dishes such as pot-au-feu or a rich black bean soup marry well with medium-intensity red wines, such as a Côtes du Rhône or Zinfandel or a red wine from Penedès, Spain. Choucroute garnie, native to Alsace, will serve as a fine match with dry Riesling or Gewürztraminer. Fish stews such as cioppino, bouillabaisse, *zarzuela*, or *zuppa di pesce* make an ideal match with medium-bodied white wines, such as Sauvignon Blanc or Friulano, or better yet, dry rosé wines, including Tavel from the southern Rhône Valley or rosé from Navarra, Spain, or the North Coast of California.

Going outside the box of tradition, why not wine and soup? If we prepare the soup to accompany a particular wine and moderate its temperature just a bit by tasting slowly, this could be a very successful and very exciting course in a multicourse meal. Soups that feature vegetables, meat, fish, legumes, fruit, and cheese are wonderful partners with wine. Think of the traditional French onion soup served with a glass of Beaujolais-Villages, a hearty bean soup served with a young red Rioja, a bouillabaisse served with a cool, dry rosé, or a cold gazpacho served with a tangy white from Rueda, Spain.

Perhaps the only caveat here is to avoid cream-based soups, bisques, and chowders. These are not really wine-friendly, as they coat the palate and kill the character of almost any wine.

Highly salted foods, especially those with intense flavors—a grilled veal steak in a chipotle chile sauce, for example—emphasize the taste of alcohol in the wine. Red and white wines that are 12 to 13 percent alcohol will taste unbalanced and overly alcoholic if the food is intensely flavored and salty. The salty taste can come from table or sea salt or ingredients such as soy sauce or anchovies. Champagne or other sparkling wines, with their cooling, refreshing acidity, do well with salty food. Good examples are Champagne and caviar, sparkling Spanish Cava with smoked foods, or Manzanilla Sherry with foods marinated in a salt brine. Smoked salmon accompanied by sparkling wine is almost a given at more formal brunches.

In recent tastings we have found that salty foods marry well with wines that have a touch of sweetness to them, creating a kind of sweet-and-sour impression on the palate. Semidry Rieslings, such as *halbtrocken* Rieslings from Germany, relieve the palate of salty flavors, as do many New World Gewürztraminers, which are rarely as dry as the classic wines from Alsace, France.

Even though the Champagne brunch is still popular in hotel dining rooms and restaurants, another problem food is the focus of those brunches: eggs. Most wines do not really enhance the flavors of most egg dishes, but light-bodied fruity whites and reds do well with omelets, as do sparkling wines. The choice of wine should be adjusted depending on the ingredients in the omelet, but try to avoid wines high in tannins. Classic egg dishes such as quiche lorraine, named for the French region of Alsace-Lorraine, bring us back to the idea of geographical matching; Riesling, Gewürztraminer, or Pinot Gris from Alsace enhance this rich egg tart.

SEASONALITY

JUST AS SERVING FOODS that are appropriate to the season has become an increasingly important part of dining in the United States, so too wines have their seasons. On a hot summer day or in south Florida in April, we may want nothing heavier than some ice-cold oysters and a salad of local greens and garden-fresh tomatoes, or a simple roast beef sandwich on good bread, accompanied by potato salad. We certainly would not be looking for a heavy, complex, tannic red wine with the latter dish, and we definitely would not be interested in an oaky, full-bodied white wine

ARE DESSERT WINES REALLY FOR DESSERT?

Dessert wines are perhaps the most controversial wines served during a multicourse, multi-wine meal. Not very popular in the United States, these sweet wines can be still, such as botrytis-affected and late-harvest styles; sparkling, such as Asti or Demi-sec Champagne; or fortified, such as Porto, Sherry, or Madeira. There are, of course, many other sweet wines in these three categories from all over the world.

These wines engender controversy because sugar, even in relatively small amounts, tends to deaden the palate, masking any flavors other than sweetness. Also, these wines, especially the fortified versions, can be high in alcohol and may be seen as the definition of "just too much" wine. Finally, perhaps the most controversial question is whether these wines really complement dessert.

Connoisseurs of sweet wines, many of whom prefer to call them by this name rather than refer to them as "dessert wines," probably will opt to drink a small glass of Sauternes from Bordeaux, Trockenbeerenauslese from the Mosel, Vendange Tardive from Alsace, or P. X. Sherry on

its own, in place of, rather than with, dessert. This makes a lot of sense, because if you pair a sweet wine with a sweet dessert, one or both of them will get lost in a swirl of sweetness. Especially if you are tasting a very special, maybe older, perhaps rare wine of great subtlety, you will lose the nuances of the wine if it is paired with a sweet dessert.

Should you decide to serve a sweet wine with dessert, a good rule of thumb is to make sure that the wine is sweeter than the dessert. Simple desserts without a pronounced sweet taste—cookies, apple tarts, dried fruit compotes—will highlight the wine nicely. Perhaps the classic example of a sweet wine paired with a simple dessert comes from Italy: Vin Santo from Tuscany, Recioto di Soave from Veneto, and Picolit from Friuli–Venezia Giulia are paired with biscotti—simple nut cookies that are often dipped in the wine. Elaborate desserts full of cream or other rich flavors, even if they are not overly sweet, still will interfere with the enjoyment of the wine.

Remember also that sweet wines vary widely in character. A fine

Sauternes will be luscious, redolent of honey and tropical fruits. For this reason Sauternes is often paired with a terrine of foie gras, leaving the diner to wonder how much silky luxury he or she can take. Sauternes is also high enough in acid to be combined harmoniously with a plate of fresh berries or a berry tart (the combination of acid and acid emphasizing the taste of the fruit in both the dessert and the wine). On the other hand, the finest sweet wines from Germany and Austria can be light and delicate, almost austere when compared to Sauternes. The sweetness of the German and Austrian wines is moderated by bracing and refreshing acidity, and so, like Sauternes, these make a brilliant complement to simpler fruit-based desserts. Of course, sparkling dessert wines such as Asti (and Brachetto d'Acqui, a red sparkler also from Piedmont, Italy) will refresh the palate with good levels of acidity and cleanse the palate with their bubbles. Finally, fortified wines, such as Portos and sweet Sherries, are probably best served with desserts such as ice cream or dark chocolate.

with the oysters and salad. However, a crisp, light, low-alcohol wine, exhibiting simple, fruity flavors and mouth-watering acidity, would be a refreshing summer wine, matching the briny flavor and shimmering textures of the oysters, as well as the fresh crunch of the greens and the sweetness and acidity of the tomatoes. Likewise, the roast beef sandwich and potato salad would happily marry with a light, fruity red wine or rosé. These low-tannin cross-over red wines work well because the cold roast beef and the potato salad are not overwhelmingly rich or fatty on the palate and so could not support a very powerful, tannic red. In the intense heat, we might want to chill the red wine (and definitely the rosé) in the refrigerator for about an hour before service, in order to emphasize its refreshing acidity and simplicity in balance with fruit, very light tannins, and moderate alcohol.

In the dead of winter, a menu as described above would hardly satisfy an appetite brought on by skiing, skating, or shoveling snow all day. In cold weather, we tend to gravitate to heartier fare, say a venison stew served with winter root vegetables, all braised in a liquid of half veal stock and half Merlot. Naturally, we will want to serve a Merlot-based wine with the dish to make for a satisfying and warming meal and a gastronomic bridge between the food and wine. In the same vein of heavier cold-weather meals, the traditional roast goose—quite a rich dish—could be served on Christmas Day with an older, full-bodied red wine that, with its warming intensity of tannin, dried fruit flavors, and high alcohol levels, is a cold-weather knockout punch.

To everything there is a season, and this includes wines. In the heat of the summer or in a climate that is warm year-round, a high-alcohol wine will cause us to sweat and make our heads swim. In a bitterly cold climate, those same wines will make us feel warm and cozy, like a roaring fire in the fireplace or woodstove. To serve a light, crisp wine with a complex cold-weather meal is to dilute the effect of heartiness that is so welcome when coming in from winter's chill.

SUMMARY

EXPLORING WINE AND FOOD is a journey that can take a lifetime. The pleasures of the table are many, but few are more satisfying than the happy union of food and wine. The ideas, guidelines, and tools presented in this chapter will help you make judgments about what wines to match with what foods. Every time you make a decision, you will be advancing your own wine and food knowledge. Whether you are planning a banquet in a hotel, giving wine advice to a party of two in an intimate restaurant setting, or just entertaining friends at home, pairing food and wine is a valuable skill.

The following are a series of theoretical regional food and wine menus from different countries of the world. Notice the use of the guidelines outlined in this chapter to match the foods and wines. First courses marry with the lightest wines, and the intensity of the wines increases as the intensity of the food increases. In some cases the flavors in the wine complement the flavors of the food, and in some cases the flavors of the food and wine contrast, creating a compelling counterpoint for the dish.

Notice also that, for each course, the first wine or wines to appear on the menu are native to the region, country, or continent, and the second wine or set of wines comes from different wine-growing regions of the world. Sometimes these wines will contain the same grapes as the native wine, sometimes not, but the style and intensity of flavor will be a good theoretical match for each dish. Often both wine choices will complement or contrast with the flavors in the food, but sometimes one of the wines will complement the flavors, while the other will contrast with the food flavors. What these menus emphasize is that while native food and wine marriages are desirable, so are the intermarriages of food and wine from different parts of the world.

There are no vintages on any of the wines, as this is not an exercise in picking the wine from the best year, but rather picking the right style of wine for each dish. Where a wine is by definition nonvintage, like many Champagnes, we have included the letters *NV*.

France
ALSACE

Tarte à l'Oignon
ONION TART

PINOT BLANC, *Hugel, Alsace*
or PINOT BIANCO, *Lageder, Alto Adige, Italy*

Escargots en Raviole aux Graines de Pavot
RAVIOLI OF SNAILS WITH POPPY SEEDS

MUSCAT, *Trimbach, Alsace*
or SAUVIGNON BLANC, *Terrunyo, Casablanca Valley, Chile*

Salade de Betteraves
BEETROOT SALAD

Choucroute Garnie à l'Alsacienne
ALSATIAN CHOUCROUTE

GEWÜRZTRAMINER, "CUVÉE MARIE," *Albrecht, Alsace*
or GEWÜRZTRAMINER, *Lenz, North Fork of Long Island, New York State*

Tarte aux Myrtilles a l'Alsacienne
ALSATIAN HUCKLEBERRY TART

RIESLING VENDANGE TARDIVE, *Domaine Weinbach, Alsace*
or RIESLING ICEWINE, *Cave Spring, Niagara Peninsula, Canada*

France

PROVENCE / RHÔNE VALLEY

Tapenade

POUNDED CAPERS, ANCHOVIES, AND BLACK OLIVES

CUVÉE GOURMANDE BLANC, *Mas de la Dame, Les Beaux de Provence*
or VINHO VERDE, *Avaleda, Minho, Portugal*

Rougets au Fenouil Sous la Cendret

MULLET WITH FENNEL BAKED IN ASHES

ROSÉ, "CUVÉE MARINE," *Domaines Ott, Bandol*
or ROSÉ OF PINOT NOIR, *Iron Horse, Green Valley of Russian River Valley, California*

Salade Aixoise

ARTICHOKE AND BEAN SALAD

Gigot d'Agneau Sauce à l'Ail

LEG OF LAMB WITH GARLIC SAUCE

CHÂTEAUNEUF-DU-PAPE, *Château Rayas, Rhône Valley*
or GRENACHE, *d'Arenberg, McLaren Vale, Australia*

Melon de Cavaillon

AU MUSCAT DE BEAUMES-DE-VENISE ET LA MENTHE

CAVAILON MELON WITH MUSCAT DE BEAUMES-DE-VENISE AND MINT

MUSCAT DE BEAUMES-DE-VENISE, *Paul Jaboulet Ainé, Rhône*
or ESSENCIA, *Quady, Madera, California*

France

BURGUNDY

Ragoût d'Asperges et Premières Morilles Printanières
RAGOUT OF ASPARAGUS WITH MOREL MUSHROOMS

CHABLIS, *Vocoret, Chablis, Burgundy*
or UNOAKED CHARDONNAY, *Kim Crawford, Marlborough, New Zealand*

Pauchose
RIVER FISH STEW

MEURSAULT 1ER CRU "PERRIÈRES," *Jadot, Côte de Beaune, Burgundy*
or FIANO DI AVELLINO, *Feudi di San Gregorio, Campania, Italy*

Pigeon de Bresse Poêlé au Vin Rouge
BRESSE PIGEON FRIED IN RED WINE

MORGON, *Jean Descombes, Beaujolais, Burgundy*
or GAMAY NOIR, *Whitecliff, Hudson River Region, New York State*

Les Fromages
CHEESES: CHAROLAIS, GRAND VATEL, AISY CENDRE, L'AMI DU CHAMBERTIN

CHARMES-CHAMBERTIN GRAND CRU, *Joseph Roty, Côte de Nuits, Burgundy*
or PINOT NOIR, "BIEN NACIDO VINEYARD," *Byron, Santa Maria Valley, California*

France

PARIS BISTRO MENU WITH LOIRE VALLEY WINES

(The wines of the Loire Valley are much appreciated in the bistros of Paris)

Huîtres Chaudes sur Endives

POACHED OYSTERS ON A BED OF ENDIVE

MUSCADET SEVRE ET MAINE SUR LIE, *Domaine Sauvion, Loire Valley*
or SAUVIGNON BLANC, *Benziger Family, North Coast, California*

Salade Maraîchère aux Truffes Fraîches

WARM GREEN SALAD WITH FRESH TRUFFLES

VOUVRAY SEC, *Marc Brédif, Loire Valley*
or CHENIN BLANC, *Chalone, Monterey, California*

Turbot Grillé avec Beurre Blanc

GRILLED TURBOT WITH A WHITE BUTTER SAUCE

SAVENNIÈRES, GRAND CRU, "CLOS DE LA COULÉE DE SERRANT," *Joly, Loire Valley*
or CHARDONNAY, *Jean Léon, Penedès, Spain*

Rouelle de Veau Braisée aux Cèpes

ET GALETTE DE POMMES DE TERRE

BRAISED VEAL SHANK WITH CÈPE MUSHROOMS AND SAUTÉED POTATO PANCAKE

CHINON, "LE PETITES ROCHES," *Joguet, Loire Valley*
or CABERNET FRANC, "BLOCK THREE EAST,"
Millbrook, Hudson River Region, New York State

Tarte Tatin

UPSIDE-DOWN APPLE TART

COTEAUX DU LAYON, "CLOS STE. CATHERINE," *Domaine Baumard, Loire Valley*
or CHÂTEAU COUTET, *Barsac, Bordeaux, France*

France

BORDEAUX / SOUTHWEST

Les Moules à l'Oseille
MUSSELS WITH SORREL

DOMAINE DE CHEVALIER, *Pessac-Leognan, Bordeaux*
or SÉMILLON, *Cousiño Maucul, Maipo, Chile*

L'Omelette aux Truffes
TRUFFLE OMELETTE

CHÂTEAU DE BELINGRAD, *Bergerac*
or BARBERA D'ASTI, "BRICCO DELL'UCCELLONE," *Braida, Piemonte, Italy*

Le Cassoulet
WHITE BEAN STEW WITH SAUSAGES, TOMATOES, GARLIC, AND MEATS

CHÂTEAU CLOS FOURTET, *St-Émilion, Bordeaux*
or CABERNET FRANC, *Rubicon Estate, Rutherford, California*

Les Fromages
CHEESES: CAMEMBERT, PONT L'EVEQUE, LIVAROT, TOMME DE CANTAL

CHÂTEAU PALMER, *Margaux, Bordeaux*
or MERITAGE, *Rappahannock Cellars, Virginia*

Les Jacques
APPLE PANCAKES

CHÂTEAU LAFAURIE-PEYRAGUEY, *Sauternes, Bordeaux*
or PICOLIT, *Livio Felluga, Friuli–Venezia Giulia, Italy*

France

CHAMPAGNE

Truite à l'Estragon

TROUT IN A COURT-BOUILLON WITH TARRAGON

BLANC DE BLANCS 1ER CRU, *Paul Goerg, Champagne NV*
or BLANC DE BLANCS, *Schramsberg, Napa Valley, California NV*

Agneau Rôti

ROAST LAMB

ROSÉ, "COMTES DE CHAMPAGNE," *Taittinger, Champagne, Vintage*
or ROSÉ, *Ferrari, Trentino, Italy NV*

Salade au Lard

GREEN SALAD WITH BACON LARDONS

EXTRA DRY WHITE STAR, *Moët et Chandon, Champagne NV*
or EXTRA DRY, PROSECCO "JEIO COLMEI," *Bisol, Valdobbiadene, Italy NV*

Les Fromages

CHEESES: CENDRÉ, BRIE, COULOMMIERS, LANGRES

BRUT, "R.D.," *Bollinger, Champagne*
or BRUT, LATE DISGORGED, *Iron Horse, Green Valley of Russian River Valley, California*

Poires à la Champenoise

PEARS POACHED IN CHAMPAGNE, BISCUITS, AND APRICOTS

DEMI-SEC, CORDON VERT, *Mumm, Champagne NV*
or MARIA GOMES ESPUMANTE, *Luis Pato, Bairrada, Portugal NV*

ITALY
Rome

CARCIOFI ALLA GIUDEA
Fried Artichokes Jewish Style

FRASCATI, *Fontana Candida, Lazio*
or RKATSITELI, *Konstantin Frank, Finger Lakes, New York State*

❧

RIGATONI ALL'AMMIRAGLIA
Rigatoni with Squid, Clams, and Mussels

MARINO SUPERIORE SECCO, "ORO," *Paola Di Mauro, Lazio*
or SAUVIGNON BLANC, *Klein Constantia, Stellenbosch, South Africa*

❧

ABBACCHIO ALLA CACCIATORA E FAVE ROMANE
Baby Lamb Cooked with Rosemary, Garlic, Anchovies, Vinegar, and Fava Beans

FIORANO ROSSO, *Boncompagni Ludovisi, Lazio*
or RESERVA, MONTECILLO, *Rioja, Spain*

❧

CREMA CARAMELLA
Caramel Glazed Custard

VELLETRI BIANCO AMABILE, *Consorzio Produttori Vini Velletri, Lazio*
or RIESLING AUSLESE, *Bernakasteler Doktor, Kerpen, Mosel, Germany*

ITALY
Tuscany

INSALATA DI FUNGHI E TARTUFI
Salad of Wild Mushrooms and Truffles

VERNACCIA DI SAN GIMIGNANO, *Teruzzi & Puthod, Tuscany*
or PINOT GRIGIO, *Benessere, Carneros, California*

❧

TONNACCIO AL PESTO E VINAIGRETTE
Grilled Tuna with a Pesto/Vinaigrette Marinade

CHIANTI COLLI FIORENTINO, *Malenchini, Tuscany*
or SANGIOVESE, *Montevina, Amador County, California*

❧

PAPPARDELLE ALLA LEPRE
Egg Noodles with Hare Sauce

CARMIGNANO, *Villa di Capezzana, Tuscany*
or PINOT NOIR, *Panther Creek, Willamette Valley, Oregon*

❧

OSSOBUCO AL VINO E TARRAGONE
Veal Shank in Wine and Tarragon Sauce

BRUNELLO DI MONTALCINO, *Biondi Santi, Tuscany*
or CHATEAU BON PASTEUR, *Pomerol, Bordeaux, France*

❧

BISCOTTI DI PRATO
Almond and Hazelnut Cookies from Prato
VIN SANTO, *Altesino, Tuscany*
or MUSCAT NECTAR, *Tsantali, Samos, Greece*

ITALY
Veneto

BROETO
Venetian Fish Soup

SOAVE CLASSICO, *Inama, Veneto*
or ALBARIÑO, *Morgadio, Rías Baixas, Spain*

INSALATA DI FUNGHI CRUDI
Salad of Raw Mushrooms

BARDOLINO CLASSICO, *Bertani, Veneto*
or BROUILLY, CHÂTEAU DE LA CHAIZE, *Beaujolais, Burgundy, France*

TORRESANI ALLA PERVERADA
Spit-Roasted Pigeons with a Sausage-Liver Herb Sauce Served on Polenta

AMARONE DELLA VALPOLICELLA CLASSICO, *Tommasi, Veneto*
or CÔTE-ROTIE, CÔTE BLONDE ET BRUNE, *Guigal, Rhône, France*

STRUCOLO
Cheese Pastry

RECIOTO DI SOAVE, "LE COLOMBARE," *Pieropan, Veneto NV*
or DEMI-SEC, *H. Piper, Mendoza, Argentina NV*

ITALY
Emilia-Romagna

FRIZON CON SALSICCIA
Vegetable Sauté

ALBANA DI ROMAGNA, *Celli, Emilia-Romagna*
or VIÑA SOL, *Torres, Catalunya, Spain*

⚬

ALI DI POLLO ALLA PARMIGIANA
Chicken Wings Parmesan

LAMBRUSCO DI SORBARA, *Fini, Emilia-Romagna*
or PERIQUITA, *J. M. Fonseca, Terras do Sado, Portugal*

⚬

FEGATO DI VITELLO ALL'ACETO BALSAMICO
Calf's Liver with Balsamic Vinegar

SANGIOVESE DI ROMAGNA RISERVA SUPERIORE, *Cesari, Emilia-Romagna*
or MERLOT, *Gamla, Galilee, Israel*

⚬

BONISSIMA
Emilian Nut Tart

MALVASIA AMABILE, *Terre Rosse, Emilia-Romagna*
or MOSCATO D'ANDREA, *Robert Pecota, Napa Valley, California*

ITALY
Piemonte

BAGNA CAUDA
A "Hot Bath" Dip of Oil, Garlic, and Anchovies Served with Crudités

GAVI DI GAVI, "WHITE LABEL," *La Scolca, Piemonte*
or SAUVIGNON BLANC, *Mulderbosch, Stellenbosch, South Africa*

RANE VERDI
Green Frog's Legs

GRIGNOLINO, *Aldo Conterno, Piemonte*
or ROSÉ OF CABERNET SAUVIGNON, *I'M, Napa Valley, California*

TAJARIN AL TARTUFO
Egg Noodles with Butter, Parmesan, and White Truffles

BARBARESCO, "MONTESTEFANO," *Produttori del Barbaresco, Piemonte*
or GIGONDAS, *Château de Montmirail, Rhône Valley, France*

CINGHIALE BRASATO AL BAROLO
Wild Boar Braised in Barolo

BAROLO, "MARCENASCO," *Renato Ratti, Piemonte*
or OPUS ONE, *Robert Mondavi/Mouton Rothschild, Napa Valley, California*

TOME
Mild Sheep's Milk Cheese from the Langhe

DOLCETTO D'ALBA, *Sandrone, Piemonte*
or CABERNET FRANC, *Schneider, North Fork of Long Island, New York State*

TORTA GIANDUJA
Hazelnut Torte

MOSCATO D'ASTI, *Saracco, Piemonte*
or TASMANIA VINTAGE CUVÉE, *Jansz, Tasmania, Australia*

ITALY
Sicily

POLIPO SICILIANO
Octopus in Garlic and Oil

ANTHÌLIA, *Donnafugata, Sicily*
or SAUVIGNON BLANC, *Cakebread, Napa Valley, California*

❧

DENTICE ALLA GRIGLIA
Grilled Red Snapper

CERASUOLO DI VITTORIA, *Planeta, Sicily*
or VALPOLICELLA CLASSICO SUPERIORE, *Masi, Veneto, Italy*

❧

INSALATA DI ARANCE, FINOCCHI, E OLIVE NERE
Orange, Fennel, and Black Olive Salad

SPEZZATINO DI MONTONE ALLA MENTA
Lamb Stew with Fresh Mint

DUCA ENRICO, *Duca di Salaparuta, Sicily*
or SYRAH, "FOLLY," *Montes, Colchagua Valley, Chile*

❧

CASSATA
Chocolate and Candied Fruit on Sponge Cake

MALVASIA DELLA LIPARI, "CAPO SALINA," *Carlo Hauner, Sicily*
or BLANC DE NOIRS, "WEDDING CUVÉE,"
Iron Horse, Green Valley of Russian River Valley, California

Spain

AND THE BASQUE REGIONS

Tapas:

TORTILLITAS DE CAMARONES GAMBAS AL AJILLO, BUÑUELOS DE BACALAO

APPETIZERS: SHRIMP PANCAKES, PRAWNS IN GARLIC, SALT COD PUFFS

MANZANILLA, "LA GITANA," *Hidalgo, Sanlucar, Jerez*
or SERCIAL, 5 YEAR OLD, *Blandy's, Madeira, Portugal*

Gazpacho Andaluz

COLD TOMATO AND VEGETABLE SOUP

TXACOLI, *Txomin Etxaniz, Guetaria (Basque Country)*
or RIESLING, *Von Kesselstatt Estate, Mosel, Germany*

Zarzuela

SHELLFISH MEDLEY

ALBARIÑO, *Morgadio, Rías Baixas*
or ALBARIÑO, "CLOVER CREEK VINEYARD," *Longoria, Santa Ynez Valley, California*

Conejo al Salmonejo y Habas con Jamón

RABBIT COOKED IN WINE AND VINEGAR WITH HERBS AND SAUTÉED LIMA BEANS WITH HAM

PESQUERA RESERVA, *Alejandro Fernandez, Ribero del Duero*
or LE PERGOLE TORTE, *Montevertine, Tuscany, Italy*

Churros

FRIED PASTRIES

SEMI SECO, "CARTA NEVADA," *Freixenet, Cava NV*
or DEMI-SEC, *Pol Roger, Champagne, France NV*

Portugal

Açorda de Mariscos
BREAD-THICKENED "DRY" SHRIMP SOUP WITH EGGS AND CORIANDER

VINHO VERDE, *Quinta da Aveleda, Minho*
or SAUMUR, *Bouvet-Ladubay, Loire Valley, France*

Sardinas Grelhadas
GRILLED SARDINES

ENCRUZADO, *Quinta dos Roques, Dão*
or TORRONTÉS, *Crios by Susana Balbo, Cafayate, Argentina*

Arroz de Pato com Choriço
E FEIJÃO VERDE COM COENTRO E ALHO
**BRAISED DUCK AND RICE WITH SAUSAGES,
AND GREEN BEANS WITH CORIANDER AND GARLIC**

QUNITA DO RIBEIRINHO PRIMEIRA ESCOLHA, *Luis Pato, Beiras*
or SYRAH, *Justin, Paso Robles, California*

Totya de Laranja
FLOURLESS ORANGE TORTE

MALMSEY, 10 YEAR OLD, *Henriques & Henriques, Madeira*
or PINEAU DES CHARENTES, *François Peyraut, France*

Germany

Heringsalat
HERRING SALAD

RIESLING KABINETT, WEHLENER SONNENUHR, *J.J. Prüm, Mosel*
or VERMENTINO DI GALLURA, *Funtanaliras, Sardinia, Italy*

— ◦ —

Nudelsoupe mit Hühner
NOODLE SOUP WITH CHICKEN

— ◦ —

Schweinebraten mit Pflaumen
MIT ROTKOHL UND KASTANIEN

**ROAST PORK WITH PRUNE STUFFING,
SERVED WITH RED CABBAGE AND CHESTNUTS**

RIESLING, BERG SCHLOSSBERG, *Georg Breuer, Rheingau*
or RIESLING, "EROICA," *Chateau Ste. Michelle, Columbia Valley, Washington State*

— ◦ —

Verweltker Kopfsalat mit Specksosse
WILTED LETTUCE WITH BACON DRESSING

SCHEUREBE SPÄTLESE, *Müller-Catoir, Pfalz*
or CHENIN BLANC, *Fleur du Cap, Stellenbosch, South Africa*

— ◦ —

Apfelalflauf
APPLE SOUFFLÉ

SILVANER EISWEIN, "PENGUIN," *Guntrum, Rheinhessen*
or RIESLING ICEWINE, *Ste. Chapelle, Idaho*

Austria

Erdbeersupe
COLD STRAWBERRY SOUP

GRÜNER VELTLINER, *Schlumberger, Wien*
or MUSCAT, *Léon Beyer, Alsace, France*

Seezungenschnitten in Weisswein
FILLET OF SOLE IN WHITE WINE

RIESLING, DE VITE, *Weinviertel, Niederösterreich*
or VIOGNIER, "WESTSIDE," *Rabbit Ridge, Paso Robles, California*

Hasenbraten mit Rahmsoss und Semmelknödel
ROAST HARE WITH SOUR CREAM SAUCE AND BREAD DUMPLINGS

BLAUFRÄNKIRSCH, *Feiler-Artinger, Neusiedlersee-Hügelland, Burgenland*
or PINOT NOIR, *Coldstream Hills, Yarra Valley, Australia*

Haselnussmakronen
HAZELNUT MACAROONS

SPÄTROT-ROTGIPGLER AUSLESE, *Franz Kurz, Gumpoldskirchen, Thermenregion*
or VIN SANTO, *Il Poggione, Tuscany, Italy*

Greece

Spaŕárangia Latholémono
ASPARAGUS MARINATED IN OLIVE OIL AND LEMON

MALAGOUSIA, *Domaine Gerovassiliou, Epanomi*
or ROERO ARNEIS, *Vietti, Piemonte, Italy*

Maritas Tighanités
TINY FRIED FISH

MOSCHOFILERO, *Domaine Tselepos, Mantinia*
or SAUVIGNON BLANC, *Shaw and Smith, Adelaide Hills, South Australia*

Gouronunópoulo tis Soúvla
SPIT-ROASTED SUCKLING PIG

XINOMAVRO, *Kir-Yanni, Naoussa*
or ZINFANDEL, *Lolonis, Redwood Valley, California*

Panzária Kritiká
BEET SALAD WITH ALLSPICE

Sika Piperáta
PEPPERED DRIED FIGS

MAVRODAPHNE, *Boutari, Peloponnese*
or ELYSIUM, *Quady, Madera, California*

A MIDDLE EAST
EASTERN MEDITERRANEAN FEAST

Ajlouke de Carrotes
TUNISIAN CARROT AND POTATO APPETIZER

CHARDONNAY, *Domaine Clipea, Mornag, Tunisia*
or SANTORINI, *Cigales, Greece*

Shorbat Ads
EGYPTIAN LENTIL SOUP

Samak Mahshi Bi Roz
SYRIAN SWEET AND SOUR FISH STUFFED WITH RICE

SAUVIGNON BLANC, *Yatir, Negev, Israel*
or GEWÜRZTRAMINER, *Navarro, Anderson Valley, California*

Djej M'qualli
MOROCCAN CHICKEN WITH PRESERVED LEMONS AND OLIVES

CHÂTEAU MUSAR BLANC, *Bekaa Valley, Lebanon*
or CHARDONNAY, *Sula, Nashik, India*

Kibbeh
LEBANESE GROUND LAMB WITH ONION, BURGHUL, AND SPICES

SYRAH, "SYROCCO," *Thalvin, Zenata, Morocco*
or MENCIA, "BALTOS," *Dominio de Tares, Bierzo, Spain*

Slat Avocado Vepri Hada
ISRAELI AVOCADO AND CITRUS SALAD

GEWÜRZTRAMINER, LATE HARVEST, "SHA'AL VINEYARD," *Carmel, Upper Galilee, Israel*
or VIGNOLES, *Baldwin, Hudson River Region, New York State*

Ayva Tatlisi
TURKISH BAKED QUINCE

COMMANDARIA ST. JOHN, *KEO, Limassol, Cyprus*
or RIESLING, LATE HARVEST
Hogue Cellars, Columbia Valley, Washington State

SOUTH AFRICA

KALTSCHALE
Curried Fish Stew

CHENIN BLANC, *Ken Forrester Vineyards, Stellenbosch*
or COLOMBELLE, *Caves Plaimont, Vin de Pays de Côtes de Gascogne, France*

BOBOTIE GEELRYS
Baked Ground Lamb Casserole with Yellow Rice and Raisins

SHIRAZ, "SOLITUDE," *Fairview, Paarl*
RUBICON, *Meerlust, Stellenbosch*
or
CROZES-HERMITAGE, "PETITE RUCHE," *Chapoutier, Rhône Valley, France*
RUBICON, *Rubicon Estate, Rutherford, California*

CARAMONGSCRAPS
Cardamom and Coconut Cookies

WEISSER RIESLING, NOBLE LATE HARVEST, *Robertson Winery, Robertson*
or MOSCATO PASSITO DI PANTELLERIA, *Pellegrino, Sicily, Italy*

SOUTH AMERICA

CEBICHE DE ATÚN
Tuna Ceviche

SAUVIGNON BLANC, *Veramonte, Casablanca, Chile*
GRAN BLANCO, *Tacama, Ica, Peru*

or

RIESLING, *Jekel, Monterey, California*
SEYVAL, *Boordy Vineyards, Maryland*

PAVO ASADO Y PURÉE DE BATATA Y JENGIBRE
Roasted Wild Turkey with Bread and Nut Stuffing
with Sweet Potato and Ginger Purée

MALBEC, "ULTRA," *Kaiken, Mendoza, Argentina*
CABERNET SAUVIGNON, "DON MELCHOR," *Concha y Toro, Maipo, Chile*

or

MERLOT, "SEVEN HILLS VINEYARD," *L'Ecole No. 41, Walla Walla Valley, Washington State*
THE McNAB, *Bonterra, Mendocino, California*

BUDIN DE SANTA ROSA
Farina and Almond Pudding with Blackberry Sauce

D'SEC, *Bodegas Chandon, Mendoza, Argentina NV*

or

CÈLEBRÉ, *Chateau Frank, Finger Lakes, New York State NV*

THE UNITED STATES
New England/Northeast

ROAST BREAST OF DUCK WRAPPED IN SMOKED BACON WITH CIDER VINEGAR SAUCE
served with Wild Rice Pancakes and Glazed Onions

PINOT NOIR, "BLOCK FIVE EAST," *Millbrook, Hudson River Region, New York State*
PINOT NOIR, *Sakonnet Vineyards, Southeastern New England, Rhode Island*

or

MERCUREY 1ER CRU MONOPOLE, "CLOS DES MYGLANDS,"
Faiveley, Côte Chalonnaise, Burgundy, France
CÔTES DU RHÔNE, "LES ABEILLES," *Colombo, Rhône Valley, France*

MIXED GREENS WITH RED ONIONS, CHIOGGA BEETS, BLUE CHEESE, AND OLIVES
SAUVIGNON BLANC, "MUDD VINEYARD,"
Channing Daughters, Hamptons Long Island, New York State

or

SAUVIGNON BLANC, "ICON," *Nobilo, Marlborough, New Zealand*

PUMPKIN PIE
RIESLING, *Red Newt Cellars, Finger Lakes, New York State*

or

MUSCAT DE FRONTIGNAN, *Domaines Gavoty, Provence, France*

THE UNITED STATES
Texas/Southwest

ANCHO NAVY BEAN SOUP

SOUTHWEST CAESAR SALAD WITH PAN-FRIED CRAB CAKES

BRUT, *Gruet, New Mexico NV*

or

BRUT, CRÉMANT D'ALSACE, *Willm, Alsace, France*

❧

TEXAS HUNTER'S QUAIL DINNER

CHARDONNAY RESERVE, *Fall Creek, Texas*
CABERNET SAUVIGNON, "RISING STAR VINEYARD," *Llano Estacado, Texas*

or

CONDRIEU, *Guigal, Rhône Valley, France*
RESERVA, *Quinta do Crasto, Douro, Portugal*

❧

BANANA SOFT TACOS WITH PAPAYA AND STRAWBERRY SALSAS

SPARKLING ROSÉ, *Cap Rock, Texas*

or

SPARKLING ROSÉ, *Croser, Clare Valley, South Australia*

THE UNITED STATES
Cajun / Creole

CRAWFISH PIE

CHENIN BLANC, *Chappellet, Napa Valley, California*

or

NAIA, *Bodegas Aldial, Rueda, Spain*

CHICKEN AND ANDOUILLE SMOKED SAUSAGE GUMBO

FUMÉ BLANC, "LA PETITE ÉTOILE VINEYARD," *Chateau St. Jean, Russian River Valley, California*
PINOT NOIR, *Wild Horse, Central Coast, California*

or

ROSÉ, MULDERBOSCH, *Stellenbosch, South Africa*
PERNAND-VERGELESSES, *Bonneau du Martray, Côte de Beaune, Burgundy, France*

GREENS IN HARD-BOILED EGG AND HOT PEPPER VINEGAR DRESSING

SAUVIGNON BLANC, *Honig, Napa Valley, California*

or

BRUT, *Parès Baltá, Cava, Spain NV*

SPICED PECAN CAKE WITH PECAN FROSTING

PORT, *Ficklin, Madera, California*

or

PORT, LBV, *Taylor Fladgate, Douro, Portugal, Vintage*

THE UNITED STATES
Spa Style

GRILLED SHRIMP AND SEA SCALLOPS
with Eggplant and Peppers

CHARDONNAY, *Inniskillin, Ontario, Canada*
or
CHARDONNAY, "LA PIETRA," *Cabreo, Tuscany, Italy*

CORNISH HENS WITH WILD RICE STUFFING AND MERLOT SAUCE

MERLOT, *Shafer, Napa Valley, California*
or
CLOS RENÉ, *Pomerol, Bordeaux, France*

WILTED SPINACH AND MUSHROOM SALAD

PINEAPPLE MADAGASCAR

ELECTRA, *Quady, Madera, California*
or
MOSCATO D'ASTI, "NIVOLE," *Chiarlo, Piemonte, Italy*

THE UNITED STATES
Vegetarian

ROASTED PEPPER AND CORN SOUP WITH BASIL

UNOAKED CHARDONNAY, *Domaine Chandon, Carneros, California*
or
CHARDONNAY, "OLD VINES," *Lenz, North Fork of Long Island, New York State*

RAVIOLI FILLED WITH EGGPLANT, ROASTED GARLIC, AND ROMANO CHEESE

PINOT NOIR, *Erath, Willamette Valley, Oregon*
or
SYRAH, "ALPHA," *Montes, Colchagua Valley, Chile*

LETTUCES, WATERCRESS, AND ESCAROLE

with Goat Cheese and Sun-Dried Tomatoes

APPLE-RHUBARB CRISP

RIESLING ICEWINE, *Peller Estates, Niagara Peninsula, Canada*
or
BRACHETTO D'ACQUI, "ROSA REGALE," *Banfi, Piemonte, Italy*

HEART

MIND

STRESS

ANTIOXIDANTS

PHENOLICS

research

MODERATION

FRENCH PARADOX

HDL

exercise

AGE

LIFESTYLE

RESVERATROL

mediterranean diet

WINE AND HEALTH

IN THE NEW TESTAMENT, Timothy, on the advice of his mentor, the apostle Paul, said to "drink no longer water, but use a little wine for thy stomach's sake and thine often infirmities." The Bible, like far more ancient civil and religious texts, is replete with references to the healing properties of wine and its positive place in spiritual life and practice. The ancients knew that drinking wine in moderation was an aid to health. They therefore encouraged, even celebrated, its use as a daily beverage.

More than two hundred years ago, Thomas Jefferson, the third president of the United States and an ardent lover of wine, spoke in support of wine as a national beverage to be consumed in moderation. Jefferson said, "No nation is drunken where wine is cheap; and none sober, where the dearness of wine substitutes ardent spirits as the common beverage. It is, in truth, the only antidote to the bane of whiskey.... Who will not prefer it? Its extended use will carry health and comfort to a much enlarged circle."

In the modern world, Timothy's dictum and Tom's declaration have been accepted as gospel by many, but questioned or rejected by many more. The entire Muslim world officially eschews the consumption of alcohol, including wine (*alcool* is Arabic for "like a monster," certainly not an incentive to imbibe). This was not always the case; the physicians of ancient Persia, Sumeria, Egypt, and Arabia prescribed wine as a tonic to help cure many ills. The oldest known pharmacopoeia, written on clay tablets by the

Sumerians and dated to 2200 B.C., cites wine as humankind's oldest documented medicine. Even after the Koran became the principal religious text of Muslims, Arab doctors continued to prescribe wine, this "device of the devil," but strictly as medicine. Other religions inveigh against the evils of drink, and even in those societies where alcohol is not banned, the secular consumption of alcohol, including wine, is often viewed as a negative trait.

Although much of the Mediterranean world is peopled by Muslims, the European sector of the Mediterranean countries—Italy, Spain, southern France, and Greece in particular—has for centuries embraced wine as a part of a healthy daily diet. These countries have rich wine histories and wine cultures and produce more wine than any other area of the world, some of it very fine. Drinking wine with meals is part of daily life in the European Mediterranean, and few doubt the overall health benefits of a glass or two of wine each day, coupled with the world's highest per capita consumption of fruits, grains, and vegetables. In this diet, most fat comes from a virtually unrestricted intake of olive oil, a largely monounsaturated fat.

In the United States, at least until recently, wine and other alcoholic beverages have been regarded with caution, with heavy emphasis placed on the dangers of overindulgence. A time when all alcoholic beverages were illegal in the United States is still within living memory for some. From 1920 to 1933 Prohibition was the law of the land,

and the production and sale of alcoholic beverages, save for religious observance, were banned. Today there are still dry towns and counties, and the nation as a whole continues to cast a wary eye on drinking, even if that drinking is largely confined to a glass or two of wine with a meal. This picture, however, is beginning to change.

As Americans have traveled more, as the culinary culture of a nation of immigrants is celebrated in restaurants and homes, and as we have developed our own American wine culture, there is strong interest in wine as part of the meal. Similarly, as Americans have become interested in healthy patterns of eating and drinking, they have looked to the Mediterranean diet as a model to follow. We know the benefits of fruits, vegetables, and grains. The consumption of olive oil is at an all-time high in the United States. Pastas (including risotto and other rice dishes) and pizzas are some of the most ubiquitous comfort foods, along with grilled or roasted vegetables. Because wine is part of the classic Mediterranean diet, it is beginning to be seen as what it always has been when consumed in moderation: a healthy beverage.

WINE AND HEALTH: THE OVERALL PICTURE

As WE LOOK at life and lifestyle in the early twenty-first century, here is what we find about the links between wine consumption and health, based on the most reliable scientific data as of 2010.

- Moderate intake of alcohol, especially wine, is associated with improved cardiovascular health.
- Alcohol exerts protective effects on the heart by raising high-density lipoprotein (HDL) cholesterol, lowering low-density lipoprotein (LDL) cholesterol, and inhibiting blood clotting.
- The antioxidant properties of the phenolic compounds in red wine, particularly a group of **FLAVONOID** polyphenols known as procyanidins, greatly reduce the risk of atherosclerosis and heart attack by a factor of as much as 60 percent.

- Moderate drinking reduces risk of both ischemic strokes and hemorrhagic strokes. People who abstain from alcohol and heavy drinkers may be at almost twice the risk for ischemic stroke as moderate drinkers.
- Excessive alcohol consumption is associated with hypertension, but low to moderate consumption (one to two drinks per day) may actually assist in lowering blood pressure and, among men, lower the risk of heart attack by a factor of 30 percent.
- Because of wine's antioxidant properties, specifically the resveratrol in red wine and the bioflavonoids in red grapes, wine may be helpful in cancer prevention and suppression. It is also useful in lowering stress in cancer patients.
- Moderate alcohol consumption leads to higher levels of cognition and memory.
- Moderate daily intake of wine, tea, and dark chocolate by elderly men and women can lead to enhanced cognition and memory.
- In several studies, light to moderate wine drinking has been shown to be highly effective in helping reduce dementia by as much as 56 percent over those who do not consume wine. Results improved when light to moderate wine drinking was part of a traditional Mediterranean diet (see opposite).
- Red wine (and tea) have shown promising results in helping patients with type 2 diabetes properly metabolize sugars and starches. Also, the antioxidant resveratrol, found in red wines, may help prevent type 2 diabetes.
- Researchers have found that starting to drink a moderate amount of wine during midlife, even after not drinking during younger years, is beneficial to the heart. In one study, wine drinkers were found to have a 68 percent less chance of having cardiovascular illness. Also, the antioxidants in red wine help improve blood circulation and improve cholesterol levels in people of all ages.
- Dry red wines made from particular grapes—Cabernet Sauvignon, Merlot, Pinot Noir, and Syrah—have been found to assist in killing harmful bacteria, including *E. coli* and *Salmonella* strains, while not killing off beneficial bacteria (probiotics). Wine consumption inhibits the growth of *Helicobacter pylori*, the bacterium that causes ulcers, with best results (30 percent less bacteria) shown among those who consumed three glasses of wine per day.

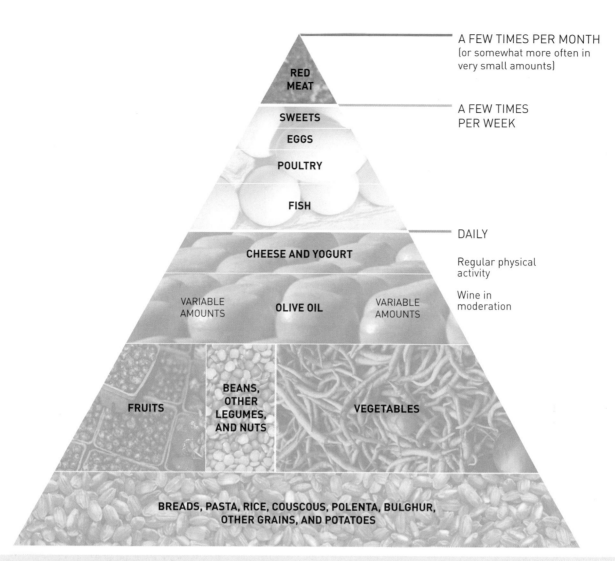

RED MEAT

A FEW TIMES PER MONTH
(or somewhat more often in
very small amounts)

SWEETS

EGGS

POULTRY

FISH

A FEW TIMES
PER WEEK

CHEESE AND YOGURT

DAILY

Regular physical
activity

Wine in
moderation

VARIABLE
AMOUNTS

OLIVE OIL

VARIABLE
AMOUNTS

FRUITS

BEANS,
OTHER
LEGUMES,
AND NUTS

VEGETABLES

BREADS, PASTA, RICE, COUSCOUS, POLENTA, BULGHUR,
OTHER GRAINS, AND POTATOES

THE MEDITERRANEAN DIET

Over the last hundred years, the industrialized world has seen a dramatic shift in the way we get sick. A century ago, most people who did not die of old age died from infectious diseases. Today, people are far more likely to die of chronic diseases—heart disease, stroke, cancer.

Diet can be a major culprit in the development of chronic diseases, and it can also be a path to better health. Fortunately, several cultural models allow us to eat a healthy diet and still enjoy the pleasures of the table. One of these is the Mediterranean diet, which calls for daily consumption of bread, pasta, and grains, as well as fruits, vegetables, legumes, and nuts. The primary source of dietary fat is a monounsaturated fat, such as olive oil, plus cheese and yogurt. Fish is consumed three or four times per week; poultry, eggs, and sweets are eaten only a few times per week. Little red meat is consumed as part of the traditional Mediterranean diet, only a few times per

month. Integral parts of this regimen are regular exercise and the consumption of wine in moderation.

The Traditional Healthy Mediterranean Diet Pyramid presents a cultural model for Americans to follow. It emphasizes grains, fruits, vegetables, legumes, olive oil, and fermented dairy products while deemphasizing foods high in processed sugars, animal proteins, and fats. Notice that the pyramid includes daily exercise and a glass of wine with meals. This pyramid was jointly developed by the World Health Organization (WHO) European Regional Office, the WHO/FAO Collaborating Center for Nutritional Epidemiology at the Harvard School of Public Health, and the Oldways Preservation and Exchange Trust in Boston (Oldways sponsors seminars and conferences about issues surrounding food, traditional diets, and sustainable agriculture). The pyramid has been endorsed by The Culinary Institute of America.

- Both white and red wine can kill streptococci, the bacteria that can cause sore throats ("strep throat"), as well as tooth decay. Scientists found that the acids present in grapes and wine (including those acids produced from malolactic fermentation) are able to kill the harmful bacteria.
- Adults who drink a glass or two of wine per day on a regular basis can cut their risk of catching a cold by as much as 50 percent, compared with adults who abstain from drinking wine or those who drink beer or spirits.
- Quercetin, an anti-inflammatory polyphenol found in red wine, has been shown to reduce the growth of prostate cancer and the replication of the influenza virus.
- Antioxidants in grape pomace (skins, pits, stems) have been shown to inhibit the growth of bacteria that cause plaque in teeth and gums.
- Moderate daily wine consumption is actually beneficial to liver health, lowering by 50 percent the incidence of nonalcoholic fatty liver disease (NAFLD).
- Light to moderate wine consumption—one to two glasses per day—results in a lower risk of kidney failure and kidney cancer than abstaining from alcohol.
- Resveratrol inhibits the growth of tumors in the prostate.
- Resveratrol has been found to enhance life and to suppress the ravages of aging, including keeping the heart, eyes, kidneys, and bones healthier.
- Resveratrol has been shown to be a useful tool in obesity research, as it prevents the development of fat cells, which can be linked to type 2 diabetes and clogged arteries.
- Moderate wine consumption may reduce the risk of rheumatoid arthritis.
- Researchers are beginning to develop resveratrol-based dietary supplements, medicines, and patches as a promising new part of the pharmaceutical industry.
- Resveratrol shows potential in attacking cancer cells, making chemotherapy more effective for cancer patients, including pancreatic cancer, which is particularly resistant to chemotherapy.

How is it that wine, which people drink mostly for pleasure or as a daily beverage to accompany meals, has become such an important focus of health research?

THE FRENCH PARADOX: THE HISTORY OF THE RESEARCH

FRANCE IS OFTEN THOUGHT to be the land of artery-clogging foie gras, rich cheeses, and buttery croissants, and in truth it is. Why, then, does France, along with the other Mediterranean nations, have some of the lowest rates of heart disease—America's number one killer—in the industrialized world? The answer may lie in a glass of wine.

Scientists and researchers in Europe and the United States have for a long time linked certain elements in alcohol with a lowered risk of heart disease and some cancers. It is a scientific certainty that for most people, one to three drinks per day are associated with improved health indices, on both the personal and the national levels. But more recently, research has begun to focus on the specific benefits of wine, especially red wine, as opposed to other alcoholic beverages.

Serge Renaud, Ph.D., now retired as director of the Nutrition and Cardiology Department of the French National Institute of Health Research, studied the relationship between alcohol, especially wine, and human health for almost sixty years and is considered a pioneer in the field. Dr. Renaud posited that the moderate consumption of wine is an important element in overall health. He

Serge Renaud, Ph.D., who retired as director of the Nutrition and Cardiology Department of the French National Institute of Health Research, is considered the father of the "French paradox."

pointed out that the French consume the same amount of dairy (and butterfat, which has a definite link to heart disease) as the British and the Americans do, if not more, yet the French are 66 percent less likely to suffer fatal heart attacks or develop heart disease. Of course, neither the British nor the Americans consume a great deal of wine on a per capita basis, and until recently, citizens of both countries preferred beer and spirits (that changed in the United States in 2008). Dr. Renaud claims that moderate consumption of wine with meals coupled with an absolute prohibition against binge drinking is a prescription for a healthy heart, lower rates of cancer and stroke, and even fewer accidents.

How much is moderate? Dr. Renaud has a surprising answer. "For every 18 milliliters [about half an ounce] of red wine you drink in a week, you decrease your risk of heart disease by 1 percent. It's only a drop of wine, just a taste, almost an empty glass. You don't have to drink it; just sniffing it is enough."[1]

In June of 1994, Arthur Klatsky, M.D., then the chief of the Division of Cardiology at Kaiser Permanente Medical Center in Oakland, California, and a pioneer in American research on the relationship between alcohol and heart disease, made a presentation in California echoing Renaud's findings. Citing data collected from more than a hundred thousand patients since 1974, Dr. Klatsky confirmed that light to moderate drinkers (less than three drinks per day, with a drink defined as 12 ounces/360 milliliters of beer,

Arthur Klatsky, M.D. (left), of the Division of Cardiology at Kaiser Permanente Medical Center in Oakland, California; Michael Criqui, M.D., M.P.H. (right), of the Department of Community and Family Medicine at the University of California, San Diego

5 ounces/150 milliliters of wine, or 1.5 ounces/45 milliliters of spirits) had a lower occurrence of heart disease and fatal heart attacks than nondrinkers or heavy drinkers. Moderate to heavy drinkers also had fewer occurrences of hospitalization than nondrinkers or very light drinkers.

Dr. Klatsky pointed out that wine drinkers fared slightly better than beer drinkers, who fared slightly better than spirit drinkers, when it comes to heart disease. He states, "We can't conclude that the wine itself gives greater protection; it may be caused by the lifestyle of wine drinkers," citing studies that found 75 percent of all wine is consumed at home and 80 percent of that consumption is with meals, about a glass and a half with each meal. Klatsky stated that "if you drink any alcohol two or more days per week, you are at lower risk for a fatal heart attack."[2]

Echoing Dr. Klatsky's findings, the American College of Cardiology, an esteemed public health group, found that "individuals reporting moderate amounts of alcohol intake—approximately one to three drinks daily—have a 40 to 50 percent reduction in coronary artery disease risk compared with individuals who are abstinent." At the organization's 1996 conference, the reporting researchers credited half of the risk reduction to the fact that alcohol consumption increases blood levels of HDL, often called "good cholesterol." Significantly, the group singled out wine as possibly more beneficial than other alcoholic beverages, reporting that red wine inhibits platelet activity—a component of the formation of plaque in the arteries.

While the world's scientists have been exploring the possibility that wine has unique health effects for at least the last thirty-five years, it was a nonscientist who captured the attention of the health-conscious, wine-drinking American public with his reports on "the French paradox." Morley Safer, a wine-loving coanchor of the television newsmagazine *60 Minutes*, posed this question in a November 1991 interview with Serge Renaud: "Why is it that the French, who eat 30 percent more fat than we do, suffer fewer heart attacks, even though they smoke more and exercise less? All you have to do is look at the numbers. If you're a middle-aged American man, your chances of dying of a heart attack are three times greater than a Frenchman of the same age."[3]

While Safer did mention that the French diet included more fruits, vegetables, and bread than the American diet, he reserved his greatest enthusiasm for red wine: "There has been for years the belief by doctors in many countries

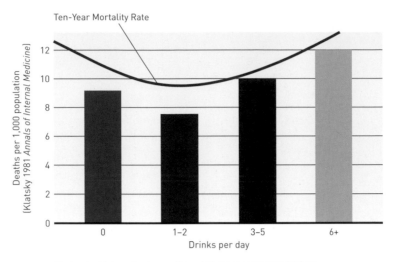

Ten-Year Mortality Rate

Moderate drinkers live longer than abstainers or heavier drinkers, according to many epidemiological studies, with the lowest risk of mortality found in those who drink one to two drinks a day.

TOTAL MORTALITY RATE COMPARED WITH ALCOHOL CONSUMPTION

that alcohol, in particular red wine, reduces the risk of heart disease. Now it's been all but confirmed."[4]

The effect of the "French Paradox" broadcast on the American wine-buying public was dramatic and measurable. The day after the broadcast, sales of red wine began to skyrocket, and for the month following the report, sales were up 44 percent (about 2.5 million bottles) over the same month of the previous year. When the report was rebroadcast in July 1992, sales of red wine went up 49 percent for that month. Sales of red wine for the entire year following the initial broadcast were up by about 39 percent.[5] It seemed as though a portion of the American public embraced red wine as the health food of the 1990s, and we've never stopped.

According to R. Curtis Ellison, M.D., chief of the Evans Section of Preventive Medicine and Epidemiology and professor of medicine and public health at Boston University School of Medicine, although per capita wine consumption is falling in France and other European countries overall, countries that consume the most wine (France, Italy, Spain, Greece, and Switzerland) have the lowest rates of heart disease, and countries that consume the least wine per capita (Scotland, Northern Ireland, Finland, New Zealand, Eastern Europe countries, the United Kingdom, the United States) have the highest rates.

Dr. Ellison, who has conducted his own research and worked with Dr. Renaud, also points out an important fact about patterns of consumption in Europe. Although overall consumption of wine is falling in France and Italy,

"death rates from heart disease in both of these countries are less than half the rate of the United States and falling." Dr. Ellison adds, "If you look at people who are in the heart disease risk group, over age 45 or so, about 80 percent of them are regular consumers of wine. All the reports I've seen indicate that it's young people who have stopped drinking, or never started. And that's not the group that has heart attacks."[6]

Dr. Ellison is perhaps the member of the scientific community who is most outspoken about the connection between moderate alcohol consumption and a lowered risk of heart disease. "Based on all of the available research data, we can conclude that abstaining from alcohol, that

R. Curtis Ellison, M.D., professor of medicine and public health at Boston University School of Medicine

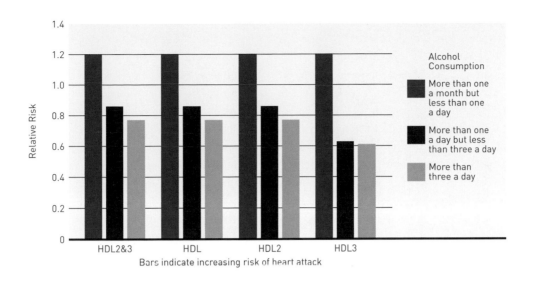

being a nondrinker, should be added to the list of important risk factors for coronary heart disease." Citing positive data from research suggesting that moderate alcohol consumption on a daily basis is good for the heart, Dr. Ellison observes "the results suggest that you should consume alcohol on a regular basis. Some might even say that it is dangerous to go 24 hours without a drink."[7]

THE CURRENT DATA

PROTECTIVE QUALITIES OF RED WINE

ALTHOUGH ALL ALCOHOLIC BEVERAGES, when consumed in moderation, protect the heart, red wine contains a number of nonalcoholic elements that have been identified by the scientific community as particularly protective for the body as a whole. These phenolic compounds, which have to do with the color and tannins in grapes, are all antioxidants. When LDL, also called "bad cholesterol," is oxidized in the blood, plaque can form on the inside of the arteries, which can lead to atherosclerosis (hardening and

clogging of the arteries) and heart disease. Antioxidants such as beta-carotene and vitamin E, along with the phenols in red wine, inhibit the oxidation of LDL and increase levels of HDL ("good cholesterol"). These antioxidants can also help prevent platelet aggregation—clumping of cells that can lead to blood clots, which in turn can lead to stroke and heart disease (see figure above). A 1990 French study indicated that only red wine, unique among other alcoholic beverages, both decreased platelet aggregation and increased HDL levels (olive oil has been shown to have the same effect).

Resveratrol is a natural fungicide found on the skin of red wine grapes (almost none is found on white wine grapes or white or red table grapes). The concentration of resveratrol in red wine is directly proportional to the amount of fungus and disease the grapes were exposed to during the growing season. Quercetin (which is also found in tea, onions, and apples) and catechin are other naturally occurring constituents of red wine grapes, and both are far more abundant than resveratrol. Catechin, quercetin, and resveratrol are all phenolic antioxidants.

Andrew Waterhouse, Ph.D., professor and chair of viticulture and enology at the University of California, Davis, believes that the phenolic antioxidants in wine can prevent atherosclerosis and inhibit LDL oxidation. Dr. Waterhouse notes that the phenols are related to astringency and bitterness in wine—the tastes of tannin. He notes that "your tongue is a good indicator of their level."[8]

Terrence Leighton, Ph.D., professor and chair of the division of microbiology and immunology at the University of California, Berkeley, has also done extensive research on the effect of quercetin on the body. He notes that this phenolic antioxidant inhibits LDL oxidation, lowers cigarette-smoke toxicity, and exhibits certain anticarcinogenic effects by inhibiting the transformation of normal cells into malignant cells. Quercetin enhances the activity of anticancer agents in the body and has been shown to inhibit mammary cancer in rats and skin cancer in mice.[9]

Both Dr. Waterhouse and Dr. Leighton cite a study by Dutch epidemiologist Michael Hertog, Ph.D., of eight hundred men over a five-year period. Those men who consumed 16 to 30 milligrams of quercetin a day, mostly from tea, onions, and apples, were found to be only half as likely to get heart disease as those who consumed smaller daily amounts of quercetin. Two glasses of red wine per day provide more than 30 milligrams of quercetin per day, as does the basic Mediterranean diet, which includes wine.

Curtis Ellison is also very impressed with the data suggesting that tannins, polyphenols, and other acknowledged antioxidants present in red wine, such as resveratrol, quercetin, and catechin, are beneficial to heart health. He cites a study conducted at the University of Wisconsin indicating that moderate intake of red wine prevents blood platelets from forming a blood clot. White wine had no such effect.[10]

In 2006, Roger Corder, professor of experimental therapeutics at the William Harvey Research Institute of London, published the book *The Wine Diet* (renamed *The Red Wine Diet* in 2007, when it was published in the United States). Corder writes that, based on his experiments with his research team, it is in fact a polyphenol in wine that is beneficial to the heart and blood vessels, but Corder also concludes from the same data that it is not resveratrol nor quercetin nor catechin that is the most important polyphenol.

According to Corder, procyanidin is the polyphenol that helps inhibit the overproduction of endothelin-1, a peptide (a limited chain of amino acids) that aids in preventing blood clots and is beneficial to the overall health of human veins and arteries. Excessive amounts of endothelin-1, however, can narrow and constrict arteries and can lead to hypertension and heart disease.

Corder, whose research was originally published in the November 30, 2006, issue of *Nature* and serialized in the British newspaper *The Daily Telegraph*, rejected the idea that resveratrol, which has been the focus of so much wine-and-health research, could possibly assist in the maintenance of a healthy heart, because the amount of resveratrol needed to do so would require the consumption of more than 200 bottles of red wine daily. On this point, most researchers, especially those who have worked with mice rather than human subjects, agree. Resveratrol is a promising antioxidant, but it must be taken in concentrations far greater than those found naturally in red wine; this is why there is a concerted effort by the pharmaceutical industry to produce a "resveratrol pill."

Corder and his team found over the course of years of research that it is procyanidin (which is also found in dark chocolate) that is able to curb the overproduction of endothelin-1 by as much as 50 percent, even in the concentrations found in red wine. But Corder went a step further in his research, a step that has caught the attention of wine consumers and producers all over the world.

Tasting wines and analyzing their levels of procyanidin, Corder and his researchers discovered that not all red wines are created equal, at least when it comes to the suppression of endothelin-1 production. Corder discovered that dry red wines with high tannin levels, mostly made in traditional ways, which includes extended skin, stem, and seed maceration during fermentation, had much higher procyanidin levels than fruit-driven, softer wines of both the Old World and New World.

Corder states that of all the hundreds of wines he tested, Madiran, a red wine from southwestern France made primarily from the Tannat grape, has the highest procyanidin levels, followed by a number of red wines produced in the Nuoro province of Sardinia, and the Gers region, also in southwestern France. (The Tannat variety is now the most important red wine grape in Uruguay; see page 224.) He also had similar findings for some Malbec wines from Argentina, red wines from Montefalco in the Italian region of Umbria, and wines from Mount Veeder in California's Napa Valley produced by The Hess Collection.

Corder found that most mass-produced "modern" wines are lower in procyanidins, due to shorter tannin-extraction times in the winery and longer ripening cycles in the vineyard, leading to higher sugars in the grapes and higher alcohol levels in the wines. The higher alcohol content can lead to an unintentional overconsumption of alcohol by the wine drinker, diminishing any health benefits from the wine.[11]

As with so many other wine-and-health researchers, Corder recommends a diet that is based on the traditional

Mediterranean model (though with a healthy daily dose of dark chocolate included), and he recommends that wine should be consumed with healthy meals. Drinking wine with meals, as part of an overall healthy lifestyle that includes exercise and fresh foods, is a thematic thread that runs through so much of this research.

PUBLIC POLICY ISSUES

MANY PHYSICIANS CONCUR that after sixty years of research into diet and heart disease, there are only two findings that consistently appear in the experimental and clinical literature: Exercise is good for human beings, and so is moderate drinking. This being the case, will doctors prescribe a glass or two of wine for their patients, much as they prescribe regular physical activity, as part of a healthy lifestyle?

Arthur Klatsky believes that because of the potential for abuse and possible hereditary tendencies toward alcoholism in some people, "indiscriminate advice to nondrinkers to take up alcohol for health reasons is inappropriate." He has said that if a patient already drinks in moderation, it is appropriate to mention that a glass of wine with a meal will do no harm. Klatsky recognizes the truth of an old German proverb: "There are more old wine drinkers than old doctors." However, he also believes that public policy surrounding wine and health is a complex and thorny issue, and he illustrates the quandary with another anonymous quote: "For every complex problem there is a solution that is short, neat, and wrong."[12]

Other physicians are far more cautious and for a variety of medical, ethical, and legal reasons will not prescribe a glass or two of wine or a drink before dinner to their patients. Dr. Ellison claims that "we've known for quite some time that alcohol tends to decrease the risk of heart disease" and says he can think of no other drug that is more effective than alcohol in protecting the heart. He admits that until recently, the medical community, for reasons of self-protection and concern for the potential of abuse by patients, has not been trumpeting the consistent results of alcohol and health studies: "We hadn't been suppressing it, but we hadn't been making it widely known either." In an interview, Dr. Ellison suggested that "if alcohol could be dispensed in a pill"—the medical model we're most comfortable with—"it would be the most-prescribed drug for avoiding fatal heart disease."[13] In the spirit of moderation, Ellison, a true pioneer in the field of wine-and-health research, believes that doctors should consider advising normally healthy, middle-aged American men to "consider the advantages of washing down their aspirin with a glass of Cabernet" to reduce their risk of heart disease.[14]

Most doctors agree that their concern for even the remote possibility of alcohol abuse outweighs the scientific evidence that light to moderate drinking is good for the vast majority of their patients. However, there are some physicians who, given the right circumstances, will mention that a glass or two of wine for people *who already drink in moderation* is perfectly acceptable. In the March 15, 1994, issue of *Wine Spectator*, as part of an issue dedicated to wine and health, Jane Shufer quotes fifteen doctors in different specialties about their attitudes toward wine. Most of the doctors, who all enjoy wine themselves, generally see little problem with recommending moderate consumption of wine to patients who are moderate drinkers.[15]

A lot of what we know about heart disease and diet is this: Men are far more likely to die of heart disease at younger ages than are premenopausal women, and both moderate alcohol consumption and exercise are good for the heart. These facts may have prompted Dr. Norman Kaplan to joke, "To live the longest, be a woman who jogs to the liquor store every day."[16]

ALCOHOL AND WOMEN

WOMEN, TOO, are candidates for heart disease, though in somewhat smaller percentags and later in life then men. Elizabeth M. Whelan, Sc.D., M.P.H., president of the American Council on Science and Health, notes that about 2.5 ounces/75 milliliters of an 80 proof (40 percent) alcoholic beverage (the rough equivalent of two glasses of wine) each day can decrease a woman's chances of dying from heart disease by 50 percent. Dr. Whelan recommends aerobic exercise as well and has said, "The best way to prevent a heart attack may be to run from bar to bar."[17]

Research on the connection between women's health and alcohol consumption is not nearly as exhaustive as studies done on men. Women metabolize alcohol somewhat

MERLOT

IINS DU

FENDANT PÉ
VINIFIÉ SU
SION APPELLATION D'OR
SWISS WHIT

LES MUI

OBERT GIL

ESTATE

COUSIÑO

LE DIX

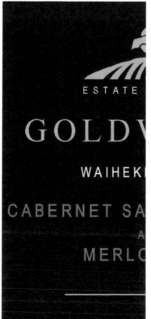

ESTATE

GOLDW

WAIHEKI

CABERNET SA

A

MERLO

PART 5
WINE SERVICE AND STORAGE

IN PART 5, WE OFFER ADVICE and suggestions on wine service, purchasing, storage, and wine lists to both consumers and professionals. The authors gratefully acknowledge the contributions of the many respected wine professionals whose insightful quotations and real-life experience enhance these chapters.

Chapter 16 details formal professional service in a restaurant setting and offers guidance for serving wine at home or in another casual setting. Note, for example, that an expensive bottle of Cabernet Sauvignon will taste harsh if served too cold. If served too warm, the bubbles of Champagne can be rough rather than pleasant. Also covered in this chapter are the dynamics of customer expectations and proper wine service in a restaurant.

We often hear feedback from students, friends, and consumers about how difficult it is to buy wine. Chapter 17 demystifies the purchasing of wine. For the majority of us who just want the best "bang for our buck," we urge our readers to go off the beaten path for value, and we give specific examples of value-driven wines at moderate prices. We also provide sample cellars that include some of those wines, and we offer lists of essential wines for the wine connoisseur or collector.

In Chapter 17, we give advice on wine storage and on keeping track of what is in the cellar. The section on inventory control, maintaining par stock, and receiving wines will be of particular interest to restaurateurs and wine retailers.

Chapter 18 offers consumers a chance to enhance their purchasing power by finding the "sweet spot" on a wine list: the price range where the markup is least egregious and most fair to the restaurant guest. For restaurateurs using the wine list as a marketing tool, there are numerous approaches and guidelines offered.

The basic information and professional insights offered in Part 5 are intended to educate our readers, enrich your experience of drinking wine, and save you money.

GLASSWARE

GUERIDON

DECANT

TEMPERATURE

APERITIF

breathing

SOMMELIER

TARTRATE
CRYSTALS

SEDIMENT

CORKSCREW

UNCORKING

RESPECT

CORKED

SCREWCAP

WINE SERVICE

THIS CHAPTER KICKS OFF with some simple service suggestion for enjoying wine in a casual setting. When you break it down, the wine-tasting experience is as much about the way we serve the wine as actually sipping it. If glasses are dirty, the wine too cold, or the company unbearable, it can ruin the experience of enjoying wine. It all comes down to seven simple steps.

SEVEN SIMPLE SERVICE STEPS

1 **SERVE THE WINE AT THE RIGHT TEMPERATURE** Sparkling, white, and rosé wines should be served well chilled. An hour or two in the refrigerator is sufficient, and an **ICE BUCKET** can keep the wine cold. Leaving one of these wines out on the table without maintaining a cool temperature will result in a wine tasting hot instead of refreshing. The reason for this is that the smooth marriage of acidity and alcohol in wine served at cool temperatures becomes rocky at higher temperatures. The opposite is true of full-bodied red wines such as fine Cabernet Sauvignon or Shiraz. Cold temperatures will accentuate the harshness of the tannins and make heavy red wines taste too bitter and out of balance. Light-bod-

ied red wines with low tannin levels, such as Valpolicella (from Italy) or Beaujolais (from France), can be served slightly chilled to accentuate their fruit. Inexpensive Zinfandels (under $15) can be served cool, while a blockbuster fine "Zin" ($35 or more) would be served at the same temperature as a Cabernet Sauvignon. (See "Serving Temperature Ranges," chart page 650.)

2 **HAVE CLEAN GLASSWARE AT ROOM TEMPERATURE** The glass should be big enough to give the wine a swirl and not have any slosh out of the glass. There are specific glasses for different grape varieties, regions, or styles of wine. (Restaurant service issues will be discussed later in this chapter.) A thin-lipped glass with a **STEM** is all you need to drink wine. The stem is useful so we do not smudge or warm the bowl of the glass with our fingers.

3 **USE A CORKSCREW TO REMOVE THE CORK** Of course, you will skip this step if you have a screwcap bottle, tetra pak, or bag-in-the-box.

4 **POUR** About 3 to 4 ounces/90 to 120 milliliters of a chilled wine is a good pour unless you are really thirsty. Being too generous with a pour will result in the wine warming up in the glass unless it is drunk quickly (rarely the case with wine). With red wines, the standard portion of 5 ounces/150 milliliters is fine.

5 **SEE.** Look at the color of the wine. The color of a wine offers some clues about its character, so take a close look at the wine by holding the glass at a tilt against a white

background (a tasting sheet or tablecloth will work). If a still white wine is watery in color with a green tinge, it is probably a light-bodied fresh wine. If the color is banana-yellow to gold, the white wine is either more powerful, perhaps from spending time in oak barrels, or older. If the wine is darker than gold with some browning, it may be too old to enjoy. (An exception to this warning sign are the fortified tawny Ports, Amontillado Sherries, Commandaria, and Madeira wines, which may have an amber color and be in great shape.) With red wines, a translucent color indicates a lighter style; an opaque deep purple color, a full-bodied wine; and, as with white wines, browning could be a sign of a wine that may be past its prime and too old to enjoy.

6 **SWIRL AND SMELL** Hold the glass by the stem and swirl it around for a few seconds to help release the aroma of the wine. If there are no warning signs with the color, have a sniff. If there are no unpleasant smells, the wine is probably sound. If there is a smell of moldy clothes, wet cardboard, or a damp basement, the wine could be "corked." (For further discussion, see page 683.)

If the idea of throwing the wine out is intolerable, there is a technique to make the wine at least drinkable again. Take a couple of large pieces of plastic wrap (about 6 inches/15 centimeters) and place them in a glass **DECANTER**. Pour the offensive wine into the decanter and shake it vigorously or leave it for a couple of hours. Remove the plastic and drink the wine if you are one of those people who hates to waste anything.

7 **SHARE** It is not the price of the wine that matters as much as the people you drink it with. Any wine tastes best when shared with people you like or love, and poor when consumed in the company of miserable people.

Another way to bring out the best in a wine is to serve it with the right foods. (For more on wine-and-food pairing, see Chapter 14, page 556.)

PROPER TEMPERATURE

FOR OPTIMAL APPRECIATION of a wine's particular qualities, it must be served at the proper temperature. (See "Serving Temperature Ranges," at right.) A good rule of thumb is that both fuller-bodied wines and older wines are served warmer than their lighter or younger counterparts in order to better appreciate the nose and taste. The vola-

tile elements are released as odors at higher temperatures, so when the wine is too cold, the aromas and bouquet are faint. Another rule of thumb is that tannin levels are a key factor in determining service temperature; lower-tannin wines are served cooler than higher-tannin wines, as serving a wine quite cold accentuates the bitter and astringent flavors, while warmer temperatures translate as increased perception of effervescence, sugars, and the "hot" feeling of acids and alcohol together. So, for example, a barrel-fermented Chardonnay, which is a tannic white wine, would be served less cold than a simple, refreshing, stainless-steel-fermented Vinho Verde from Portugal.

In the past, red wines were served at room temperature, but now there is widespread agreement that cellar temperature—slightly cooler than the dining room—is more appropriate. If there is a point of differentiation in the service of reds, it is that lighter, fruitier red wines may be served with a slight chill; full-bodied, tannic reds are served at about 62°F/16.7°C. An example of this would be to serve a Valpolicella light-bodied red cooler than a full-bodied Barolo, also from Italy.

Also, a wine consumed at a summer barbecue might be refreshing served cool, but during the winter at a formal dinner, the same wine will taste better served at room temperature. Consider that room temperature during

SERVING TEMPERATURE RANGES

- Sparkling wines: 41° to 47°F / 5° to 8°C
- Dry whites and rosés: 44° to 54°F / 6.6° to 12°C
- Light-bodied reds: 50° to 55°F / 10° to 12.75°C
- Medium-bodied to full-bodied reds: 55° to 62°F / 12.75° to 16.7°C
- Sweet wines: 41° to 47°F / 5° to 8°C (but sweet, fortified wines, such as vintage Portos, should be served at room temperature)

More complex wines within each category are served less cool to retain aromatics and flavors, which are more difficult to discern at colder temperatures. For example, an estate-bottled Chardonnay from the Green Valley subregion of the Russian River Valley in Sonoma would be served less cold than a commercial Chardonnay labeled as "California."

January a century ago in a French château in Bordeaux was closer to the 55°–60°F/12.75°–15.5°C common in cellars today, whereas nowadays room temperature implies 65°–70°F/18°–21°C. The server could ask the guest what temperature the guest prefers, if there is a question of chilling the wine.

Some guests (and almost all winemakers) prefer their complex, fuller-bodied white wines, including Champagne or other sparkling wine, served at or close to cellar temperature (55°F/13°C), while simple, lighter-weight, fruity white wines can do with more chilling (44°F/6.6°C). Many Americans like their wines, especially whites, served very cool, while some do not. Whites, reds, rosés, and all sparkling wines are accompanied by an ice bucket, filled with ice and enough water to slide the bottle in easily, though use of an ice bucket, once commonplace in restaurant service, has now become something of a controversy for table wines. If an ice bucket is used, there should also be a clean, neatly folded napkin draped over the bucket or around a handle. Tabletop chillers made of clay, marble, or plastic, which maintain the temperature of a refrigerated wine without the danger of numbing it, are gaining in popularity but are no substitute for a real ice bucket. Again, certain types of wine need to be kept cold in a real ice bucket to ensure that their acidity is perceived as refreshing. Acid and alcohol taste hot on the palate in a wine served at warmer than proper temperature.

Fortified sweet wines are higher in alcohol than dessert table wines and are not served chilled. There are a couple of exceptions to this rule. Porto, Madeira, and Sherry are all fortified wines that are produced in hot growing regions. Drinking these wines outdoors may be a good enough reason to give a light chill to a Pedro Ximénez Sherry, Malmsey Madeira, or tawny Port.

All glassware should be at room temperature. A very warm glass is the wrong choice for a chilled white, and a cool glass is wrong for a full-bodied tannic red or Porto, which is served at higher temperatures. Never refrigerate a Champagne glass, as the moisture that forms on the glass will dilute the wine and lessen the *perlage* (the upward stream of bubbles).

A wine served at 44°–59°F/6.6°–15°C warms up one degree Fahrenheit or a half degree Celsius about every seven minutes in the glass until it reaches room temperature; a wine served at 39°–44°F/4°–6.6°C gains about a degree every four minutes. As mentioned earlier, the palm or fingers of the hand can also warm the bowl of the glass.

Serving wine quite cold will accentuate the bitter and astringent flavors in the wine. Sweetness, alcohol, acidity, and effervescence are all exaggerated at warm temperatures.

RESTAURANT SERVICE = RESPECT, SKILLS, AND KNOWLEDGE

THE STANDARDS AND ETIQUETTE for restaurants provided here can always be trumped by house rules, but there are certain expectations customers have, whether they are at a fine-dining restaurant, a diner, or a nightclub.

The most important elements of a server's or sommelier's skills are knowledge about the wines of an establishment and high service standards, as well as the humility to interact with the customers in a positive manner.

Let's address respect for the customer first.

Servers cannot assume they have a customer "pegged." Twenty years ago, sommeliers worked mostly at very expensive restaurants with dress codes. They might have assessed their clients by their suits, dresses, or shoes, and treated some clients with more deference than other guests.

Today, the rules have changed, and someone in blue jeans, T-shirt, and sandals may be the client willing to pay a couple of hundred dollars or more for a bottle of wine. Or that person may start off with a simple glass of rosé, then order a finer wine. A client who prefers a glass of White Zinfandel should be treated with the same respect as someone who orders a glass of red Zinfandel. The hint of sweetness, not the color, is the reason some servers can put on airs. Customers deserve respect regardless of the style or price of the wine ordered.

A server can guess at, but not be sure of, the occasion that brought the diners to the restaurant. A woman and a man, two women, or two men could be having a business meeting, a friendly get-together, or a romantic encounter.

The server should respect the privacy of the guests and not be obtrusive. A pet peeve of many customers is the server who keeps reaching over the table to remove glasses as quickly as possible or fill up the water glass, even if

WINE SERVICE AND STAFF TRAINING

Service is all about exceeding the unspoken want and need. It's not about us, it's about the guest. How a guest feels when they sit in our restaurant is the point of everything we do—the product research, costing, training, and service execution. The primary focus of a superlative restaurant professional, be it sommelier, chef, bartender, restaurant manager, or busser, is pleasing the guest.

Ask yourself, is your venue truly guest-friendly? Is a beautifully prepared dish easy to eat? Are the wine glasses a comfortable size and weight? Is the wine list easy to read?

No matter how committed we are to the quality of our products, if they are not presented with the ease and satisfaction of the guest in mind, they will fail to create an indelible experience. It's the pleasurable memory that will draw a guest back to a dining venue.

The sommeliers on staff are service leaders. Their tone of voice and body language will be closely observed and imitated, especially by the young front-of-the-house staff. And principles of service are the same whether a restaurant's check average is $20 or $200. One man's $35 bottle of wine is another man's $100 selection. All beverages, from light beer on up to mature red Bordeaux, should be handled with

respect, both for the product and for the guest that it's being served to.

Keep beverage training simple. Speak to the least knowledgeable people in the room, not the wine geeks; they will take care of themselves. The staff members who do not ask questions are often your most solid servers but the least confident. And they touch many more guests than one sommelier does! Stress the obvious: how to open a bottle of champagne (gracefully and safely), how (and when) to decant, the importance of pristine glassware, how to carry a bottle through a room. Guests fully expect competence from a full-time sommelier. They are most impressed when servers execute wine service with practiced confidence.

In terms of product knowledge, what does the staff actually need to know? The primary terminology on a wine label needs to be defined. What are the grape name and the growing region? The style of a wine should be simply stated in "real life" terms that a guest can relate to. Don't forget to cover pronunciation! Servers will avoid selling a bottle because they can't pronounce the name of the wine. No one enjoys appearing ignorant.

Be generous with your knowledge. Look for opportunities to give it away. The deepest service

compliment a sommelier or restaurant owner can receive is about an experience when you were nowhere near the building! Make peace with the inevitability that service training will never end, and that attention to details will fall through the cracks without relentless, albeit cheerful, follow-through.

Madeline Triffon,
MS, Wine Director,
Matt Prentice Restaurants,
Detroit, Michigan

Madeline Triffon was the first female American Master Sommelier (MS). She lectures on hospitality and wine at festivals and for her restaurant group in Detroit. Madeline has shared her knowledge with thousands of servers, sommeliers, managers, and restaurant owners.

it is only missing a couple of ounces. Servers must respect the customers' space and not be too intrusive. They must sense how much or how little interaction the guests at each table want.

Before suggesting wines the servers are excited about, they must respect the customers' taste by asking some questions to find out what style of wine those guests are interested in.

If food has been ordered prior to taking a wine order, the server can suggest a couple of different styles of wines that work with the foods and watch the reaction of the guests to those suggestions.

Listening and watching the body language of the guests as they respond to wine suggestions is one way of respecting them. It should ensure guests will be pleased with their wine selection. Once a style of wine has been determined, the server should suggest wine at different price points. If a full-bodied red wine seems to be the customer's preference, the server can discreetly point first to a wine, say, at $44, then a

Wine service, like all service in the hospitality industry, centers around the needs of the customer. Simple rules paired with common sense and the willingness to give the customer the personalized care he deserves will ensure a gratifying experience for all. Having the knowledge of the wine list and the menu allows the sommelier to be well informed and to answer any question pertaining to wine and the wine's harmony with food.

Roger Dagorn,
MS, Porter House Restaurant, New York, New York

Roger Dagorn is a Master Sommelier (MS). He has been a mentor to many young sommeliers.

I strongly believe that wine education is critical to any server's constant and daily work environment. A professional restaurant offers to servers the chance to increase their knowledge and abilities: Expanding a server's skill set is often a greater incentive than money. But regardless of a server's bank of information about wine, it is a server's ability to make a guest feel at ease that is any server's most important asset. Servers should be measured first by their skill in creating happy customers, secondly by the sales, and lastly, by their knowledge.

Doug Frost,
MW And MS, Author, Consultant,
Kansas City, Missouri

Doug Frost is one of a handful of people to have attained both the Master Sommelier (MS) and Master of Wine (MW) certifications. He writes and lectures about wine, and his enthusiasm is infectious.

second at $29, and a third at $75. The prices used to illustrate the example are not as important as respecting guests by giving them the option to choose a price point they are comfortable with. The guests are more likely to order a second bottle of a wine that is in their budget. Nobody enjoys being coerced to spend more than they intended, and even though they may not verbally complain, it is unlikely that they would return to the restaurant.

It seems that many servers and sommeliers are motivated by the "quick hit," up-sell approach to get the customer to pay more, thereby increasing their tip. It is important

to establish a level of trust between server and diner, and down-selling occasionally is vital to establishing a loyal base of clientele. In a resort area that has no problem filling seats during the season, it is the faithful locals that will keep a restaurant afloat. In a city where diners have so many choices, it is the fair and respectful nature of service staff that may be the key factor in a customer's choice of restaurant.

If a customer asks the sommelier or server for some information, it is best to describe a wine by its style, not by some score it received in a magazine or book. The guest needs to know a wine's level of sweetness, acidity, body,

SOMMELIERS

A sommelier is a wine steward whose role in a dining room is assisting guests with choosing wines and then opening and pouring them (see photos on page 665).

A complete knowledge of the menu items and their ingredients and flavors is essential for the sommelier to collaborate with the chef and be able to suggest wines that will not be lost or overwhelm food but enhance it.

A trial tasting of the food and wine pairings is often organized for staff or with a potential banquet customer to ensure success. The duties of a sommelier may also include selecting and ordering wines for the list, as well as organizing the wine cellar. The title cellar master, wine director, or chef sommelier is sometimes used for sommeliers whose responsibilities include the layout and maintenance of the cellar and the systems of controls to track sales and inventory. A sommelier will also train fellow workers to make them more familiar with the products the establishment carries as well as proper service techniques.

Sommeliers have the task of studying the wine regions of the world and keeping current on how the wines are being shaped by the producers and the effects of climate from vintage to vintage.

A sommelier or wine director may also be in charge of other beverages such as sake, beer, spirits, and nonalcoholic "mocktails."

and a couple of descriptors about its aromas and flavors, which should be sufficient. Again, watching the reaction of the customer will indicate how much information they are receptive to. "This dry wine has ripe red fruit flavors, crisp acidity, and is medium-bodied" is sufficient information for most guests. Other diners may ask more specific questions about the vintage conditions of the wine, or about the different grapes used in a blend. For some customers, telling a story about the family who own the winery, the history of the wine, or a personal experience with the wine will resonate more than technical data about *batonnage* or barrel-aging. The sommelier or server is a professional who must know the wines on the list but never show off that knowledge and be tiresome.

Many of the professionals quoted in this chapter remind sommeliers and servers how important their deportment is. A jocular attitude by a server may be appropriate for some establishments, but in other restaurants, it could make a guest angry. "Can I get you guys some wine?" or "How you guys doin'?" is never a respectful way to address a table of guests, yet it occurs far too often. It is even more disrespectful when one of the guests is not a guy, but a woman. When speaking with repeat customers, it is correct to address the client as "Ms." or "Mr." and more respectful to ask if they are enjoying their specific beverage than to ask, "How's the wine?"

It is imperative that the waitstaff and sommelier be well groomed. A body odor of cigarettes, perfume, or cologne

> The major cornerstones of proper wine service have always been wine and food knowledge, basic wine presentation and preparation skills, honesty, and above all the ability of the wine server to make the customer feel comfortable.
>
> **Joseph Delissio,**
> *Wine Director, The River Cafe, Brooklyn, New York*

> The most important element of the dining experience is good service. An attitude of generosity and helpfulness is a primary condition for a waiter or a sommelier, but beyond that it is training, training, training.
>
> **Larry Stone,**
> *MS, General Manager, Rubicon Estate,*
> *Rutherford, Napa Valley, California*

may lead to the loss of a sale if the customers cannot wait for the server to leave the table. Chipped fingernail polish or dirty hands are unacceptable under any circumstances.

Respect the customer's needs by having a sense of urgency. Far too often, a guest orders a wine and the food comes before the wine. Many diners will not begin to eat unless the wine is in front of them as well. To remind a server that the wine has been ordered, and then watch the server go to another table and talk with them instead of addressing the issue, is seen as a sign of disrespect by the client. Ultimately it will diminish the appreciation of the course being served and the overall impression of service at the restaurant or bar.

Respect a guest's opinion about a wine and do not argue with them at the table over what the guest perceives as a bad wine they are unhappy with. (See "Refused Bottles," page 662.)

It is unfortunate that some servers, whether they be maître d's, captains, sommeliers, or waitstaff, fantasize that they are superior to the guests they are serving.

Though a restaurant may have terrific food, an engaging menu and wine list, beautiful decor, and lovely ambience, an otherwise enjoyable meal can be marred or even ruined by poor service. Restaurant guests deserve the best in professional service, and as discussed earlier in this chapter, servers should endeavor to provide the highest possible level of attention to a guest's needs. Proper wine service is a customer's right and a service professional's duty and pleasure.

Sommeliers today realize they have to offer the highest possible level of service and professional counsel to the dining public. As with any true professional, the best sommeliers are in demand at large hotels and restaurants. However, with a growing trend toward more informal dining and the customer's interest in the perception of value

as part of the successful dining experience, the role of the sommelier is often filled by an energetic, friendly, helpful, and informed member of the waitstaff. Be they owners, hosts, servers, captains, maître d's, or managers, the folks who fill the role of wine service professional are eager to give the pleasure of good service and, just as important, to learn as much as they can about wine, the wine list, and wine's relation to food.

SETTING THE TABLE: GLASSWARE

THE TABLE MAY BE PRESET with an all-purpose wineglass or with glasses for sparkling, white wine, and red wine. Wineglasses must be clear, colorless, and unadorned, so that the true color of the wine may be appreciated.

The glasses should be rinsed and hand-polished with a lint-free cloth (a clean cotton napkin is ideal) so that there is no soapy residue. The advantage of presetting the table with the wineglasses is that it allows time for better

LEFT: *Wine service tools (clockwise, from top left): basket or cradle (used to transport old red wines to the table), candle (used for decanting old red wines), wine chiller (maintains temperature without ice), decanting funnel, thermometer, sparkling wine pliers, cork retriever, sparkling wine cap or preserver, cork retriever,* TASTEVIN, *and thermometer.* RIGHT: *A preset table with wineglasses. The first glass to be used is placed above the knives. Subsequent glasses are placed to the left or above the original glass.*

service, especially when the restaurant and its staff are busy, and it sends a message to the guest that wine is an integral and essential part of the meal.

The type of glass used affects the taster's perception of the wine. A proper glass should be large enough to hold 3 to 4 ounces/90 to 120 milliliters of wine and still have enough space at the top to allow swirling the glass to release the nose. The glass should have a stem long enough to be held, so that the bowl of the glass is not warmed by the hands and no fingerprints are left on the glass to mar appreciation of the wine's color. The lip should not be too thick, and the glass should be widest at the bowl, narrowing to a smaller diameter at the rim. Restaurants have the option of using one glass for sparkling wine and one all-purpose glass for still wines, or they may opt to have a range of glassware for the different types of wine. (See the discussion of tasting in Chapter 3, page 87.) Extensive research has proven that using a specific glass for different regions, grape varieties, or styles of wine can greatly affect the appreciation of those wines. Savvy restaurateurs may endear their establishment to wine lovers by offering varietal or regional wine-specific or finer-quality glasses on the table.

Most restaurants mark up a wine somewhere between two and a half and five times the wholesale price. Customers expect a proper glass, a knowledgeable server, and proper service for the premium price they are paying for a wine.

On the flip side, restaurants make a major financial investment in the purchase, storage, and maintenance of the wines in their cellar. Other restaurant costs include staff training, sommelier's salary, ice buckets, preservation systems, refrigerated wine cabinets, special dishwashing machines, and glassware. The breakage of glassware is a devastating sound to proprietors and nothing to clap about. Refused bottles of wine are another potential loss for a restaurant. (See "Refused Bottles," page 662.)

PRESENTING AND DISCUSSING THE WINE LIST

THE WINE LIST is not only a listing of the wines available but also a marketing tool for the restaurant and a statement of its image. Obviously, the list should be free from stains and should not appear dog-eared, old, or overused. All of the wines listed should be available. The best way to make sure that the list is current and clean is to print it from a computer. Printing one's own list allows the restaurateur to select a type style and colors that reflects the appropriate image. Computerizing the wine list also allows the restaurateur to coordinate the printed list with cellar inventory, sales records, and wine ordering. While large restaurants and hotels print the lists daily or every few days, this may not be appropriate for smaller operations. However the list is produced, whether by hand or by computer, it must be accurate and up-to-date. (For a full discussion of wine lists, see Chapter 18, page 695).

The wine list may be presented at the same time as the menus, which again emphasizes that wine is an integral part of the dining experience. Many restaurants have a short wine list printed with the food menu and notify the guest that a more extensive list is available on request.

Unless one guest asks for the list, it should be placed toward the center of the table, opened to the first page, or presented to the host. The first page often presents sparkling wines, Champagnes, or premium wines by the glass, a mission statement, or a table of contents for extensive lists. If the server presents the list with the menu, the customer is more likely to begin considering wine either as an aperitif or as an accompaniment to the first course of the meal. In general, wine contains less alcohol than spirit-based drinks and is more effective as an appetite stimulant.

When the server approaches the table to take the order, he or she should not interrupt a conversation. Speaking in a clear and friendly voice, the server might ask, "May I help you with a wine selection?" or "Will you be having wine this evening?" A more assertive statement, such as "Which wine have you chosen to enjoy with your meal?" may be in order. The service professional establishes a rapport with the host at the table and, whenever possible, addresses the host by name. The server should not assume that a male is the host. While it is important to acknowledge all the guests at the table, it is the guest who orders the wine whom the server should approach to continue the meal's wine service (by bringing a second bottle or suggesting a different wine).

The service staff must understand what is happening at the table and suggest wines that fit the situation. As discussed earlier in this chapter, people dine out for many reasons. The guests may be celebrating a special occasion or, at the other extreme, conducting business during the meal. While an anniversary or birthday dinner may call for a festive bottle of Champagne, a working lunch may be alcohol-free. On the other hand, some business dinners involve entertaining a special client, so a more expensive bottle of wine may be appropriate. When conferring with the host or any guest, staff should not discuss price directly unless requested; instead, direct the guest's attention to where the prices are on the wine list.

The server must determine the style of wine and price range each customer prefers and also be sensitive to how the wine will perform with the menu items the guests have chosen.

Wine aficionados offered an exciting wine list may wish to sample and compare smaller portions of different wines just as gourmets love to graze and share a number of smaller portions of food. Many restaurants offer a 3-ounce/90-milliliter taste, a 5-ounce/150-milliliter standard pour, and a "quartino," which is about 9 ounces/266 milliliters of wine. Some restaurants specialize in a large selection of half bottles of wine. Finally, a flight of wine may be presented with small portions of three or four different wines—for example, four Pinot Noir wines, including one from the Russian River Valley in California, one from the Willamette in Oregon, one from Martinborough in New Zealand, and one from Chambolle-Musigny in Burgundy, France. Or a "century of Porto" with an ounce each of 10, 20, 30, and 40 Year tawny Port. (For an example of flights of wines specifically paired with cheeses, see page 724.)

PRESENTING THE WINE

PROPER WINE SERVICE dictates that the wine server approach the table, show the label on the bottle to the person who ordered the wine, and quietly announce the product name, producer, and vintage. Any special attributes of the wine such as "Reserva," "Grand Cru," "Classico," "Colheita," "Late Harvest," or "Icewine" should also be announced to the guest.

This allows the guest to verify the selection or to make a change. Sometimes, especially when ordering varietal-labeled wines, some confusion can occur in ordering. For example, a guest may order a Zinfandel, a red wine, but

really means to order a White Zinfandel (a blush or rosé wine). Or if a savvy guest chooses a Riesling for their appetizer, they would recognize that a late-harvest version would be an inappropriate wine because it is sweet.

Presenting the wine to the guest allows the server to verify the order before the wine is opened; in some cases a completely different wine than the one the customer ordered is brought to the table. For example, the customer ordered a bottle of Barbaresco (an Italian wine named by its origin), and the server shows up with a bottle of Barbera instead (an Italian grape variety).

The bottle should be opened in view of the table, and if possible, the bottle should never leave the sight of the host during the meal, unless requested. It is common practice in many fine restaurants today to open the wine and taste it to ensure it is sound before bringing it to the customer. House rules prevail when it comes to where to uncork the wine. However, in states where it is legal to take a partial bottle of wine home after finishing a meal, the cork (or screwcap) should always be available to the customer.

Before opening the bottle, the server should have ready a corkscrew, preferably the classic "waiter's tool" (see photos on page 660), and a napkin that is damp at one end. The dining room staff must work as a team, and the wine waiter or captain should always check the table first to see if empty glasses should be removed, ashtrays changed, or crumbs cleaned off the tablecloth.

The best place to open wine is on a side stand or cart, sometimes called a gueridon. Red wines may be opened on the table, while whites and rosés are opened in the ice bucket or chiller if one or the other is being utilized. Sparkling wines may be opened either in or out of the ice bucket or chiller.

Common sense and house policies will usually win over steadfast rules, but opening still wines in the air, without surface support, is the least desirable choice, especially for older red wines, whose sediment can be jostled. A crowded table in a corner may leave the server no alternative but to open a wine in the air, but let common sense prevail. It is easier for a server to correctly remove a cork without breaking it when using a stable surface.

The server should check older red wines for ULLAGE (see photo in Chapter 17 on page 681), seeing if the bottle fill is lower than normal so that oxygen may have deteriorated the wine. This is rare and usually occurs with reds after more than a decade in the bottle. Not all wines with ullage are spoiled, but the server should be prepared for that possibility and may advise the maître d' or manager before presenting the wine to the guest.

Because sediment in older red wines could be shaken and dispersed, some restaurants may employ **WINE CRADLES**, or baskets, for transporting the wine to the table.

UNCORKING THE WINE

TO OPEN THE WINE, the server uses the broad part of the knife blade on the corkscrew to cut the foil or plastic **CAPSULE** at the lower lip of the bottle neck, to ensure a clean, uniform cut. The foil or cap is sometimes removed by pulling a tab provided on the capsule. The cap should be placed in the server's pocket, not in the ice bucket or in any other receptacle. Some wine bottles do not have a capsule but rather a flanged neck with a small beeswax capsule just over the cork. The server can remove the disk with the blade of the corkscrew or just insert the corkscrew through the center of the beeswax disk and remove it with the cork. Once the cork has been removed, the bottle lip should be wiped with the moist end of the napkin if necessary. (Steps for opening a bottle are illustrated on page 660.)

Many wines not intended for aging come in screwcap-topped bottles or in tetra paks, and these bottles are easiest to open.

We would not present a screwcap to the taster at a table. The tradition of presenting the cork is not common practice anymore. The presentation of the cork is an awkward moment for both the server and the guest. Sommeliers do

not smell a cork and neither should a guest, unless he or she wishes to do so. Guests can inspect the cork to make sure it is not dry and crumbly or wet from bottom to top. Those conditions could be warning signs that the wine is flawed due to poor storage conditions. It makes

Tartrate crystals may be visible on the corks of some wines. They are tasteless and harmless. This example is from a Shafer Cabernet Sauvignon from Napa, California.

sense to present a cork of an older bottle of fine wine to ensure that the cork is sound. Perhaps it is sufficient to ask the guest ordering an older bottle of wine if they wish to inspect the cork. Most knowledgeable clients would defer to the sommelier or captain, who should advise them if the cork exhibits a potential flaw in the wine.

Some guests want to look at the cork to ensure that the vintage or name of the producer on the cork is the same as the information on the wine bottle. Since many customers think that the cork presentation is an important part of the ritual of wine service, the server can inform the guest that house rules are not to present the cork unless requested. That way the guest does not feel slighted.

CONTINUING SERVICE

THE SERVER SHOULD POUR from the right of the guests in a clockwise fashion. In a mixed group, women are to be served first, then men, and finally the person who ordered the wine (see the photos on page 665). A standard glass of wine is a 5-ounce/150-milliliter pour, but a full bottle of table wine could be perfect for a table of six or eight if that is what the person who orders the wine desires. A sweet dessert wine, for which a 2- or 2.5-ounce/60- or 75-milliliter pour is adequate, is usually poured for six from a half bottle.

The server should pour the wine in a firm and steady motion with the bottle opening placed just over the glass but not touching it. After pouring, the bottle neck should be lifted, twisted a half turn, and then dabbed clean with the napkin, ensuring that no wine drips on the table or customers' clothes. When pouring, the server should hold the bottle near the bottom so that the label is visible to the guests.

The server should ask the person who tasted the wine if corks and finished bottles may be removed. Also, the server should ask a guest's permission before pouring more wine or when removing a glass containing wine from a previous bottle, even if there is only a small amount left. Fresh glasses should always be offered for each new bottle presented, unless it is a large banquet setting where replacing all glassware for the exact same wine is impractical.

The server may also inquire after a bottle is finished if the guests are enjoying the wine and would like to continue with more of the same or try something different.

CORK: IS THE HONEYMOON OVER?

Some traditionalists like the romance of a true cork in the bottle. The authors are nonplussed about the resistance to screwcaps. We have endured too many faulty corks and spoiled bottles to have reverence for a cork. About 8 to 12 percent of all wines sealed with a cork have been contaminated by 2,4,6 trichloroanisole or TCA, a chemical compound that in its early stages robs the wine of some of its flavors and later in its development makes a wine smell musty or moldy.

The $4 billion annual sales of cork is certainly motivation for those in the cork industry to take steps to improve the consistency of their product. They cite evidence that the amount of air in a cork protects a wine from unpleasant reductive smells and that cork has a track record for wines that have been cellared for decades. Considering that most wines are meant to be drunk within three years of their harvest, perhaps corks should be reserved for the small number of wines meant to be reserved, or aged for a long period of time. There are both fierce defenders and detractors of cork.

The authors and other wine lovers will surely hear a lot more pro and anti cork trial results in the next few years. Today, there are many alternatives challenging cork's supremacy. Aside from screwcaps and plastic corks, some sparkling wine producers opt for a **CROWN CAP**, figuring if it is good enough for cola, why not for wine?

Vino-Seal (known as Vino-Lok in Europe) uses an attractive glass closure; Zork is made of polymers; ProCork is a traditional cork layered with polymers.

There is also a cork that has been ground up and bombarded with carbon dioxide to remove any TCA. The cork particles are reconfigured into a cylinder and bound with polymers. This closure is known as Diam for still wines and Mytik for sparkling wines. (The cork and closure issue is also discussed in Chapter 17, page 683.)

Respected Burgundian wine *négociant* Jean-Claude Boisset packages some of his wines in aluminum bottles and others in plastic. The winery does not believe that any flavor will be leached into the wine from the plastic. Are baby boomers ready for wine in a plastic bottle?

Bag-in-the-box packaging that holds 101.6 ounces/3 liters is convenient and is no longer just used for domestic "Chablis" or "Burgundy" but also for varietal wines such as Chardonnay, Merlot, or Shiraz.

Single-portion and larger-format tetra paks are being used for both simple and fine wines. For example, the esteemed Restaurant Daniel in New York City, which garnered three stars from the Michelin Guide, its highest honor for a restaurant, serves "Dtour," a Chardonnay from the Mâcon-Villages appellation of Burgundy, France, produced by winemaker Dominique Lafon, chef Daniel Boulud, and sommelier Daniel Johnnes, in a tetra pak.

A new wine is offered through the wine list or by verbal suggestion, but it is usually best to bring the list to the table and point out the price of the new wine to the host, so there is no confusion on the issue. In some situations, the host may not want to be bothered with seeing each wine and price on the list and will allow the server to pick appropriate wines within a certain price range. The server or sommelier must accept that each table and occasion is a distinct situation that requires sometimes more, sometimes less interaction with the host.

A service professional will be sensitive to the ambience of the restaurant and to the particular guests he or she is serving. When walking the fine line between familiarity and formality, it is always best to maintain a professional but friendly attitude. Service professionals not only respond to their guests' requests but also *anticipate* their guests' needs.

DECANTING

RED WINES ARE FERMENTED with their skins, which contribute both pigments and tannins. Over time the pigments and tannins form sediment. The process of **DECANTING** older red wine is done to separate the sediment from the wine before serving it to the guests.

A server should ask the guest if she or he prefers to have the wine decanted. Older bottles of fine red wine are

TOP ROW, FROM LEFT TO RIGHT: *Present the bottle with the label facing the taster. Declare the name of the producer and product and the vintage of the wine. Cut the foil or capsule at the lower lip of the bottle neck. Use the edge of the corkscrew knife to remove the cap.* SECOND ROW, FROM LEFT TO RIGHT: *Insert the worm of the corkscrew near the center of the cork. Twist the corkscrew in a clockwise motion until just one spiral of the worm is showing. Tilt the corkscrew back so the lever or foot may be placed on the lip of the bottle.* THIRD ROW, FROM LEFT TO RIGHT: *Place the foot on the lip of the bottle. Ensure that the foot is flush with the lip; if not, lift the foot and twist the corkscrew in reverse a half turn and try again. Bracing the foot with a finger or thumb, pull straight up with the corkscrew. Age-worthy wines with long corks may require a second series of turning and lifting. Once most of the cork is visible, grip the cork at the end near the bottle and jiggle it out.* BOTTOM ROW: *The server should hold the lower half of the bottle to pour. The bottle is positioned just above the glass with the label facing the guest. Do not pick up the glass to pour.*

Great wine service is not just wine knowledge, but it definitely helps. The key element is the ability to understand what the guest wants and translate it within the confines of the wine program. To do this, one must understand the taste of wine and the styles of wine from different regions of the world, in addition to making the guest feel comfortable about expressing their taste and knowledge of wine.

In other words, if a guest explains that they like "a dry wine like a White Zinfandel," they are providing a multitude of clues in terms of what they like and dislike. In this case, they have indicated that they prefer sweet wine, they don't normally spend a lot on a bottle of wine, and they probably prefer California wines over wines from other parts of the world.

So what if there is no White Zinfandel in the house? A sweeter-style Riesling or Chenin Blanc or Pinot Gris will probably make them just as happy as that White Zinfandel. This scenario is the ultimate in wine service. When a recommendation leads to a new, pleasurable wine experience, in some cases the guest may remember this even more than the food they ate.

Bob Bath, Educator
MS, Consultant, Wine Importer, Wine Educator,
St. Helena, California

Staff support and wine training are very important. Many places that have a sommelier depend heavily on that one person, leaving an uncomfortable void when he or she is unavailable. Enthusiasm is the most important and basic component that comes from the staff when learning about wine. I have trained staff members who initially knew very little about wines but have gone a long way with their energy and enthusiasm. I have found that daily wine tastings (four or five times a week at the preservice meeting) work better than a one-hour tasting once a week; I get higher attendance. I can always sell off the other glasses left after the tasting, regaining my cost. I use maps, information from the distributors, and stories about the area or particular vineyard site and about the producers to help demystify the wine or a wine-producing area. Staff and customers love information that personalizes a particular wine.

Beth Von Benz,
Sommelier, Consultant, New York, New York

Great wine service to me means the wine comes to the table and is presented at the appropriate temperature for the wine's style, in stemware that shows the wine to its best advantage. Additionally I look for waitstaff to make the customer feel comfortable during the wine-ordering process, to pronounce the wine on the list correctly, and to understand the wine being ordered without pointing to the bin number. If I am speaking to a sommelier, he or she should be able to discuss the producer's styles, the flavor or profile benchmarks for the region, the vintages, and how the wine tastes right now in a succinct, confident—not arrogant—way.

Jennifer Simonetti,
MW, Rémy Amerique, New York, New York

decanted as an extra touch of service, but some customers do not want to draw attention to their table and just ask for the bottle to be poured slowly so that the sediment is not agitated too much. (Tools used for decanting are illustrated on page 655, and the method illustrated on page 664.)

The bottle may be brought to the table in a basket unless it has been ordered in advance and has been standing up to allow the sediment to settle to the bottom. The cork is removed. A light source, such as a **CANDLE**, is positioned just under the neck or shoulder area of the bottle. The server pours in a steady, continuous motion into a glass decanter. The server watches the neck and stops transferring the wine if sediment or haze appears in the neck. It is important for the server not to stop in the middle of transferring the wine, for the rocking motion will cause the sediment to be stirred up in the wine. If the server gets through only one-half or two-thirds of the bottle before the haze or sediment appears, the wine should be left for a half hour or more, if possible, before attempting to decant again. The server should respectfully ask the guests

not to pick up the wine bottle, as the sediment would be disturbed, while assuring the guests that the sediment is not harmful and is a natural part of the wine.

Many guests do not want their wines decanted. Some experts say French Burgundy wines are best not decanted, but Bordeaux wines, which are made with thicker-skinned grapes, should be decanted.

It is best to allow the guest the option. The other reason a wine may be decanted is to **AERATE** it. Young, tannic red

REFUSED BOTTLES

When wine is being served, the person who ordered the bottle is offered a chance to inspect the cork. If the cork is dry on both ends, the wine probably was not stored on its side, which is not a problem for a young, simple wine.

However, if the cork feels very dry and crumbles a bit, air may have invaded the wine through the cork, and the wine could be bad. A cork that is wet on both ends suggests a similar problem. Both cases warrant suspicion, but the guest should still smell the wine. If the smell is very unpleasant (the smell of rotten eggs or of a moldy cork), the guest may ask the server to taste it or may refuse the bottle outright.

A guest has the right to refuse a bottle of bad wine. Although it is not proper for a guest to return a bottle simply because he or she does not like the style of the wine, the old adage "the customer is always right" may hold true. A hospitality business can ill afford to alienate its guests, whether they are technically right or wrong about the wine. As always, house policies apply, but a server facing an unpleasant situation should try to be as diplomatic and gracious as possible. Of course, it is proper procedure for the server to involve the restaurant manager in any decision concerning a refused bottle. While restaurant guests do occasionally refuse wines, modern winemaking has resulted in the majority of the world's wines being clean, sound, and enthusiastically welcomed at the table.

A restaurant that carries very expensive older wines, which sell for $200 to $2,000 per bottle or even more, may print a disclaimer on its wine list stating, "Not responsible for the condition of wines over $500." Of course, an occasional guest may test the staff by ordering and refusing a very expensive wine, but it is more likely that a valued patron may, with the best of intentions, order a fine, older wine yet be unhappy with its condition. Each situation requires a decision by the manager or owner that she or he believes is fair to both the guest and the establishment.

In a perfect world, the sommelier is your champion, and you are at the restaurant to enjoy the food and wine, and he is there to help you, no? Sometimes, I am afraid, no. I am not saying that he may be trying to prevent you from enjoying the wine with food. I'm just saying that his idea of wine-with-food enjoyment may be different from yours. And that is why, upon starting the process at an unknown restaurant, with an unknown sommelier, I always initiate a phase I call "Test the Sommelier." No, I do not ask him to name the *grands crus* of Burgundy. But I will throw out a preliminary question that gives me a pretty good idea if he's on my beam or his.

"Would love to start with a really crisp, dry white wine that's a great refresher. Not looking for a wine with an excess of anything," I'll say. If he says something like, "I've got this Grüner Veltliner from Weinvert that's like a laser beam," he has won me over. I'm ready to rock. I'm oeno-putty in his hands. If he says, "I've got a dynamite Chardonnay from Napa Valley," I sigh, take out my flashlight, and get to my lonely work.

David Rosengarten,
Author, Consultant, Ultimate Munch, New York, New York

---

wines are less harsh after **BREATHING**. The bottle opening is small, allowing very little of the wine to be in contact with oxygen; it takes only a few seconds to pour a young red into a decanter, thereby exposing all the wine to oxygen. The merits of allowing young reds to aerate is another subject without one correct answer. Franco Biondi-Santi, of Brunello di Montalcino in Italy, insists his *riserva* needs twenty-four hours to open up and reveal itself at its best, while many other wines have been proven to taste best when freshly opened. A vintage Madeira that has been purposely oxidized for twenty years can be opened a day or two before service.

Although it is not common practice, complex ageworthy white wines consumed young may be decanted to aerate. The interaction with oxygen allows the wine to show off more of its scents and flavors. For example, a very young Corton-Charlemagne *grand cru* white Burgundy or an Alsace *grand cru* Riesling wine that have great potential to age could be candidates for decanting. In Champagne, France, the dessert-style demi-sec wines are sometimes decanted at the end of an all-Champagne dinner. A reason to decant the last wine is to have less fizzy pressure on the stomach at the end of a meal. It is not done at all fine restaurants in Champagne, but it is worth mentioning to give the option to the restaurant patron.

SPARKLING WINE

A STANDARD BOTTLE of sparkling wine served at 45°F/7.2°C has 6 to 8 atmospheres of pressure (1 atmosphere equals 14 pounds per square inch) and so must be treated with caution and respect. Warm sparkling wines are liable to foam over the lip of the bottle when opened and go flat quickly, so *sparkling wines should always be well chilled before they are opened* (see "Serving Temperature Ranges," page 650). Twenty minutes in ice and water chills the champagne properly. Many restaurants keep sparkling wines refrigerated and ready to serve.

The bottle should be handled carefully during transit from the cellar to the table. A bottle that has been swung about or bumped is more likely to explode when the cage is removed or to foam over when the cork is removed.

As with all wines, the bottle is presented to the person who ordered it (see photos on page 665). Sparkling wines may be opened either in or out of the ice bucket. Many sparkling wines have a pull strip that can be used to remove the foil. If there is no pull strip, the server should first pull the hasp of the metal cage out and down, then twist the hasp about five times to unwind it, and finally pull the cage outward and upward to remove both the cage and the foil that surrounds it. Some people believe it is best to remove the

Did you know that customers who complain are really doing you and the restaurant a favor? Studies show that for every customer who voices a complaint, there are likely at least twenty-five others who have had a similar problem but didn't say anything about it. Maybe they didn't want to make a fuss or make you uncomfortable. Customers like that may be easier to wait on, but they're not likely to come back or talk the restaurant up to their friends if they encountered a food or service issue and it went unresolved.

By having the courage to speak up when something isn't right, guests who complain are really giving us information we desperately need and giving us a chance to correct the situation. In fact, handling minor glitches or even major screwups the right way can earn you more customer loyalty than if everything went "right." Here are some quick tips on turning problems into opportunities:

SHOW EMPATHY

- There is absolutely no need to get defensive when a food or service problem is brought to your attention. Not only is it unnecessary, but it will give your guest another justified reason to get upset. Apologize immediately and do not assign blame. Don't think of apologizing as an admission of wrongdoing in a legal sense. Think of it as an expression of sympathy for an unfortunate occurrence. Even if you know the problem wasn't your fault, say you're sorry anyway.

ASSESS THE SERIOUSNESS OF THE SITUATION

- The urgency of corrective action is best determined by the person on the front lines. Even if your manager is the one who will handle making amends, they will need to know from you how big a problem it is.
- Be honest—downplaying the seriousness of an issue will not reflect well on you in the big picture. Determine how big a problem it is by putting yourself in the guest's shoes—how upset would you be if the same thing happened to you? If the guest perceives an issue as either a threat to their health or if there was damage to their property, that's more serious than if they waited too long for coffee or got the wrong salad.

TAKE IMMEDIATE STEPS TO MAKE THINGS RIGHT

- Every restaurant is different in their policies, so this may mean informing a manager, ordering a replacement item or comping something. Some restaurants even empower their service staff to make amends on the spot, up to the full cost of dinner. Make sure you know how your establishment handles issues and what steps you are authorized to take when something goes wrong.
- A prompt and heartfelt apology will take the sting out of almost any problem.
- Taking steps to fix it, or at least to invite the guest back for a fresh start, can turn a public relations nightmare into a success story.

Marnie Old,
Author, Consultant, Educator, Philadelphia, Pennsylvania

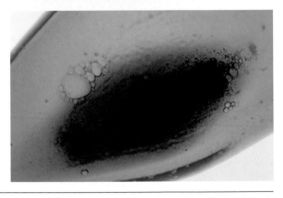

The first step in decanting an older wine taken from the cellar, where it has been lying on its side, is to open it in a cradle. The next step is to pour the wine with a steady motion, using a candle as a light source. The wine is poured until some sediment is viewed. When decanting old red wines, the server watches for sediment and avoids transferring it to the decanter.

entire cage, while others simply loosen it and keep a thumb on top of the cage to avoid a flying cork, a safe alternative.

Once the cage has been loosened or removed, the bottle is ready to be opened. Place a napkin on top of the cork, exerting slight downward pressure. Hold the bottle at about a 45-degree angle, supporting the bottom with one hand. With the other hand, twist the bottle in one direction while holding the cork steady. Do not twist the cork, because the "mushroom"—the top half of the cork—can break off from the bottom half, and because it is easier to apply force to the larger bottle than to the smaller cork.

The formal way to open a bottle of sparkling wine is to avoid making a loud pop. The desired sound is the slightest hiss, a soft "sigh," which allows surface carbon dioxide to escape gently and helps maintain the *perlage*, the small **BEAD** of bubbles. On certain occasions, such as New Year's Eve, loud pops may be encouraged to add to the festivities, and with a very inexpensive product, that's fine. When opening a fine sparkler or true Champagne, however, stay away from popping.

The lip of the bottle should be wiped off with the napkin and the cork presented. The server should dry off the bottle if it was opened in the bucket. The bottle should be held in a similar manner as a still wine bottle, with the label exposed. Some servers place their thumb in the **PUNT**, or indentation, under the bottle, but this is not recommended. Not all sparkling wines have a punt, and it is also a very unwieldy practice for larger-size bottles.

The server should pour about 1 ounce/30 milliliters into a clean, dry tulip- or flute-shaped glass for the host or the person designated to be in charge of the wine ordering.

The saucer-shaped sorbet glasses so popular at catered events allow too many bubbles to escape. A sparkling wine's first sensory appeal is the hissing sound of the wine being poured into the glass, then the color of the wine and movement of the bubbles in the glass. When sparkling wine is poured, a foam, or mousse, rises toward the top of the glass.

Once the host approves the wine, the guests at the table are served. Sparkling wine should be poured in two

Taking the order, opening, decanting, and serving a young and tannic California Cabernet Sauvignon for aeration TOP ROW, FROM LEFT TO RIGHT: *Presenting the wine list. Presenting the bottle.* SECOND ROW, FROM LEFT TO RIGHT: *Opening the bottle. The taster inspects the cork.* THIRD ROW, FROM LEFT TO RIGHT: *The wine is poured into a glass decanter to aerate, rather than to remove sediment.* BOTTOM LEFT: *The aeration from decanting and the larger glasses make a young Cabernet Sauvignon less harsh and more enjoyable. A tasting portion is offered.*

motions. The first ounce or so provides a base, and when the mousse settles after the first pour, the wine is poured again, until the glass is about two-thirds full. After all the guests are served, the wine bottle is then placed back in the ice bucket or cooler with a draped napkin, so the server can dry off the bottle next time the sparkling wine is poured.

SERVING FORTIFIED WINES

PORT

VINTAGE PORTO and some late-bottled vintage Ports must be decanted, as they may contain sediment. Tawny, ruby, or white Ports do not require decanting.

Wines may have a metal or plastic cap over the cork, but some vintage Porto from Portugal has sealing wax covering a driven cork. The blade of the corkscrew must be used to scrape the wax off the top so that the cork is exposed. A damp napkin is used to clean off any bits of hardened wax. Vintage Porto is intended to age for a long time in the bottle, so corks are quite long. A good tool to have for opening vintage Porto is a corkscrew with two "feet," or an alternative opener such as a screwpull or "ah-so," which grips the sides of the cork. Another option is an opener that injects nitrogen through a needle to force the cork up. Proceed with the service of Port as you would with any other still wine.

Vintage and late-bottled vintage Ports are served at the same temperature as full-bodied reds, while tawny Ports may be served just slightly cooler than, but not as cold as, a white Port. A serving of 2 to 2.5 ounces/60 to 75 milliliters in a Port glass or small tasting glass is standard.

SHERRY, MADEIRA, AND MARSALA

SHERRY, MADEIRA, AND MARSALA may have plastic-capped cork stoppers, so they can be opened without any special tools. The exception would be the finest vintage

TRAINING PRACTICES FOR WINE SERVICE STAFF: WHAT WORKS, WHAT DOESN'T, AND WHY

There is no more effective way to build server knowledge and thereby increase sales (whether wine-, beverage-, or cigar-related) than through training.

Engage your staff to speak about wine in a fun and simple manner. If you spend twenty minutes speaking about the winemaking process and refer to terms such as malolactic fermentation and clonal selection, you will most likely lose them. You can motivate your staff by demonstrating a vibrant knowledge of wine without pretension.

What style of food is the restaurant serving and at what price point? Explain to them why the wines were chosen for that particular culinary concept and the thought process behind pricing. Then allow them to taste some of the wines with food, and identify the special attributes that arise from the pairings.

What is the demographic profile of your restaurant's employees? Are they predominantly newer or seasoned staff, young or older team members? Clearly a staff with lower turnover will typically be better trained than one with high turnover.

Younger employees usually have had less exposure to wine. Wine training should be tailored to the tenure of the team members. Do not allow employees with more wine knowledge to intimidate those who are still trying to learn. This can lead to withdrawal of novice staff and generate their negative perceptions of wine.

Select wines that are unique and not case-stacked at the local grocery store. The server will feel more confident about quality of the selections and take more pride in recommending them.

Allow the staff to participate in the selection of all wines by the glass, before implementation. Every wine by the glass in each of our restaurants is first tasted and approved by that outlet's staff. In some restaurants, this tasting is done blind. Employees will take greater ownership of the wine list knowing they have helped create it.

Make sure your servers take their wine training very

seriously. Wine notes for each wine should be drafted in advance and then distributed to the team. Then, the wine servers should be tested. I do not believe in giving out prizes for high scores. Doing well on the exam is simply a part of the job.

Empower the staff to make decisions. If allowing a guest to taste a wine can assist in facilitating its sale, then encourage them to do it.

Explain glass sizes and portion sizes. Glassware used today is better than what was offered in the past. If your restaurant sells 6-ounce/180 milliliter pours in a 22-ounce/650- milliliter glass, guests may think that they have been shorted. Explain that a bottle of wine only holds 25.4 ounces/750 milliliters to begin with, and ensure that the employee is comfortable explaining why the portion appears to be smaller than it actually is.

Make a sale that is optimal for the guest. Teach the staff that honesty builds trust with the customer and will go a long way. Wine should always be sold to complement the dish and not just be based upon price.

WHO IS RESPONSIBLE FOR TRAINING, SPECIFICALLY WINE TRAINING?

Wine training should be each staff member's responsibility. Realistically, we know this cannot always happen. At The Breakers, the sommelier team and the restaurant's management teams are responsible for wine training. This can be a rather challenging task at our property, since we have eight restaurants and 450 employees.

Some of the ways we have structured and conduct our wine training:

- A comprehensive, sixteen-week class is offered once a year in the spring. Every major wine region is covered, and employees taste between six and seven wines per class. For employees working at L'Escalier, our AAA Five Diamond restaurant and a *Wine Spectator* Grand Award winner, attendance and a passing grade of 85 points are required. Otherwise, the course is optional and available to all hotel employees, including those outside the food and beverage division. If an individual in our Information Technology department is interested in joining the class and space is available, they are more than welcome to attend. You never know when an employee in one department may find their interest in food and wine

to be so strong that they consider changing careers. (This has happened!)

- Wine and beverage training is conducted during the pre-shift at least three to four times per week. I have found that bringing a supplier during pre-meal periods to discuss and taste the wine firsthand is an excellent training technique. At that time, if the supplier wants to kick off an incentive program, we apprise the staff of the contest rules and prizes involved. I have found every incentive contest to be extremely beneficial to all sides concerned: guests, wine and restaurant staff, and the wine vendor and distributor alike.

- Articles from *Wine Spectator, Decanter, Wine & Spirits, Wine Enthusiast,* and other publications can be distributed at pre-meal training sessions and discussed. Seeing the information in writing allows the employee to absorb the content better. I also make it a point to let them know that I am not a big fan of points, puffs, glasses, etc. Wine tasting is subjective, and what makes one wine great in one person's opinion is simply that—one person's opinion.

- We send a new employee who is struggling to open, decant, or pour wine to work a shift or two in our banquet division. By the time they finish opening thirty bottles for a party, they will be much more comfortable!

- We invite winery reps to conduct seminars and tastings. The wines can be from just one winery or a varietal comparison from different portfolios. Invite employees from any of the restaurants to attend. I have found this technique to be very successful and appreciated by staff members.

- Mentor others. Surround yourself with knowledgeable staff. Not only does your job become easier, but the reward and enjoyment in mentoring others is unequalled.

Virginia Philip,
*MS, The Breakers Hotel,
Palm Beach, Florida*

SPLIT

nebuchadnezzar

BOUQUET

BALTHAZAR

hygrometer

JEROBOAM

ULLAGE

PAR STOCK

CULT WINES

BIN NUMBER

INVENTORY

HUMIDITY

DUMB STAGE

FUTURES MARKET

AUCTIONS

MAGNUM

PURCHASING AND STORING WINE

Perhaps the most helpful piece of information in this chapter is the fact that wines are often priced on their ability to age. It makes no sense to purchase a wine that is priced for the pleasure it can deliver in a decade if the customer intends to drink that wine the same week they buy it. This is how most of us buy wine. In this chapter, we offer a list of best value wines for drinking in the short term, as well as a list of collectible wines that will improve over time.

For wine collectors, retail shops, and restaurants, we provide important information about setting up and maintaining a wine cellar.

Just as the concept of a restaurant having an open kitchen creates theater for the dining room, so a creative display of wine brings attention to the fact that wine is an integral part of the dining experience. Shopping for that wine should be a positive experience and not a chore that provokes anxiety. Proper storage, too, is a vital element in protecting your wine investment. After all, wine is a perishable product.

WHY START A CELLAR?

The word *cellar* can refer either to the collection of wines or to the place where the wines are stored; sometimes it alludes to both. The following discussion refers to both the selection of wines for the cellar and the techniques of cellaring and proper storage.

A consumer may get started by purchasing a case of assorted wine to avoid repeated trips to the store. A favorite wine may be purchased by the case to save money or as a way to chart its evolution by trying bottles over a period of time. The first cache for a collector may be a cool, dark corner of a basement or closet. As the number of bottles increases, so does the need for space to properly store the wine and a system to record its costs and how it tasted.

TYPES OF CELLARS

There are various types of cellars: the home, wine shop, or restaurant cellar and the investor or collector cellar. The main differences between the two are purpose and scope of inventory.

Home, Wine Shop, or Restaurant

This cellar usually has three categories of wines: a great many wines purchased at relatively low prices to use as a casual beverage or to accompany a simple meal; fewer moderately priced wines for more elaborate lunches or

dinners; and a small number of expensive wines for "laying down" or for special occasions.

A wealth of well-made wines are available at less than $20 a bottle, so there can be great variety within the first category. The moderate range goes from $21 to about $50 at the retail level, while the premium wines and rarities of the world command higher prices. Within the price categories, the types of wine in the cellar may change with the seasons. The warmer months and lighter fare of summer may require a cellar to have more light whites, rosés, and sparklers, while the approach of winter signifies a time to stock up on hearty reds that better match the heavier dishes consumed during the cooler months.

Investor or Collector

This cellar requires a different strategy. The majority of wines purchased will be not for casual use but for the potential value or worth of the wines sometime in the future. The reasons for creating this type of cellar are for the investment, for the enjoyment of collecting exclusive or rare items, and for the pleasure of drinking a great wine at its peak. Powerful wines achieve more harmony over time,

and as the majority of a specific wine is usually consumed prematurely, the remaining stock increases in value.

A wine's price can be attributed to consumer awareness and acceptance, the complexity of the wine, the amount of wine produced, and the wine's predicted longevity. For example, Chardonnay is the most popular white grape, and when produced in ideal vintages and locations, it has the ability to age over two decades. The Chardonnay-based *grand cru* Montrachet in France can come only from a specific area of 20 acres/8 hectares, and the limited supply increases its value over other Chardonnay-based wines. Expect to pay about $1,000 in a restaurant for a young bottle of Montrachet.

The most popular French white wine in American restaurants is Pouilly-Fuissé, another Chardonnay-based wine from Burgundy. Because of its popularity and the fact that it can age for five to eight years, it costs about $55 in a restaurant. The lesser-known neighboring town of St-Véran makes a wine that is very similar to Pouilly-

TOP: *The wine cellar at Aureole Restaurant in Las Vegas, with a "wine angel" suspended by cables, retrieving a bottle*   BOTTOM: *Temperature-controlled wine storage at The Culinary Institute of America's American Bounty restaurant*

Fuissé but only costs about $35. St-Véran is ready to drink younger than Pouilly-Fuissé, so we suggest *Exploring Wine* readers save $20 and choose St-Véran or a Macon Villages from the same area.

Throughout the world, there are many other examples of affordable wines that are ready to drink in their youth. In Italy, consider buying Rosso di Montalcino for about $22 retail instead of Brunello di Montalcino for $75 (or more) or Nebbiolo del Langhe for $22 instead of the pricier Barolo or Barbaresco. The Rosso and Nebbiolo are admittedly not as complex as their noble brethren, but they share many of their flavors and can be very effective substitutes in food pairings.

Perhaps Champagnes could be considered an investment category by some people, but we always find occasions to consume them.

The leading wines for financial speculation continue to be the highest-quality Pinot Noirs from Burgundy, France; Cabernet Sauvignon– or Merlot-based wines from the New World or Old World; and the Super Tuscans from Italy. Some collectors specialize in a particular grape or an area that produces complex wines. For example, an investor may seek out Shiraz from Australia, Syrah from the Rhône, Priorato or Ribera del Duero from Spain, Douro from Portugal, or Barbaresco or Barolo from Italy.

For sweet wines, the most esteemed wines are true Porto from Portugal; Sauternes, such as the famous Château d'Yquem and very old bottles of vintage Madeira from Portugal or Tokaji Aszú from Hungary.

The bottom line is that it takes money to make money. The blue-chip cult Cabernet Sauvignons and châteaux from Bordeaux are the most expensive wines to purchase and also the most likely to increase in value. Expect to pay from $2,000 to $35,000 a case for these wines.

Some collectors are nondrinkers and collect wine purely for financial reasons, while other collectors devote

One of the world's most impressive cellars is at Bistro à Champlain in Sainte Marguerite-du-Lac-Masson in the Laurentian mountains of Quebec. Owner Champlain Charest's wine list has over 4,000 wines, with many available in the Methuselah (eight-bottle) format.

only a portion of their cellar to long-term aging and investment. Just as the racetrack and stock market present perilous gambles, so does wine speculation. It is as difficult to predict a wine's character twenty years from its birth as it is a person's. Educated guesses for both are based on ancestry, place and time of birth, and upbringing. As discussed in Chapter 1, factors such as low yields in the vineyards and various techniques in the winery can be used to extend the life of a wine.

DECISIONS AND DIRECTIONS ON BUYING WINE

SOME MAY CHOOSE a bottle because of an attractive label or name and take their chances, but there are methods that can help the wine buyer. Following simple guidelines and knowing where to find specialized information can be useful, whether buying an expensive bottle or case or trying to find a decent inexpensive wine.

SHOP AROUND BEFORE BUYING

PRICE, ALTHOUGH IMPORTANT in any transaction, is not the sole consideration when buying wine. Finding a store with a knowledgeable salesperson who makes the customer feel at ease is a key factor in building a relationship of trust with that establishment. Just as snooty attitudes and intimidation by servers should not be tolerated in a restaurant, these same characteristics should not be acceptable in a wine shop or wine section of a grocery store. As a good sommelier would take time to determine each guest's personal preferences in wine style and price, so a store's staff should be sensitive to the shopper's needs. Many stores keep a profile of customers' purchase preferences and send out newsletters alerting those customers of sales and tastings focusing on specific wines. Laws vary from state to state, but there are opportunities to buy wines online directly from wineries or retailers and have them shipped to your home.

TRY BEFORE YOU BUY

PROSPECTIVE MUSIC BUYERS can usually listen to tunes before buying compact discs, just as car buyers usually have a chance to take a test drive before they make a commitment. Why not use the same strategy in buying wine? Retail shops frequently offer in-house tastings, which are a fine opportunity to evaluate the wines. The producer or representative of the winery may be presenting the tasting and is therefore available to answer questions on the production methods or the anticipated maturity of the wines.

Another way to sample wines without having to buy a bottle is to try a tasting or a glass of wine at a wine bar or restaurant known for offering wines by the glass.

GET EXPERT ADVICE

THERE IS A VARIETY of methods to gain knowledge of wines. Advice from a salesperson is helpful, as is shopping with a knowledgeable acquaintance or friend. Participation in wine festivals and winemaker-sponsored nights at restaurants are other avenues. A collector or business ready to invest a large amount of money may find it more efficient and cost-effective to pay a professional consultant, whose purpose is to objectively evaluate and purchase wines on behalf of clients.

The same magazines, newspapers, and journals that offer schedules for seminars on food and wine have sections devoted to reviewing wines. Obviously, if the publication accepts advertising, the reader must be aware that the advertising could affect the reviews. The power of some of these publications and the subsequent demand for the wines they review have affected the prices of the wines. Books with tasting notes on specific wines and assessments of regions by vintage are available. Be sure to refer to the most recent editions of such books. Tasting notes on the character of a wine tasted a decade ago cannot describe the present state of the wine (though such notes usually indicate when a wine would be at its prime). The concept of rating wines numerically is certainly controversial; one person's 90 may be another's 75. The idea of placing a wine on a 100-point scale is more difficult than using a simpler five-star system, such as is used for films or hotels. The American author Robert Parker Jr. and *Wine Spectator* magazine both use the 100-point system, and their high

THE MOST IMPORTANT BUYING TIP

It is essential for consumers to understand that a wine rated 19 or 20 points out of a possible 20, or a wine that is a five-star wine on a vintage card will be given that high rating because of its value as an investment. The wines are bestowed high marks not for the pleasure they may give today but the profit they will bring the investor after a decade or more.

As stated at the beginning of this chapter, most people buy wine when they need it. They will purchase a couple of bottles of wine to drink that night or the next day. It is ridiculous to pay top dollar for a wine that will be at its prime in ten years if you are going to drink it in the next ten hours or days.

Another factor to consider is the "dumb stage," sometimes called "closed" or "shy," which refers to wines that are not showing their flavors or aromas well because they are in an awkward youthful stage of their lives. The dumb stage can last a few months or a few years. Inexpensive wines meant for early consumption do not pose this problem; it is only wines with a fine pedigree that can be capricious.

Be adventurous and try wines from lesser-known grape varieties and lesser-known areas. The best values are found off the beaten path.

Here is a short list of some great off-the-beaten-path values:

NEW WORLD SIX-PACK OF WHITE WINES A Verdelho or Sémillon from Australia, Torrontés from Argentina, Riesling from New York State, Washington, or Ontario, Marsanne from California, Pinot Gris from Oregon or British Columbia

OLD WORLD SIX-PACK OF DRY WHITE WINES Godello-based Ribeiro from Spain, Vermentino from Italy, Arinto-based Bucelas from Portugal, Assyrtiko-based Santorini or Moschofilero from Greece, Sauvignon Blanc–and Semillon-based Entre-Deux-Mers from France

NEW WORLD SIX-PACK OF DRY RED WINES Grenache and Grenache blends from Australia or Washington, Mourvèdre from California, Tannat from Uruguay, Malbec from Argentina, Carmenère from Chile, Syrah-Grenache "Rhône style" blends from South Africa

OLD WORLD SIX-PACK OF DRY RED WINES Aglianico from Basilicata, Italy, Monastrell from Jumilla or Yecla, Spain, Dão or Alentejo blends from Portugal, Nemea from Greece, Cahors from France

SWEET SIX-PACK FROM AROUND THE WORLD Moscato d'Asti from Italy, Muscat of Samos from Greece, Moscatel de Setúbal or Vintage Character Port from Portugal, Pedro Ximénez Sherry from Spain, Commandaria from Cyprus

endorsement of a wine has a strong impact on consumers; their ratings or reviews are often placed on the shelves next to the respective wines in retail shops or on wine lists. The Beverage Testing Institute in Chicago has a five-level approach, with wines obtaining a point score under 80 rated "not recommended," wines with an 80 to 84 score "recommended," those with 85 to 89 points "highly recommended," those with 90 to 95 "exceptional," and those scoring 96 to 100 "superlative." The British publication *Decanter* rates wines from one star, "acceptable," to five stars, "award," while *Wine & Spirits* magazine uses the point system supported with selections of value (great wines for the price). Ultimately, consumers and professionals should be guided by their own preferences, as the opinions printed in the aforementioned publications are just that.

Vintage charts can relieve the burden for consumers who have no desire to memorize the weather patterns of the major wine-growing regions for the past few decades. Such charts are widely available.

We all taste things differently, and one person's favorite selection may be a barely tolerable wine for the next. A group of knowledgeable writers at the same tasting often disagree among themselves as to which wines are best and why they are deserving of praise. One of the pleasures of wine for the beginner and the seasoned taster alike is supporting claims for individual preferences. Tasting terminology, discussed in Chapter 3, abounds in professional tasting reviews but may boil down to "I just think that wine is delicious." Reviews and opinions can be helpful in selecting wines for a cellar. A bottle of highly touted wine that lives up to expectations or reviews can be the inspiration to begin collecting and cellaring wines.

SHOP TALK

There's never been a better time to be a wine consumer. Ever. In terms of price, availability, and diversity, there are good and great wines out there for everyone at every budget—from "Two Buck Chuck" to a first-growth Bordeaux. With modern technology and winemaking know-how, it is quite difficult to produce a poorly made wine. It is a buyer's market.

On the other hand, with *so* many countries producing *so* much wine, the number of selections can be dizzying, with emerging regions battling classic estates for your attention, and grapes you love competing on store shelves against lesser-known regions and varietals.

Here are a few tips to make shopping for wine more fun and less frustrating, ensuring you go home with something delicious (almost) every time:

- Use your words: Just like a restaurant, a quality wine shop will have a well-trained staff of employees capable (and excited) about helping you choose the right bottle. The best way to find a new and exciting wine, a surefire crowd-pleaser, or the best value in the store is to make sure you engage the people who are there to help you. What is the season, cuisine, or occasion? This can be a launch pad (or a crush pad) for inspiration. Establish a relationship with the employees at your local wine shop. Be a loyal customer. Make a point to remember the sales clerks' names and have a dialogue with them about wines they've recommended in the past. Did you like the style, or not...and why? Sip and speak!
- Change is good: No matter how serious and frequent a wine drinker you are, you can always be surprised. For many the joy and pleasure of wine is the adventure in experiencing something new. Ever have a Cabernet Sauvignon from China, or a Tannat from Uruguay?
- Fear commitment: Never buy a case until you have tried a bottle.
- Mix it up: If you've developed a good relationship with a clerk who understands your wine preferences, consider going all the way—buy a mixed case rather than just a bottle or two. If you want to try a number of wildly different wines, or different styles of the same grapes, this is a great way to build your wine knowledge. Most wine shops also offer discounts of up to 20 percent when you purchase wine by the case, so assuming you'll drink another twelve bottles of wine in your life (or this month), it's a good investment.
- Avoid being a weekend warrior: Try not to shop for wines on Saturday during the day, or Friday evening when many folks are looking for wine—and advice. The salespeople will never be able to truly make time for you with throngs of thirsty oenophiles clamoring for help behind you. Try shopping on weekday mornings if you are able.
- Leave the calculator at home: No matter how tempting it may be to gravitate toward those little numbers (aka numerical ratings) and simply select the wine with the highest point rating, you should never let a numerical value be the arbiter of your taste.

Michael Green,
Consultant, Wine Writer

BUYING WINE AT AUCTION: STRATEGIES FOR THE CONSUMER AND THE SOMMELIER

Fine and rare wines have appeared at auction since James Christie's first sale in 1766, and auctions are now becoming a mainstay for wine lovers of all stripes.

Auction houses function by sourcing collections of fine and rare wine and establishing to the best of their ability the quality and provenance of the wines. A catalogue of the wines is produced and a sale date is set. Estimates that indicate a range of prices that the wines may sell for are included in the catalogues.

In a soft market, wines can go for less than the low estimate, while in boom times, they often exceed the high estimate. Factors that influence this include the rarity, condition, and provenance of the wines. In general, full cases sell for more per bottle than single bottles, and cases still in their original wooden case (OWC) command the greatest premium.

On sale day, clients bid on wines either by leaving an absentee bid, bidding in the room, or bidding over the telephone; some auction houses are equipped to enable bidding on the Internet in real time. The successful bidder then pays the hammer price and a premium (usually around 20 percent) to the auction house. Although the system seems difficult to navigate, auction house department specialists are always on hand to assist buyers with their transactions.

Charles Curtis,
MW, Vice President, Head of North American Wine Sales,
Christie's Wine Auctions

· ·

There are thousands of good wines available at any given moment, and good merchants spend considerable time and effort sifting through the available bottlings to select their favorites. It pays to take advantage of their efforts. When knowledge of your taste is interwoven with their understanding of the market, the result can be a delight to your palate. When you find a merchant with an honest desire to explore wines with you, reward his or her interest and efforts with your business. You'll find that it will reduce the stress and uncertainty that clouds your wine-purchasing decisions.

Wayne Belding,
MS , Wine Merchants, Boulder, Colorado

· ·

Wine purchasing on the retail level has become an increasingly more challenging position as the average consumer becomes not only educated about wine but more in tune with what they like. Unique from the on-premise side, not every customer is assisted or even has the desire to be assisted with their selection, which stresses the importance of the correct product mix. Not only is the buyer responsible for maintaining stock, but they must find a harmonious balance between wines that can sell themselves and wines they love to sell.

Rebecca Martin,
Specialty Associate Team Leader,
Whole Foods Market

In terms of buying strategies for today's consumer, I would recommend looking south of the border to countries like Chile, Argentina, and even South Africa. All three regions have benefited from a wave of modernization and investment in their wine industries and offer tremendous value in terms of pleasure-per-dollar for the wines they're putting on the market. You'll have a hard time going wrong with a $10 bottle of crisp and mouthwatering Sauvignon Blanc from Chile's Casablanca Valley or a richly fruited Argentine Malbec.

As a retail buyer, I'm looking beyond the bottle and trying to connect wines with specific occasions, particularly meals. More and more consumers are including wine in their lives on a regular basis, and we need to recognize that it's not enough to simply recommend a wine on its own merits; we're looking to move beyond the perception of wine as a cocktail beverage and towards its becoming an integral part of a good meal.

Alexander Joerger,
Wine Director and Category Manager,
A&P–Best Cellars

FUTURES MARKET

THE TERM *futures* refers to a purchasing strategy that involves buying cases of a wine after the harvest but before it is bottled. A certificate of purchase is the buyer's proof of ownership. The bottled wine is shipped to the broker or middleman, who closes the deal between winery and customer. Speculators gamble that the wine will increase in price during the aging period. French Bordeaux is the commodity most commonly sold this way, but other rarities, such as fine California Cabernet Sauvignons, are also available through this system. Sometimes portions of futures may be resold a half dozen times in the few years before the wine leaves the winery.

TERMINOLOGY USED IN WINE AUCTIONS

OWC	The wine being auctioned is in its original wooden case.
OC	The wine being auctioned is in its original carton.
WC	The wine comes in a wooden case.
DOZ.	dozen bottles
hf.bt.	half bottle (.375 liter)
bt(s).	bottle(s) (.750 liter)
mag.	magnum (1.5 liters)
d.mag.	double magnum (3 liters)
jero.	Jeroboam (3 liters)
reho.	Rehoboam (4.5 liters)
imp.	Imperial (6 liters)
meth.	Methuselah (6 liters)
salm.	Salmanazar (9 liters)
balth.	Balthazar (12 liters)
nebu.	Nebuchadnezzar (15 liters)
ULLAGE ABBREVIATIONS	
u.	ullage
n.	neck, within the neck of the bottle—normal for young wines
bn.	bottom neck—acceptable and proper ullage
vts.	very top shoulder—also acceptable ullage
ts.	top shoulder—acceptable level for wine aged over 12 to 15 years
hs.	high shoulder—acceptable level for aged wine over 15 years of age
ms.	middle shoulder—red flag; caution is advised
ls.	low shoulder—red flag; caution is strongly advised
bs.	below shoulder—avoid

VISIT A WINERY

GOING TO THE SOURCE, the winery, is an excellent way to learn about and evaluate wines.

Many wineries are open to the public for tours and have a tasting room where a small portion of their wines are poured either for free or for a small charge. The wineries may sell bottles of their own wines at reduced prices, and some may send the wine to the customer's home or business, where permitted by law. (Each country and state has its own laws to control the import of wines.) Currently, it is a crime for a winery to ship directly to some states.

Wineries that do not have regular business hours for tours and tasting may be available to visit by writing and phoning in advance. Some wineries maintain a mailing list of customers and send free newsletters that describe the wines currently available, the growing season, or promotional events. For example, many famous Cabernet Sauvignon producers in Napa and other parts of California give "first dibs" on purchasing their wine to their club members. Some producers with very small amounts of wine sell only to select restaurants and their mailing list. Other wineries are publicly held and offer stock as an incentive or give special discounts on wine to stockholders. Robert Mondavi, Ravenswood, Beringer, Constellation, R. H. Phillips, and Willamette Valley Vineyards are some of the domestic wineries traded on the stock market.

OTHER OPTIONS

OTHER VENUES for trying wines are tastings organized by local wine and food societies or government trade commissions. Listings for these events are generally found in local or national food and wine publications.

Wine can be purchased at auction, either at the actual event or by submitting bids prior to the event. American sources for buying wine at auction include Morrel and Company, Christie's, Sherry-Lehmann, Sotheby's, Zachy's, Acker Merrill, Chicago Wine Company, and Butterfield and Butterfield.

The telephone directory used to be the way to "let your fingers do the walking," but today, access to wine information and purchasing is available on the Internet. There are literally thousand of web sites related to wine tastings,

	BURGUNDY	BORDEAUX	CHAMPAGNE	PORTO
Half bottle (hf.bt.)	0.375	0.375	0.375	0.375
Imperial pint (imp.pt.)	0.568	0.568	0.568	0.568
Half liter (hf.ltr.)	0.5	0.5	0.5	0.5
Bottle(s) (bt(s).)	0.75	0.75	0.75	0.75
Liter (ltr.)	1	1	1	1
Magnum (mag.)	1.5	1.5	1.5	1.5
Marie-Jeanne (m-j.)	–	2.5	–	–
Double magnum (d.mag.)	–	3	–	3
Jeroboam (jero.)	3	5	3	–
Rehoboam (reho.)	–	–	4.5	–
Imperial (imp.)	–	6	–	–
Methuselah (meth.)	6	–	6	–
Salmanazar (salm.)	–	–	9	–
Balthazar (balth.)	–	–	12	
Nebuchadnezzar (nebu.)	–	–	15	

Modified with permission from The River Cafe Wine Primer. *Copyright © 2000 by Joseph Delissio. Boston: Little, Brown.*

"Ullage" is the term used to describe the space between the top of the wine and the cork. The Mayacamas Cabernet Sauvignon on the right may described as having some ullage because of its lower level, or fill. This is because the wine on the right is twenty-five years older than the wine on the left.

auctions, and commerce. Some state laws prohibit delivery of wine from Internet sources into the state, though the state does not directly regulate the sale.

STORING WINE

WINE IS A PRODUCT that is sensitive to changes in temperature, humidity, light, and vibration. Taken to the extreme, these conditions can ruin a wine. Terms such as "bottle shock," "COOKED," or "light-struck" are used to describe wines that taste bad or have been ruined by fluctuations in these conditions. Some wines suffer from being shipped and stored in transit at too high a temperature. Moderately priced wines so affected can usually be returned to the source for credit or refund. There are indicators that a wine may be bad without opening the bottle or tasting it. A lot of ullage—the term for the air space between the top of the wine and the bottom of the cork (see photo at left)—could be the result of a low bottle fill or some other problem. It is not certain that the wine with more ullage is bad, but it's enough to raise concern over the wine's quality. Rare wines with greater ullage sell for less than those with a higher fill. If a sealed case of wine contains bottles of different ullage, it is advisable to drink

STORING AND PURCHASING WINE

There are many wine-storage facilities in North America. A relatively new service some provide is the opportunity to taste and sell to other members of the wine-storage facility. The owners of the storage company will put potential buyers and sellers together and charge a small percentage on the deals. This is a good opportunity to find rare or older bottles of wine not generally available in retail stores.

WINE NOTES: A PERSONAL JOURNAL

The study of wine is never-ending. No one in the wine trade would presume to say they know all about wine, regardless of how much they have studied and tasted.

Figuring out what grape varieties, regions, and producers of wine you, your family, and friends like drinking is a lot easier.

Make a few simple notes when you find a wine you truly enjoy or dislike. A positive description could be as simple as "Riesling, Salmon Run, New York, 2008: semidry, fruity, tart, and inexpensive."

Or it could include the food you had it with. For example, "Great with spicy Thai Shrimp Curry."

A negative remark could be as simple as "Merlot, Poppycock, California, too light, flat, and boring" or "Stinky, yuck."

Once you start tracking your own preferences, a pattern will emerge. Sometimes it is a grape type such as Riesling, sometimes it is an area such as Priorato in Spain, sometimes it is a producer of organically grown grapes such as Lolonis, Robert Sinskey, or Benziger of California.

In each major wine-growing region of the world, we have wineries we trust to make the best wines they can. When the vintage conditions are difficult, they often declassify their wines to second labels or sell them off to another winery.

Remember, these tasting notes are for your benefit, so any system you devise or terminology you use is totally correct.

the wines with the greatest ullage first, as they mature more quickly. A cork that is pushing the capsule over the bottle lip is another sign of trouble, as is a bottle with evidence of liquid that has seeped from the top capsule. Another problem occurs with faulty corks.

Wine storage systems are available through specialty shops and catalogs. Some are built to offer temperature control as well as to meet organizational or structural needs. There are also professional storage facilities available for rent; these are listed in the telephone directory, in wine publications, and on the Internet. Some restaurants and country clubs have small storage facilities where patrons can keep a few bottles of special wine to be enjoyed with their meals. Restaurants or country clubs that offer that service may charge an annual fee or a corkage charge.

STORAGE CONDITIONS

THE PRIVATE CONSUMER should not be too concerned about a wine's stability if the wine is intended for drinking in the near future. However, wines that require years of cellaring to mature and develop balance tend to be expensive and well worth protecting.

Assuming the wine is sound, the ideal conditions for temperature, humidity, light, vibration, oxygen, and water are as follows:

Temperature

A constant temperature of 55°F/13°C is considered best for keeping wines. An area that heats up to 75°F/24°C in the day and chills down to 35°F/2°C at night is not a good location. It is better to have a more consistent temperature, slightly lower or higher than the ideal, than to have severe fluctuations. Cellars that are too cold retard a wine's maturation, whereas hot temperatures, over 75°F/24°C, can cause a wine to taste hot as well; such a wine is described as "cooked," and there is no way for it to recover. Thermometers are common equipment in wine cellars, as are air conditioners. A business should have a power generator as a backup to the regular power source in case of an outage; however, temperatures several degrees higher or lower than 55°F/13°C or minor fluctuations would not warrant the expense or energy usage of an air conditioner.

CORK, THE CONTROVERSIAL STOPPER

Cork is the most popular stopper used for quality wines. Cork's elasticity has made it the preferred protector of liquids in bottles, protecting the bottle's contents from the smells, molds, bacteria, and oxygen outside the bottle.

Portugal is the world's leading grower and producer of cork, with 1.65 million acres/670,000 hectares of the *Quercus suber* type of oak, from which cork is taken. Spain has 1.18 million acres/480,000 hectares, and Algeria, Tunisia, and Morocco are also major growers that export cork to be processed in Portugal.

A cork tree is first stripped of its outer bark when it reaches twenty-five years. Cork trees usually live for more than a century and a half and are stripped once every nine years. The long strips, after they are dried outdoors, are boiled, dried again, and shaped. Traditionally the corks were bleached for appearance and sanitary reasons. Unfortunately, the chemical compound 2,4,6 trichloroanisole (TCA) can result from the bleaching process, and it tends to remain in the cork. When this happens, it causes an unpleasant moldy smell in the bottle, which is referred to as "corked." Research is under way to offer alternative methods to sanitize and preserve the cork's natural flexibility and avert problems related to molds or bacteria.

To facilitate their insertion into and extraction from bottles, corks are usually coated with wax or another lubricant. Corks are often stamped with the name of the wine producer and may also carry the symbol or name of the cork producer. The cheapest corks are made from dust or small bits of cork formed into the cork shape and are called "agglomerate." Corks for sparkling wine, which have to be wider and able to withstand more pressure than those used for still wines, are often made from agglomerate with disks of whole cork at the bottom.

Simple wines for early consumption may have corks as short as 1 inch/2.5 centimeters. The finest wines that are intended for long aging use whole cork with few markings. These corks can be up to 2.3 inches/6 centimeters long. A winemaker purchasing corks in advance would do best to store them at temperatures of 59°–68°F/12°–15°C, with humidity under 70 percent, as there is much less chance of mold at that level.

Cork's ability to allow small amounts of air into the bottle can be seen as both positive and potentially damaging. Cork is about 80 percent oxygen, and there is much debate about whether a small amount of oxygen entering the wine is beneficial or detrimental. Detractors of screwcaps say that the lack of oxygen in the wine can lead to unpleasant reductive, rubbery smells.

Warmer temperatures in a cellar cause expansion of both the wine and the air in the bottle. Air expands thirty-two times more than water and much more than the glass bottle. Cork is able to resist slight temperature variations but usually succumbs to large swings in temperature, allowing wine to leak out of a bottle laid on its side or air to enter the bottle. Even if there is no great temperature change, oxygen may also enter through the cork because of the difference in pressure outside and inside the bottle. The longer the cork, the more resistant it is to such conditions.

Bottles in a wine cellar are laid on their side so that the cork is in contact with the wine. If the bottle were stored standing straight up, the cork could dry out and deteriorate, allowing excess air to enter.

Debate continues over the use of stoppers other than cork, and some wineries have begun to use synthetic cork, screw tops, crown caps, glass closures, or corks covered with polymer. About a third of the wine consumed in America today is from a bag-in-the-box carton or a tetra pak container.

Both consumers and wineries want reliable stoppers, but there is a feeling expressed by consumers and some winemakers that wines with real corks are more authentic and will age better than those with metal crown caps (as on beer bottles) or screwcaps. The cork industry has made some real progress in reducing the number of corks attacked by TCA, but a good estimate is that somewhere between 8 and 12 percent of all wines with a cork are affected, either at a stage when the wine starts to lose its personality or the advanced stage when it smells moldy.

Perhaps there is a certain romance associated with cork, but for those who have been let down by the natural cork plug one time too many, it is a source of frustration. (To learn about alternatives to cork, see "Cork: Is the Honeymoon Over?," page 659.)

Humidity

The best level of humidity for storing wine is around 70 to 75 percent. Mold is less likely to form when the humidity is under 80 percent. (See the discussion in "Cork, The Controversial Stopper," page 683.) However, higher humidity reduces the risk that some of the wine in the bottles will evaporate and be replaced with oxygen, which makes the wine mature faster and may cause spoilage. A cork that is wet on both ends and increased ullage are warning signs of excessive evaporation. Many European or Old World companies put the capsule on over the cork just before shipping, so sometimes the consumer will see a small amount of mold on the top of the cork after removing the capsule on such wines. (In contrast, most New World wineries put the capsule on the bottle prior to storage.)

A hygrometer, a device used for measuring relative humidity, can be found at hardware stores and wine shops. A way to increase humidity in a very dry commercial cellar is to spread a bed of stones or gravel on the floor and intermittently sprinkle the floor with water. Conversely, an electric dehumidifier can be used for overly damp conditions. A solution of half propylene glycol and half distilled water in an open jug can also diminish humidity. To get rid of mildew on the walls—a common problem in very moist environments—a solution of one part water to one part laundry bleach can be used. To avoid loss through evaporation, wineries often store barrels at close to 90 percent humidity.

Light

Light can harm a wine in several ways. First, exposure to direct sunlight can increase the wine's temperature, affecting it negatively; also, alternating between the warmth of direct sunlight and the cool of darkness sets up temperature fluctuations that can damage wine. Ultraviolet light from direct sunlight can give wine unpleasant aromas and may potentially ruin it. Sparkling wines are especially susceptible to this problem. Most sparkling wine producers are moving away from clear glass and to green, except for their rosés and Blanc de Noirs, where they want to show off the attractive color of the wine. The clear glass bottle of Louis Roederer's Cristal Champagne comes individually wrapped in golden-yellow plastic for protection, and many other producers are using similar paper protectors, which should be left on until service. Technological advances in the 1990s have allowed for the production of green-colored CHAMPAGNE BOTTLES that are 90 percent effective in blocking ultraviolet rays. A brown-colored bottle is 100 percent effective but is not seen as something consumers would find attractive.

Fluorescent lights are thought to be more harmful to wine than mercury vapor, sodium, or incandescent lights. Some retailers are switching to those lighting alternatives. Consumers shopping in a wine store with fluorescent lights may choose to buy the bottle that is stored below, behind, or under the one on display, as that display bottle will be receiving the most fluorescent light.

Vibration

Excessive vibration may disturb a red wine's sediment and possibly the wine itself. Some jostling of a bottle will not destroy a wine, but those in earthquake-prone areas, such as California, should take precautions. Wine bottles may be surrounded by plastic bubble wrap or some other protective material.

Oxygen

As discussed earlier in this section, oxygen can accelerate the maturing of a wine or ruin it completely. An oxidized wine such as a Madeira may be stored upright. Traditionally, all wines are stored on their side (see photo on page 675), but recent research suggests that sparkling wines may be stored upright. Some producers of sparkling wine are now experimenting with storing bottles vertically.

Water

This is another potential hazard, although not as directly harmful to wine as other environmental factors. It is best not to set bottles or cases of wine directly on the floor, as dampness tends to collect there. Moisture on the outside of the bottle may not harm the wine, but it can ruin the label, making the bottles less attractive for home consumption or sale. Wood pallets can be used to raise a case off the floor.

KEEPING A CELLAR BOOK

HAVING A RECORD of which wines are in the cellar and how much they cost is a starting point for organizing your cellar. A scrapbook that includes notes of how a wine tasted and which friends or business clients enjoyed it is also useful. Comments on the wine may be a few simple words, such as "dry, green apple smell; tastes tart and not too heavy in the mouth." A more rigorous system using tasting sheets such as the ones shown on pages 104–107 could also be warranted for the serious collector or for business needs.

Charting a wine's character over time is important. Perhaps a specific white wine is beginning to brown on the rim, indicating full maturity. An owner of several cases of the wine should not panic but may wish to plan an event to use the wine in the near future. On the other hand, if a red was opened and it was opaque, black cherry in color, and very astringent on the palate, the owner would not use any more of this wine in the immediate future, as it will improve in balance with age. Another consideration is that many fine wines go through a *dumb stage*, a period during which a wine seems to close up, showing limited complexity in aromatics or flavor. The owner of a case of dumb or overly tannic red wine has the luxury of trying another bottle a year or two later and then waiting for the optimal time to serve the remainder.

The cellar book, whether an actual log book or a computer software program, can function as a business tool when it helps maintain inventory, but wine that is shared is also a source of pleasure to be remembered. To that end, the label of a wine may be soaked and peeled off the bottle to be pasted in a book. Another memento could be photographs of the foods served and people attending when the wine was enjoyed. If a menu was printed that included the wines served, this could also be placed in a cellar book. There are no steadfast rules of what must be included in a cellar log book.

A wine cellar can be an underground space, or an above-ground refrigerated unit, or somewhere in between. It should be cool and dark and not near anything that vibrates a lot. The cooler the cellar, 55° to 65°F, the longer you can keep your wines.

One mistake people make is to put wines in their cellar and then forget to take them out and enjoy them! One way to stay on top of your collection and also learn about aging is to get three or six or twelve bottles of a certain wine, and then pick a familiar day to taste a bottle. That day might be New Year's Day or your birthday, etc. Taste one bottle, making a note of the date tasted, and making notes on the color, aroma, and flavor. The following year, try another bottle and make notes again. After a couple of years, you will begin to see the evolution of the wine and how your cellar affects that wine. Try it with both dry and sweet wines. It will become an invaluable learning experience.

Harriet Lembeck,
CWE, CSS, President, Wine and Spirits Program Inc.,
Author, Educator, New York, New York

Proper storage of wine should be foremost in the minds of restaurateurs seriously considering a wine program. In fact, wine storage should be approached with the same consideration as the storage of meat, fish, or produce, and for the same reasons. Loss of revenue due to wine storage is equally, if not more, damaging to your finances than food spoilage, and it is more easily avoided. Therefore, no serious wine program can be developed if the wines are unable to maintain or achieve their optimal character, which is gained only by proper cellaring. The same holds true for the connoisseur or collector of wine. Nothing can be more disappointing than opening a serious bottle only to find its pleasures have succumbed to the lack of proper storage.

Tim Buzinski,
Proprietor, Beacon Wine Shop,
Beacon, New York

In the past ten years, the value of a quality wine program has dramatically increased in the minds of restaurant proprietors. Because of this, we can expect to see more world-class wine programs.

In the case of Aureole in Las Vegas (see photo on page 674), the architect's mindset was to create for the wines the greatest on-premises marketing tool. Although I believe this was accomplished, there were a variety of challenges that had to be dealt with if a forty-two-foot tower was to be efficient and functional. Although climate was not an issue, since there were four massive cooling and humidifying units on each level, retrieving and stocking the bottles while dangling four stories above the ground did pose a few issues. After the logistics of a bin-numbering system for the ten-thou-sand-plus bottles and the writing of a job description for a "wine angel" were conquered, the only true storage issues were those of light contact and what to do with the wines throwing sediment. Solving the latter prob-lem was simple enough; we built a rare-wine cellar on the ground. A bit more troublesome was the problem of light. Since there is a real concern of spoilage when light comes into contact with wine, both from the UV rays in sunlight and, to a lesser degree, from artificial lighting, before the first bottle was placed in the tower all the windows were covered with screens providing 100 per-cent UV blockage. Furthermore, a second, total-blackout screen was applied to finish the job. This was not part of the original design, but we felt it was vital enough to make the change. Voilà—mission accomplished.

Every storage facility will inevitably have a logistical challenge of some sort. The key is to care enough about the way the wine is handled in your establishment to do something about it. Start by serving and storing your wines at the right temperatures and continue from there.

Steven A. Geddes,
MS, Former Director of Wine, Aureole,
Las Vegas, Nevada

ESTABLISHING INITIAL INVENTORY

ALTHOUGH A PRIVATE CONSUMER may keep records for his or her personal pleasure and information, the business operator has a large investment in wine, which demands a more stringent system of organization and planning.

A wine shop or restaurant stocks wines to supply its customers. (Wine list strategy is explained in Chapter 18.) A wine shop develops its catalog of wines based on infor-mation gleaned from periodicals and tastings, the personal preferences of the managers and owners, and the needs of the targeted clientele. The demographics of the area served by the business may point the way to including more wines from specific areas or at higher or lower ends of the price range. A store must decide how much space to devote to low-end, medium-range, and high-priced wines, just as a restaurant does. The business must also decide whether to offer a wide range of products or to be known more as a specialist in a particular country's wines.

Questions that a business must address include what percentage of the investment should be in expensive wines requiring cellar time before they can be sold, or whether it may be better to forgo the expensive wines and take ad-vantage of the discounts available when purchasing mul-tiple cases of inexpensive and moderately priced wines.

The four possible contributors to the cost of maintain-ing a cellar are:

1 **COST OF THE FACILITY** A wine cellar takes up space that could be used by a restaurant for seating customers and bringing in more revenue, or by a shop for inexpensive inventory that is going to move more quickly. In high-rent areas, a business may opt to devote a minimum of space to on-premise storage of wines and keep the majority of stock off the premises at a less expensive warehouse.

2 **LABOR** The more extensive the cellar, the higher the labor cost to maintain the facility. Software track-ing systems must be backed up by periodical physical inventories.

3 **COST OF INVENTORY** The funds tied up in inventory are not available for speculative investments that could be more lucrative, or for other needs such as promotion of the business.

4 **TAXES** Some states in the United States charge a tax on alcohol held in inventory, which adds to the costs.

There has been so much written about building a successful wine program. Usually the focus is wine list construction, what wines to include, and the importance of staff training in selling. What is rarely discussed is the challenge of just getting the wine. Many of the small independent suppliers that took pride in customer service and made their own deliveries have been swallowed up by larger companies that often fail to provide the same level of service. Because the focus has been shifted so blatantly from small customer service–oriented companies to huge profit-focused entities, errors are frequent.

It is so important to have a system in place to avoid the headaches of being strapped with incorrect and damaged items. Put a system in place for yourself or for your staff if you do not do the receiving yourself. If someone other than you is receiving the order, make sure they are trained to spot damaged goods. A purchase order or similar document for each distributor you have ordered from should be readily available for reference at the receiving area. The information on it should include:

- Name of distributor
- Name of producer, such as Wild Horse
- Varietal, blend, or proprietary name such as Pinot Noir, Meritage, or Alluvium Blanc
- Any specific region or subregion, such as Rutherford, Napa Valley
- Any special attributes, such as Reserve or Late Harvest
- Any vineyard designation, such as Mitsuko's Vineyard
- Include whether the wine is Vintage (1997), Nonvintage (NV), or Late Bottled Vintage (LBV 1998)
- Bottle size, such as 750ml, 1.5 liter
- Number of bottles or cases expected, such as 3c/12 (3 cases, each containing 12 bottles)
- Distributor code number for each item, if available
- Your inventory code or bin number

As the orders are checked in, they should also be inspected for flaws like damaged or missing labels, broken or empty bottles, leaking bottles, and signs of oxidation, especially in white wines. Any incorrect or damaged items should be sent back to the warehouse on the truck. Any differences in the order should be noted on the receiving document for tracking and reference purposes.

Having a receiving system in place and a knowledgeable person to handle it is worth the extra effort and money. Without it, a wine program can't be successful.

Noelle Guagliardo, CHE
Manager, Beverage Operations, and Adjunct Wine Instructor,
The Culinary Institute of America, Hyde Park Campus, New York

Most wines do not increase very much in value, and the small amount saved on multiple-case purchases of inexpensive wines may not be the best financial return. The expensive "cult" wines of the world may increase in value, but they are an expensive investment. The greatest possible gains come from rare wines, but these also offer the most risk. Wine is a perishable commodity, and, just as when playing the stock market, the investor has to know the background information on the wine and its potential in order to determine when to buy or sell. When dealing with imported wine, another factor to consider is the fluctuation of the dollar against foreign currency such as the euro.

Just as a restaurant tracks its sales of food products, so must a business check wine sales and inventory to be able to replenish stock and assess a product's popularity.

A number of software programs are available for use in updating wine lists and figuring out sales and percentages of costs versus income on items, as well as scheduling reorders of wines.

PAR STOCK

BEFORE SCHEDULING THE REORDER, it is important to establish par stock. Par stock is the set amount or the maximum number of each wine that should be kept on hand. The par stock for a popular, inexpensive Chardonnay will be much higher than that of a more expensive, lesser-known wine. New businesses make an educated guess when setting the initial par stock levels for each item. Then the levels are adjusted as the sales data are recorded. A par stock should

POST OFFS

VERTICAL FLIGHT

CORKAGE FEE

SLIDING SCALE

off the beaten path

MARKUP

QUARTINO

horizontal flight

STYLE

theme

DEPTH

CONSISTENCY

WINE LISTS

THIS CHAPTER WILL SERVE the needs of both professionals and consumers. For the consumer, there are tips to simplify the selection of wine and to get the best value for the money. For those in the hospitality business, the chapter offers guidelines for the selection and pricing of wines, ways to organize them on the list, and possible designs or style of the list. A wine list, just like a menu, should evolve to reflect the seasons, trends, sales analysis of specific wines, and feedback from the customers. Wine directors, sommeliers, restaurant managers, food and beverage managers, or proprietors undertake this important task of implementing, maintaining, and updating exciting wine lists that will reflect the food, ambience, and location of their respective establishments.

From its inception, the wine list should be an integral marketing tool that will make a restaurant or catering facility a destination for customers. This chapter also includes quotes and advice that offer the valuable expertise of many respected and successful professionals in the wine and hospitality industry.

Just as there is no single approach to growing grapes because there are numerous varieties and a myriad of possible growing conditions, there is no one recipe for an infallible wine list. The list needs to be one piece in an overall management concept that emphasizes wine as an essential part of the total dining experience. If a wine list, by its use or misuse, projects a notion that wine is for special-

occasion dining only, then wine sales will suffer. The list must reflect the fact that the restaurant, its managers, and its staff expect the customer to order wine. (Professionals reading this chapter should refer to Chapters 14, 16, and 17 for discussions of food pairing, wine service, and purchasing.) The cliché is correct: the chain is only as strong as its weakest link. To create an appropriate wine list and not be wholeheartedly behind the education of the staff serving the wines and to exclude them from the process of selection is a mistake.

The "back" and "front" of the house (kitchen and dining room, respectively) must have mutual respect and maintain dialogue so that the team will have access to information and opportunities for input to ameliorate the wine program.

The commitment of making a major financial investment in wine must be coupled with having a proper facility to store it. Unless there is a system in place to monitor inventory and order replenishments in a timely manner, the credibility and quality of a beverage program will be undermined. The person in charge of receiving deliveries must have the knowledge to refuse orders if the wine is not exactly what was ordered. It is frustrating for customers to settle on a wine choice and then be told that the item is out of stock, and if a second choice is also out of stock or a different single vineyard or vintage, the customer will think the wine program is "bush league."

MEET CUSTOMER EXPECTATIONS

CUSTOMERS OFTEN have preconceived expectations when they enter a restaurant. A Spanish tapas restaurant that does not have a broad selection of Cava, Sherry, and still wines would be a disappointment to the guest. A French bistro with an all-American wine list? Not cool, but an American bistro with an all-American wine list is fine.

Demographic information and culinary profiles of guests can help the restaurant understand what customers want to eat and drink, how they want it presented and served, and how much they are willing to pay for it. This information is readily available from organizations such as the National Restaurant Association and local chambers of commerce and is often published in trade journals such as *Wine & Spirits, Decanter, Santé, Wine Spectator, Saveur, Wine Enthusiast,* and *Restaurant Business.*

These magazines chronicle what is "hot" and what is not. Cabernet Sauvignon is still the most popular red, with "food friendly" Pinot Noir in second place, while Syrah and Zinfandel compete for third. Who knows how long the much-maligned Merlot will remain in the doghouse?

In addition, climate can affect local wine preferences, as warmer areas generally consume more whites, rosés, light reds (which can be chilled), and sparkling wines than cooler areas. A winter wine list could show a heavier emphasis on red wines than a summer list.

> Prejudiced though I may be, I am a firm believer that no cook can become a great chef without a solid understanding of the role wine plays in the kitchen and at the table. Wine is both a garnish and a condiment for food, changing and enhancing the way the diner tastes the finished product.
>
> Danny Meyer,
> *Co-Owner, Union Square Cafe, Gramercy Tavern, Eleven Madison Park, Tabla, The Modern, Maialino, Shake Shack, and Blue Smoke, New York, New York*

Restaurants in areas with a large ethnic population will support those wines. For example, in San Juan, Puerto Rico, and Miami, Spanish and South American wines rule. In Montreal, it is French wines, while in Newark, New Jersey, Portuguese wines do well, just as Astoria in New York is great for Greek wines. Italian wines are the most popular imports, but in neighborhoods with a large Italian-American base, they vie with California for most popular status.

Someone dining in a fine restaurant on Long Island, New York; in Portland, Oregon; or in the wine country of Canada would want to see a few local wines on the list.

If the average price of a main course is $18, it would be ridiculous for the least expensive wine on the list to be $39. At a special-occasion formal restaurant, a customer might be disappointed if there was an absence of an expensive Champagne, or white or red wine over $100.

Whether it be an $18, $180, or $1,800 bottle, the wines must be fairly priced. Never underestimate how savvy customers are. They may be very familiar with retail prices of wines and can be so turned off by excessive markups that they will skip the wine as a matter of principle.

ADVICE FOR CONSUMERS: HOW I BEAT THE SYSTEM

CONSUMERS CAN READ this entire chapter and glean information about how wine lists are set up while gaining insight on the pricing strategy that many restaurants and catering firms use. Here are some basic tips on getting the best-value wine selections and navigating a wine list.

First, try to find a couple of popular wines that you are familiar with and know the retail price of. Say the retail price of one wine is $20. That means that the probable wholesale cost is about $13.50, about a third less than retail. If that wine is under $40 on the list, it means that the markup is no more than triple wholesale, which is average. If it is $35, then the mark up is only two and a half times, which is of course better. Time to relax and choose a wine. If the wine sells for $60, *caveat emptor*—buyer beware!

> When designing a wine list, there are certainly many factors to consider, but none is more important than the cuisine of the restaurant. It is the sommelier's duty, then, to create a wine list that enhances the dining experience by complementing the cuisine of the chef. Better yet, think of the wine program as a condiment, just as you would think of mustard. Wine should not dominate the meal; rather, it should help make the food taste better, thereby contributing to the overall dining pleasure. Wine is food, and wine's place is on the table with food.
>
> Steven Olson,
> *Proprietor, AKA Winegeek Beverage Consultants, New York, New York*

The customer must proceed carefully to find a less popular wine that may not be priced as aggressively.

The blue-chip wines such as red Bordeaux or Burgundy from France, Cabernet Sauvignon or Merlot from Napa, Super Tuscans or Brunello di Montalcino from Italy, and cult wines from elsewhere will never be the best values on a wine list. For those empowered to order those wines at whatever price, we say "Cheers!" For the majority of restaurant patrons, we want good wine at a fair price most days and for special occasions great wine that is undervalued on a list. The way to accomplish this is to look for the "other grape varieties." Although there are some yummy Chardonnays and Cabernets out there, they are rarely the best-value wines or the most adaptable with diverse foods. There are great values to be had in lesser-known areas of well-known wine-producing countries such as the United States, Australia, France, Italy, Chile, and Spain. Want to get even wilder? Check out wines from Portugal, Greece, Uruguay, Argentina, Israel, Lebanon, and New Zealand. Rosé wines are always a bargain, many are bone dry, and most are easy to quaff as a cocktail or pair with food.

Here is a list of some off-the-beaten-path wines to check out.

NEW WORLD

DRY SPARKLING WINES

U.S.A. Sparkling wines from New Mexico, New York State, Washington State, and Oregon

DRY WHITE WINES

U.S.A. Sémillon, Marsanne or Marsanne-Roussanne blends, Viognier, Pinot Blanc, and Albariño

AUSTRALIA Wines based on Verdelho, Sémillon, or Sémillon-Sauvignon blends

NEW ZEALAND Viognier and Pinot Gris

ARGENTINA Torrontés

DRY RED WINES

U.S.A. Mourvèdre, Grenache, or Mourvèdre-Grenache-Syrah blends; Carignan, Petite Sirah, Zinfandel blends, Charbono, Barbera, Gamay, and Tempranillo; Lemberger from Washington State; Cabernet Franc from New York State

CANADA Pinot Noir

AUSTRALIA "GSM": Grenache-Syrah-Mourvèdre blends

NEW ZEALAND Pinot Noir

ARGENTINA Bonarda or Malbec

CHILE Carmenère

SOUTH AFRICA Syrah blends

OFF-DRY OR SEMISWEET WINES

U.S.A. AND CANADA Chenin Blanc, Riesling, and Gewürztraminer

NEW ZEALAND Riesling and Gewürztraminer

SOUTH AFRICA Steen (Chenin Blanc)

OLD WORLD

DRY SPARKLING WINES

SPAIN Cava

ITALY Prosecco

FRANCE Crémant d'Alsace and Blanquette de Limoux

PORTUGAL Espumante

GREECE Moschofilero-based sparkling wine from the Peloponnese

DRY WHITE WINES

ITALY Vermentino, Falanghina, Vernaccia di San Gimignano, Tocai, Ribolla Gialla, Verdicchio, Greco di Tufo

FRANCE Entre-Deux-Mers, Muscadet Sèvre-et-Maine, Quincy, Jasnières, Menetou-Salon, Aligoté, Rully, Sylvaner, Pinot Blanc, Les Baux de Provence, St-Joseph

SPAIN Rueda, Rioja, Ribeiro, Rías Baixas, Albariño, Valdeorras, Penedès

PORTUGAL Vinho Verde, Alvarinho, Bucelas, Bairrada, Dão, Terras do Sado, Douro, Alentejo

GREECE Moschofilero, Malagousia, Roditis, Athiri, or Robola single-grape variety wines or blends from Santorini, Drama, Rhodes, Amyndeo, and Peloponnese

GERMANY Ruländer (Pinot Gris)

HUNGARY Furmint

AUSTRIA Grüner Veltliner

DRY RED WINES

ITALY Aglianico del Vulture, Salice Salentino, Nero d'Avola, Cannonau di Sardegna, Primitivo, Refosco, Teroldego Rotaliano, Lagrein, Ruché, Sagrantino di Montefalco, Morellino di Scansano, Inferno, Valtellina, Ghemme, Spanna, Nebbiolo delle Langhe, Barbera d'Asti, Barbera d'Alba

FRANCE Minervois, Faugères, Fitou, Côte du Roussillon-Villages, Caramany, Costières du Nimes, Collioure, Coteaux du Tricastin, La Clape, Corbières, Madiran, Côtes du Marmandais, Les Baux de Provence, Rasteau, Gigondas, Vacqueyras, Chinon, Bourgueil, Fronsac, Cahors, Collioure, Cairanne, St-Aubin, Santenay, Mercurey

SPAIN Garnacha, Tempranillo, or Monastrell single-variety or blends from Penedès, Campo de Borja, Jumilla, Yecla, Toro, Montsant, Ribera del Guadiana, Cariñena, Navarra, Costers del Segre, Castilla y León, and La Mancha; Prieto Picudo from Tierra de León

PORTUGAL Single-varietal Touriga Nacional, Tinta Roriz, Castelão, Trincadeira, Baga, Jaen, Sousão, blends from Douro, Dão, Beiras, Bairrada, Tejo, Alentejo, and Lisboa

GREECE Xinomavro or Agiorgitiko single-variety or blends from Naoussa, Nemea, Rapsani, Drama, Epanomi, and Goumenissa

SWEET WINES

ITALY Moscato d'Asti and Vin Santo

FRANCE Muscat de Rivesaltes, Jurançon, and Maury

SPAIN Pedro Ximénez from Montilla-Moriles or Jerez

PORTUGAL Moscatel de Setúbal, Reserve Porto, and 5 Year Malmsey Madeira

GREECE Commandaria from Cyprus, Muscat of Samos, Vinsanto, and Mavrodaphne

Find the Sweet Spot on the Wine List

The least expensive wine on a wine list and a house wine are often the worst value. Since the restaurant sells so many of those wines, they may mark them up four to five times the wholesale price. To entice customers to spend more money, restaurants may only multiply the wholesale price by two and a half times for wines in the $45 to $85 price range. Pricy wines at some restaurants may be marked up less than twice wholesale.

For example, if a restaurant buys a bottle that costs them $5 and sells the wine for $25, they have a final cost of only 20 percent, but they only generate $20 profit. If they buy one for $30 and sell it for $75, their final cost is 40 percent but they have $45 profit. Finally, if the restaurant buys a wine for $200 and sells it for $300, they have a 75 percent final cost but get $100 profit. Believe it or not, there are cases of restaurants just across the street from each other where a $200 wholesale wine is priced at $300 in one restaurant and $600 in the other.

Different restaurants have different sweet spots. One way to find the best-value area is to ignore the few inexpensive and expensive wines and figure out the range of prices where most of the wines fall. At many restaurants it may be $29 to $55. Find the middle ground or average of those prices, and that $42 point and up is likely to be the price level where best values begin.

Go online and research the restaurant wine list. Whenever possible, check it out. That way, you and your guests will know you are not walking into a trap, where the wines are priced too high.

Most servers and sommeliers really want to please you and find the best wine for your palate and your foods, so let them know some of the styles of wine you like. The more information you share with the sommelier or server, the more likely it is that she or he will bring you a wine you enjoy.

Never, ever, be embarrassed to set a price point that is your limit. No server should intimidate you into spending more than you want to.

THE WINE LIST

THEME AND STYLE

A WINE LIST is a marketing tool used to inform and sell, and it must be user-friendly. Whether there are helpful maps, background information about a winery or a region, flavor profiles of wines, or food and wine suggestions, the information should never be given in a pedantic manner. A light-hearted approach or one that celebrates the pleasures of enjoying wine and food is the best way to entertain and educate guests.

The wine list should be consistent with the level of service; decor; style of plates, cutlery, and glassware; music; and of course, the food.

Wines listed on a chalk board, on laminated paper table tents, or as a handwritten sheet are fine for a casual restaurant. The list could even be printed daily and given to customers to keep as a souvenir. It could include promotions for upcoming events at the restaurant, such as a dinner paired with the wines of a guest winemaker or a week when the wines of a specific region are featured or discounted.

A white-tablecloth or formal restaurant's wine list will probably be lengthier and presented in a more elegant fashion than a list for a casual spot. We applaud restaurants that have a well thought-out short wine list that is part of the food menu. Such menus may have a statement letting customers know there is another larger "reserve" or "captain's" wine list available upon request.

Some restaurants offer diners a computer containing the list, which gives diners a chance to link up to the wineries' websites to obtain more information on specific wines. In short, the wine list must reflect the restaurant's ambience.

Many customers are overwhelmed by large wine lists and prefer a short list of, say, fifty to eighty wines, so they can spend their time conversing with their dining companions. For some wine lovers, an exciting and extensive wine list will make that restaurant destination a pilgrimage they obsess about.

There is no one formula for how many wines should be on such a list. Usually it is the large upscale restaurants that have extensive lists, yet an intimate restaurant could have a large selection if finances and storage space permit. A restaurant with a smaller footprint can have an exten-

> In my experience, the design of the wine list is almost as important as the content. Here are some wine-list features that increase sales:
> - One-page format. It is easy to use, less intimidating, and you can deliver one to every table. If guests have to ask for the wine list, chances are they won't bother.
> - By-the-glass prices listed next to the bottle price. One-step shopping is easier and faster.
> - Wines arranged by style, from light to full body. This is really a handy format for servers to know how one wine differs from another.
>
> **Andrea M. Immer Robinson,**
> *MS, Consultant, Author*

sive wine list by using off-premise storage for the bulk of their wines, while keeping a small par stock of each wine at the restaurant.

Once the people in charge have decided on the physical format or style of the wine list and the number of wines to be included, the selection process can begin.

SELECTION

THE WINE SELECTION should reflect the restaurant's ambience and food. A Tuscan trattoria with a fairly large list of one hundred wines should have some depth in its selection of Tuscan wines (perhaps twenty-five wines), while one or two Tuscan wines might be sufficient for a Continental restaurant trying to show breadth with a general sampling of the major wine regions of Europe. When a restaurant's cuisine is based on an area without quality wine production, Vietnamese or Swedish for example, the strategy should be to choose wines that will partner well with the foods in a range of prices appropriate to the menu.

An American restaurant showcasing regional foods may not require any European wines. It can still create excitement by offering a diverse selection of grape types with different styles of each. For example, the restaurant could list stainless-steel-aged and oak-aged Chardonnays in both current and older vintages and from both cool and warm regions. It also may offer a flight (smaller portions of a few selections served simultaneously). A horizontal flight, for example, might include several 2009 Chardonnays from different

No matter how much I have learned about wine, I've never been comfortable with long, encyclopedic wine lists. They make me feel like a restaurateur has just thrown money at the wine problem instead of providing a service to the customer. The best list provides a selection of wines thoughtfully tailored to the food; such a focused selection rarely needs to be more than fifty wines. Anything more than that can effectively appear on a reserve list, which still should be chosen to complement the food. If this emphasis on style and compatibility sounds so obvious, then why are there so many lists made up primarily of Cabernet and Chardonnay?

Joshua Greene,
Publisher, Wine & Spirits *Magazine*

WINE LIST PHILOSOPHY

I believe all menus, whether food or wine, should tell a "story." Not a prosaic story as such, but a story that inherently, by its offerings and descriptions, subtly imparts a sense of place and a sense of the person who wrote the menu. The best menus and lists should have a personal aspect to them. A well thought-out wine list is not just a compendium of good-tasting wines. I see hundreds of wonderful wines that I do not buy. There needs to be a relationship between each entry in a category. As the wine director of the Wentworth by the Sea Hotel, my wine list reflects some of my favorite wines, some of the wine regions I have traveled to and hold special, some of the winemakers I have met and most admire, and some of the "gems" or "good buys" I have procured—all in the context of what matches our dining room's cuisine and style.

Michele Duval,
Wine Director, Wentworth by the Sea Hotel, New Hampshire

producers, while a vertical flight would sample three or four vintages from the same Chardonnay producer.

Another strategy is to avoid the ubiquitous Chardonnay-dominated lists. It is not uncommon to see wine lists with thirty dry white wines and twenty-five are Chardonnay. Some white wine alternatives are Marsanne, Roussanne, Pinot Blanc, Pinot Gris, Malvasia, Sémillon, Albariño, Chenin Blanc, Gewürztraminer, Riesling, and Sauvignon Blanc (also known as Fumé Blanc). Instead of just having a list dominated by Cabernet Sauvignon, Syrah (also known as Shiraz), Merlot, Pinot Noir, and Zinfandel, consider offering some other fine red grape varieties or blends. Grenache, Petite Sirah, Charbono, Barbera, Mourvèdre, and Tempranillo are just some of the other fine red wines California has to offer. We are not suggesting that wine lists should not have a decent representation of Chardonnays, just that a customer may be delighted to have other options. Those other options may very well end up being the perfect choice for the foods of that restaurant.

A restaurant that specializes in spicy hot food should definitely be lighter on the tannic Chardonnay and Cabernet Sauvignon selections in their wine-list mix. It is more important for that restaurant to feature lower-alcohol, lighter-style wines with forward fruit flavors. For white wines, Vinho Verde from Portugal, Riesling from Germany or the New World, Galestro from Italy, Sylvaner from France, and Moschofilero from Greece are good choices. Rosé still and sparkling wines, and light-bodied, fruity reds are good choices for restaurants with spicy foods. (For more on pairing, see Chapter 14, page 555.)

Likewise, a restaurant with a preponderance of seafood items should avoid having a lot of tannic red wines on its list. A large selection of Pinot Noir wines and other lighter red wines would be more appropriate for a menu with mostly seafood or one with lighter fare.

A rib shack or steak house is the place where full-bodied red wines should dominate its list. Aside from these extreme examples, a restaurateur should figure out the percentage or ratio of red meat, white meat, game, seafood, and vegetarian items on the menu and allot wine selections accordingly. As mentioned earlier in the chapter, during spring and summer there could be more white, sparkling, and rosé wines on a list, and wintertime could signal a shift to more warming reds.

The focus should be on wines that can best complement the food, and there is no substitution for the staff actually tasting the dishes with the wine. If a proprietor

SWEET WINES WE LOVE WITH SPICY DISHES

19752	Pichot, Domaine le Peu de la Moirette Vouvray, 2006	Loire Valley	$29
19611	Michele Chiarlo Moscato d'Asti "Nivole," 2006	Piedmont	$27
19339	Snoqualmie "Naked" Riesling (organically grown grapes), 2006	Columbia Valley, WA	$27

YES...! YOU CAN DRINK RED WITH FISH

19701	J. Lohr "Wildflower" Valdigue, 2006	Arroyo Seco	$23
9962	Château Thivin, 2006	Côtes de Brouilly	$29

GREAT SHELLFISH WINES

Muscadet			BOTTLE	GLASS
19454	Michel Delhommeau "Cuvée Harmonie," 2006	Loire Valley	$25	$6.95
Albarino				
9262	Martin Codax, 2006	Rías Baixas, Spain	$27	$7.95
19174	Condes de Albarei, 2006	Rías Baixas, Spain	$29	
Chenin Blanc				
19823	Savennières, Damien Laureau "Genets," 2004	Loire Valley	$39	

The Legal Sea Food restaurant chain organizes wine by grape variety but also has specialty categories at the bottom of each page.

or manager makes all the decisions and tells the staff it is their duty to sell the wines he or she has chosen, servers will not have the enthusiasm generated by personal involvement in the selection process.

Another factor to consider in the selection of wines is the demographics of an area. A restaurant in a higher-income area can have affordable wines in different styles, but should offer a more extensive selection of higher-priced wines than a family-style establishment or a restaurant in a college town.

Demographics may also allow for a list with more off-the-beaten-path wines. Older clientele may have settled in a comfort zone with some tried-and-true wines from traditional grape varieties and popular wine-growing regions. Certain areas of Florida with large retirement communities may have to include the three P's and C's on their list: Pouilly-Fuissé, Pinot Grigio, and Piesporter Goldtröpfchen; and Chianti, Cabernet Sauvignon, and Châteauneuf-du-Pape.

We are not suggesting that all older clientele are conservative, but rather that a younger or upwardly mobile customer base opens up the possibilities to promote up-and-coming wines. Restaurants with a varied menu, exotic decor, and cutting-edge music can feature a more diverse, unusual wine selection. While some well-known standards could be included on the list, such a concept calls for a host of wines from lesser-known grape varieties or off-the-beaten-path regions.

Here are ten examples of grape types we are happy to find on a wine list: Sémillon from Australia, Riesling from Canada, Torrontés from Argentina, Moschofilero from Greece, Tannat from Uruguay, Aglianico from Italy, Touriga Nacional from Portugal, Monastrell from Spain, Grenache from California or Washington, and Pinot Noir from New Zealand.

There is a combination of pride and excitement generated when one person in a group of friends or colleagues can recount a restaurant experience where they got turned on to a new wine. Sharing that discovery is one of the pleasures wine lovers enjoy.

Today, restaurants with small plates, tapas, or *mezze* are very popular. Some guests order a series of appetizers to share instead of main courses. A way to enliven a wine list is with various bottle sizes, so customers can "graze" on the menu and the beverage list. A half bottle or a "quartino" (8.48 ounces/250 milliliters in a CARAFE), for example, are well suited to a table of two. A series of 2-ounce/60-milliliter tasting portions may be ideal for a solitary diner, while a Jeroboam (the equivalent of four bottles, or about twenty glasses) is the perfect size for a table of fourteen. The guests may then keep the empty bottle as a souvenir. Serving wines by the glass from a Magnum (equivalent of a double bottle) is perceived as festive by some and dramatic by others. This too can be indicated on the wine list.

A traditional restaurant with formal service must meet customer expectations on a wine list. It is impossible to have a fine Italian restaurant and exclude Barolo, Chianti, and Pinot Grigio wines, for example. Likewise, when a customer sees a Graves white Bordeaux on the list, he or she expects to see whites from Burgundy, Alsace, and the Loire as well. A list with white Bordeaux should also include red Bordeaux as well as some Rhônes and Burgundies and perhaps a few wines from the up-and-coming appellations within Roussillon, Languedoc, and Provence.

Note that this rule of representing the classic wine-producing zones applies mainly to still table wines. A wine list could have international representation in its sparkling, aperitif, and dessert categories without representing those nations in the still wine categories. For example, the only true high-quality Madeira, Sherry, or Porto wines come from Iberia, and a list could include those products

WINE	GLASS	BOTTLE

Champagne "Agua de Bilbao" NV Paul Laurent Brut, Epernay ·········· 12

NV Alfred Gratien Brut Classique, Epernay ················· 130

WHITE

2008 Ameztoi, Getariako Txakolina, Hondarribi Zuri, Beltza ·········· 12 ·········· 48

2008 Castillo de Monjardin, Navarra, Chardonnay ········· 8 ·········· 32

2007 Chateau Jolys, Jurançon Sec, Gros Manseng, Petit Manseng········· 34

2008 Vega Sindoa, Navarra, Viura, Chardonnay ··········· 30

* 2007 Gaba do Xil, Valdeorras, Godello ·········· 36

2008 Txomin Etxaniz, Getariako Txakolina, Hondarribi Zuri, Beltza ·········· 54

2008 Itsas Mendi, Bizkaiako Txakolina, Hondarribi Zuri ·········· 42

2008 Ostatu, Rioja Alavesa, Viura, Malvasia········· 36

* 2008 Zarate, Rías Baixas, Albariño ········· 56

2007 Ilori, Irouleguy, Gros Manseng, Petit Courbu ·········· 48

ROSÉ

2008 Enanzo, Navarra, Garnacha ·········· 7 ·········· 28

2008 Lezaun Egiarte Rosado, Navarra, Garnacha ·········· 28

2008 Viña Sardasol Rosado de Lagrima, Navarra, Garnacha ·········· 28

* 2008 Monte Castrillo Rosado, Ribera del Duero, Tempranillo ·········· 30

2008 Señorio de Sarria #5, Navarra, Garnacha ·········· 38

RED

2007 Seis de Azul y Garanza, Navarra, Cabernet Sauvignon, Merlot·········· 11 ·········· 44

2006 Beronia Crianza, Rioja, Tempranillo, Garnacha, Mazuelo ·········· 10 ·········· 40

2008 El Chaparral, Navarra, Garnacha ·········· 9.5 ·········· 38

2006 Biga, Rioja Alavesa, Tempranillo ·········· 46

** 2003 Baron de Ley Reserva, Rioja, Tempranillo ·········· 60

* 2005 Finca Villacreces, Ribera del Duero, Tempranillo, Cabernet Sauvignon ·········· 80

2005 Señorio de Sarria #7, Navarra, Graciano ·········· 36

* 2007 Errazuriz, Aconcagua Valley, Chile, Carmenère ·········· 40

2004 Baron de Oña, Rioja Alavesa, Tempranillo ·········· 50

2003 Monje Ameztoy, Rioja Alavesa, Tempranillo ·········· 72

2000 Contino Reserva, Rioja Alavesa, Tempranillo, Graciano, Mazuelo, Garnacha ·········· 84

1996 Contino Gran Reserva, Rioja Alavesa, Tempranillo, Graciano, Mazuelo ·········· 120

2003 Remírez de Ganuza, Rioja Alavesa, Tempranillo, Graciano, Garnacha ·········· 140

2007 Artazuri, Navarra, Garnacha ·········· 32

* 2003 Viña Cubillo Crianza, Rioja Alta, Tempranillo, Garnacha, Graciano, Mazuelo ·········· 50

2005 Pago de Larrainzar, Navarra, Merlot, Cabernet Sauvignon, Tempranillo, Garnacha ·········· 88

* 2005 Dehesa Gago "G", Toro, Tinto de Toro ·········· 78

* 2006 Auroch, Toro, Tinto de Toro ·········· 35

2008 Doniene Gorrondona, Bizkaiako Txakolina, Hondarribi Beltza ·········· 56

SWEET WINES

2006 Aliaga Vendimia Tardia, Navarra, Moscatel ·········· 13

* 2007 Errazuriz, Chile, Late Harvest Sauvignon Blanc ·········· 13

* Basque Heritage winemakers producing outside Euzkadi

** DO Rioja from Navarra

An example of a small, effective wine list at the Basque restaurant Txikito in New York City.

Cave Spring Whites

	2 oz.	5 oz.	½ LITRE	BOTTLE
2007 Riesling Dry	$2.60	$6.50	$22.50	$30.00
2007 Riesling	2.60	6.50	22.50	30.00
2007 Riesling Dolomite	3.00	7.20	25.00	34.00
2006 Riesling Estate	3.50	8.50	28.50	41.00
2007 Riesling CSV				55.00
2004 Riesling CSV				70.00
2006 Sauvignon Blanc Estate	3.50	8.50	28.50	41.00
2007 Chenin Blanc				50.00
2006 Chardonnay	2.60	6.50	22.50	30.00
2007 Chardonnay Musque	3.00	7.20	25.00	34.00
2006 Chardonnay Estate	3.70	9.20	33.00	45.00
2007 Chardonnay CSV				60.00
2004 Chardonnay CSV				70.00

Other Canadian Whites

	BOTTLE
2006 Fielding Estate Gewürztraminer	$40.00
2002 Legends Chenin Blanc	35.00
2006 Peninsula Ridge Sauvignon Blanc McNally Vineyard	50.00
2006 Calamus Pinot Gris	35.00
2006 Creekside Pinot Grigio	40.00
2002 Stoney Ridge Charlotte's Chardonnay Unoaked	65.00
2002 Peninsula Ridge Inox Chardonnay	70.00
2003 Pelee Island Barrique Chardonnay	40.00
2003 Henry of Pelham Barrel-Fermented Chardonnay	45.00
2005 Hidden Bench Vieilles Vignes Chardonnay	85.00
2002 Harbour Estates Chardonnay Reserve	50.00
2002 Sandstone Chardonnay Reserve	55.00
2005 Creekside Chardonnay Reserve	45.00

All wines VQA Niagara Peninsula unless otherwise noted.

Cave Spring Wine Cellars was the first Canadian winery to establish a fine-dining restaurant to showcase their wines as well as others from the Niagara Peninsula region of Ontario and around the world. Their Inn on the Twenty restaurant in Jordan, Ontario, features local fare and dishes influenced by the Pennachetti family's Italian heritage.

without featuring table wines from Spain or Portugal (although some customers might be disappointed to not find wines from those nations on the list). Unique fortified wines could be excluded from the main wine list if the restaurant has a separate by-the-glass list for aperitif or dessert wines.

Multiple lists can be very effective, from a tabletop card with Champagnes and sparkling wines by the bottle, glass, and aperitifs (perhaps with a house special that changes nightly) to separate lists for appetizers and desserts in addition to the main list.

All dessert wines should be available by the bottle or glass, as a couple may only require two 2-ounce/60-milliliter portions, while full bottles would be appropriate for a larger party.

PRICING

General Pricing Strategies

A criticism of some establishments is that their wine list prices are too high. Restaurants have closed because of their refusal to accept that customers will simply not pay for overpriced food and wine. The perception of being "ripped off" is increased when the high price is not offset by other factors, such as quality glassware, that enhance the nose and flavor of the wine, as well as knowledgeable staff who can explain the wine's flavors or affinities with food. It is essential to keep certain styles of wines well chilled, and the absence of a true ice bucket in a restaurant bewilders and frustrates many customers. A clay or marble chiller that is supposed to maintain the temperature of the wine is just not good enough for many restaurant patrons.

The range of prices charged for wines baffles most consumers. Why is it that a particular wine may be sold for $85 in one restaurant and $135 in another nearby restaurant and $200 in another?

Possible reasons for price variations include whether the wine was bought at the lower-than-current futures price in advance of its release or in large quantity for a discount. If the wine was bought at a lower price than the current rate, is the buyer willing to sell those wines based on their purchase price or should the price be based on their replacement cost? Is a wine buyer justified in making a profit on his or her long-term investment? (For a discussion of purchasing, see Chapter 17, page 676.)

I think about the guest at the outset. Will the selections make sense in terms of compatibility with the menu? Will the list be easy and fun to read, and will the guest be able to effortlessly find the style of wine that is most appealing to them and will best pair with the food that they order? Next I consider the service staff. Are they going to be able to use the list as a tool that will guide the guest? I like to see a lot of white space on a menu, readable print, clear guidelines as to predominant flavor and style. I want to have a healthy mix of interesting and obscure, as well as reliable and established. I want to excite the guest and the service staff by changing things up on a regular basis and encouraging experimentation with glasses and tasting flights. And, above all, I want to offer the bottles at tempting, if not ludicrously low, prices to engender a glow of happiness that will sweeten the entire dining experience.

Sandy Block,
MW, Vice President, Legal Sea Foods, Boston, Massachusetts

Señora Martinez is a tapas restaurant in the artsy Urban Design District of Miami. The wine list is 100 percent Spanish, with only 75 labels. Miami has an influential Latin community, so Spanish wine sells! But most drinkers are familiar with the big name reds like Rioja and Ribera del Duero. The big names are big names for a reason, and I personally love Rioja and consider it one of the best red wine values in the world. Our backbone is Rioja and Ribera del Duero, the classics, with vintages dating back to 1964. We also offer upcoming regions, like whites from Ribeiro, Txakoli by the glass, and powerful reds from Jumilla and Murcia. Most of the wines at Señora Martinez range from $35 to $60 per bottle. All wines by the glass are $11 and under, including eight Sherries. The price point is approachable, so people feel more comfortable ordering a second bottle or having that third glass of wine.

Allegra Angelo,
Sommelier, Michy's, Señora Martinez, Miami, Florida

We suggest using a sliding scale of markup. Restaurants strive to have a lower final cost percentage on high-volume, inexpensive wines. Often, the least expensive Chardonnay on a list will be marked up three to five times. To generate more revenue, the markup on more expensive wines may be only two and a half times or a fixed amount.

For example, a Chardonnay with a wholesale price of $6 may sell for $25, an $11 version may sell for $33, a $30 wine for $75, and a $120 wine for $225. Consumers may find they get more "bang for their buck" in the mid-price range of a wine list.

The saying goes, "You don't take percentages to the bank." As an incentive to sell all the wines on the list and attract the clientele who can afford expensive wines, truffles, and caviar, do not be greedy. Instead, operators must be motivated by low percentage cost on their "house" and inexpensive wines and by generating revenue on the high end. The sales mix of such a program generally aims to keeps wine cost between 33 and 39 percent. (See "Pricing Individual Wines," on page 710.)

We include a sample grid from the Wentworth on the Sea resort in New Hampshire. A grid such as this can be very helpful, but we find that many restaurants price wines not only based on cost but on their particular appeal. For example, a restaurant will take a bigger profit on a popular Pinot Grigio Italian white wine than they will a more obscure Fiano di Avellino.

Some restaurants have a small wine list with only one price, say $30. That restaurant will likely look for a less expensive White Zinfandel, Cabernet Sauvignon, or Chardonnay that costs about $5 a bottle, while a less popular Mourvèdre that wholesales for $8 won't affect the overall final cost percentage too much because of the sales mix.

Wine list prices cannot be based solely on the wines' wholesale price. The sales mix will determine how aggressively to mark up specific wines. High-volume sellers such as White Zinfandel, Pinot Grigio, and Chardonnay are bought at a lower final cost percent than a lesser-known varietal such as Barbera or region such as Alentejo. The incentive to increase revenue and sell more expensive wines means being less aggressive on their markup. Finally, having a few good "steals" on the list will please knowledgeable customers seeking value.

WINE COST PERCENTAGE FROM WENTWORTH BY THE SEA

BOTTLE PRICING GUIDELINE

BOTTLE COST	MARKUP	SELL RANGE
Up to $8	Up to 4 x bottle cost	Up to $32
$8.01 to $12	Up to 3.5 x bottle cost	$30 to $45
$12.01 to $15	Up to 3 x bottle cost	$39 to $48.75
$15.01 to $25	Up to 2.75 x bottle cost	$45 to $75
$25.01 to $50	Up to 2.5 x bottle cost	$69 to $137
$50.01 to $75	Up to 2.25 x bottle cost	$125 to $187
$75.01 to $100	Up to 2 x bottle cost	$168 to $225
Above $100	Up to 1.75 x bottle cost	$200++

GLASS WINE GUIDELINE

Based on 6–8 oz pour Graduated Pricing matrix
($5 bottle price x 1 – 1.25% = glass price;
graduating to $25 bottle price x .65–.85% = glass price)

WINE	BOTTLE COST	MULTIPLIER	RETAIL GLASS PRICE
Canyon Road Chardonnay	$5.00	1 – 1.25	$5.00 – 6.25
Clos Du Bois Chardonnay	$8.50	.95 – 1	$8.00 – 8.50
White Haven Sauv. Blanc	$10.00	.85 – .95	$8.50 – 9.50
Kendall Jackson Cabernet	$12.00	.75 – .85	$9.00 – 10.25
Stone Street Merlot	$16.00	.65 –.75	$10.50 – 12.00

Supplied by Michele Duval, Sommelier at Wentworth by the Sea Hotel, New Hampshire

A wine list is just that, a list. But it does set the tone for the overall image of the restaurant. The style, size, and pricing philosophy go a long way in telegraphing that image to the guest. Value or elite? Easy, fun, or respectful contemplation? The wine list's intent should dovetail naturally and easily with the restaurant's menu and clearly defined mission statement.

Regardless of the size or content, the structure of the wine list should be translucent, easy to comprehend. Can a guest locate the white Burgundy section with ease? Is it evident if a Riesling is dry or sweet? Can a guest remember their selection from page 1 by the time they get to page 25? If not, they may just give up and order a beer.

No one can deny the important role that wine and all alcoholic beverages play in the financial success of a restaurant. You don't have to slice it, dice it, heat it up, or toss it out after a week. But how much wine is too much wine? As a business, it is important to turn the inventory unless the owners are willing to sit on 25 percent of their wine investment for five years or more. Are verticals of Cabernet Sauvignon important to the restaurant's long-term success? They may be essential in a casino hotel but an utter indulgence in a neighborhood venue. And, on a totally prosaic note, how much storage space do you really have?

The basic pricing philosophy needs to be clearly defined with whomever you are accountable to. Where does wine fit into the larger scheme of things? Are you going for volume or high check average? What kinds of numbers does your employer need to run on a P and L statement? The more you understand the business as a whole, the more easily you can make a case for changes in budgeted cost of goods.

Wine pricing is all about perceived value. If the guest feels good about what they are paying, they'll be more inclined to buy another bottle, or two—and maybe one to go! There's no one absolutely correct way to price restaurant wine. But it is important that you feel confident in the pricing structure of your list.

When guests question the markup, can you reply with openhearted honesty? The wine consumer has immense knowledge at their fingertips. Will your pricing bear examination when cross-referenced with other lists online? Do you care? Is it important to undercut the competition, or is your market segment so strong that you can cull more dollars without risking the loss of cover counts?

Balance is the name of the game. A dynamic wine program has something for everyone who walks in the door. Do you have enough selections in the important price windows? Know your market. If your guests use the establishment as an upscale family restaurant, they will tend toward more-comfortable price points. If destination dining is your game, the clientele may expect wines with limited availability at higher price points.

The easiest way to achieve balance is through progressive pricing: wines-by-the-glass are aggressively purchased and costed, the middle tiers are moderate, and the ultra-premiums are attractively modest in markup. The skill of the buyer comes into important play particularly in selecting glass pours. These should affect the blended cost of goods most dramatically without negatively impacting guest perception.

In costing out a program, consider an attitude switch from "What can we get away with charging?" to "How can we make our beverage program irresistible?" Think of "inclusive pricing" versus "exclusive pricing." Inclusive pricing makes great wine accessible, at a fair price. Exclusive pricing can lead to a lot of window dressing and not enough meat on the bones.

If quality, price-value, and your guests' pleasure determine the wine program, success will surely follow. At the very least, you won't be stuck with cases of bad judgment that make you wince.

Madeline Triffon,
MS, Wine Director, Matt-Prentice Restaurant Group, Detroit, Michigan

TABLE OF CONTENTS	PAGE

Champagne & Sparkling Wine

Argyle "Brut"	$ 30
Ariola Malvasia NV Italy	30
Bollinger "Special Cuvée" NV	72
Bollinger "Grande Année" 1999	190
Gruet "Blanc de Noirs" NV New Mexico	25
J 2000 Russian River	32
Gosset Grand Rosé NV	75
Krug "Clos du Mesnil" Blanc de Blancs 1992	750
Nicolas Feuillatte "Brut" NV	45
Nicolas Feuillatte "Cuvée Palms d'Or" 1996	200
Laurent Perrier "Brut" NV	60
Laurent Perrier "Grand Siècle" NV	125
Roederer "L'Ermitage" 2002 Anderson Valley	72
Salon "Clos de Mesnil" Blanc de Blancs Brut 1996	295
Veuve Clicquot Ponsardin Brut NV	54

Here are the opening pages of the wine list of one of the Plumpjack restaurants of San Fransisco. Notice that a table of contents is provided and the wines are very fairly priced.

BECCO WINE LIST We created this wine list to remove the inhibition and confusion of price from your wine selection. We encourage you to explore the many styles and great values here.

ALL SELECTIONS · $25

ITALIAN RED WINES

LIGHT BODIED

399 Langhe Nebbiolo 2006, Produttori del Barbaresco *(Piemonte)*

206 Erta e China 2005, Masi *(Toscana)*

228 Sangiovese di Romagna Superiore "Maestri di Vigna" 2006, Fattoria Paradiso *(Emilia-Romagna)*

205 Nero d'Avola "Poggio Bidini" 2005, Valle dell'Acate *(Sicilia)*

209 Cirò Classico 2005, Librandi *(Calabria)*

233 Friuli Rosso 2004, Palmadina *(Friuli)*

251 Valpolicella Classico Superiore 2005, Le Salette *(Veneto)*

265 Marzemino 2004, Battistotti *(Trentino)*

379 Negroamaro "Solyss" 2004, La Corte *(Puglia)*

291 Teroldego Rotaliano 2005, Cantina Rotaliano di Mezzolombardo *(Trentino)*

216 Canavese Rosso 2005, Ferrando *(Piemonte)*

499 Rosso di Montefalco 2005, Milziade Antano *(Umbria)*

232 Dolcetto d' Alba "Vigneto Loreto" 2006, De Forville *(Piemonte)*

386 Monica di Sardegna "San Bernardino" 2005, Cantina Il Nuragne *(Sardegna)*

202 Nero d'Avola "Contempo" 2004, Santa Anastasia *(Sicilia)*

MEDIUM BODIED

247 Morellino di Scansano "I Perazzi" 2006, La Mozza *(Toscana)*

230 Capitel dei Nicalò 2004, Tedeschi *(Veneto)*

355 Rosso di Montepulciano 2006, La Calonica *(Toscana)*

201 Syrah 2005, Roccaperciata *(Sicilia)*

227 Valpolicella Classico Superiore 2005, Brigaldara *(Veneto)*

271 Primitivo di Salento 2006, Caleo *(Puglia)*

221 Rosso di Toscana 2004, Monte Antico *(Toscana)*

203 Carignano de Sulsis "Grotta Rossa" 2003, Santadi *(Sardegna)*

250 Moratèl 2004, Cesconi *(Trentino)*

249 Uva di Troia "Vigneto del Melograno" 2005, Santa Lucia *(Puglia)*

366 Dolcetto d'Acqui "L'Ardi" 2005, Vigna Regali *(Piemonte)*

281 Nero d'Avola "Capo Soprano" 2005, Fazio *(Sicilia)*

277 Ripasso di Valpolicella 2004, Le Ragose *(Veneto)*

287 Sine Cura 2006, Martinetti *(Piemonte)*

320 Umbria Rosso 2005, Poggio Muralto *(Umbria)*

395 Barbera d'Alba 2006, De Forville *(Piemonte)*

387 Sangiovese di Marche 2006, Mojo

293 Aglianico d'Irpinia 2006, Terradora *(Campania)*

364 Nero d'Avola "Scurati" 2006, Ceuso *(Sicilia)*

365 Barco Reale di Carmignano 2006, Ambra *(Toscana)*

FULL BODIED

324 Oltrepo Pavese Rosso "Pezzalunga" 2006, Vercesi del Castellazzo *(Lombardia)*

299 Rosso di Sicilia 2005, Colosi *(Sicilia)*

231 Turlo 2004, Salviano *(Umbria)*

120 Aglianico del Vulture "Il Viola" 2004, Tenuta le Querce *(Basilicata)*

397 Dolcetto d'Alba "Vilot" 2005, Ca' Viola *(Piemonte)*

226 Barbera d'Alba "Annunziata" 2004, Rocche Costamagna *(Piemonte)*

290 Rosso di Toscana "Casamatta" 2005, Bibi Graetz *(Toscana)*

244 Perdera 2006, Argiolas *(Sardegna)*

351 Ramitello 2004, Di Majo Norante *(Molise)*

285 Dolcetto d'Alba "Vigneto della Chiesa" 2006, Seghesio *(Piemonte)*

282 Rosso Conero "Julius" 2005, Silvio Strologo *(Marche)*

298 Rosso Piceno "Il Brecciarolo" 2004, Ercole–Velenosi *(Marche)*

229 Rosso Orvientano "Rosso di Spicca" 2005, Tenuta Le Velete *(Umbria)*

329 Barbera d'Alba "Tre Vigne" 2004, Vietti *(Piemonte)*

Becco, an Italian restaurant in Manhattan, provides quite an impressive example of a single-priced wine list that is well suited not only to their prix fixe lunch and dinner menu options but also to the pocketbooks of their customers. The wines are organized by weight (or body). We include the red wine portion of the list as an example of the format.

PRICING INDIVIDUAL WINES BY THE SLIDING SCALE

The most important aspect of pricing is that more expensive wines should have a smaller markup than less expensive wines. There are several approaches to pricing the wines on the list. The most common are:

- Straight percent markup
- Straight dollar markup
- Sliding-scale markup (percent or dollar)
- Fixed-price markup

On the sale of any bottle of wine, whether it costs $5 or $50 wholesale, there is a predetermined markup that needs to be added to cover storage, labor, equipment, glasses, and overhead. Any additional markup is profit.

A standard percent markup applies a straight markup percentage to every item on the wine list. The result is an unjustifiable amount of profit on more expensive wines. If, for example, your standard markup is 300 percent, the selling prices on $5 and $50 bottles of wine would be as follows:

$5 wholesale cost × 300% = $15 selling price
$50 wholesale cost × 300% = $150 selling price

Not only would it be fairer to the customer to offer the expensive bottle at a reduced percentage markup, but it most likely will result in greater sales, thus increasing the wine's profitability.

In the standard dollar-markup approach, the restaurant determines how much money it needs to generate from the sale of one bottle to cover all its costs and still leave some profit. It then uses that dollar figure as the markup on every bottle of wine. If, for example, your restaurant finds that a $15 profit per bottle sold is enough to cover costs plus residual profit, then the wine prices in the above example would be:

$5 wholesale cost + $15 markup = $20 selling price
$50 wholesale cost + $15 markup = $65 selling price

The sliding-scale method applies a reduced markup to higher-cost items; the markup can be a standard percentage or dollar amount. For example:

$5 wholesale cost × 350% = $17.50 selling price or
$5 wholesale cost + $13 markup = $18 selling price
$50 wholesale cost × 150% = $75 selling price or
$50 wholesale cost + $20 markup = $70 selling price

Here are ten situations the person in charge of a wine list may encounter:

1 **BOTTLE AGING** If a wine has been bought and cellared to mature for a few years, should the wine be priced at current value or should the savings be passed on to the customer, who will recognize a great value? It seems reasonable to base the price somewhere between the original cost of the wine and its current value.

2 **PRICING THE LESS-COMMONLY AVAILABLE WINE** If a wine is on allocation and cannot be replaced, should the establishment take more profit on a wine that is not easily found at other restaurants? There are so many great wines available today that other wines could replace it, so charge a fair price.

3 **CONSIDER THE COMPETITION** Should the prices of restaurants that compete with your establishment be taken into account when setting prices? One example is the lowest price of wines by the glass at a restaurant. In a college town, if the competitor's cheapest glass is $7 and there is a possibility of selling a glass for $5, it makes sense to offer wines at that price point.

4 **SHOULD LOCAL WINES BE OFFERED AT A LOWER MARKUP?** If so, those associated with the wineries will frequent the restaurant with guests, and locals who know the price of the wine from the winery will not feel ripped off.

5 **WATCH PRICING ON LOCAL FAVORITES** Popular wines that sell at local grocery stores or wine shops cannot be priced too aggressively. For example, a popular Pinot Grigio that sells for $20 retail should not cost more than $40 on a wine list. Customers can buy chicken for $2 a pound at a grocery and will not feel cheated paying $20 for a main course with chicken, yet the same is not true of wine. This is yet another reason to feature off-the-beaten-path wines.

6 **THE ECONOMY** Sommeliers often recount how a wine selling for $19 was a dud and once it was raised to $22, sales increased. Perhaps pretentious people were worried about being seen drinking inexpensive wine. In today's economy, we suggest that unless the restaurant or catering establishment is very expensive, customers are searching for restaurants with affordable wines. Finding an inexpensive wine at $19 or $25 will make the customers more relaxed and more likely to order that second or third bottle for the table.

7 **POST-OFFS** A savvy wine buyer can take advantage of "post-off" wines—those sold at reduced prices by wholesalers with the aim of moving those particular wines. The savings can be passed on to restaurant patrons as "specials" or used to enhance bottom-line profit.

8 **CUSTOMERS WHO RESIST CHANGE** Just as some chefs would love to ditch an appetizer or main course and replace it with a new creation, wine directors must also find a balance when adding new wines to the list and maintain a core list of favorites that their clientele is hooked on.

9 **CORKAGE** Some restaurants will allow customers to bring their own bottle of wine and charge a fee for the opening and service of the wine. House rules may be that the wine cannot be one that is on the restaurant's wine list. Another stipulation restaurants may tell the guest is that they must tip the sommelier, captain, or server accordingly. Corkage fees range from $10 to as high as $150 a bottle. If a guest comes in with a fine old bottle of red wine that must be decanted and has a wine list value of $500, a 15 or 20 percent tip on a $20 corkage fee would be only $3 or $4, an insufficient amount.

BYOB (bring your own bottle) restaurants have the advantage of lower financial investment since they do not have to purchase wine, and they have more space for tables because there is no wine cellar. Other benefits include being considered a destination restaurant because of the lower cost of dining there without the wine markup, and the onus of wine-and-food pairing is on the customers so there are less staff training costs. Montreal and Philadelphia are two cities that have lots of successful BYOB restaurants. In some states, such as New York, it is illegal for a restaurant without a wine list to charge a corkage fee.

10 **A POLICY ON THE RETURN OF EXPENSIVE WINES** If a restaurant has wines that cost hundreds or thousands of dollars, they may include a statement on the wine list such as, "The restaurant is not responsible for the condition of wines that cost over $500."

Some guests have ordered a wine for $2,000 and returned it even though it was not flawed. In one case, the guests were amused at an opportunity to do something so outlandish. A guest might be in a bad mood and feel the need to exercise their power. The rule in the hospitality business is that the guest is always right. (The returned-bottle issue is covered in Chapter 16, on page 662.) If the bottle is in fine shape, the written statement is a form of protection for the restaurant, and they may choose to charge for the wine.

In a country club or resort area, if a time-honored guest refuses an expensive bottle one time, the house may have to absorb some of the cost of the loss. If it is in good shape, the wine can still be sold by the two-ounce taste or glass to other customers.

Pricing is one of the most crucial elements of wine list development and one of the more difficult to get right. I appreciate lists that are priced on a sliding scale, with the lower-end wines having a higher markup and higher-end wines a lower markup. Every restaurant should have one or more cash cows on its list, wines that wholesale for four to six dollars a bottle, can be marked up four to five times, and generate a lot of cash. At the same time, every restaurant should offer one or more big, prestige wines at a very fair price, the kind of wines that look good on the list and are priced to move.

Mark Vaughan,
Editor and Publisher, Santé Magazine, *Bennington, Vermont*

The most reasonable approach to wine pricing is to have a sliding scale. In today's market, it is difficult to maintain a set markup. The top-quality wines are expensive, and with a multiple of three over cost, the wine appears on the list at a very high price. At a two-times markup, the expensive wines sell faster, the clientele is happier, and the restaurant still makes a healthy profit. Extremely hard-to-find wines may require a hardier markup in order to prevent them from selling too quickly. Lower-end wines can handle a higher percentage markup, between two and a half and three times. This commonsense approach drives accountants crazy. But in the end, remember, you are in the hospitality business. Satisfy the customer, and eventually the accountant will thank you.

Daniel Johnnes,
Wine Director of Dinex (Daniel Boulud's Restaurant Group), New York, New York

VINS DE FRANCE – *Bourgogne Rouges*
Suite VOSNE-ROMANÉE GRANDS CRUS

LA TACHE	1994	DOMAINE DE LA ROMANÉE-CONTI	
LA TACHE	1995	DOMAINE DE LA ROMANÉE-CONTI	
LA TACHE	1995	DOMAINE DE LA ROMANÉE-CONTI	*1.5 LITERS*
LA TACHE	1996	DOMAINE DE LA ROMANÉE-CONTI	
LA TACHE	1997	DOMAINE DE LA ROMANÉE-CONTI	*1.5 LITERS*
LA TACHE	1998	DOMAINE DE LA ROMANÉE-CONTI	
LA TACHE	1998	DOMAINE DE LA ROMANÉE-CONTI	*1.5 LITERS*
LA TACHE	1999	DOMAINE DE LA ROMANÉE-CONTI	
LA TACHE	2000	DOMAINE DE LA ROMANÉE-CONTI	
LA TACHE	2001	DOMAINE DE LA ROMANÉE-CONTI	
LA TACHE	2002	DOMAINE DE LA ROMANÉE-CONTI	
LES RICHEBOURG	1969	CHARLES NOELLAT	
LES RICHEBOURG	1971	CHARLES NOELLAT	*1.5 LITERS*
RICHEBOURG	1970	DOMAINE DE LA ROMANÉE-CONTI	
RICHEBOURG	1976	DOMAINE DE LA ROMANÉE-CONTI	*1.5 LITERS*
RICHEBOURG	1983	DOMAINE DE LA ROMANÉE-CONTI	
RICHEBOURG	1985	DOMAINE DE LA ROMANÉE-CONTI	
RICHEBOURG	1991	DOMAINE DE LA ROMANÉE-CONTI	
RICHEBOURG	1992	DOMAINE DE LA ROMANÉE-CONTI	
RICHEBOURG	1993	DOMAINE DE LA ROMANÉE-CONTI	
RICHEBOURG	1993	DOMAINE DE LA ROMANÉE-CONTI	*1.5 LITERS*
RICHEBOURG	1994	DOMAINE DE LA ROMANÉE-CONTI	
RICHEBOURG	1995	DOMAINE A. F. GROS	
RICHEBOURG	1995	DOMAINE DE LA ROMANÉE-CONTI	
RICHEBOURG	1995	DOMAINE DE LA ROMANÉE-CONTI	*1.5 LITERS*
RICHEBOURG	1996	DOMAINE A. F. GROS	
RICHEBOURG	1996	DOMAINE DE LA ROMANÉE-CONTI	
RICHEBOURG	1996	DOMAINE JEAN GRIVOT	
RICHEBOURG	1996	DOMAINE JEAN GRIVOT	*6 LITERS*
RICHEBOURG	1997	DOMAINE DE LA ROMANÉE-CONTI	
RICHEBOURG	1998	DOMAINE DE LA ROMANÉE-CONTI	
RICHEBOURG	1998	DOMAINE DE LA ROMANÉE-CONTI	*1.5 LITERS*
RICHEBOURG	1998	DOMAINE JEAN GRIVOT	
RICHEBOURG	1998	DOMAINE JEAN GRIVOT	*6 LITERS*
RICHEBOURG	1999	DOMAINE DE LA ROMANÉE-CONTI	
RICHEBOURG	1999	DOMAINE DE LA ROMANÉE-CONTI	*1.5 LITERS*

ABOVE: *Bistro à Champlain, located in the Laurentian mountains of Quebec, has one of the world's largest cellars (see page 675), and this is a page of its Burgundy wines. Perhaps because French is the dominant language of the area, the bin numbers are not as important for their wine list (prices not shown by request).* OPPOSITE: *L'Escalier restaurant in the Breakers Hotel in Palm Beach has an impressive collection of Chardonnay-based white Burgundies arranged by classification. Notice that all the Meursaults are grouped together, as are wines from other sites. L'Escalier provides bin numbers to the left of their selections to facilitate ordering the wines.*

French White—Burgundy
Côte de Beaune
<small>Appellation d'Origine Contrôlée</small>

BIN		VINTAGE	BOTTLE
5920	Bourgogne Blanc, Domaine Leflaive	2002	83
5965	Chassagne-Montrachet, Joseph Drouhin	2005	120
5968	Chassagne-Montrachet, Alex Gambal	2005	96
5994	Chassagne-Montrachet, Louis Latour	1999	86
5956	Meursault, Robert Ampeau	1994	151
5952	Meursault, Joseph Drouhin	2002	91
5954	Meursault, Louis Jadot	2005	96
5953	Meursault, "Labarre," François Jobard	2001	104
5823	Meursault, Labouré-Roi	2001	84
5951	Meursault, Louis Latour	2002	62
5941	Meursault, Domaine Matrot	2002	80
5939	Meursault, "Cromin," Domaine Moret-Nominé	2005	125
5940	Pernand Vergelesses, Domain Guyon	1997	114
5961	Puligny-Montrachet, Joseph Drouhin	2004	110
5959	Puligny-Montrachet, Louis Jadot	2004	106
5958	Puligny-Montrachet, Louis Latour	2004	73
5981	Puligny-Montrachet, Olivier Leflaive	2003	111

PREMIER CRU

BIN		VINTAGE	BOTTLE
5997	Beaune, "Clos Saint-Landry," Bouchard	1999	103
5992	Chassagne-Montrachet, "Caillerets," Blain-Gagnard	2003	116
5898	Chassagne-Montrachet, "Caillerets," Joel-Gagnard	2005	240
5974	Chassagne-Montrachet, "Morgeot," Clos de la Chapelle Domaine du Duc de Magenta/Jadot	2003	146
5984	Chassagne-Montrachet, "Morgeot," Domaine Leroy	1997	256
5986	Chassagne-Montrachet, "Les Ruchottes," Domaine Ramonet	2004	188
5963	Meursault "Charmes," Domaine Leroy	1999	221
5976	Meursault "Poruzots," Domaine Leroy	1966	696
5960	Puligny-Montrachet "Clavoillon," Domaine Leflaive	2005	265
5962	Puligny-Montrachet "Les Pucelles," Domaine Leflaive	1998	414
5845	Saint-Aubin "Le Charmois," Château de Chassagne-Montrachet	2000	77

GRAND CRU

BIN		VINTAGE	BOTTLE
5977	Bâtard-Montrachet, Domaine Leflaive	2004	631
5978	Bienvenues-Bâtard-Montrachet, Ramonet	1997	367
9008	Bienvenues-Bâtard-Montrachet, Sauzet	2000	499
5971	Corton Charlemagne, Bonneau du Martray	2002	236
5945	Corton Charlemagne, Bouchard	2002	244
5985	Corton Charlemagne, Louis Latour	1990	416
5987	Corton Charlemagne, Louis Latour	1993	236
5988	Corton Charlemagne, Louis Latour	1995	276
5989	Corton Charlemagne, Louis Latour	1996	221
5970	Corton Charlemagne, Louis Latour	2000	181
5995	Chevalier-Montrachet, Georges Deléger	1997	357
5967	Chevalier-Montrachet-Demoiselles, Louis Latour	1996	433
5966	Chevalier-Montrachet-Les Cabottes, Bouchard	2000	536
5980	Montrachet, Domaine de la Romanée-Conti	1999	3,000
5975	Montrachet, Marquis de Laguiche, Joseph Drouhin	1999	527
5979	Montrachet, Marquis de Laguiche, Joseph Drouhin	2000	960

Côte de Nuits
<small>Appellation d'Origine Contrôlée</small>

BIN		VINTAGE	BOTTLE
5853	Hautes Côtes de Nuit, Mommessin	2005	52
6428	"Clos du Prieure" Vougeot Blanc Monopole, Domaine de la Vougeraie, Vougeot	2001	251

Prices subject to service charge and sales tax

BREADTH AND DEPTH

A WINE LIST that has *breadth* offers an extensive, even inclusive, range of wines from the regions of the countries represented (see wine list on page 708). In other words, a wine list with breadth contains a wide array of wines and represents all the major wine regions of, for example, France, as well as some of its lesser-known regions.

A wine list that has *depth* offers several different vintages of many of the individual wines on the list (see wine list on page 712), for example, a list that offers Cakebread Cellars Cabernet Sauvignon wines in 1987, 1990, 1994, 1998, 2001, 2004, and 2007 vintages.

WINE LIST CONCERNS

PRESENT THE LIST EARLY

OF ALL THE PROBLEMS that are associated with wine lists, one of the most common is that the list is not available or is not presented to the diner.

Today, many customers will order a glass of wine rather than a spirit-based drink as a cocktail. A list of the wines by the glass should be either on the table as a tent card or presented along with the menus when the guest are seated.

If a consumer has to ask (and wait) for the list, they may have a negative image of the restaurant, especially of its service, and the restaurant could lose a wine sale. By not presenting the wine list, the total revenue for the restaurant is reduced, the tip-earning potential of the service staff is diminished drastically, and the food will not be enhanced by a proper wine pairing.

Assuming that the wine list is available to the customer, the most frequently voiced concerns about restaurant wine lists revolve around the issues of information presented, organization, selection, and pricing.

> A wine list is the most fundamental communication between sommelier and customer. It must both mirror the way the former thinks about wine and present it in a way that is easily comprehensible to the latter. In the interest of clear, direct, and friendly conversation, then, everything must be taken into account: from color and appellation to typeface and font size.
>
> Rajat Parr,
> *Wine Director, Michael Mina Group*

INFORMATION PRESENTED ON THE WINE LIST

AT A MINIMUM, a wine list should include the following elements:

CATEGORIES The most common categories are color (white, rosé, red) grape type (Zinfandel), region (Mendocino), nation (Portugal), and wine style (light-bodied sparkling wine). Unfortunately one person's perception of a light to medium- bodied wine may be another's medium- to full-bodied wine.

Subcategories may be appropriate for large lists or to make a small list less intimidating to the guest. For example, the heading may be California, the subheading Sonoma, and a subsubheading for the Russian River Valley.

BIN NUMBERS Bin (identification) numbers enable customers to order wine without fear of mispronunciation. They also minimize mistakes by the wait staff, as many wines sound similar. Such identification numbers make it easier to distinguish between Muscadet and Muscat, for example, or Pouilly-Fuissé and Pouilly Fumé. A different bin number is used for not only each wine, but each size of bottle (a half bottle would have a different bin number than a magnum of the same wine) and each vintage. As prices vary greatly by size and vintage, the bin numbers help avoid costly errors. It is important to leave gaps in the numbering system—especially between major categories—to provide room for future additions. For example, all sparkling wines could be in the 100–150 series, dry whites 200–250, and so on.

Many restaurants overlook the importance of bin numbers to put their guests at ease when ordering wine, and the result is a loss of sales and satisfaction for the guest.

PRODUCT NAME Examples include Chardonnay (varietal), Rioja (place), Vernaccia di San Gimignano (varietal and place), Insignia (proprietary/fantasy), Brut (dry sparkling), Fino (dry sherry), 10 Year Tawny (aged sweet Porto), and 5 Puttonyos Aszú (sweetness of Tokaji).

Special information and attributes: Barrel-fermented, Late Harvest, Proprietor's Reserve, Bin 707, Gran Reserva, Garrafeira, Recioto, and Grand Cru are examples.

PRODUCER NAME The estate, winery, cooperative, for example.

VINTAGE DATE Either a year or nonvintage notation (NV).

REGION Regional names must be included if they are not used as categories. For example, Côte de Nuits, Redwood Valley, Dão, Pirque-Maipo Valley, Marlborough, Coonawarra.

COUNTRY For example: U.S.A., Canada.

PRICE For example: $18, $108.

A lack of information on the wine list will probably not deter educated consumers from ordering the wine they want, but for the customer who is just getting to know wines, small snippets of useful information and general descriptive phrases can easily result in the sale of a glass or bottle of wine from a higher price bracket than originally intended.

Food-and-wine matching suggestions are a great tool for hesitant or less-knowledgeable customers. Hints about which wines go well with a spicy seafood or a delicate vegetarian appetizer enable customers to make a comfortable choice about wines to complement their meal.

CONSISTENCY

REGARDLESS OF THE NUMBER of wines on the list, the amount of information included, and the organizational structure, wine lists always work best when the information is presented consistently.

For example, if the list has the headings of "Red Wines" and "White Wines," with the selections coming from France and North America, the order of the regions must be the same in each section. In addition, if France is fur-

ther subdivided into Burgundy, Bordeaux, the Loire Valley, and Alsace, and North America into California, New York, Oregon, and Washington, the sequence of regions must be the same in the red and white sections. The first wine (and grouping) on a list sets the standard. The same holds true for the order in which the information is presented for each wine selection.

CORRECT EXAMPLE:

UNITED STATES CALIFORNIA WHITE WINES

BIN#		PRICE
10	Reserve, Chardonnay, Cakebread, Napa Valley, 2008	$108
11	"The Fumé," Sauvignon Blanc, Murphy-Goode, Alexander Valley, 2008	$40

INCORRECT EXAMPLE:

UNITED STATES CALIFORNIA WHITE WINES

BIN#		PRICE
10	Reserve, Chardonnay, Cakebread, Napa Valley, 2008	$108
11	Sauvignon Blanc, Murphy-Goode, "The Fumé," 2008, Alexander Valley	$40

Note that in the correct example above, both wines are listed the same way: special attribute, product or wine name, producer, region, and year. This is not the case with the incorrect example.

ORGANIZATION

CONSUMERS HAVE SEVERAL CONCERNS regarding the organization of wine lists. First, a major problem arises with extensive wine lists that do not include a table of contents or some other device to assist the client's search.

An intimidated restaurant guest who has to wade through an overly long wine list is likely to become frustrated and perhaps forgo the wine.

A second problem arises when the wine list is inconsistently organized. Even knowledgeable wine consumers can become irritated by a list that presents wines in no particular order or that jumps from category to category. The end result is that customers may not find the kind of wine they are looking for, and at worst, may develop an

south food + wine bar

white

> We list our Aussie + Kiwi wines by style and personality rather than grape or region. That way, you can choose a wine based on your mood, your food, the weather, or whatever!

> If you love the wine you're drinking, chances are we sell it at our online bottle shop, www.southwineclub.com.

> And every month we send out two of our faves for the south wine club. If you sign up today, you'll get 50% off your first bottle in the restaurant! Ask your server for more info.

sparkly   Glass / Bottle

Lindauer, Brut, Marlborough, NV ··· $ 8 / 30

Taltarni, Clover Hill, Brut, Tasmania, 2003 ··· 68

Jansz Rose, Tasmania, NV ··· 13 / 49

crisp

Grosset, Polish Hill, Riesling, Clare Valley, 2007 ·· 79

Tim Adams, Riesling, Clare Valley, 2005 ··· 32

Howard Park, Riesling, Great Southern, Western Australia, 2006 ································· 45

Tohu, Sauvignon Blanc, Marlborough, 2007 ··· 9 / 35

Isabel Estate, Sauvignon Blanc, Marlborough, 2007 ··· 44

Chalice Bridge, Semillon Sauvignon Blanc, Margaret River, 2007 ······························· 10 / 39

Margan, Semillon, Hunter Valley, 2004 ··· 37

Tyrells, Vat 1, Semillon, Hunter Valley, 2000 ·· 84

Peter Lehmann, Semillon, Barossa Valley, 2003 ·· 31

Robert Oatley, Pinot Grigio, South Australia, 2008 ··· 9 / 35

fruity

B3, Unoaked Chardonnay, Barossa Valley, 2007 ··· 10 / 39

Villa Maria, Private Bin, Unoaked Chardonnay, Hawkes Bay, 2006 ································ 41

Leasingham, Magnus, Riesling, Clare Valley, 2006 ·· 7 / 28

Muddy Water, Riesling, Waipara, 2006 ··· 48

Forrest Estate, Riesling, Marlborough, 2004 ··· 30

Tahbilk, Marsanne, Nagambie Lakes, Victoria, 2006 ·· 37

Millton, Te Arai, Chenin Blanc, Gisborne, 2006 ·· 45

Aurum, Pinot Gris, Central Otago, 2006 ··· 8 / 31

Borthwick, Paper Road, Pinot Gris, Hawkes Bay, 2006 ·· 44

Brancott Vineyards, Patutahi Estate, Gewurztraminer, Gisborne, 2003 ·························· 56

Lawson's Dry Hills, Gewurztraminer, Marlborough, 2007 ·· 45

Vinoptima, Reserve, Gewurztraminer, Ormond, 2004 ··· 89

The Gorge, Viognier, Hunter Valley, 2006 ··· 10 / 39

creamy

Yalumba, Virgilius Viognier, Eden Valley, 2004 ··· 65

Shaw & Smith, M3 Vineyard, Chardonnay, Adelaide Hills, 2006 ·································· 62

Nautilus, Chardonnay, Marlborough, 2005 ··· 49

Giant Steps, Sexton Vineyard, Chardonnay, Yarra Valley, 2003 ································· 12 / 45

Felton Road, Chardonnay, Central Otago, 2005 ·· 59

Moss Wood, Chardonnay, Margaret River, 2003 ·· 69

Leeuwin Estate, Art Series, Chardonnay, Margaret River, 2001 ································· 130

20% GRATUITY APPLIES TO PARTIES OF SIX OR MORE

South food + wine bar   330 Townsend St. #101   San Francisco, CA 94107   t. 415 974 5599   www.southfwb.com

---

South food + wine bar in San Francisco serves exclusively wines from Australia and New Zealand. The wines are organized by style and within those categories by grape variety.

antagonistic attitude toward the restaurant and its staff. A popular solution is to begin the list with a short statement of the restaurant's philosophy in choosing wines or an explanation of how the list is organized.

It is wise to group the wines on the list into categories, not only to break up the print but also to make it easier to find specific items. The categories may be driven by your target customer's expectations, the number of wines on the list and their origins, current trends, the culinary emphasis of the menu, or the ambience of the restaurant.

Most commonly, the items are grouped by grape variety, region, wine style (for example, weight, sweetness, unoaked or oaked white wines), food affinities, or price range.

"Wines by the glass" or "Sparkling wines" are usually the first page of wine choices on a list.

If the wine list is short enough and the selection of wines makes it possible, it is acceptable to group by grape variety only. If there are Meritage-style blends of Cabernet Sauvignon, Merlot, Cabernet Franc, Malbec, Petit Verdot, and Carmenère, the heading could be "Meritage" or "Cabernet" or "Bordeaux-style blends." Similarly, a blend featuring the grape varieties Syrah, Grenache, and Mourvèdre can list those three as a heading or can be labeled "Rhone Ranger" or "Rhône-style blends."

An American regional restaurant may choose to feature only American wines, grouped by state or region. Likewise, a wine list that incorporates wines from many countries may be grouped by geographic unit. It makes sense to do that because many Old World wines are labeled by a place name, such as Barolo, Bordeaux, or Douro. However, how helpful is it for a wine enthusiast to see a list grouped by place names if they do not know the style of wines produced in those regions?

The restaurant must also decide whether to cluster all of the whites together, subdivided by region or grape, and then all of the reds, also subdivided, or to list each country's white, rosé, and red wines before going to the next country. In some cases it is preferable to group by region and list the whites and reds separately under that geographic heading.

Humorous or whimsical headings are also appropriate for some restaurants.

Most restaurants try several organizational styles before they decide on one that is clean, uncluttered, easy to follow, visually attractive, and fits best onto the page space available. A wine list with few white spaces is intimidating to the customer.

Organize by Essential Category

The most basic categories are sparkling wines, white wines, red wines, rosé wines, fortified wines, and dessert wines. This gives the customer a starting point.

Organize by Body

Lists can be organized by body, with dry, light-bodied white wines preceding fuller-bodied whites. The heading could be just that—"Dry, Light-Bodied White Wines"—or, under the heading of "New York Dry White Wines," selections could be listed from lightest to fullest by body. Thus, customers are more likely to order lesser-known wines because they can estimate their body and degree of sweetness. This type of organization also facilitates the pairing of food and wine for both the customer and the server, as references to specific menu items can be included under the appropriate category of relative richness and intensity on the palate.

Remember that the way in which the first wine is listed sets the standard for the rest of the list. For example, if under the first heading, "Dry, Light-Bodied Sparkling Wines," the sequence is established as French wines before American—with each wine listed with information about product, producer, special attribute (such as *reserva*, which indicates a superior quality due to longer aging in an Iberian wine), region, nation, and vintage, in that order—then the wines in each category should also follow that sequence.

Women Winemakers We Love

This is a man's world, but it would be nothing, nothing without a woman to care.
— *James Brown (1933–2006)*

Follow the Moon...Biodynamics.

Coined in the 1920s by Austrian scientist and philosopher Rudolph Steiner, biodynamic farming's core philosophy demands a respect and understanding of the soil, the animals that inhabit it, and the natural cycles that shape them both. The whole vineyard is viewed as a living, interconnected organism. Biodynamic vineyard work is timed to coincide with the Earth's natural rhythms, determined by the position of the sun, the moon, and the planets. Balanced and self-sufficient, these vineyards do not require synthetic fertilizers, weed-killers, or insecticides. Composts are made of grape skins, animal manure and vegetables. Vintage after vintage, this sensible farming system ultimately enhances the vineyard's health, which, in turn, provides less costly, larger, and more healthful yields in a balanced environment.

WHITE WINE

NEW WORLD
Araujo "Eisele Vineyard" Sauvignon Blanc, Napa Valley, California, 2007 · 96
Bonny Doon Vineyard "Ca' del Solo Vineyard," Muscat Giallo, Monterey County, California, 2007 · · · · · · 36
Bonny Doon Vineyard "Ca' del Solo Vineyard," Albariño, Monterey County, California, 2007 · · · · · · · · · · 38
Grgich Hills Fumé Blanc, Napa Valley, California, 2006 · 52

OLD WORLD
Domaine Leflaive, Puligny-Montrachet, France, 2004 · 182
Domaine Leflaive, "Clavoillon" 1er Cru, Puligny-Montrachet, France, 2005 · · · · · · · · · · · · · · · · · · · 278
Huet "Le Mont" Demi-Sec, Vouvray, France, 2002 · 69

RED WINE

NEW WORLD
Araujo "Altagracia" Red Wine, Napa Valley, California, 2005 · 192
Benziger "Tribute" Cabernet Sauvignon, Sonoma Mountain, California, 2005 · · · · · · · · · · · · · · · · · · 138
Grgich Hills "Estate Grown" Zinfandel, Napa Valley, California, 2005 · 62
Grgich Hills Merlot, Napa Valley, California, 2004 · 75
Quintessa, Rutherford, California, 2005 · 265

OLD WORLD
Chapoutier "Le Meal," Hermitage, France, 1999 · 495
Domaine Dujac "Clos de la Roche" Grand Cru, Morey-St.-Denis, France, 2004 · · · · · · · · · · · · · · · · · · 326
Domaine Dujac "Clos de la Roche" Grand Cru, Morey-St.-Denis, France, 2005 · · · · · · · · · · · · · · · · · · 495
Domaine Dujac "Les Gruenchers" 1er Cru, Chambolle-Musigny, France, 2004 · · · · · · · · · · · · · · · · · · 275
Domaine Dujac "Les Gruenchers" 1er Cru, Chambolle-Musigny, France, 2005 · · · · · · · · · · · · · · · · · · 420
Domaine de la Romanéc-Conti, "La Tâche" Grand Cru, 2002 · 2,018
Movia "Villa Marija" Merlot, Brda, Slovenia, 2003 · 28

The Martini House Restaurant wine list in Napa Valley offers a quote from Ernest Hemingway that sets the tone for its patrons: "In Europe we thought of wine as something as healthy and normal as food and also a great giver of happiness and well being and delight. Drinking wine was not a snobbism nor a sign of sophistication nor a cult; it was as natural as eating and to me as necessary."—from A Moveable Feast. *Two other features of the list we appreciate are pages devoted to "Women Winemakers We Love" (opposite page) and "Follow the Moon: Biodynamism" (above).*

Organize by Grape Variety

Americans seem to be most comfortable ordering varietal-labeled wines. Thus under the heading "Chardonnay" the wines could be organized by weight (as previously stated) or by area, since Chardonnays from different regions have different flavor profiles. An extensive list could also subdivide alphabetically or by vintage. For example:

CHARDONNAY

BIN #		PRICE
201	Lolonis, Organically Grown, Redwood Valley, Mendocino, California, USA, 2008	$39
202	Gustavo-Thrace, Napa Valley, California, USA, 2008	$66

CHARDONNAY

BIN #		PRICE
203	Benziger, Carneros, California, USA, 2008	$43
204	Millbrook, Reserve, Hudson River Region, New York, USA, 2008	$33
205	Rosemount, Southeast Australia, 2008	$22
206	Chablis, Domaine Laroche, Burgundy, France, 2007	$40
207	Meursault, O. Leflaive, Côte de Beaune, Burgundy, France, 2007	$90
208	Gaia & Rey, A. Gaja, Piemonte, Italy, 2007	$180

Note in the next example that Zinfandel is the sub-heading under the headings "Red Wines," "U.S.A.," and "California"; it is not necessary to repeat those terms in the product description. The list therefore looks less cluttered and intimidating.

RED WINES
USA
California
ZINFANDEL

BIN #		PRICE
31	Cakebrook, "Red Hills," Lake 2007	$82
32	Eberle, Paso Robles 2008	$34
33	Preston, Dry Creek 2008	$41

The example above shows how the grape variety can be used to group wines from various areas. Grape-variety groupings have the advantage of being immediately recognizable to consumers. It may also be advantageous to list the proprietary wines and lesser-known varietals before the popular Chardonnays or Cabernet Sauvignons so that

A wine list can be judged with parameters and prioritized differently for a final decision. These parameters can include breadth (total number of wines, different varieties, countries, styles, etc.), depth (range of prices, number of producers), ratings, name recognition (producer, variety, region), appropriateness with food of the restaurant, and fit with the restaurant style (expense, decor, theme).

The prioritization of these will vary by person and by type of restaurant.

In a broad-market, national-chain restaurant, I would expect to see a wine list primarily with great name recognition with limited breadth and depth. However, in an ultra chic, white-tablecloth, fine dining restaurant, I would expect large variety in breadth and depth, in keeping with the restaurant's style. Personally, for buy-the-glass lists, I've been prioritizing the breadth of grape varieties, showing a range of profiles (delicate and light-bodied to intensely aromatic to full-bodied, etc.).

Once you have clarity on your prioritization (keeping in mind your type of restaurant and customer), make it clear in how the list is organized. A key to a great wine list is making it easy to read and sort through, no matter how many pages.

Jennifer Simonetti,
MW, Wine Educator, Rémy Amerique, New York, New York

customers are drawn further into the list. Promoting lesser-known varieties or regions could endear your restaurant to the customer, making it a wine destination spot.

A disadvantage is that the list becomes cluttered if, for example, there is only one Pinot Gris and one Sémillon and each wine has a separate heading. An alternative heading, such as "Other Whites" "Oddball Whites," "Misfits," or "Exotic Whites," is useful when there are not enough wines in a category to warrant its own heading.

A second disadvantage of grouping by grape type is that it is impossible to use for wines from France, Italy, Spain, and Portugal that are blends of several grape types.

Headings could also feature the major grape types of a blend used in an area.

CABERNET SAUVIGNON

Luce Abbey Estate, 2003, *St. Helena* . . . . $ 230

Meander, 2003, *Napa Valley* 120

Mount Eden, "Old Vine Reserve," 2000, *Santa Cruz Mountains* 110

Mount Veeder, 2004, *Napa Valley* 66

Narsai, 2000, *Napa Valley*. 98

O'Shaughnessy, 2004, *Howell Mountain* 150

Oakville Ranch, 1998, *Napa Valley* 100

Paradigm, 2003, *Oakville* 116

Phelan, 2000, *Napa Valley* 120

Pine Ridge, 2005, *Rutherford*. 102

Provenance, 2005, *Rutherford* 70

Revana Family, 2002, *Napa Valley* 179

Ridge, "Monte Bello," 1990, *Santa Cruz Mountains*. 430

Riscow, "Quinta de Pedras Vineyard," 1998, *Napa Valley* 120

Robert Mondavi, 2002, Stags Leap District, *Napa Valley*. 11

Robert Pecota "Kara's Vineyard," 2003, *Napa Valley*. 65

Rombauer, 2004, *Napa Valley* 75

Rudd, "Estate," 2002, *Oakville* 250

Ruston, 2001, *St. Helena* 80

Screaming Eagle, 1996, *Napa Valley*. 1200

Showket, 2004, *Oakville* 150

Silver Oak, 2003, *Alexander Valley* 130

Stag's Leap Wine Cellars, "Artemis," 2005, *Napa Valley*. 110

Sterling Reserve, 2004, *Napa Valley*. 200

Tedeschi Family Winery, 2003, *Napa Valley*. 90

V Madrone, 2004, *St. Helena, Napa Valley* 150

Veraison, "Stagecoach Vineyard," 2001, *Napa Valley*. 96

Vineyard 29, 1999, *Napa Valley*. 275

Von Strasser, 2001, *Diamond Mountain, Napa Valley* 120

Napa Valley is a major tourist destination, and for Cabernet Sauvignon lovers it is heaven. It makes sense for the Greystone restaurant to organize its list of wines by varietal and have breadth and depth in the Cabernet offerings. In addition to the example above, there are pages that list vertical selections from famous wineries such as Shafer, Opus One, and Bryant Family.

GOING, GOING, GONE!

AMERICAN BOUNTY'S LIMITED SELECTION LIST

These wines have been enjoyed by many of our guests before, and now they are almost gone.
Don't miss the opportunity to treat yourself to something special before they disappear.

Wedding Cuvée, Iron Horse, Green Valley, Sonoma County, California, 2003 – – – – – – – – – – – – $ 68

Chardonnay, Jordan, Russian River Valley, California, 2005– 60

Merlot, Duckhorn, Napa Valley, California, 2005 – 80

Insignia, Joseph Phelps, Napa Valley, California, 2003 – 250

Opus One, "20th Anniversary Release," Mondavi-Rothschild, Napa Valley, California, 1998 – – – – – – – 175

Opus One, Mondavi-Rothschild, Napa Valley, California, 1996 – – – – – – – – – – – – – – – – – 250

Opus One, Mondavi-Rothschild, Napa Valley, California, 1995 – – – – – – – – – – – – – – – – – – 275

Cabernet Sauvignon, Spottswoode Estate Vineyards and Winery, St. Helena, California, 1995 – – – – – – 150

Cabernet Sauvignon, Diamond Creek Vineyards, Gravelly Meadow, Napa Valley, California, 1992 – – – – – 300

Cabernet Sauvignon, Diamond Creek Vineyards, Gravelly Meadow, Napa Valley, California, 1998 – – – – – 250

Cabernet Sauvignon, Ridge Montebello, Santa Cruz Mountains, Napa, California, 1997 – – – – – – – – 200

Cabernet Sauvignon, Robert Mondavi Family Winery, Napa, California, 1995 – – – – – – – – – – – 225

Cabernet Sauvignon, Robert Mondavi Family Winery, To-Kalon Vineyards, Napa, California, 1997 – – – – 200

Cabernet Sauvignon Reserve, Robert Mondavi Family Winery, Napa, California, 1997 – – – – – – – – 150

Due to the fact that this is a limited selection list, some selections and vintages may
not be available at the time of your visit..

---

*A restaurant has an opportunity to sell wines they have in limited stock by having a page such as this one from American Bounty, the
Culinary Institute of America's restaurant in Hyde Park, New York.*

Organize by Place

The majority of European wines are labeled by place name, so it makes sense to group them that way. An extensive list could then employ subheadings for wine names. For example, a Tuscany heading could be divided into Chiantis, Brunello di Montalcinos, Vino Nobile di Montepulcianos, Morellinos and perhaps Super Tuscans (see Chapter 8, pages 388–391) for wines labeled by proprietary name. Bin numbers are especially important when organizing a list in this manner, because they help lessen the customer's anxiety about mispronouncing foreign wines. For example:

RED WINES · ITALY
Tuscany

BIN #		PRICE
250	Chianti, Badia a Coltibuono, Riserva, 2007	$63
255	Brunello di Montalcino, Banfi, Poggio all'Oro, 2004	$265
260	Aprelis, San Luigi, 2005	$47

Organize by Style

Another way to group wines is by style, using such descriptive headings as "Light, Dry, Tart Whites," "Light, Dry, Soft Whites," and "Light, Fruity, Slightly Sweet Whites." Each category could also include food pairing suggestions. For example:

LIGHT, FRUITY, SLIGHTLY SWEET WHITES

BIN #		PRICE

Our light, fruity, slightly sweet whites make a nice complement to our red snapper with papaya salsa or pork tenderloin with red cabbage and spaetzle. They also provide a soothing contrast to our spicy Szechuan shrimp or curry mussel appetizer.

| 210 | Riesling, Cave Spring Cellars, Beamsville Bench, Niagara Peninsula, Ontario, Canada, 2008 | $32 |
| 211 | Wehlener Sonnenuhr, Riesling, J.J. Prum, Kabinett, Mosel, Germany, 2008 | $67 |

Organize by Food Affinities

A list might also be organized by the wines' food affinities. "Shellfish Wines," "Appetizer Wines," "Wild Game Wines," or "Dessert Wines" would be appropriate headings. Note that with dessert wines and dry fortified wines such as

Manzanilla Sherries (see Chapter 9, page 439) the portion size is usually 2 to 2.5 ounces rather than the standard 5 ounces for table wines. The smaller portion size may be indicated on the list.

PAIRING WINE AND CHEESE

First, let me ruin one myth: The biggest red on the table may NOT be the best choice for the cheese course. In my experience, whites are much more versatile with cheeses than reds. Three things need to be considered when pairing wine and cheese. First, sweet versus salty: The saltier the cheese, the sweeter the wine should be. Think about Roquefort and Sauternes. Second, acidity: A high-acid cheese should get a high-acid wine. Try a fresh goat milk cheese with a Sancerre. Third, body: Cheese has body levels just like wine, and they should be in balance. A very heavy cheese will overpower a light-bodied wine and vice versa.

Over the past several years, I have seen a tremendous change in the way people order wine in a restaurant. It seems with the increased knowledge of the American public, wines are taking a much more important role in their meal. Consumers are not willing to settle for a mediocre wine.

What used to be a very intimidating task is becoming easier as knowledge increases. The best advice for the novice is ask for help. When talking to a sommelier, it is important to be honest; tell him how much you want to spend and what you are looking for. If you don't know the terminology, don't worry: Sommeliers are trained to ask the right questions. When you are dining in a top restaurant, the responsibility falls on the sommelier to provide you the best wine possible. No sommelier worth anything will sell you anything different. After all, we are just a bunch of wine geeks who love to talk about wine and introduce our guests to something new and special.

Jason Miller,
Manager, Picholine Restaurant, New York, New York

The Cheese Plate by Country $20
Three tasting wines to match $20

CHEESE	WINE
SPAIN	
Majorero	VINA MEIN (Treixadura Blend) 2005 Ribeiro
Valdeón	RIBERA DEL DUERO 2004 Tinto Pesquera
Roncal	LUSTAU Moscatel "Emilín"
SWITZERLAND	
Krûmmensiler Fürsterkäse	CHARDONNAY Sbragia Family 2005 Dry Creek Valley
Hoch Ybrig	RIESLING Schmitt-Wagner "Longuicher Maximiner Herrenberg" Spätlese 2005 Mosel
Gruyère	BRUNELLO DI MONTALCINO 2001 La Fornace
ENGLAND	
Spenwood	POUILLY-FUMÉ 2004 Marc Deschamps
Montgomery's Cheddar	PINOT NOIR Taz 2005 Santa Barbara County
Colston Bassett Stilton	TAWNY PORT Graham's 20-year
FRANCE	
Bonde de Gâtine	POUILLY-FUMÉ 2004 Marc Deschamps
Le Moulis	CHASSAGNE-MONTRACHET ROUGE 2004 J. N. Gagnard
Carles Roquefort	SAUTERNES 2003 Château Sudutraut
USA	
Constant Bliss	VINA MEIN (Treixadura Blend) 2005 Ribeiro
Uplands Pleasant Ridge	GRUNER VELTLINER 2005 S. Donabaum
Bartlett Blue	MER ET SOLEIL "Late Harvest" 2002 Monterey
ITALY	
Robiola Rocchetta	SAVENNIÈRES 2003 Nicolas Joly
Taleggio	GEWÜRTZTRAMINER 2005 Hugel
Piave	BRUNELLO DI MONTALCINO 2001 La Fornace

Flights specifically chosen to accompany cheeses at Picholine Restaurant in New York City (See quote on pairing wine and cheese from manager Jason Willer on page 723.)

WHITE WINE, LUSH & TROPICAL

CÔTES DE PROVENCE Domaine De La Sauveuse "Cuvée Carolle" Provence, France 2007	$26
LOUREIRO Quinta Do Ameal Ponte De Lima, Portugal 2006	29
RIBOLLA GIALLA Radikon Venezia Giulia, Italy 2003	75 *500ml*
RIESLING KABINETT Weingut F. G. Zilliken "Ockfener Bockstein" Saar, Germany 2001	33
TORRONTES Tomero Salta, Argentina 2007	26

WHITE WINE, LUSH & TELLURIC*

BOURGOGNE BLANC Domaine Roulot Burgundy, France 2006	$54
CHARDONNAY White Helix "Cuvée Chalk Plus" Paso Robles, California 2006	60 37 *375ml*
CHARDONNAY Littorai "Mays Canyon" Russian River Valley, California 2006	104
LANGHE BIANCO Roagna "Solea" Piedmont, Italy 2003	53
MEURSAULT Domaine Michel Caillot Côte De Beaune, France 2005	75
RETSINA Malamatina Thessaloniki, Greece	10 *500ml*
RIOJA RESERVA R. Lopez De Heredia "Viña Tondonia" Rioja Alta, Spain 1989	73
SOAVE CLASSICO Vigneti Di Foscarino "Inama" Veneto, Italy 2005	38

* Telluric: of or pertaining to the earth

What is this life you are so sure about ? A flame that kindles, flashes, and goes out, the unchanging heaven and the eternal sea serve but to mock our mutability. And you before this wine who hesitate for what, I ask you frankly, do you wait?

—Li Po

Chinese poet, 8th century

The eclectic wine list at Bussaco restaurant in Brooklyn, New York, is organized by style and offers thoughtful quotations.

A GOOD WINE LIST IS ONE THAT IS EASY TO READ

Contrary to popular belief, a good wine list is not determined by its gigantic size or the number of expensive, exclusive wines on it.

That's a dangerous idea that has been perpetuated by magazines and award programs. In fact, from the perspective of both restaurant patrons and restaurant owners, the best wine list is the one that can sell the most wine with the fewest possible wines.

Essentially, a wine list must cover all the bases, offering a full spectrum of wine styles in an appropriate variety of price ranges for its level of service and type of cuisine. Wine lists with fewer choices are more work to maintain, but make for less "work" on the part of the guest making the decisions. A good wine list should be, first and foremost, easy to use. It should also be clean, legible, and balanced among wine styles and prices.

But a great wine list is one that is so well organized that it can both forestall some guest questions and act as a subliminal staff-training tool. Wine lists are not read with rapt attention like novels; people are often splitting their attention between conversation and food ordering.

Categories and headings are of particular importance and should make no assumptions about wine knowledge. Wine names are unfamiliar territory for most guests, so maintaining clear and consistent patterns in presenting them is important. Some standards to bear in mind are:

IDENTIFYING WINES WITH 'BIN NUMBERS' IS A GOOD IDEA.
These code numbers help speed wine service, prevent mix-ups, and provide your guests with something 'pronounceable' to order.

DON'T SCRIMP ON HEADINGS, SUBHEADINGS, OR PAGE NUMBERS.
Ordering wine is "work" for guests, so make it as easy as possible. Not everyone knows Pinot Gris is white and Tempranillo is red, so make sure every page is clearly identified at the top.

LEGIBILITY IS EVEN MORE IMPORTANT FOR WINE LISTS THAN MENUS.
Despite this we tend to use smaller fonts and forgo negative space. Make sure the wine list can be read comfortably in low light. No one feels sexy pulling out their reading glasses on a date.

LEAD WITH THE FAMILIAR OVER THE UNKNOWN.
To put guests at ease, put the grape or appellation first on the line instead of a brand name wherever possible. This makes them feel smart and in control. Unfamiliar lead words, like winery names, can be disorienting and stressful.

AVOID UNPLEASANT SURPRISES BY PRINTING CRITICAL INFORMATION ON THE LIST.
Nonstandard wines shouldn't lurk like landmines. Make a special notation for wines with unexpected characteristics. If a wine is sweet, pink, bubbly, or screwcapped, be sure to let guests know. Use positive language, like "cork-free."

DON'T LIST BY PRICE!
Use sequence to convey something more useful. This common practice sends a subliminal message that how much guests spend on wine is what the restaurant sees as most important. Your guests already know how to count, so listing by price is a missed opportunity for communicating something else.

USE THE INTUITIVE "PROGRESSIVE WINE LISTING" FORMAT.
List from lightest to heaviest among styles (e.g. Sparkling before White), among categories (e.g. Riesling before Chardonnay), and within categories (e.g. Chablis before Napa Valley Chardonnay). Every server will then be able to say something useful when asked about the difference between any two wines, whether or not they've tried them.

LIST HALF-BOTTLES AMONG NORMAL WINES, JUST CLEARLY MARKED.
When segregated, only half-bottle shoppers find them. Mix them in and you might score a "one and a half-bottle" sale.

Marnie Old,
Author, Consultant, Educator,
Old Wines LLC

Organize by Selling Price

As a more radical departure, some restaurants have successfully increased wine sales by grouping the wines according to price range. A modest list containing thirty-six selections might employ a three-tier system featuring a couple of sparkling wines, a rosé, four whites, four reds, and a sweet white in each of three price ranges (say, $23, $36, and $55), with a diversity of styles in each. Another option is to have categories such as "Sparkling Wines from $20 to $50," "Sparkling Wines from $50 to $100," and "Sparkling Wines over $100."

Organize by Humorous Headings

Humorous headings may be appropriate at some restaurants to demystify wine. "Sparkling Wine" as a heading, for example, could be replaced with "Putting on the Spritz," "Bubbles = No Troubles," "Bubble Up," "Foamy and Frothy," "Naked Chardonnays," and so on.

The options for organizing a wine list are almost endless, and there is no one right answer. The format selected will depend on the restaurant style, the range of foods, and the customer base. The most important consideration in deciding on the format and organization is that the list should make the process of choosing a wine understandable for the customer.

WINES BY THE GLASS AND HALF BOTTLE

MANY SUCCESSFUL RESTAURANTS agree that much of their success and profit lies in the strength of their wine program. This includes offering an extensive selection of half bottles or wines by the glass. Consumers prefer to enjoy several different wines with their meal rather than a whole bottle of wine.

Automated dispensing/preservation systems have revolutionized the selling of wines in restaurants because they keep the wine in good condition for a month or more, allowing them to be sold by the glass. As wine is dispensed from the bottle, the empty space is filled with argon gas to prevent air from mixing with the wine, thus preventing oxidation and loss of flavor and character. In fact, some restaurants argue that dispensing machines are a major promotional asset, since the machine itself can be a focal point in the restaurant. Vacuum systems are another alternative to preserve wine. The inexpensive stoppers and pump available for home use are decent, but the professional versions that cost a few hundred dollars are much more effective.

Selling wines by the glass can lead to increased sales and revenue and higher numbers of repeat customers. The diner perceives that a greater selection is being offered, guests can enjoy wines that complement their specific food choices rather than all sharing the same bottle of wine, and customers may feel more confident about ordering a whole bottle of a higher-priced wine if they can try a glass of it beforehand. Dispensing systems have also made possible a relatively new concept in restaurants: the wine bar. Wine bars enable customers to sample several different wines of a favorite varietal or region during a meal.

A busy restaurant may not even require a dispensing system if there are just a dozen wines by the glass. Partial bottles may be used for educational tastings for the staff or to offer tastes to frequent guests as a courtesy. In addition, the by-the-glass program can be an important tool for phasing out remainders of wines, featuring wines bought at a favorable discount, or offering a taste of local wines. A restaurant might also test-market a new wine that is being considered for the main list by first offering it by the glass, then tracking sales and soliciting guests' opinions of the wine.

One of the more exciting applications of by-the-glass wine sales has been in the area of sparkling wines. They are an ideal way to begin a meal and are certainly food-friendly. For years restaurateurs argued that sparkling wine could not be sold by the glass because the wine would lose its effervescence. Likewise, it is not possible to put bottles of sparkling wine, which contain carbon dioxide gas, into a dispensing system that is designed to fill the empty space in the bottle with argon gas. However, any high-quality sparkling wine that has been chilled and opened properly (without a loud pop) and kept cold after opening (preferably with a clamped stopper in the bottle) will maintain its effervescence for at least several hours. A motivated and educated service staff can sell a case or two of sparkling

THE VINTAGE

No wine is rarer or more sought-after than vintage Port. At most, it constitutes a mere 2% of production. They are the quintessence of Port wine. These Ports are only declared when various factors combine to make an exceptional year. Intensely powerful and concentrated, these wines are adapted to age in bottle, developing over the years and releasing a complex variety of flavors.

	VINTAGE	BOTTLE (750ml)
Quinta do Crasto, *Susana Esteban*	2003	250
Quinta do Cotto, *Miguel Champlimaud*	2001	120 (375 ml)
Quinta do Vale Meao, *Francisco Olazabal*	2000	200
Caves Santa Marta	1998	200
Ferreira, *José Maria Soares Franco*	1997	250
Dow's, *Peter & Charles Symington*	1996	120 (375 ml)
Quinta do Infantado, *João Roseira & L. Duarte*	1995	275
Qta da Eira Velha, *Jim Reader*	1995	290
Krohn, *Antonio Cid*	1994	170
Taylor's Qta das Vargelas, *David Guimaraens*	1991	120
Feist, *Jose Manuel Soares*	1987	175
Kopke	1987	175
Fonseca & Guimaraens, *David Guimaraens*	1986	300
Krohn, *Antonio Cid*	1982	220
Ferreira, *José Maria Soares Franco*	1980	350
Noval Nacional, *António Agrellos*	1975	900
Delaforce	1970	600
Taylor's, *David Guimaraens*	1970	650
Graham's, *Peter & Charles Symington*	1970	650
Warre's, *Peter & Charles Symington*	1960	900
Croft, *Nicholas John Delaforce*	1960	950

Magnum (2 x bottle = 1500 ml)		**1500 ml**
Graham's, *Peter & Charles Symington*	1994	900
Dow's, *Peter & Charles Symington*	1977	900

Chiado in Toronto, Canada, is a Portuguese restaurant that honors the winemakers represented by including their names.

SOOKE HARBOUR HOUSE

Table of Contents

The cellar at the Sooke Harbour Hotel in British Columbia is one of the finest in Canada. In the table of contents, local wines are well represented, as well as international wines.

ICE WINES FROM THE NIAGARA PENINSULA, ONTARIO AND NOVA SCOTIA, AND ICE CIDER FROM QUEBEC

Canadian $

HENRY OF PELHAM, CABERNET FRANC
2006 Short Hills Bench -- 200 ml --------- 95

CAVE SPRING, RIESLING
1998 --- 375 ml --------- 145
1990 --- 375 ml --------- 145

HENRY OF PELHAM, RIESLING
2004 --- 375 ml --------- 130
1998 --- 375 ml --------- 145
1995 --- 375 ml --------- 90
1990 --- 375 ml --------- 125

PILLITTERI, RIESLING
2001 --- 200 ml --------- 75
1999 --- 200 ml --------- 70
1996 --- 200 ml --------- 85

THIRTY BENCH, RIESLING
1999 Special Select ----------------------------------- 375 ml --------- 165
1999 --- 375 ml --------- 165
1998 --- 375 ml -------- 155

OTHER RIESLING ICE WINE
2003 Misek Vineyard, Malivoire ------------------------- 200 ml -------- 90
2002 Paul Bosc Estate Vineyard, Château des Charms --------- 375 ml ------- 145

INNISKILLIN, VIDAL
1998 --- 375 ml --------- 90
1996 --- 375 ml --------- 90

KONZELMANN, VIDAL
2000 --- 375 ml -------- 150
1997 --- 375 ml -------- 150

MAGNOTTA, VIDAL
2005 --- 375 ml --------- 90
2004 --- 375 ml --------- 90

OTHER VIDAL ICE WINE FROM ONTARIO
1996 Stonechurch -------------------------------------- 375 ml --------- 95
1989 St. Urban Vineyard, Vineland Estates -------------------- 375 ml -------- 185

VIDAL ICE WINE FROM NOVA SCOTIA
1999 Jost Vineyards ------------------------------------ 375 ml --------- 75

ICE CIDER FROM QUEBEC
NV Crémant de Glace, Verger du Minot, Hemmingford --------- 375 ml --------- 75
2004 Domaine Pinnacle, Frelighsburg ------------------------ 375 ml --------- 75

Sooke Harbour's dessert offerings include native Icewines, which are among the finest sweet wines of the world, as well as a couple of sweet apple ciders from Québec.

wine per night in a restaurant that previously sold only a case of whole bottles per month.

Wines offered by the glass must be easily identifiable as such by the customer. This may mean listing all by-the-glass offerings on a separate list or placing them in a prominent position, such as on the first page or at the top of the list. These strategies make it possible to promote the by-the-glass selections and to point them out to customers.

The choice of how many wines to offer by the glass will depend on the type of restaurant and customer expectations. There are famous examples of restaurants with extensive lists that boldly offer to open any wine on the list if a customer will order two glasses.

As with all sales in the restaurant, the major consideration is that by-the-glass sales be profitable. In addition, the selling price of a wine by the glass must bear some relation to that of the bottle. Some restaurants keep their by-the-glass prices exactly relative to the bottle price. For example, if a bottle sells for $25 on the list and the restaurant offers that wine by the glass in a 5-ounce portion, the glass of wine will sell for $5, since a 25.4-ounce/750-milliliter bottle contains approximately five 5-ounce portions. The majority of restaurants, however, insist that selling wines by the glass requires more labor; they therefore charge more by the glass than by the bottle. Exactly how much more is largely subjective, and the final decision may simply be an assessment of how much more a customer would be willing to pay. Thus the wine in the above example may be priced anywhere from $5.50 to $7. Unfortunately, we have seen far too many bars, restaurants, and clubs where the wholesale price of the glass equals the cost of the entire bottle.

An alternative to offering numerous wines by the glass is to have a good selection of half bottles. We suggest at least three different price points in the categories of sparkling, dry and semidry whites, dry light- and heavy-bodied reds, and sweet wines.

SUMMARY

A RESTAURATEUR TAKES A CALCULATED RISK with her or his wine list. It is important to view all wine lists as temporary. Management and staff must listen to their patrons' comments, monitor the sales mix, and adjust the list accordingly. Wines that lag in sales may be boosted by a price adjustment, promotion by the glass, or inclusion in a fixed-price food-and-wine tasting. An analysis of the types of wine that are moving well, together with patrons' comments, will influence the choice of which wines to add to the list.

The willingness and flexibility to constantly change and update the list is also important. Computers enable restaurants to control their wine lists in ways that were previously unimaginable. Many establishments now change the list (along with the menu) on a regular basis—perhaps monthly or seasonally. The evolution of the list is dependent on such forces as customer and staff feedback, sales analyses, and trends.

A wine list does not have to be a work of art. In fact, as important as the visual aspect may be, it is worthless if the content does not provide the selection that the customer is looking for.

Finally, although a good wine list is a valuable sales tool, it must be complemented by an educated and enthusiastic service staff who have tasted and can accurately describe the majority of wines on the list.

APPENDIX A: CONVERSION TABLES

VOLUME

Standard wine bottle = .75 Liter (l)/750 milliliters (ml)/75 centiliters (cl)

1 liquid pint = .473 liter	1 liter = 2.114 liquid pints
1 quart = .946 liter	1 liter = 1.057 quarts
1 gallon = 3.785 liters	1 liter = 0.264 gallon

1 hectoliter (hl) = 100 liters = 26.4 gallons

1 barrique = 60 gallons = 225 liters = 300 bottles

1 tonneau = 4 barriques = 900 liters = 1,200 bottles

BOTTLES (SIZES AND EQUIVALENTS)

Half-bottle = 375 milliliters = 12.7 fluid ounces

Bottle = 750 milliliters = 25.4 fluid ounces

Magnum = 1.5 liters (2 bottles) = 50.8 fluid ounces

Double magnum (Bordeaux) = 3 liters (4 bottles) = 101.6 fluid ounces

Jeroboam (Burgundy/Champagne) = 3 liters (4 bottles) = 101.6 fluid ounces

Jeroboam (Bordeaux) = 4.5 liters (6 bottles) = 152.4 fluid ounces

Rehoboam (Champagne) = 4.5 liters (6 bottles) = 152.4 fluid ounces

Impériale (Bordeaux) = 6 liters (8 bottles) = 203.2 fluid ounces

Methuselah/Methusalem (Champagne) = 6 liters (8 bottles) = 203.2 fluid ounces

Salmanazar (Champagne) = 9 liters (12 bottles) = 304.8 fluid ounces

Balthazar (Champagne) = 12 liters (16 bottles) = 406.4 fluid ounces

AREA

1 acre = .405 hectare	1 hectare = 2.47 acres

10 hectares is nearly 25 acres (1 hectare = 10,000 sq. meters = 2.47 acres)

10 acres is just over 4 hectares (1 acre = 4,840 sq. yards = 0.405 hectare)

5,000 vines per hectare is approximately 2,000 per acre

YIELD (PRODUCTION PER ACRE)

45 hectoliters per hectare (average standard yield) is equivalent to 3 tons of grapes per acre, which yields about 6,000 bottles per hectare, or 2,430 bottles per acre

TEMPERATURE

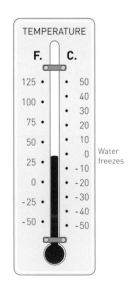

	DEGREES CENTIGRADE	DEGREES FAHRENHEIT
To Convert	× 9/5 and add 32	Subtract 32 and × 5/9

APPENDIX B: HOW TO READ A WINE LABEL

AMERICAN GENERIC/SEMI-GENERIC WINE LABEL

1. Name of producer.
2. Name of wine. "Mountain Chablis" is a generic, also known as semi-generic, white wine label, as Chablis is a famous white wine region in Burgundy, France. Other generic labels include Champagne, Burgundy, Sherry, and Chianti, all of them famous wine regions, but none of them located anywhere in the United States. Generic/semi-generic labels are legal in the United States, except for the states of Oregon and Washington, which forbid their wines to be labeled generically. By international agreement, as of March 2006, no new wine brands may be labeled as generic/semi-generic wines, but those already in existence may continue to do so.
3. Appellation. According to U. S. wine law, if the name of a state appears on the label as the sole appellation, 75 percent of the grapes for that wine must have been grown in that state. Some states, such as California, Oregon, and Washington, have opted for 100 percent when the state name appears on the label.
4. "Vinted and bottled by" could mean that the producer made wine from its own grapes or purchased grapes, or blended wine from finished wines delivered to its facilities. We only know for sure that the producer bottled the wine.
5. Address of producer and legally required alcohol percentage.

Note: Generic/semi-generic wines are usually not vintage-dated, although there is no prohibition to include a vintage date on the label.

AMERICAN VARIETAL LABEL: STATE APPELLATION

1. Brand name for a line of wines, in this case moderately inexpensive wines produced by a larger winery (see 5, below).
2. The varietal. According to U. S. wine law, at least 75 percent of the grapes in this wine must be Chardonnay.
3. Appellation. According to U. S. wine law, if the name of a state appears on the label as the sole appellation, at least 75 percent of the grapes for that wine must have been grown in that state. Some states, such as California, Oregon, and Washington, have opted for 100 percent when the state name appears on the label.
4. The phrase "produced and bottled by" means that the winery made the wine and bottled it but probably purchased grapes from other growers to make the wine, the grapes were grown by the producer on leased land, or the wine was bottled outside the appellation. It is not, according to law, estate-bottled.
5. The name of the producer.
6. Alcohol percentage is legally required.

Note: This wine would normally include a vintage date on the label. The vintage date is the year in which the grapes were harvested. In the United States, if a vintage date appears on a wine label, a minimum of 95 per cent of the grapes were harvested in that year.

Pinot Noir ①
Willamette Valley ②
DOMAINE SERENE
RESERVE ③

PRODUCED AND BOTTLED BY DOMAINE SERENE
CARLTON, OREGON, USA ⑤
ALC. 12% BY VOL. ⑥

NAPA VALLEY ①
PINOT NOIR ②
RESERVE ③
④ UNFILTERED
ROBERT MONDAVI WINERY ⑤
ALCOHOL 14.2% BY VOLUME ⑥

AN OREGON VARIETAL WINE LABEL

1. The varietal, in this case Pinot Noir. In Oregon, if a varietal name appears on the label, at least 90 percent of the wine must be made from those grapes. This is true for all grapes except Cabernet Sauvignon, for which 75 percent is required. Oregon wine law supersedes U. S. wine law, which mandates at least 75 percent for any single-varietal label.
2. The American Viticultural Area (AVA), in this case the Willamette Valley. In Oregon and Washington State, if a wine label includes any appellation—AVA, county, state, etc.—100 percent of the grapes must have been grown and harvested in that appellation. Oregon and Washington State's wine law supersedes U. S. wine law, which mandates at least 85 percent for any AVA.
3. The term "reserve," although a special attribute, simply means that the wine must be a vintage-dated varietal wine; other than that, it has no legal meaning under U. S. wine law. For some producers, the term is used strictly for marketing the wine. For other producers, the term has ethical meaning, at least—one of the best wines made in that vintage.
4. The phrase "produced and bottled by" means that the winery made the wine and bottled it but probably purchased grapes from other growers to make the wine, the grapes were grown by the producer on leased land, or the wine was bottled outside the appellation. It is not, according to law, estate-bottled.
5. The name and address of the producer.
6. Alcohol percentage is legally required.

Note: This wine will always include a vintage date on the label. The vintage date is the year in which the grapes were harvested. In the United States, if a vintage date appears on a wine label, a minimum of 95 percent of the grapes were harvested in that year.

AMERICAN VARIETAL LABEL WITH SPECIAL ATTRIBUTES

1. The American Viticultural Area (AVA). According to U. S. wine law, at least 85 percent of the grapes in this wine must have been grown and harvested in the Napa Valley.
2. The varietal. According to U. S. wine law, at least 75 percent of the grapes in this wine must be Pinot Noir.
3. The term "reserve," although a special attribute, simply means that the wine must be a vintage-dated varietal wine; other than that, it has no legal meaning under U. S. wine law. For some producers, the term is used strictly for marketing the wine. For other producers, the term has ethical meaning, at least—one of the best wines made in that vintage.
4. "Unfiltered" is another special attribute. It implies that the producer chose not to filter the finished wine in order to improve the color, flavor, and complexity of the wine.
5. Alcohol percentage is legally required.
6. Name and address of producer.

Note: This wine will always include a vintage date on the label. The vintage date is the year in which the grapes were harvested. In the United States, if a vintage date appears on a wine label, a minimum of 95 percent of the grapes were harvested in that year.

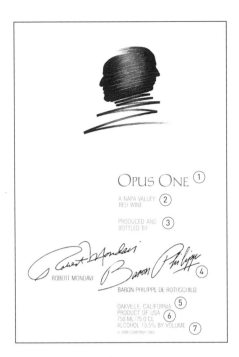

AMERICAN VARIETAL LABEL: ESTATE BOTTLED, SUB-AVA, SINGLE VINEYARD

1. Name of producer.
2. The American Viticultural Area (AVA). According to U. S. wine law, at least at least 85 percent of the grapes in this wine had to come from the Napa Valley. However, because the wine is estate-bottled, 100 percent of the grapes must have been grown and harvested in the Napa Valley (see 6, below).
3. The sub-AVA. Howell Mountain is one of several subappellations of the Napa Valley American Viticultural Area. According to U. S. wine law, at least 85 percent of the grapes in this wine must be grown and harvested in the Howell Mountain AVA. However, because the wine is estate-bottled, 100 percent of the grapes must have been grown and harvested not only in the blanket AVA, Napa Valley, but entirely in the Howell Mountain AVA.
4. The varietal. According to United States wine law, at least 75 percent of the grapes in this wine must be Merlot.
5. The name of a single vineyard of high quality, in this case Bancroft Ranch. a special attribute. According to U. S. wine law, if a single vineyard name appears on the label, at least 95 percent of the grapes in the wine had to be grown and harvested in that vineyard.
6. The phrase "estate-bottled" means that the same company (in this case, Beringer Vineyards) grew the grapes, made the wine, and bottled the wine. According to law, it also means that Beringer Vineyards owns the land on which the grapes were grown, and that all of its facilities—the vineyards, the winery, and its bottling plant—are located in the appellation of origin (in this case, the blanket appellation, Napa Valley and/or the sub-AVA, Howell Mountain).
7. The phrase "grown, produced, and bottled" in this case reiterates that the wine is estate-bottled by Beringer Vineyards.
8. Alcohol percentage is legally required.

Note: This wine will always include a vintage date on the label. The vintage date is the year in which the grapes were harvested. In the United States, if a vintage date appears on a wine label, a minimum of 95 percent of the grapes were harvested in that year.

AMERICAN PROPRIETARY LABEL

1. The name of the wine, in this case the proprietary name Opus One. This allows the producer the freedom to not adhere to the "75 percent law" governing American varietal labels.
2. The American Viticultural Area (AVA). According to U. S. wine law, at least 85 percent of the grapes in this wine had to be grown and harvested in the Napa Valley. Also, an optional descriptor of the wine is provided.
3. The phrase "produced and bottled by" means that the Opus One winery made the wine and bottled it, but may have purchased grapes from other growers to make the wine, or the grapes were grown by the producer on leased land, or the wine was bottled outside the AVA, Napa Valley. It is not necessarily estate-bottled.
4. The (optional) signatures of the producers. Opus One is a joint venture by the Robert Mondavi winery and the estate Château Mouton Rothschild of Bordeaux, France.
5. Oakville is a sub-AVA of the Napa Valley AVA and is where the Opus One winery is located.
6. Bottle size is legally required.
7. Alcohol percentage is legally required.

Note: This wine will always include a vintage date on the label. The vintage date is the year in which the grapes were harvested. In the United States, if a vintage date appears on a wine label, a minimum of 95 per cent of the grapes were harvested in that year.

AMERICAN NONVINTAGE SPARKLING WINE

1. The phrase *"méthode champenoise"* indicates that the sparkling wine was made by the classic Champagne method, with the second fermentation and aging of the wine occurring in the bottle at hand.
2. Style of sparkling wine; in this case, Brut, a relatively dry style.
3. Name of the producer, Domaine Carneros.
4. The American Viticultural Area (AVA) and optional statement of wine type (sparkling). According to U. S. wine law, at least 85 percent of the grapes in this wine had to be grown and harvested in the Carneros AVA.
5. The phrase "produced and bottled by" means that the Domaine Carneros winery made the wine and bottled it, but may have purchased grapes from other growers to make the wine, or the grapes were grown by the producer on leased land, or the wine was bottled outside the AVA, Carneros. It is not necessarily estate-bottled.
6. A restatement of the AVA and the address of the producer, Domaine Carneros. Carneros is a shared AVA between Napa and Sonoma counties. The winery is located on the Napa side of Carneros. The Napa information is not required.
7. Kobrand is the distributor of the wine
8. Bottle size is legally required.
9. Alcohol percentage is legally required.

VINTAGE *CUVÉE DE PRESTIGE* CHAMPAGNE LABEL

1. Name of the producer; in this case, Taittinger.
2. Proprietary name of the Champagne, in this case, Comtes de Champagne. Proprietary names are often reserved for the best and most expensive wine produced by the Champagne house, its *cuvée de prestige*.
3. The word *millésime* refers to the vintage, the year in which the grapes were picked. In this case the vintage year is 1993.
4. Style of the Champagne; in this case, Brut, a relatively dry style.
5. The city of Reims, along with Epernay and Ay, is a major center for Champagne production. The Taittinger winery is located in Reims.
6. The phrase "Blanc de Blancs" indicates that the Champagne is made only from white grapes. By law, the only legally permitted white grape in Champagne is Chardonnay, so this Champagne is 100 percent Chardonnay.
7. Appellation of origin *(Appellation d'Origine Contrôlée)*, Champagne is the only approved appellation that does not legally require the phrase "appellation d'origine contrôlée" on the label, although this label includes the phrase.
8. Kobrand is the importer of the wine
9. Alcohol percentage is legally required.
10. Bottle size is legally required.

NEW WORLD BLENDED VARIETAL LABEL (ARGENTINA)

1. The grapes for this wine are "estate grown"; all of the grapes were grown and harvested in the producer's vineyards, and none were purchased elsewhere.
2. The name of the producer, Santa Julia.
3. Mendoza is the appellation of this wine, the *denominación* of the vineyards for this wine.
4. The blend of grapes and in what percentage. Legally, the percentage need not appear, but the dominant grape must be listed first.
5. The phrase "grown, produced and bottled by" indicates that the producer grew the grapes and made and bottled the wine. Very close in meaning to estate-bottled.
6. Country of origin; in this case, Argentina.
7. Bottle size is legally required.
8. Alcohol percentage is legally required.

Note: This wine will always include a vintage date on the label. The vintage date is the year in which the grapes were harvested.

FRENCH *VIN DE PAYS* VARIETAL LABEL

1. Name of the producer, in this case Vichon Mediterranean.
2. Name of the varietal. If the name of a sole varietal appears on any French wine label, the wine must be made from 100 percent of that varietal.
3. *Vin de pays.* Wines from six very large wine-growing regions, mostly in the south of France. Pays d'Oc is one such region, located in the Languedoc-Rousillon area of Mediterranean France.
4. Alcohol percentage is legally required.
5. Vichon was at one time owned by the Robert Mondavi winery in California; it no longer is. There is quite a bit of foreign investment in the *vin de pays* regions.

Note: This wine will most often include a vintage date on the label. The vintage date is the year in which the grapes were harvested.

TYPICAL *APPELLATION D'ORIGINE CONTRÔLÉE* **FRENCH WINE LABEL**

1. The label of the importer; in this case, Frederick Wildman and Sons Ltd.
2. The name of the wine. In this case it is named for the Crozes-Hermitage district in the northern Rhône Valley. This is typical of many of the *appellation d'origine contrôlée* (AOC) wines of France.
3. Name of a vineyard site owned by the producer, in this case the Domaine Raymond Roure. The vineyard is the source of the grapes for this wine.
4. Bottle size is legally required.
5. Alcohol percentage is required.
6. Indicates that the wine is bottled by the producer Paul Jaboulet Aîné, whose headquarters are in the town of La Roche de Glun in the Rhône Valley.

Note: This wine will always include a vintage date on the label. The vintage date is the year in which the grapes were harvested.

ITALIAN WINE LABEL: *DENOMINAZIONE DI ORIGINE CONTROLLATA* **(DOC)**

1. Name of the producer; in this case, Renato Ratti.
2. Proprietary vineyard name or single vineyard site name. The name Torriglione loosely translates as "warm hill."
3. DOC (*denominazione di origine controllata*), a controlled place name. In this case, the DOC is a grape and place name: Barbera d'Alba, one of more than forty DOC zones in the Piedmont region of Italy.
4. The wine is bottled by the producer at the Renato Ratti winery in La Morra. The wine is not necessarily estate-bottled.
5. Bottle size is legally required. The letter **e** indicates that this wine is legal for sale in the member countries of the European Union. Normally, this letter would not appear on a bottle destined for sale in the United States.
6. Alcohol percentage is legally required.

Note: This wine will always include a vintage date on the label. The vintage date is the year in which the grapes were harvested.

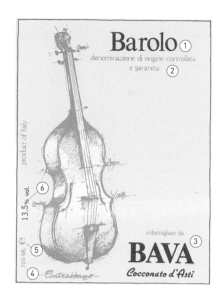

ITALIAN WINE LABEL: *DENOMINAZIONE DI ORIGINE CONTROLLATA E GARANTITA* (DOCG)

1. Name of the wine, which is also the name of the appellation of origin; in this case, Barolo, a wine village in the Piedmont region of Italy. By law, Barolo, a red wine, must be made from 100 percent Nebbiolo grapes.
2. Indicating that the wine is from the highly respected DOCG zone Barolo.
3. Bottled by the winery Bava. Not estate-bottled.
4. Bottle size is legally required.
5. The letter **e** indicates that this wine is labeled for sale in the member countries of the European Union.
6. Alcohol percentage is legally required.

Note: This wine will always include a vintage date on the label. The vintage date is the year in which the grapes were harvested.

ITALIAN WINE LABEL: SUPER TUSCAN *VINO DA TAVOLA*

1. Proprietary name of the wine, named for the estate on the Tuscan coast where the grapes for this wine grow. Ornellaia, one of the first nontraditional Super Tuscans, is a blend of Cabernet Sauvignon, Merlot, and Cabernet Franc.
2. The vintage. Year in which the grapes were harvested. In this case the vintage year is 1991.
3. Name and address of the producer and the Ornellaia estate.
4. The wine is estate-bottled.
5. Indicating that the wine is not IGT, DOC, or DOCG, but a *vino da tavola*, a table wine, albeit a very expensive one. This wine reflects its age; as of 1996, the overwhelming majority of expensive *vino da tavola* wines were reclassified as IGT (*indicazione geografica tipica*). A select few, such as the iconic Sassicaia, have become DOC (*denominazione di origine controllata*) wines. Many of these elite "table wines" were made for long aging, such as this 1991 Ornellaia.
6. Alcohol percentage is legally required.
7. Bottle size is legally required.

ITALIAN WINE LABEL: SUPER TUSCAN, *INDICAZIONE GEOGRAFICA TIPICA* (IGT)

1. Vintage; year in which the grapes were harvested. In this case, the vintage year is 1997.
2. Proprietary name of the wine, named for the estate in Tuscany where the grapes for this wine grow. Solaia is primarily a blend of Cabernet Sauvignon and Sangiovese.
3. Name and address of the producer, Marchese Antinori, in *Firenze* (Florence).
4. Region is *Toscana* (Tuscany).
5. Indicating the wine is not DOC or DOCG, but IGT (*indicazione geografica tipica*). Note that after the 1996 vintage, virtually all of the Super Tuscans, which had been categorized as *vino da tavola*, were certified as IGT, or in a few select cases, as DOC (*denominazione di origine controllata*).
6. The wine is estate bottled in Casciano, a village in Tuscany.
7. Bottle size is legally required.
8. Alcohol percentage is legally required.

GERMAN WINE LABEL: RIESLING, *QUALITÄTSWEIN* LEVEL

1. Name of producer or wine broker. In this case, Joh. Jos. Christoffel Erben is a winemaker who produces wines from only single estates (see 2, below).
2. VDP, Verband Deutscher Prädikatsweingüter, is a voluntary group of traditional German wine producers committed to producing high-quality Riesling wines from single estates, with no chaptalization, lower yields from fine vineyard sites, and sustainable agriculture practices.
3. Christoffel Erben is the name of the wine estate.
4. Name of the varietal (in Germany, optional, but almost always appears on a Riesling label).
5. *Qualitätswein* indicates that the wine is a wine of high quality from a specific wine-producing region. In this case, that wine region, or *Anbaugebiet*, is Mosel-Saar-Ruwer (now known as Mosel).
6. *Gutsabfüllung* means that the wine is estate-bottled by a winemaker who holds a degree in enology.
7. The name and address of the winery and estate, the *Weingut*.
8. Bottle size is legally required.
9. Name of the *Anbaugebiet* or wine region, Mosel-Saar-Ruwer (now Mosel).
10. Alcohol percentage is legally required.
11. The *Prüfungsnummer*—a number assigned to quality German wines by each of the thirteen regional bureaus of the federal Amtliche Prüfstelle (the State Institute for Quality Control). This A.P. number indicates that the Mosel-Saar-Ruwer (now Mosel) bureau approved this wine as being free of chemical and sensory defects.

Note: This wine will always include a vintage date on the label. The vintage date is the year in which the grapes were harvested.

GERMAN WINE LABEL: RIESLING, *QUALITÄTSWEIN MIT PRÄDIKAT* **(NOW** *PRÄDIKATSWEIN***),** *KABINETT* **LEVEL**

1. Name of the wine producer.
2. *Weingut*, a wine estate (winery and vineyards).
3. The word *Rüdesheimer* means "from Rüdesheim," the village (*bereich*) in which the grapes were grown.
4. Berg Roseneck is the name of the vineyard in Rüdesheim, in this case an *Einzellage*—a single-vineyard site.
5. Name of the varietal (in Germany, optional, but almost always appears on a Riesling label).
6. *Kabinett* is one of six *Prädikatswein* special attributes. *Kabinett* indicates grapes from a normal harvest. Other special attributes that could appear on this label, in ascending order of sugar level in the grapes, are *Spätlese, Auslese, Beerenauslese, Eiswein*, or *Trockenbeerenauslese*.
7. *Qualitätswein mit Prädikat* (QmP: quality wine with special attributes) has, since August 2007, been renamed as *Prädikatswein*. All wines labeled in this way must list the special attribute (see above).
8. *Erzeugerabfüllung* means "bottled by the producer," near-synonymous with the term "estate-bottled."
9. The *Prüfungsnummer*, a number assigned to quality German wines by each of the thirteen regional bureaus of the federal Amtliche Prüfstelle (the State Institute for Quality Control). This A.P. number indicates that the Rheingau bureau approved this wine as being free of chemical and sensory defects.
10. Alcohol percentage is legally required on the label.
11. Bottle size is legally required. The letter **e** indicates that this wine is legal for sale in the member countries of the European Union. Normally, this letter would not appear on a bottle destined for sale in the United States.
12. The address of the wine producer.
13. Rheingau is the *Anbaugebiet*, one of thirteen German wine regions.

Note: This wine will always include a vintage date on the label. The vintage date is the year in which the grapes were harvested.

GERMAN WINE LABEL: RIESLING, *QUALITÄTSWEIN MIT PRÄDIKAT* **(NOW** *PRÄDIKATSWEIN***),** *SPÄTLESE* **LEVEL**

1. Name of the wine producer, Kruger-Rumpf. Weingut is a wine estate (winery and vineyards).
2. The word Münsterer meands "from Münster," the village in which the grapes were grown.
3. Rheinberg is the name of the vineyard in Münster, in this case, an *Einzellage*, or single-vineyard estate.
4. Name of the varietal (in Germany, optional, but almost always appears on a Riesling label).
5. *Spätlese*, which means "late harvest," is the special attribute of this wine. Normally this wine is moderately sweet, with balanced acidity.
6. Nahe is the *Anbaugebiet*, one of thirteen German wine regions.
7. *Qualitätswein mit Prädikat* (QmP: quality wine with special attributes) has, since August 2007, been renamed as *Prädikatswein*. All wines labeled in this way must list the special attribute (see 5, above).
8. The *Prüfungsnummer*, a number assigned to quality German wines by each of the thirteen regional bureaus of the federal Amtliche Prüfstelle (the State Institute for Quality Control). This A.P. number indicates that the Nahe bureau approved this wine as being free of chemical and sensory defects.
9. Alcohol percentage and bottle size are legally required.
10. *Gutsabfüllung* means that the wine is estate-bottled by a winemaker who holds a degree in enology.
11. The name and address of the wine producer.

Note: This wine will always include a vintage date on the label. The vintage date is the year in which the grapes were harvested.

GERMAN WINE LABEL: RIESLING, *QUALITÄTSWEIN MIT PRÄDIKAT* (NOW *PRÄDIKATSWEIN*), *AUSLESE* LEVEL

1. Name of the wine producer, Karlsmühle. *Weingut* is a wine estate (winery and vineyards).
2. The word *Lorenzhöfer* means "from Lorenzhöf," the village in which the grapes were grown.
3. Name of the varietal (in Germany, optional, but almost always appears on a Riesling label).
4. *Auslese* is one of six special attributes. This wine is quite sweet with high levels of acidity.
5. *Qualitätswein mit Prädikat* (QmP: quality wine with special attributes) has, since August 2007, been renamed as *Prädikatswein*. All wines labeled in this way must list the special attribute (see 4, above).
6. *Gutsabfüllung* means that the wine is estate-bottled by a winemaker who holds a degree in enology.
7. The address of the wine producer.
8. The *Prüfungsnummer*, a number assigned to quality German wines by each of the thirteen regional bureaus of the federal Amtliche Prüfstelle (the State Institute for Quality Control). This A.P. number indicates that the Mosel-Saar-Ruwer (now Mosel) bureau approved this wine as being free of chemical and sensory defects.
9. Alcohol percentage is legally required.
10. Bottle size is legally required. The letter **e** indicates that this wine is legal for sale in the member countries of the European Union. Normally, this letter would not appear on a bottle destined for sale in the United States.
11. Mosel-Saar-Ruwer (now Mosel) is the *Anbaugebiet*, one of thirteen German wine regions.

Note: This wine will always include a vintage date on the label. The vintage date is the year in which the grapes were harvested.

GERMAN WINE LABEL: RIESLING, *QUALITÄTSWEIN MIT PRÄDIKAT* (NOW *PRÄDIKATSWEIN*), *EISWEIN* LEVEL

1. Name of the wine producer, Koehler-Ruprecht.
2. The word *Kallstadter* means "from Kallstadt," the village in which the grapes were grown.
3. Saumagen is the name of the vineyard in Kallstadt, in this case, an *Einzellage*, or single-vineyard estate.
4. Name of the varietal (in Germany, optional, but almost always appears on a Riesling label).
5. The term *Eiswein* refers to the special attribute of this wine. *Eiswein* is made from grapes frozen on the vine and then harvested. Since only the water in the grape freezes, the sugars remain high and concentrated. The wine features searing acidity. *Eiswein* is made only in exceptionally cold vintages.
6. *Gutsabfüllung* means that the wine is estate-bottled by a winemaker who holds a degree in enology.
7. *Qualitätswein mit Prädikat* (QmP: quality wine with special attributes) has, since August 2007, been renamed as *Prädikatswein*. All wines labeled in this way must list the special attribute (see 5, above).
8. The *Prüfungsnummer*, a number assigned to quality German wines by each of the thirteen regional bureaus of the federal Amtliche Prüfstelle (the State Institute for Quality Control). This A.P. number indicates that the Pfalz bureau approved this wine as being free of chemical and sensory defects.
9. Alcohol percentage is legally required.
10. Pfalz is the *Anbaugebiet*, one of thirteen German wine regions.
11. Bottle size is legally required.

Note: This wine will always include a vintage date on the label. The vintage date is the year in which the grapes were harvested.

GERMAN WINE LABEL: RIESLING, *QUALITÄTSWEIN MIT PRÄDIKAT* (NOW *PRÄDIKATSWEIN*), *TROCKENBEERENAUSLESE* LEVEL

1. Name and address of the wine producer, J.u.H.A. Strub. *Weingut* is a wine estate (winery and vineyards).
2. The term *Niersteiner* means "from Nierstein," the village in which the grapes were grown.
3. Orbel is the vineyard in Nierstein, in this case a *Grosslage*, or a collective vineyard site.
4. Name of the varietal (in Germany, optional, but almost always appears on a Riesling label).
5. The term *Trockenbeerenauslese* refers to the special attribute of this wine. *Trockenbeerenauslese* indicates grapes totally affected by botrytis, producing singular wines of incredible richness, sweetness, complexity, and depth, with high acidity levels. *Trockenbeerenauslese* is made only in exceptional vintages.
6. *Qualitätswein mit Prädikat* (QmP: quality wine with special attributes) has, since August 2007, been renamed as *Prädikatswein*. All wines labeled in this way must list the special attribute (see 5, above).
7. The *Prüfungsnummer*, a number assigned to quality German wines by each of the thirteen regional bureaus of the federal Amtliche Prüfstelle (the State Institute for Quality Control). This A.P. number indicates that the Rheinhessen bureau approved this wine as being free of chemical and sensory defects.
8. *Gutsabfüllung* means that the wine is estate-bottled by a winemaker who holds a degree in enology.
9. Alcohol percentage is legally required.
10. Bottle size is legally required.
11. Rheinhessen is the *Anbaugebiet*, one of thirteen German wine regions.

Note: This wine will always include a vintage date on the label. The vintage date is the year in which the grapes were harvested.

SPANISH WINE LABEL: RIOJA RESERVA

1. The short name or acronym of the producer, in this case Cune (see 4 below).
2. The word *reserva* indicates that this is a red wine from Rioja that has been aged at least three years, including at least one year in barrel, the remainder in bottle. The wine cannot be released until the fourth year following the harvest.
3. Indicates that the wine is an approved *denominación* or appellation. Rioja is currently one of only two *denominaciónes de Origen Calificadas* (DOCa) among the sixty demarcated regions (*denominaciónes*). The other DOCa is Priorato. Each of the remaining appellations is certified as *denominación de origen*.
4. The full name of the producer (see 1 above).
5. The seal of the Rioja *consejo regulador*, the regional control bureaucracy of the federal *denominación de origen* (appellation of origin) wine control board.
6. Alcohol percentage is legally required.
7. Bottle size is legally required.

Note: This wine will always include a vintage date on the label. The vintage date is the year in which the grapes were harvested.

SHERRY

1. The name of the producer, Lustau.
2. The term *solera* refers to the fractional blending system used in making Sherry.
3. *Palo cortado* is the style of Sherry, a relatively dry fortified wine. Other popular Sherry styles include *fino*, *manzanilla*, *amontillado*, and *oloroso*.
4. Península is the proprietary name for this wine.
5. An optional description of the Sherry. This is an export label, as the description is in English.
6. The place that the Sherry was produced, the Jerez region of Spain.

Note: Sherry is most often a nonvintage wine.

PORTUGUESE WINE LABEL: *DENOMINAÇÃO DE ORIGEM CONTROLADA*

1. The name of the producer. *Quinta* is similar to the French *château*, indicating an estate-bottled wine.
2. *Vinho Tinto* means "red wine."
3. Alcohol percentage is legally required.
4. Bottle size is legally required.
5. Not a legal term, but the producer's term for its top wine.
6. The wine is produced from grapes grown in the demarcated region, Douro.
7. This phrase indicates that this is a vintage-dated wine made from traditional grapes.
8. Estate-bottled.
9. Name of the company that owns the estate.

Note: This wine will always include a vintage date on the label. The vintage date is the year in which the grapes were harvested.

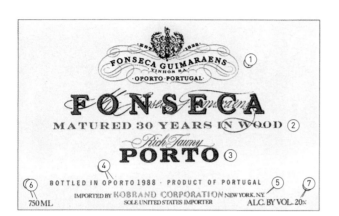

INDICATED AGE TAWNY PORT LABEL

1. Name and location of the producer, Fonseca.
2. Indicating a thirty-year-old tawny Port, meaning that the wines in the blend of this fortified wine were aged in wood for an average of about thirty years. A very smooth and mellow wine.
3. Name of product is Tawny Porto. "Rich" is an optional descriptor.
4. Bottling date in Oporto, the center of the Port trade in the Douro Valley.
5. Name of U.S. importer.
6. Bottle size is legally required.
7. Legally required alcohol percentage. Since Porto is a fortified wine, it will always be high in alcohol.

Note: This is a nonvintage wine.

VINTAGE PORT LABEL

1. Name of producer, Taylor Fladgate
2. The vintage. All of the grapes in the wine must have been harvested in 1977.
3. Name and style of the product.
4. Official name of producer.
5. Vintage Port must be bottled between the second and third year from the harvest of the grapes. Oporto is the famous port from which the wine is shipped.
6. Obviously bound for the United States, because the label reads "Contains Sulfites." Legally, all wine sold in the United States must have this phrase printed on the wine label.
7. Legally required alcohol percentage. Since Porto is a fortified wine, it will always be high in alcohol.
8. Bottle size is legally required.

APPENDIX C: AMERICAN APPELLATIONS (AVAs)

There are thirty-one states where American Viticultural Areas (AVAs) are located. This table lists the states and the AVAs located, in whole or in part, in those states.

The Upper Mississippi Valley AVA is the largest demarcated wine region in the world (29,914 square miles/77,477 square kilometers) and spans parts of four states: Iowa, Illinois, Minnesota, and Wisconsin. The Ohio River Valley AVA also contains parts of four U.S. states: Indiana, Kentucky, West Virginia, and Ohio.

There are fourteen multistate viticultural areas. These are Central Delaware Valley (NJ, PA); Columbia Gorge (OR, WA); Columbia Valley (OR, WA); Cumberland Valley (MD, PA); Kanawha River (OH, WV); Lake Erie (NY, OH, PA); Mesilla Valley (NM, TX); Mississippi Delta (LA, MS, TN); Ohio River Valley (IN, KY, OH, WV); Ozark Mountain (AR, OK, MO); Shenandoah Valley (VA, WV); Southeastern New England (CT, MA, RI); Upper Mississippi Valley; and Walla Walla Valley (OR, WA).

Augusta, MO, was the first recognized American Viticultural Area (T.D. ATF-72 published 45 FR 41632, effective date June 20, 1980).

Napa Valley soon followed and was the first California Viticultural Area established (T.D. ATF-201; published 49 FR 9061, effective date January 1, 1983).

PACIFIC NORTHWEST AVAs

IDAHO
Snake River Valley (shared with Oregon)*

OREGON
Applegate Valley
Chehalem Mountains
Columbia Gorge (shared with Washington)*
Columbia Valley (shared with Washington)*
Dindee Hills
Eola-Amity Hills
McMinnville
Red Hill Douglas County
Ribbon Ridge
Rogue Valley
Snake River Valley (shared with Idaho)*
Southern Oregon
Umpqua Valley
Walla Walla Valley (shared with Washington)*
Willamette Valley
Yamhill-Carlton District

WASHINGTON
Columbia Gorge (shared with Oregon)*
Columbia Valley (shared with Oregon)*
Horse Heaven Hills
Lake Chelan
Puget Sound
Rattlesnake Hills
Red Mountain
Snipes Mountain
Wahlike Slope
Walla Walla Valley (shared with Oregon)*
Yakima Valley

EAST COAST AVAs

CONNECTICUT
Southeastern New England*
Western Connecticut Highlands

MARYLAND
Catoctin
Cumberland Valley*
Linganore

MASSACHUSETTS
Martha's Vineyard
Southeastern New England*

NEW JERSEY
Central Delaware Valley*
Outer Coastal Plain
Warren Hills

NEW YORK
Cayuga Lake
Finger Lakes
Hudson River Region
Lake Erie*
Long Island
Niagara Escarpment
North Fork of Long Island
Seneca Lake
The Hamptons, Long Island

NORTH CAROLINA
Yadkin Valley

OHIO
Grand River Valley
Isle St. George
Kanawha River*
Lake Erie*
Loramie Creek
Ohio River Valley*

PENNSYLVANIA
Central Delaware Valley*
Cumberland Valley*
Lake Erie*
Lancaster Valley
Lehigh Valley

RHODE ISLAND
Southeastern New England*

VIRGINIA
Monticello
North Fork of Roanoke
Northern Neck George Washington Birthplace
Rocky Knob
Shenandoah Valley*
Virginia's Eastern Shore

WEST VIRGINIA
Kanawha River
Ohio River Valley*
Shenandoah Valley*

CENTRAL AVAs

ARIZONA
Sonoita

ARKANSAS
Altus
Arkansas Mountain
Ozark Mountain*

COLORADO
Grand Valley
West Elks

ILLINOIS
Shawnee Hills
Upper Mississippi Valley*

INDIANA
Ohio River Valley*

IOWA
Upper Mississippi Valley*

KENTUCKY
Ohio River Valley*

LOUISIANA, MISSISSIPPI, AND TENNESSEE
Mississippi Delta

MICHIGAN
Lake Michigan Shore
Leelanau Peninsula
Old Mission Peninsula

MINNESOTA
Alexandria Lakes
Upper Mississippi Valley*

MISSOURI
Augusta
Hermann
Ozark Highlands
Ozark Mountain*

NEW MEXICO
Mesilla Valley*
Middle Rio Grande Valley
Mimbres Valley

OKLAHOMA
Ozark Mountain*

TEXAS
Bell Mountain
Escondido Valey
Fredericksburg in the Texas Hill Country
Mesilla Valley*
Texas Davis Mountains
Texas High Plains
Texas Hill Country
Texoma

WISCONSIN
Lake Wisconsin
Upper Mississippi Valley*

Multistate viticultural area

CALIFORNIA VITICULTURAL AREAS BY COUNTY

Of the 204 American Viticultural Areas already established, 107 of them are entirely contained within the state of California. California has the most viticultural areas of all the states.

Napa County leads all California counties with sixteen AVAs located at least partially within its boundaries.

Sonoma County has fourteen AVAs wholly or partially within its boundaries.

ALAMEDA
Central Coast*
Livermore Valley

AMADOR
California Shenandoah Valley
Fiddletown
Sierra Foothills*

CALAVERAS
Sierra Foothills*

CONTRA COSTA
Central Coast*

EL DORADO
California Shenandoah Valley
El Dorado
Fair Play
Sierra Foothills*

FRESNO
Madera*

HUMBOLDT
Willow Creek*

LAKE
Benmore Valley
Clear Lake
Guenoc Valley
High Valley
North Coast*
Red Hills Lake County

LOS ANGELES
Leona Valley
Malibu-Newton Canyon
Saddle Rock-Malibu

MADERA
Madera*

MARIN
North Coast*

MARIPOSA
Sierra Foothills*

MENDOCINO
Anderson Valley
Cole Ranch
Covelo
Dos Rios
McDowell Valley
Mendocino

Mendocino Ridge
North Coast*
Potter Valley
Redwood Valley
Yorkville Highlands

MONTEREY
Arroyo Seco
Carmel Valley
Central Coast*
Chalone*
Hames Valley
Monterey
San Antonio Valley
San Bernabe
San Lucas
Santa Lucia Highlands

NAPA
Atlas Peak
Calistoga
Chiles Valley
Howell Mountain
Los Carneros*
Mt. Veeder
Napa Valley
North Coast*
Oak Knoll District of Napa Valley
Oakville
Rutherford
St. Helena
Spring Mountain District
Stags Leap District
Wild Horse Valley*
Yountville

NEVADA
Sierra Foothills*

PLACER
Sierra Foothills*

RIVERSIDE
Cucamonga Valley
South Coast*
Temecula Valley

SACRAMENTO
Alta Mesa
Borden Ranch*
Clarksburg
Jahant*
Lodi*
Sloughouse*

SAN BENITO
Central Coast*
Chalone*
Clenega Valley
Lime Kiln Valley
Mt. Harlan
Pacheco Pass
Paicines
San Francisco Bay*

SAN BERNARDINO
Cucamonga Valley

SAN DIEGO
Ramona Valley
San Pasqual Valley
South Coast*

SAN FRANCISCO
Central Coast*
San Francisco Bay*

SAN JOAQUIN
Borden Ranch*
Clements Hills
Cohumnes River
Jahant*
Lodi*
Mokelumne River Junction
Tracy Hills*

SAN LUIS OBISPO
Arroyo Grande Valley
Central Coast*
Edna Valley
Paso Robles
Santa Maria Valley*
York Mountain

SAN MATEO
Central Coast*
San Francisco Bay*
Santa Cruz Mountains*

SANTA BARBARA
Central Coast*
Happy Canyon
Santa Maria Valley*
Santa Ynez Valley
Sta. Rita Hills

SANTA CLARA
Central Coast*
San Francisco Bay*
San Ysidro District

Santa Clara Valley
Santa Cruz Mountains*

SANTA CRUZ
Ben Lomond Mountain
Central Coast*
San Francisco Bay*
Santa Cruz Mountains*

SISKIYOU COUNTY
Seiad Valley

SOLANO
Clarksburg
North Coast*
Solano County Green Valley
Suisun Valley
Wild Horse Valley*

SONOMA
Alexander Valley
Bennett Valley
Chalk Hill
Dry Creek Valley
Green Valley of Russian River Valley
Knights Valley
Los Carneros*
North Coast*
Northern Sonoma
Rockpile
Russian River Valley
Sonoma Coast
Sonoma Mountain
Sonoma Valley

STANISLAUS
Diablo Grande
Salado Creek
Tracy Hills*

TRINITY
Willow Creek*

TUOLUMNE
Sierra Foothills*

YOLO
Capay Valley
Clarksburg
Dunnigan Hills
Merritt Island

YUBA
North Yuba
Sierra Foothills*

* Multicounty AVAs

GLOSSARY

A

ABBOCCATO Italian. Semidry, also AMABILE.

ABOCADO Spanish. Semidry.

ACACIA Chemical used for clarifying and stabilizing wine.

ACERBIC A bitter, unpleasant taste from unripe grapes.

ACESCENCE Vinegar-like smell and taste due to bacterial spoilage.

ACETALDEHYDE Formed when carboxylase, an enzyme, acts on pyruvic acid, producing acetaldehyde and carbon dioxide. Colorless, soluble, volatile liquid. During final stage of fermentation it is reduced to ethyl alcohol, but a small quantity remains, adding flavor to the wine. Vinegar-like odor in large amounts.

ACETIC Used to describe wine that has gone sour due to prolonged exposure to oxygen. Acetic acid combines with ethyl acetate to give the vinegary smell and taste that a spoiled wine emits.

ACETIC ACID Colorless, volatile acid found in all wines. Normally present in small quantities, and if there is excessive development of it, the wine turns to vinegar. Key ingredient of vinegar.

ACETOBACTER Airborne, aerobic microorganism that causes the oxidation of alcohol, primarily to acetaldehyde by prolonged exposure to oxygen. Oxygen is essential for its formation: Barrels should be kept full and air spaces in bottles kept to a minimum.

ACIDIFICATION The addition of acid to wine, during or after fermentation, to adjust or improve balance and flavor.

ACIDITY Quality of tartness or sharpness to the taste due to the presence of pleasant fruit acids. Contributes flavor and freshness to wine when it is in proper balance, and contributes to its controlled aging. The principal acids found in wine are tartaric, citric, malic, and lactic.

ACIDULOUS Describes wine that displays an unpleasant, sour taste due to high acidity, often more than 1 percent of total acid.

ACTIVATED CHARCOAL Assists precipitation of solids during fermentation. Clarifies and purifies wine. Removes excess color in white wine.

ADDITIVES Collective name for a group of materials added to wine to improve or preserve it. Some additives are colors, flavors, acids, vitamins, minerals, yeast, and bacterial inhibitors.

ADEGA Portuguese. A winery.

ADULTERATION Treating wine with unauthorized or prohibited ingredients, or excessive levels of a permitted substance.

AERATION Allowing a wine to come into contact with air. Swirling wine already present in a glass.

AEROBIC FERMENTATION Fermentation conducted in the presence of oxygen.

AFTERTASTE Flavor that lingers or remains in the throat or on the tongue after wine is swallowed.

AGING Period of storage in oak barrels or bottles to develop character and palatability.

AGUARDENTE Portuguese. Grape-based distilled spirit used to fortify Porto and Madeira.

ALBARIZA Spanish. White chalky soil in vineyards between Jerez de la Frontera and Sanlúcar de Barrameda.

ALBUMEN Egg whites used as a fining agent, mostly in winemaking.

ALCOHOL Colorless, volatile, flammable liquid that is the intoxicating agent in all beverages that are fermented or distilled. Ethyl alcohol is a preservative and the intoxicating constituent of wine.

ALCOHOLIC Term used to describe a wine that has too much alcohol for its body and weight, making it unbalanced.

ALDEHYDE Colorless, volatile fluid with a distinct odor that is a natural by-product of fermentation and increases in concentration as a wine ages. One of the organic chemical ingredients of wine formed by the partial oxidation of alcohol.

ALLIER French. Small forest centered the city of Moulins, noted for its production of wood barrels. Wood has a medium-tight grain, with moderate oak flavor and tannin extractions, displaying an intense, earthy component and a floral perfumed character.

ALLUVIAL Type of soil made of mostly sand and clay, formed by gradual deposits in the bottomlands along a river by the currents of moving water, as along a riverbed or a lakeshore.

ALMACENISTA Spanish. Grape growers and winemakers who produce Sherry wine to be sold by licensed wineries.

AMABILE Italian. Semidry to semisweet.

AMBER Golden tints reminiscent of the color amber. Color change results from oxidation of the anthocyanins. Color often describing Sherries.

AMERICAN OAK Often considered higher than European oak in the aromas of vanillin and related compounds. As barrels, used for fermenting and aging wines.

AMERICAN VITICULTURAL AREA (AVA) Delimited, geographical grape growing area that has officially been given appellation status by the Alcohol and Tobacco Tax and Trade Bureau.

AMONTILLADO Style of Sherry that has more color and body than *fino*, with a dry taste and nutty flavor.

AMPELOGRAPHY Descriptive study and identification of grapevines; grapevine botany.

AMPHORA Ancient vessel, often of ceramic or earthenware, usually with two handles, which was used as a container for wine.

AMTLICHE PRÜFUNGSNUMMER German. AP number that appears on some wine labels. It certifies that the wine has met all legal requirements and has passed a series of laboratory and sensory tests.

AMYLASE Enzyme that converts starch to sugar.

AÑADA Spanish. Year of harvest. Youngest wine in a Sherry solera.

ANAEROBIC FERMENTATION Fermentation without oxygen.

ANBAUGEBIET German. Wine-producing region.

ANGULAR Wines without much delicacy, often referred to as being stiff or hard, with bitter or tart flavors.

ANTHOCYANINS Phenolic compound of wine that gives it its red color. The purple-red color of a young wine is caused by unstable anthocyanin molecules that, during aging, combine with tannins to give the wine its ruby red color.

ANTIOXIDANTS Phenolic compounds present in grape color and tannin that provide protection to the human body, inhibiting LDL cholesterol and stimulating HDL cholesterol.

APERITIF French. Alcoholic beverage taken before meals to stimulate the appetite.

APPEARANCE Refers to clarity, color, and brilliance of a wine. Wines should usually be free of cloudy and suspended particles when evaluated in a glass.

APPELLATION CONTROLÉE French. Wine laws ("AC laws") specific to each of the wine-producing regions of France. Laws govern each of the defined areas, the varietals that can be used to produce each wine, minimum alcohol for each wine, and maximum yields per hectare.

APPELLATION D'ORIGINE French. Created by the French authorities in 1935 to establish areas of production and wine laws for each area.

APPELLATION D'ORIGINE CONTROLÉE (AOC OR AOP) French. Higher-quality wines from a controlled area.

APPLE Odor detected in certain wines, like Chardonnay and Riesling. Also a taste detected in some wines due to high levels of malic acid.

APRICOTS Odor present in wines affected by *Botrytis cinerea* (noble rot), which totally masks the varietal character and substitutes an odor reminiscent of apricots.

AQUEOUS Watery. Detected in appearance and in taste of some lighter wines.

ARENAS Type of soil found in approximately 17 percent of the Sherry region of Spain. It consists of about 80 percent sand, red-yellow in color, with alumina, silica, and clay. Produces more coarse wines than either ALBARIZA or BARROS soils.

AROMA A particular smell, odor, or fragrance of a specific grape used to produce the wine.

AROMATIC Describes wines that have intense aromas of fruits, herbs, or other odors either directly from the grape or developed by the winemaking process.

AROMATIZED WINE Fortified wine with a wide variety of related aromatic plants or bitter herbs, roots, bark, or other plant parts infused into its bouquet. An example of an aromatized wine is vermouth.

ASPERSION French. A continual misting of the grapes with water so they are protected from damage by frost.

ASSEMBLAGE Blending of various cuvées in the making of a wine; often applied to the blending process in the making of Champagne.

ASTRINGENCY Tactile, bitter sensation that makes the mouth pucker. Wines with high levels of astringency may be described as coarse, harsh, and rough. Also describes wines with too much tannin.

ATMOSPHERE In physics, a unit of pressure equal to 14.69 pounds per square inch. Champagne is bottled under five to six atmospheres.

AUSLESE German. A *Prädikat* wine made from very ripe, selected late-harvest bunches of grapes. These wines are full, rich, and sweet, unless they are vinified as *trocken* (dry).

AUTOLYSIS Self-destruction of yeast cells over time, which contributes complexity and richness to a wine.

AWKWARD Describes a wine that has poor structure or is out of balance.

AZIENDA AGRICOLA Italian. Commercial association, usually a farm or agricultural holding, involved in the production of an agricultural product.

B

BAC À GLACE Shallow brine bath used to freeze the necks of champagne bottles prior to dégorgement.

BACCHUS Roman god of wine.

BACKBONE Descriptive term indicating a firm structure that is able to support the fruit character of the wine.

BACTERIAL SPOILAGE Damage caused by bacteria that attack must or wine during and after fermentation. Often due to formation of mold from improperly cleaned equipment, lack of sterile conditions, and faulty sanitation procedures.

BAG-IN-BOX Package for wine consisting of a plastic membrane, closed by an air lock, and then placed in a cardboard box, which acts as a label for the wine and a holder for the plastic bladder.

BAKED A negative smell or flavor in wine—warm, cooked, or roasted—often resulting from extremely ripe grapes grown in hot climates.

BALANCE Pleasant harmony of the elements and components of a wine. A balanced wine is one whose components —sugar, fruit, tannin, acid, alcohol, wood, and extract—are evident, but do not mask or dominate each other.

BALLOON GLASS Oversized wine glass whose bowl has a capacity of between 10 and 26 fluid ounces/290 and 800 milliliters.

BALTHAZAR Oversized Champagne bottle, equal to sixteen 750 ml bottles, or 12 liters/1.5 gallons.

BARREL AGING Process of mellowing wine through extraction, as the alcohol dissolves flavor-affecting chemicals present in the wooden barrels. The wine extracts certain aroma and flavor elements present in the wood.

BARREL FERMENTATION The process of fermenting in wooden barrels rather than stainless steel. Extractables of tannin, color, and various odors and flavors are leached into the wine, creating more complexity and depth.

BARRICA Spanish. Small oak barrel.

BARRIQUE French. Small oak barrel.

BARROS Spanish. Heavy, dark soil with some chalk, but mostly made of clay and sand.

BASKET PRESS A wooden tub with slotted sides. Grapes are put in and pressure is applied by means of a large screw, which presses the grapes and allows the juice to run out through the slots.

BATF Bureau of Alcohol, Tobacco, and Firearms.

BÂTONNAGE French. Stirring the lees in a barrel to impart rich, creamy flavors into the wine.

BAUMÉ French. Term used to measure the level of unfermented sugar present in the grapes or must. If degrees Baumé are multiplied by 1.8, the result is degrees BRIX.

BEAD Describes the chain of tiny bubbles found in sparkling wines, formed by the presence of carbon dioxide.

BEERENAUSLESE German. Wines made from overripe grapes partially affected by *Botrytis cinerea*, picked individually and produced in very small quantities.

BELL PEPPER Odor characteristic of bell peppers sometimes detected in Cabernet Sauvignon, Sauvignon Blanc, and certain other grape varieties.

BENCH GRAFT A graft done in a nursery, as opposed to the vineyard (a "field graft"). Grafted grapevines of a desired fruiting species on rootstocks resistant to phylloxera or nematodes.

BENEFICIO Portuguese. Quality rating system that ranks Douro vineyards by points and also sets production limits.

BENTONITE Fining agent. Clay originating from the state of Wyoming and containing montmorillonite, produced from the decomposition under water of volcanic glass.

BEREICH German. Wine subregion, or district, within a region (*Anbaugebiet*).

BERRIES Fruity characteristic often linked with young red wines, such as Beaujolais.

BERRY SET Successful pollination of grape flowers. The pollinated grape blossoms start to develop, with each flower in the floral cluster transformed into a miniature grape berry about the size of a small BB.

BIG Rich, powerful, full-bodied and intensely flavored wine. Big wines are generally high in alcohol, tannin, and extract.

BIN Where bottles of wine are stored, usually by number ("bin number").

BITTER Taste sensed by the taste buds most often at the back of the tongue. Easily detectable in tonic water because of the presence of bitter-tasting quinine. In wine, usually caused by the presence of tannins and accompanied by astringency. A wine that is quite high in tannin may be negatively described as "bitter" by a taster with a low tannin threshold.

BLANC DE BLANCS White wine made only from white grapes.

BLANC DE BLANCS (CHAMPAGNE) French. Made exclusively from Chardonnay grapes, resulting in the most delicate of Champagnes.

BLANC DE NOIRS White wine made only from black or red grapes.

BLENDING Marrying wines to obtain a desired quality and style.

BLIND TASTING System of evaluating wine without knowledge of the grape, the producer, the country of origin, the vintage year, and so on.

BLOOM When young flowers open and caps fall from the flowers.

BLUSH White wine made by limited skin contact with red grapes, extracting a hint of color. Also used to describe pink wines made by limited skin contact, or pink wines made by blending.

BOCKSBEUTEL Short, flat-sided, flask-shaped bottle used in parts of Germany, Chile, and Portugal.

BODY Tactile sensation of weight or fullness on the palate, usually from a combination of alcohol, extracts, glycerin, tannin, and other physical components in wine.

BONBONNES French. Glass carboy protected by a wicker or wooden crate.

BORDEAUX BOTTLE Bottle shape originating in Bordeaux, France. Easily recognized by its regular cylindrical form. Characterized by a short neck and high shoulders.

BOTA Spanish, Portuguese. Bag made of goatskin from which wine is squirt into the mouth.

BOTRYTIS CINEREA Mold that develops on grapes. Depending on the grape variety, the time of year, and climatic conditions, it can greatly enhance or severely damage the grapes in a vineyard. (See NOBLE ROT and EDELFÄULE.)

BOTTLE Glass container that typically holds 750 ml.

BOTTLE AGING Aging process that takes place in the bottle at the winery or in private cellars.

BOTTLE FERMENTATION Refers to sparkling wines. Means that the secondary fermentation took place in the bottle rather than in a large vat.

BOTTLE SHOCK Stage that can affect a wine just after bottling. During bottling, the aroma, flavor, and/or balance of a wine may be temporarily diminished. Also known as bottle sickness.

BOTTLE VARIATION Differences detected, bottle by bottle, in the appearance, nose, and taste of the same wine.

BOUCHON DE TIRAGE French. Temporary cork sometimes used to close the bottle during second fermentation of sparkling wines.

BOUCHON D'EXPÉDITION French. Final cork used in a finished bottle of sparkling wine.

BOUQUET Various fragrances noted by smell, created by a wine's development and imparted to the wine from the fermentation and aging process, whether in barrel or bottle.

BRANDY Spirit made by distilling wines or the fermented mash of fruit, which may be aged in oak barrels.

BREATHING Practice of allowing air to reach wine by uncorking and pouring it. Dispels unpleasant odors and brings out aroma and bouquet.

BRICK Shade of red-brown often found in well-aged, mature red wines or slightly old red wines.

BRIGHT Descriptive term for a clear wine, or a wine with fresh, bright colors.

BRILLIANT Quality of a wine when it is free from any visible suspended solids or haziness.

BRIX Measurement of the sugar content of the grape.

BROWNING Oxidation's effect on the color, odor, and taste of a wine which is past its prime, or has been carelessly exposed to a prolonged period of aeration.

BRUT Champagne, France. Very dry.

BUD Compressed shoot located at the node of a cane.

BUD BREAK Natural forcing open of the bud by the increasing pressure of sap in a grapevine.

BUNG Plug that fits into the opening at the top of a barrel for a tight seal. Can be cork, wood, or silicon.

BURGUNDY BOTTLE Bottle of conical shape, not regular in form, with a fat belly. Bottle is used to house both red and white wines of Burgundy, France.

BURNT Wine having cooked or baked characteristics.

BUTT Barrel used to store or ship ale, Sherry wine, or other wines.

BUTTERY Descriptor of odor and/or taste; creamy.

C

CALCAIRE/CALCAREOUS French. Limestone soil.

CALCIUM CARBONATE Reduces the excess natural acids in high-acid wines.

CANDLING Action to determine clarity in wine, by holding a bottle in front of light source to see if any sediment or haze is present.

CANE PRUNING At pruning time extra growth is cleared away, leaving only the strongest. The remaining canes are, tied to support wires.

CAP Grapeskins, stems, and seeds that rise to the top of the tank or barrel and harden during fermentation of a red wine. For maximum flavor extraction and the release of carbon dioxide gases, the cap must be broken up several times a day.

CAPSULE Cover placed over the cork to protect the wine and improve the appearance of the bottle. Can be made of plastic, lead, or aluminum.

CARAFE French. Decanter or glass bottle for serving wines.

CARBON DIOXIDE Odorless, colorless gas that is a by-product of wine fermentation. Creates effervescence.

CARBONIC MACERATION Intracellular fermentation. Whole uncrushed clusters of grapes are placed into a stainless steel fermenter; the tank is filled with carbon dioxide and sealed. The lack of oxygen causes skin cells to die, releasing an en-

DENOMINAZIONE DI ORIGINE CONTROLLATA E GARANTITA (DOCG OR DOP) Italian. Designation given to wines that are considered to be of a higher quality than DOC wines and made under even stricter guidelines.

DEPTH Wine with intense complex flavors that seem to fill the mouth from front to back. Subtle layers of flavor that are long-lasting.

DIATOMACEOUS EARTH Filtering agent used in the production of some alcoholic beverages. Pure silica mined from the sea.

DOLCE Italian. Sweet.

DOMAINE French. Wine estate.

DOSAGE Addition of a mixture of sugar syrup, grape concentrate, or brandy to Champagne or sparkling wines before recorking. Corrects the sweetness in the final product.

DOUX French. Sweet.

DRAINAGE After the primary fermentation of red wines, the juice is drained off and the skins, which are still heavily laden with juice, are sent to a press for further juice extraction.

DRIP IRRIGATION Slow, frequent, precise application of water directly to the plant through devices known as emitters. The emitters are placed on the soil or just below the surface of the soil.

DRY Wine with little or no noticeable residual sugar.

DULCE Spanish. Sweet.

DULL Wine that lacks brilliance in its appearance.

DUMB Wine with potential, but not developed enough to offer its full character.

DWI Driving while intoxicated.

E

EARTHY Describes scents or odors reminiscent of soil or the earth in which grapes are grown.

EC/EEC/EU European Community / European Economic Community / European Union. The political and economic federation of European countries.

EDELFÄULE German. Noble mold responsible for Beerenauslese and Trockenbeerenauslese wines.

EDELZWICKER An Alsatian wine that is a blend of noble grape varieties.

ÉGRAPPAGE French. Separation of the grapes from the stalks before pressing and fermenting.

EINZELLAGE German. Single vineyard.

EISWEIN German. Specific classification of wine made from grapes that are harvested and pressed frozen. Produces a sweeter and more concentrated wine.

ELEGANT Wine with dignified richness, grace, and refinement.

ÉLEVE EN FUTS French. Labeling that indicates oak aging.

ENFORCADO Portuguese. Term used for forcing the vines upwards, often on tree trunks, and then stretching them across branches to other trees.

ENGARRAFADO NA ORIGEM Portuguese. Estate bottled.

ENOLOGIST Wine technician, or an expert in viniculture (winemaking).

ENOLOGY Science or study of wine and winemaking.

ENOPHILE One who loves wine and wine lore.

ENRICHMENT See CHAPTALIZATION.

EN TIRAGE French. Refers to second fermentation in the bottle during sparkling wine production, most often Champagne.

ERZEUGERABFÜLLUNG German. Bottled by the producer.

ESPUMANTE Portuguese. Term used in Portugal and Brazil for sparkling wine.

ESTATE BOTTLED May be used by a bottling winery on a wine label only if the wine is labeled with a viticultural area appellation of origin and the bottling winery (1) is located in the labeled viticultural area; (2) grew all of the grapes used to make the wine on land owned or controlled by the winery within the boundaries of the labeled viticultural area; (3) crushed the grapes, fermented the resulting must, and finished, aged, and bottled the wine in a continuous process.

ESTERS Organic, volatile compounds, which contribute fruity aromas to wines and distilled spirits.

ESTUFA Portuguese. Large heating chambers or ovens used to make Madeira.

ETHANOL/ETHYL ALCOHOL Principal alcohol found in all alcoholic beverages.

EUCALYPTUS Odor of an evergreen species occasionally found in some California Cabernet Sauvignon or Pinot Noir wines.

EXTRA BRUT (Brut Sauvage or Ultra Brut) French. Champagne products that are bone dry, with 0 to 6 grams of sugar added per liter.

EXTRA DRY Term used for a Champagne that is not as dry as brut, but drier than sec.

EXTRACT Nonvolatile, soluble solids present in a wine.

F

FADED Wine that has lost its bouquet, character, and definition, generally through age.

FAT Heavy, intense wine that has a higher-than-average glycerin level.

FATTORIA Italian. Farm or estate.

FERMENTATION Conversion of sugar in the grapes into ethyl alcohol or ethanol and carbon dioxide. Yeast is needed to begin the process. Fermentation stops when the sugars are depleted or when the alcohol level reaches about 15 percent and kills the yeast.

FERMENTATION LOCK Low-pressure valve made of glass or plastic that seals a barrel or other container of fermenting wine from the outside air while permitting carbon dioxide given off during fermentation to escape through sulfited water.

FERMENTATION TANK Barrel, stainless steel tank, concrete vat, or other type of container utilized for the primary fermentation of grapes and grape juice into wine.

FERMENTED IN THE BOTTLE Terminology used for sparkling wines produced using the transfer method. The second fermentation takes place in a bottle, but not this bottle.

FERMENTED IN THIS BOTTLE Terminology used for sparkling wines produced using the *méthode champenoise*. The second fermentation takes place in the bottle in which the wine is sold.

FEUILLETTE French. A 33-gallon/132-liter cask.

FIASCO Italian. A name for the flask-shaped bottle in a wicker basket that was at one time popular for shipping Chianti.

FIELD BLEND Practice of growing several varieties of grapes in the same vineyard and combining them to make one wine.

FILL LEVEL The point in the bottle neck to which the wine is filled.

FILTERING Mechanical process by which wine is forced through a porous filtering medium.

FINING Process of clarifying a cloudy or hazy wine to brilliance by adding a colloidal agent to remove suspended particles.

FINISH Tactile and flavor impressions left in the mouth after the wine is swallowed.

FINO Spanish. The driest Sherry.

FLAVONOIDS Flavoring compounds, phenols, found in the skins of grapes and extracted into wines.

FLINTY Aroma and flavor of dry, usually white, wines, similar to the smell of two flints being rubbed together or struck with steel.

FLOR Spanish. Yeast-like substance that forms a white film on the surface of certain Sherries.

FLUTE Elongated V-shape glass used for serving Champagne and sparkling wine. (See TULIP.)

FLÛTE / FLÛTE DU RHIN Elongated wine bottle used in Alsace, France, and in Germany. Also used for wines from other countries made in German or Alsace style.

FOIL CUTTER Semi-cylindrical instrument used to cut the foil or plastic cover on the bottle so the cork can be removed.

FORTIFICATION / FORTIFIED WINE Addition of distilled spirits to a wine to arrest fermentation and leave some residual sugar or to give better keeping properties.

FOUDRE French. Large wood cask.

FOXY Grapy aroma and flavor of native American grapes, especially *Vitis labrusca*.

FREE-RUN JUICE Initial juice released by the grapes by the sheer weight or pressure of the mass, before the press is used.

FRESH Describes younger white or lighter red wines displaying a youthful, lively, fruity aroma and clean, acidic taste.

FRIZZANTE Italian. Spritzy.

FRUCTOSE Simple sugar. Generally found in fruits.

FRUITY Describes wines that have a pleasant aroma and flavor of grapes or other fresh fruits.

FUDER German. Large barrel with a capacity of 250 gallons/1,000 liters. Mostly used in the Mosel region.

FULL-BODIED Describes mouth-filling capacity of a beverage. Usually refers to beverages with high extracts and levels of glycerin.

FUNGICIDE Chemical substance used to control the growth, infection, and spread of fungi on plants.

G

GARRAFEIRA Portuguese. Specially aged wine, similar to Reserva.

GARRIGUE French. Term used for the dry land and typically scrubby vegetation of southern France.

GAY-LUSSAC, JOSEPH-LOUIS Famous French chemist who correctly devised the overall equation for fermentation in 1810.

GENERIC Designation of a particular class or type of wine of limited quality. Wine can be named or labeled after a wine-producing region—Burgundy, Chablis, Champagne, etc.—but rarely do these wines resemble the wines from the region for which they are named.

GLUCO-OENOMÈTRE French. Instrument that measures the amount of sugar needed to produce the required bubbles for Champagne production.

GLYCERIN By-product of the fermentation of grapes into wine. Increases the feeling of fatness in the mouth, giving the wine a soft, almost oily tinge on the tongue and palate.

GOBLET Bowl-shaped glass with a stem and a base.

GOÛT DE TERROIR French. The flavors imparted by the complexity of the *terroir*—the geography, soil, and the weather conditions—in which the wine is grown.

GOVERNO Italian. Process sometimes used to produce Italian wines. During refermentation 5 to 10 percent stronger, riper grape musts are added to produce a roundness and liveliness in the wine.

GRAFTING Viticulture technique that joins a bud or other part of one grapevine to a portion of another so that their tissues unite.

GRAND CRU French. A vineyard designated as a "great growth"—the best vineyards in Burgundy, also Alsace and Loire. Champagne vineyard rated at 100 percent, assuring highest price for the grapes.

GRAND CRU CLASSÉ French. A great growth that is a legal grade of quality in areas of Bordeaux. The Médoc, for example, established five levels of *grand cru classé* in 1855.

GRANDE ESCOLHA Portuguese. Sometimes used for a producer's choice, or top selected wine.

GRANDES MARQUES French. Long-established firms that are legally required to have a presence in the international market.

GRAN RESERVA Spanish. Red wines that have been aged in small oak barrels—*barricas*—for a minimum of two years, followed by three years in the bottle, and may not leave the *bodega* until the sixth year after the vintage. Whites are aged a minimum of four years before release, with at least six months in *barrica*. Produced only in the best years.

GRAPE Juicy, round, smooth-skinned, edible fruit, generally green, red-purple, or sometimes black, grown in clusters on a woody vine.

GRAPPA Italian. Distillate made from the stems, pulp, skins, and seeds of grapes. A pomace brandy.

GREEN Immature, underdeveloped wine that usually displays an austere, somewhat sour taste. Also, term for unripe grapes.

GROSSLAGE German. Composite, collective vineyard made up of numbers of individual vineyards within subregions.

GYPSUM Calcium sulfate.

H

HALBTROCKEN German. Semidry ("half dry") German wine. Maximum of 0.6 ounce per quart/18 grams per liter of residual sugar.

HEAT SUMMATION Geographic classification of regions in terms of heat—specifically, degree days during the growing season. Used to determine vineyard sites for appropriate grapes.

HECTARE Metric measure equal to 10,000 square meters of land or 2.471 acres.

HECTOLITER Metric measurement equal to 100 liters or 26.418 gallons. Wine production in Europe is often referred to in hectoliters per hectare.

HERBACEOUS Describes the odor or taste. Grassy or vegetal smell may be contributed by the varietal character of certain grapes.

HERBICIDE Chemical substance used to destroy plants or weeds or to check their growth.

HOGSHEAD Barrel used in many wine-producing countries, where its capacity varies from region to region.

HOT Highly alcoholic wines with heady odors. Burning qualities noticed in the smell and back of the throat when swallowing.

HOT ZONE The price range in which the overwhelming majority of wines on a restaurant wine list are priced.

HYBRIDS Cross between two grape species, generally between *Vitis vinifera* and any of the North American species such as *Vitis labrusca*.

HYDROMETER Cylindrical glass instrument of various lengths with a scale running along its length and a bulbous weighted end. Measures density of a liquid, and so can be used to determine alcohol or sugar density by comparing the liquid to the density of water.

I

ICE BUCKET Metal vessel that contains ice and water for the chilling of bottles of white wine and sparkling wine.

INDICATED-AGE TAWNY PORTO Portuguese. Wines with an average of ten, twenty, thirty or forty years prior to bottling.

INDICAZIONE GEOGRAFICA TIPICA (IGT OR IGP) Italy. One quality level above *vino da tavola*. Replaced *vino tipico* in 1992, when DOC wine laws were overhauled. Many non-traditional but expensive premium wines, especially from Tuscany, are IGT wines.

IMPÉRIALE Oversized bottle equivalent in capacity to eight 750 ml bottles or 6 liters.

INSTITUT NATIONAL DES APPELLATIONS D'ORIGINE (INAO) French. The governmental agency that regulates the production and labeling of wines.

INTEGRATED PEST MANAGEMENT A progressive agricultural practice that encourages the growth and maintenance of certain beneficial pests to control diseases and dangerous pests.

IRRIGATION System that applies water to grapevines.

ISINGLASS Protein fining agent derived from dried sturgeon air bladder.

J

JACKETED TANK Mechanized system that circulates hot or cold water, or a cooling agent such as glycol, around a tank, enabling the temperature of the grape must to be controlled.

JEROBOAM Oversized bottle with a capacity of four standard 750 ml bottles (3 liters) in Champagne and Burgundy, six standard 750 ml bottles (4.5 liters) in Bordeaux.

JUG WINE Inexpensive wine of no particular breed or quality; usually sold in quantity.

K

KABINETT German. Driest level of the highest grade of wines.

KICKER Term for an expensive wine outside the hot zone of a wine list. By definition, many vintage Champagnes are kickers.

KOSHER WINE Wine made under strict rabbinical supervision and suitable for Jewish religious practice.

KWV Antiquated South African wine cooperative to which all the nation's wine producers used to belong.

L

LACTIC ACID Organic acid that appears during the malolactic fermentation of the wine, when malic acid changes into carbon dioxide and this smooth acid.

LAGARE Portuguese. Trough used for foot pressing of grapes.

LANDWEIN German. Category of wines defined according to the 1982 wine laws as a step above *Tafelwein* in quality. *Landwein* may be chaptalized.

LATE-BOTTLED VINTAGE Portuguese. Porto from a single vintage, bottled between July 1 of the fourth year and December 31 of the sixth year after the vintage.

LATE-HARVEST Denotes wines made from very ripe grapes that have been picked or harvested later than usual. They are often shriveled, resembling raisins, and often make sweeter wines, due to their increased sugar levels. Dry late-harvest wines are usually high in alcohol.

LEAKAGE Loss of wine through the cork due to improper storage or a faulty cork.

LEATHERY Odor occasionally found in red wines rich in tannin; similar to rawhide.

LEES Dead yeast cells and, in the case of red wines, pulp, skins, seeds, and other solids that settle to the bottom of a barrel or tank during and after fermentation.

LEGS Trails or streaks of a transparent liquid apparent on the inner walls of a wine or brandy glass that run downward after it has been swirled. Substantial legs indicate high levels of glycerin, and relatively high alcohol or sugar.

LIEUX-DITS French. Specific name of a vineyard site, often mentioned on the label of wines from parts of southern France.

LIGHT Term used to describe a pleasant, refreshing wine, lacking in body, color, or alcohol.

LIMOUSIN OAK Soft oak with loose grain used to make barrels for wine. Made from wood grown in the Limousin forest near Limoges, France.

LIQUEUR DE TIRAGE French. Mixture of yeast cells and sugar added to still wine to begin secondary fermentation in order to produce a sparkling wine.

LIQUEUR D'EXPÉDITION French. Final DOSAGE in Champagne that determines its relative dryness. Usually consists of a mixture of wine and sugar.

LITER Metric unit of capacity equal to 1,000 cubic centimeters at 20°C or 33.814 fluid ounces at 68°F.

LIVELY Describes white wines that are young and fresh with plenty of zestiness, acidity, and fruit with a small amount of SPRITZ.

LUSCIOUS Soft, sweet, fat, and fruity.

M

MADERIZED Wine that is past its prime. Excessive heat and poor storage cause the wine to oxidize prematurely and turn a brownish tinge. Does not apply to Madeira wines.

MADURO Portuguese. Well matured.

MAGNUM Bottle of wine equivalent in capacity to 50.8 fluid ounces/1.5 liters or two 750 ml bottles.

MAÎTRE DE CHAIS French. Employee in charge of the cellar who is responsible for the vinification and aging of all wines.

MALIC ACID Principal acid of apples and second major acid in grapes. Tart, astringent taste. Decreases in grapes as they become fully ripe.

MALOLACTIC FERMENTATION Bacterial fermentation, converting malic acid to lactic acid while releasing carbon dioxide. Has four major effects on wine: (1) changes a harsh acid to a smooth acid, making the wine softer and more pleasant to drink; (2) lowers overall acidity; (3) increases biological stability in the wine by assuring that a malolactic fermentation will not take place in the bottle; and (4) increases the sensory quality, complexity, and flavor of the wine.

MANZANILLA Spanish. Palest and driest fino Sherry, produced and aged in Sanlúcar de Barrameda.

MARITIME CLIMATE Regions close to water with a narrow range of temperature variations.

MARQUE D'ACHETEUR (MA) French. The initials will appear on the labels of brands produced for buyers.

MARQUES French. Companies that own some vineyards but purchase the majority of the grapes they use for blending.

MARQUES AUXILIARE French. Term used for secondary brand name.

MAS French. Vineyard site on the label.

MATURE Stage in the aging of wines when they have developed all of their characteristic qualities in harmony.

MECHANICAL HARVESTER Large machine that mechanically removes grapes from clusters by gently shaking the vines. Once picked, the machine helps sort leaves from grapes and stems.

MEDITERRANEAN CLIMATE Warmer growing region.

MENISCUS Curved upper surface of a column of liquid. The "rim" of the wine in a wine glass.

MERITAGE Wines made in the United States predominately from a blend of the traditional Bordeaux grape varieties: Cabernet Sauvignon, Merlot, Cabernet Franc, Petit Verdot, and Malbec, for red wine; Sauvignon Blanc and Sémillon for white.

MÉTHODE CHAMPENOISE French. Fermented wine is bottled with yeast cells and sugar to induce a secondary fermentation. When fermentation is complete, the wine is aged, and the yeast sediment is removed.

METHUSELAH / METHUSALEM Oversized bottle. Equivalent to eight 750 ml bottles or 6 liters.

MICROCLIMATE Climate of a small, distinct area that has either slightly or greatly varying degrees of difference from the general climate of the larger area.

MILDEW Fungal disease that attacks grapevines in rainy or damp seasons. Must be treated or it will cause crippling damage to tissue and the fruit.

MILLÉSIMÉ French. Dated or vintage wine. Term is mostly used to indicate a vintage Champagne.

MINT Describes odor or taste of fresh green mint.

MIS EN BOUTEILLES AU CHÂTEAU Bordeaux, France. Estate bottled.

MIS EN BOUTEILLES AU DOMAINE Burgundy, France. Estate bottled.

MIS EN BOUTEILLES DANS NOS CAVES Burgundy, France. "Bottled in our cellars."

MISTRAL French. The powerful cold winds that sweep through the valley, which can blow hard enough to strip vines of their shoots, leaves, and fruit.

MOËLLEUX French. Sweet.

MOLDY The indication, usually by smell, of bacterial spoilage in a wine.

MONOCRU French. Wine made from a single commune.

MONOPOLE French. In Burgundy, a vineyard with one owner.

MOUSSE French. Froth or foam on the surface of a glass of sparkling wine.

MUST Unfermented juice or any mixture of juice, pulp, skins, and seeds from fruit, berries, or grapes. The must is fermented to make wine.

MUST WEIGHT The difference, in grams, between one liter of the must and a liter of distilled water. Sugar has a higher specific gravity than water, so the must weight indicates the amount of sugar present in the must.

MUSTY Describes odor or flavor in wine, similar to a moldy smell.

MUTAGE Process of retarding fermentation of grape juice by adding brandy or other distilled spirits.

N

NATURAL North American designation for bone-dry sparkling wines.

NEBUCHADNEZZAR Large bottle with a capacity of twenty 750 ml bottles. Used almost exclusively for charity events and festivals.

NÉGOCIANTS ÉLEVEURS France. Merchants who may purchase grapes or wines from growers which will be aged and bottled in the cellars of the merchants.

NÉGOCIANTS-MANIPULANTS France. Middlemen who operates between grower and shipper. The négociant is at the center of the wine trade in France.

NEVERS OAK French. Named after the French city. Hardwood with fine, medium grain from which barrels are made.

NITROGEN Naturally occurring gas needed by yeast cells to multiply. Since nitrogen is an inert gas, it can also be used to provide a blanket of gas to cover a wine in storage to prevent oxidation; used in restaurant wine-dispensing systems for the same reason.

NOBLE ROT *Botrytis cinerea*. Gray, hairy mold present in most vineyards. Affected berries look like cracked raisins, but do not resemble them in taste. Needs humid climate to grow. If the mold attacks desirable varieties, the affected grapes are handpicked to produce a very sweet, expensive wine.

NONVINTAGE Term applied to sparkling wines whose cuvées contain wine from previous vintages. Also applies to any wine blended from two or more vintages.

NOSE Aroma and bouquet of a wine.

NOUVEAU / NOVELLO French/Italian. New wine, usually first wine of the vintage.

NUTTY Describes odor and flavor of Madeira, Marsala, Sherry, or other oxidized, fortified wines.

O

OAK Species of hardwood trees used for aging wine.

OAK CHIPS Pieces of oak often used when aging inexpensive wines in stainless steel vats, to provide the essence that oak barrels impart to the wine.

OAKY Odor or taste of wines fermented or aged in oak.

OECHSLE German or Swiss. Specific gravity of must. Scale to determine level of sugar present in the must. Named after chemist who invented method, Christian Ferdinand Oechsle.

OENOLOGY Science or study of wine and winemaking.

OFF Term used to describe wines that display undesirable attributes.

OIDIUM European name for powdery mildew, a mold that can prove fatal to grapevines if not prevented or controlled.

ORGANICALLY GROWN Grown without potentially harmful chemical sprays.

ORGANIC WINES Wines made from organically grown grapes, vinified naturally with absolutely minimum addition of sulfites.

ORGANOLEPTIC Analytical evaluation of wine, using all of the senses.

OVERCROPPING Growing more grape clusters than a grapevine can bring to maturity at normal harvest time, leading to diluted levels of sugar and nutrients.

OXIDATION Chemical change in wine due to exposure to oxygen during any phase of production, aging, or storage.

P

PAGO Spanish. A single vineyard estate.

PALATE The combined sensory organs of the mouth, detecting tastes and textures.

PALO CORTADO Spanish. A high-quality specialty Sherry.

PASSE-TOUT-GRAINS French. Red Burgundy wine made from a blend of Pinot Noir with Gamay or other lesser grapes.

PASSITO Italian. Sweet wine made from overripe grapes that have been allowed to dry in the sun, or on drying racks indoors, increasing sugar levels.

PEPPERY Describes smell or taste, usually in full-bodied red wines, reminiscent of black pepper, herbs, or spices.

PERFUME Refers to floral smells encountered in the aroma and bouquet of some white wines.

PESTICIDE Chemical compounds used to kill insects.

PÉTILLANT French. Spritzy.

PH A measure of the relative ACIDITY of grape musts and finished wines.

PHENOLS ANTIOXIDANT compounds that occur naturally in wine grapes. Often referred to as tannins.

PHYLLOXERA VASTATRIX Latin. Aphid-like insect, a plant louse. Lives on grapevines and burrows through the plant, eating its roots. Kills VITUS VINIFERA varieties when the insect's waste is injected into the vine's root system.

PIÈCES French. Small barrels that are commonly used for aging in the northern part of France.

PIERCE'S DISEASE Virus spread by a form of leafhopper insect and found in many vineyards around the world. Causes leaves to yellow along the veins, edges to burn, fruit to wilt, the vine to put out dwarfed shoots, and the vines to die in one to five years.

PINOT Name of grape family. Includes Blanc, Gris, Noir.

PIPE 145.2-gallons/550 liters barrel used to store and ship Sherry, Madeira, Marsala, Port, and other fortified wines.

POLISHING FILTER Ultra-fine filtering medium used to clarify wine just prior to bottling.

POMACE Skins, stems, and seeds remaining after the grapes have been pressed. A very compact mass often referred to as "cake."

POURRITURE NOBLE French for *Botrytis cinerea*.

POWDERY MILDEW Fungal disease that retards grapevine growth and interferes with winter hardiness.

PREMIER CRU French. Burgundian labeling representing the town name followed by the name of an approved classified vineyard site, or CLIMAT.

PRESS WINE Portion of wine that is pressed from the skins and pulp under pressure, after the free-run wine has been drained off. Concentration of color, flavor, and harshness is found in this wine, which if used at all, is used for blending.

PRIMARY FERMENTATION First stage of FERMENTATION in which the yeast begins to metabolize the sugar, converting it into alcohol and carbon dioxide.

PRIMEUR French. New wine.

PRISE DE MOUSSE Strain of yeast particularly suited to sparkling wine production.

PRODUCED AND BOTTLED BY Label term used by U.S. producers and bottlers if they have made at least 75 percent of the wine in a particular bottle (fermenting the must and clarifying the wine).

PROHIBITION Eighteenth Amendment to the U.S. Constitution, which repealed the right to manufacture, sell, transport, import, and export alcoholic beverages in or from the United States. Passed in 1919, repealed in 1933.

PROPRIÉTAIRE-RECOLTANTS France. Independent winegrowers who sell under their own label.

PRUNING Removal of the previous year's growth to leave a predetermined number of buds on the canes of the vine. The number of buds will determine the number of bunches produced in the current year.

PUMPING OVER During the fermentation of red wines, the cap of skins must be redistributed with the juice, in order to release carbon dioxide and to allow for optimum extraction of flavors and pigmentation from the skins. The wine is pumped from the bottom of the tank over the cap several times a day. In France, called *remontage*.

PUNT Dome-shaped indentation found on the bottom of some wine bottles. Serves to strengthen the bottle. Most pronounced in Champagne bottles.

PUTTONYOS Hungarian buckets used for measuring quantity of selected grapes used in sweet Tokaji Aszú wine. Labels read 3 Puttonyos, 4 Puttonyos, etc.

Q

QUALITÄTSWEIN German. Classification for quality table wines. This and the following (QmP) classification may be grouped as Geschützte Ursprungsbezeichnung in 2011.

QUALITÄTSWEIN MIT PRÄDIKAT (QmP) German. Former designation reserved for highest-quality wines. Chaptalization is prohibited at the QmP level. Every QmP label must include the class of the wine, based on the ripeness of the grapes at harvest (e.g., *Auslese*). Now Prädikatswein.

QUINTA Portuguese. Wine estate.

QUINTAL Metric measurement of weight equal to 100 kilograms/220.46 pounds.

R

RACKING Moving wine from one barrel or tank to another in order to separate the wine from the sediment that has fallen to the bottom of the container, and to aerate the wine.

RAINWATER Portuguese. Type of Madeira made for the British market.

RANCIO Spanish. Describes odor and taste of wine as Sherry-like, especially as it applies to older, often fortified wines that are intentionally oxidized.

RAPÉ French. Declassification of wines used to ensure that the less ripe grapes are not used.

RECENTLY DISGORGED After extra aging on its LEES, a bottle of sparkling wine or Champagne undergoes disgorging shortly before release, often resulting in richer, fuller flavors. (See DÉGORGEMENT.)

RECIOTO Italian. Semidry or sweet wine made from the ripest grapes, the *recie* (ears) of the bunch. The *recie* grapes are partly dried and used to make sweet, sparkling, or dry wines. The term applies most often to wines from the Veneto province.

RÉCOLTANTS MANIPULANTS French. Producers or farmers who make wine from their own grapes, but purchase up to 5 percent of the grapes from another source.

REFRACTOMETER Measures sugar content of grape juice by refracting light. The higher the degree of refraction, the denser the juice, and the higher the sugar content.

REGIÃO DEMARCADA Portuguese. An outdated term for an appellation or wine region of Portugal.

REHOBOAM Large bottle with a capacity of six 750 ml bottles or 1.2 gallons.

RÉMUAGE/RIDDLING Process used as part of the *méthode champenoise* to move sediment from the side of the bottle into the neck of the bottle after the second fermentation; can be done by hand or by machine.

RESERVA Spanish, Portuguese. Term indicating that wine from an exceptional harvest has been aged longer. There are specific legal minimum aging requirements.

RESERVE In the United States, any vintage-dated and varietally labeled wine, but without minimum aging requirements or any other quality requirement.

RESIDUAL SUGAR (RS) Natural grape sugar intentionally left in the wine after fermentation to make a sweeter wine.

RESIN Added to Greek table wine in powder form to create Retsina.

RICH Describes wine mouthfeel, bouquet, and flavors.

RIM The outer edge of wine in a glass. Color of rim helps determine age of wine. Sometimes called the MENISCUS.

RIPE Describes wines that have reached their full term of aging or have achieved desired bouquet and flavor, or fully "ripe" flavors.

RISERVA Italian. Term indicating that wine from an exceptional harvest has been aged longer. There are specific legal minimum aging requirements.

ROBE French. Term that refers to color and other visual aspects of a wine.

ROBUST Describes flavor and mouthfeel of wine. Full-bodied.

ROOTSTOCK Vines specially developed to be resistant to diseases, pests, and extreme weather conditions. They are used to form the root system of a vine. A vinifera bud is grafted onto the rootstock to form the fruit-producing part of the vine.

ROSÉ Wine made from red grapes that have limited contact with the skin. Wine made from a combination of both red and white wines.

ROT Wet conditions in the vineyard at harvest time that cause the grapes to rot. Also, decomposition of wine due to bacteria.

ROUGH Describes young, immature wines that are unbalanced and very astringent, often due to high levels of tannin.

RUBY PORTO Portuguese. A blend of Porto from different vintages, usually of less than six years old.

S

SACCHAROMYCES CEREVISAE The dominant yeast strain used in making wine.

SACK Old English term for Sherry.

SACRAMENTAL WINE Wines used during religious ceremonies.

SAIGNAGE French. "Bleeding" process used to make red and rosé wines. By drawing off some of the liquid, the remaining must will have more skin contact and make a darker-colored red wine.

SALMANAZAR Large bottle with the capacity of twelve 750 ml (2.4 gallons) bottles generally used for Champagne.

SCION Shoot or bud to be grafted onto rootstock.

SEC French. Dry.

SEDIMENT Precipitation of tannins, tartrates, and pigments as the wine ages in the bottle. Red wines high in tannins will create sediment in the form of brownish solids.

SEEDS Pit in the grape berry.

SEKT German. Sparkling wine.

SÉLECTION DE GRAINS NOBLES French. Designation for wines made with botrytis-affected grapes to produce a very concentrated sweet wine. Similar to Germany's *Beerenauslese*.

SERCIAL Portuguese. Grape variety used to make a pale, dry style of Madeira. Also used as the name of the wine on the label.

SERVING TEMPERATURE Best temperature for serving wine.

SHERRY Spanish. Fortified wine produced in Jerez, Spain. Produced using the SOLERA system. Traditionally contains 15–22 percent alcohol.

SHOOT Living growth from a grapevine. Bears leaves and tendrils and possibly fruit.

SITE SELECTION Process of locating and planning a vineyard, based on weather patterns, heat summation, soil types, etc.

SKIN Outer covering of grape containing pigments, tannins, and other phenolic compounds. Yeasts are also found on the skin of the grape.

SKIN CONTACT Refers to grape skin contact with the juice before or during fermentation. Lends color, flavor, complexity, and longevity to the wine. Most often an important part of red wine production.

SMOKY Describes odor present in bouquet of wines fermented in charred oak barrels.

SNIFTER Balloon-shaped brandy glass.

SOFT Describes the mouthfeel of wine. Smooth, without harshness.

SOLAR OR PALÁCIO Portuguese. Vineyard and fine house similar to the French château.

SOLERA Spanish. System used to produce Sherries. Series of old white American oak barrels set up in tiers, eight- to fifteen rows. The wine in the bottom barrel is removed for bottling and replaced by the tier above and so on, so that the older wines are refreshed, and the younger wines gain complexity. Wine sold is from the bottom, but no more than 33 percent of the bottom barrel is removed.

SOMMELIER Individual in charge of the wine, wine service, the wine list, and the wine cellar in the restaurant.

SPÄTLESE German. Means "late picking" or "late harvesting," as determined by the sugar content of the grapes at harvest.

SPECIFIC GRAVITY Density of a substance compared with the density of a standard substance, such as water.

SPICY Describes odor and/or taste that resembles spices.

SPRAYING The application of liquid fungicides and insecticides to combat pests and diseases.

SPRITZ Light, pleasant effervescence created by carbon dioxide in the wine.

SPUMANTE Italian. Sparkling wine.

STABILIZERS Various additives used to retard deterioration of the wine.

VINHO REGIONAL Portuguese. Regional wines from large areas such as Alentejano, Beiras, Lisboa, or Ribatejo.

VINICULTURE Theory, art, and science of making wine.

VINIFERA Latin. Species of grapes for making wine.

VINIFICATION Process of converting grapes into wine.

VIN JAUNE French. This Jura wine is made from late harvested Savagnin grapes. The fermented "yellow wine" spends at least six years in oak, with air contact, before it is released.

VINO DA TAVOLA Italian. Table wine under DOC wine laws.

VINO DE CALIDAD Spanish. Quality wine under DO wine laws.

VIN ORDINAIRE French. Everyday wine.

VINOSITY Refers to wine-like aroma and flavor of wine due to its alcohol level.

VINSANTO Italian. An oxidized style of wine, most often sweet.

VIN SANTO Greek. A sweet wine made from dried grapes on the island of Santorini.

VINTAGE The year the grapes were harvested.

VINTAGE PORTO Portuguese. Porto from a single vintage, produced in years determined by producers to be the best quality. Rarest and most expensive style of Porto, aged in cask for two to three years before bottling. The wine must age in the bottle for many years to achieve harmony, balance, and complexity.

VINTNER Grower, blender, and seller of grapes and wines.

VISCOUS Describes full-bodied wines that taste "fat," usually full-bodied reds or sweet dessert wines.

VITICULTURE Theory, science, study, and practice of growing grapes.

VITIS LABRUSCA Latin. Eastern North American species of grapevines, such as Concord and Niagara.

VITIS RIPARIA Latin. North American species of grapevines.

VITIS ROTUNDIFOLIA Latin. North American species of grapevine found predominately in the southern Atlantic states, such as Muscadine and Scuppernong.

VITIS VINIFERA Latin. European species of grapevine. Translates as "grapes to make wine."

VOLATILE ACIDITY (VA) Total combination of acids in wine that are considered to be volatile, i.e., can be separated easily from the wine, usually by distillation. High levels of volatile acidity in wine are considered a defect and are usually detected as the vinegary smell of acetic acid, or the plastic, nail-polish aroma of ethyl acetate.

VOSGES Forest located in the Vosges Mountains near Alsace. Vosges oak features a tight grain with neutral flavor and medium tannin extraction.

W

WEINGUT German. Wine estate.

WELL BALANCED See BALANCE.

WILD YEAST Yeasts indigenous to certain vineyards that collect on the skin of grapes around harvest time and can be used to start the fermentation process.

WINE Alcoholic beverage produced from fermenting fruit juice (generally grapes).

WINE CRADLE Basket designed to hold a bottle of mature wine that contains sediment. Keeps the bottle in a semi-horizontal position to minimize disruption of the sediment.

WINEMAKER Individual in charge of producing wine in a winery.

WINERY Building where grape juice is fermented into wine.

WOODY Describes odor and taste of some wines aged in wood barrels for an extended period of time.

Y

YEAST Brings about fermentation of grape juice to wine by secreting the enzyme zymase, which converts sugar to ethyl alcohol and carbon dioxide.

YEASTY Describes odor in wine as that of freshly made bread.

YIELD Refers to the production from an acre or hectare of land.

BIBLIOGRAPHY

Adams, Leon. *The Wines of America.* New York: McGraw-Hill, 1990.

Amerine, Maynard. *Table Wines: The Technology of Their Production in California.* Berkeley: University of California Press, 1951.

Amerine, Maynard. *The Technology of Wine Making.* Westport, CT: Avi Publishing, 1980.

Amerine, Maynard, and M. A. Joslyn. *Table Wines: The Technology of Their Production.* 2nd ed. Berkeley: University of California Press, 1970.

Amerine, Maynard, and C. S. Ough. *Wine and Must Analysis.* New York: John Wiley & Sons, 1974.

Amerine, Maynard, and Edward B. Roessler. *Wines: Their Sensory Evaluation.* 2nd ed. San Francisco: W. H. Freeman, 1983.

Anderson, Burton. *The Simon & Schuster Pocket Guide to the Wines of Italy.* New York: Simon & Schuster, 1993.

Anderson, Burton. *Treasures of the Italian Table.* New York: Morrow, 1994.

Anderson, Burton. *Vino: The Wines and Winemakers of Italy.* Boston: Little, Brown and Company, 1980.

Anderson, Burton. *The Wine Atlas of Italy.* New York: Simon & Schuster, 1992.

Anderson, Stanley, and Raymond Hull. *The Art of Making Wine.* New York: NAL-Dutton, 1991.

Asher, Gerald. *On Wine.* New York: Random House, 1982.

Asher, Gerald. *Vineyard Tales.* San Francisco: Chronicle Books, 1997.

Ausmus, William. *Wines and Wineries of California's Central Coast: A Complete Guide from Monterey to Santa Barbara.* Berkeley: University of California Press, 2008.

Bastianich, Joseph, and David Lynch. *Vino Italiano: The Regional Wines of Italy.* New York: Clarkson Potter, 2005.

Belfrage, Nicolas. *Barolo to Valpolicella: The Wines of Northern Italy.* London: Mitchell Beazley, 2004.

Belfrage, Nicolas. *Brunello to Zibibbo: The Wines of Tuscany, Central and Southern Italy.* London: Mitchell Beazley, 2003.

Benson, Jeffrey, and Alastair Mackenzie. *The Wines of Saint-Émilion and Pomerol.* London: Sotheby's Publications, 1990.

Bespaloff, Alexis. *The New Frank Schoonmaker's Encyclopedia of Wine.* New York: Morrow, 1988.

Blue, Anthony Dias. *Anthony Dias Blue's Pocket Guide to Wine 2007.* New York: Fireside, 2006.

Broadbent, Michael. *The Great Vintage Book.* New York: Alfred A. Knopf, 1981.

Broadbent, Michael. *Michael Broadbent's Guide to Wine Vintages.* New York: Simon & Schuster, 1993.

Broadbent, Michael. *Michael Broadbent's Pocket Vintage Wine Companion.* New York: Harcourt, 2007.

Broadbent, Michael. *Michael Broadbent's Vintage Wine.* New York: Harcourt, 2002.

Broadbent, Michael. *Michael Broadbent's Wine Tasting.* London: Mitchell Beazley, 2003.

Broadbent, Michael. *The New Great Vintage Wine Book.* New York: Alfred A. Knopf, 1991.

Broadbent, Michael. *The Simon & Schuster Pocket Guide to Wine Tasting.* New York: Simon & Schuster, 1988.

Brook, Stephen. *The Complete Bordeaux: The Wines, the Chateaux, the People.* London: Mitchell Beazley, 2007.

Brook, Stephen. *Liquid Gold.* New York: William Morrow, 1987.

Brook, Stephen. *Sauvignon Blanc and Sémillon.* London: Viking Penguin, 1993.

Buller, Michael. *The Winemaker's Year: Four Seasons in Bordeaux.* New York: Thames & Hudson, 1991.

Buller, Michael. *The Winemaker's Year in Beaujolais.* New York: Thames & Hudson, 1993.

Campbell, Christy. *The Botanist and the Vintner: How Wine Was Saved for the World.* New York: Algonquin, 2006.

Casas, Penelope. *Foods and Wines of Spain.* New York: Alfred A. Knopf, 1982.

Cernilli, Daniele, and Marco Sabellico. *The New Italy: A Complete Guide to Contemporary Italian Wine.* London: Mitchell Beazley, 2008.

Chelminski, Rudolph. *I'll Drink to That: Beaujolais and the French Peasant Who Made It the World's Most Popular Wine.* New York: Gotham, 2007.

Clarke, Oz. *Oz Clarke's Bordeaux: The Wines, the Vineyards, the Winemakers.* New York: Harcourt, 2007.

Clarke, Oz. *Oz Clarke's Encyclopedia of Grapes.* New York: Harcourt, 2001.

Clarke, Oz. *Oz Clarke's New Encyclopedia of Wine.* New York: Harvest Books, 2003.

Clarke, Oz. *New Essential Wine Book: An Indispensable Guide to the Wines of the World,* 3rd ed. New York: Fireside, 2005.

Livingstone-Learmonth, John. *The Wines of the Northern Rhône*. Berkeley: University of California Press, 2005.

Loubère, Leo. *The Wine Revolution in France*. Princeton: Princeton University Press, 1990.

Lynch, Kermit. *Adventures on the Wine Route*. New York: Farrar, Straus & Giroux, 1990.

MacDonogh, Giles. *Portuguese Table Wines*. London: Grub Street, 2001.

MacNeil, Karen. *The Wine Bible*. New York: Workman, 2001.

Manessis, Nico. *The Illustrated Greek Wine Book*. Corfu: Olive Press, 2000.

Maresca, Tom. *Mastering Wine: A Learner's Manual*. New York: Grove-Atlantic, 1992.

Maresca, Tom. *The Right Wine*. New York: Grove-Atlantic, 1992.

Markham, Dewey, Jr. *1855: A History of the Bordeaux Classification*. New York: Wiley, 1998.

Matasar, Ann. *Women of Wine: The Rise of Women in the Global Wine Industry*. Berkeley: University of California Press, 2006.

Matthews, Thomas. *A Village in the Vineyards*. New York: Farrar, Straus & Giroux, 1993.

Mayson, Richard. *Port and the Douro*. London: Mitchell Beazley, 2005.

Mayson, Richard. *Portugal's Wines and Winemakers*. San Francisco: Wine Appreciation Guild, 1992.

Mazzeo, Tilar. *The Widow Clicquot: The Story of a Champagne Empire and the Woman Who Ruled It*. New York: Collins Business, 2008.

McCoy, Elin. *The Emperor of Wine: The Rise of Robert M. Parker, Jr., and the Reign of American Taste*. New York: Harper Perennial, 2006.

McGee, Harold. *On Food and Cooking: The Science and Lore of the Kitchen*. New York: Scribner, 2004.

McGovern, Patrick. *Ancient Wine: The Search for the Origins of Viniculture*. Princeton: Princeton University Press, 2007.

McWhitter, Kathryn, and Charles Metcalfe. *Encyclopedia of Spanish and Portuguese Wines*. New York: Simon & Schuster, 1991.

Norman, Remington. *The Great Domaines of Burgundy*. New York: H. Holt, 1996.

Norman, Remington. *Rhône Renaissance*. San Francisco: Wine Appreciation Guild, 1996.

Novitski, Joseph. *A Vineyard Year*. San Francisco: Chronicle Books, 1983.

Olney, Richard. *Ten Vineyard Lunches*. New York: Interlink Books, 1988.

Olney, Richard. *Yquem*. London: Dorling Kindersley, 1985.

Osborne, Lawrence. *The Accidental Connoisseur: An Irreverent Journey Through the Wine World*. San Francisco: North Point Press, 2005.

Parker, Robert. *Bordeaux*. New York: Simon & Schuster, 2003.

Parker, Robert. *Parker's Wine Buyers Guide No. 7*. New York: Simon & Schuster, 2008.

Parker, Robert. *Wines of Burgundy*. New York: Simon & Schuster, 1990.

Pellechia, Thomas. *Wine: The 8,000-Year-Old Story of the Wine Trade*. Philadelphia: Running Press, 2006.

Penin, José. *Penin Guide to Spanish Wine 2009*, 18th ed. Madrid: Grupo Pein, 2008.

Penning-Roswell, Edmund. *Wines of Bordeaux*. San Francisco: Wine Appreciation Guild, 1983.

Peppercorn, David. *Bordeaux*. London: Faber and Faber, 1991.

Perdue, Lewis. *The French Paradox and Beyond: Live Longer with Wine and the Mediterranean Lifestyle*. San Francisco: Renais, 1992.

Peynaud, Emile. *Knowing and Making Wine*. New York: John Wiley & Sons, 1984.

Peynaud, Emile. *The Taste of Wine*. San Francisco: Wine Appreciation Guild, 1987.

Pigott, Stuart. *Riesling*. London: Viking Penguin, 1993.

Pinney, Thomas. *A History of Wine in America, vol. 1, From the Beginnings to Prohibition*. Berkeley: University of California Press, 2007.

Pinney, Thomas. *A History of Wine in America, vol. 2, From Prohibition to the Present*. Berkeley: University of California Press, 2005.

Pitte, Jean-Robert. *Bordeaux/Burgundy: A Vintage Rivalry*. Berkeley: University of California Press, 2008.

Prial, Frank, ed. *The Companion to Wine*. New York: Prentice Hall, 1992.

Radford, John. *The New Spain: A Complete Guide to Contemporary Spanish Wine*. London: Mitchell Beazley, 2004.

Read, Jan. *Chilean Wine*. London: Sotheby's Publications, 1988.

Read, Jan. *The Wines of Portugal*. London: Faber and Faber, 1982.

Read, Jan. *Wines of Spain*. London: Faber and Faber, 1986

Read, Jan. *Wines of the Rioja*. London: Sotheby's Publications, 1984.

Ribérau-Gayon, Pascal, ed. *The Wines and Vineyards of France.* New York: Viking Penguin, 1990.

Richards, Peter. *The Wines of Chile.* London: Mitchell Beazley, 2007.

Robertson, George. *Port.* London: Faber and Faber, 1978.

Robinson, Jancis. *The Great Wine Book.* New York: Morrow, 1982.

Robinson, Jancis. *How to Taste: A Guide to Enjoying Wine.* New York: Simon & Schuster, 2008.

Robinson, Jancis. *Jancis Robinson's Food and Wine Adventures.* London: Headline, 1987.

Robinson, Jancis. *Jancis Robinson's Guide to Wine Grapes.* London: Oxford University Press, 1996.

Robinson, Jancis. *Jancis Robinson's Wine Course.* New York: Abbeville Press, 2006.

Robinson, Jancis, ed. *Oxford Companion to Wine*, 3rd ed. Oxford: Oxford University Press, 2006.

Robinson, Jancis. *Questions of Taste: The Philosophy of Wine.* London: Oxford University Press, 2007.

Robinson, Jancis. *Vines, Grapes, and Wines.* London: Mitchell Beazley, 1992.

Robinson, Jancis. *Vintage Timecharts: The Pedigree and Performance of Fine Wine to the Year 2000.* New York: Weidenfeld & Nicolson, 1989.

Rogov, Daniel. *Rogov's Guide to Israeli Wines, 2010.* New Milford, CT: Toby Press, 2010.

Root, Waverly. *The Food of France.* New York: Random House, 1992.

Rosengarten, David, and Joshua Wesson. *Red Wine with Fish: The New Art of Matching Wine with Food.* New York: Simon & Schuster, 1989.

Sichel, Peter M. F. *Which Wine?* New York: Harper & Row, 1975.

Sichel, Peter M. F. *The Wines of Germany: Frank Schoonmaker's Classic,* rev. ed. New York: Hastings House, 1980.

Simon, André. *The History of Champagne.* New York: Octopus Books, 1971.

Simon, André. *Wines of the World.* New York: McGraw-Hill, 1972.

Siler, Julia Flynn. *The House of Mondavi: The Rise and Fall of an American Wine Dynasty.* New York: Gotham, 2008.

Simon, Joanna. *Discovering Wine.* New York: Simon & Schuster, 1995.

Smith, Brian H. *The Sommelier's Guide to Wine: Everything You Need to Know for Selecting, Serving, and Savoring Wine like the Experts,* 2nd ed. New York: Black Dog and Leventhal, 2008.

Sokol Blosser, Susan. *At Home in the Vineyard: Cultivating a Winery, an Industry, and a Life.* Berkeley: University of California Press, 2006.

Spurrier, Steven. *Académie du Vin Concise Guide to French Country Wines.* New York: Perigree Books, 1983.

Spurrier, Steven. *Académie du Vin Guide to French Wines.* Topsfield, MA: Salem House, 1986.

Spurrier, Steven, and Michael Dovaz. *Académie du Vin Complete Wine Course.* New York: Macmillan, 1991.

Standage, Tom. *A History of the World in Six Glasses.* New York: Walker, 2006.

Steinberg, Edward. *The Vines of San Lorenzo.* Hopewell, NJ: Ecco Press, 1992.

Sterling, Joy. *A Cultivated Life: A Year in a California Vineyard.* New York: Random House, 1993.

Stevenson, Robert Louis. *Napa Wine.* San Francisco: Westwind Books, 1974.

Stevenson, Tom. *Sotheby's World Wine Encyclopedia*, 4th ed. New York: Dorling Kindersley, 2007.

Stevenson, Tom. *Wine Report 2009.* New York: Dorling Kindersley, 2008.

Sullivan, Charles L. *A Companion to California Wine: An Encyclopedia of Wine and Winemaking from the Mission Period to the Present.* Berkeley: University of California Press, 1998.

Sullivan, Charles L. *Zinfandel: A History of a Grape and Its Wine.* Berkeley: University of California Press, 2003.

Sutcliffe, Serena, ed. *Great Vineyards and Winemakers.* New York: Rutledge, 1981.

Swinchatt, Jonathan, and David G. Howell. *The Winemaker's Dance: Exploring Terroir in the Napa Valley.* Berkeley: University of California Press, 2004.

Taber, George M. *Judgment of Paris: California vs. France and the Historic 1976 Paris Tasting That Revolutionized Wine.* New York: Scribner, 2006.

Taber, George M. *To Cork or Not to Cork: Tradition, Romance, Science, and the Battle for the Wine Bottle.* New York: Scribner, 2007.

Thomas, Tara . Q. *The Complete Idiot's Guide to Wine Basics,* 2nd ed. New York: Alpha, 2008.

Unwin, Timothy. *Wine and the Vine.* London: Routledge, 1991.

Vaynerchuk, Gary. *Gary Vaynerchuk's 101 Wines: Guaranteed to Inspire, Delight, and Bring Thunder to Your World.* New York: Rodale, 2008.

Wagner, Philip. *Grapes into Wine: The Art of Winemaking in America.* New York: Alfred A. Knopf, 1976.

Wallace, Benjamin. *The Billionaire's Vinegar: The Mystery of the World's Most Expensive Bottle of Wine.* New York: Crown, 2007.

Wasserman, Sheldon. *White Wines of the World.* New York: Stein and Day, 1978.

Wasserman, Sheldon, and Pauline Wasserman. *Italy's Noble Red Wines.* New York: Macmillan, 1992.

Watson, Jeremy. *The New and Classical Wines of Spain.* Barcelona: Montagud Editores, 2002.

Waugh, Alec. *Wines and Spirits.* New York: Time-Life, 1968.

Whitten, David N., and Martin R. Lipp. *To Your Health: Two Physicians Explore the Health Benefits of Wine.* San Francisco: Harper Collins West, 1994.

Willinger, Faith. *Eating in Italy.* New York: Hearst Books, 1989.

Willinger, Faith. *Red, White, and Green.* San Francisco: HarperCollins, 1996.

Winkler, A. J., James A. Cook, M. W. Kliewer, and Lloyd A. Lider. *General Viticulture,* 2nd rev. ed. Berkeley: University of California Press, 1974.

Wolfert, Paula. *The Cooking of the Eastern Mediterranean.* New York: HarperCollins, 1994.

Wolfert, Paula. *The Cooking of Southwest France: Recipes from France's Magnificent Rustic Cuisine.* Hoboken, NJ: Wiley, 2005.

Wolfert, Paula. *Mediterranean Clay Pot Cooking.* Hoboken, NJ: Wiley, 2009.

Wolfert, Paula. *The Slow Mediterranean Kitchen: Recipes for the Passionate Cook.* New York: Wiley, 2003.

Zraly, Kevin. *Kevin Zraly's American Wine Guide: 2009.* New York: Sterling, 2008.

Zraly, Kevin. *Windows on the World Complete Wine Course: 2010 Edition.* New York: Sterling, 2009.

bottle shock, 72
Bouchet grapes, 307
Boulud, Daniel, 549, 659
bouquet *vs* aroma, 95–97
Bourboulenc grapes, 338, 339, 342, 345
Bourgogne Côte Chalonnaise appellation, France, 326
Bourgueil appellation, France, 266, 270–271
Boutari, Yiannis, 534
Boutari winery, Greece, 534, 535, 539, 540, 541, 542
Bouzeron appellation, France, 312, 326
"box wines," 114, 128, 181
Brachetto d'Acqui wine, 363, 398–399, 404
Brachetto grapes, 48, 363
Brancellao grapes, 426, 452
branding, in wine industry, 126
Braquet grapes, 348
Brazil, 11, 207, 223–224, 595
breast cancer, 642
breathing, 662
Breede River Valley wine region, South Africa, 248, 249
Brézème appellation, France, 337
Bricco Rocche vineyard, Italy, 399
Brillat-Savarin, Jean Anthelme, 99
Britain. *See* England
British Columbia wine regions, Canada, 22, 26, 28, 203, 204–205
Brix scale, 55
Broadbent, Michael, 523
Bronco Wine Company, 126, 127
Brotherhood winery, New York, 188
Brouilly appellation, France, 330
Brounstein, Al, 149
Brounstein, Boots, 100, 149
Brown-Forman, 127
Brunello di Montalcino wine, 36, 47, 362, 385, 391–392, 675, 691
brut, 84, 285, 528
Bruwer, Aubrey, 250
de Brye family, 125
Bual grapes (Boal), 33, 481, 482
Bucelas DOC, Portugal, 449, 476
Buck, John, 243
Buena Vista Winery, California, 122, 123, 125
Bugey appellation, France, 331
Buil & Giné winery, 435
Buitenverwachting winery, South Africa, 251
Bulgaria, 36, 39, 520, 524
Bullas DO, Spain, 423, 437
"Bull's Blood wine (Egri Bikavér), 522
Bureau of Alcohol, Tobacco, and Firearms (BATF), 117, 155
Burgenland wine region, Austria, 511–512
Burgess, Tom, 124
Burgess Cellars, California, 124
Burgundy wine, 115, 136
Burgundy wine region, France, 261, 311–327
    appellation/classification system in, 314–316
    business practices in, 313–314
    Chablis, 21, 312, 316–318
    clonal variation in, 11–12
    Côte Chalonnaise, 312, 326–327
    Côte d Or, 312, 318–326
    food/wine pairing, 609
    grape varieties in, 21, 40–41, 313
    Mâconnais, 21, 312, 327
    map of, 312

    soil and climate of, 312–313
    winemaking practices in, 314, 317
buying wine. *See* purchasing wine
Buzbag wine, 544
Buzet appellation, France, 310
Buzinski, Tim, 685

C

Cabardès appellation, France, 311, 343
Cabernet d'Anjou wine, 268
Cabernet Franc grapes, 11, 35, 46, 69, 115, 117, 119, 134, 187, 292, 307, 308, 521
Cabernet Sauvignon grapes, 34–37, 69, 115, 118, 119, 122, 146, 147, 153, 177, 211, 213, 229–230, 238, 247, 260, 291, 347, 390, 431, 493, 521
Cabernet Sauvignon wine, 65, 91, 102, 113, 116, 117, 124, 126, 133, 134, 136–137, 141, 142–143, 144, 145, 147, 148, 154, 156, 159–160, 191–192
Cachapoal Valley wine region, Chile, 217
Cahors appellation, France, 261, 310
Le Cailleret vineyard, France, 324, 325
Les Caillerets vineyard, France, 324
Cain Cellars, California, 146
Caiño grapes, 426
Cajun food/wine pairing, 596, 629
Cakebread, Delores, 102
Calabria wine region, Italy, 357, 361, 370, 372, 376
Calatayud DO, Spain, 423, 424, 425, 430
Calaveras County AVAs, California, 183, 747
calcareous soil, 7
calcium carbonate, 67
California, 109, 121–183
    biodynamic viticulture in, 17
    climate change in, 128–129
    degree days in, 119
    grape varieties in, 29, 30, 31, 33, 46, 47, 48, 49
        Cabernet Sauvignon, 35, 36–37
        Chardonnay, 21–22
        Gewürztraminer, 28
        Italian varietals (Cal-Italians), 162, 180
        Merlot, 39
        Pinot Noir, 41
        Rhone Ranger (Rhône-style), 150, 161, 173, 176
        Sauvignon Blanc, 24
        Syrah/Shiraz, 43
        Zinfandel, 43–45
    history of winemaking, 121–129
    Internet sales of wine, 128
    map of, 130
    organic viticulture in, 15
    in Paris wine tasting (1976), 126, 136
    phylloxera in, 10–11, 124, 150, 170–171
    Pierce's Disease in, 173, 177, 178, 179
    viticultural areas (by county), 747
    wine brands in, 126–128
    wine exports of, 126
    wine labels in, 117
    wine production of, 131
    wine regions of, 120–121, 129–183, 747
        Central Coast, 121, 130, 168–177
        Central Valley/Interior, 130, 179–182
        by county, 183, 747
        map of, 130
        North Coast, 121, 129–168
        South Coast, 130, 177, 179

    wood aging in, 120
California Certified Organic Farmers (CCOF), 15
Calistoga AVA, California, 132, 149
Cal-Italian grapes, 162, 180
Callaway winery, California, 179
calço, 456
Camarate grapes, 472
Campania wine region, Italy, 357, 361, 364, 367, 370, 372, 377–378
Campo de Borja DO, Spain, 423, 424, 425, 430
Canada
    grape varieties in, 22, 26, 28, 37, 203
    hybrid grapes in, 12
    wine laws in, 203
    wine regions of, 203–205
Canaiolo grapes, 363, 384, 386
Canandaigua Wine Company, New York, 187
Canary Islands wine region, Spain, 425
cancer, and alcohol/wine consumption, 634, 636, 642
cane pruning, 18, 19
Can Feixes winery, Spain, 433
Cannonau di Sardegna wine, 375
Cannonau grapes, 36, 45, 46, 375
Canon-Fronsac appellation, France, 308
canteiro method, 483, 484, 485
Canterbury wine region, New Zealand, 244–245
Cape Agulhas District, South Africa, 249, 252
Capezzana vineyards, 393
cap of grape, 64–65
Caprai, Arnaldo, 384
carbon dioxide, 57, 94, 101
carbonic maceration, 66–67, 328, 338, 341, 343, 344, 432, 472
Carcavelos DOC, Portugal, 449
Caribbean food/wine pairing, 595–596
Carignan grapes, 48, 338, 339, 343–344, 345, 346, 347, 375
Cariñena DO, Spain, 423, 424, 425, 430
Cariñena grapes, 48, 421, 430
Carmel Valley AVA, California, 130, 169
Carmenère grapes, 48, 211, 213
Carmen winery, Chile, 218
Carmignano wine, 47, 363, 385, 393
Carneros AVA, California, 130, 132, 138–139, 152
Carpy, Charles, 125
Casablanca Valley wine region, Chile, 209, 216
Casa de Santar estate, Portugal, 473
Casa Lapostolle winery, Chile, 213
Casa Pedro Domecq company, in Mexico, 202
Cassis appellation, France, 343, 347
casta, 456
Castelão grapes, 452
Castello Banfi winery, Italy, 391
Castilla La Mancha wine region, Spain, 425
Castilla y Léon wine region, Spain, 425
Castro, Alvaro, 474
Catalonia wine region, Spain, 425, 432–436
Cataluña DO, Spain, 424, 425, 432, 433
Catamarca wine region, Argentina, 209, 222
Catarratto grapes, 373
catechin, 639–640
Catena, Nicolas, 220, 222
Catoctin AVA, Maryland, 202
cava, 529
Cava DO, Spain, 420, 424
Cavas de San Juan Winery, Mexico, 202
Cava wine, 420, 425, 432–433

Colchagua Valley wine region, Chile, 217
Coldstream Hills winery, Australia, 234
Cole Ranch AVA, California, 163, 165
colheita Tawny Porto, 464
colheita wines, 455, 481, 484
collector wine cellar, 674–676
Colli Asolani Prosecco Bianco wine, 367
Collio Orientali del Friuli wine region, Italy, 370, 410
Colli Orientali del Friuli Picolit wine, 367, 409
Collioure appellation, France, 343, 344
Collio wine region, Italy, 410
colloids, 65
Colombard grapes, 33
Colombo, Jean Luc, 337, 338
Colorado AVAs, 37, 746
Colorino grapes, 386, 387
color of wine, 52–53, 57, 65, 68, 88–89, 91, 92, 93, 649–650
Color Wheel, 93
Columbia Gorge AVA, Oregon, 192, 198
Columbia Gorge AVA, Washington State, 192–193, 194
Columbia Valley AVA, Oregon, 192, 198
Columbia Valley AVA, Washington State, 192–193
Comité Interprofessionel des Vins de Champagne (CIVC), 280
Commandaria wine, 543
Commonwealth of Independent States (CIS), 524–525
comparative tasting, 102
complementing flavors, in food/wine pairing, 558–559
compost, 15
Comté Rhodaniens IGP, France, 264
Comté Tolosan IGP, France, 264
Conca de Barberà DO, Spain, 424, 425, 436
Concannon winery, California, 173
concentrateur, 292
Concha y Toro winery, Chile, 208, 212, 214, 218
Concord grapes, 188
Condado de Huelva DO, Spain, 425, 445
Conde de Valdemar winery, Spain, 431
Condrieu appellation, France, 332, 334
Cònero wine, 365, 382
Connecticut AVAs, 746
Cono Sur winery, Chile, 218
Conseil Interprofessionel du Vin de Bordeaux (CIVB), 289
consejo regulador, 417, 439
consorzio system, 362
Constantia wine region, South Africa, 249, 250–251
Constellation, 124, 125, 127, 181, 212
Contra Costa AVAs, California, 168, 169, 170, 183, 747
contrasting flavors, in food/wine pairing, 558–559
Controguerra DOC, Italy, 381
cooking method, and food/wine pairing, 557, 564–567, 599–600
cooking wine, 599
Coonawarra wine region, Australia, 228, 230, 232, 238
Cooper Mountain Vineyards, Oregon, 17
copita, 442
Coppola, Francis Ford, 69, 123, 125, 156
Corbières appellation, France, 343, 344–345

Corder, Roger, 640–641
Cordillera wine, 213
cordon-spur pruning, 18
corkage fee, 711
corked, 650
corks
    dry/wet, 662
    production of, 683
    for sparkling wine, 79, 84, 284
    synthetic, 659, 683
    tartrate deposits on, 94, 658
    TCA contamination of, 97, 659
    uncorking, 649, 658, 660
corkscrew, 649, 657, 658, 660, 666
Cornas appellation, France, 332, 337
Cornell University, Agricultural Experiment Station, Geneva, N.Y., 11, 12, 15
Coro Mendocino wines, 164
Corsica, wine regions of, 261, 348–349
Cortes de Cima winery, Portugal, 478, 479, 480
Cortese di Gavi wine, 366, 399, 405
Cortese grapes, 33, 366
Corton-Charlemagne vineyard, France, 321, 322
Corvina grapes, 48, 364, 407
Corvo winery, Italy, 373
cosecha wines, 419
Cosentino, Mitch, 135
Costers del Segre DO, Spain, 425, 436
Costières de Nîmes appellation, France, 339–340
Côteaux d'Aix-en-Provence appellation, France, 343, 347
Coteaux de l'Aubance appellation, France, 266, 269
Coteaux Champenois appellation, France, 286
Coteaux du Giennois appellation, France, 266, 273
Coteaux du Languedoc appellation, France, 343, 345
Coteaux du Layon appellation, France, 265, 266, 269, 270
Coteaux du Loir appellation, France, 266, 271
Coteaux de Pierrevert appellation, France, 332, 348
Coteaux de Saumur appellation, France, 270
Coteaux du Tricastin appellation, France, 332, 339
Coteaux Varois appellation, France, 343, 347
Coteaux du Vendômois appellation, France, 266, 271
Côte des Bar wine region, France, 278, 282
Côte de Beaune appellation, France, 21, 40, 312, 315, 318, 321, 322–326
Côte de Beaune-Villages appellation, France, 322
Côte des Blancs wine region, France, 278, 281
Côte de Brouilly appellation, France, 330
Côte Chalonnaise wine region, France, 41, 312, 326–327
Côte de Nuits appellation, France, 40–41, 312, 318–322
Côte d'Or region, France, 40–41, 312, 316, 318–326
Côte de Provence appellation, France, 343, 347
Côte Roannaise appellation, France, 273
Côte-Rôtie appellation, France, 332, 335
Côtes de Bergerac appellation, France, 309
Côtes de Bordeaux Blaye appellation, France, 288, 290, 297, 308
Côtes de Bordeaux Cadillac appellation, France, 288, 300, 308–309

Côtes de Bordeaux Castillon appellation, France, 288, 308
Côtes de Bordeaux Francs appellation, France, 288, 297, 308
Côtes de Bordeaux Saint-Macaire appellation, France, 288, 300
Côtes de Bourg appellation, France, 288, 290, 297, 308
Côtes de Duras appellation, France, 309
Côtes du Forez appellation, France, 273
Côtes du Frontonnais appellation, France, 310
Côtes du Jura appellation, France, 330–331
Côtes du Lubéron appellation, France, 332, 339
Côtes de la Malepère appellation, France, 311, 343
Côtes du Marmandais appellation, France, 309–310
Côtes de Meliton AOC, Greece, 533, 535–536
Côtes de Millau appellation, France, 311
Côtes du Rhône appellation, France, 62, 332, 333, 338
Côtes du Rhône-Villages appellation, France, 333, 338 339
Côtes du Roussillon appellation, France, 343–344
Côtes du Roussillon-Villages appellation, France, 343, 344
Côte de Sézanne wine region, France, 278, 281
Côtes du Ventoux appellation, France, 332, 339
Côtes du Vivarais appellation, France, 332, 339
Cot grapes, 48
Coulée de Serrant, France, 16–17, 268
Counoise grapes, 341
Cousiño-Macul winery, Chile, 216, 218
Covelo AVA, California, 164
cover crops, 15, 16
Craig, Robert, 144
Crawford, William, 165
cream sherries, 443
Crémant d'Alsace wine, 277
Crémant de Bourgogne appellation, France, 327
Crémant du Jura wine, 330
Crémant de la Loire appellation, France, 269, 270
Creole food/wine pairing, 596, 629
Crépy appellation, France, 331
Crete AOC, Greece, 532, 533, 540–541
Crew Wine Company, California, 181
crianza wines, 419
Criots-Bâtard-Montrachet vineyard, France, 325
Criolla grapes, 122, 202
Croatia, 113
Croser, Brian, 196
crossbreeding, 9, 10, 12
cross-pollination, 11
crown caps, 659, 683
Crozes-Hermitage appellation, France, 332, 337
cru, 265, 280, 285, 294
cru Beaujolais wines, 329–330
cru bourgeois, 295
crushing, 63, 461
crusted Porto, 463
cryoextraction, 68, 76, 292, 472
Cucamonga Valley AVA, California, 177, 179, 183
Culinary Institute of America, Greystone campus of, 123, 143, 149
Cumberland Valley AVA, Maryland, 202
Curicó Valley wine region, Chile, 209, 217
Curtis, Charles, 678–679
customer complaints, handling, 663

Merlot grapes, 35, 37–39, 69, 115, 117, 118, 119, 122, 134, 139, 142, 154, 177, 231, 289, 291, 293, 307–308, 310, 384, 515, 521
Merlot wine, 113, 116, 140, 156, 191–192, 211, 223, 230, 289, 293, 308
Merritt Island AVA, California, 180
Merseguera grapes, 422
Meseta wine region, Spain, 422, 424, 437–439
Mesilla Valley AVA, New Mexico and Texas, 200
mesoclimate, 6
Messenikola grapes, 536
Messinia *Vin de Pays*, Greece, 538
méthode champenoise (Champagne method), 78, 80–84, 277, 284, 327
méthode dioise ancéstrale, 338
méthode Gaillaçoise, 310
méthode rurale, 311
Methusaleh bottle, 680, 681, 691
Meursault appellation, France, 312, 324
mevushal kosher wines, 545, 546
Mexico, 37, 43, 202
Meyer, Danny, 696
Michael, Peter, 159–160
Michele Chiarlo winery, 401
Michigan AVAs, 189–190, 746
microclimate, 6
Middle Eastern wine regions. *See* Mediterranean (Eastern) wine regions
Middle Rio Grande Valley AVA, New Mexico, 200
Midwest (U.S.) wine regions, 189–190, 746
Millbrook Vineyards, New York, 188, 189
Miller, Jason, 723
Mimbres AVA, New Mexico, 200
mineral content of soil, 6, 7–8
Minervois appellation, France, 343, 346
Minho wine region, Portugal, 449, 465, 468–470
Minnesota AVAs, 746
Mission grapes, 202
Mission San Juan Capistrano, California, 121–122
Missouri AVAs, 746
Mittelburgenland DAC, Austria, 511, 512
Mittelrhein wine region, Germany, 500, 507
moëlleux (sweet) wines, 268, 271, 272
Moët & Chandon, 283, 284, 285
Moldova, 39, 520, 525
Molette grapes, 331
Molinara grapes, 407
Molise wine region, Italy, 357, 360, 370, 379, 380, 382
Monastrell grapes, 46, 421, 437
Monbazillac appellation, 309
Monção, 469
Mondavi, Cesare, 123
Mondavi, Peter, 123
Mondavi, Robert, 24, 114, 123, 125, 126, 148, 181, 272
Mondavi (Robert) Winery, California, 123, 125, 142, 212, 734
Mondéjar DO, Spain, 423, 425
Mondeuse grapes, 331
Monemvasia grapes, 532
monoterpene compounds, 54
Montagne de Reims wine region, France, 278, 281
Montagne-St-Émilion appellation, France, 288, 306–307
Montagny appellation, France, 326–327
Montana Winery, New Zealand, 244

Montefalco Sagrantino wine, 364, 384
Montepulciano d'Abruzzo Colline Teramane wine, 365, 381
Montepulciano d'Abruzzo wine, 365, 380, 381
Montepulciano grapes, 365, 382
Monterey AVA, California, 130, 150, 168, 170–172
Monterey County AVAs, California, 169, 170–172, 183, 747
Monte Rosso Vineyard, California, 133, 153, 154
Monterrei DO, Spain, 423, 424, 425
Montes, Aurelio, 216, 218, 220
Montevina Winery, California, 162
MontGras winery, Chile, 216, 217
Monthélie appellation, France, 324
Monticello AVA, Virginia, 201
Montilla-Moriles DO, Spain, 423, 424, 425, 444–445
Mont La Salle Vineyards, California, 143
Montlouis appellation, France, 266, 271
Montrachet vineyard, France, 316, 324–325, 674
Montravel appellation, France, 309
Montsant DO, Spain, 424, 425, 435
Monvedro grapes, 474, 476
Morellino di Scansano wine, 47, 362, 385, 393
Moreto grapes, 475
Morey-St-Denis appellation, France, 312, 319, 321
Morgado de Reguengo vineyard, Portugal, 479–480
Morgon appellation, France, 329
Moristel grapes, 421, 430
Mornington Peninsula wine region, Australia, 232, 234
Morocco, 527, 548, 595
Morse, Barbara, 644
Moscadello di Montalcino wine, 392
Moscatel de Setúbal wine, 453, 474, 475, 485
Moscatel grapes, 443, 453, 482
Moscatel Roxo grapes, 475
Moscatel Sherry, 443
Moscato d'Asti wine, 366, 399, 405–406
Moscato di Noto wine, 371
Moscato di Pantelleria wine, 371
Moscato di Scanzo wine, 364
Moscato di Siracusa wine, 371
Moscato grapes (Muscat), 31, 277, 338, 346, 349, 371, 405, 475, 532, 540, 543
Moschofilero grapes, 531, 538
Moschofilero wine, 538–539, 540
Mosel-Saar-Ruwer wine region, Germany, 25
Mosel wine region, Germany, 25, 492, 499, 500, 501–504
Moueix, Christian, 148, 308
Moueix family, 308
Moulin-à-Vent appellation, France, 329
Moulis appellation, France, 288, 304
Mount Barker wine region, Australia, 239–240, 241
Mount Benson wine region, Australia, 229, 232
Mount Harlan AVA, California, 130, 172
Mount Veeder AVA, California, 132, 143–145, 640
Mourvèdre grapes, 42, 45, 46–47, 230, 338, 339, 340, 341, 344, 345, 346, 347, 421
Mouton-Cadet wine, 289
Mtsvani grapes, 524–525
mugron system, 208, 210
Müller, Antoine, 80, 284

Müller, Hermann, 31, 492
Müller-Thurgau grapes, 31–32, 410, 412, 492, 502, 504
multivintage wines, 54
Munksgard, Dave, 158
Murcia wine region, Spain, 423, 424, 425
Murietta's Well winery, 170, 174
Murphy, Sean, 669
Murray Darling wine region, Australia, 231, 232, 234
Muscadelle grapes, 33, 291
Muscadet grapes (Melon de Bourgogne), 32, 266–267, 313
Muscadet wine, 62, 91, 267, 559
Muscardin grapes, 341
Muscat appellation, France, 346
Muscat de Cap Corse appellation, France, 349
Muscat grapes (Moscato), 31, 277, 338, 346, 349, 371, 405, 475, 532, 540, 543
Muscat Lunel grapes, 521
Musigny vineyard, France, 319
Muskotály grapes, 521, 522
must, 57

N

Nagyréde winery, Hungary, 522
Nahe wine region, Germany, 500, 507
naming systems. *See* appellation systems
Nantes wine region, France, 266–267
Naoussa AOC, Greece, 533, 534–535
Naoussa wine, 534
Napanook vineyard, California, 148
Napa Valley AVA, California, 183, 747
    AVA status, 120–121
    boundaries of, 130, 131
    climatic zones, 133
    historical background, 122, 125, 126
    in London/Napa wine tasting (2006), 136–137
    map of, 132
    Meritage-style wines of, 134
    in Paris tasting (1976), 136
    phylloxera in, 10–11, 124, 150
    Pierce's Disease in, 178
    production of, 131
    replanting program in, 150
    reputation of wines, 133–134
    soils of, 131, 133
    subappellations of, 121, 129, 138–149, 151
    and wine labels, 117
Nashik wine region, India, 550, 551
National Cancer Institute, 642
Navarra DO, Spain, 423, 424, 425, 430–431
Navarro Vineyards, California, 165
Nebbiolo d'Alba wine, 402
Nebbiolo grapes, 47, 118, 363, 364, 395, 397, 400, 401, 402
Nederberg Estate, South Africa, 251
négociants, 289, 294, 300, 313, 314
négociants-manipulants, 285
Negoska grapes, 535
Negra Mole grapes, 476, 482
Négrette grapes, 310
Negroamaro grapes, 49, 377
Nelson wine region, New Zealand, 244
Nemea AOC, Greece, 533, 539
Nero d'Avola grapes, 49, 365, 371, 373, 374
Neuchâtel wine region, Switzerland, 514, 517
Neuquén wine region, Argentina, 222

FIGURE AND PHOTOGRAPHY CREDITS

Photographs have been taken by the authors unless otherwise credited below.

FOREWORD

1, Andy Katz

CHAPTER 1

8 *(right)*, 30 *(top)*, 45, Luis Castañeda; 10, John Rizzo; 17, 19 *(top row, bottom, center and right)*, Kristin H. Stangeby, Pebble Ridge Vineyards and Wine Estates; 19 *(bottom left)*, 31 *(left and right)*, 46 *(bottom)*, Conseil Interprofessionel des Vins de Bordeaux; 20, 27, Ron Watts/Corbis; 23, 25, Bryan Peterson/Corbis; 28 *(top)*, Tracey Kusiewicz/Foodie Photography/Jupiterimages; 29, Diana Healey/Jupiterimages; 34, ImageSource/Jupiterimages; 38, Ben Fink/Jupiterimages; 40, 44, Jack K. Clark/Corbis; 42, Lance Nelson/Corbis

CHAPTER 2

79, Veuve Clicquot-Ponsardin; 81, 82 *(top and bottom, right and left)*, The Champagne Institute; 84, Nick Pavloff

CHAPTER 3

93, 96, American Journal of Enology and Viticulture; 92, 95, 97, The Culinary Institute of America, Iron Horse Ranch and Winery

CHAPTER 4

155 *(top)*, Matanzas Creek Winery; 155 *(bottom)*, Vérité Wines; 160, Anakota; 171, Carmel Road Winery

CHAPTER 5

193, John Rizzo; 195 *(top and bottom)*, 196, 197 *(right and left)*, Patrick Prothe/Oregon Wine Board

CHAPTER 6

208, Concha y Toro Winery; 215, Errazuriz Winery; 223 *(left)*, Panceri Winery; 236 *(top left)*, 239, 241, Australian Wine & Brandy Corporation

CHAPTER 7

283 *(top right)*, The Champagne Institute; 334 *(top)*, Isabelle Desarzens; 334 *(bottom)*, 336, 339, 341, Christophe Grilhé

CHAPTER 8

353 *(top and bottom)*, Michael Belardo/Tre Vasselle Museum, Torgiano; 375, 377, 381 *(top)*, 384, 386 *(top, right and left)*, 393, 395, 410, 411, 412, Michael Belardo; 391, Castello Banfi

CHAPTER 9

416 *(left and right)*, ICEX—Wines of Spain; 421 *(left)*, Carlos Navajas ICEX; 421 *(right)*, Juan Manuel Sanz ICEX; 424, Wines of Spain, Trade Commission of Spain, New York; 426, 434 *(bottom right)*, Classical Wines from Spain, Ltd.; 434 *(left)*, Marti Mensa

CHAPTER 10

448, 457, 464, Quinta do Crasto; 451, 452, ViniPortugal; 461 *(top)*, Quinta do Vale do Meão; 461 *(top and bottom)*, Symington family; 483, J. M. Fonseca

CHAPTER 13

531, 541 *(right)*, 542 *(top)*, All about Greek Wine, www.allaboutgreekwine.com

CHAPTER 15

638 *(top)*, Michael H. Criqui/University of California, San Diego, School of Medicine; 643, F. Forrest et al., British Medical Journal, 1991

CHAPTER 16

638 *(top)*, Michael H. Criqui/University of California, San Diego, School of Medicine; 643, F. Forrest et al., British Medical Journal, 1991

CHAPTER 17

674 *(top)*, Aureole Restaurant; 674 *(bottom)*, The Culinary Institute of America; 675, Bistro à Champlain